The Duchess of Malfi's Apricots,
and Other Literary Fruits

The Duchess of Malfi's Apricots, and Other Literary Fruits

Robert Palter

University of South Carolina Press

© 2002 University of South Carolina

Published in Columbia, South Carolina, by the
University of South Carolina Press

Manufactured in the United States of America

06   05   04   03   02   5   4   3   2   1

Library of Congress Cataloging-in-Publication Data

Palter, Robert.
  The Duchess of Malfi's apricots, and other literary fruits / Robert Palter.
    p. cm.
  Includes bibliographical references (p.) and index.
  ISBN 1-57003-417-6
  1. Fruit in literature. 2. Fruit. I. Title.
PN56.F76 P35 2001
809'.93364—dc21

                                        2001003346

Dedicated to the hardworking, ill-rewarded,
and often unjustly maligned guild of translators,
without whom much of what follows
could not have been written

BRIEF TABLE OF CONTENTS

ANALYTICAL TABLE OF CONTENTS

LIST OF FIGURES

LIST OF PLATES

ACKNOWLEDGMENTS

For their assistance in this undertaking, I wish especially to thank the Trinity College librarians: in collection development, Doris Kammradt; in circulation, Alice Angelo, Helen Canzanella, Renee Counts, and Howard Barry Hannah Jr.; in interlibrary loan, Mary Curry; in reference, Janice Adlington, Pat Bunker, Lorraine Huddy, and Rebecca Wondriska; in periodicals, George Graf; in the Watkinson Library, Sally Dickinson, Jeffrey Kaimowitz, Peter Knapp, and Alesandra Schmidt; in information systems and services, Vincent Boiselle.

Several bookstores, whose stocks of titles—some newly published, some old and out-of-print—provided me with many opportunities for discovering literary fruit episodes: in Connecticut, Barnes & Noble (Farmington), the Bookstore on the Road (Canton), Borders (Farmington), Brick Walk (West Hartford), and Gallows Hill (Hartford); in Montreal, The Double Hook; in New York City, Hacker Art Books, Kitchen Arts and Letters, and the Strand Bookstore.

For their help in finding and interpreting literary episodes about fruit, I wish to thank Jenny Allan, Beverly Bardsley, Dr. Robert M. Bedard, Julie Berman, David Blitz, Pat Bunker, Jeffrey Kaimowitz, Arnold Kerson, Mary Lefkowitz, Annes McCann-Baker, Douglass Parker, Marie-Claire Rohinsky, Natasha Roklina, Abner Shimony, and Howard Stein.

For information on the biology of fruit, I appreciate the assistance of Craig Schneider and Scott Smedley of the Trinity College Biology Department.

For advice on copyright law, I wish to thank Lewis Kurlantzick and Stephen Utz of the University of Connecticut Law School.

For the preparation of photographs and slides, I wish to thank Phil Duffy; for assistance with computers, ZIP drives, and color copying, Curt Leonard, Adam Palter, Jude Russell, and Ron Spencer.

For invaluable assistance in obtaining permission to quote copyrighted literary materials, I wish to thank Nan Taylor. For advice on obtaining permissions to reproduce copyrighted works of art, I thank James Ganz and Linda Henderson, and for invaluable assistance in obtaining those permissions, Jenny Allan.

James A. Miller (once my colleague at Trinity College and now a professor of English and American Studies at George Washington University) brought my manuscript

xviii   to the attention of Barry Blose (acquisitions editor of the University of South Carolina Press), whose enthusiasm, together with that of two anonymous readers, was critical in the editorial decision to publish my book.

At the University of South Carolina Press, I thank copyeditor Tracy Bealer and managing editor Barbara Brannon for helping to transform a complicated manuscript into a book, and Sandi Frank, for her index.

Finally, I express thanks to my children (Alixe, Geoffrey, Jennifer, Nicholas, and Adam), Anne Lundberg, and Susan Pennybacker, for encouragement and moral support; and to Sue Kamell, for invaluable advice on literature and art, but above all for her love and her support in hard times.

The Duchess of Malfi's Apricots,
and Other Literary Fruits

INTRODUCTION

While I was reflecting, some twenty-five years ago at the University of Texas at Austin, on how to construct a course introducing the humanities to undergraduates, I hit on the idea of taking the human body as my principle of organization. Successive sections of the course were designed to emphasize the bodily aspects of food, sexuality, clothing and cosmetics, illness and death, architecture, language, movement and gesture, performances (real and staged), and history. In the first section, on food, students were introduced to some illustrative literary episodes by Chekhov, Proust, and Kafka. For successive versions of the course, I found fresh literary food episodes. One thing I quickly learned was that food (or cooking or eating) in literature usually stands for something else—love, religion, politics, time, often literature itself—as in the following examples: Levin likening adulterous love to stealing rolls during his dinner with Oblonsky in an elegant Moscow restaurant in the first part of Tolstoy's *Anna Karenina;* Emily Dickinson's frequent invocation of bread as an intimation of divinity; Jacques Prévert's "Lazy Morning" and Pablo Neruda's "The Great Tablecloth," two politically inspired poems about hunger; Keith Douglas's poem "Time Eating." There were also endless comparisons of writing to cooking, from the comedies of Plautus to the satires of Horace and Martial to the prologue of Rabelais's *Gargantua and Pantagruel* to Ben Jonson's masque *Neptune's Triumph* to the first chapter of Fielding's *Tom Jones* to numerous passages in Proust's *Search for Lost Time.* And then there were the literary fruits: the Duchess of Malfi's apricots, Prufrock's peach, Krapp's bananas, and many more.

At about this same time, I heard the late Paul Schmidt read his brilliant account of cookbooks as literature (subsequently published as "'As If a Cookbook Had Anything to Do with Writing.'—Alice B. Toklas," in *Prose* [1974]). So stimulated, I began seriously collecting food episodes in literature, from all periods and in all accessible languages. In an attempt to bring some order into my collection, I composed a lecture called "Reflections on Food in Literature" (subsequently published in *The Texas Quarterly* [1978]). At Trinity College (Hartford), in the late 1980s, the organization and teaching of an undergraduate course on food stimulated further efforts on my part to find interesting and unusual food episodes in literature. More recently, the completion of

2   several pieces of scholarly research with intensely controversial intellectual and political overtones found me eager to return to the (for me) more relaxed theme of food in literature. I envisaged a short essay on fruit in literature, covering perhaps a dozen examples. But even after casual research, examples began to accumulate at an alarming rate. Not an essay, then, but a short book. Or, after a year of concentrated effort, a somewhat longer book. And now, finally, *this* book. But not *finally*, because I have come to realize that my project is inherently open-ended: in effect, I have been studying (admittedly in very partial fashion) certain pervasive and persistent themes in the history of culture, together, of course, with the corresponding genres, styles, and tropes. My study is ongoing, and this book represents in a way only an interim report. Thus, for example, while I have cited—not counting wine episodes—only a couple of fruit episodes from Arabic poetry, I have unquestionably missed many similar episodes; for, as a recent book on food in classical Arabic literature states in its introduction, "Relatively little attention is given . . . to the numerous epigrams on kinds of fruit" (van Gelder, *God's Banquet* [2000]).

The book I offer here deploys many hundreds of literary fruit episodes, illustrated with images from the visual arts, and drawn from a substantial fragment of the history of culture two-and-a-half millennia in duration and stretching westward from Palestine and Egypt to the Americas. The entire range of literary genres is represented (poetry, drama, novel, short story, parable, fairy tale, nursery rhyme, personal memoir, horticultural manual) in some twenty-five languages (Arabic, Chinese, Czech, Dutch, Egyptian, English, French, German, Greek, Hebrew, Hungarian, Italian, Latin, Latvian, Norwegian, Polish, Portuguese, Rumanian, Russian, Serbian, Slovene, Spanish, Swedish, Turkish, Yiddish). Although the book may resemble an anthology of annotated texts on the theme of fruit, it is really both less and more than an anthology. Less, because only some of the episodes (primarily short poems) are reproduced in their entirety; and more, because some of my critical comments are quite extensive. All foreign-language texts are reproduced in English translation; occasionally, in the case of some of the more familiar languages (French, German, Italian, Latin, Spanish), the original is also provided. I am aware of the profound and difficult issues, both practical and theoretical, involved in the translation of literary texts, and this awareness is, I hope, reflected both in my choice of translations (sometimes more than one for a given original) and in my occasional discussion of problems in the translation of specific texts. The few unattributed translations are my own.

In examining literary fruit episodes, we may distinguish at least three relevant issues. These relate to, first, the defining characteristics of the fruit, including how it grows and is harvested; second, the phenomenology of consuming, or otherwise interacting with, the fruit; and third, the cultural roles of the fruit.

THE DEFINING CHARACTERISTICS OF FRUIT

Botanical definitions of fruit usually run something like this: "the edible part of a plant developed from a flower" (*Random House Dictionary*), or "the organ derived from the ovary and surrounding the seeds" (McGee, *On Food and Cooking*). But tomatoes, nuts, cucumbers, and olives, for example, though satisfying the definitions, are not generally considered fruits in contemporary usage, whereas rhubarb, clearly a fruit in contemporary usage, just as clearly violates the definitions. (It may be noted that the ancient Greeks and Romans often grouped nuts, cucumbers, and olives with their apples and pears.) Definitions, in a subject like this, will not take us very far, so let us now simply assume that we can with some confidence recognize a considerable range of fruits and ask how we may usefully distinguish them.

Fruits differ from one another in the following ways: their physical properties (taste, odor, color, size, shape, weight, surface texture, internal structure); their chemical properties (sugar and acid content, nutritional value); their biological identity (genus, species, variety); and their modes of propagation and growth, which may be natural (say, by the scattering of seeds) or artificial (say, by grafts on trees). Propagation and growth include planting, germinating, leafing, budding, blossoming, pollination, fruiting, and ripening, this last process followed by rotting, fermenting, or being eaten (raw or cooked) and metabolized. Each of the three post-ripening processes involves a particular species of organism, such as bacteria, worms, birds, or mammals. (It is salutary to recognize that there exist fruits undreamed of within my selected culture areas. Thus, as Salve Millard explains, in the Philippines there is a fruit called "santol": "It's a big yellow fruit with seeds inside. You chew the seeds and throw the fruit away, except for the skin, which you can eat." None of my fruits is like that!)

It may come as a surprise to some—it did to me—but I have found literary fruit episodes exemplifying just about every one of the above properties and processes, including such obvious properties as shape and size but also most of the subtler stages of growth such as ripening. Consider, to begin with, shape. In his entry on "Pomology" in *The Oxford Companion to Food* (1999), Ian Jackson explains how "shape is a more significant element in folk-pomology than colour" and illustrates with a sample of shape-based names for fruit:

> To the Talentiaion pear of Theophrastus, so called from its resemblance to the metal weights of the balance, add the gourd-shaped Calebasse, the quoin-shaped or wedgelike Quining, the nippled Téton, the barrel-shaped Tonneau, the Sugarloaf pippin, the many egg plums and pears, the bagpipe-shaped Musette, the spindlelike Fusée, the Sheep's Nose apple, the Bishop's Thumb, and the many Ladies' Finger fruits.

The Calebasse, Quining, Téton, Tonneau, Musette, Fusée, and Bishop's Thumb are all varieties of pears. As for size, I once guessed that the relatively small size of cherries and grapes made it likely (always excepting the connection of grapes with wine) that these fruits would be associated primarily with insubstantial, fleeting, even superficial human experiences. This assumption was certainly at first borne out by most of my examples, but then I came across two poems (each in a highly traditional form) that compelled me to reconsider: a narrative of 110 lines of blank verse by Anthony Hecht, in which grapes are invested with cosmic significance; and a poem of four strictly rhymed and regularly accented quatrains by Donald Davie, in which cherries and grapes convey deep and poignant meanings about art. (The poems will be discussed in chaps. 17 and 18.) My guess about the metaphorical significance of these small fruits has been not so much refuted as rendered nugatory by the unexpected imaginative flights of two resourceful poets.

Consider next the ripening of fruit, a process of particular interest to most of us owing to its promise of gustatory delights but also (for some of us) owing to its interestingly complex biochemistry; on both of these topics the food writer Jeffrey Steingarten has condensed a good deal of information in his short essay "Ripeness Is All." Since his main objective is to guide his readers in selecting the most delicious fruit, Steingarten develops a fivefold classification of fruits using as a criterion the ability of the fruit to ripen—that is, to improve its color, odor, flavor, and juiciness—after it is picked: fruit that cannot ripen at all after it is picked (citrus fruits, for example), fruit that can only ripen after it is picked (uniquely, avocados), fruit that can improve in juiciness but not in color or flavor after it is picked (such as peaches), fruit that can improve in flavor and juiciness but not in color after it is picked (such as apples), and fruit that can improve in all respects after it is picked (uniquely, bananas). This classification, though valuable while shopping in the supermarket, has not yet been very useful to me in the study of fruit episodes in literature—with at least one exception, as we shall see, in the form of Derek Walcott's remarkable poem "In a Green Night," which exploits the color changes in oranges and the underlying biochemistry.

CONSUMING FRUIT

The range of experiences expressed in literary renditions of our transactions with fruit I have found to be very wide, even, I venture to say, open-ended. Therefore I do not find very helpful Harold McGee's claim that the etymology of the words "vegetable" (from the Latin verb *vegere,* to animate or enliven) and "fruit" (from the Latin verb *frui,* to enjoy or to delight in) is reflected in contemporary usage, where "by and large, we refer to fruits when we want to convey praise, and to other plant products in order to disparage." McGee's examples of certain common English expressions, such as "That job is a real plum" and "That show was pure corn," do certainly support his point. But *literary* fruit episodes cannot be so neatly categorized, as we shall find instances of such episodes exhibiting love, hate, joy, erotic arousal, religious fervor, guilt, embarrassment, disgust, horror, fear, anger, resentment, curiosity, remorse, nostalgia, and a host of less easily named feelings. And the representation of even the most elusive of such feelings in literary episodes involving fruit is facilitated by the subtleties of our actual transactions with fruit. Compare, for example, the experience of eating cherries or grapes with the experience of eating berries. All three types of fruit are usually small enough to be eaten one at a time from the hand, but there are significant differences: in contrast to the relatively impermeable skin of cherries and grapes, the porous surface of most berries permits the juice to escape and stain one's hands and face; in contrast to the relatively tiny seeds of most berries (hardly impeding mastication), the pits of cherries must be deliberately disposed of and the seeds of most seeded grape varieties must either be deliberately disposed of or deliberately crunched. People will respond differently to the slight discomfort or inconvenience of the berry stains on their hands and face and the pits or seeds in their mouth—indeed, some people may positively enjoy these vivid physical experiences.

THE CULTURE OF FRUIT

The cultural roles of fruit are expressed in myths (the apple of Genesis), rituals (the tossed apple as a love-token), social mores and conventions ("as American as apple pie"). One of my general hypotheses, however, is that in the case of literary episodes involving fruit eating, we might expect relatively diminished cultural complexity, at least, as compared with the eating of other foods—and this for several reasons: fruit is often eaten raw, so cooking and kitchens are dispensable (conversely, in Claude Lévi-Strauss's terms, when we cook, or ferment, we acculturate); many fruits may be eaten from the hand, so dishes and cutlery are dispensable; and fruit is frequently eaten outside the setting of a meal, thereby dispensing with mealtime conventions—a point confirmed by Margaret Visser's *The Rituals of Dinner: The Origins, Evolution, Eccentricities, and Meaning of Table Manners* (1991), where the incidence of fruit is almost negligible. And my hypothesis is, I believe, further confirmed by the relatively enhanced cultural complexity of such episodes as the baked apples in chapter 27 of Jane Austen's *Emma* (see the "Cooked Apples" section of chapter 1); the strawberries and cream in Robert Herrick's "The Lilly in a Christal" (see chapter 4); and many episodes of wine drinking (see chapter 19). It must be remembered, of course, that literary fruit episodes frequently do not allude to eating at all, and about such episodes no clear-cut generalizations regarding degrees of cultural complexity have occurred to me.

ORGANIZATION OF THE BOOK

The overall organization of my book is by type of fruit, beginning with chapters on apples and figs and ending with a chapter on berries, each of the intervening chapters (with a few exceptions) being devoted to a specific fruit or class of fruits. This organization reflects my general hypothesis that each type of fruit will tend to be employed for a unique range of literary uses. (The hypothesis does not emerge entirely unscathed from its confrontation with my own empirical evidence in the form of literary episodes.) The sequential order of the fruit chapters is largely arbitrary, but the location of apples and figs at the beginning and berries at the end is deliberate, for apples and figs represent perhaps the oldest continuously domesticated fruits (from ancient times to the present) and berries (especially the wild varieties) represent a special treat for twentieth-century urban dwellers sated with domesticated fruits, who perhaps long

6   to recapture the remembered pleasure of childhood berrying expeditions. The striking cultural significance of apples on the one hand, and of wild berries on the other, is nicely illustrated by two pieces in *Harper's Magazine* for October, 1999: a long essay on apple growing in the state of Washington by David Guterson, and a previously unpublished discussion by Thoreau of wild huckleberries; the two texts will be discussed in my first and last chapters respectively.

The motivation of each of the several exceptional chapters should be mentioned. In the chapter on "The Flowering Plum: A Chinese Interlude"—which briefly summarizes the fascinating millennium-long role of the flowering plum in Chinese culture—I seek to underline the absence of any such wide-ranging pomological culture-marker in Western literary and artistic traditions. Given the great popularity of its subject, chapter 19, "Wine," is inevitably the most deficient in coverage in the book. A late addition—for I had initially decided to eschew what I mistakenly expected to be no more than a series of tedious tributes to boozing—the chapter touches on some high points in a long and complex cultural history, beginning with ancient Egypt and ancient Greece, selecting a few striking passages from the Jewish and Christian Bibles, pausing for a sustained look at ancient Rome and medieval Latin Europe, noting the extraordinary traditions of vinous poetry in Arabic and Hebrew, sampling some choice writings, in various languages, from fifteenth- through nineteenth-century Europe, and concluding with a handful of poems from the twentieth century. The chapters "Orchards, Groves, and Gardens" and "Fruit, Conjoined and Disjoined" interrupt the sequence of chapters on particular types of fruit to address certain matters pertaining to fruit in general or to physical or conceptual combinations of different fruits. The chapter on "Enemies and Friends of Fruit" deals with the strange and puzzling phenomena of pomophobia and pomophilia.

Some of the longer chapters—including those on apples, figs, quinces and pears, citrus fruits, and wine—have been organized into subsections for easier comprehension; the remaining chapters are composed less systematically. Within each chapter, a wide variety of literary critical approaches are deployed, including the teasing out of structures of imagery and sound, the analysis of narratological techniques, and the identification of historical and cultural contexts. Sometimes the approach will range over a group of texts, arranged either chronologically or thematically; sometimes the approach will focus on the explication of a single text; and sometimes a text will be simply quoted without much comment at all.

If my book may be said to possess any single objective, it would have to be to entertain and stimulate the reader with the pleasurable diversity, both of matter and form, belonging to my collection of texts and pictures. I do not assume that all these texts and pictures are of equal aesthetic value, but I believe that each is sufficiently good of its kind to be worth some sustained attention. I should add that in some of my digressions presenting elementary facts about fruit, more information has been provided than is strictly required for understanding any of the texts or pictures cited; such information may be of interest in its own right but I am also anticipating attempts by readers (myself included) to understand newly discovered fruit episodes (and even attempts by some readers to create fruit episodes of their own).

The visual material in the book is of several kinds: literary episodes which are themselves pictures or diagrams (so-called pictorial, or concrete, poetry); pictures selected to illustrate or complement literary episodes discussed in the text; pictures of exotic or unusual fruit presented for information or sheer delectation. The single best place to begin a study of "pure" still life paintings of fruit is probably the German art historian Sybille Ebert-Schifferer's *Still Life: A History* (1999), which—beginning with antiquity and ending with the late twentieth century—contains a reliable text as well as almost three hundred beautiful reproductions (including dozens of fruit still lifes). One might turn then to the catalogue of an outstanding exhibition, *Still-Life Paintings from the Netherlands, 1550–1720* (1999), together with its companion volume, *Still Lifes: Techniques and Style* (1999), for an account of some of the newer approaches to the study of still-life painting.

NOTE ON DATES AND SOURCES

At first mention of an author or artist, life dates, when available, are provided in parentheses; at first mention of a literary work, the date of first publication, or sometimes of first publication in book form, is provided in parentheses after the title. The indexes of names and titles may be consulted to find the first mention of each author, artist, or title. As for works of art, the date of completion is provided in parentheses after its title and then the medium and size (height, width, depth) in inches. Bibliographical data on sources of quotations are listed at the end of the book in the order of their occurrence in the text. This sequential arrangement of citations forgoes ease of source location in favor of a clear text without distracting notes or numerals. It should be noted that the bibliographical data on translated passages often includes a source in the original language.

1

APPLES

No other fruit unites the fine qualities of all fruits as does the apple [*melon*]. For one thing, its skin is so clean when you touch it that instead of staining the hands it perfumes them. Its taste is sweet and it is extremely delightful both to smell and to look at. Thus, by charming all our senses at once, it deserves the praise that it receives.

Plutarch, Table-Talk

SOME APPLE FACTS

To contrast with the fine tribute to apples by Plutarch (b. before 50; d. after 120 C.E.), another Greek text, perhaps half a millennium earlier, may be quoted from an even more prestigious source—if it is indeed by Plato (ca. 429–327 B.C.E.), as the (doubtful) traditional attribution would have it:

> I am an apple [*malon*] tossed by one who loves you.
> Say yes, Xanthippê, we both decay.

(The shift from eta to alpha in the Greek word for apple is a matter of dialect.) This epigram from the *Greek Anthology* (5.80) has been translated many times; my own version, pieced together from translations by Dudley Fitts and Peter Jay, has the virtue of being briefer than any of the half-dozen English translations known to me.

A few words are in order about the *Greek Anthology* (or, as it is sometimes called, the *Palatine Anthology*), which I shall be citing on many more occasions: this is a collection of several thousand epigrams put together by Byzantine scholars in the tenth century C.E., and which may be succinctly characterized, in the words of Alan Cameron, the leading contemporary specialist on the Anthology, in his entry on the topic in the *Oxford Classical Dictionary* (1996), as "one of the great books of European literature, a garden containing the flowers and weeds of fifteen hundred years of Greek poetry, from the most humdrum doggerel to the purest poetry." Cameron is, of course, alluding to the etymology of the Greek word "anthology" (*anthos,* flower).

The point of the above epigram depends on the fact that apples decay, which is used to support the blunt admonition to eat and make love before it is too late. This decay, and some other facts about apples, are worth recounting before we proceed any further. As to the process of decay itself: the exposed flesh of an apple will always eventually show the telltale brownness, resulting from an enzymatic process of oxidation promoted by the opening or bruising of the apple, which brings into contact two chemical substances previously segregated in the intact fruit. (Most other fresh fruits and vegetables exhibit this same browning process; citrus fruits, melons, and tomatoes are exceptions.) According to Harold McGee (in his *The Curious Cook* [1990]), the tendency to brown varies considerably among different varieties of apples; for some common contemporary varieties the order, from slower to faster, is Golden Delicious, Jonathan, Granny Smith, Gravenstein, Red Delicious.

The number of apple cultivars (or cultivated varieties) is very large; thus, in 1905 the New York State Department of Agriculture published *The Apples of New York,* by S. A. Beach, listing and describing in minute detail some seven hundred cultivars (with long lists of synonyms) and containing many illustrations, of which over eighty are in color. (At the outset, Beach explains that the only species of apples indigenous to North America is crab apples.) It is not always recognized that by limiting himself to apples grown in New York, Beach was omitting many southern varieties. The extent of the omission may now be estimated from the work of Creighton Lee Calhoun Jr., whose *Old Southern Apples* (1995) lists about 1,600 varieties, almost 1,400 of which originated in the southern United States. In the course of his research, Calhoun also discovered a virtually unknown cache of over seven thousand fruit paintings commissioned by the Division of Pomology in the United States Department of Agriculture during the years 1885–1930. Forty-eight of the more than three thousand paintings of apples are reproduced in color in Calhoun's book.

As for Europe, in 1988 an English horticultural artist published a volume containing her paintings together with identifying descriptions of 122 of the apple cultivars now available in Britain (Rosanne Sanders, *The Apple Book*); unfortunately for American readers, many of the most popular varieties in the United States (such as Baldwin, Cortland, Macoun, Northern Spy, Rome Beauty, and Winesap) are missing. Commenting, in Sanders's book, on the indefinitely large variety of apple cultivars, the horticulturist H. A. Baker explains that "because of its complex parentage, and the wealth of genetic material within its make-up, the apple shows more variability in its progeny than any other major fruit." This variability extends to the season in which a particular cultivar ripens, which, in England for example, includes every month except June and July. (See Edward A. Bunyard, *The Anatomy of Dessert* [1934], for an enthusiastic description of the best English apple varieties month by month.)

Another English publication describes in detail over 2,100 varieties of apple (including all the American varieties mentioned above), each of them corresponding to a cultivar in the Apple Collection at Brogdale in Kent, England: *The Book of Apples* (1993), by Joan Morgan and Alison Richards, with paintings by Elisabeth Dowle. Only little of this variety seems to be reflected in Euro-American literature, with a few notable exceptions: Herman Melville (1819–1891) included Spitzenberg apples in "Bartleby the Scrivener" (1856); James Joyce (1882–1941) placed American apples in the great feast episode in "The Dead" (1914) and Australian apples near the beginning of the "Lestrygonians" chapter of *Ulysses* (1922); Ernest Hemingway (1899–1961) described the Wagener apple in an early short story, "The Three-Day Blow" (1925); and Robert Frost (1874–1963) features an apparently imaginary variety of apple in his narrative poem "The Gold Hesperidee" (1936). But while it is generally true that for most earlier authors an apple is an apple is an apple, in numerous twentieth-century American poems (as we shall see) specific varieties of apple do appear. In any case, one may consult an alphabetized list of ninety North American varieties, with brief descriptions and beautiful, life-sized pictures, in Roger Yepsen's *Apples* (1994). Few of these, though, are easily available to consumers, and the unusually large number of varieties (twenty-two) I found a few years ago in Central Market in Austin, Texas, should be compared with the forty-seven described in an apple cookbook (Mark Rosenstein, *In Praise of Apples: A Harvest of History, Horticulture, and Recipes* [1996]).

The immense variety of apple cultivars is reflected in their wide range of tastes. But the language of taste is notoriously meager, so it is not surprising that terms from wine tasting have been enlisted to describe the taste of apples—terms such as "*rich, aromatic, vinous, nutty, spicy,* and *perfumed*" (Edward Behr, *The Artful Eater* [1992]). I have found few literary allusions to the tastes of specific apple varieties.

But why an apple rather than, say, a pear, in the epigram quoted above? After all, we have it on the word of an earlier Greek poet, Praxilla (5th cent. B.C.E.), that for Adonis in the underworld both pears and apples are recalled as delectable fruits (in David Campbell's translation):

> The most beautiful thing I leave behind is the sun's light; second, the
> shining stars and the moon's face; also ripe cucumbers [or "figs"] and
> apples and pears.

This fragment has survived only as a quotation in the *Proverbs* of Zenobius (2d cent. C.E.), where we are told that the proverbial saying "sillier than Praxilla's Adonis" was used of stupid people, "for anyone who lists cucumbers and the rest alongside sun and moon can only be regarded as feeble-minded." Does the proverb reflect the attitudes of some early enemies of fruit? Or, perhaps, merely indignation at anyone who was not sufficiently respectful of the traditional divinity of the heavenly bodies? In any case, a modern Turkish poet, Nazim Hikmet (1902–1963), finds it natural to take a cucumber as the harbinger of spring and hope and love, in his "The Cucumber," date-lined "March 1960 Moscow." (Hikmet had been exiled from Turkey for his Communist affiliations and was living in Moscow.) At the beginning of the poem it is snowing hard outside, but "On the table, on the oilcloth, spring— / on the table there's a very tender young cucumber, / pebbly and fresh as a daisy" (translated by Randy Blasing and Mutlu Konuk).

In this context, one should also recall Homer (ca. 725 B.C.E.), who, in the *Odyssey* (11.588–590), depicts Tantalos in the land of the dead, burning with thirst, surrounded with water but unable to drink, his torture intensified by the presence of ripe fruit forever just out of reach (translated by Robert Fitzgerald):

> Boughs, too, drooped low above him, big with fruit,
> pear trees, pomegranates, brilliant apples,
> luscious figs, and olives ripe and dark;

The delectability of pears was perhaps enhanced by their perishability, this latter quality presumably explaining why, for the ancient Greeks, "the pear was a metaphor for the fleeting ripeness of youthful beauty" (Andrew Dalby, *Siren Feasts: A History of Food and Gastronomy in Greece* [1996]). A good example of this view of pears occurs in *Idyll* 7 of the Greek poet Theocritus (early 3d cent. B.C.E.): "the all-too-attractive Philinus . . . already as ripe as a pear, nearly rotten" (translated by Daryl Hine). But for that very reason "Plato's" choice in his epigram could not have been the pear: ripe pears, unlike ripe apples, bruise easily and hence are not very suitable for tossing— unless, that is, one wishes to exploit the splattering effect of using a ripe pear as a missile. Such an exploit is part of a "culinary event" by performance artist Bobby Baker (*Kitchen Show,* first performed in 1991 in London). Lucy Baldwyn, a critic of Bobby Baker's work, has commented on the throwing of a pear:

> The action involves taking a ripe pear and throwing it against a cupboard door. . . . The destruction of the hapless pear was such a fine expression of pent-up tension. The soft explosion of the pear is a comic fantasy moment during which an unspoken anger is acceptably vented. . . . The pear, however, leaves behind a provocation—how may a woman show anger in public? Since then I have secretly admired pears, weighing their explosive potential should the need arise.

THE CLASSICAL TRADITION

Apples as Love Tokens

The motif of the tossed apple as a love token recurs in Theocritus, *Idylls* 5 and 6, though now it is shepherdesses who throw the apples, pelting the flocks of their laggard goatherd lovers. The Latin poet Propertius (ca. 50–ca. 16 B.C.E.) wrote a brilliant variation on the apple-tossing theme, with the apple handler drunk, the recipient asleep, and the apples gently placed on her recumbent body. The first seven lines of the forty-six line elegy describe three different mythical sleeping women; then, in the next three lines, the actual lover, Cynthia, makes her appearance, "her head pillowed on a cushion of her hands" (1.3.8, translated by G. P. Goold). The speaker has just returned from a night of carousing and he recounts how he hovered over his slumbering lover, transferred the garlands from his brow to hers, played with wisps of her hair, and, "then with hollowed palms I stealthily gave you apples" (1.3.24, translated by Goold). The Latin of this last line consists of six words: "nunc furtiva cavis poma dabam manibus" (now, stolen/stealthy, hollow, apples, I-gave, to-hands/with-hands/from-hands). As usual in Latin, the meaning is not uniquely determined by the word order, which helps to explain the substantial variation in these different English translations by Ronald Musker, J. P. McCulloch, and Guy Lee, respectively:

> Now covertly in the hollow of your hand
> I tried to plant apples
>
> ~
>
> & bestow secret fruit on your ungrateful sleep
> with hollowed hands
>
> ~
>
> Or to cupped hands gave stolen fruit

Evidently, Goold and McCulloch take the hollowed hands (palms) to be those of the speaker, rather than (as with Musker and Lee) those of the sleeping Cynthia; McCulloch imports the word "ungrateful" (*ingrato*) from the next line. The word *furtiva* also receives quite different interpretations: for Goold and Musker, the word modifies the act of giving; for McCulloch and Lee, it modifies the fruit itself. Finally, Goold and Musker translate *poma* as "apples," while McCulloch and Lee prefer the less specific "fruit."

The fate of the fruit is also quite different for the four translators, the Latin line (1.3.26) "munera de prono saepe voluta sinu" (gifts, down-from, tilted, often, rolled, breast/lap/pocket) being variously translated: "repeatedly rolled down from your lap" (Goold); "rolled / down the slope of your breast" (Musker); "a wealth of gifts poured down" (McCulloch); "Gifts rolled from my pocket often as I leant" (Lee). Lee chooses not to connect the apples deposited in Cynthia's hands with those rolling out of the speaker's pocket (*sinu* can mean "the hanging fold of the toga"); he also associates *prono* with the (leaning) speaker, rather than with the (falling) apples. Goold's vagueness about just which region of Cynthia's body receives the apples enables him to have them roll down from Cynthia's lap (another possible meaning of *sinu*). Musker's choice of a different portion of Cynthia's anatomy, her breast (yet another meaning of *sinu*), is in keeping with the apples being deposited in her hands (under her head and hence not far from her breast). Finally, McCulloch inverts the order of the two lines we have been considering, so that, first, "as I bent over you / a wealth of gifts poured down," and only then is the fruit bestowed on Cynthia. Each of the four translations presents a vividly realized action, reflecting some insight into Propertius's original text. I might add that Cynthia eventually wakes up—not from the ministrations of her lover but from the light of the moon in her eyes. What follows are a dozen lines full of Cynthia's bitter complaints, on which note the poem ends.

That the association of apples with love was still alive almost two millennia later is clear from a scene in the great film *La Grande Illusion* (1937), directed by Jean Renoir

(1894–1979). Toward the end of the film, the two escaped French prisoners of war, Maréchal (Jean Gabin) and Rosenthal (Dalio), are taken in by a German war widow, Elsa (Dita Parlo). Following the Christmas celebration devised by the two Frenchmen for Elsa's five-year-old daughter, Maréchal enters his bedroom, and the film script describes the action (translated by Marianne Alexandre and Andrew Sinclair):

> When he has closed the door, he turns his head towards the dresser. On the dresser is a tray full of apples set out to dry. He takes one and begins eating it, as he walks about the room. Follow him to show at the same time as he notices it, that the door leading from his room to the dining-room is ajar. In the background, Elsa is still standing where he left her. Maréchal, surprised, goes up to her very slowly until he is standing right next to her. She raises her face and he takes her in his arms.

The apple as a kind of anti-love token occurs in a *dizain* (a traditional ten-line stanza, with the rhyme scheme *ababbccdcd*) by the sixteenth-century French poet Maurice Scève (ca. 1501–1563). In 1544, Scève wrote a sequence of 449 such *dizains* (introduced by an eight-line *huitain*), *Délie, objet de plus haute vertu* (Delia, object of highest virtue), addressed to an idealized lover named Delia (whose name is conceivably an anagram of *l'Idée*). The apple poem begins chattily with the line (in Geoffrey Brereton's translation): "While we were chatting one evening, my lady said to me" (En devisant un soir me dit ma Dame). The speaker's lady then offers him an apple to cool off his excessive ardor, apples being "cold by nature" (de froide nature). To which the speaker responds with a rebuke to his lady: she is herself "so cold" (si froide), "you will quench my fire better than the apple" (Tu éteindras mon feu mieux que la pomme).

It is worth noting that the alleged coldness of the apple's nature was not something invented by Scève; rather, he could scarcely have avoided familiarity with the idea from an authoritative Italian health manual first published (in Latin) in 1470 and appearing in French translation no less than eight times between 1505 and 1539 (two of these editions were published in Scève's own city, Lyons): *On Right Pleasure and Good Health,* by Platina (1421–1481). Situated as he was in southern France and deliberately imitating Italian literary models, Scève would surely have known Platina's popular book. Later, in chapter 22, "Enemies and Friends of Fruit," we shall discuss Platina's work in greater detail; here, I wish only to note how he emphasizes the coldness and wetness of apples: "It is . . . understood that apples are cold and damp because their juice easily turns to vinegar when pressed out of them. Because of this, some think that fruit of this kind does not harm a healthy stomach before a meal, because it moistens the belly and cools the insides" (translated by Mary Ella Milham).

Mythological Apples
There is a further significance to the tossed apple, which is the implicit association of apples with Aphrodite, as in a fragmentary poem by Sappho (ca. 620–ca. 550 B.C.E.). In Barbara Hughes Fowler's version:

14
>
> Come to me from Crete, down from heaven,
> come, for here your shrine in a charming
> grove of apple trees keeps its altars
> smoking with incense.
>
> Here the water, cool through the apple
> boughs, is babbling; shadowed with roses
> all the grove. From shimmering leaves sleep,
> drifting, will come down.

Half a millennium later, Aphrodite and her apples are alluded to by way of a marvelously compressed simile in a love poem by Catullus (84–54 B.C.E.). The poem (no. 2) is about his sweetheart's pet sparrow and it consists of a single sentence of thirteen lines, beginning with an initial section of ten lines addressed to the sparrow; I quote the last five lines in the close English translation of G. P. Goold:

> to be able to play with you, as does your mistress,
> and allay the sad cares of my heart
> would be as welcome to me as they say
> was to the swift-footed girl that golden apple
> which loosed her long-tied girdle.

The swift-footed girl is Atalanta, committed to marrying any man who can outrun her; success comes to a suitor assisted by Aphrodite, who gives him a golden apple— three in the usual versions of the story—to throw in Atalanta's path, thereby slowing her down so that, apparently not unwillingly, she loses the race. It must be noted that most editors of Catullus regard the terminal three line simile ("tam gratumst mihi quam ferunt puellae / pernici aureolum fuisse malum, / quod zonam soluit diu ligatam") as a separate fragment (2b). Its self-containment is evidenced by the English version of Jane Wilson Joyce (1995):

> I'm pleased as the little maid in the fable,
> the sprinter who picked up the gilded pippin
> that loosened her ceinture, so long tight-laced.

Ovid (43 B.C.E.–17 C.E.) gives a full account of Atalanta's swiftness of foot in the tenth book of his *Metamorphoses* (ca. 7 C.E.), though ignoring other sides of her athletic prowess: she killed the vicious so-called Calydonian boar and once outwrestled Achilles's father Peleus! I want to quote some of Ovid's lines about the golden apples in a translation by Charles Boer (1989), which announces itself as intending to bring out "the harsher, violent subtexts" of Ovid's poem. Ovid's narrative strategy is to imagine Venus telling the tale of Atalanta to her lover Adonis. At a certain point in the narrative (10.600), Hippomenes looks at Atalanta and decides to race her and risk the death which comes to losers; she looks back at him and almost wishes she might lose the race. But Hippomenes prays to Venus for help and the goddess, with little time to improvise, picks three golden apples (*aurea poma*) in a nearby field consecrated to her worship; she gives them to Hippomenes, explaining their use, and the race begins (10.664–680):

> Neptune's offspring throws one apple;
> the astonished girl wanting shiny fruit turns
> off course to get the golden rolling thing;
> Hippomenes ahead: applause resounds at the sight;
> she quickly makes up time, leaving
> boy again behind; a second apple toss
> for her to chase; delayed, but she passes boy again;
> last part of race: 'Now be with me,
> goddess, giver of the gift!' he throws shiny gold
> way off course to slow her down
>
> girl seems to hesitate: should she get it?
> I force her to: & add weight to the fruit;
> hinder her with heaviness & delay; but, my story
> shouldn't be slower than the race: girl beaten;
> winner takes his prize.

Ovid is, of course, especially interested in what occurs next: the married couple make love in a temple of Jupiter or Cybele (the mother-goddess of Anatolia) and are punished for their desecration by being transformed into a pair of lions.

Ezra Pound (1885–1972) insisted many times that the Elizabethan translation of Ovid's *Metamorphoses* (1567) by Arthur Golding (ca. 1536–1605) was the most beautiful book in the language, and while not many other critics have shared this opinion, at least one eminent American poet and translator, John Frederick Nims, believes that "in its racy verve, its quirks and oddities, its rugged English gusto, it is still more enjoyable, more plain fun to read, than any other *Metamorphoses* in English." Here, therefore, is Golding's version of the above passage:

> Then *Neptunes* imp her swiftnesse too disbarre,
> Trolld [rolled] downe at oneside of the way an Apple of the three.
> Amazde thereat, and covetous of the goodly Apple, shee
> Did step asyde and snatched up the rolling frute of gold.
> With that *Hippomenes* coted [passed] her. The folke that did behold
> Made noyse with clapping of theyr hands. She recompenst her slothe
> And losse of tyme with footemanshippe: and streight ageine outgothe
> *Hippomenes,* leaving him behind: and beeing stayd agen

With taking up the second, shee him overtooke. And when
The race was almost at an end: He sayd: O Goddesse, thou
That art the author of this gift, assist mee freendly now.
And therwithall, of purpose that she might the longer bee
In comming, hee with all his might did bowle the last of three
A skew at oneside of the feelde. The Lady seemde too make
A dowt in taking of it up. I forced her too take
It up, and too the Apple I did put a heavy weyght,
And made it of such massinesse shee could not lift it streight.
And least that I in telling of my tale may longer bee
Than they in ronning of their race, outstripped quight was shee.
And he that wan her, marying her enjoyd her for his fee.

Golding's fourteeners seem clogged with words. By contrast, Boer's laconic six-beat lines use scarcely more words than Ovid's Latin. The version (1997) by Ted Hughes (1930–1998), on the other hand, though it seems at first deliberately stripped-down (no allusion to Neptune, for example), adds flourishes absent from the Latin (the rocky, thorny gulley, for example) and ends up using over a hundred more words than Boer's:

"This was the moment
For flinging one of my apples out past her—
He bounced it in front of her feet and away to the left.

"Startled to see such a gorgeous trinket
Simply tossed aside, she could not resist it.
While she veered to snatch it up
Hippomenes was ahead, breasting the crest
Of the crowd's roar.

"But Atalanta came back in with a vengeance.
She passed him so lightly he felt to be stumbling.
Out went the second apple.
As if this were as easy she swirled and caught it
Out of a cloud of dust and again came past him.

"Now he could see the flutter of the crowd at the finish.
'O Venus,' he sobbed, 'let me have the whole of your gift!'
Then with all his might he hurled
The last apple
Past and beyond her—into a gulley

"Choked with tumbled rock and thorn. She glimpsed it
Vanishing into a waste

Of obstacles and lost seconds.
With two gold apples heavier at each stride
And the finish so near, she tried to ignore it.

"But I forced her to follow. And the moment she found it
That third apple I made even heavier.
Lugging her three gold prizes far behind
Her race was lost. Atalanta belonged to the winner.

Somewhat surprisingly, after Apollodorus (ca. 180–ca. 120 B.C.E.) wrote down what must have been one of the first full accounts of the myth, subsequent Greek and Roman writers and artists did not pay much attention to Atalanta's golden apples. Madeleine Jost's assertion (in her entry "Atalanta" in the *Oxford Classical Dictionary,* 2d ed.)—"The episode of the foot-race is not found in art"—does, however, require some qualification, since Atlanta and Hippomenes appear on at least one ancient Greek vase of around 420 B.C.E. and on at least a few Roman vessels (one clay, two glass) of the second to third centuries C.E. (See the monumental compendium of the iconography of Classical mythology, *Lexicon Iconographicum Mythologiae Classicae* [1984].) Since the Renaissance large-scale revival of ancient mythology, there have been numerous representations of the Atalanta-Hippomenes race in a variety of media, including literature, painting, sculpture, music, and dance. Thus, in the entry "Atalanta" in the survey of the afterlife of Classical mythology, *The Oxford Guide to Classical Mythology in the Arts, 1300–1990s* (1993), edited by Jane Davidson Reid and Chris Rohmann, over two dozen paintings of the race are listed. The earliest dates from the fifteenth century, the latest from the nineteenth. I mention here only a single example, a particularly beautiful work by the Bolognese baroque painter Guido Reni (1575–1642): *Atalanta and Hippomenes* (1618–19), now in the Prado, Madrid (oil on canvas, 81 x 117 in.; there is an identical painting in Naples, now generally considered a copy). Guido chooses to represent the moment when Atalanta is stooping to pick up one of the golden apples with her right hand; she already holds one in her left hand. Hippomenes meanwhile seems to be pausing for a moment as he turns his head back towards her and gestures theatrically with his right hand. Both figures are nude except for some wisps of flying drapery designed to satisfy Counter-Reformation standards of modesty. The picture is an impressive study in the thrusts of diagonalized limbs, most notably in the crossing of Atalanta's left leg and Hippomenes' right. (For a reproduction, see D. Stephen Pepper, *Guido Reni, A Complete Catalogue of His Works* [1984]; or the catalogue of a major exhibition in 1988–89, *Guido Reni, 1575–1642* [1988], which reproduces also the Naples copy of the painting.)

For Natale Conti (1520–1582), author of an extremely popular manual of mythology—there were no less than thirty-one editions between 1531 and 1669—the main interest of the Atalanta-Hippomenes episode was its "moral": "For Atalanta indeed is the pleasure which we seek out through not a few things dangerous to our life. Whenever someone pursues her or pleasure, with no reverence for either God or

18   law, they no longer retain a human form of mind or way of thinking, but are transformed into ferocious brutes, as were Atalanta and Hippomenes." Conti is here alluding to that later incident in which the married couple are transformed into lions as a punishment for violation of a religious sanctuary.

Hermetic interpretations of ancient myths were developed—almost in tandem with the new sciences of Galileo and William Harvey—in the sixteenth and seventeenth centuries, and even such a minor figure as Atalanta did not escape the attention of the occult-minded. Thus, beginning with the assumption that "the ancient philosophers were admirable for their ability so dexterously to cover over all their science with the pleasant veil of poetical fables," Henri de Linthaut, in his French *Commentary on the Treasure of Treasures of Christophe de Gamon* (1610), provides an alchemical interpretation of Atalanta's race with Hippomenes: "With Atalanta they covered our Mercurial water, quick and fugitive, whose race is arrested by the golden apples thrown by Hippomenes, which are our fixing and coagulating Sulphurs" (translated by John Leavitt).

Just a year before de Linthaut's work appeared, Francis Bacon (1561–1626) published his own interpretation of the ancient myths in 1609, *De Sapientia Veterum* (On the wisdom of the ancients), a brief Latin treatise popular enough to be reprinted during his lifetime as well as translated into English and Italian. Bacon strongly disapproved of occult readings of myth; as he writes in his preface: "the Alchemists more absurdly still have discovered in the pleasant and sportive fictions of the transformation of bodies, allusions to experiments of the furnace." Bacon's own mode of rationalizing the myths turns them into truths exemplifying—in the words of Bacon's nineteenth-century editor and translator James Spedding—"Bacon's own thought and observation upon the nature of men and things, and replete with good sense of the best quality." Specifically, in chapter 25, "Atalanta, or Profit," after retelling the Atalanta story, Bacon writes:

> The story carries in it an excellent allegory, relating to the contest of Art with Nature. For Art, which is meant by Atalanta, is in itself, if nothing stand in the way, far swifter than Nature and, as one may say, the better runner, and comes sooner to the goal. For this may be seen in almost everything; you see that fruit grows slowly from the kernel, swiftly from the graft. . . . But then this prerogative and vigour of art is retarded, to the infinite loss of mankind, by those golden apples. For there is not one of the sciences or arts which follows the true and legitimate course constantly forth till it reach its end; but it perpetually happens that arts stop in their undertakings half way, and forsake the course, and turn aside like Atalanta after profit and commodity, —
>
> Leaving the course the rolling gold to seize.
>
> And therefore it is no wonder if Art cannot outstrip Nature, and according to the agreement and condition of the contest put her to death or destroy

her; but on the contrary Art remains subject to Nature, as the wife is subject to the husband.

I confess to being rather surprised when I came across a contemporary American short story based on Atalanta's race with Hippomenes: "Ordinary Apples" (1998), by Ron Nyren. Set in contemporary Connecticut in the imaginary town of Baldwin (named, we are told, after Baldwin apples), the story takes the form of a reminiscence by the narrator, Vaughn, about the Apple Harvest Festival of his senior year in high school. Vaughn's Latin teacher, Mr. Kintner, decides to stage the race of Atalanta and Hippomenes out of doors as part of the festivities. The only three students in the senior Latin class make up the cast: Melissa and Roger—who have been flirting with each other all semester—play Atalanta and Hippomenes, while Vaughn plays Atalanta's father. The main props are the three apples, which have been covered in glue and gold sparkles. The performance goes well until Melissa abruptly leaves the defined theatrical space in search of the third golden apple, which Roger has flung off into the surrounding audience. She never finds the apple and never returns to her role. Afterwards, Vaughn observes Mr. Kintner triumphantly presenting the third golden apple to Melissa (though Vaughn later changes his mind about the apparent flirtatiousness of the gesture). Vaughn then obtains one of the golden apples from Roger, and peels and eats it; Roger follows suit with the second golden apple.

The narrator considers the possible "symbolic" meaning in this shared consumption of once-golden apples and finds none; and yet the whole sequence of events has marked a coming of age for him: "We weren't eating the apples of the Tree of Knowledge, we were eating a couple of McIntoshes, we were eating the apples of stupidity, we were eating ordinary apples. They tasted good. When we had finished, we threw the cores into some evergreen bushes. It was my last October in Baldwin."

There are some incidental but attractive features of the story having to do with the apples themselves. First is the information about Baldwin apples: "one of the most commercially successful varieties of the nineteenth century; our founders must have felt it would have lasting resonance. However, though the Baldwin survives shipping well, its trees bear fruit only every other year. New annual varieties began to supersede it around the turn of the century. Now you hardly see the Baldwin anywhere." Beach confirms all these details—except the supersession of the Baldwins, which had not yet begun while he was writing—in his *Apples of New York,* even including two photographs of thriving Baldwin apple orchards in New York State, as well as two color plates of Baldwin apples. Finally, in his description of the apple festival, Nyren devotes an entire paragraph to the apple-based foods on sale at the festival:

> From the booths you could buy every kind of apple concoction imaginable: apple cider, apple crisp, apple cake, apple pie, apple rhubarb pie, apple-and-green-tomato pie, apple cupcakes, apple brown betty, apple slump, apple pandowdy, baked apples, caramel apples, mint apple jelly, maple apple

custard, apple chutney, apple soufflé. You could buy plain apples from the three huge Kintner Orchards booths, which sold Gravensteins and McIntoshes. No Baldwins, though. They didn't ripen until November.

Golden apples also figure in one of the labors of Hercules: he is required to steal them from a tree guarded by a fierce dragon in a garden belonging to the African King Atlas and his daughters, the Hesperides (named after their mother, Hesperis, whose name was in turn derived from her father, Hesperus). The story is retold by the minor Italian Renaissance writer Pietro Andrea di Bassi (ca. 1375–1447), in his "Le Fatiche d'Ercole" (Labors of Hercules), composed around 1431, and extant in an illuminated manuscript now in the Houghton Library at Harvard. It seems that Juno, in a scheme to destroy Hercules, has presented Atlas with a tree bearing golden apples (translated by W. Kenneth Thompson):

> [Juno] secretly caused a marvellous golden apple tree to spring forth from the floor of the banquet hall. As the tree grew, and spread its delicate golden boughs, which were laden with perfectly formed apples of the purest gold, Juno gazed upon it with delight, and graciously thanked Earth for such a beautiful gift. Then, turning to Atlas, she prayed him to take the golden tree into his custody and to keep it safe, out of love for her.

Hercules despatches the guardian dragon with a single blow of his club and proceeds to pluck every one of the golden apples, thereby acceding to the demands of King Eurystheus, who had asked Hercules "'to bring to Us as many of those golden apples as you are able.'"

Statues of Hercules with the golden apples—as also, drawings and engravings after the statues—became extremely popular throughout Europe after the discovery of the so-called Farnese Hercules in Rome around 1546. This gigantic marble statue (over ten feet tall) is probably an enlarged third-century-B.C.E. Roman copy of an ancient Greek sculpture of Hercules. (For a picture of the Farnese Hercules and a detailed scholarly discussion, see Francis Haskell and Nicholas Penny, *Taste and the Antique* [1982].) With a relatively tiny head and enormous muscle-bound limbs, the graceless figure is represented leaning to the side with his left arm around his club and with his right hand, grasping several apples, behind his back. (See Haskell and Penny's book for an engraving by the Dutch artist Hendrik Goltzius [1588–1617] of the statue viewed from the rear.)

A superb rendition of Hercules with the golden apples—called *Hercules Pomarius*— by Willem Danielsz Van Tetrode (ca. 1525–1580) was included in the exhibition on Vermeer and the Delft School at the Metropolitan Museum of Art in 2001. Van Tetrode was one of the outstanding Dutch artists of the sixteenth century (though an iconoclastic crusade drove him out of his native Delft in 1573). He followed the Italian mannerist style, having studied with Benvenuto Cellini (1500–1571) and other Italian masters. His Hercules statue (completed some time between 1545 and 1565) was highly influential among northern artists; as James David Draper explains, in the catalogue edited by Walter Liedtke, *Vermeer and the Delft School* (2001), "it apparently circulated in plaster and bronze replicas that were presumably cast in the north." (Four bronze replicas are known; the one on view at the Metropolitan Museum belongs to the Hearn Family Trust.) The work is in a different medium (bronze) and on a different scale (h. 15 ⅜ x w. 5⅛ x d. 9⅛ in.) from the Farnese Hercules; and the figure also has a different pose: legs wide apart, Hercules wields his club with his right hand and holds his left hand grasping the apples behind his back (see the Liedtke catalogue for a picture of the sculpture).

The youthful Tennyson (1809–1892)—he was around twenty-two—published a poem called "The Hesperides" (1831), prefixed by an epigraph by John Milton (1608–1674) from *Comus* (1634): "Hesperus and his daughters three, / That sing about the golden tree"(ll. 982–3). (As noted above, the three daughters of Hesperis are actually granddaughters of Hesperus.) After a brief introduction, Tennyson's poem is an extended "song" of some hundred lines; the opening and closing lines are especially evocative of the apples:

> The golden apple, the golden apple, the hallowed fruit,
> Guard it well, guard it warily,
> Singing airily,
> Standing about the charmèd root.
>   [. . . . .]
> All round about
> The gnarlèd bole of the charmèd tree.
> The golden apple, the golden apple, the hallowed fruit,
> Guard it well, guard it warily,
> Watch it warily,
> Singing airily,
> Standing about the charmèd root.

With an oblique allusion to the golden apples of the Hesperides, Emily Dickinson (1830–1886) compares the shapes of individual human lives to the shapes of apples, in a poem of around 1866:

> Except the smaller size
> No lives are round—
> These—hurry to a sphere
> And show and end—
> The larger—slower grow
> And later hang—
> The Summers of Hesperides
> Are long.

The most momentous golden apple in Greek mythology was, of course, the one that, in effect, launched the Trojan war. This piece of legendary history consists of a

sequence of episodes beginning with the wedding of Thetis and Peleus (she a goddess, he a mortal—Achilles was their son), continuing with the judgment of Paris, and
concluding with the abduction of Helen. Many of these episodes do not occur in
Homer and are known only from surviving fragments of the so-called epic cycle, a
series of mediocre epic poems dating from perhaps the second half of the sixth century B.C.E. (For a brilliantly compressed account of a very controversial subject, see
Malcolm Davies's *The Epic Cycle* [1989].) One of these epics, the *Cypria*, may have
been composed primarily to serve as a history of the events leading up to the Trojan
war, and its account may be supplemented by Apollodorus and Proclus (of unknown
date but probably earlier than the fifth century C.E. neo-Platonist philosopher of that
name). Drawing on these literary sources and many others, Natale Conti composed a
not entirely coherent account in chapter 23 ("Paris"), book 6 of his *Mythologies* (translated by Anthony DiMatteo):

> All the Gods were fabled to have gathered to celebrate the marriage of
> Peleus and Thetis, with the exception of Discord, whom no one had
> invited. Taking this badly, she hurled among the guests a most elegant and
> sumptuous apple of gold inscribed with the words, "To the fairest I
> belong." It was Mercury who picked it up and read the words. . . . Then,
> with many Goddesses at first seeking it, great discord and contention
> developed among the three Goddesses, with all others relinquishing claim,
> and Jupiter ordered the dispute brought before the man purported to be
> the most just of mortals then alive, Paris. . . . The three Goddesses each
> plied him with magnificent gifts, Juno promising him rule over Asia and
> Europe, Pallas vowing to make him the wisest man in all of Greece, but
> Venus said she would grant him the most beautiful woman in the world
> if he would rule her the most beautiful of the three, as Ovid touches upon
> in the "Epistle of Paris." . . . Many writers have represented these alterna-
> tives which Euripides so plainly articulates in his *Trojan Women* (in the
> words of Helen). . . .
>
> At the time of the judgment, Helen had the reputation of being the
> most beautiful woman of all of Greece, surpassing all others in riches and
> nobleness of birth.
>
> [. . . . .]
>
> It so happened that Paris was sent to Greece as an ambassador with
> twenty triremes to demand the restoration of his aunt, Hesione. . . .
> Menelaus, who had won the favor of marrying Helen (and by this time
> had become king of Lacedaemon, succeeding Tyndarus), received Paris
> with a gracious display of hospitality. . . . Paris, disregarding customs of hos-
> pitality and the friendliness of Menelaus, is said to have made off with that
> strumpet Helen along with a great amount of gold and silver and a mass

Fig. 1: Frans van den Wyngaerde, *Marriage of Peleus and Thetis,* ca. 1640

of the royal household's belongings, as the anonymous author of the "Song of Cypria" and Herodotus in Book 2 of his *Histories* write.

That Conti cites Paris as an outstandingly just man is very strange. Also, Conti quotes from *Trojan Women,* by Euripides (ca. 485–407/6 B.C.E.), Athena's promise to lead Paris in victory over Greece, without bothering to resolve—or, indeed, even to notice—the discrepancy with his earlier account of Athena's proffered bribe to Paris.

Such an intellectually cultivated artist as Peter Paul Rubens (1577–1640) would have been well acquainted with Conti's *Mythologies,* and would no doubt have consulted it when he was commissioned by Philip IV, in 1635, to design decorations on Classical themes for the walls of a new hunting lodge, the Torre de la Parada, outside Madrid. Rubens actually made only oil sketches, for some sixty-one or sixty-two paintings, which were then executed by other less distinguished artists. (For black and white reproductions of the more than fifty surviving sketches, see Julius Held's catalogue, *The Oil Sketches of Peter Paul Rubens* [1980].) Another Flemish artist, Frans van den Wyngaerde (1614–1679), made engravings following the sketches, probably after Rubens's death. One of Rubens's subjects was the marriage of Peleus and Thetis; his sketch (1636) is now in the Art Institute of Chicago (oil on panel, 10½ x 16½ in.) The corresponding painting was executed by Jacob Jordaens and is now in the Prado, Madrid. Van den Wyngaerde's engraving (12½ x 16½ in.) is reproduced as figure 1.

The first thing to note about van den Wyngaerde's engraving is how all the characters are gesturing with their left hands—a consequence of the left-right reversal inherent in printmaking. Most of the characters can be fairly easily identified: Jupiter is handing the apple to Mercury, while Winged Discord hovers behind them. Jupiter's spouse Juno is on his right, with Venus and Minerva directly across the table. Thetis and Peleus are off to the left, not looking very joyful on their wedding day. Of the three contending goddesses in the engraving, only Venus is unclothed. In three painted versions of *The Judgment of Paris,* by Rubens, on the other hand, all three goddesses are nude: in two paintings in the National Gallery in London (ca. 1600 and 1632–5, each on an oak panel) and a third in the Prado (1639, on canvas). In all of these, Paris holds an apple in his extended right hand.

The judgment of Paris and its consequences is the theme of the most grandiose of all baroque operas, *Il pomo d'oro* (The Golden Apple), by the Italian composer Marc Antonio Cesti (1623–1669), first performed in Vienna in 1668. Cesti was a Franciscan monk, a tenor in the papal choir, court conductor to Emperor Leopold I of Austria, and a leader of the Venetian school of opera. The opera was commissioned by the emperor to celebrate his marriage, but the technical demands of staging the work were so great that the first performance had to be delayed for a year and a half (until the occasion of the Empress Margarethe's birthday) while a new theater was being constructed. The opera was in five acts and sixty-seven scenes and required no less than twenty-four different sets (located in heaven, earth, and hell). The treatment of the ancient myths was ironic, with a running commentary by the court jester. At the conclusion of the opera, the golden apple was conveyed by Jupiter's eagle to the Empress, a sign that she united in herself the principal virtues of all three goddesses who had competed for the prize. As for Cesti's music, Paul Henry Láng says, in his *Music in Western Civilization* (1941) that "it was he who contributed greatly to that melodic quality which makes Italian music irresistible in its sensuous beauty." (For further details, see Láng's book and also János Malina's discussion of the opera in a volume edited by András Batta, *Opera: Composers, Works, Performers* [2000], which contains three pictures of contemporary colored engravings representing some of the original stage sets.)

Another late-antique motif—that of the three Graces (or Charites)—also came to be associated with golden apples (though there is no warrant for this association in the earliest literary allusions to the Graces), perhaps through a conflation with the Judgment of Paris motif. The representation by Raphael (1483–1520) of the three Graces (ca. 1504; oil on wooden panel, 6¾ x 6¾ in.), in the Condé Museum, Chantilly, has each of the Graces holding a golden apple in one hand. (For a reproduction of the painting, see *Raphael* [1983], by Roger Jones and Nicholas Penny.) All this helps to explain the connection between the apples and the Graces in a lovely little poem, "Offering" (1846), by Eduard Mörike (1804–1875), translated from the German by Christopher Middleton:

Peeled by dexterous hands, three little apples, so delicate,
    Hung on a single twig still with a circlet of leaf;
White as wax their flesh suffused with a shimmer of rose,
    Close together they cling, naked and eager to hide.
Do not be bashful, sisters, it was a girl who undressed you;
    And to the Graces Three [*Chariten fromm*] he brings you, a poet demure.

So far as I know, Mörike has created in his three peeled apples still attached to a twig a wholly original image; and the notion of peeling as undressing also seems original.

Women and Apples

Identifying women with apples, as we shall soon see, is a very old conceit by Mörike's time; an ancient instance is a fragmentary poem by Sappho (105a, here translated by Barbara Hughes Fowler) comparing a young woman to a particularly tempting but inaccessible apple (*melimela,* sweet apple):

> Like the sweet apple that reddens on the topmost bough,
> at the top of the topmost—the apple pickers forgot it.
> No, they did not forget it. They could not get it.

The association of girl and apple occurs in a poem by Catullus (65), which, like the poem discussed earlier (2), concludes with an extended simile. The poem was written to Catullus's friend, Quintus Hortensius Hortalus (a distinguished orator, the chief rival of Cicero), to accompany a translation from the Greek poet Callimachus. Catullus first expresses his grief at his brother's recent death and then his concern that Hortalus might think his words had (in Goold's translation):

>   slipped from my mind,
> as an apple, stealthily sent as a gift from her lover,
>   rolls out from a chaste maiden's bosom (for she forgets,
> poor thing, that it is hidden beneath her soft gown) and is
>   shaken out when she starts up at her mother's coming;
> and flung headlong it tumbles to the ground,
>   while over her sorry face spreads a guilty blush.

Catullus would very likely have known the writings of Theocritus, whose seventh Idyll contains the line: "All of you Loves with your blushing complexions like ripening apples" (7.114). And this is far from the last time we shall find lovers' blushes associated with apples. I might just add that my friend Jeffrey Kaimowitz has pointed out to me numerous echoes of this poem by Catullus in the elegy by Propertius (1.3) discussed above in "Apples as Love Tokens"; Propertius would certainly have known Catullus's work.

The Roman poet Martial (ca. 38–101 C.E.) probably delighted in subverting our gender expectations in *Epigrams* 3.65.1, which begins with the line: "Quod spirat tenera malum mordente puella" ("The fragrant breath of a lovely young girl's / bite on an apple"; translated by Smith Palmer Bovie). This turns out to be the first in a list of ten especially fragrant items (occupying altogether eight lines): the aforementioned apple-scented breath, saffron (or crocus), early white grapes, sheep-cropped grass, myrtle, spices gathered by an Arab, rubbed amber, burning frankincense, earth moistened by summer rain, and spikenard. Finally, in the last two lines of the poem, we learn that the speaker has all along been addressing a young boy lover: his kisses are fragrant all right (like the items in the list)—if only he would grant them *sine invidia* (without the spitefulness)!

The woman/apple Ur-metaphor was adopted and elaborated by later writers, notably, in Longus's "romance," or novel, *Daphnis and Chloe,* written probably in the eastern Greek settlement of Lesbos (the setting of the work) around 200 C.E. Longus's life dates are unknown, but there is evidence that narrative fiction in prose was an innovation that appeared in the Greek literary tradition sometime between the first century B.C.E. and the first century C.E. As for apples, Longus explains in his very first section how "it was from passion that the apples [*mela*] were falling to the ground." The translator Christopher Gill comments in a note: "Longus suggests, rather preciously, that one could imagine that the apples fell not from natural causes but from a passionate attraction to the ground, in harmony with the erotic atmosphere of the season." A little later, Longus describes the innocent exchanges of the lovers: "Sometimes they threw apples at each other, and tidied themselves up by combing each other's hair. She said his hair was like myrtle berries, because it was dark; he said her face was like an apple, because it was pink and white."

A more extended apple episode takes place one day when, after completing their farmyard chores (he is a goatherd and she a shepherdess), Daphnis and Chloe wander the fields looking for ripe fruit:

> There was plenty available because it was the time of the year when everything is ripe. There were lots of wild pears and lots of cultivated ones; lots of apples, some of which had already fallen, some still on the trees. Those on the ground were more fragrant; those on the branches were fresher in color. The former smelt like wine; the latter shone like gold.

> One apple tree had been stripped and had neither fruit nor leaves; all the branches were bare. But it still had one apple hanging at the very top of the highest branches—a big and beautiful one, and one that by itself had more fragrance than all the rest put together. The apple picker must have been frightened to climb up there and failed to take it down; also, perhaps, the lovely apple was being preserved for a shepherd in love.

Daphnis, against Chloe's advice and to her annoyance, climbs the tree and picks the apple; he then presents it to Chloe by placing it in her bosom, and she rewards him with "a kiss that was better than an apple—even a golden one." This paradigmatic incident involving a lone apple would very likely have been familiar to a cultivated reader in 200 C.E., perhaps as a recollection of Sappho, fr.105a (see above), or of a similar passage from some more contemporary author. Also, the allusion to the golden apple would remind such a reader of the Atalanta story, which we have found Catullus using two and a half centuries earlier. The frequency of such allusions to the Classical literary tradition, as well as other textual subtleties, in many of the extant ancient Greek novels have helped to persuade the scholar J. R. Morgan that these works are "better regarded as off-duty amusement for the highly literate than as a product aimed at those with lower grades of taste and education."

Also notable in the passage quoted from Longus is the careful observation evident in the description of a winy smell in apples on the ground and of the superior appearance of apples still on the bough. Such realistic touches could have served for ancient readers to enhance the verisimilitude of an otherwise fantastic narrative. Finally, the lone apple incident, occurring, as it does, just after the respective foster fathers of Daphnis and Chloe have agreed to their marriage, puts a seal on the asymmetrical relationship which must now replace the earlier symmetry between the two lovers: Daphnis must be bolder, and indeed he has just recently been initiated into sex by an older woman, while Chloe remains cautious (though ardent) and virginal.

The image of an inaccessible apple at the very top of a tree has a long history; for Emily Dickinson it symbolized heaven, as in this quatrain (the first of three) in a poem of around 1861:

> "Heaven"—is what I cannot reach!
> The Apple on the Tree—
> Provided it do hopeless—hang—
> That —"Heaven" is—to Me!

One of the more recent occurrences of the lone apple—completely divorced, needless to say, from a Classical context —is in the lyrics by Lorenz Hart (1895–1943) for the titular number in the musical comedy *On Your Toes* (1936; music by Richard Rodgers):

> See the pretty apple, top of the tree,
> The higher up, the sweeter it grows.
> Picking fruit you've got to be
>   Up on your toes!

> See the pretty penthouse, top of the roof,
> The higher up, the higher rent goes.
> Get that dough, don't be a goof;
>   Up on your toes!

Here the apple is a metaphor for social class, with the "pretty penthouse" equated to the "pretty apple." A fair assumption would be that many in the audience for *On Your*

Toes, in mid-Depression America, enjoyed themselves by identifying with the upwardly mobile characters—at the same time wishing they could afford a more expensive (if not higher!) apartment. In this respect that thirties audience would have perhaps differed from the audience for *Daphnis and Chloe,* "whose lives," according to J. R. Morgan, "had settled into a comfortable but boring routine, which they had no desire to change but could supplement imaginatively."

The association between an apple and an attractive woman may be direct rather than involving the intermediary of an apple tree; as Gavin Ewart (1916–1995)—never one to mince words—uses the peeling-undressing metaphor in the limerick "Eve and the Apple" (1986):

> A young girl whose life-style the malicious
> described, loosely, as too meretricious,
> said "When the boys peel me
> and delightfully feel me,
> I just feel like a Golden Delicious!"

The "Eve" of Ewart's title is simply a generic name for a woman but no doubt possesses still a trace of the biblical meaning.

Women's Breasts as Apples

It may be conjectured that the metaphoric coupling of a temptingly inaccessible apple with a temptingly inaccessible woman had its origin in the metonymic association of a woman with her breasts together with the metaphoric coupling of apples with women's breasts. Though I know, in fact, of no evidence for the metonymic usage in question—which, for example, does not seem to be present in American slang—the breast-apple coupling goes back, in the Classical tradition, at least to Aristophanes (ca. 450–ca. 386 B.C.E.). In his *Lysistrata* (411 B.C.E.), he refers to Helen's breasts in line 115 as "apples" (*mala*), repeating the usage in *Ecclesiazusae* (The Congresswomen) (904), of 392 B.C.E. In fact, Jeffrey Henderson, a leading student of obscenity in ancient Greek literature, has found (in *The Maculate Muse* [1991]) that the metaphor of breasts as apples "seems to have been a standard image throughout Greek erotic literature." Thus, in the third century B.C.E., in a poem erroneously included by ancient editors in the works of Theocritus (*Idyll* 27), we find the following exchange (as translated by Thelma Sargent):

> GIRL: What are you doing, young satyr? Why are you touching my breasts?
>
> DAPHNIS: I'm teaching these ripe apples [*mala*] of yours their first lesson.

Many centuries later, Rufinus wrote a group of erotic poems, thirty-six of which were subsequently included in the fifth book of the *Greek Anthology* (and thereby preserved, even while the very century of the author's birth—somewhere between the second and fifth centuries C.E.—has been lost to us); two of these poems make use of the breast-apple metaphor. One of the two (5.60) is here translated by Alan Marshfield:

> a silvertoed virgin
>   was washing her body
>   drenching the golden
> apples of her breasts
>   their flesh like yogurt
> the plump cheeks of her bum
>   tossed against one another
> as she swung about
>   flesh as lithe as water
> a hand spread down
>   to cover
>   much swollen
>   the fairflowing conduit
> not the whole thing
>   but as much as she could

The phrase "fairflowing conduit" corresponds to "Eurotas" (the name of the river along which ancient Sparta was located) in the original Greek; other modern translators simply repeat the place-name (for example, a prose translation by W. R. Paton, or a metrical translation, which follows Paton very closely, by Barbara Hughes Fowler). This difference in the translation of a proper name reflects a larger difference in the very presuppositions and objectives of translation from an ancient language. Thus, Peter Jay, in the introduction to his *Greek Anthology,* criticizes the procedure of substituting modern proper names for ancient ones on the ground that such modernization foolishly assumes "that the reader has no imaginative historical sense at all," and yet Jay includes in his anthology the above translation of Rufinus, which eliminates altogether the name of an ancient river, while substituting a different (although admittedly related) metaphor. In this case, though the intended anatomical locus of "Eurotas" is clear from the context, someone not familiar with the history and geography of ancient Greece might not even suspect that "Eurotas" refers to a river.

Another poem by Rufinus (5.62, translated by Fowler), lacking one of its six lines in the version preserved in the *Greek Anthology,* also equates breasts with apples:

> Time has not quenched your beauty. Much of your bygone prime
>   survives. Your charms have not aged, nor has
> the loveliness left those gleaming apples of yours or your rose.
>   How many did that divine blossom burn
> to ashes before . . . .
>   . . . .

The rhymed translation by Robin Skelton (b. 1925) is more compressed (twenty-six words rather than forty) and simply ignores the missing line:

> Time has not withered you; in age
> your shining apples, your moist rose,
> retain that beauty that has burned
> more hearts to ashes than it knows.

Women's breasts—or parts of them—have also been associated with other fruit—pears or melons or grapes—and, in *Bech at Bay* (1998), by John Updike (b. 1932), with apricots. Bech is engaged in postcoital conversation with one of his lawyers, "touching two fingers to the erectile tip—the color of a sun-darkened, un-sulphur-treated apricot—of her nearest breast." I assume Updike is referring here to dried apricots which have not been treated—as all dried apricots used to be—with preservative sulphur dioxide; such un-sulphur-treated apricots became widely available in the late twentieth century. Whether the color of such apricots is plausibly attributable to a woman's nipple is a question on which I bow to Updike's expertise. And women's breasts have even been associated with pineapples, by an American artist, Susan Hauptman (b. 1947), in a 1991 self-portrait (charcoal and pastel on paper, 48 x 32 in.), now in a private collection. The subject is standing, nude to the waist, and holding a large pineapple in front of each breast, while balancing a bowl of fruit on her head. (For a reproduction, see the catalogue of a show at the California Center for the Arts Museum in Escondido, California: *Narcissism: Artists Reflect Themselves* [1996].)

A good example of a nonspecific fruit/breast metaphor occurs in the medieval Latin satirical poem *Architrenius* (Arch-weeper), dating from around 1185, by Johannes de Hauvilla (d. ca. 1210), who was probably born in Normandy and taught in the important cathedral school of Rouen. The poem resembles a traditional epic in its hexameter verse, its great length (nine books, 4, 361 lines), and its story of a young student, the Arch-weeper—so called because of his extended lament for the state of the world—engaged in a cosmic quest for moral enlightenment. Johannes's treatment of the theme, however, is hardly epical in the traditional sense, for the focus is on the ills of church, court, and schools in his own time; more specifically, in the words of his translator Winthrop Wetherbee, "Johannes is the poet *par excellence* of the capitalist-careerist mentality."

The Arch-weeper's quest ends when (in book 6) he reaches the Earthly Paradise, referred to as "Thylas" and characterized, in traditional terms, by "an eternizing power, a deity native to the place, [which] ensures the perennial flowering of its youthful spring." Here the Arch-weeper encounters a personified Nature, who, after teaching him about the moral and cosmological order of the universe (in books 7–9), offers him the beautiful maiden Moderation as a bride.

Returning now to the beginning of the Arch-weeper's journey (in book 1) for our example of a fruit-breast metaphor, we note how he comes upon the golden palace of Venus, with one among the goddess's handmaidens being singled out for her

beauty in an extraordinary sequence of 194 lines (book 1, ll.365–487; book 2, ll.1–71),
of which no fewer than twenty-nine are devoted to her torso. Wetherbee provides a
rich prose translation of the nine lines about her budding breasts:

> Her breasts, small, restrained, and clearly defined, do not overflow her
> bosom like those of an old woman, but hold their position with a firm-
> ness proper to her tender years. Each little sphere puts forth a tender bud.
> This, since there is as yet no infant for whom it must weep milky tears,
> remains closed, a tight little node set in ivory. A valley divides the twin
> fruits (*pomula*) of her breasts like a straight and level furrow, descending
> unhindered until a nice sense of proportion gives rise to her stomach, and
> the modest swell of her smooth womb ascends to meet it.

The breast-apple comparison has had a very long run in European thought; for
purposes of illustration, a few examples (in four different languages) will have to suffice. At the beginning of the seventh canto of *Orlando Furioso* (1516; 1521; 1532), by
Ludovico Ariosto (1474–1533), there is a description of the evil sorceress, Alcina,
including the following words: "due pome acerbe, e pur d'avorio fatte" (7.14). In a
modern translation by Barbara Reynolds, this reads: "Two ivory breasts, firm as young
fruit." A nineteenth-century English version by William Stewart Rose translates
"pome" as "apples": "fresh and firm, two ivory apples." Later in the poem, one of the
two main heroines, Angelica, is described as she appears to Ruggiero: chained to a rock,
her nude body like a statue of alabaster or marble, her only sign of life a tear "bedew-
ing the young fruit, so firm and fair" (10.96), in Reynolds's translation. It is worth noting that the adjective modifying *pome* is now *crudette*—literally, "raw"—rather than, as
before, *acerbo*—literally, "sour."

Later in the sixteenth century, Pierre de Ronsard (1524–1585) writes as follows,
in the fifty-fifth sonnet of his first book dedicated to Helene (1578):

> J'entre-vy dans son sein deux pommes de beauté,
> Telles qu'on ne voit point au verger d'Hesperide.

which has been translated by Humbert Wolfe as:

> I saw the apples of her breast as fair
> as orchard-fruit of the Hesperides.

By 1629, there was an apple cultivar in England called "Womans Breast," which
was characterized as "a great Apple" by John Parkinson (1567–1650), the renowned
seventeenth-century apothecary and botanist (see Stuart Peachey's *Fruit Variety Register,
1580–1660*).

Finally, in part 1 of *Faust* (ca. 1800), by Goethe (1749–1832), in the Walpurgis
Night scene, a pair of apples on a tree stands in for a woman's breasts, in the following exchange between Faust and the Young Witch (in Stuart Atkins's version):

Fig. 2: Hans Baldung Grien,
Fall of Man, 1511

FAUST

One day I had a lovely dream,
in which I saw an apple tree
and on it saw two apples gleam;
they tempted me to climb the tree.

YOUNG WITCH

You men have always craved that fruit
since it first grew in Paradise.
I quiver with delight to know
that in my orchard apples grow.

This passage from *Faust* was associated with a dream by a patient of Freud's, as recounted in *The Interpretation of Dreams* (1900). Freud knew that the patient had recently broken off a love affair with an actress and, after quoting the two quatrains, he writes: "There cannot be the faintest doubt what the apple-tree and the apples stood for. Moreover, lovely breasts had been among the charms which had attracted the dreamer to his actress." Does the comment seem irritatingly redundant only because on such matters we are all Freudians today?

A vivid realization of the breast-apple comparison may be seen in a chiaroscuro woodcut (14⅞ x 10⅛ in.) by Hans Baldung Grien (1484/5–1544), *Fall of Man* (1511), where Adam, standing just behind Eve, grasps one of her breasts with his left hand while extending his right hand to grasp an apple on a branch high above him. (See fig. 2.) The woodcut has a special theological interest because, as James H. Marrow and Alan Shestack explain, "For apparently the first time in art, the Fall is represented as an overtly erotic act." (For further discussion of the woodcut, see Marrow and Shestack's catalogue of Baldung Grien's prints and drawings and H. Diane Russell's catalogue of a fascinating exhibition, *Eva/Ave: Women in Renaissance and Baroque Prints* [1990].)

Apples for breasts is now established American slang, according to the *Random House Historical Dictionary of American Slang*. One might have thought, however, that no self-respecting twentieth-century author would dare to use such a hackneyed comparison. But Colette (1873–1954) so dares and brings it off, in her final novella *Julie de Carneilhan* (1941); her trick, of course, is to put the words in the mouth of one of her characters. The eponymous protagonist is of a type familiar enough in Colette's fiction: a twice divorced woman of forty-five, born an aristocrat but now living alone in shabby-genteel poverty in a small Paris apartment. (As has been pointed out by some critics, Julie's initials are the reverse of Colette's when she was married to Henry de Jouvenel many years before.) Julie is perpetually anxious about her next meal, and this anxiety reaches a fever pitch each month as her funds dwindle in the days just before the small monthly stipend from her first husband is due to arrive. She could, of course, easily receive virtually unlimited funds from wealthy admirers, but refuses, less out of pride than out of selfishness—she will not tolerate men in control of her life (though, in reality, the main movements of her life are often controlled by men, in particular—as we shall see in chapter 21, "Fruit, Conjoined and Disjoined"—by her second husband, for whom she retains an ambivalent regard). The paragraph of interest at this point describes the naked Julie looking at herself in a mirror as she converses on the telephone with a female acquaintance (translated by Patrick Leigh Fermor):

> In the looking-glass opposite, a tall, naked woman was watching her. From her feet to her small head with its golden-beige hair she was the colour of a yellow tea-rose, with the rather spare, flat belly of a barren woman, a pretty navel placed high at her middle and breasts that had lost none of their fineness, except in her own severely critical eyes. "Just a shade more like jelly-fish than apples cut in half these days," was her verdict. ["Ils sont un brin plus méduses que demi-pommes, a présent," jugea-t-elle.]

With her passion for food and her relatively impoverished imagination, the breast-apple comparison is perfectly in character for Julie, and her "apples cut in half" may even introduce an original note of her own (as her "jelly-fish" certainly does!).

Anne Sexton (1928–1981) also puts a remark about women's breasts and apples in the mouth of one of her characters—the character is Jesus and he is talking about his mother—in the opening lines of the first poem ("Jesus Suckles") of "The Jesus Papers" (1972): "Mary, your great / white apples make me glad."

The Australian Marjorie Barnard (1897–1987), in a brief impressionistic sketch called "The Persimmon Tree" (1943), compares a woman's breasts to persimmons. Looking at the window of a flat across the street from her own, belonging to a woman she has seen but never met, the unnamed narrator, one early spring morning, notices "a row of persimmons set out carefully and precisely on the sill, to ripen in the sun. Shaped like a young woman's breasts their deep, rich, golden-orange colour, seemed just the highlight that the morning's spring tranquillity needed." The persimmons, she reasons, "must have come, expensively packed in sawdust, from California or have lain all winter in storage. Fruit out of season." The persimmons remind her of the vivid experience of a grove of persimmon trees in her childhood neighborhood:

> In the autumn they had blazed deep red, taking your breath away. They cast a rosy light into rooms on that side of the house as if a fire were burning outside. Then the leaves fell and left the pointed dark gold fruit clinging to the bare branches. They never lost their strangeness—magical, Hesperidean trees. When I saw the Fire Bird danced my heart moved painfully because I remembered the persimmon trees in the early morning against the dark windbreak of the loquats. Why did I always think of autumn in springtime?.

In fact, the narrator herself is a woman out of season, first, because she is recovering from a serious illness and cannot face meeting any new people—indeed, even any old friends—and, second, because—though this is only implied—she is attracted only to women. The story ends on a bleak note, as the woman of the persimmons stands curtained behind her window and drops her gown, while the narrator watches and despairs: "I turned away. The shadow of the burgeoning bough was on the white wall [of the narrator's flat]. I thought my heart would break."

Another association from American slang is "melons," according to *The Oxford Dictionary of Modern Slang* (1992): "A woman's breasts; esp., large breasts." This meaning of melons has been exploited by the British artist Sarah Lucas (b. 1962) in her assemblage *Au Naturel* (1994), included in "Sensation," the sensational exhibition at the Brooklyn Museum in 1999–2000. Lucas's work (33 x 66 x 57 in.) consists of an actual mattress on which are arranged, on the left, a pair of melons and a water bucket, and on the right, two oranges and an upright cucumber. (For a photograph, see the catalogue of the exhibition, *Sensation* [1997]. Another work by Lucas in the same exhibition, by the way, consists of a wooden table on which are suggestively arranged two fried eggs and a kebab.)

We return to apples and women's breasts with a pictorial poem by the Czech writer Jaroslav Seifert (1901–86), "Abacus of Love" (1925), in a version by Dana

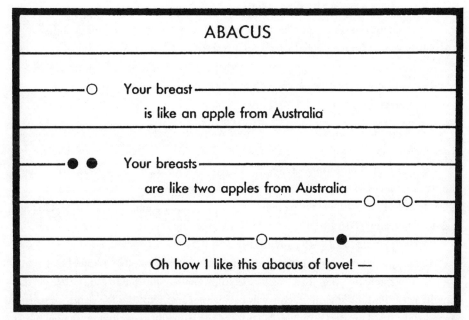

Fig. 3: Jaroslav Seifert, "Abacus of Love," 1925

Loewy. (See fig. 3.) Seifert had a long, eventful and, in certain ways, exemplary career as a writer (eventually winning a Nobel Prize in 1984), and later in this chapter we shall glance at the political and cultural contexts of his later, more complex, poetry. This youthful poem presupposes no acquaintance with such contexts; some of the circumstances surrounding the initial publication of the volume containing "Abacus of Love," *On the Waves of TSF* (1925), are, nevertheless, intriguing. (The volume, incidentally, also contained a poem called "Guillaume Apollinaire," and Seifert must certainly have derived the idea of "Abacus of Love" from the shaped poems of *Calligrammes* [1918], by Apollinaire [1880–1918].) In his reminiscences, *All the Beauties of the World* (1981), Seifert recalls first of all the origin of the title: the initials "TSF" are derived from the French initials for *telegraphie sans fil,* or what came to be called radio. At the time, there were no radios in Czechoslovakia and no Czech word for them. As for the book itself, Seifert explains: "The titles and texts of the poems were in the most varied type faces. Every poem was set differently. Some pages were horizontal, others vertical. The old printer in Vyskov shook his head over this manner of doing things, but he let us have our way." Finally, Seifert tells us something about the availability of Australian apples in Czechoslovakia at the time he was writing the poem:

> In those days, gourmet shops sold Australian apples in the winter. The
> apples did not have a very pronounced taste, because they ripened while

they were being shipped. But they were very beautiful. Each apple was wrapped in fine silk paper, and Mr. Paukert, who owned a gourmet shop on National Street, placed them on a platter in the window of the store, each one unwrapped a little bit, so that people could see their unusually beautiful coloring. They were rare and expensive. But that has nothing to do with my poem.

Looking for a moment outside Euro-American artistic traditions, I note that in a painting of a nude woman (oil on canvas) by Tang Muli (b. 1947)—a survivor of the Chinese Cultural Revolution—the seated figure has her hand on a basket of apples. The painter was obviously influenced by the traditional Euro-American motif, though his *Nude with Apples* (1979) was painted before he studied abroad at the Royal College of Art in London. (For a reproduction of the painting, see Joan Lebold Cohen, *The New Chinese Painting, 1949–1986* [1987].)

Breasts are emphatically present but the apple only implied in a staged black and white photograph by Man Ray (1890–1976), *Ciné-sketch: Adam et Eve* (1924): the frontally presented nude woman conceals her genital area with her left hand, while her cupped right hand proffers an invisible apple to the frontally presented nude man, who conceals his genital area with something like a large leaf; the faint image of a snake is barely visible above Eve. Adam, by the way, is the painter Marcel Duchamp and Eve an artist's model named Broina Perlmutter. (For a reproduction, see *Man Ray,* ed. Manfred Heiting [2000].)

Finally, there is a powerfully disturbing photograph of missing women's breasts, by Frédéric Brenner (b. 1959), included in his volume of photographs, *Jews/America/ A Representation* (1996). The photographs are black and white, mostly of blatantly staged groups of people—not quite all of them Jews—against highly improbable or surprising backdrops: a Sukkah on top of the Empire State building, taxicabs on the beach at Coney Island, a large oriental rug hovering over a road, a display of mattresses in a store. Almost all the people depicted are named; at the end there are some celebrities. Some of the reproductions are on gatefolds and these are about twenty-seven inches wide and about eight inches high; of the latter, one is labeled *Survivors, Los Angeles, California, 1994.* When we unfold the page we see a long, narrow table covered with a cloth and a white brick wall as backdrop. In the shallow space between table and wall six women are sitting facing the camera with their arms on the table, holding hands and nude to the waist. The women are survivors of mastectomy, one of a double mastectomy. The table is mostly bare except for a centered overflowing bowl of fruit.

How are we meant to look at Brenner's photographs, and why are they so compelling? Well, at first what we seem to be looking at are either staged versions of traditional rituals (a Passover seder in a women's prison) or invented actions that look like rituals (the survivors holding hands). But on second thought we realize that the only rituals really on view are those involved in the very photographic act itself. Has photography become a surrogate for our waning ritual traditions?

Apples in the Song of Songs

In the passage cited above from Goethe, a fleeting allusion to Paradise (following, of course, a long tradition of biblical interpretation) was combined with the Classical apple-breast metaphor. Apples are explicitly associated with love in another book of the Hebrew Bible, the Song of Songs (which in its present form probably dates from a century or so after Plato). We must face the fact, though, that apples may not have been known in Palestine at the time the Song of Songs was composed, so that the Hebrew word, *tappuach,* usually rendered "apple" in translations of the Song of Songs, may have referred to some other fruit. What could it have been? In the most recent English version of the Song of Songs, by Ariel and Chana Bloch, the translators (following Harold and Alma Moldenke's *Plants of the Bible* [1952]) opt for the apricot (in their note on verse 2.3). Here, in the Blochs' translation, are the four occurrences of apricots (2.3, 2.5, 7.9, 8.5), which, of course, are apples in most other translations:

[she speaks]

2.3   And my beloved among the young men
      is a branching apricot tree in the wood.
      In that shade I have often lingered,
      tasting the fruit.

~

2.5   Let me lie among vine blossoms,
      in a bed of apricots!
      I am in the fever of love.

~

[he speaks]

7.9   And oh, may your breasts be like clusters
      of grapes on a vine, the scent
      of your breath like apricots,
      your mouth good wine—

~

[she speaks]

8.5   There, beneath the apricot tree,
      your mother conceived you,
      there you were born.
      In that very place, I awakened you.

In following the Moldenkes the Blochs were, in fact, relying on outdated evidence in their choice of the apricot rather than the apple as one of the fruits in the Song of Songs. Consider, for example, the evidence in certain third millennium B.C.E. Akkadian texts from Mesopotamia, in which one of the most prominent fruits has until recently resisted secure identification. Usually interpreted as apples, allusions to the fruit in question as dried and strung had convinced some scholars that the texts must be referring to apricots. However, dried and strung apples have now been found in graves of the period, which, together with strong etymological indications, suggest that apples may indeed be the correct identification (see J. N. Postgate's "Notes on Fruit in the Cuneiform Sources" [1987]). Furthermore, Dalby explains that "the only early archaeological finds of cultivated apple pips are from Iraq, before 2000 b.c., and later Israel." And finally, the absence of the apricot in early Classical sources again suggests apples as the fruit called *tappuach* in the Song of Songs (see M. A. Powell's "Classical Sources and the Problem of the Apricot" [1987]).

If one half of the breath-apricot (apple) simile is uncertain, so is the other, with Marvin Pope's adventurous Doubleday Anchor Bible translation reading: "The scent of your vulva like apples" (Song of Songs 7:9).

Whatever the word *tappuach* may have meant in ancient Palestine, by the time Jerome (ca. 347–419) composed a Latin version of the Song of Songs—"produced," as Pope points out, "by Saint Jerome in a few days in the year 398"—it was translated (in the above four passages of the Song of Songs) as *malum,* which certainly meant apple in Jerome's Latin. (For the so-called Vulgate text of the *Cantica Canticorum*—the Latin Song of Songs—see E. Ann Matter, *The Voice of My Beloved: The Song of Songs in Western Medieval Christianity* [1990].) This Vulgate Song of Songs, or "Canticles," was a popular text for allegorical interpretation during the Middle Ages, as evidenced by the almost one hundred extant Latin commentaries and homilies from the period 700–1400 c.e. (for discussion of which, see Matter's book); and by the late Middle Ages secular vernacular poetry began to be influenced by this Song of Songs tradition.

Christian writers generally interpreted the Song of Songs as an epithalamion composed for the marriage of Solomon but also simultaneously as an allegory of the spiritual marriage of Christ (the Bridegroom) with his spouse (the Church). Individual writers could then work out their own personal ideas of the ways in which each detail of the Song of Songs anticipated some element of Christian belief. In Stanley Stewart's monograph on "the enclosed garden" in seventeenth-century English poetry (1966), which pays special attention to the allegorical tradition of the Song of Songs, he points out that "though that tradition finds its clearest expression in the sermons and treatises on the Canticles, it extends also into the graphic arts, into architecture, and into gardening." Our primary concern will be the apples and apple trees of the Song of Songs as they appear in certain religious lyrics—a tiny sample, it should be noted, from an enormous corpus—many of which were scored for musical performance.

Consider first the minor English poet Francis Quarles (1592–1644), whose book of moralized and illustrated Bible stories, *Emblemes, Divine and Moral* (1635), continued to be popular for centuries after its first publication (I quote from an edition of 1845). *Emblemes* 5.2 is based on Canticles 2:5: "Stay me with flowers, and comfort me with apples, for I am sick of love." The poem consists of five nine-line stanzas, the second and third of particular interest here:

> Ye blessed maids of honour, that frequent
>   The royal courts of our renown'd Jehove,
> With flowers restore my spirits faint and spent;
>   O fetch me apples from love's fruitful grove,
> To cool my palate, and renew my scent,
>   For I am sick, for I am sick of love:
>   These will revive my dry, my wasted powers,
>   And they will sweeten my unsav'ry hours;
> Refresh me then with fruit, and comfort me with flowers.
>
> O bring me apples to assuage that fire,
>   Which, Ætna-like, inflames my flaming breast;
> Nor is it every apple I desire,
>   Nor that which pleases ev'ry palate best:
> 'Tis not the lasting deuzan I require:
>   Nor yet the red-cheek'd queening I request:
>   Nor that which first beshrew'd the name of wife,
>   Nor that whose beauty caus'd the golden strife;
> No, no, bring me an apple from the tree of life.

The term "deuzan"—sometimes written "deusan" or "duzing" or "deux-ans"—refers to an apple variety that one seventeenth-century pomologist described as "a delicate fine fruit, well relished when it beginneth to be fit to be eaten, and endureth longer than any other apple" (quoted by Peachey in his *Fruit Variety Register*). The "queening"— or "queen"—"is a fair red striped Apple, and beautiful in its Season, being a king of winter fruit" (once again, as quoted by Peachey). Quarles's point, of course, is that somehow the mortal apples are transmuted into life-sustaining apples. Succinctly, in the words of the extremely influential Jesuit neo-Latinist poet—"the Polish Horace," as he was called—Mathias Casimire Sarbiewski (1595–1640), "The Apple ripe drops from its stalke to thee, / From tast of death made free." The translation of Ode 4.21 is from G. Hils's selection of "The Odes of Casimire" (1646). In the Latin—published in 1625—Sarbiewski's language is even more succinct: "Ipsa tibi, leti succos oblita priores, / Mitia poma cadent."

Canticles 2:3 mentions the apple tree, here quoted from the King James Bible: "As the apple tree among the trees of the wood, so is my beloved among the sonnes. I sate down under his shadow with great delight, and his fruit was sweete to my taste." This became a fertile source of religious verse with the apple tree interpreted as the Bridegroom, as in these two popular songs (1683), by the seventeenth-century English poet John Mason:

My Jesus is an Apple-Tree,
　　And others Barren Wood.
He is a Shadow from the Heat
　　Of Conscience, Wrath and Hell.

～

What are the common Trees o'th'Wood
　　Unto the Apple Tree?
What is the Rich and Noblest Blood,
　　My lovely Lord, to Thee?

I sate Rejoycing in Times past
　　Under his cooling Shade
His Fruit was sweet unto my Tast,
　　O what a Feast I made!

　　Many striking variations on themes from the Song of Songs may be found in the verse of Edward Taylor (ca. 1642–1729), now generally considered America's greatest colonial poet. Taylor was born in England but came as a young man to America, where, after graduating from Harvard, he became the minister of a newly established Congregational church in the frontier settlement of Westfield, Massachusetts, serving in this capacity for some fifty years. Taylor wrote well over two hundred poems, almost all on religious themes; he published none of them and forbade his heirs from publishing them, but manuscript copies of the poems were preserved (and have been in the Yale University Library since 1883). The first publication of a selection of Taylor's poems was in 1937 and the first complete edition (ed. Donald E. Stanford) in 1960. In his foreword to Stanford's edition, Louis Martz characterizes the poetry, beginning with the fact that Taylor was deeply influenced by George Herbert (1593–1633). As for Taylor's language, it is a "peculiar mixture of the learned and the rude, the abstract and the earthy, the polite and the vulgar; for such distinctions do not exist in the wilderness"; more specifically, Martz refers to Taylor's "bold and often unseemly use of common imagery." To appreciate Taylor's subject matter one must understand that he is writing about "a world where the Puritan doctrine of Grace operates to consecrate, within the soul of one of the Elect, every object, every word, every thought that passes through his anguished, grateful, loving mind."

　　The bulk of Taylor's verse belongs to two series of so-called "Preparatory Meditations," each poem citing as text a particular biblical passage. In the second series, no fewer than sixty poems (out of 165) take off from a line in Canticles. I want to look at Meditation 161, where the text is, once again, Canticles 2:3. Meditation 161 actually exists in two versions, dated 1722 (A) and 1723 (B), which, like all the Meditations, use the six-line iambic pentameter stanza (*ababcc*) of George Herbert's long poem, "Church-porch" (1633). Version B is longer than A by eight lines but has six incomplete lines, while version A has one stanza lacking the final couplet. Consider the third and fourth stanzas of 161A:

> Thou art as Apple tree 'mong sons of man
> > As was the Apple tree amonge the trees
> That many are, (the Worlds geese are white swans
> > In its account.) but thou excellest all these
> > Ten thousand times bearing on every limb
> > All golden apples; ripest grace that springs.

> Not like the tree that once in Eden grew
> > Amongst whose fruits the serpent old soon lops
> And in his very teeth the poison threw
> > Into our Mother Eves her sorry Chops.
> > Nor like the Serpents Egge the Squerill held
> > Secur'd itself from th'venom that on it fell.

Understandably dissatisfied with the parenthetical remark in stanza 3, Taylor omitted it from his second version but apparently could think of nothing better, for the third and fourth lines now read: "The world * * * in envy's eyes / But thou these White * * * thou tellst." (The asterisks are Taylor's.) The "Squerill" allusion in stanza 4 is unintelligible without further explication, so Taylor adds a further stanza in his later version:

> Not like the tree that once in Eden grew
> > Out of whose bows th'old serpent drops
> Into our Mother Eve's lap the apple threw
> > The which she quickly mumbled in her Chops.
> > That tree of Life god's Paradise within
> > That healing fruite brings froth to heale 'gainst sin.

> Its better far then was the snakes eges found
> > By the poore squerrell, and did arm itselfe
> Therewith held in its teeth when th'Snake did round
> > Assault it who held them unto this Elfe.
> > She tendered the Eggs held in its mouth strange fate
> > And so repelld away the Rattle Snake.

The image of a squirrel holding a rattlesnake's eggs in its mouth as a defensive measure certainly qualifies as an instance of Martz's "bold and . . . unseemly use of common imagery." (Stanford quotes Taylor's prose version of the anecdote from another manuscript, also in the Yale University Library.) In any case, Taylor's theological point seems to be that a spiritually transformed variety of the very apples that led to the fall can save us (or, at least, those of us who are among the Elect), this being spelled out in the last three stanzas of Meditation 161; the A and B versions differ in detail but not in doctrine, so I quote one stanza from each version:

> Lord shake their bower and let these apples fall
> Into my Wicker basket and it fill.
> Then I shall have rich spirituall food for all
> Occasions as they essences do still
> And I shall feed on their rich grace my fare
> As they drop from thy Apple tree most rare.
>
> Lord serve up in thy Saphire Charger bright
> A service of these golden Apples brave
> Whose sight and sent will fill me with delight
> As they come tumbling * * * Wave,
> My food will Food and Med'cine to mee bee
> Which Grace itselfe cooks up aright for mee.

I might just add that a concordance to Taylor's verse finds some thirty occurrences of "apple" or cognates in at least a dozen poems.

Edenic Apples in Biblical Contexts

We must now turn to another part of the biblical apple story. There are, of course, no identifiable apples in Genesis, only the special tree, whose fruit Adam is forbidden to eat. It seems, though, that as early as the fifth century C.E. some Christian writers had begun to use the Latin words *pomum* (fruit) and *malum* (apple) interchangeably in their accounts of the Fall. (It has been suggested that some Christian Latin writers confused the two meanings of *malum* —"apple" with a long *a,* "evil" with a short *a*—but this is disputed by modern scholars; see Monika Brazda's *Zur Bedeutung des Apfels in der Antiken Kultur* [1997]). There is also a fascinating retelling of the Genesis temptation story (with significant changes) in a fragmentary Old Saxon poem dating from probably the late eighth century and usually called "the Saxon Genesis." According to A. N. Doane, in *The Saxon Genesis* (1991), the poem is "one of the most original and striking vernacular productions of the earlier Middle Ages." In any case, one manuscript of the poem (Bodleian Library, Junius 11), probably written in southern England shortly after 1000 and now called "Genesis B," contains a couple of lines (636–7) that refer to one apple in Eve's hand and another by her heart (for the text and a glossary, see Doane's book). The actual phrase of interest is: "æppel unsælga" (unblessed, or unwholesome, apple).

In the late twelfth century, the apple seems clearly identified as the forbidden fruit in the anonymous Anglo-Norman mystery play about Adam and Eve, *Le Mystère d'Adam,* where one finds the word *pomum* in the Latin stage directions and the word *pome* in the French dialogue. (See *Medieval French Plays* [1971] for an English translation of the play, by Richard Axton and John Stevens.) In this play, as in "the Saxon

Genesis" just mentioned above—but unlike the Bible—Satan first offers the apple to
Adam and, only after he refuses it, to Eve.

In a Latin verse parody of a biblical feast, the so-called Arras *Cena* (Feast), datable
to about 1300, there is, once again, an allusion to the apple of Genesis. The anonymous poem in 160 octosyllabic quatrains—clearly incomplete in the only known manuscript version (written in the city of Arras)—is notable, according to the medieval
scholar Martha Bayless in her *Parody in the Middle Ages* (1996), for the way it "recounts
biblical history as a coherent narrative in which the characters respond rationally to
events and to each other." Something on the order of one hundred leading Old and
New Testament characters sit down to a nuptial feast arranged by King Joel, but "the
virgin" (*uirgo*)—who can be identified with Eve—prematurely "assaults the soup [law]
of the meal." Bayless explains: "When Eve violates the *ius,* the law and the soup, the
pun points up the fact that the first sin was a transgression born of gluttony." It may
be noted, though, that according to a very influential treatment of the cardinal sins—
that of Gregory the Great (d. 604)—*pride* stands at the root of all the other six sins,
including gluttony. After Eve's transgression, the guests must leave the table and work
for their food, corresponding to Adam's sentence to labor by the sweat of his brow.
And, then, when the feast resumes (in stanza 88):

> Primus minister pestifer
> Apponit pomum coluber;
> Adam cum Eua coniuge
> Accelerat comedere.

~

> The first attendant, the deadly serpent, serves an apple; Adam with Eve,
> his wife, makes haste to eat.

Dating from about a century after the Arras *Cena* is a vernacular dramatic trilogy, surviving in a unique manuscript (Bodley 791) and consisting of some 8,600 lines
of stanzaic verse. Usually called *The Cornish Ordinalia,* the first part is devoted to events
of the Old Testament, beginning with Genesis. Written in Middle Cornish, a Celtic
language closely related to Welsh and Breton, the text also contains short passages in
Latin, French, and Middle English. Documentary evidence indicates that the plays
were staged on fixed earthworks, known as "rounds." According to Markham Harris
(who has translated the entire cycle into modern English), "its lengthy roster of speaking parts and procession of scenes quite literally runs the gamut from the ever sublime
to the occasionally ridiculous." Somewhere between the sublime and the ridiculous is
this exchange between Eve and the Serpent in the temptation scene, which elaborates
a bit on Genesis:

EVE

> I'm almost out of my mind, trying to figure what to do about the apple,
> as much as anything because I'm afraid there might be some trick.

SERPENT

Let the risk be mine, then. Go ahead, pluck and have done, and include your husband while you're at it.

EVE

If I'm going to reach the branches, you'll have to bend them toward the ground.

SERPENT

All right, but no more quibbling. Pick a handful and be on your way.

The easy, conversational tone prepares one for the hilarious negotiation, after the expulsion, between Adam and God the Father about how much earth Adam is to be allotted for cultivating his grain: God's initial offer of "a full spade's length" is increased at Adam's insistence to "as much of the world as you desire"!

A perfectly straightforward account of the Edenic apple may be found in the very first piece in Quarles's *Emblemes,* composed on a text from James 1:14—"Every man is tempted, when he is drawn away by his own lust, and enticed"—and taking the form of a dialogue between the Serpent and Eve. The accompanying "emblem" is a small woodcut of Eve and the Serpent (curled around an apple tree). The poem begins:

> *Serp.*　Not eat? not taste? not touch? not cast an eye
> 　　　　Upon the fruit of this fair tree? and why?
> 　　　　Why eat'st thou not what Heav'n ordain'd for food?
> 　　　　Or cans't thou think that bad which Heav'n call'd good?

After almost fifty more lines, Eve is finally persuaded:

> *Eve.*　'Tis but an apple; and it is as good
> 　　　　To do as to desire. Fruit's made for food:
> 　　　　I'll pull, and taste, and tempt my Adam too
> 　　　　To know the secrets of this dainty. *Serp.* Do.

The Edenic apple is, of course, most grandly displayed in Milton's *Paradise Lost* (1667; 2d ed., 1674). It is not until late in the poem (book 9 in the twelve-book second edition) that the apple tree is introduced, and we see it only through the eyes of the Serpent (which are, presumably, the eyes of Satan). Speaking to Eve, the Serpent describes his initial glimpse of the tree:

> Till on a day roving the field, I chanced
> A goodly tree far distant to behold
> Loaden with fruit of fairest colours mixed,
> Ruddy and gold: I nearer drew to gaze;

When from the boughs a savoury odour blown,   *45*
Grateful to appetite, more pleased my sense
Than smell of sweetest fennel, or the teats
Of ewe or goat dropping with milk at even,
Unsucked of lamb or kid, that tend their play.
To satisfy the sharp desire I had
Of tasting those fair apples, I resolved
Not to defer; hunger and thirst at once,
Powerful persuaders, quickend at the scent
Of that alluring fruit, urged me so keen.

The Serpent—who is, after all, speaking with Satan's voice—may not, of course, be telling the truth but we may assume that the smell (of fennel) and the taste (of ewe's or goat's milk) are designed to appeal to Eve, and, of course, they do.

Edenic Apples in Nonbiblical Contexts

In a variety of medieval contexts, apples are, unsurprisingly, associated with sinful desires, even—or perhaps especially—in children. One instance occurs in the popular thirteenth-century compendium of natural history, *De proprietatibus rerum* (On the properties of things), by Bartholomaeus Anglicus. An English translation of the treatise by John Trevisa was completed in 1398/9 but not widely circulated until it was printed around a century later; in book 6, chapter 5 ("On Children"), we find the following remarks: "And they louen an appil more than gold. . . . And wepith more for the losse of an appil thanne fore the losse of theire heritage." Bridget Henisch has cited this passage in her book *The Medieval Calendar Year* (1999) as supporting evidence for her claim that "apples and children were always paired together" in medieval calendar illustrations. (She actually cites only one such illustration, from a sixteenth-century Flemish manuscript, in which a woman is offering a newly picked apple to a young child.)

I want now to look at a few of the ways in which an explicitly Edenic apple functions in nonbiblical literary contexts, and first in a couple of English poems, each of which is in some sense a Christian epic. In his "Letter" appended to the first edition of *The Faerie Queen* (1590–1596), Edmund Spenser (ca. 1552–1599) emphasizes the allegorical and historical (we would say "legendary") character of his work, but he also at one point specifies that the hero of the first book, the Knight of the Redcrosse, is meant to "express Holynesse," and, indeed, at the very beginning of that book we read: "But on his brest a bloudie Crosse he bore, / The deare remembrance of his dying Lord" (1.2.1). Now, book 1 culminates with the Knight of the Redcrosse's slaying of the dragon (standing for Sin and Death, and perhaps also Roman Catholicism), and it is here that Spenser transposes the Tree of Life from the Genesis story into an instrument of the knight's victory. The knight has fallen for the second time but, providentially, he lands in "A trickling streame of Balme" (11.48.2) from the Tree of Life, which has itself been described two cantos earlier (11.46–7):

> There grew a goodly tree him faire beside,
>> Loaden with fruit and apples rosie red,
>> As they in pure vermilion had beene dide,
>> Whereof great vertues over all were red [known]:
>> For happie life to all, which thereon fed,
>> And life eke everlasting did befall:
>> Great God it planted in that blessed sted
>> With his almightie hand, and did it call
> *The tree of life,* the crime of our first fathers fall.

Spenser is being loose in his interpretation of Scripture when he identifies the Tree of Life as an apple tree and as responsible for the fall; what Genesis actually says (3.22) is that Adam and Eve ate fruit from the Tree of the Knowledge of Good and Evil, and this led God to punish them by banishing them from Eden *in order to prevent them from eating fruit from the Tree of Life* (because eating such fruit would have had the unacceptable consequence of conferring immortality on them!). In any case, in the very next stanza, almost as an afterthought, Spenser recalls that "Another like faire tree eke grew thereby / Whereof who so did eat, eftsoones did know / Both good and ill: O mornefull memory: / That tree through one mans fault hath doen us all to dy" (11.47.6–9). This confusion between the two trees, though not uncommon, is rarely as blatant as in this instance. What I find interesting is the way in which Spenser adapts a biblical episode to the plot of his own story.

Though *The Faerie Queen* is one of the longest poems ever written in English, its six books correspond to only half of Spenser's original plan. By contrast, "The Progress of the Soule," or "Metempsychosis" (1601), by John Donne (1572–1631) is just an extended fragment—fifty-two stanzas (or cantos) completed of the "First Song," for a total of 520 lines. In his epistle preceding the poem, Donne explains his subject: the transmigrations of a soul in "all her passages from her first making when she was that apple which Eve eat, to this time when she is he, whose life you shall find in the end of this book." Possible candidates whom Donne is supposed to have considered for the latest reincarnation of the wandering soul were Calvin and Queen Elizabeth—which may help to explain why the work was never completed. What Donne did write was a remarkably lively and fanciful narrative of the embryonic development of mandrakes, sparrows, fish, whales, mice, wolves, apes, and, finally, Themech, the sister and wife of Cain. (Most discussions of Donne's poetry ignore "The Progress of the Soule," but a detailed and appreciative account may be found in John Carey's *John Donne: Life, Mind, and Art* [1990].) Our concern is with an early canto (9) describing the fatal tree, which Donne calls "the forbidden learned tree":

> Prince of the orchard, fair as dawning morn,
> Fenced with the law, and ripe as soon as born
> That apple grew, which this soul did enlive,

Till the then climbing serpent, that now creeps
For that offence, for which all mankind weeps,
Took it, and to her whom the first man did wive
(Whom and her race, only forbiddings drive)
He gave it, she to her husband, both did eat;
So perished the eaters, and the meat:
And we (for treason taints the blood) thence die and sweat.

It may be noted that Donne was eighteen years old at the time of the first publication of *The Faerie Queen,* whose chauvinistic English sentiments and anti-Catholicism he would presumably have found abhorrent. (Donne's family was Roman Catholic and his younger brother had died, in 1593, while in prison for his religious beliefs. It was not until 1615 that Donne took Anglican orders.) But surely Donne must have been familiar with Spenser's impressive and popular poem and perhaps "The Progress of the Soule" was his riposte. After all, for his own version of a Christian epic (or anti-epic) Donne invented a variant of the Spenserian stanza: *aabccbbddd,* instead of *ababbcbcc,* in each case with a hexameter (or Alexandrine) as the last line.

Another instance of confusing or conflating the two special trees of Genesis occurs in a version of the Adam and Eve story by the Marrano, Antonio Enríquez Gómez (ca. 1600–1663), who left Spain for France in midcareer for fear of being persecuted for judaizing. Among his writings published in Rouen was "The Sin of the First Pilgrim" (1644), the first part of which consists of a dialogue between Adam and Eve. According to his editor and translator, Timothy Oelman, the poem is most notable for its "use of biblical sources—Job, Ecclesiastes, and Song of Songs—in a manner which by its literalness appears to pay homage to the very language of the source and which breathes new life into the poetic conventions of the Golden Age." Here is part of the passage in which Adam explains to Eve about the apple (*manzana*) growing on "the tree of life" (*el árbol de la vida*):

> Although it appears fair to you,
> this apple of a pallid hue,
> it contains a worm within it
> which toils to make a grave for you.
> If we do not ever touch
> its skin which shines aglow with rouge
> we shall live on eternally
> in this forest hallowed of God.

> ~

> Aunque le ves hermoso,
> su pálida manzana
> tiene un gusano dentro
> que tu sepulcro labra.

Si no tocamos nunca
su tez arrebolada,
viviremos eternos
en esta selva sacra.

Oelman notes that *pálida* can mean "yellowish" as well as "pale," thereby suggesting a yellow fruit. The other color word, however, definitely makes the fruit red, since *arrebolada* means "rouged," "suggesting a woman's face, made up to be superficially attractive." Also worth noting is how a worm stands in for the serpent. This worm-in-apple motif recurs with some frequency, as we shall see, in secular contexts.

Robert Graves (1895–1985) thought, and wrote, a lot about Edenic and many other varieties of mythical apples; his contexts included the biblical but were much broader. I cite him here not for what he thought he was providing—some sort of key to world mythology—but rather for the constructive power of his own personal poetic imagination. Here, to begin with, is an excerpt from his introduction to *The Greek Myths* (1955):

> The so-called Judgement of Paris, where a hero is called upon to decide between the rival charms of three goddesses and awards his apple to the fairest, records an ancient ritual situation, outgrown by the time of Homer and Hesiod. These three goddesses are one goddess in triad: Athene the maiden, Aphrodite the nymph, and Hera the crone—and Aphrodite is presenting Paris with the apple, rather than receiving it from him. This apple, symbolizing her love bought at the price of his life, will be Paris's passport to the Elysian Fields, the apple orchards of the west, to which only the souls of heroes are admitted. A similar gift is frequently made in Irish and Welsh myth; as well as by the three Hesperides, to Heracles; and by Eve, "the Mother of All Living," to Adam.

Graves has discovered—or invented—a connection between biblical and Greek myth; in the following passage from *The White Goddess* (1966), he does the same for biblical and Irish myth:

> In the Cuchulain version of the [Samson] story, Blodeuwedd is named Blathnat and extracts from her husband King Curoi—the only man who ever gave Cuchulain a beating—the secret that his soul is hidden in an apple in the stomach of a salmon which appears once every seven years in a spring on the side of Slieve Mis (the mountain of Amergin's dolmen). This apple can be cut only with his own sword. Her lover Cuchulain waits for seven years and obtains the apple. Blathnat then prepares a bath and ties her husband's long hair to the bedposts and bedrail; takes his sword and gives it to her lover who cuts the apple in two. The husband loses his strength and cries out: "No secret to a woman, no jewel to slaves!" Cuchulain cuts off his head.

Finally, here is the poem "Apple Island" (1975), by Graves himself, proclaiming—or inventing—a synthesis of apple myths:

> Though cruel seas like mountains fill the bay,
> Wrecking the quayside huts,
> Salting our vineyards with tall showers of spray;
>
> And though the moon shines dangerously clear,
> Fixed in another cycle
> Than the sun's progress round the felloe'd year;
>
> And though I may not hope to dwell apart
> With you on Apple Island
> Unless my breast be docile to the dart—
>
> Why should I fear your element, the sea,
> Or the full moon, your mirror,
> Or the halved apple from your holy tree?

Edenic Apples in Art

Early medieval artists, with rare exceptions, had little concern for exact representations of flora or fauna, but what look like stages in the visual evolution of the forbidden fruit may be reflected in the following sequence of medieval illuminations, all tempera on parchment (the first two are Spanish, the others English, French, and Flemish). We begin with a superb—but highly unrealistic—rendition of the Fall of Adam and Eve by a late-tenth-century Spanish artist (Escorial Beatus, fol. 18, 13¼ x 8⅞ in.), where the forbidden fruit are red and three-lobed. (For a reproduction, see John Williams's *Early Spanish Manuscript Illumination* [1977] or the exhibition catalogue *The Art of Medieval Spain* [1993].) By circa 1175, in a Spanish illuminated Bible (whose artistic style has been likened to that of the English Winchester school), now in the Provincial Library of Burgos (MS. 846, fol. 12v, 20½ x 14 in), the forbidden fruit has become a tiny colorless disc in Eve's hand, while the tree under which she and Adam stand seems to have no recognizable fruit at all hanging from its highly stylized branches. (For a reproduction, see *The Art of Medieval Spain*.)

Our third example is the Paris Psalter, circa 1250, now in the Bibliothèque Nationale (MS. lat. 10434, fol. 10, 15¼ x 12 in.), where the forbidden fruit are tiny red discs in the hands of Adam, Eve, and the Serpent, with, however, none growing on the forbidden tree. (For a reproduction, see Jean Porcher's *French Miniatures* [1960].) Next, there is a French book of Old Testament miniatures, circa 1250, now in the Morgan Library (MS M.638, fol.1v, 15¼ x 12 in.), where the forbidden fruit in the hands of Adam and Eve and hanging on the forbidden tree are discs colored pale red, dark red, and green. (See plate 1.) The miniatures are discussed in Sydney C. Cockerell's *Old Testament Miniatures* (1975).

From early in the fourteenth century comes a superb though fragmentary English manuscript, now in the British Library (MS Arundel 83 II), the Psalter of Robert de Lisle (1288–1344), one of whose folios (128v, 13 ¼ x 9 in.) represents the so-called Tree of Vices. The "tree" is highly schematic and "the vices hang down like fruit clusters from the seven sinuously curving branches of the symmetrical tree," in the words of Lucy Freeman Sandler. The three branches on the left represent avarice, anger, and gluttony (with many subsidiary vices) and the three on the right represent envy, vanity, and sloth (with many subsidiary vices), while the trunk extends from pride at the base up to lust at the top. At the base stand Adam, about to eat an apple, and Eve, grasping an apple in the mouth of the serpent curled about the trunk. Two more apples hang on branches just above Adam and Eve. Adam's apple is colorless, the other three are bright red (the same red that appears on the tri-lobed leaves throughout the tree). Also, the apples are not mere discs—they are clearly furnished with stems and tips. (See plate 2.) The entire manuscript has been published, with illustrations, in Sandler's *Psalter of Robert de Lisle* (1983).

Perhaps a century later, we find a depiction of the Garden of Eden and the expulsion from Paradise by the Flemish artists Paul, Herman, and Jean Limbourg (all d. after 1416) in *Très Riches Heures* of Jean, Duke of Berry, dating from 1413–1416 (MS 65, Musée Condé, Chantilly, 11 ½ x 8 ¼ in.), where the apples are gilded discs with traces of three-dimensional modeling. (For a reproduction, see Jean Longnon and Raymond Cazelles, *The* Très Riches Heures *of Jean, Duke of Berry* [1969].) Contemporary with the Limbourgs' work, there is the magnificent Adam and Eve, circa 1415, by the Boucicaut Master, in an illuminated manuscript of a French translation of a work by Boccaccio (1313–1375), *De cas de nobles hommes et femmes* (MS 63, 16 ¾ x 11 ⁹⁄₁₆ in., Getty Museum, Los Angeles), in which both the apple held by Eve and the apples on the forbidden tree are reasonably realistic. (See plate 3.) For an essay on the manuscript by Thomas Kren, see *Apollo* (Sept. 1996).

It should be noted that the paintings in the above sequence, with the exception of the first two, are from northern Europe. A fuller study of medieval representations of the forbidden fruit would, of course, have to look at other regions and at other media, such as stained glass or wooden panel paintings. Thus, in a window from the southern side aisle of the nave in Chartres Cathedral (ca. 1205–1215) one or two tiny red discs may be observed in the green foliage of the forbidden tree, while in a painting of the Fall from the ceiling of the monastery of St. Michael's in Hildesheim, Adam and Eve each hold a small white disc containing a colored core and are framed by a red circular background decorated with scores of similar discs (tempera on oak panel from a Lower Saxon workshop, ca. 1240). (Reproductions of these two pictures may be found in a volume edited by Ingo Walther, *Painting of the Gothic Era* [1999]).

It may be instructive to examine some paintings of the forbidden fruit from Italy, and first from that greatest shrine of early Renaissance Italian painting, the Brancacci Chapel in Florence. Here we find in Masolino's representation from the 1420s of *The*

Temptation of Adam and Eve (fresco, 82 x 34 ½ in.) a tree "whose leaves are those of a fig," according to Andrew Ladis's study (*The Brancacci Chapel, Florence* [1993]). Ladis does not commit himself as to the identity of the fruit on the tree, which in reproduction, at least, look too red, too spherical, and too big to be figs (see the illustration in Ladis's book). On the other hand, the fruit in Eve's right hand is brown, nonspherical, and about the size of a fig. And, indeed, Perri Lee Roberts's monograph on Masolino (1993) says that "Eve is shown holding the fruit of temptation (a fig)." Later, in chapter 2, "Figs," we shall identify an Eastern Christian tradition in which the forbidden fruit is the fig. Was Masolino simply playing it safe by including both apple and fig in the same picture? In any case, almost a century later we find what looks like that same fig in the hand of Eve in a painting by Raphael, *Adam and Eve on the Brink of Disobedience* (ca. 1508–9). Including Raphael's first female nude since his *Three Graces,* this painting is on the ceiling of the Stanza della Segnatura of the Vatican Palace in Rome—a small element in the vast decorative scheme of ceiling and walls, which is one of the defining works of the High Renaissance in Italy. In his monograph *Raphael: The Stanza della Segnatura* (1993)—which is well illustrated with many details of the frescoes—James Beck writes that "Eve holds a tiny fig, which is interpreted here as the fruit, rather than the apple, which caused the first children's disobedience."

The iconography of the fig as the forbidden fruit has been transmitted down the centuries at least in part through the medium of reproductive prints, as in engravings of Raphael's *Adam and Eve on the Brink of Disobedience,* by Nicolas Bocquet (late 17th cent.) and Joseph-Théodore Richomme (1784–1849). Both artists worked in Paris, and their respective engravings (1690–1, 12 x 10 ½ in.; 1814, 15 x 12 in.) were included in an exhibition, in Nice, of prints from the Bibliothèque Nationale (see *Adam et Eve de Dürer à Chagall* [1992]).

It seems that it took visual representations by late fifteenth and early sixteenth century northern European artists—especially Hugo van der Goes (1420?-1482), Albrecht Dürer (1471–1528), Lucas Cranach the Elder (1472–1553), and Hans Baldung Grien (1484–1545)—possibly introducing the apple as simply the most familiar fruit they knew—to make the apple forever after an indispensable part of the iconography of the Fall. Cranach, for example, painted, between 1526 and 1537, nine—and possibly as many as seventeen—representations of Adam and Eve containing easily recognized apples, according to the Friedländer-Rosenberg catalogue of Cranach's paintings.

There is an extraordinary painting by Baldung Grien, *Eve, the Serpent, and Death* (ca. 1510–1512), in the National Gallery of Canada, which contains two apples, one held coyly behind her back by Eve and one held triumphantly aloft by Death—unless this latter apple is being picked, in which case the figure of Death may be doubling as Adam. (See plate 4.) This small oil on wood panel (2 x 1 ft.) is also notable for its replacement of the traditional skeletal figure of death by a realistically rendered corpse with peeling and rotting flesh, and for its replacement of Eve's traditional fig leaf by a forthright depiction of her pubic hair. This last detail supports Robert Koch's comment that "the image barely qualifies as a *memento mori,* a pious exhortation to think of death; it becomes instead a profane exhortation, in the spirit of classical antiquity and the new thinking of the Renaissance in Italy, to make the most of youth."

The opposite relation between Eve's apple and the Classical tradition may be observed in another small oil on wood panel (2.75 x 2.1 ft.) in the National Gallery in London. (See plate 5.) Painted by Lucas Cranach the Elder sometime in the 1530s, this *Cupid Complaining to Venus* gratuitously adds an apple tree to a purely Classical tale (the nineteenth idyll of Theocritus); the result, as Alistair Smith puts it, is that Cranach "complicates his subject-matter, subtly introducing suggestions of original sin—his Venus poses beneath an apple-tree like a menacingly erotic Eve." And indeed this same Venus figure occurs as Eve in Cranach's panel painting of Adam and Eve (1526) in the Courtauld Collection in London (for a reproduction, see the catalogue of *The Courtauld Institute Galleries* [1990]); though their poses are somewhat different, each figure grasps an overhanging branch of the apple tree with an identical gesture of her left hand. In all of these paintings (as in many others) the Classical and biblical traditions may be vividly experienced in creative interaction.

Now, three asides. First, painted representations of the Edenic apple were not restricted to wood panel and canvas but included, for example, paintings on ceramics. Thus, a traditional image of the Fall (a human-headed serpent coiled around an apple tree flanked by Adam and Eve) may be found on ceramic pieces from the Italian Renaissance, such as a dish (1500–1510) from the great center of majolica production at Siena, now in the Hermitage, St. Petersburg; and a bowl (ca. 1535) from a minor center of majolica production at Rimini, now in the Louvre, Paris. (For color reproductions of the two images, see, respectively, Mikhailova and Lapkovskaya's *Italian Majolica, Fifteenth to Eighteenth Centuries* [1976], and Liverani's *Five Centuries of Italian Majolica* [1960].)

Second, representations of the Edenic apple were not restricted to painting. Consider, for example, three thirteenth-century painted wooden sculptures of the Virgin and Child (each somewhat less than three feet in height) in the National Museum of the Art of Catalonia, in Barcelona. In all three, Mary is holding a sphere in her right hand; one of the spheres is gilded, the other two possess traces of red paint. The Museum's *Romanesque Art Guide* (1998)—which includes pictures of two of the sculptures—says that the spheres may represent Edenic apples or "a symbol of power." Also from the thirteenth century is a superb French Virgin and Child (ivory with traces of polychromy and gilding, 7½ in. high), in which the Child is holding a sphere in his left hand. The work is now in the Metropolitan Museum of Art, New York (see the Museum publication, *Recent Acquisitions: A Selection, 1998–1999* [1999]).

Consider next representations of Adam holding an apple by two exactly contemporary artists, one from Germany and one from Venice: Tilman Riemenschneider's (ca. 1460–1531) Adam is a brilliantly executed miniature sculpture (ca. 1495–1505) of pearwood (9½ in. high) now in the Kunsthistorisches Museum in Vienna, while

Tullio Lombardo's (ca. 1455–1532) *Adam* is an equally brilliantly executed over-life-
size sculpture (ca. 1490–95) of marble (77 in. high) now in the Metropolitan Museum
of Art. Next, I cite two sculptures from the seventeenth century. The first is a small
bronze statuette (h. 9 in.) of Adam and Eve (ca. 1620) that has been attributed to
Nicolò Roccatagliata (active 1593–1636), a Genoan who was trained in Venice. That
the scene depicted is the expulsion from Paradise is clear from the pose and expression
of each of the two figures: Adam is wringing his hands with a pained, despairing look
on his face; Eve looks sadly down at the apple in her right hand, while her left arm
embraces Adam as she leans her head on his shoulder. Finally, in the Morgan Collection
of the Wadsworth Atheneum, Hartford, there is an anonymous German-Austrian
mid-seventeenth-century ivory relief sculpture of *The Fall of Man* (12 $^{11}/_{16}$ x 6 $^{3}/_{4}$ in.), in
which Eve holds an apple in each hand. (For pictures of the four works, see *Tilman
Riemenschneider: Master Sculptor of the Late Middle Ages* [1999], *Italian Renaissance Sculpture*
[1985], by John Pope-Hennessy, *Renaissance Master Bronzes* [1986], by Manfred Leithe-
Jasper, and *J. Pierpont Morgan, Collector* [1987], by Linda Horvitz Roth).

Rainer Maria Rilke (1875–1926) wrote a pair of sonnets (1908) about the statues
of Adam and Eve on the main facade of Notre-Dame de Paris; here are the opening
lines of "Eva" (in German and in M. D. Herter Norton's translation), containing the
marvelous word-coinage "Apfelpose" (apple-pose):

> Einfach steht sie an der Kathedrale
> grossem Aufstieg, nah der Fensterrose,
> mit dem Apfel in der Apfelpose,
> schuldlos-schuldig ein für alle Male

> ~

> Simply she stands on the cathedral's
> great ascent, close to the rose window,
> with the apple in the apple-pose,
> guiltless-guilty once and for all

My third aside concerns William Blake (1757–1827), who characteristically
reverts to an early-medieval representation of apples as flat, nondescript, vaguely pinkish
ovals in his pen and watercolor illustrations for Milton's *Paradise Lost*. Blake actually
made two series of these illustrations, one approximately 10 x 8 in. in size, dating from
1807 (now in the Huntington collection, in San Marino, California), and one approximately twice as large, dating from 1808 (now in the Boston Museum of Fine Arts);
both sets include *Raphael Warns Adam and Eve* and *The Temptation and Fall of Eve*. Plate
6 reproduces the former subject from the Huntington collection. In the picture, the
centrally placed bowl of fruit reflects the fruitarian meal that Milton has Eve prepare
for Raphael (to be discussed in chapter 21, "Fruit, Conjoined and Disjoined"). Robert
Essick, in his catalogue *William Blake at the Huntington* (1994), even describes the fruit
on the tree as "figlike," though, of course, Milton specifies apples.

New motifs involving the Edenic apple were introduced by post-Renaissance painters. Thus, Rubens painted an Immaculate Conception of the Virgin (now in the Prado) for a Spanish patron while he was on a diplomatic mission to Madrid in 1628–89. The Virgin is standing on the moon but at the same time trampling underfoot a snake whose jaws are holding by its stem a rotting apple. To understand this imagery one must first realize that the belief that Mary had been miraculously conceived without sin was highly controversial in the Catholic Church during the seventeenth century (and indeed remained controversial throughout the next two centuries, with the Thomists opposing and the Franciscans supporting the belief, until the dogma of the Immaculate Conception was finally proclaimed by Pope Pius IX in 1854). In the seventeenth century, the Immaculate Conception was most popular in Spain, where both church and royal family were deeply committed to the belief. The image of Mary standing on the moon was derived from an account, in Revelation 12:1, of "a woman clothed with the sun, with the moon under her feet, and on her head a crown of twelve stars." Also, in Spain, it was customary in pictures of the Immaculate Conception to depict Mary without her child. What, though, of the snake and the apple? Here, the reference is to Mary as the new Eve, shown triumphant over the snake of Eden.

One of the most splendid paintings of the Immaculate Conception is by Giambattista Tiepolo (1696–1770), dating to 1734–5 and now in Vicenza. (For a reproduction, see the catalogue, *The Glory of Venice: Art in the Eighteenth Century* [1994].) The apple in this painting looks fresh and inviting, but while it is provided with a leafy stem, the snake grasps the apple in its mouth rather than by the stem. (There is another, very similar—but, I think, inferior—painting by Tiepolo in the Prado.) Not all Spanish representations of the image of Mary Immaculate included the snake and apple, which are, for example, omitted in the six versions of the subject (dating from the 1630s to the 1660s) included in the 1987–88 Francisco de Zurbarán (1598-1664) retrospective in New York and Paris (see the catalogue of the exhibition, *Zurbarán,* ed. Jeannine Baticle [1987]). In other religious paintings, the symbolic snake and apple may occur detached from one another, as in *Allegory of the Faith* (1670–72) by Johannes Vermeer (1632–1675). The setting includes a painting of the Crucifixion in the background and an altar on which rest a crucifix, a Bible, and a chalice (a reminder perhaps of the sort of clandestine chapel to which Dutch Catholics had to resort, public worship being outlawed; Vermeer, of course, was himself a Catholic convert). The central figure is a fashionably dressed woman (representing the Catholic faith) with her right foot resting on a terrestrial globe. On the marble floor in the foreground is a snake being crushed by Christ, in the guise of, literally, a cornerstone of the Church. As if it had just rolled onto the scene, an inconspicuous and apparently intact apple is resting on the floor at some distance from the bloody snake. So different in subject matter from most of Vermeer's paintings, this late work has been underrated by modern critics, according to Walter Liedtke, who provides a detailed account and an excellent reproduction of the painting in the exhibition catalogue he edited, *Vermeer and the Delft School* (2001).

Edenic Apples Allegorized

If the artists and the poets have reached a consensus on the apple as the key allegorical fruit of Eden, they have, of course, never achieved any consensus on the precise meaning of the allegory. This is illustrated by an anthology of poems in English inspired by the Bible: *Chapters into Verse* (1993), in two volumes, edited by Robert Atwan and Laurance Wieder. Somewhat disappointingly for my purposes, although there are over two dozen poems about Eden, only four—by Milton, Abraham Cowley (1618–1667), Keats (1795–1821), and Philip Booth (b. 1925)—actually mention apples. The apple in Milton's *Paradise Lost* has already been discussed and the apples in Keats's ode "To Autumn" will be discussed below. The other two poems provide some captivating novelties. Abraham Cowley's "The Tree of Knowledge" (1656) begins with a characteristic metaphysical conceit: the tree of knowledge identified with "Porphyry's tree" of logic (as illustrated, for example, when the term "man" is defined by the sequence substance-living-animal-biped-rational), named after a neo-Platonist philosopher of the third century C.E.:

> The sacred *Tree* midst the fair *Orchard* grew;
> The *Phœnix Truth* did on it rest,
> And built his perfum'd Nest.
> That right *Porphyrian Tree* which did true *Logick* shew,
> Each *Leaf* did learned *Notions* give,
> And th' *Apples* were *Demonstrative.*
> So clear their *Colour* and divine,
> The very *shade* they cast did other *Lights* out-shine.

This promising start is followed, however, by a pedestrian, though occasionally witty, exposition of orthodox Christian sentiments—including the inferiority of women ("and she / Who tempted him to this, grew yet more blind than he")—quite unrelated to the initial conceit. We must be grateful, though, for the splendid line "And th' apples were demonstrative."

Philip Booth's "Original Sequence" (1957) also has a single conceit running through it: the apple eaten by Eve and Adam represents temporality, that is, clock time as opposed to eternity: "Time was the apple Adam ate. / Eve bit, gave seconds to his mouth." The secondary meaning of "seconds" (secondhand goods) works beautifully. During the rest of the poem the consequences of temporality are represented by the bruising and decaying of apples:

> Hands behind him, walking
> to and fro, he counted how
> the fruit fell, bruised on frozen sod.

This was his orchard, his to pace;
the day was cool, and he was God.

Old Adam heard him humming, talking
to himself: *Winesap, King,*

ripen in sun,

McIntosh and

Northern Spy

fall one by one,

ripen to die.

There is, by the way, no single apple variety called "King"; Morgan and Richards, *Book of Apples,* list at least ten different "Kings."

"A Symposium: Apples," a delightful variant on the Edenic apple theme by Linda Pastan (b. 1932), first published in her volume *Aspects of Eve* (1975), is in what might be called the *domestic* mode, with allusions to aprons, lunchpails, and iceboxes; it must be quoted in full to be appreciated:

Eve   Remember a season
of apples, the orchard
full of them, my apron
full of them. One day
we wandered from tree
to tree, sharing a basket
feeling the weight of apples
increase between us.
And how your muscles ripened
with all that lifting.
I felt them round and hard
under my teeth; white
and sweet the flesh
of men and apples.

Gabriel   Nameless in Eden,
the apple itself
was innocent—an ordinary
lunchpail fruit.
Still it reddened
for the way it was used.
Afterward the apple
chose for itself
names untrusting
on the tongue: stayman

>   gravenstein,
>   northern spy.
>
> *The Serpent*   Ordinary, innocent
>   yes. But deep
>   in each center of whiteness
>   one dark star. . .
>
> *Adam*   In the icebox
>   an apple
>   will keep
>   for weeks.
>   Then its skin
>   wrinkles up
>   like the skin of the old man
>   I have become,
>   from a single
>   bite.

Pastan has subsequently written many more poems about Eve and the apple in Paradise, culminating in a sequence of eleven poems called "The Imperfect Paradise," in a volume of the same title (1988). (It should be noted that three of these poems are omitted from Paston's selected poems, *Carnival Evening*.) The apple motifs in this sequence range from stockpiled apples in barns ("Fruit of the Tree") to an apple in the mouth of a suckling pig ("The Animals"), and the forms range from free verse to sonnets. "On the Question of Free Will" is the shortest of these paradisical apple poems:

> Sometimes,
> noticing the skeleton
> embossed
> on every leaf
>
> and how
> the lion's mouth
> and antelope's neck
> fit perfectly,
>
> I wonder
> at God's plan
> had Eve refused
> the apple.

Resembling Pastan's sequence "The Imperfect Paradise" is the sequence "Paradise Illustrated" (1978), by English poet D. J. Enright (b. 1920), consisting of thirty-four poems, the tone and technique of which are well illustrated by this one (the eleventh) involving apples:

> Eve chomped at the apple
> (Her teeth were white and strong:
> There was no such thing as decay).
> The juice ran down her chin.
>
> She ate it all
> (There was no worm at the core:
> There was no core).
> The juice ran down her breasts.
>
> "I have done something original,"
> She told herself.
> "But I mustn't be selfish."
> She plucked a second for Adam.

A later and much darker poem about the apple of Paradise is "In a Corner" (1991):

> Hunched in a corner of the garden, behind an innocent tree, the two of
> them tickling the back of their throats with blades of grass. Both of
> them bent over, side by side, retching, heaving, hoping, despairing. It is
> the eleventh hour, they must clear themselves of the deed. Coughing,
> spluttering, hiccuping. Trying to disgorge their last meal, trying to spew
> up the apple.

An updated approach to the Genesis story is "In the Orchard" (1976), by Robert Friend (1913–1989). The setting is an apple orchard in Cambridge, where the narrator is drinking tea with a woman friend. No "master" of the languages of love, he is nevertheless pulled up short:

> Master or not, was she not signaling?
> And was I not interpreting her eyes?
> For suddenly I felt it like a sting:
>   Why, this was Paradise!
>
> and almost dropped my cup. Something was slithering.
> Well, here was one man it could not deceive.
> I laughed—as if I hadn't heard a thing.
> And she laughed back—as if her name were Eve.

Jorie Graham (b. 1950), on the other hand, in her "Self-portrait as the Gesture between Them [Adam and Eve]" (1987), sees Eve not as a temptress but as engaged in a metaphysical leap for freedom: "So it was to have freedom she did it." Her interest, however, is in the pressure behind the gesture, which is described in terms of the growth of the fruit on the apple tree:

12
as the apple builds inside the limb, as rain builds
in the atmosphere, as the lateness accumulates until it finally
is,
as the meaning of the story builds,

Graham then describes the delicate equilibrium between Eve and Adam—she the "question," he the "answer"—and Eve's feeling of empowered satisfaction with the very "error" of her ways:

24
the balance like an apple held up into the sunlight

25
then taken down, the air changing by its passage, the feeling of being capable,

26
of being not quite right for the place, not quite the thing that's needed,

27
the feeling of being a digression not the link in the argument,
a new direction, an offshoot, the limb going on elsewhere,

28
and liking that error, a feeling of being capable *because* an error

A similar attempt to construe Eve's consumption of the apple as something predominantly, if not wholly, positive, at least for women, may be found in a poem by a Spanish poet: "Impertinent Exhortation to My Sister Poetesses" (1950), by Angela Figuera (1902–1984). Eve does not appear until the last four of the forty-three lines (translated by John Wilcox):

Eve wanted the fruit to bite it. So bite it.
And sing the fate of her long,
painful and glorious lineage. Because, girls, that's what life's about:
everything that frightens and dumbfounds you.

~

Eva quiso morder en la fruta. Mordedla.
Y cantad el destino de su largo linaje

dolorido y glorioso. Porque, amigas, la vida
es así: todo eso que os aturde y asusta.

The phrase "porque, amigas" in the penultimate line echoes a phrase in the challenging admonition at the beginning: "For, friends, your problem is that you live life / as if you were paying it a courtesy call," emitting "little rhymed sighs, like silly birds."

A more irreverent allusion to the Adam and Eve story is that by another Spanish poet, Gloria Fuertes (b. 1918), in her "Another Version" (Otra version, 1981; translated by Wilcox):

> In the beginning.
> It was the age of paradise.
>
> They played in the vales,
> climbed the cliffs,
>
> and all was possible,
> all allowed.
>
> And Adam became [Adam's] apple
> and Eve was converted to Catholicism.

~

> Al principio.
> Era la era del paraíso.
>
> Jugaban por los valles
> trepaban por los riscos,
>
> y todo era posible,
> y todo permitido.
>
> Y Adán se convirtió en manzana
> y Eva se convirtió al catolicismo.

One may wonder whether either Figuera or Fuertes knew the brief poem about Adam and Eve by Federico García Lorca (1898–1936), "Initium" (A beginning), which, though written during the period 1921–23 was not published until 1983 in the posthumous *Suites*. García Lorca's poem is a good example, as Christopher Maurer expresses it, of the "new era . . . in Spanish poetry: the poets of the Hispanic world had discovered the short poem (*cante jondo* lyrics, and, more important, haiku) and, like the English and American Imagists, the central importance of metaphor." In Jerome Rothenberg's translation:

Adam & Eve.   *61*
The serpent cracked
the mirror
in a thousand pieces,
& the apple
was his rock.

Rhina P. Espaillat (b. 1932) is more sanguine than some of our other poets about the first couple's departure from Eden, which she sees as their only hope of warding off boredom. Born in the Dominican Republic, Espaillat came to the United States in 1939 and now writes chiefly in English; her sonnet "If You Ask Me" (1998) concerns the Fall:

"If you ask me," said the snake, "this couple's doomed:
they started naked, not a thing to need,
a thing to wonder at, since orders boomed
over the speaker. Every day they weed
a little, see what's ripe and pluck it off,
eat this, no don't eat that. Now I'm not blind:
I see her fidget with her hair and cough
that nervous cough; she's bored out of her mind.
I see him gawk at birds and flap in vain;
then his blank eyes cloud over with the sky
and circle his estate, so green, so plain.
She's ripe to risk herself; they need to die;
unbanished, he's an ornament, a brute.
We're neighbors; I'll go visiting, with fruit."

For another contemporary American poet, Maurya Simon, the original sin of Adam and Eve was greed, ingeniously figured by the punctuation mark indicating possession, in "Claiming the Apostrophe" (which is the ninth and penultimate poem in a sequence entitled "A History of Punctuation" [1999]). The first two (out of five) stanzas—which happen to be the stanzas featuring the paradisiacal apple—are fresh and unpredictable:

Was it the keen Serpent who first saw how
Possessiveness could snare people's hearts,
Making their fingers close like vises around
A perfect apple, or their lovers' wrists?

No, it was Eve, I think, who first witnessed
How loss gives rise to greed—who saw that
The fruit she offered Adam bore her mouth's
Perfect teeth marks, a cage of apostrophes.

Unfortunately, the speaker's very next assertion—"We all know the story"—turns out to be only too accurate, as we hear, predictably, about "Eve's birth pains, Adam's lost Eden, Abel's heart; / Cain's knife—and all bearing God's thumbprint." Lots of apostrophes but nothing very demanding, either intellectually or emotionally.

In a rowdy poetic variant on the Fall theme, "Apple Tragedy" (1971), by Ted Hughes, we find the serpent resting on the seventh day and God a kind of cosmic jokester, who produces intoxicating cider by simply squeezing an apple, and then manages to get all three of the other participants in the drama dead drunk! A similarly rowdy rendition of the serpent—with a watering can held in its tail—is to be found in a lithograph, *Greenfinger* (1973), by the English artist, Ronald Searle (b. 1920), where the biblical tale is reduced to just a gardener-serpent and a single tree bearing copious bunches of colorful fruit of many kinds. (See plate 7.)

Apples and cider function very differently in Keats's ode, "To Autumn" (1820). The personified season in the poem lacks God's magic touch and the cider in the poem presumably remains unfermented and unintoxicating. Also, unlike the supremely active God of Genesis and of Hughes's poem, Keats's Autumn simply watches passively as the cider-press oozes apple juice. Helen Vendler explains why apples must replace grapes in Keats's representation of the harvest: following Milton, Keats with his "characteristic sobriety . . . refuses Venus and Bacchus as progenitors of mirth." It is not entirely clear, however, why unfermented grape juice would not do for Keats, unless it is the fact that fermented apple juice generally has a lower alcoholic content (2 to 7 percent) than fermented grape juice (6 to 12 percent), as reported by John Ehle in his *Cheeses and Wines of England and France* (1972); I should add that literary episodes involving cider will be discussed later in this chapter.

The view of a sober Keats has been challenged by Anya Taylor, who couples Keats with Coleridge in their attitudes toward drinking (though, of course, they only met once and never drank together); she writes: "Of possible pleasures Coleridge and Keats most consistently chose drink. Both appreciated tavern life and tavern songs and thought of themselves as participating in an old English tradition" (1994). In chapter 13, "Wine," we will return to Keats and some of his friends.

Not only Autumn—apostrophized but never named—but the full round of the seasons is contained in Keats's ode: Summer is named in stanza 1, Spring in stanza 3, and approaching Winter makes its menacing presence felt offstage in stanza 4. Whatever redemption there can be from the inevitable darkness of the "soft-dying day," whatever recovery from the irretrievable loss of the harvest's bounty, must come from within the natural processes of the seasonal cycle, perhaps through some form of human art (agriculture, music, poetry itself); there is no scope for anything transcending the natural realm (such as intervention by a supernatural divinity). And when Keats does choose to write about the traditional Edenic apple it is, significantly, in the rollickingly lighthearted style of the poem he enclosed in a letter to his friend, J. H.

Reynolds, of 31 January 1818; the third and last of the five stanzas playfully invoke the apple:

> O sigh not so! O sigh not so!
>   For it sounds of Eve's sweet pippin;
> By those loosen'd hips, you have tasted the pips,
>   And fought in an amorous nipping.
>   [. . . . .]
> There's a sigh for yes, and a sigh for no,
>   And a sigh for I can't bear it!
> O what can be done? Shall we stay or run?
>   O cut the sweet apple and share it!

With the last line of the poem we are back in the world of Plato's epigram.

An equally playful representation of the Edenic apple theme may be found in Emily Schlesinger's acrostic, "An Allegory" (1981), based on *A* as the obligatory first letter of each word; here is the first paragraph:

> Adam and alert associate, agreeably accommodated, aptly achieved accord and amiability—ample ambrosias available, and arbors alone adequate against ambient airs. Ah, auspicious artlessness! Adversity and affliction attacked appallingly, as avowed antagonists, Adonai, almighty Author, announced, and Apollyon, archangel-adder, asserted. "Avoid apples and abide amid abundance," admonished Adonai. "Admire apples and acquire acumen," advised Apollyon. Alas! Apollyon attained ascendancy. Ancestor Adam's attractive associate ate, arch and alluring against an antinomian apple-tree. Adam ate also, amoral although aware. Abruptly, arteries and arterioles achingly awash, an ashamed and amorous Adam advanced and *****.

The second (and concluding) paragraph contains this sentence: "Adam, antique addlepate, accumulated arguments, and afterward appraised adders as abominations, apples as aphrodisiacs, and ardor as artful ambush."

A poetic exercise of another kind is Anne Sexton's poem about Adam and Eve in her *The Death Notebooks* (1974), "Rats Live On No Evil Star." The epigraph following the title explains that it was "A palindrome seen on the side of a barn in Ireland," and the challenge must have been to retell the story of Adam and Eve in such a way as to incorporate the rats and the star. This is attempted only in the second half of the forty-nine line poem. First, though, "Eve came out of that rib like an angry bird," while "Adam sat like a lawyer / and read the book of life." Then the apple appears:

> Only later did Adam and Eve go galloping,
> galloping into the apple.

They made the noise of the moon-chew
and let the juice fall down like tears.

Because of this same apple
Eve gave birth to the evilest of creatures
[. . . . .]
she gave birth to a rat.
[. . . . .]
and when it died before its time
she placed its tiny body
on that piece of kindergarten called a STAR.

Now, we all die before our time and are put on "the RAT'S STAR." But redemption
is possible, after all, and the smiling watermelon has—and is—the last word:

We are put there beside the three thieves
for the lowest of us all
deserve to smile in eternity
like a watermelon.

Edenic Apples Demystified

Suppose the imaginative world of a poet were divested entirely of the supernatural,
including even Keats's largely allegorical creatures of myth; what then might the Adam
and Eve story look like? The Polish poet Tadeuz Rózewicz (b. 1921) has written a
poem, "The Apple," which answers that question (translated by Czeslaw Milosz):

Give me an apple
said the husband
and stretched out his hand

from a clay bowl
a snake was sipping milk
a domestic gentle snake
black with orange
lightning

in the cradle a little man
was sucking the big toe of his foot
larger
than the flower called "lady's slipper."

A spider tied together
the hands of the clock

which ticked out eternity
to the happy

and when the weak thread snapped
the wife handed the red apple
to her husband
and quiet
sat down on the threshhold
of the family nest

Milosz characterizes Rózewicz's persona as "a nihilistic humanitarian, constantly searching for a way out of his negation which is mitigated only by pity." This corresponds precisely to the thrust of the poem. The simple domestic act of a wife handing her husband a requested apple (first stanza) can only be completed (last stanza) after a few things have been cleared up, or cleared out (the intermediate stanzas): the beautiful snake must be accepted as a member of the family; the baby must behave like a normal baby rather than like some miracle-worker; and eternity must be replaced by ordinary time.

Mark Twain (1835–1910) in a way anticipated Rózewicz's nontheistic or humanistic version of the Adam and Eve story in a little-known work published near the beginning of the twentieth century. The work first appeared in two parts: *Extracts from Adam's Diary, Translated from the Original MS* (1904), which reveals Adam's chief characteristics to be physical and mental indolence, if not lethargy; and *Eve's Diary, Translated from the Original MS* (1906), which reveals Eve's chief characteristics to be curiosity and adventurousness. Adam's very first entry (on a Monday) records the arrival in Eden of a new creature, who talks; on Tuesday, the new creature starts to name all the animals; by Wednesday, Adam is complaining about the incessant talking; on Saturday, he writes that "the new creature eats too much fruit" and on Sunday that "the new creature [is] trying to clod apples out of that forbidden tree." (No explanation of the forbidden tree is provided and Eve apparently does not succeed initially in obtaining any of its fruit.) Finally, the new creature says its name is Eve and that "it is a She." Eve befriends the snake, who talks, and this gives Adam a welcome respite from conversation. Eve reports that "the snake advises her to try the fruit of that tree, and says the result will be a great and fine and noble education." Adam is very doubtful about this because he has been told—we do not learn from whom—that eating the apples will bring death into the world. But Eve is *interested* in death because it would enable her to "save the sick buzzard, and furnish fresh meat to the despondent lions and tigers." In any case, Adam and Eve eat the apples and are banished from Eden.

Ten days after they have left Eden, Adam notes that Eve accuses *him* of having precipitated their departure from Eden by perpetrating the First Chestnut (meaning "an aged and mouldy joke"); the Serpent—suddenly renamed by Adam—had told her that chestnuts, not apples, were the forbidden fruit. Adam's diary ends with an entry ten years later, mentioning Cain and Abel and some unnamed girls, and concluding: "It is better to live outside the Garden with her than inside it without her. . . . Blessed be the chestnut that brought us near together and taught me to know the goodness of her heart and the sweetness of her spirit!"

So much for Adam's diary. Eve's is more lyrical, more full of enthusiasm, more wide-eyed with wonder, as she makes one discovery after another; one such discovery is fire, which turns out to improve the taste of apples. Eve's diary ends forty years after the departure from Eden with a prayer that she and Adam will die together, but, if not, that she will die first because "he is strong, I am weak, I am not so necessary to him as he is to me"—though, in Twain's account, Eve did well enough on her own in Eden. But Twain lets Adam have the last word, at Eve's grave: "Wheresoever she was, *there* was Eden."

The comments of Ursula K. Le Guin (b. 1929) on Mark Twain's Adam and Eve story in her introduction to an edition of the work (1996)—the first edition, by the way, to include both parts in a single volume—deserve quotation:

> The nerve of the man, the marvelous, stunning independence of that mind! in pious, prayerful, censorious, self-righteous Christian America of 1896, or 1996 for that matter, to show God as an unnecessary hypothesis, by letting Eve and Adam cast themselves out of Eden without any help at all from him, and really none from the serpent either—to put sin and salvation, love and death, in our own hands, as our own, strictly human business, our responsibility—now that's a free soul, and a brave one.

THE SECULARIZATION OF BIBLICAL APPLES

In European Hebrew poetry of the Middle Ages, both religious and secular, the Song of Songs was highly influential, with, for example, the Spanish Jewish poet, Moses Ibn Ezra (ca. 1055–d. after 1135), maintaining, as Dan Pagis puts it, that "the metaphorical language of The Song of Songs sanctions the writing of love poems." One of Ibn Ezra's quatrains, beginning with the line, "v'tappuach emes el lo b'ror'o," may be translated (very literally) as follows:

> And the apple truly was not by God created
> Only to delight those who smell and fondle it.
> I imagine, seeing green and red
> Joined in it, the faces of beloved and lover.

(For the original Hebrew and a rather different translation, which unaccountably ignores the Hebrew word *lo* [not] in the first line, see T. Carmi's *Penguin Book of Hebrew Verse* [1981]). Now, first of all, the colors mentioned in the poem seem to confirm that the apple is indeed the intended fruit. Next, if we look at the Hebrew text, we see that the poem has the rhyme scheme *abcb;* the rhyming words are, in transliterated Hebrew, *noshéyk* and *choshéyk,* meaning, respectively, "fondle" and "(male) lover," while the last words of the first and third lines are "created" and "red." It is also important to note that the last two words of the third line are "green and red," while the last two words of the fourth line are "(female) beloved" and "and (male) lover." Assuming that the order of the Hebrew words for green and red should agree with the order of the Hebrew words for the respective female and male lovers, we must conclude that the beloved's face is green (her youthfulness and inexperience?) and the lover's face is red (his passion?). This interpretation—suggested by my friend Howard Stein—seems to me more persuasive than that of T. Carmi, who sees the beloved's face as blushingly red and the lover's face as wanly green (see his translation cited above). Also to be noted are the resounding vowel shifts in the two Hebrew words for beloved and lover: in transliterated Hebrew, *chashúk* and *choshéyk,* from a/u to o/ey. After mentioning two of the pleasurable physical properties of apples—their smell and their feel (which might include both shape and texture)—Ibn Ezra creates a lovely metaphor for the faces of the lovers by having them blend into one another the way the red and green of the apple blend into one another.

Moses Ibn Ezra wrote another quatrain about his beloved—conventionally named *Ophrah,* meaning female gazelle or fawn—in which she does "blush" (in biblical Hebrew the verb means "is shamed," as in Jer. 10:14). In fact, the verb occurs twice in the poem, as the rhyming words in lines 2 and 4, meaning respectively "blushes" and "dries up" (in this case, with respect to tears). This repetition of the same word with two quite different meanings (homonymy) is common in medieval Arabic poetry, which Ibn Ezra is here imitating. (For the Hebrew text and English translation of Ibn Ezra's poem, see Solomon Solis-Cohen's *Selected Poems of Moses Ibn Ezra* [1945], where, however, for some reason the author translates as "pomegranate" what was, by this time, the usual Hebrew word for apple, *tappuach*.)

Solomon Ibn Gabirol (1021/2–ca. 1055), a younger contemporary of Moses Ibn Ezra, was born in Malaga, lived most of his short life in Saragossa, and died in Valencia. Ibn Gabirol draws on the Jewish mystical tradition as well as on neo-Platonic cosmology and Muslim astronomy in his theoretical works in prose and poetry, but he also wrote beautiful love lyrics, like "An Apple for Isaac" about a blushing apple (as translated by David Goldstein):

> My lord, take this delicacy in your hand.
> Perceive its scent. Forget your longing.
> On both sides it blushes, like a young girl
> At the first touch of my hand on her breast.
> An orphan it is without father or sister,
> And far away from its leafy home.
> When it was plucked, its companions were jealous,
> Envied its journey, and cried aloud:
> "Bear greetings to your master, Isaac.
> How lucky you are to be kissed by his lips!"

A more recent, and somewhat different, translation of this poem may be found in Peter Cole's *Selected Poems of Solomon Ibn Gabirol* (2001), which includes also two other astringent lyrical poems about apples. I should add that Cole explains how "in many of the apple poems, the bite into the apple is associated with a kiss, as the two words involved in the association—*nashakh* (bit) and *nashaq* (kissed)—differ in one [Hebrew] letter only, which also look like one another."

Men are not normally likened to apples but the complexion of a man—especially a young man—may be, as in this characterization by Guillaume de Lorris (first half of the thirteenth century) of the figure called Diversion, at the very beginning of the long (almost 22,000 lines) allegorical poem in old French, *The Romance of the Rose* (Le Roman de la Rose; 1230–1275): "His face, like an apple, was red and white all over [La face avoit, con une pome, / vermeille, et blanche tot entor]" (translated by Charles Dahlberg).

But if a face can blush like an apple, an apple can also be flushed like a face, as in the first two lines of "Red" (1948), by Rafael Alberti (1902–1999), one of his "homage to painting" poems (translated by Ben Belitt):

> 1
>
> Lucho en el verde de la fruta y venzo.
> [I strike through the greens of the fruit, and prevail.]

> 2
>
> Pleno rubor redondo en la manzana.
> [The apple's full flush in the round.]

A slightly younger contemporary and friend of Moses Ibn Ezra was Judah (or Jehudah) Halevi (b. before 1075–d. after 1141), usually considered the finest of the medieval Spanish school of Hebrew poets. Among his love poems is "By an Apple Tree" (translated by Nina Salaman):

> I lift my greeting on the wings of the wind
> To my friend, when the heat of the day beginneth to cool.
> I ask him nought but to remember the day of our parting,
> When we made a covenant of love by an apple tree.

The rhyme scheme of the original Hebrew poem is *aaba;* the rhyming lines end with the sound *u-ach,* and the final word, is, of course, *tappuach* (apple). The question of the gender of the (male) speaker's "friend" is controversial; many of Halevi's (and his contemporaries') love poems are grammatically addressed to a male beloved—whether this was a mere convention or reflected actual behavior in the society of the time is not easy to say. (For a probing discussion, see Dan Pagis, in his book referred to above, *Hebrew Poetry.*) In any case, in Halevi's poem the lovers' vows are sealed under an apple tree; in another short poem by him, "The Apple," (translated by David Goldstein), they part and he must "console [himself] with a rosy apple":

Whose scent is like the myrrh of your nose and your lips,
Its shape like your breast, and its colour
Like the hue which is seen on your cheeks.

Once again, we find the reversal noted above: instead of "my beloved resembles—but far surpasses—this apple" we have "this apple resembles—but falls far short of—my beloved"; in other words, while the beloved is usually thought of as present and the apple only imagined, in Halevi's poem the apple is thought of as present and the beloved only imagined. Dan Pagis comments on this reversal as follows:

Samuel Hanagid likens a woman to an apple:

Scented like its fragrance, sweet like its taste,
smooth like its skin, beautiful like its shape.

Later, Halevi reversed the comparison, with perhaps humorous overtones, and compared an apple to a woman, his unfaithful mistress. She has left him, he can find nothing as perfect, and so he must be content with what at least brings her to mind:

Since we parted I have found no one as beautiful as you.
So I find comfort in a reddish apple, ripe and lush;
its fragrance is like your breath . . .
Its shape like your breasts, its color like your blush.

(Pagis's translation of the lines from Judah Halevi's poem may be compared with that of Goldstein above.) Hanagid (993–1056), by the way, was the earliest of the four outstanding Jewish poets of the so-called classical period in Muslim Andalusia (10th to 12th cent. C.E.); one of the first authors of secular Hebrew poetry since biblical times, he was also one of the most extraordinary figures of early medieval Europe. He was a great Talmudist and Jewish statesman, and as vizier to the Berber ruler of Granada he led the armies of Granada in victorious campaigns against Seville and her allies. (Not surprisingly, Hanagid was the only one of the Spanish Hebrew poets to write poems about war.) He actually went so far as to have his young sons edit his poems as part of their education, and, as Raymond Scheindlin sees it, "The inclusion of secular poetry in the conception of Jewish education was itself a notable innovation within Judaism, having arisen in direct imitation of the Arabic cultural model."

Almost half a millennium before Hanagid, a Byzantine court official called Paul the Silentiary (6th cent. C.E.) used the displacement we have noted above—of the beloved by an apple—in this epigram from the *Greek Anthology* (5.290, translated by Robin Skelton):

Under her mother's nose
and avoiding her eye,

she slipped me a pair
of apples; as she pressed
them in my hands, Love rose
and made me curse
two apples in my grip
and not two breasts.

Apples can be like women and women can be like apples, but in the world of folklore and fairy tale an apple can *become* a woman and vice versa. (Usually, if the metamorphosis works in one direction, it will also work, under the right circumstances, in the other.) There is a Tuscan folktale in which the dual change occurs; Italo Calvino (1923–1985) retells it after a story collected in 1876 in Florence. In "Apple Girl" (translated by George Martin) a queen gives birth to an apple "redder and more beautiful than any you ever saw." In seclusion, the apple changes into a beautiful girl, who "neither ate nor talked; she only bathed and arranged her hair." When stabbed by a jealous stepmother queen the apple bleeds "a rivulet of blood," and subsequently when sprinkled with a magic powder," The apple burst open, and out stepped the maiden in bandages and plaster casts." In conclusion, she explains to the king who is in love with her that she has been under a spell (we never learn why) and that "If you like, I will be your bride." The contrast between the apple—most traditional of fruits—and the bandages and plaster casts—signifying modern medicine—lends an extra piquancy to the tale.

SECULARIZED APPLES

Lacking the rich cultural resources of Classical and biblical apple episodes, the author of a purely secularized apple episode is necessarily more attentive to what might be called "apple culture," that is, the physical qualities, structure, and growth of apples. (Recall the blushing apples of the previous section.) With this in mind, and following my general scheme for the classification of fruit episodes (formulated in the introduction), with a few adjustments, we come up with the following taxonomic scheme for secularized apple episodes.

The fruit
> Varieties: wild, cultivated
> Parts: stem, skin, flesh, core, pips
> Properties: color, odor, taste, shape, size, weight, number
> Physically transformed: peeled, sliced
> Chemically transformed: eaten, cooked, fermented, rotted, poisoned
> Sheer appleness: banal, philosophical

The trees
> Parts: root, trunk, twig, bud, blossom, leaf, fruit

Growth: budding, blossoming, leafing, fruiting, ripening, windfall
Aggregations: wild groves, cultivated orchards

It must be understood that these rubrics are intended only for the convenience of grouping literary apple episodes in potentially illuminating ways; I make no pretense that there are uniquely insightful ways of doing this. Any particular apple episode will generally exemplify various rubrics in the scheme. But there are some fairly pure cases. Thus, on one occasion, Samuel Hanagid must have improvised a group of fifteen "riddle-like poems" about apples that, as Peter Cole says, "seem to be about the ornamental aesthetic of the Andalusian court." Cole has translated six of the fifteen, of which I quote the first three (respectively, about the color, the texture, and the odor of apples):

> An apple filled with spices:
>   silver coated with gold.
> And others that grow in the orchard,
>   beside it, bright as rubies.
>
> I asked it: Why aren't you like those?
>   soft, with your skin exposed?
> And it answered in silence: Because
>   boors and fools have jaws.
>
> The grape was created for gladness,
>   to banish our grief;
> and virgin oil—for pleasure,
>   and the apple—to sniff.

The occasion for Hanagid's improvisation would have been one of those wine parties on which Hanagid wrote numerous poems and which we will look at in chapter 19, "Wine."

Secularized Apples in Art

The secularized apple occurs in perhaps its purest form in still life painting, so it will be useful now to return to the point where we terminated our earlier history of the Edenic apple in medieval manuscript illumination. Illuminated manuscripts were supplemented, and eventually supplanted, by printed books with printed illustrations starting in the sixteenth century, but there appeared, in a great burst of artistic creativity toward the end of that century, the *Mira Calligraphiae Monumenta,* a calligraphic manuscript inscribed by the Hungarian Georg Bocskay (d. 1575) and illuminated by the Fleming Joris Hoefnagel (1542–1601). The manuscript (now in the Getty Museum, Los Angeles) consists of some 150 folios, mostly vellum, a few paper (6 %₁₆ x 4 ⅞ in.). There are really two books bound together: a book of calligraphy (intended for display rather than instruction) by Bocksay and another unknown scribe dating from 1561–62 and illuminated by Hoefnagel, using watercolor and gouache together with gold and silver paint, in the late 1590s; and a book of so-called constructed alphabets, of unknown date and authorship, also illuminated by Hoefnagel in the 1590s. Hoefnagel's illuminations are unrelated to the written texts. But, as Thomas Kren explains, "The manuscript stands at an art historical crossroad. It constitutes one of the last important monuments in the grand tradition of medieval European manuscript illumination. In addition to its meticulous studies of flora and fauna, however, it points directly to the emergence of Dutch still life painting, an essentially new artistic genre of the seventeenth century." Among the many flora represented are fifteen kinds of fruit: apple, pear, cherry, apricot, currant, medlar, orange, fig, quince, pomegranate, grape, blackberry, peach, mulberry, and tomato. In addition to faithfully depicting the external aspects of Hoefnagel's specimens, according to Lee Hendrix, "the surfaces of natural elements are consistently peeled away to reveal their hidden internal fabrics in minuscule detail. . . . Hoefnagel rediscovered the latent strangeness of quotidian objects . . . which display their contents as if revealing occult secrets. Pears, figs, and other familiar fruits shown from odd angles take on an aura of the exceptional." In the case of the apple, the pear, and the orange, we get to see the fruit sliced open with its internal structure fully on view (see plates 8 and 9 for pictures of a sliced-open apple—exposing its double core—and a sliced-open pear).

If Hoefnagel's paintings are backward-looking—reminding us of the tradition of medieval illumination on vellum for noble patrons—there is a roughly contemporary corpus of some 1, 800 botanical watercolors on paper (averaging 17¾ x 11¾ inches), of unknown provenance and date but which are known to have belonged to a leading Netherlandish pharmacist named Theodorus Clutius (1546–1598) and to have been used by him as teaching aids for medical students at the University of Leiden. These drawings are now in the Jagiellon University Library in Kraków, Poland, comprising thirteen volumes (*Libri picturati* A.18–A.30). Many of the watercolors are extremely beautiful, to judge by the sample of 142 of them reproduced in *The Clutius Botanical Watercolors* (1998), edited by Claudia Swan; there are paintings of plum, apple, sour and Cornelian cherry, red and black currant, strawberry, and melon. The attention to relevant botanical detail in these watercolors is remarkable; as Swan explains: "In most cases the plants are shown in full and actual size and are arranged with care on the sheets, so that their various surfaces—the backs and fronts of leaves and the variegated forms of stems, petals, leaves—are all fully visible. Generally, root structures are as painstakingly described as other features." Clearly, this is the direction which "scientific" illustration was to take in the seventeenth and later centuries.

Independent still life painting—often including representations of fruit—seems to have originated at about the same time, the 1590s, in Spain, Italy, and the Low Countries (as appears from histories of the genre, such as that by Norbert Schneider [1994]). Hoefnagel may have played a role in this development, since the earliest surviving Netherlandish examples of the new genre are by Roelandt Savery (1576?-1639), who, like Hoefnagel, was one of Rudolf II's court painters in Prague. (See Thomas Da Costa Kaufmann's discussion in his *The Mastery of Nature: Aspects of Art, Science, and Humanism in the Renaissance* [1993].) As examples of these earliest still lifes, outstanding paintings of a quince by Juan Sánchez Cotán (1560–1627), of a basket of fruit by Michelangelo Merisi Caravaggio (1573–1610), and of oranges by Francisco de Zurbarán will be mentioned in the appropriate chapters (respectively, 13, 21, and 15).

Sánchez Cotán, Caravaggio, and Zurbarán were none of them devoted exclusively to still life painting (though Zurbarán had a son, Juan [1620–1649] who was; for reproductions of six of his fruit paintings and discussion, in both Spanish and English, see *Zurbarán Al Museo Nacional D'Art de Catalunya* [1998]). Less well known today (though widely admired in her own time—her patrons included the Medici in Florence) is the extraordinary still life painter Giovanna Garzoni (1600–1670), whose "finest work," in the words of Ann Sutherland Harris's entry in *The Dictionary of Art* (1996), "is a splendid synthesis of art and science rivalled by few specialists in this genre." One of Garzoni's works is an illustrated herbal, now in the Dumbarton Oaks Museum, Washington D.C., which includes as a frontispiece a self-portrait in red and black chalk (ca. 1650) characterizing herself as a "miniatrice," or miniaturist. In Gerardo Casale's catalogue (1991) of her paintings—some 136 are definitely attributed—there are a couple of religious paintings, some portraits, and—the vast majority—studies of flowers and fruit (including figs, pears, peaches, cherries, grapes, plums, pomegranates, berries, and the occasional apple). Garzoni's medium was old-fashioned (watercolor on parchment) but perhaps her technique (tiny stippled dabs of color) was not. (For reproductions of many of Garzoni's paintings, see Casale's book and the superb picture book by Silvia Meloni Trkulja and Elena Fumagalli [2000].) I should add that there is something mysteriously exciting about Garzoni's fruit and vegetable paintings, "with" (in Gillian Riley's words) "their manic perspectives and surreal backgrounds"; a good instance is *Still Life with Fruit and Birds* (undated, 10 x 16 ⅔ in.), now in the Cleveland Museum of Art. (See plate 10.) Though Garzoni's name may not yet be a household word, some of her images of fruit are becoming widely distributed: several such images on pillow covers may now be ordered over the Internet from a company in Australia!

Still lifes of fruit continued to be painted throughout Europe after the seventeenth century, occasionally reaching great heights, as in the work of Chardin (1699–1779) and Luis Meléndez (1716–1780) in the eighteenth century (for reproductions, see Pierre Rosenberg, *Chardin, 1699–1779* [1979], and William B. Jordan and Peter Cherry, *Spanish Still Life from Velázquez to Goya* [1995]). The genre was revitalized in certain nineteenth-century paintings, among which Courbet's (1819–1877) studies of fruit are exceptional, including, as they do, perhaps the first monumental still lifes of apples. These paintings were among the series of fruit and flower studies which occupied Courbet in 1871–2, while he was serving a six-month prison sentence for his actions in support of the Paris Commune of 1870; the fruit which served as models—including apples, pears, and pomegranates—was brought to him in prison by his sister. (Courbet and the Commune has been the subject of an exhibition at the Musée d'Orsay in Paris. The catalogue of the exhibition [2000] contains reproductions of seven Courbet fruit still lifes; see also Sarah Faunce and Linda Nochlin's catalogue, *Courbet Reconsidered* [1988].)

Linda Pastan has written a poem about her father's attempt "To lift himself from one of his depressions" by taking up oil painting; his subjects were still lifes of fruit, mostly apples, occasionally peaches. The first two five-line stanzas of her "Courbet's 'Still Life with Apples and Pomegranates'" (1995) are devoted to memories of her father, the third stanza reacts to the painting referred to in the title (reproduced in Faunce and Nochlin's catalogue), while the fourth (and concluding) stanza returns to her father; here are the last two stanzas:

> Courbet's fruit have so much roundness,
> such warmth and homeliness beside the pewter tankard,
> you could almost say they had humanity,
> if apples could be human.
> And as I stand in this crowded museum,
>
> all these years after my father's death,
> they make me grieve for him
> and his precise, mistaken apples,
> not for his failures;
> for how stubbornly he tried.

Around the time of Courbet's death, in 1877, Paul Cézanne (1829–1906) began painting what many critics believe to be the greatest representations of apples in the history of art. Some indication of the excitement generated by Cézanne's apple paintings is apparent from the following account by Virginia Woolf (1882–1941), in a letter of 15 April 1918 to Nicholas Bagenal, of a visit to the home of John Maynard Keynes. Keynes had just returned from Paris with a small painting of apples by Cézanne, *Still Life with Apples,* which he had purchased at an auction of the works of art belonging to the recently deceased Degas:

> Nessa left the room and reappeared with a small parcel about the size of a large slab of chocolate. On one side are painted 6 apples by Cezanne. Roger [Fry] very nearly lost his senses. I've never seen such a sight of intoxication. He was like a bee on a sunflower. Imagine snow falling outside, a wind like there is in the Tube, an atmosphere of yellow grains of dust, and us all gloating upon these apples. They really are very superb. The longer one looks the larger and heavier and greener and redder they

become. The artists amused me very much, discussing whether he'd used veridian or emerald green, and Roger knowing the day, practically the hour, they were done by some brush mark in the background.

The painting in question (oil on canvas, 7½ x 10½ inches and dating from around 1878) is now on loan from the Keynes Collection of Kings College, Cambridge University, to the Fitzwilliam Museum in Cambridge. (For further information about the painting, see John Rewald, *The Paintings of Paul Cézanne: A Catalogue Raisonné* [1996]; for a colored reproduction, see Françoise Cachin et al., *Cézanne* [1996].) Woolf carelessly refers to six rather than seven apples. She seems to have been not only amused but bemused at the responses of her friend, the art critic and painter Roger Fry, who was more concerned with pigments and brush strokes than with the representational qualities which impressed Woolf.

Like Woolf, W. H. Auden (1907–1973) had a hard time appreciating apple still lifes, writing in "Letter to Lord Byron" (1936): "All Cézanne's apples I would give away / For one small Goya or a Daumier." "A Cart with Apples" (1975), by Christopher Middleton (b. 1926), however, provides a beautiful verbal equivalent of a painting of apples—full of colored apples and colored shadows, with the apples and the shadows endlessly reflecting each other:

> In the blue shadow
> alone with its rose
> and full of fields
> round ones and yellow ones
> an apple stands
>
> a blue apple stands
> in the field of yellow
> alone with its cart
> and round of roses
> full ones and shadow ones
>
> and full of yellow
> the shadow stands
> alone with an apple
> a rose one a round one
> in a blue field
>
> and in the apple shadows
> blue ones and yellow ones
> a cart stands

> alone with its field
> and full of rounds
>
> but in the field of roses
> and full of apples
> yellow ones and round ones
> a blue cart stands
> alone with its shadow

The Australian poet, Les Murray (b. 1938), has written a set of five poems, collectively titled "Five Postcards" (1998), with each poem consisting of six to eight short lines and conceived as a message on the back of a picture postcard. The second of the poems is imagined to be fronted by a painting of apples by Cézanne:

> Cosmic apples by Cézanne:
> their colours, streaming, hit
> wavelengths of crimson and green
> in the yellowy particle-wind.
> Slant, parallel and pouring,
> every object's a choke-point of speeds.

Auden might have changed his mind if he had been able to read the brilliant analysis by Meyer Schapiro (1904–1996) of Cézanne's apple oeuvre—"The Apples of Cézanne: An Essay on the Meaning of Still-life" (1968)—in which Schapiro contends that a purely formalistic interpretation of Cézanne's paintings of apples is inadequate. To begin with, Schapiro suggests that "in [Cézanne's] persistent choice of the apples we sense a personal trait." Furthermore, the very details of Cézanne's representations of apples set him apart from his contemporaries, such as Courbet, in whose paintings of apples "the fruit is not only strikingly larger than Cézanne's, but retains a stem and leaves that give to the whole the aspect of a living segment of nature." Not that Cézanne's apples are unrelated to "living nature"—indeed, Schapiro goes so far as to suggest that "the apple was for him an equivalent of the human figure." But this meaning of apples, owing to its sexual content, was repressed or sublimated; and here Schapiro cites as a key piece of evidence the *Still-life with Plaster Cast of Amor* (ca. 1895), now in the Courtauld Institute Galleries in London, about which he comments as follows: "We may regard [the] free and perhaps unreflective association of apples, Cupid and a suffering nude man as an evidence of the connection of the apples and the erotic. . . . In the Courtauld canvas the apples are grouped with onions—contrasted forms as well as savors, that suggest the polarity of the sexes." (For a reproduction of the Amor painting, oil on canvas, 28 x 22 ½ in., see Schapiro's *Modern Art* [1978], plate 1.) But Schapiro had formulated a brief, brilliant, and almost entirely formal analysis of this painting—in terms of coloristic and geometric considerations—some sixteen years earlier, in his *Paul Cézanne* (1952), an analysis which, surprisingly enough, he never refers to in the "Apples of Cézanne." We are touching here, of course, on one of the more perplexing problems in the criticism of the arts: how to combine convincingly analysis of the "form" and analysis of the "matter" in a given work.

Schapiro, of course, sees nothing idiosyncratic in Cézanne's linking of apples with sex, nor does he wish to ignore Cézanne's conscious interest in the literary tradition of pastoral where this link is prominent. On these two counts, Schapiro appeals first to Classical writers of pastoral verse for whom "since Theocritus the apples are both an offering of love and a metaphor of the woman's breasts," and then reminds us that the *Eclogues* (34–38 B.C.E.) of Virgil (70–19 B.C.E.) remained a favorite of Cézanne's ever since his Latin studies in school. Schapiro also quotes Cézanne's remark: "Avec une pomme, je veux étonner Paris," commenting:

> [Cézanne] declares to the admiring critic, Geffroy, that he wishes to astonish Paris with an apple. In this pun—really no strict pun—he plays on the theme of his career, fusing in the name "Paris" both the hoped-for success of his art and the myth of fortune that delivers the prize of Helen to the judge of beauty. (Did he perhaps think also that he would surprise with an apple Zola, the friend who first brought him to Paris from Aix?)

It might be added that Émile Zola (1840–1902) was also the friend to whom Cézanne had once brought a gift of apples when they were in school together. Also, it should be emphasized that, according to Schapiro, the sexuality of apples by no means exhausts their significance for Cézanne:

> In paintings of the apples [Cézanne] was able to express through their more varied colors and groupings a wider range of moods, from the gravely contemplative to the sensual and ecstatic. In this carefully arranged society of perfectly submissive things the painter could project relations of human beings as well as qualities of the larger visible world—solitude, contact, accord, conflict, serenity, abundance and luxury—and even states of elation and enjoyment.

Another less well known Classical writer, of special interest for the tradition of painting in which Cézanne deliberately and proudly located himself, is also cited by Schapiro: the Greek Sophist Philostratus the Elder (3rd cent. C.E.), whose *Imagines* consists of a series of descriptions of paintings, whether actual or imagined is uncertain. Among the descriptions, there is one (1.6) called *Erotes* (Cupids), in which winged infants of both sexes are gathered, eating and playing with apples in a garden of Venus. Schapiro offers a summary of Philostratus's rather wordy exposition:

> The Cupids have laid on the grass their mantles of countless colors. Some gather apples in baskets—apples golden, yellow and red; others dance,

wrestle, leap, run, hunt a hare, play ball with the fruit and practice archery, aiming at each other. In the distance is a shrine or rock sacred to the goddess of love. The Cupids bring her the first-fruits of the apple trees.

And Schapiro then refers to a painting by Titian (ca. 1477–1576), *The Worship of Venus,* dating to 1518–24, which seeks to realize Philostratus's description. This work by Titian, now in the Prado in Madrid, is perhaps the most extraordinary painting of apples prior to Cézanne. (For a color reproduction, see David Rosand, *Titian* [1978].) To begin with, the sheer variety of the cupids' antics and their highly charged sexuality are astonishing. Also, one delightful detail in Titian's picture which Schapiro omits to mention—and which is in Philostratus—is the presence of four cupids flying and picking fruit among the branches of the large apple tree occupying the entire upper left hand region of the painting. It is also of great interest that Titian's painting was copied by Rubens—incidentally, one of Cézanne's greatest heroes in the history of painting—with a few telling changes. As Julius Held explains in his essay, "Rubens and Titian," the alterations include the transformation of the sex of the cupid who is the target of the (male) cupid about to discharge his arrow: the target cupid is male for Titian (thereby countenancing homosexual sex?) but female for Rubens. Held also notes a more subtle difference in the two paintings: "With Titian the symbolic activity of gathering apples (fruits of delight) is a rather serious business; Rubens's children evidently have more fun." Finally, Rubens seems to have replaced some of the apples with grapes. It is worth quoting Christopher White's judgment, in his *Peter Paul Rubens: Man and Artist* (1987), that "although unashamedly Titianesque in inspiration, the picture is an entirely personal re-creation." (The Rubens copy, probably made in the 1630s, from a copy of Titian's painting, is now in Stockholm in the National Museum; for a color reproduction, see White's book.)

One twentieth-century artist, Cuno Amiet (1868–1961), painted apple trees obsessively and wonderfully during his long life; in George Mauner's words, they "recur like leitmotifs throughout his career." Born in Solothurn, Switzerland, Amiet studied painting in Munich and Paris, was a member of the Brücke group for a year or so, and visited the great Cézanne exhibition of 1907 in Paris. It is, unfortunately, almost impossible to see any of Amiet's work outside Switzerland, nor are there reproductions of his work in standard histories of art. Even Peter Selz—who goes so far as to say, in his *German Expressionist Painting* (1974), that "because of his own background [Amiet] was able to help the Brücke evolve from a provincial group of German artists to a movement of European importance"—does not reproduce any of Amiet's work. In Lothar-Günther Buchheim's fundamental work on the Brücke, there is one (black and white) reproduction of a painting by Amiet, *The Apple Harvest* (an oil of 1912; no dimensions or location given). In 1974, however, the Museum of Art of Pennsylvania State University organized an exhibition of three Swiss painters, one of whom was Amiet; the exhibition was also shown in three other American museums. George Mauner's catalogue of this exhibition—which includes numerous reproductions of Amiet's art—is my main source of information about Amiet and his work.

Some of Amiet's apple paintings are religious, some secular. Thus, in an early painting, *Garden of Eden* (1894–5), the entire upper half of the canvas is devoted to a densely fruited apple tree, whose trunk bisects the picture. Eve stands directly in front of the trunk and is handing an apple to the kneeling Adam. (The medium is tempera on paper, 40 x 38 in.; privately owned in Solothurn, the painting is reproduced in black and white in the Mauner exhibition catalogue, no. 6.) *Apple Harvest* (1907), on the other hand, is painted in oil on a square canvas (40 x 40 in.) and is almost entirely given over to an enormous green oval dotted with red discs representing the foliage and fruit; the oval is supported by a short and slender trunk at the base of which is a pile of apples. This painting won a gold medal at the Munich International Exhibition in 1913 and is now in a private collection in Solothurn. (For a color reproduction, see Mauner's catalogue, No. 24.) Amiet returned to the apple tree motif many times—including posters for exhibitions of his own art in 1902 and 1958, and a monumental graffito on the outside wall of an art museum in Bern in 1936—but his definitive version of 1912 was one of some fifty of his paintings tragically destroyed in a fire in a Munich museum in 1931. One other painting (also in a private collection in Switzerland) may be mentioned: an oil on canvas (15 x 18 in.) self-portrait (ca. 1895–6), whose wooden frame (some four inches wide) was decorated by Amiet with green leaves and yellow-golden apples. (For a color reproduction, see Mauner's catalogue, no. 9.)

In 1897, Amiet met Oscar Miller, his first collector and patron. Miller wrote about aesthetics, and in the fourth edition of his book, *Von Stoff zu Form* (From matter to form; 1913), an analogy is drawn between the unity of an apple tree and the unity of a work of art (quoted and translated by George Mauner):

> A work: The life of the apple tree
>> One volume of it: The apple tree in blossom
>> One chapter of it: A simple apple blossom.
>
> In one blossom lives the richness, the fullness of the flowering tree, as does the whole life of the tree. At the same time, one blossom is a creation, a world in itself, unconcerned with where it came from and what will grow from it.
>
> So, in art, total beauty functions through particular beauty, and still the particular beauty is a creation in itself, a world, an eternity.

A better-known contemporary of Amiet's—the Austrian painter Gustav Klimt (1862–1918)—also was attracted to apple trees, producing no less than three versions of this subject during the last dozen years of his career. The earliest, *The Golden Apple Tree* (1903), was destroyed by fire in 1942, while the two later paintings, *Apple Tree I* (ca. 1912) and *Apple Tree II* (ca. 1916), are now in the Österreichische Gallerie in Vienna (oil on canvas; respectively, 43 x 43 in. and 31 ½ x 31 ½ in.). (For reproductions of the two paintings, see Catherine Dean, *Klimt* [1996].) Dean says "It is unclear whether these held any private symbolism for Klimt; however, his repeated attention to the motif makes it likely that he associated the tree with particular qualities."

At the time Amiet was painting his early pictures of apple trees, the self-styled "pictorialist" photographers in the United States (led by Clarence White) were arguing that photography must "elevate a mechanized and commercial craft to the status of art" (in the words of Bonnie Yochelson). One beautiful early example (1902) by White himself is *The Orchard* (platinum print, 9¾ x 7 ¹¹⁄₁₆ in.), in which two women clothed in long dresses are picking fruit from a mostly hidden tree in the upper left corner of the picture, while in the foreground a third similarly clad woman is stooping and picking up what appears to be an apple. (For a reproduction, see *Pictorialism into Modernism* [1996], ed. Marianne Fulton.) As in other pictorialist photographs, the soft focus lends a mysterious "poetic" aura to the unknowable events, which the picture implies have just happened or are just about to happen (or both). Many, perhaps most, photographs exhibit this narrativity without narrative (a phrase modeled after "purposiveness without purpose," the term Kant uses to differentiate works of art from other artificial objects). In pictorialist photographs, the mysteriousness of this narrativity is enhanced, if not by soft focus, then by composition, angle of shot, or the subject matter itself. A very different photographic style is represented by Man Ray's untitled image (1931) of an apple with a small screw where its stem should be (black and white, 8½ x 7 in.). Usually classified as an early Surrealist photograph, it was included by K. G. Pontus Hultén in his important exhibition at the Museum of Modern Art in New York, "The Machine as Seen at the End of the Mechanical Age" (1968), with the following comment (in the famous catalogue with the metal covers): "Man Ray must have retained some love for machines. In this image of sadistic love-making, it is not altogether clear whether he is on the side of the apple or of the screw—though obviously he gives the latter a chance." (For a reproduction of the photograph, see Pontus Hultén's catalogue or *Man Ray, 1890–1976* [2000], ed. Manfred Heiting.)

History and Apples

It can come as no surprise that Americans, given their relative remoteness in space and time from both the Classical and biblical culture areas, have tended to adopt a secularized view of apples. But the extraordinary enthusiasm of Americans for apples demands explanation, which would seem to be partly a matter of biology and partly of culture. It is a historical fact that American apple horticulture in colonial times was often based on seeds (rather than, as in Europe, on grafts), thereby, in effect, exploiting a fuller range of genetic diversity in the initial apple stocks. Listen, for example, to Adriaen van der Donck, the seventeenth-century Dutch author of a book on the region that was to become roughly the state of New York:

> The Netherlands settlers, who are lovers of fruit, on observing that the climate was suitable to the production of fruit trees, have brought over and planted various kinds of apple and pear trees, which thrive well. Those also grow from the seeds, of which I have seen many, which, without grafting, bore delicious fruit in the sixth year.

(The translator is Jeremiah Johnson.) And it did not take long for the English especially to recognize just how favorable the American environment was for growing apples; as Ann Leighton explains in her *American Gardens in the Eighteenth Century* (1976):

> Small wonder, then, that the discovery in the eighteenth century that apples would grow better in the New World than ever they had in the Old, and that all the old sorts would combine and multiply into new sorts, was heralded in the English-speaking world. That new sorts could be fixed by grafting their scions on others and the results named for their discoverers or places of origin made the fruit-growing world look to the central Atlantic states and New England for what was flourishing in apple culture.

As the United States expanded westward, it was discovered that most of the new environments encountered were favorable for growing apples: today, apples are grown in practically all states (Hawaii has too little winter, Alaska too much); commercial production of apples occurs in some thirty-five states, with Washington, Michigan, and New York leading the way. However, the very familiarity of apple trees in the rural landscapes of the American past and the very abundance of fresh apples in American supermarkets today have tended to detach the fruit from the cultural traditions in which it had been traditionally embedded; nowadays, writers in the United States can, if they choose, use apples or apple imagery for their own individual, even idiosyncratic, purposes with no hint of Classical or biblical associations. But let us begin by looking at what some leading nineteenth-century authors in the United States had to say about apples.

An obvious starting point is the legend of Johnny Appleseed. The many versions of his story all seem to agree that his real name was John Chapman and that he was born in 1775 in or around Springfield, Massachusetts, and died in 1845, in Indiana; for other details I follow the account of a woman named Rosella Rice, whose home in Ohio was visited by Johnny many times (see the compilation edited by Catherine Peck, *A Treasury of American Folk Tales* [1998]). Around the turn of the century, Johnny moved to Pennsylvania, where he started a nursery business, eventually specializing in apple trees. He was a Swedenborgian and claimed to converse with spirits and angels. Obtaining his apple seeds from the cider mills of western Pennsylvania, he became an itinerant vendor:

> Sometimes he carried a bag or two of seeds on an old horse, but more frequently he bore them on his back, going from place to place on the wild frontier, clearing a little patch, surrounding it with a rude enclosure and planting seeds therein. He had little nurseries all through Ohio, Pennsylvania and Indiana. If a man wanted trees and was not able to pay for them, Johnny took his note, and if the man ever got able and was willing to pay the debt, he took the money thankfully; but if not, it was well.

Rice recalls Johnny's eloquence on the subject of apples:

> On the subject of apples he was very charmingly enthusiastic. One would
> be astonished at his beautiful description of excellent fruit. I saw him once
> at the table when I was very small, telling about some apples that were new
> to us. His description was poetical, the language remarkably well chosen.
> It could have been no finer had the whole of Webster's Unabridged, with
> all its royal vocabulary been fresh upon his ready tongue. I stood back of
> mother's chair, amazed, delighted, bewildered, and vaguely realizing the
> wonderful powers of true oratory. I felt more than I understood.

Even before Johnny Appleseed, Americans were being admonished, in the first
cookbook written by an American, to plant apple trees. Here is what Amelia Simmons
says about apples in the first edition (1796) of her cookbook, published in Hartford,
Connecticut, by Hudson & Goodwin (publisher of Noah Webster's dictionary):

> Apples are still more various [than pears], yet rigidly retain their own
> species, and are highly useful in families, and ought to be more universally
> cultivated, excepting in the compactest cities. There is not a single family
> but might set a tree in some otherwise useless spot, which might serve the
> two fold use of shade and fruit; on which 12 or 14 kinds of fruit trees
> might easily be engrafted and essentially preserve the orchard from the
> intrusions of boys, &c. which is too common in America. If the boy who
> thus planted a tree, and guarded and protected it in a useless corner, and
> carefully engrafted different fruits, was to be indulged free access into
> orchards, whilst the neglectful boy was prohibited—how many millions of
> fruit trees would spring into growth—and what a saving to the union.
> The net saving would in time extinguish the public debt, and enrich our
> cookery.

The cookbook—only some forty-seven pages in length—sold out in just a few months
and had to be reprinted; in the new edition, for some reason Simmons repudiates and
eliminates the first seventeen pages of the first edition, including the passage on apples.

Not economics but aesthetics is the focus of a lecture on apples delivered at the
Concord Lyceum in 1860 by Henry David Thoreau (1817–1862) and subsequently
published as "Wild Apples" in the *Atlantic Monthly* (November 1862). Thoreau loves
apple blossoms, "perhaps the most beautiful of any tree's, so copious and so delicious
to both sight and scent," and he loves the myths and folk rituals associated with apples,
some of which he recounts, but especially he loves the wild apples (from ungrafted
trees), which he describes with regret as rapidly vanishing from the New England
landscape. Most memorable is Thoreau's attention to the tangy tastes of wild apples
("racy and wild American flavors") and to their colors, more lovingly described than
by any of the poets:

Painted by the frosts, some a uniform clear bright yellow, or red, or crimson, as if their spheres had regularly revolved, and enjoyed the influence of the sun on all sides alike, —some with the faintest pink blush imaginable, —some brindled with deep red streaks like a cow, or with hundreds of fine blood-red rays running regularly from the stem-dimple to the blossom-end, like meridional lines, on a straw-colored ground, —some touched with a greenish rust, like a fine lichen, here and there, with crimson blotches or eyes more or less confluent and fiery when wet, —and others gnarly, and freckled or peppered all over on the stem side with fine crimson spots on a white ground, as if accidentally sprinkled from the brush of Him who paints the autumn leaves. Others, again, are sometimes red inside, perfused with a beautiful blush, fairy food, too beautiful to eat,— apple of the Hesperides, apple of the evening sky! But like shells and pebbles on the sea-shore, they must be seen as they sparkle amid the withering leaves in some dell in the woods, in the autumnal air, or as they lie in the wet grass, and not when they have wilted and faded in the house.

What remained of those wild apples almost fifty years after Thoreau's pomaceous raptures was closely observed by Henry James (1843–1916) during a visit to New England—his first in two decades—during the autumn of 1904:

> The apple-tree, in New England, plays the part of the olive in Italy, charges itself with the effect of detail, for the most part otherwise too scantly produced, and, engaged in this charming care, becomes infinitely decorative and delicate. What it must do for the too under-dressed land in May and June is easily supposable; but its office in the early autumn is to scatter coral and gold. The apples are everywhere and every interval, every old clearing, an orchard; they have "run down" from neglect and shrunken from cheapness—you pick them up from under your feet but to bite into them, for fellowship, and throw them away; but as you catch their young brightness in the blue air, where they suggest strings of strange-coloured pearls tangled in the knotted boughs, as you note their manner of swarming for a brief and wasted gaiety, they seem to ask to be praised only by the cheerful shepherd and the oaten pipe.

Is the, so to speak, lower temperature of James's response compared with Thoreau's attributable to temperament or to pomological degeneration? Unlike Thoreau, James finds little to enjoy in the flavors of wild apples but their appearance seems to have remained magical, James's "strange-coloured pearls" replacing Thoreau's "shells and pebbles."

In the year before James visited America he had published a biography, *William Wetmore Story and His Friends* (1903). James had been persuaded by the subject's family— against his better judgment, for he was not very fond of Story (1819–1895)—to write a life of the recently deceased American emigré poet and sculptor, who had spent most of his life in Rome. Of course, as James's biographer, Leon Edel, reminds us, "the Bostonian-Roman sculptor was an archetypal Jamesian subject—the American expatriate with a penchant for the artist life," and James chose tasting apples as the central metaphor in a passage commenting on the circumstances of a crucial turning point in Story's life. The time was the summer of 1854 and Story had just left Rome for home, deeply disappointed with an artistic career that failed to take off. Within two years Story was to return to Rome, taking up residence with his family in an apartment (consisting of over forty rooms) in the Barberini Palace. Anyone familiar with James's late novels will easily reconize their convoluted style in the following excerpts from the Story biography (written in just two months during the early stages of composition of James's last novel, *The Golden Bowl* [1904]):

> He was not to know till he had tried a second winter there how little his Roman doubts mattered. He might live as an anxious, even as a misguided, artist, but he could not, apparently, live as anything more orthodox. The anxiety, at least, might, so to speak, still be beguiled, but the habit of conformity was not to be acquired, was not, at any rate, to be found bearable. . . . Very special and very interesting to catch in the fact—even if not of the order of things "eternal"—is the state of being of the American who has bitten deep into the apple, as we may figure it, of "Europe," and then has been obliged to take his lips from the fruit. The intensity of the case depends of course on the inward energy of the bite and the kind of susceptibility involved in the act of tasting. There are small kinds and there are great kinds, and when these latter have been engaged the subsequent sense of privation is of course proportionate. The apple of "America" is a totally different apple, which, however firm and round and ruddy, is not to be (and above all half a century ago was not to have been) negotiated, as the newspapers say, by the same set of teeth. The inward drama of this perception on the part of the repatriated pilgrim has enacted itself in thousands of breasts and thousands of lives, and doubtless goes on doing so without coming to light—that is to any such light as permits us, as we say of dramas that are typical, to assist at it. It has never been noted, reported, commemorated in a manner worthy of its intrinsic interest.

Here, a straightforward "firm and round and ruddy" apple is the apt vehicle for James's metaphorical allusion to the unbridgeable gap between Europe and America.

American painters during the nineteenth century were no less attentive to apples than the writers. In a remarkable exhibition, in 1993—accompanied by Bruce Weber's valuable catalogue—the Berry-Hill Galleries, in New York City, revealed some of the richness of American apple paintings. More than fifty painters were represented, the earliest William Coxe (1762–1831), the latest William McCloskey (1859–1941); I would like to single out the little-known, slightly mysterious Joseph Decker (1853–1924). His *Green Apples* (oil on canvas, 10 ¼ x 20 in.), painted ca. 1883–1888, combines probing naturalism with artful composition. (See plate 11.)

Behind New England apples were, of course, the apples of Britain, and some apple episodes drawn from English texts from a variety of genres should serve to remind us of this. The use of apple trees as a marker of family history may be found in a poem by Thomas Philipott (ca. 1616–1682), a minor seventeenth-century metaphysical poet who seems to have specialized in elegies and other types of poems about death. Philipott's subject is a farmer who lost five of his children to the plague, and the poet wishes to memorialize (with a poem) the farmer, who has himself memorialized (with apple trees) his children. The last eleven of twenty-two heroic couplets from "On a Farmer, who having buried five of his children of the Plague, planted on each of their graves an Apple-tree" (1646) describes this act:

> To preserve life in their remembrance, hee
> Establishes on each grave an apple-tree,
> By that quaint Hieroglyphick to declare
> He was their tree, and they his apples were,
> Which in his estimate did farre outvie
> In tendernesse the apple of his eye;
> And though sterne death had been so much unkind,
> To pluck the fruit and leave the tree behind,
> Yet in that action, he did but show,
> That they untimely to their graves did go:
> To shew in time, what we must likewise do,
> Branches, Trunk, Root, and all must follow too.

The long history of apples in Britain (and, indeed, in northern Europe generally) is reflected in many aspects of folk culture, such as nursery rhymes. Apples turn out to be the commonest fruit in English nursery rhymes, so that, for example, in two standard collections by Iona and Peter Opie, totaling some thousand items (*The Oxford Nursery Rhyme Book* [1955] and *A Family Book of Nursery Rhymes* [1964]), there are no less than thirty-one rhymes in which apples appear; ten of these are entirely about apples. (Only plums rival apples in their frequency: some twenty occurrences, with five entirely about plums.) Two of the more striking apple rhymes go like this:

> Here's to thee, good apple tree,
> Stand fast at root,
> Bear well at top,
> Every little twig
> Bear an apple big,
> Every little bough
> Bear apples enow,

Hats full! Caps full!
Three score sacks full!
Hurrah, boys! Hurrah!

~

Up in the green orchard there is a green tree,
The finest of pippins that you may see;
The apples are ripe, and ready to fall,
And Robin and Richard shall gather them all.

There is also in Britain, as Iona Opie explains in *The People in the Playground* (1993), a perennial skipping game called "Apple, apple," where "the skipper says 'Apple, apple, choose your apple, Call in ——,' and the person she calls in has to chase her over and around the rope. The one being chased can call out 'Reverse,' and chase the chaser. Whoever is caught becomes the next skipper." ("Skipping" is usually called "jump rope" in the United States.)

If apples are frequently present in English nursery rhymes, children's stories, and games, apple trees have always been common in English orchards and nurseries (the botanical ones), and this is reflected, among other places, in the novels of Jane Austen (1775–1817), which are full of country estates said to be famous for their apple orchards, such as Woodston of *Northanger Abbey* (1818), and Abbey-Mill-Farm and Donwell of *Emma* (1816). None of these orchards is described in any detail, however, and we must await our later discussion of a book-length elaboration (by Eleanor Farjeon) of a nursery rhyme theme about apples for a substantial description of an English apple orchard.

Contemporary American poets continue the nineteenth-century tradition of extraordinary enthusiasm for apples, as in this example by the New England poet Robert Francis (1901–1987), for whom apples possess such overwhelmingly positive associations that, in "Remind Me of Apples" (1960), recital of apple names gives him hope, during the summer lull when they are temporarily unavailable, of their providential autumn return:

When the cicada celebrates the heat,
Intoning that tomorrow and today
Are only yesterday with the same dust
To dust on plantain and on roadside yarrow—
Remind me, someone, of the apples coming,
Cold in the dew of deep October grass,
A prophecy of snow in their white flesh.

In the long haze of dog days, or by night
When thunder growls and prowls but will not go

Or come, I lose the memory of apples.
Name me the names, the Goldens, Russets, Sweets,
Pippin and Blue Pearmain and Seek-no-further
And the lost apples on forgotten farms
And the wild pasture apples of no name.

Equally enthusiastic are the opening stanzas of "Apple" (1999), by Susan Stewart (b. 1952), with its baker's dozen of apple varieties:

If I could come back from the dead, I would come back
for an apple, and just for the first bite, the first
break, and the cold sweet grain
against the roof of the mouth, as plain
and clear as water.

Some apple names are almost forgotten
and the apples themselves are gone. The smokehouse,
winesap and York imperial, the striped
summer rambo and the winter banana, the little
Rome with its squat rotunda and the pound apple

that pulled the boughs to the ground.
The sheep's nose with its three-pointed snout,
the blue Pearmain, speckled and sugared.
Grime's golden, cortland, and stayman.
If an apple's called "delicious," it's not.

Two of the names ("smokehouse" and "pound") are indeed missing from all of the contemporary books on apples I have been able to consult, but Beach's *Apples of New York* comes to the rescue (see the "Index to Varieties" in vol. 1). I should add that there are twenty-three more stanzas to Stewart's poem, with many references to biblical apples, to the golden apples of Greek myth, to the folklore of apples, to apple pests; and, three stanzas from the end, the first stanza is repeated with some small changes. I believe the stanzas I have quoted above constitute a much shorter, and better, poem.

An impatience with the relatively small range of apple varieties available to most of us today and a nostalgia for the unimaginably rich variety of apples we have lost are well captured by David Guterson in an essay in *Harper's Magazine* for October 1999. In the fall of 1998, Guterson did a survey of commercial apple production in the eastern half of his home state of Washington (once the leading apple-producing region in the leading apple-producing nation in the world, now being rapidly overtaken by expanding Chinese production). Exploring the operations, first, of a conventional apple-grower and then of an organic one, Guterson turns finally to Doyle and Tye Fleming, who are interested in developing apple varieties with improved tastes (such as the new "Cameo," which was "mildly tart and aromatic, had a fine firm texture, creamy white flesh, and an exquisitely subtle sweet taste"). At the end of his visit, Guterson is introduced to

> the Flemings' personal breeding plot, where about 4,000 apple varieties grow in crowded rows. None of the fruit here has a name, and we wander among it with our pocketknives open, sampling like connoisseurs, seeking the proper descriptive language, and pondering whether anything we've tried might be worth grafting to rootstock and peddling in the marketplace. The range of fruit is beyond imagining—a kingdom of varied treasures. I try an apple that tastes like a banana, a timid apple, an apple of spice, an apple that smells like watermelon. One is no bigger than the common plum; another is as big as a coconut. One has a waxy, bitter skin; another is tough and coarse in the mouth; a third, dry and pungent, musty; a fourth, delicate, ethereal. Russeted like a small mosaic, surprisingly weighty in the palm of the hand, potato-fleshed, mealy, invigorating, fine-grained, piquant, astringent, a spitter. Doyle chews and wipes juice from his chin with a slightly crazy grin on his face, barely containing his ecstasy, his exultation. The world seems a fine place to the three of us just now. There is nothing in it but apples.

Apples have also been used by American writers to help them deal with historical issues. Thus, in "Winesaps" (1985), by the American poet Dave Smith (b. 1940), the locale is specified as "the Shenandoah hills" (in Virginia) and the memory of the poet's widowed grandmother stands in for a family whose men have been lost fighting for the Confederacy in the Civil War ("Nothing moves in boxwood / where gray soldiers lie"). The poet thinks of horses fed on apples: "those stallion-feeders, / little red handfuls of joy!" Gathering apples in "the arthritic orchard," exploring the basement, where apples used to be stored, in his grandparents' now unpeopled home, the speaker's constricting family memories trouble him: "Why is it we keep what we cannot bear / to use, and can't escape, shoving / ourselves into shrunken rooms?" Finally, his fingers clenching, the poet cries out in futile invocation of the women in his family with their intoxicated, and intoxicating, mendacities:

> I hold every
> core peeled on this slab.
> My fingers claw the meat
> of family stillness,
> parting all the way to seeds.
>
> Oh widows of the air,
> fill me with your
> cidery, useless lying,

> those bladed hours
> you fed me the dark
> rotting dreams of your love.

A very different but equally personalized vision of American history is adumbrated in a poem called "History as Apple Tree" (1972), by Michael S. Harper (b. 1938). Specifically, the poem's persona is a "black man" in Providence, Rhode Island (where, incidentally, Harper has been teaching since 1971), whose ancestors escaped into a local Indian tribe in the village of Cocumscussoc. From the chief of this same tribe Roger Williams obtained "his tract of land" and "founded Providence Plantation." After twenty-eight lines recounting these historical episodes, the speaker tries to connect himself with his history by means of an old legend:

> In your apple orchard
> legend conjures Williams' name;
> he was an apple tree.
> Buried on his own lot
> off Benefit Street
> a giant apple tree grew;
> two hundred years later,
> when the grave was opened,
> dust and root grew
> in his human skeleton:
> bones became apple tree.
>
> As black man I steal away
> in the night to the apple tree,
> place my arm in the rich grave,
> black sachem on a family plot,
> take up a chunk of apple root,
> let it become my skeleton,
> become my own myth:
> my arm the historical branch,
> my name the bruised fruit,
> black human photograph: apple tree.

We are left wondering whether such an act of self-imagining could possibly succeed.

Another American poet, Brendan Galvin (b. 1938), in his "Brother Francisco Anthony Eats an Apple" (1999), imagines an English "monk and pomologist" who can detect an entire strand of British history in the taste of a Suffolk apple:

> he could taste dispersals in
> that golden apple, a hint
> of thatch afire, smoke funneling

> to the sky, a channel crossing
> in a bowman's sack.
>
> He saw a Norman fletcher
> pluck it on the road to St.-Malo, 1065,
> then tribal palimpsests, migrations,
> horsemen, their blades flashing back
> across the dark of Europe into
> the wild groves of the Caucasus:
> Alma Alta, "Father of Apples," its trees
> hung with shapes as various as
> the faces of those who journeyed there
> to twist fruit from the branches
> and sugar their bitter lives.

And then Brother Francisco reaches back even further into history, all the way to Genesis:

> He saw
> that apple fallen from a suddenly
> fatal hand. The print of perfect teeth
> skewed and began to brown
> in its flesh, a white mouth whispering
> rot among the roots. *Their choice*
> *was immortality,* he said, *or never*
> *to have tasted this fruit.*

Let us look now at some apple episodes by writers from (northern) continental Europe. Just a few years before Henry James was observing the apples of New England, the Russian writer Ivan Bunin (1870–1953) had published a short story in which the fragrance of apples is all-pervasive. "Apple Fragrance" (1900) is an impressionistic, virtually plotless series of reminiscences of life in the country. Bunin's narrator begins (the translation is Olga Shartse's), "I remember a fine, early autumn," and then, a few sentences later, continues: "I remember a crisp, clear morning. . . . I remember a big, golden orchard, rather dry, with thinning trees. I remember the walks lined with maples, the subtle fragrance of fallen leaves and the smell of Antonovka apples—a smell of honey and autumn freshness." (The variety, Antonovka, is similar to Golden Delicious; more specifically, Morgan and Richards characterize it as "Large, milky white, classic Russian apple. Sharp, refreshing, juicy, crisp flesh. . . . Esteemed for 'perfumed, vinous' flavour.") And a few sentences later: "the trading gardeners . . . with the help of hired peasants, were loading apples on to the carts to send to town that very night. . . . A peasant loading apples would eat one after another with a juicy crunch, but that was one of the unwritten laws—the employer would never cut him short." Spotted throughout the story are several more references to the fragrance or taste of these apples. It is worth remarking that this is not a case of the narrator's memory being stimulated by the fragrance of apples (and other fragrances) but rather a case of the fragrance being an essential part of what is remembered; as Hans Rindisbacher sees it in his discussion of Bunin's story: "A whole era, a whole way of life becomes thus infused with and described as a collage of odors. This use of olfaction lies somewhere between the strictly realist on the one hand, with scents clinging to and emanating from objects or persons in the actual fictional reality of the text . . . , and a use . . . of scents for the very creation of a fictional reality of the second order."

In Jaroslav Seifert's poem, "Moscow" (1926)—I quote from Ewald Osers's translation—he writes about the reminders of the Russian tsarist past which haunt the imagination of a visitor to Moscow: "The display cases in the old palace," "the Kremlin's bloodstained wall," "Rotten rings, a mildewy diadem," "Suits of armour, empty like golden nutshells." Perhaps the most explicit statement of Seifert's theme occurs in the fifth of the six quatrains:

> The orb, symbol of power, lying on the ground,
> an apple worm-eaten and rotten.
> All's over, all is over under the golden domes,
> death is guarding history's graveyard.

Dana Loewy's translation of the stanza reads somewhat differently:

> On the floor lies the czar's orb, emblem of authority,
> rotten and worm-eaten.
> This is the end, it is over under golden domes,
> death guards the burial grounds of history.

We wonder: does the apple occur in the Czech original, or not? Loewy provides the answer in a note: "The Czech word for 'orb' is the same as for 'apple.'" But why Moscow? To answer this question, we must know something of Seifert's personal history.

To begin with, George Gibian explains, "Seifert's mother was Catholic and his father an atheist and socialist" and "Seifert felt warmly towards both of them." Seifert became one of the founders of the Czech Communist Party in 1921, and worked for Communist newspapers, reviews, and publishers; in 1925 and 1928, he traveled in the Soviet Union. On the other hand, by 1929, Seifert, along with eight other prominent Czech Communist writers, had signed a letter protesting the dogmatic new Communist Party line on culture, leading to their expulsion from the party. As for poetry, Seifert's earliest style—a simple and direct "worker's poetry"—was soon replaced, in the 1920s, by a style deeply influenced by Apollinaire and by Apollinaire's nineteenth-century predecessors and early-twentieth-century successors. In Seifert's version of this modernist poetic style, straightforward, even banal-sounding, passages are abruptly

92   enlivened by unexpected, even surreal, imagery. An example is "An Apple Tree with Cobweb Strings" (1926), a poem contemporary with "Moscow," and also alluding to that city; the first three stanzas (translated by Loewy) invoke apples and apple trees.

> Ruddy apples
> have bent the regal stem like a harp,
> autumn has draped it with cobweb strings,
> wail and play
>   my player!
>
> We are not from that land where oranges ripen,
> where grapevine twines around Ionic columns,
> its grapes sweeter
>   than the mouths of Roman women;
> we only have the apple tree, warped severely
>   by fruit and age.
>
> And beneath this apple tree would sit he,
>   who perhaps had seen
> Parisian nights, Italian afternoons
>   or the moon above the Kremlin,
> home he returned all this to remember.

The historical perspective here is obviously far wider than that of a simple memory of a recent visit to Moscow. And, then, suddenly, in the remainder of the poem, the point of view shifts from a poet involved in the objective processes of history to a poet inwardly contemplating the small triumphs and losses of his own personal life:

> It is after noon,
>   one fruit I will pick from the apple tree
>   and long smell at it.
>   [. . . . .]
> For the idle beauty of foolish women
>   an apple is wasted.

Apples: Shape and Weight

The roughly spherical shape of apples is all that Jonathan Swift (1667–1745) could rely on when he associated "A ball of new-dropped horse's-dung" with apples, in his "On the Words 'Brother Protestants and Fellow Christians'" (1734). The politico-religious background of this intensely polemical poem is suggested by Swift's notation below the title: "So Familiarly Used By The Advocates For The Repeal Of The Test Act In Ireland, 1733." In brief, Swift was indignant at attempts by the Presbyterians (concentrated mainly in Ulster) to make common political cause with the established church by appealing to their shared Christianity. Our concern is with just the first fourteen (of sixty-four) lines, in which Swift recounts a traditional fable about apples and horse dung:

> An inundation, says the fable,
> O'erflowed a farmer's barn and stable;
> Whole ricks of hay and stacks of corn,
> Were down the sudden current borne;
> While things of heterogeneous kind,
> Together float with tide and wind;
> The generous wheat forgot its pride,
> And sailed with litter side by side;
> Uniting all, to show their amity,
> As in a general calamity.
> A ball of new-dropped horse's-dung,
> Mingling with apples in the throng,
> Said to the pippin, plump, and prim,
> "See brother, how we apples swim."

(One version of the traditional fable may be found in the entry "apple 1" in the *Random House Historical Dictionary of American Slang,* vol. 1.)

Any cross section through a sphere is a circle. The American poet Paul Zimmer (b. 1934) is applying this bit of geometry when he writes, in his "In Apple Country" (1983):

> Baseballs, acorns, bags of marbles,
> Tulip bulbs, yo-yo's, dandelions—
> But ripe apples sliced across always
> Make the most perfect circles of all.

Zimmer tells us in his poem how he grew up fascinated by circles; he tells us (in the commentary accompanying his poem) how he grew up fascinated by apples. In his poem, though, he worries that apples may die when they are picked, and that this may be a sign of something lethal they convey when we eat them. But, then, with some dubious arithmetic, he concludes:

> If all the apples ripening
> On one fall day and all the circles
> Ever grown in these orchards
> Draped across the driftless hills,
> Were counted by a great master,
> They would total the number of stars
> In western skies on an autumn night.

And finally, perhaps too complacently, the poet "lean[s] back in his garden chair" and contemplates the harvest of apples ("Red, yellow, green, their blemishes and tiny wormholes"), while at the same time—and now with some dubious geometry—he is contemplating "the round ends of the universe." Zimmer has placed "In Apple Country" at the conclusion of his volume of selected poems, *Crossing to Sunlight* (1996), and another apple poem, "Apple Blight" (1967), at the beginning. "Apple Blight" we will discuss in chapter 22, "Enemies and Friends of Fruit."

The rotundity and gravity of apples are invoked in the slight poem "Gift" (Regalo), by the Chilean poet Jorge Teillier (b. 1935), here translated from the Spanish by Mary Crow:

> A friend from the South
> has sent me an apple
> too beautiful
> to eat right away.
> I hold it in my hands:
> It is heavy and round
> like the Earth.
>
> ~
>
> Un amigo del sur
> me ha enviado una manzana
> demasiado hermosa
> para comerla de inmediato.
> La tengo en mis manos:
> es pesada y redonda
> como la Tierra.

Teillier's heavy, round apple, "like the Earth," must remind us of the second most famous apple in Euro-American cultural history: the apple in the garden of Sir Isaac Newton (1642–1727), whose fall—so the legend goes—somehow inspired him to formulate his law of gravitation. Four different individuals claimed to have heard the story from Newton himself near the end of his life. One account, by William Stukeley (1687–1765), goes like this:

> After dinner, the weather being warm, we went into the garden and drank thea [*sic*]· under the shade of some appletrees, only he and myself. Amidst other discourse, he told me, he was just in the same situation, as when formerly, the notion of gravitation came into his mind. It was occasion'd by the fall of an apple, as he sat in a contemplative mood. Why should that apple always descend perpendicularly to the ground, thought he to him self. Why should it not go sideways or upwards, but constantly to the earths centre? Assuredly, the reason is, that the earth draws it. There must be a drawing power in matter: and the sum of the drawing power in the matter of the earth must be in the earths center, not in any side of the earth. Therefore dos this apple fall perpendicularly, or towards the center. If matter thus

draws matter, it must be in proportion of its quantity. Therefore the apple draws the earth, as well as the earth draws the apple. That there is a power, like that we here call gravity, which extends its self thro' the universe.

Newton scholars today are disposed to believe the anecdote of Newton's falling apple but to doubt that the incident made any substantial contribution to his discovery or demonstration of the law of universal gravitation.

The first publication of the apple incident, by the way, was in several works by Voltaire (1694–1778), who claimed to have heard the story, while visiting London, from Newton's niece, Catherine Barton Conduitt. Here is a modern translation of the anecdote from Voltaire's *Lettres philosophiques* (published in 1734, a year after the publication of the English version, "Letters Concerning the English Nation"): "Having withdrawn in 1666 into the country near Cambridge, one day as he walked in his garden and noticed fruit falling from a tree [fruits tomber d'un arbre] he drifted off into deep meditation on that problem of gravity." In Voltaire's first published version of the story in *Epick Poetry of the European Nations from Homer Down to Milton* (1727) and in the version published in his *Elements of the Philosophy of Newton* (1738), the fruit is an apple (*pomme*).

The apple incident is memorialized in the form of a spray of apple blossoms on a British one-pound note and in the form of an apple on an eighteen pence British postage stamp, both issued in 1987 to commemorate the three hundredth anniversary of the publication of Newton's *Principia*. (See plate 12.) The actual tree from which the apple is imagined to have fallen has also not been neglected: scions from the supposed tree (which was taken down in 1814) have produced apples in Britain, the United States, and New Zealand, recognizable as Flower of Kent (a variety known in Britain since the seventeenth century). It is even possible that a descendant of the original tree still survives in Newton's garden at Woolsthorpe Manor (near Grantham, in Lincolnshire); at least, so I am informed by Peter Joyce, the present custodian of the manor, now a National Trust.

A notable poetic rendition of Newton's falling apple occurs in the first stanza of the tenth canto of *Don Juan* (1823), by Lord Byron (1788–1824):

> When Newton saw an apple fall, he found
> > In that slight startle from his contemplation—
> 'Tis *said* (for I'll not answer above ground
> > For any sage's creed or calculation)—
> A mode of proving that the Earth turned round
> > In a most natural whirl, called "Gravitation";
> And this is the sole mortal who could grapple,
> Since Adam—with a fall—or with an apple.

Since Newton's law of gravitation accounted for the orbital motion of Earth about the Sun—rather than for the daily rotational motion of Earth suggested by Byron's "turn[ing] round / In a most natural whirl"—one might question the poet's physics. Byron's very next stanza, however, contains an unmistakable reference to Earth's orbit, in the course of reassuring us that man's biblical fall is redeemed by his evolving knowledge (and Byron even hints that applied science—in the form of the steam engine—may soon get man into the heavens):

> Man fell with apples, and with apples rose,
>> If this be true; for we must deem the mode
> In which Sir Isaac Newton could disclose
>> Through the then unpaved stars the turnpike road,
> A thing to counterbalance human woes;
>> For ever since immortal man hath glowed
> With all kinds of mechanics, and full soon
> Steam-engines will conduct him to the Moon.

At the time of composition of *Don Juan,* by the way, turnpikes had not yet begun to be replaced by railways but Byron was evidently alert to the potentialities of early-nineteenth-century technological advance.

The Russian poet Vladimir Soloukhin (b. 1924), like Byron, accepts the legend of Newton's apple but, unlike Byron, Soloukhin professes to favor the apple's horticultural and alimentary roles as compared with its intellectual role in "The Apple" (quoting Daniel Weissbort's translation):

> I am convinced that finally
> Isaac Newton ate
> The apple that taught him
> The law of gravity.
>
> The apple, born of Earth and Sun,
> Came into being,
> Sprang from the seed,
> Ripened
> (And before this bees flew to it,
> Rain fell and a warm wind blew),
> Not so much that it might drop
> And by its direct motion demonstrate
> That gravity exists,
> But to become
>> heavy and sweet,
> Beautiful, juicy,
> To be admired and picked,
> Its scent enjoyed—
> And with its sweetness
> To delight a Man.

Soloukhin subscribes to the ideology of Pamyat'—a Russian political party with a seemingly contradictory mixture of slavophilic, culturally preservationist, and socially reactionary impulses—though whether (and if so how) his politics influences his view of Newton's apple is unclear to me.

Another contemporary Russian poet, the Jewish emigré Lev Mak (b. 1939), refers to "Newton-apples" in his "Eden" (1979). Mak was trained as an engineer but expelled from Russia in 1974 after the confiscation of all his writings; he now lives in the United States. His political point of view is obviously drastically different from Soloukhin's, and includes deep feelings for his lost Eden (in Daniel Weissbort's translation): "What have they done with your peoples, garden, / My homeland, where have they been hidden?"—lines from the second half of the poem, which, in a way, brings the ancient myth of the first half up to date. Thus, the first half of the poem describes the apple tree of Eden:

> Do not forget, Temptation has its price,
> And the fruit on the apple tree is from the Serpent:
> On the graftings of knowledge and retribution,
> Newton-apples hang from the Tree of Evil.

A more muted political significance is conveyed by the weightiness of apples in two enigmatic poems by the Latvian writer Imants Ziedonis (b. 1933), both translated by Inara Cedrins. One of the poems, "I Love an Apple," begins:

> I love an apple in the night, that floats
> without any branch and without any tree.
> I love an apple tree in night, that floats,
> bending its branches in the dark, without roots.

The two remaining stanzas leave the apple behind, now applying to the "whole earth" and to individual persons the phraseology already used to describe the apple: the speaker loves them—only?—when they are floating and unrooted. It is curious, then, that in "Try to Find" Ziedonis insists that all apples are heavy, which somehow proves that "neutral" (that is, unrooted?) apples are impossible:

> try to find
> a neutral apple
>
> they've all struggled heavily
> against the heavy earth
> and have fallen heavily
>
> those green grafted branches
> are witness
> that a neutral apple
> isn't possible.

John Hollander (b. 1929) contrasts Granny Smiths with American apple varieties, while alluding in passing to the fall of Newton's apple, in his "Granny Smith" (1971): the principal action in the poem is the falling of a Granny Smith apple, "green levin, to her grave / From Newton's skyward tree." Granny Smith apples—and ripe green apples ("greenings") in general—were rare in the United States in 1971 (less so in England, where Granny Smiths were introduced from Australia in the 1930s), and the archaic term "levin" (meaning lightning) strikes an appropriately exotic note. It is curious that Hollander refers, like Soloukhin, to "apples of the earth and sun," which he takes to include all the more ordinary apple varieties: "Bright Americans fallen or / Plucked."

Another American poet, Charles Simic (b. 1938), has written a poem "Dear Isaac Newton" (1982), explicitly about Newton's apple, which is from the start identified with the Edenic apple:

> Your famous apple
> Is still falling.
>
> Your red, ripe,
> Properly notarized
> Old Testament apple.

Simic's main conceit is that Newton's apple—identified as "The famous *malus pumila*," meaning crab, or dwarf, apple—has never stopped falling despite all our attempts "to cause her to stay up there." I cannot say I find the chattiness or affected jauntiness of some the lines very attractive: "(Is she suffering for us, Isaac, / In some still incomprehensible way?)"; "And wasn't that one of her / Prize worms / We saw crawling off / Into the unthinkable?" One other interrogatory stanza—the penultimate one—incorporates the pun on "fall" that seems to be the point of the poem:

> O she's falling lawfully,
> But isn't she now
> Perhaps even more mysterious
> Than when she first started?

Apples can also defy gravity, as in a prose poem by David Young (b. 1936)—one of "Four about Apples" (1977)—where apples fly (and also take part in human rituals).

The apple in the tree; the tree within the apple. Apple of the desert, desert of the apple. The apple in the body, pulsing; the body in the apple, cursing. The tower with its high room where an apple rests on the table next to a dark green bottle. The apple with wings, escaping through the casement, soaring out over the cemetery, resting-place of flesh and seeds, the

same place where, next to a freshly-dug grave, a coffin full of apples waits
for burial.

Even more radically, in numerous paintings by the Belgian surrealist René Magritte
(1881–1967)—almost all in private collections—apples are liberated from many of the
constraints consequent on their being members of the plant kingdom: apples defy
gravity (*The Post Card* [1960], reproduced in David Larkin's *Magritte* [1972] and in Suzi
Gablik's *Magritte* [1976]), swell to enormous size (*The Listening Room* [1958], reproduced in Larkin and in Jacques Meuris's *Magritte* [1994]), or replace a man's head (*The
Idea* [1966] reproduced in Gablik). Why, I cannot help wondering, are there apples in
so many of Magritte's paintings (I know of over a dozen) and why are they mostly
greenings? (Pears also appear occasionally in Magritte's paintings—accompanied by
apples in the two examples I know, which will be discussed in chapter 13, "Quinces
and Pears.")

A swelling apple also appears in a sequence of twelve photographs (11 x 14
inches, black and white) by the American Hollis Frampton (1936–1984), in collaboration with Marion Faller, where the increasing size of the apple as one moves from
upper left to lower right, against an unvarying background grid, must be read as an
advance of the piece of fruit toward the camera (in the penultimate photograph the
apple intersects the frame, while the last photograph is completely black). This work,
Apple Advancing [var. *"Northern Spy"*], is the last of sixteen identically formatted
sequences entitled *Sixteen Studies from Vegetable Locomotion* (1975). The subjects of these
studies—an obvious takeoff on Eadweard Muybridge's photographic studies of human
and animal locomotion in the late nineteenth century—include gourd, four kinds of
squash, sunflower, cabbage, radish, pumpkin, tomato, watermelon, corn, dill, beet, and
carrot. (For reproductions of all sixteen sequences, see Bruce Jenkins and Susan Krane,
Hollis Frampton: Recollections, Recreations [1984].)

Sheer Number of Apples

Because of their ubiquity in the temperate zones of Europe and America, apples have
frequently been used in those areas of the world for the verbal formulation of elementary algebraic problems. This pedagogical practice goes back at least to late antiquity.
Thus, in the *Greek Anthology* (14.117–119) one finds a set of three so-called arithmetical epigrams attributed to Metrodorus (4th cent. C.E.?), which are stated in terms
of apples. (There are also twenty-eight similar epigrams not involving apples attributed
to the same shadowy individual.) The six lines of Greek verse of 14.118 have been
literally rendered by W. R. Paton:

> Myrto once picked apples and divided them among her friends; she gave
> the fifth part to Chrysis, the fourth to Hero, the nineteenth to Psamathe,
> and the tenth to Cleopatra, but she presented the twentieth part to

Parthenope and gave only twelve to Evadne. Of the whole number a hundred and twenty fell to herself.

The solution is 380 (76+95+20+38+19+12+120). Robin Skelton has even produced a rhymed translation with Anglicized proper names.

It may not seem immediately obvious but, as with other discrete physical objects, an interest in mere numbers of apples may far transcend the trivial applications of a Metrodorus. Thus, I want to consider four poems about apples by Jean Follain (1903–1971): "Vie" (1953), "La Pomme rouge" (1953), "Eve" (1964), "Ces Trois pommes dernières" (1967), translated respectively by Waldrop, Gavronsky, McHugh, and Merwin. Like most of Follain's poems, each of the four consists of ten or twelve short lines almost totally lacking in punctuation. "Vie" (Life) is about a soldier who dies at the age of fifty; the most memorable event in his life was when he "set on the ground / a heavy sack of apples / two or three of which rolled out." "La Pomme rouge" (The red apple) is about change and permanence: Tintoretto and his daughter die, the earth's surface is altered by transportation systems, and voices change; "the Renaissance resists / in the chiaroscuro of museums," "but the red apple remains." "Ces Trois pommes dernières" (These last three apples) is about a man who buys the last three apples in a shop and a woman who also wanted the apples; she remarks that "there is always someone to buy what's left," which leads the loveless man "that evening with the fruit in hand / straight to his death." Finally, "Eve" explains an alternative to the biblical account of Eve's origin: her name comes from the Hebrew word *haya,* meaning "to live," and now "creatures / sure of their existence" transmit the truth about "human passions" to all girls, the youngest of whom "holds a blond apple / on a worn sill / and does nothing else / before she sleeps."

It looks as if the first three Follain poems bear little sign of Classical or biblical apple lore—indeed the very absence of such traditional lore may contribute to the flat, rather impersonal, "objective" effect. As for the last poem, the blond apple that finally makes its appearance seems to be doing little else than surviving (like the eponymous red apple of the earlier poem). The four poems may be said to constitute a set of variations on the contribution of sheer *number* to the significance of apples in literary contexts: the loose numerosity of the apples in the sack, the specificity of exactly three apples in the shop, the stark singularity of each of the two lone apple survivors. What is entirely missing from the four poems—presumably a deliberate choice—is any trace of the more sensuous properties of apples, such as their taste, odor, shape, and heft.

Can there be a surfeit of apples? Two different answers to this question have been provided by the New England poet Robert Frost and the Chilean poet Pablo Neruda (1904–73). Already in his great early collection, *North of Boston* (1914), Frost had a dark and difficult poem, "After Apple-picking," forty-two lines of irregularly varying length with an irregular rhyme scheme, in which the speaker attempts to come to terms with the impact on his inner fantasy life of the immense number of apples he has personally harvested. Having just finished his apple picking for the season—some ten thousand fruit, he tells us—we hear him anticipating how his dreams will be full of the smells, sights, touches, and sounds associated with apple-picking. He desperately needs sleep but as he is dozing off he cannot help raising the disturbing question of exactly what kind of sleep can come after the fatigue of such heroic apple picking. Two possible answers are suggested:

> One can see what will trouble
> This sleep of mine, whatever sleep it is.
> Were he not gone,
> The woodchuck could say whether it's like his
> Long sleep, as I describe its coming on,
> Or just some human sleep.

The woodchuck's hibernation is certainly very different physiologically and behaviorally from ordinary human sleep and the implication seems to be that the former is somehow to be preferred—it is not immediately clear why. In his book on Frost's poetry, Richard Poirier suggests a reason: "His [the apple picker's] sleep will be human precisely because it will be a disturbed, dream- and myth-ridden sleep. Human sleep is more than animal sleep for the very reason that it is bothered by memories of what it means to pick apples." Perhaps the apple-picker is—impossibly—longing for the untroubled sleep of the woodchuck (in Poirier's terms, for return to a pre-Fall consciousness).

Not surprisingly for anyone who is acquainted with some of his yea-saying poetry, Neruda is much more enthusiastic than Frost about the superabundance of apples in the world, which, indeed, Neruda appeals to in order to communicate a simplistic, almost sloganistic, "one world" ideology. Neruda begins his "Ode to the Apple" (1957) by celebrating the fruit (in Maria Jacketti's translation) as "always / newly fallen / from Paradise: / simple / and pure / rouged cheek / of dawn!"—deliberately rejecting the religious association of apples with sin. The apple is then exalted above all other fruits ("grapes in their cells," "gloomy / mangos," "bony plums," "figs / in their underwater world") culminating in the highest praise for any food—a comparison with bread and cheese: "You are pure pomade, / fragrant bread, / the cheese / of vegetables." The poem then concludes with a rather limp political message:

> I crave
> your absolute
> abundance,
> your family
> multiplied.
> I want a city,
> a republic,
> the Mississippi river rolling
> with apples,
> and along its banks,
> I want to see

> the population
> of the entire world,
> united, reunited,
> enjoying the simplest act on Earth:
> eating an apple.

It is of considerable interest, I believe, to see what a biologist can contribute to the question of apple numbers. Bernd Heinrich (b. 1940) begins his discussion of the question with an account of apple blossoms:

> As Robert Frost and others have long noted, their sudden appearance is startling and beautiful. When the thick buds at the ends of the apple tree's twigs open to reveal five or six flowers, they also quickly unfurl six to seven small, mouse ear-size leaves. The unfurling of the flowers takes precedence over the leaves. Among the flowers on any one bud, the central one surrounded by five others is the first to open. The other five follow so quickly that the tree seems almost to erupt in its blazing show of pink.

Heinrich's next observation is that "each bud yields one twiglet with flower and leaves. I counted on average eight twiglets with 6 blossoms on every one-eighth-inch diameter twig. Could such a small twig support forty-eight apples?" In fact, "about 96.5 percent of the fruit is aborted early in development. The small number of maturing fruits relative to what might be produced is not a failure of the tree. It is instead a triumph of adaptation. Trees regulate their own reproduction to produce only what they can support."

Apples, Peeled and Sliced

One might doubt that in contemporary Israeli literature it would be possible to evade the traditional associations of apples. Yehuda Amichai (1924–2000) does manage to write a purely secular Hebrew love poem, "With Her in an Apple" (1989), involving apples by a most untraditional concentration on the peel, but tellingly includes a biblical allusion to prophecy and an apocalyptic-sounding allusion to scorched fields (here translated by Benjamin and Barbara Harshav):

> You visit me in an apple.
> We listen together to the knife
> Paring all around us, carefully
> Not to tear the peel.
>
> You speak to me, I can trust your voice,
> It holds pieces of hard pain
> As real honey holds waxen pieces
> Of honeycomb.
>
> With my fingers I touch your lips.
> This too is a gesture of prophecy.

> Your lips are red, as a scorched field is black.
> Everything comes true.
>
> You visit me in an apple.
> And you stay with me in the apple
> Till the paring knife finishes its work.

The English poet Charles Tomlinson (b. 1927), in an early poem, "Paring the Apple" (1955), dwells on the artistry of producing that "spring of concentric peel / Unwinding off white"—an artistry in no way inferior to that which produces portraits and still lifes:

> There are portraits and still-lifes
> And the first, because 'human'
> Does not excel the second, and
> Neither is less weighted
> With a human gesture, than paring the apple
> With a human stillness.

Not only the process of paring but the product—"apple-rind / Compelling a recognition"—takes its place (in the last words of Tomlinson's preface) in "the song of a universe that offered an otherness that was both concrete and inexhaustible."

The enormous versatility of apple imagery is well illustrated by a radically different use of apple peel in the memoir of Frank McCourt (b. 1930) and his family in New York and Ireland, *Angela's Ashes* (1996). At one point, after his family has returned to Limerick in the 1930s, against a background of harrowing disease and extreme hunger, McCourt tells of a favorite game played by a sadistic teacher:

> It is torture to watch Mr. O'Neill peel the apple every day, to see the length of it, red or green, and if you're up near him to catch the freshness of it in your nose. If you're the good boy for that day and you answer the questions he gives it to you and lets you eat it there at your desk so that you can eat it in peace with no one to bother you the way they would if you took it into the yard. Then they'd torment you, Gimme a piece, gimme a piece, and you'd be lucky to have an inch left for yourself.
>
> There are days when the questions are too hard and he torments us by dropping the apple peel into the wastebasket.

A little later in McCourt's narrative, these painful school episodes are balanced by an idyllic passage recounting an escape from school discipline by the ten-year-old Frank and his pal Paddy; the two boys skip school (thereby missing lunch) and wander into an apple orchard.

> We stuff apples into our shirts till we can barely get back over the wall to run into a long field and sit under a hedge eating the apples till we can't

swallow another bit and we stick our faces into a stream for the lovely cool water. Then we run to opposite ends of a ditch to shit and wipe ourselves with grass and thick leaves. Paddy is squatting and saying, There's nothing in the world like a good feed of apples, a drink of water and a good shit, better than any sangwidge of cheese and mustard and Dotty O'Neill can shove his apple up his arse.

Finally, the boys discover a cow, drink milk directly from her teats, and escape from an irate farmer; whereupon Frank wonders "why anyone should be hungry in a world full of milk and apples."

The peeling of an apple has also been likened to poetic composition in "Apple Peeler" (1953), by Robert Francis:

> Why the unbroken spiral, Virtuoso,
> Like a trick sonnet in one long, versatile sentence?
>
> Is it a pastime merely, this perfection,
> For an old man, sharp knife, long night, long winter?
>
> Or do your careful fingers move at the stir
> Of unadmitted immemorial magic?
>
> Solitaire. The ticking clock. The apple
> Turning, turning as the round earth turns.

Connected with this poem is an anecdote involving Robert Francis's friend and mentor, Robert Frost. In the following, I draw on the account in Lawrance Thompson and R. H. Winnick, *Robert Frost: The Later Years, 1938–1963* (1976). When Frost encountered Francis's "Apple Peeler" on its first publication, he assumed, apparently mistakenly, that the "trick sonnet" in the poem was Frost's own sonnet, "The Silken Tent," and that the "old man" in the poem must be Frost himself. In revenge, Frost wrote a quite nasty poem about Francis, "On the Question of an Old Man's Feeling," which he never showed to Francis and never published—and which remains unpublished, not even being included in the Library of America volume, *Robert Frost: Collected Poems, Prose, and Plays* (1995). Thompson and Winnick do print some lines from Frost's poem, of which the following triplet particularly demonstrates the poet's hurt feelings:

> He found fault with an aging friend for reeling
> A sonnet off with skill for lack of feeling
> In one unbroken length like apple peeling.

Often before eating an apple one slices it, usually into halves, a practice explored for some of its metaphorical possibilities by the Italian poet Biancamaria

Frabotta (b. 1946), in a poem from her first collection, *Il rumore bianco* (White noise, 1982):

> The apple you teach me is to double the half [*metà*] of self.
> Life you teach me is the slices of the apple
> the ambition [*meta*] of the regrettable circumstance
> the mirror which doubles the head of good hope
> the head split in two by a fog walking by
> two halves in one, the complete apple, copulation [*una copula*] of poor taste.

I would prefer the literal meaning of *meta* (goal or purpose) and of *copula* (conjunction). The translator, Catherine O'Brien, tells us that in the poems of *White Noise* the idea of "psychological division" recurs, which puts a name to the halved apple metaphors without really explaining them.

The merely imagined halving of an apple may serve to symbolize an underlying unity, whether of two people or of individual and community, as in a short poem by Nazim Hikmet (1902–1963); the poem is one in a sequence called "9–10 P.M. Poems," written while he was a political prisoner and addressed to his wife (translated by Blasing and Konuk):

> 27 *October 1945*
> We are one half of an apple,
>   the other half is this big world.
> We are one half of an apple,
>   the other half is our people.
> You are one half of an apple,
>   the other half is me,
>   us two . . .

This is a case, I think, when a poetic image is saved from banality by the known circumstances of its composition: real bars separate what the two imagined halves of the apple stand for.

Eaten Apples

In the twentieth century, the usual motive for eating an apple is its taste. In her "Green Apple," the American poet Elinor Wylie (1883–1928) uses various elements in the taste of a green (presumably unripe) apple to evoke a "personal emotional experience"— the phrase is that of Jane D. Wise, who transcribed the poem from Wylie's undated manuscript and then published it posthumously (1943). Like all Wylie's verse, the poem is traditional in both form and content: six rhymed, metrically regular quatrains on the—obliquely but unmistakably expressed—theme of love. Beginning unpromisingly with one of William Blake's most famous lines, the poem's successive characterizations of the apple's savor (flavor plus odor) include references to nectar, brine, honey, lilacs, salt, juniper and balsam trees, thorn, and nuts. The last stanza stands somewhat apart, not least by its last line—with four accents (to match the first three lines) rather than the two accents of previous stanzas; here are the first and last stanzas:

> In England's green and pleasant land
> I plucked an apple greener still;
> I took the apple in my hand
> As women will.
>   [. . . . .]
> Some love the saps of west and south
> And some the apple sharp and cold
> And may it come to as fair a growth
> As those who planted it foretold.

Wylie's poetry is no longer highly regarded, or even much read, but it continues to be anthologized, as in the first volume of the Library of America collection, *American Poetry: The Twentieth Century* (2000), which includes one of Wylie's best poems, "Wild Peaches" (to be discussed in chap. 21, "Fruit, Conjoined and Disjoined").

Perhaps not many Americans have seen in apple growing (as Amelia Simmons does) a solution to their society's economic problems, but eating apples has certainly been touted as medicinally valuable, if not quite in the same class as chicken soup. This association of apples and good health informs the Shirley Kaufman (b. 1923) poem, "Apples" (1973), about her mother's illness. The poet remembers from her childhood her mother's phrase (always accompanying the offer of apples), "eat and be well," and the poet repeats the phrase when she brings the apples she has picked to her mother's sickbed. Three of the eight stanzas stand out for the freshness of their perceptions, first of picking apples, then of opening them:

> I stretch my arms for apples
> anyway, feel how the ripe ones
> slide in my hands like cups
> that want to be perfect. Juices
> locked up in the skin.
>
> She used to slice them in quarters,
> cut through the core,
> open the inside out. Fingers
> steady on the knife, expert
> at stripping things.
>
> Sometimes she split them sideways
> into halves to let a star break
> from the center with tight seeds,

> because I wanted that,
> six petals in the flesh.

Kaufman has recalled her mother's special ways of slicing apples to show off the symmetry of their internal structure. The last two stanzas return us from the past to her mother's sickbed and are less perceptive—it is far from felicitous, for example, to characterize pieces of apple as "celery white" and the poem ends with a rather trite comparison: "swallowing / apples, swallowing her life."

Another American poet, Roger Weingarten (b. 1945), writes, in "Apples" (1986), about subsisting on apples as he builds himself a house after his divorce: "a local orchard / kept me alive with Yellow Transparents / and Paula Reds." The house burned down but he "can still taste / Seek No Further, Sheepsnose, Roxbury / Russet and that one reeling / monk of a Winesap." After the quotidian details of the first two-thirds of the poem—sawdust, plumb bob, hammer, and apples—Weingarten treats us to two fantasies:

> If I were a worm
>
> I'd tunnel into the core, curl up
> and dream that I was the first
> Red Delicious to cultivate the concupiscent
>
> eye of the woman who wrote the first
> independent clause in the history of love.
> If I were the world, I'd metamorphose
>
> into the mature ovary
> of an apple tree, into the almond-sweet
> cyanide of its seed, into its vermilion
>
> red envelope, into the snowstorm
> of its hard flesh, and rot
> in the palm of God's hand
>
> as He regards His handiwork
> breaking up into continents, sinking
> into oceans, with no little satisfaction,
>
> awe and lust *si señor.*

Just as Weingarten slides easily from carpentry to wormy apples to God, so other contemporary poets present the eating of an apple as a generic metaphor for sin or temptation. The Canadian poet Ralph Gustafson (b. 1909) joyfully celebrates the act of biting into an apple in "My Love Eats an Apple" (1972):

> She bites into the red skin
> Of the white hard apple in bed
> And there is joy in heaven
> [. . . . .]
> God sits up there amongst
> His shamefully nude nudgers,
> Praising sin,
> The juice of the plucked
> Happy apple
> In great psalms and paeans
> Dripping down His testamentary beard.

The American poet Cary Waterman (b. 1942) presents us, in her "Temptation" (1980), with a narrative about a recumbent young woman holding an apple in her hands and facing a seated nude little girl. The title of the poem derives from the title of a painting of 1880 (oil on canvas, 38 3/16 x 51 3/16 in.) by William Bouguereau (1825–1905), which, we are told in the epigraph, inspired the poem. The exact nature of the temptation in the painting is unclear, perhaps unknowable; one Bouguereau specialist, Robert Isaacson, thinks "the provocative title may refer to nothing more than the woman, perhaps the mother, trying to coax the child to take the painter's desired pose." In the poem's first stanza, the narrator asks us to imagine the painter either setting out for the locale represented in the painting—a patch of green sward jutting out into a pond—or simply unrolling in his studio a painted backdrop in the form of a piece of oilcloth. (For a reproduction of the painting, which is in the Minneapolis Institute of Arts, see the catalogue *William Bouguereau, 1825–1905* [1984], or Fronia Wissman's *Bouguereau* [1996].) Given what is rather definitively known of Bouguereau's painting procedures (which were those of traditional French academic painters), it is highly improbable that Bouguereau ever left his studio while, in the words of Waterman's poem, "carrying / that dented paint box / and a lightweight, brand-new easel," since, outside his studio, Bouguereau made only "thumb nail sketches" (*croquis*), either in pencil or ink. (On Bouguereau's working methods, see Mark Steven Walker, "Bouguereau at Work" [1984].) The three middle stanzas of the poem, constituting some two-thirds of the lines, formulate an accurate verbal equivalent of the painting, spiced with some conjecture as to the relationship between the two figures: "the child turns to the woman / who is perhaps an older sister / or a maid from the kitchen / who has been given the afternoon off." What follows next is the narrator's interpretation—or, better, rejection—of original sin; for we are told that these same two figures

> know that all our sins
> are original and that
> there is no temptation here
> but to eat a late summer apple,

> teeth thundering through
> the red skin and white juice
> to reach the seeds at the center
> while a foolish man stands
> with his back to all the light.

The foolish man is of course the painter, and the final stanza finds him retiring for "a supper of boiled cabbage / and thin slices of tender lamb," as he abandons his painting together with his two models. The choice of lamb for the painter's meal is presumably to assure us that, just as there is no meaning for original sin, so too the lamb is altogether secular (no Lamb of God). The reader, though, is left with the problem of the narrator: is she foolish too?

Perhaps one might even ask if the simple act of eating an apple can ever be foolish. One Italian poet of the turn of the twentieth century certainly thought so. Indeed, Guido Gozzano (1883–1916) created a poetic persona with "the uncanny ability to come away from any experience a frustrated fool" (in the words of his translator, Michael Palma). The poem I have in mind is a sonnet called "Parable," from Gozzano's first book, *The Road to Shelter* (1907); this was published a few years before his more important book of poetry, *The Colloquies* (1911), which opens with the Prufrockian lines:

> Twenty-five years old! . . . I'm old, I'm old!
> The prime of youthfulness has passed me by
> and left its gift (and left me in the cold).

The early sonnet I want to quote is at least proto-Prufrockian, most notable for its mundane—and entirely untraditional—subject matter: the unceremonious consumption of an utterly demythologized apple. Palma's translation of "Parable" cleverly captures many of the Italian rhymes, such as "the happy apple" for *la bella mela:*

> Through tiny fingers he looks to see
> the happy apple he clutches tight:
> he waits—it's perfect and so bright—
> before he inflicts the injury.
>
> He hurries once he starts to bite:
> now the apple sits insipidly
> in the eye ambitious for delight . . .
> Already it's half what it used to be.
>
> He bites and then he bites some more—
> each time the look before the tooth—
> until he stops when the core arrives.

"Hardly a taste and here's the core!"
the boy thinks . . . The ambitious eyes
have pulled each pleasure to the mouth.

Cooked Apples

The simplest way to cook an apple is to bake it, but not even every middle-class household in eighteenth-century England possessed an oven; this fact is of some importance in Jane Austen's *Emma,* a novel that Maggie Lane sees as "uniquely laden with references to food." The missing oven emerges in the course of an extended monologue (in chapter 27) by Miss Bates, whose position and character may be adequately summed up in a few of Austen's phrases from the beginning of the novel (chap. 3): "a most uncommon degree of popularity for a woman neither young, handsome, rich, nor married"; "a great talker upon little matters." Miss Bates lives with her mother and niece, Jane Fairfax, an impoverished and sickly orphan, who is also an attractive and talented young lady. The main topic of Miss Bates's monologue—one might almost call it a harangue—is Jane's favorite (indeed, almost her only) food: baked apples. The apples are generously supplied by George Knightley—the man Emma will eventually marry—from his own orchard and the gift is so discreetly managed that, in Lane's words, "Mr Knightley is giving Emma—and us—an example of how to do good by stealth." But Miss Bates is communicating much more than a moral lesson for Emma's (and the reader's) edification; she is also shrewdly characterizing many of the nodes in the complex network of exchanges by means of which Mr. Knightley's apples are transferred from one character to another, at some point cooked, and then eventually consumed by Jane Fairfax. For one thing, Knightley's servants are involved, including William Larkins, who is pleased when he brings the last of the season's apples to the Bateses because he has already managed to sell so much of the crop for his master's profit, and Mrs. Hodges, who is displeased because she will not be able to make any more of her master's favorite apple tarts. For another thing, the apples are baked by the town baker as a favor to the Bateses even though the Bateses buy little of the baker's bread. Finally, there is the question of Jane's severe loss of appetite (perhaps more than a touch of what we would today call anorexia nervosa).

We find a speaker preparing some apples for baking in the first part of the prose poem "Apples" (1979), by the American poet Margaret Gibson (b. 1944):

I am peeling the apples making a note to replenish
the cinnamon. The knife pares in circles. The smell
of the peeling teases the air.

As she works, she looks out the window at an empty road and the sense of a deeply felt loss overwhelms her: "A soldier in brown, this man who has always been missing in action." The second (and concluding) part of the poem asserts, not very convincingly, a connection between baking apples and the presumed death of the missing man. Thus, the speaker places the apple peelings around her arms, calling them "little slave bracelets," and even identifies the man with "the knife that whistles at the core."

Finally: "I whistle. White wedges of apple bake in the oven. Death is the heat. I will sugar them, glaze them, serve them and eat."

Apples may also be baked in a pie, and an apple pie is the recurring image in an anonymous little alphabet book (4⅝ x 6 inches) first published over a century and a half ago in New York (and reprinted in New York in 1973), *The Adventures of A, Apple Pie, Who Was Cut to Pieces and Eaten by Twenty Six Young Ladies and Gentlemen.* Versions of this apple pie alphabet go back to at least the seventeenth century in England (see Gloria Delamar's *Mother Goose, from Nursery to Literature* [1987]). The Opies, in their monumental *Oxford Dictionary of Nursery Rhymes* (2d ed., 1997), add the further information that in 1742 this alphabet "figured in the Coopers' enlightened spelling book *The Childs' New Play-thing,* and it was common in the latter half of the century in the chapbook series. . . . The rhyme was a favourite for ABC instruction in the nineteenth century. Kate Greenaway made a book of it, *A Apple Pie,* which is still reprinted."

In the booklet I described above, each letter of the alphabet is assigned a separate page, always with the colored image of an immense apple pie occupying center stage (the illustrations in the early editions would have been hand-colored). Here are the texts accompanying the first four and the last four letters:

> a   apple pie.
> b   bit it.
> c   curtsied for it.
> d   dreamed of it.
>   [. . . . .]
> w   watched it.
> x   storm'd for a share,
>   Like a vixen so bold
>   You'd have thought had you seen her
>   'Twas Xantippe the scold.
> y   yeomaned it,
> z   mounted his zebra,
>   And said with a zest.
>   Though his share was the last.
>   Yet he liked it the best.

An amusing set of recommendations on how to make a good apple pie, "Of Apple-Pyes," was composed in 1704 by Leonard Welsted (1688–1747), an English civil servant and occasional poet. Consisting of seventy-seven lines of heroic couplets, the poem purports to recount the evolution of apple pie from a crude dish to its present refined form. Among the recommended ingredients are quinces, cloves, and orange water. (The text has been reprinted in *Petits Propos Culinaires* [2000].)

An elegant variation on apple pie is the Italian pastry which the American poet Jane Hirshfield (b. 1953) deems worthy of a short poem, entitled "Mele in Gabbia" (1997):

The pastry
is dusted with sugar.
The slices of apple inside,
just sour enough.

The name,
"apples in a cage."

I eat them
in this good place—
the pastry warm,
a little bit chewy,
the linen
impeccably white—
and consider.

Apple pie occurs memorably as a prop in the quite dreadful scenario of an early short story by Raymond Carver (1938–1988). In "Bright Red Apples" (1967) we encounter a paradigmatic dysfunctional family living on what appears to be a non-functioning farm: feeble elderly father, long-suffering mother striving against the odds to hold the family together, brain-damaged and passive elder son, and the central character, an angry high school dropout younger son named Rudy. The only thing that briefly calms Rudy's homicidal fury against the members of his family is apples, whether in the form of pie, trees, or windfall. At the end of the story Rudy positions himself, rifle in hand with the crosshairs fixed on the porch, "behind an apple tree a hundred years from the house." When no one from the family appears, while "A small band of California mountain quail began to work their way down through the orchard, stopping every now and then to pick at a fallen apple," Rudy finally can stand it no longer. The story ends as, "With a last, forlorn glance at the empty porch, he placed the shiny, recently blued barrels of the 12–gauge double into his mouth." There are odd—but presumably deliberate—gaps in the narrative structure of the story, as when Rudy first notices the smell of his mother's freshly baked apple pie in the kitchen, and is then, without further explanation, discovered devouring half an apple pie in the barn. The case of Rudy's firearms is even more disconcerting: within what seems to be an interval of just a few minutes, he wields a Smith & Wesson .38 service revolver, a Colt .45, a BAR (Browning automatic rifle), and a 12-gauge shotgun. Carver's writing here is almost as erratic as Rudy's behavior. (Perhaps this is what Carver's widow, Tess Gallagher—who reluctantly decided to reprint this piece of Carver juvenilia—had in mind when she wrote that "'Bright Red Apples' . . . doesn't seem to know what it's about.")

Carver's propensity for associating domesticity with doom never went away. In his poem, "My Daughter and Apple Pie" (1985), he is served a piece of freshly baked

apple pie by his daughter and, silently noting her dark glasses, thinks with pain of the
man she loves. In another poem of the same period, "To My Daughter," Carver refers
explicitly to the dark glasses which hide her "beautiful bruised eyes."

The meaning of Carver's bright red apples and freshly baked apple pies are only
too obvious: they are soothing, reassuringly domestic, even potentially life-enhancing—
which is also precisely the effect of the apples in a grotesque story by the British
writer, Sara Maitland (b. 1950). Maitland's "Gluttony" (1988) is one of seven brief
pieces by seven different authors in a collection on the traditional deadly sins. There
are three different "voices" in Maitland's piece: first, a collection of recipes for four
apple desserts; next, the first-person narrative of an unnamed woman, born in 1950,
married with a six-month-old daughter, and speaking to an unidentified friend; and,
finally, the second-person narrative about Mother Angela, a seventy-year-old nun
obsessed with the sinfulness of her own gnawing hunger. There are fourteen (unnumbered) sections in all; the first is a recipe for "Classic Baked Apple," the last is a meditation by Mother Angela on Eve and the apple in Eden. The recipes form an escalating
series, steadily richer and more elaborate (more eggs, more butter, more sugar), from
the aforementioned baked apples to "Krapfen" (fried dough containing beer and
grated apples) to "Hot apple flan with calvados" to "Alsatian apple tart." The mother
is a gourmand (a "foodie" in contemporary slang), who tells in great detail of her
ecstatic food experiences; presumably, the apple dessert recipes are hers. Her mood
increasingly apologetic, she finally reveals her secret: in an uncontrollably gluttonous
act she has consumed her baby: "I ate my baby, à la tartare. It was the best meal I had
ever had. Simply delicious. I loved her. I loved her and I ate her." The last voice in the
story, as noted above, is that of Mother Angela, meditating on *her* mother—*everyone's*
mother—Eve:

> This was the original sinless apple, round and smooth and smelling of the
> first long perfect summer in all creation. She was overwhelmed with long-
> ing. She ate the apple. Genesis got it wrong. It wasn't pride, it wasn't desire
> for knowledge, it wasn't even competition with God. It was greed. The
> apple beguiled her and she ate.

We are back with Plutarch's apple, now not only physically but also morally and
metaphysically perfect. Is the message one of women's liberation or is this a warning
that without a moral discipline based on the idea of sin even cannibalism becomes
acceptable?

Fermented Apples: Cider

Jean Le Houx (1545/6–1616), a lawyer in the small town of Vire, in Normandy, composed, according to his editor and translator, James Patrick Muirhead, "a collection of
considerably more than one hundred songs, of which, amid all their diversity of treatment and expression, the dominant theme is the praise of cider, of wine, and of good-
fellowship." Here, in translation, are two of the cider songs:

Some men, in their foolishness,
>   Make it quite the common way
Rather to be stripped of dress,
>   Than at drinking-bout to stay.
Cider good [*Bon pommé*], shalt thou be lost?
Rather let us drink thee most!

To dissimulate our thirst
>   Is shame or hypocrisy;
But to go away is worst,
>   Spurning such a courtesy.
Chorus.

When I see thee, I am blest;
>   My throat waits thee cider [*sildre*] good,
As the bird which, in the nest,
>   Waiteth for its little food.
Chorus.

~

I will drink the good apple-trees' health!
For this year they will yield cider-wealth
At a pot for six farthings; whereby
Thirst will surely be ruined and die.
>   [. . . . .]
They will get but a penny, to fell
A whole bushel of fruit ripened well,
And they cannot get rid of the pears
Therefore who to mix water now cares?
>   [. . . . .]
If you'll give them but one empty cask,
They will fill you another, and ask
Nothing more; so good times, never fear,
Have come back. Bless the plentiful year!

Then rejoice, merry comrades all round!
For again shall your melodies sound
And again, as gay chorus ye sing,
Shall the fame of your Vaux-de-Vire ring.

Sixteen hundred and twelve was the timer
When a good cider-lad made this rhyme:

All the neighbours, their homage to pay,
Come to visit him throned on the way!

By the nineteenth century, cider was a major agricultural product in France. Thus, in conveying to us the "scientific" ethos of the provincial pharmacist Homais (in *Madame Bovary* [1857]), Flaubert (1821–1880) has his character boast of having written (in Francis Steegmuller's translation) "a rather considerable little treatise—a monograph of over seventy-two pages, entitled: *Cider: Its Manufacture and its Effects; Followed by Certain New Observations on This Subject*"; and for this Homais has been rewarded with membership in "the Agronomical Society of Rouen . . . Agricultural Section, Pomology Division." Finally, it must be noted, that France is still the world's largest producer of cider (though most of it is turned into apple brandy).

Cider has long occupied a prominent place in the English potatory imagination, patriotic imbibers having no alternative but to reconcile themselves to the sobering fact that the English environment supports excellent apples but only mediocre wine grapes, the problem being not the cold winters but rather the deficit of summer warmth and sunshine for ripening the grapes. That is why, as James Galloway explains, "although quite common, medieval English wine-making seems to have been generally small-scale and unreliable as to quality, production of wine alternating with that of verjuice (the juice of unripe grapes, used in cooking) and vinegar." (On verjuice, see also chapter 18, "Grapes.")

No less a figure than Isaac Newton was concerned with the quality of the cider served at Cambridge University (where he had been appointed Lucasian Professor of Mathematics in 1669). In a letter of 2 September 1676 to the secretary of the Royal Society, Henry Oldenburg, Newton discusses at some length the question of which are the best cider apples for growing in Cambridge. It seems that "Red Streaks (the famous fruit for cyder in other parts) will not succeed in this country. The tree thrives well here, and bears as much fruit, and as good to look as in other countries; but the cyder made of it they find harsh and churlish, and so this fruit begins here to be generally neglected." (A late-seventeenth-century text, cited by Stuart Peachey, characterizes "Red Strake" apples as follows: "greenish, striped all over with red; this is a good Sider Apple.") Newton then continues: "The ill success of Red Streaks here, I perceive, is generally imputed to the soil; but since the tree thrives, and bears as well here as in other parts, I am apt to think it is in the manner of making the cyder." In particular, Newton suggests that the mixing of Red Streaks with other apple varieties *in the proper proportions* may be what is required for making the best cider:

What sort of fruit are best to be used, and in what proportion they are to be mixed, and what degree of ripeness they ought to have? Whether it be material to press them as soon as gathered, or to pare them? Whether there be any circumstances to be observed in pressing them? or what is the best way to do it? If you can direct us to, or procure for us a short narrative of the way of making and ordering cyder in the cyder countries, which takes in a resolution of these, or the most material of these queries, you will oblige your humble servant.

Newton's concern for mathematical exactitude was, of course, a dominating feature of his approach to nature. It may be worth mentioning that in the months just before and just after writing the above letter, Newton was engaged in research on mathematics, on experiments regarding a quantitative theory of spectral colors, and on a quantitative approach to alchemy. Indeed, in a letter of 14 November 1676 to Oldenburg, Newton's opening paragraph is, once again, about cider, after which he turns to mathematics. As to the cider, Newton is eager to obtain some grafts from the apple trees of Ralph Austen (d. 1676), a famous Oxford horticulturist, who, unfortunately, had just died without an heir to take over his horticulture business. The garden historian Mavis Batey has written about Austen:

> Profits and Pleasures was stamped on the title page of Ralph Austen's *The Spiritual Use of an Orchard or Garden of Fruit Trees,* published in Oxford in 1653. The first part of the book gave clear instructions for planting based on experimental methods and the second part of the book was aimed at promoting Puritanism. Austen had his own nursery in Oxford and academics started their own orchards. So great was his trade that he estimated that he could sell 20,000 plants a year from his seedlings and grafts.

(We will take a look at Austen's "Profits and Pleasures" in chapter 22, "Enemies and Friends of Fruit.")

A considerable English literature in praise of cider developed in the seventeenth century, culminating with John Philips (1676–1709) and his Miltonesque epic in two books, *Cyder* (1708), with its triumphalist conclusion:

> where-e'er the *British* spread
> Triumphant Banners, or their Fame has reach'd
> Diffusive, to the utmost Bounds of this
> Wide Universe, *Silurian* Cyder borne
> Shall please all Tasts, and triumph o'er the Vine.

Philips's poem includes many lengthy digressions—on such topics as the praise of women and of Queen Anne in particular—interspersed among the passages on how to graft apple trees and on the best varieties of apples for making cider. It is difficult to credit the opinion of Dr. Johnson (1709–1794) that *Cyder* was not only Philips's "greatest work" but "as an imitation of Virgil's Georgic . . . needed not shun the presence of the original." It is true, however, that Johnson also thought Philips had chosen the wrong poetic style for his poem: blank verse was too elevated for the subject matter and rhymed couplets would have been more appropriate.

One of Philips's digressions is on the wonders of pear cider—also known as "perry"—(if only, Philips laments, it were free of sediment!): "Chiefly the *Bosbury,* whose large Increase, / Annual, in sumptuous Banquets claims Applause. / Thrice acceptable Bev'rage! could but Art / Subdue the floating Lee, *Pomona's* self / Would dread thy Praise, and shun the dubious Strife." Finally, though, in a version of what seems to be a traditional competition between apples and pears—a competition to which we shall return later in chapter 13 on pears—the champion apple variety wins out:

> Let every Tree in every Garden own
> The *Red-streak* as supream; whose pulpous Fruit
> With Gold irradiate, and Vermilion shines
> Tempting, not fatal, as the Birth of that
> Primæval interdicted Plant, that won
> Fond *Eve* in Hapless hour to taste, and die.
> This, of more bounteous Influence, inspires
> Poetic Raptures, and the lowly Muse
> Kindles to loftier Strains; even I perceive
> Her sacred Virtue. See! the Numbers flow
> Easie, whilst, chear'd with her nectareous Juice,
> Hers, and my Country's Praises I exalt.
> [. . . . .]
> What shou'd we wish for more? or why, in quest
> Of Foreign Vintage, insincere, and mixt,
> Traverse th' extreamest World? Why tempt the Rage
> Of the rough Ocean? when our native Glebe
> Imparts, from bounteous Womb, annual Recruits
> Of Wine delectable, that far surmounts
> *Gallic,* or *Latin* Grapes.

In modern times, the English fondness for cider appears in a relatively late poem by Thomas Hardy (1840–1928), "Great Things" (1917). The poem is in ballad form; the first stanza particularly extols the glories of cider:

> Sweet cyder is a great thing,
> > A great thing to me,
> Spinning down to Weymouth town
> > By Ridgway thirstily,
> And maid and mistress summoning
> > Who tend the hostelry:
> O cyder is a great thing,
> > A great thing to me!

The next two stanzas describe, respectively, two more "great things" (dancing and love) while the last stanza, in typical Hardy fashion, alludes to the poet's inevitable oblivion, and then reassures us that "Joy-jaunts, impassioned flings, / Love, and its ecstasy, / Will always have been great things, / Great things to me!" But surely there is cold comfort in the future perfect tense of "Will always have been."

A poem full of multiple pomaceous allusions is "Eve's Apple" (1992), by Peter Redgrove (b. 1932); the dominant images are of apple cider (occurring explicitly in five of the seven stanzas) but there are also apple peel, apple trees, apple juice, Eden, and the snake in the apple. A clear line of development from beginning to end is difficult to make out, so I will quote three stanzas, each of which seems to make sense on its own:

> I
>
> The sunbather in the sunshine, her body
> Slowly browning, as though carved out of the white flesh
> Of many apples; and she sips strong cider
> In the sun, and through her peel sweats alcohol.
>
> II
>
> Peeling an apple with a silver knife
> In one continuous strip, he looks
> As wise or wiser than anyone who peers
> Round the stinking bowl of some Sherlock pipe.
>
> [. . . . .]
>
> V
>
> Every one of the linked organs of the body
> Brims with its own apple-spirit, like heavy jugs
> Of cider, just as the crushed ghosts of apple-trees
> Poured from jug to jug fill the farmhouse kitchen and
> Gnarled fruiting trees bend over our table; this is
> My Eden-haunt, and the woman pours for us.

Imperfect Apples: Cores and Rot

In contrast to Plutarch's view of the apple as the most nearly perfect fruit, some writers have focused on the apple's imperfections, such as its nasty, inedible core or its inherent tendency to rot—and thereby to rot its neighbors, as in the proverb: "One rotten apple spoils the barrel." Thus, in the novel *L'Assommoir* (1876), by Émile Zola, the moral corruption of Nana by the young girls with whom she works in an artificial flower workshop is said to be "just like those baskets of apples in which one or two have started to go" (Leonard Tancock's translation). In English literature, perhaps the best-known allusion to a rotten apple occurs in an aside by Bassanio in act 1, scene 3, of Shakespeare's *The Merchant of Venice* (1598):

> The devil can cite Scripture for his purpose, —
> An evil soul producing holy witness

Is like a villain with a smiling cheek,
A goodly apple, rotten at the heart.
O, what a goodly outside falsehood hath!

Bassanio produces the rotten apple metaphor in response to Shylock's lengthy and slightly obscure comparison between his own loaning of money at interest and Jacob's breeding of his uncle Laban's sheep (in Genesis). The devil's association with the forbidden apple gives an extra edge, of course, to Bassanio's remark. I cannot help expressing a little indignation, though, at the way Shakespeare has set Shylock up for Bassanio's aside. The point of Shylock's biblical midrash is, admittedly, uncertain (see John Russell Brown's note on the passage [1977], in which he summarizes four different interpretations). Shylock has been saddled with a tendentious rationalization that seems to be sheer invention on Shakespeare's part (according to Brown, there are no sixteenth-century books on usury which mention the Laban story).

It is interesting that in a couple of poems by Clarence Major (b. 1936) and David Ignatow (1914–1997) addressing these pomaceous imperfections—for they are, indeed, characteristic of the other pome-like fruits, pears and quinces—each poet leaves us in the end with an image of the apple as an integral part of the living natural world (represented in one case by a bird, in the other case by—yet again!—a horse). First, Major's poem "Apple Core" (1990), in which what is inedible for the speaker becomes a tasty treat for the bird:

Up the road
I saw black birds
on the edge of a pine box.
When I got there
the birds flew a few feet away,
to the other side.
I looked down in the box.
There were red apples,
ripe, with stems still on them.
A sign on the box said Take One.
So I took one.
My, it was heavy,
and when I bit into it,
you would not believe
such sweetness. I walked on,
eating it down to the core.
When I finished, I threw the core
out over a cornfield.
A bird flew to catch it
before it hit the ground,

but it fell anyway.
The bird followed.

And I stood there,
not seeing anything
but the stalks moving
in the morning wind.
I waited, and the bird
came up, carrying the core.
He flew off across the field,
carrying this thing,
about the size
    of his own head.

From the point of view of the apple itself—if one can imagine such a thing—possessing a core may not seem like a failing; thus, in a 1977 prose poem by David Young, an apple being interviewed on television "replies with genuine candor about its prejudices ('You can't deny tomatoes lack a core'), its hopes (reparations for Genesis), its justified pride in that ancestor who took such careful aim at Newton." And an apple core occurs in the first line of Philip Larkin's (1922–1985) brief and brilliant poem "As Bad As a Mile" (1960), consisting of two tercets, rhyming *aaa* and *bbb,* in which the career of an apple—standing in for the unlucky failure who consumes it—is traced backwards in time from where the "shied core" lands on the floor after "striking the basket," to the "arm," the "unraised hand," and finally "the apple unbitten in the palm."

Ignatow's poem "To an Apple" (1964) explicitly addresses the ambivalence of a rotten apple:

You were rotten
and I sliced you into pieces
looking for a wholesome part,
then threw you into the street.
You were eaten by a horse,
dipping his head to nibble
gently at the skin.
I heard later he became violently ill,
died and was shipped off
to be processed. I think about it
and write of the good in you.

The Czech writer Ludvík Vaculík's (b. 1926) brilliant little piece of prose called "Cidering" (1981) is centered around a disturbing rotten apple episode. The narrator has just harvested some beautiful "Blenheim Cox" apples and is taking three sacks of the less than perfect ones to a cidering shed. While he waits his turn, a boy and his grandmother arrive with a wagonful of apples:

> The apples appear unusually large, green, of smooth complexion with an incredibly regular round shape, as from a factory. With permission I take one in my hand, then another . . . the defect is hidden in the hollow by the stem: a cut-out hole reaching far inside. "There, you see," the woman says, "such nice apples and all rotting at the stem, even while on the tree!" I ask what kind they are. She answers, "Mazánek's Miracle!" I nod in sympathy, but in my mind I am rejoicing at the prospect of writing it here.

Someone now approaches the narrator with a letter for him to sign requesting the release of certain prisoners awaiting trial. The narrator refuses, either (one guesses) because he thinks the effort futile, or because he is afraid, or both. (The poem is dated October 1981—a time when Vaculík's writings had been banned in Czechoslovakia.) The last paragraph begins with the remark: "I don't see what sense it makes to go on blabbering here about apples." And a note by the translator(s)—"Slavic 116, UC/Berkeley"—informs us that "this article is printed without the knowledge of the author." The politics and ethics of writing and keeping silent have been likened to the doomed project of attempting to produce a crop of perfect apples.

Rotten apples also figure memorably in an early poem by William Empson (1906–1984), "Value Is in Activity" (1928), but it is the breeding inside (and outside) the apple that constitutes the central imagery of the poem. (The title is derived from Aristotle's definition of happiness, in his *Ethics*, as "an activity in accordance with virtue," which was used as epigraph in an early version of the poem.) The poem begins:

> Celestial sphere, an acid green canvas hollow,
> His circus that exhibits him, the juggler
> Tosses, an apple that four others follow,
> Nor heeds, not eating it, the central smuggler.

Five apples are being juggled by a circus performer inside a spherically shaped canvas tent, which seems to be referred to in the opening words—the syntax is not entirely clear—as a "Celestial sphere"; yet another sphere is implied by the fact that the tent is resting on the spherical earth. The juggler performs inside one of these spheres, stands on another, and tosses five others. The nature of the "central smuggler" is only revealed in the first line of the next stanza:

> Nor heeds if the core be brown with maggots' raven,
> Dwarf seeds unnavelled a last frost has scolded,
> Mites that their high narrow echoing cavern
> Invites forward, or with close brown pips, green folded.

Yet one more sphere has been introduced in the form of the (possibly) brown cores of the apples together with their maggoty contents; further contents of some of the other spheres appear in the form of seeds, mites, and pips. Finally, outside the tent we are apprised of the rapid breeding activity of some beetles, inside the earth, who compete for nourishment with fungi growing presumably on the roots of trees:

> Some beetles (the tupped females can worm out)
> Massed in their halls of knowingly chewed splinter
> Eat faster than the treasured fungi sprout
> And stave off suffocation until winter.

One "activity of value" in the poem is certainly the juggler's, but the value of juggling is presumably minimal—mere repetition, mere show—as compared with the activity of the beetles with their fertile "tupped females." Now, in his note to the poem, Empson tells us that "The beetles . . . inside the globe of the earth . . . are only compared to the creatures that may be in the apple; hence to the juggler." Thus, the beetles feeding inside the earth are compared to the maggots feeding inside the apple and the breeding activity of the former suggests that of the latter. When we notice, in addition, the at least potential breeding capacities of the seeds, mites, and pips, we realize that we are being presented, in effect, with a great chain—not of *being*—but of *breeding.* With respect to size, the apples are in the middle, intermediate between the tent and the earth on the one hand and the maggots, mites, beetles, and fungi on the other. The apples will also represent human knowledge, in the form of objects essential to the exhibition of the human skill of juggling; and, following the Genesis story, such knowledge is represented as dishearteningly rotten at the core. The human prospect seems bleak, however much creaturely breeding goes on.

Empson's poem is obscure owing to both its language and its syntax. If the role of the rotten apple in *The Metamorphosis* [Die Verwandlung] (1915) by Franz Kafka (1883–1924) is as obscure as most other elements in the story, that has to be in spite of the unusual clarity and simplicity of Kafka's diction and style. The very first sentence (here translated by Stanley Corngold) is typical: "When Gregor Samsa woke up one morning from unsettling dreams, he found himself changed in his bed into a monstrous vermin." The manager of Gregor's place of business arrives to inquire why Gregor, a traveling salesman, has missed the morning train. Gregor emerges from his bedroom to attempt an explanation, and is injured when his father, brandishing a heavy newspaper and a cane, drives him back into the bedroom. Some weeks later Gregor again emerges from his bedroom and this time his father pelts him with apples:

> He had filled his pockets from the fruit bowl on the buffet and was now pitching one apple after another, for the time being without taking good aim. These little red apples rolled around on the floor as if electrified, clicking into each another [sic]. One apple, thrown weakly, grazed Gregor's back and slid off harmlessly. But the very next one that came flying after it literally forced its way into Gregor's back.

A month later, "the apple remained imbedded in his flesh as a visible souvenir since no one dared remove it." Eventually, the apple rots; Gregor dies, perhaps as much from his refusal of food as from the inflamed area on his back. Freudian critics have had a field day with these apple episodes; thus, among the critical essays included by Corngold in the volume containing his translation of *The Metamorphosis,* one by Hellmuth Kaiser, "Kafka's Fantasy of Punishment" (first published in a leading psychoanalytic journal, *Imago* [1931]), includes this comment: "The fruit which the father employs while maltreating him—the apple—is indeed the typical, proverbial reward of the child, as it recurs, for example, in 'moralizing tales,' not to speak of its significance in the biblical fall of man." Kaiser then proposes a psychoanalytic interpretation, according to which "the lodging of the apple in the back of the 'insect' also signifies a wish fulfillment—namely, by this coitus to gain the father's penis as a substitute for his own missing member." This—and similar interpretations in several other critical essays in Corngold's book—sometimes sound like parodies and tempt one to quote Empson's remark, in his review of the first American edition of *The Metamorphosis,* "A Family Monster" (1946), that "this brief masterpiece is so direct, so like a punch on the jaw, that there should be little to say about it." In accord with Empson's usual critical approach, he raises straightforward, even literal-minded, questions, such as how a ripe (and hence presumably soft) apple can cause so much damage to a hard insect carapace; "no doubt," he adds, "it is the apple of Adam, but one wants the details more convincing."

That it is possible to interpret *The Metamorphosis* sensibly and persuasively in psychological terms is clear from a brilliant essay by David Eggenschwiler, "*Die Verwandlung,* Freud, and the Chains of Odysseus" (1978), which claims that "the concerns of Freudian and formalist must converge in this story, that they are not merely equal but also inseparable." Eggenschwiler is especially perceptive about Kafka's sense of humor, as in this analysis of the apples episode:

> As horrified as Gregor feels, as symbolic as this confrontation may be, the scene is a bit silly. . . . The description suggests some kind of children's game. And if we are to take the apples as particularly symbolic, as some commentators have done without irony, the scene becomes even more ridiculous. If these apples have been imported from Eden and if they symbolize the instrument by which the original Father expelled his son from paradise, then Kafka has turned [Freud's] *Moses and Monotheism* into a travesty a quarter of a century before it was written.

Worms in Apples

In a really nasty poem, "Clinical Bulletin," by the Chilean Gonzalo Millan (b. 1947) the speaker's fury at a woman's rejection of him generates the revolting image of a worm bitten from an apple (translated by John Upton):

pfelApfelApfelApfei
felApfelApfelApfelApfelA
felApfelApfelApfelApfe
ApfelApfelApfelApfelApfi
pfelApfelApfelApfelApfel
lApfelApfelApfelApfelApfe
pfelApfelApfelApfelApfel
ApfelApfelApfelApfelApfe
felApfelApfelApfelApfel
pfelApfelApfelApfelApf
elApfelApfelApfelWurmAp
felApfelApfelApfelApfel
pfelApfelApfelApfel
felApfelApfelA
felApfelA

Fig. 4: Reinhard Döhl, "Wurm in Apfel," 1965

Hour after hour, every day
in yellow, foaming urine
I expel the rotten little eggs
and the worm I bit from your apple:
Leather-hearted lady, well-thumbed
and greasy card
from a second-hand deck.

The wormy apple motif is realized typographically by Reinhard Döhl (b. 1934) in one of his so-called concrete poems (1965), using just two German words: "Wurm" occurs once in the lower right-hand portion of an apple-shaped region composed of parallel lines of "Apfel"'s. (See fig. 4.) In Döhl's poem, many of the lines of type constituting the image of the apple have their bounding letters partly sliced away so as to form a smooth contour, and if we think about the process of construction, it seems clear that the poem must have been simply cut out of a sheet printed with many—at least sixteen (corresponding to the vertical height of the apple)—lines of type, each of them repeating the word "Apfel" many times—at least seven (corresponding to the maximum width of the apple)—and such that each line is horizontally displaced by two spaces with respect to the lines immediately above and below it. The procedure in question is very different from one in which the shape has been built up by simply juxtaposing lines of type of the appropriate lengths. Thus, the mutilated letters forming the contours of the apple suggest a certain brutality, softened perhaps by the fact that no "meaning" has been lost—there are, after all, plenty of intact "Apfel"s; in a distinction drawn from contemporary linguistic philosophy (*type* vs. *token*), while some of the tokens of "Apfel" have been damaged, the type remains untouched. The highly cerebral character of the poem seems oddly to cancel out any feelings of disgust.

A more lighthearted version of the worm-in-apple motif occurs in a tiny fable entitled "The Worm" by the distinguished French poet Eugène Guillevic (1907–1997), from his *Fabliettes* (1981). His translator, Norman R. Shapiro, comments that the volume, "brilliantly illustrated in its original edition (in the 'Folio Benjamin' series for children) by California artist Laurie Jordan, contains thirty-eight unnumbered, unpaginated verses":

> Worm was in apple, sun
> Was overhead.
>
> As soon as day was done,
> Apple was dead.
>
> ~
>
> La ver était dans le fruit,
> Le soleil à la porte.
>
> Lorsque arriva la nuit,
> La pomme était morte.

Not lighthearted at all are the opening lines of Pastan's "Routine Mammogram" (1985), which compare the mammogram procedure to "looking for a worm / in the apple." After some reflections, first on the topography of the X-ray photographs of her breasts, and then on one-breasted Amazons, the poem returns to the doctor who "smiles, / as if he could give innocence back, / as if he could give back / to the apple / its spiraled skin." Once again, the peeled apple, but now in a medically sinister context.

Who would have thought that anyone might want to use the worm in an apple as the basis for a moral parable? This is what the American poet Sue Owen does in her third book of poetry, *My Doomsday Sampler* (1999). (Other poems in the book take off from traditional fables of the ant and the grasshopper, and the spider and the fly.) In the third quatrain (out of seven) of "The Worm in the Apple" (1999), the ravenous worm

> never thinks of the harm
> it does to that earth of apple,

> how rot will set in
> like a slow death to follow
>
> it and that the heavy tree
> the two of them belong
> to is weighted by the worm's
> travels and ambition,
>
> and is that much sadder.

And then comes the rather obvious moral of the last stanza:

> Isn't selfishness like that,
> feeding on itself until
> all the thoughts grow fatter?

Poisoned Apples

Dante Gabriel Rossetti (1828–1882) introduced lethal apples in a grim poem about that favorite figure of both the Romantics and the pre-Raphaelites—the femme fatale, *la belle dame sans merci* (who could appear in various guises, natural and preternatural). "The Orchard-Pit" is fragmentary and undatable; it was published posthumously by the poet's brother, William M. Rossetti, together with Dante Gabriel's lengthy summary of the proposed theme of the never-completed poem. The five-quatrain fragment is often reprinted but not the four-page "argument," which begins like this:

> Men tell me that sleep has many dreams; but all my life I have dreamt one dream alone.
>
> I see a glen whose sides slope upward from the deep bed of a dried-up stream, and either slope is covered with wild apple-trees. In the largest tree, within the fork whence the limbs divide, a fair, golden-haired woman stands and sings, with one white arm stretched along a branch of the tree, and with the other holding forth a bright red apple, as if to some one coming down the slope. Below her feet the trees grow more and more tangled, and stretch from both sides across the deep pit below: and the pit is full of the bodies of men.
>
> They lie in heaps beneath the screen of boughs, with her apples bitten in their hands; and some are no more than ancient bones now, and some seem dead but yesterday. She stands over them in the glen, and sings for ever, and offers her apple still.
>
> This dream shows me no strange place. I know the glen, and have known it from childhood, and heard many tales of those who have died there by the Siren's spell.

There follows a long section set in waking reality, including this passage:

> One day at table my love offered me an apple. And as I took it she laughed, and said, "Do not eat, it is the fruit of the Siren's dell." And I laughed and ate: and at the heart of the apple was a red stain like a woman's mouth; and as I bit it I could feel a kiss upon my lips.

Returning to his dream, the dreamer now finds himself accompanied by his love, who tries, unsuccessfully, to save him from his encounter with the Siren in her apple-tree. The dream ends and the dreamer awakens:

> And one kiss I had of her mouth, as I took the apple from her hand. But while I bit it, my brain whirled and my foot stumbled; and I felt my crashing fall through the tangled boughs beneath her feet, and saw the dead white faces that welcomed me in the pit. And so I woke cold in my bed: but it still seemed that I lay indeed at last among those who shall be my mates for ever, and could feel the apple still in my hand.

With this introduction, we may look at the first two of the five stanzas:

> Piled deep below the screening apple-branch
>   They lie with bitter apples in their hands:
> And some are only ancient bones that blanch,
> And some had ships that last year's wind did launch,
>   And some were yesterday the lords of lands.
>
> In the soft dell, among the apple-trees,
>   High up above the hidden pit she stands,
> And there for ever sings, who gave to these,
> That lie below, her magic hour of ease,
>   And those her apples holden in their hands.

Who is this golden-haired Siren offering men "bright red" but deadly apples? One does not have to be a confirmed (Melanie) Kleinian to detect a predatory mother in the recurring dream.

An interesting textual point has been raised about the word "bitter" in the second line of Rossetti's poem. Oswald Doughty, in his edition of a selection of Rossetti's poetry, tells us that J. W. Mackail—who was in a position to know—believed "bitter" in William Rossetti's printed text of "The Orchard-Pit" to be a misprint for "bitten" in the original manuscript—which would seem to be confirmed by the word "bitten" in the third paragraph of the prose version of "The Orchard-Pit," quoted above.

Attractive but poisonous apples which kill can hardly help reminding us of the poisonous apple that (temporarily) kills Snow White in the Grimms' fairy tale; this hardly needs retelling but let us recall the final ruse of the wicked stepmother Queen disguised as an old woman (translated by Jack Zipes):

> "Are you afraid that it might be poisoned?" said the old woman. "Look, I'll cut the apple in two. You eat the red part, and I'll eat the white."
>
> However, the apple had been made with such cunning that only the red part was poisoned.

Here, the apple is an explicit embodiment of duplicity: Snow White dies for her disobedience in accepting the apple from the old woman but is magically resurrected when an accidental stumble by one of her coffin bearers dislodges the fatal piece of apple from her throat. It may be noted that in some retellings of the tale for young children the binary coloration of the poisonous apple is omitted; in other versions of the tale the binary coloration is shifted from red-white to red-green, presumably in the interest of verisimilitude.

In her poem, "Snow White" (1977), Olga Broumas (b. 1949) is not so much retelling or updating the fairy tale as simply identifying the wicked stepmother of the tale with her own real mother, "flesh / of your woman's flesh, your fairest, most / faithful mirror." Her mother comes to visit the now married narrator:

> A curious
>
> music, an un-
> catalogued rhyme, mother/daughter, we lay
> the both of us awake
> that night you straddled
> two continents and the wet
> opulent ocean to visit us, bringing
> your gifts.
>
> Like two halves
> of a two-colored apple—red
> with discovery, green with fear—we lay
> hugging the wall between us, whitewash
> leaving its telltale tracks.
> Already
> some part of me had begun
> the tally, dividing
> the married spoils, claiming
> your every gift.

Here we have a new use of the poisoned fairy tale apple as it models the fraught mother/daughter relationship.

The fairy tale poisonous apple of Snow White appears in an all too real context in a twentieth-century Slovenic poem by Alojz Ihan (b. 1961) from, and about, war-torn former Yugoslavia. (The author is a doctor and a research fellow at the Institute of Microbiology, University of Ljubljana; his poetry has been translated into Serbo-Croatian and Macedonian.) At the beginning of "Apple," a Slovene-speaking soldier is on guard duty and a little Albanian girl throws him an apple; here is how he reacts (translated by Tom Lozar):

> She swung her arm and threw the apple toward me. I jumped
> behind a shelter, hugged my automatic, waited ...
> There was no explosion. I lowered the barrel. "I won't
> shoot the little girl," I told myself, "she doesn't understand."
> Then I watched the apple, big, red, it looked totally authentic.
> I made a threatening motion in the little girl's direction,
> she became frightened and began to run away. I didn't know what
> to do with the apple. It could have been injected
> with poison, if I bit into it, I might die or at least fall asleep,
> and then the irredentists would cross the ditch, and butcher me.
> I didn't know if the poison worked at the mere touch, and so
> as a precaution, I did not touch the apple, nor did I kick
> it into the ditch, I just stood there and waited, helpless.

Is the soldier being paranoid, or is he merely being sensible when he treats even apples thrown by little girls as sinister during a war whose cruelties are exacerbated by bitter ethnic animosities? In any case, the traditional, folkloric practice of throwing apples as love-offerings is here painfully negated.

Apples, Blossoming and Falling

The two termini of the process of apple growth—the blossoming and the falling of the mature fruit—seem to have elicited the strongest responses from writers and artists. Thus, John Clare (1893–1864) wrote a sonnet, "The Crab Tree" (sometime between 1822 and 1833), about the regretful pleasures of spring and how seeing crab apple blossoms enables him to recapture the purer joys of his boyhood:

> Spring comes anew & brings each little pledge
> That still as wont my childish heart deceives
> I stoop again for violets in the hedge
> Among the Ivy & old withered leaves
> & often mark amid the clumps of sedge
> The pooty shells I gathered when a boy
> But cares have claimed me many an evil day
> & chilled the relish which I had for joy

> Yet when crab blossoms blush among the may
> As wont in years gone bye I scramble now
> Up mid the brambles for my old esteems
> Filling my hands with many a blooming bough
> Till the heart stirring past as present seems
> Save the bright sunshine of those fairey dreams.

Eric Robinson and Geoffrey Summerfield include this poem in their selection of Clare's writings but explain that the "appeal [of Clare's sonnets] lies in their freshness"; "one would not expect, and generally does not find, any great weight of thoughts in the sonnets, but they are a series of images." This sonnet, however (as Robinson and Summerfield might agree), is exceptional in its subtle phenomenology of interpenetrating present and past experiences. The subject matter is also unusual—not the violets and not the "pooty" (or girdled snail) shells but the crab apple blossoms. For if one peruses Clare's writings on natural history, one finds a surprising dearth of references to fruit trees—or, indeed, any trees—except as habitats for birds. (An exception will be noted in chapter 13, in the "Pears and Apples" section.) The very opposite, by the way, seems to be true of Thoreau, who is interested in birds primarily as dispersers of seeds.

There is a pair of interestingly contrasting poems involving apple trees and apple blossoms by two Victorian poets, Christina Rossetti (1830–1894) and William Morris (1834–1896). (The two were well acquainted, as Christina's brother became the lover of Morris's wife.) Rossetti's "An Apple-Gathering" (1857) supplements the traditional practice of apple picking with the picking of apple blossoms in order to add resonance to a personal lament about disappointed love, while Morris's "Pomona" (1883) invokes the traditional goddess of fruit trees to assure us that even in an age bereft of myth it still makes sense to invest nature with transcendent powers. Rossetti's poem begins:

> I plucked pink blossoms from mine apple tree
> And wore them all that evening in my hair:
> Then in due season when I went to see
> I found no apples there.

There follow six more stanzas, each with three iambic pentameter lines and a concluding dying fall of a trimeter line; the fourth and fifth stanzas continue the meditation on apples and love:

> Plump Gertrude passed me with her basket full,
> A stronger hand than hers helped it along;
> A voice talked with her thro' the shadows cool
> More sweet to me than song.

> Ah Willie, Willie, was my love less worth
> Than apples with their green leaves piled above?

I counted rosiest apples on the earth
    Of far less worth than love.

Morris's "Pomona" was written for, and first reproduced on, a large (118⅛ x 82¾ inches) tapestry woven by Knight, Sleath, and Martin in 1884–85 for the firm of Morris & Co. The tapestry (now in the Whitworth Art Gallery, Manchester) was designed by Edward Burne-Jones (1833–1898) and manufactured of wool, silk, and cotton; in it, Pomona's gown contains apples in its lifted folds, while Morris's two quatrains (one alluding to apple blossoms) form the borders at top and bottom of the tapestry (for a reproduction, see Oliver Fairclough and Emmeline Leary, *Textiles by William Morris and Morris and Co., 1861–1940*). Morris eventually published the following poem in 1891:

        I am the ancient Apple-Queen,
        As once I was so am I now.
        But evermore a hope unseen,
        Betwixt the blossom and the bough.

        Ah, where's the river's hidden Gold?
        And where the windy grave of Troy?
        Yet come I as I came of old,
        From out the heart of Summer's joy.

Christina Rossetti, incidentally, wrote another poem, "A Birthday" (1857), whose third and fourth lines are: "My heart is like an apple tree / Whose boughs are bent with thickset fruit." Other fruits occur in the poem—pomegranates, and gold and silver grapes—depicted as embroidered on a silk-covered dais raised in celebration: "Because the birthday of my life / Is come, my love is come to me." So, Rossetti imagines embroidery depicting fruit, while Morris supervises the production of an actual piece of such embroidery.

In a late painting by Christina Rossetti's brother Dante Gabriel, *A Vision of Fiammetta* (1878), the three-quarter, frontal figure of the young woman is surrounded by apple blossoms, as she holds a branch of the blossoms in each hand. (The painting, 36 x 55 in., oil on canvas, is now privately owned; for a reproduction, see Alicia Faxon's *Dante Gabriel Rossetti* [1989].) Fiammetta was Boccaccio's name for Maria d'Aquino, whom he is supposed to have met on the day before Easter, 1336, in a church in Naples; she died young and Boccaccio wrote several sonnets memorializing her, which Rossetti translated for his volume *The Early Italian Poets* (1861). Rossetti had difficulty in painting the apple blossoms (which presumably allude to the spring season when Boccaccio first met Fiammetta), and he wrote several letters in April 1878 to his friend and student, the artist Frederic Shields, requesting that "if you know any means of sending me good blossom, I would pay anyone well to bring me as much as possible daily, for some days to come," and, again, "What I want is a full-coloured red and white blossom, of the tufted, rich kind." Shields seems to have obliged by sending Rossetti some watercolor representations of apple blossoms of his own (one of which is illustrated in Faxon's book on Rossetti).

Rossetti also wrote his own sonnet describing his painting of Fiammetta; it begins:

> Behold Fiammetta, shown in Vision here.
> Gloom-girt 'mid Spring-flushed apple-growth she stands;
> And as she sways the branches with her hands,
> Along her arm the sundered bloom falls sheer,
> In separate petals shed, each like a tear.

An early poem by William Carlos Williams (1883–1963), "Portrait of a Lady" (1920), begins with apple trees and apple blossoms: "Your thighs are appletrees / whose blossoms touch the sky." As Linda Wagner observes, the poem "illustrates [Williams's] use of mock conversation in dialogue, here between the hesitating, self-conscious romantic and his antagonistically literal other self." Thus, the lines just quoted are followed by: "Which sky? The sky / where Watteau hung a lady's / slipper." And again, in the last eleven lines, romantic assertion is followed by disenchanted questioning:

> it is
> one of those white summer days,
> the tall grass of your ankles
> flickers upon the shore—
> Which shore?—
> the sand clings to my lips—
> Which shore?
> Agh, petals maybe. How
> should I know?
> Which shore? Which shore?
> I said petals from an appletree.

Wagner also points out how the romantic lines (such as the opening two) can be slightly altered to yield perfect examples of iambic meter—an arrangement Williams may have deliberately considered and then eschewed. As for the allusion to Watteau (1684–1721) and a subsequent allusion to Fragonard (1732–1806), Litz and MacGowan refer us to Fragonard's *The Swing,* presuming, I take it, that Williams somehow confused the two painters. Now, there are, in fact, two paintings by Fragonard with the "swing" motif in public collections, which would have been accessible to Williams. Only one of the paintings, however, includes the striking detail of the swinger's slipper hanging in the sky (having flown off her foot); this is *The Happy Hazards of the Swing* (1767) in the Wallace Collection, London. (The other painting, *The Swing* [1778–80], is in the National Gallery, Washington D.C.; for reproductions of the two paintings, see Jean-Pierre Cuzin, *Jean-Honoré Fragonard: Life and Work* [1998].) Finally, I cannot help wondering if Williams's poem was not perhaps conceived as a riposte to T. S. Eliot's (1888–1965) "Portrait of a Lady," published three years earlier (in 1917); we know, after all, that Williams strongly disapproved of Eliot's poetry at this time.

Another American poet, James Wright (1927–1980), in his "The Revelation" (1959), uses the imagery of apple branches and apple blossoms to describe a confrontation with his father, writing, in the first stanza, of the angry division between the two men—reflected in "The apple branches dripping black / Divided light across his face"—and then, in the last (of six) stanzas, of a reconciliation—reflected in "The apple branches, dripping black, / Trembled across the lunar air / And dropped white petals on his hair." Another of Wright's poems "Two Horses Playing in the Orchard" (1963), proceeds quietly with two horses, a mare and a stallion, eating in the dusk the last few apples of late autumn, and then, after two and a half stanzas, comes this "moral":

> I let those horses in to steal
> On principle, because I feel
> Like half a horse myself, although
> Too soon, too soon, already. Now.

An early poem by Robert Frost, "The Cow in Apple Time" (1914), finds not a horse but a solitary cow consuming windfall apples. "Her face is flecked with pomace and she drools / A cider syrup." Once having tasted the fruit, she cannot resist: "She runs from tree to tree where lie and sweeten / The windfalls spiked with stubble and worm-eaten." And the upshot of her drunken spree is that "her udder shrivels and the milk goes dry."

Apple blossoms can be used to point all sorts of morals. Thus, Linda Pastan's "The Apple Shrine" (1995) is in two parts, with the second devoted to a vague and rather platitudinous moral lesson about the mysteriousness of healing and "how quickly / everything can change." I like better the beginning of the first part about the use of one tree's blossoms to pollinate other trees:

> Last week you gathered armfuls of apple blossoms
> from trees along the roadway, and a few
> from the bent Cortland down the street
> to place beneath our nameless apple tree
> for pollination, you said, so we'd have fruit
> next winter.

The American Janet Holmes features windfall apples in the last two poems of her sequence "Seven Lyrics of Autumn" (1993). First, a three-line poem in the form of a near-haiku (one extra syllable in the first line):

> Equinox-night orchard:
> apples crushed on the roadway—
> delicious cool rot!

134   Other windfall fruits (peaches and plums) are then introduced in the middle of an eleven-line poem—rather slackly composed compared to the preceding poem—that ends like this:

> each tree
> carrying more than it wants to hold
> and spilling windfalls into the grass, carrying
> more than even the birds will eat
> and still full of fruit,
> bearing, bearing.

Finally, a more complex poem about windfall apples, "Long After the End of Fall" (1988), the fifth of six poems in a sequence entitled "Leaves from an Almanac," by John Hollander. The first poem, "Something for the Fall Wind," sets the bleak tone of the whole sequence with its cold summer, whose falling pome fruits (these would probably be pears) and berries are little more than anticipations of the "fall" to come:

> Comforting me with pomes and drupes whose falling
> Song comes down to a whispering in the grass,
> I patch together scraps of the appalling
> Year that I brought to such a scattered pass.

The first eight lines of "Long After the End of Fall," turning a "dead tree" into a "man in black," dismiss the anticipated spring, which will not, after all, revive *everything*. The last twelve lines about windfall apples are notable for the brilliance—an oxymoron?—of their unrelieved gloom:

> The rotten, unsustaining windfalls, scattered
> Underfoot, unreadable for the deep
> Meanings that shade the surfaces of apples,
> The flecked originals of all the fallen,
> Stand in for us when dead trees can no more.
> Death will bite into us now, one by one,
> Like apples plucked that never should have been,
> Like apples all that never were intended
> To be devoured, but for admiring time
> Only to study, only to regard
> With such a deep absorption it could never
> Remember to take up its fell work again.

Apple Orchards

In her two long poems about gardens and orchards, the English writer Vita Sackville-West (1892–1962) has some memorable lines about apple orchards. Both *The Land* (1923–26) and *The Garden* (1939–45) are divided into "seasons," and composed of alternating passages of traditional blank verse and rhymed pentameters or tetrameters. In "Spring" of the earlier poem there is an extended passage (forty-four lines) on orchards, which includes these lines on an apple orchard in blossom:

> Sometimes in apple country you may see
> A ghostly orchard standing all in white,
> Aisles of white trees, white branches, in the green,
> On some still day when the year hangs between
> Winter and spring, and heaven is full of light.

The ghostliness of these massed white blooms had been noted a decade earlier by Robert Frost in "A Prayer in Spring," published in his first book, *A Boy's Will* (1913): "Oh, give us pleasure in the orchard white, / Like nothing else by day, like ghosts by night."

In "Winter" of Sackville-West's later poem a gardener plans an apple orchard:

> The gardener dreams his special own alloy
> Of possible and the impossible.

> He dreams an orchard neatly pruned and spurred,
> Where Cox' Orange jewels with the red
> Of Worcester Permain

The two apple varieties mentioned are colored, respectively, orange with a red flush and bright red; they are also England's two most popular commercial varieties (see the entries in Morgan and Richards, *The Book of Apples*).

We turn next to a remarkable early-twentieth-century English children's book set in an apple orchard: *Martin Pippin in the Apple Orchard* (1921), by Eleanor Farjeon (1881–1965). The book, it must be said, was not originally intended for children; in a memoir of Edward Thomas (1878–1917), Farjeon explains how she sent successive portions of the manuscript to a soldier in the trenches during the First World War and she professes surprise that children enjoy it. The book is, in fact, among other things, a complicated exercise in narratology, with its framing narrative dominated by the Wandering Minstrel, Martin Pippin, surrounded by "six young milkmaids, sworn virgins and man-haters all," whose names are Joan, Joyce, Jennifer, Jessica, Jane, and Joscelyn, and its six inner narratives—one for each milkmaid—consist of wonderfully imaginative love stories resembling certain types of traditional fairy tales. Also, Martin the narrator is extremely sensitive to any sign of disapproval from the members of his audience and frequently interrupts his narration to argue with them; occasionally, he is persuaded to elaborate some episode or even to alter the conclusion of one of his stories.

As Martin spins a tale on each of six successive evenings, five of the girls always sit in branches of the centrally located and largest tree of a great apple orchard (in Sussex), while the sixth sits in a swing attached to a branch of that same tree. Three meals of apples and bread are consumed during each of the six days; in between the meal-times, the girls dance and sing, accompanied by Martin on his lute, and play at games like see-saw. Telling the tales has a therapeutic purpose: they are designed to be overheard by Gillian Gillman, who has been imprisoned by her father (the milkmaids' master) in his Well House to deter her from starving herself to death as she pines away in forbidden love for the young farmer, Robin Rue. In the interlude after the fifth tale—there is an interlude after each tale—with only Joscelyn (tallest, bossiest, and least amiable of the girls) left to take her turn sitting in the swing, Martin insists that each girl must eat an apple before he will begin his tale: Joan chooses a Cox's Pippin, Joyce a Beauty of Bath, Jennifer a Worcester Pearmain, Jessica a Curlytail, Jane a Russet. Joscelyn refuses to choose an apple but Martin chooses for her—"a King of Pippins, the biggest and reddest in the orchard." (Each of these, needless to say, is a real English apple variety; see the alphabetical listing in Morgan and Richards, *The Book of Apples*.). Martin peels each apple but before eating it each girl twirls the peel three times round her head and throws it onto the grass behind her, where it takes the form of a letter: C for Joan, M for Joyce, T for Jennifer, O for Jessica, J for Jane, and H for Joscelyn. It is understood by all that the letters stand for the first initial of the name of each milkmaid's future lover. Martin himself then repeats the ritual six times, once for each of the six apple varieties, and obtains a J each time; and then "little Joan slipped away and came back with the smallest, prettiest, and rosiest Lady Apple in Gillman's Orchard, and said softly, 'This one's for you.'" Repeating the peeling ritual, this time Martin obliterates the letter before the girls can read it, and tosses the apple away. After the sixth tale, Gillian, revived by the stories and rescued by Martin with the aid of the swing, goes off to join her beloved. In the postlude Martin gives a party; the food is described, in a long paragraph, beginning, of course, with the apples: "In the middle was a great heap of apples, red and brown and green and gold; but besides these there was a dish of roasted apples and another of apple dumplings, and between them a bowl of brown sugar and a full pitcher of cream." Finally, in something of a surprise ending, Martin discovers Gillian and Robin Rue, unmarried. Robin explains that he is not a husband "worthy" of her (he belongs to the wrong social class is what he means), and so Martin goes off with Gillian, explaining to her, among many other things, how the peeling of his Lady Apple had in fact formed the letter G.

I must emphasize that I have not discussed at all what occupies the bulk of the book—the six lengthy and wonderfully unpredictable meandering love stories told by Martin—but I will add that I wholeheartedly subscribe to Naomi Lewis's characterization of Farjeon's book as "unique, puzzling, magical." Similarly magical is a watercolor (13 ¾ x 10 ¼ in.) by Samuel Palmer (1805–1881), in the Fitzwilliam Museum, Cambridge, entitled *The Magic Apple Tree*. (See Sally Twiss's *Apples: A Social History* [1999] for a reproduction.) It is worth noting that Palmer was painting in Kent, a neighboring county to Farjeon's Sussex.

Of the two principal sites in Maine of John Irving's (b. 1942) novel *The Cider House Rules* (1985), one—Ocean View—is a large commercial apple orchard and the other—St. Cloud's—is an orphanage cum lying-in and abortion facility. As the plot unfolds, the two sites, which had initially seemed poles apart, come to resemble each other in certain respects, in a process which constitutes one of the more interesting aspects of the novel. Thus, many of the leading characters move back and forth between the two sites, while apple trees are planted on the hillside behind St. Cloud's and an abortion is performed at Ocean View. I want to cite two brief episodes—the first at St. Cloud's, the second at Ocean View—in which the convergence in question takes place at a more symbolic level. In chapter 9, "Over Burma," "Homer entrusted Nurse Edna with the care of the hillside orchard. He explained that the wire-mesh sleeves around the trees could not be wrapped so tightly that they didn't permit the trees to grow—but also not so loosely that the mice could girdle the trees." In chapter 10, "Fifteen Years," Homer receives a doctor's bag from his mentor and vicarious parent: "And the thing about a good doctor's bag is that it's comfortable to carry. That was why he took it with him to the cider house. The bag was empty, of course—which didn't feel quite right to Homer—so he picked some Gravensteins and a couple of early Macs on his way to the cider house and put the apples in the bag. Naturally, the apples rolled back and forth; that didn't feel quite authentic."

Something of the magic of apples and apple orchards is well captured in two American poems about pomological duplicity or doubleness: "The Crossed Apple" (1929), by Louise Bogan (1897–1970), and "Pomology" (1996), by Rachel Hadas (b. 1948). In each poem the speaker addresses a woman: in Bogan's, an unnamed "maiden"; in Hadas's, the poet Sappho. Both poems are technically brilliant: Bogan's use of accentual meter and Hadas's use of syllabics, and the effective contrast in both poems between long and short lines. Best of all, both poems use the idea of an imaginary apple taxonomy as a means for integrating in powerful and unexpected ways many of the elements—sensuous, mythical, pomological—we have been encountering in earlier literary episodes.

Bogan's poem "The Crossed Apple"—in its diction, its fairy tale echoes, its botanical allusions—reminds me of *Martin Pippin*. Bogan herself relates the poem to Snow White, "the fairy story of a witch who brings a young girl an apple, one side of which is poisoned" (on a recorded reading by Bogan, reported by Jacqueline Ridgeway). There are eight quatrains, in each of which the first and third lines are in iambic pentameter, the second and fourth lines in iambic dimeter, with the rhyme scheme: *abab* (except for the initial stanza where the first and third lines do not rhyme but instead end with the key words "orchard" and "apples").

> I've come to give you fruit from out my orchard,
> Of wide report.
> I have trees there that bear me many apples
> Of every sort:
>
> Clear, streakèd; red and russet; green and golden;
> Sour and sweet.

This apple's from a tree yet unbeholden,
Where two kinds meet, —

So that this side is red without a dapple,
And this side's hue
Is clear and snowy. It's a lovely apple.
It is for you.

Within are five black pips as big as peas,
As you will find,
Potent to breed you five great apple trees
Of varying kind:

To breed you wood for fire, leaves for shade,
Apples for sauce.
Oh, this is a good apple for a maid,
It is a cross,

Fine on the finer, so the flesh is tight,
And grained like silk.
Sweet Burning gave the red side, and the white
Is Meadow Milk.

Eat it; and you will taste more than the fruit:
The blossom, too,
The sun, the air, the darkness at the root,
The rain, the dew,

The earth we came to, and the time we flee,
The fire and the breast.
I claim the white part, maiden, that's for me.
You take the rest.

    Bogan's biographer Elizabeth Frank writes (1985) that in "The Crossed Apple" the poet "mixes Yankee and Baroque sensibilities to perfection, blending the traditional fairy tale with a plainly worded yet ecstatic vision of earth, and setting forth the apple as both an archetypal symbol of temptation and fall, and a matter-of-factly observed object in nature, much as Thoreau himself might have discussed it." And Frank adds that Bogan may well have been reading Thoreau's essay "Wild Apples" during the period when she was writing the poem. Finally, Frank thinks "the surprising end . . . is gloriously mean-spirited."

    Hadas's poem has six quatrains, each consisting of three eleven-syllable lines followed by a five-syllable line, with, of course, no rhymes. If Bogan's speaker is initially duplicitous in her offer of a crossed apple—she peremptorily demands the white half back for herself—Hadas's speaker is equally brusque in her dismissal of Sappho's famous lone apple—inaccessible but presumed delicious— at the very top of the tree (fragment 105a; discussed earlier in this chapter). Instead, we are told, the important principle for classifying apples is how early they ripen and how easily they fall, and this system yields two basic kinds (which, of course, are not varieties in either the ordinary or the botanical sense), one straightforward and one duplicitous:

> Sappho, of the numberless kinds of apples
> we have two, and one of them ripens early,
> striped with sweetness, fragrant and lambent, by mid-
> > August already
>
> falling even on utterly windless days
> > [. . . . .]
> > > Our other apples
> cling to the branches. Pick them—you clutch at twigs and
> leaves, or just as likely you find that you are
> > hoisted and dangling
>
> from the bough. So that by late September,
> when the soft fruit long has let go and fallen,
> the stern tough tree's loaded with glossy apples,
> > hard, dry, and woody
> to the tooth; to the eye, globed, rosy beauties.

The unpicked autumn-ripening apples are beautiful to look at, all right; but, far from being rare, they are myriad; and far from being especially delicious, they are inedible. The moral: virginity is overrated.

> All the pitiful few we could reach we've picked, but
> seen from the roadside the tree is untouched, a virgin
> > beaming sheer ripeness.

Another American poet prefers the apples that do not fall of their own accord; the second half of "Apples in August" (1995), by Angie Estes, communicates the preference:

> The apples I like best stay on the tree
> and wait, although I've heard them stumble
>
> to the ground at night when they think
> that no one is near. Of the ones
>
> that remain, most will be content
> to drop in the hand when called.

> I try not to feel slighted by those
> who refuse; they have mulled it over
>
> and decided to let only the days
> lengthen around them, untouched
>
> by gravity and all that it desires,
> tightening in their own fragrant heat.

Finally, I want to quote for its technical brilliance a youthful poem by James Merrill (1926–1995), with an extended apple orchard conceit that reminds one of seventeenth-century English metaphysical poetry. First published in *Poetry* (1956) but not reprinted by Merrill in either of his two volumes of selected poems (1982, 1992), "For a Second Marriage" was undoubtedly one of the poems whose writing he later characterized as "having fed / Feelings genuine but dead / With language quick but counterfeit" (quoted by John Hollander in his memorial tribute to Merrill). On the other hand, three American poets, Donald Hall, Robert Pack, and Louis Simpson, judged the poem worthy of inclusion in their anthology, *New Poets of England and America* (1957), which is where I first read it. (The poem is included in McClatchy and Yenser's edition of Merrill's collected poems [2001] under a slightly altered title, "Upon a Second Marriage.") The poem almost seems to have been written in deliberate defiance of the famous strictures which Dr. Johnson (in his life of Abraham Cowley) placed on metaphysical verse:

> The fault of Cowley, and perhaps of all the writers of the metaphysical race, is that of pursuing his thoughts to the last ramifications, by which he loses the grandeur of generality. . . . Thus all the power of description is destroyed by a scrupulous enumeration, and the force of metaphors is lost, when the mind by the mention of particulars is turned more upon the original than the secondary sense, more upon that from which the illustration is drawn than that to which it is applied.

In "For a Second Marriage," the "illustration" is apple orchards, "that to which it is applied" is second marriages.

> Orchards, we linger here because
> Women we love stand propped in your green prisons,
> Obedient to such justly bending laws
> Each one longs to take root,
> Lives to confess whatever season's
> Pride of blossom or endeavor's fruit
> May to her rustling boughs have risen.

But autumn reddens the whole mind.
No more, each swears, the dazzle of a year
Shall woo her from your bare cage of loud wind,
    Promise the ring and run
  To burn the altar, reappear
With apple blossoms for the credulous one.
    Orchards, we wonder that we linger here!

    Orchards we planted, trees we shook
To learn what you were bearing, say we stayed
Because one winter twilight we mistook
    Frost on a bleakened bough
  For buds of green, and were afraid
To miss the old persuasion, should we go.
    And the spring came, and discourse made

    Enough of weddings to us all
That, loving her for whom the whole world grows
Fragrant and white, we linger to recall
    As down aisles of cut trees
  How a tall trunk's cross-section shows
Concentric rings, those many marriages
    That life on each live thing bestows.

Johnson, though, might have approved of the regular versification of the four stanzas, since, in his view (expressed, again, in his life of Cowley), "The great pleasure of verse arises from the known measure of the lines, and uniform structure of the stanzas, by which the voice is regulated, and the memory relieved." Merrill has even carefully chosen by the indention of his lines to indicate the metrical pattern of tetrameters, pentameters, and trimeters rather than the more easily apprehended rhyme scheme: *abacbcb.*

THE RESANCTIFICATION OF APPLES

Some modern poets have been writing about apples in ways which attempt to revivify the religious associations of the fruit, not in terms of the images of traditional myth or religion but rather in terms of the more universal spiritual ideas which they attempt to distill from the traditional images. Two such poets are the Welshman Vernon Watkins (1909–1967) and the American Jim Harrison (b. 1937). Thus, in his difficult "Music of Colours—White Blossom . . ." Watkins writes of the whiteness of apple (and cherry and pear) blossoms:

> Buds in April, on the waiting branch,
> Starrily opening, light raindrops drench,
> Swinging from world to world when starlings sweep,
> Where they alight in air, are white asleep.

Such whiteness is utterly ephemeral, for "White flowers die soonest." The source of true whiteness lies in the miraculous cleansing power of "the Nazarene" (who is mentioned in the very first line of the poem):

> If there is white, or has been white, it must have been
> When His eyes looked down and made the leper clean.
> White will not be, apart, though the trees try
> Spirals of blossom, their green conspiracy.
> She who touched His garment saw no white tree.

The key to personal salvation seems to be the recognition that "I know nothing of Earth or colour until I know I lack / Original white."

Jim Harrison's "Suite to Appleness" (1968) is mostly about the growing and harvesting of apples, dwelling on such details as bags of fertilizer and irrigation systems. Images of violence occur throughout the poem: "their heads, soldiers', floating as flowers," "If Christ offends you tear him out," a girl "throwing herself from the asylum roof," a boy with "a green / apple he picked to throw at starlings," the narrator "in recoil moving backward, crushing / the fallen apples with my feet." There are also two more idyllic, even quietly ecstatic, episodes in the apple orchard, each involving an escape (from chores in the first case, into drunkenness in the second):

> The old tree, a McIntosh:
> 68 bushel last year,
> with 73 bushel the year before that,
> sitting up within it on a smooth branch,
> avoiding the hoe, invisible to the ground,
> buoyed up by apples . . .
>   [. . . . .]
> Or in the orchard that night
> in July: the apple trees too thick
> with branches, unpruned, abandoned,
> to bear good fruit—the limbs
> moving slightly in still air with my drunkenness;

But the poem returns to violence at the end, with a reflexive Christ ("Christ bless torn Christ") and "all things bruised or crushed / as an apple."

BANAL, OR PHILOSOPHICAL, APPLES

Apples devoid of culturally sanctioned associations can easily lapse into banality, reduced to arbitrarily selected bits of quotidian reality with little resonance of any kind, as in the

poem of Edna St. Vincent Millay (1892–1950) titled "Recuerdo" [Memory] (1920), 143
about riding the ferry all night with a companion: "And you ate an apple, and I ate a
pear, / From a dozen of each we had bought somewhere." Nor is the banality of the
apples and pears redeemed in the poem when the couple present the unconsumed
fruit to a poor old woman. The poet Amy Clampitt (1920–1994), however, has quoted
some lovely lines about apples from a posthumously published journal by Millay:

> Now, I could very easily tell
> An apple-orchard by the smell,
> And in my mind's eye see again
> The rough bark blackened by the rain
> And glistening, and the hardy big
> Red and white blossoms on the twig.
>
> But nothing could recall the sound
> Of apples falling on the ground . . .

The very banality of ordinary apples may be precisely what permits them to
enter that class of commonsensical pedagogical paradigms (including white envelopes,
red tomatoes, and brown sticks) so much favored in epistemological exercises designed
to distinguish "the real" from mere simulacra, illusions, or—a late-twentieth-century
technological wrinkle—holographs. It may occasion some surprise, though, that the
notion of such a "philosophical" apple goes back at least as far as the Roman writer
Macrobius in the early fifth century C.E., in whose *Saturnalia,* written for the edification of his son, Eustachius, Macrobius concludes the fifteenth and penultimate chapter
of the seventh and last book with an analysis of reason and the senses as sources of
knowledge (translated by Percival Vaughan Davies):

> The reason does not always find the evidence of a single sense enough to
> establish the identity of an object; for, if I see from afar an object with the
> shape of the fruit called an apple, it does not necessarily follow that the
> object is an apple—it might have been made from some material to
> resemble an apple. I must therefore call for the advice of a second sense
> and let smell judge. But, if the object had been placed in a heap of apples,
> it could have acquired the smell of an apple, and so at this point I must
> consult my sense of touch, which enables me to judge by the weight. But
> there is a risk that this sense too may itself be deceived, should a cunning
> craftsman have chosen a material equal in weight to an apple's. I must
> therefore have recourse to my sense of taste, and, if the taste of the object
> agrees with its appearance, then I have no hesitation in regarding the
> object as an apple.

Whether philosophically sound or not, it should be deeply satisfying to all pomophiles
that the ultimate criterion of the apple's reality is said to be its *taste.*

But the contemporary Norwegian poet Arild Nyquist (b. 1937) tries to write a poem, "Apple Stealing," in which apples are minimally present, appearing only, so to speak, at the last possible moment, without actually being *in* the poem, whose final line is, in a real sense, "No, said I" (translated by Martin Allwood):

> This is a poem.
> It came to me last night.
> It came on a billow
> and walked slowly across the paper
> with small, delicious steps.
> Must I walk straight? said the poem.
> No.
> Is it very far to Africa? said the poem.
> Well, rather.
> What time is it? said the poem.
> Five minutes after four.
> Are you all right, Arild?
> No, said I.
> I will give the last word to apple stealing, said the poem
> happily.

It seems appropriate to conclude our literary apple episodes with one in which an apple, like Lewis Carroll's Cheshire cat, gradually disappears, leaving, instead of the cat's smile, the apple's pips. "Promenade de Picasso" (1949), by Jacques Prévert (1900–1977) is concerned with attempts by a "painter of reality," faced by an apple posing "on a very round plate of real porcelain," to capture "the apple as it is." The painter fails, of course, as he "finds himself the sad prey / of a numberless crowd of associations of ideas." And we are then treated to a selection of some of these ideas, real ones mixed indiscriminately with absurd ones (here translated by Lawrence Ferlinghetti):

> the earthly Paradise and Eve and then Adam
> a watering-can a trellis Parmentier a stairway
> [*l'arrosoir l'espalier Parmentier l'escalier*]
> Canadian Hesperidian Norman apples Reinette apples and Appian apples
> the serpent of the Tennis Court and the Oath of Apple Juice
> [*le serpent du Jeu de Paume le serment du Jus de Pomme*]
> and original sin
> and the origins of art
> and Switzerland with William Tell
> and even Isaac Newton
> several times prizewinner at the Exhibition of Universal Gravitation

("Parmentier"—the name of the man who popularized potatoes in France—refers to
a kind of potato dish.)

Picasso then comes along:

> and Picasso eats the apple
> and the apple tells him Thanks
> and Picasso breaks the plate
> and goes off smiling
> and the painter drawn from his dreams
> like a tooth
> finds himself all alone again before his unfinished canvas
> with right in the midst of his shattered china
> the terrifying pips of reality.

The apple as a marker, symbol, or evidence of reality occurs with telling effect in a scene in the film *Sunset Boulevard* (1950), directed by Billy Wilder (b. 1906). Joe Gillis (played by William Holden) and Betty Schaefer (played by Nancy Olson) are eating apples as they wander around an empty movie set late one night, three quarters of the way through the film. She is explaining how she spent her childhood on these sound stages, and how her first screen test showed she needed a nose job, while her second (after the plastic surgery) showed she looked fine but couldn't act. With no regrets, she became a script-reader with aspirations of becoming a scriptwriter. Joe is a failed scriptwriter, who is being kept by the aging silent film star Norma Desmond (played by Gloria Swanson) in return for his sexual favors and his willingness to rewrite her absurd film script about Salome. Both Joe and Betty, in other words, are uncritical and enthusiastic participants in Hollywood's dream-factory; only the apples are real.

The apples in *Sunset Boulevard* also function as love tokens: when we first see an apple in the film, it is sitting, half-eaten, on Betty's desk; later in the scene, when Joe refuses to collaborate with Betty on the rewriting of his old film script, she picks up the apple and almost throws it at him. His response is to suggest a title for the new script: "An Apple For the Teacher." Later, in the scene referred to above, where both Joe and Betty are eating apples, he finishes his and throws the core off into the night— a not very subtle anticipation of his later rejection of Betty's love. This gesture by Joe may have been improvised during shooting; it is, in any case, missing from the published screenplay of *Sunset Boulevard* (which was written by Charles Brackett, Billy Wilder, and D. M. Marshman, Jr.).

Probably the most notorious philosophical—more specifically, epistemological— modern painting must be Magritte's *The Treachery of Images,* a picture of a pipe with a caption painted in script beneath it reading "Ceci n'est pas une pipe" (This is not a pipe). There are several versions; the best known is of 1928–9 (oil on canvas, 24½ x 32 inches), now in the Los Angeles County Museum of Art. Not as well known is

146   Magritte's much later painting (in a private collection) called *This not an Apple* (1964), where the caption painted in script above the image of an apple with a leafy stem reads "Ceci n'est pas une pomme" (This is not an apple); for reproductions of both pipe and apple paintings, see Meuris, *Magritte.*

2

FIGS

SOME FIG FACTS

The ubiquity of apples in the modern world is paralleled in large tracts of the ancient world by the central importance of figs as a basic source of nutrition (though not as a literary subject). According to one pair of food historians, Don and Patricia Brothwell, figs "constituted a very important article of food in early Mesopotamia, Palestine, Egypt and Greece"; Lyn Foxhall, a Classical archeologist, writes even more emphatically, in the *Oxford Classical Dictionary* (1996), that "the fig-tree is an underrated food source in antiquity, producing more calories per unit area than any other crop: 15,000, 000 kilocalories per hectare" and that figs "feature in the diet of slaves in the Linear B tablets from Pylos." Figs, indeed, were—along with olives, dates, pomegranates, and grapes—among the first fruits domesticated (sometime around 4000 B.C.E. in southwest Asia's Fertile Crescent); whereas apples (along with pears, plums, and cherries) were only domesticated in later times. (For a brief introductory discussion of plant domestication, with references, see Jared Diamond's *Guns, Germs, and Steel: The Fates of Human Societies* [1997].)

Three small but telling bits of evidence will illustrate the importance of figs in the ancient world. The first two are from the proceedings of a symposium on food in antiquity, edited by John Wilkins et al. (1995): (1) a poetic fragment from Ananios (6th cent. B.C.E.) reads: "If a man were to lock up in his house a large amount of gold, a few figs and two or three men, he would find out how much better figs are than gold"; (2) a text from the Mishnah (second cent. C.E.) advises Jews on how an absent husband is obliged to provide for his wife (*Ketubot,* or Marriage Documents, 5.8); the foods mentioned include wheat, chickpeas and lentils, olive oil, and dried figs, with the figs, by modern calculations, comprising some 14 to 16 percent of the estimated calorific value of the total food ration. For the third example, we turn to Philostratus the Elder (*Imagines,* 1.31, "Xenia") for his description of a still life picture in which the lengthiest passage is devoted to figs (with briefer allusions to chestnuts, pears, apples, cherries, grapes, a honeycomb, cheese, and milk; the translator is Arthur Fairbanks):

> It is a good thing to gather figs and also not to pass over in silence the figs
> in this picture. Purple figs dripping with juice are heaped on vine-leaves;

and they are depicted with breaks in the skin, some just cracking open to disgorge their honey, some split apart, they are so ripe. Near them lies a branch, not bare, by Zeus, or empty of fruit, but under the shade of its leaves are figs, some still green and "untimely," some with wrinkled skin and over-ripe, and some about to turn, disclosing the shining juice, while on the tip of the branch a sparrow buries its bill in what seems the very sweetest of the figs.

There are good reasons for the great success of fig culture; in the words of a modern manual of fruit growing (1987) by Barbara Ferguson, "In warm regions the fig bears big, juicy fruit in early summer, then sets a heavier crop of small fruit, perfect for drying, in the fall. It lives for many years, loves clay soil if drainage is good, and needs next to no attention." But figs are also fascinating organisms from a purely biological point of view, particularly with respect to their reproductive mechanisms, aspects of which have occasionally been exploited for literary ends. It must be understood that all the hundreds of (humanly) edible fig cultivars—their colors include black, brown, red, purple, green, yellow, and white—belong to just two species, *Ficus carica* (the common fig) and *Ficus sycamorus* (the Egyptian fig), which are in important respects not typical of the over 900 other species of the genus *Ficus* (which includes such plants as the rubber and banyan trees). I should like to begin, therefore, by explaining a few fundamental biological characteristics shared by all figs and then go on to discuss what is peculiar about the edible ones.

Most species of *Ficus* are tropical plants, which may be trees, shrubs, or vines. In the tropical rain forest, for example, figs grow on vines (rooted in the ground but climbing up trees) and on epiphytes (rooted in the bark or soil of the rain-forest canopy); during the dry season, figs may be the only edible fruit available to small rain-forest mammals. As for reproduction, almost none of these fig plants is self-pollinating; rather, like many plants, figs require insects for pollination, specifically, tiny fig wasps (around a millimeter in size, almost invisible to the naked eye), each species of fig generally being associated with its own unique species of wasp. This association between figs and wasps has been known since antiquity but its full elucidation is quite recent, with some details not yet understood. A female wasp, loaded with fig pollen, penetrates a tiny opening (the ostiole) in the inner rind at the base of an unripe fig and delivers the pollen to the hundreds of tiny female (or pistillate) flowers lining the internal spheroidal cavity, the fertilized flowers then becoming seeds. (These flowers, it must be understood, are little more than sexual organs; there are, for example, no petals.) The wasp also lays her own fertilized eggs in as many as half of these flowers, and each resulting wasp larva is nourished by a developing seed. The female wasp then dies but after a month or so her eggs hatch into (wingless) male and (winged) female wasps, which mate. By this time, male (or staminate) flowers (also rudimentary) have matured inside the fig and these furnish the new female wasps with pollen. All the male wasps inside a given fig now together chew a hole in the fig wall, which enables the mated female wasps, bearing fig pollen, to leave the fig and search for new figs to penetrate. The subsequent history of the figs and fig trees is well summarized in the course of a lucid review essay, entitled "How to Be a Fig" (1979) by Daniel H. Janzen:

> The figs newly vacated by the pollinating wasps ripen rapidly and are avidly eaten by many species of vertebrates. These digest the fruit wall and the florets from which the wasps have exited, but the seeds undamaged by the wasps usually survive the trip through the gut. . . . Mature fig trees are most common in moderately disturbed sites such as riparian edges, tree crowns (as epiphytes), tree falls, secondary agricultural regeneration, and old landslides. Their life spans are unknown, but probably do not exceed several hundred years in the wild state.

At the end of his essay, Janzen remarks that "Figs turn out to be very different from other plants. They deserve careful study for reasons besides the details of their peculiar pollination or their direct value as bat food. They are almost everywhere in the tropics and are often left standing even when the forest is cut. They should quickly provide that animal-plant interaction in the tropics about which we know the most."

Many people, as we shall see, have mixed feelings about figs. There is, for example, the American Frances Mayes, who bought a house in Cortona on whose terrraces fig trees were found to be growing, as she recounts in her book, *Under the Tuscan Sun: At Home in Italy* (1996). "I'm mixed on figs," she writes. "The fleshy quality feels spooky. In Italian, *il fico,* fig, has a a slangy turn into *la fica,* meaning vulva." She then provides a brief but accurate summary of fig pollination and concludes: "Is this appetizing, to know that however luscious figs taste, each one is actually a little graveyard of wingless male wasps? Or maybe the sensuality of the fruit comes from some flavor they dissolve into after short, sweet lives."

Very different is the point of view of the scientist Richard Dawkins (b. 1941). In one of his popular expositions of Darwinian evolution, *Climbing Mount Improbable* (1996), Dawkins, who occupies an Oxford chair in the Public Understanding of Science, begins and ends with figs because "the fig story is among the most satisfyingly intricate in evolution." Dawkins reserves his version of the fig story for his last chapter, "'A Garden Inclosed,'" whose title consists of a phrase from the Song of Songs 4:12 in the King James translation. (The Revised Standard Version substitutes "locked" for "inclosed.") Dawkins defends his choice of title for the chapter as follows:

> Look at a garden through the eyes of the insects that pollinate its flowers. A garden, on the human scale, is a population of flowers covering many square yards. The pollinators of figs are so tiny that, to them, the whole interior of a single fig might seem like a garden, though admittedly a small, cottage garden. It is planted with hundreds of miniature flowers, both male

and female, each with its own diminutive parts. Moreover the fig really is an enclosed and largely self-sufficient world for the minuscule pollinators.

But, of course, the "flowers" inside a fig do not resemble ordinary flowers in one respect unmentioned by Dawkins, namely, the absence of petals. However, Dawkins is simply using a metaphor, as he is the first to admit. (Indeed, the very title of his book points to Dawkins's central metaphor for explaining how such improbable events as the emergence of new species can occur.) My only objection to Dawkins's attitude is that he does not extend his tolerance of his own metaphors to other writers. Thus, he begins his book by pouring scorn on "a certain kind of literary mind":

> I have just listened to a lecture in which the topic for discussion was the fig. Not a botanical lecture, a literary one. We got the fig in literature, the fig as metaphor, changing perceptions of the fig, the fig as emblem of pudenda and the fig leaf as concealer of them, "fig" as an insult, the social construction of the fig, D.H. Lawrence on how to eat a fig in society, "reading fig" and, I rather think, "the fig as text."

Dawkins sees himself, by contrast, as telling the "true"—that is, scientific—story of the fig. This includes, of course, the reproductive wiles involved in the fig-wasp pairing, but also an entire "rich and writhing Lilliputian fauna" that inhabit the interior of the fig, including minute beetles, moths, flies, mites, worms, and even what Dawkins calls "freeloader" parasitic wasps which contribute nothing obviously beneficial to the fig. What fascinates Dawkins most, however, is the special case of a fig-pollinator system in which there are exclusively male and exclusively female fig trees, and he devotes the last nine or so pages of his book to dealing with the challenges presented by such a system to strictly Darwinian explanations; here is Dawkins's summary of the extraordinarily complex situation (he acknowledges he is following the work of two leading British biologists):

> We can expect both male and female fig trees to do all in their power to lure wasps into their own kind of fig. And we can expect the wasps to struggle to tell the difference between male and female figs, to enter the first and shun the second. Remember that "struggle" means that, over evolutionary time, they will come to possess genes that confer a predilection for male figs. More contortedly, we shall also find that both male and female fig trees should have an interest in fostering wasps that enter figs of the *other* sex.

Let us return to ordinary, humanly edible figs, which come in two species, well summed up by Hilary Wilson in her pamphlet, *Egyptian Food and Drink* (1988):

> Among ancient Egyptian food plants, fruit trees were very important. The most significant was the sycamore fig (*Ficus sycamorus*), also known as the

wild fig. The leaves, unlike the lobed leaves of the true fig (*Ficus carica*), are oval. The fruits grow in twos and threes from separate stalks, while true figs grow singly from leaf nodes on the main stem. Sycamore figs are smaller, yellower and have a more astringent taste than ordinary figs but were a most popular dessert fruit from very early times. . . . The tree was held sacred to the goddess Hathor, who was known as "Lady of the Sycamore."

In the Metropolitan Museum of Art, in New York, there is a wooden model of an enclosed garden from the tomb of a high-ranking Egyptian official (ca. 2010 B.C.E.) containing a small grove of sycamore fig trees. (For a picture of the model, see Karen Polinger Foster's "The Earliest Zoos and Gardens," in *Scientific American* [1999].)

Another thing to note about many of varieties of edible figs is how they can thrive in either subtropical or temperate climates and even survive severe cold, as explained in this dramatic description (in *Pomona* [1996], the quarterly publication of North American Fruit Explorers, or NAFEX) of how one amateur horticulturist protects his fig tree from the frost of a Kentucky winter:

> My fig tree is planted against the south side of my house. When the leaves drop in the fall I push it down, weight it with boards, and cover it with leaves. In the fall of 1995 it got so big, with the largest trunk 12 feet high and 3 inches in diameter, that I had to sit on it and ride it down, then tie the trunks to stakes. After getting all parts down, I put several stakes around the perimeter and ran a couple of wires around them to form a sort of fence to contain the leaves. . . .
>
> The fig tree tends to spring back, needing only a little pulling to tie it to stakes to get it upright. The wood is limber, easily manipulated, and does not break when I put the tree to bed or get it up.

Edible fig varieties fall into three different fruiting classes: those that require pollination (Smyrna figs); those that are self-pollinating (Common figs); and those that can set a secondary (so-called *breba*) crop without pollination but which require pollination to set the main crop (San Pedro figs). (See the exterior and interior views of two varieties of figs, painted by Deborah G. Passmore [1840–1911], published as a colored lithograph by the U. S. Department of Agriculture in 1897; the images are approximately life-sized [plate 13].) In the self-pollinating varieties, the female and male flowers inside the fig simply mature at the same time, so fertilization (and thereby seed production) can occur directly without the intervention of any other organism. The other two classes of figs are fertilized by wasps that grow not within the edible fig itself but within figs of a different species, so-called caprifigs. Caprifigs are themselves inedible (by humans) but their male flowers, with the aid of appropriate wasps, can furnish the pollen required to fertilize the edible figs. In practice, fig growers cultivate their caprifig trees and their edible fig trees some distance apart; they then collect their caprifigs just before the wasps emerge and place a few in each of their Smyrna or San

Pedro fig trees, repeating the procedure several times during the fig growing season, a process known as caprification. (For a beautiful picture of a caprifig and its associated wasp, see plate 14, an unsigned drawing from the *Pomona italia* [1817], vol. 1, by Giorgio Gallesio [1772–1839].)

Caprification was known in the ancient world (and indeed named by the Romans). An early literary allusion to caprification occurs in *The Birds* (414 B.C.E.), by Aristophanes. An Athenian, Pisthetairos, is explaining the advantages of replacing the traditional gods by birds (in William Arrowsmith's translation):

> Why, enormous plagues of locusts will not infest their vines:
> a single regiment of our Owls will wipe the locusts out.
> And the gallfly and the mite will no longer blight their figs
> since we'll send down troops of Thrushes to annihilate the bugs.

There is confusion here, presumably deliberate, about the respective roles of gallflies (wasps) and mites, since it was known in Aristophanes's time that the former are somehow positively involved in fig culture (caprification), while the latter attack the gallflies.

It is interesting to compare the detailed account of caprification by Pliny the Elder (23–79 C.E.) in his posthumously published *Natural History* with our own understanding of what is going on (translated by H. Rackham):

> A remarkable fact about the fig is that this alone among all the fruits hastens to ripen with a rapidity due to the skill of nature. There is a wild variety of fig called the goat-fig [*caprificus*] which never ripens, but bestows on another tree what it has not got itself, since it is a natural sequence of causation, just as from things that decay something is generated. Consequently this fig engenders gnats which, being cheated out of nutriment in their mother tree, fly away from its decaying rottenness to the kindred tree, and by repeatedly nibbling at the figs—that is by feeding on them too greedily— they open their orifices and so make a way into them, bringing with them the sun into the fruit for the first time and introducing the fertilizing air through the passages thus opened. . . . Because of this in fig-orchards a goat-fig is allowed to grow on the windward side, so that when a wind blows the gnats may fly off and be carried to the fig-trees.

For Pliny, the role of the "gnats" is simply to open up the figs to the "fertilizing air," and, of course, some plants are indeed fertilized by air-borne pollen. Presumably, if Pliny had been familiar with the internal flowers of figs, he would have mentioned them. By the end of the nineteenth century, such familiarity was presupposed by Samuel Butler (1835–1902) in his novel *The Way of All Flesh* (1903), where we find the narrator using his hero Ernest's ignorance of this peculiar feature of figs as an example of defective education:

Another time he preached upon the barren fig-tree, and described the
hopes of the owner as he watched the delicate blossom unfold, and give
promise of such beautiful fruit in autumn. Next day he received a letter
from a botanical member of his congregation who explained to him that
this could hardly have been, inasmuch as the fig produces its fruit first and
blossoms inside the fruit, or so nearly so that no flower is perceptible to an
ordinary observer.

In our own time, anyone unaware of the fact that, as mentioned earlier, some fig trees
bear two crops a year, is likely to miss the meaning of the reference in the poem, "Late
August" (1990), by Marilyn Hacker (b. 1942), to "the second fruit [of the fig tree],
ovarian, purple, splitting to scarlet."

BIBLICAL FIGS

References to figs are not numerous in the Bible, but there are some memorable ones.
The earliest such reference, of course, is to fig leaves, which Adam and Eve fashion
into genital covers (Gen. 3:7). And here it must be noted that, according to an Eastern
Christian tradition of biblical interpretation, the fruit that tempts Eve was a fig rather
than an apple. A famous visual representation of this interpretation is to be found in
the great mosaics of San Marco in Venice (1220s–1290s) in the so-called Creation
cupola. (For a colored reproduction of the entire cupola, see Penny Howell Jolly, *Made
in God's Image? Eve and Adam in the Genesis Mosaics at San Marco, Venice* [1997]; the figs
that Eve plucks and offers to Adam are visible in an enlarged black and white detail.)
I might add that this traditional identification of the Edenic fruit seems to be preserved
among certain groups of Jews. Thus, the Portuguese Sephardic Jew, Victor Perera
(b. 1934), in his book *The Cross and the Pear Tree* (1995), tells of his mother's saying,
"This will cost us what the fig cost Adam the First Man."

An explicit reference to figs occurs in a passage in Jeremiah 24:1–10, apparently
communicated to the prophet in a vision or dream:

> Yaweh pointed it out to me—and there, arranged in front of the temple
> of Yaweh were two baskets of figs. . . . In one basket the figs were excel-
> lent, like early-ripening figs. In the other basket the figs were extremely
> bad, so bad, indeed, as to be inedible.

Yaweh goes on to explain that the good figs represent the Israelites who have been
deported from Jerusalem by the Babylonian King Nebuchadnezzar, while the bad figs
represent the collaborators with the king who have remained in Jerusalem. (The historical event referred to by Jeremiah is Nebuchadnezzar's conquest of Jerusalem in 597 B.C.E.)

Given the widespread presence of figs in the ancient world, it is understandable
that the development of the fig tree and its fruit was sometimes used as an index of
the seasons. Thus, Hesiod (ca. 700 B.C.E.) explains a sign of the spring sailing season:
"At that point, when you first make out / on the topmost branches / of the fig tree,

a leaf as big as the print / that a crow makes / when he walks; at that time also the sea is navigable / and this is called the spring sailing season" (Richmond Lattimore's translation).

Again, in the Song of Songs 2:11–13, spring is heralded by, among other things, the sweetening of the green figs: "Look, winter is over, / the rains are done, / wildflowers spring up in the fields. / . . . The fig tree has sweetened / its new green fruit / and the young budded vines smell spicy." This association of figs and the seasons is found also in Mark 13:28, when Jesus is telling his disciples how to recognize the signs of the coming fall of Jerusalem: "From the fig tree learn its lesson: as soon as its branch becomes tender and puts forth its leaves, you know that summer is near." Also, in Matthew 7:16 the sentence "You will know them by their fruits" is immediately followed by the rhetorical question "Are grapes gathered from thorns, or figs from thistles?" Later in Matthew, an incident centered on a fig tree reveals something that may be seen—controversially, I know—as centrally important about Jesus, that is, his occasional manifestations of some of the nastier sides of his human nature. In the incident in question, the hungry Jesus comes upon a fig tree with leaves but bare of fruit, and he curses it: "'May no fruit ever come from you again!' And the fig tree withered at once." His disciples seem disconcerted, though not apparently so much at Jesus' vindictiveness as at his miraculous powers. Jesus then draws the moral for his disciples: those who have faith will possess equally miraculous powers, and "whatever you ask in prayer, you will receive, if you have faith." The incident also occurs, with some elaboration, in Mark 11:12–26, but is absent from Luke.

There is, however, a parable involving a fig tree in Luke 13:6–9 that is not found in any of the other gospels. A man decides to cut down a fig tree in his vineyard which has not borne fruit in three years, but the vinedresser advises him to spare the tree: "'Let it alone, sir, this year also, till I dig about it and put on manure. And if it bears fruit next year, well and good; but if not, you can cut it down.'" This incident has been interpreted as an expression of Jesus's growing impatience with the rejection of his prolonged ministry (three years?) in Jerusalem: the fig tree stands for the city, which Jesus grants a reprieve of one more year from its imminent destruction. Can it be mere coincidence that the age of the fig tree reflects the following passage (19:23–5) in Leviticus?

> When you come into the land and plant all kinds of trees for food, then you shall count their fruit as forbidden; three years it shall be forbidden to you, it must not be eaten. And in the fourth year all their fruit shall be holy, an offering of praise to the Lord. But in the fifth year you may eat of their fruit, that they may yield more richly for you: I am the Lord your God.

The fig reference in Luke is taken up by the minor seventeenth-century poet, Mildmay Fane, Earl of Westmorland (1602–1666), in his consciousness-of-sin poem "Shamed by the Creature" (1648). For Fane, as Alistair Fowler explains in his anthology of seventeenth century verse, "nature was a matter for religious meditation." The matter about which Fane meditates in this poem is the nature cultivated by the farmer and the vinedresser, exemplified by the vine, which responds to cultivation with a harvest of grapes: "So doth the youthful vine those prunings own, / Whenas her blossoms are to clusters grown"; as for himself, "This vegetable lecture may indeed / Cast a blush o'er me, whose return for seed / So far fall short." The fig tree occurs in the last of the twenty-four lines of the poem:

> And for my fruits, ere ripeness is begun,
> Abortive-like, they wither in the sun
> Of self-conceit. Lord, prune once more this vine,
> And plough this ground, lest the fig-tree's doom be mine.

It is understandable that many Christian commentators much prefer Luke's fig tree story to Matthew's and Mark's, and there have, of course, been attempts to explain away the unpleasantness of the latter story. Thus, in a recent dictionary of the Bible (1996), edited by W. R. F. Browning, we read that Jesus' "condemnation of the [fig] tree must be regarded as symbolic of a disillusionment with Israel." On the other hand, in the early poem "A Small Fig Tree," by Donald Hall (b. 1928), the condemned fig tree is personified and made to utter deeply heretical thoughts:

> I am dead, to be sure,
> for thwarting Christ's pleasure,
> Jesus Christ called Saviour.
>
> I was a small fig tree.
> Unjust it seems to me
> that I should withered be.
>
> If justice sits with God,
> Christ is cruel Herod
> and I by magic dead.
>
> If there is no justice
> where great Jehovah is,
> I will the devil kiss.

In one of the letters (addressed to British workingmen) of *Fors Clavigera* (no. 20, 3 July 1872), John Ruskin (1819–1900) describes an incident involving figs and relates it to several biblical passages. The incident, he tells us, took place on a Venetian quay just as he began to write the letter in question. Hearing what sounded like "a large new steamer coming in from the sea" but which turned out to be just "a little screw steamer . . . not twelve yards long"—but extremely noisy—Ruskin leaves off writing to go and look:

The cry of a boy selling something black out of a basket on the quay became so sharply distinguished above the voices of the always debating gondoliers, that I must needs stop again, and go down to the quay to see what he had got to sell. They were half-rotten figs, shaken down, untimely, by the midsummer storms: his cry of "Fighiaie" scarcely ceased, being delivered, as I observed, just as clearly between his legs, when he was stooping to find an eatable portion of the black mess to serve a customer with, as when he was standing up. His face brought the tears into my eyes, so open, and sweet, and capable it was; and so sad. I gave him three very small halfpence, but took no figs, to his surprise: he little thought how cheap the sight of him and his basket was to me, at the money; nor what this fruit "that could not be eaten, it was so evil," sold cheap before the palace of the Dukes of Venice, meant, to any one who could read signs, either in earth, or her heaven and sea.

At this point Ruskin adds an asterisked footnote: "'And the stars of heaven fell unto the earth, even as a fig-tree casteth her untimely figs, when she is shaken of a mighty wind.'—Rev. vi.13; compare Jerem. xxiv. 8, and Amos viii. 1 and 2." In Revelation 6:13, figs drop "untimely" through the "mighty wind" of God's wrath. The passage from Jeremiah we have already considered: the rotten figs stand for the bad Israelites. Finally, Ruskin follows many Bible commentators in taking figs, in Amos 8:1–2, to be the "summer fruit" that God shows the prophet Amos to signify the end of the people of Israel (in Hebrew, *qayits* is "summer fruit," and *qets* is "end"), the reason for God's curse on Israel being the prevailing social injustice.

To understand, now, why Ruskin found the sudden apparition of rotten figs so apt, one must be aware of his highly agitated state at the time of writing owing to the presence of steam-driven boats in the Venetian canals and, more generally, to what he saw as the wanton destruction of both the pristine natural environment and the beauties of Venetian architecture, as well as the general decay of modern society. As Wolfgang Kemp puts it in his commentary on the passage: "Ruskin 'reads' the boy fig seller and the fruit he sells as an apocalyptic emblem." What I find surprising is Ruskin's failure to include among the biblical references he cites the passages from Matthew and Mark in which Jesus curses the fig tree, particularly since the announced topic of Ruskin's letter is precisely the significance of blessing and cursing. I must emphasize that we have been considering only the very beginning of a long and complex essay that many Ruskin critics place among his most original writings; for a sustained analysis of the essay, see the ten-page discussion by Kemp.

CLASSICAL FIGS

In Classical literature ripe figs (*sykon* in Greek) are often employed as double entendres for the female pudenda and fig trees for the male genitals (for some examples of the former, see Henderson's *The Maculate Muse*). But at least one early literary occurrence

of a fig tree, in the epigram "On a Willing Woman," by Archilochus (ca. 680–640
B.C.E.), has feminine sexual associations (Lattimore's translation):

> Wild fig tree of the rocks, so often feeder of ravens,
> Loves-them-all, the seducible, the stranger's delight.

Dried figs, owing presumably to their cheapness, are often used to suggest something
nugatory. Instances involving both ripe and dried figs occur toward the end of Aristophanes's *Peace,* chronologically the second of his peace comedies and dating from 421
B.C.E., when the war of Athens with Sparta had been going on for some ten years. In
fact, peace negotiations had started the year before, and the play reflects the playwright's
mood of hopeful anticipation. (As it turned out, the war was still going on ten years
later, the date of *Lysistrata,* and ended only in 404 with the defeat of Athens.) The plot
of the play is simple: Trygaeus, an old farmer, makes his way to Olympus on the back
of a dung beetle in an effort to bring Peace (personified as a statue) back to Greece.
His eventual success leads to complaints from the war-profiteers. Here is part of the
exchange between Trygaeus and an arms dealer (translated by Jeffrey Henderson):

TRYGAEUS
All right, what will you take for this pair of crests?

ARMS–DEALER
What's your offer?

TRYGAEUS
My offer? I'm embarrassed to say, but considering the workmanship of
the fastening, I'd offer three quarts of dried figs for the pair.

ARMS–DEALER
Done; go in and fetch the figs.

TRYGAEUS *goes inside.*

(*to a companion*) It's better than nothing, my friend.

TRYGAEUS *comes out.*

TRYGAEUS
Get these the hell out of here, get them away from my house! They're losing their hair, they're worthless. I wouldn't even pay a single fig for them.

At the very end of the play, when the feast in celebration of Trygaeus's marriage
to Cornucopia (one of the handmaids of Peace) is starting, the Chorus Leader chants:

CHORUS LEADER
You will live happily,
and free of troubles
gather in your figs.
[. . . . .]
His fig is big and ripe,
hers is nice and sweet!

About the last two lines Henderson makes the witty comment that this "is a case of brachylogy for the sake of parallelism."

Sextus Propertius (54/47–2 B.C.E.) ends his lengthy ode to a bawd (4.5), appropriately enough, with a wild fig tree (caprificus) marking her grave, but not just marking it—bursting it with the downward thrust of its roots; two contrasting translations of the last four lines may be quoted, the first in highly literal prose (by G. P. Goold), the second more ambitiously poetic (by John Warden):

Let the bawd's tomb be an old wine-jar with broken neck, and upon it, wild fig-tree, exert your might. All ye that love, pelt this grave with jagged stones, and mingled with the stones cast curses!

~

And for your burial place

a wine jar
with a broken neck

where the fig tree grows
to crack your bones

and lovers pelt
your tomb with muck

and mingle curses
with the stones.

The wood of the fig tree was considered as inferior for construction as the fig itself was for food. Evidence of this was the use of fig tree wood to make statues of Priapus, the lowliest of the gods. The last of the Classical pantheon to become a cult figure, beginning around 400 B.C.E., probably in the city of Lampsacus, Priapus was the offspring of Dionysus and Aphrodite (or a nymph) and rejected from birth by his mother because of his deformed—immensely large and perpetually erect—phallus. One of his main roles in the Roman world, as Maurice Olender explains, was "that of a god who protects small farms against thieves or the evil eye by threatening sexual violence against anyone who came close to the property that he guarded." To this end, a statue of Priapus cradling fruit in his rolled-up tunic—thereby exposing his phallus—

was often placed in a Roman garden. That these statues were usually of the crudest character, Olender explains, is clear from numerous "Greek and Latin epigrams [in which] the ithyphallic effigy of the god, often crudely carved out of cheap fig tree wood and carelessly daubed with red, assumes a voice to utter obscene threats." An instance of vocalization from the fig tree wood occurs in the opening lines of *Satire* 1.8 (ca. 30 B.C.E.) by Horace (65–8 B.C.E.; the translation is by W. H. Parker):

> A fig tree once I was, which useless wood
> The carpenter in doubt was if he should
> To a priapus turn, or to a chair.
> He chose the god, and so my job's to scare
> Away the thieves with penis painted red
> From loins erect; the wreath upon my head,
> From gardens new deters the birds.

Surviving statues of Priapus from antiquity are rare; for a discussion illustrated with images of Priapus, see Parker's *Priapea* (1988) and Peter Stewart's "Fine Art and Coarse Art: The Image of Roman Priapus" (1997). A picture of a splendid Renaissance example, in bronze, may be found in Charles Avery's *Bernini, Genius of the Baroque* (1997). (Avery's characterization of the dimensions of the work is confined to the term "statuette"; its provenance is listed only as "formerly Adams Collection, London.") A wonderful description by Giorgio Vasari (1511–1574) of a painted Priapean scene featuring figs may be found in his life of Giovanni da Udine (1494–1564), a student of Giorgione's and assistant of Raphael's, famous for his depictions of birds, fruit, and flowers, and for his discovery of the formula for ancient stucco. The painting in question, dating from circa 1518, is part of the decoration of the Loggia of Psyche, in the Villa Farnesina, in Rome. Here is the passage from Vasari (in a translation quoted from an essay by Leonard Barkan):

> Above the figure of Mercury who is flying, he made to represent Priapus,
> a gourd entwined in bind-weed, which has for testicles two egg-plants,
> and near the flower of the gourd he depicted a cluster of large purple figs,
> within one of which, over-ripe and bursting open, the point of the gourd
> with the flower is entering; which conceit is rendered with such grace, that
> no one could imagine anything better. But why say more?

(For a color reproduction of this painted detail, see Jones and Penny, *Raphael*.)

The Roman poet Martial uses figs in one of his satires (7) for setting up an opposition between his own biting epigrams and the rather tame ones of an unnamed contemporary (translated by Olive Pitt-Kethley):

> The epigrams you write are full of grace,
> More dazzling than a white-enamelled face;
> No grain of salt, no drop of bitter gall—
> You're mad to think they will be read at all.

> Sharp vinegar improves the appetite,
> No face without a dimple will delight.
> Give children figs and apples without zest—
> For me strong figs of Chios taste the best.

The Latin of the two punch lines which end the poem reads as follows: "Infanti melimela [apples] dato fatuasque mariscas [figs]: / Nam mihi, quae novit pungere, Chia sapit." Here, the word *mariscas* is unusual, and seems to mean an especially large variety of fig; the ordinary Latin word for fig is *fico*.

A famous allusion to figs near the end of Plutarch's *Life of Marcus Cato* (27.1) is presumed to be a summary of the longer account in the *Natural History* of Pliny the Elder. In the course of his discussion of figs, Pliny remarks (14.74–5, translated by John F. Healy):

> The variety called "African" by Cato reminds me that he used this fig for an important demonstration. For, burning with a deadly hatred of Carthage and troubled with anxiety about the safety of his descendants, Cato used to shout at every meeting of the Senate: "Carthage must be destroyed!" Now one day he brought into the Senate House an early ripe fig from Africa, showed it to his fellow senators and said: "I ask you, when do you think this fig was plucked from the tree?"
>
> All agreed that it was fresh, so he said: "Know this, it was picked two days ago in Carthage; that's how near the enemy are to our walls!" Immediately they began the Third Punic War, in which Carthage was destroyed.

Since Cato lived from 234 to 149 B.C.E., Plutarch and Pliny were writing at least two centuries after the alleged incident. A careful analysis of the relevant information on such matters as the keeping qualities of fresh figs, the strength and direction of prevailing winds between Italy and the northern coast of Africa, and the maximum speeds of sailing ships in Cato's time, has convinced a modern scholar that Cato's figs could not possibly have come from Africa. F. J. Meijer estimates the sailing time from Africa to Rome as at least six days and concludes that "A voyage of six days would make it impossible, and even after only three days it would be highly unlikely, for the figs displayed by Cato to give any impression of freshness." But the story need not therefore be wholly false: "Most senators would probably have seen through Cato's fig performance and realized that he was displaying African figs from his own estate. Only a minority of them would have disapproved of such behaviour." That Cato's figs actually helped bring on the Third Punic War is, of course, a much more dubious idea.

THE FIG GESTURE

Our next fig episode, from Dante (1265–1321), requires some preliminary explanation. Dante and Virgil, in canto 24 of the *Inferno* (ca. 1310), have arrived at the seventh subdivision (or chasm) of the eighth circle of Hell, the region reserved for the punishment of thieves. (I cite Charles Singleton's prose translation throughout.) The canto begins, in its second tercet, with a delicate and melodious account of an early spring "hoarfrost [that] copies on the ground the image of his white sister" (quando la brina in su la terra assempra / l'imagine di sua sorella bianca). Given the horrors to come in this and the next canto, one might ask: why such an opening? One answer is that theft is itself a form of deception, analogous to the deceiving of the peasant in the very next tercet, who initially mistakes the hoarfrost for snow. Another answer is that the human-serpent metamorphoses of cantos 24–25 are so shocking precisely because they involve such an extreme instability of appearances. (Both these answers may be found in Joan M. Ferrante's brilliant commentary, "Canto xxiv, Thieves and Metamorphoses" [1998].) In any case, after a strenuous climb and a brief rest sitting down—but not before Virgil has admonished Dante that he must overcome sloth and exert himself to seek fame— Dante is ready to encounter the resident sinners, and Virgil leads him to a place where they can see a ditch containing "a fearful throng of serpents, of kinds so strange that the memory of it still chills my blood." And here Dante's diabolical imagination reaches an extreme limit, for these serpents not only torture the sinners but also *are* the sin-ners (with the loss of self-identity becoming the justly compensatory punishment for the losses inflicted on the thieves' victims, though the full horror of this metamor-phosis of serpents into sinners and vice versa only emerges in the next canto). Dante notices one sinner nearby, hands bound behind him by means of a coiled and knot-ted serpent threaded through his loins: the man is attacked by another serpent and instantly—"never was *o* or *i* written so fast as he took fire and burned"—reduced to dust, at which point the whole cycle is repeated. During a short lull in the cycle, Dante has a chance to question this sinner; he turns out to be Vanni Fucci, from Pistoia, whose crime was the theft of beautiful adornments from the sacristy of a church. The canto ends with Fucci deliberately discomforting Dante by prophesying Florence's defeat at the hands of Pistoia in the ongoing war between the two cities.

Canto 24 has ended and the next canto begins, but there is no lapse at all in the narrative continuity. This kind of rhetorical enjambment has not happened before in the *Inferno,* and indeed, in a brilliant commentary by Anthony Oldcorn on canto 25, we read that "the transition from Canto xxiv to Canto xxv is one of the most sur-prising and cleverly handled in the entire *Comedy.*" Canto 25 opens with these explo-sively blasphemous lines:

> At the end of his words the thief raised up his hands with both the
> figs, crying, "Take them, God, for I aim them at you!"
>
> ~
>
> Al fine de le sue parole il ladro
>   le mani alzò con amendue le fiche,
>   gridando: "Togli, Dio, ch'a te le squadro!"

It will be noted that Fucci's hands have been conveniently unbound by Dante (the author) so Fucci can make the "fig," an obscene gesture with the fist in which the

162   thumb is placed between forefinger and middle finger. Performing the gesture with both fists seems to have been especially popular at Pistoia; thus, the fourteenth-century chronicler Villani tells of a tall stronghold in Pistoia on top of which were "two marble arms that made the *fiche* toward Florence with their hands" (quoted by Singleton in his commentary on the Inferno). One final point about the two cantos is that their content and form depend heavily on a—presumably benevolent—form of theft: Dante's borrowings from Virgil, Ovid, and Lucan (39–65 C.E.), the two last mentioned by name as rivals Dante has overcome or "silenced" (Canto 25.94, 97; see the essays by Ferrante and Oldcorn).

     Manuscripts of the *Divine Comedy* began to be illuminated in the fourteenth century, and many later artists have illustrated Dante's work. In Eugene Paul Nassar's book (1994) on the illustrations for the *Inferno,* the earliest for cantos 24–5 are some illuminations dating from around the middle of the fourteenth century. As for Vanni Fucci, the earliest picture of him reproduced by Nassar is in a fresco by Nardo di Cione (also known as Bernardo Orcagna; 1320–1365/6) in the cathedral of S. Maria Novella in Florence (Strozzi Chapel, ca. 1350s). Later pictures of Vanni occur in two Florentine manuscripts, one of circa 1390–1400 in the Vatican (Biblioteca Apostolica, Ms lat. 4476), and another of circa 1420 now in Paris (Bibliothèque Nationale, MS. it. 74). Fucci can also be seen just left of center at the bottom of one of Botticelli's great set of drawings (1485–1495) for the *Divine Comedy.* Nassar includes further renditions of Fucci by a nineteenth-century disciple of Gustave Doré, Yan Dargent (1879), and by the twentieth-century Italian artist Renato Guttoso (1969). In the last three representations, Fucci is engulfed and almost disappears in the crowd of surrounding sinners.

     The representation of Fucci by William Blake is quite different. Blake made a watercolor representation of the Fucci episode as part of his uncompleted project for illustrating the entire *Divine Comedy.* Commissioned in 1825–27 by Blake's patron John Linnell, the drawings were designed for eventual engraving. Blake learned some Italian so he could read Dante's text, but mostly he relied on Henry Cary's English translation (published in 1814). Blake was mortally ill during this period and many of the drawings must have been made while he was in bed. (As Blake explained in a letter to Linnell, he could draw in bed but not engrave; only seven engravings were completed.) Of the 102 surviving drawings, many were never finished; one finished drawing is for *Inferno,* canto 25, and shows the figure of Fucci, facing us and extending his arms up to heaven as he makes the figs with both hands. Fucci is of noble stature, taller than Virgil or Dante, who are the only other figures in the picture. All this reflects Blake's personal theology, according to which any rebel against the traditional Judeo-Christian God must be a hero. (The drawing is now in the National Gallery of Victoria, Melbourne; for a black and white reproduction, see Milton Klonsky's *Blake's Dante* [1980]; for a color reproduction, see David Bindman, *William Blake, The Divine Comedy* [2000].)

     A contemporary counterpart, in a way, of Blake's drawing of Fucci is a print made by the English artist Tom Phillips (b. 1937), the second of four plates for canto 25 of the *Inferno* and one of 139 colored lithographs and screenprints made for his own limited edition of the work (1983), which also includes his own English translation. Phillips's Fucci illustration looks roughly like this: against a brick wall as background, one notices first a pair of forearms emerging from the lower left and lower right corners of the picture; one of these arms terminates in a figged fist, while the other terminates in an ugly face with its long red tongue sticking out. Above the arms, at the very center of the picture, is a square containing a stylized hand with two fingers making another obscene gesture. (Phillips explains all this in his notes on the plates.) But more details become visible on closer scrutiny, such as the faint graffiti of human genitals covering the brick wall. Equally important, however, in plate 25/2, are some small passages of type just above the central square: the word "fig" occurs twice and there are several obscenities. These words are the residue after Phillips has painted over most of the print on a page from the popular Victorian novel, *A Human Document* (1892), by W. H. Mallock (1849–1923). Phillips bought a copy of the novel by chance in 1966 and used it initially to generate first the title and then the text of an illustrated book called *A Humament,* which has now been published in two versions (1980, 1987); more are promised. Phillips has also used the same technique to generate other texts, paintings, and even an opera (libretto, score, staging, and costumes) called *Irma* (the name of Mallock's original heroine). The few words, then, in plate 25/2 serve, among other things, to relate this illustration to almost all the other *Inferno* illustrations—the exception is the frontispiece, independently created by Phillips—and to much of Phillips's rich and ever-expanding artistic oeuvre.

For the place of *A Humament* in the twentieth-century tradition of artists' books, see Johanna Drucker's *The Century of Artists' Books* (1995); her view of Phillips's achievement in that book—or series of books—certainly applies equally to his *Inferno,* and is worth quoting at length:

> The work is infinitely varied, the range of opacity and translucency permitting the Mallock work differing degrees of preservation. In terms of stategies of representation, each page and each opening makes visual interventions at different levels of literalness and illusion—either using the page as the support for a visual image, a pattern, or taking its typographic layout as the basis of a design. The work is impossible to pigeonhole—its visual and textual interventions are not strictly pop, conceptual, or pointed by a particular agenda. It is rather a full-scale work of invention and variation— an obsessive doodle onto a framework which repaid this labor with a rich harvest of discoveries. Let free of the responsibility of making a new invention the book artist is able to allow associative processes free reign, to let the work happen—which is not to discount either labor or intention in the process, merely to point out their framework.

A couple of centuries after Dante, we find Rabelais (ca. 1490–1553) using the fig gesture in chapter 4.45 of his *Gargantua and Pantagruel* (1534/5; 1546; 1548; 1552); the chapter is titled "How Pantagruel went ashore on the island of the Popefigs" (translated by Donald Frame). It seems the inhabitants of an imaginary island were subjects of a people who supported the pope. After an incident in which the subjected islanders offended their masters by making the sign of the fig at a portrait of the pope, the "Popefigs" were punished by the "Papimaniacs"; and the punishment was the same as that meted out to the Milanese by the emperor Frederick Barbarossa—which enables Rabelais to tell what purports to be a historical episode:

> The Milanese had rebelled against him and driven his wife the empress out of the city, ignominiously mounted on an old mule named Thacor [Hebrew: a fig in the fundament] wrong way round, that is to say with her ass turned toward the head of the mule and her face toward the crupper.
>
> Frederick, on his return, after subjugating and taking back the city, made such a thorough search that he recovered the famous mule Thacor. Thereupon, in the middle of the great Brouet [the marketplace of Milan], on his orders the hangman placed a fig in the pudenda of Thacor, in the presence and sight of the captive townsmen, then proclaimed on behalf of the emperor, to the sound of the trumpets, that any one of them who wanted to escape death must publicly take the fig out with his teeth, then put it back in the right place without using his hands. Anyone who refused would be hanged and strangled on the spot. Some of them felt shame and horror at such an abominable penalty, put it beyond the fear of death, and were hanged. In others the fear of death won out over such sense of shame. These, after pulling out the fig with their teeth, displayed it clearly to the hangman, saying *Ecco lo fico* [Behold the fig].

Since the emperor in question lived some three centuries before Rabelais, this story must be considered one of those legends—sometimes aggrandizing, sometimes (as in this case) belittling—that accumulate around powerful men. Frederick's political influence extended into southeastern France (his wife was Beatrice of Burgundy, and her family had title also to Provence), and Rabelais, of course, was a professor not too far away, at the University of Montpellier, where he would have become aware of local legends. As for Milan, the conflict there seems to have been a purely local affair, which accounted, in Geoffrey Barraclough's words, for "the intransigence of Milan's hostility, and this intransigence . . . provoked on Frederick's side an inveterate hostility to Milan, which far outstepped what was politically desirable."

The origin of the fig gesture is disputed. Shakespeare (1564–1616), for one, uses, in *Henry V* (1600), a variant of the well-known phrase, "the Spanish fig" (3.6.56–8):

> *Pistol.* Die and be damned, and *fico* for thy friendship!
> *Fluellen.* It is well.
> *Pistol.* The fig of Spain!

In fact, the fig gesture as such goes back to antiquity, apparently originating as an apotropaic charm to ward off evil, as in this passage (5.433–34) from Ovid's *Fasti* (ca. 8 C.E.): "he makes a sign with his thumb in the middle of his closed fingers, lest in his silence an unsubstantial shade should meet him." At some point, the gesture acquired an obscene connotation and an association with figs. Presumably, also, the association (noted by Rabelais) between the fig gesture and the mule was mediated by Priapus, who was often associated with that lustful but sterile animal. It is worth noting that one lexicographer has derived the expressions "not to care a fig" or "give a fig" for someone from the obscene meaning of fig, a derivation which seems to conflate the latter meaning with the meaning of a (dried) fig as something of little value. (See the entry "fig" in Eric Partridge's *A Dictionary of Slang and Unconventional English* [1961].)

The Puritan Edward Taylor was presumably unaware of the obscene connotations of figs when he wrote his poem "A Fig for thee Oh! Death" (undated). In fifty-six heroic couplets, Taylor describes graphically the terrors of death and then concludes:

> Why camst thou then so slowly? Mend thy pace.
> Thy Slowness me detains from Christ's bright face.
> Although thy terrours rise to th'highst degree,
> I still am where I was, a Fig for thee.

A full discussion of "the fig hand" (*mano in fica*) is found in a curious book by the Neapolitan priest and classical archeologist Andrea Vincenzo de Jorio (1769–1851): *Gesture in Naples and Gesture in Classical Antiquity* (1832), which, in the view of its modern translator Adam Kendon, "remains one of the most complex treatises on the subject ever published and it is the first ever to present a study of gesture from what today would be called an ethnographic point of view." De Jorio recognizes three different meanings for the fig gesture, which he designates "amulet," "serious insult," and "obscene invitation." "Bear in mind," he tells us, "that when it is used in the first and third meanings, the gesture is always accompanied by a joyful, gay, or mild expression, with modifications that convey differences in meaning, however always with an erotic implication. The second meaning however, that of insult, is accompanied by an indignant, vindictive, or violent expression." De Jorio cites, of course, canto 25 of Dante's *Inferno*, but also ancient bronzes and vase paintings.

MODERN POETIC FIGS

The description of a particular hand gesture as "the fig" owes something presumably to a resemblance between a human fist and a fig, but for a consideration of figs in their own unique shape and form we may turn to one of the unrhymed (or free verse) poems by D. H. Lawrence (1885–1930), "Figs," one of the sequence of six poems about fruit that opens *Birds, Beasts, and Flowers!* (1923). It is clear that Lawrence knows something about the unusual way in which fig trees are pollinated (though he never refers to fig wasps) and that he has carefully observed both figs and people eating them:

> The proper way to eat a fig, in society,
> Is to split it in four, holding it by the stump,
> And open it, so that it is a glittering, rosy, moist, honied, heavy-
> petalled four-petalled flower.
>
> Then you throw away the skin
> Which is just like a four-sepalled calyx,
> After you have taken off the blossom with your lips.
>
> But the vulgar way
> Is just to put your mouth to the crack, and take out the flesh
> in one bite.

There follows an extended discourse on the fig as a "secretive fruit" (alluding to those concealed flowers); and this "flowering all inward and womb-fibrilled; / And but one orifice" identify the fig definitively as female for Lawrence. The next third of the poem plays brilliant variations on the theme: "the female should always be secret," beginning with some observations of the public, on-view character of other fruit tree blossoms (the "adventurous rosaceæ"—peaches, medlars, and sorb-apples are Lawrence's examples) as contrasted with the fig flower, "Its nakedness all within-walls, its flowering forever unseen"; and then, at season's end:

> the fig has kept her secret long enough.
> So it explodes, and you see through the fissure the scarlet.
> And the fig is finished, the year is over.

Unfortunately, Lawrence proceeds to insist heavy-handedly on figs as the "fruit of the female mystery" and on women as dying of the "rottenness" arising from excessive self-consciousness about their "secret" and their "nakedness." Lawrence's stale and tiresome ideology about the necessity for passive women is blatantly and offensively summed up in the last four lines of his poem:

> Honey-white figs of the north, black figs with scarlet inside, of the south.
> Ripe figs won't keep, won't keep in any clime.
> What then, when women the world over have all bursten into self-assertion?
> And bursten figs won't keep?

In his 1969 film adaptation of Lawrence's *Women in Love* (1920), Ken Russell (b. 1927) elaborates an early scene from the novel and invents a speech for one of the central characters incorporating the lines of the poem we have just been discussing. The setting is a lunch on the lawn outside the house belonging to Hermione Roddice, two of the guests being Ursula and Gudrun Brangwen (chap. 8). Lawrence does not specify any of the food served but Russell provides a large bowl of fruit. From this bowl Hermione takes a fig, cuts it into quarters, and starts to eat it. Immediately, Hermione's lover, Rupert Birkin, repeats the opening lines of Lawrence's fig poem (about the "proper" way to eat a fig), then himself picks up a fig and eats it in one bite, as he repeats the appropriate lines (about the "vulgar" way to eat a fig). (Of course, in the film Rupert does not sound as if he is reciting a poem.) While Rupert is speaking, the camera dwells successively on each of the spellbound faces of those around the table. The poem's sentiments are quite appropriate at this point, for Rupert is becoming disenchanted with Hermione's fake spirituality and aggressive femininity and will soon turn to Ursula.

Lawrence's "Figs" has elicited the indignant response "To D. H. Lawrence" (1998) from Michael Burns:

> The female should always be secret, you said.
> Women, like figs—rotten
> when open.
>   Your mother, the moment
> she contorted to conceive
>   and to send—
>
> the inward-growing flower
>   that pushed itself open
>   to give you your life—
> Rotten!
>
> That's how you've named it. Shameful.
>
> Was it her doing when you passed through?
>   Is it *she* who puts
> shame on you?

Lawrence also wrote a poem, "Bare Fig-Trees" (1930), comparing the trees, aptly enough, both to a "strange and sweet-myriad-limbed octopus" and to a "many-branching candelabrum . . . / where every twig is the arch twig, / Each imperiously over-equal to each."

The peculiar non-flowering of the fig tree—more precisely, its concealed, interior flowering—must be very tempting to writers of a certain cast of mind. In his curious early book, *Les Nourritures terrestres* (Fruits of the Earth; 1897), André Gide (1869–1951) described the phenomenon as follows (in Dorothy Bussy's translation):

> I sing the fig, said she,
> Whose loves are hidden,

Whose flowering is folded away.
Closed chamber where secret nuptials are celebrated;
No perfume betrays them.
As nothing of it evaporates,
All its perfume turns to succulence and savour.
Flower without beauty; fruit of delights;
Fruit which is but the ripened flower.

In 1912, Rilke wrote the first three-quarters of "Duino Elegies, 6"; the first ten lines (in a prose translation by Leonard Forster) demonstrate Rilke's fascination with the interior flowering of the fig tree:

> Fig-tree [*Feigenbaum*], for a long time now I have found meaning in the way you almost entirely overleap the stage of blossom and thrust your pure mystery, unsung, into the early set fruit! / Like the pipe of a fountain your bent branches carry the sap downwards and up again: and it leaps out of sleep, hardly awake yet, into the bliss of its sweetest achievement. Look, like Jupiter into the swan. . . . We, alas, take our time, for it is praiseworthy for us to bloom and we enter into the belated core of our finite fruit and find ourselves betrayed.

The remainder of the poem—alas, thirty-four more lines—is devoted to a long disquisition on heroes in general and on Samson in particular. Rilke's "meaning," however, is already stated succinctly but adequately in the last sentence of the quotation, another rendition of which, by A. Poulin Jr., runs like this: "But we linger; / oh, we glory in our flowering, and so we come to / the retarded core of our last fruit already betrayed." What follows the first ten lines is supererogatory.

I want now to consider three poems about fig trees that are as compressed as Rilke's is distended. In his "Bacchus," one of the "Three Portraits with Shading" in *Canciones* (Songs; 1921–24; published 1927), Federico García Lorca manages to allude to three different stories about the god in just six couplets. García Lorca himself summarizes the stories in his lecture on Góngora: "In mythology, Bacchus suffers three passions and deaths. He is first a goat with twisting horns. For love of his dancer Cyssus, who dies and is turned into ivy, Bacchus changes into a vine. Lastly, he dies, and is turned into a fig tree" (cited by Christopher Maurer in the notes to his volume of García Lorca's verse in English). The first and last couplets of "Bacchus" allude to the fig tree story (here quoted in Alan Trueblood's translation, followed by the Spanish):

> Green sound intact.
> The fig tree's arms open to me.
> [. . . . .]
> . . . And the fig tree shouts and comes at me
> in frightful proliferation.

~

Verde rumor intacto.
La higuera me tiende sus brazos.
[. . . . .]
...Y la higuera me grita y avanza
terrible y multiplicada.

One surprising thing about these lines on the fig tree is the introduction of "sound" (which, by the way, in Spanish is *sonido; rumor* is literally "rumor" or "murmur").

Exceptionally pared down is another Spanish poem about a fig tree (*la higuera*), by Miguel Hernández (1910–1942), the largely self-educated shepherd boy from Orihuela (Alicante), who was deeply influenced by Neruda and other modernist poets on his visits to Madrid in 1931 and 1934. "Like a Young Fig Tree" was included in the collection, *The Songs and Ballads of Absence* (1939), written during Hernández's first stay in prison. In striking contrast to the baroque elaboration and surrealist imagery of his early verse—see a lemon poem in chapter 15, "Citrus Fruit"—Hernández is now writing poems in which, according to Geraldine Nichols's book, *Miguel Hernández* (1978), "the change of one word or one verb tense constitutes the only development from one stanza to the next," "the effect of repeating a stanza with only one change [being] to concentrate the reader's attention on the significance of that one change." Such repetition is found in Hernández's poetic fig tree metaphor (in Timothy Baland's translation followed by the Spanish text):

You were like a young fig tree
in the craggy gorges.
And when I walked by
I heard you in the rocks.

Like the young fig tree
radiant and blind.

You are like a fig tree.
An old fig tree.
I pass by and am greeted
by silence and dry leaves.

You are like a fig tree
made old by lightning.

~

Como la higuera joven
de los barrancos eras.

Y cuando yo pasaba
sonabas en la sierra.

Como la higuera joven
resplandeciente y ciega

Como la higuera eres.
Como la higuera vieja.
Y paso y me saludan
silencio y hojas secas.

Como la higuera eres
que el rayo envejeciera.

Comparing original and translation should further concentrate the reader's attention. I would note first of all that what may appear to be small changes in word order and diction in the translation are not really necessary. Thus, the first two lines could be: "Like a young fig tree / were you in the ravines." Again, I see no compelling reason for varying the translation of the definite article: why not "a" in the fifth line? The eighth and ninth lines might as well be "Like an old fig tree" and "And I pass by and am greeted." As for the symbol of the fig tree, Nichols points out that in Hernández's early writing, the fig tree stands for masculinity and lust (and figs for testicles). In his war poetry, fig trees continue to be associated with masculinity but now more specifically with the masculinity of the Republicans, whose side Hernández passionately supported. So, "Like a Young Fig Tree" may have a decidedly political application.

The third of our short poems is "Figtrees," by the Hungarian, Ágnes Nemes Nagy (1922–1991), in a version by Bruce Berlind:

Stunted
Figtrees
Motionless moonshine
Under the trees under the moon
A flock of belled goats presses on
Now even the figs are bells
The seeds jingle in their cells
Just the black-bronze boom
Of the vast sky is quiet

From metal
Pulsates the
Hush

A fig tree can also serve as a bridge between cultures, as in the poem, "My Father
and the Fig Tree" (1980), by Naomi Shihab Nye (b. 1952), whose father is a Palestinian
from Jerusalem; she writes in English and lives in San Antonio. Her poem begins with
a memory:

> For other fruits my father was indifferent.
> He'd point at the cherry trees and say,
> "See those? I wish they were figs."

And then:

> At age six I ate a dried fig and shrugged.
> "That's not what I'm talking about!" he said,
> "I'm talking about a fig straight from the earth—
> gift of Allah!—on a branch so heavy it touches the ground.
> I'm talking about picking the largest fattest sweetest fig
> in the world and putting it in my mouth."
> (Here he'd stop and close his eyes.)

But for years he never plants a fig tree; finally:

> The last time he moved, I got a phone call.
> My father, in Arabic, chanting a song I'd never heard.
> "What's that?" I said.
> "Wait till you see!"
> He took me out back to the new yard.
> There, in the middle of Dallas, Texas,
> a tree with the largest, fattest, sweetest figs in the world.
> "It's a fig tree song!" he said,
> plucking his fruits like ripe tokens,
> emblems, assurance
> of a world that was always his own.

In a poem by Felix Stefanile (b. 1920), also about a filial relationship, the speaker
marvels at the continuing life of a fig tree planted by his father in some rubble; I quote
the first and last of four stanzas from "A Fig-Tree in America" (1962):

> They hang full jewel, clusters of ripe figs
> on the soft vine, and stir like pregnant women,
> bothered by a breeze toward new discomforts:
> in a keen ache of fulness slowly stir.
>   [. . . . .]
> And here I stand, amid the brick and business,
> over the ultimate exile of his grave,

to marvel at my mortal foreigner,
who struck a flag that still can fly so green.

The contrast between ripe and dried figs has been cleverly employed by Francis Ponge (1899–1988) in his book, *Comment une figue de paroles et pourquoi* [How a fig of words and why] (1977), a late work in which he sets forth his ideas on the epistemology and ontology of poetry. The book (some two hundred pages in length) takes the form of a compilation of handwritten and typewritten texts, often fragmentary and overlapping, and of differing dates, but incorporating numerous variants of several short essays on the relations between "la figue sèche" (the dried fig) and "l'art poétique" (the poetic art). The book remains untranslated into English, and all I would like to do here is to offer translations of two characteristic passages, one on dried and one on fresh figs. I must first explain, though, that even to begin to grasp what Ponge is saying, one must be aware that most of his own poems—all are prose poems—deal with objects or things, mostly small by human standards, such as pebbles, bread, sponges, snails, apricots, oranges, and blackberries. (The three fruit poems will be discussed in later chapters.) Thus, it is plausible that what Ponge says about figs may apply to the subject matter—and even the style—of his own poems. Here are the two passages, on the dry and the fresh fig, respectively:

> The form of this fruit is by no means perfect, by no means a masterpiece. No, it is withered and grotesque, it evokes a certain mode of growing old—ugly enough and pitiable: a little like jowls, with many wrinkles. A form a little formless [Une form un peu informe], loose, drooping (Yes, like drooping breasts), something withered, subsided, collapsed—but not too much: just enough for one to bite it shamelessly. . . .

> But I acknowledge that the fig (fresh) disgusts me a little: there is in it, in a form so very common (simplified and lumpish), and not so far from the form of a pear or of a sack of excrement, so much softness and lack of resistance that it is intolerable and something like a sugary liquid; soon sticky and easily soiling the hands; a little ignoble. An indefinable color; I acknowledge that it is rare, most certainly, but also without sincerity, one would say a little shameful.
>
> The fresh fig is in a wretched state of transition, I would say, an ungrateful age.

"A form a little formless" is, of course, only the most obvious of Ponge's allusions to his own poetic tastes (recall his preference for prose poems and small, self-contained objects as subject matter).

The Chilean writer Gabriela Mistral (1889–1957) presents a very different view of figs in her prose poem "The Fig." Born Lucila Godoy Alcayaga in the Elqui valley of northern Chile, she brought together Basque ancestry on her mother's side, Indian and possibly Jewish ancestry on her father's. She became a schoolteacher but published widely, her poetry characterized by modernism and her prose by radical social ideas. Her first book of poetry, *Desolación* (1922), was published by the Hispanic Institute of New York under the pen name Gabriela (the archangel Gabriel) Mistral (the strong hot wind of Provence). Widely traveled in Europe and the Americas, Mistral won the Nobel prize for literature in 1945, the first woman and the first Hispano-American writer to do so. She eventually became Chilean delegate to the United Nations. Forced to resign because of ill health, Mistral continued to live in New York until her death.

Mistral was surrounded by fig trees where she grew up and her prose poem alternates between sensuous metaphors and allusions to exotic cultures (the Congo, Palestine, the Greeks). I much prefer the former portions of the text, here quoted in Maria Giachetti's translation:

> Touch me: it is the softness of good satin, and when you open me, what an unexpected rose! Do you not remember some king's black cloak under which a redness burned?
>
> I bloom inside myself to enjoy myself with an inward gaze, scarcely for a week.
>
> [. . . . .]
>
> If I spill my pressed flowers into your hand, I create a dwarf meadow for your pleasure; I shower you with the meadow's bouquet until covering your feet. No. I keep the flowers tied—they make me itch; the resting rose also knows this sensation.
>
> I am also the pulp of the rose-of-Sharon, bruised.

MODERN FICTIONAL FIGS

Probably the best known figs in modern fiction in English appear in James Joyce's *A Portrait of the Artist As a Young Man* (1916). The figs are dried and occur in the fifth, and last, chapter of the book, in which the main dramatis personae are Stephen Dedalus and his fellow students at the university. One of these students, Cranly, enters the novel with a question posed by Stephen: "Why was it that when he thought of Cranly he could never raise before his mind the entire image of his body but only the image of the head and face?" The face is "priestlike" and indeed Stephen freely confesses to Cranly his loss of faith. During the conversation Cranly chews on dried figs, continually replenished from the supply in his pocket. Finally, Stephen admonishes him: "— Don't, please. You cannot discuss this question with your mouth full of figs." And Cranly's response is this:

> Cranly examined the fig by the light of a lamp under which he halted. Then he smelt it with both nostrils, bit a tiny piece, spat it out and threw the fig rudely into the gutter. Addressing it as it lay, he said:
>
> —Depart from me, ye cursed, into everlasting fire!
>
> Taking Stephen's arm he went on again and said:

—Do you not fear that those words may be spoken to you on the day
of judgment?

Cranly has mockingly cursed the fig and implicitly each of its sensory qualities
(look, smell, taste) in a kind of analogue of Jesus's cursing the barren fig tree in the
gospels of Matthew and Mark. Later, Stephen speculates about Cranly's parents and
decides he is a "child of exhausted loins," which reminds Stephen of the elderly parents (Elizabeth and Zachary) of St. John the Baptist. And Stephen finds his speculation confirmed by Cranly's eating preferences, which are analogous to those of St.
John in the wilderness: "Item: he eats chiefly belly bacon and dried figs. Read locusts
and wild honey." ("Locusts and honey" is a reference to Matthew 3.4.) St. John, of
course, baptized Jesus and since Cranly is trying to persuade Stephen at least to go
through the motions of Catholic ritual, it seems that Stephen becomes the analogue
of Jesus (a conclusion Stephen never explicitly draws). Stephen's previous metonymic
identification of Cranly with his head fits in nicely with the image of a decapitated
St. John. It may be noted, finally, that in the early version of Joyce's novel, *Stephen Hero*
(1904–5), the corresponding episode alludes to Cranly's fondness for bacon with no
mention of figs.

Figs also figure prominently in the novel *The Bell Jar* (written in 1961), by Sylvia
Plath (1932–1963). The figs actually occur twice, some twenty-five pages apart. In the
first occurrence, the narrator, Esther Greenwood, reads a story in a volume sent her by
the editors of the woman's magazine on which she has been serving as an intern. The
story is about a Jewish man and a nun who meet regularly at a fig tree to pick the ripe
fruit, until one day they inadvertently touch hands, and the nun appears no more.
Esther then reflects:

> I thought it was a lovely story, especially the part about the fig tree in winter
> under the snow and then the fig tree in spring with all the green fruit. I
> felt sorry when I came to the last page. I wanted to crawl in between those
> black lines of print the way you crawl through a fence, and go to sleep
> under that beautiful big green fig tree.

A short time later, Esther, mulling over her own inadequacies, makes a list of the many
skills she lacks: cooking, shorthand, dancing, singing, gymnastics, horseback riding, ski-
ing, foreign languages, geography. Forced to think about her life after school, Esther is
reminded of the fig tree, with each fig now standing for a possible "wonderful future."
So she compiles a new list, this time not of skills but of roles: housewife and mother,
poet, professor, editor, lover, Olympic crew champion. Unable to select any particular
fig—that is, any particular role—she arrives at a dispiriting conclusion:

> I saw myself sitting in the crotch of this fig tree, starving to death, just
> because I couldn't make up my mind which of the figs I would choose. I
> wanted each and every one of them, but choosing one meant losing all

the rest, and, as I sat there, unable to decide, the figs began to wrinkle and go black, and, one by one, they plopped to the ground at my feet.

Esther's radical indecisiveness at this point prefigures her crippling depression in the rest of the novel.

Why a fig tree? In her book about the novel, Linda Wagner-Martin can suggest only, very tentatively, that the fat purple figs are "phallic, perhaps." My conjecture would be that what captured Plath's attention about fig trees was the isolation of each individual fig (there are no clusters); like the flowers that in a sense they are, each fig is directly attached to a branch by a heavy stem. Also, the strikingly regular branching of a fig tree (which Lawrence noticed)—corresponding, in a way, to the structure of branching lines called a "decision tree" in the mathematical discipline known as decision theory—may have suggested to Plath the baffling alternation of choices confronted by her leading character.

While Plath was writing her only novel, in 1961, Katherine Anne Porter (1894–1980) was, in the very same year, rediscovering the lost manuscript of a story she had written some two decades earlier. "The Fig Tree" is, in fact, part of a sequence of seven stories, first published (without "The Fig Tree") in *The Leaning Tower* (1944). The stories concern four generations of the Gay family, spanning the years roughly from the 1830s to the turn of the century. The family starts out in Kentucky, moves to Louisiana, and ends up in Texas; a country house in or near Austin and a farm some five hours away (by horse and wagon) are the main locales of the stories. The principal characters are three: Grandmother; her exact contemporary and slave (later ex-slave), Nannie; and Grandmother's granddaughter, Miranda. Grandmother is Miranda's father's mother; Miranda's own mother died young, and the child—youngest of three —has been brought up by her grandmother. (Incidentally, one of Porter's most notable short novels, *Pale Horse, Pale Rider* [1964], concerns the later life of Miranda, during the First World War.)

As "The Fig Tree" opens, Grandmother is preparing to depart for her regular summer visit to her old farm (now occupied by Grandmother's eccentric sister, Eliza, devoted to the pursuit of microscopy and astronomy), to be accompanied by Harry (her son), Nannie, Jimbilly (Nannie's husband), and Miranda. (Miranda's older brother and sister have already arrived at the farm.) Miranda's exact age is unspecified: she is clearly a young child—certainly under nine years of age, since she is nine in the next story, "The Grave," in which Grandmother is already dead. The two-horse "carry-all" is made ready and Miranda approaches it, "down the crooked flat-stone walk hopping zigzag between the grass tufts"; she arrives at "her favorite fig tree where the deep branches bowed down level with her chin, and she could gather figs without having to climb and skin her knees."

Miranda recalls how Grandmother seemed not to notice how superior the figs were here at home, "black and sugary," while those at the farm were "big soft greenish white ones." Here, the chickens were always escaping to the fig grove to eat the figs on the ground; and, indeed, at this very moment, "One mother hen was scurrying around scratching and clucking. She would scratch around a fig lying there in plain sight and cluck to her children as if it was a worm and she had dug it up for them." Miranda is now arrested by the sight of one little chicken which is not moving: "'Lazy,' said Miranda, poking him with her toe. Then she saw that he was dead." Since her practice is always to bury with some ceremony any dead animal, she hurries back into the house, finds a shoe box in one of her bureau drawers, wraps the chick in tissue paper, digs a hole, and buries it. But as Aunt Nannie calls, Miranda suddenly hears "a very sad little crying sound. It said Weep, weep, weep, three times like that slowly, and it seemed to come from the mound of dirt." She is swept up and into the wagon by the impatient adults, and then, desperate to release the chick but unwilling to explain the source of her desperation to her puzzled father and grandmother, Miranda finally "had to stand up to cry as hard as she wanted to." To distract her, Aunt Nannie offers "some nice black figs," which she has brought along, clearly remembering Miranda's fondness for these homegrown figs. To the child, Nannie's "face was wrinkled and black and it looked like a fig upside down with a white ruffled cap." Miranda politely but firmly refuses Nannie's offer. But figs put in one more appearance in the story. Out walking, Miranda and her Great-Aunt Eliza

> took the dewy path through the fig grove, much like the one in town, with the early dew bringing out the sweet smell of the milky leaves. They passed a fig tree with low hanging branches, and Miranda reached up by habit and touched it with her fingers for luck. From the earth beneath her feet came a terrible, faint troubled sound. "Weep weep, weep weep . . ." murmured a little crying voice from the smothering earth, the grave.

Miranda is terrified until Eliza explains that the "weep weep" sounds emanate from the summer's first tree frogs and foretell rain. The last sentence of the story has Miranda thanking Eliza "through her fog of bliss at hearing the tree frogs sing, 'Weep weep. . . .'"

Facts—specifically, scientific facts—have exorcised one of Miranda's deepest fears, and the fig tree—the one Miranda touched for luck—has played its part, even if its fruit is inferior to that at home. Figs have served to identify Miranda with the stern but loving Nannie and the knowledgable, kindly Eliza (rather than with her passive, insensitive father or her stern, unloving grandmother). Neither Classical nor biblical associations with figs seem to play any part in the story.

Another short story titled "The Fig Tree," by V. S. Pritchett (1900–1997), was first published in the *New Yorker* (1979). One of Pritchett's longest stories and also one of his most widely praised, its plot involves the gradual and subtly paced exchange of roles of husband and lover in a middle-class marriage in post–World War II London. The husband, Duggie, in his late fifties, travels regularly to Brussels on business; the lover, Teddy, a widower in his early forties, runs a nursery; the wife, Sally, in her late thirties, likes to garden. The story is told by Teddy and is framed by an initial section of some three and a half pages and a final section of some four lines, which together constitute an interrupted account of a visit of Teddy and his mother to the house of Duggie and Sally. The remaining larger portion of the story consists of Teddy's memories of the past, as he traces the stages of the aforementioned shift in roles.

During the visit of Teddy and his mother to Duggie and Sally's, the following conversation takes place in the garden:

> "It's doing well," [Duggie] said in a loud confidential voice, nodding at the fig tree by the south wall, close to us.
>
> "What a lovely tree," Mother said. "Does it bear? My husband will only eat figs fresh from the tree."
>
> "One or two little ones. But they turn yellow and drop off in June," said Sally.
>
> "What it needs," Duggie said, "is the Mediterranean sun. It ought to be in Turkey, that is where you get the best figs."
>
> "The sun isn't enough. The fig needs good drainage and has to be fertilized," Mother said.
>
> "All fruit needs that," said Duggie.
>
> "The fig needs two flies—the Blastophaga and, let me see, is it the Sycophaga? I think so—anyway, they are Hymenoptera," Mother said.
>
> Duggie gazed with admiration at my mother. He loves experts. He had been begging me for years to bring her over to his house.
>
> "Well, we saved its life, didn't we, Teddy?" he said to me and boasted on his behalf and mine. "We flagged the area. There was nothing but a lake of muddy water here."

We learn subsequently, in the course of the long flashback, that Teddy, on his first visit to Sally and Duggie's, had noticed how

> The damp yellow leaves of the fig tree hung down like wretched rags, and the rest had fallen flat as plates into a very large pool of muddy water that stretched from one side of the garden to the other. Overnight, in November, a fig collapses like some Victorian heroine. Here—as if she were about to drown herself. I said this to Duggie, who said, "Heroine? I don't follow."

Teddy is then employed by Sally and Duggie to lay flagstones on the part of their garden near the fig tree. The workmen discover a buried concrete air-raid shelter. Sally is depressed by the entire operation and vows never to enter her garden again. But Teddy drops by one day unannounced (Duggie is not at home) with the gift of "a small strong magnolia, a plant three feet high and already in bud," its "swollen rusty-pink and skin-white buds . . . as bright as candles in the darkness of the van." Teddy persuades Sally to watch him place the magnolia in its tub near the fig tree, promising: "It will be in full bloom in ten days. . . . It will cheer up the fig tree. It's trying to bud." A day

178   later, Sally and Teddy become passionate lovers. Finally, Duggie—whose firm has transferred him to Brussels—persuades Teddy to take on Sally as an assistant in the nursery; she quickly takes over the administrative side of the business, and in the process "the roles of Duggie and myself were reversed: when Duggie came home once a week now from Brussels, it was he who seemed to be the lover and I the husband."

Duggie and Sally's garden may remind us of the Garden of Eden but there are certain striking differences: Sally is self-exiled from her own garden but returns through the sexual potency of Teddy (symbolized by his gift of the sensual magnolia plant)—a clear reversal of the Genesis tale in which the discovery of sex is followed by exile. And what are we to make of Duggie? Well, he is anhedonic, nonsexual, and manipulative, which might identify him as the secularized counterpart of God! As for the two trees, they are pretty clearly gendered (a collapsed fig is said to resemble a Victorian heroine and the buds of the magnolia are said to resemble candles). I would only add that there is somewhat more to the story than my bare outline suggests; thus, Duggie and Sally's daughter, Judy, thirteen or fourteen years old, plays a minor though not insignificant role in the plot.

Pritchett's editor at the *New Yorker*, Roger Angell (b. 1920), in some reminiscences about Pritchett, remarks on a fig tree that once belonged to him and his wife: "A temperamental fig tree that used to stand in the back garden of the V. S. Pritchetts' house in Regents Park Terrace—I can recall Victor complaining about having to sweep up its huge yellow leaves each November—also droops and drops its leaves in 'The Fig Tree.'"

3

MISSING FRUIT

Sometimes when I look at a literary work or a particular corpus of works I am surprised by the relative absence of food episodes or of food episodes of a particular kind. I want to explore some striking instances of missing or marginalized fruit, and first in a beautiful Hebrew poem by Yehuda Amichai, "The Singer of the Song of Songs" (1999), which begins (in the translation of Chana Bloch and Chana Kronfeld):

> The singer of the Song of Songs sought his beloved so long and hard that
> he lost his mind and went out to find her with the help of a simile map
> and fell in love with the images he himself had imagined.

Amichai's theme is the singer as wanderer, so naturally the "simile map" contains mostly place-names: her hair is like a flock of goats moving down Mount Gilead, her nose is like a tower in Lebanon, and so on. Thus, for good reasons, most of the items in the Song of Songs inventory of the beloved are ignored, including some memorable fruit similes: her breasts like clusters of grapes, the scent of her breath like apples (or apricots), her mouth like sweet wine, her cheek like a pomegranate. And, too, no doubt for his own reasons, Amichai ignores the fact that modern interpretations of the Song of Songs read it as a dialogue between lover (male) and beloved (female).

In another poem, "A Thousand Raindrops" (1999), by Charles Tomlinson, real fruit is missing and metaphorical fruit is prominent, the point being that both kinds of fruit may be understood as products of sunlight and rain. There are four brief, sparkling stanzas: in the first we see rainbow-hued waterdrops on a pane of glass, in the second the waterdrops are understood as potential symbols, in the third the waterdrops are compared to fruit, and in the fourth the waterdrops are extinguished while their symbolism (content unspecifed) endures. I quote the third stanza:

> these berries of light
> no branch sustains:
> they are the fire's fruit,
> fruit of the rain's:

CLASSICAL GREEK LITERATURE

A good indication of the infrequency of fruit in classical Greek literature is the relative scarcity of references to fruit in the great compendium of food episodes from that literature, *The Deipnosophists* (The Sophists at Dinner), in fifteen books (some 1,250 authors are cited), by Athenaeus (ca. 200 C.E.). Thus, examining the extensive index of a one-thousand-page mid-nineteenth-century translation of the work by C. D. Yonge or the two-hundred-and-fifty-page index in the last volume of Charles Burton Gulick's translation, one finds only a scattering of references to fruit. (There are, though, many references to wine). Furthermore, one of these references includes Aristophanes's assertion (in a lost work called *The Seasons*) that "all the fruits were to be found in Athens throughout the year." This last quotation confirms, of course, what we already know: that fresh fruit was admired and eaten with pleasure in ancient Greece—at least by those who could afford it, but this must have included most writers and readers. Yet as Andrew Dalby points out, "The *Odyssey*, for example, with all its set-piece descriptions of meals, never depicts the eating of a fruit." How can this be accounted for?

In Dalby's detailed analysis of ancient Greek cuisine, we learn that a proper ancient Greek meal had three components: *sîtos,* that is, the staples: lentils, barley, or wheat; *ópson,* that is, accompaniments of the staples: vegetables, cheese, eggs, fish, and, less frequently, meat (from sheep, pigs, or goats); *oînos,* that is, wine, accompanied by cakes, sweets, nuts, fresh and dried fruits. Appetizers, selected from among the more piquant constituents of the *ópson,* often preceded the meal itself; these included the less sweet fruits, such as apples, quinces, plums, sour cherries, certain varieties of melon, and cucumbers. The main fresh fruits in the *oînos*—sometimes also referred to as the "second tables"—included pears, figs, pomegranates, and grapes. Dalby's explanation of the dearth of fruit in Greek literature is, then, that this particular food was relegated by the Greeks to the less important parts of the meal, either before or after the main course; and, for the explanation to be valid, I think one must add that the principal traditional Greek genres (epic, tragedy, comedy, and lyric with its various sub-genres) were not very receptive to the depiction of conventionally *complete* meals. An intriguing comparison could be made here, by the way, with James Davidson's discussion, in his *Courtesans and Fishcakes* (1998), of "the fish missing from Homer."

CLASSICAL ROMAN LITERATURE

Both the culinary and the literary situations were quite different in Rome from what we found in Greece. In her book-length analysis of food in ancient Roman literature (1993), Emily Gowers describes the structure of a proper Roman meal as consisting of an initial "tasting" or *gustatio* (roots, vegetables, fish, eggs), the meal proper or *cena* (meat, poultry, fish), and finally so-called second tables or *secundae mensae* (fruit, nuts, and other delicacies). Gowers says there is no single literary source for this menu, but she ignores the fact that all the elements can be assembled from the meal described in the Baucis and Philemon episode in the *Metamorphoses* (8.637–678) of Ovid (to be discussed later on in chapter 21, "Fruit, Conjoined and Disjoined"). Gowers suggests the following historical interpretation of the traditional Roman meal:

> The structure of the Roman meal . . . begins to look like a commemora-
> tive history of eating habits, a way of classifying food so that it becomes

steadily more "civilized": it begins with the *gustatio,* the initial tasting of pure roots, vegetables, fish and eggs (the containers of early life); culminates with the *cena* proper, with its "sacrificial" meat; then either atones by returning to nature in the form of fruit and nuts (fruition), or declines further into the superfluities of the *secundae mensae.*

Gowers's main concern in Latin literature is with the genre of satire for, as she suggests, "Food is in the guts of Roman satire, not just because of its laughable qualities and its capacity for grabbing at our most basic instincts of revulsion: the very name, 'satire,' is culinary by origin." Gowers generalizes so far as to assert that "when food appears in Roman literature, it always has some connection with the style of the work to which it belongs." (She is not, of course, disputing the presence of connections of a nonliterary sort.) But prepared, or cooked, dishes offer far richer possibilities for satire than simple dishes, such as raw fruit; as Gowers puts it (referring to Horace), "A metaphor of simple and innocent food would be inappropriate for satire, the mess-making form." Indeed, it seems to me that in Latin literature, especially in Roman satire of the early imperial period, fresh fruit sometimes signifies most when it is absent. More specifically, for such writers as Horace, Petronius (1st cent. C.E.), Martial, and Juvenal (ca. 55–ca. 140 C.E.), the presence or absence of fresh fruit in a meal is often what separates traditional and wholesome fare from exotic and expensive gorging. Let me illustrate with some examples.

Horace's eighth satire of his second book is an account of a dinner given by a wealthy parvenu in Rome. The food is described in detail and includes boar, oysters, fillets of plaice and turbot, lamprey with prawns, crane, goose liver, hare, blackbirds, and pigeons, many of the dishes being served with special sauces. Fruit is mentioned just once, when someone remarks that (in Niall Rudd's translation) "the apples [*melimela*] were red because they'd been picked / by a waning moon." Clearly, the apples are there as just another instance of foolishly pretentious food (because of the way the apples were harvested), thereby adding one more barb to the satirical depiction of the meal; what is striking is the virtually complete absence of fresh fruit, which we know was highly valued and readily available to those who could afford it.

The intent of the fourth satire of Horace's second book is more difficult to assess; thus, Bovie sees it as "an inspired plea for finer eating and more technical cooking," where Rudd sees "parody and pedantry." (They may both be right.) As far as fruit goes, though, the main point to notice is that the poem is about cooking, making fresh fruit more or less irrelevant. Two fruits are, in fact, mentioned (in Rudd's translation): "black mulberries / picked from the tree before the sun is unpleasantly hot"; "Apples from Tivoli are inferior in taste to those of Picenum, / which is odd, for they look nicer." (The word translated as "apples" is *poma,* which usually refers to any orchard fruit.) Horace, then, is concerned with the quality of the berries and the other fruit. (And I would assume he thought that sunlight, unlike moonlight, really did affect that quality!)

One may wonder whether fresh fruit has the same significance for Martial as for Horace. Let us examine the lengthy epigram 5.78, in which Martial invites his friend

182   Toranius to dinner; in the very first lines promising only simple food, Martial formulates the following menu: cheap Cappadocian lettuces, smelly leeks, tunny with hard-boiled eggs (*gustatio*); cabbage-sprouts, sausage and porridge, beans and bacon (*cena*); withering (meaning preserved) grapes, Syrian pears, and roasted chestnuts for dessert (*secundae mensae*). And, Martial adds, if you're still hungry after all that, there will be olives, hot chickpeas, and warm lupins. (For the Latin text and a straightforward prose translation, see D. R. Shackleton Bailey's Loeb Library edition; a racier translation by Peter Whigham is in the volume edited by him and J. P. Sullivan, *Epigrams of Martial Englished by Divers Hands* [1987].) What is one to make of this repast? The food is certainly simple by Roman standards; the *cena* could be that of a Roman peasant. Gowers, however, sees "a jostling queue of good and bad elements" in the menu. She also senses double entendre and "apparent innocence" throughout, suggesting that both the cabbage-sprouts (which she calls "broccoli") and the sausage and porridge may well have sexual connotations. As for the only fresh fruit in the promised meal, the "Syrian pears," they are tainted because Syrians are usually slaves. Gowers's interpretation is ingenious and documented in detail; it treats the epigram as an elaborate joke, not just on the presumed recipient of the invitation but also on Martial's readers, who are expecting a brief poem and instead get thirty-two lines (just as the food turns out to be plain but plentiful).

Much of the menu of *Epigrams* 5.78 is repeated in 10.48, where Martial is issuing a dinner invitation to a group of six (named) friends; there are, however, what appear to be certain critical additions: kid, leftover chicken, and ham, in the *cena,* and, "when my guests are satisfied," ripe fruit and wine for dessert. But the phrase translated by Shackleton Bailey as "ripe fruit," *mitia poma* —which, Gowers notes, echoes the same phrase in *Eclogues* 1.80 of Virgil—she unaccountably translates as "sweet apples." (Guy Lee's late-twentieth-century English version of the *Eclogues* also translates the phrase in question as "ripe fruit.") In any case, Gowers takes this fruit to be just the last and wholly supererogatory item in an "unabashedly makeshift dinner . . . [that] piles up dishes without discrimination, jumbling the relics of pastoral with the remains of yesterday's dinner into a muddle of surprises and inconsistencies." On Gowers's interpretation, then, Martial's menu once again includes fresh fruit only, so to speak, as an afterthought.

Finally, what one might call the null case: in *Epigrams* 1.43, Martial tells of attending a dinner along with a large crowd of other people (literally, "twice thirty"), where all that is served is a small boar, (in Bovie's translation) "suited / to be slaughtered by an unarmed dwarf"—and even that is only meant to be *looked at*. The bulk of the fourteen-line poem is devoted to what was *missing* on the occasion: grapes (*uvae*), must-apples (*melimela*), pears (*pira*), pomegranates (*Punica grana*), cheese, and olives:

> None of those grapes left to ripen on the vine;
> none of those must-apples that taste as sweet
> as a honeycomb; none of those pears, hung up

to ripen on a twig of broom plant; none of those
pomegranates the color of summer roses;

(See Shackleton Bailey's Loeb again for the Latin and a more literal English translation; and for the sometimes difficult identification of the various foods, see Peter
Howell, *A Commentary on Book One of the Epigrams of Martial* [1980].) After confronting
so many of Gowers's subversive readings of Latin texts on food, it may seem naive to
suggest that Martial means it when he emphasizes the desirability of really fresh fruit;
and, sure enough, in connection with some other poems by Martial, Gowers refers to
"the exaggerated clichés of describing food fresh from the tree."

Juvenal's eleventh satire deals with one of his favorite subjects, the inferiority of
his own time to an earlier age when, in Rolfe Humphries's translation, "everything
[was] perfectly simple, / Furniture, household, food." Included in the poem is a dinner
invitation to a friend, with the menu specified as fat and tender kid, wild asparagus,
fresh eggs together with the chickens that laid them, and then:

> We'll have grapes kept part of the year, but fresh as they were on the vines,
> Syrian bergamot pears, or the red ones from Segni in Latium;
> In the same basket with these the fragrant sweet-smelling apples
> Better than those from Picenum. Don't worry, they're perfectly ripened,
> Autumn's chill has matured their greenness, mellowed their juices.

Humphries comments that the mellifluous quality of the Latin hexameters in the
above passage is not typical of Juvenal's style—but appropriate enough given Juvenal's
unwontedly relaxed and amiable attitude in this portion of his poem.

Complementary to Juvenal's eleventh satire is his fifth, which describes a dinner offered by a mean host named Virro, whose meagre fare reaches its nadir with
the dessert course (in translations by Rolfe Humphries and Peter Green, respectively):

> To himself and the rest of the Virros
> Fruit [*poma*] will be served. Such fruit you'd be happy with even a smell of,
> Fruit such as grew in the days when Autumn was never-ending,
> Fruit you would think had been robbed from the girls of the Golden
>   Orchards.
> You get a rotten old apple [*malum*], the kind that is given a monkey
> All rigged out with a helmet and shield . . .

> ~

> To himself, and his fellow-tycoons,
> Virro has choice fruits [*poma*] served, their scent a feast in itself,
> Fruit such as grew in Phaeacia's eternal autumn,
> Or might, you feel, have been rifled from the Hesperides.
> For yourself, a rotten apple [*malum*], only fit to be munched
> By those performing monkeys you see along the Embankment . . .

(Phaeacia was a legendary kingdom visited by Odysseus and the Hesperides were the guardians of the golden apples.)

Contemporary with the writings of both Martial and Juvenal is the most memorable of all literary Roman banquets—that of Trimalchio in Petronius's *Satyricon*. To those familiar with the story it will come as no surprise that the freedman, parvenu host has little interest in fresh fruit as a food with which to impress his guests. Fruit is present on two occasions during the banquet (I follow J. P. Sullivan's translation): first, one of the extravagant hors d'oeuvres consists of "steaming hot sausages . . . on a silver gridiron with damsons and pomegranate seeds underneath" (31.11); and, second, a tray of cakes is brought in with its center "occupied by a Priapus made of pastry, holding the usual things in his very adequate lap—all kinds of apples and grapes" (60.4). Neither the damsons and pomegranate seeds, nor the grapes and apples, are meant to be eaten, for the former are merely intended to simulate a fire beneath the griddle and the latter (presumably made of pastry) constitute an obscene practical joke (they emit a cloud of irritating saffron when touched). Presenting fruit to his guests—like most of the food Trimalchio offers—is not designed for nutrition or even for pleasure but rather as a mode of exhibitionistic behavior. It is perhaps worth adding that not too long after the pastry-Priapus episode a drunken guest named Habinnas arrives with his wife, Scintilla, and, in response to Trimalchio's question, recounts in detail—but with no distinctions among the courses—the food served at a dinner party he has just left: sausages, blood-pudding, giblets, beetroot, wholemeal bread, cold tart, a wine and honey concoction, chickpeas, lupins, nuts, apples, bear-meat, cheese basted with wine, snails, chitterlings, liver, eggs in pastry hoods, turnips, mustard, tunny, and pickled cumin seeds. The food seems to have been plentiful but not nearly as pretentious as Trimalchio's. Habinnas mentions that he took two apples and still has them "tied up in a napkin, because if I don't take something in the way of a present to my little slave, I'll have a row on my hands" (66.4). For characters like Habinnas and Trimalchio, simple and unadorned apples are worthy only of slaves.

DANTE

Three occasions of missing fruit in *The Divine Comedy* are of considerable interest, for each must reflect a deliberate—a deeply pondered—choice on Dante's part. At the beginning of canto 13 of the *Inferno*, Dante and Virgil enter a pathless wood (I again use Charles Singleton's translation): "No green leaves, but of dusky hue; no smooth boughs, but gnarled and warped; no fruits [*pomi*] were there, but thorns with poison" (13.4–6). Since this is the first—and, it will turn out, the only—vegetation encountered by Dante and Virgil in Hell proper, it is not surprising that Dante is "bewildered" as they enter the wood and are surrounded by wailing voices—bewilderment expressed even in Dante's locution, "I believe that he believed that I believed" (13.25). Soon Dante discovers that each tree is a soul who has committed violence against himself or his possessions, so the lifeless trees constitute a perfect measure of the wanton rejection of human life. As for the *pomi* that are absent, Charles Singleton's commentary points out that these must include not only edible fruit but fruit or seeds of any kind.

At the beginning of canto 28 of the *Purgatorio,* Dante has left Virgil behind and again entered a forest, now "green and dense," but also "divine" (28.2), in accord with Virgil's assurance in the previous canto: "That sweet fruit [*dolce pome*] which the care of mortals goes seeking on so many branches, this day shall give your hungerings peace" (27.115–17). In fact, Dante is in Eden, the "place chosen for nest of the human race" (28.78), and which contains "fruit that yonder is not plucked" (e frutto ha in sé che di là non si schianta; 28.120), "yonder," of course, being the earth. This characterization of Edenic fruit—by negation—must be taken, according to Singleton's commentary, as referring not only to the two special trees of Genesis but to many other "varieties of fruit that are not known to us here. A principle of plenitude would require this to be so."

In canto 32 of the *Purgatorio,* Dante, still in Eden, encounters "a tree stripped of its flowers and of its foliage in every bough" (una piana dispogliata / di foglie e d'altra fronda in ciascun ramo; 32.38–9). Fruit is not specifically mentioned in the passage but surely, says Singleton, we are to understand the tree as having also been stripped of its fruit as a result of the Fall, for this is the tree of the knowledge of good and evil (see Singleton's commentary on the *Purgatorio*). An elaborate allegorical performance is now enacted—the wooden pole (actually the Cross) of the chariot bearing Beatrice is bound to the stripped tree by the griffin (symbolizing Christ) that has been pulling the chariot—but its complex and in part obscure significance cannot be pursued here.

In each of the three passages we have been examining, fruit—or, at least, certain types of fruit—are characterized by their total absence, first from the infernal wood, then from the entire terrestrial region, and finally from a very special tree in Eden. Later in *Purgatorio* (32.74–5), Dante introduces fruit in a more positive way, though only as fruit tree blossoms and only in the form of a simile. The allegorical performance alluded to above has overwhelmed Dante and, indeed, put him to sleep. It then takes no less than three tercets, incorporating an extended simile, for Dante to wake up (here cited in the verse translation by Allen Mandelbaum):

> Even as Peter, John, and James, when brought
> to see the blossoms of the apple tree [*melo*]—
> whose fruit [*pome*] abets the angels' hungering,
>   providing endless wedding-feasts in Heaven—
> were overwhelmed by what they saw, but then,
> hearing the word that shattered deeper sleeps,
>   arose and saw their fellowship was smaller—
> since Moses and Elijah now had left—
> and saw a difference in their Teacher's dress;
>   so I awoke and saw, standing above me,

> she who before—compassionate—had guided
> my steps along the riverbank.

The New Testament allusion in the simile is to Matthew 17:1–8, where Christ leads Peter, John, and James up a high mountain "and was transfigured before them. And his face shone as the sun, and his garments became white as snow" (quoted by Singleton from the Latin Vulgate Bible). It is impossible to enter here into the likely moral and allegorical meanings of Dante's simile, but his idea of the importance of the passage from Matthew may be gauged from the fact that he discusses it in two of his other writings.

4

STRAWBERRIES (AND CREAM)

In poetry, as occasionally in real life, the mere sight of certain fruits can be intoxicatingly pleasurable. This happens for Robert Herrick (1591–1674), in his poem, "Upon the Nipples of *Julia's* Breast" (H-440, 1648), when he sees a cherry placed at the center of a lily or a strawberry "halfe drown'd" in cream. These combinations—as well as other such artful juxtapositions as an arrangement of white and red roses or of pearls and rubies—all remind him of "each neate Niplet of her breast." The first four couplets of the poem constitute a tissue of artifices, and so it is not too difficult to accept the comparison with Julia's breast in the last couplet as just another artifice. A closely similar poem by Herrick, "Fresh Cheese and Cream" (H-491, 1648), is more outrageous:

> WO'd yee have fresh Cheese and Cream?
> *Julia's* Breast can give you them:
> And if more; Each *Nipple* cries,
> To your *Cream,* her[e]'s *Strawberries.*

The juxtaposition of real milk products—or, at least, a real source of such products—with metaphorical strawberries leaves us disoriented and disconcerted, and to no discernible purpose. To any lingering embarrassment still associated with nipples in today's culture of exposure, there is added the embarrassment of detecting a misconceived metaphor. (On the topic of embarrassing nipples, see Christopher Ricks's *Keats and Embarrassment* (1974). Though he refers to Herrick as "the diminutive precursor of Keats," Ricks does not discuss these two poems.)

Strawberries and cream also occur in Herrick's "The Lilly in a Christal" (H-193, 1648), which may be read as an exposition of what has been termed (by J. B. Broadbent in the *TLS*) his "aesthetics of concealment." The central idea of Herrick's poem must have been suggested by two poems of Martial: 4.22, which Herrick translated as "Upon Julia washing herself in the river" (H-939); and 8.68, which describes an orchard under glass (cited later in chap. 20, "Orchards, Groves, Gardens"). The thesis of "The Lilly in a Christal" is clear enough: the beauty of a woman, no matter how white her complexion, may be enhanced by veiling or partly concealing it. Herrick's probative instances include roses under fine linen ("cobweb-lawn"), lilies within crystals, cloudiness inside amber, grapes or cherries behind glass, but not—as one might have expected—strawberries partly concealed in cream; rather, after the pattern has been established with roses and lilies in the first stanza, comes this:

> You see how *Creame* but naked is;
>> Nor daunces in the eye
>> Without a Strawberrie:
>> Or some fine tincture, like to this,
>> Which draws the sight thereto,
> More by that wantoning with it;
>> Then when the paler hieu
>> No mixture did admit.

It is the cream, then, and not the strawberry, that is said to be naked. In arguing for the integrity—indeed, the profundity—of the poem, J. B. Broadbent notes (but only parenthetically) that "the cream-strawberry demonstrates the topic by inverting it"; he is much more interested in hurrying on to the multiple meanings of concealment in the poem, culminating in his argument that Herrick is suggesting "a ritual for dealing with the constitutional problems of the century [by] wrap[ping] power up in worship."

It may be worth noting that somewhat more than a century after Herrick's strawberry poems, in the *Encyclopédie* of Diderot and D'Alembert (1757), as the conclusion of a lengthy entry on "fraisier [strawberry plant]," there appear the following remarks: "The strawberry [la fraise] is a small red or white fruit; it resembles the tip of a wet-nurse's breast; it is the earliest and one of the most delicious of springtime fruits: one knows it is ripe and ready to eat when it leaves its stem without difficulty."

Strawberry cultivation goes back many centuries in England, as is evident from the remarks of Thomas Tusser (1524?–1580) in his much reprinted long poem, *Five hundreth pointes of good husbandry united to as many of good huswifery* . . . (1st ed., 1573). The first two of the following quatrains are instructions for September, the last for December:

> Wife, into thy garden, and set me a plot,
>> with strawbery rootes, of the best to be got:
> Such growing abroad, among thornes in the wood,
>> wel chosen and picked proove excellent good.
>
> The barbery, Respis [raspberry], and Goosebery too,
>> looke now to be planted as other things doo:
> The Goosebery, Respis, and Roses, al three,
>> with Strawberies under them truly agree.
>> [. . . . .]
> If frost doe continue, take this for a lawe,
>> the strawberies looke to be covered with strawe.

Laid overly trim upon crotchis [crutches] and bows [boughs],
　　　and after uncovered as weather allows.

Some two-and-a-half centuries after Tusser, we find, in chapter 42 of Jane Austen's *Emma,* a brilliant and stylistically inventive passage about picking strawberries. George Knightley has invited a party to visit his estate, Donwell, renowned for its strawberries, and to pick and eat the delicious fruit. Here is how Austen summarizes half an hour's conversation:

> "The best fruit in England—every body's favourite—always whole-some.—These the finest beds and finest sorts.—Delightful to gather for one's self—the only way of really enjoying them.—Morning decidedly the best time—never tired—every sort good—hautboy infinitely superior—no comparison—the others hardly eatable—hautboys very scarce—Chili preferred—white wood finest flavour of all—price of strawberries in London—abundance about Bristol—Maple Grove—cultivation—beds when to be renewed—gardeners thinking exactly different—no general rule—gardeners never to be put out of their way—delicious fruit—only too rich to be eaten much of—inferior to cherries—currants more refreshing—only objection of gathering strawberries the stooping—glaring sun—tired to death—could bear it no longer—must go and sit in the shade."

On the one hand, this could be a simple transcription of the author's notes for some dialogue that never got written but, on the other hand, there is almost the suggestion of a stream of consciousness (except, of course, that what we seem to have is the inter-section of several different individual streams of consciousness).

In North America vast acres of wild strawberries resulted from the very con-quest and settlement of the land; strawberry plants thrived, Peter Hatch explains, "as a pioneer species when Indians or Europeans cleared or burned the forests, or when exhausted tobacco fields were abandoned. Like all wild fruits, the strawberry responded to the additional light that resulted from the disturbance of the native for-est by bearing more and larger berries on a rich green carpet of leaves." The great American naturalist William Bartram (1739–1823), traveling through western North Carolina in 1776, came upon vast fields of wild strawberries—"Elysian fields," he calls them—and his idyllic description is not to be missed:

> Proceeding on our return to town, continued through part of this high for-est skirting on the meadows: began to ascend the hills of a ridge which we were under the necessity of crossing; and having gained its summit, enjoyed a most enchanting view; a vast expanse of green meadows and strawberry fields; a meandering river gliding through, saluting in its various turnings the swelling, green, turfy knolls, embellished with parterres of flowers and

fruitful strawberry beds; flocks of turkies strolling about them; herds of deer prancing in the meads or bounding over the hills; companies of young, innocent Cherokee virgins, some busy gathering the rich fragrant fruit, others having already filled their baskets, lay reclined under the shade of floriferous and fragrant native bowers ... whilst other parties more gay and libertine, were yet collecting strawberries, or wantonly chasing their companions, tantalising them, staining their lips and cheeks with the rich fruit.

Bartram and his companion "accepted a basket, sat down and regaled ourselves on the delicious fruit." It should be added that Bartram greatly admired the Cherokee and, indeed, all the Indians he encountered, their government being, in his view, "the most simple, natural, and rational that can be imagined or desired."

By the mid-nineteenth century in Europe and America strawberries had begun to be cultivated on a large scale; in an American fruit growing manual by Patrick Barry (1816–1890) of the mid-nineteenth century, for example, no less than twenty-six varieties of strawberries are listed. Today, special varieties of strawberries have been developed for different regions of the United States, and Barbara Ferguson's fruit growers' manual lists well over fifty varieties. New varieties keep appearing, and there seems to be no overlap between the nineteenth- and twentieth-century lists. Already in the nineteenth century, then, eating strawberries was no longer a marker of high social class. Wild strawberries, however, must have remained a special treat, as appears from an incident in John Ruskin's autobiography, *Præterita* (1885–89). Ruskin and his parents were visiting the Continent in 1842 and stopped at Fontainebleu. Ruskin was feverish that night and feared he was coming down with a serious illness. Toward noon, however, "the inn people brought me a little basket of wild strawberries; and they refreshed me, and I put my sketch-book in pocket and tottered out." And then Ruskin has what can only be called an epiphany, as he lies supine by the side of a road and sketches an aspen tree against the blue sky; he has discovered the true beauty of natural forms, whose delineation becomes the defining task of his life:

> But that all the trees of the wood (for I saw surely that my little aspen was only one of their millions) should be beautiful—more than Gothic tracery, more than Greek vase-imagery, more than the daintiest embroiderers of the East could embroider, or the artfullest painters of the West could limn, —this was indeed an end to all former thoughts with me, an insight into a new silvan world.

Something of the magical character of Ruskin's wild strawberries is captured in a poem by Gabriela Mistral, included in the collection of her children's poems, *Ternura* (Tenderness; 1924; 4th ed., 1945). Mistral rounded out this collection with an essay expounding her views on European children's folklore—especially Spanish, Provençal, and Italian—in which she took a deep interest. The author of a monograph on Mistral's poetry, Margot de Vazquez, points out that "the wide publication of the lullabies, rounds, and games in this book is evidence of their success." But this success is not achieved by writing down to children: "Gabriela is not guilty of becoming artificially child-like, of abandoning the adult point of view, nor of using the silly language that adults presumptuously attribute to children." At the same time, there is a pedagogical aim in many of the poems insofar as "almost all of them embody a moral teaching or attempt to develop in the student specific attitudes, inclinations, and sentiments: love for nature and country, respect for animals, attention to the miracles of creation, brotherly union, the encouragement of fantasy and of the aesthetic sense." "The Wild Strawberry" demonstrates the sophistication of Mistral's poems for children (translated by Maria Giachetti):

> The wild strawberry, set apart
> in a leafy tent,
> gives off fragrance before she is picked.
> Before she is seen, she blushes . . .
> Untouched by birds,
> it is heaven's dew
> that moistens the wild strawberry.
>
> Do not bruise the earth;
> do not squeeze the sweet one.
> For her love, lower yourself,
> inhale her, and give her your mouth.

Today, it is the consumption of *fraises des bois*—so-called wild or Alpine strawberries—that marks the elite, as in the poem "Dinner Guest: Me" (1965), by Langston Hughes (1902–1967), where he finds the other guests at the dinner party on Park Avenue "murmuring gently / Over *fraises du bois,* / 'I'm so ashamed of being white.'" The bitterness over racism in American society evident in the poem should be assessed against a background of Hughes's preoccupations at the time it was first published in the *Negro Digest* for September 1965. During that year, Hughes hailed President Johnson's endorsement of the Civil Rights Act of 1965, denounced racism in his column in the *New York Post,* and gave lecture-readings of his poetry, sponsored by the U.S. Department of State, on visits to France, Germany, and Denmark (see Rampersad's chronology in his edition of Hughes's poetry). The misspelling of *fraises des bois* in the poem may be a typographical error (Hughes did, after all, spend some time in French-speaking countries like France and Haiti).

One irony concerning so-called wild strawberries is that often they are not really wild at all; Eleanor Perényi (b. 1918), in her acclaimed book on gardening, *Green Thoughts* (1981), explains:

> The Alpine strawberry . . . has been in cultivation since the eighteenth
> century. These and other European strawberries resemble the wild not

because they have been plucked from some woodland habitat but because they don't hybridize well. . . .

So why grow them in preference to the big, luscious natives? Snobbery pure and simple, and I speak with authority because I must have been among the first to respond to those classy ads for *fraises* the White Flower Farm ran, and still runs, in *The New Yorker.* . . . And what of the taste? A dish of *fraises,* rustling like taffeta and with a squeeze of orange over it, brings coos of delight from those who have eaten them, preferably under a pergola, in some foreign restaurant: pleasure by association. Their flavor isn't a patch on that of a fat, home-grown strawberry of American ancestry. And the gardener who serves them, whether he mentions it or not, has gone through hell to harvest them. Eternities pass on hands and knees before enough are assembled to make a dessert for six.

The English cookery writer Jane Grigson (1928–1990), on the other hand, in her book on fruit cooking (1982), has a very different slant on the wood strawberry:

The wood strawberry has been taken as a bright relic of our time, in a humorous and ironic poem by Jacques Prévert. He wrote as an archaeologist of the twenty-fifth century, living at a time when nothing grew any more and making what he could of the twentieth century from the few bits and pieces dug up in the Champ de Mars (the site of the Eiffel Tower):

> Behind a triple wall of glass
> in the great museum of machines
> in a little block of ice
> a wood strawberry is shown
> the whole world crowds in to look at that strawberry
> charts show the height of the tree that gave
> such fruit
> nine hundred feet

He tries to fit everything in, picturing the Eiffel Tower tree hung with dentist's drills—*fraises* in French—and wood strawberries, and interprets it as a relic of the time when they were only just beginning to tar over the great oases of Africa.

Returning to the nineteenth century, consider one of its greatest naturalistic novels: *L'Assommoir* (1876), by Émile Zola, is about Parisian workers living in poverty and squalor during the years 1850–1869, and in particular about the long descent into alcoholism of two of the chief characters (the laundress Gervaise and her roofer husband, Coupeau). The whole of chapter 7, situated exactly halfway through the thirteen chapters of the book, is devoted to the planning, preparation, and consumption of the great dinner, for fourteen guests plus four children, celebrating Gervaise's saint's day. She and her friends "started discussing the party a month in advance, thinking out dishes and licking their chops in anticipation" (Leonard Tancock's translation). The cooking begins on the Sunday afternoon prior to the day of the party, and at the last minute Gervaise has to pawn her best black silk dress and her wedding ring to pay for the wine. The dining room is the laundry shop itself and the table at which the guests eat is, significantly, the very structure on which the laundresses iron clothes. The courses are, in order, noodle soup, boiled beef, blanquette of veal, stewed chine of pork with boiled potatoes, peas and bacon, and—the pièce-de-résistance—roast goose, all accompanied by huge amounts of bread, lettuce salad, and wine. Next comes the dessert, lovingly described by Zola:

> The sweet was now on the table. In the centre was a Savoy [sponge] cake in the shape of a temple, with a dome made of sections of melon, and on the dome was an artificial rose, near which hovered a silver paper butterfly on a wire. Two drops of gum in the heart of the flower represented dewdrops. Then on the left there was a piece of cream cheese [*fromage blanc,* which is a skim-milk cheese different from our own cream cheese] on a dish, and on the right, in another dish, a pile of huge strawberries, crushed and running with juice.

The guests continue to drink wine and this encourages some of them to regale their companions with sentimental or comic songs, and the meal ends with the serving of coffee. (We shall return to the wine drinking in chapter 19, "Wine.") The critic David Baguley sees the dinner as "clearly the pivotal event of the novel, both the summit of Gervaise's success and the turning point in her fortunes. Indulgence replaces industry in the very workplace itself."

We know that Gervaise and Coupeau's daughter, Nana, gets her share of the strawberry dessert at her mother's saint's day dinner but this does not stop her from being terribly excited when she is somewhat older, in chapter 6 of *Nana* (1880), at her first glimpse of strawberries growing at the country estate bought for her by one of her admirers (the banker, Steiner). By the time of the novel's opening, Nana has become an actress and courtesan, and indeed the first chapter is devoted to her starring role in a musical play called *The Blond Venus,* in the third act of which Nana makes a sensational nude appearance. In the midst of the highly successful theatrical run, Nana (in chap. 6) absconds from Paris and arrives at the estate in the country on a rainy September night, accompanied only by her maid, Zoé. After her arrival (in Douglass Parmée's translation):

> In the pouring rain she continued to inspect the kitchen garden and the orchard, stopping at every tree, bending down to examine each vegetable plot. Then she ran over to take a look down the well, lifted up a frame to

see what was underneath and became lost in contemplation of a giant pumpkin. [. . .]It was raining harder than ever but she didn't notice; her only regret was that it was growing dark. She could no longer see things clearly, she had to feel them to discover what they were. Suddenly, in the dim light, she caught sight of some strawberries. She became a child again.

"Strawberries! strawberries!" she exploded. "They've got strawberries, I can feel them! . . . Zoé, bring a plate. Come and help me pick strawberries."

Nana dropped her sunshade and squatted down in the mud, letting the rain soak her. She started picking strawberries, groping under the leaves with her wet hands.

The combination of cream cheese and strawberries in *L'Assommoir* may remind readers of Proust of a passage in the "Combray" section of *Swann's Way* (1913), where the narrator compares pink hawthorn flowers to reddened cream cheese: "I set a higher value on cream cheese when it was pink, when I had been allowed to tinge it with crushed strawberries" (Kilmartin and Scott-Moncrieff translation).

Whatever the intense pleasures of eating strawberries, with or without cream, it seems it is possible to lose one's taste for them; so we learn, in "Erdbeeren, Fragole, Fraises" (1996), by Alistair Elliot (b. 1932), which begins with an epigraph:

qui legitis flores et humi nascentia fraga
Virgil, Eclogues, 3

We notice that the title and epigraph ("who are picking flowers and earth-born strawberries") together present us with no less than four words for "strawberry" (in German, Italian, French, and Latin), which seems to promise a learned, possibly bucolic, treatment of the subject; what we get instead is a thoroughly mundane account of how the speaker may have acquired his great fondness for strawberries from an antenatal experience of his mother's when she gorged herself on (Scottish) strawberries. His mother sickened at the time and acquired an aversion for the fruit, while for the speaker, "Strawberries were his treat / And still are, still with feelings of a birthday, / Though sugared, in lemon-juice, the Italian way." So, in this, the last, line of the poem we do finally get something slightly exotic—both the fruit (lemons don't grow in Britain) and the method of serving strawberries (Italian).

The German term for strawberries, *Erdbeeren* (literally, earthberries), suggests an earthy quality to the fruit, and indeed this arises from the fact that strawberries grow close to the ground, on so-called runners (the botanical term is "stolon") sent out by the strawberry plant. This characteristic of strawberry growth is referred to at the very beginning of a vividly direct and straightforward poem about strawberries, "The Strawberry Plant" (1966), by the English poet Jon Silkin (1930–1997):

The rootless strawberry plant
Moves across the soil. It hops

Six inches. Has no single location,
Or root.
You cannot point to its origin,
Or parent. It shoots out
A pipe, and one more plant
Consolidates its ground.
It puts out crude petals, loosely met.
As if the business of flowering
Were to be got over. Their period is brief.
Even then, the fruit is green,
Swart, hairy. Its petals invite tearing
And are gone quickly,
As if they had been. The fruit swells,
Reddens, becomes succulent.
Propagation through the devouring
Appetite of another.
Is sweet, seeded, untruculent;
Slugs like it, all over.
It is nubile to the lips,
And survives even them. And teeth,
Insane with edible fury,
Of the loving kind.

The same unusual feature of strawberry plant growth is the theme of another poem, by the Australian John Kinsella (b. 1963), "In the Best Interest of Strawberries" (1989); what Silkin terms "hops," Kinsella terms a "creep, in bursts":

Not at all predictable, strawberries.
Begun earlier, this would have been
   nothing out of the ordinary,
   nothing more than a justification
for the slow creep of a not so long ago
   dormant strawberry. Though now,
after abstinence, brought about
in uncertainty and delay, they have
begun their creep, in bursts. Transplanted,
they shall reach the edge of grass, the
threat of tangling, eventual choking.
We can only survey their movements, attempt
   to curb frustration with our coaxings.
If we do not witness, a hope should be
   held in their eventual fruiting.

An old conjectural etymology by Walter Skeat, incidentally, suggests that "strawberry" (which comes from Old English) may be derived from the verb "strew" referring to the plant's runners: "straw-berry. (E.) A. S. *streaw-berige,* straw-berry; perhaps from its propagation by runners; cf. *strew.*" And this feature of strawberry growth figures in a folktale, "Strawberries" (1988), as retold by native Cherokee storyteller Gayle Ross. The first man and woman—husband and wife—quarrel, and she walks away. A spirit offers to help recover the man's wife, provided he promises never to quarrel with her again. The spirit then makes some huckleberry bushes along the woman's path burst into blossom and ripen into fruit; she ignores the bushes. Other berries are then made to ripen and fruit, with the same result. "And again, the spirit waved his hand, and, one by one, the trees of the forest—the peach, the pear, the apple, the wild cherry—burst into bloom and ripened into fruit. But still, the woman's eyes remained fixed, and even still, she saw nothing but her anger and pain. And her footsteps didn't slow." Finally, then, the spirit creates an entirely new fruit:

> A thick green carpet began to grow along the trail. Then the carpet became starred with tiny white flowers, and each flower gradually ripened into a berry that was the color and shape of the human heart.
>
> As the woman walked, she crushed the tiny berries, and the delicious aroma came up through her nose. She stopped and looked down, and she saw the berries. She picked one and ate it, and she discovered its taste was as sweet as love itself. So she began walking slowly, picking berries as she went, and as she leaned down to pick a berry, she saw her husband coming behind her.

Husband and wife are reconciled and the new fruit becomes known as "the berries of love."

The intense excitement of discovering this newly created species of fruit was repeated each spring for Thoreau, as he explains at the very beginning of his book-length unpublished manuscript, "Wild Fruits" (1859–62). To begin with, "the strawberry is our first edible fruit to ripen," usually around the first days in June. Furthermore, it is not easy to find these earliest berries: "They are at first hard to detect . . . amid the red lower leaves, as if Nature meant thus to conceal the fruit, especially if your mind is unprepared for it. The plant is so humble that it is an unnoticed carpet. No edible wild fruit . . . lies so close to the ground as these earliest upland strawberries." Finally, there is the earthy taste, which sends Thoreau into ecstasies:

> What flavor can be more agreeable to our palates than that of this little fruit, which thus, as it were, exudes from the earth at the very beginning of the summer, without any care of ours? What beautiful and palatable bread! I make haste to pluck and eat this first fruit of the year, though they are green on the underside, somewhat acid as yet, and a little gritty from

lying so low. I taste a little strawberry-flavored earth with them. I get
enough to redden my fingers and lips at least.

Strawberries even from a single plant can vary considerably in size and shape;
occasionally, owing presumably to mutated genes or environmental trauma, a particular strawberry may be highly distorted and never really ripen. According to Marguerite
Young, it was just such a berry that apparently stimulated the writing of "Nevertheless" (1944), one of the best-known poems of Marianne Moore (1887–1972); Moore
sometimes referred to the poem as "my strawberry," according to one of her biographers, Laurence Stapleton. In Young's words: "there was the occasion when Marianne
Moore found, in a box of strawberries, a flat, green, disc-shaped strawberry which with
[*sic*] its seeds sticking out. It was almost all seeds and no strawberry. 'Here's a strawberry
that's had quite a struggle,' she said—and wrote one of her most beautiful poems with
that image in mind." The poem opens with a strawberry and ends with a cherry,
touching along the way on apple-seeds, hazel-nuts, *kok-saghyz* leaves, prickly-pear
leaves, carrots, and grape-tendrils:

> you've seen a strawberry
>   that's had a struggle; yet
>   was, where the fragments met,
>
> a hedgehog or a star-
>   fish for the multitude
>   of seeds.
>   [. . . . .]
>   What is there
>
> like fortitude! What sap
>   went through that little thread
>   to make the cherry red!

Ruth Pitter (1897–1992) has written, in "The Strawberry Plant" (1936), a poem
very different from Moore's, celebrating not the struggle but the easy grace of the
strawberry's growth; fittingly, Pitter's poetic form is traditional blank verse. The first ten
of twenty-two lines expresses her theme nicely:

> Above the water, in her rocky niche,
> She sat enthroned and perfect; for her crown
> One bud like pearl, and then two fairy roses
> Blanched and yet ardent in their glowing hearts:
> One greenish berry spangling into yellow
> Where the light touched the seed; one fruit achieved

198   And ripe, an odorous vermilion ball
        Tight with completion, lovingly enclasped
        By the close cup whose green chimed with the red,
        And showered with drops of gold like Danaë.

And Pitter's "moral"—unlike Moore's celebration of "Victory"—lies in the noninvasive contemplation of her last line: "Perfection's self, and (rightly) out of reach."

Grace Paley (b. 1922) is more succinct in her untitled poem about wild strawberries—three lines for the appearance of the plant, three lines for the application to her own life:

    When the wild strawberry leaves turn
    red and show the dark place of the strawberries
    it is too late

    I know this has a
    meaning inside my own life
    inside dark life

The culturally richest literary use of strawberries I know of is by the Russian poet Marina Tsvetaeva (1892–1941), who, on numerous occasions, evokes powerful childhood experiences of picking and eating them. We may begin with her memoir "The Kirillovnas" (1934), where she reminisces about her childhood stay in the town of Tarusa, not far from Moscow. The title refers to a religious sect consisting of a single young man, named "Christ," and some thirty women, each between thirty and forty years old, who shared not only the same clothing but even the same name, Mary (or Masha), and the same patronymic, "Kirillovna" (though they did not, of course, all have the same father). Behind their backs, the members of the sect were called "flagellants." Among the remarkable characteristics of the Kirillovnas for Marina was that in their garden, "all the berries ripened at once: strawberries, for example, and ashberries. . . . Where all you have to do is enter (but we never went in!) and everything is right at your fingertips: strawberries and cherries and currants and, especially, elderberries!" (Collyer Bowen's translation). Every so often, two of the Kirillovnas would bring Marina and her family a gift of strawberries:

  while they poured the berries from the colander into a basin, Kirillovna
  (which one? they were all alike! all thirty faces the same, under all thirty
  kerchiefs!), with her eyes still lowered, but not letting Mother's departing
  back out of sight, calmly and unhurriedly fed berry after berry into
  the nearest, most daring and hungriest mouth (most often mine!), like a
  bottomless pit.

At the end of her memoir Tsvetaeva tells us she "would like to come to rest in the flagellants' graveyard in Tarusa, under an elderberry bush, in one of those graves with a silver dove on it, where the reddest and largest strawberries in those parts grow." And in a short untitled poem of seven quatrains (1913), Tsvetaeva had already made use of this motif of wild strawberries in a cemetery, as she speaks from her own grave to a passerby; I will quote the last three stanzas in Pamela Chester's translation (in her essay on the significance of strawberries and chocolate for Tsvetaeva and Mandelstam):

> Pick yourself a wild stem
> And a berry with it, —
> There's nothing bigger and sweeter
> Than a wild strawberry from the cemetery.
>
> Only don't stand there gloomily,
> With your head sunk to your chest.
> Think lightly of me,
> Lightly forget me.
>
> How the sunbeam illuminates you!
> You're all covered in golden dust . . .
> —And may my voice from beneath the earth
> Not trouble you.

Chester points out that the wild strawberries [*zemlianika,* "earthberry"] of this poem are different from the much larger, cultivated strawberries [*klubnika*] of Tsvetaeva's memoir of Tarusa.

The chocolate of Chester's essay is connected with the poet Osip Mandelstam (1891–1938), Tsvetaeva's exact contemporary and close friend. As Chester explains, in a memoir about Mandelstam, "History of a Dedication" (1931), Tsvetaeva recalls his visit to see her, in a village near Tarusa, in the spring of 1916. On one occasion during the visit Mandelstam complains that the only chocolate in the household is reserved for Tsvetaeva's young nephew Andrei, with the result that he is forced to have jam rather than chocolate with his tea. For Tsvetaeva, Mandelstam, native of a manufactured city, St. Petersburg, prefers a manufactured food, chocolate, while she, native of a naturally evolved (we might say, an organic) city, Moscow, prefers to be associated with a natural food, strawberries; and indeed she begins her memoir as follows: "a balcony, and on the balcony on a small pink tablecloth—an enormous dish of strawberries and a notebook with two elbows. The strawberries, the notebook, the elbows are all mine." Later in the memoir, Tsvetaeva interprets a poem that Mandelstam dedicated to her, "Not Believing in the Miracle of Resurrection" (1916), and shows how it reflects in many details the visit described earlier in the memoir. One irony of this memoir is that Tsvetaeva wrote it (like "The Kirillovnas") in exile in Paris, while Mandelstam never left Russia. Tsvetaeva eventually returned to Russia; she hanged herself after the arrest of her husband and daughter. Mandelstam died during his second stay in a Soviet prison camp.

Finally, we may return to strawberries and cream in the rapturous words of that great American preacher, Henry Ward Beecher (1813–1887):

> And this harvest of strawberries,—what visions of bliss lie in the near future! They shall be picked in great, cool dishes, before the sun rises, with dew fresh on their blushing cheeks! They shall be pulled by delicate fingers; heaped up in saucers forever too small,—great berries,—each one a mouthful,—some to be eaten just as they are, while the red multitude are to be overpoured with cream.... Cream that is neither young nor old, but a term midway between both,—take this, O inquisitive reader! and let your hand be liberal toward the saucer-full of Jenny Lind, Triumph de Gand, Bartlett's Seedling, or Lanier's Madison, and then, with sweet bread and butter, and your friends around you, eat, and pity the gods that sit above the clouds where they can't have cows or strawberries!

It is not too hard to find luscious paintings of strawberries; here are three of my favorites, one from each of the eighteenth, nineteenth, and twentieth centuries. First, there is the *Basket of Wild Strawberries* (1761) by Chardin—now in a private collection in Paris (oil on canvas, 15 x 18 in.)—which is, as Pierre Rosenberg says, "one of his most beautiful still lifes." Next, there is *Strawberries and Cream* (1818), by (in J. Carter Brown's words) "America's first professional still-life painter and one of the finest artists of the new nation," Raphaelle Peale (1774–1825); the painting (oil on panel, 13⅛ x 9½ in.) is now in the Mellon Collection in Upperville, Virginia. And finally, there is *Fraises* (1920) by Pierre Bonnard (1867–1945), in the Phillips Collection, Washington, D.C. (oil on canvas, 10⅝ x 9⅞ in.). For reproductions, see Rosenberg's *Chardin, 1699–1779* (1979) or Conisbee's *Chardin* (1985); Cikovsky's *Raphaelle Peale Still Lifes* (1988); and de Looper and Grogan's *Pierre Bonnard* (1979).

If I were given just a single choice, however, I would have to select as my favorite painted strawberries those by Hieronymus Bosch (ca. 1450–1515) in the central panel (oil on wood, 86⅝ x 76¾ in.) of a triptych (ca. 1500), now in the Prado, Madrid. The interpretation of this central panel—usually called *The Garden of Earthly Delights*—is controversial. (Uncontroversially, the left panel represents the Garden of Eden and the right panel Hell.) What we see in the central panel is "an extensive park-like landscape teeming with nude men and women who nibble at giant fruits, consort with birds and animals, frolic in the water and, above all, indulge in a variety of amorous sports overtly and without shame" (Walter Gibson, *Hieronymus Bosch* [1973]). Is the subject matter here the apotheosis of sin or a celebration of the heights of innocent human pleasure? One thing is clear in the painting: the spectacular abundance of fruit. There are oversized cherries and blackberries and, most notably, numerous oversized strawberry plants, as well as several scenes incorporating gigantic strawberries—one such berry being carried on someone's back, one being nibbled at by a lone individual, one being offered by a man to a woman, and one surrounded by a seated throng

of people. (For reproductions of original-size details of these four strawberry scenes,   *201*
see John Rowland's *The Garden of Earthly Delights, Hieronymous Bosch* [1979]). We
need not agree—few Bosch scholars do—with Wilhelm Fränger's arguments for the
innocent-pleasure interpretation to appreciate what he has to say about Bosch's giant
strawberries:

> The [element] earth is represented by the symbol constantly recurring all
> over the panel, the strawberry. The strawberry belongs to the rose-family,
> which means that it belongs to the botanical retinue of Aphrodite, the
> goddess of love. Containing all the sweetness and fragrance of the aphro-
> disian spring-time, with its mild flame-colour and, above all, its spherical
> form, and sprinkled with innumerable grains of seed, it represents the
> essence of earthly voluptuous delight.

PLUMS

Compared with strawberries, plums are in all respects a rather modest kind of fruit; and yet, that very modesty seems to have freed some writers' imaginations, enabling them to create out of plums a surprising variety of fruit episodes. Consider, for example, Keats's "On Fame" (the later-written of two sonnets with the same title, both dating to 30 April 1819). As numerous critics have noted, Keats transcends his nominal subject to comment more generally (in the first four lines) on the fatal tendency of human beings to live in the feverish pursuit of externally imposed goals (such as fame). The next eight lines of the sonnet suggest how one ought to live, with Keats enlisting the aid of three similes of growth and movement—involving, respectively, a rose, a plum, a lake—each of which functions first negatively and then positively:

> It is as if the rose should pluck herself,
>> Or the ripe plum finger its misty bloom,
> As if a Naiad, like a meddling elf,
>> Should darken her pure grot with muddy gloom;
> But the rose leaves herself upon the briar,
>> For winds to kiss and grateful bees to feed,
> And the ripe plum still wears its dim attire,
>> The undisturbed lake has crystal space.

This idea of a reflex action on the part of rose or plum or lake in which each is somehow complicitous in its own ruination seems to me quite original, as are also the adjectives "misty" and "dim" applied to the plum.

The plum—more precisely, the wild plum—becomes both a marker of low social class and a tempting forbidden fruit in a brief story, "Wild Plums" (1929), by the American writer Grace Stone Coates (1881–1976). The setting is farm country and the plot involves two neighboring families, one in which the parents are utterly conventional and stuffy, the other, the Slumps, who are poor, ignorant, shiftless—and, to the young girl narrator, endlessly fascinating. Her parents see the Slumps as hopelessly déclassé, as, for example, when the entire Slump family sets out to pick wild plums and her father has only this to say to them: "If you happen on a plum thicket, an outcome highly unlikely, you still face the uncertainty of finding plums. The season has been

too dry. And should you find them, they will prove acrid and unfit for human consumption." On returning from one such expedition, the young Slump son tosses handfuls of wild plums out onto the road in front of the narrator's house. She gathers them
in her apron and brings them home to her mother, who professes to be horrified at
the idea of eating them, but finally relents, with severe admonitions to wash the plums
thoroughly, to avoid the skin, and to eat only a few. The story then ends with these
words:

> They were strange on my tongue as wild honey, holding the warmth of
> sand that sun had fingered, and the mystery of water under leaning
> boughs.
>
> For I had eaten one on the road.

I'm not sure why this story was selected by John Updike and Katrina Kenison as one
of the best American short stories of the past century: the prose style is certainly undis-
tinguished; and was not the theme—a repressed child eager to share in the forbidden
adventures of another family, less inhibited than her own—already familiar by the
1920s?

William Bartram, by the way, a century and a half before Coates's story, had
commented in his *Travels* (1791) on the sour and yet not unpleasant taste of the wild
plums he found growing luxuriantly on an island in the Pearl river in Alabama:

> Manured fruit trees arrive in this island to the utmost degree of perfec-
> tion, as Pears, Peaches, Figs, Grape Vines, Plumbs, &c.; of the last men-
> tioned genus, there is a native species grows in this island, which produces
> its large oblong crimson fruit in prodigious abundance; the fruit, though
> of a most enticing appearance, is rather too tart, yet agreeable eating, at sul-
> try noon, in this burning climate; it affords a most delicious and reviving
> marmalade, when preserved in sugar, and makes excellent tarts; the tree
> grows about twelve feet high, the top spreading, the branches spiny and
> the leaves broad, nervous, serrated, and terminating with a subulated point.

A wonderful picture of wild plums (*Prunus Americana*) may be found in a lithograph by Joseph Prestele (1796–1867), one of many he prepared for a book on the
forest trees of North America, by Asa Gray (1810–1888), America's leading botanist of
the time. The projected publication by the Smithsonian Institution, however, was never
realized. Prestele was a German-born artist who emigrated to New York State in 1843.
Working for Gray, Prestele engraved, printed, and colored the lithographs, which were
mostly based on drawings by Isaac Sprague (1811–?). The wild plum lithograph, made
in 1851, shows leaves, blossoms, and a pit. (For a reproduction, see Charles Van Ravenswaay's *Drawn from Nature: The Botanical Art of Joseph Prestele and his Sons* [1984].)

Next, we look at a sonnet about plums by the Yiddish poet Mani Leyb
(1883–1953), who emigrated to America from the Ukraine in 1905 and settled in

New York City. "A Plum" is one of a sequence of sonnets written during the last two decades of Leyb's life, published posthumously in 1955 (translated by John Hollander):

> In the cool evening, the good provider plucked
> From off a tree a fully ripened plum,
> Still with its leaf on, and bit into some
> Of its dewy, blue skin. From there, unlocked,
>
> The long-slumbering juice came leaping up,
> Foaming and cool. In order to make use
> Of every single drop of all that juice,
> Slowly, as one walks bearing a full cup
> Of wine, he brought a double handful of plum
> To his wife, and gently raised it to her mouth,
> Whereupon she could lovingly begin—
>
> "Thanks," she said—to gnaw the plum from out
> Of his hands, until those hands held only skin,
> And pit, and flecks of overbrimming foam.

Here, within the strict confines of a Petrarchan sonnet, we find a small ritual being enacted in the form of a double-hand-cupped walk from plum tree to wife, followed by what can only be imagined as a rather messy consumption of the plum's flesh, with the residual skin and pit left in the cupped hands. Part of the impact of the poem for many readers will come from the surprise of a Yiddish *sonnet,* producing a certain tension between, on the one hand, what is perceived as a verse form alien to Jewish culture and, on the other hand, such emphatically Jewish allusions as the "good provider" (*baleboss*) and "a full cup of wine" (it will be recalled that a full cup of wine is always prepared for Elijah the Prophet at the Passover seder). It must be understood, of course, that Leyb, like most of his fellow emigré Yiddish poets, was ambivalent about the religion of his childhood. After his arrival in New York he never attended religious services until the Rosh Hashanah (New Year) just before his death; on the other hand, one of his last poems was a sonnet called "Inscription on My Tombstone" in which he describes his own traditional Jewish burial—and the sonnet was read at his traditional Jewish burial. (The first Yiddish sonnets, by the way, seem to have been composed by Fradl Shtok [1890–1930], writing in New York City around the time of the First World War. But Hebrew sonnets were already written by the Jewish poet Immanuel of Rome around 1300—the first non-Italian sonnets after the Italians invented the form.)

Leyb's sonnet about plums was probably written not too many years after our next example, a well-known poem first published in 1934 by William Carlos Williams (Leyb's exact contemporary).

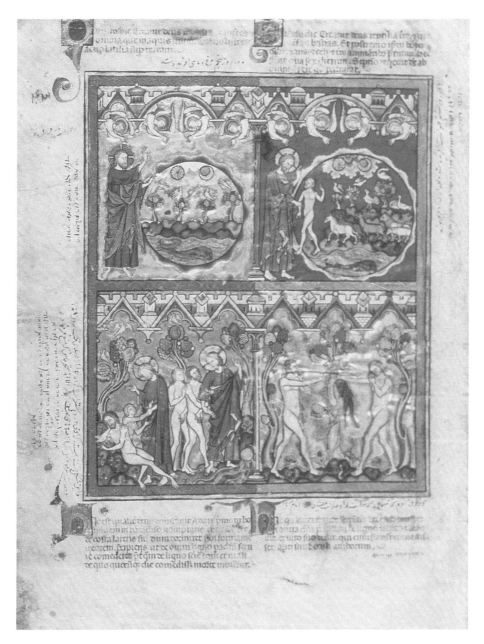

1. "The Fall," Pierpont Morgan Old Testament, ca. 1250 [p. 49]

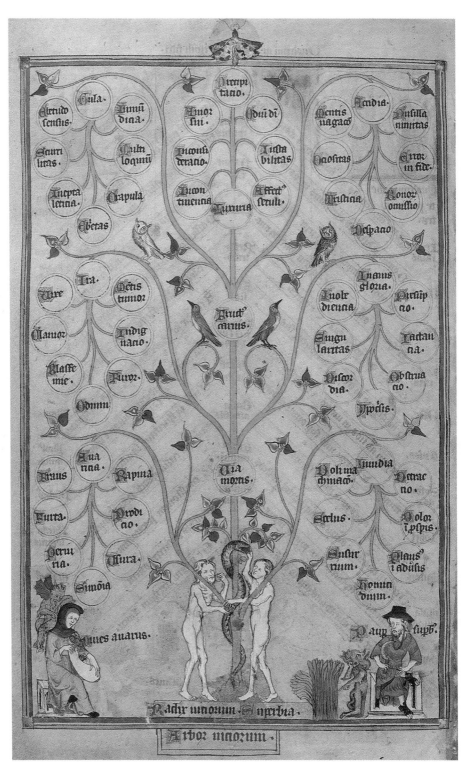

2. "Tree of vices," De Lisle Psalter, early 14th century [p. 50]

3. Boucicaut Master, "Adam and Eve," ca. 1415 [p. 50]

4. Hans Baldung Grien, *Eve, the Serpent, and Death,* ca. 1510–12 [p. 51]

5. Lucas Cranach the Elder, *Cupid Complaining to Venus,* 1530s [p. 52]

6. William Blake, *Raphael Warns Adam and Eve,* 1807–08 [p. 53]

7. Ronald Searle, *Greenfinger,* 1973 [p. 62]

8. Joris Hoefnagel, common apple, two cores, *Mira Calligraphiae Monumenta*, late 1590s [p. 72]

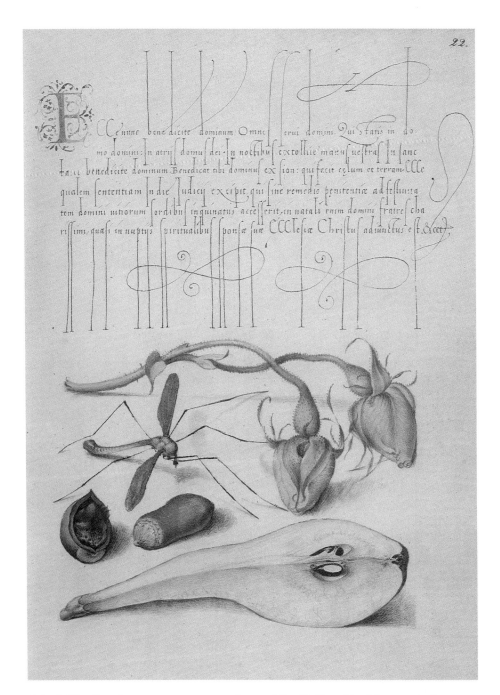

9. Joris Hoefnagel, common pear, gourd type, *Mira Calligraphiae Monumenta,* late 1590s [p. 72]

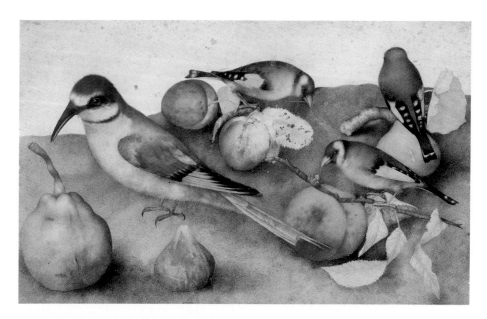

10. Giovanna Garzoni, *Still Life with Fruit and Birds,* 17th century [p. 73]

11. Joseph Decker, *Green Apples,* 1883–88 [p. 85]

12. Postage stamp, Newton's *Principia* tricentennial, 1987 [p. 95]

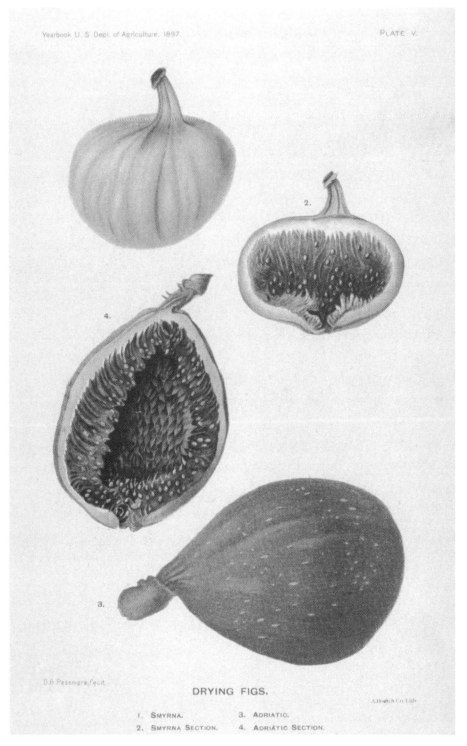

DRYING FIGS.

1. Smyrna.	3. Adriatic.
2. Smyrna Section.	4. Adriatic Section.

13. Deborah G. Passmore, "Drying Figs," 1897 [p. 151]

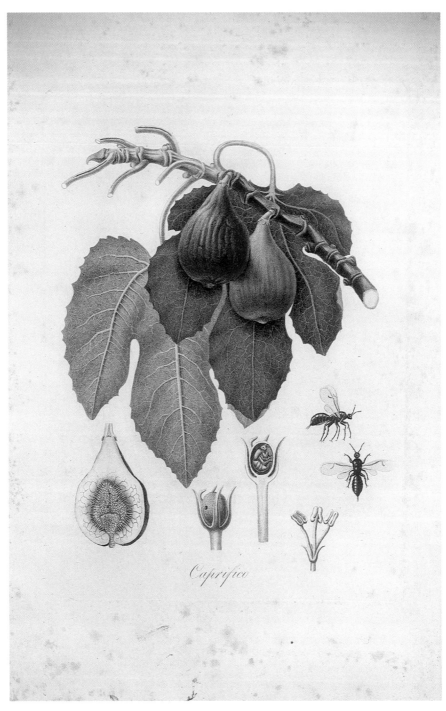

14. "Caprifico," Giorgio Gallesio, *Pomona italia,* vol. 1, 1817 [p. 152]

INFLUENCE OF PRECOOLING ON PEACHES.

[Fig. 1.—Hard ripe Early Crawford peach delivered at New York in sound condition by precooling and ordinary icing.   Fig. 2.—Early Crawford peach from California, picked green and shipped to New York under ordinary icing in the usual way.]

15. Deborah G. Passmore, "Influence of Precooling on Peaches," 1909 [p. 230]

16. "Golden Rareripe," Ebenezer Emmons, *Agriculture of New-York,* vol. 4, 1851 [p. 232]

EARLY CRAWFORD

17. "Early Crawford," U. P. Hedrick, *The Peaches of New York,* 1917 [p. 233]

ELBERTA

18. "Elberta," U. P. Hedrick, *The Peaches of New York,* 1917 [p. 233]

THIS IS JUST TO SAY

I have eaten
the plums
that were in
the icebox

and which
you were probably
saving
for breakfast

Forgive me
they were delicious
so sweet
and so cold

This is a note to his wife, identifiably "poetic" by the regular arrangement into three four-lined stanzas, in which the poet asks forgiveness for having consumed some plums that he assumes she had intended to serve at breakfast; he simply ate them, presumably the night before. The autobiographical status of the poem was confirmed by Williams himself when he converted a real note from his wife, Florence ("Flossie"), into a poem intended as a response to "This Is Just to Say" (see Litz and MacGowan's comment on the poem). Nevertheless, there is something to be made of the distinction between the poet and the note writer: for one thing, the first line of the printed text is the title of a poem for the poet but the first line of a note for the note writer. For my rather restricted purposes here the distinction will not need to be systematically insisted on.

In the poem, there is no expression of regret, far less of remorse; just a statement of fact, a hypothesis about intentions, a request for forgiveness, and a reference to enjoyment. The flat literalness of the diction makes the evident power of the poem somewhat perplexing. Other than the pleasure in eating the plums the only other feeling that seemingly animates the poem is a mild sense of guilt. Or, at least, we may say that asking forgiveness *usually* implies a sense of guilt; in this case, one cannot be so sure—perhaps the note writer is simply repeating a meaningless/meaningful form of words to ease his relationship with his wife. The phrase "forgive me" may also be viewed from the perspective of the illocutionary act its utterance performs—that is, the act of apology achieved through its very utterance (whether the apology is accepted is another question). (See the perceptive comments of Charles Altieri, "Presence and Reference in a Literary Text: The Example of Williams's 'This is Just to Say'" [1979]). If, however, it seems reasonable to posit a minimal sense of guilt on the note writer's part as at least a partial explanation of his apologetic impulses, it must still be remembered that these impulses are to be understood as by no means inconsistent with his full, uninhibited enjoyment of the plums; the phrase "guilty pleasures" would be quite out of place in describing his feelings (though perhaps "forbidden pleasures" would not). One achievement of the poem is the way it holds in equilibrium such normally conflicting feelings as the tranquil selfishness of eating the plums and the equally tranquil unselfishness of asking forgiveness.

The contrast in the men's behavior in their eating of the plums is so evident in the poems of Leyb and Williams as to be hardly worth mentioning: Leyb takes a bite, immediately remembers his wife, and brings her the remainder of his half-eaten plum; Williams consumes all the plums with presumably scarcely a thought of his wife until he has finished eating and writes her a note. But there may be more than a revelation of individual character here; there may be a revelation of deeper paradigms of conduct stemming from deeply contrasting cultures and occupations. For what it is worth, Williams—a secular humanist who practiced family medicine in two small towns of northern New Jersey, not far from New York City—was a close friend and supporter of many a Jewish writer (some of whom he told of his Jewish grandfather) but also an occasional uneasy purveyor of ugly Jewish and other ethnic stereotypes (see the index under "Jews" in Paul Mariani's *William Carlos Williams: A New World Naked* [1981]), while Leyb—a skilled bootmaker in New York City—was a non-observant Jew who never lost his feeling for Jewish life and ritual. (Neither poet is likely to have known the work of the other.)

Some other features of the two poems are perhaps less obvious, and worth noting. Each poem is strongly gendered in that it is very difficult, if not impossible, to imagine the wife and husband in either poem exchanging their roles. In "This Is Just to Say," it is reasonable to assume that the relationship between the note writer and his wife is characterized by the conventional asymmetry of American middle-class domesticity; after all, it is *she* who was planning the breakfast menu for *him* (or for them). In Leyb's poem, on the other hand, a Jewish husband initiates the action and then co-opts his wife—gently enough, to be sure—to join him in completing it. There is, of course, a relative dearth of rituals for women in traditional Judaism, and it is perhaps not easy to imagine a traditional Jewish wife creating a new ritual on her own.

In another Williams poem written around the same time as, and perhaps forming a pendant to, "This Is Just to Say," a woman gets to eat and enjoy a plum:

TO A POOR OLD WOMAN
munching a plum on
the street a paper bag
of them in her hand

They taste good to her
They taste good
to her. They taste
good to her

You can see it by
the way she gives herself
to the one half
sucked out in her hand

Comforted
a solace of ripe plums
seeming to fill the air
They taste good to her

Once again, the title may also be taken as the first line of the poem; if one does this, the poem consists of four stanzas of four lines each. No ritual, no interpersonal situation here, just a lone individual enjoying the taste of a ripe plum and even enjoying—or, at least, putting up with—the messiness of sucking it out of her hand (which, of course, must remind us of the wife in Leyb's sonnet eating a plum from her husband's cupped hands). But yet the old woman's comfort and solace are not hers alone because her experience has a public aspect, "seeming to fill the air." What is most memorable about the poem, however, is not the poor old woman munching her plums but rather the continual intrusion of the selective process involved in writing the poem: the ambiguity of the title; the fourfold repetition, with varying lineations, of the words "They taste good to her"; and the cluster of subtly different meanings associated with the words "comforted" and "solace." (In its original publication, the first line of the last stanza read: "Comforted, relieved"; evidently, Williams decided that "relieved" is not sufficiently differentiated in meaning from "comforted" and "solace" to justify its presence.)

That Williams had long been as enchanted with the sight of plum blossoms as he was with the taste of plums appears from two earlier poems, published in 1921. "Spring" is slight—just two lines: "O my grey hairs! / You are truly white as plum blossoms." "The Widow's Lament in Springtime" is more substantial; its voice is that of Williams's widowed mother. The key lines, near the middle of the poem, are about plum and cherry blossoms:

Thirtyfive years
I lived with my husband.
The plumtree is white today
with masses of flowers.
Masses of flowers
load the cherry branches
and color some bushes
yellow and some red
but the grief in my heart
is stronger than they

for though they were my joy
formerly, today I notice them
and turn away forgetting.

Another Yiddish poem involving plums forms a fascinating contrast with both Leyb's and Williams's spousal plum poems; the author is Moshe-Leyb Halpern (1886–1933), who came to America in 1908 and settled in New York City (translated by Sarah Betsky):

NEVER AGAIN WILL I SAY
There are people who perhaps would say
it is not polite to crowd around a dray
of onions and cucumbers and plums.
But if it is polite to trail after a hearse, in the middle of the street,
dressed all in black, and moreover weep,
then it is a sin to say
it is not polite to crowd around a dray
of onions and cucumbers and plums.

Maybe we shouldn't scramble so and fight;
we could at least shove quietly around the dray
of onions and cucumbers and plums.
But, since even a whip could chase not one of us away
because the tyrant of this earth's creatures, the stomach,
wants it so—you'd have to be a villain to say
it is not polite to crowd around a dray
of onions and cucumbers and plums.

For that very reason I'll never again say
it is not polite to crowd around a dray
of onions and cucumbers and plums.
However strongly such jostling may torment and trouble me
I will bow my head and bear it patiently.
I will weep perhaps—but I'll never again say
it is not polite to crowd around a dray
of onions and cucumbers and plums.

On first reading the title, one may mistake it for a line of the poem, especially if one has recently been looking at Williams's "This Is Just to Say." In fact, the poem initially appeared, with the title "Around a Wagon," in one of the earliest issues of *Die Freiheit* (the Communist Yiddish newspaper) in the spring of 1922 in New York City; only when the poem was reprinted two years later in one of Halpern's collections did it receive the title used above. In any case, as soon as one gets into the body of the poem, it becomes apparent that the title cannot reasonably be attached to the first stanza. Eventually, one discovers that the title is just a phrase quoted from the third stanza of the poem. But it is not only in terms of syntax that Halpern's title differs from Williams's, for the effect of the latter title is to play down the importance of what is said in the ensuing poem, while the effect of the former title is to anticipate the sweeping statements of the ensuing poem, with the phrase "never again" (*keynmol shoyn*) so pregnant with the possibility of universal meanings (as in its—much later—application to the Holocaust). Though Halpern is here confronting society's conventionalized responses to death with the unruliness of living (in the guise of the tyrannical stomach), this is one of the less savage and nihilistic of his poems.

In its original Yiddish, Halpern's poem consists of three eight-line stanzas, of varying line lengths, with the rhyme scheme *aabaaaab.* The recurring "a"-rhyme is the syllable *-ogn,* which appears five times as *zogn* (say) and seven times as *vogn* (dray, or wagon). The climax of the poem comes exactly halfway through with *mogn* (stomach), the rhyme word of the fifth line of the second stanza. The six-times repeated line ends with the word "plums" (*floymn*), which, along with onions and cucumbers, are easily recognizable as among the more popular items for sale in the horse-drawn wagons, so common and so welcome, especially in the summertime in certain neighborhoods of New York City during the years before World War II. It is obvious even in the English translation that the word "plums" is very prominent in the poem. And yet plums (as well as onions and cucumbers) hardly correspond to the imperious demands of the "tyrant stomach." In other words, there seems to be a discrepancy between the gentleness of some of the imagery and the ruthlessness of the intended social commentary. This is interesting in view of Ruth Wisse's interpretation in her critical biography of Halpern, where the poem is seen as a commentary on the poet's role in revolutionizing society:

> Dragging into his poem the cacophony of the marketplace, the poet hawks his wares like any vegetable monger who has to keep himself and his customers alive. How can the artist, because of his thin-skinned intolerance for noise and rudeness, deny the dominion of the stomach? The poet may be disheartened by the barbarity of the material struggle, but it forces its terms on him and on anyone who pretends to deal in truth.

Wisse suggests that Halpern's emphasis on the material basis of social relations satisfied the Communist editors of *Die Freiheit.* Inevitably, after a year or two, Halpern and *Die Freiheit* were to part company; perhaps those plums should have warned the editors.

Bertolt Brecht (1898–1956) might have been thinking about the diffident character of plums—and plum trees—when he wrote his children's song, "The Plum-Tree" (Der Pflaumenbaum), during his first year of exile in 1934. The song was for

Brecht's son Stefan and it was set to music by Hanns Eisler (1898–1962) and later again by Paul Dessau (1894–1979); an English version by Edwin Morgan goes like this:

> The back-yard has a tiny plum-tree,
> It shows how small a tree can be.
> Yet there it is, railed round
> So no one tramps it to the ground.
>
> It's reached its full shape, low and meagre.
> O yes, it wants to grow more, it's eager
> For what can't be done—
> It gets too little sun.
>
> A plum-tree no hand's ever been at
> To pick a plum: it strains belief.
> It is a plum-tree for all that—
> We know it by the leaf.

Earlier—to be precise, on 21 February 1920, at 7 P.M., on the train to Berlin—the twenty-two-year-old Brecht had composed a poem with the title, "Sentimental Song no. 1004," later retitled "Remembering Marie A." (Erinnerung an die Marie A.), in which a plum tree figures as the sentimental accompaniment of a fleeting romance with a girl from Brecht's hometown of Augsburg. In the poem, the strict iambic pentameter and regular rhyme scheme of the three stanzas are at odds with the nontraditional, antisentimental content. Brecht does not remember the face of the girl he kissed under a young plum tree (unter einem jungen Pflaumenbaum)—though he does remember her name—and he only recalls kissing her at all because he remembers the cloud that happened to float by just at that moment; for all he knows, the plum trees may have been chopped up for firewood—or, then, again they may still be blooming and Marie A. may have seven children by now! As Willett, Manheim, and Fried—the editors of a collection of English versions of Brecht's poetry—explain, Brecht is deflating, parodying, and transcending the kind of sentimental self-pity typical of a certain tradition of love poetry (as one might put it: poems in which the lover kisses his beloved under a blossoming tree).

But Brecht was hardly one to remain fixed in a single attitude toward love (or any other experience), and one of his responses to his experience of exile was a distinctly sentimental poem about someone absent. The poem is a sonnet of 1934, "Buying Oranges" (Der Orangenkauf), set in London, and in it Brecht's fumbling attempt to buy an orange "in yellow fog along Southampton Street" suddenly brings home to him the fact "that you are not here with me in this town" (Naomi Replansky is the translator). The "you" was Margarete Steffin, Brecht's chief assistant during his Danish exile, from 1933 to 1939.

It is possible to go much further than Brecht in neutralizing—or, indeed, negating—the lore, at once reassuringly homely and excitingly exotic, associated with plums, plum trees, and plum blossoms. Consider "Plum," by the American poet William Dickey (1928–1994), in his volume *The Education of Desire* (1996). To begin with, when we read W. D. Snodgrass's foreword to the volume, we learn that these are the last poems Dickey wrote before he died of AIDS and also that "Plum" belongs to a group of poems about death. The poem itself is recognizably a vil lanelle, beginning:

> Now the plum blossoms on its Chinese branch
> argues in spring across the waterless country.
> Spring as a fist. Its delicacies clench.

In a strict villanelle the first and third lines would now be repeated alternately in the next four stanzas, and the two lines would occur together in the last, four-lined, stanza. Dickey, instead, uses variants of the first and third lines when they recur in the remaining five stanzas, but the variant lines always end with "branch" or "clench," except for the last stanza where one of the end-words is "stench" rather than "branch." Crucial to the understanding of the poem, I believe, is the phrase "Spring as a fist" in the first stanza, which becomes "a fist in spring" in the third stanza, "spring comes as a fist" in the fifth stanza, and "the fingers of the plum blossom" in the last stanza; for the fist is one of the preferred anatomical parts in certain forms of gay male sex. (For the slang meaning of "fisting," see the *Random House Historical Dictionary of American Slang*.) If there are any doubts about this interpretation, they can be dispelled by two lines of the third stanza: "forcing their unlubricated entry, / a fist in spring & the bruised membranes clench / & convulse." The artificial, painted, Chinese plum blossoms become, or are contrasted with, the projected "missile" of "the fire's blossom," which transforms the (other) body into a "beggar," a "zero," a "rotted petal." One thing seems clear about the poem: its subject matter is always on the verge of shattering the clenched delicacies of the traditional villanelle form.

Jon Silkin has even written a poem called "The Plum-tree" (1976) about the Holocaust. It seems to me a puzzling combination of conversational tone and pretentious diction: on the one hand, "Yes, I said, / I believe," "I speak of the six million / and do not shave," "We consider, and feed / the excellence of three cats," "I talk with the plum-tree"; on the other hand, "iso-rhythmic / evennesses of mind," "the blithe compliant ratchets of industry," "in the dene where mild limestone / kneels to the ice-floe," "The tree's / incipience of fruit makes plump / the maidenly flowers," "if beauty affirm the techniques / work anneals," and—the concluding lines of the poem— "Barren are the plum-tree's flowers / fleshed as they glisten." One feels Silkin is straining too hard to invent phrases commensurate with his subject. His worry that "afraid I insult my God / of my poems I'll say little" might better have been translated into the precept that about the Holocaust, less is more.

It is time for some women to be heard from on the subject of plums. Let us begin not with a poem but with a memoir by Helen Thomas (1877–1967) of a summer holiday she and her husband, the poet Edward Thomas, together with their children, spent with Robert Frost and his family. The time was August 1914, just after the British declaration of war, and the place was a remote farm in Herefordshire, near Ledbury, in western England. Although Helen Thomas published two books of memoirs (1926, 1931), she chose to publish her account of "Poets' Holiday in the Shadow of War" in 1963 in the London *Times*. Here is what she remembers seeing on the first morning after her arrival at the farm:

> In the farmhouse orchards the choicest of dessert plums grew, each hanging in its own muslin bag to protect it from insects. These plums had to be without blemish and they were packed for Covent Garden, each in its own compartment of cotton wool. Near the farmhouse hung delicious fruit which we were allowed to pick—greengages and large golden, rosy or black plums.

Helen Thomas goes on to recount how Frost had encouraged her husband to become a poet, how Edward had enlisted in the Artists' Rifles in July 1915, and how he was killed in action at Arras in April 1917. Now, among the poems Thomas wrote in July 1915 was one called "Two Houses," about the farmhouse he and his family occupied the summer before and about another, much older, destroyed farmhouse whose foundation stones must have been visible in the vicinity. Two brief stanzas are alloted to each house; here is the second stanza devoted to the farmhouse they lived in:

> Not far from the road it lies, yet caught
> Far out of reach
> Of the road's dust
> And the dusty thought
> Of passers-by, though each
> Stops, and turns, and must
> Look down at it like a wasp at a muslined peach.

Helen Thomas would, of course, have known this poem but apparently still remembered plum trees. It seems quite possible that the poet preferred peach to plum for the rhyme but it is also possible that Helen Thomas confused the vividly colored plums she picked with muslined peaches nearby.

In his prose poem "Plums" (1994), Jay Meek (b. 1937) appreciatively summarizes Helen Thomas's memoir and then comments: "But someone had cared for the plums. Someone before all those blasted years of devastation and mass murder had gone into the orchard to coddle them with gauze, believing this made a difference, like the cotton wool they were packed in to arrive at Covent Garden without blemish. It seems almost precious now." At this point one should not resist quoting some lovely lines by Edward Thomas about damson plums, from a twenty-line poem, "There's nothing like the sun," written in November 1915:

> November has begun,
> Yet never shone the sun as fair as now
> While the sweet last-left damsons from the bough
> With spangles of the morning's storm drop down
> Because the starling shakes it, whistling what
> Once swallows sang.

Here now are some poems about plums by women; first, "Conservancies," dating from 1974, by Josephine Miles (b. 1911):

> Plums on the ground
> Lay with a soft sound
> And the sweet sense of dissolution they have.
> She used to pick them up
> With a scoop, thickened with bees.
> She would carry away into bottles what she could save
> And the cinnamon worked in the kitchen
> Saying *save.*
>
> Now when the lingering fresh breezes
> Flurry in the field rows
> Some sifts of clear summer air,
> She pickles the puffs in clear jars,
> Brings them out
> In winter scarcity,
> Gives everybody on his plate of malathion
> A rich spoonful of air.

Playing on the words of her title, Miles refers in the first stanza to plum "conserves" and in the second to the "conservation" of the natural resource of pure air. Malathion is an insecticide, whose traces presumably linger on into winter, and the maker of real plum conserves of the first stanza has become in the second stanza a wholly imaginary would-be restorer of the environment.

Concerned more with the absence than the abundance of plums is "The Pernickety Plum Tree," by Marge Piercy (b. 1936), in which the narrator muses on the failure of the plum tree she has planted to yield significant numbers of fruit:

> The fourth year after we planted it
> the Shiro plum tree gave us
> two perfect plums

Until now, we have encountered no references to particular plum varieties (despite the fact that of all stone fruits the plum has the most cultivars). The Shiro is a round, medium to large, yellow plum that is supposed to produce heavily, so the narrator has good reason to be disappointed at the paucity of fruit:

> From a thousand flickering leaves,
> from a hundred white blossoms
> falling like stars on the path,
> two plums

Finally, the narrator concludes that perhaps she has been victimized by "our own gullibility / strung along with two plums." The repetition of the phrase "two plums" no less than four times in the twenty-five lines of the poem has a distinctly comic effect.

If there is a dearth of plums in Piercy's poem, there is a superfluity in "Plums" (1967), by the Anglo-Canadian poet Robin Skelton. Skelton is writing about the obsessive picking of plums by a seventy-three-year-old man, as he ascends higher and higher:

> upon his long green ladder,
> pulls through leaves
> and gaps of sky and
> knuckled twigs and pulls
> all afternoon

The onlookers' anxiety for the old man is well expressed, as also is their empathy with what he is learning about risks and fear:

> One branch more
> is just beyond him still,
> lumped huge with plums
> he nods with, sways with,
> tugging ripeness free
> for all our hesitations
> and our love,
> still learning how it feels,
> how plum trees feel
> and fingers on the plums

And why does the picker persist so stubbornly? Because

> it makes
> the world redeemable;
> he just can't stop.
> When you grow plums
> you have to get them down.

In "The Plum's Heart" (1985), by the American poet Gary Soto (b. 1952), a boy is lifted into a plum tree by his father. This is the third poem in Soto's volume *Black Hair* (1985), and like the first two poems it dwells on the death of his father. Once he is in the tree,

> My hands
> Opened like mouths,
> The juice running
> Without course down
> My arms, as I stabbed
> For plums, bunched
> Or half-hidden behind
> Leaves.
>   [. . . . .]
> I climbed searching
> For those red globes,
> And with a sack filled,
> I called for father
> To catch—father
> Who would disappear
> Like fruit at the end
> Of summer, from a neck
> Wound some say—blood
> Running like the juice
> Of these arms. I
> Twisted the throat
> Of the sack, tossed
> It, and started down
> To father, his mouth
> Already red and grinning
> Like the dead on their
> Rack of blackness.

The last three lines quoted (the poem continues for five more lines) presumably constitute a retrospective view of the missing father—or is the speaker supposed to be actually remembering how his father looked that day of plum picking?

Here are three more poems about plums by American poets, the first, "Plum" (1997), by Faye George (b. 1933):

> Everything that flowers
> flowers for itself.
> The flesh of the plum
> swells sweet,

> capsuled in its royal wrap.
> All that preparation
>
> just to be.
>
> And when I have finished,
> nothing left
> but the liberated seed,
> green tongue coiled within,
> waiting for a chance
> to taste the bitten earth.

The very texture and sound of the poem enact its subject: the becoming of the verbal pattern which is the poem echoes the becoming of both the plum's flesh and its means of renewing that flesh (the pit). If the plum flowers for itself, so does the poem, at least insofar as the sounds of the words possess a certain independence of their meanings. Thus, in the six short lines of the first stanza we are treated to a veritable showcase or anthology of the possible kinds of harmony in verse, each involving the repetition of some ordered combination of consonant and vowel sounds: ver/wer; th/th; er/or; fl/lf; fl/pl; sw/sw; r/wr; pre/par; cap/rap/that. The poem then momentarily pauses—or, better, hovers—on the isolated line "just to be," in which the sound repetition is reduced to t/t, scarcely audible, as the two t's tend to merge in the pronouncing. And then with the new stanza the too-easy idyll of word-sounds truly independent of meaning vanishes, as we are shaken by the brutal fact of the plum's disappearance, its being consumed shockingly signalized by the extra space between the lines. It is natural to expect that the poem will end with the consumption of the plum, as is forcibly suggested by the words "finished / nothing left." But we have forgotten the pit, "liberated" in the act of eating and ready to adopt its new role as "seed." The rhymes are simpler in this stanza—often simple pairs of vowels or consonants (i/i; a/a; ee/ee; f/f; l/l; w/w; t/t)—and the movement of the verse accelerates, culminating in the exuberant and rather daring metaphor of the seed as a "green tongue . . . waiting . . . to taste the bitten earth."

Next, "It Is the Ripe Red" (1998), by Alan Shefsky, whose entire attention is focused on the sensual aspects of eating a plum; here are the first two and the last (of six) stanzas:

> It is the ripe red
> plum she prefers,
> she tears into it with
> the sharp fingernail
> of her right thumb.
>
> She loves even
> the mess of it, the red-yellow

juice that washes
her hand and wrist,
falls to her dress.
    [. . . . .]
All is yellow-red
and tart, all is sweet
and wine-red; all is
flesh and tender
and plum and heart.

Finally, a Stevensian poem, "Plums" (1979), by a great admirer of Wallace Stevens (1879–1955), the American Robert Winner (1930–1986), who, like Stevens, spent all of his working life in the business world:

Their excellencies the plums
plumped into dignity
announce themselves

Your amiable servants
the plums with their hats off
persuasive in their glowing skins

declare their readiness
to sing on your teeth.
Enclosed in flesh, in vests of sanity

juicy insinuations proclaim themselves—
The yes, the yes of the surprised senses
burst from a stone
A wintering sensation kept
alive in its depths
A stubborn magnified ideal of itself.

The deliberately assertive idiosyncrasy of these last three plum poems (and of so many poems like them in the Euro-American tradition) is in sharp contrast to the conventional and repetitive literary and artistic devices and images of even the most original work in such a cultural tradition as that of the Chinese flowering plum, to which we now turn.

THE FLOWERING PLUM
A Chinese Interlude

The flowering plum tree's blossoms (*meihua*) have been for close to a thousand years a favorite theme of Chinese poets and painters, and beyond that the basis for an entire aesthetic (including the design of everyday objects), and even a guide to an idealized way of life. (In the 1930s, the *meihua* was selected as the national emblem of China.) There is nothing remotely comparable in Euro-American culture, but for that very reason it may, by contrast, illuminate Euro-American fruit episodes to look at the role of *meihua* in Chinese culture. (I follow here the splendid catalogue of an exhibition in the Yale University Art Gallery: *Bones of Jade, Soul of Ice: The Flowering Plum in Chinese Art,* ed. Maggie Bickford [1985].)

The flowering plum (*mei; Prunus mumae*) is, in fact, closer botanically to the apricot (*Prunus armeniaca*) than to the plum (*Prunus domestica*); its fruit has been described by the botanist Hui-Lin Li as "a globose drupe, about 2–3 cm. across, yellowish green, slightly pubescent, and with the flesh adhering to a pitted stone." Is the fruit edible? Hui-Lin says "scarcely," but this holds only for the raw fruit, whereas in various pickled, candied, dried, honeyed, and smoked forms the fruit has been of central importance as a relish in the Chinese culinary tradition, and remains to this day an important economic crop. None of these uses of the *mei* fruit is alluded to by Chinese poets or artists, but, complains Craig Clunas in his 1996 book on Chinese gardens, that is no reason why historians of Chinese gardens should ignore its culinary status. Indeed, Clunas sees "the oblivion of the flowering plum's edibility as being . . . grounded in the larger trend towards an exclusively aestheticized understanding of Chinese garden culture." Be that as it may, one of the greatest flowering plum cultists of all, Lin Hong (13th cent. C.E.), wrote a manual for conducting life in accordance with the flowering plum aesthetic in which he recommends, among other things, making plum-blossom wafers and serving them in chicken-noodle soup. (See Hui-lin Li's essay for a photograph of flowering plum blossoms, and Maggie Bickford's book, *Ink Plum: The Making of a Chinese Scholar-Painting Genre* [1996], for the recommended soup.)

What Chinese poets and artists have seized upon has been the flowering plum blossoms, which are extraordinary in that they appear, before the leaves, in winter, near the time of the Chinese New Year. The blossoms are five-petaled—extremely important because five is a lucky number in Chinese culture—and their color varies from deep pink through a range of pale colors to white, with white being favored by the flowering plum connoisseur. Also, the blossoms are slightly fragrant, delicate, and short-lived in the wintry environment. By contrast, flowering plum trees are, as Bickford explains, long-lived: "Rough and twisted, splotched with moss, its battered trunk and broken boughs bear the scars of a hundred winters" (Maggie Bickford, "The Flowering Plum: Literary and Cultural Traditions," in *Bones of Jade, Soul of Ice*).

The physical properties of the flowering plum had already been exploited by poets during the Late Northern Song period (ca. 1100) but it was only during the Southern Song period (1128–1279) that the flowering plum motif really took off—in poetry and prose, in painting and the decorative arts, in garden design. An important stimulus to this great cultural efflorescence was the loss of the northern portion of the Chinese Empire to the Jurchen barbarians and the consequent shift of the Chinese capital and court to a location in the south. In the southern environment flowering plum trees flourish in far greater numbers and varieties than in the north. Also, while the flowering plum had always been associated with feelings of nostalgia and the pain of exile (whether for southerners living in the north or northerners living in the south), in the new and politically vulnerable southern empire these feelings were intensified and, as Bickford writes, "gave added resonance to the theme of transience embodied in falling plum blossoms" (*Bones of Jade, Soul of Ice*). More specifically, *meihua* came to be associated with two different personae: the Plum-Blossom Beauty (for example, an abandoned lover) and the Flowering-Plum Recluse (for example, an exiled government official or a scholar in self-imposed isolation). Thus, the treatment of individual types in *meihua* poetry and painting is rigorously gendered. As Bickford explains in her *Ink Plum*:

> Basic to the dichotomous development of pathetic and heroic *mei* modes—blossoms and branches, beauties and hermits—is their temporal orientation. . . . For flowers and women blossom only once, while old trees—and old men, who are like them—come back again and again. It is these fundamentally opposed conceptions of time—linear and terminal for blossom and beauty, cyclical and self-renewing for tree and hermit— that permit the *meihua* issues of isolation and adversity to pass from the debit to the credit side of the symbolic ledger as the page is turned from female to male accounts.

The images of both types share a certain austerity, simplicity, and purity, which reaches its culmination, during the Yuan dynasty (1279–1368), in the painting genre called *momei,* or "ink plum." Ink plum is confined to black ink on paper—a monochromatic genre in sharp contrast to older Chinese painting in which the medium was often polychromatic paint on silk. A full historical account of ink plum is now available in the superb book by Maggie Bickford; here, we must turn to some of the literary manifestations of *meihua*.

The earliest extant poem associating a woman with *mei* —though, in this particular example, not with *meihua*—is anonymous and can be dated only roughly to around the eleventh century to seventh century B.C.E. (translated by Hans Frankel):

> Falling are the plums,
> Seven are left.
> You young men who seek me,
> Seize the auspicious time!
>
> Falling are the plums,
> Three are left.
> You young men who seek me,
> Seize the present moment!
>
> Falling are the plums,
> With slanting baskets we scoop them.
> You young men who seek me,
> Seize the chance to speak up!

A poem by the statesman Wang Anshi (1021–1086), translated by Hans Frankel, incorporates the man/woman dichotomy described above:

> The flowering plums on Lone Hill, what are they like,
> Half blossoming, half fading, midst briars and thorns?
> A lovely woman, desolate, among grasses and trees?
> A high-minded gentleman, thwarted, amidst brambles and weeds?
> Straight upright, their forsaken beauty carries the wintry sun;
> Quiet and silent, their fragrance spreads through the wilds with the wind.
> They missed their chance to be transplanted, now their roots are aging;
> They turn their heads toward the Imperial Park—their beauty wasted.

The last couplet is predicated on a contrast between "wild" and "official" plum, two of the ten kinds of plum described in a plum painting manual of the mid-fourteenth century; the others are old/young, sparse/luxuriant, garden/mountain, river, and withered (for a discussion, see Bickford's *Ink Plum*).

Finally, here is a pair of poems by Li Qingzhao (1084–d. after 1151), again translated by Frankel, writing of her loneliness, exiled in the south after her husband's death:

> Last night I was very drunk and careless in undressing,
> Flowering-plum calyxes remained stuck in my hair.

As I awake, the stench of wine ruins my spring sleep,
The dream is receding, I can't get back to it.

People are still,
The moon is stationary,
The kingfisher curtain hangs.
I just crush the stamens,
Just to wring out a little more fragrance,
Just to prolong the time.

~

Year after year when it snowed
I'd often stick plum blossoms in my hair and get drunk;
I'd crush the plum blossoms with ill will
And get my clothes all drenched with pure tears.

This year, out of the way at the edge of sea and sky,
The hair on both my temples blossoms white.
I see the evening wind is so strong,
It will be hard to find plum blossoms.

Even in translation, one can appreciate, I believe, how the same few elements of plum blossom lore have been deployed with slight variations to express subtly different feelings. One pinnacle of flowering plum art is the earliest extant illustrated text on the subject, Song Boren's *Meihua xishen pu* (Register of plum-blossom portraits). The author was a minor official in salt administration, and his masterpiece, dating from circa 1238, consisted of one hundred woodblock pictures of plum blossoms at various stages of development, each picture accompanied by a poem, with "visual and verbal elements so [manipulated] as to call for dynastic renovation, renewal, and reunification" (*Ink Plum*). According to Maggie Bickford, however, "The same ardor that fueled the Song plum cult also exhausted its creative resources. How could the blossoms withstand this onslaught of admiration in which individual poets composed suites of plum poems comprising ten or a hundred or eight hundred verses, and pairs of poetic friends matched each other verse for verse through a hundred different themes on the flowering plum?" (*Bones of Jade, Soul of Ice*). It must be remembered, though, that at the very time that plum poetry was beginning to lose its creativity, ink plum was rising to its greatest heights, while in the decorative arts (ceramics, metalwork, textiles, lacquerware, wooden furniture, architectural ornament) the *meihua* theme retained its vitality right through the Qing dynasty (1644–1911).

To illustrate the striking diversity in continuity of the long flowering plum tradition in Chinese art and literature, one other outstanding artist may be mentioned: Jin Nong—also transliterated Chin Nung—(1687–d. after 1764). Jin Nong's century,

222   as Bickford explains, "was a time of consolidation, proliferation, and new beginnings for the flowering-plum tradition" and the ink-plum tradition was even "codified . . . in analytic diagrams which, disseminated on an unprecedented scale, made that literati art available to painters denied the privilege of individual instruction or access to the classical models in private painting collections" (*Bones of Jade, Soul of Ice*). In this period, the emperor himself was an amateur artist and the leading collector of the empire. As for the contribution of Jin Nong, this was, in Bickford's words, "systematic construction of an individual plum language based on his thorough integration of painting, idiosyncratic calligraphy, and seals. . . . He developed a repertory of form-types and compositions, along with stock poetic and prose inscriptions, which he combined and recombined in work after work. No matter how often he used them the result always seemed intended for the recipient alone" (*Bones of Jade, Soul of Ice*). Commenting on one of Jin Nong's paintings—"Branches of Blossoming Plum" (1759), in the Freer Gallery of Art, Washington, D.C. (ink and color on paper, 51 x 11 in.)—another historian of Chinese painting, James Cahill, points out that "we have tended to read the conventional meaning into the image and pay little attention to the inscription. But when we *do* read it, we learn that Chin did the painting to congratulate a friend who had acquired a lovely new concubine, likening the red color of the blossoms to her rouged cheeks, but also calling up the more conventional associations of the subject to felicitate his friend's continuing virility." (For a reproduction of the painting, see Cahill's *The Painter's Practice: How Artists Lived and Worked in Traditional China* [1974].)

I want to emphasize that, compared with the flowering plum in Chinese culture, no motif in the traditions we are studying has ever achieved such high incidence together with such specificity and variety of meanings during such a prolonged time span. (The closest Euro-American parallel is perhaps the two-and-a-half-millennium history of the nude, but this is pretty much restricted to the visual arts.) Thus, when, say, plum blossoms or apple blossoms appear in American poetry, they can have little of the resonance of *meihua* in Chinese poetry. Recall William Dickey's villanelle, "Plum," with its allusions to Chinese plum blossoms: even if one knows something of the history of plum blossoms in Chinese poetry—or, more generally, in Chinese culture—that knowledge can contribute little to the effectiveness of the poem, in which painted plum blossoms simply stand in for "culture" as opposed to the "nature" of the thrusting fist. And even the apple blossoms in James Wright's "The Revelation," as they fall on his father's head, possess a largely private significance internal to the poem itself.

PEACHES, MANGOES, AND OTHER JUICY FRUITS

We look first at an Italian poem that pictures a small, almost trivial, episode involving peaches and other juicy fruits—one of a set of poems titled "Poems for a Print-collector"—by Roberto Roversi (b. 1923). The poem is called "Afternoon" and is here translated by William Weaver; the reader is thrust at the outset *in medias res:*

> Suddenly the ball goes flying
> beyond the hedge and the field,
> beyond the gate of the neighboring villa;
> fallen into the garden
> red with soft, sweet-smelling peaches.

Several girls have been playing with the ball and one of them, Gioietta, runs to retrieve it:

> And here, Gioietta returns with the ball
> and peaches, apples and pears in her skirt
> which she offers like a goblet.
> Each of them seizes a fruit and she too
> bites with her white talons
> a fruit that breaks open,
> fearful, bitten, and the juice
> runs to her chin in a flaming river.

A storm follows, reducing the girls to passive observers:

> The swift rain falls
> and the motionless girls,
> some lost in thought, others smiling,
> throw down the fruit and, awe-stricken, gaze
> at the unfolding boughs, the leaves
> that are suddenly dark.

Finally, "the girls, with happy cries, / under the rain, run and disappear"—washed clean of fruit juice, presumably, by the rain.

　　　It is this juice, I believe, that makes T. S. Eliot's Prufrock ask: "Do I dare to eat a peach?" ("The Love Song of J. Alfred Prufrock," 1910–11; published 1915). What is daring, we may well ask, about eating a peach, and—apart from the rhyme—wouldn't a plum do just as well? To begin with, it must be recalled that, by the time we encounter the peach (near the end of a fairly long poem), we know that, by his own confession, Prufrock is a vain, timorous, cautious, and indecisive man, racked by self-doubt, and sure that the mermaids who are "singing each to each" will not sing for him. His fear of eating a peach—which might be said to sum up and epitomize his entire spiritual life—has, one may surmise, two aspects, one inner and private, the other outer and public: on the one hand, the sensuous experience might be too unsettling for him, and, on the other hand, he might make a spectacle of himself because of the messiness involved in biting and masticating something so juicy. A smaller fruit, such as a plum or an apricot, or a less juicy fruit, such as an apple, would hardly serve to make Eliot's point.

It is true, though, that when Saul Bellow (b. 1915) and Isaac Rosenfeld (1918–1956) composed a Yiddish parody of "The Love Song of J. Alfred Prufrock" sometime in the 1940s they replaced the peach by a plum; the poem is hilarious and a few lines must be quoted (translated by Mark Shechner):

> I grow old, I grow old,
> And my navel grows cold.
> Shall I comb out my hair,
> May I eat a prune?
> I shall put on white pants
> And walk by the sea.
>
> ~
>
> Ikh ver alt, ikh ver alt
> Un der pupik vert mir kalt.
> Zol ikh oyskemen di hor,
> Meg ikh oyfesen a flom?
> Ikh vel onton vayse hoysn
> Un shpatsirn by dem yom.

Incidentally, "flom" should be "floym," which, of course, would not rhyme exactly with "yom"; the word *floym* usually designates a plum but perhaps the juicy fruit so embarrassing to Prufrock was aptly replaced by a prune in the English translation.

A parody, "J. Alfred's Appetite" (1985), by Christopher Driver (1932–1997), proposes a solution to Prufrock's gustatory dilemma:

> Prufrock, as he takes a peach,
> Fingers the bloomy fuzz, and peels.
> When fruit is ripe, the skin is trash:
> He needs a knife throughout his meals.

There is another peach in a later poem by Eliot, "The Hippopotamus" (1920), a humorous poem on a serious theme—the relation between the "True Church" and its flesh and blood representatives. The fourth stanza (of nine) mentions the peach and two other juicy fruits, the mango and the pomegranate:

> The 'potamus can never reach
> The mango on the mango-tree;
> But fruits of pomegranate and peach
> Refresh the Church from over sea.

Oranges can also be messy to eat and, indeed, I know of two literary episodes that feature the messiness of eating oranges. The first episode, by Elizabeth Gaskell (1810–1865), occurs toward the beginning (chap. 3) of her novel *Cranford* (1851–53), when the narrator informs us that the Jenkyns sisters have a peculiar way of consuming their dessert oranges:

> Miss Jenkyns did not like to cut the fruit; for, as she observed, the juice all ran out nobody knew where; sucking (only I think she used some more recondite word) was in fact the only way of enjoying oranges; but then there was the unpleasant association with a ceremony frequently gone through by little babies; and so, after dessert, in orange season, Miss Jenkyns and Miss Matty used to rise up, possess themselves each of an orange in silence, and withdraw to the privacy of their own rooms, to indulge in sucking oranges.

This behavior by the Jenkyns sisters illustrates to perfection the way in which their conventionality is often a mere cover for deeply eccentric behavior, in this case an astonishing sensuality (sucking juice from oranges is implicitly compared to babies nursing). The narrator's response to the sisters' behavior is also astonishing: she attempts to prevail on them to stay in the dining room and suck their oranges, while she holds up a screen to avoid seeing them. (Though she cannot, of course, help hearing them!)

The early orange episode should also prepare us for a series of shocking episodes that punctuate the novel: far from being "charming, kindly, ironically humorous and easy to read"—to quote a characterization of *Cranford* by Graham Handley—the novel seems to me disturbing, cruel, bitterly humorous, and sometimes painful to read. Just consider the following: a cat swallows a valuable piece of lace that has been soaking in some milk and is dosed with an emetic until she vomits the lace up (chap. 8); the amiable Mrs. Brown tells of her successive loss of six children in India (chap. 11); Miss Matty is financially ruined when her bank fails (chap. 13). Most terrible of all, however, is another early scene (in chap. 6) in which the Jenkyns sisters' young brother, Peter, as a joke disguises himself as a woman (with a pillow standing in for a baby) and is publicly caned by his father, the Rector, in front of a crowd of townspeople. The boy immediately leaves home, never to return while his parents are still alive, thereby blighting the remainder of their lives. Charming, kindly, ironically humorous?

My second orange-eating episode involves a much more self-confident fictive character than Prufrock—the narrator of a novel, *The Sea, the Sea* (1978), by Iris Murdoch (1919–1999), who is obsessed with preparing and consuming food. Concerned about the messiness of eating oranges, his solution is, like that of the Jenkyns sisters, to eat in private: "Oranges should be eaten in solitude and as a treat when one is feeling hungry. They are too messy and overwhelming to form part of an ordinary meal."

John Keats, for one, was not only unafraid to eat a peach but once consumed one (actually, a nectarine) with great gusto while writing a letter to his friend Charles Dilke (22 September 1819). About halfway through the letter comes this passage: "Talking of Pleasure, this moment I was writing with one hand, and with the other holding to my Mouth a Nectarine—good god how fine—It went down soft pulpy, slushy, oozy—all its delicious embonpoint melted down my throat like a large beatified Strawberry." The letter—never sent, by the way, though it eventually ended up in Dilke's possession—was written at Winchester, where Keats was living with his friend, Charles Brown; they were, as always, sorely in need of money (hence the letter to Dilke announcing Keats's decision to rent rooms in London and earn money as a journalist). It is also worth recalling that just three days earlier (19 September 1819) Keats had written the last of his odes, "To Autumn" (in which, it will be recalled from an earlier discussion above, apples are the only fruit to appear).

Where did Keats get his nectarine? Probably from some acquaintance's garden— at least that was his source back in London, as appears in a letter written a month earlier (28 August 1819), to his sister, Fanny. After two weeks, Keats reports, he is thoroughly enjoying Winchester, especially the weather; and, he goes on, "Give me Books, fruit, french wine and fine whether [*sic*] and a little music out of doors . . . and I can pass a summer very quietly." A few sentences later the allusion to fruit is amplified: "I should like now to promenade round you[r] Gardens—apple tasting—pear-tasting— plum<b>-judging—apricot nibbling—peach sc[r]unching—Nectarine-sucking and Melon carving—I have also a great feeling for antiquated cherries full of sugar cracks— and a white currant tree kept for company."

Nectarines, of course, are closely related to peaches, but though peaches go back to antiquity, nectarines seem to have been first recognized as a distinct species in the sixteenth century; the Latin name for peaches, *Amygdalus persica,* reflects European belief as to the origin of the fruit. By the middle of the seventeenth century at least a dozen varieties of nectarines were known in England (Bastard Red, Cluster, Roman Red, Elruge, Green, Little Dainty Green, Little Green, Murry, Muske, Russet, Tawney, White, Yellow), while at this same period, over fifty varieties of peaches were known (see Peachey, *Fruit Variety Register, 1580–1660*). It is obvious that the two species of fruit are closely related: their flesh possesses the same range of colors (white, red, or yellow); they possess similar (though not identical) tastes; their pits can be either clingstone or freestone. These similarities were noted by Charles Darwin (1809–1882) in the course

of analyzing the rather puzzling genetic connections between peaches and nectarines   227
in chapter 10 of his *Variation of Animals and Plants under Domestication* (1883):

> We have excellent evidence of peach-stones producing nectarine-trees,
> and of nectarine-stones producing peach-trees—of the same tree bearing
> peaches and nectarines—of peach-trees suddenly producing by bud-variation
> nectarines (such nectarines reproducing nectarines by seed), as well as fruit
> in part nectarine and in part peach—and, lastly, of one nectarine-tree first
> bearing half-and-half fruit, and subsequently true peaches.

If Keats is enthusiastic about nectarines, Wallace Stevens is equally enthusiastic
about peaches in one of his so-called still life poems, "A Dish of Peaches in Russia"
(1942), but he is less relaxed and less vivid than Keats:

> The peaches are large and round,

> Ah! and red; and they have peach fuzz, ah!
> They are full of juice and the skin is soft.

> They are full of the colors of my village
> And of fair weather, summer, dew, peace.

It must be added that Stevens's poem—which is about exile and self-identity—ends
with a surprising eruption of violence:

> I did not know

> That such ferocities could tear
> One self from another, as these peaches do.

Like many other fruits, peaches were once available only to the affluent. Thus,
Massimo Montanari, in his *The Culture of Food* (1994), tells of a fourteenth-century
Italian novella by Sabadino degli Arienti (d. 1540) in which a peasant is finally caught
after regularly stealing peaches from his master's garden. Captured in an animal trap
and punished by a bath of boiling water, the peasant is admonished: "'In future leave
my fruit alone and eat your own foods which are turnips, garlic, leeks, onions and shal-
lots with sorghum bread.'" Montanari comments that "the recurring behaviour of the
peasant is clearly intended to be transgressive, confrontational and challenging." The
scarcity of fresh fruit in the medieval peasant's diet held for England as well, though
contemporary sources mention some limited consumption of apples, cherries, pears,
and plums (see P. W. Hammond's *Food and Feast in Medieval England* [1995]). People
living in English towns had easier access to fruit (grown often in town gardens) provided they could afford to buy it.

228   With the emergence of still life as a distinctive—though always low status—genre of painting in late-sixteenth-century Europe, all kinds of fruit became popular subjects. (This international artistic phenomenon can be studied to advantage in Ebert-Schifferer's *Still Life,* part 3, "The First Modern Still Lifes, Around 1600.") In Italy, for example, the Milanese painter Ambrogio Figino (1548–1608) was enthusiastically praised for his *Still Life with Peaches,* among the very first Italian still lifes. Figino's picture, painted between 1591 and 1594, is now in a private collection in Bergamo (oil on panel, 8¼ x 11¾ in.); it was the subject of the madrigal "On the Painting of Certain Very Naturalistic Peaches" (1594), by the painter's good friend Gregorio Comanini (ca. 1550–1607), here translated by Helen Langdon in her *Caravaggio: A Life* (1999):

> Nature was mother to us
> On the second bough
> Now we are sons to Painting
> Fruits in unfruiting wood behold us here.
> Not only will you be persuaded by the colour,
> But scent too emanates from what you see.
> Sweet, soft and mellow,
> Your eye devours us all,
> What gentle skill
> Guided the hand that immortalised this fragile
> beauty.

(For a black and white reproduction of Figino's painting of peaches, see Jordan and Cherry's *Spanish Still Life* or Ebert-Schifferer's *Still Life;* for a color reproduction, see Roberto Paolo Ciardi's monograph on Figino [1968].)

Another Lombard painter, in the generation after Figino, Fede Galizia (1578?–ca. 1630), "developed her own compositional style. She always placed her carefully stacked fruits in round bowls, either plain or footed, on the front edge of a wooden table or stone slab" (according to Ebert-Schifferer). A particularly luscious example of her work is *Peaches in a White Ceramic Basket* (ca. 1600–1605), which is in a private collection in Campione (oil on panel, 11¾ x 16¾ in.; for a reproduction, see Ebert-Schifferer).

Probably the best peaches in seventeenth-century Europe were grown in Montreuil, a suburb of Paris, where a tradition of carefully nurturing fruit trees had developed among the local farmers. Frederic Janson relates the following fascinating details:

> Eventually these methods became a secret knowledge guarded by 12 jealous,
> vain clans sharing in the profitable monopoly of producing every year up
> to 100,000 perfect peach specimens. The methods, ideally producing a V-
> shaped trunk dotted with fans and fans of fans to cover a wall, had been

passed from father to son for about six generations. Nothing seems to have been written down. Fierce dogs guarded the enclosed fruit walls to prevent spying and theft of fruit or bud wood. Off and on, envious neighbors started rumors of sorcerers at work, but the peach-enamored Sun King wanted no court case.

The whole question of secret—even disreputable—horticultural methods was referred to by the French Jesuit René Rapin (1627–1687) in the fourth book (on orchards) of his *Hortorum Libri IV* (Four books of gardens), first published in Latin (1661) and then several times reprinted and translated into French, German, Italian, and English. Here, in a translation by James Gardiner (1st ed., 1706), is the relevant passage:

> His strange Increase the Neighbourhood alarms,
> And Envy blackens him with magick Charms.
> How by bad Art the secret Powers he knew
> Of Herbs that on his native Mountains grew,
> And thence with Hands impure forbidden Plenty drew.
> The Charge was mov'd in Court, the Judges sate,
> And heard the Pris'ner in Arrest of Fate:
> He reaching from the Bar the shining Blade,
> Of his old pruning Knife, his Hook and Spade,
> Worn bright with Use, "Behold my magic Spells,
> By these I force my Fruit, by these my Crop excels."
> His Sun-burnt Arms he stretch'd out to the Crowd,
> And his rude Spouse and homely Daughter show'd,
> Each an Accomplice in the guiltless Feat,
> Harden'd with Labour, and imbrown'd with Sweat.
> The honest Countryman obtain'd his Cause,
> And Industry was crown'd with just Applause.

In the next century, the Parisian Abbé Roger Schabol was so impressed with the peaches of Montreuil farmers that he studied their horticultural methods for some twenty-eight years, finally publishing his findings in a French journal in 1755. And Schabol managed, in a way, even to surpass the Montreuil farmers by imprinting the royal initials on the skins of his peaches! This he ingeniously accomplished by a procedure that is explained by Janson: "While still on the tree, these peaches had been wrapped in oiled paper on which the designs were drawn, then cut out to be colored by the sun, a kind of natural anthocyanin trademarking popular in Japan."

Good-sized peaches must have been available in England in the seventeenth century, since, in 1629, referring to the peaches being cultivated by contemporary English farmers, John Parkinson writes: "sometimes as great as a reasonable Apple or Pippin (I speake of some sorts; for there be some kindes that are much smaller)"

230   (quoted by Peachey in his *Fruit Variety Register, 1580–1660*). A century later, we know that Dr. Johnson frequently consumed large peaches. According to his longtime and close friend, Mrs. Thrale, "He usually eat seven or eight large peaches of a morning before breakfast began, and treated them with proportionate attention after dinner again, yet I have heard him protest that he never had quite as much as he wished of wall fruit." ("Wall fruit," by the way, was from trees grown against a wall for support or on south-facing walls for extra reflected warmth.)

What finally made fresh peaches (and other fresh fruit) widely available were certain technological developments in the nineteenth century. In Georgia and South Carolina, for example, where peach horticulture had flourished between 1850 and 1870, economically critical expansion of production was limited by the problem of transporting perishable fruit to distant markets. Railroads with refrigerator cars and the new hardier Elberta peach saved the day. (See Waverly Root and Richard de Rochemont, *Eating in America: A History.*) Later on, peaches flourished in the favorable climate of California, which now grows half the peach crop of the United States. By the early twentieth century, a special method of precooling peaches before they were shipped in ice made transportation feasible even for long distances. The dramatic effects of precooling are illustrated in two contrasting pictures of early Crawford peaches transported from California to New York, painted by Deborah G. Passmore and published as a color lithograph by the United States Department of Agriculture in 1909; the images are approximately life-sized (see plate 15).

Peaches also flourish in central Texas in the so-called hill country around Fredericksburg; hence Naomi Shihab Nye's poem "Going for Peaches, Fredericksburg, Texas" (1986). The speaker, out with some elderly aunts for a drive to the town to buy some peaches, begins:

> Those with experience look for a special kind.
> *Red Globe,* the skin slips off like a fine silk camisole.
> Boy breaks one open with his hands. Yes it's good,
> my old relatives say, but we'll look around.

When they finally do buy some peaches,

> One aunt insists on reloading into her box
> to see the fruit on the bottom.
> One rejects any slight bruise.
> But Ma'am, the seller insists, nature isn't perfect.
> Her hands are spotted, like a peach.

And then the return home and the division of the spoils: the teleology of peach buying has defined a day:

> Everything we have learned so far,
> skins alive and ripening, on a day

> that was real to us, that was summer,
> motion going out and memory coming in.

A pertinent allusion to the geographical distribution of American peach horticulture occurs in the novel *American Pastoral* (1997) by Philip Roth (b. 1933):

> A railroad line used to run up into Morristown from Whitehouse to carry the peaches from the orchards in Hunterdon County. Thirty miles of railroad line just to transport peaches. Among the well-to-do there was a peach craze then in the big cities and they'd ship them from Morristown into New York. The Peach Special. Wasn't that something? On a good day seventy cars of peaches hauled from the Hunterdon orchards. Two million peach trees down there before a blight carried them all away. But he could himself tell her about that train and the trees and the blight when the time came, take her on his own to show her where the tracks used to be. It wouldn't require Orcutt to do it for him.

There are three layers of narration in the novel and all three narrators are showing off their acquaintance with certain details of the local history of Morris County, New Jersey: the Jewish son of immigrants, Seymour Levov ("Swede")—the central character of Roth's novel—is thinking, in the quoted passage, of how he could tell his daughter Merry about an interesting aspect of the history of the county where she has grown up and do so without appealing to the man who is cuckolding him, the architect Orcutt, whose roots in the county go back to Revolutionary times; Roth's fictional creation, the novelist Nathan Zuckerman, in writing about his revered old high school acquaintance, Swede, wants us to recognize that he has done his homework so well that he can at least give the illusion of getting inside Swede's mind; and Roth himself is intent on proving that he can measure up to any other contemporary American novelist in his eye for telling historical detail.

My guess is that we can count on the accuracy of Roth/Zuckerman/Swede's account of peach-growing, at least as far as it goes. There is, however, a long and fascinating history of peaches and their cultivation in the United States stretching back to colonial times, a history recounted by Peter Hatch in his book on the fruits of Jefferson's Monticello (1998). It seems that peaches were used not only for eating but for making brandy and feeding livestock, while peach trees furnished both timber and firewood and also served as boundary markers. All these uses depended on the ease with which peach trees can be grown, providing

> a kind of instant gratification unique among tree fruits by bearing after two or three years, particularly in the sunny microclimate of the [Monticello] south orchard. Their quick growth suggests a perennial vegetable rather than, for example, a venerable, centuries-old apple. Peaches are also easy to propagate; they sprout readily from the stone, and Jefferson himself

232   distinguished the peach as one of the few fruits whose seedling would produce a faithful copy of the original.

On the other hand, as Hatch explains, "the success of American peaches degenerated with cultivation, the depletion of virgin soils, and the ravages of three virulent plagues: peach yellows, plum curculio, and peach tree borers." The first of these plagues is a virus, the second and third are insects. The eventual defense against all of these plagues came with the development of pesticides and new disease-resistant peach varieties.

By the early eighteenth century, pictures of peaches (along with those of many other fruits) began to appear in printed books (though similar books on flowers were much more numerous). Some of the illustrations were in hand-painted color. A survey with catalogue raisonné of the first century of such books may be found in chapter 7, "Prints of Fruit," of Gordon Dunthorne's *Flower and Fruit Prints of the Eighteenth and Early Nineteenth Centuries* (1938).

According to the historian of American horticulture U. P. Hedrick (1870–1951), there appeared in the middle of the nineteenth century a book whose "discussions of insects and fungi of fruit crops were the fullest and most accurate that had yet been published in America." The book was part of an extensive survey of the natural history and agriculture of the state of New York, published between 1842 and 1896 in thirty quarto volumes at a cost of over a million dollars. Part 5 of the survey, edited by Ebenezer Emmons (1799–1863), in an edition of three thousand copies, was called *Agriculture of New-York* and consisted of five volumes: volume 1, geology and soils (1846); volume 2, plant crops (1849); volume 3 fruit (1851); volume 3, fruit illustrations (1851); volume 5, insects (1854). (There seems to be no volume numbered 4).

Emmons lists some sixty varieties of peaches, with twenty-eight singled out for more detailed description. Typical is the "Early Crawford," a freestone variety: "Fruit very large, roundish oval; pointed at the apex; suture shallow. Color yellow; cheek red. Flesh juicy and rich, slightly acid. Ripens at the beginning of Autumn. Late production." The Early Crawford is not one of the eleven peaches and nectarines depicted in the fruit plate volume, which contains over one hundred life-sized hand-colored lithographic illustrations (mostly apples and pears, and, in addition to the peaches, a few plums, cherries, currants, and berries). Not surprisingly, there is considerable variation in the quality of the plates in different copies (I have personally inspected three copies). Emmons himself was dissatisfied with the color plates, complaining in the preface to the plate volume that "both paper and printing are of that character that it was impossible to color the plates, handsomely." (Plate 16 reproduces Emmons's plate of a Golden Rareripe peach, which incorporates in tiny print the words "On Stone by Swinton" in the lower left and "R. H. Pease Lith. Albany" in the lower right.)

The culmination of all the attention devoted to peach-growing by nineteenth-century American horticulturists came with Hedrick's publication, in 1917, of a great quarto volume, *The Peaches of New York*. (This was the fifth in a series; earlier volumes were on apples, grapes, plums, and cherries, and two later volumes were on pears and small fruits.) The scope of the volume is not, in fact, limited to New York State because, as the author explains, *all* varieties of peaches "might be grown in New York and are therefore of interest to the peach-growers of the State." Several hundred peach cultivars—including the leaves and blossoms as well as the pits and fruit—are meticulously described, and there are over eighty excellent life-sized colored illustrations. Just two of the cultivars may be singled out here as examples: the Early Crawford (developed, Hedrick tells us, in New Jersey in the early nineteenth century) and the Elberta (developed in Georgia in 1870). Of the former, we read that "in its season, when well grown, it is unapproachable in quality by any other peach and is scarcely equalled by any other of any season," while of the latter we read that "it leads all other peaches in number of trees in New York and in America." The two varieties are described in minute detail (like each of the other principal varieties); of the more than three hundred words describing the tree, leaves, blossoms, and fruit of the Early Crawford (which may be compared with Emmons's brief description quoted above), I quote just a few about the skin and flesh of the peach: "color golden-yellow, blushed with dark red, splashed and mottled with deeper red; pubescence thick; skin separates from the pulp; flesh deep yellow, rayed with red near the pit, juicy, tender, pleasantly sprightly, highly flavored; very good in quality." (See plates 17 and 18 for reproductions of the Early Crawford and Elberta peaches from Hedrick's volume.) The Elberta from Georgia remains today, in the words of Flowerdew's 1995 guide to fruit growing, "the most popular peach in America." (The peaches of Georgia are memorialized, by the way, on the 1999 United States quarter commemorating the state.)

The mode of reproduction of the color plates in all of Hedrick's volumes issued by the New York Agricultural Experiment Station was color photo-engraving, and this, of course, insured uniformity of quality. Nevertheless, Hedrick is not entirely satisfied, even while claiming that the reproductions of his peaches are more accurate than the reproductions in his earlier volumes on apples, grapes, plums, and cherries; his remarks are worth quoting:

> Although most carefully selected, an illustration of one or two fruits does not give an adequate picture of a variety. Neither does the camera take colors quite as the eye sees them nor can the plate-maker quite reproduce what the camera takes. The illustrations are of life-size as the peaches grow on the grounds of this Station and represent specimens of average size and color. The fruits, as shown in the plates, look small for the reason that a flat picture of a round object minifies size.

The motivation of Hedrick's reproductions of peaches—practical utility for fruit-growers—contrasts sharply, of course, with the motivation of a still life painter. Consider, for example, that almost exactly a century before Hedrick's peach volume

234 appeared, Raphaelle Peale was painting pictures of isolated, individual peaches. We know this, first of all, from a letter of 6 September 1816 in which Peale explains to one of his patrons that an attack of gout in both his hands is preventing him from painting: "I therefore fear that the Season will pass without producing a single Picture, I meant to have devoted all my time, Principally, to Painting of fine Peaches & instead of whole Water Melons, merely single Slices on which I could bestow a finish that would have made them valuable." Also, half a dozen paintings by Peale titled "Still-Life—Peach(s)" are listed (all for sale) in the catalogue of an exhibition of 1817 at the Pennsylvania Academy of the Fine Arts, in Philadelphia. Two of these paintings may well correspond to two paintings (7⅜ x 9 and 7⅜ x 8⅜ in., respectively) now in the San Diego Museum of Art, each depicting a single peach with a leafy twig (figs. 43 and 70 in Nicolai Cikovsky's *Raphaelle Peale Still Lifes;* see plate 19). Cikovsky interprets such paintings—with "the impeccably careful, sensitively balanced, and measured placement of their objects and the geometric purity of their form"—as, on the one hand, responding to Peale's inner need of "some psychological compensation for the instability and disorderliness of his real life" and, on the other hand, responding—in their challenge to the traditional hierarchy of painted subjects—to a "profound and pervasive remaking of political, social, economic, and intellectual order that was the central condition of Raphaelle Peale's age." As for artistic style, Peale was able to draw on Netherlandish still life, which "held an aptness of meaning for an American painter . . . working at a time of high national consciousness and democratic feeling—because of the political and social pertinence of its associations with republican government and middle-class culture."

One foreign observer who understood that even Americans of low income towards the end of the nineteenth century could afford to eat fresh fruit was Matthew Arnold (1822–1888). In his essay "Civilisation in the United States," composed in January 1888—four years after his lecture tour of the United States—Arnold praised the political institutions and the social egalitarianism of the country but deplored its "civilisation" (what today might be called its "culture"). Whatever the superficiality of Arnold's views—for which he was roundly criticized by numerous American writers —we can perhaps rely on his observation that "even luxuries of a certain kind are within a labouring man's easy reach. . . . The abundance and cheapness of fruit is a great boon to people of small incomes in America." One may, however, reasonably resist his further admonition not to "believe the Americans when they extol their peaches as equal to any in the world, or better than any in the world; they are not to be compared to peaches grown under glass." As an amateur fruit-grower himself, Arnold should have known better than to prefer hothouse fruit to the real thing!

An American professional peach grower in the late twentieth century has written a book about his experiences as a small family farmer in California. David Mas Masumoto (b. 1954) is a third generation Japanese American who, after graduating from college, took over his father's fifteen-acre orchard of 1,500 peach trees in the San

Joaquin Valley. But his book, *Epitaph for a Peach: Four Seasons on My Family Farm* (1995), begins with an account of the bulldozing in 1987 of all the remaining 350 of these trees. The problem was that the particular variety of peach Masumoto grew could no longer command a market: Sun Crests "turn an amber gold rather than the lipstick red that seduces the public" and furthermore possess an unacceptably brief shelf life. On the other hand, according to Masumoto, "Sun Crest is one of the last remaining truly juicy peaches."

The bulk of Masumoto's book explains what he does as a peach farmer during each season of the year; with some simplification, the seasonal activities may be described as *thinning* in spring, *picking* in summer, *pruning* (and occasional *planting* of new peach trees) in winter. What about autumn? This would be the time when the farmer decides to eliminate an "obsolete" peach orchard. It is also the season when cover crops—vetches, clovers, and wildflowers—are planted. I would like to quote a few of Masumoto's more eloquent and informative passages about each of the first three activities.

> In the spring I hired thinners to enter my orchards and destroy over half the Spring Lady crop. They climb ladders and knock off thousands of the tiny peaches with their fingers. The earth is covered with these little peach corpses, they crunch beneath your feet as you walk. The sound of a crew thinning peaches reminds me of a thunderstorm, the falling fruit knocking against ladder steps and pattering on the ground, building from a light tapping to a dazzling crescendo as the crew picks up speed.

Masumoto is of two minds about all this destruction: fewer peaches may represent lower profits but more peaches may reduce size and therefore marketability. Eventually, he opts for "only a single peach per hanger, or stem, about two hundred peaches per tree."

Next comes summer picking:

> Peaches are picked in "rounds," beginning at the top of the tree, where the fruit ripens first. Pickers work their way down a tree with each round. Three to four times we will enter a field, glean the best, and leave the rest to mature and grow. It may take up to two weeks to complete the harvest. The first round produces some of the best fruit, though it's expensive for a large crew to harvest them. Most of a laborer's time is spent moving from branch to branch and tree to tree, searching for the ripe fruit.

Finally, when the peach trees are entirely bare in winter, the pruning occurs:

> My best pruning efforts seek order out of the rank growth while acknowledging the seeming disorder nature has left me. Each tree will have branches I don't like. Some are too horizontal, with flat surfaces begging to be burned in the summer sun. Others may fork too close to a neighbor

and will compete for sunlight. A few thick and vigorous shoots push straight upward from the main trunk, and I'll have to trust the weight of the fruit to pull and bend the branch down into a graceful, natural bow shape. A good pruning job forces me to acknowledge and live with the wild. . . .

The best pruners dance with their shears, slicing and cutting and snipping with a cadence. Their eyes guide their movements, building to a crescendo where enough space is opened between hangers and the pruning feels complete.

Among the many Americans eating all those peaches in the nineteenth century, millions belonged to the middle class, and many of them were growing increasingly anxious about their appearance while eating fresh fruit. One late-nineteenth-century American guide to manners, James Bethuel Smiley's *Modern Manners and Social Forms* (1889), offers this advice for eating fruit: "It is always better to use a fork, even at the peril of seeming affected than to offend the taste of another by making a mess with the fingers, as some careless people often do." Smiley's qualms about the proper way to eat fruit were anticipated by an anonymous early-eighteenth-century French author whose concerns did not reach to the juiciness of the eaten fruit:

You should not throw bones or eggshells or the skin of any fruit onto the floor.

The same is true of fruit stones. It is more polite to remove them from the mouth with two fingers than to spit them into one's hand.

Another possible explanation for Prufrock's hesitation about eating a peach might be the rarity and high cost of the fruit in the England of 1911, when Eliot completed the final version of the poem. (It is true that Eliot wrote most of the poem in Munich, but the tea and marmalade identify the setting as English.) It would seem that peaches were also rare in England after World War II, for Ted Hughes writes, in the last six lines of "Fulbright Scholars" (1998), that he tasted his first fresh peach in the year Sylvia Plath arrived in England as a Fulbright scholar (1955):

Was it then I bought a peach? That's as I remember.
From a stall near Charing Cross Station.
It was the first fresh peach I had ever tasted.
I could hardly believe how delicious.
At twenty-five I was dumbfounded afresh
By my ignorance of the simplest things.

In these lines—the last five of the initial poem of a book devoted to his relationship to Sylvia Plath—Hughes seems eager to characterize himself as youthful and inexperienced, using a peach to do it, freshness being ascribed both to the peach and to Hughes's response to the taste of the peach. This presentation of a passive and

"dumbfounded" self persists throughout the book, as several of the early reviewers
have complained.

Peaches must have become more familiar in England by 1961, which was the year that Roald Dahl (1916–1990) published his first children's book, *James and the Giant Peach,* in Britain and the United States. (A film based on the book appeared in 1996.) In the story, James Henry Trotter's entry into the peach "almost as big as a house" is dramatic:

> The tunnel was damp and murky, and all around him there was the curious bittersweet smell of fresh peach. The floor was soggy under his knees, the walls were wet and sticky, and peach juice was dripping from the ceiling. James opened his mouth and caught some of it on his tongue. It tasted delicious.
>
> He was crawling uphill now, as though the tunnel were leading straight toward the very center of the gigantic fruit. Every few seconds he paused and took a bite out of the wall. The peach flesh was sweet and juicy, marvelously refreshing.

Later, after the creatures who inhabit the interior of the giant peach accept James's suggestion that they avoid starvation by eating their surroundings, the exuberant Centipede "with his mouth full of peach and with juice running down all over his chin, suddenly burst into song." What he sings is a kind of ode to the peach, including six stanzas describing delectable nonesense foods (such as "jellied gnats and dandyprats and earwigs cooked in slime" and "Hot noodles made from poodles on a slice of garden hose") and concluding with this paean to the peach:

> "Now comes," the Centipede declared, "the burden of my speech:
> These foods are rare beyond compare—some are right out of reach;
> But there's no doubt I'd go without
> A million plates of each
> For one small mite,
> One tiny bite
> Of this FANTASTIC PEACH!"

An appearance of peaches in popular culture is the cover song "Peaches" (1995) by a rock group called the Presidents of the United States of America. Here are the three refrains:

> I'm moving to the country
> I'm gonna eat (me) a lot of peaches.
>
> If I had my little way
> I'd eat peaches every day.
>
> Millions of peaches, peaches for me
> Millions of peaches, peaches for free.

A rather different experience of the messiness which Prufrock feared, Keats and James Henry Trotter enjoyed, and Ted Hughes probably ignored is conveyed by Christina Rossetti in her magical long poem, "Goblin Market" (written 1859; published 1861). The poem is about two sisters, one of whom, "sweet-tooth Laura," is tempted to buy the fruit of some "goblin men," which includes apples, quinces, lemons, oranges, cherries, melons, raspberries, peaches, mulberries, cranberries, crabapples, dewberries, pineapples, blackberries, apricots, strawberries, grapes, pomegranates, dates, bullaces (a kind of plum), pears, greengages, damsons, bilberries, currants, gooseberries, barberries, figs, and citrons (ll. 5–29). (One fruit not mentioned in this large compendium is the banana, presumably because it was not yet obtainable in Britain at the time Rossetti was writing. Even in the northern markets of the United States it was not until the 1880s that bananas began to become available—see W. J. Rorabaugh's essay, "Beer, Lemonade, and Propriety in the Gilded Age" [1987].)

As payment for their fruit, the goblin men exact a lock of Laura's golden hair:

> She clipped a precious golden lock,
> She dropped a tear more rare than pearl,
> Then sucked their fruit globes fair or red:
> Sweeter than honey from the rock.
> Stronger than man-rejoicing wine,
> Clearer than water flowed that juice;
> She never tasted such before,
> How should it cloy with length of use?
> She sucked and sucked and sucked the more
> Fruits which that unknown orchard bore;
> She sucked until her lips were sore;
> Then flung the emptied rinds away
> But gathered up one kernel-stone,
> And knew not was it night or day
> As she turned home alone.

Laura is unable to find the goblin men again and is unsuccessful in her attempt to get the single pit she has saved to germinate; her hair turns gray and she dwindles away to the point of death. Her sister Lizzie is determined to obtain more of the goblin fruit to revive Laura, but the goblin men, after accepting her "silver penny," try to persuade Lizzie herself to eat the addictive fruit. Finally, in exasperation, the goblin men, with horrific violence, squash the fruit all over Lizzie's face, while she clenches her teeth against the assault. But though kicked, knocked, mauled, and mocked, Lizzie stands her ground, "Like a fruit-crowned orange tree / White with blossoms honey-sweet / Sore beset by wasp and bee"; she even

> laughed in heart to feel the drip
> Of juice that syrupped all her face,

> And lodged in dimples of her chin,
> And streaked her neck which quaked like curd.

Returning home all sticky, Lizzie implores her sister to

> Hug me, kiss me, suck my juices
> Squeezed from goblin fruits for you,
> Goblin pulp and goblin dew.
> Eat me, drink me, love me;
> Laura, make much of me;

Laura does as she is told and is saved. Eventually, we are told, both girls grow up to have children of their own, and Laura entertains them with the story of her rescue by heroic Lizzie, the final moral being: "there is no friend like a sister."

There have been many divergent interpretations of Rossetti's poem, some as an allegory (which Rossetti herself denied), others, more literal, in terms of some species of love between the sisters. In a useful critical summary of this wide range of interpretations, Ellen Moers makes clear her own preference for reading "Goblin Market" as "a poem . . . about the erotic life of children." Moers, however, ignores a vital piece of evidence: the pit (or "kernel-stone") that Laura futilely plants and waters with her tears. Clearly, eating the goblin fruit—or, perhaps more precisely, exchanging her lock of hair for the goblin fruit—has aged Laura and made her sterile. Imbibing goblin fruit juices—or, perhaps more precisely, being fed goblin fruit juices by her sister— restores Laura's youth and permits her eventually to bear children.

Other interpretive hypotheses for "Goblin Market" have suggested that the opposition between the wayward Laura and the saintly Lizzie reflects Rossetti's great interest in fallen women (D. R. M. Bentley), or that Laura's pattern of bingeing on fruit and then fasting reflects the high incidence of eating disorders among Victorian women (Paula Marantz Cohen). But neither of these hypotheses requires that the food consumed in the poem be fruit. Richard Menke, on the other hand, calls our attention to the economics of fruit in mid-nineteenth-century Britain, specifically, to the development of techniques for insuring a steady supply of fruit by "forcing" in hot-houses. (Menke even suggests that Laura's failure to get her kernel-stone to grow points to a failure in horticultural technique!) Rossetti would certainly have been aware of the necessity for growing fruit out of season to satisfy the rapidly increasing demands of the domestic market, since the weeks just before the date written on the manuscript of "Goblin Market" (27 April 1859) had witnessed a disastrous spring frost: "Given the destruction of the new fruit crop and the subsequent scarcity of imported fruit, England in late April 1859 must have been a particularly fruit-less place." Menke's larger claim—that "*Goblin Market* may not offer an analysis of the commodity form as Marx does, but it incisively locates the play of surface and secret in the commodity and suggests the perils presented by its inarguable allure"—I cannot pause to evaluate here.

240   It is fascinating to consider the lengths to which a gardener must go in forcing the growth of hothouse fruit; the entire process may be followed in detail in the diary kept by William Taylor, the Marquess of Bath's head gardener at Longleat. Perhaps most surprising at first sight is the *danger* of too much sunshine, as appears from some of the observations Taylor recorded in January of 1875 (quoted here from the excellent book by Joan Morgan and Alison Richards, *A Paradise out of a Common Field* [1990]):

> We have actually had a whole day's sunshine, a blessing not to be lightly esteemed. I was a little timid in the morning, anxious to make the most of every ray of light, but half afraid that tender Vine leaves which had never seen real daylight before, would not bear such an abundance of it. Peaches, too, with flowers fully expanded under adverse circumstances, would they bear it?

During the morning the outside air must be gradually admitted to prevent the temperature from rising too much but then by noon the ventilation must begin to be reduced so the temperature will not drop too low:

> . . . all excepting the Peach house are entirely closed soon after one o'clock. Were the peaches a little forwarder, and fairly commenced swelling they would be closed up too; but probably all the flowers are not yet fertilised, and during the process of fertilisation a close atmosphere is not good for them.

We have earlier discussed the possibility that "Goblin Market" is, in some obscure hesitant way, about female fertility, and this hesitancy is concretely exemplified in Rossetti's descriptions of peaches. These are, indeed, perceptively characterized as "bloom-down-cheeked" (l. 9) and "with a velvet nap" (l. 178); and, of course, like all the the fruit, the peaches are described as succulent and sweet to the taste. What is missing is the erotic suggestiveness of the peach's *shape*—precisely what is fastened on by Erica Jong (b. 1942) in her untitled poem (1974) about "Adam naming the fruit / after the creation of fruit." (In Genesis 2.20, it will be recalled, Adam names only the animals.) Omitting Jong's description of Adam naming the pomegranates, quinces, plums, watermelons, pumpkins, and tomatoes, I cite only the lines about peaches:

> the tip of his penis licking
> the cheeks of the peach,
> [. . . . .]
>
>   peach
>   peach
>   peach

peach
peach

he sighs

to kingdom come.

Jong's erotic peach has been anticipated by the Italian Renaissance writer Pietro Aretino (1492–1556) in the last of his six dialogues (1536) on the (sexual) ways of women. The point of Aretino's satire is all too obvious: women—whether nuns, wives, or whores—living in a perpetual state of sexual excitement are uncontrollably promiscuous, as illustrated by a seemingly endless (and soon tiresomely repetitious) sequence of obscene episodes. Here is the prologue to the last of the dialogues:

> The next day they arrived as planned and sat down under the peach tree. The midwife sat between the wetnurse and Nanna, while like a gallant Pippa sat opposite the midwife. Just at that point a large peach, which had remained on the tree, fell on the midwife's head, and the wetnurse said, while laughing: "Now you can't deny that when men made you give them the peaches of your ass, you didn't like to."

The translation (1971) is by Raymond Rosenthal, who tells us in his preface that the Italian text he used was that "recently published [1969] by Laterza in Italy under the title *Sei Giornate* and edited by the Renaissance scholar, Giovanni Aquilecchia." Unfortunately, the passage I have quoted about peaches is not present in Aquilecchia's text, nor in another critical edition by Giuseppe Guido Ferrero (1970), which I have consulted. Perhaps Rosenthal found the peaches passage in some early edition of Aretino's dialogues. I might add that a similar passage in the first dialogue (about the sexual prowess of nuns and priests) *is* present in Aquilecchia's Italian text, where the conversation is said to take place under a fig tree, and while no allusion to figs occurs in the dialogue itself, this was undoubtedly because the significance of figs would have been perfectly clear to the intended readers.

Interestingly, in D. H. Lawrence's "Peach"—belonging to the sequence of six poems about fruit in his *Birds, Beasts, and Flowers!*—peach stones are characterized not in terms of female fertility but as possible missiles, hence as aggressive objects, which, given Lawrence's well-known views, we can safely take to be male: "Would you like to throw a stone at me? / Here, take all that's left of my peach." If (plausibly enough) the speaker is taken to be a man and the "you" being addressed a woman, *he* is demanding that *she* be aggressive only on *his* terms. This becomes even clearer in the last two lines of the poem: "And because I say so, you would like to throw something at me. / Here, you can have my peach stone." This view of the relations between the sexes is Lawrence at his least appealing. And here is Lawrence's image of the peach:

Why the groove?
Why the lovely, bivalve roundnesses?
Why the ripple down the sphere?
Why the suggestion of incision?

The extreme anthropomorphism of the metaphor makes it precisely *not* an instance of what the editors of Lawrence's collected poems (de Sola Pinto and Roberts) call "the immediate apprehension of the flux of life, especially of sexual life, in non-human organisms."

Philip Roth prefers the nectarine, or hairless peach, but the same portion of the anatomy in characterizing the woman Portnoy calls "the Monkey": "She has an ass on her with the swell and the cleft of the world's most perfect nectarine." That women are now beginning to claim their own rights in these matters may be inferred from "Ass" (1987), a poem by the American Sandra Cisneros (b. 1954), containing these lines: "Pomegranate and apple / hath not such tempting / allure to me / as your hypnotic / anatomy." The anatomical feature on which Lawrence, Roth, and Cisneros dwell is present, of course, in all human beings—but also, Francis Ponge suggests, in angels; the thought occurs in his prose poem "The Apricot" (1942, translated by John Montague):

> The only possible division that presents itself is into halves: it's an angel's backside turned round, or that of Baby Jesus on a napkin fold.
>
> ~
>
> Nulle autre division n'y est d'ailleurs préparée, qu'en deux: c'est un cul d'ange à la renverse, ou d'enfant-jésus sur la nappe.

Here, the diminished size of the fruit (apricot instead of nectarine) suggests a physically diminished—but also infinitely more exalted!—vehicle for the metaphor.

But let us return to the extreme juiciness of certain fruits and consider the mango. Sometimes referred to as "the peach of the tropics," mangoes are increasingly available outside the tropical regions where they are grown. A brief description of the mango tree from *Taylor's Guide to Fruits and Berries* is worth quoting:

> Mango trees (*Mangifera indica*) are evergreens that usually reach about 20 to 30 feet tall in cultivation. They have a wide-spreading crown and dense, narrow leaves, with new growth often tinged red. Creamy yellow to red flowers are borne in long sprays at the end of each branch, with hundreds of flowers in each cluster. The fruits dangle on long "strings," an eye-catching arrangement.

The mango is believed to have been cultivated in India as long as 4, 000 years ago and both twigs and blossoms from the mango tree are used in Hindu ceremonial rites. It is possible that an independent origin of the mango was in Southeast Asia; in any case, in his foreword to an old bibliography of writings on the mango (1950), J. J. Ochse of the University of Miami tells of an old Javan myth involving the mango:

> In the native Javan myth of Surya Bai, the daughter of the sun was pursued by a witch (Surya—in the poetic Javanese language, the sun is still "suria"). In order to escape from her, she disguised herself in a gold lotos. The King fell in love with this beautiful flower, which was thrown into a fire by the witch because of envy. A mango tree grew out of the ashes, and the King fell first in love with the flowers and then with the fruit. When the last fruit ripened and fell on the ground, the daughter of the sun appeared again in her real form and was recognized by the prince as his wife, whom he had thought lost a long time before.

No trace of these Asian associations of the mango seems to be present in the mango episodes we are about to examine from the Caribbean culture area. What does always seem to be present in these episodes is an emotional attachment to the fruit every bit as powerful as the North American attachment to apples.

The juiciness of mangoes is used by the Guyanese writer John Agard (b. 1949) to mark a profound cultural difference between his native country and England (where he has resided since 1977), in his poem "English Girl Eats Her First Mango (a kind of love poem)" (1983). Consisting of ninety-six brief, unpunctuated, occasionally rhyming lines, the poem opens with a dazzling evocation of juiciness:

> If I did tell she
> hold this gold
> of sundizzy
> tonguelicking juicy
> mouthwater flow
> ripe with love
> from the tropics
>
> she woulda tell me
> trust you to be
> melodramatic
>
> so I just say
> taste this mango

When the English girl asks how to eat a mango, the poet replies:

> do like me mother
> used to do
> and squeeze

till the flesh
turn syrup
nibble a hole
then suck the gold
like bubby
in child mouth
squeeze and tease out
every drop of spice

sounds nice
me friend tell me

and I remind she
that this ain't
apple core
so don't forget
the seed
suck that too
the sweetest part
the juice does run
down to you heart

Having eaten her mango, the English girl now asks to borrow a hanky to wipe the sticky juice from her fingers; the poet replies:

what hanky
you talking bout
you don't know
when you eat mango
you hanky
is you tongue

man just lick
you finger
you call that
culture
lick you finger
you call that
culture

unless you prefer
to call it

colonization
in reverse

Another celebration of the messy juiciness of mangoes—this time by a Cuban American writer—is found in a prose poem by Richard Blanco (b. 1966), "Mango, Number 61" (1998). Blanco spends the first quarter of his poem explaining the origin of "number 61." It seems that in the neighborhood where he grew up—according to a biographical note at the end of his book, this was in Miami—when placing bets or selecting lottery numbers one uses a system correlating numbers (from one to one hundred) with important objects or events. Thus, in one such system, *dinero* (money) was ten, *coco* (coconut) was seventy, *melón* (melon) was eighty-nine, and *mango* (mango) was sixty-one. There follows a series of propositions about mangoes:

Mango was fruit wrapped in brown paper bags, hidden like ripening secrets in the kitchen oven. Mango was the perfect housewarming gift and a marmalade dessert with thick slices of cream cheese at birthday dinners and Thanksgiving. Mangos, watching like amber cat's eyes. Mangos, perfectly still in their speckled maroon shells like giant unhatched eggs. . . . Mango was *Abuela* [Grandmother] and I hunched over the counter covered with the Spanish newspaper, devouring the dissected flesh of the fruit slithering like molten gold through our fingers, the nectar cascading from our binging chins, *Abuela* consumed in her rapture and convinced that I absolutely loved mangos. Those messy mangos. Number 79 was *cubano*—us, and number 93 was *revolución,* though I always thought it should be 58, the actual year of the revolution—the reason why, I'm told, we live so obsessively and nostalgically eating number 61's, *mangos,* here in number 87, *América.*

But a poet writing about mangoes need not dwell on their juiciness. Here, for example, is the Haitian poet Duracine Vaval (1879–1952) offering a gift of a basket of mangoes to an unnamed recipient in "The Mangoes," with mention of mango juice—*sève* (literally, sap)— deferred until the very last line of the sonnet (translated by Donald Devenish Walsh):

To intoxicate you with the wine of things,
Might I not offer you a pale bouquet where roses fail?
A poem pleasing in its even rhythms?
I send you then a basket of mangoes.
[Or, je t'envoie une corbeille de mangos.]

Desire clings to their yellow tawny flesh.
The savour of the soil lies deep within them.
Their dusky tang of camphor or of muscatel
Filters scent-born into the very soul.

And these mangoes, honey-sweet, that decked the hedge,
[Et ces mangos de miel qui pavoissaient la haie,]
They are fragrant with black shadow, with the sun,
Fragrant with a true and love-provoking breath.

In the orchard that bleeds in its vermilion cloak
The golden mango surpasses in prime sweetness
[La mangue couleur d'or passe en douceur première]
Our royal fruits swollen with juice and light!
[Nos fruits royaux gorgés de sève et de lumière!]

Stories about cravings for mangoes (and lemons) during pregnancy are the subject of "Mangos y limones" (1996), by the American writer Pat Mora (b. 1942). Mora explains in a note that she was told these stories by a Salvadoran woman now living in California with three children back home in El Salvador. The first stanza tells of eating an entire jar full of "*mangos,* gold / flesh fermenting in salt water," and the third of eating twenty-five lemons, "tart yellow moons she dug into salt / in her palm, chewing lemon after lemon on the bus home"; the fourth, concluding, stanza contains the woman's reminiscences:

The mother thinks of them back in El Salvador,
when she slices *limones* or peels *mangos.* Yellow
scents pucker her memory, awaken her mouth then
and its cravings, the aching for fruit and hunger
for grains of sweet salt. Her body thicker now,
she slides a slice of *mango* between her lips,
laughs about once eating twenty-five frosted lemons,
her mouth full of her own stories.

Two other short stories featuring mangoes further support my decision to give the fruit equal billing with peaches in the title of this chapter. One story, "Tales Told under the Mango Tree" (1990), is by Judith Ortiz Cofer (b. 1952) and concerns a magical mango tree which serves as a "throne" for her grandmother, "Mamá," as she spins tales about the legendary feats of "a girl who was so smart that she was known throughout Puerto Rico as María Sabida." Cofer's story actually begins with one of María Sabida's exploits and only after three-and-a-half pages do we meet Mamá herself when she announces the end of *her* story with a nonsense phrase, "colorín, colorado este cuento se ha acabado" (this story has ended). The voice then shifts to that of the primary narrator (hard to distinguish from the author), who begins by describing Mamá's mango tree:

I remember that tree as a natural wonder. It was large, with a trunk that took four or five children holding hands to reach across. Its leaves were so thick that the shade it cast made a cool room where we took refuge from the hot sun. When an unexpected shower caught us there, the women had time to gather their embroidery materials before drops came through the leaves.

So, the mango tree protects against heat and storm. But it is also empowering, for "it was under that mango tree that I first began to feel the power of words." And though there is something potentially dangerous about the mango tree—it is located, after all, behind barbed wire "on land that belonged to 'The American,' or at least to the sugar refinery that he managed"—nevertheless, "during mango season we threw rocks at the branches of our tree, hanging low with fruit. Later in the season, a boy would climb to the highest branches for the best fruit—something I always yearned to do, but was not allowed to: too dangerous." And soon, the primary narrator recalls, she began to make up stories of her own about María Sabida, "listening all the while to that inner voice which, when I was very young, sounded just like Mamá's when she told her stories in the parlor or under the mango tree." Thus, in the penultimate sentence of Cofer's story her protagonist comes to realize that the mango tree is not essential to story-telling (the parlor, for example, will do) and she can conclude: "As I gained more con-fidence in my own ability, the voice telling the story became my own." We have witnessed the coming of age not just of a woman and not just of a writer but of a woman-writer.

The Cuban American writer Vivian Leal (b. 1965) begins her story, "Mangoes" (1996), with a little essay:

Ah, to bite into the ticklish flesh of a ripe red and yellow mango. One has to be careful with mangoes: If they ripen too long on the tree, the birds will come and peck at them. The trick is to pluck them from the tree a hot day away from their lusty red ardor. Left unrefrigerated, they remember their tree-bound passion so that their light pink blush continues to deepen into full embarrassment. If you don't eat them then, they rot.

The story that follows centers on Margarita, the matriarch of a family of Cubans in exile (in the United States, most likely Miami). Margarita has had a stroke, is speech-less, barely able to walk by herself. Her family home was the lavish estate of Torrecillas, "mansion of thirty-two rooms, fragrant wicker, silver and crystal, inherited jewels, and ceremony," rumored to be occupied at present by Raúl Castro. She now inhabits a cramped "rotting house"—all her unemployed, alcoholic husband, Fausto, can man-age. At least, outside the house is a mango tree, though its fruit is far inferior to that of Torrecillas, "the best in the country, much smoother than the ones Luz so frantically collected, sliced, and serves to her now for breakfast." Luz—the Dominican maid—is catering to Margarita's one surviving passion—for mangoes—but Margarita is never permitted to walk outside and pick the fruit herself. The climax of the story occurs when Luz and her lover are discovered one night stealing money from under Fausto's

248   bed. The thieves get away even though Margarita has succeeded in waking her husband. The next day Margarita, unattended, is able to fix Fausto a scotch and then wander, "out the door, down the lawn stairs, up the street . . . pajama-clad," until she
triumphantly reaches the treeless, crime-ridden park, where "she could still hear her
mangoes drop—those juicy sounds, like the watery thud of lifeless bodies falling to the
ground." I should add that my outline of the plot ignores many members of three generations of Margarita's extended family whose personalities and foibles enhance Leal's
portrait of the lifestyles of this particular Cuban emigré family.

The contrast between two different kinds of mangoes becomes, at the hands of
the Chinese-Malaysian-American writer Shirley Geok-lin Lim (b. 1944), a way of characterizing her own mixed and deeply divided identity. In her "Mango" (1998), there is,
first, "A mango at the New York A.&P. / at eighty-nine American cents each, / heaped
by apples: a stony red, puffy / hybrid all the way from Acapulco," and then, "Crescent
mangoes like smooth-thighed trailer- / girls from Siam." On her return to Malaysia, the
speaker eats one of the latter mangoes, "Solid, / sour, it cuts the back of the throat, torn
/ taste, like love grown difficult or separate," and is moved to her concluding question:

> Where do we go from here, carrying
> those sad eyes under the mango trees,
> with our sauces, our petty hauntings?

The mango—or, at least, eating it in a certain way—has been identified with
poetry itself by the Jamaican writer Lorna Goodison (b. 1947), in her "The Mango of
Poetry" (1999). She associates the mango tree with her prematurely dead father:

> The tree by way of compensation
> bears fruit all year round
> in profusion and overabundance
> making up for the shortfall
>
> of my father's truncated years.
> I'd pick this mango with a cleft stick,
> then I'd wash it and go to sit
> upon the front wall of our yard.
>
> I would not peel it all back
> to reveal its golden entirety,
> but I would soften it by rolling
> it slowly between my palms.
>
> Then I'd nibble a neat hole
> at the top of the skin pouch

and then pull the pulp
up slowly into my mouth.

I'd do all this while wearing
a bombay-colored blouse
so that the stain of the juice
could fall freely upon me.

And I say that this too would be
powerful and overflowing
and a fitting definition
of what is poetry.

Like other fruits, the mango can be invoked as a source of spiritual or psychological insight, as in "Mangoes" (1992), by the American poet Laurie Kutchins. Watching her mother eating mangoes induces fear—fear that being born is just a prelude to
being consumed by her mother. But by learning to eat mangoes herself the daughter
begins to realize her power to strike out on her own, in the last words of the poem,
"leaving her [mother] behind." If it is true, as Neal Bowers says in his foreword to
Kutchins's volume *Between Towns* (1992), that "central to her endeavor is . . . a wonderful relinquishing of self to participate in something larger and more important than
the individual ego," then "Mangoes" is an exception: both its strengths and its weak-
nesses are bound up with a brooding self-absorbedness. The best lines, for me, come
in the first stanza:

I learned to eat mangoes from my mother.
I learned to eat them from a small plate
under the bedside light when it was late and the moon
and I were sleepless.
I watched her suck and slurp the mango's beauty,
as if she were eating the moon or her own children.
She carved and devoured
the agreeable pulp and I feared her
hunger, the imprint of teeth in skin.
I eat mangoes for the sound through my lips is a lullaby,
the sweet juice is an ointment, a slick thread
I lick and erase
between her chin and mine.

The expression of what might be called mango-ecstasy can reach too high a
register—a voice which becomes both too shrill and too predictable, as in these
excerpts from the most recent of the poems in my mango collection:

> I take this champagne mango
> entering the monastery
> of its plump flesh peel by peel,
> crescent by crescent sliding
> lush gold into my mouth,
>   [. . . .]
> the juice drips down my chin,
> between my breasts, essence
> of mango my barest wish.
>   [. . . .]
>   I say *mango*
> as if it were prayer and orchard,
>   [. . . .]
> Add mango to the list of all that is
> too wonderful for me.

I put my hand on my mouth and bow down.

The lines are from "Mango" (1999), by Margaret Gibson, in *The Georgia Review* (1999).

Is there anybody who really dislikes peaches or mangoes? (Not Prufrock, of course.) Well, consider the short essay, "The Last Peach," published in *The London Magazine* for April 1825, by Charles Lamb (1775–1834), which begins: "I am the miserablest man living. Give me counsel, dear Editor. I was bred up in the strictest principles of honesty, and have passed my life in punctual adherence to them. Integrity might be said to be ingrained in our family. Yet I live in constant fear of one day coming to the gallows." The writer goes on to explain that he works in a banking-house and fears he may be tempted someday to "commit a forgery, or do some equally vile thing." Now, anyone reading this at the time would have been immediately reminded of the notorious case of a banker named Henry Fauntleroy, convicted of forgery, and hanged just a few months earlier (on 30 November 1824). But what exactly is worrying the writer? He explains in a long paragraph which constitutes the real point of the essay:

> When a child, I was once let loose, by favour of a nobleman's gardener, into his lordship's magnificent fruit garden, with full leave to pull the currants and the gooseberries; only I was interdicted from touching the wall fruit. Indeed, at that season (it was the end of Autumn), there was little left. Only on the south wall (can I forget the hot feel of the brickwork?) lingered the one last peach. Now, peaches are a fruit which I always had, and still have, an almost utter aversion to. There is something to my palate singularly harsh and repulsive in the flavour of them. I know not by what demon of contradiction inspired; but I was haunted with an irresistible

desire to pluck it. Tear myself as often as I would from the spot, I found myself still recurring to it; till, maddening with desire (desire I cannot call it), with wilfulness rather, —without appetite, —against appetite, I may call it, —in an evil hour I reached out my hand, and plucked it. Some few rain-drops just then fell; the sky (from a bright day) became overcast; and I was a type of our first parents, after the eating of that fatal fruit. I felt myself naked and ashamed, stripped of my virtue, spiritless. The downy fruit, the sight of which rather than its savour had tempted me, dropped from my hand, never to be tasted. All the commentators in the world cannot per-suade me but that the Hebrew word, in the second chapter of Genesis, translated "apple," should be rendered "peach." Only this way can I reconcile that mysterious story.

Lamb has produced a version of the pear theft scene (to be discussed in chapter 13, "Pears") in the *Confessions* (397–400 C.E.) of St. Augustine (354–430). Lamb even makes explicit the analogy with the temptation in Eden, so it is hard to believe the echo of Augustine was inadvertent. As for the Fauntleroy case, Lamb was rather obsessed with it, as appears from several letters to his friends.

My second case of dislike for—or, at least, indifference to—peaches occurs in "Peaches" (1998), by the American poet Jack Gilbert (b. 1925). Finding himself—in the words of the second and third lines of the poem—"at the edge / of emptiness, absence and heat everywhere," the speaker for no particular reason begins to remember peaches:

> A strange, almost gray kind
> that had little taste when he got them home, and that
> little not much good. But there had to be a reason
> why people bought them. So he decided to make jam.
> When he smelled the scorching, they were already tar.
> Scraped out the mess and was glad to have it over.
> Found himself licking the crust on the spoon. Next day
> he had eaten the rest, still not sure whether he liked
> it or not. And never able to find any of them since.

The conventional pleasurable associations of peaches form a proper foil to the deso-lation expressed in the first six lines of the poem. The speaker seems barely capable of activity of any kind, and when he does act he is indecisive, blundering, and ineffec-tual. Is there an unspoken assumption that anyone who cannot appreciate peaches must be doomed?

The distaste of another American poet, Rita Dove (b. 1952), for peaches—more precisely, for a particular peach orchard on a particular occasion—is very different from Gilbert's rather unfocussed uneasiness. In "The Peach Orchard" (1999), the speaker is suffering from a common complaint—the loss of a lover: "he's / gone, just like the wind / when the air stands still." Her loss is characterized as dehumanizing and "shameful"; she is "drifting speechless and pale" like the petals of the peach trees' blossoms. But in a kind of masochistic frenzy she is is driven to the peach orchard, with its "stone floor" (the ground littered with peach stones?). I must say I find the last of the six five-line stanzas extremely irritating—but perhaps that's the point:

> O these
>
> trees, shedding all
> over themselves.
> Only a fool
> would think such frenzy
> beautiful.

For yet another American poet, Dave Morice (b. 1946), peaches seem to be simply one more topic for a perfunctory poem, since his "Peaches" (1973) was one of a thousand poems he wrote "from 10:00 A.M. to 10:00 P.M., March 3, 1973—the 100th anniversary of the typewriter" (on topics such as hats, memory, the exclamation point, and fans in winter):

> as the sun sets in the peach,
> the icebox rises in the west.

In the picture that accompanies his poems, showing Morice in action, he seems, by the way, to be writing by hand on an enormous roll of paper.

A brief poem is not necessarily, of course, a perfunctory poem (Chinese and Japanese examples spring to mind). Consider "Peaches" (1975) by the American poet Siv Cedering (b. 1939):

> There was a contest
> once
> for the best picture
> of a peach
>
> in China
>
> Madame Ling
> or was it Ching
> sat in some yellow
> pollen
>
> then
>
> carefully, again

> she sat upon
> a piece of white
>
> paper

The feelings generated by the lines "Madame Ling / or was it Ching" seem to me to clash with the mood of the rest of the poem: what should have been a gently humorous image of a woman sitting in some pollen is soured by the trace of xenophobia in the unthinking confusion between the two Chinese names. Another poem by Cedering —the title poem of her collection *Mother Is* (1975)—sustains throughout a carefully modulated tone of near-hysteria, beginning with the title:

> MOTHER IS
> in an asylum, "obsessed with sexual fantasies."

People bring the mother things which upset her because of their sexual charge—hot dogs and umbrellas and cucumbers. Then her daughter comes:

> I bring her peaches; she scolds: "No. Take them
> away. Uptight peaches from a store
> cannot come into my mouth with the sweet juices of orchards.
> I want ripe ones I can peel, feel my tongue
> follow that ridge. I want to smell of persimmons."

Though the mother is now beginning to make some sense, her daughter is frightened:

> I am a good daughter—the peach tree bloomed again
> this spring—but I fear
> inheritance. It hurts me to slice the cucumber
> and scares me to suck the juice of purple
> plums.

In the final stanza, the daughter is almost paralyzed by her fear of madness, both for herself and her own daughters:

> My daughters do the harvesting. I tell them
> to be careful. They are laughing
> in the kitchen. I read recipes
> and sterilize
> jars.

It takes some doing to plausibly associate juicy fruit with madness.

8

BANANAS

The first banana in England was obtained by the apothecary and herbalist Thomas Johnson in 1633. Johnson was a friend of John Tradescant (1608–1662), Keeper of the Gardens, Vines, and Silkworms of King Charles I, at Oatlands Palace, in Surrey. The dramatic event is described by Prudence Leith-Ross in her biography of John Tradescant and his father (also John, and like his son a gardener and importer of exotic plants):

> Tradescant's friend, Thomas Johnson, received from Bermuda a plant with unripe green fruit. "This stalke with the fruit thereon I hanged up in my shop, where it became ripe about the beginning of May, and lasted until June: the pulp or meat was very soft and tender, and it did eate somewhat like a Muske-Melon," Johnson declared. It must have caused considerable interest hanging in the apothecary's shop on Snow Hill and, from whomever it was acquired, Tradescant evidently found a means of preserving one as a banana is listed in the *Musaeum Tradescantianum*.

Jeanette Winterson (b. 1959), in the opening pages of her novel *Sexing the Cherry* (1989), elaborates on the arrival of that first banana. Thomas Johnson is supposed to be "trying to charge money for a glimpse of the thing," but the archetypal matriarch narrator—"Dog-Woman" as she calls herself—will have none of it and she forcibly removes the concealing cloth, revealing something "yellow and livid and long." The following dialogue ensues:

> "It is a banana, madam," said the rogue.
>
> A banana? What on God's good earth was a banana?
>
> "Such a thing never grew in Paradise," I said.
>
> "Indeed it did, madam," says he, all puffed up like a poison adder. "This fruit is from the Island of Bermuda, which is closer to Paradise than you will ever be."
>
> He lifted it above his head, and the crowd, seeing it for the first time, roared and nudged each other and demanded to know what poor fool had been so reduced as to sell his vitality.

"It's either painted or infected," said I, "for there's none such a colour that I know."

Johnson shouted above the din as best he could . . .

"THIS IS NOT SOME UNFORTUNATE'S RAKE. IT IS THE FRUIT OF A TREE. IT IS TO BE PEELED AND EATEN."

At this there was unanimous retching. There was no good woman could put that up to her mouth, and for a man it was the practice of cannibals.

The novel continues in this vein: beginning each episode with a modicum of facts—drawn from, say, the history of seventeenth-century Britain or the grafting of trees or modern astrophysics—Winterson spins occasionally exhilarating but too often incoherent fantasies. (Later in the novel, Jordan, the Dog-Woman's adopted son, is present when the first pineapple arrives in England—an episode we will glance at in chapter 14.)

Bananas (including plaintains) seem to have originated in Southeast Asia; in the words of the two scholars De Langhe and de Maret—who base their conclusions on a combination of botanical, genetic, linguistic, anthropological, and archeological evidence—"the species in its wild state covers a huge area, from New Guinea in the east to Myanmar [Burma] in the west." Initial domestication of bananas "started well before 4500 BP [before the present]" and "plaintains reached Africa by 3000 BP." After the discovery of the banana in West Africa by fifteenth-century Portuguese explorers and its introduction a century later to the Americas, it was sometimes speculatively identified as the forbidden fruit of Genesis, as in the Belgian Jesuit Frans van Sterbeeck's (1631–1693) *Citricultura* (1682), a book on citrus fruits and other exotic trees. (For the unsigned engraved illustration [8 x 6 in.] of the banana plant, see figure 5.) As late as 1736 Linnaeus (1707–1778) took note of this identification of the banana as the forbidden fruit in his first botanical monograph, *Musa Cliffortiana*. "Musa" was the name of the banana in the Middle East, while "Cliffortiana" referred to Linnaeus's Anglo-Dutch patron, George Clifford, in one of whose hothouses the banana was first induced to flower by dint of "setting it in a rich soil, keeping it quite dry for some weeks, and then deluging it with water in imitation of tropical storms" (quoting from Wilfrid Blunt's biography of Linnaeus). The particular species of banana thought to be the forbidden fruit was the plantain, hence its botanical name, *Musa paradisiaca*. The genus *Musa* is, botanically speaking, a perennial herb rather than a tree. It should be noted that there is some inconsistency in the names for the cultivars of the genus *Musa* because they are sterile (seedless) hybrid forms and hence necessarily lack exact species names.

Bananas are celebrated as one of many tropical fruits—"Delicious, and of flavour exquisite; / Fruits not unworthy Europèan soils"—by John Singleton in his long poem in four books and over two thousand lines, *A General Description of the West-Indian Islands* (1767). Little is known of Singleton beyond the fact that he was a member of

Fig. 5: Banana plant,
Frans van Sterbeeck,
Citricultura, 1682

a professional acting company—the first in America—that performed in the North American colonies before touring Jamaica and the eastern Caribbean islands in the 1760s. (Singleton's poem was first published in Barbados; later, in 1776, an abridged version was published in London.) In the first book of *A General Description,* almost a hundred lines are devoted to fruit (and nuts), leading up to the main subject of the book: a barbecue. I will quote here the passage on plantains and bananas (and in later chapters, the passages on pineapple and citrus fruit), including Singleton's lively annotations:

> Courting the taste, the luscious plantane* here
> Within its yellow coat his tribute brings;
> And sweet bananas (kindred fruit) their pulp
> Luxuriant yield in rich abundant store,
> By superstitious bigots sacred held.†

*It has been objected, that the plantane ought not to be admitted into the catalogue of fruits, because it is served to table as a kind of bread. It is granted, when half grown and roasted, it makes very good food; but that ought rather to add to its value, nor can it in any way lessen our approbation of it as an excellent fruit when ripe.

†Some of these people fancy that the resemblance of a cross appears on every slice of the banana, and therefore will not cut it.

In "Silva to Agriculture in the Torrid Zone" (1826), written and published in Spanish by the Venezuelan Andrés Bello (1781–1865) while he was on a diplomatic mission in London, numerous tropical plants are singled out for special praise, including sugar cane, indigo, pineapple, yucca, potatoes, and cotton. But there is an extended tribute to the banana (here quoted in a translation kindly provided for me by Arnold L. Kerson):

> For you [the Torrid Zone] the banana tree
> droops under the oppressive weight of its sweet offering.
> The banana tree, first of all the wondrous gifts
> that divine wisdom has generously bestowed
> upon the peoples of the blessed Equator.
> Human skill is not needed
> to cultivate its abundant fruit.
> Its clusters owe nothing
> to the pruning hook or plow.
> It asks for very little care, and thus eases the burden
> of the slaves who harvest it.
> It grows rapidly, and when, wholly spent, its life ceases,
> a full grown tree has replaced it.

What seems to have impressed Bello most about bananas was the non-labor-intensive character of their cultivation. This would be in acccord with the didactic thrust of the last half of his poem, which deals with peace, honest work, virtue, reconciliation with Spain, and the political unity of Spanish America. Bello's poetic form, the *silva,* is a revival of a relatively free form of the seventeenth century (itself originating in Italy), lacking both a regular rhyme scheme and fixed strophes. (A full translation of Bello's poem is available in a volume of selections from his writings by Frances M. López-Morillas.)

George Clifford's hothouse bananas in the eighteenth century may remind one of the opening pages of *Gravity's Rainbow* (1973), by Thomas Pynchon (b. 1937), where readers are introduced to Capt. Geoffrey ("Pirate") Prentice, famous all over England for his Banana Breakfasts. (The comic values of the extended banana episode may be appreciated quite apart from the convoluted structure of the novel as a whole, as revealed, for example, in the book-length commentary of Steven Weisenburger's *Companion* [1988].) Pirate grows his bananas in the rich topsoil of a glass hothouse he has built on the roof of a maisonette situated near the Chelsea Embankment in London. On the particular morning of the opening episode of the novel—the date is 18 December 1944—Pirate needs to distract himself from the thought of the German rocket he knows has just been fired at London from Holland. Pirate proceeds to his hothouse "bananery" and picks bananas, some as much as a foot and a half in length. The next few pages include hilarious interludes like the drunken Teddy Bloat slipping on a banana peel and then, as he sits on the floor, "working the banana peel into a pajama lapel for a boutonniere." Another minor character, Osbie Feel, sings a banana song to welcome the dawn, while "holding one of the biggest of Pirate's bananas so that it protrudes out the fly of his striped pajama bottoms":

> Time to gather your arse up off the floor,
>   (have a bana-na)
> Brush your teeth and go toddling off to war.
> Wave your hand to sleepy land,
> Kiss those dreams away,
> Tell Miss Grable you're not able,
> Not till V-E Day, oh,
> Ev'rything'll be grand in Civvie Street
>   (have a bana-na)
> Bubbly wine and girls wiv lips so sweet—
> But there's still the German or two to fight,
> So show us a smile that's shiny bright,
> And then, as we may have suggested once before—
> Gather yer blooming arse up off the floor!

Finally, all the preparations completed, comes the great climactic meal:

> banana omelets, banana sandwiches, banana casseroles, mashed bananas molded in the shape of a British lion rampant, blended with eggs into batter for French toast, squeezed out a pastry nozzle across the quivering creamy reaches of a banana blancmange to spell out the words *C'est magnifique, mais ce n'est pas la guerre* (attributed to a French observer during the Charge of the Light Brigade) which Pirate has appropriated as his motto . . . tall cruets of pale banana syrup to pour oozing over banana waffles, a giant glazed crock where diced bananas have been fermenting since the summer with wild honey and muscat raisins, up out of which, this winter morning, one now dips foam mugsfull of banana mead . . . banana croissants and banana kreplach, and banana oatmeal and banana jam and banana bread, and bananas flamed in ancient brandy Pirate brought back last year from a cellar in the Pyrenees also containing a clandestine radio transmitter . . .

Another twentieth-century novel, *A Question of Upbringing* (1951), by Anthony Powell (1905–2000), also features in its opening pages an incident involving a banana. The scene is Eton in the summer of 1921, in a shop where some students are drinking lemonade. One of the students, Budd, the captain of the Eleven (the soccer team), throws a "skinned banana" at someone but misses his target and hits Widmerpool, a little-liked and little-respected student. Widmerpool will become one of the principal characters in the sequence of twelve novels (of which *A Question of Upbringing* is the first), called collectively *A Dance to the Music of Time* (1951–75); indeed he will come to be recognized (in the second novel, *A Buyer's Market* [1952]) by Nick Jenkins, the narrator of the entire story, as "one of those symbolic figures, of whom most people possess at least one example, if not more, round whom the past and the future have a way of assembling." The incident in question is being told to Jenkins: "It was a bull's-eye. The banana was over-ripe and it burst all over his face, knocking his spectacles sideways. His cap came off and he spilt most of the lemonade down the front of his clothes." The importance of the incident lies in Widmerpool's reaction: "an absolutely *slavish* look came into Widmerpool's face" as he professed to Budd not to mind at all, one of Widmerpool's defining traits being the way he fawns on his superiors and lords it over his inferiors. A very similar incident occurs at a dinner-dance some years later in London, in the first chapter of *A Buyer's Market*. This is the "sugaring" of Widmerpool by a woman with whom he is in love, which reminds Jenkins twice of the banana incident, as Widmerpool is once again observed "grovelling before someone he admired." And this later incident becomes a key reference point throughout the remaining novels.

At the very end of the early novel *As I Lay Dying* (1930) by William Faulkner (1897–1962), bananas are being eaten by the pregnant Dewey Dell and her little brother Vardaman, who have just arrived in Jefferson along with their older brothers, bearing their mother Addie's body in order to bury her where she was born. As they look out of the wagon in which they are sitting, their father Anse with his newly acquired "duck-shaped" wife walks down the street (at this point, the eldest son, Cash, is narrating): "And there we set watching them, with Dewey Dell's and Vardaman's mouth half open and half-et bananas in their hands and her coming around from behind pa, looking at us like she dared ere a man." The bag of bananas has been given to Vardaman to keep him quiet by Macgowan, the man who is having sex with Dewey Dell in exchange for some pills to abort her fetus. The critic Olga Vickery sees the bananas—along with the new wife and the portable gramophone she is carrying—as signifying "a shift in the family's focus of consciousness" enabling them "to avoid too close, protracted, and painful a scrutiny of the meaning of life and death." This sounds a trifle too portentous: I see merely the final grotesque incident in a book full of—composed of—such incidents.

Bananas have attracted some attention from poets, though it may be that Erica Jong is right when she remarks, in her own (untitled) prose poem about bananas, that "the poem about bananas has not yet been written." Perhaps not *the* poem; but there is, for example, "Rotten Bananas" (1978), by the Brazilian poet Ferreira Gullar (b. 1930), an interesting poem of some eleven stanzas and over 150 lines. Gullar makes of the rotting bananas on a fruit stand, in the words of the translators, Emanuel Brasil and William Jay Smith, "a symbol for the 'afternoon's ulcer,' and the scene of poverty from which the poet cannot escape." The most explicit passage about bananas is the first stanza:

260

> Like a gold watch the blight
> hidden in the fruits
> on the counter (still honey
> under the skin
> in the pulp which will turn to water) was
> still golden
> muddy sugar
> from the ground
> > and now
> look: black bananas
> > like soft bags
> > where a bee hovers
> > and spins
> > a watch hand spinning in the golden universe
> > (early afternoon)
> in April
> > while we live our lives.

Bananas rot quickly in the afternoon sun, and the result is a rich, sickly-sweet, smelly, liquescent pulp: what other fruit could rival rotten bananas as a symbol of social corruption?

Another poem about bananas is "Flipochinos" (1986), by the Philippine American poet Cyn. Zarco (b. 1950):

> when a brown person
> gets together
> with a yellow person
> it is something like
> the mating of a chico and a banana
> the brown meat of the chico
> plus the yellow skin of the banana
> take the seed of the chico for eyes
> peel the banana for sex appeal
> lick the juice from your fingers
> and watch your step

A chico, to my knowledge, is a shrub of the western United States: successfully crossing it with a banana is probably biologically impossible (which does not seem to be the point of the poem!).

Michael Benedikt (b. 1935) has written a prose poem concerning the sexuality of bananas, "The Moralist of Bananas" (1976), in which a certain Saint preaches sermons to bananas "about the suggestiveness of their shapes." This "Moralist of

Bananas" objects also to the colors of bananas: "'O bananas, not only are you shaped in a bodily fashion, but you even ripen by turning from an innocent canary yellow, to bright yellow, to orange, and then to bright skin pink! And some of you, losing all control, even turn bright red, with flesh-tones of jet black!'" One thing the Saint succeeds in doing is to drive away all the lovers, who "have gone down among the pomegranates, hid among the permissive persimmon groves, or left for the grapes." One is left wondering why these other fruits are so much less sexy than the banana.

The sex appeal of bananas is, in an oblique way, part of the subject of Wallace Stevens's "Floral Decorations for Bananas," from his first collection, *Harmonium* (1923). Reading the poem through, one is immediately struck by the slightly awkward combination of discipline and freedom in the verse. The poem consists of four stanzas, the first two of six lines and the last two of seven lines, all in iambic trimeter. In each stanza there is a single pair of rhyming lines immediately preceding the last line, while in the second stanza the first and last lines also rhyme; in addition, there are various assonances and consonances scattered throughout. The location of the rhyming lines seems arbitrary, thereby introducing a discordant note into the very framework of a poem whose subject matter is precisely a certain discordancy in the structure of the world. That latter discordancy is the incongruous appearance of bunches of bananas in a room occupied by "the women of primrose and purl, / Each one in her decent curl." More appropriate than bananas—with their "insolent, linear peels / And sullen, hurricane shapes," their "blunt yellow" color—would have been "plums tonight, / In an eighteenth-century dish, / And pettifogging buds." In the second half of the poem, an alternative scenario is proposed, either with a different group of women or with the original group somehow transformed: "The women will be all shanks / And bangles and slatted eyes." The bananas are retained but now piled on planks rather than on the table and they are decked in banana leaves—fibrous, purple, oozing—matching if not surpassing the grotesqueness of the bananas themselves.

The grotesqueness of Stevens's bunches of bananas is transformed into an almost surreal apparition in "The Banana Dwarf" (1985) by Laurence Lieberman (b. 1935), a long poem consisting of seven stanzas each of thirteen unrhymed lines. Lieberman writes in what has been called "patterned free forms," which means that in a given poem the visual shapes of all the stanzas are identical. In the poem we are considering, for example, each stanza has long lines at the beginning, middle, and end, with much shorter lines in between—more specifically, the first, sixth, eighth, twelfth, and thirteenth lines are long, while the intervening lines are short—all the lines being centered about the same vertical axis. Each stanza, then, appears to be a highly stable structure with a long, flat top and bottom and a bulge around the middle. Less steady is the puzzling structure that appears in the second stanza: "Is it a crane, two blurred yellow derrick beams / swung on each side / of the advancing figure / or apparatus— / but not mowing down the crush of bodies / it plows across?" The place is a crowded street in Santo Domingo, Dominican Republic, and the yellow structure turns out to be two tall stalks of bananas, each suspended from a wooden pole and carried by a "spry, red-cheeked midget." Here is what happens next:

> Though I walk jauntily toward him, I seem
> to stand still, to hang
> in a pool
> of banana fluff, banana
> yellow light emitted from the stalks:
> a cloud, in which I float, weightless, tongueless,
> wanting to speak—to beg a choice
> ripe banana to eat. *He flies. He sings the all-*
> *saving nutrients,*
> *blessings of the Banana*
> *God.* He plucks
> a sample banana here, a sample there, peels
> one, offers a munch to each of several passersby

The speaker buys some bananas: "a nine-banana spiral draped over my wrist, the coil / and whorl of the golden cluster symmetrical / as a pineapple, my small vine- / twist of fruit / wee replica of the many-tiered, / many-wreathed stalks of banana garlands / slung from the Banana Apostle's shoulders."

Lieberman has composed another exuberant celebration of bananas, "The Banana Madonna" (1985), where he finds himself in the countryside surrounded by the green, unpicked fruit: "the thousands of green firm tubes wrapped / in bundles, thousands / of green hands upon hands upon hands— / fingers woven together, wound / about the stalks and vines ... It's the great *Siesta* / of banana trees." Responding to the surroundings, "Banana images, profuse in local Church / Art, glut our talk." The glut of bananas enforces a banana aesthetic: "the marvelous flowing banana forms, arched like horseshoes, / boomerangs, erect phalluses— / but always, the banana is the norm all bold variations branch / away from or return to." The climax comes with the apparition of a stained-glass Banana Madonna in a church near some banana plantations: "faces and busts / of baby, Madonna, seem a tapestry woven of banana vines, half-open / banana peels. Silhouettes of bulky unpeeled bananas, / winding around frames / of glass panels, overspill their outlines."

The Jamaican writer Evan Jones (b. 1926) celebrates banana-pickers in his dialect poem "The Song of the Banana Man" (1971); here is the fourth of seven stanzas:

> 'Banana day is me special day;
> I cut me stems an' I'm on me way;
> load up de donkey, leave de lan',
> head down de hill to banana stan';
> when de truck comes roun', I take a ride

all de way down to de harbour side.
Dat is de night, when you, touris' man,
would change you' place wid a banana man.

'Yes, by God an' me big right han',
I will live an' die a banana man.'

In her book *Bananas: An American History* (2000), Virginia Scott Jenkins lists in an appendix over five dozen popular songs about bananas, reflecting the ubiquity of the fruit in American life, bananas having "become as 'American' as apples or strawberries despite the fact that virtually all our bananas are imported from the countries of the Caribbean basin." Pound for pound, today bananas are, indeed, the most popular fruit among American consumers.

Stevens's purely aesthetic approach to bananas brought out the absurdity of their appearance, but there are other equally humorous aspects of the fruit. The two main things we ordinarily associate with bananas are, first, a coarse, ludicrously obvious eroticism, and second, the broadly humorous banana peel induced pratfalls of circus clowns and silent film comedians. As to the first, we may cite Jong again: "According to Freud, girls envy bananas." More interesting is the amusing photograph, "Buy Some Bananas" (1972) by Linda Nochlin (b. 1931), showing a nude young man holding a tray of bananas just below his genitalia. (Nochlin's photograph was a response to a photograph entitled "Buy Some Apples" in a nineteenth-century popular French magazine, showing a nude young woman holding a tray of apples just below her breasts; for both pictures, see Nochlin's "Eroticism and Female Imagery in Nineteenth-Century Art" [1972]) Exactly the same banana motif occurs in a work by the American artist Alexis Smith (b. 1949), *Me Tarzan, You Jane* (1985), which consists of two mixed-media collage panels (each 19 x 15½ in.), one of them showing a naked, squatting, stereotypical bodybuilder of a young man with a bunch of three bananas in front of his crotch, and the other the torso of a pretty, blond, young woman in a pink bra, her cleavage emphasized by a dangling necklace with cherry pendants.

The identification of penis and banana occurs to shocking effect in the concluding line of the Hebrew sonnet "Finding It Hard to Fall Asleep" (1994; translated by Peter Cole), by Israeli poet Aharon Shabtai (b. 1939):

Finding it hard to fall asleep, my mind
slips from the day's refuse and manages to find
a trough between the legs of a rider across from me;
it dreams it's plowing into her thick, hairy

muff, the softer down on her lip my clue
to what eluded my stare on its way into

hiding, deep in the recesses of her white groin.
Whoever you are, wherever, I have no way of knowing. . . .

If they opened my head, in its cells they'd find your pussy
which, in my mouth, just now is speaking through me
like a stolen fetish overcoming the thief in his ploy—

it orders you to retaliate, instantly,
and you swallow his cock, taking it into your hand
like a ripe banana to the mouth of a lazy boy.

But, of course, women can also make use of the erotic banana motif. Thus, the American dancer Josephine Baker (1906–1975) was famous throughout her career for her banana costume, first worn in her debut at the Folies-Bergère in Paris, in 1926; as her biographer Phyllis Rose explains: "She was wearing nothing but a little skirt of plush bananas. It was the outfit she would be identified with virtually for the rest of her life, a witty thing in itself and wittier still when Baker started dancing and set the bananas in jiggling motion, like perky, good-natured phalluses." The character of the costume changed, however, over the years: "She wore the banana skirt again in a more spangled, hard-edged version. It was the fate of those bananas to become ever harder and more threatening with the years, so that at last they looked like spikes." (For photographs of Baker in her earlier and later banana costumes, see Rose's book.) What is surely a descendant of Baker's costume occurs in an early (black and white) Elvis Presley vehicle called *King Creole* (1958), one of the last films of director Michael Curtiz (1888–1962). For me, the only thing in the production worthy of the director of *Casablanca* (1942) is a brief number ("Banana") performed by a chorus girl with a French accent in a New Orleans night club. She is wearing a scanty dress that looks as if it is made of banana skins; dangling from the dress are real bananas, which she pulls off and tosses to members of the audience. Even cruder is a picture postcard (ca. 1930) with a photograph of a nude young woman dangling a banana before her smiling mouth (see Michael Koetzle, *One Thousand Nudes, Uwe Scheid Collection* [1994]).

As for banana peel, Marina Warner, in her book *No Go the Bogeyman: Scaring, Lulling, and Making Mock* (1999), has this deep interpretation: "The banana skin, which remains after the fruit has been consumed, presents, in metonymy, an image of the return of the repressed." On the other hand, Philip Levine (b. 1928), in a poem about his immigrant mother's arrival at Ellis Island, "The Mercy" (1999), has her simply remembering "trying to eat a banana / without first peeling it."

Warner also comments on the banana peel caper in connection with a film by Buster Keaton (1895–1966): "By the early 1920s the banana-skin joke was already so hackneyed that it was mocked, with understated skill, by Buster Keaton in his twenty-minute short *The High Sign* (1921)." She goes on to describe the successive roles of the main prop in the film, a banana that is substituted for a policeman's gun and later peeled and eaten. But no one falls or even slips on the peel—though Buster comes close. The banana peel caper has even penetrated the world of television advertising: a television commercial some years ago featured a business-suited man miming some complicated financial transaction by carefully hopping his way among an extended array of closely spaced banana peels. Again, Clive Hart explains how the risk of slipping on a banana peel is used by James Joyce in section 9, chapter 10 ("Wandering Rocks") of *Ulysses* "to make a crucial distinction between our responses to the superficially similar Lenehan and M'Coy" when the latter, as Joyce tells us, "dodged a banana peel with gentle pushes of his toe from the path to the gutter. Fellow might damn easy get a nasty fall there coming along tight in the dark."

Both of the above associations of bananas are exploited by Samuel Beckett (1906–1989) when he introduces bananas as key props in the opening, wordless section of *Krapp's Last Tape* (1958). This I want to look at in some detail. When the lights go up in a staging of the play, viewers are confronted with a feeble old man (it can be calculated, but we are never directly informed, that he is sixty-nine years old) sitting behind a small table and facing the audience. According to the elaborate stage directions, Krapp resembles a conventional clown: white face, purple nose, black trousers too short, black waistcoat with oversized pockets, enormous dirty white boots. After a motionless interval, he gets up, opens a drawer in the table, and extracts a banana. After first stroking the banana, he peels it, drops the peel on the stage at his feet, inserts the end of the banana in his mouth, and stares off into space. He then proceeds to eat the banana as he paces across the stage in front of the table. At one point he slips on the banana peel, rights himself without falling, and pushes the peel with his foot over the edge of the stage. (Beckett later revised these stage directions and had Krapp toss the peel backstage left). After a short time Krapp extracts a second banana from the drawer, strokes it, peels it, tosses the peel backstage left, inserts the end in his mouth, and again stares off into space. And here comes a critical change in stage directions: whereas in the original version, Krapp never eats the second banana but rather places it with the tip protruding in one of his waistcoat pockets, in later versions Krapp eats a mouthful (or none) and then tosses the banana backstage left. In any case, at this point the interaction with the tape recorder begins and Krapp finally speaks.

Before proceeding, I might just recall Buster Keaton's *The High Sign,* in which, as we have seen, the banana peel caper is deliberately omitted. Beckett would certainly have known this film, since, as Hugh Kenner tells us, "Buster Keaton [was] a hero of [Beckett's] from the 1920s." (And, of course, in 1964 Keaton played the only—but doubled—role in the silent movie, *Film,* from a script by Beckett.) Beckett, as we have seen, permits Krapp to slip on a banana peel without actually falling.

In certain productions of *Krapp's Last Tape* that Beckett himself directed and in his notebook for one of these productions (at the Schiller-Theater Werkstatt, Berlin, 1969), we find Beckett softening both the erotic and the comic aspects of the entire pre-tape-recorder episode. (For details, see *The Theatrical Notebooks of Samuel Beckett*

[1992], edited by James Knowlson; volume 3 is on *Krapp's Last Tape*.) We have already noted how the protruding tip of the second banana in Krapp's pocket is eliminated; the stroking of the bananas is also eliminated. Krapp himself no longer has a purple nose, his clothes are more ordinary, and in at least one production directed by Beckett himself the boots are replaced by slippers. Most important, in none of Beckett's stage directions and in no production directed by Beckett himself does Krapp eat more than one banana (together with perhaps a single bite out of a second banana). I have seen and read of productions in which the actor playing Krapp gorges on bananas; this gets laughs but is clearly contrary to Beckett's intention.

Reviews of a couple of recent productions of *Krapp's Last Tape*—one in Greenwich Village (1993) and one at Stratford-upon-Avon (1997)—suggest that in both of these stagings Krapp consumes more than one banana. Thus, Michael Feingold reports (with enthusiastic approval) of Krapp "letting the bananas hang in his mouth erotically" and Gabriel Egan remarks that Krapp "steps away from the desk to eat bananas." For what it is worth, I believe Beckett would have disapproved, and, again, it must be emphasized that Beckett was extremely concerned about the details of these banana props. At one time he suggested one small banana and one large one but eventually rejected that idea. Another time—this was the important Schiller production—the bananas were small and green. He certainly was aware that the bananas used as props must not be too ripe or too long, or they may break off as they dangle from the actor's mouth. In the end, Beckett suggested, with some attempt at precision, bananas of a moderate size which could be consumed in three mouthfuls.

It is time to look at the significance of bananas in the spoken portion of *Krapp's Last Tape,* that is, in Krapp's (tape recorded) accounts of events in his past together with his present comments on the earlier accounts. Very near the beginning of the long excerpt from his thirty-ninth-birthday tape that Krapp listens to initially, we hear: "Have just eaten I regret to say three bananas and only with difficulty refrained from a fourth (*He grunts.*) Fatal things for a man with my condition. (*Vehemently*) Cut 'em out!" The condition Krapp refers to, we learn somewhat later, is constipation; in Krapp's odd phrase, "unattainable laxation," or, more explicitly, "iron stool." Now, we know that bananas are extremely nourishing and, in fact, constitute a principal food staple for many tropical and semitropical societies, which means Krapp is addicted to a nourishing but—at least in his view—constipating food. Must not this tell us something about Krapp's spiritual state? It is only too easy at this point to begin to talk about Krapp's state of spiritual constipation, but that will only do—or begin to do—if we recognize that there must also be something (spiritually) well-nourished about that state. Finally, if as one critic (Jim McCue) asserts, "the banana routine . . . stands for all the clowning in life," then the rest of Beckett's play will have to stand for whatever is the opposite of clowning in life, with the connotations of bananas perhaps shifting from comic to tragic during the course of the play.

Beckett explained his use of green bananas as props in *Krapp's Last Tape* by saying—in jest?—that perhaps Krapp couldn't wait for them to ripen (as reported by Knowlson in *Theatrical Notebooks of Samuel Beckett*). Bananas for human consumption, we know, *must* be picked while still green and allowed to ripen before eating them. That is why the color green is so prominent in some novels in which banana plantations form the essential background of the action. Let us look first at *Viento Fuerte* (Strong wind; 1950), by the Nobel prize–winning Guatemalan writer Miguel Angel Asturias (1899–1974). *Strong Wind* was the first book of a "banana trilogy" about the exploitative role of the United Fruit Company—lightly disguised as "Tropical Banana, Inc."—in Guatemala. (The United Fruit Company was actually incorporated in 1899 to grow bananas for export from Central America, Ecuador, and Colombia, at a time when consumption of bananas in the United States, in particular, was sharply rising.) Asturias's plots are melodramatic stories of political and personal corruption and betrayal. Americans and Guatemalans are evenhandedly included among both the heroes and villains but always in the background is the systematic and massive exploitation of the peasants. Perhaps in quest of something like ethnographic authenticity, Asturias frequently introduces elements of Mayan folklore, resulting in a not very convincing mixture of realism and myth. There are, though, some effective passages (here translated by Gregory Rabassa). At one point, for example, banana picking is transformed into a green crucifixion:

> The movements of the cutting crew at the foot of a banana tree which looked like a green cross resembled those of Jews with ladders and spears as they tried to lift down a green Christ who had been changed into a bunch of bananas which descended among arms and ropes and was received with great care, as if it were a case of an overdelicate being, and carried off in small carts to receive its sacramental bath and be placed in a bag with special cushions inside.

Again, when a Guatemalan couple from the mountains see a coastal banana plantation for the first time, they are overwhelmed:

> Bastiancito could not finish the word because he had opened his mouth and become one with his wife, both of them unable to take a step, wounded by a sort of rain of machete blows given by some leaves of a most beautiful green in color, not the green of mountain vegetation, not the green of parrots, not the green of a forest, but a green made from the mixture of the green of the sea and the green which was carried down by the golden light above the leaves and the deep and fleshy, light emerald green of the blue water flowing under the leaves. The sunlight, as if it were passing through torn canopies, was like a clustering of diamonds in the dark shadows. Rows of banana trees on both sides, in movement, and motionless, as they continued on their way toward Semírames.

And, in the second book of Asturias's banana trilogy, *El Papa verde* (The green pope; 1954), also translated by Gregory Rabassa, the most striking feature of a banana plantation (other than its color)—its rigid geometric structure—is described as follows:

> The lewd silence of the green flesh, hopeful in its sprouts, twigs, leaves, bunches. The geometric lines, logical and single, of the rows of banana trees broken at the horizon by confused, disorderly woods, the authentic breathing of the land enclosed in the plantations, held down, imprisoned, condemned to what could be extracted from it up to the last drop of life.

The title of the novel, by the way, is an epithet that refers to the president of Tropical Banana as the "Pontiff of the Caribbean banana groves, worthy of wearing the Great Emerald on his finger." The central character of *The Green Pope* aspires to this presidency; he is an American named Geo Maker Thompson who at one point fantasizes about the possibility "that there be added to the glorious American flags the no less glorious one of our Fruit State, consisting of a green background and in the center a pirate skull and crossbones over two bunches of bananas." According to Richard J. Callan, "Geo Maker," to be understood as "Earth Maker," "is connected with the creator gods, who in Maya Quiché theology, are also called Makers, inasmuch as their creation was not *ex nihilo*" (1970). Unfortunately, in the English translation of *The Green Pope* "Geo" comes out "George."

Needless to say, there is nothing either erotic or funny about bananas in Asturias's novels; and this is equally true of an utterly different type of novel in which a banana plantation forms the setting: *La Jalousie* (Jealousy; 1957), by Alain Robbe-Grillet (b. 1922). An unnamed, disembodied narrator tells the story but he reports only what he can directly observe (primarily through his senses of sight and hearing) or immediately infer from his observations. The narrator is a banana planter with a wife, A, and a friend Franck, also a banana planter. The narrator reports conversations between A and Franck, never anything he himself has said, but what makes the entire narrative so strangely forbidding and foreboding is that the narrator never *responds* to anything he reports (including an automobile trip by A and Franck into town, where they are forced by engine trouble to stay overnight). In the very first pages of the novel, we learn of A's "light-colored" dress, her "black curls," her "pale blue" letter paper, and of the location, size, and orientation of her room. We also learn that the house is surrounded by a garden on three sides and a courtyard to the north, and (in the translation by Richard Howard):

> On all sides of the garden, as far as the borders of the plantation, stretches the green mass of the banana trees.
>
> On the right and left, their proximity is too great, combined with the veranda's relative lack of elevation, to permit an observer stationed there to distinguish the arrangement of the trees; while further down the valley,

the quincunx can be made out at first glance. In certain very recently replanted sectors—those where the reddish earth is just beginning to yield supremacy to foliage—it is easy enough to follow the regular perspective of the four intersecting lanes along which the young trunks are aligned.

The second section of *Jealousy* opens with an extended account—some seven pages of French text, almost four in the English translation—of the geometrical structure of the banana plantation, specifying the dimensions and shapes of various sectors, the numbers of trees in various rows, and the sizes of various patches of trees of different ages. (When the novel was first published, this section of it was read mockingly over the radio by hostile critics. Only the English translation, by the way, contains a helpful—some would say, indispensable—diagram of the house and plantation.) But the form of the plantation and its sole product—green bananas—are not seen to have any effect on the members of the ménage à trois. And though the novel is nominally about sexual jealousy, any erotic feelings associated with bananas seem to have been deliberately anesthetized. Sometimes a banana is not even a banana!

APRICOTS,
RIPE AND UNRIPE

The allusion to ripe or unripe fruit as a metaphor for qualifying human action or decision is so trite that most authors today instictively avoid it, and yet a notable instance occurs in Shakespeare's *Hamlet* (1599–1601)—only, however, in the play within the play (in scene 2 of act 3). The Player Queen has just declared with great vehemence that should her husband die she would never marry again, and the Player King responds in a lengthy speech (3.2.174–203) that begins:

> I do believe you think what you now speak;
> But what we do determine oft we break.
> Purpose is but the slave to memory,
> Of violent birth, but poor validity;
> Which now, like fruit unripe, sticks on the tree,
> But fall unshaken when they mellow be.

Shakespeare commentators have duly noted the ungrammatical shift from the singular "sticks" to the plural "fall" (see, for example, the note to the passage in G. R. Hibbard's Oxford Shakespeare edition of the play [1987]). Now, the referent of "which"— namely, "purpose"—is singular, but "fruit" can be either singular or plural, so Shakespeare has simply split the difference, and employed one verb of each form!

Except for bananas, unripe fruit tends to have negative connotations in literary food episodes. As an example, a poem by C. J. Driver (b. 1939), titled "A Psalm" (1996) —although "anti-psalm" might be more apt—runs like this in the first four of its twelve (numbered) lines:

> 1. Who shall be cursed for kindness: or who praised for favours?
> 2. The eye-servers are turned into statues: the men-pleasers are haggard
> in the late autumn.
> 3. They shall get none of what they desire: they shall be offered long
> words on flimsy paper.
> 4. They shall be paid with false money: and fed with unripe fruit.

In a commemorative sonnet in Dutch by Constantijn Huygens (1596–1687), there is play in the first three lines on the greenness, ripeness, sourness, and rottenness of some unnamed, generalized fruit, standing in for the offspring of a close friend of Huygens's, Madame Tesselschade (who translated Tasso into Dutch and whose subsequent conversion to Catholicism Huygens deeply deplored). But who was Constantijn Huygens? Simply, a "polymath, poet, composer, statesman and translator," almost none of whose writings are currently in print in the Netherlands and whose "name is known only to a very few English-speaking readers as a historical figure, as the father of a more famous son [Christaan], or as the friend and translator of John Donne." I have been quoting Peter Davidson and Adriaan van der Weel, from their preface to a selection of Huygens's poetry published in the four-hundredth anniversary year of his birth. The poem I alluded to above is called "On the Death of Tesselschade's Eldest Daughter, and on Her Husband Thereafter Bleeding to Death" (1634). The first four lines (here in English and Dutch) focus on the distasteful unripe fruit:

> The fruit more green than ripe, more ripe than sour,
> The first fruit all of fruits of Tessel's scions
> Rotted with smallpox; God has plucked it up
> To raise its best part to the immortal throng.

~

> De groener vrucht als rijp, de rijper vrucht als wrang,
> De voor-vrucht in de rij van Tessels echte planten
> Verrotte van quaed vier: God raeptes' uijt het sand, en
> Verhief 'er 'tbeste van in 'theilighe gedrang.

We shall have occasion in chapters 19 and 20 to consider a couple of other poems by Huygens.

The ripeness of apricots is particularly problematic, as is indicated already by the etymology of their name. In seventeenth-century English, the fruit was called "apricock," derived probably from Portuguese or Spanish and ultimately from the Latin term for "early ripening," *praecox;* our present "apricot" derives from the French *abricot.* (The dated instances of usage in the *OED* suggest that by the nineteenth century "apricot" had replaced "apricock.") It is worth quoting some of what John Parkinson says about apricots in his great quarto volume of some 1,755 pages, titled *Theatrum Botanicum: The Theater of Plants; or, An Herball of a Large Extent* (1640):

Malus Armeniaca sive præcocia. The Apricocke tree.

> . . . the flowers are white and like the [plum] but larger, the fruit that followeth is round, with a cleft or open furrow in the middle, somewhat like unto a Peach, of a pale yellowish Colour on the outside, as well as on the inside, and a little reddish on a side in most, yet whiter in some, and of

differing sizes also, some smaller or greater; of a firmer or faster close substance then any of the Plummes; a smooth flattish stone in the middle,
great or little, according to the fruite, which ripen with or before the earlier
sort of Plummes (and likely long before any of our earely sorts were
known in former times) which was the cause of the name, and a sweete
kernell within it, yet it is said there is one that hath a bitter kernell, which
I have not seen.

A poem that deftly reverses the negative connotations of unripe fruit is "Upon
two greene Apricockes sent to *Cowley* by Sir *Crashaw*" (written probably in the 1630s),
by Richard Crashaw (1612?-1649). Crashaw was older than Abraham Cowley by
some half dozen years, and his poem is a gracefully composed tribute to the precocity
of his younger friend, who had published three volumes of poetry by the time he was
nineteen. The point of the poem (which we are to understand as accompanying the
gift of fruit) is that Crashaw had wished to send Cowley some early apricots—a highly
prized fruit in seventeenth-century England (as indicated, for example, by Titania's
feeding her beloved Bottom apricots, along with dewberries, grapes, figs, and mulberries, in *A Midsummer Night's Dream* [3.1.144]). Now, it is a horticultural fact that apricot
blossoms appear early in English springs, resulting in the special vulnerability of
the fruit to spring frosts. The fruit itself does not ripen until August, as is reported by
seventeenth-century observers (see Peachey's *Fruit Variety Register, 1580–1660*). Hence,
we must imagine the time of composition of Crashaw's poem as being early summer,
when only green apricots would have been available. (The "April" mentioned in line
15 of the poem is an allusion to Cowley's precocity.) Crashaw makes the lack of ripe
apricots his central conceit: whatever slight traces of redness exhibited by the apricots
accompanying his poem, he insists, must be owing to their shame at the maturity or
ripeness of the youthful Cowley's poetry:

> the blush to thee they ow.
> By thy comparrison they shall put on
> More summer in their shames reflection,
> Than ere the fruitfull *Phœbus* flaming kisses
> Kindled on their cold lips.

Later, Crashaw alludes wittily to the title of Cowley's first book of poems, *Poetical
Blossoms* (1633): "'Twas only Paradice, 'tis onely thou, / Whose fruit and blossoms both
blesse the same bough." The allusion is to a belief (which we will encounter again) in
the perpetual spring of paradise, manifested in the simultaneous appearance of flowers and fruit on the trees. For a painting roughly contemporary with Crashaw's poem
depicting this idea, see the *Garden of Eden* by Jan Brueghel the Elder (1568–1625) in
the Victoria and Albert Museum, in London (a reproduction is in Prest's *Garden of
Eden* [1981].)

Next comes the poem's most convoluted thought, expressed in its most convoluted syntax:

> No fruit should have the face to smile on thee
> (Young master of the worlds maturitie)
> But such whose sun-borne beauties what they borrow
> Of beames to day, pay back againe to morrow,
> Nor need be double-gilt. How then must these,
> Poore fruits, looke pale at thy Hesperides!

Double-gilding was apparently a technical process for coating a surface with a double layer of gold.

No doubt it was lines like these that so discouraged Emma, the "very average anthropologist," who is the protagonist of Barbara Pym's (1913–1980) *A Few Green Leaves* (1980). At one point, she discovers an anthology of seventeenth-century verse, marked at Crashaw's poem, in the cottage rented by Graham, her departed one-time lover of the recent past. (I have been unable to find an anthology of seventeenth-century poetry containing the Crashaw poem in question.) What was Graham doing with such a (for him) unlikely book; why was it marked at such an obscurely metaphysical poem; and what, anyway, did the poem mean? It turns out the book had been borrowed from the rector, a bachelor friend of Emma's but no real friend of Graham's, and the rector even hints that Graham's borrowing of the book might have been connected with a letter Graham had received from his wife. All this adds further dimensions to the small mystery. One thing Emma is too inhibited to think of in this connection is Graham's earlier rather ungrateful response to the groceries she has had sent over to his cottage from the local shop: "I just thought it seemed odd to have tinned vegetables in the country—I'd imagined produce from people's gardens, even yours." All Emma says in reply is that she does not grow vegetables, while "feeling nettled (surely that was the appropriate word?)"; she is much too polite to let her witticism be heard. Emma's and Graham's feelings for each other turn out to be as unfresh as the tinned vegetables—"Did I once love this man? Emma asked herself"; instead of Crashaw's eloquent apology for his gift of green apricots, there is Graham's boorish complaint about Emma's gift of tinned food. Of course, Graham's expectation of fresh produce in the country, though based on an ignorance of contemporary country life, is not unworthy, and, indeed, his taste in food is not notably inferior to that of many of the other characters in a novel dense with food episodes. But, then, whether in their tastes in food or in any other aesthetic or moral perceptions, there are no heroes or villains in the novel.

One thing we do learn about the borrowed book is how it serves to introduce the topic of marriage into a conversation between Emma and the rector, when he mentions the fact that his deceased wife had liked the metaphysical poets. And the novel ends with Emma determined to remain in the village and to "embark on a love affair which need not necessarily be an unhappy one." So, we have here an instance of a second-order literary use of fruit, Pym using Crashaw's poem about fruit as a means of advancing her own plot, though at the same time as a source of unanswered questions about the inner lives of some of her main characters.

Apricots as agents of discovery—more specifically, as a pregnancy test—occur in an early episode of *The Duchess of Malfi* (1611–12), by John Webster (1580?–1625?). But while the act of discovery is conclusive (for Bosola, evil servant of the Duchess's two evil brothers), we eventually realize that there are no real consequences for the plot, thus making the episode in a sense otiose. Whether one decides that this reflects the fecklessness of the author or his deliberate contrivance—say, to create suspense—will depend on one's assessment of the play as a whole. The episode in question serves to interrupt an exchange between the Duchess and her steward, Antonio, to whom she is secretly married (whether legitimately—either legally or theologically—married is one crux of the play). The Duchess has been arguing that it is mere convention for courtiers to uncover their heads in the presence of the monarch, and she asks that Antonio be the first to violate this convention at her court. Antonio demurs, and before she can respond Bosola offers her what he has already divulged to the audience during a soliloquy: "some apricocks, / The first our spring yields" (2.1.70–1); what follows is a complicated set of physical and verbal transactions, involving deception of several kinds and on all sides.

The Duchess accepts the apricots with thanks; her "color rises," thinks Bosola (2.1.131), thereby raising the question of whether the apricots' color has yet risen. She says the apricots taste of musk. Bosola counters this sexual innuendo with a scatological remark: the apricots should have been peeled because the gardener used horse dung to make them ripen early. (As we have already noted, apricots in England normally ripen only in August.) Bosola's nasty joke here echoes his earlier remark to Ferdinand, the Duchess's brother, who has just bribed him with an offer of the position of provisorship of the horse in order to get Bosola to spy on the Duchess: "Say then, my corruption / Grew out of horse-dung: I am your creature" (1.1.286–7). The Duchess responds in a similarly joking manner by offering some of the apricots to Antonio; again, he refuses a request from his sovereign (and wife), to which she soothingly replies, "Sir, you are loth / To rob us of our dainties:—'tis a delicate fruit, / They say they are restorative" (2.1.142–4). Does the Duchess truly believe that even in her pregnant state apricots are restorative, or, does she, believing otherwise (like Bosola), eat the apricots simply because she cannot resist?

Bosola next speaks of the "pretty" art of grafting, which can produce such monstrosities as "a pippin grow upon a crab, / A damson on a blackthorn" (2.1.146–7)—a veiled allusion to the liaison he suspects between the Duchess and her (unidentified) lover. The Duchess begins to feel ill—in the Cheek by Jowl production of 1995–96 she actually "chokes up the fruit with such violence that it is a wonder she doesn't knock someone out with the effort," as she is carried off the stage (see the review by Ian Sansom in the *TLS* and the essay by John Russell Brown)—blaming "this green fruit" (2.1.154); without a word Bosola exits, followed by the Duchess with her ladies, as she goes into labor. Left alone on the stage, Antonio and his friend Delio agree that in order to hide the impending birth, they will put out a rumor that the Duchess has been poisoned by Bosola and will refuse all physicians, on the ground that the latter are also suspects. Immediately, at the opening of the next scene, Bosola draws his conclusion: "So, so: there's no question but her tetchiness and most vulturous eating of the apricocks are apparent signs of breeding" (2.2.1–3). But the father is unknown to Bosola, and remains unknown even after two more children have been born (sometime between acts 2 and 3), so that in terms of advancing the plot, the apricots episode, as already noted, really accomplishes very little. However, a critical approach to *The Duchess of Malfi* that sees in Bosola the pivotal character of the play might well argue that his apricot test on the Duchess tells us something significant about his own moral psychology. (It should be noted that there is some tenuous evidence that Webster did see Bosola in this way: Bosola's name is first in the list of actors' names printed in the first edition of the play in 1623. See John Russell Brown's note to this effect in his edition.)

There has been deception all around in the apricots episode, and the dramatist compounds the duplicity by leaving us in the dark as to whether Bosola's apricots are ripe or green; perhaps the likeliest possibility is that the apricots are ripe and the Duchess declares them green to disguise the real reason for her adverse reaction to eating them. Some important traits of the Duchess's character have indeed been revealed in the scene: her irreverence for custom and fashion, her lusty nature, and her delight in embarrassing, even tasteless, jokes. But all of these traits have already appeared in the prolonged and extraordinary marriage scene, where the Duchess cajoles, tempts, and finally tricks Antonio into marrying her (1.3). It is true, though, that the horror and revulsion of the rest of the play are foreshadowed in the apricot episode by, for example, Bosola's loathsome image of highly prized fruit covered with manure.

Now, it must be acknowledged that in at least two modern critical editions of *The Duchess of Malfi* and in several collections of critical essays on the play, there are no discussions or annotations of the apricots scene. For that very reason, though, it may perhaps be worth saying a little more about the context of that scene. To begin with, in the first two acts of the play there are numerous allusions to fruit: plum trees (Bosola in 1.1), apricots, pippins, damsons, and crab apples (Bosola, the Duchess, and Delio in 2.1; Antonio in 2.3), lemons (the Duchess in 2.1), and orange trees (Bosola in 2.2). Bosola is the one who mentions most of these fruits (indeed, all of them except for the lemons): the comparison of the Duchess's brothers to plum trees; the apricot pregnancy test; the insinuation about grafting pippins, damsons, and crab apples; the comparison of women's lust to orange trees. The Duchess, on the other hand, recoils in disgust from the lemony breath of one of her ladies (one wonders why—is she allergic to the smell of lemons?). In any case, *all* the fruit in these first two acts has deeply negative connotations. And one wonders about this reversal of the usual connotations of fresh fruit. In fact, however, these negative connotations are just the prelude to the even more repellent and violent character of the animal imagery that pervades the play (and culminates in the lycanthropy of Ferdinand). From all this I conclude that, thematically, the apricot episode contributes something essential to the overall atmosphere of the play—an atmosphere characterized by John Russell Brown in an essay on the play (1998) as "a dark sensationalism and menace, contrasted with softness, intrigue, madness, moral sayings."

Looking to the theatrical world beyond the play, the immediate comparison that suggests itself is the pregnancy test in a play first performed some ten years later: *The Changeling* (1623–4) by Thomas Middleton (1580–1627) and William Rowley (1585?–1626). In that play, the recipes for both a pregnancy test and a virginity test are discovered by the heroine Beatrice in a medical manuscript owned by Alsemero, the man she is to marry (4.1). After checking the reliability of the virginity test on her waiting-woman, she arranges to take the test herself before Alsemero (4.2). Neither test is ever specified beyond the drinking of liquids identified only as "C" and "M" in the play. Bosola's apricots are certainly more persuasive, realistically reflecting, as they do, widespread folk beliefs about pregnant women. Such beliefs, for example, may be found in Shakespeare's *Measure for Measure* (first recorded production, 1604), where Pompey the clown says of Elbow the constable's wife: "Sir, she came in great with child, and longing, saving your honour's reverence, for stewed prunes" (2.1.86–7).

By contrast with Bosola's apricot pregnancy test, apricots form an extended political metaphor in lines 3.4.29–66 of Shakespeare's *Richard II* (1597). The speakers are a gardener and his assistants (overheard by the queen and her ladies), and the discourse, which takes place in the Duke of York's garden, begins with an observation about the apricot trees, gradually shifts to a mixed horticultural/political mode, and concludes with language that is almost purely political:

> Go, bind thou up yon dangling apricocks,
> Which, like unruly children, make their sire
> Stoop with oppression of their prodigal weight;
> Give some supportance to the bending twigs.
> Go thou, and like an executioner
> Cut off the heads of too fast growing sprays
> That look too lofty in our commonwealth:
> All must be even in our government.

Later, the discourse moves in the opposite direction, from politics back to horticulture, and then reverts once more to politics.

> Bolingbroke
> Hath seiz'd the wasteful king. O, what pity is it
> That he had not so trimm'd and dress'd his land
> As we this garden! We at time of year
> Do wound the bark, the skin of our fruit trees,

Lest, being over-proud in sap and blood,
With too much riches it confound itself;
Had he done so to great and growing men,
They might have liv'd to bear, and he to taste
Their fruits of duty.

Apricots occur in a purely domestic context early on (chap. 6) in Jane Austen's *Mansfield Park* (1814). The scene is a dinner at Mansfield Park; present at the table are (by my count) ten members of the extended family—including Lady Bertram and three of her four children (Edmund, Maria, and Julia), Mrs. Norris, Fanny Price, Dr. and Mrs. Grant, Mary and Henry Crawford—and one guest, Maria Bertram's suitor, Mr. Rushworth. The main conversational theme of the entire chapter—horticulture and agriculture—is initiated by the foolish Rushworth, who is bent on "improving" his estate. Not to be outshone, the insufferable Mrs. Norris, in the longest speech of the chapter, explains all that she and her deceased husband were planning by way of improving the Parsonage (presently occupied by the Grants). She concludes: "It was only the spring twelvemonth before Mr. Norris's death, that we put in the apricot against the stable wall, which is now grown such a noble tree." Dr. Grant, however, responds by "regretting that the fruit should be so little worth the trouble of gathering." To which Mrs. Grant retorts: "Sir, it is a Moor Park, we bought it as a Moor Park, and it cost us—that is, it was a present from Sir Thomas, but I saw the bill—and I know it cost seven shillings, and was charged as a Moor Park." At this point, Mrs. Grant remarks that her husband could hardly be acquainted with the taste of their apricots because "what with early tarts and preserves, my cook contrives to get them all." Each assertion by each participant in this little apricot episode is exquisitely in character: the penurious and bitter Mrs. Norris, the pretentiously arrogant Dr. Grant, the tactful Mrs. Grant. Maggie Lane, however, sees the incident as much more than a way of reinforcing our grasp of the character of each of the conversationalists; the tree stands for nothing less than Fanny Price herself:

> Transplanted from one part of the country to another, rather tender, with aspersions cast upon its pedigree, the Moor Park apricot is like the sapling Fanny. Mrs. Norris is the prime mover in the acquisition of both, but the bill for the fruit tree (seven shillings, for like Fanny, it has a Price) is paid by Sir Thomas, as the whole of Fanny's maintenance is to be. To Dr. Grant's coarse and over-indulged taste, the fruit is insipid and not worth gathering. Just so is Fanny considered by almost everybody through the greater part of the book. In fact, Fanny has been transplanted to a spot that suits her: she thrives: and with the 'stable wall' of Mansfield tradition and Edmund's love to support her, the novel sees her grow into a 'noble' woman.

Lane might have added that a comment by Mary Crawford later in the chapter echoes this concern with "price." Mary is bored with all the talk of horticultural

278   improvement and to change the subject remarks to Edmund that her harp will arrive
the next day—laughably, in her brother's barouche, since she has been unable to hire
a horse and cart. Edmund patiently explains that it is harvest time and farmers have
other uses for their horses, to which Mary replies: "I shall understand all your ways
in time; but, coming down with the true London maxim, that everything is to be
got with money, I was a little embarrassed at first by the sturdy independence of
your country customs." We cannot be sure whether Mary is being ironic here or
whether her embarrassment will eventually lead her to reconsider the truth of the
"London maxim" (she never does); nevertheless, one might already at this point in the
novel entertain some doubts about Lionel Trilling's claim that "Mary Crawford is
conceived—is calculated—to win the charmed admiration of almost any reader."
Claudia Johnson is perhaps closer to the mark when she characterizes Mary and her
brother as "citified siblings . . . stock figures." Neither Trilling nor Johnson refers to the
"London maxim," about which, however, Tony Tanner remarks that "much of the
novel is implied here." Neither Trilling nor Johnson nor Tanner so much as mentions
the apricot episode, which is also missing from a first-rate 1999 film adaptation
(directed by Patricia Rozema).

Something must be said about Moor Park apricots. This superior variety of apricot had been developed by Lord Anson from an imported stone he planted in 1760
on his estate, Moor Park, in Hertfordshire. (*Mansfield Park* is set some twenty-five years
later.) In Barry's mid-ninteenth-century horticultural manual, the Moor Park—one
of seven recommended apricot cultivars—is described as follows: "One of the largest
and finest apricots, yellow, with a red cheek, flesh orange, sweet, juicy and rich, parts
from the stone; growth rather slow, but stout and short jointed; very productive." The
Moor Park remains today a prime apricot cultivar (it is the one that Vaughan and
Geissler choose to illustrate in their *New Oxford Book of Food Plants* [1997]) but there
are many other varieties (some two thousand in China alone).

The entry "Apricots" in Flaubert's *Dictionary of Accepted Ideas* reads in its entirety:
"'None to be had again this year.'" (The *Dictionary* was only one of several similar collections compiled by Flaubert during his lifetime; all were left unfinished at his death
in 1880.) The reason for this relative scarcity of apricots depends, as already observed,
on their vulnerability to late spring frosts, as noted by Alexandre Dumas *père* (1802–1870)
in his own "dictionary" (which Flaubert must have known, since it was published in
1873): "Such an early fruit that there are few springs when one does not hear people saying: 'There will be no apricots this year, they've all been caught by the frost.'"

One way of insuring a supply of ripe apricots in early spring—and "what could
be more thrilling / than ripe apricots out of season"—is to get them from warmer
climes. This is the strategy of the speaker in "Consolations of Apricots" (1998) by
Diane Ackerman (b. 1948), whose "sense-ravishing apricots" are imported from
Morocco. But before an apricot is actually consumed, the poem systematically surveys
the fruit's sensuous qualities. First, an anticipatory readying of the palate:

Apricots, Ripe and Unripe

Somewhere between a peach and a prayer,
they taste of well water
and butterscotch and dried apples
and desert simooms and lust.

Sweet with a twang of spice

Next, there are the apricot's shape (its "two hemispheres," its "continuous curve"), its feel ("velvety sheen / . . . shorter / than peach fuzz, closer to chamois"), and its color ("Tawny gold with a blush on its cheeks, / an apricot is the color of shame and dawn"). Waiting for the perfect moment ("at twilight" "while a trail of bright ink tattoos the sky"), the reader is finally admonished, in the last line of the poem, to "sink [our] teeth into the flesh of an apricot."

   An entirely different strategy for taking literary advantage of the beauty of an apricot tree is used by the Hungarian writer Gyula Illyés (1902–1983) in his poem "The Apricot Tree," where the speaker personifies the tree as a young woman offering her fruit (here brilliantly translated by Christine Brooke-Rose):

> The apricot tree
> shoulder-high or less—
> look! An apricot
> at branch-tip ripens.
>
> Stretching, straining,
> holding out a prize,
> the tree is a maiden
> offering her closed eyes.
>
> You stand and wonder,
> will she bend and sway
> her slender waist or
> step back, run away . . .
>   [. . . . .]
> This garden, a ballroom,
> she gazes about,
> anxiously, constantly,
> wants to be sought out.

In the second half of the poem, the speaker becomes passionately involved with the tree and yet at the same time conscious of his own poetic conceit:

> She rustles softly
> when I salute her.

It seems my poetry
can still transmute her.

Then, at a still higher level of fantasy, the speaker dreams of the tree and concludes by adressing her:

Since that dream I glance
towards you, flushing.
Please look at me too,
askance and blushing.

A dream of an apricot tree is the culminating image in the story "Portrait of the Yellow Apricot Tree" by Norman Manea (b. 1936), translated from the Rumanian by Cornelia Golna. The setting is a high school classroom but the students are adults, the grown-up classmates of the narrator. The psychological status of the succession of brief episodes is unclear: dream predominates (the word is used several times), but memory and fantasy seem also to be involved. One thing is clear—the threat of violence that hovers over the entire narration. There are allusions to sentries, barracks, terror; there is a frequent coupling of "examination" with "execution"; and at one point the sadistic teacher appears in a military uniform. A little over halfway through the story, the narrator notices that one of the students has copied from the blackboard into his notebook the teacher's chalked words: "PORTRAIT OF THE APRICOT TREE." The narrator then scrutinizes the blackboard closely and finally discerns, "standing out in relief on the blackboard, the apricot tree," which the teacher has drawn in colored chalk. As he continues to stare at the image, he says, "it rained luminous apricots, small, golden balls, the branches arched and sprang back, whipping the air." His focus then drifts away to "those suddenly all-too-short afternoons before the examinations, the executions," and then:

The apricot tree had revealed itself once more; again there were the reassuring yellow circles that lit the sky with the gold of firm, dense fruit. As I ventured into the depths of the blackboard, the relief opened up protectively with a murmur of invisible waters that cooled my brow.

But the picture of the apricot tree is perhaps only a ruse—it was, after all, created by the teacher—and, unable "to free myself of the apricot tree," the threatening teacher approaches; as the story ends, "He was shaking me, but I could not get up. I was trying with all my strength to gain some time, to put off the moment."

Still-life painters of fruit—or perhaps their patrons and customers—seem not to have favored pictures of apricots (after all, apricots are not as large as peaches, as shapely as pears, or as crisp as apples). One picture of apricots worth mentioning is by the French painter Jacques Linard (ca. 1600–1645), who specialized in still life and was prestigious enough to serve as *valet de chambre* to Louis XIII. In his *Apricots and Moths*

(1631), Linard artfully arranges twenty-eight ripe apricots on a large platter with one of them split open to reveal the pit; hovering just above the fruit are two moths, which in the words of Jacques Thuillier "evoke from a dish of fruit . . . that delicate and somewhat melancholy poetry we find in his Vanitas pictures." (The painting, oil on canvas, 17 x 24½ in., is in a private collection in Paris; there is a reproduction in Thuillier and Châtelet, *French Painting from Le Nain to Fragonard* [1964].)

An exact contemporary of Linard's was Louise Moillon (1615-16–after 1674) —in Christopher Wright's opinion, "the greatest still-life painter of the French seventeenth century"—who also painted numerous still lifes of apricots. Michel Faré's monumental work on French seventeenth-century still life painting refers to (and reproduces in black and white) three paintings of apricots by Moillon: *Bowl of Apricots* in a private collection in Paris (oil on canvas, 13¾ x 20½ in.), *Apricots on a Blue Porcelain Plate* in the De Boer collection in Amsterdam (oil on canvas, 13 x 20½ in.), and *Basket of Apricots* in the F. Heim collection in Paris (oil on canvas, 15¾ x 20½ in.). It is apparently the latter painting about which Christopher Middleton has written an eloquent essay (1983), "Louise Moillon's Apricots (1635)." Middleton sees "each apricot with its twin rondures meeting in the tender sweep of its crease, even though not many display this crease, so as to discourage any donjuanesque counting of the apricots." But Middleton is not discouraged: he counts the apricots and finds twenty-nine, attaching some mysterious significance to the number's primeness, or, as he puts it, "one of those that are not divisible without a rupture of number into fractions." He also carefully records the "lining, or nest, of leaves," some looking wilted, in which the heap of apricots rests, as well as, on the table top, the two purple plums, the five drops of water (one of them being sipped by a fly), and the single apricot that has been opened. Dominating Middleton's interpretation of the picture, though, is the idea of the apricots as deeply erotic: "the seductively edible, creased and golden fruits are for all the world like virgin quims, waiting to enjoy and to be enjoyed."

My own favorite representation of apricots is *Apricot Branch* (ca. 1630) by the German painter Georg Flegel (1566–1638), now in the Darmstadt Museum (oil on panel, 19¼ x 13 in.; see plate 20). The author of the catalogue (1999) of Flegel's still life paintings, Kurt Wettengl, arguing for the painter's originality and power of invention, asserts that no comparable work is known either in Flegel's oeuvre or in contemporary Dutch still life painting. Ebert-Schifferer's comment, in her *Still Life,* is also worth quoting: "Flegel's branch of fruit is set in a jar like a bouquet, without regard to the laws of gravity, which normally would cause the jar to tip over. Although the precisely rendered differences in the ripeness of the fruits and the onset of drying in the leaves celebrate the beauty of nature and exhibit the painter's botanical precision, the carefully chosen motif conveys a more complex message."

PITS AND SEEDS

THE PERILS OF PITS

Let us begin by looking at a little Yiddish story called "The Search" (or, in another translation, "A Yom Kippur Scandal") by Sholom Aleichem (1859–1916); the text of the English version by Norbert Guterman is just a scant five pages in length. That the story is about Yom Kippur should occasion some surprise, for in the *shtetl* setting of Sholom Aleichem's world everyone would be fasting on Yom Kippur, and fruit (or any other food) would be significant presumably only by its absence. There is, in fact, suspense in the telling of the story and an unresolved mystery at the end, and I want to suggest that the story is not only, as Irving Howe and Eliezer Greenberg put it, "a complex story about the relationship between worldly and other-worldly values in *shtetl* society" (1973), but also a virtuoso exhibition of narrative technique. I will begin with the core narrative and then proceed to the framing narrative at the beginning and end of the story.

A stranger from Lithuania—known for its pious Jews—appears in Kasrilevke just in time for the evening Yom Kippur service. Just before the service begins, the stranger, who insists on concealing his name, makes very generous contributions to the synagogue and to the town's beggars. When the final prayer is over and all are about to return home for their first meal in twenty-four hours, the stranger suddenly cries out, faints, and, on being revived, explains that he had secretly hidden eighteen hundred rubles in his prayer stand for safekeeping and the money has disappeared. The rabbi proposes that each member of the congregation, beginning with himself, empty his pockets. One young man refuses when it comes his turn; though not a native of Kasrilevke, he is exceptionally learned and the son-in-law of the rich man of the town. The young man is forcibly searched, revealing in his pockets "guess what?—chickenbones and a dozen plum pits; everything was still fresh, the bones had recently been gnawed, and the pits were moist." Confirmed in their suspicions that the young man is not really a pious Jew despite all his intellectual accomplishments (which are listed in great detail), the worshippers take a malicious delight in his disgrace; only the rabbi feels shamed.

The preceding core narrative is enclosed at its beginning and end by a few lines of framing narrative: an anonymous narrator, who has been "sitting in a corner by the window, smoking and taking in stories of thefts, holdups, and expropriations," offers to tell a good story about a theft in a synagogue. He begins by identifying his hometown as Kasrilevke (which makes him, like the Litvak, a stranger in town); at one point, partway through his narrative, he is described as looking at his audience to see what kind of an impression he is making; finally, when he stops talking and resumes smoking his story is over. But Sholom Aleichem's story is not over; it continues for a few more lines:

> "And what about the money?" we all asked in one voice.
>
> "What money?" the man said with an uncomprehending look as he blew out the smoke.
>
> "What do you mean, what money? The eighteen hundred—"
>
> "O-o-o-oh," he drawled. "The eighteen hundred? Vanished without a trace."
>
> "Vanished?"
>
> "Without a t–r–a–c–e."

It is compatible with what we read in the text of "The Search" that its author, Sholom Aleichem, had been a member of the anonymous narrator's audience in the unidentified town (one of the members of the audience collectively identified as "we" in the above quotation) or, alternatively, that Sholom Aleichem had heard the anonymous narrator's story from someone who had heard it firsthand. On the other hand, the anonymous narrator from Kasrilevke could be Sholom Aleichem himself, who just happens to be visiting the unidentified town; after all, the name "Sholom Aleichem" is a pseudonym referring to an inhabitant of the imaginary town of Kasrilevke. We might even note that early in the story the first words uttered by the Litvak are "Sholom aleichem" (an entirely appropriate greeting, of course)—which is very much like Alfred Hitchcock placing himself, as himself, in a scene in one of his own films. In any case, it is clear that just as the anonymous narrator from Kasrilevke has been seemingly cavalier in deflecting the attention of his listeners away from the potentially exciting story of a theft of eighteen hundred rubles in a synagogue to the petty story of some furtive mouthfuls of chicken and plum, so the author of "The Search" has been shrewd in deflecting the attention of us, his readers, away from his failure to enact narrative closure and onto the plight of the miserable young man. And our interest in the young man's plight has been sharpened by a full page of praise for his learning, both sacred and secular, culminating in the phrase, "in short, a man with all seventeen talents." Now, *seventeen* is an odd number, in both senses. Though it does not quite reach the magnitude of the *Eighteen* Blessings of the daily prayer—which, in fact, are really nineteen—or of the *eighteen*-headed man whose brilliance is sometimes even surpassed by that of the rabbi, or of the *eighteen* hundred rubles, it certainly surpasses the *dozen* plum pits, and possesses, furthermore, a wonderful air of randomness and arbitrariness. "The Search" is about tradition and modernity in *shtetl* culture but it is also about narrative strategies, how to extract humor from numbers, and the literary uses of plum pits!

In the first nine lines of "Family Portrait" (1958), by Irving Layton (b. 1912), the Canadian poet confronts a family consisting of a wealthy father together with his offspring, three "slobs with a college education," all eating watermelon in a hotel dining room. He then makes the following observations:

> With the assurance of money
> in the bank
> they spit out the black, cool, elliptical
> melonseeds, and you can tell
> the old man has rocks
> but no culture: he spits,
> > gives the noise away free.
>
> The daughter however is embarrassed
> (Second Year Arts, McGill) and sucks harder
> to forget.
>
> They're about as useless
> as tits on a bull,
> and I think:
> "Thank heaven I'm not
> Jesus Christ—
> I don't have to love them."

Apricot pits figure in a powerful episode in Flaubert's *Madame Bovary*. We recall, first of all, how a gift of apricots signalizes the end of Emma Bovary's affair with Rodolphe (part 2, sect. 13). Rodolphe has decided to break off the affair and he cruelly informs Emma of this on the day before their planned elopement, adopting his usual means of secret communication with Emma: a note buried at the bottom of a basket of special seasonal food, in this case freshly picked apricots. Emma frantically empties the basket on to the sideboard and opens the letter just as her husband arrives home. She retreats to the attic, where she reads the note and nearly commits suicide by leaping out the window. In a trance she comes back downstairs and sits through an agonizing dinner with Charles: "She unfolded her napkin as though to inspect the darns, and began really seriously to devote her attention to it and count the stitches" (translated by Steegmuller). Mentioning Monsieur Rodolphe but oblivious that his wife has turned scarlet, Charles asks the servant for the apricots (now returned to the basket) and proceeds to eat one. Emma refuses his offer of the basket of apricots: "'Smell them: such fragrance!' he said, moving it back and forth before her." And Charles continues to eat, "spitting apricot pits into his hand and transferring them to his plate." For a moment all is calm, but then Emma recognizes Rodolphe's carriage driving by and falls to the floor in a faint. A couple of chapters later she has recovered and is ready to have another affair, this time with her old friend Leon, just returned from Paris.

In Flaubert's description of the events just summarized his style gives an impression of being absolutely pared down to essentials; it is Flaubert, in his own words, at his most "realistic" or "scientific." But, of course, in passages like those quoted it is Flaubert's selectivity—of words, of images, of physical details—that counts. The two most vivid and memorable images of Emma and Charles in the episode are of her counting the stitches in the darns of her napkin and of him spitting apricot pits into his hand. Emma, as usual, is engaged in a desperate but futile search for something she can hardly imagine, while Charles, as usual, complacently and repellently feeds his senses. Emma may be the more sympathetic character—if we feel we must take sides—but is not there something to be said for enjoying fresh apricots, and is there any politer way than Charles's to dispose of the pits?

A final note about this apricot episode: one may wonder why Charles finds Rodolphe's apricots so irresistible; after all, he must have a supply of his own, at least if we can rely on our earlier information (part 1, section 5) that Charles's "long narrow garden ran back between two clay walls covered with espaliered apricot trees." And Charles seems to be a good gardener, for the local marquis himself, no less, "asked Charles for a few grafts [for his cherry trees]" (part 1, section 7).

For another view of the "irksome" apricot pit, we may return to Ponge's prose poem about apricots, cited in chapter 7, "Peaches, Mangoes, and Other Juicy Fruits" (translated by John Montague):

> Here, no doubt at all, is a fruit for the right hand, made to be carried immediately to the mouth.
>
> You could eat it in one bite, but for this very hard and relatively irksome pit, which makes you take two, or at most, four.

~

> Voici, n'en doutons pas, un fruit pour la main droite, fait pour être porté à la bouche aussitôt.
>
> On n'en ferait qu'une bouchée, n'était ce noyau fort dur et relativement importun qu'il y a, si bien qu'on et fait plutôt deux, et au maximum quatre.

A DIGRESSION ON NATURE FROM WITHIN

In his "Stone Fruit," Les Murray attempts to imagine the fruit of the title from within. To begin with, it must be understood that his poem is included in a collection called *Translations from the Natural World* (1992; dedicated "to the glory of God"), where most of the poems are about personified animals and plants, often from the double perspective, first, of a speculative consideration of the inner life of various living organisms

286   (such as eagles, dogs, foxes, cattle, elephants, pigs, sea lions, DNA, sunflowers, sperm whales, bees, cuttlefish, and possums)—relying for the most part on ideas and language derived from our own inner life—and, second, of the direct physical encounters between those organisms and ourselves. One of the few poems about a plant is "Stone Fruit," a virtuoso performance taking the form of a single sentence of thirteen lines. The term "stone" does not occur in the poem, but what I take to be a synonym—"crack seed"—does. No particular kinds of fruit are anywhere specified, but we are naturally led to think of peaches, plums, apricots, or cherries when we read the following lines:

> I am streamy inside, taut with sugar meats, circular,
> my colours are those of the sun as understood by leaf liquor cells
> and cells of deep earth metal, I am dressed for eyes by the blind,
> perfumed, flavoured by the mouthless, by insect-conductors who kill
> and summon by turns.

Each of the sensory qualities mentioned or implied—taste, shape, color, odor—depends, of course, on an interaction of appropriate fruit cells with an appropriate sense organ. The "insect-conductor" presumably refers to the bees and other insects responsible for the pollination of many stone fruit trees. A different type of interaction occurs when the fruit is engulfed by an animal, both nourishing the eater and at the same time helping the tree to reproduce itself: "I am / the animals of my tree, appointed to travel and be eaten / since animals are plants' genital extensions." But Murray is especially interested in the stone fruit's "inner world," a phrase that occurs in the initial and final lines of the poem:

> I appear from the inner world, singular and many,
>   [. . . . .]
>   I emerge continually
> from the inner world, which you can't mate with nor eat.

Among the messages from the inner world is this: "I'm to tell you there is a future and there are / consequences, and they are not the same." This slightly cryptic saying seems to be drawing a distinction between mere physical nature—the realm of cause and consequence—and some other realm, perhaps one of unrealized potentialities.

Murray's poem—and, indeed, his entire volume of *Translations from the Natural World*—raises the question of how much sense it makes to write about the "inner world" of plants or animals. Rather than taking up this philosophical issue (or pseudo-issue?) as such, I prefer to cite as a cautionary reminder the vehemently skeptical views on this topic of the Portuguese poet Fernando Pessoa (1888–1935), or, rather, of one of Pessoa's three principal personae (his term is "heteronyms"), Alberto Caeiro, in poem 28 of his *The Keeper of Flocks* (1911–12; translated by Keith Bosley):

> One has to be ignorant of flowers and stones and rivers
> In order to speak of their feelings.

> To speak of the souls of stones, of flowers, of rivers,
> Is to speak of oneself and one's delusions.
> Thank God that stones are only stones,
> And that rivers are nothing but rivers,
> And that flowers are merely flowers.
> As for me, I write the prose of my poetry
> And I rest content,
> For I know that I understand Nature from without;
> And I don't understand it from within
> Because Nature has no within;
> Otherwise it would not be Nature.

But perhaps the false and perverse anthropocentrism to which Alberto Caiero objects can be evaded by a different approach to the self, say, that of the Belgian writer and painter Henri Michaux (1899–1984), who believed that, in the words of his translator Richard Ellmann: "we are multiple, carried this way or that by influences of different intensity from various sources, 'born,' as he puts it, 'of too many mothers.' 'There is no one self. There are no ten selves. There is no self. SELF is only a position of equilibrium. (One among a thousand others continually possible and always ready).'" In any case, one of the many non-human beings into which Michaux imagines projecting himself is an apple (others include an ant, a boa, a bison, and a saucer). Some excerpts from the first section of Michaux's prose poem, "Magie" (Magic)—included in a collection aptly titled *Lointain Intérieur* (The far-off inside; 1938; translated by Richard Ellmann)—imagine the speaker within an apple:

> I used to be very nervous. But I have started on a new road
>   I put an apple on my table. Then I put myself into the apple. How peaceful!
>   [Je mets une pomme sur ma table. Puis je me mets dans cette pomme. Quelle tranquillité!]
>   That may look very simple. And yet I have been trying for twenty years; and I would not have succeeded if I had wanted to begin with that. Why not? Maybe I thought I might be humiliated, considering its small size and its opaque and slow life [sa petite taille et sa vie opaque et lente]. That is possible. The thoughts of the lower layer are rarely beautiful.
>   I therefore started on a new tack and united myself to the river Sheldt.
>   [. . . . .]
>   I come now to the apple. Here too there were gropings, experiments; a long story. It's not easy to start, nor to explain either.
>   But I can tell it to you in one word. The word is *suffering*.
>   When I arrived inside the apple, I was frozen.

The fourth section of the poem explores a way of eliminating suffering (in the form of a toothache and an earache) by focusing all one's attention on it, and concludes with a sense of triumph: "Because of this discipline I now have a better and better chance of never coinciding with any mind at all and of being able to move about freely in the world." Why does the sufferer come back to the apple after abandoning the initial experiments with it? For no special reason at all, I would say—any more than it was essential to begin with an apple.

PITS AND GAMES

One thing one can do with pits (or fruit stones) is to play games with them. A traditional French children's game, called "La Fossette aux Noyaux," consists simply of attempting to throw the pits into a small hole in the ground. The game is the sixteenth (out of fifty) in *Les jeux et plaisirs de l'enfance* (1657) by Jacques Stella (1596–1657); each game is explained by a picture of *putti* at play, with a verse caption underneath. The engravings are by one of Stella's pupils, his niece, Claudine Bouzonnet Stella (1636–1697). The verse caption for "La Fossette aux Noyaux" describes the game (translated by Stanley Appelbaum):

> Although these cherrystones for them
> Are worth a precious diadem,
> These hopeful youngsters bravely toil
> To throw their treasures in a pit;
> But I'd say on the face of it,
> They're being sown in barren soil.
>
> ~
>
> Quoy qu'ilz estiment ces Noyaux
> autant que de riches Ioyaux,
> ce Cadet qui d'espoir se flatte
> les jette en terre asseurement
> mais j'apprehende aucunement
> qu'il ne les Seme en terre jngratte.

It should be noted that "noyaux" does not necessarily refer to a cherrystone; the stones being tossed by the *putti* in the engraving could be the pits of any small stone fruit; see the entry "Noyau" in Randle Cotgrave's *A Dictionarie of the French and English Tongues* (London, 1611): "The stone of a Plum, Cherrie, Date, Olive, &c."

Another kind of game is played with fruit pits and seeds in "Eating Your Words" (1982), by Sandra Gilbert (b. 1936), which begins with the sourness of love misspoken —first he says he loves her, then he denies his words, even says he could eat them— and ends with the fantasied pleasures of *her* eating *his* words of love. The clever twist of the poem is to savor not only the banal fruitlike juiciness of the uttered words themselves but also the (inedible) kernels of meaning wrapped up in the flesh of the words:

> I knew just how they'd
> taste, how they'd

feel on my tongue, in my
dry throat, each of your

words small and round and complete,
a grape, a plum, a nectarine
tense with its own sweetness,
half drowned in the liquid

of its own desire, each word
wrapped around a seed of meaning
marvelous as a meteorite
from light years away.

I'd swallow the meat of your words,
I'd collect the beautiful seeds
and make them into buttons and earrings
and glittering stones for my fingers.

From Layton's spitting of watermelon seeds as a marker of sociocultural class to Gilbert's metaphorical seeds of meaning is a long stretch but perhaps as good a way as any of illustrating, once again, the extremely wide semiotical reach of literary fruit episodes.

MEDLARS,
THE RIPE AND THE ROTTEN

The ripening of fruit—with its often dramatically palpable changes—has long been a fertile paradigm for students of human development (physical, moral, or social). Consider, for example, what commentators have made of the famous passage in Matthew (7:18–20): "A sound tree cannot bear evil fruit, nor can a bad tree bear good fruit. . . . Thus you will know them by their fruits." *The Abingdon Bible Commentary* (1929), in an entry by J. Newton Davies, explains just how apt is Matthew's comparison of moral character to fruit: first, the fruit is the end or purpose of the tree; second, fruit occurs in a great variety of forms; third, each variety of fruit possesses its own specific goodness or beauty; and finally, it takes time for fruit to ripen and mature. No mention, not surprisingly, of how fruit can be expected to decay. One may wonder, though, whether any reader of Matthew, in the first century C.E. or at any later time, was really capable of keeping completely at bay all associations with such familiar physical characteristics of many fruits as the propensity to turn brown when cut open and eventually to rot. Indeed, already in the Old Testament, the imminent decay of summer fruit was used as a metaphor by the prophet Amos (8:1–2) in his account of God's prediction of the imminent destruction of a sinful Israel: "Thus the Lord God showed me: behold, a basket of summer fruit [*qayits*]. And he said, 'Amos, what do you see?' And I said, 'A basket of summer fruit.' Then the Lord said to me, 'The end [*qets*] has come upon my people Israel.'" All commentators notice the near coincidence of the Hebrew terms for "summer fruit" and "end," and also the implicit assumption of the ripeness of the summer fruit.

In a secular context, Ludovico Ariosto makes good literary use of rotting fruit in an extended simile toward the end of canto 7 of his *Orlando Furioso*, when Ruggiero, the main pagan hero of the work, with the aid of a magic ring finally sees his lover, the evil sorceress Alcina, for what she is (in Barbara Reynolds's translation):

> And as a boy who hides a fruit away
> And then goes off, forgetting all about it,
> On finding it long afterwards one day

Within a drawer or cupboard where he'd put it,
Astonished at the sight of such decay,
Is more than willing now to do without it,
And takes the putrid thing, with mould encrusted,
And flings it far away from him, disgusted,

So did Ruggiero, when his former lover
Was altered by the ring.

About this simile, A. Bartlett Giamatti makes the interesting observation that it is

the only heroic simile in the entire Alcina episode, [which] underscores
the revelation and solemnizes its meaning. The simile, of the little boy and
the once prized, now rotten and rejected fruit, is literally apt. Ruggiero has
been a little boy, innocent and uneducated, naïve and trusting, and the fruit
which seemed so fine and is now so rotten that the boy spurns it, is precisely Alcina, that fair-seeming but actually much-handled delicacy of the
deceptive earthly paradise.

Turning to northern Europe, we may note that the God-fearing Dutch in the
seventeenth century had a motto: "Soon ripe, soon rotten" [*vroech rijp, vroech rot*]. For
an engraved illustration of the motto (1614) by Roemer Visscher (1547–1620), featuring a bowl of fruit, see Schneider, *Still Life: Still Life Painting in the Early Modern
Period*. And closer to home we may recall Wallace Stevens's challenge to the Christian
idea of heaven in "Sunday Morning" (1923): "Is there no change of death in paradise?
/ Does ripe fruit never fall?"

Now, it happens that there are certain species of fruit—notably, the sorb apple
and the medlar—that require for edibility a lengthy process of decomposition (sometimes called "bletting") after they are picked and before they are ready to eat. For bletting to occur successfully the fruit must first mature fully on the tree, which means
picking should be delayed until the leaves start to fall off. From the biochemical standpoint, the process of bletting involves an increase in sugars and a decrease in acids and
tannins; colloquially, the process is usually described as rotting or decaying—see standard
dictionary entries on "medlar": "It is eaten only when decayed" (*Shorter Oxford English
Dictionary*); "not edible until the early stages of decay" (*Random House Dictionary of the
English Language*). Or, note this recipe (accompanied by a copper-plate engraving of
medlars) from the anonymous *A book of fruits and flowers*, published in London in 1653
(2nd ed., 1656): "To make a Tart of Medlers. Take *Medlers* that be rotten, and stamp
them, and set them upon a chafin dish with coales, and beat in two yolks of Eggs,
boyling till it be somewhat thick, then season it with *Sugar, Cinamon,* and *Ginger,* and
lay it in paste." C. Anne Wilson, in her introduction to a facsimile edition (1984) of
what she refers to as "one of the most attractive of early English household books,

with its unusual illustrations, and its higgledy piggledy mixture of recipes for cooking, confectionary, preserves and medicines," points out that this recipe for medlar tarts goes back to at least 1596.

The sorb apple—the European serviceberry—is not an apple though it belongs to the genus *Pyrus;* its fruit is berrylike in size. As for the medlar, it must be understood that several different kinds of fruit are sometimes referred to by that name; here we are speaking of a fruit, well known at least as early as the Middle Ages (in western Europe) and botanically denominated *Mespilus germanica.* Today, the adventurous horticulturist Lee Reich deems the medlar "uncommon," and clearly has sought familiar terms in which to describe it (in his *Uncommon Fruits Worthy of Attention* [1991]): "The fruits resemble small, russeted apples, tinged dull yellow or red, with their calyx ends (across from the stems) flared open. . . . Inside, the flesh is as soft as a baked apple. The flavor has a refreshing briskness with winy overtones, like old-fashioned applesauce laced with cinnamon. Embedded in the pulp are five, large, stonelike seeds." For such a now increasingly unfamiliar fruit, it is worth quoting from Vaughan and Geissler another description of one of its most remarkable features: "The five seed vessels are visible in the eye of the fruit, for the fruit is set in the receptacle as in a gaping cup, around the rim of which stand the five conspicuous calyx lobes." Beautifully rendered paintings of two medlars (along with a poppy anemone and a common pear) may be found in one of the folios of Joris Hoefnagel's *Mira Calligraphiae Monumenta* (see plate 21).

In England in the eighteenth century medlars must have been familiar enough for Dr. Johnson to remark, during an argument with Sir Joshua Reynolds about the effects of drinking on character, "that there are some sluggish men who are improved by drinking; as there are fruits which are not good till they are rotten. There are such men, but they are medlars."

Medlars were obviously still familiar enough to Vita Sackville-West in the England of the 1940s to enable her (in the "Autumn" section of *The Garden*) to formulate this rather overwrought description:

> And that true child of Fall, whose morbid fruit
> Ripens, with walnuts, only in November,
> The Medlar lying brown across the thatch;
> Rough elbows of rough branches, russet fruit
> So blet it's worth no more than sleepy pear,
> But in its motley pink and yellow leaf
> A harlequin that some may overlook
> Nor ever think to break and set within
> A vase of bronze against a wall of oak,
> With Red-hot Poker, Autumn's final torch.

But D. H. Lawrence, perhaps predictably, revels in the rottenness of bletted fruits. From the more than fifty lines of his "Medlars and Sorb-apples" (1923) I quote a few typical passages:

I love you, rotten,
Delicious rottenness.

I love to suck you out from your skins
So brown and soft and coming suave,
so morbid, as the Italians say.
   [. . . . .]
What is it?
What is it, in the grape turning raisin,
In the medlar, in the sorb-apple,
Wineskins of brown morbidity.
Autumnal excrementa;
What is it that reminds us of white gods?
   [. . . . .]
Medlars, sorb-apples,
More than sweet
Flux of autumn
Sucked out of your empty bladders

And sipped down, perhaps, with a sip of Marsala
So that the rambling, sky-dropped grape can add its savour to yours,
Orphic farewell, and farewell, and farewell
And the *ego sum* of Dionysos
The *sono io* of perfect drunkenness
Intoxication of final loneliness.

When eating a medlar its seeds naturally present a problem of disposal. Or—as in the following enthralling account (1986) of eating medlars—an opportunity for inventing a family game, observed by the American Mary Simeti (b. 1941) during her stay with Sicilian relatives:

> Eating a medlar entails a long run for a short slide: there is only a thin layer of sweet, tangy flesh between the skin and the shiny brown seeds the size of a slightly flattened marble, so that small mountains of skin and seeds accumulate on our plates at the end of dinner. The Everest that Tonino's grandfather would produce in his passion for medlars is legendary in the Simeti household, while Tonino has passed on to Francesco his own child-hood taste for shooting the smooth-skinned seeds across the room with thumb and forefinger. At least once each spring, dinner degenerates into outright warfare, with Natalia and me pretending to be above such non-sense while taking surreptitious aim at the men who circle the table carry-ing their munitions in a glass of water to make them squirt better. The rule is that they must sweep up afterward, but now and then throughout

the summer and into fall the odd medlar pit will roll out from under the furniture.

There is also a traditional Italian game played with medlars on the so-called Ventura (10 November, the feast of St. Martin) to help celebrate the opening of the new wines. The game is described by Giacomo Castelvetro (1546–1616) in the essay "The Fruits, Herbs, and Vegetables of Italy" (1614), in Italian, he dedicated to Lucy, Countess of Bedford. Castelvetro was born in Modena but became a Protestant sympathizer as a teenager and therefore chose to spend much of the rest of his life outside Italy, the last three years in England (where he even taught Italian for a term at Cambridge University). Castelvetro's purpose was to encourage his English hosts to eat more fresh fruits and vegetables. His lists are arranged by seasons; the "autumn" items include "medlars," beginning as follows (translated by Gillian Riley):

> Medlars are gathered at the end rather than the beginning of autumn. They ripen, as the proverb says, with a little time and a little straw. Medlars are quite well known in England, and well liked for their pleasant flavour. They are eaten raw after meals, with or without sugar.

There follows Castelvetro's account of the medlar game:

> And so, when this special evening arrives, the father of the family settles himself by the fire and has a basket brought to him. In it he puts as many pairs of medlars as there are people under his roof, and one extra for the poor. Then he covers the basket with a cloth so that he can hide three small coins in three of the fruit, gives the basket a good shake, and announces: "Let it be known to one and all that I have put three coins inside these fruit—a *denaio,* a two-*denaio* piece and a *soldo.* Whoever finds the smallest of them shall win one *scudo,* the next size up wins one half of one, and the largest he keeps and gets a third of a *scudo* as well."
>
> Then he calls his youngest child to him and says: "Put your hand into the basket and take out two medlars for the poor and put them on the table," making sure the child does not peep to see if they have any money in them. This continues until the child has distributed all the medlars, except the last two, which it keeps for itself. Then everyone looks inside their fruit, and if there is any money in the ones for the poor, it will be given to the first beggar who knocks on the door the next morning. Then follows a big celebration, tinged for some with sadness at not winning the *Ventura,* and with noisy merriment for others. I well remember the indescribable joy I felt on finding the money in a fruit.
>
> When this cheerful commotion has died down, the medlars are eaten and the wines sampled.

Medlars go back deeply into English literary history. Thus, in the Reeve's Prologue (ll. 3869–3875) of *The Canterbury Tales,* by Geoffrey Chaucer (early 1340s–1400), there is a passage in which the narrator compares himself in his old age to an "open-ers" (open-arse), the vulgar English name for a medlar:

> This white top writeth myne olde yeris [age];
> Myn herte is also mowled [mouldy] as myne heris,
> But if I fare as dooth an open-ers, —
> That ilke fruyt is ever lenger the wers,
> Til it be roten in mullok [rubbish] or in stree [straw].
> We olde men, I drede, so fare we:
> Til we be roten, kan we nat be rype;

We shall encounter this play on the words "rotten" and "ripe" again, and more specifically, the proverbial saying that for some person or thing the latter condition presupposes the former.

Contemporary with Chaucer, an anonymous poem (probably by a woman), "The Flower and the Leaf," contains the following lines (in Walter Skeat's modernized English):

> And as I stood and cast aside mine eye,
> I was 'ware of the fairest medlar tree
> That ever yet in all my life I see,
> As full of blossoms as it might be
> Therein a goldfinch leaping prettily
> Fro' bough to bough; and as him list he eet
> Here and there of buds and blossoms sweet.

John Dryden (1631–1700) composed a version of this poem, "The Flower and the Leaf; or, the Lady in the Arbour: A Vision" (along with selections from *The Canterbury Tales*) for his volume of *Fables* (1700), which included also translations from Homer and Ovid. Dryden smoothes out the couplets and slightly elaborates the language of the anonymous poem, producing a polished and thoroughly delightful work of some 618 lines. Here is Dryden's version of the lines already quoted:

> Thus as I mused, I cast aside my eye,
> And saw a medlar-tree was planted nigh.
> The spreading branches made a goodly show,
> And full of opening blooms was every bough:
> A goldfinch there I saw with gaudy pride
> Of painted plumes, that hopped from side to side,
> Still pecking as she passed; and still she drew
> The sweets from every flower, and sucked the dew

I might just add that the narrator (the lady in the arbor) is a witness to a "vision" or "fairy show," at the end of which she learns the identities of the Lady of the Leaf (she is Diana, and her chaste followers are clothed in white and attended by the

296   nightingale) and of the Lady of the Flower (she is Flora, and her pleasure-seeking followers are clothed in green and attended by the goldfinch).

Goldfinches were often taken as symbols of fertility in medieval thought. Such a goldfinch perched in a medlar tree may be found in the second panel of the Unicorn Tapestries (Brussels ?, ca. 1500; The Cloisters, New York), just to the left of the unicorn (see the color plate in Margaret B. Freeman, *The Unicorn Tapestries* [1976], or in Adolfo Salvatore Cavallo, *The Unicorn Tapestries at the Metropolitan Museum of Art* [1998]). Also, in both the third and fourth panels of the set of seven tapestries, there is a medlar tree, which, as Margaret Freeman explains, "appears in almost every list of trees to be cultivated in medieval orchards."

Not surprisingly, the medical writers had strong views concerning medlars, as in this English version of an anonymous versified Latin treatise, *The Englishman's Doctor* (1607):

> Eat medlars if you haue a a looseness gotten,
> They bind, and yet your vrine they augment,
> They haue one name more fit to be forgotten,
> While hard and sound they be they be not spent,
> Good *Medlars* are not ripe till seeming rotten,
> For meddling much with *Medlars* some are shent [disgraced, ruined].

There are four allusions to medlars in Shakespeare; the more interesting ones are in two plays dating from the 1590s, *Romeo and Juliet* and *As You Like It*. The allusion in the former play occurs at the opening of act 2 during an exchange between Romeo's two friends, Benvolio and Mercutio, whose mission is to remove Romeo from the dangerous environs of Juliet's garden. Failing to locate Romeo (who is in fact hiding among the trees in the darkness) Mercutio recites some characteristically mocking and obscene lines—lines, it may be noted, which set the stage, by contrast, for the next scene's tender balcony duet between the lovers:

> If love be blind, love cannot hit the mark.
> Now will he sit under a medlar tree
> And wish his mistress were that kind of fruit
> As maids call medlars when they laugh alone.
> O Romeo, that she were, O that she were
> An open-arse and thou a poperin pear!

A couple of textual notes gleaned from Brian Gibbons's edition of the play are illuminating: "open-arse" is a reading of the two different expressions in the two quarto versions of *Romeo and Juliet:* "open Et cetera" (Q1), and "open, or" (Q2). As for "poperin," it embodies "bawdy quibbles on (i) the *name* of a kind of pear from Poperinghe, near Ypres, and (ii) (*poperin*=pop her in) on its *shape,* resembling the male genitalia."

In *As You Like It,* during a witty exchange between Touchstone the fool and Rosalind (disguised as a young man, Ganymede), the former mocks the verses in her own praise Rosalind has been reading aloud from a paper found on a tree, saying "Truly the Tree yields bad Fruit." To which Rosalind replies: "I'll graff it with you, and then I shall / graff it with a Medler: then it will be the / earliest Fruit i'th' Country; for you'll be / rotten ere you be half ripe, and that's the / right Virtue of the Medler" (3.2.124–28). It is worth noting that not too long before the medlar passage (specifically, in 2.7.26–27), Jaques, like Rosalind, recites aloud before the exiled Duke a passage composed by Touchstone and which Jaques takes to apply to himself, including the lines: "And so from Hour to Hour, we ripe, and ripe, / And then from Hour to Hour, we rot, and rot"; and, a little later, Orlando admonishes the Duke in these words: "But forbear, I say; / He dies that touches any of this Fruit / Till I and my Affairs are answered" (2.7.97–99). Fruit, ripeness, and rottenness form a pattern of telling images in this part of the play—a play in which, more generally, "the number of food and taste similes . . . is remarkable" (Spurgeon, *Shakespeare's Imagery and What It Tells Us* [1935]).

Medlars make an appearance once more in *Bussy D'Ambois* (1604), by George Chapman (1559–1634), at the beginning and at the conclusion of a sustained and highly obscene passage of some forty lines (3.2.228–68). The passage takes the form of an exchange between the three villains (the king's brother Monsieur, the Duke of Guise, and the Count of Montsurry) and two lady's maids (Charlotte and Pero). The topic of the witty repartee is women's chastity: the men are, in fact, attempting to learn about the sexual liaisons of the man they wish to destroy, the upstart Bussy D'Ambois. The men open the conversation by alluding to the ways in which women conceal their sexual desire, and the following dialogue ensues:

> *Char.* We be no windfalls my Lord; ye must gather us with the ladder
> of matrimony, or we'll hang till we be rotten.
> *Mons.* Indeed that's the way to make ye right open-arses. But alas ye
> have no portions fit for such husbands as we wish you.

Pero then formulates a riddle about the "portions" women really do possess, which turns out to be their chastity, and after the women exit, Monsieur says, "Farewell Riddle," Guise says, "Farewell Medlar," and the Count says, "Farewell Winter Plum" (3.2.267–69). According to the editor Nicholas Brooke's note, the last phrase refers to "fruit which ripens very late, or possibly never, thus contrasting with 'Medlar.'" I might just add that earlier in *Bussy D'Ambois,* the ripe/rotten imagery has occurred in connection with Bussy's boast to some court ladies that he is perfectly capable of becoming a courtier, to which one of the ladies responds: "Here's a Courtier rotten before he be ripe" (1.2.85).

It is worth recalling that ripe fruit may be blighted by frost as well as by rot, as in the concluding lines of the beautiful sonnet "The Frailty and Hurtfulness of Beauty" (first published 1557), by Henry Howard, Earl of Surrey (1517–1547):

> Ah, bitter sweet! infecting as the poison,
> Thou farest as fruit that with the frost is taken:
> Today ready ripe, tomorrow all to-shaken.

The most poignant occurrence of the ripe/rotten imagery—but now with practically all traces of the underlying fruit paradigm eliminated—must be in the last act of *King Lear* (1606), during an exchange between the blind Gloucester and his son Edgar:

> Glo. No further, sir; a man may rot even here.
> Edg. What, in ill thoughts again? Men must endure
>   Their going hence even as their coming hither:
>   Ripeness is all. Come on.
> Glo. And that's true too.

12

POMEGRANATES

The pomegranate was a highly prized fruit in the ancient world; the earliest pictures of pomegranates occur in Egyptian tombs, and in Deuteronomy 8:8 (mid-13th cent. B.C.E.) pomegranates are singled out—along with figs, vines, and olives—as belonging to the rich resources that the Israelites, after crossing the Jordan, will find in the Promised Land. Also, in the period 1650–1050 B.C.E. certain Cyprian sculptured ivory pinheads (1½ in. in height) were being produced in the form of pomegranates (for pictures, see *Ancient Art from Cyprus: The Cesnola Collection* [1999], ed. Vassos Karogeorghis). The pomegranate—especially its interior—is also visually intriguing, and it is often included in still life paintings of fruit. There is, for example, a representation of pomegranates in a wall painting from Pompeii now in the Museo Nazionale, Naples (29½ x 45½ in., dining room, house of Julia Felix, 1st cent. C.E.), where a single split pomegranate rests on a raised block next to a large glass bowl containing apples, grapes, figs, and pomegranates. (For a reproduction, see *A Handbook of Roman Art* [1983], edited by Martin Henig, or the 1978 catalogue of an exhibition of Pompeiian archeological finds that was shown in four American museums in the years 1978–79.)

By the time of the Renaissance, pomegranates often appear in paintings as symbols of the Virgin's chastity or, when held by the infant Christ, as symbols of the resurrection (see the entry "Pomegranate" in James Hall's *Dictionary of Subjects and Symbols in Art* [1979]); one outstanding example is the tondo *Madonna of the Pomegranate* (ca. 1487) by Botticelli (1444/5–1510), in the Uffizi in Florence. (For a reproduction, see Alexandra Grömling and Tilman Lingesleben's *Alessandro Botticelli* [1998].)

In our own century, one of the more interesting pictures of pomegranates is the *Still Life with Pomegranates* (1917), by the Russian painter David Shterenberg (1881–1948), now in the S. A. Shuster and Ye. V. Kryukova Collection. The oil on canvas is oval-shaped (24¾ x 20½ in.), and it depicts one intact and one split pomegranate, the former resting on a bluish, oval-shaped platter and the latter resting on a flat, yellowish surface (tabletop or floor), all with a greenish backdrop; the space of the picture is deliberately puzzling, uneasily combining extreme emphasis on the picture plane with a hint of perspectival depth. (For a reproduction, see David Elliott and Valery Dudakov's *One Hundred Years of Russian Art* [1989].) Shterenberg studied and exhibited in Paris;

300   after returning to Russia during the Revolution, he became a leading bureaucrat of
the arts and produced dreary socialist realist paintings.

Dictionary definitions of pomegranates often rise to near-poetic heights: "a cham-
bered, many-seeded, globose fruit, having a tough, usually red rind and surmounted by
a crown of calyx lobes, the edible portion consisting of pleasantly acid flesh developed
from the outer seed coat" (*Random House Dictionary of the English Language*). The pomegranate's size, shape, and external color (golden, red, green, or white) often resemble
those of an apple; its internal structure is more complex than any of the fruits we
have so far considered, and it was possibly this complexity that helped make the pomegranate a prominent fruit both in ancient Greek mythology (the "Homeric" *Hymn to
Demeter,* 7th cent. B.C.E.) and in the Hebrew Bible (the Song of Songs). Echoing the
former, pomegranates have come to stand for fertility (both vegetable and human), and
echoing the latter, they have come to stand for love. In the *Hymn to Demeter* we learn
of the abduction of Demeter's daughter, Persephone, by her uncle Hades, Zeus's
brother and king of the underworld. In angry response, Demeter refuses to return to
Olympus and vows to prevent Earth's grain from ever sprouting again. Since this
would encompass the destruction of the human race and the dishonoring of the gods,
Zeus sends Hermes to persuade Hades to release Persephone. Hades agrees but before
Persephone leaves he slyly feeds her "a honey-sweet pomegranate seed" (l. 372) that
compels her to return to the underworld for a third of each year. The beginning of
spring each year is associated with Persephone's return to Earth and thereby with
Persephone's special fruit, the pomegranate.

The *Hymn to Demeter* survives in just a single imperfect manuscript from the
early fifteenth century C.E., discovered in 1777 in a Moscow stable. But this does not
mean the myth of Persephone and Demeter was not popular; it is just that so many
authors were busy composing their own versions of the myth that nobody bothered
to preserve copies of the earliest version. We have, for example, copies, sometimes fragmentary, of over twenty Greco-Roman versions of the myth, by such eminent authors
as Euripides (ca. 485–407/6 B.C.E.), Cicero, Virgil, Lucan, and Ovid. (For a list of these
versions, see Helene P. Foley's *The Homeric "Hymn to Demeter"* [1994].) Some authors
omit the pomegranate episode; others, like Ovid, alter that episode in more or less significant ways. In Ovid's influential retelling of the myth in his *Metamorphoses* (5),
pomegranate seeds make their appearance and Persephone seems to eat them volun-
tarily (translated by A. D. Melville): "The girl had broken her fast / And wandering,
childlike, through the orchard trees / From a low branch had picked a pomegranate /
And peeled the yellow rind and found the seeds / And nibbled seven." The number
seven seems inexplicable and, indeed, in another work, his *Fasti* (4.607), Ovid has
Persephone eat three seeds, one for each of the winter months that she will annually
spend in Hades.

The Demeter-Persephone myth, in one form or another, has continued to stimulate the imaginations of writers in the Euro-American tradition right on up to the

present. (My own collection of examples is, of course, considerably narrowed down by the requirement that the pomegranate play a significant role.) For a long list of late-nineteenth and twentieth-century literary versions of the myth in English, encompassing a variety of genres—poems, plays, novels, and stories—see Foley's book referred to above. A novel that appeared too late for mention by Foley is *Babel Tower* (1996), by A. S. Byatt (b. 1936), in which a character called Hugh Pink writes what he conceives of as "a rich red honeycomb of a poem about a pomegranate"; the poem—alluding in vague terms to the Persephone myth—when we finally get to read it, is dreadfully bad (though Byatt may not think so, since in her novel she has it, improbably, published in *The New Statesman*). In any case, the poem is sent to Frederica (the central character of the novel) together with a letter from her friend Hugh, and the ensuing events have "changed Frederica's marriage": her bullying husband has deeply and inexcusably offended her by mockingly reading the poem aloud (even while nevertheless "getting the stresses automatically right"). It is not clear what function, if any, the Persephone myth plays in the novel, which is mostly a fairly gripping account of England in the 1960s.

In the Song of Songs there are allusions to pomegranate trees in bloom, to the wine made from pomegranate juice, and, most strikingly, in two places, to the face of the (female) lover: "the curve of your cheek / a pomegranate [*rimmon*] / in the thicket of your hair [or: in your thicket of hair]" (4.3, 6.7). This last simile (in the Blochs' translation) must remind us of Herrick's "The Lilly in a Christal," discussed above in chapter 4, "Strawberries (and Cream)." But just here the Blochs' translation differs significantly from both the Authorized (King James) Version and the Revised Standard Version. Thus, the Authorized Version reads: "Thy temples are like a piece of a pomegranate within thy locks," while the Revised Version reads: "Your cheeks are like halves of a pomegranate behind your veil." For the pomegranate/cheek (temple) image to work in these last two English versions it would seem that one must forget about the look of the exposed inner portion of the pomegranate. Poets, of course, are expecting us to forget things all the time; it is just harder to accomplish with something as memorable as the interior of a pomegranate. So, the Blochs' version makes things easier for the reader, but at the expense of fidelity to the Hebrew text. They do provide a literal translation of the passage in a note: "like a slice of pomegranate is your *raqqah*." The only doubtful word here, as they point out, is "raqqah," which usually means a part of the face or head, such as cheek, temple, or forehead; the phrase they translate "like a slice" is *ke-felach* in the Hebrew (where *ke* means "like" and *felach* means "slice").

The art historian James Elkins has discussed the above passage from the Song of Songs in the course of his analysis of how we see faces:

> If I read a close description of a face and attend to it very carefully and try to construct it in my mind, I end up with something monstrous. If I read 'Your parted lips behind your veil are like a pomegranate cut open' (from the Song of Songs), I imagine a pomegranate with its wet white seeds and

their deep red pulp, and then I think of small teeth gleamimg in red gums—
the picture is a little nauseating, since pomegranate seeds are too small to be
teeth, and if teeth were jumbled like pomegranate seeds the mouth would be
frightening. So I know not to think that closely but to extract a more poetic
image of sweet wetness and smooth whiteness and to leave it at that.

Elkins perhaps increases the repellent character of the central image by turning the cheek
into lips—though it is true there is an allusion to teeth (compared to a flock of ewes) in
the immediately preceding verse (6.6)—but his point is the same as my own. Later, he
somewhat recklessly speculates: "Did the author of the Song of Songs secretly hate the
woman he was describing? Could he open her mouth with his fingers while thinking
of ripping a pomegranate? Could he look at her and see pomegranate teeth in juicy red
gums?"

The Vulgate Latin text of the two passages is of no help at all; it reads (with Matter's
translation):

> sicu fragmen mali punici ita genae tuae
> absque eo quod intrinsecus latet
>
> ~
>
> like grains of pomegranates so your cheeks
> besides that which lies within

> sicut cortex mali punici genae tuae
> absque occultis tuis
>
> ~
>
> like the skin of a pomegranate your cheeks
> besides your hidden things

We notice that the two identical Hebrew passages in 4.3 and 6.7 have been rendered
quite differently, with the piece of pomegranate once rendered "grains" (*fragmen*) and
once "skin" (*cortex*), and the word for hair/veil converted into mystifyingly nonsensi-
cal Latin.

The passages from the Song of Songs we have been discussing were provided
with homiletic interpretations by Jewish and Christian commentators; one midrash, for
example, applies the split pomegranate to Israel, with the seeds counting as good deeds
(as the biblical scholar Marvin Pope explains). An annotated English translation of a
late medieval Hebrew commentary on the Song of Songs, by Levi ben Gershom, or
Gersonides (1288–1344), was published in 1998, and I want to quote his interpretation
of the pomegranate passage. Gersonides was not only a leading Jewish philosopher and
theologian but he was also an outstanding astronomer, inventing an important instrument, the Jacob's staff, to measure the angular distance between stars. Menachem Kellner
characterizes him as follows:

Gersonides stands at the intersection of three worlds. A learned and devoted Jew, his major philosophical-scientific teachers were Muslims, although he worked in close scientific (astronomical and astrological) cooperation with Christians and was, at the very least, aware of some developments in Latin philosophy. He is almost a perfect case study in the acculturation of mid-fourteenth-century Provençal Jews, providing a window into the life and thought of his Jewish contemporaries.

Written in 1325, Gersonides's commentary takes two things for granted: that the subject matter of the Song of Songs is the ultimate felicity of a human being—which is to know God insofar as that is possible for human beings—and that the proper methodology to use in interpreting any biblical text is Aristotelian. As in all scholastic commentaries, much of the argument proceeds by way of citing earlier authorities; for Gersonides, these include forty-nine citations of Aristotle but only twenty-nine citations of the Bible and seven of rabbinical texts. Kellner finds something deeply paradoxical about the commentary, such as Gersonides's conclusion that the extolling of passionate love in the Song of Songs is in actuality an argument for the necessity of overcoming all physical passions. More generally, Kellner tells us that for himself "the most amazing thing about this commentary . . . is the way in which Gersonides' approach, absurd on the face of it as an attempt to explicate the true meaning of the text as intended by its author, becomes more and more convincing as one goes along." Unfortunately, my quotation of just a single passage from Gersonides's commentary may tend to emphasize the absurdity at the expense of the convincingness. With some apologies, then, here is Gersonides's explication of the pomegranate passage (in Kellner's translation):

Thy temples are like a pomegranate split open behind thy veil (6:7)

This verse accords with the allegory alone, indicating her beauty and modesty. The ordering of her praises in this place is different from the previous one; he did not move in a step-by-step fashion, ordering her praises below her head, as he did in the previous apprehension, because in this apprehension one moves—in some fashion—from the prior, for example, the study of physics. This is so because that which is investigated first is prior in some fashion to that which is investigated later, for the general things investigated first are prior to the specific things, whether it be material priority, as is the case with the remote matter, or priority by way of efficient cause, formal cause, and final cause as is the case with the remote mover, as has been made clear in the *Metaphysics* [of Aristotle]. His praises of her did not pass below her head since movement in this science is not from prior to posterior, that is, that one investigates in it each of the actually existent, natural, specific things, but rather the movement toward apprehending them is through the sense apprehension of things posterior to them, they being the accidents and attributes, as will be explained below.

According to Marvin Pope, the Christian interpretations of the pomegranate passage were even more imaginative—not to say far-fetched—than the Jewish ones:

> Aponius saw the cheeks as belonging to those who fall into post-baptismal sin, and, being washed anew with the tears of repentance, beautify the Church with the ruddy blush of shame. Philo of Carpasia saw in the pomegranate the mingled glow of faith and hope in every holy soul that serves the Lord, and the numerous seeds within he likened to the good works and devout thoughts hidden behind the rough rind, one day to be revealed by the Bridegroom who alone knows them at present. Cardinal Hugo compared the pomegranate to the preachers of the Church because of the firm rind and many seeds; the red and white which vie in the cheeks of the pomegranate representing fervor and purity, and the hidden insides, the precious inner devotions.

Pope also points out that many recent interpretations of the Song of Songs even— if not especially—by religiously committed scholars (including Protestants, Catholics, and Jews) have tended to stress human sexuality as central to the meaning of the work. But there are some holdouts. Thus, in the ArtScroll bilingual edition of the *Tanakh* (the twenty-four books of the Hebrew Bible), edited by Rabbi Nosson Scherman for orthodox Jews, readers are informed that "in the interest of accuracy, our translation of the Song is different from that of any other ArtScroll translation of Scripture. Although we provide the literal meaning as part of the commentary, we translate the Song according to Rashi's allegorical translation." Following the great Jewish commentator, Rashi (1040–1105), then, Song of Songs 4:3 becomes "As many as a pomegranate's seeds are the merits of your unworthiest within your modest veil," and we must look to a note on the facing page for the literal translation: "Your cheeks are like a slice of pomegranate, from behind your veil." It seems that today only orthodox Jewish interpretors of the Song of Songs can be counted on to defend what Pope calls "the allegorical charade" that has "persisted for centuries with only sporadic protests."

Returning from biblical hermeneutics to poetry, we may note that near the end of the fifteenth century, the Italian poet Jacopo Sannazaro (1458–1530) composed a Latin poem (*Elegies* 2.10) to accompany a gift of pomegranates to his Neapolitan friend Andrea Matteo Acquaviva d'Aragona (referred to in the poem as simply "Acquaviva"). In Ralph Nash's book (1996) on Sannazaro's poetry, there are both poetic and prose translations of the elegy to Acquaviva. Sannazaro imagines the pomegranates themselves to be speaking; at the outset they are assuring a sailor that he need not risk trips to foreign lands to find exotic riches, for pomegranates will do:

> As lustrous gems our tender skins enclose
> as any that the Red Sea margin owes,
> whether of hyacinth's rose-purple shine,
> or amethyst, that hates the god of wine,
> or ruby's flame, like torches blazing bright,
> or topaz gentle with diffused light.

(The allusion to the amethysts' hatred of Bacchus is based on a traditional etymology, which derives "a-methyst" from the Greek for "not drunken.") There follows a fairly conventional denunciation of the moral dangers of wealth, which the pomegranates say,

> lack the twin gifts that nature us supplies,
> to quench men's thirst and slow their gazing eyes.

Finally, the recipient of the gift of pomegranates is addressed directly:

> You (Acquavive) with double laurel crowned
> —alike for arms and poetry renowned—
> receive our gift; and wearied with the strain
> (whether of study or the long campaign)
> quenching your thirst with us, profusely poured,
> refresh your vigor at the festive board.

There is little trace here of pomegranate imagery from either Greek myth or the Bible; instead, Sannazaro dwells on the faceted look of pomegranate seeds and the refreshing taste of their juice. The almost complete absence of both Classical and biblical imagery is perhaps surprising in a poet who is imitating a classical Roman elegy and whose most important Latin poem is "On the Virgin's Childbearing." Sannazaro does use the phrase "jewel-laden sea" *(gemmiferi . . . maris),* which comes from Propertius 3.4.2. On the other hand, Sannazaro is much more than a mere reviver of ancient Latin forms and motifs; indeed, Richard Jenkyns, in *Virgil's Experience* (1998), sees Sannazaro—not Virgil—as the inventor of Arcadia (understood as a bucolic land of poetry and love).

The idea of a pomegranate seed as a gem *(gemma)* can also be found in "Bermudas" (1653), by Andrew Marvell (1621–1678): "And does in the pom'granates close / Jewels more rich than Ormus shows." (Ormus, or Hormuz, was on the Persian Gulf.) And the jewel metaphor persisted, so that Dumas *père* quotes a certain M. Cohier de Lompier as saying (translated by Alan and Jane Davidson):

> "There are no beautiful dessert fruit baskets without pomegranates; likewise there are none without oranges. A pomegranate which has been cut open, looking like a rich treasure of rubies or sparkling garnets, is one of the most beautiful jewels of our majestic fruit baskets. Nothing else can equal the effect of a few half-open pomegranates on the sides of a pyramid of fruit."

In *Fruits of the Earth* André Gide describes pomegranates—like the figs in a passage already quoted in chapter 2—in the same intensely evocative prose poetry (again from Dorothy Bussy's version):

> Their juice is tart like like unripe raspberries.
> Their flowers look made of wax;
> They are coloured like the fruit.
>
> Guarded treasure, honeycomb partitions,
> Richness of flavour,
> Pentagonal architecture.
> The rind splits; the seeds fall—
> Crimson seeds in azure bowls,
> Or drops of gold in dishes of enamelled bronze.

~

> Leur jus est aigrelet comme celui des framboises pas mûres.
> Leur fleur semble faite de cire;
> Elle est de la couleur du fruit.
>
> Trésor gardé, cloisons de ruches,
> Abondance de la saveur,
> Architecture pentagonale.
> L'écorce se fend; les grains tombent,
> Grains de sang dans des coupes d'azur;
> Et d'autres, gouttes d'or, dans des plats de bronze émaillé.

Gide writes of "treasure" but not of jewels. "Rubies" (*rubis*) and "gems" (*gemmes*) recur in an octosyllabic sonnet, "Pomegranates" (1920), by Paul Valéry (1871–1945), here translated by David Paul:

> Tough pomegranates half-opening
> Yielding to your intemperate seeds,
> I see you as brows of sovereign minds
> Bursting with their discoveries!
>
> If the suns that you've endured,
> Oh pomegranates agape,
> Have made you overworked with pride
> Crack open your partitioned rubies,
>
> And if the parched gold of the rind
> Responding to a certain force
> Explodes in gems ruddy with juice,

That illuminating rupture
Recalls a dream to a soul I had
About its secret architecture.

Valéry's rhyme scheme—*abab cddc eef gfg*—is ignored by the translator, who prefers to preserve closely both the diction and the syntax of the original text. It is interesting, though, to look at another translation (Rachel Hadas, 1994), which, while compressing the French tetrameters into English trimeters, also employs rhyme (though hardly that of the original):

Oh pomegranates! Seeds
So pack your tough, taut rind
They burst it like a mind
Drunk with discoveries.

The sun that works its will
To bring you to fruition
Softens your hard gold shell
And there begins to spill

Obedient to some power
Bright red through each partition,
Each drop a scarlet jewel.

The wound's illumination
Allows me to envision
Your secret inmost bower.

The gem metaphor is expanded and intensified in the first stanza of "The Pomegranate" (1952), by the Canadian poet Louis Dudek (b. 1918):

The jewelled mine of the pomegranate, whose hexagons of honey
The mouth would soon devour but the eyes eat like a poem,
Lay hidden long in its hide, a diamond of dark cells
Nourished by tiny streams which crystallized into gems.

The next stanza continues a description of the hidden and mysterious metabolic activities that generate the pomegranate "gems":

The seeds, nescient of the world outside, or of passionate teeth,
Prepared their passage into light and air, while tender roots
And branches dreaming in the cell-walled hearts of plants
Made silent motions such as recreate both men and fruits.

Then, after a stanza which moves from the hidden growth of the plant to the actual presence of the piece of fruit itself ("broken by my hand"), in the fourth (and centrally located) stanza there is a sudden allusion to a wedding, which can only refer to Persephone and Hades. We are then returned, in the penultimate stanza, from the world of myth to the excitement of contemplating the opened pomegranate, and the final stanza reaches—not very successfully, I think—for cosmic implications:

> As now, the fruit glistens with a mighty grin,
> Conquers the room; and, though in ruin, to its death
> Laughs at the light that wounds it, wonderfully red,
> So that its awful beauty stops the greedy breath.
>
> And can this fact be made, so big of the body, then?
> And is beauty bounded all in its impatient mesh?
> The movement of the stars is that, and all their light
> Secretly bathed the world, that now flows out of flesh.

The most recently published occurrence of the gem-pomegranate metaphor I have encountered is in the slender volume *Movin': Teen Poets Take Voice* (2000), by teenage poets from New York City. "Pomegranate," by Kellyn Bardeen, contains the phrases "Faceted crimson / gemstones" and "stones / more beautiful than rubies."

We consider next a modern Hebrew poem, "To the Pomegranate Tree" (1961), by the Israeli poet T. Carmi (b. 1925), who, like Sannazaro, avoids the pomegranate's heavy freight of Classical and biblical associations and yet writes a poem of great originality and force (translated by Stephen Mitchell):

> Go away. Go.
> Go to other eyes.
> I wrote about you yesterday.
>
> I said green
> to your branches bowing in the wind,
> and red—red—red—
> to your fruit shining like dew.
> I called light to your dank
> obstinate root.
>
> Now you don't exist.
> Now you're blocking the day
> and the moon that has not yet arisen.
>
> Come, beloved
> (I wrote about you two days ago,
> and your young memory
> stings my hands like nettle),

come look at the strange pomegranate tree:
its blood is in my veins, on my head, on my hands,
and it still is planted in its place!

The Hebrew text of this poem has been translated literally and analyzed in some detail by an Israeli scholar, Harold Schimmel, in a volume of which Carmi himself is one of the co-editors, *The Modern Hebrew Poem Itself* (1966). If Schimmel is right (and presumably Carmi would have corrected any misinterpretation), there are few biblical (and no Classical) allusions in the poem; an exception is the thrice-repeated "red" in the sixth line, which "echoes the praise of the seraphim in the heavenly spheres . . . of the Hebrew Prayerbook." To appreciate this last point, one must know that in Hebrew "red" is *adom,* that the song of praise for the Lord of Hosts begins with the thrice-repeated word "holy" (*kadosh*), and finally that both Hebrew words are bisyllabic with the accent on the second syllable. Another critical analysis of Carmi's poem is by M. L. Rosenthal:

> The speaker had at first thought the pomegranate tree merely a source of vivid impressions. Now he sees it possessing his whole being . . . Carmi's preoccupation is with the way passionately regarded external reality invades his own very nature. Like an Israeli Lawrence, he has his pomegranate personify a world of fierce knowledge, blood-drenched, sexual and intractable.

Rosenthal suggests also how—to paraphrase him—the pomegranate tree may be functioning as an insistent reminder of the historical landscape in the modern state of Israel. It seems to me that this idea is supported when the speaker says that even the very recent memory of his beloved "stings my hands like nettle." How much more stinging, then, must be the ancient memories associated with the pomegranate tree (as in the Song of Songs)? And the speaker answers by telling his beloved that the blood of the tree touches him intimately in his veins, his head, and his hands, and that the tree remains "planted in its place," which is to say, in its proper place as part of the historical landscape. Why else choose a pomegranate? For the sanguinous association, a native blood orange would do just as well, but the resonance of the pomegranate tree for an Israeli Jew must far transcend the easy identification of pomegranate juice with blood.

The Mexican writer Octavio Paz (b. 1914) has actually composed a love poem, "A Tree Within" (1987), in which both the pomegranate and the blood orange appear as fruits on a tree growing within his head (the tree thereby symbolizing the poet's imagination, just as in Carmi's poem):

A tree grew inside my head.
A tree grew in.
Its roots are veins,

> its branches nerves,
> thoughts its tangled foliage.
> Your glance sets it on fire,
> and its fruits of shade
> are blood oranges
> and pomegranates of flame.
>   Day breaks
> in the body's night.
> There, within, inside my head,
> the tree speaks.
>   Come closer—can you hear it?

It is worth pointing out that the English translation (by Eliot Weinberger) necessarily fails to capture the parallel between the Spanish terms for "blood oranges" and "pomegranates of flame": *naranjas de sangre* and *granadas de lumbre*. Also, it is curious how in Carmi's poem the beloved is asked to *look* at the tree, while in Paz's poem the beloved is asked to *listen* to the tree.

Just a year before Carmi's pomegranate poem was published, another Israeli poet, Rukhl Fishman (1935–1984), published her first volume of Yiddish verse, containing "Full as a Pomegranate" (1960). Having lived in Philadelphia and Los Angeles, Fishman emigrated to Israel when she was nineteen. Her poem of some three dozen short lines begins with this stanza (translated by Seymour Levitan):

> I'm full
> not of good deeds
> but of appetites,
> full as a pomegranate,
> and red laughter
> is about to spurt
> through my skin.

After a sustained comparison of her blood cells to the cells of a pomegranate, in the last stanza she invokes an old Jewish legend that there are 613 seeds in a pomegranate (corresponding to the number of biblical *mitsvot*—often translated "commandments"—of which 365 are prohibitions and 248 are positive precepts):

> 613 sweet sins
> 613 luscious joys
> for both of us
> I gather
> as I gather the fruit.

David Roskies, who introduces the volume of Fishman translations, points out that "a pair of rhymes, reserved for the poem's finale, carries the weight of her delicious subversions. *Klayb ikh mit di peyres*, 'I gather together with the fruit,' rhymes with *TaRYaG zise aveyres*, '613 sweet sins,' just as *freydn*, 'joys,' rhymes with *far undz beydn*, 'for both of us.'" (This irreverent use of the number 613 is matched, in one of Yehuda Amichai's poems, "Jerusalem" [1999], by the 613 springs in the mattress of two lovers!)

It should come as no surprise that pomegranates in contemporary Greece have special mythical and ritualistic connotations, which reach a peak at New Year's. Patricia Storace—a Greek-speaking American, who spent a year in Greece and wrote a book about it—describes the ubiquity of the pomegranate in the days leading up to New Year's; gift packages, for example are

> fastened with a tiny ceramic pomegranate, the key image of this season here, and a measure of the emotional difference between the Eastern and Western holidays. The fruit sellers at the farmer's markets display pomegranates dyed gold on their tables, along with branches of gold- and silver-dyed leaves. Flower sellers offer pomegranates wrapped in silver foil for you to smash against your threshold with all your force on New Year's Eve, to spread the seeds of good luck, and to have an abundant year, and gift shop tables are covered with brilliant red candles in the shape of pomegranates. In jewelry shop windows, there are pomegranate-shaped pendants, and silver pomegranates to give as gifts, cast open to show their abundant silver seeds.

Storace goes on to speculate about the dual significance of the pomegranate:

> Here, of course, the pomegranate is the fruit of Persephone, or at least, I realize, in this dual-natured country, half of it is. The other half belongs to Hades, since this fruit is also the King of the Dead's, which he offers in order to ensure that she will remain with him in the kingdom of the dead—the pomegranate is a fruit neither of death nor life, but of the inseparability of the two.

Finally, Storace notes "that the dream pomegranate of both the Greeks of antiquity and the modern Greeks is an ambiguous fruit" implying, as in modern dream books, either "charming and pleasant erotic adventures, because it is a symbol of the return of spring and fertility," or "a sign that your life is in danger, that some underworld force may be reaching out to seize you."

One of a sequence of dramatic soliloquies, "Persephone" (1965–70), by the Greek poet Yannos Ritsos (b. 1909), occupies a pivotal place—it is the eleventh of seventeen poems—in his volume, *The Fourth Dimension* (1972). As the translators of the volume, Peter Green and Beverly Bardsley, say in their introduction, in this poem "the various tensions and antitheses of the earlier poems—between speech and silence, involvement and withdrawal—are explored at their most fundamental level as the choice between Eros and Thanatos." Without attempting to delve into the complex mixture of ancient myth, modern history, and autobiography which makes up Ritsos's poem, I want simply to point to the crisis (occurring somewhat before the middle of the poem) when Persephone asks her uncle-husband (Hades in the myth but unnamed in the poem) to heal her divided self by retaining her once and for all in his realm; central to the passage is a pomegranate:

> He washed a pomegranate for me with his own hands.
> His fingers grew still blacker. The pomegranate seeds gleamed dazzlingly
> like glass phials fillled with blood. He fed me from his palm
> amid the great jars and the stone stools, lest I forget
> and not retun to him again. How could I not return? This sea
> shakes its glitter at you, splinters of glass in your eyes, your mouth,
> your shirt, your sandals.
>   "Keep me," —I said to him—
> "let me be only one—even half—the whole half (whichever it is),
> not two, separate and unmingled, for nothing is left to me
> but to be the cut—that is, not to be—
> only a vertical knife-slash and pain to the core—,"
> nor will even the knife be your own. "I can't resist," I said to him—
>   "keep me."

Most of the text of Ritsos's "Persephone" is spoken by the eponymous heroine, but this is preceded by a short passage in prose, describing her presence on the earth in third-person narrative. It is summer and "she has returned, as every summer, from the strange dark region, to her large family home in the country," where her only companion is the water nymph, Cyane, who protects Persephone from the harsh light. In the prose passage that concludes the poem, Persephone suddenly throws open the shutters, and stands "in the blinding light, like a statue slowly coming to life." She looks out the window at the sea with its "boatful of young swimmers" and at the shore road with its "large black dog . . . holding in his teeth a basket of multicolored fruit." This last image is most telling because Persephone has encountered just such a dog (Cerberus in the myth)—his mouth containing, however, not fruit but only "crooked teeth"—in her uncle's relatively unfertile region, where the vegetation consists of "a few poplars only, ash-gray in the underground garden, / black cypresses, sterile willows, wild mint, / and some pomegranates." Persephone is poised to choose between Eros and Thanatos.

Cutting open a pomegranate can be an exciting act, as one exposes the marvelously reticulated structure while the intensely red juice flows, coloring whatever it reaches; in his "Pomegranate" (1996), the American poet Bruce Bond likens this structure to a honeycomb: "a stain running out of a maze, / its honeycomb filled with dead sweet bees." Like Ritsos, Bond introduces no names but the presence of the ancient myth is unmistakable, and the "you" of the poem is clearly intended to refer to a modern incarnation of Persephone. Bond's poem is composed of five five-line unrhymed stanzas (except for a prominent rhyme in the last stanza); the poem ends like

Ritsos's "Persephone" with an image of the heroine—and I use the ancient Greek term advisedly—looking out an open window:

> And now wherever you leave, it's winter.
> You go to the window and wait, stare, turn away,
>
> and the long night trails you like a gown.
> Even in March as you return to all
> your name's sake, what flowers you see are the tips
> of buried fingers, each red flame bursting
> through the earthly crust, calling you down.

In the haiku "Young Fate" (1940), by another modern Greek poet, George Seferis (1900–1972), pomegranate seeds become stars (instead of gems, glass phials filled with blood, or dead bees), in the Keeley-Sherrard translation:

> Naked woman
> the pomegranate that broke
> was full of stars.

Yet a third modern Greek poet, Odysseus Elytis (1911–1996), included a poem about pomegranates in his first collection, *Orientations* (1939). "The Mad Pomegranate Tree" has six stanzas, each of six lines, and a double epigraph: "Morning high spirits as questions / *à perdre haleine* [on getting out of breath]." One clause, echoing the first epigraph, recurs no less than eight times throughout the poem, at least once in each stanza: "tell me, is it the mad pomegranate tree?" The question seems almost always to be raised at dawn, and of the dawn, as in the first stanza:

> tell me, is it the mad pomegranate tree
> That quivers with foliage newly born at dawn
> Raising high its colors in a shiver of triumph?

In the second stanza the pomegranate tree, presumably by means of its colors, "combats cloudy skies of the world"; in the third stanza the pomegranate tree "cries out the new hope now dawning"; in the fourth stanza the pomegranate tree is "waving in the distaance, / Fluttering a handkerchief of leaves of cool flame"; in the fifth stanza the pomegranate tree "spreads far as can be the saffron ruffle of day" and "hastily unfastens the silk apparel of day"; in the sixth stanza the pomegranate tree, "spilling in the sun's embrace intoxicating birds / . . . opens its wings on the breast of things / On the breast of our deepest dreams." Whatever else the pomegranate tree may represent, it is associated with a breathless, dreamy kind of freedom, with a potential to shatter the usual constraining patterns of sky, atmosphere, and sun. That in the poem "a girl turns into a pomegranate tree," as Jeffrey Carson (along with Nikos Sarris, the translator of Elytis's collected poems) affirms, is not at all obvious to me.

Pomegranate seeds occur at the very center of a long book-length poem, in thirty-one numbered sections, called *Love* (1986), by Aharon Shabtai. The poem begins with a brutal negation of the subject matter announced in the title (translated by Peter Cole):

> I'm a man
> who murdered love
>
> simply
> with his own two hands

Shabtai proceeds to characterize himself as a man of extremes: for many years a totally faithful husband, he now, for his old flame, D., would go "Even into apostasy / even into the PLO"; and again, he wishes he could say: "'D., look— / here's the mezuzah, / bore / the awl through my ear.'" The sixteenth section—exactly halfway through the poem—ends with these lines:

> D.,
> listen to what my dream is, my every dream:
>
> to put the ring on your finger
>
> and the pomegranate seed in your mouth
>
> Here are the little children
> who escort the bride and groom
>   on their eternal journey
>
> Do they realize that Aharon is Hades
> and D.—Persephone?

At this point it is worth recalling that Shabtai is the foremost translator of ancient Greek literature (including some fourteen volumes of Greek tragedy) into Hebrew.

Just ten years earlier, Shabtai had published another long poem, this one titled "The Domestic Poem" (1976), which celebrates his then six-and-a-half-year-old marriage in all its dimensions, including wife, six children, and household items (furniture, kitchen, water supply, food, clothing). The poem consists of fifty-eight numbered sections, of which some seven are about fruit. I quote four, omitting the mixed fruit (22), the winter orange (24), and the vine (43):

> 10.
> Fruit chewed in the mouth
>
> (mentioned by Valéry
> in "The Cemetery by the Sea")

orange pulp an acid rich
in Vitamin C

rich in bubbles
of pure saliva
and not at all repulsive
. . . .
19.
There's an apple in the
southern part of the apartment

the space is divided
to ward off boredom

the frying pan has a handle
to ward off boredom

36.
Jam's
concocted from quince

at one and the same time
the belly arouses

52.
I'm a chemist
    of bananas

I vaporize
I secrete
    pepsin

(The passage from Valéry alluded to in section 10 of Shabtai's poem will be quoted and discussed in chapter 21, "Fruit, Conjoined and Disjoined.") Notable by its absence in this poem is the pomegranate, presumably because it is not a proper domestic fruit.

After all these pomegranate poems by men it is of considerable interest to see what a woman might make of the Demeter-Persephone myth. The Irish poet Eavan Boland (b. 1945), in "The Pomegranate" informs us right from the start that this is "The only legend I have ever loved," her reason being "I can enter it anywhere. And have." That is, Boland can identify either with Persephone—as a child, Boland was "exiled" to "a city of fogs and strange consonants" (presumably London)—or with Persephone's daughter (here called by her Roman name, Ceres):

> I walked out in summer twilight
> Searching for my daughter at bedtime.
> When she came running I was ready
> To make any bargain to keep her.
> [. . . . .]
> I was Ceres then and I knew
> Winter was in store for every leaf
> On every tree on that road.

Having analyzed the myth into its two leading female roles, Boland then proceeds to dissect the word "pomegranate" into its two component words, while stretching the etymology to the breaking point, in the course of the longest and syntactically most complex sentence in the poem. The sentence extends over nine lines (only one other sentence in the poem extends over as many as five):

> She put out her hand and pulled down
> The French sound for apple and
> The noise of stone and the proof
> That even in the place of death,
> At the heart of legend, in the midst
> Of rocks full of unshed tears
> Ready to be diamonds by the time
> The story was told, a child can be
> Hungry.

Now, "pome" is French all right, while "granate," though it *means* "seeds" or "grains," *sounds* like "grenade" and "granite" (hence, "the noise of stone" and perhaps even the subsequent "rocks").

But though the mother cannot shield her daughter forever from knowledge of the inevitability of hunger, cold, and, most of all, death, retelling the legend communicates its truths only insofar as the way is opened for the daughter to live the legend herself:

> The legend must be hers as well as mine.
> She will enter it. As I have.
> She will wake up. She will hold
> The papery, flushed skin in her hand.
> And to her lips. I will say nothing.

The final image of the poem is a marvel of compressed meanings: the pomegranate's pulpy reticulated network is a "papery, flushed skin"—like the medium on which the poem itself is inscribed. The child lifts this skin—this poem—to her lips, while her mother "will say nothing"—nothing, that is, beyond the words of the poem.

Disregarding the complexities and ambiguities of the Persephone myth, the Spanish poet Concha Méndez (1898–1986) used the mere appearance of an opened

pomegranate as a simile for female sexuality in a tiny but vivid poem (translated by
John Wilcox), "Just Like a Pomegranate" (1928):

> My heart has opened up on me
> just like a pomegranate.
>
> And I feel its blood falling
> —my blood—in crystal drops.
>
> ~
>
> El corazón se me ha abierto
> lo mismo que una granada.
>
> Y siento caer su sangre
> —mi sangre—cristalizada.

According to John Wilcox, the great fame and talent of the male Spanish poets of the
1920s have caused the female poets of the period (like Méndez) to be "marginalized
by the canonical anthologies and histories of Spanish literature," and in Méndez's case
her early poetry has often been unfavorably contrasted with what she wrote after meeting the poet she was to marry in 1932. In any case, the early pomegranate poem above
is written in a manner that Wilcox believes is crucially different from that of Méndez's
contemporary male writers in at least five respects: presentation of a female persona,
concern with desire, gynocentric style, nontranscendental subject matter, and subversion of masculine ideals.

Another Spanish-language poet, Gabriela Mistral, totally eschews sexual connotations in writing about pomegranates, as she creates a magical children's tale called
"Mother Pomegranate" (like "The Wild Strawberry," quoted in chapter 4, one of the
poems in Mistral's volume, *Tenderness*) using as her point of departure simply the physical structure of the pomegranate as it appears on a majolica plate. There are nineteen
short stanzas, of which the first five and the last three celebrate the color and bounty
of the pomegranate (in Giachetti's translation):

> I'll tell you a story in majolica;
> purplish red and red come alive
> in my majolica, the tale
> of Mother Pomegranate.
>
> Mother Pomegranate is old
> and toasty like a French roll,
> but her faithful crown consoles her,
> the insatiable bounty of her tree.
>
> Her deep house is divided
> by slim lakes

where her children caper in ships
dressed in red, in scarlet.

With red passion, she adorns them,
using the same chasuble-skin;
and to prevent fatigue, Mother Pomegranate
never names or counts her seeds.

The overcrowded one
leaves her door ajar,
and the hemmed-in multitude breaks free;
she grew weary of sustaining their mansion.
     [. . . . .]
And Mother Pomegranate begins counting
and continues wondrously counting;
the children erupt in laughter
and she splits open with their guffaws.

The pomegranate split open
in the orchard
is a complete feast of fire;
we slice her and keep
the heart of hearts under her crown.

We place her on a white plate;
her blush of dreams
sounds an alarm.
Now I've told her story,
in shades of red,
in scarlet.

A short poem, "Pomegranates" (1973), by Siv Cedering, describes a technique for shared consumption of the fruit by two lovers while, at the same time, tracing the love-sustaining juice of the fruit back to the water and soil in which the pomegranate tree grows:

you take me to the woods
where the sun is still warm
on brown leaves
you show me how to squeeze
the fruit
bite a small hole
and suck

fresh water sifted in soil
drawn by roots to rise
in the trunk
to be red and sweet
in the fruit
and yet sweeter
in my mouth
before I give you
to drink

The bright red lips of Proserpine (a variant of "Persephone") in Dante Gabriel Rossetti's painting (1874; oil on canvas, 49¾ x 24 in., Tate Gallery, London) match in hue the pomegranate she holds in her left hand; a portion of the skin of the fruit has been removed to expose the seeds, which she is clearly supposed to have been eating. (For a reproduction of *Proserpine,* see *Essential Pre-Raphaelites* [1999], by Lucinda Hawksley and Juliet Hacking.) Rossetti worked on as many as eight versions of this subject over a period of ten years (1872–82), and the vicissitudes of the paintings—some were lost, some damaged, during shipment to various patrons—seem to reflect his troubled liaison with Jane Morris (William's wife), who was the model for Proserpine. As Virginia Surtees comments in her catalogue raisonné of Rossetti's art, "the subject of Proserpine bound to her husband except for a few short periods of escape, would seem to bear an analogy to the circumstances of their own two lives." The Tate version of *Proserpine,* though dated 1874, is in fact a copy of one in private hands, completed in—and dated—1877. (This latter painting is reproduced in Alicia Faxon's *Dante Gabriel Rossetti* [1989].) Rossetti's own Italian sonnet about the Proserpine myth appears in the upper-right-hand corner of both of these paintings. In a letter quoted by Surtees, Rossetti writes that Proserpine "is represented in a gloomy corridor of her palace, with the fatal fruit in her hand. As she passes, a gleam strikes on the wall behind her from some inlet suddenly opened, and admitting for a moment the light of the upper world; and she glances furtively towards it, immersed in thought." For his last version of the subject, completed just a few days before his death, Rossetti translated the sonnet into English; one line reads: "Dire fruit, which, tasted once, must thrall me here." Rossetti was very fond of these paintings—clearly among his best—on which Hawksley makes an apt comment: "The symbolism in the painting is poignantly indicative of Proserpine's plight, and also of that of Jane herself, torn between her husband (and the father of her two adored daughters) and her lover."

It is interesting now to look at a more extended example of how the pomegranate can function in a literary context outside the Classical and biblical cultural traditions. *The Arabian Nights* is a compilation of stories first written down in Arabic during the latter half of the thirteenth century but based on much older, orally transmitted Arabic and Persian stories. The stories include fables, fairy tales, romances, and comic and historical anecdotes; the narrator of all the stories is Shaharazad, and her life-and-death challenge is to keep up King Shahrayar's interest in listening from night to night and thereby deflect him from his practice of deflowering and then immediately executing his sexual partners (see the introduction to Husain Haddawy's English translation of *The Arabian Nights* [1990], and for a fuller account, Robert Irwin, *The Arabian Nights: A Companion* [1994]). "The Story of the Three Apples" is begun on one night (seventieth) and continued on the next; it is then interrupted by the much longer "The Story of the Two Viziers" (seventy-second through one-hundred-and-first nights), at which point the first story is finally concluded. Apples are important in the first story, pomegranates in the second.

Here is a brief summary of the first story. A young man goes to great lengths—a two-week journey from Baghdad to Basra—to satisfy the craving for apples of his ailing wife. Somehow, one of the three apples he brings back ends up in the hands of a slave and the husband, apprised of this, becomes convinced that his wife has had an illicit liaison with the slave. The husband stabs his beloved wife to death and, unaccountably, dismembers her, but then learns that the slave had actually snatched the apple from the couple's eldest son. Both the slave and the young man are brought before the caliph. At this point (on the seventy-second night), Shaharazad makes her usual claim that the story just told will be surpassed by the one she is about to tell. (The narratological situation is more complicated than I have indicated because the second story is being told by Shaharazad in the voice of a character in the first story.) The second story (about the two viziers) has innumerable twists and turns in which the main goal of the narrative is constantly thwarted—that goal being to unite in marriage the daughter and son, respectively, of two brothers who are joint viziers of Egypt. At the outset, the brothers quarrel; the younger one leaves Cairo and travels to Basra, where he eventually becomes vizier. God arranges for the brothers to marry on the same day; the older brother's wife bears a daughter, Sit al-Husn, the younger brother's wife bears a son, Badr al-Din, and it is these two cousins who must somehow be united in marriage.

With the aid of a helpful Jewish merchant and two demons, one male and one female, the cousins are eventually united, but the story is circuitous and twenty-four nights are consumed in the telling. Briefly, Badr al-Din is magically transported from Basra to Cairo just in time to attend the wedding of Sit al-Husn to a hunchback (at the king's command). The bride is introduced in a public ceremony during which she appears in a succession of differently colored wedding dresses, the sixth (and last) of which is green.

> She surpassed every fair woman in the world and broke every heart, as the poet said of one like her:
>
> > There was a maid with such polish and grace
> > That e'en the sun seemed borrowed from her face.
> > Bedecked in green she came, fair to behold,
> > As a pomegranate bud the green leaves unfold.

And when we asked, "What do you call this dress?"
She answered in sweet words meant to impress,
"Since I have tortured many with my arts,
In this dress, I call it Breaker of Hearts."

By a ruse, Badr al-Din is substituted for the hunchback, consummates the marriage, and impregnates his cousin, after which, in his sleep, he is magically whisked off to Damascus by the she-demon; there he is adopted by the proprietor of a cookshop. Meanwhile, Sit al-Husn has given birth to a son, 'Ajib, and when 'Ajib is twelve, he, his mother, and his grandfather set off for Basra to find Badr al-Din. On the way, they stop off in Damascus and 'Ajib unknowingly befriends his own father, Badr al-Din, who has inherited the cookshop. 'Ajib and his eunuch servant are offered by Badr-al-Din "a sizzling bowl of pomegranate seeds conserved with almonds and sugar, and they ate and found it extremely delicious." On a later visit, they are treated to another "pomegranate-seed dish, preserved in almonds and sweet julep and flavored with cardamom and rosewater." When they return home, 'Ajib's paternal grandmother—who has also arrived in Damascus from Cairo—offers them a pomegranate-seed dish, which 'Ajib finds insipid; he tells his grandmother that "we have just now found in the city a cook who had prepared a pomegranate-seed dish whose aroma delights the heart and whose flavor stimulates the appetite. Your food is nothing by comparison." The eunuch is sent to buy some of the cookshop's pomegranate dish. When 'Ajib's grandmother "tasted the food and noticed its excellent flavor, she knew who had cooked it, shrieked, and fell down in a swoon . . . and when she came to herself, she said: 'If my son Badr al-Din is still in this world, none has cooked this dish but he.'" This is an instance of Aristotle's *discovery* and *peripeties* via pomegranate: the taste of a prepared pomegranate dish has served, at long range, to reveal the identities of several people to one another and to reverse the direction of the plot. So, after further trials and afflictions, Basr al-Din is reunited after twelve years with his wife, Sit al-Husn, and the rest of his family. Finally, the caliph in the first story frees the slave and bestows on the murderer "one of his choice concubines" and "a sufficient income."

Like the apple, the pomegranate has occasionally figured in arguments about the nature of knowledge, for no other reason, I suppose, than its ready recognizability. In the life of the Stoic philosopher Sphaerus, by Diogenes Laertius (early 3rd cent. C.E.), we learn that Sphaerus once engaged in a philosophical discussion with King Ptolemy Philopator (222–205 B.C.E.). Sphaerus having maintained that a wise man could never permit himself to hold mere opinions, the king attempts a refutation by deceiving Sphaerus with some waxen pomegranates. Diogenes then reports the following exchange (translated by R. D. Hicks):

Sphaerus was taken in and the king cried out, "You have given your assent to a presentation which is false." But Sphaerus was ready with a neat answer. "I assented not to the proposition that they are pomegranates, but to another, that there are good grounds for thinking them to be pomegranates. Certainty of presentation and reasonable probability are two totally different things."

QUINCES AND PEARS

PYRUS FRUITS

It is time to take stock of our fruits. A botanical inventory suggests that outside of bananas, grapes, citrus fruits, pineapples, figs, pomegranates, and melons, most of the fruits we consume today belong to the rosaceous (or rose) family; the defining characteristic of these fruits is that their blossoms share with roses a corolla of five broad petals. The rosaceous family includes the genus *Prunus* (stone-bearing fruits, such as peaches, plums, apricots, and cherries), the genus *Pyrus* (apples, pears, quinces—so-called pome fruits), and the genus *Rubus* (strawberries, raspberries, and blackberries—but not blueberries, which belong to a different genus). Robert Frost pokes some fun at this botanical taxonomy in a slight poem called "The Rose Family" (1928):

> The rose is a rose,
> And was always a rose.
> But the theory now goes
> That the apple's a rose,
> And the pear is, and so's
> The plum, I suppose.
> The dear only knows
> What will next prove a rose.
> You, of course, are a rose—
> But were always a rose.

A few years before this poem by Frost, D. H. Lawrence wrote a much more serious poem, "Grapes" (1923), which begins by setting "the universe of the unfolded rose"—in all of its manifestations, including "apples and strawberries and peaches and pears and blackberries"—in opposition to another universe, "of which . . . the vine was the invisible rose." Most of the rest of the unrhymed poem is devoted to describing the "pristine" universe of the vine, which is "dusky, flowerless, tendrilled," and ruled by "instinct." Aside from providing a conception of that more vital universe which Lawrence thinks we are losing, the poem has, I think, little to recommend it.

Apples, figs, strawberries, *Prunus* fruits, bananas, medlars, and pomegranates we have already encountered in many literary episodes; there remain the quinces, pears, pineapples, citrus fruits, melons, cherries, grapes, and berries. As for quinces, I have come across just a few extended literary episodes involving the fruit and one extraordinary painting. First, however, some basic information from *Taylor's Guide to Fruits and Berries* about a fruit that may not be very familiar today:

> When they hear "quince," many gardeners think immediately of the lovely Japanese or flowering quince. . . . The true or orchard quince, *Cydonia oblonga,* is a small tree with interesting crooked branches and the less distinctive habit of flowering from the tips of its leafy stems. It has been cultivated for its fragrant, golden fruit for thousands of years.
>
> The fruits of the true quince are large (up to 5 inches), firm, and shaped like apples or pears. Quince usually tastes better cooked than raw, although some cultivars, such as "Champion," are sweet enough to enjoy fresh. The round, white-fleshed "Pineapple" has a tart, fruity taste for zesty fresh eating. Quinces can be simmered for preserves and jellies, or baked like apples, with brown sugar and lemon.

The name for the quince in classical Latin is derived from the city of Cydonia, on the north coast of Crete, which produced outstanding quinces; the Greek name was later Latinized to "cotonea." Brief literary allusions to quinces are not uncommon, from Propertius's reference (3.13.27) to the happy young men of an older and better age for whom a gift might be (in Goold's translation) "quinces shaken down from the bough" (illis munus erat decussa Cydonia ramo), to line 44 at the beginning of book 4, chapter 3, of Johannes de Hauvilla's *Architrenius* (translated by Wetherbee)—"the quince, jacketed in a yellow that is almost gold" (Et tunicata croco germanaque coctanus auri), to Thoreau's entry on quinces in his "Wild Fruits" manuscript—"Their fragrance is the best part of them, and for this they may be worth raising: to scent your chamber," to the lines in "The Owl and the Pussy Cat" (1871), by Edward Lear (1812–1888)—"They dined on mince, and slices of quince, / Which they ate with a runcible spoon."

More arresting are two quince poems about love, the first by an ancient Greek poet and the second by a medieval Arabic poet. The former is by Ibycus of the late sixth century B.C.E., who was born in Rhegium, on the southern tip of Italy, and later lived on the island of Samos. Several ancient writers report that Ibycus was murdered by thieves and that he was wild about young boys. What survives from his seven books of poetry are mostly fragments but the following poem, as quoted by Athenaeus (and translated by David Campbell), seems to be complete. Athenaeus precedes his quotation with the remark, "And the man of Rhegium, Ibycus, shouts and screams":

> In the spring flourish Cydonian quince-trees, watered from flowing rivers where stands the inviolate garden of the Maidens, and vine-blossoms growing under the shady vine-branches; but for me love rests at no season: like

the Thracian north wind blazing with lightning rushing from the Cyprian
[Aphrodite] with parching fits of madness, dark and shameless, it powerfully shakes my heart from the roots [or: devours my heart completely].

The opposition between a rhythmically but calmly changing Nature (as exemplified
by the quince trees) and the stormy, omnipresent sexual passion of the poet is quite
memorable. And, of course, we must remember that the quince was highly prized in
antiquity.

The author of the medieval Arabic love poem referred to above is an early Hispano-
Arabic writer named al-Mushafi (d. 982), who served as vizier at the court in Cordoba. The great Spanish scholar Emilio García Gómez (1905–1995), who discovered,
in 1928, an eighteenth-century copy of an anthology of Hispano-Arabic poems (dating from the tenth to the thirteenth centuries), eventually published numerous editions of his own Spanish prose versions of over a hundred of these poems, including
"The Quince," by al-Mushafi. (Some leading modern Andalusian poets—notably
Rafael Alberti and Federico García Lorca—were deeply influenced by these translations in the 1930s.) Christopher Middleton and Leticia Garza-Falcón have translated
the al-Mushafi poem, in their collection *Andalusian Poems* (1993):

> Yellow its color
> As if it wore
> A daffodil slip
> A perfume
> Penetrating as musk
>
> Perfumed and hard of heart
> As that woman I want
> Mine its color, lover-color
> Passionate, strong
>
> It is pale with a pallor
> Loaned from the midst of me
> And when she breathes
> She breathes its deep odor
>
> It had grown on a branch
> Ripe in its odor
> And leaves by then had woven
> Brocade for its mantle
>
> Hand outstretched
> Gently I picked it

In the middle of my room
I placed it with reverence
A censer

Rolled
In ashes, fuzz
Its golden body

Naked in my hand
Under its daffodil slip

It made me think of her
I cannot name
I was breathing so hard
My fingers crushed it

Obviously, the double translation—from medieval Arabic to Castilian Spanish to modern English—raises many questions, to which Middleton tries to supply some answers in his "Introduction." Relying on the sound Hispano-Arabic scholarship of García Gómez and others and on an "unswerving fidelity to the Spanish," he nevertheless concedes that "we were aiming at vivid and believable English versions of poems in a language imaginable but unknown to us." As for this particular poem, Middleton explains that the original Arabic texts generally had no titles. ("The Quince" is simply a translation of García Gómez's title, "El Membrillo"; no quince is ever mentioned in the poem.) Perhaps a more troubling liberty that has been taken in translating Mushafi's poem is the substitution of a *crushed* for a *withered* piece of fruit. Also, of course, as Middleton admits, he and his cotranslator Garza-Falcón have "only an inkling of the tools (the exact and complex prosodic and rhetorical conventions of Arabic) with which the older artists went to work." All this said, *Andalusian Poems*—and "The Quince" in particular—remains a substantial and exhilarating achievement. (Some additional Hispano-Arabic poems will be cited in chapter 19, "Wine," and chapter 20, "Orchards, Groves, Gardens.")

Pictures of isolated quinces do not seem very common in the history of Euro-American art, which makes even more precious the following three representations of the fruit. The first is a tin-glazed terra-cotta sculpture, some six inches in height, probably from one of the Della Robbia workshops in Florence (ca. 1500–1520), and now in the Ashmolean Museum at Oxford. Such terra-cotta fruits seem to have been popular in Renaissance Florence, but very few have survived. (There is also in the Ashmolean a somewhat larger terra-cotta citron.) It appears from the illustration to an article by Jeremy Warren (in *Apollo,* 1997) that the color of the quince is a rich yellow, with green leaves.

My second example of a quince representation is García Lorca's dedicatory drawing of two pale yellow quinces, in ink and colored pencils, on the title page of a copy of one of his books, *Romance de la Luna, Luna* (Ballad of the moon, moon; 1930). That copy is now in the collection of the National Museum of Fine Arts of Cuba, in Havana; for a reproduction of the drawing, see the volume devoted to García Lorca's drawings by Mario Hernández, translated by Christopher Maurer as *Line of Light and Shadow, the Drawings of Federico García Lorca* (1991).

The extraordinary painting of a quince to which I alluded earlier occurs in Sánchez Cotán's *Still Life with Quince, Cabbage, Melon, and Cucumber* (ca. 1600), now in the San Diego Museum of Art (oil on canvas, 27 x 33½ inches). In the painting, on the left a quince and a cabbage hang by strings from an invisible support, while to the right on a table rest, in order, a cut melon, a slice of the melon, and a cucumber. There is nothing else in the painting and the background is simply undifferentiated blackness. It is obvious even at first glance that the five objects are arranged according to some mathematical scheme (a hyperbola, says Martin Soria; "a perfect parabola," says Gillian Riley—but neither explains how this can be known). For a reproduction of the painting, see Jordan and Cherry, *Spanish Still Life* (1995), or Ebert-Schifferer, *Still Life*.

THE TASTE OF, AND FOR, PEARS

We found it expedient to draw some comparisons of pears with apples in chapter 1, where it was noted how pears are less firm-fleshed and more perishable; we may add that pears tend to be more shapely and, in the past, harder to come by and therefore more highly prized. On a more subjective matter, the taste of pears, the best discussion I know—virtually the only serious discussion—is by Edward Bunyard:

> The Pear flavour must stand as a basis upon which may be laid the various overtones of flavour and acidity, and this basal flavour is experienced in all its simplicity in any of the early pears, such as the Chalk, Madeleine, and the like. In eating them you say, "Yes, this tastes like a pear"—and no more. The presence of acid, that oboe of the Pyrian orchestra, gives a zest and at once raises the mere Pear to a higher plane. The next addition is the musk, which Williams has in such notable quantity: a quality to be used with a sparing hand. . . . we feel that musk predominating is a facile and suspect quality; it requires great discretion in its disposal.
>
> What are the other flavours which we can distinguish in our best pears? Some will detect an almond flavour, others a vinous quality, and I find even a "parfum excitant" in one French author. We also have the perfumes of the rose (in Thompson's Pear), a "parfum enivrant," of honey, noyau, and so on.

Unfortunately, to appreciate Bunyard's distinctions requires that we have available for tasting the varieties of pears he takes as touchstones (Chalk, Madeleine, Williams, Thompson).

328 Already in antiquity pear varieties are singled out, as in Virgil's *Georgics* (29 B.C.E.): "the Crustamine pear, the bergamot and the pound-pear" (translated by C. Day Lewis). Pears continued to be much admired throughout the Middle Ages and Renaissance. Consider, for example, a passage about pears from the beginning of book 4 of Johannes de Hauvilla's *Architrenius* (translated by Wetherbee), where the eponymous hero has just arrived at the Mount of Ambition, partly characterized by traditional garden imagery, including allusions to a variety of fruits (figs, peaches, quinces), with one remarkable sequence of eleven lines mentioning six varieties of pears (pirus):

> Et pirus, huicque sacrum tituli dat Regulus omen,
> Et pirus, hancque vole plenus denominat orbis,
> Et pirus, huicque dedit matrina angustia nomen,
> Et pirus, Augusto que patrinante vocatur,
> Et pirus, hec nota est et filiolata Roberto,
> Et pirus, est huius alius baptista Iohannes,
> Et pirus a quovis precio signata, vel oris
> Cena vel aspectus; coit uno quelibet arbor
> Ambiciosa sinu, quo picte prodiga forme
> Ambiciosa sinu, quo picte prodiga forme
> Rumpitur in vernos montis lascivia risus.

~

And there are pears: that on which Regulus conferred the sacred token of his own title; and that round fruit which is named for the hollow of the palm; that to which the narrow passage of motherhood gives its name; and that for whose naming Augustus stood as godfather; that which was acknowledged and christened by Robert; that one whose baptizer was a second John; and pears distinguished by all sorts of attributes, whether of taste or of appearance. The ambitious tree generates any and all kinds in its single womb, so that a wanton profusion of bright shapes bursts forth into the merry springtime of the mountain.

The allusions in these lines are not easy to make out and, while Wetherbee has some suggestions, he is "willing to leave for future study the question of just what six varieties of pear are referred to."

Equally enthusiastic is the allusion to pears in a neo–Latin Renaissance poem "Iolas" (published 1530), by the distinguished Venetian literary diplomat Andrea Navagero (1483–1529). According to Fred Nichols, "Navagero's poetry was admired and imitated throughout Europe in the [sixteenth] century; not the least of his admirers was Joachim Du Bellay." In the poem, the shepherd Iolas addresses (to his sheep and dog!) a long lament for his lost love, Amaryllis, praising her beauty in extravagant terms, including the following: "As much as the lovely spring is more pleasant than the gloomy winter, as much as the ripe pear is sweeter than even the sorb apple, as much as the bristly she-goat is shaggier than her kid, as much as dawn arising at the reddish break of day is brighter than the nightly shadows of the dark evening, so, Amaryllis, you are dearer to me than other girls." (The sorb apple we have already encountered in chapter 11, along with medlars.) All four comparisons involve directly observable aspects of nature, and Nichols suggests that Iolas's "love is itself an integral part of the order of nature, as much as the shepherd is rooted in his natural context."

A theologico-botanical exaltation of the pear appears in the simile comparing the generation of Christ from a virgin with the generation of a pear from a pear tree in a Latin Christmas song, "On the Nativity of the Lord," appearing in a sixteenth-century collection:

> Behold, a new joy,
> Behold, a new wonder!
> A virgin gives birth to a son,
> She who has not known a man,
> But as the pear-tree brings forth the pear,
> The clod [of earth] the rush,
> The flowering lily.
> Behold that nature
> Changes its laws!
> A virgin pure gives birth to
> The Son of God.

This is the first of three stanzas (in a translation by Jeffrey H. Kaimowitz).

The praise of the bride in the tenth stanza (there are twenty-two in all) of "A Ballad upon a Wedding" (posthumously published in 1646), by Sir John Suckling (1609–1642), is of course entirely secular and, literally, superficial (describing her complexion in terms of a particular variety of pear):

> Her cheeks so rare a white was on,
> No daisy makes comparison,
>   (Who sees them is undone);
> For streaks of red were mingled there,
> Such as are on a Katherine pear,
>   (The side that's next the sun).

The Katherine pear is listed in several books about fruit by seventeenth-century English writers (John Parkinson, John Evelyn, Gervase Markham); Stuart Peachey quotes Parkinson: "known to all I thinke to be a yellow red sided peare, of a full waterish sweete taste, and ripe with the foremost [i.e., early ripening]." (In his sixth stanza, by the way, Suckling had used another fruit metaphor to praise the bride: "No grape,

330   that's kindly ripe, could be / So round, so plump, so soft as she, / Nor half so full of
juice.")

In 1690, the monumental treatise on fruit and vegetable gardens, *Instruction pour
les jardins fruitiers et potagers* (Instruction for fruit and vegetable gardens) by Jean de La
Quintinie (1626–1688), chief gardener for Louis XIV in France, was published
posthumously. (The king, as Frederic Janson explains, "paid royal tribute with a bronze
statue in the garden of Versailles portraying a youthful La Quintinye with a twig in
one hand, pruning knife in the other.") Three years later the book was published in
an English version of some three hundred thousand words under the title *The Compleat
Gard'ner . . . in Six Books;* though the translator is given as John Evelyn (1620–1706)—
a friend of the author's—he almost certainly had assistance. Our concern here is with
what La Quintinie says about growing pears—or, rather, with a tiny sample of what
he says, since he devotes three long, and exceptionally long-winded, chapters to the
topic. First, in the section prefacing part 3, La Quintinie argues for the supremacy of
the pear tree in fruit gardens, on the following grounds: "If it be well ordered, its top
or spreading cannot well grow monstrous enough to be any Nuisance; but, on the
contrary, may be agreeable, and give pleasure all the Year long, either by its Earliness,
Plenty and considerable Goodness of its *Fruit,* or by its round, open and well ordered
Figure, which lasts in all Seasons." La Quintinie then proceeds to explain, first for dwarf
pear trees (chaps. 1–2) and then for standard pear trees (chap. 3) which of some 240
varieties of pears are the best to plant. But La Quintinie's horticultural pedantry has to
be read to be believed: he actually provides an ordered list of no less than *five hundred*
names of pear varieties (first for dwarf trees, then again for standard trees) for fruit
gardens of increasing size! His chapter titles explain his procedure: chapter 1: "Of the
Choice of a Dwarf-tree to be Planted alone; Or, To be the first in any other Gardens,
where there are more than one," and chapter 2: "Concerning the Choice of a Second
Dwarf-pear-tree, and after that, concerning the Choice of a Third, Fourth, Fifth and
Sixth of the same, &c." Naturally, (as we shall see) many of the names are repeated
many times. To be fair to La Quintinie, one must recognize his legitimate concern to
arrange for pears to be ripening through as many months of the year as possible.

To conserve space (and patience), let me report only on what La Quintinie says
in defense of his supreme pear, the Winter Boncretien (or "good Christian"). To begin
with, this pear is very old, known to the Romans "under the name of *Crustumium* or
Volemum." (We may guess that the former Latin name was familiar to La Quintinie
from Virgil's *Georgics.*) In addition, the very name suggests an appropriateness for
Christian gardeners. More to the point, this pear is outstanding in its shape, size, color,
and long-lastingness (both on the tree and after picking), and here La Quintinie is
worth quoting at some length (though he does go on):

> It must be confessed, That among Kernel-Fruits, Nature presents us noth-
> ing so Beautiful, nor so Noble to behold as this *Pear,* whether we consider

its shape which is long and pyramidical, or its bigness, which is prodigious, as being for Example three or four Inches thick, and five or six long, and very commonly of a pound weight or more, nay, and some times exceeding two pounds, which is certainly a truth of rare and singular Remark; Or particularly, if we cast our Eyes upon its lively Carnation Colour, with which the ground of its natural Yellow is so charmingly set off, when it grows in a favourable Sun and advantageous Exposition, that it attracts the Admiration of the whole World: Add to this, That it is the *Pear* which of all others gives the longest pleasure, as well upon the Tree, upon which it continues still increasing to the view of the Eye from *May* till the End of *October,* as in the Fruit-Magazine; where easily preserving its self for four or five Months together, it daily pleasures the sight of the Curious that have a mind to look upon it, as much as the view of a Jewel or a Treasure rejoyces the Master that possesses it. It is the *Pear* that does the greatest Honour at all Tables, and which in all Countries, and principally in *France,* where the Gardens produce a wonderful quantity of them has acquired the greatest Reputation: It is that which is most commonly made use of when any considerable Presents of Fruits are made, and especially such as are sent to remote places, either within or without the Kingdom; and lastly, it is the *Pear* for the Beauty of which, the ablest Gard'ners have always Laboured with the greatest Passion, and that which yields the greatest profit to those which cultivate it only to expose to Sale.

("Kernel-fruits," by the way, are those containing seeds rather than stones, and include apples, pears, and quinces.) But what about the taste of the Winter Boncretien? La Quintinie admits that this pear is not of the first class with respect to taste, for it is not "buttery"; still, it is "often tender enough, with an agreeable Taste, and a sweet sugred Juice, indifferently abundant, and a little perfum'd." It must be reported that in La Quintinie's list of five hundred dwarf pear trees the Winter Boncretien occupies the rank of twenty-fourth, thirty-seventh, forty-ninth, fifty-fourth, sixty-fourth, eighty-first, one hundred and twenty-third, one hundred and twenty-sixth, one hundred and fifty-first, etc., etc., for a total of some forty-one Winter Boncretiens in the grand total of five hundred dwarf pear trees.

In his next (fourth), very brief, chapter on apples, La Quntinie considers only some twenty-seven varieties—around a tenth as many as the number of pear varieties—on the grounds that "there is no great difference among them in goodness"—a statement which will outrage apple-lovers. Similar but less detailed recommendations are then formulated for fig, peach, plum, cherry, and mixed orchards. Clearly, for La Quintinie, writing in 1690, pears have overwhelming pride of place.

In the eighteenth century, La Quintinie's exalted opinion of pears (and his correlative downgrading of apples) were, like so much else, authoritatively codified and

332   canonized in the *Encylopédie* of Diderot and d'Alembert. It will suffice to quote the
second paragraph from each of the entries by the naturalist Daubenton (1703–1776)
on "*Poirier* [Pear tree]" and "*Pommier* [Apple tree]," from the twelfth and thirteenth volumes (1757, 1765) respectively. Daubenton, by the way, "was subdelegate, lieutenant
general of police, and mayor (1756–68, 1772–76) of Montbard, where, from 1760, he
created a tree nursery of international repute" (according to Terence Russell and Ann-
Marie Thornton, in their book of translations of all the entries on gardens and landscapes from the *Encylopédie*).

> The pear is the most prized 'pip-fruit' tree and the most commonly culti-
> vated fruit tree in the fruit and kitchen gardens of the wealthy, while apples
> abound in the orchards of common people. The reason for this last pref-
> erence is that the acid which dominates in apples, especially rennets which
> are the most widespread, means that they keep longer and may be eaten
> before they are ripe, because the acid corrects their greenness, whereas
> pears are edible only when they are more or less ripe. But good pears, by
> their variety, different ripening seasons, and the rich and refined flavour of
> the majority, are infinitely superior to the finest apples.

> ∼

> The apple tree is the most commonly cultivated fruit tree and produces
> the main fruit crop of an orchard. However, it is inferior to the pear tree
> with regard to flavour, fragrance, and number of cultivars, though apples
> have one advantage which is more to the taste of common people: they
> are long keeping and can be eaten before they are ripe when they are no
> worse than green, whereas unripe pears are intolerably tart. Moreover, the
> apple tree grows more quickly, fruits more reliably, and, since it flowers
> a fortnight later than the pear tree, is less vulnerable to unpredictable weather
> during the change of season. Finally, apple trees require less warmth than
> pear trees, and it has even been observed that apple trees planted in espaliers
> of a favourable exposure do not always bear fine fruit.

Several decades later (1805), in America, a prize pear from Ipswich, Massachusetts,
weighing thirty-seven-and-a-half ounces was commemorated by a carved and painted
wooden sculpture (see the account in William H. Gerdts, *Painters of the Humble Truth:
Masterpieces of American Still Life, 1801–1939* [1981]). By 1864, when Wesley Vernier
was commissioned to paint a portrait of a prize-winning pear weighing four pounds,
pears had become the most fashionable fruit in the United States; the painting, titled
The Great California Pear (16 x 12 in., oil on canvas), is now in the Los Angeles County
Museum of Art (for a reproduction, see Gerdts, *Painters of the Humble Truth*). A leading
historian of United States horticulture, U. P. Hedrick, sums up what he calls a "mild
mania" as follows:

From about 1820 to 1870, the pear was the most popular fruit in the orchards of "gentleman farmers," and nearly as popular as the peach and the apple in commercial orchards. The center of interest in pear culture was eastern Massachusetts, with the Massachusetts Horticultural Society, founded in 1829, as the clearing house for information and exhibits of the fruit. . . .

There had been much interest in growing this fruit in Belgium, France, and England, beginning about 1785, and from these countries came the urge to plant pears. The man most responsible for the popularity of this fruit in two continents was Jean Baptiste Van Mons, born in Brussels in 1765, who became a student of plants and plant breeding, beginning his work with pears about 1785. . . . Van Mons' pears began to reach America in 1825, sent to American nurserymen, and brought over by two of his disciples, Parmentier and Berckmans.

It should come as no surprise, then, that in many nineteenth-century printed treatises on fruit, written for an elite, cultivated audience, pears occupy a privileged position; as Sandra Raphael explains: "In most of the general fruit books there are more pears than any other fruits, with flocks of varieties for different seasons. Once again they may have a special appeal to the connoisseur, if only because they must be picked and eaten at their peak of perfection to be tasted at their best, and that moment is easily missed." Even the rather modest book on fruit growing to which we have referred several times (by Patrick Barry of the Mount Hope Nurseries in Rochester, New York) lists 133 varieties of apples and 182 varieties of pears.

One great mid-nineteenth-century study of pears must be briefly discussed even if we cannot do full justice to its superb combination of beauty and botanical detail. This is the work of Joseph Decaisne (1807–1882), whose treatise on pears comprises the first six volumes of his nine-volume *Le Jardin fruitier du Museum* (The fruit garden of the museum); the remaining volumes deal with peaches, nectarines, plums, apricots, strawberries, and currants. The work was published in 129 parts in 1857–78 and later compiled as books. Decaisne describes well over 250 varieties of pears, each illustrated, life-sized, with a fine color plate (11 ½ x 8 in.), and lists many synonyms for each variety. (In Decaisne's time, the Jardin des Plantes—the great botanical garden in Paris—contained over fourteen hundred varieties of pears.) The plates far surpass in quality the (far fewer) plates of pears in the *Agriculture of New-York,* by Decaisne's contemporary Ebenezer Emmons, while Hedrick's *Pears of New York* (published in 1921) illustrates only eighty main varieties. One of Decaisne's varieties is the Bon-Chrétien (see plate 22), which La Quintinie so admired, but Decaisne remarks that posterity has not ratified this opinion. Another of Decaisne's varieties is named "Louis-Philippe"—synonym "Grand Salomon"—presumably after the king who ruled France during the years 1830–1848 (see plate 23).

In the contemporary United States, pears are as easily available and as inexpensive as apples; indeed, pears are ordered by the case in Jane Hirshfield's "Heart Grown Stubborn on Nectar" (1997), where the fruit becomes an ingredient in all the courses of a meal, from salad to entrée to dessert:

> The kitchen has ordered
> a case of pears, and so it begins:
> pear pancakes,
> pear upside-down cake,
> pear pudding, stewed chicken with pears.
>
> After a few days,
> the jokes turn to complaints.
>
> Then the pyramid
> of centerpiece-pears grows smaller—
>
> Pear salad with endive,
> pears poached in red wine,
> a pear course with cheeses.
> Delicious; and yet.

There follow four more stanzas, ten lines in all, that seem to have strayed in from some other poem—gnomic assertions about an "old woman, / who remembers much and says little," and "greedily eats." I prefer to recall for comparison the long list of apple dishes for sale at the apple festival in Nyrens's "Ordinary Apples" and the even longer list of banana dishes in Pynchon's *Gravity's Rainbow.*

PEARS AND APPLES

Nothing could seem more natural than the juxtaposition of the two foremost pome fruits, apples and pears, as in this passage intended for, but not included in the published version of, John Clare's "The Flitting" (1832):

> Yet can I sit me in my corner chair
> & welcome pleasure as a daily guest
> For what can be more pleasant even there
> Then see the trees in natures beauty drest
> The apples blushing blossoms—& more fair
> The delicate blooming of the leaning pear

The phrase "the leaning pear" is explained by an entry in one of Clare's natural history notebooks (Peterborough MS A46), where he records that "there is a pear tree & like all pears which I have noticed it leands towards the west—but so much so as tho it wanted a prop—it seems the only tree that excaped the perils of the bill hook & there fore might wish to fly away & be at rest—I have always noticed that these trees have some inclination more or less towards the west."

More often, however, apples and pears are not treated evenhandedly. Perhaps it should come as no surprise, given Henry Thoreau's enthusiasm for apples (noted in chapter 1), that he did not share the pear mania of his time. Thus, in his journal for 11 October 1860—repeated with slight changes in his "Wild Fruits" manuscript— Thoreau contrasts pears and apples:

> They [pears] are a more aristocratic fruit. How much more attention they get from the proprietor! The hired man gathers the apples and barrels them. The proprietor plucks the pears at odd hours for a pastime, and his daughter wraps them each in its paper. . . . They are spread on the floor of the best room. They are a gift to the most distinguished guest. Judges and ex-judges and honorables are connoisseurs of pears, and discourse of them at length between sessions. . . .
>
> Pears, it is truly said, are less poetic than apples. They have neither the beauty nor the fragrance of apples, but their excellence is in their flavor, which speaks to a grosser sense. They are *glouts-morceaux*. Hence, while children dream of apples, ex-judges realize pears. They are named after emperors and kings and queens and dukes and duchesses. I fear I shall have to wait till we get to pears with American names, which a republican can swallow.

The notion of apples as plebeian and pears as aristocratic seems to go back a long way, as in this remark by the great seventeenth-century French cook de La Varenne: "The pear is the grandfather of the apple, its poor relation, a fallen aristocrat . . . pre- serving the memory of its prestige by its haughty comportment" (quoted as an epi- graph by Victor Perera in his book *The Cross and the Pear Tree: A Sephardic Journey*). The status competition between apples and pears crops up in some unexpected places; it may, for example, be at work in *The Harvesters* (1565), that great painting by Pieter Bruegel the Elder (ca. 1525–1569), in the Metropolitan Museum of Art in New York City (oil on wood, 45 ⅞ x 62 ⅞ inches; for a reproduction of the painting, see *From Van Eyck to Bruegel: Early Netherlandish Painting in the Metropolitan Museum of Art* [1998]). The left-hand half of the painting is dominated by wheat fields, which peasants are engaged in harvesting; the right-hand half of the painting, depicting levelled wheat fields, is dominated by a tall pear tree, which is cut off by the top margin of the paint- ing, thereby enhancing the apparent height (and importance) of the tree. Under the pear tree, some nine peasants are eating, drinking, or napping. The only food visible is a loaf of bread and four or five pears resting on a small white cloth on the ground. Further back than the pear tree and cut off by the right-hand margin of the painting is an apple tree in the lower branches of which someone is shaking down apples, some seven or eight of which can be observed falling; beneath the tree are a basket, a ladder, and two peasants picking up the fallen apples. Was Bruegel deliberately showing his peasants eating aristocratic pears instead of plebeian apples? Well, if he was, it was probably not to celebrate the life of the peasant, for, as Mary de Jesus remarks, "Bruegel was hardly a propagandist for peasant virtue or the joys of the yeoman's life." Just why Bruegel might have painted a picture in this way is almost entirely a matter for conjecture, since, according to Nadine Orenstein, "the relative paucity of documents concerning the artist's life and, more important, his beliefs has left the nature of his intentions open to interpretation." In a book dealing with the meaning of Bruegel's art, *Pieter Bruegel: Parables of Order and Enterprise* (1999), Ethan Kavaler remarks about *The Harvesters* that "growth, harvest, work, and rest are all shown as integral elements in a divinely ordained system." The remark implies an absence in the painting of what really interests Kavaler (according to his introduction): "Paintings, drawings, and prints . . . presenting the world as a place of conflict, of opposing values, forces, and natural drives." At the very least, I find represented in *The Harvesters* a contrast—even some tension—between the wheat crop (and bread), on the one hand, and the apples and pears, on the other.

An exalted status for pears (and an ensuing rivalry with apples) seems, once again, to be reflected in one of the poems by Jules Renard (1864–1910), in his *Histoires Naturelles* (1896). The sequence "Au Jardin" (In the garden) takes the form of a series of tiny dialogues among spade, pick, and watering can; sunflower, rose, raspberry, thistle, violet, leek, scallion, garlic, asparagus, and potato; carp, hornet, and bee; and, finally, between apple and pear tree (translated by Richard Howard):

The Apple Tree (To the Pear Tree Opposite): It's your pear, your pear, your pear . . . , it's your pear I want to grow.

~

LE POMMIER, *au Poirier d'en face.*
—C'est ta poire, ta poire, ta poire . . . , c'est ta poire que je voudrais produire.

The apple-pear rivalry is perhaps also reflected in the book *Apples and Pears and Other Stories* (1984), by Guy Davenport, one of whose stories is titled "Erewhonian Apple, New Harmony Pear." It must be said, however, that the significance of apples and pears (and many other fruits) in Davenport's densely allusive text is not at all easy to make out. (At least one extended critical analysis of the book, by Bruce Bawer, does not even mention the fruit.) We shall have to be content, then, with simply quoting two stanzas (out of four) embedded in the story called "Quagga" (which begins with the phrase, "A basket of summer fruit"):

Build me a high house,
Angels at the eaves.

> Grow me an apple tree
> With a thousand silver leaves.
>
> Grow me a pear tree,
> A daughter of the sun.
> Put yellow pears upon it
> And bless them every one.

This seems to rate pears (golden) above apples (silver) in the hierarchy of fruits. And Davenport has returned to the theme in a later book, *Objects on a Table* (1998), concerned primarily with still life painting. Among his findings are the "pyriform and pomenoid shapes that turn up in the eyes and parts of the body" in a suite of Picasso drawings of the 1950s, "The Human Comedy," and "a Picassoid romp of apples and pears" in a pencil drawing of 22 February 1933.

With appropriate contextualization, a pear can shed its elitist associations and even serve as reminder of our common humanity, specifically, the sour taste of defeat and the stubborn insistence on sharing that taste with our fellow-sufferers. At least, so I interpret "Montana Pears" (2000), by the American poet Patricia Goedicke (b. 1931), beginning:

> In the middle of Montana, eating.
> What the man sliced for them, two pears on a plate
> sprinkled with bottled lime juice
> and sugar.
>
> His fork. Then hers. Spearing up
> naked, white-to-sour-green
> chunks of moonless November's
> cold orchards.

In the twelve stanzas that follow, we learn that the couple is elderly, tired, and cheaply dressed; that they are sitting on a "part nylon / and part wool sofa," listening to some popular music for electric guitar and acoustic bass, each reading a book; and that—as the culmination of the eating of the two pears—"the man forks up / the last piece of pear and puts it / in the woman's mouth." In the sixth and last stanza, the speaker addresses us—the audience for this impoverished little scene—directly:

> You, out there in the dark,
> don't be afraid.
> See, they're all lit up for you, do you
> know them? I don't,
> and I'm stage manager here. In fact,

I'm one of the actors.

. . . .

Doesn't anyone
recognize them? You, out there in the dark,
look in at the two of them,
glowing.

And that glow, we are to understand, is not just stage lighting.

The juxtaposition of apple and pear occurs in unexpected places, like the satirical drawing of Julia Child by David Levine (b. 1926), for the *New York Review of Books* (see his 1999 calendar). The cookbook writer's face is distinctly pear-shaped and she is holding a platter on which there lies a book, in the pages of which an apple has been embedded.

René Magritte also has painted a couple of still lifes (now in private collections) featuring apples and pears: the two fruits, with mottled, plaster-like surfaces, nestled together against a background of cloudy sky (*Memory of a Journey* [1952], reproduced in *Painters of the Mind's Eye: Belgian Symbolists and Surrealists* [1974]; some apples next to a footed bowl of pears, both resting on a framed blank canvas, which is itself resting on a tabletop (*Common Sense,* reproduced in Gablik's *Magritte*). Also, a film by Luc de Heusch, *Magritte or the Object Lesson* (1960), in one sequence shows Magritte himself arranging the fruit for his own still life *Common Sense;* another film by Jean Dypréau, *Magritte* (1983), in one sequence shows Magritte himself holding an apple up before his face. (For some stills from the two films, see Gablik's or Meuris's volumes on Magritte.)

Apples and pears have even been fashioned in bronze, as in some works by the Italian sculptor Giacomo Manzù (1908–1991): a chair on whose seat are resting an apple and a pear separated by a stalk of celery, the chair being life-size and the fruit oversized; a basket of fruit (9 7/8 x 19 11/16 inches), containing an apple, pear, lemon, and what appears to be a fig. The former dates from 1960, and is discussed and illustrated by E. H. Gombrich in his essay "Tradition and Expression in Western Still Life" (1963); the latter dates from 1985 and was exhibited in the Tasende Gallery in La Jolla, California, in 1989.

Finally, we may note that in British slang, the phrase "apples and pears" is used to mean "stairs," as in "he was shoved down the apples and pears"; according to Eric Partridge, the expression goes back to at least 1859.

THE SHAPES OF PEARS

Along with taste, shape is the most obvious distinguishing mark of the pear, though not all fruits botanically classified as pears are "pear-shaped." Thus, so-called Asian pears are generally shaped like apples, but also some apples are long and conical, like our paradigmatic pears; indeed, already by the end of the sixteenth century, we find the Swiss naturalist Jean Bauhin (1541–1613) distinguishing his pictures of pears and apples by a convention regarding the orientation of their stems: pears stem up, apples stem down. (See Stephen Jay Gould's essay, "When Fossils Were Young" [1999].) This convention was adopted by John Parkinson in his important treatise *Paradisi in sole paradisus terrestris* (1629), where the punning Latin title—the text itself is in English—means "Park in Sun's [Parkinson's] Earthly Paradise"! The convention was also adopted in the great (posthumously published) treatise on plants by Bauhin and his son-in-law Jean Henri Cherler (ca. 1570–ca. 1610), *Historia plantarum universalis* (1650–1). This extraordinary work in three quarto volumes—the full title is "Universal History of Plants, New, and with Complete Consensus and Dissent About Them"—begins with fruit. In the first book, chapter 1 on apples and chapter 4 on pears are, respectively, twenty-seven and twenty-five pages in length; there are sixty-two life-sized woodcuts of apples, all depicted with their stems down, and thirty-three of pears, all with their stems up (see figs. 6–7). Many later representations of apples and pears adopt the same convention (see figs. 8–9). Nevertheless, the notion of a pear shape does seem to possess an unambiguous meaning, as in the following short poem, "Pears" (1980) by Linda Pastan, in which a pear is compared to no less than three utterly different things (a womb, a cello, and a woman's breasts):

> Some say
> it was a pear
> Eve ate.
> Why else the shape
> of the womb,
> or of the cello
> whose single song is grief
> for the parent tree?
> Why else the fruit itself
> tawny and sweet
> which your lover
> over breakfast
> lets go your pear-
> shaped breast
> to reach for?

In another poem about pears, "Espaliered Pear Trees" (1995), Pastan calls attention to the shape of the tree itself:

> You tack the pear trees to the wall
> in a mime of crucifixion—
> their limbs splayed flat,
> their leafed backs toward us—
> and water them with a hose.

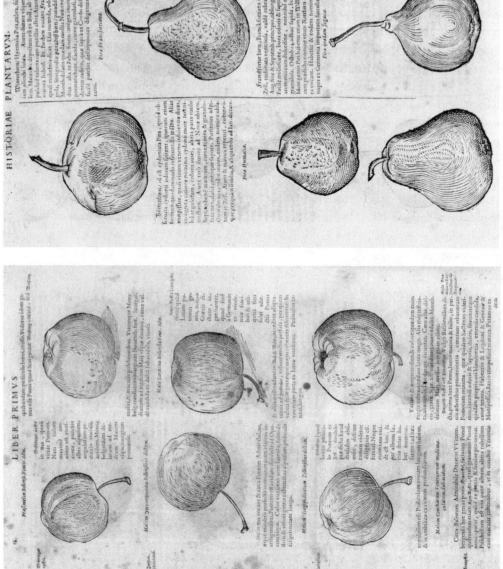

Fig. 6: Apples, Jean Bauhin and Jean Henri Cherler, Historia plantarum universalis, 1650–51

Fig. 7: Pears, Jean Bauhin and Jean Henri Cherler, Historia plantarum universalis, 1650–51

In addition to these forms and their various modifications, some varieties are

Figs. 42 to 47, forms of apples. 42, round. 43, conical. 44, ovate. 45, flat ~., oblong. 47, ribbed.

Angular, having projecting angles on the sides.
One-sided, having one side larger than the other.
Ribbed (47), when the surface presents a series of ridges
    and furrows running from eye to stem.

FORMS OF APPLES.

Round or Roundish (fig. 42).—When the outline is
    round, or nearly so, the length being about equal
    to the breadth.
Flat (fig. 45).—When the ends are compressed, and the
    width considerably greater than the length.
Conical (fig. 43).—In the form of a cone, tapering from
    the base to the eye.
Ovate, or *egg-shaped* (fig. 44).
Oblong (fig. 46).—When the length is considerably greater
    than the width, and the width about equal at both
    ends, not tapering as in the conical.

Fig. 8: "Forms of Apples," Patrick Barry, *The Fruit Garden,* 1855

Turbinate or *top-shaped*.—The sides somewhat rounded and tapering to a point at the stem (fig. 52).

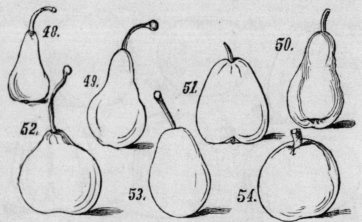

Figs. 48 to 54, forms of pears. 48, pyriform. 49, long pyriform. 50, obtuse pyriform. 51, obovate. 52, turbinate. 53, oval. 54, round.

Oval.—Largest in the middle, tapering more or less to each end (fig. 53).

Round.—When the outline is nearly round (fig. 54).

FORMS OF PEARS.

It has been remarked that the pyramidal form prevails in pears; but they taper from the eye to the stem, which is just the reverse of the tapering form in apples. Their forms are designated thus—

Pyriform.—When tapering from the eye to the base, and the sides more or less hollowed (concave) (fig. 48).

Long Pyriform.—When long and narrow, and tapering to a point at the stem (fig. 49).

Obtuse Pyriform.—When the small end is somewhat flattened (fig. 50).

Obovate or *egg-shaped*.—Nearly in form of an egg, the small end being nearest the stem (fig. 51).

Fig. 9: "Forms of Pears," Patrick Barry, *The Fruit Garden*, 1855

After a glance at how growing things are shaped in other cultures (Japanese bonsai trees, Chinese women's bound feet), we are returned to the garden—to its soil, to its weeds—and finally to the taste of pears:

> Here in the garden,
>
> where the cost of beauty
> is partly pain, we kneel
> on the resilient ground
> trying to befriend the soil
> we must become.
>
> Long after Eden,
> the imagination flourishes
> with all its unruly weeds.
> I dream of the fleeting
> taste of pears.

In the opening stanza of his "A Study of Two Pears" (1942), Wallace Stevens also mentions three things that are "pear-shaped" (viols, nudes, bottles) even as he rejects all pear metaphors involving shape:

> Opusculum paedagogum.
> The pears are not viols,
> Nudes or bottles.
> They resemble nothing else.

It is somewhat surprising to be told, in this "little pedagogical work," that pears resemble nothing else, especially in light of what Stevens was to say five years later when he gave a talk at Harvard ("Three Academic Pieces") in which he asserted, "Poetry is a satisfying of the desire for resemblance." Consistently enough, however, in the next four stanzas of this poem we find no metaphors, but rather a sequence of descriptions of pears using only simple abstract nouns (such as "forms," "curves," "round," "tapering") and simple adjectives (such as "bulging," "flat," "curved," "hard," "dry"). Color words are especially prominent: "yellow," "red," "blue," "Citrons, oranges and greens." In the last stanza, noticing the shadows of the pears on some green cloth, we have involuntarily left the realm of abstractions and returned to reality (even if only the reality of shadows):

> The shadows of the pears
> Are blobs on the green cloth.
> The pears are not seen
> As the observer wills.

The lesson is that we cannot, after all, choose not to see things in terms of their resemblances—in this case, the resemblance between the solid physical presences of the pears and their bloblike shadows. The impulse to notice or create resemblances *is* poetry, whose "singularity is that in the act of satisfying the desire for resemblance it touches the sense of reality, it enhances the sense of reality, heightens it, intensifies it." In order to accomplish this act of intensification, of course, the resemblances must not be tied to a narrowly perceptual basis; the resemblances may, in fact, be far-fetched indeed. (Stevens's ideas in this regard are further explored in the next chapter, on pineapples).

"A Study of Two Pears" may remind some readers of a less well-known Stevens poem, one of those added, a decade earlier, to the enlarged edition of *Harmonium:* "In the Clear Season of Grapes" (1931). Here the poet is impressed by the contrast between a mere domestic still life—"the table that holds a platter of pears, / Vermilion smeared over green, arranged for show"—and the grand sweep of the autumnal landscape—"This conjunction of mountains and sea and our lands." The pears are even a little contemptible: "this gross blue under rolling bronzes / Belittles those carefully chosen daubs. / Flashier fruits!" In "A Study of Two Pears," Stevens is willing to settle for the "daubs" of the still life painter and to eschew any larger, cosmic questioning.

The American poet Gabriel Preil (1911–1993) must have been well acquainted with Stevens's "A Study of Two Pears" when he wrote (in Hebrew) his own poem, "A Pear, for Instance" (1980). Though he made several trips to Israel, Preil lived in the United States after immigrating from Estonia when he was eleven; he wrote poetry in both Hebrew and Yiddish and translated Edwin Arlington Robinson, Robinson Jeffers, and Robert Frost into Hebrew. Furthermore, the title of Preil's pear poem is Stevensian and so also in some respects is the poem itself, while another of Preil's poems, "Record," is about the experience of listening to Stevens read his own poetry. Constituting twelve lines of free verse in the original Hebrew, here is an English version of Preil's pear poem by Robert Friend:

> Waves of fearful knowledge in print, in the air,
> a flowering that is a sun-setting, the windows bewildered,
> and within—the stormy reticence of a poem,
> its winy strength, the fragility of its meanings—
> like those, perhaps, of a fruit, of a pear, for instance,
> with flashes of tawny-gold, hints of reddish-green,
> and something autumnal and like a violin
> going through it, as if in this world
> invitations were still extended
> to come and sample tables of aromas.
> Nor do you stumble, these late afternoons,
> on angles sharp and unexpected,
> some yards away from a smoking hand-grenade.

The idea in this work, as in many of Preil's other poems, is to convey the contradictory attitudes and feelings involved in the process of its own composition: "knowledge in print" and "in the air," "flowering" and "sun-setting," "windows bewildered" [and also presumably transparent], "stormy reticence," "strength" and "fragility"—all these "perhaps" like the equally contradictory "tawny-gold" [tawny is dull, gold glitters] and "reddish-green" of a pear. More consistent than contradictory, however, are "autumnal" and "like a violin"—at least, if one focuses on the sound rather than on the shape of the instrument. In any case, it seems the world is not so inhospitable to poetry-making after all; indeed, the world *appears* to be sufficiently orderly and civilized for us to appreciate the subtlety of its "aromas" without worrying that a nearby pear may turn out to *be*—and not just to *resemble*—"a smoking hand-grenade." Coming right at the end of Preil's poem, this hand-grenade threatens to explode what has been up until that point a finely wrought and delicate structure. It may be recalled that the last stanza of Stevens's poem about pears also threatens to overturn the ideas of the earlier stanzas, though the threat there comes from insubstantial shadows rather than from an act of violence.

A narrowly geometrical image of pears may be found in a poem about contemporary America, "Prelude I" (1962), by the Russian poet Andrei Voznesensky (b. 1933), expressing "his ambivalent feelings about its technology and its hectic tempo" (the words are those of his editors, Blake and Hayward). Written after his visit to the United States in 1961, the poem's most vivid image is that of a "triangular pear" (translated by William Jay Smith):

> I peel the skin from the planet,
>   sweep away mold and dust;
> Cut through the crust
>   and go down
>   into the depths of things
> As into the subway.
>
> Down there grow triangular pears;
>   I seek the naked souls they contain.
>
> I take the trapezoidal fruit, not to eat
> Of it; but to let its glassy core
> Glow with an altar's red heat.
>
> Pry into it incessantly,
>   do not relent;
> Do not be misled
> If they say your watermelon's green when in fact it's red.

Finally, a poem about a misshapen pear: "A Pear Like a Potato" (1985), by John Updike. The speaker is holding a pear and reflecting, in one long sentence, on its resemblance to a potato:

> Whatever the reason, the pear
> fresh-plucked from my tree where it leans and struggles
> in the garden's dappled corner
> is a heavy dwarf-head whose faceless face
> puckers and frowns around a multitude of old problems,
> its furrowed brow and evil squint and pursy mouth
> and pinched-in reptilian ear rescrambling,
> feature for feature, as I rotate
> this weight in my hand, this
> friendly knot of fruit-flesh, this
> pear like a potato.

After some strained references to the nature of teratological anomalies and to Plato's theory of ideas, the poem—from first to last plainly that of a prose writer—ends with the eating of the pear:

> this poor pear
> that never would do at the supermarket,
> bubble-wrapped with symmetrical brothers, but
> has given me a snack,
> a nibble here and there, on my own land,
> here in the sun of a somewhat cloudy morning.

PEARS AS SEXUAL OBJECTS

The shape of pears has also been seen as providing a source of male sexual imagery complementary to the female sexual imagery of apples. Thus, an ingenious (anonymous) Middle English poet uses the ripening of pears as a source of sexual innuendo:

> I have a newe garden,
>   and newe is begunne;
> Swych [such] another garden
>   know I not under sunne.
>
> In the middës [midst] of my garden
>   is a perer [pear-tree] set,
> And it wil non pere bern [bear]
>   but a pere-jonet [early pear].
>
> The fairest mayde of this toun
>   prayëd me

For to griffen her a gryf [plant her a graft]
　　of myn pery-tre.

When I hadde hem griffëd [planted]
　　alle at herë wille,
The wyn and the alë
　　she dide in fille [poured out].

And I griffëd here
　　right up in here home [deep inside her]
And be that day twenty wekes [weeks]
　　it was quik in here womb.

That day twelvë month
　　that mayde I met,
She said it was a pere Robert
　　but non pere Jonet.

　　It is not possible to determine the exact date of the poem; the date of the manuscript is around 1400–1450 but the poem may be considerably earlier. To interpret the poem, one must understand that a "pere-jonet" is a pear that ripens by St. John's day (24 June), that is, an early ripener. (This is confirmed by Peachey's *Fruit Variety Register*, where the seasonal chart for some two hundred varieties of pears from the period 1580–1660 shows that ripening before August is rare.) Duncan also explains that the speaker is presumably named "Jonet," so that when, in the last stanza, the maiden denies that the pear is a "Jonet" and proclaims it instead a "Robert," she is saying something about the paternity of her child. Finally, according to Duncan, the poem appears in "a small, pocket-sized manuscript with all the appearance of a minstrel's song book, and although lacking musical notation, many of its [fourteen] lyrics seem eminently singable."

　　More or less contemporary with "I have a new garden" are two structurally similar tales of amorous intrigue, each involving a pear tree, by, respectively, Boccaccio and Chaucer; each tale is highly entertaining and each has been read in recent years as a narrative far transcending simple entertainment. First, in the *Decameron* (ca. 1350) of Boccaccio, the ninth story of the seventh day incorporates an old fable about a sexual encounter in a pear tree between a young wife—who is the instigator throughout—and her youthful servant. Variants of this fable depend on the variety of tricks by which the young lovers manage to deceive the husband, who is standing directly under the tree. In Boccaccio's version, Lydia (the wife) gets Nicostratus (her husband) and Pyrrhus (the young servant) to accompany her into the palace garden. Expressing a great craving for pears, Lydia asks Pyrrhus to climb up the pear tree and throw down some fruit. He does what he is told but then pretends to recoil in horror from what he loudly describes as sexual activity between Lydia and Nicostratus. The latter denies the act but is moved to climb the tree himself to discover if it is enchanted. Lydia and Pyrrhus then go to it, much to the chagrin of Nicostratus up in the tree. When he returns to earth, the two lovers persuade him that (in the translation of G. H. McWilliam) "whatever it is that is distorting our vision, it must emanate from the pear-tree." Lydia then orders Pyrrhus to chop the tree down. All three return to the palace, "within whose walls it thenceforth became easier for Pyrrhus and Lydia to meet, at regular intervals, for their common delight and pleasure. May God grant that we enjoy a similar fate!" (A fifteenth-century manuscript, in the Bibliothèque de l'Arsenal, Paris, MS. 5070, contains illustrations of a French *Decameron* including one hundred miniatures painted between 1430 and 1440 by two Flemish artists; for a picture of Pyrrhus in the pear tree and the married couple underneath, see Edmond Pognon, *Boccaccio's Decameron: Fifteenth-Century Manuscript* [1978].)

Chaucer may have been influenced by the above story when he came to write his Merchant's Tale (1392–95), the last part of which consists of another variant on the pear tree fable (though scholars have identified many other possible sources in Italian, French, and Latin, for other parts of the Merchant's Tale). Leaving aside the Merchant's Prologue—important as it may be for an adequate interpretation of the subsequent tale—here is a bare outline of the plot. Once again, there is a triangle consisting of an aged husband, January (who has married late in life in order the better to satisfy his carnal desires), his young wife, May, and the couple's young servant, Damyan, who, naturally, is in love with May. To communicate his love—and, significantly, here the man is the instigator—Damyan slips May a note, which she reads and disposes of in the privy. She replies with an ardently loving note of her own; what one recent interpreter has called "literary foreplay" is indeed present throughout the tale (see Eric Jager, *The Tempter's Voice: Language and the Fall in Medieval Literature* [1993]). At this point in the story January suddenly loses his sight, thereby presumably matching his physical blindness with his psychological—even spiritual—blindness. Now more jealous than ever, January rarely takes his hands off May; he also frequently retreats with her to his locked garden for sexual play, and one morning he awakens her with words that recall the Song of Songs (ll. 2138–2149):

> "Rys up, my wyf, my love, my lady free!
> The turtles voys is herd, my dowve sweete;
> The wynter is goon with alle his reynes weete.
> Com forth now, with thyne eyen columbyn!
> How fairer been thy brestes than is wyn!
> The gardyn is enclosed al aboute;
> Com forth, my white spouse! out of doute
> Thou hast me wounded in myn herte, O wyf!
> No spot of thee ne knew me I al my lyf.
> Com forth, and lat us taken oure disport;

I chees thee for my wyf and my confort."
Swiche olde lewed wordes used he.

The occurrence of this clear biblical echo helps to justify the appeal to Augustinian interpretative ideas in recent discussions of the Merchant's Tale.

Returning to the plot: with a duplicate key for January's locked garden, Damyan and May devise a plan. Undetected by January, Damyan enters the garden and, at a signal from May, climbs up into the pear tree. May then pleads for a pear; in an effort to pick one, she ends up standing on January's back as he clasps the trunk of the tree. Then comes the climax (in all senses): "And sodeynly anon this Damyan / Gan pullen up the smok, and in he throng [thrust]" (ll. 2352–3). (For a fifteenth-century woodcut representing this amazingly uncensored image of sexual desire, see illustration 7 in Jager's book.) Pluto and Proserpina, depicted as quarreling fairies, have been loitering about in the garden, and now intervene: January recovers his eyesight (courtesy of Pluto) just in time to witness the erotic behavior of May and Damyan, and May is granted (courtesy of Proserpina) the ability to persuade January that her "struggle with a man upon a tree" (l. 2374)—as she so euphemistically puts it—was precisely what cured her husband's blindness. He is reluctantly persuaded, and they are reconciled as the tale ends. An epilogue, emphasizing the misogynous moral of the tale, refers to the "sleightes and subtilitees" (l. 2421) of women—though Lee Patterson sees "the *Tale* as a whole . . . underwritten by a well-disguised but nonetheless profound belief in the liberating power of the feminine."

Few modern Chaucer scholars (so Larry Benson tells us) have been content to interpret the Merchant's Tale as simply "a rather lighthearted jape at women and human folly." For Jager, the pear tree in January's garden leads us back inescapably to the episode in St. Augustine's *Confessions,* which itself leads us back to the Garden of Eden: "the main precedents for January's garden are biblical and patristic ones, including the Garden of Eden, the *hortus conclusus* of the Canticle, and Augustine's gardens in the *Confessions.*" As for the pear tree, it is presumed to possess both sacred and secular significance: on the one hand, "of course a sign 'charged' with far more than just its actual fruit, since it figures a long series of typological trees going back to the Tree of Knowledge in the first Garden," and on the other hand, "although medieval tradition usually associated the forbidden fruit, typically an apple, with Eve's breasts, here the 'smale peres grene' desired by May suggest instead the male sexual organs, a metaphor having precedent in medieval art." It should be added that Jager constructs an extended interpretation—well over fifty pages—of the Merchant's Tale in Augustinian hermeneutical terms (chap. 6, "The Carnal Letter in Chaucer's Earthly Paradise").

A much more straightforward use of the sexual connotations of pears occurs when in the opening pages of *Anna Karenina* (1878), by Leo Tolstoy (1888–1910), Stiva Oblonsky returns from the theater "with a huge pear for his wife in his hand" (Joel Carmichael's translation). Why a pear? Presumably because that is the fruit which was

350   available and perhaps also because pears were particularly prized at the time in Russia; of course, the implicit sexual connotations would certainly be pertinent in the case of a man who has lost erotic interest in his wife. Unfortunately for Stiva, the gift of a pear hardly compensates for his wife's discovery earlier in the day of his recent affair with the French governess. A Russian folk song, by the way, confirms the association of pears with masculinity:

> In the green garden a pear tree
> > Began to rustle, to rustle.
> Why in the garden has the pear tree
> > Begun to rustle, to rustle?
> And the sharp, wild winds,
> > Little winds begun to blow.
> In Mixail's home there was joy,
> > There was joy.
> In Ivanovich's home there was joy,
> > There was joy.
> Why in his home
> > Was there joy, was there joy?
> His young wife a son
> > Has borne, has borne,
> And the sweet Theodosia-darling a son
> > Has borne, has borne,
> Sweet Petrovna—darling a son
> > Has borne, has borne.

But what of the most famous pears in the postclassical Euro-American literary tradition—pears stolen by Augustine in his sixteenth year, an incident which, according to some critics, forever looms over (or, better, lurks within) all later writings in that tradition? The incident in question is analyzed in depth in book 2 of the *Confessions*. About the incident one feels compelled to wonder whether or not its implications are sexual. Augustine's biographer, Peter Brown, answers: "Augustine . . . treats [the sins of concupiscence] as not very important: in his eyes they paled into insignificance before a single act of vandalism. The pointless robbing of a pear-tree is what really interests this great connoisseur of the human will: he will analyse this one incident with fascinated repulsion; 'For what could I not have done, seeing that I could enjoy even a gratuitous act of crime?'" Those who are tempted to think that the stealing of the pears might be just a metaphor for sexual sin must engage with a careful commentator on the *Confessions*, James J. O'Donnell, who argues that taken literally as an act of theft "the case is logically simpler than any fornication could have been. Of no sexual transgression could he have unequivocally said (or had any hope of convincing us) that what appealed to him was not the thing itself but wrongness itself" (1992). And indeed

Augustine labors hard to make the act in question appear wholly gratuitous: "I stole
something which I had in plenty and of much better quality" from "a pear tree near
our vineyard laden with fruit, though attractive in neither colour nor taste" and "carried off a huge load of pears . . . not for our feasts but merely to throw to the pigs"
(translated by Henry Chadwick). Most commentators see a deliberate parallel being
drawn by Augustine between his theft and the eating of the forbidden fruit in Eden—
a type of interpretation which, when applied to the two Testaments, has been called
typological (and is fully discussed by O'Donnell). One difference is that Eve is furnished by the author of Genesis with no less than three reasons for eating the fruit: it
is good for food (somehow Eve knows that *all* fruit in Eden is edible), it is pleasant to
look at, and (according to the serpent) it makes one wise; Augustine, on the other
hand, assures us that his pears are both unattractive to look at and lacking in flavor.
(Another apparent parallel with the Garden of Eden occurs toward the end of book
8 of the *Confessions* when Augustine has his great conversion experience under a fig
tree in his garden.)

The visual association of pears and apples with male and female sexuality, respectively, seems to have been especially favored by Lucas Cranach the Elder. In his representations of such sexually charged subjects as Adam and Eve in the Garden of Eden,
Samson and Delilah, and the Golden Age, one finds prominent pictures of apple and
pear trees laden with fruit. (For reproductions of two paintings of each of these subjects, see Friedländer and Rosenberg's *Paintings of Lucas Cranach*.)

Freud recounts a dream of pears that a thirty-five-year-old man remembered
having had at the age of four. The little boy's father had just died and the lawyer in
charge of his father's will appeared in the dream with two large pears. The boy was
given one of the pears and the other one lay on a windowsill. With no associations
forthcoming from the dreamer, Freud decides he has "a right to attempt an interpretation by symbolic substitution," and he concludes that the pears represent the breasts
of the dreamer's mother; specifically, "The dream must be translated: 'Give (or show)
me your breast again, Mother, that I used to drink from in the past.' 'In the past' was
represented by his eating one of the pears; 'again' was represented by his longing for
the other. The *temporal repetition* of an act is regularly shown in dreams by the *numeri-
cal multiplication* of an object." Thus, Freud plays no favorites as between apples (recall
"Women's Breasts as Apples" in chap. 1) and pears, citing a dream apiece for each type
of fruit.

PEARS AS LITERARY DEVICES

That the pear can be much more than a simple sexual symbol is amply illustrated by
a variety of literary and artistic examples. A pear stands in for a multitude of different
ideas in the following series of prose fictions and poems: a premature act, a human victim, a process of cosmic decay, some failed hopes, a narrative hook, a comic prop, a
mere image, a childhood scenario. In Charles Dickens's *David Copperfield* (1849–50)

352   Uriah Heep compares the premature announcement of his intention to marry Agnes Wickfield to the picking of an unripe pear. The use of such a metaphor is highly unusual in Uriah's idiolect—which consists largely of flat, literal declarations—but the occasion is an emotional one (for both Uriah and David). David's first encounter—he is fifteen—with Uriah is in chapter 15, and, of course, David finds him immediately execrable. Considerably later, in chapter 25, David learns that Uriah has become the business partner of Mr. Wickfield and also that Uriah hopes to marry Agnes. Appalled, but previously instructed by Agnes not to insult Uriah, David actually invites him home for coffee and suffers the indignity of having Uriah sleep on the floor of his lodgings. Then, in chapter 39, Uriah provokes a violent reaction in Mr. Wickfield by announcing his intentions vis-à-vis Agnes. The next morning Uriah seeks David out in a departing stagecoach and this exchange occurs—the concluding passage of the chapter:

> "I suppose," with a jerk, "you have sometimes plucked a pear before it was ripe, Master Copperfield?"
>
> "I suppose I have," I replied.
>
> "*I* did that last night," said Uriah; "but it'll ripen yet! It only wants attending to. I can wait!"
>
> Profuse in his farewells, he got down again as the coachman got up. For anything I know, he was eating something to keep the raw morning air out; but, he made motions with his mouth as if the pear were ripe already, and he were smacking his lips over it.

I can almost imagine that Dickens introduced the pear metaphor just for the sake of alluding to the revolting action of Uriah's mouth and lips.

In "The Pear," by the Brazilian writer Vinícius de Moraes (b. 1913), a pathetic pear seems to have no role beyond self-sacrifice (by contrast with the banana or the apple in the poem), and the human application is almost immediate. Both the translation by Ashley Brown and the original Portuguese are quoted in order to exhibit the rhymes and also because so many of the key Portuguese words are English cognates.

> As if of wax
> And by chance
> Cold in the dish
> Growing late
>
> The pear is a fruit
> Burnt offering
> To life, like
> A breast exhausted
>
> Among bananas

Extraneous
And apples, candid

Ruddy, content
The poor pear:
Who brings it to be?

~

Como de cêra
E por acaso
Fria no vaso
A entardecer

A pêra é um pomo
Em holocausto
À vida, como
Um seio exausto
Entre bananas
Supervenientes
E maçãs lhanas

Rubras, contentes
A pobre pêra:
Quem manda sera?

The translation does not attempt to capture all of the Portuguese end-rhymes but does include "offering/exhausted" and "bananas/candid." A more accurate rendering of *vaso,* though, would be "bowl" rather than "dish."

A younger Brazilian writer—whose rotten-bananas poem we have already encountered—has written a poem, "The Pears," in which the decay of pears stands for the downward trend of all cosmic processes. Ferreira Gullar begins with his pears on a plate (*prato*)—just as de Moraes begins with his pear in a bowl (*vaso*)—but whereas the latter's pear is passive and cold, Gullar's pears are glowing and self-consuming (translated by Emanuel Brasil and William Jay Smith):

On the plate the pears
decay.
The clock above them
measures out
their death?
Let us stop the pendulum: Would
we thus postpone
the death of the fruit?

Oh, the pears have tired
of their shape and
sweetness! The pears
have spent themselves
in the final glow of preparation
for oblivion.
   The clock
does not measure. It works
in a void: its voice glides
forth from the bodies of the fruit.

Everything tires
of itself. The pears are consumed
in their golden
repose. The flowers, in their everyday
flowerbed, burn,
burn in reds and blues. Everything
glides forth and yet remains intact.

It seems, by the last line of the poem, that song can ward off—or, perhaps, merely distract us from the sense of—decay: "sing- / ing, the cock / knows no death."

Pamela Stewart (b. 1946) prefaces her poem "The Pears" (1980) with an epigraph consisting of some lines from Delmore Schwartz's (1913–1966) poem, "All of the Fruits Had Fallen": "And the pears were useless and soft / Like used hopes, under the starlight's / Small knowledge . . ." The occasion of Stewart's poem is the death of the speaker's father, and the speaker is addressing the three children of her father's second marriage, to an Asian woman. The failed—or "used"—hopes of the speaker refer to the fact that her father left her mother ("a girl from Boston") immediately after the speaker's birth. The formal structure of the poem consists of seven unrhymed stanzas of unequal length (from three to ten lines), each enjambed. For me, the more interesting segments of the poem are those containing the pears, as in these lines, from the beginning (setting the scene) and the end (reiterating the failed hopes):

At noon the wasps clink and whir
Under the pear trees like bits
Of brown and yellow fruit rising sharply
Back into the leaves; they
Dive again where the soft pears
Flatten in the grass.
. . . .

        Perhaps,
You've finally learned of me, the facts of death

Not included in his life. You might think of me, then,
As a blonde working in a dress-store—as impossible

As halves of a pear—left out
To be shared
By an odd number of difficult children.

Pears may also be represented as simply an especially colorful, luscious, and tasty fruit, as in the following piece by the Austrian author Konrad Bayer (1932–1964). Bayer wrote experimental poems, stories, and plays after the Second World War. His prose poem, "the pear" (1965), consists of an unparagraphed, uncapitalized, and unstopped sequence of well over a thousand words. Here, in Christopher Middleton's translation, is the opening:

> and he bit into a pear a golden yellow pear as they say precisely that yellow
> pear so juicy the water ran from the corners of his mouth which the day
> before had lain so far forward on frau jekel's open fruitstand

The prose narrative now moves backward in time, with the history of that individual yellow pear providing the narrative thread on which is strung selected incidents from the lives of many people, all connected in some way with the pear: the seventy-four–year-old Ferdinand Nevosad, who picks the pear from one of the pear trees belonging to his old friend and employer, Wawerka, and Ferdinand's wife Marie; the individuals involved in the transport and sale of the pear, including Gredler, Remesberger Junior, Ellsler, and Frau Jekel; Stefan Kronik; Lorenz Vutz; Reinhold Ponzer; and the (unnamed) narrator who has taken a bite out of the pear. At the very end of the piece, we return to the narrator and the bitten pear:

> and then he put the pear down again bitten into it as it was and the flies
> settled on it and the next day he looked at it again and thought the flies
> have settled on it because it has been bitten into and i did not go on
> eating anymore that one anyhow does taste bitter

Bayer's stylistic flourishes mostly take the form of syntactical embeddings, such as those in the following passage (continuing on from "fruitstand" in the first passage quoted above):

> and then he had come by he had been on his way to the museum and
> he could not resist buying this juicy 24 decagram pear for one schilling
> twenty groschen that very pear itself cheap at the price which with many
> others about 2 tons of golden yellow if this description is permitted pears
> had been delivered on monday october 14

I can discover nothing in the entire piece that requires that the fruit be a pear rather than some other tree fruit. In our next example, by contrast, the pear's self-identity as a particular material object is essential.

In the later of the two great comic novels by Niccolò Tucci (1908–1999), *The Sun and the Moon* (1977), the action is restricted to just nine days in the year 1902. The place is Rome, and the plot revolves about the efforts of a poor provincial doctor, Leonardo, from a small town in Apulia, to woo an immensely wealthy Russian named Mary. (Both Leonardo, thirty-two years old, and Mary, twenty-three, are already married.) On the fourth day—subject of the fourth part of the novel—lunch is being served in the palace belonging to Sophie, Mary's domineering mother. Leonardo is altogether bewildered by Rome on this, his first visit, and, on this occasion, in particular, by the array of knives, forks, and dishes, not to mention the critical murmurs (in German!) of the server, Bernhard, and the bullying and sarcastic remarks of another guest, the eighty-two-year-old Jew, Mr. Schultz, a close friend and adviser to Mary's family. It is time for dessert and Leonardo is preoccupied with "two large pears he had put on his plate and was extremely impatient to eat." The problem is how to consume the pears in the least embarrassing way:

> Pears in March were a contradiction in terms, he had never seen any, although he knew winter pears existed up North, but they had never reached Apulia. Now, pears are eaten whole, skin and all, after spitting on them and drying them on the seat of your pants to wipe off the dirt. He was never going to do that, because he was now a man of the world, but he was going to wash them in the nice little crystal bowl Bernhard had put on his plate, and he was going to dry them on his own napkin.

Leonardo prepares to carry out the above operation on the pears but suddenly Sophie

> paralyzed Leonardo just as he was plunging the first pear into the crystal bowl and turning it, so that the water began to splash all over the tablecloth. He looked at her plate, and saw that the bowl had been removed from the center of it and was now standing on the side, for God knows what purpose. But what alarmed him even more was that she too had taken a pear and was peeling it with a small knife he had already used for the fish, but she was also using a fork of the same make and size to keep the pear in a standing position, and the whole operation reminded him of his first lesson in surgery, as delivered by a famous professor of the University of Naples. She wasn't even looking, but her knife cut through the white substance with not a second's hesitation. Leonardo had reached the same complete self-control on the bodies of his patients, but the mere thought of peeling a pear in front of this great teacher was too much for him. Could he remove the pear from the bowl and the bowl from the plate, and replace the pear on the plate?

Adding to Leonardo's woes is the fact that "Mr. Schultz also began to take an active interest in his plight, and he was speaking about his rich friends in their rich New York palaces, as if they were all in that bowl, swimming around that pear, or perhaps inside it." There is, of course, nothing very original about making fun out the plight of an awkward country bumpkin translated to a sophisticated urban setting, but some of Tucci's details are delicious, especially the fork holding the pear upright and the surgical analogy.

A Japanese Canadian poet, Roy K. Kiyooka (1926–1994), composed an interrelated set of poems called "The Pear Tree Pomes" (1982–5), which was first published with original illustrations by David Bolduc in 1987. Kiyooka's point of departure is an old pear tree outside his house:

> tall as a telephone pole and as old as the oldest house on
> the block the pear tree lights up the whole sky above our alley
> every spring and every fall it's a pear a day for every kid
> who saunters down the alley—something round to bite into some-
> thing ripe to splatter the nearest garage door with.

Though the tone of the poem is consistent enough—at different times folksy-conversational and ecstatic-visionary—there are unfortunately severe lapses in the intensity and freshness of perception, with the pears sometimes becoming too easy metaphors for the body of the beloved ("these words mime / the exactitude of your scent—even as they reach out to / cup the ah cool tingle of your pear-shaped breasts"), and the writing sometimes degenerating into rather banal lists ("there will always be pears to look up at and pears to preserve / pears to bite into and toss and last but not least there'll / always be pears rotting into the ground to nourish the seed of a / small pome"). Wallace Stevens is nervously invoked several times ("ask wallace stevens if an ode to an old pear tree sounds too / trifling to thrill the air of our well-being"). A departed lover is repeatedly addressed: "you know that i know a pear tree isn't / anybody's property. and if i may say so, neither are you. nor i." Kiyooka relies heavily on his loquacity and yet is at his best when he uses words sparingly, as in these two little poems:

> moment-
> arily   air
> borne
>
> another
> mottled pear
> slides—
>
> down
> an   unseen
> draft
>
> to touch
> earth
> home—free

~

> pied
> pear
>
> i love
> you
>
> pith
> stem
>
> seed
> un–
>
> voiced
> sun

In the brilliantly compressed story of the planting of his mother's pear tree "beyond the last trolley-stop / when the century was young," Stanley Kunitz (b. 1905) manages to retrieve the feelings of his young boyhood self as he stretches physically—and, more subtly, mentally—to live up to his mother's expectations. The poem "My Mother's Pears" (1995) consists of thirteen three-line stanzas, of which the first three and the last two invoke the delicacy of the pears and the hardiness of the pear tree:

> Plump, green–gold, Worcester's pride,
>   transported through autumn skies
>   in a box marked Handle With Care
>
> sleep eighteen Bartlett pears,
>   hand–picked and polished and packed
>   for deposit at my door,
>
> each in its crinkled nest
>   with a stub of stem attached
>   and a single bright leaf like a flag.
>   [. . . . .]
> I summon up all my strength
>   to set the pear tree in the ground,
>   unwinding its burlap shroud.
>
> It is taller than I. "Make room
>   for the roots!" my mother cries,
>   "Dig the hole deeper."

Perhaps this is as good a place as any to record a remark by Colette, in a letter to a friend in September 1912, after some difficult times with Henry de Jouvenel (her lover and soon-to-be husband): "Rest assured, I am a pear bitten by the frost; you know that if it doesn't rot them, they become riper and sweeter-tasting, beneath their little scars, than other pears" (translated by Yvonne Mitchell).

PEARS AS VISUAL METAPHORS

Any sustained thought about pears in European culture will have to include the notorious woodcut caricature by Charles Philipon (1806–1862), published in 1831, trading on the similarity between the shape of a plump pear and the jowly face of the reigning French monarch, Louis-Philippe. As John Merriman explains, in his introduction to the catalogue (1991) of an exhibition of pear caricatures, "The image of Louis-Philippe as a pear, a soft and bulbous piece of fruit that rots quickly, became both an emblem and a metaphor. . . . The poire as an image was also commonly taken to be obscene; its phallic associations, linked to prostitution, were understood by the middle-class market for political caricature." Adding to the fun was the fact that *poire* is French slang for simpleton or dope, and yet another pun was on *pair* [peer]. Literary allusions to the pear began to accumulate and, as Robert Justin Goldstein explains, "One Frenchman, Sebastien Peytel, even wrote a book in 1832, entitled *Physiology of the Pear,* which amounted to a grand collection of all puns and other variations on the pear theme." Fueled by the increasing unpopularity of Louis-Philippe, the pear caricature quickly caught on, with Grandville, Daumier, and other artists each elaborating his own version of the image, which—Goldstein again—"survived Louis-Philippe and entered French history as one of the dominant images of his reign." Many of the satirical images were published in newly established periodicals such as *La Silhouette* and *La Caricature* (both founded in 1830) and *Le Charivari* (founded in 1832). Two choice instances of the pear motif are the untitled depiction of two men and a boy pulling on a rope as they hang a pear (1832), by Honoré Daumier (1808–1879) and "Les Favoris de la Poire" (1833), by Auguste Bouquet (1800–1846). Both pictures were published in *La Caricature* and both are lithographs. (My own copies of each—the Bouquet in a hand-colored version—are illustrated in fig. 10 and plate 24.) The Bouquet print involves an elaborate pun on "favoris," which means both "favorites" and "whiskers." As Elise K. Kenney explains in a catalogue entry:

> In *Les Favoris* are two of the king's ministers, Argout the censor with his scissors, and Barthe, the Minister of Justice who administers punishment. Both snuggle up to the fleshy substance of Louis-Philippe's pear-body, as though to caress it and be sheltered by it. In fact, they become his whiskers. . . . On the floor are scraps of censored documents with the words, *"La Caricature"* and *"Etat de siège,"* on them.

One of the more striking versions of the image was the typographical pear, in which lines of type were printed in the shape of a pear. In the last issue of *La Caricature*

Fig 10: Honoré Daumier,
untitled, 1832

(27 August 1835) before it closed down to protest the recently enacted censorship laws, the very texts of those laws were printed in the shape of a pear, with the caption "AUTRES FRUITS DE LA RÉVOLUTION DE JUILLET" (Other fruits of the July revolution). (For illustrations of the latter and of many other pear caricatures of the time, see the book already mentioned by Goldstein as well as Elise K. Kenney and John M. Merriman's *The Pear: French Graphic Arts in the Golden Age of Caricature* [1991].)

Philipon's was not the first printed instance of a pear used in political caricature, for on 23 June 1820 the pear caricature of King George IV and Queen Caroline, by George Cruikshank (1792–1878), was published in London, in the form of a hand-colored etching (see plate 25.) Rather than caricaturing the shapes of the king and queen, Cruikshank depicts each of them enclosed up to the neck in a large green pear-shaped bag, which is designed to remind the viewer of the customary receptacles for conveying legal documents (in this case documentary evidence of adultery on the part of the queen to be presented to Parliament, and presumed evidence of the king's well-known adulteries—which was not, of course, to be presented to Parliament). The caption of the caricature, punning on pair/pear, was "Ah! sure such a pair was never seen so justly form'd to meet by nature," from a much-quoted song in the comic opera *The Duenna* (1775), by Richard Sheridan (1751–1816).

pair g.
rl au pair
ɔair girl au
au pair girl
ɹu pair girl a.
ırl au pair girl a
ɔair girl au pair gir.
ɟirl au pair girl au pair
ɔair girl au pair girl au pa
air girl au pair girl au pair
pair girl au pair girl au pa
ɹu pair girl au pair girl aı
ʼirl au pair girl au paiʼ
ʼirl au pair girl ⌐

Fig 11: Ian Hamilton Finlay,
"au pair girl"

Ian Hamilton Finlay (b. 1925) has incorporated both a visual and a verbal pun on pear/pair in one of his concrete poems, where a pear shape is defined by the contours of fourteen lines of type, each of them consisting entirely of repetitions of the phrase "au pair girl." (See fig. 11.) As in Reinhard Döhl's "Worm in Apple," so here, in many of the lines constituting the pear the bounding letters are partly sliced away; what was said earlier about the effect of a mutilation of certain letters applies equally in this case.

Finally, there is the notorious reference to the shape of a pear in the title of a suite of brief piano duets by Erik Satie (1866–1925). Satie's "Trois Morceaux en forme de poire" (Three pieces in the shape of a pear, 1903), consists, in fact, of seven pieces, none of which has anything to do with the fruit of the title. In fact, the title probably constitutes Satie's facetious response to a criticism by Debussy of some of Satie's earlier compositions to the effect that they lacked "form." (For a discussion of the Debussy incident, see Alan M. Gillmor's *Erik Satie* [1988].) Presumably the distinctive shape of the pear accounts for Satie's choice of fruit—in his title, if not in his music.

14

PINEAPPLES

The Spanish Jesuit Father Joseph de Acosta (1540–1600) spent some seventeen years in the West Indies and Peru and then wrote an account of the flora, fauna, and native inhabitants of the places he had explored. Here are some excerpts from Acosta's description of the pineapple, first published in Latin in 1588 and then in Spanish in 1590 (the quotation is from an English translation of 1604 by Edward Grimston):

> It is a fruite that hath an excellent smell, and is very pleasant and delight-full in taste, it is full of iuyce, and of a sweete and sharp taste, they eate it being cut in morcells, and steeped a while in water and salt. Some say that this breedes choler, and that the vse thereof is not very healthfull. But I have not seene any experience thereof, that might breede beleefe. . . . They grow one by one like a cane or stalke, which riseth among many leaves, like to the lilly, but somewhat bigger. The apple is on the toppe of every cane, it grows in hote and moist grounde.

And here is a modern, scientific description of the pineapple by Vaughan and Geissler:

> The plant [*Ananas comosus*] is a perennial or biennial, up to 1.5 m in height, with tough, spiny leaves which can cause difficulties during culti-vation.
> . . . Pineapple's inflorescence consists of up to 200 reddish–purple flowers. . . . The fruit (about 20 cm long and 14 cm in diameter) normally develops by parthenocarpy (no pollination). . . . It is a compound fruit (a sorosis) where the axis thickens and the small berry-like fruits fuse. . . . On the top of the fruit is a "crown" of leaves which, together with the "slips" (shoots below the fruit) and "suckers" (shoots below in the leaf axils), can be used for propagation.

Acosta dwells on the unusual odor and taste of pineapples (and on possible ill effects of consuming them), Vaughan and Geissler on the pineapple's unusual structure and mode of reproduction: from either point of view the plant is a remarkable one. Dutch explorers encountered pineapples in Brazil in the early seventeenth century, and one of them, Prince Johan Maurits of Nassau-Siegen, commissioned the Dutch painter

Albert Eckhout (ca. 1610–1665/6), during an expedition to Brazil in 1637–1644, to make a painted record of the local fruit. (See the reproduction of *Pineapples and Papayas* [1640s] in Chong and Kloek's *Still-Life Paintings from the Netherlands;* the oil on canvas, 37½ x 35 in., is now in the National Museum of Denmark, Copenhagen.) The prince wrote, in a letter of 1679 to Louis XIV, that the "pineapple, the best fruit in all of Brazil, . . . tastes like musk."

Soon, pineapples began to appear in Europe. Thus, John Evelyn reports in his diary for 9 August 1661: "I first saw the famous *Queene-pine* brought from *Barbados* presented to his *Majestie,* but the first that were ever seene here in England, were those sent to *Cromwell,* foure-yeares since"; and several years later he reports at some length in his diary for 14 August 1668 of another species of pineapple called the "Kinge-Pine," which he actually got to taste:

> Standing by his *Majestie* at dinner in the Presence, There was of that rare fruite called the *King-Pine,* (growing in *Barbados* & W. Indies), the first of them I had ever seen; His Majestie having cut it up, was pleasd to give me a piece off his owne plate to tast of, but in my opinion it falls short of those ravishing varieties of deliciousnesse, describ'd in *Cap: Liggons* history & others; but possibly it might be, (& certainely was) much impaired in coming so farr: It has yet a gratefull accidity, but tasts more of the Quince and Melon, than of any other fruite he mentions.

European gardeners also attempted to grow pineapples at home. The Dutch seem to have been the first to succeed; according to Sandra Raphael, the Dutch gardener Agnes Block "had a ripe pineapple in her estate of Vijverhof [in 1687]. She even had a special medal struck to mark the occasion of the first fruit." The Dutch gardeners used heated greenhouses, and their techniques were introduced to England with the arrival of a Dutch king, William III, in 1688. A picture painted between 1668 and 1677 and attributed to the Dutch painter Hendrik Danckerts has been supposed to show the first pineapple grown on English soil being presented to King Charles II by his gardener John Rose, but the depicted pineapple was almost certainly imported from Holland. In Winterson's *Sexing the Cherry,* this painting is the point of departure for an imaginary and gratuitously bizarre incident:

> The pineapple arrived today.
>
> Jordan carried it in his arms as though it were a yellow baby; with the wisdom of Solomon he prepared to slice it in two. He had not sharpened the knife before Mr Rose, the royal gardener, flung himself across the table and begged to be sawn into bits instead. Those at the feast contorted themselves with laughter, and the King himself, in his new wig, came down from the dais and urged Mr. Rose to delay his sacrifice. It was, after all, only a fruit. At this Mr Rose poked up his head from his abandonment amongst the dishes and reminded the company that this was an historic

occasion. Indeed it was. It was 1661, and from Jordan's voyage to Barbados the first pineapple had come to England.

As late as 1716 Lady Mary Wortley Montagu (1689–1762) was evidently seeing her first European pineapples on a visit to Germany, as she reports in a letter of 17 December 1716 to her sister Frances back home in England:

> I had more reason to wonder that night at the king's table. There was brought to him from a gentleman of this country, two large baskets full of ripe oranges and lemons of different sorts, many of which were quite new to me; and, what I thought worth all the rest, two ripe ananas [the Latin name], which, to my taste, are a fruit perfectly delicious. You know they are naturally the growth of Brazil, and I could not imagine how they could come there but by enchantment. Upon enquiry, I learnt that they have brought their stoves to such perfection, they lengthen the summer as long as they please, giving to every plant the degree of heat it would receive from the sun in its native soil. The effect is very near the same; I am surprised we do not practice in England so useful an invention.

By 1720 what may have been the first pineapple grown in England was memorialized in a painting by Theodore Netscher (now in the Fitzwilliam Museum in Cambridge) including a Latin inscription, translated by Miles Hadfield: "To the perpetual memory of Matthew Decker, baronet, and Theodore Netscher, gentleman. This pineapple, deemed worthy of the Royal table, grew at Richmond at the cost of the former, and still seems to grow by the art of the latter. H. Watkins set up this inscription, A.D. 1720." Decker was a Dutchman living in England and the secret of his gardener, Henry Telende, explains Hadfield, "was the use of a hot-bed made of tanner's bark. The brick-lined pit was rather more than 5 feet deep; it was 11 feet long and 7 ft. 6 in. wide, glass-covered. At its bottom was a foot of hot dung, upon which was laid 300 bushels of tanner's bark. Made early in February, the bed was hot in fifteen days, and would last until October."

Bernard Mandeville (ca. 1670–1733), expatriot Dutchman living in England, introduced a tribute to Decker in the second part of his *Fable of the Bees* (1729), where the description of the pineapple is as tempting as any I know:

> It excells every thing; it is extremely rich without being luscious, and I know nothing, to which I can compare the Taste of it: to me it seems to be a Collection of different fine Flavours, that puts me in mind of several delicious Fruits, which yet are all outdone by it.
>
> The Scent of it likewise is wonderfully reviving. As you was paring it, a Fragrancy I thought perfum'd the Room that was perfectly Cordial.
>
> The Inside of the Rind has an Oyliness of no disagreeable Smell, that upon handling of it sticks to ones Fingers for a considerable time; for tho'

now I have wash'd and wiped my Hands, the Flavour of it will not be
entirely gone from them by to-morrow Morning.

By the early decades of the eighteenth century, the pineapple—often under its
Latin name, *Anana*—had seized the European imagination, as writings began to pro-
liferate on the horticultural and medical aspects of the fruit, and as painted, sculpted,
and literary renditions of it began to appear. As G. S. Rousseau explains in his "Pineapples,
Pregnancy, Pica, and *Peregrine Pickle*" (1971), "The cultivation of pineapples in the third
and particularly the fourth decades of the eighteenth century became a hobby—
not quite a popular sport—among expert gardeners and aristocrats." Alexander Pope
(1688–1744), for example, was eager to grow pineapples at his Thames-side villa at
Twickenham, and we learn from a letter to William Fortescue (22 March 1734/5) of
the successful attempt of Pope's gardener, John Searle: "I am building a stone obelisk,
making two new ovens and stoves, and a hot-house for anana's, of which I hope you
will taste this year." The pineapple receives a succinct tribute in *The Seasons,* by James
Thomson (1727–1730):

> Winess, thou best Anana, thou the Pride
> Of vegetable life, beyond whate'er
> The Poets imag'd in the golden Age:
> Quick, let me strip thee of thy tufty Coat,
> Spread thy ambrosial Stores, and feast with *Jove!*

Some years later, in 1761, one of Thomson's fellow Scotsmen, the fourth Earl of
Dunmore, commissioned an architect to celebrate the pineapple in a folly on the earl's
estate near Stirling in Scotland: "The architect, about whom nothing is known, paid
the most eloquent homage to the fruit by reproducing it with astonishing realism and
on an enormous scale as the roof to a charming pavilion," as Sylvia Saudan-Skira and
Michael Saudan explain, with some excellent photographs, in their book, *Orangeries:
Palaces of Glass* (1998). (See plate 26.)

Though we may wonder how many pineapples Thomson had actually handled
(and eaten), we cannot doubt that John Singleton had plenty of firsthand experience
of the fruit when he was traveling in the West Indies, as his tribute to the pineapple
attests (from his *General Description of the West-Indian Islands,* ll. 184–95):

> —And last,[†] though first in praise,
> The luscious pine, of humble growth indeed,
> But of majestic form, its mitred head
> Uprears; ambrosial fruit its sculptur'd coat,
> Diversify'd by Nature's hand, contains,
> All fruits compriz'd in one; its flavours rich
> By Heav'n upon itself alone bestow'd.
> Not those which in Alcinous' garden bloom'd,

> Nor those which grace our Europèan soil,
> And ripen, beauteous, on the sunny wall,
> When Sol, with Virgo riding, autumn brings,
> Could e'er the royal Indian pine excel.

†There are some other fruits, but they are not so generally esteemed as those I have particularised, viz. The soursop, the mammee, sugar, custard, and monkey apples, dunks, bullyberries, pimploe and prickly pears, &c.

A fondness for pineapples was accompanied—if not caused—by the increasing incidence of fruit in the European diet during the seventeenth and eighteenth centuries. But, as so frequently with fruit, there was some ambivalence, in this case taking the form of a firm belief on the part of many doctors and their patients that eating pineapple could lead to miscarriage. The case of the pineapple as an (unintended) abortifacient was part of a much larger controversy on the role of the mother's imagination in "marking" the baby, and specifically in producing monstrous births. One of the more interesting literary manifestations of the belief in question occurs in chapter 5 of *Peregrine Pickle* (1751), by Tobias Smollett (1721–71). Mrs. Pickle is pregnant and when she announces that "she had eaten a most delicious pine-apple in her sleep" her sister-in-law, Mrs. Grizzle, immediately sets off to procure for her some of the rare fruit: "During three whole days and nights, did she, attended by a valet, ride from place to place without success, unmindful of her health, and careless of her reputation, that began to suffer from the nature of her inquiry." Part of the fun is that the mother-to-be is only trying to annoy her sister-in-law; indeed, on the evening before her pineapple dream Mrs. Pickle had "observed that she herself never could eat pine-apples, which were altogether unnatural productions, extorted by the force of artificial fire, out of filthy manure." Mrs. Grizzle, on the other hand, was following the latest medical advice for pregnant women and "restricted [Mrs. Pickle] from eating roots, pot-herbs, fruit, and all sort of vegetables; and one day when Mrs. Pickle had plucked a peach with her own hand, and was in the very act of putting it between her teeth, Mrs. Grizzle perceived the rash attempt, and running up to her, fell upon her knees in the garden, intreating her, with tears in her eyes, to resist such a pernicious appetite."

Still later in the eighteenth century, Richard Sheridan, in his comedy *The Rivals* (1775), introduced the pineapple in one of Mrs. Malaprop's speeches, as she responds to Captain Absolute, who has been criticizing "our ladies":

> *Abs.* . . . like garden-trees, they seldom shew fruit, till time has robb'd them of the more specious blossom.—Few, like Mrs. Malaprop and the Orange-tree, are rich in both at once!
>
> *Mrs. Mal.* Sir—you overpower me with good-breeding.—He is the very Pine-apple of politeness!

It was a nice idea on Sheridan's part to use oranges—another highly prized fruit in
England at the time—as a foil for Mrs. Malaprop's phrase "Pine-apple of politeness,"
which is, in fact, a brilliant coinage, even if she presumably intends "pinnacle."

By 1779, William Cowper could count on his readers appreciating the allusion
to pineapples in one of his characteristic moralistic fables, in which nature is invoked
as a source of lessons in good behavior. The occasion for writing "The Bee and the
Pine Apple" (published 1782) seems to have been a gift, during the winter of 1778, of
six pineapple plants, which would have been flowering in the spring of 1779 along
with Cowper's peaches and apricots. The poem exists in two versions; the presumed
earlier one (which Cowper never published), a dozen lines shorter than the published
version, is found in two holographs. I prefer the earlier version because the moral is
less distended:

> A Bee allur'd by the Perfume
> Of a rich Pine Apple in Bloom,
> Found it within a Frame inclosed,
> And Lick'd the Glass that interposed,
> Blossoms of Apricot and Peach,
> The Flow'rs that Blow'd within his Reach,
> Were arrant Drugs compar'd with That
> He strove so vainly to get at.
> No rose could Yield so rare a Treat,
> Nor Jessamine was half so Sweet.
> The Gard'ner saw this Much Ado,
> (The Gard'ner was the Master too)
> And thus he said—Poor restless Bee!
> I learn Philosophy from Thee—
> I learn how Just it is and Wise,
> To Use what Providence supplies,
> To leave fine Titles, Lordships, Graces,
> Rich Pensions, Dignities and Places,
> Those Gifts of a Superior kind,
> To those for whom they were design'd.
> I learn that Comfort dwells alone
> In that which Heav'n has made our Own,
> That Fools incur no greater Pain
> Than Pleasure Coveted in vain.

The pineapple comes up again in chapter 22 of *Northanger Abbey* (1803; published
1818), by Jane Austen, where General Tilney is showing Catherine Morland around

his estate under the misapprehension that she is a great heiress who might marry his son. They enter the kitchen-garden:

> The walls seemed countless in number, endless in length; a village of hot-houses seemed to arise among them, and a whole parish to be at work within the inclosure. . . . He loved a garden. Though careless enough in most matters of eating, he loved good fruit—or if he did not, his friends and children did. There were great vexations however attending such a garden as his. The utmost care could not always secure the most valuable fruits. The pinery had yielded only one hundred in the last year.

The walls in the garden are, of course, used for growing fruit trees, while the pinery refers to a hothouse for growing pineapples—one hundred in a year sounds like a typical piece of boasting on the general's part. As with food and its preparation in general, Austen finds no moral fault in a simple love of good fruit; excessive interest is what she objects to, especially when that interest overrides other more important human interests or ignores the claims of individuals to whom one is morally obligated. Besides, the general's language is morally corrupt; as Maggie Lane puts it, "In what he says about eating, and all the paraphernalia that goes with that activity, he is untruthful and insincere."

In nineteenth-century provincial France, on the other hand, pineapples were not readily available to such families as the Bovarys, for Emma "had never seen pomegranates or eaten pineapple" (Steegmuller's translation), both served at the marquis's dinner.

Writing poetic tributes to exotic fruits was commonplace in Latin America in the eighteenth century. Among the more famous of these tributes is "A la piña" (To the pineapple), an ode to the pineapple, written probably in the late eighteenth century by the Cuban soldier and poet Manuel de Zequeira y Arango (1760–1846) but first published in New York in 1829. The Spanish text is most easily available in the anthology of Latin American literature edited by Enrique Anderson Imbert and Eugenio Florit: *Literatura Hispanoamericana* (1960); here is, I believe, the first published English translation, by Jeffrey H. Kaimowitz:

> From the fertile breast of mother earth
> erect in posture stands the graceful
> pineapple clothed in splendor,
>   full of rich adornments.
>
> From its birth, bountiful Pomona
> protects it with a deep green mantle,
> until Ceres embroiders its garment
>   with golden stars.
>
> Even before its birth, its stately mother
> readies its dominion among the plants

and with royal heraldry encircles the great
diadem with emeralds.

As with some graceful young lady,
who stands out among her serving women,
the magnificent crest that covers it
glitters amid divers fruits.

Its presence is an honor to gardens,
rural obelisk that rises in
Amalthea's flowery precinct
to make glorious her altars.

The fragrant juices of the flowers,
the essences, the balms of Arabia,
and all perfumes of nature are
concentrated within it.

To our fields from sacred Olympus
Ganymede, Jove's cupbearer, rushes forth
and returns with the fruit which the gods
await for their banquet.

In the heavenly mansion it was
received with universal joy and,
stripped of royal vesture, it perfumed the
firmament with its scent.

In the sacred cup ambrosia
lost its merit: the divinities are inflamed
with the fragrance of the honeyed juice
of the American sherbet.

After the divine Orpheus partook of it,
accompanied by his well-tuned lyre,
swelling heaven with his music,
he sang its praises.

When mother Venus put the nectar
to her ruby lips, she became intoxicated
by its alluring pleasure, and gaily
cried to Ganymede:

"The pineapple," she said, "the fragrant pineapple,
let it be cultivated in my gardens
by the hands of my nymphs, yes, let its
    balm flow in Idalia."

Hail, o fortunate soil, where mother
nature offers in abundance the pungent
smelling plant that one can smoke!
    Hail, o fortunate Havana!

The lovely flowers in your fiery region,
gathering fragrant substances,
temper the sweltering heat of summer
    with fresh pineapples.

Spring crowned with flowers, rich autumn,
and gentle breezes in a thousand
twitterings and joyful choruses
    proclaim its merit.

All the gifts and all delights that nature
in her workshop manufactures
in the sugared nectar of the pineapple
    find themselves united.

Hail, divine fruit! With the oil
of your essence perfume my lips:
have my muse, worthy of praising you,
    make known your fragrance.

Thus may Jove the merciful, the powerful,
never allow from a dark gray cloud
a swift bolt, crackling with thunder,
    to strike your crown.

Thus may the mild Zephyr in your environs
never tire of beating his wings,
freeing you from the harmful insect
    and the blustery North Wind.

And thus may Dawn with her divine breath
producing pearls that she condenses on her bosom

preserve your splendor, that you may be the
glory of my country.

As for philosophy, the pineapple can boast of guest appearances in the two greatest of English philosophical treatises: *An Essay Concerning Human Understanding* (1690), by John Locke (1632–1704), and *A Treatise of Human Nature* (1739–40), by David Hume (1711–1776). Locke referred to pineapples in his important chapter on "the names of simple ideas." There, the taste of the pineapple is introduced as an instance of a simple idea, which, like all simple ideas, is irreducible to other ideas, and can hence only be apprehended by actually tasting the fruit:

> He that thinks otherwise, let him try if any words can give him the taste of a pine-apple, and make him have the true idea of the relish of that cele-brated delicious fruit. So far as he is told it has a resemblance with any tastes whereof he has the ideas already in his memory, imprinted there by sensible objects not strangers to his palate, so far may he approach that resemblance in his mind. But this is not giving us that idea by a definition, but exciting in us other simple ideas by their known names; which will still be very different from the true taste of that fruit itself.

Hume mentions the pineapple at the very beginning of his treatise (part 1, sect. 1, "Of the Origin of our Ideas"), asserting (as he echoes Locke) that "we cannot form to our-selves a just idea of the taste of a pineapple, without having actually tasted it."

When Wallace Stevens appeared at Harvard in 1947 he delivered "Three Aca-demic Pieces," consisting of a philosophical lecture on resemblance and two poems, one called "Someone Puts a Pineapple Together." Later, he referred to this poem as "that poem about the pineapple" (in "As You Leave the Room," a poem concerning his life's work and written probably during the last year of his life). There can be little doubt, then, of the importance Stevens attributed to his pineapple poem. It begins, just like his poem about two pears, with some Latin, presumably a measure of Stevens's seriousness (or, is it mock-seriousness?): "O juventes, O filii . . ." The subject of the poem is "man and his endless effigies," which we are to think of as belonging to a realm governed by some third "planet" different from the sun or moon; the prime element of this third realm on display in the poem is, or is generated by, a pineapple resting on a table. In the second part of the poem we read that "There had been an age / When a pineapple on the table was enough"; this portion of the poem is pointedly populated not by poets, but by "captious" scholars. The third part is devoted to the "endless effigies" of the pineapple:

> Divest reality
> Of its propriety. Admit the shaft
> Of that third planet to the table and then:
>
> 1. The hut stands by itself beneath the palms.
> 2. Out of their bottle the green genii come.

3. A vine has climbed the other side of the wall.

4. The sea is spouting upward out of rocks.
5. The symbol of feasts and of oblivion . . .
6. White sky, pink sun, trees on a distant peak.

7. These lozenges are nailed-up lattices.
8. The owl sits humped. It has a hundred eyes.
9. The coconut and cockerel in one.

10. This is how yesterday's volcano looks.
11. There is an island Palahude by name—
12. An uncivil shape like a gigantic haw.

This assortment of one-liners is followed by a single brilliant and sinuous sixteen-and-a-half-line sentence, describing in varying terms "the tropic of resemblance." There then follow, by way of "philosophical" conclusion, two short sentences:

> This is everybody's world.
> Here the total artifice reveals itself
>
> As the total reality.

But Stevens will not end on such an abstract note; the remaining eight and a half lines return to the pineapple: "the odor of this fruit" and its "geometric glitter."

About this extraordinarily rich and difficult poem I want to ask only a simple question: Why a pineapple? Two obvious answers would be, first, that Stevens was always partial to tropical fauna and flora, and second, that the complex appearance and structure of pineapples were conducive to that "profusion of metaphor" invoked already in the third line of the poem (though a poet who could invent thirteen ways of looking at a blackbird could probably have said what he wanted to say about resemblance in terms of a less convoluted fruit than the pineapple!). One wonders also if Wallace Stevens knew Zequiera's poem (he does refer to the pineapple as "This husk of Cuba, tufted emerald" in the first part of his pineapple poem).

One critical remark on the pineapple poem by a Stevens specialist will have to suffice. In her *Wallace Stevens' Experimental Language* (1999), Beverly Maeder explains what she calls the "strategy" of the poem: "The hope for metaphor is not to find new words, new illustrations, or new transfers; rather it lies in the changes that take place between a poem's point of departure and its point of arrival, the path the poem takes. It becomes a metaphor for the poem itself." Not very helpful, I would say, though Maeder does inform us of an earlier piece by Stevens, which is "another pineapple poem." This is a short poem from *Parts of a World* (1942), "Poem Written at Morning," with some wonderful lines characterizing pineapples:

> Thus, the pineapple was a leather fruit,
> A fruit for pewter, thorned and palmed and blue,
> To be served by men of ice.
>   The senses paint
> By metaphor. The juice was fragranter
> Than wettest cinnamon. It was cribled pears
> Dripping in a morning sap.

And here Maeder's comments are helpful:

> This is a visually and auditively exciting pineapple, a highly crafted, if over-domesticated one. Both signifieds and signifiers become overfull. English no longer suffices. The pears are "cribled"? This too is domesticated, of course, by the English past suffix, yet is still foreign: the French *cribler* (to grade fruit according to size; or to riddle with holes) has no English cognate in the *Oxford English Dictionary*. The pears are high quality; the language is *recherché*. This is Stevens at his most epicurean.

CITRUS FRUITS

CITRON OR ETROG

The Latin term *citrus* comes from the Greek *kedros,* which meant any tree (such as pine or cypress) which smelled like a cedar. In consequence, for a long time there was confusion between the Latin names for two types of trees, *cedrus* and *citrus,* both derived from the Greek name. Also, owing to an association in Greek mythology with the golden apples of the Hesperides, the term "Hesperidean" eventually came to be applied to all citrus fruits. In fact, however, the only citrus fruit known in the ancient world of Greece and the Middle East was the citron (Hebrew: *etrog*), not edible but—for that very reason?—an important Jewish ceremonial fruit for *Sukkot* (the Feast of Tabernacles). Here is how Roger Holmes's handbook of fruit characterizes the citron:

> The citron is a small, thorny, open shrub that doesn't match other citrus as an ornamental. It is most often grown for the aroma given off by the lemonlike fruit's thick rind, a fragrance that can fill a room. The fruit produces little juice, but the mildly sweet rind can be candied or pickled. Citron is very sensitive to frost and can be grown only in the mildest areas, in portable containers, or protected locations.

The continuing prominence of the etrog in the Jewish religious imagination (as well as, of course, in Jewish ritual) is evidenced by a brief tale recorded by a Czech Hasid named Jiri Langer in 1937, and available in an English version by Harold Schwartz. The Reb of Kamionka comes at the time of Sukkot to visit his teacher, Reb Sholem of Belz, but though he can hear Reb Sholem's voice in the synagogue, he cannot see him. After a while the disciple realizes that

> somehow Reb Sholem had entered entirely into an etrog, an etrog so perfect that it could only have been a gift of heaven. . . . As he peered at it, the etrog began to glow. It became transparent in his vision, and he saw that the source of its light was within, and that it was the light of Reb Sholem, who filled the shell of the etrog.
>
> The Rabbi of Kamionka closed his eyes for an instant and still saw the glowing etrog as clearly as when his eyes were open. He marveled at this,

and when he opened his eyes again, he saw Reb Sholem standing before
the Ark, with the light of the etrog glowing from his face and the fruit
itself cradled in his hand.

Schwartz remarks that "Great emphasis is put on having a beautiful fruit for the festival, often at great expense, since the fruit has to be imported. Those who have succeeded in obtaining such a beautiful etrog for Sukkot are likely to appreciate it, or, as
in this tale, make it an object of contemplation."

A spectacularly beautiful painting of two citrons from the early seventeenth century is by the Italian painter Fillipo Napoletano (ca. 1585/90–1629) and is now in the
Botanical Museum of the University of Florence (oil on canvas, 20¼ x 24¼ in.).
According to Ebert-Schifferer, "Napoletano's portrait of the citron, with its characteristic wrinkled skin, combines both artistic interest and scientific curiosity. Napoletano,
himself a collector of plant specimens, was clearly painting directly from the fresh fruit,
as natural scientists of the day required their illustrators to do." (For a reproduction, see
Ebert-Schifferer's *Still Life*.)

CITRUS TREES: BLOSSOMS AND FRUIT

Citrus trees flourish in subtropical climates, but are also viable in tropical climates. Like
many trees native to these climatic zones, citrus trees do not shed their leaves each fall
but bear green leaves all year round (some of the leaves even persisting for an entire
year). Furthermore, the flowering and fruiting cycles of citrus trees overlap, resulting
in the simultaneous presence of blossoms and fruit (though the presence of fruit on a
particular shoot may inhibit the development of flowers on that shoot). When orange
trees were first grown in Europe in the seventeenth century, the phenomenon of flowers
and fruits on the same tree "raised it to Edenic status," to quote John Prest's intriguing account of this cultural phenomenon. But John Webster has Bosola, in *The Duchess
of Malfi*, turn the same phenomenon into a metaphor insinuating an unpleasant slur
on women: "The orange tree bears ripe and green fruit, and blossoms all together: and
some of you give entertainment for pure love; but more, for more precious reward"
(2.2.14–17). Some thirty years later, Edmund Waller (1606–1687) was still writing, in
his "The Battle of the Summer Islands" (1645), as if this botanical phenomenon only
occurred in the tropics (canto 1, ll. 40–43):

> For the kind spring, which but salutes us here,
> Inhabits there, and courts them all the year.
> Ripe fruits and blossoms on the same trees live;
> At once they promise what at once they give.

By the eighteenth century, however, the Edenic—and, of course, the tropical—connotations of orange trees had begun to fade, and are absent, for example, from this youthful imitation (before 1709), by Alexander Pope, of Abraham Cowley's "The Garden"
(1667):

376

> Here *Orange*-trees with blooms and pendants shine,
> And vernal honours to their autumn join;
> Exceed their promise in the ripen'd store,
> Yet in the rising blossom promise more.

Another English poet, Ruth Pitter, over two centuries later, celebrates the orange tree in the same terms as Pope but with a strong tinge of nostalgia for a lost or distant terrestrial paradise, which she (and we) know all along to be a mere figment of her poetic imagination; the excerpt is from her wonderful long (191 lines) poem, "Other People's Glasshouses" (1941):

> But look where Orange-trees in fruit and bud
> Bless our cold eyes, and stir nostalgic blood
> To pine, as ever, for their odorous groves,
> Their fireflies, and their Mediterranean loves!

It is not even a fancied Eden that Yehuda Amichai has in mind when, in his "Poem in an Orange Grove" (1968), he writes: "Blossoms and fruit were on one and the same tree, / Above us, in that double season" (translated by Assia Gutmann). The doubleness—distinct and yet merged, as in spring-summer—can refer to God and to the poet's father, each of whom forgot him, according to the first four lines of the poem; to the language with "that foreign / And strange accent of those who will die" and some other language representing that which will live on (religion? poetry?); perhaps even to his father's—and hence also his own—dual status as an Israeli and a Diaspora Jew. One thing is clear about the poem: its tone is that of a lament not for anything as remote as a lost Eden but simply for the lost "scent of orange groves in blossom" and the lost "Hands sticky / With juice and love."

Poet James Merrill introduces the citrus fruit/blossom motif as an emblem accompanying "rings exchanged for life" and "lovers' lips" near the end of a long journey that has started with death (the signing of his will). These three lines begin the last section of "The Will" (1976):

> Already thickskinned little suns
> Are coming back, and gusts of sharp cologne
> —Lemon trees bearing and in bloom at once.

THE GENUS *CITRUS*

The details of citrus fruit reproduction are exceedingly complex, so that classifying citrus fruits by modern taxonomic methods does not lead to unequivocal conclusions. There does seem to be a consensus, however, on the existence of just three true species: pummelo, mandarin, and citron (using the common names). Pummelo (also called shaddock) is similar to grapefruit (except for a green rind and a much larger size) and is currently widespread in Java, Malaysia, Thailand, and Fiji; mandarin is also called tangerine. The citron is believed to have originated in northeastern India, the other two true species in southern China. The remaining five familiar kinds of citrus fruit are all thought to be hybrids, involving the crossing of two or even three species: sour and sweet orange=mandarin x pummelo; lemon and lime=citron x pummelo x *Microcitrus* (a genus closely related to *Citrus*); grapefruit=pummelo x sweet orange. There are far fewer significant cultivars of citrus fruit species than of, say, peaches: on the order of a dozen or so cultivars each for orange, mandarin, pummelo, and lemon, and far fewer for grapefruit and lime. (For further details, see Spiegel-Roy and Gold-schmidt, *Biology of Citrus* [1996].) Spontaneous hybridization occurs among different species of the genus *Citrus,* but in Calabria in southern Italy, where (in Waverly Root's words) "every citrus fruit you ever heard of is grown . . . and probably one or two of which you have not," two deliberately contrived varieties are especially interesting:

> The *megalolo* is a lemon grafted onto a bitter-orange tree, which enhances its flavor. The *verdello* is an ordinary orange, but one which is produced by a process of forced growth. The roots are uncovered and left bare under the hot sun "to make the tree thirsty." They are then covered up again, watered abundantly, and heavily manured. The sap rises rapidly and the tree flowers overnight. This gives extremely highly flavored very soft oranges—indeed, a little too soft for eating, but they are not designed for that. They are used for making perfume.

One thing we all know about citrus fruits today is that they contain substantial amounts of vitamin C and thereby can prevent scurvy. How this was first discovered is a fascinating story, admirably told in Kenneth Carpenter's book *The History of Scurvy and Vitamin C* (1988). The symptoms of scurvy—primarily sore gums and swollen limbs—began to appear with alarming frequency among sailors as soon as fifteenth-century European navigators began to spend long periods at sea. The first serious attempt to discover a cure for the disease was made by the British naval surgeon James Lind (1716–1794) when he conducted a well-designed trial (in 1747) on a group of twelve sailors who had scurvy. Over a period of fourteen days, all were put on identical diets except for the addition of six different ingredients (each tested on two sailors): cider, *elixir vitriol* (sulphuric acid), vinegar, sea water, oranges and lemons, a medicinal paste (composed of garlic, mustard seed, tree resin, dried radish root, and gum myrrh). Those sailors receiving cider were somewhat improved; those receiving citrus fruit were much improved. Unfortunately, Lind's results were ignored. Over three decades later, during the American Revolution, the Scottish Sir Gilbert Blane (1749–1834) was serving as personal physician to the admiral of the West Indies Fleet when nearly sixteen hundred men died during a single year, mostly from scurvy. Returning to London, Blane wrote a report containing the following recommendation (as quoted by Carpenter):

378   Scurvy, one of the principal diseases with which seamen are afflicted, may be infallibly prevented, or cured, by vegetables and fruit, particularly oranges, lemons, or limes. These might be supplied by employing one or more small vessels to collect them at different islands: policy, as well as humanity, concur in recommending it. Every fifty oranges or lemons might be considered as a hand to the fleet, inasmuch as the health, and perhaps the life, of a man would thereby be saved.

This too was at first ignored by the British Admiralty but Blane persisted, and during the Napoleonic Wars lemon juice finally began to be issued on a regular basis to British sailors—no less than 1.6 million gallons during the years 1795–1814. Blane admitted that he had no idea why citrus fruit was effective, and, indeed, as late as 1905 expert medical opinion was divided on the etiology of scurvy (food poisoning and infection were still seriously considered, as well as environmental stress and mental depression). Finally, in the early 1930s, after intensive biochemical experimentation the active antiscorbutic factor in lemon juice (as measured in guinea pigs), initially designated "Vitamin C," was synthesized as ascorbic acid. The eventual discovery of small concentrations of vitamin C in apples, potatoes, cabbage, and other foods helps to explain why even traditional peasant diets could have been antiscorbutic. (For details, see Carpenter's chapter 8, "Guinea Pigs and the Discovery of Vitamin C, 1905–1935.")

Patrick O'Brian (1914–2000), in his *Desolation Island* (1978)—the fifth in his Aubrey/Maturin series of twenty novels about the British navy in Napoleonic times—provides a vivid description of the symptoms of scurvy:

It was within three days . . . that the first cases of scurvy appeared in the sickbay. All four of them were prime seamen, broad-shouldered, long-armed, powerfully-built, responsible men, cheerful in an emergency, valuable members of the crew. Now they were glum, listless, apathetic. . . . Stephen pointed out the physical symptoms, the spongy gums, the offensive breath, the extravasated blood, and in two cases the old reopening wounds; but he insisted even more upon the gloom as the most significant part of the disease.

It turns out that these men have been trading their mandatory "sovereign lime-juice" (mixed in with their diluted rum, or grog) for tobacco; when forced to drink their "citreous drench," their physical symptoms disappear (but not their gloom).

One of the first systematic treatises on citrus fruit was written by the distinguished Neapolitan diplomat and humanist Giovanni Pontano (1429?–1503). In Latin verse, *De hortis hesperidum libri duo* (On the garden of the Hesperides in two books; 1500; published 1505, Venice) was dedicated to the Marquess of Mantua, Francesco Gonzaga. Full of advice on how to plant, irrigate, prune, and pick the flowers and fruit, the treatise also explains how to cultivate citrus in cold climates. On this last topic, Frederic Janson provides a summary:

For "regions where citrus trees cannot be grown because of the cold," Pontano suggests planting lemons, citrons, and (bitter) oranges in wheel-mounted boxes called "rhaedis" after a traveling carriage used by the Gauls. The trees could be moved to shelters in inclement weather or around banquet tables as a pick-your-own dessert course. This was less involved—but also less ingenious—than Leonardo da Vinci's scheme of the same period. He suggests planting citrus trees near the run-off of a natural spring. In winter, a fan operated by the water flow would create a temperate micro-climate around the trees.

The different species of citrus fruits, by the way, vary in their cold hardiness in the following order (from least to most): lime, lemon, pummelo, grapefruit, orange, mandarin, kumquat. (This is beautifully illustrated with a color photograph of the seven fruits in Lance Walheim's *Citrus* [1996].) Kumquats are not strictly citrus fruits but they belong to the closely related genus *Fortunella* and breeders have crossed them with true citrus fruits, the resulting hybrids—limequats, orangequats, lemonquats, citrangequats, etc.—possessing the desirable property of being highly resistant to cold. The English food writer Alan Davidson (b. 1924) explains that the kumquat has "been assigned to a genus of its own because of the simpler structure of its fruit. In particular, its attractive golden rind is not a distinct, pithy covering like that of a true citrus fruit, but is thin, soft, and pulpy. This is all to the good because the rind is therefore edible, and the fruit can be eaten whole, although the taste of most kinds is rather too sour for the average palate" (see the entry "Kumquat" in *The Oxford Companion to Food* [1999]). The distinctive structure of the kumquat underlies the main theme of the single kumquat literary episode I have come across.

A Kumquat for John Keats (1981), by the English poet, dramatist, and filmmaker Tony Harrison (b. 1937)—consisting of 124 iambic pentameter lines, for the most part arranged in couplets—has been elegantly printed by Bloodaxe Books (fourth impression, 1995) in the form of a little booklet, with delicate kumquat decorations on the covers and on the versos of each of the (unnumbered) text pages. The verse is conversational, jaunty, and funny—quintessential light verse—but serious underneath, for the kumquat has become the poet's favorite fruit in the prime of his life (at forty-two) owing to its quality of mixed sweetness and tartness (mirroring "life," of course):

> For however many kumquats that I eat
> I'm not sure if it's flesh or rind that's sweet,
> and being a man of doubt at life's mid-way
> I'd offer Keats some kumquats and I'd say:
> *You'll find that one part's sweet and one part's tart:*
> *say where the sweetness or the sourness start.*
> I find I can't, as if one couldn't say
> exactly where the night became the day,

380

> which makes for me the kumquat taken whole
> best fruit, and metaphor, to fit the soul
> of one in Florida at 42 with Keats
> [. . . . .]
> Then it's the kumquat fruit expresses best
> how days have darkness round them like a rind,
> life has a skin of death that keeps its zest.

I should add that less than a decade later Harrison wrote an even longer poem in (tetrameter) couplets about his favorite fruit—or, at least, his favorite breakfast fruit—the papaya (see chapter 16, "Melons and Papayas").

During his Italian sojourn, Goethe noticed that citrus trees in winter were treated differently in Rome than back home in Germany (letter of 13 December 1786). W. H. Auden and Elizabeth Mayer are co-translators of Goethe's "Italian Journey":

> Here you do not notice the winter. The only snow you can see is on the mountains far away to the north. The lemon trees are planted along the garden walls. By and by they will be covered with rush mats, but the orange trees are left in the open. Hundreds and hundreds of the loveliest fruits hang on these trees. They are never trimmed or planted in a bucket as in our country, but stand free and easy in the earth, in a row with their brothers. You can imagine nothing jollier than the sight of such a tree. For a few pennies you can eat as many oranges as you like. They taste very good now, but in March they will taste even better.

On a second stay in Rome, Goethe again took note of the lemon trees (April 1788):

> In our garden, an old secular priest looked after a number of lemon trees of medium height, planted in ornamental terracotta vases. In summer these enjoyed the fresh air, but in winter they were kept in a greenhouse. When the lemons were ripe, they were picked with care, wrapped singly in soft paper, packed and sent off. They were particularly choice specimens and much in demand on the market. Such an orangery was regarded by middle-class families as a capital investment which would pay a certain interest every year.

One biological peculiarity of citrus fruits is their high rate of mutation, which affects such economically important traits as time of ripening, color, degree of acidity, and seedlessness. Citrus fruits also exhibit an astonishing teratological proclivity, that is, a tendency to generate "monsters" (fruit with a highly distorted form) and "chimeras" (such as a single fruit which is half orange and half lemon). We now know that this tendency arises from genetic factors or from floral disorders induced by a certain wormlike mite, *Acerius sheldoni* (see Spiegel-Roy and Goldschmidt's *Biology of Citrus,* chapters 5–6). One of the earliest serious examinations of citrus fruit teratology was by a Jesuit professor of Hebrew in Rome, Giovanni Batista Ferrari (1583–1655), in his *Hesperides sive de Malorum Aureorum Cultura et usu* (Hesperides, or the culture and use of golden apples; Rome, 1646). The *Hesperides* is divided into four books, the first devoted to citrus lore and each of the remaining three presided over by one of the daughters of Hesperus: Aegle presides over citrons, Arethusa over lemons, and Hesperthusa over oranges. Ferrari's volume contains 101 splendid etched and engraved plates. Citrus species and cultivars are depicted in eighty of these plates, almost all of them by Cornelis Bloemaert (1603–?1684), a Dutch printmaker working in Rome; each fruit is shown in natural size, whole and halved, with foliage and sometimes blossoms, and with its Latin name inscribed on a ribbon winding across the picture. The plates include representations of eight citrons, thirty-nine lemons, four limes, twenty oranges, and nine monstrous fruits grouped with the lemons. There are an additional twenty-one plates, including several allegories involving citrus fruits, also mostly by Bloemaert. (All 101 plates are reproduced in David Freedberg and Enrico Baldini, *The Paper Museum of Cassiano dal Pazzo, Series B, Natural History, Part One, Citrus Fruit* [1997].)

The man responsible for the preparatory drawings for the illustrations in Ferrari's *Hesperides* was Cassiano dal Pazzo (1588–1657), an important art patron in seventeenth-century Italy (he commissioned more than forty paintings by Nicolas Poussin). He was also a member of the first scientific academy in Europe, the Academy of the Lynxes, and thereby a friend of Galileo. (For a portrait of Cassiano, see Francis Haskell and Henrietta McBurney's general introduction in *The Paper Museum of Cassiano dal Pazzo.*) Cassiano commissioned Vincenzo Leonardi (d. 1646) to do the drawings on which the *Hesperides* illustrations were to be based. These drawings, some 118 of them—most on paper—are in color, whereas the printed versions are, of course, in black and white. The drawings receive high praise from David Freedberg: "Very little in the history of botanical illustration prepares one for the sumptuousness and refinement of Vincenzo Leonardi's drawings of citrus fruit," which, Freedberg believes, were likely examined by Ferrari while he was preparing his text. Some of the sumptuousness of the originals is captured in the catalogue raisonné of the drawings that Freedberg has edited—one of the earliest volumes to appear in what will eventually be a thirty-volume publication of the roughly seven thousand drawings in Cassiano's so-called Paper Museum. (Two of the drawings, incidentally, may be by Giovanna Garzoni, since they are on vellum, her preferred medium.)

Many of Leonardi's citrus fruit drawings—including several depicting anomalous specimens—were not represented by a plate in Ferrari's volume, but Freedberg suggests a special interest in such taxonomically recalcitrant specimens on the part of both Cassiano and Ferrari because of their concern for the formulation of valid general taxonomic principles for plants. Ferrari, of course, was unable to make any real sense of these biological anomalies, so after some speculation in terms of the special fertility of the ground or a special generative vigor in the trees, he turns to metamorphosis myths of his own invention; in Freedberg's words: "The poetic imagination, harnessed by

382   the rules of rhetoric, became a heuristic tool to supplement empirical logic and the limited evidence of the eyes." Here is where the engraved allegories come in: each corresponds to a climactic moment in one of Ferrari's complex etiological narratives designed to account for the appearance of some particular anomalous specimen of citrus fruit. Freedberg says that Ferrari's baroque Latin prose is untranslatable, but he does provide a detailed summary of a couple of Ferrari's narrative inventions.

One of Ferrari's narratives involves a beautiful young boy named Harmonillus, endowed with a beautiful voice. Sent by Apollo to a school for training young male singers, Harmonillus was—and here I omit much detail—attacked by the fierce old women in charge of the school:

> At the very moment in which the women pounce on poor Harmonillus, as is clear from the illustration commissioned from Sacchi, he begins to weep profusely, calling upon his old tutor Cleomedes to come and rescue him. Cleomedes rushes forward, but—too late! Watered by the abundant flow of tears, Harmonillus begins to turn into a citron tree. His feet turn into roots, his arms into branches; but by the greatest miracle of all, his very hands turn (as is clear from Sacchi's illustration of the story) into digitated fruit.

But the story is not yet over. A servant of Harmonillus's mother, Tirsenia, brings back the bad news, which she communicates by handing Tirsenia a piece of fruit from the citron tree into which Harmonillus has been metamorphosed. This citron turns out to be "pregnant," that is, it contains within itself some miniature lemonlike fruits (analogous to our navel oranges), which reminds Tirsenia of Harmonillus in her womb. At this point Tirsenia herself is transformed into a lemon tree! An engraved illustration of *The Transformation of Tirsenia* accompanies Ferrari's account.

James Thomson celebrates all three principal citrus fruits in these lines from *Summer:*

> Here, in eternal Prime,
> Unnumber'd Fruits, of keen delicious Taste
> And vital Spirit, drink amid the Cliffs,
> And burning Sands that bank the shrubby Vales,
> Redoubled Day, yet in their rugged Coats
> A friendly Juice to cool its Rage contain.

> Bear me, *Pomona!* to thy Citron-Groves;
> To where the Lemon and the piercing Lime,
> With the deep Orange, glowing thro' the Green,
> Their lighter Glories blend.

It is worth mentioning that the four books of *The Seasons* were initially published independently; *Summer* first appeared in 1727 but received major revisions when it became part of the combined edition of 1744. The scheme of *Summer* is to follow the course of a summer's day, from sunrise to night, with loosely related interpolations of various kinds; in particular, at "raging Noon" (1. 432) Thomson takes us to the tropics and proceeds to recount the horrors of those regions (venomous serpents, predatory beasts, plagues, droughts, famines, earthquakes, and tremendous storms). One of Thomson's most significant revisions of this section of the poem for the 1744 edition was to add some sixty-nine lines about a third of the way into the book and just preceding the tropical horrors. These lines (629–897) were designed to balance somewhat the horrors to come with "the Wonders of the *torrid Zone*" (1. 632). In the lines quoted above, we are to imagine the narrator sitting in a shady spot, commenting on the variety of tasty tropical fruits and then invoking Pomona, the goddess of fruit trees. The citrus groves represent one of the more benign and soothing manifestations of tropical excess, and Thomson's point is subsequently reinforced with additional allusions to tropical fruits, including tamarind, fig, coconut, palm, pomegranate, berries, and "anana" (pineapple). (The passage about pineapples has already been quoted above, in chapter 14.)

Not surprisingly, John Singleton is careful to expound the varied virtues of citrus fruits (*General Description of the West-Indian Islands,* ll. 119–28):

> There juicy grape-fruits, burnish'd by the sun,
> With rich forbiddens, grace the golden grove:
> The bulky shaddock, and the citron green,
> Which chearful dames in dainty pastries mix,
> When, at the holy season, they regale,
> And celebrate with joy a Saviour's birth.
>
> Cool water-lemons to the fev'rish guest
> Hold forth their grateful moisture, and invite
> The gath'rer's hand; whilst, yielding to the touch,
> The scented fruits enrich their bending vines.

Two immediate questions arise: What are "forbiddens," and what happened to the oranges? Well, if we look up "forbidden" in the *Oxford English Dictionary,* we find, under the illustrative phrase "forbidden fruit," the following: "hence, a name given to several varieties of *Citrus,* esp. *C. decumana.*" Now, *decumana* means "large" (from the Latin) and though the term seems not to be standard botanical usage today, we do find in contemporary citrus taxonomy the term *C. maximus* for pummelo (or shaddock). What we do not find in the *OED* is any reference to Singleton's apparent coinage of the noun "forbiddens."

As for oranges, Singleton does finally get to them—after the granadilla (passion fruit), melon, pomegranate, avocado, tamarind, and cocoa tree (ll. 163–65):

> But let us turn to yonder fragrant grove,
> Where hangs the orange, rich in burnish'd gold,
> And by the fair seems eager to be pluck'd.

384 Singleton then offers his versified account (ll. 175–79) of Francis Bacon's allegorical interpretation of the Atalanta race (which we have already encountered in chapter 1):

> Thus ART and NATURE ever will contest
> In vain: She, steady goddess, perseveres
> In her wise course, nor ever turns aside;
> Whilst ART, still stooping to some luring bait,
> Like ATALANTA, labours still behind.

ORANGES

Citrus fruits are thought to have spread, during the first centuries B.C.E. and C.E., from China and India to Rome and subsequently to the rest of the Mediterranean world. That the details of this historical process have yet to be definitively established is a result in part of the biological complexities to which we have already alluded. (For some of the evidence—not always entirely reliable—from botany, written sources, and the visual arts, see the early chapters of S. Tolkowsky, *Hesperides: A History of the Culture and Use of Citrus Fruits* [1938].) An extraordinarily vivid medieval Hispano-Arabic poem, "The Orange," composed almost entirely of fresh and unexpected metaphors, is by Ibn Sara (d. 1123) of Santarén (Portugal), here translated from the Spanish version of Emilio García Gómez by Jeffrey H. Kaimowitz and myself:

> Are they red-hot coals that show their lively colors over the branches, or cheeks which appear among the green curtains of the palanquins?
>
> Are they branches which rustle or delicate forms, for love of which I am suffering what I suffer?
>
> I see that the orange shows us its fruits, which look like tears reddened by the torments of love.
>
> They are frozen; but if they melted, they would be wine. Some magic hands shaped the earth to form them.
>
> They are like balls of carnelian in branches of topaz, and the zephyr strikes them with mallet fingers.
>
> At times we kiss them, at times we inhale them, they are, alternately, damsels' cheeks or fruity perfumes.

The other poems by Ibn Sara in García Gómez's collection—"The Brazier," "Zephyr and Rain," "The Fleeting Star," "A Pool with Turtles," "The Eggplant," "The Thimble" —are equally brilliant and certainly justify the words he uses to describe the poet's style: "audacious metaphorist and enemy of frigidity."

A notable fourteenth-century literary occurrence of oranges is in the introduction to the "Third Day" of Boccaccio's *Decameron* as part of the description of the walled garden alongside a great palace (translated by G. H. McWilliam):

> In the central part of the garden (not the least, but by far the most admirable of its features), there was a lawn of exceedingly fine grass, of so deep a

green as to almost seem black, dotted all over with possibly a thousand different kinds of gaily-coloured flowers, and surrounded by a line of flourishing, bright green orange- and lemon-trees, which, with their mature and unripe fruit and lingering shreds of blossom, offered agreeable shade to the eyes and a delightful aroma to the nostrils.

By the early Italian Renaissance, citrus trees and their fruits, especially oranges, are common in Italian paintings: for example, the well-known masterpieces of Giovanni di Paolo (1399–1482), *Creation of the World and Expulsion of Adam and Eve* (1445) and *Paradise* (1445), in the Metropolitan Museum of Art, New York; and that of Botticelli (1444/5–1510), *Primavera* (ca. 1482), in the Uffizi, Florence.

Occasionally, the orange was even identified as the fruit of the tree of knowledge, probably by confusion with the Jewish ceremonial citron; by the sixteenth century, though, Italian painters such as Titian and Tintoretto (1518–1594) were following their northern counterparts in depicting the fruit of the tree of knowledge as apples (see Tolkowsky's *Hesperides* and Moldenke and Moldenke's *Plants of the Bible*). With the development of independent still life painting, isolated images of oranges became of interest in their own right. One out of many candidates for the most memorable of such images occurs in Zurbarán's *Still Life with Basket of Oranges* (1633), now in the Norton Simon collection in Pasadena (oil on canvas, 24½ x 43 inches). Flanked by a tray of lemons (or possibly citrons) on the left and a tray with a cup and a single rose on the right, the basket of oranges—dramatically lighted from the left—is located exactly at the center of the painting. The picture is certainly, in the words of Jordan and Cherry's book on Spanish still life painting, the "masterpiece [of] the greatest of all non-specialist still-life painters in Spain" (the book contains an excellent reproduction). There is something haunting about each object in the still life—"an almost surreal isolation," in Christopher Wright's phrase. In modern times, the most memorable mound of oranges—actually, mandarins—in a painting must be those in a glass compote in the last great masterpiece by Edouard Manet (1832–1883), *A Bar at the Folies-Bergère* (1881), now in the Courtauld Institute Galleries, London. (For a reproduction of the painting—oil on canvas, 37¾ x 51¾ in.—see the catalogue of the 1983 Manet retrospective at the Metropolitan Museum of Art.)

A new play, *Blue/Orange,* by Joe Penhall, which opened at the Cottesloe Theater in London in the 2000 season, features a bowlful of oranges at the center of an otherwise clinically white stage set. As the *TLS* reviewer, William McEvoy, explains, one of the three characters is a young black African imprisoned "for lewd behaviour with an orange." The other two characters are psychiatrists, and they argue about whether the patient is psychotic: he believes the oranges in the bowl are blue, says one psychiatrist; he grew up in colonial Uganda, says the other psychiatrist, at a time when *Tintin and the Blue Oranges* was popular, and, besides, there is a line by the French surrealist poet Paul Eluard which says "la terre est bleue comme une orange" (The earth is blue like an orange). The Belgian Hergé (1907–1983)—creator of the world-renowned cartoon character Tintin—never, in fact, wrote a book about blue oranges, but there is a

386 film called *Tintin et les oranges bleues* (1964), in which the plot revolves around a mysterious variety of blue orange capable of growing in the desert. (An illustrated book in English was published in 1967 based on André Barret's script for the film.) I might just add that the American artist John Baldessari (b. 1931) created a suite of "millennium" photographs in 1999, including images of a blue apple and an orange-colored orange (for reproductions, see the photography magazine *Blind Spot* [1999]).

Rather more dada than surreal was an intervention involving real oranges some years ago in New York City. Jack Bankowsky, the editor of *Art Forum,* reports on the episode in the list of his favorite art/culture happenings of the 1990s: "Honorable mention[s] to Gabriel Orozco for putting those oranges on the window sills of that beige brick apartment building across from MOMA (we've all looked out over the sculpture garden at those rounded bays, but Orozco's discreet intervention made the everyday strange and left us at once more self-conscious and somehow lighter on our feet)."

Returning to the sixteenth century, we may note that oranges (for those who could afford them) were increasingly eaten and used as flavoring for other foods; orange blossoms and orange water were increasingly prized for their scent; and orange trees were increasingly deployed for decorative purposes, outdoors in mild climates and indoors in the form of heated orange-houses, or orangeries, in severe climates (see Tolkowsky's seventh chapter). Ample traces of all this production and consumption of oranges can be found, needless to say, in the vast corpus of Euro-American literature and art. A culmination of sorts was reached when a bronze sculpture of an orange tree in a monumental vase was erected, in 1683, in the marketplace of a town in Germany called Oranienbaum (for a photograph of the monument, see Tolkowsky, *Hesperides*). Here, I should like to refer to a much smaller—but nevertheless significant—example.

In some letters of Dorothy Osborne (1627–1695), from her family's estate, Chicksands (some fifty miles northwest of London), to William Temple (1628–1699), in London, we find her asking him to send her some orange-flower water. Osborne and Temple had first met in 1648 and were to marry in 1654; the letters in question date from the spring of 1653. In a letter of 19/20 March, she writes: "When you goe into the Exchange, pray call at the great Shop above, (The Flower Pott). I spoke to Heam's the man of the Shop, when I was in Towne for a quart of Oringe flower water, hee had none that was good then, but promised to gett mee some, pray putt him in mind of it, and let him show it you before hee sends it mee, for I will not altogether trust to his honesty." By 23/24 April, Osborne must have received the water, because she writes: "But I shall talk treason by and by if I doe not look to my self, tis saffer talking of the Oringe flower water you sent mee." And a month later, on 21/22 May, Osborne writes: "Bee it what it will that displeased you, I am glad they did not fright you away before you had the Orange flower water for it is very good, and I am soe sweet with it a day's that I dispise Roses."

Temple purchased in 1680 an estate called Moor Park, to which he retired when his political career was over; his time was now devoted to writing and fruit-growing (especially grapes, apricots, and cherries). In 1689, the youthful Jonathan Swift, a relative of Temple's, became his secretary, continuing in this post off and on for the next ten years. When Temple died in 1699, Swift returned to his native Dublin, where at some point he composed a culinary tribute to oranges as part of some undatable verses imitating (Dublin?) street cries: "Verses Made for the Women Who Cry Apples, etc." After referring to apples, asparagus, onions, oysters, and herrings, Swift concludes with oranges:

> Come, buy my fine oranges, sauce for your veal,
> And charming when squeezed in a pot of brown ale.
> Well roasted, with sugar and wine in a cup,
> They'll make a sweet bishop when gentlefolks sup.

"Bishop" is a kind of punch.

Dr. Johnson seems to have been very fond of oranges, and he also retained the dried peel for a purpose he refused to reveal to Boswell, who artfully constructs from a few bare facts an enthralling little episode (1 April 1775). Boswell begins with an account of a small bet he won from Lady Diana Beauclerk (the second wife of Johnson's good friend Topham Beauclerk): "It seems [Johnson] had been frequently observed at the Club to put into his pocket the Seville oranges, after he had squeezed the juice out of them into the drink which he made for himself." Boswell bets Lady Diana that he will dare to ask Johnson the reason. He asks—thereby winning the bet—but Johnson will answer only that he scrapes the peels and dries them for some purpose he will not divulge. Here is how Boswell reports the remainder of the conversation: "BOSWELL. 'Then the world must be left in the dark. It must be said (assuming a mock solemnity,) he scraped them, and let them dry, but what he did with them next, he never could be prevailed upon to tell.' JOHNSON. 'Nay, Sir, you should say it more emphatically:—he could not be prevailed upon, even by his dearest friends, to tell.'"

It is difficult to believe that Boswell did not learn the answer to his question sometime during the ten remaining years of Johnson's life, but the Hill-Powell edition of Boswell's *Life of Johnson* provides an explanation: "Twenty years earlier he had recommended to Miss Boothby, as a remedy for indigestion dried orange-peel finely powdered, taken in a glass of hot red port." Miss Boothby, as Bruce Redford explains in his edition of Johnson's letters, was Hill Boothby, "a pious and learned spinster whom SJ had known since 1739" and "'the most probable candidate' for the woman SJ was considering as his second wife." The pertinent letter to Hill Boothby—written on 31 December 1755 when she was seriously ill (she died two weeks later)—provides a detailed recipe for this medicinal use of dried orange peels:

> Give me leave, who have thought much on Medicine, to propose to you
> an easy and I think a very probable remedy for indigestion and lubricity
> of the bowels. Dr. Laurence has told me your case. Take an ounce of dried

orange peel finely powdered, divide it into scruples [one scruple equals one twenty-fourth of an ounce], and take one Scruple at a time in any manner; the best way is perhaps to drink it in a glass of hot red port, or to eat it first and drink the wine after it. If you mix cinnamon or nutmeg with the powder it were not worse, but it will be more bulky and so more troublesome. This is a medicine not disgusting, not costly, easily tried, and if not found useful easily left off.

Johnson adds that Boothby should attempt this remedy only with her physician's permission but should not divulge its source because "physicians do not love intruders," and he concludes: "I love you and honour you, and am very unwilling to lose you." It seems that Johnson was not at all squeamish about mentioning intimate details of his bodily functioning when it came to helping a sick friend; or did he simply become more squeamish with age?

In certain eighteenth-century circles an inordinate fondness for oranges was apparently considered reprehensible. Thus, Guffroy and Fréron both report disapprovingly in their hostile sketches of Maximilien Robespierre (1758–1794) of his passionate taste for oranges (see J. M. Thompson, *Robespierre,* vol. 1), and Fréron adds (according to Norman Hampson) "that he always had in front of him a pyramid of oranges which the Duplays dared not touch." (The Duplays were the genial family who furnished Robespierre with room and board during the last three years of his life.)

The orange tree itself can be invested with magical dimensions, as in a fairy tale by Marie-Catherine Le Jumel de Barneville, Comtesse d'Aulnoy (ca. 1650–1705), "The Bee and the Orange Tree." It should first be explained that Mme d'Aulnoy conducted a salon in which it was customary, as Jack Zipes informs us, "to recite fairy tales and on festive occasions to dress up like characters from fairy tales. She herself became one of the most gifted storytellers at her salon." Mme d'Aulnoy's collections of fairy tales—which, it must be emphasized, were not originally written for children—were published in numerous volumes in the years 1696–1698. The first three-quarters of "The Bee and the Orange"—some sixteen pages in Zipes's English version—deploys a fairly conventional plot in the course of which two royal cousins, Aimée and Aimé, after being independently shipwrecked (she as an infant, he as a young man), meet in a land dominated by horrible, one-eyed ogres, whose favorite food is human flesh. Aimée has been brought up in the ogre family and at first cannot communicate with Aimé, but with the aid of a magic wand she learns his language. The wand also helps them to escape from the ogres, but only after Aimée transforms herself into a bee and Aimé into an orange tree. At this point, the plot becomes a traditional love triangle. First, Aimée "shut herself up in one of the largest flowers as though in a palace, and true love, which is never without its consolations, found some even in this union." Enter a lovely princess named Linda, who is delighted by the "delicious scent" of the orange tree and attempts "to gather a few of the blossoms." The bee drives her off with severe stings, leading Aimé to question Aimée's cruel behavior, and the following dialogue ensues:

> "But," he said, "you see [the blossoms] fall without being distressed. Wouldn't it be just the same to you if the princess adorned herself with them, if she placed them in her hair or put them in her bosom?"
>
> "No," the bee said, "it's not at all the same thing to me. I know, ungrateful one, that you feel more for her than you do for me. There's also a great difference between a refined person, richly dressed and of considerable rank in these parts, and an unfortunate princess whom you found covered with a tiger's skin, surrounded by monsters who could only give her crude and barbarous ideas, and whose beauty is not great enough to enslave you."
>
> And then she cried, as much as any bee is capable of crying. Some of the flowers of the enamored orange tree were wetted by her tears, and his distress at having disturbed his princess was so great that that all his leaves turned yellow, several branches withered, and he thought he would die.
>
> "What have I done, my beautiful bee? What have I done to make you so angry? Ah, doubtless, you'll abandon me. You're already weary of being linked to one so unfortunate as I."

One more trial of the two young lovers must be endured before they can be united in marriage. Linda dons a suit of armor, and then "she entered the garden, followed by all her ladies, who were armed like she was and who called this fete the 'Battle of the Bees and Amazons.'" One of the orange tree's branches is broken, and blood flows, but the bee flies to Arabia for some healing balm. And then, finally, love can conquer all.

"The Bee and the Orange Tree" is typical of d'Aulnoy's tales insofar as (citing Zipes once again) it is "filled with violence and violation" perpetrated on people who "must live under laws that they do not always understand and under fairy powers who are arbitrary, not unlike Louis XIV and his ministers," and replete with an extensive "repertoire of tortures and bestial transformations." Finally, Zipes speculates that the fairy tales "were a means of confronting the frustrating conditions under which [d'Aulnoy] lived and of projecting possibilities for change."

Another bit of social and cultural history relating to oranges—amusing but also enlightening—can be inferred from the fact that in February 1663 the Kings Company (one of two licensed theater companies in Restoration London) granted to Mary Meggs (later famous as "Orange Moll") the right to sell in its new theater "oranges, lemons, fruits, sweetmeats, and all manner of fruiterers and confectioners wares" (as we read in John Harold Wilson's biography of Nell Gwyn, the notorious mistress of Charles II). The price of a "China" orange was sixpence, half the price of admission to the cheapest seats in the upper galleries—which tells us something about who could

390   afford to eat oranges at the time. (For the prices, see Wilson's book and Arthur Bryant's *The England of Charles II* [1934].) Orange Moll (one of whose first "orange-girls" was the thirteen-year-old Nell Gwyn) was noticed by Samuel Pepys (1633–1703) during a performance of *Henry IV* on 2 November 1667, rescuing from choking "a gentleman of good habitt, sitting just before us eating of some fruit" by "thrust[ing] her finger down his throat." It can be tempting to go on recounting one such racy incident after another. But amusing though they may be, isolated incidents like these hardly contribute to genuine historical understanding. Let me illustrate with another incident involving oranges.

In his lively little book about oranges (originally an article in the *New Yorker*), John McPhee (b. 1931) traces the Lombard invasion of Italy to the delectability of Italian oranges. Thus, he writes, "After the fall of Rome, oranges played a part in the great Lombard invasion. A Byzantine governor of Rome, enraged at being summarily called back to Byzantium, sent an embassy with a selected display of Italian oranges to Alboin, King of the Lombards, inviting him to overrun Italy, which Alboin did." McPhee cites no sources, but a few pages earlier he had made clear his indebtedness for historical information to the already-cited book by Tolkowsky, where we find the following:

> Narses, infuriated, . . . sent messengers to the Lombards in Pannonia bearing some of the fruits of Italy and inviting them to enter the land which bore such goodly produce. Hence came the invasion of Alboin in 568. . . . Leo of Ostia, in his chronicle of the monastery of Monte Cassino, says, no doubt on the strength of some old tradition, that it was "cedar apples"— a term by which any citrus fruit may have been meant—that Narses sent to the Lombards in order to tempt them to come to his assistance.

Now, let us turn to Edward Gibbon's account of the episode in question (chap. 45, *Decline and Fall of the Roman Empire* [1788]):

> The destruction of a mighty kingdom established the fame of Alboin. . . . But his ambition was yet unsatisfied; and the conqueror of the Gepidæ turned his eyes from the Danube to the richer banks of the Po and the Tyber. . . . his subjects . . . were encouraged by the spirit and eloquence of Alboin; and it is affirmed, that he spoke to their senses, by producing, at the royal feast, the fairest and most exquisite fruits that grew spontaneously in the garden of the world.

Gibbon later remarks that "(if any credit is due to the belief of the times) Narses invited the Lombards to chastise the ingratitude of the prince and the people [by invading Italy]." In his annotated edition of Gibbon's *Decline and Fall*, J. B. Bury comments on this last passage that Gibbon's "evidence does not establish a presumption of [Narses's] guilt, but shows that very soon after the event it was generally believed that he was in collusion with the invaders." The sequence of events as recounted by Gibbon is rather different from that stated or implied by Tolkowsky and McPhee: Alboin had already decided to invade Italy by the time of his feast featuring choice Italian fruits, and Narses did not provide those fruits, the identity of which is in any case left unspecified; nor is there any compelling evidence that Narses ever invited Alboin to invade Italy. Neither Gibbon nor Bury, by the way, ever refers to the twelfth-century chronicle of Leo of Ostia (composed some five hundred years after the invasion of Alboin and first published in the seventeenth century), and both historians were masters of the relevant sources.

What is at stake here is not the truth of some minor—even trivial—episode in the social history of citrus fruits; what is at stake is the very way we are to understand history, whether as a succession of amusing anecdotes centered on striking personalities or as the complex interweaving of long-term socio-economic and political forces with a variety of individual human agents. Tolkowsky and McPhee reduce history to titillating stories, deflecting attention away from the essential historiographical issues. Narses and Alboin are, indeed, colorful historical figures—the former a great Byzantine general and (not irrelevant to his career) a eunuch, the latter a ruthless Germanic military leader who married the daughter of one of his conquered enemies only to be murdered by her. But even to begin to understand the actions and motivations of these figures one must examine the political and military situations in which they found themselves, and one might begin by reading Gibbon's account (at the beginning of his chapter 45) of Byzantium and Italy at the time of Alboin's invasion of Italy in 567 C.E. The Byzantine emperor Justinian had died a couple of years earlier and the new emperor, Justin, was weak in his foreign policy and unresponsive to domestic problems. Narses had not endeared himself to the people of Italy in his position as exarch, or governor, for fifteen years, and he had been replaced by a successor wholly ignorant of conditions in Italy. Furthermore, the dismissal of Narses had been accompanied by an insulting allusion, from the empress Sophia, to his being a eunuch, and he refused to return home to Byzantium. Alboin, on the other hand, fresh from one notable conquest, was eager for more, and he probably guessed—correctly, as it turned out—that no Roman army would oppose him in Italy. As for the incident concerning the feast Alboin provided for his soldiers, no specific source is mentioned by Gibbon; given his usual scrupulousness with documentation, however, we may be reasonably certain he had a source (and we know in general that he had several sources for the period in question contemporary with the events they describe). If there were any oranges at the putative royal banquet—and there may well have been—they could scarcely have played a decisive role in Alboin's invasion of Italy.

Further evidence that Narses's oranges are the stuff of legend rather than history is the fact that the same story has been repeated for a later invasion of southern Italy. Waverly Root recounts the story while sensibly casting doubt on its veracity, in his book *The Food of Italy* (1971): "There is a story which attributes the Norman conquest of southern Italy and Sicily in part to a present of oranges sent to the Duke of Normandy in the 11th century by a prince of Salerno, which tempted the Normans to acquire the land producing such treasures—the same story told about the Longobards [Lombards] five centuries earlier." But let us return to literature.

Two lyrics with orange trees as their nominal subject matter, composed some seventy-five years apart, nicely illustrate the outer limits of style and approach that had emerged in Spanish poetry of the seventeenth century. The great dramatist Lope de Vega Carpio (1562–1613), according to the critic Elias L. Rivers, also wrote "folkloric lyrics [which] are unexcelled . . . often indistinguishable from those of the anonymous tradition" (1974). One of those lyrics is an untitled eighteen-line poem, which begins and ends with this quatrain:

> Naranjitas me tira la niña
> en Valencia por Navidad,
> pues a fe que si se las tiro
> que se le han de volver azahar.

In between is a ten-line stanza, with the two last lines repeating the two last lines of the quatrain. Though the quatrain is unrhymed, the middle stanza rhymes (*abba accd ed*). There is a single conceit: if the little oranges thrown at the speaker are thrown back to the girl—such, presumably, is her innocence and beauty—they will be metamorphosed into orange blossoms. The Spanish text is plain and unadorned, so J. M. Cohen's literal prose translation can adequately convey the sense of the poem:

> The girl throws me little oranges in Valencia at Christmas, but I swear that if I throw them at her they will be sure to turn back into blossom.
>
> I went out to a masquerade and stopped at her window; her morning dawned and I saw the sun in her eyes. She frantically flung little oranges from there; as she knows nothing of love she thinks that everything is a joke. But I swear that if I throw them at her they will be sure to turn back into blossom.
>
> The girl throws me little oranges in Valencia at Christmas, but I swear that if I throw them at her they will be sure to turn back into blossom.

At the other stylistic extreme is our second example, by a fairly obscure author, Salvador Jacinto Polo de Medina (1603–1676), who wrote a prose work on gardens containing several poems, one entitled "Los naranjos" (The orange trees). Consisting of twenty-four lines, with a few irregularly spaced end-rhymes, the poem is an exercise in Góngoran poetics: no line—indeed, no word—is repeated (except for the copula and two forms of *fragante* [fragrant]); the impression is one of verbal richness, even excess, with more than a touch of the outrageous. Again, surprisingly, a good deal of this verbal play is conveyed by a literal prose translation (again, by J. M. Cohen):

Those lovely orange-trees whose flowers breathe amber on the meadows are pomanders in the sun's brazier: a perpetual and lovely emerald, in which the loquacious nightingale with harmonious voice tells us a thousand tales; among whose tender leaves the flowers which April shaped from short-lived stars of snow are fragrant clusters: the metamorphoses of time which will sweetly transform what are diamonds to-day into topazes to-morrow; to whose green liveries crystal twigs give handsome ornaments and a most fragrant whiteness: rich mine of the valley where shy January gave us free gold and showy May free silver.

What Rivers says about Góngora seems to apply equally to this poem: "The world of Góngora's major poems is a material world of solid substances and glittering colors in which the poet, using words, attempts to rival the artificiality of nature, *Natura Artifex*, herself."

On a smaller scale than anything we have yet considered is this *copla*, in the shortest of the standard *cante flamenco* forms (varying from three to six lines):

> A branch of orange blossom:
> What a little thing it is
> But how many oranges it gives.
>
> ~
>
> Una ramita de azahar:
> qué poquita cosa es
> pero cuántas naranjas da.

Like all *coplas*, this one (translated by Paul Hecht) is anonymous and undatable; it belongs to that minority of *coplas* that are not about love. The tiny song—just twelve words—expresses surprise at the smallness of the blossomed branch compared with the bulk of the oranges it will produce. In a little more than twice as many words, A. R. Ammons (1926–2001), in "Communication," expresses his similar surprise at the fertility of an orange tree:

> All day—I'm
> surprised—the
> orange tree, windy, sunny,
> has said nothing:
> nevertheless,
> four ripe oranges have
> dropped and several
> dozen
> given up a ghost of green.

In the case of two of García Lorca's early poems previously discussed—one about Adam, Eve, and the apple, the other about a fig tree—it is easy to make out the influence of

394   *cante jondo,* or flamenco, lyrics. This influence is equally evident in his numerous early (1921–24) poems about oranges. (I use Alan Trueblood's English versions.) Thus, one of the so-called *Andalusian Songs* ("Adelina Out Walking") begins: "The sea has no oranges / nor Seville any love." And six lines later, the words are repeated: "The sea has no oranges. / Oh the pity, love. / Nor Seville any love!" In one of the *Moon Songs* ("The Moon Appears"), the third of four stanzas reads:

> No one eats oranges
> in the full moon's light.
> Fruit must be eaten
> green and ice-cold.

Another *Moon Song* ("Two Evening Moons, 2") is dedicated to García Lorca's sister, Isabelita:

> The evening is singing
> a *berceuse* to the oranges.
>
> My little sister is singing:
> The earth is an orange.
>
> In tears, the moon says:
> I want to be an orange.
>
> No way, my child,
> even if you turned rosy.
> Not even a nice lemon.
> Oh, what a pity!

And, finally, here is the first stanza (which is repeated as the fourth and last) of one of the *Songs to End With,* "Song of the Dead Orange Tree":

> Woodcutter.
> Cut down my shadow.
> Deliver me from the torment
> of bearing no fruit.

The word translated "fruit" is *toronjas;* the Spanish word for "orange" appears only in the title, never in the poem itself—clearly a way of further emphasizing the oranges missing from the tree. *Toronja,* by the way, means grapefruit in Latin American Spanish, while grapefruit is *pomelo* in Spain. García Lorca could have used *frutas* for fruit; I assume he preferred *toronjas* because of its extra syllable.

Orange blossoms may even have political connotations, as in this expression of nostalgia for a lost Palestinian homeland by an Arabic poet born in Haifa and now living in Syria. The poet is Hasan al-Buhairi (b. 1921, whose work has been characterized by Salma Jayyusi as preferring "the old style of poetry with its symmetrical, two-hemistich forms, its terse constructions, and its strong echoing resonances" (1992). In an English translation by Salwa Jabsheh and John Heath-Stubbs, "Orange Blossoms (A Palestinian Song)" consists of four quatrains, the first three interrogative in form, the last declarative; here are the first and last stanzas:

> Do you ask about the orange blossom,
> its charm, and all its magical delight?
> How dawn arrests the caravan of morning
> to catch perfection of it, shimmering bright?
> [. . . . . . .]
> It was *our* sky that warmed and fostered them
> with purest sunshine that could give them birth
> and that which nourished all their grace and beauty
> and all their fragrance—was our native earth.

It must be emphasized that there is nothing intrinsically "scaled"—and, in particular, diminutive—about orange imagery. Thus, Neruda begins his "Ode to the Orange" (1957) with the bald assertion (translated by Jacketti):

> Orange,
> the world
> was made
> in your image

For us, Neruda is implying, the most important parts of the world are the sun and the earth, and both are said to to resemble oranges—the sun presumably because of its color and the earth because of its structure, "with trains and with rivers / achieving / the extraordinary unity of an orange." One might recall García Lorca's poem of some thirty years earlier, in which his little sister is singing: "The earth is an orange." Also, the unity induced by travel reminds us of the political unity stressed in Neruda's "Ode to the Apple," and indeed Neruda goes on to write, in what is probably the best image in the poem:

> Beneath your rind,
> countries come together
> unified
> like sections of a single fruit.
>
> ~
>
> En tu piel se reúnen
> los países
> unidos
> como sectores de una sola fruta,

396 The trouble is that Neruda does not stop there, and the poem ends with fatuous lines invoking

> the heart of humans,
> piquant-sweet sections—
> a spring
> capable of preserving
> the mysterious simplicity
> of the Earth
> and the impeccable unity
> of an orange.

Similar in their limpid simplicity to a *copla* are some of the love lyrics of Jacques Prévert, in which the beloved is sometimes associated with a piece of fruit. "Alicante," from *Paroles* (1946–7), serves as an example:

> An orange on the table
> Your dress on the rug
> And you in my bed
> Sweet present of the present
> Cool of night
> Warmth of my life.
>
> ~
>
> Une orange sur la table
> Ta robe sur le tapis
> Et toi dans mon lit
> Doux présent du présent
> Fraîcheur de la nuit
> Chaleur de ma vie.

(Alicante is a province in southeastern Spain, which is, along with adjoining Valencia, the principal citrus-producing region of Spain.) The almost word-for-word translation by Ferlinghetti cannot capture the sound repetitions *doux/du* in line four and *fraicheur/chaleur* in lines five and six.

As already noted, tangerines are closely related to oranges, and Prévert has compared a lover also to a tangerine (in another poem from *Paroles,* "Tangerine"). And once again, her dress falls to the floor (translated by Teo Savory):

> The heat-lightning forked down your loins
> at the very center of shadow
> the happy storm of your waiting body
> has suddenly burst
> Your dress falling on the waxed floor

makes no more of a sound
than the rind of an orange falling on the rug
But under our feet
little pearl buttons crack like seeds
Tangerine
pretty fruit
the tip of your breast
has traced a new fate line
in the palm of my hand
Tangerine
pretty fruit

Sun in the night

There is, of course, nothing intrinsically gendered about tangerines, so it should come as no surprise to find Jack Gilbert treating them as masculine objects in his "The Four Perfectly Tangerines" (1962). Employing diction and syntax that recall e.e. cummings (1894–1962), Gilbert's poem is at the same time both lighthearted and metaphysically preoccupied. The first and last stanzas make up twenty-one of the thirty-eight lines:

The four perfectly tangerines were a
clue
as they sat
singing
(three to one)
in that ten-thirty
am room
not unhappily of
death
singing of how they were tangerines
against white
but how
against continuous orange
they were only
fruit.
    [. . . . . .]
So
I opened the one
and the odor of his breaking
was the sweet breasts
of being no longer
only.

398   The references to color and odor of the tangerines are separated (in the unquoted intervening lines) by references to "inside / green" seeds and to a "God / of . . . eight thousand green faces." But the definiteness of sense qualities and the precision of numbers are upset by the equivocal syntactical and lexical status of the final "only."

With a passion equaling Prévert's, Francis Ponge has directed his attention, not to love or any other human emotion, but rather to "things," more specifically—in the words of his first collection's title—to "le parti pris des choses" (taking the side of things). About these "things"—which can include oysters as well as candles, water as well as a piece of meat, a young mother as well as a pebble—Ponge composes prose poems involving sophisticated puns and etymologically based wordplay. Thus, the first sentence of Ponge's "The Orange" (1942) reads: "Comme dans l'éponge il y dans l'orange une aspiration à reprendre contenance après avoir subi l'épreuve de l'expression," which can mean (in Lane Dunlop's translation) either "As in the sponge [*éponge*], there is in the orange [*orange*] an urge to fill up again after having been squeezed" or "As in the sponge, there is in the orange an urge to regain countenance after expression." Ponge's verbal pyrotechnics succeed in capturing in amazing ways certain prominent properties of oranges, both the fruit and the word, as witness the third paragraph of his poem:

> But it is not enough to have noted the orange's particular way of scenting the air and delighting its torturer. One must stress the glorious color of the resultant liquid which, more than lemon juice, obliges the larynx to open wide for the saying of the word as for the swallowing of the liquid, with no apprehensive grimace of the mouth in front, whose papillae it does not make bristle.

The fourth paragraph, about the peel of the orange, begins with the words: "Et l'on demeure au reste sans paroles pou avouer l'admiration qui mérite l'enveloppe du tendre, fragile et rose ballon ovale"; which Dunlop translates: "And one remains without words to express the admiration merited by the envelope of the soft, fragile and rose oval balloon." Now, the English phrase "one remains" corresponds to the reduplicated French locution, "l'on demeure" followed by "au reste." Far from being "without words" Ponge has found two different ways of expressing the same thing! But, of course, attempting to say the same thing in two different ways may also be a sign of an inability to say something adequately in even one way. Perhaps more to the point, Ponge has made the interesting assertion that the phrase "au reste" was intended to suggest the word "zeste," the thin outer skin of the orange (nowhere mentioned in the poem). (See the report of a conversation with Ponge by Ian Higgins, in his edition of *Le Parti pris des choses* [1979].)

Finally, in the fifth and last paragraph of "The Orange" Ponge turns to the pips, which are

> found, after the sensational explosion of the Chinese lantern of tastes, colors and scents that constitute the fruity balloon itself, the relative hardness

and greenness (not entirely tasteless, besides) of wood, of the branch, of
the leaf: a small thing, to sum up, yet surely the fruit's reason for being.

In the same conversation referred to above, Ponge has asserted that in the penultimate
phrase of the poem, "the sounds of 'somme toute petite quoique avec certitude' are
intended to convey the acidity of the fruit." Whatever the success of Ponge's semantics of sound in this particular case, we have been reminded that his concerns are at
least as much with *language*—especially written language—*as object,* as with objects in
the ordinary sense.

Perhaps the most extended recent literary tribute to the orange is *The Orangery*
(1978), by Gilbert Sorrentino (b. 1929); appropriately enough, the book's binding is
orange, its endpapers are orange, and a picture of an orange-tree branch decorates its
title page. The book consists of seventy-seven fourteen-line poems and one twenty-
eight line poem, mostly unrhymed, all sparingly punctuated, some titled and some not,
all more or less sonnetlike. The allusions to oranges run all the way from the word (in
English, in Spanish, in French) to the color (of clothes, of sunsets, of hair, of lampposts,
of marmalade), to the fruit itself. There is even one poem ("Across this water sits a
shore") lacking the obligatory allusion—until the penultimate word of the last line: "I
forgot orange. There." One of the poems ("That the mouth speak not daggers") is
about oranges and the past:

> That the past
> be not illumined but allowed
>
> to blaze forth the brilliance
> proper to it.
>
> What is the past of orange?
>
> Oranged.
>
> The orange's past is green
> hard and sour, a plain fruit
> splendid in its ripeness
> as splendid in its salad days
>
> light amid the green daze
> of the groves
> (ll. 3–14)

The implication here that green oranges are always hard and sour is mistaken; as John
McPhee explains, "The color of an orange has no absolute correlation with the maturity of the flesh and juice inside. An orange can be as sweet and ripe as it will ever be
and still glisten like an emerald in the tree. Cold—coolness, rather—is what makes an

400   orange orange." The fact that, unlike most other fruits, the citrus does not exhibit ripening in the form of abrupt changes in fruit texture and composition (e.g., softening of the flesh) has even led some biologists to prefer the term "maturation" for the process, which involves a gradual decline in citric acid and a gradual increase in sugars. This process occurs while the citrus fruit is still on the tree and is not directly correlated with changes in the color of the peel; indeed, as Spiegel-Roy and Goldschmidt explain, "During maturation peel and pulp behave in most respects as separate organs, although some coordination does exist." The rates of both peel and pulp development depend on temperature: thus, tropical climates slow the loss of chlorophyll and the buildup of colored pigments in the peel, and increase the soluble solids (mostly sugars) in the juice; subtropical climates have the opposite effects. This explains why tropically grown citrus fruit is preferable for processing, while the more vividly colored subtropically grown citrus fruit is preferable for the fresh fruit market. Subtropical regions, such as Florida, experience occasional frosts, which can damage, or even destroy, the citrus fruit. Damage consists in a reduction in the amount of juice together with a lowering of both the sugar and the acid content. Destruction of the fruit occurs when frozen water inside the fruit causes rupture of the cells.

To return to Sorrentino's poem, since he emphasizes the importance of the sheer factuality of the past, insisting that the past not be illuminated from without (say, by the present?) but shine rather in its own unique way, one may legitimately demand of him that he get the horticultural facts right about the past, present, and future of individual oranges. That he does not, in my view, fatally weakens his poem. The last two lines, by the way, echo—whether deliberately or not, it is hard to say—a memorable pair of lines from Marvell's "Bermudas":

> He hangs in shades the orange bright,
> Like golden lamps in a green night

These lines may themselves have been inspired by a passage (canto 1, ll. 4–7) in Edmund Waller's mock-epic, "The Battle of the Summer Islands":

> Bermudas, walled with rocks, who does not know?
> That happy island where huge lemons grow,
> And orange trees, which golden fruit do bear,
> The Hesperian garden boasts of none so fair

In another poem from *The Orangery* ("Remember the story of Columbus and the orange?"), Sorrentino begins by citing a bit of pseudohistory: "Remember the story of Columbus and the orange? / He impressed Isabella with a demonstration." Now, there *is* no story of Columbus and an orange; presumably Sorrentino has misremembered the story of Columbus and the egg, itself almost certainly a piece of biographical fabrication, conflated perhaps with the equally false idea that Columbus had to persuade Isabella and Ferdinand that Earth was round. If one objects that the success of the poem does not depend crucially on the truth of its historical assertions—"After all, it's only a poem"—I would ask whether the poem would not seriously falter if the allusion to "the bloody North of Ireland" (in the eighth line) were imaginary or if the "clarinet marmalade" of the penultimate line were not plausibly described as "black and orange." My thinking here reflects an essay by Christopher Ricks on "Literature and the Matter of Fact" (1996) in which at one point he sums up the "writer's responsibility": "You can't both lean upon historical or other fact (this being not only permissible but indispensable to many kinds of literary achievement) and at the same time kick it away from under you. You can't get mileage from the matter of fact and then refuse to pay the fare."

George MacBeth (1932–1992) has the speaker in "The Orange Poem" fantasize about becoming known as "the orange poet" (though surely MacBeth himself did not wish to become known primarily as the author of this poem!). The poem is reflexive in the sense that it refers to the act of its own writing, but while it will do as a piece of pure whimsy, it is not nearly as challengingly outrageous as some of MacBeth's more serious poems.

For an example of abysmal failure in a piece of fictional whimsy featuring orange trees, we may take a look at *The Orange Tree* (1993), by Carlos Fuentes (b. 1928), translated by Alfred MacAdam. Generally considered one of the most important contemporary writers of Mexico—indeed, of Latin America—Fuentes, in this group of five loosely connected stories, has produced a set of variations on the real and fantasized history of the connection between Spain and the New World. Orange trees occur in all five of the stories. Thus, in the first story, "The Two Shores," the narrator—an actual historical figure, Jerónimo de Aguilar, a shipwrecked Spaniard who has spent eight years as a captive of the Aztecs—eventually becomes a translator for Cortés. On his first encounter with Cortés, Aguilar is concerned to come off as a real Spaniard and—here the fiction begins—uses an orange as evidence:

> As luck would have it, in my old mantle I'd kept one of the oranges, the fruit of the tree Guerrero and I planted here. I showed it to him as if for a moment I was the King of Coins in our Spanish playing cards: I had the sun in my hands. Could any image verify a Spaniard's identity better than the sight of a man eating an orange? I sank my teeth avidly into the skin until they found the hidden flesh of the orange, her flesh, the woman-fruit, the feminine fruit. The juice ran down my chin. I laughed, as if saying to Cortés, What better proof could you want that I'm a Spaniard?

Fuentes also invents the idea that Aguilar in his capacity as translator deliberately misled Cortés with the object of helping to prepare for an eventual Aztec expedition to conquer Spain, the (counterfactual) event with which Aguilar's narrative ends.

Skipping over the next three stories, let us turn to the last one, which is about Columbus. We must recur first of all to how the idea dies hard that Columbus was

402   unusual in late-fifteenth-century Europe in believing the earth to be round; the belief in a spherical earth goes back, of course, to ancient Greece and was taken for granted by virtually all serious thinkers during the Middle Ages and Renaissance in Europe. In Fuentes's story, however, we find repeated the same old myth about Columbus with a new twist: "From the cradle," Fuentes's Columbus tells us, "I had a carnal impression of the roundness of the earth" because of the rotundity of his mother's and his wet-nurses' breasts. So, this is why Columbus—identified as a Sephardic Jew—came to believe in the rotundity of the earth (though how his infantile experience was different from any other baby's is never explained). In fact, in Fuentes's story Columbus actually imagines the earth as a pear, "the nipple being the highest part and closest to heaven." When he arrives in the New World, Columbus tells us, he planted the orange seeds he had brought with him from Spain. The resulting orange trees "grew better in Antilia than in Andalusia," and Columbus "finally had a garden of perfect breasts, suckable, edible, renewable." Fuentes also has Columbus recount the apocryphal anecdote about standing an egg on its end. But let us not pursue any further details of a boring and silly book.

A deliberate juxtaposition of the intensely pleasureable associations of oranges with a sudden eruption of terror and death is the perhaps too obvious device of the Irish writer David Park in his short story, "Oranges From Spain" (1988). A Northern Irish man of unspecified name and age—we do learn that he is at present married—relates an incident which occurred when he was sixteen. The first fifteen or so pages serve to locate the scene in Belfast in Gerry Breen's fruit shop, where the narrator has a summer job. On the last page of the story Mr. Breen will be shot dead because the Protestants "needed a Catholic to balance the score." First, however, Park attempts to enhance the poignancy of his ending by a conversation in which Mr. Breen says, "You asked me what I'd do if I won the jackpot—well, I've got it all thought out. I'd go to every country whose fruit I sell, go and see it grow, right there in the fields and the groves, in the orchards and the vineyards. All over the world!" Four days later, Mr. Breen has just brought a tray of Spanish oranges out from the back of the store when he is shot by a man in a black motorcycle tunic, wearing a blue crash helmet, with a green scarf covering the lower half of his face: "Blood splashed his green coat, and flowed from the dark gaping wound, streaming across the floor, mixing with the oranges that were strewn all around us. Oranges from Spain." The narrator kneels beside Mr. Breen, praying for his survival, praying God would "let Gerry Breen live to build his ark and bring abroad the fruit of the world. All the fruit of the world safely stored. Oranges from Spain, apples from the Cape—the sweet taste of summer preserved for ever, eternal and incorruptible." All I can say is that ending the story with fruit as the symbol of eternity and incorruptibility is not very convincing.

Another novel featuring oranges, *Tropic of Orange* (1997), by Karen Tei Yamashita (b. 1951), takes place in Los Angeles in the near future. The front cover of the book consists of an aerial view of a burned-out section of Los Angeles on which a large orange is superimposed; on the back cover there is a quite decent summary of the techniques and plot of the novel.

> Irreverently juggling magical realism, film noir, hip hop, and chicanismo, Karen Yamashita presents an L.A. where the homeless, gangsters, infant organ entrepreneurs, and Hollywood collide on a stretch of highway struck by disaster. The Harbor Freeway crisis becomes the apex of events —caused by an orange, which has been brought to L.A. from just north of Mazatlan, dragging with it the Tropic of Cancer.

Inside the book we find a table of contents with seven sections—labeled "Monday" through "Sunday"—each composed of seven chapters. This is followed by a diagram called "HyperContexts," consisting of a seven-by-seven matrix assigning seven chapters to each of the seven main characters: an English-speaking Mexican woman with a small son; her husband, "Chinese from Singapore with a Vietnam name speaking like a Mexican living in Koreatown [in L.A.]"; a Japanese American television news producer; a middle-aged homeless male African American; a psychotic homeless Japanese American composer; a young Chicano newspaper reporter; and a miracle-working performance artist of unknown origins.

The faintly absurd but moderately absorbing plot involves these orangey elements: a lone orange growing on a tree located exactly on the Tropic of Cancer in Mexico; the arrival of that one orange in L.A. and its infection of all the city's oranges, causing an outbreak of fatal cancers; the confiscation of all the oranges in L.A. except one, which is pursued by an angry crowd. As for Yamashita's style, the frenetic pace of her prose (presumably reflecting her hip-hop inspiration) is somewhat at odds with the strict symmetries of her novel's structure. I will add only that it was a disappointment but perhaps not too much of a surprise to find the old Columbus story about the spherical earth repeated yet again. At least this time it is called a myth (in the poem at the beginning of Yamashita's thirtieth chapter): "The myth of Columbus: / . . . making his case / for a round world."

With a sense of relief, I turn from historical or futuristic fiction to a real personal experience of oranges—disenchanted, though it is—"The Orange Picker" (1961) by David Ignatow:

> I was tempted to the grove by its odor;
> the tang lingered over the whole countryside,
> and from the hilltop where I stood orange
> was the banner laid out like a signal.
> I had no exact notion, but of itself
> it seemed a goal: to be overwhelmed
> in its odor.
>   I came downhill,
> and saw these men at work,

> on ladders to pick oranges;
> they were not tall enough;
> and as I watched I too was drawn in.
> And now as I labor, the days going by redolent—
> I have breathed in them too long to be curious—
> these oranges have failed me.
>
> c. 1940

One at first puzzling feature of the poem is the missing "of" phrase that usually follows the word "redolent," but the line-ending dash supports a reading of the line as having been abruptly terminated by the disenchantment of the narrator. The poem is admirable in its objectivity and honesty.

Equally honest and yet utterly subjective in its response to some citrus fruit is a poem by Diane Wakoski (b. 1937), "Image is Narrative," in which the narrator free-associates, or improvises, in front of a still life painting by Francisco de Zurbarán (which Wakoski calls *Still Life: Lemons, Oranges and a Rose* and which we have already discussed in chapter 13 under its usual title, *Still Life with Basket of Oranges*). After making assorted desultory comments about the objects in the painting and even querying why a cup in the painting is omitted from the title, the narrator finally notices that the entire ground of the painting, including the surface of the table on which the still life rests, is black. The blackness seems to free her imagination and the painting now begins to function almost like a psychological projection test:

> Black as a night in the garden
> when the young bride is wearing her wreath of orange blossoms,
> having been married to someone she's never met,
> who now is drunk and pinching her breasts
> like those oranges, those juicy
> lemons, the rose from her hair,
> fallen to the ground,
> and there is only night ahead. Night
> to be gotten through, now that the
> guests are gone,
> and all the cups are empty.
>
> I do not need a single human
> in the picture
> to tell me this story.
> (ll 53–66)

Professing to challenge "a speech-based poetics" and traditional ideas of "reference," a group of so-called Language, or language-oriented, poets have attempted to exploit the "polysemantism" of language and the reader's share in creating "meaning."

In a manifesto for this kind of poetry Ron Silliman (b. 1946) has written that "any new direction would require poets to look (in some ways for the first time) at what a poem is actually made of—not images, not voice, not characters or plot, all of which appear on paper, or in one's mouth, only through the invocation of a specific medium, language itself." Other Language poets trace their practice back to Gertrude Stein (1874–1946). Leafing through Silliman's large anthology (1986), I came across this short, untitled poem (1981), by John Mason:

> Red Fred exhumed the orangepeels.
>
> He was very interested in the designs.
>
> What a fortunate wisdom!
>
> His bicycle sang when the garage was full.
>
> He stood in the doorway when the earth shook.
>
> He excoriated an orange.

What caught my attention initially was, of course, the two occurrences of "orange" on the page. The next thing I noticed was the wide spacing between the printed lines and the rhyme between the first two words, "Red" and "Fred." Proceeding, then, to read the entire poem, I discovered that each line consisted of a single complete sentence and quickly decided that it was reasonable to assume—in spite of the apparent isolation of the lines—that Fred was the center of attention in all six sentences. "Red" bothered me: it could have a political meaning ("Communist") or it could refer to Fred's hair color. My initial idea that Mason's poem was "about" oranges seemed to stand up to further scrutiny; after all, the two crucial action verbs associated with Fred have him digging up orange peels in the first line and producing orange peels in the last. Also, the two verbs in these lines not only have identical prefixes but also have similar pairs of literal/metaphorical meanings: "exhume" (dig up/revive); "excoriate" (peel/denounce). About Fred we know that he's interested in certain designs (of the orange peels?), that he has a bicycle, and that he is prudent (standing in doorways during earthquakes). It is not clear what the garage is full of (orange peels?) or in what sense Fred's bicycle sings (the sound of the wheels turning as Fred rides when there is no room for his bicycle in the garage?). This about exhausts my efforts to "read" the *words* of the poem (as opposed to "reading" the poem in conventional fashion).

Whatever the merits of Mason's poem as an example of Language poetry, its considerable residue of traditional semantics makes it a far cry from the verbal antics of Gertrude Stein. The best way of seeing this is simply to quote a stylistically exemplary sample of Stein's prose/poetry. Since one of the main surface features of Stein's style is the apparent homogenization of subject matter, so that nothing at first stands out beyond the individual words themselves, we might as well quote Stein on "oranges." In *Tender Buttons* (1912; published 1914) the second and longest of the three sections, labeled "Food Studies in Description," is positioned between sections labeled "Objects" and "Rooms." (There is evidence that the last section was the first composed and that it represents a preliminary formulation of the ideas in the first two sections; see Lisa Ruddick, *Reading Gertrude Stein: Body, Text, Gnosis* [1990].) Within this central section there occurs a set of four successive prose poems about oranges:

Orange.

Why is a feel oyster an egg stir. Why is it orange center.

A show at tick and loosen loosen it so to speak sat.

It was an extra leaker with a see spoon, it was an extra licker with a see spoon.

Orange.

A type oh oh new new not no not knealer knealer of old show beefsteak, neither neither.

Orange.

Build is all right.

Orange In

Go lack go lack use to her.

Cocoa and clear soup and oranges and oat-meal.

Whist bottom whist close, whist clothes, woodling.

Cocoa and clear soup and oranges and oat-meal.

Pain soup, suppose it is question, suppose it is butter, real is, real is only, only only excreate, only excreate a no since.

A no, a no since, a no since when, a no since when since, a no since when since, a no since when since a no since when since, a no since, a no since when since, a no since, a no, a no since a no since, a no since, a no since.

As throughout *Tender Buttons,* the vocabulary is plain and predominantly Anglo-Saxon and monosyllabic (though with occasional coinages and occasional puns on French words); the syntax is uncomplicated but frequently ambiguous or punning ("polyvalent" or "polysemous" are the terms preferred in some recent criticism of Stein).

To begin with, two phrases in the first poem seem related to the juiciness of oranges: "leaker with a see spoon" and "licker with a see spoon" (but who eats oranges with a spoon?), though the point of these phrases may lie not only in their denotative meanings but also in such visual and auditory parallelisms as "leaker" and "licker." There are numerous puns and near puns throughout the poems: "egg stir"/"extra," "see spoon"/"tea spoon," "knealer"/"kneeler" (and possibly "annealer"—since "knealer" is not a proper English word), "orange in"/"origin," "a no since"/"innocence," "no since"/"no sins." Some of these are proposed by Lisa Ruddick, others are my own conjectures.

Ruddick, however, is more interested in the thematic interpretation of Stein's text, which she (along with some other critics) understands as a discourse on patriarchy (not for Ruddick, however, a simple attack on patriarchy). In particular, oranges stand in the first instance for the mother—"another round thing with a hidden, soft, seed-filled interior"—while the beefsteak stands for the father. Though "Orangemother seems to be utterly favored over beefsteak-father," any straightforward polarization is, according to Ruddick, rejected in the phrase "neither neither," which ends the second poem (and is perhaps confirmed by the brief third poem: "Build is all right"?). The fourth poem is the longest and the most obviously complex of the orange poems. Notable here is Stein's coinage of "excreate," which might mean the opposite of "create" but also suggests, Ruddick reminds us, "excrete" and "excrement." It may be, then, that Stein "subversively reinterprets the theological term innocence, to mean a return to an excremental source." The body—in particular, the female body—is then reinstated at the center of our consciousness after its displacement and repression by patriarchy's sham "spiritualism."

A later poem, "linguistically innovative" in the Steinian sense, is "Lure, 1963" (1993), by the English writer Denise Riley (b. 1948), which exploits brilliantly the fact that the names for certain fruits may also serve as color words. Such words (in English) include "apricot," "peach," and "plum," but Riley restricts herself to the citrus fruits. (In the course of the poem, each of the spectral colors in the conventional list of seven—a list, incidentally, traceable backward to the enormously influential *Opticks* [1702] of Isaac Newton—is also mentioned at least once, along with pink, black, white, and gray.) The poem begins:

> Navy near-black cut in with lemon, fruity bright lime green.
> I roam around around around around acidic yellows, globe
> oranges burning, slashed cream, huge scarlet flowing
> anemones, barbaric pink singing, radiant weeping When
> will I be loved?

The poem is about "a crimson / kid that you won't date"—she is fifteen, if the year in the title can be taken as designating a year in Riley's life—who is desperately attempting to attract some "Pear glow boys"; the luridly contrasting colors suggest a fish lure. Ten lines follow and then this conclusion (with what seems to be a pun on "wearing"):

Oh yes I'm the great pretender. Red lays a stripe of darkest
green on dark. My need is such I pretend too much, I'm
wearing. And you're not listening to a word I say.

From our encounter with a variety of strenuous linguistic strategies, let us turn
now to the enchantingly lyrical early poem by Derek Walcott (b. 1930), "In a Green
Night," the title poem of a volume published in 1962. The title, of course, comes from
a line in Marvell's "Bermudas" (quoted earlier in this section). Both poems are in
iambic tetrameters. Marvell's is in couplets, with, in effect, ten four-line stanzas, while
Walcott's consists of eight four-line stanzas, rhyming *abab;* in neither poem is there any
enjambment between stanzas. Furthermore, each poem has a pair of framing—first
and last—stanzas. In short, the two poems have a deep formal affinity. As for the circumstances of the speaker vis-à-vis his poem, again there is a deep analogy: Marvell's
speakers deliberately compare their island home (England) to Bermuda ("an isle so
long unknown, / And yet far kinder than our own"), while Walcott, a native of St.
Lucia (in the chain of islands, once British and French colonies, called the Lesser
Antilles), deliberately imitates the formal structure of Marvell's poem while writing
about an Atlantic island thousands of miles to the northwest. And both poems celebrate the wonders of nature: Marvell's "eternal spring" and the "splendours" of Walcott's oranges.

There are, to be sure, important differences between the poems. Except for its
framing first and last quatrains Marvell's poem is supposed to be a song sung to the
rhythm of rowing by the oarsmen of a small boat; the song celebrates the natural wonders of Bermuda (and, ultimately, of nature's God). Oranges appear in just a single pair
of lines. Walcott's theme, on the other hand, is a celebration of the growth of oranges,
in terms of their changing color. And unlike Marvell's benevolent God (mentioned
only pronominally), the "cyclic chemistry" of these color changes is said to be
"strange"—referring, I believe, to the fact already noted earlier in this chapter, that the
color of the fruit on an orange tree depends on the surrounding temperature: cool
weather turns the fruit orange, warmer weather turns it green (though, of course, the
sun is necessary for the fruit to ripen in the first place). And, the poem adds, aging
mottles the skin of the fruit. All of this is summed up in the third and fourth stanzas:

> For if by night each golden sun
> Burns in a comfortable creed,
> By noon harsh fires have begun
> To quail those splendours which they feed.
>
> Or mixtures of the dew and dust
> That early shone her orbs of brass,
> Mottle her splendours with the rust
> She sought all summer to surpass.

The sixth stanza speaks of "the darkening fear that grieves / the loss of visionary rage" but the seventh, more hopefully, asserts that "Not the fierce noon or lampless night / Can quail the comprehending heart." So far, we have not considered the first or last stanza, each of which seems to encapsulate the "moral" of the poem. The two stanzas are in fact identical except for what seems like a small difference in the second line. The first stanza reads:

> The orange tree, in various light,
> Proclaims perfected fables now
> That her last season's summer height
> Bends from each overburdened bough.

The last stanza is the same except for the second line, which becomes "Proclaims that fable perfect now." In the first stanza the "fables" would seem to be the oranges themselves, but the singularity of "fable" in the altered line suggests that now it refers to something else, perhaps to the entire process of the growth and maturing of the oranges. Or, is the difference in the two lines just a slip?

The volume *In a Green Night* contains numerous poems which are "imitations" or "mimickings"—the differing connotation of the two terms is a crux for many critics —of poems or poets in the traditional English-language canon, and this has occasioned intense debate over the underlying politico-cultural issues. It would seem hard to deny that the poem "In a Green Night," in particular, constitutes a tribute to "Bermudas." What else can been said about the relation between the two poems? In a book on Walcott's poetry, Rei Terada says that "Walcott's lyric seems to reprove Marvell's by pointing out that religion, nature, and art alike are perishable." But here Terada seems to have misunderstood Marvell's phrase "eternal spring," which, given the poet's Christian beliefs, could hardly be intended to deny that religion, nature, and art are perishable. I would guess that the lines "this eternal spring / Which here enamels everything" are simply calling attention to the mild, subtropical climate of the Bermuda islands (warmed by the Gulf Stream) and, more specifically, to the simultaneous presence of blossoms and fruit on the same tree (recall the second section of this chapter, "Citrus Trees: Blossoms and Fruit"). As for the first and last stanzas of Walcott's poem, Terada suggests that these constitute a means for "enclosing the poem in a sphere (like an orange) inside which the body of the poem reveals mortal imperfection." But if Walcott is not attempting to rebut Marvell, why would he bother with such a trite theme as mortal imperfection? Furthermore, Terada gives no reason why Walcott's first and last stanzas are (slightly) different—another sign of mortal imperfection perhaps?

As further indication of the wide range of literary uses to which oranges can be put, here are some highly diverse twentieth-century episodes. In his foreword to an anthology of contemporary Hebrew poetry, published in 1938, Asher Barash compares the collection to an orange grove:

410

And it is indeed possible to view [this] book as the orange grove of our poetry, with its great and little trees, a grove whose earth is also covered with shrubs, flowers, and weeds. A spirit of sadness stalks the garden, and the gay sound of birdsong is heard there only seldom. But many are the paths of the orange grove, royal roads and side paths, mountain ranges and valleys, and it is full of breezes and pleasant odors, sights, and colors that take the breath away and that expand the mind.

In *Death of a Salesman* (1949), by Arthur Miller (b. 1915), there is a metaphorical orange in Willy Loman's desperate, near-hysterical speech in act 2, pleading not to be fired from his job with the firm where he has worked for thirty-four years: "You can't eat the orange and throw the peel away—a man is not a piece of fruit!" Most of the language of Miller's play is doggedly literal; in her dismissive review of the first New York production (1949), Eleanor Clark refers to "the colloquial but unimagized language of the play." Thus, Willy's orange metaphor comes as something of a surprise and yet its triteness only serves to reinforce our sense of his severely impoverished imagination.

In "Reasons for Happiness in San Francisco" (1989), Alistair Elliot begins his poem of some hundred lines like this:

> Breakfast can always be the same.
> The mind in the morning likes to hover
> Over its habits: food as happiness,
> Opening an orange as a form of power.

Next, consider the richly evocative poem "Oranges," by James Merrill (posthumously published in 1998). Like Sorrentino, Merrill plays with the entire range of associations of the term "orange": the odor (of orange blossoms), a kind of building (the Orangerie in Paris), an orange grove (with its vulnerability to cold), the fruit itself (taste, segmentation, juice, rind), a kind of cat (marmalade), the name of a military herbicide (Agent Orange). The poem consists of six iambic pentameter quatrains with the rhyme scheme *aaba* and its subject seems to be a youth's difficult childhood: in the first quatrain he is obsessed with a photograph of his mother wearing a crown of orange blossoms, which effectively distances her, "as in a fairy tale," from her child; in the last quatrain "the marmalade / Deathmask tomcat Agent Orange" leaves home after "Jim's"—his own?—death, and returns only when the period of mourning is over. In two of the four intervening quatrains the child's feeble attempts to gain his mother's love are matched with the losing struggles of a freezing orange to achieve maturity: "that sweetness just beneath the skin / A single night of frost undid"; "each night he lit / His sorry smudge-pot in the shivering grove." As we noted above, a frost will generally lower both the sugar and the acid content of an orange, while perhaps enhancing its orange color. The fifth stanza sounds like a final coming to terms with the child's own mortality:

Segment by segment, nonetheless a mind
Made up of taste and sunlight. May the blind
Gods who drink its juice be satisfied,
Disposing gently of the empty rind.

Gabriela Mistral used to tell an incident about herself involving *missing* oranges. Beginning in 1912, Mistral was teaching in a girls' school in Santiago, and in the patio of the school there was an orange tree. "Looking at it one day," in the words of her friend Margot de Vazquez, who heard Mistral tell the story, she "gave orders that not a single orange was to be touched. She wished to come every afternoon to delight in its beauty." But the next morning all the oranges are picked and then eaten for dessert at the school lunch; "late in the afternoon Gabriela returned to the garden and sat down facing the tree with the same rapture as on the preceding day. . . . The real tree had disappeared: in its place Gabriela kept seeing only the beautiful image of the orange tree with its golden, rounded fruit."

Mistral (as we have seen in chapters 4 and 12) loved children's poetry and poetry about children. "Oranges" (1985), by the American poet Gary Soto (b. 1952), is about an incident in the life of a twelve-year-old boy and is perhaps a poem for modern children. The speaker tells the story of his first date. He sets out with two oranges in his jacket and a nickel in his pocket. When his girl chooses some chocolate worth a dime, he has the wit to offer one orange plus the nickel to the saleslady, who silently accepts. And the poem ends:

I took my girl's hand
In mine for two blocks,
Then released it to let
Her unwrap the chocolate.
I peeled my orange
That was so bright against
The gray of December
That, from some distance,
Someone might have thought
I was making a fire in my hands.

I want to describe two pieces of art featuring oranges. The first is an enormous mixed-media collage on painted canvas backdrop (22 x 64 ft.) prepared by Alexis Smith (and assistants) to hang in the lobby of the Brooklyn Museum on the occasion of her retrospective in 1987. The work was called *Same Old Eden* and showed orange groves stretching away to distant hills. On the right-hand side was an orange-tree branch from which hung one immense orange together with orange blossoms; on the left-hand side was a road running back into the hills but becoming an immense coiled snake in the foreground. The orange—cultivated on a very large scale in southern California—has

412   been turned into the forbidden fruit. (For a picture of the painting, see Richard Armstrong's *Alexis Smith*.)

The second artwork, *Fanfare for an Orange* (2001), is a quilt (48 x 77 in.) consisting of twelve panels in a four-by-three grid representing successive stages in the peeling and consumption of an orange: the left uppermost panel depicts an orange sliced in half, while the right lowermost panel depicts only some orange peel. The quilter is Barbara Barrick McKie of Lyme, Connecticut, who is also a jewelry and clothing designer. The work, one of fifteen winners in an international contest sponsored by the Museum of Folk Art in New York City, is pictured in the Fall 2001 issue of *Folk Art* and described as "computer-altered images disperse dyed on polyester and hand-dyed silk; machine appliquéd, pieced, and quilted."

As a transition to literary lemons, I introduce "Drei Orangen, zwei Zitronen" (Three oranges, two lemons; 1953), by Karl Krolow (b. 1915). What one notices first about the poem is the way in which its first four strictly rhymed quatrains *(abac)* clash with the surrealistic imagery and syntax; and then there is the fifth (and last) stanza with its extra, unrhymed line. As to the rationale for introducing citrus fruits at all, their presence seems to derive from the so-called word problems used in teaching elementary algebra ("Suppose one buys three oranges and two lemons, and the oranges cost two-and-a-half times as much, etc., etc."). Mathematics is explicitly mentioned in the first and last stanzas (the following English translation is Patrick Bridgwater's):

> Drei Orangen, zwei Zitronen:—
> Bald nicht mehr verborg'ne Gleichung,
> Formeln, die die Luft bewohnen,
> Algebra der reifen Früchte!
>   [. . . . .]
> Drei Orangen, zwei Zitronen:—
> Mathematisches Entzücken,
> Mittagsschrift aus leichten Zonen!
> Zunge schweigt bei Zunge. Doch
> Alter Sinn gurrt wie ein Tauber.

~

Three oranges, two lemons—equation that will soon no longer be secret, formulae that dwell in the air, algebra of ripe fruits! . . .

Three oranges, two lemons—mathematical delight, midday-script from light zones! Tongue is silent by tongue. Yet old meaning coos like a cock-pigeon.

LEMONS

Let us look first at what might be termed a minimalist Spanish poem (untitled) about lemons: the fruit is simply present but utterly featureless—no golden color, no tangy odor, no sexy shape, no delicate blossoms. We are presented nevertheless with a vivid and unforgettable image set off by some conventional props in the form of a rose garden on the bank of a river, a singing nightingale, and a young woman gathering lemons (translated by J. M. Cohen):

> In the garden is born the rose. I want to go there to see the nightingale,
> how he sings.
>   On the banks of the river, the maiden gathers lemons. I want to go
> there, to see the nightingale, how he sings.
>   The maiden was gathering lemons to give to her love. I want to go
> there to see the nightingale, how he sings.
>   To give them to her love in a hat of silken stuff. I want to go there to
> see the nightingale, how he sings.

The author of this image of a young woman presenting to her lover a silken hat full of the lemons she has gathered is Gil Vicente (1465?–1537), a Portuguese dramatist, who wrote a few poems in Spanish.

Instead of a gift of lemons, an exchange: Philip Levine tells the story of how he traded his copy of T. S. Eliot's *Selected Poems* "for a pocket knife and two perfect lemons." The transaction took place in Genoa, where Levine had arrived by ship from Barcelona (a seaport located some two hundred miles north of the heart of Spanish citriculture). In the last lines of "The Trade," the traveler himself, with his lemony scent, becomes a "gift" to his fellow travelers:

> Two lemons, one
> for my pocket, one for my rucksack, perfuming
> my clothes, my fingers, my money, my hair,
> so that all the way to Rapallo on the train
> I would stand among my second-class peers, tall,
> angelic, an ordinary man become a gift.

Next, emphasizing the lemon's shape, the fourth of "Six Poems for Poetry Chicago," with its stress on the unfortunate shape of lemons (and with its unfortunate misuse of the apostrophe), by the San Francisco Renaissance writer Jack Spicer (1925–1965):

> The rind (also called the skin) of the lemon is difficult to understand
>   It goes around itself in an oval quite unlike the orange which, as anyone
> can tell, is a fruit easily to be eaten.
>   It can be crushed in canneries into all sorts of of extracts which are still not
> lemons. Oranges have no such fate. They're pretty much the same as they were.
> Culls become frozen orange juice. The best oranges are eaten.
>   It's the shape of the lemon, I guess that causes trouble. It's ovalness, it's rind.
>   This is where my love, somehow, stops.

414   And now a particularly haunting reference to the taste of lemons in a sonnet, "Delphica," first published in 1845, by Gérard de Nerval (1808–1855): the critical image is that of a woman biting a lemon, but the surrounding context, though containing some conventional props, is surpassingly rich and deep (the translation is by Peter Jay):

> Do you recognize, DAPHNE, the old refrain,
> At the sycamore's foot, by the white laurels, below
> The olive, myrtle or the trembling willow,
> The love-song . . . always starting up again!
>
> Remember the TEMPLE, its endless colonnade,
> The bitter lemons printed with your teeth?
> And, fatal to rash visitors, the cave
> Where sleeps the conquered dragon's ancient seed.
>
> They will come back, those gods you always mourn!
> Time will return the order of old days;
> The land has shivered with prophetic breath . . .
>
> Meanwhile the Sibyl with the latin face
> Still sleeps beneath the arch of Constantine:
> —And nothing has disturbed the austere porch.

~

> La connais-tu, DAFNÉ, cette ancienne romance,
> Au pied du sycamore, ou sous les lauriers blancs,
> Sous l'olivier, le myrthe ou les saules tremblants,
> Cette chanson d'amour . . . qui toujours recommence!
>
> Reconnais-tu le TEMPLE, au péristyle immense,
> Et les citrons amers où s'imprimaient tes dents?
> Et la grotte, fatale aux hôtes imprudents,
> Où du dragon vaincu dort l'antique semence.
>
> Ils reviendront ces dieux que tu pleures toujours!
> Le temps va ramener l'ordre des anciens jours;
> La terre a tressailli d'un souffle prophétique . . .
>
> Cependant la sibylle au visage latin
> Est endormie encor sous l'arc de Constantin:
> —Et rien n'a dérangé le sévère portique.

We are about to isolate for interpretation the sixth line of this sonnet—but as if such an apparent critical gaffe were not bad enough, the fact must be faced that this sonnet is the fifth in a sequence of twelve sonnets, on closely related themes, that Nerval published as *Les Chimères* in 1854 (though all of the sonnets were originally published separately during the decade prior to 1854, and in a chronological order bearing no significant relation to the order in *Les Chimères*). But then the sonnets are so resistant to interpretation that no approach should be ruled out in advance; or, in the words of Norma Rinsler in her 1973 edition, "The reader is . . . at liberty to invent his own sequence, or to follow Nerval's; indeed, he should do so, for no one account of these poems can claim to be definitive, and whatever the reader can bring to them in the way of relevant understanding will help to illuminate their mystery."

One characteristic of the sonnets that should be mentioned at the outset is their surface clarity: no esoteric diction, no twisted syntax. The difficulties arise because separate assertions, each of which is reasonably clear, are often simply juxtaposed with no evident clue as to how they are to be related. One might, for example, have thought that the meaning of the important term "chimeras" was reasonably clear (namely, illusion or error, either in love or in religion) but even here perplexities emerge when one realizes that these two types of chimera are not really distinct for Nérval, and also that, for him, chimeras may embody perfectly acceptable beliefs. (For a discussion, see Rinsler's *Les Chimères*.) Some admirers of the sonnets have been so repelled and frustrated by the sheer volume and apparent incoherence of the criticism initiated by the centenary of Nérval's death, in 1955, that they have proposed the extreme measure of avoiding all interpretation in favor of exclusive attention to the sheer sounds of the verse. The variety of interpretations is, indeed, daunting; one French critic has drawn up the following list of methodological approaches adopted by different interpreters: occultism (alchemy, astrology, and the Tarot), esotericism (history and bibliography), spiritual symbolism (religious myths), crypto-psychology, and literary (Jungian) psychoanalysis. Perhaps no interpreter would disagree, but it is still worth citing Rinsler's emphasis on the importance of the intimate interaction among *all* the words and images in a given sonnet, an interaction "reinforced by the limited compass of the sonnet form, which enables the elements of the poem to make their effect on the reader almost simultaneously."

To turn now to "Delphica": grammatically, the two quatrains are interrogatory, while the two tercets are declarative, with the latter pair obliquely answering the former. The questions are being asked not *by* Daphne but *of* Daphne. Who is asking the questions? One interpretor, J. W. Kneller, identifies her as "'Delfica,' a priestess invented by the author." Questions and answers taken together express a kind of nostalgia for the vanished ancient world, evoked by allusions to Daphne, a colonnaded temple, the dragon in a cave, the gods, a Sibyl, and the arch of Constantine. But something important, perhaps even essential, associated with that vanished world—a love song—persists; or—which is not at all the same thing—it begins again and again (and is perhaps never concluded?). What must be added is that Daphne is physically present only in the sixth line of the sonnet, through her act of biting some bitter lemons. Now, Richard

416   Holmes—who says, "The line has always fascinated me, and I have thought about it for years"—like a jazz musician plays some riffs on that sixth line.

First, Holmes translates the line: "And the bitter lemons bitten/printed/punctured by your teeth," and comments that "the image arrives with a clean, sharp physical impact. You can almost taste it. You can certainly hear it, with its sudden little moaning rhyme, coming unexpectedly from the inside (but invisible to the naked English eye!)—*citrons/dents*. [Norma Rinsler says, in her edition of *Les Chimères*, that "the consonants seem to bite into the fruit."] But the sensation is complicated—bitterness and lusciousness combined, desire and regret."

Next, Holmes remarks that lemons and teeth have specific symbolic meanings in various folkloric and mythological traditions. Generally speaking, lemons stand for "the powers of life and healing" and teeth stand for "some kind of talisman, linked with luck and fortune, and especially with the sexual appetite." Then, after adducing further associations of Daphne with the return of the Golden Age, Holmes traces the image of a woman biting into a lemon back to two earlier writings by Nérval. The first of these writings is a letter of November 1834 to his friend Théophile Gautier, in which Nérval mentions two details concerning a sea voyage he took from Naples to Marseilles: meeting a very pretty woman on the ship and carrying a suitcase containing two lemons. This incident is then elaborated during the years 1842 to 1854 into Nérval's story "Octavie," of which Holmes translates this pertinent passage: "The young English woman was on the bridge, pacing up and down with rapid strides. As if impatient with the slow progress of the ship, she bit into the flesh of a lemon with her ivory-white teeth." There is the further detail, as noted by Norma Rinsler, that "the scene of the poet's encounter with Octavie is set largely in and near Naples, where the legendary tomb of Virgil stands under a laurel tree on Posilipo"—the laurel being, of course, associated with Daphne.

Derek Walcott, in his "Sunday Lemons" (1976), uses "Desolate lemons" with their "acid silence" to express the nuances of a "woman's remembering / Sundays of other fruit." The poem is a stylistic marvel, consisting of a single sentence winding its way through eleven three-line, three-stress stanzas. There are numerous rhymes and near-rhymes at the ends of lines ("glare/armour," "apples/waxen," "bees/sweetness," "demands/candles," "damp/lamp"), as well as numerous internal rhymes, and a proliferation of l's in the last stanza:

> of the evening that blurs
> the form of this woman lying,
> a lemon, a flameless lamp.

Lemony traits alluded to in the poem include taste ("bitter flesh"), optical reflectivity ("lemon glare," "inflexible light"), and shape ("phalanx of helmets"). The Sunday lemons somehow provide illumination "as the afternoon vagues / into indigo," mysteriously constituting "still life, but a life / beyond tears or the gaieties / of dew."

The most tenuous literary allusion to lemons I know of is Abraham Cowley's love poem "Written in Juice of Lemmon" (1647). The conceit here is that Cowley is writing with invisible ink, requiring heat to make the words appear; the source of the heat is then identified successively with the fire of the last judgment, the fire in which heretics are burned, the fire of love, the fire of the sun, and the fire that may consume the actual piece of paper on which the poem is written. More modest and less extravagant than some of Cowley's other metaphysical efforts, the poem is written in an easy and informal style, as the first three (of eight) stanzas show:

> Whilst what I write I do not see,
> I dare thus, even to *you,* write *Poetry.*
> Ah foolish Muse, which do'st so high aspire,
> And know'st her judgment well
> How much it does thy power excel,
> Yet dar'st be read by, thy just doom, the *Fire.*

> Alas, thou think'st thy self secure,
> Because thy form is *Innocent* and *Pure:*
> Like *Hypocrites,* which seem unspotted here;
> But when they sadly come to dye,
> And the last *Fire* their Truth must try,
> *Scrauld* o're like thee, and *blotted* they appear.

> Go then, but reverently go,
> And, since thou needs must *sin, confess* it too:
> Confess't, and with humility clothe thy shame;
> For thou, who else must burned be
> An *Heretick,* if she pardon thee,
> May'st like a *Martyr* then *enjoy* the *Flame.*

Undercutting—or, better, ignoring—most of the usual associations of citrus fruits, Alain Bosquet (1919–1998) composed a pair of parallel poems about lemons in an early collection called *Master Object* (1962). The book is divided into three sections: "Slave Objects," "Fellow-Creatures," and "Free Objects." The twelve "objects" of the first and last sections are identical, consisting of, in order: trees, stools, horsewhips, lemons, news, nothings, boots, saxophones, lamps, waterfalls, hummingbirds, and telephones; while the eleven "objects" of the middle section include "In the neuter," "In the imperative," "In the passive," and "In the collective." The very titles tell us that Bosquet is attempting to break down—or ignore—conventional distinctions between animate and inanimate objects or between concrete objects and abstractions. Now, at first glance this seems also to be the modus operandi of Francis Ponge in *his* prose poems about things. But how close really are Ponge's *choses* and Bosquet's *objects*?

We may take it for granted that before Bosquet published his own "object" poems (in 1962) he knew Ponge's "thing" poems, which had been published twenty years earlier (in 1942); there is also a twenty-year difference in their ages. It would be surprising if Bosquet were not attempting something quite different from Ponge. Briefly, we know that Ponge speaks of "la qualité différentielle," a phrase which has been interpreted by Ian Higgins, in his edition of Ponge's *Le Parti pris des choses,* as "the essential difference . . . which gives a particular thing its individuality." Such an "essential difference"—even when it is relativized by Ponge in terms of the particular set of things with which the targeted thing is compared—is foreign to Bosquet. Thus, in a brief preface to his book, Bosquet begins by saying, "Everything is permitted the imagination, which is not embarrassed by meanings. I therefore invent an origin of the world, peopled by objects." I think it would be fair to say that Ponge *discovers* and Bosquet *invents* (though such a simple formula will not take us very far in understanding their respective poems).

Our next question is whether, for Bosquet, there can be any intrinsic difference between slave objects and free objects; more specifically, between slave lemons and free lemons. Formally, the lemon poems are identical, each consisting of four quatrains, rhymed *abab* (the first translated by Susan Alliston, the second by Edward Lucie-Smith):

> Tonight the moon is carnivorous,
> And the lemons are quarreling.
> Six dead already! Who mourns them?
> The medlar rots at the core.
>
> To be the pulp, the citrus?
> An archipelago hatches the fruits
> Of its shipwreck. A fox sniffs
> A sacred mango. Demolished,
>
> All the gardens! The sun stays
> In its room, playing poker . . .
> Is this why the rind, the pith,
> Will be green even in November?
>
> Tonight the moon is an apple;
> Cannibal, it has the right
> To take on a human fate.
> And the lemons shake with cold.

> ～

> Lemon looks and lemon faces,
> They have suffered, they have loved,

> They live in the neighbourhood.
> Larynx lemons, they have mimicked
>
> Man until they're human now,
> Bourgeois lemons wearing suits,
> Very solemn ones who're called
> Q.C. lemons. What alibi,
>
> Vertebrate lemons, what excuse?
> Notary object, tailor object,
> A fruit argues, a fruit is busy
> Inventing itself a better fate.
>
> OK! We will take your place
> On the lemon-tree; you'll be us,
> And we'll be hanged. Boldness
> Will favour you, lemon knees.

("Q.C." means "Queen's Counsel"—a very "solemn" position.) The most obvious difference between the two poems is that the "slave" poem is dominated by allusions to fruit—the pulp, the rind, the pith of the lemons themselves, as well as short episodes involving a rotting medlar, a sacred mango, and a lunar apple—whereas the "free" poem is dominated by allusions to human beings. But in both cases, the lemons can communicate: as enslaved, they can quarrel; while as free they can negotiate "a better fate": "you'll be us, / And we'll be hanged." Appropriately enough, the last glimpse we have of the enslaved lemons finds them shaking with cold, while the last glimpse we have of the free lemons finds them favored with, or by, boldness.

In a trilogy of later volumes of poems, Bosquet reconfigures the field of objects and subjects: the former are now auxiliary to the presentation of the latter. In the first of these volumes, *Cent notes pour une solitude* (One hundred notes for a solitude, 1970), the subject (in William Frawley's words) is "a simple *agent* (that is, someone whose sole aspect is 'the doing of things') as a unique, observable participant in situations which ostensibly demand his interaction with objects and animals." The poems are written in the third person singular ("il"); the two succeeding volumes are, respectively, in the second person singular ("tu") and the first person plural ("nous"). Lemon trees are important in this untitled poem from the first volume (translated by Frawley):

> He would give orders
> to the old hired sun.
> He would be the monarch of typhoons.
> The best lemon trees [Les meilleurs citronniers]
> would offer him their dreams [songes].
> But no lunacy

runs to seed!
He will be sentenced to become a mask.

Prévert, as we have seen, invokes oranges and tangerines in his celebration of consummated love; in contrast, among the early poems of Miguel Hernández are classical sonnets, featuring citrus fruits, about the pains of unconsummated love. The opening lines of two of these sonnets, in Spanish and in Robert Bly's English, demonstrate this connection: "Me tiraste un limón, y tan amargo [You threw me a lemon, oh it was sour]"; "Tu corazó, una naranja helada [Your heart?—it is a frozen orange]." The first of these sonnets has been translated into English by many authors; of the three versions with which I am familiar, Edwin Honig's is somewhat woodenly literal, Willis Barnstone' is far too free for my taste though it preserves the rhyme scheme, and Robert Bly's—which I prefer, with reservations—is fluent but closely rendered. I think it should be of considerable interest from the point of view of the theory and practice of translation to compare these versions with one another and back against the original Spanish.

Hernández:

> Me tiraste un limón, y tan amargo,
> con una mano cálida, y tan pura,
> que no menoscabó su arquitectura
> y probé su amargura sin embargo.
> Con el golpe amarillo, de un letargo
> dulce pasó a una ansiosa calentura
> mi sangre, que sintió la mordedura
> de una punta de seno duro y largo.
> Pero al mirarte y verte la sonrisa
> que te produjo el limonado hecho,
> a mi voraz malicia tan ajena,
> se me durmió la sangre en la camisa,
> y se volvió el poroso y áureo pecho
> una picuda y deslumbrante pena.

Bly:

> You threw me a lemon, oh it was sour,
> with a warm hand, that was so pure
> it never damaged the lemon's architecture.
> I tasted the sourness anyway.
> With that yellow blow, my blood moved
> from a gentle laziness into an anguished
> fever, for my blood felt the bite
> from a long and firm tip of a breast.

Yet glancing at you and seeing the smile
which that lemon-colored event drew from you,
so far from my dishonorable fierceness,
my blood went to sleep in my shirt,
and the soft and golden breast turned
to a baffling pain with a long beak.

Honig:

Your hand that tossed me such a bitter lemon
was so warm and was so pure,
it did not mar the architecture,
and yet I tasted all its bitterness.
One yellow nip and my blood switched
from sweet and slow to racing hot
and writhing. The big hard pointed teat
had bitten me straight back.
When glancing up to catch your smile,
innocent of my sly voracity,
at my lemonry in action,
I felt the blood slump in my vest,
and all that porous golden breast
became a sharp and dazzling pain.

Barnstone:

You threw a lemon at me so austere
and bitter, with your hand of warmth so pure,
it hardly shattered its architecture
as I explored its bitterness so near.
Stunned with a yellow blow of lethargy
and softly slipping into anguished heat,
my blood experienced the sudden bite
of a hard breast, a nipple large and free.
And as I looked at you and saw your smile
that gave you meadows of a lemon nest,
my blood fell dead asleep under my shirt,
paralyzed far from my voracious bile.
Then entering my pocked and golden chest
came pain, a pointed glow beyond all hurt.

We might begin by listing some of the extra words in Barnstone's version, none
of which corresponds to a word in the Spanish: "austere" (not really a metaphorical

422 correlate of "bitter"), "free," "meadows," "nest," and "beyond." Three of these additions supply rhymes, but, more deeply, all five seem to reflect Barnstone's attempt to intensify the surrealistic tendencies of the poem, in accord with his view that "the mixture of formalism and extravagantly fantastic imagery that is Góngora is found almost uniquely in Hernández's rigorously formal sonnets with their fantastic and surreal images." On the other hand, Barnstone's "glow" and Honig's "dazzling" for *deslumbrante* seem more accurate than Bly's "baffling," while the challenge of perhaps the most fantastic fruit image in the poem—*el limonado hecho*—is met in interestingly different ways: "lemon-colored event"; "lemonry in action"; "meadows of a lemon nest."

Hernández grew up in the province of Alicante in southeastern Spain, an area of large-scale citriculture; he also died in Alicante, as a political prisoner in one of Franco's jails. Italy's greatest twentieth-century poet, Eugenio Montale (1896–1981), spent his early years in and around Genoa on the shores of the Ligurian Sea, where he would have seen citrus trees growing (though, of course, the main citrus-producing region in Italy is much further south, in Sicily, which has the same latitude as Alicante). Furthermore, we know there was a greenhouse on the grounds of the Montale family villa (see the account by Montale's sister, Marianna, quoted in Jonathan Galassi's *Eugenio Montale: Collected Poems, 1920–1954* [1998]), where citrus trees might have been cultivated. In any case, Montale wrote two important poems about lemons: the earlier, "I limoni" (The lemon trees, or The lemons; 1922), published in his first volume of poetry, *Cuttlefish Bones* (1925), and the later, "Nella serra" (In the greenhouse; 1945), published in what many critics see as his culminating volume of poetry, *The Storm and Other Things* (1956).

I should begin by explaining that in my comments on Montale's lemon poems I shall be relying on—in addition to the Italian text—three English translations of each poem: those by Irma Brandeis, William Arrowsmith, and Jonathan Galassi for the earlier poem, and those by James Merrill, Arrowsmith, and Galassi for the later one. Both Arrowsmith and Galassi copiously annotate their respective translations and I have also consulted a half-dozen books on Montale's poetry by other critics. I make no pretense of providing a full interpretation of either poem—at best, just a few prolegomena to such an interpretation.

Consistent with my usual approach to literary fruit episodes, I will focus on the lemons (or lemon trees: *limoni* has both meanings). All critics seem to agree that the earlier poem is, in Galassi's phrase, "about poetics," presumably an immediate deduction from the allusion to the rejected "i poeti laureati" (the poets laureate) in the very first line of the poem. Now, I do not want for a moment to question this assumption; I only want to emphasize that the poem is, after all, *also* about lemons and other elements of Montale's youthful environment, such as eels.

Let us look more closely at both the syntactic positioning and the semantic charge of the lemons in Montale's poem. The phrase *dei limoni* (of the lemon trees, or of the lemons) occurs in the first, second, and last of the four stanzas of "I limoni"; furthermore, the phrase terminates each of the first two stanzas. Of the three translators, only Brandeis conveys this thrice-repeated syntax in her English version (though once she replaces "of the lemon trees" with "of the lemon blaze"); Arrowsmith twice translates "of the lemon trees" and once "among the lemon trees," while Galassi twice translates "of the lemons" and once "among the lemon trees." Some commentators see the lemons as transformed in meaning during the course of the poem, but the critical terms in which these transformations are formulated differ widely. Thus, Glauco Cambon characterizes the strategic location of *limoni,* in its first two occurrences, as follows:

> The two preceding stanzas ended on the word "limoni" (lemons), an identical rhyme well attuned to the happily literal drift of the first half of the poem: it's as if the rhyme said, just by being there, that lemons are lemons and nothing else, nor do they need to be anything else, for their significance is in their reality, in their presence.

The final presence of *limoni,* in the fourth stanza, Cambon supposes to be accompanied by a major shift in the meaning of lemons:

> By contrast, the "Divinità-solarità" rhyme of the last two stanzas introduces a semantic swerve into the unpredictable; even if it is "illusion" (as the first line of stanza 4 says), the epiphany favored by the twilight's silence and lemon aroma, which activate the mind in a contemplative direction, suspending the quotidian, will have given us a spiritual break, and we shall then be able to recognize the fullness of reality ("solarità") without having recourse to mere "shadows."

For another critic, Joseph Cary, Montale first "opposes his personal emblem, the *limoni* discovered in a humble truck-garden, to the official boutonnières involving laurel, privet, acanthus." Later, the *limoni* become "a talisman affording a glimmer of another order of reality at certain unpremeditated occasions," and "the significance of what originally seemed a 'literary' choice . . . has come to have extraordinary 'metaphysical' implications."

Finally, Claire Huffman rejects any idea of a temporal development in the poem:

> The moments in the poem are not sequential; they are different approaches to a central problem. The whole poem breaks down, then, into a series of tentative approaches to the exceptional objects, a series of almost entirely discrete variations: the walk of the first stanza and the movement of sensations and mind in the two long central stanzas, in which the poet attempts to quell his ultimately undefined emotions, to replace them by sensations, chiefly of smell, and to arrive at the essential meaning of the lemons by transcending these sensations. . . .
>
> "I limoni" is, finally, an "adventure" in language and not in life, as the first stanza suggests it will be: the lemons cause the release of sensations that are semantic as much as physical.

Let us examine the smell of Montale's lemons more closely. In the second stanza, the lemons' odor (*odore*) is marvelously characterized: "this odor / inseparable from earth, / and rains an unquiet sweetness in the breast" (Brandeis); "that smell / inseparable from earth, / that rains its restless sweetness in the heart" (Arrowsmith); "this smell / that can't divorce itself from earth / and rains a restless sweetness on the heart" (Galassi). Later in the stanza, we are told that "here"—presumably among the orchards of lemon trees referred to at the end of the first stanza—"even we the poor share the riches of the world— / the smell [*odore*] of the lemon trees" (Arrowsmith). (Poor in what sense, we want to ask, but I have yet to discover where we might turn for an answer.) In the third stanza, lemons go unmentioned but their "perfume [*profumo*] that gets diffused [*dilaga*]" (Galassi) is also subtly diffused into the entire stanza. This stanza is the one Cambon calls "epistemologically oriented," and, in it, inhaling the lemons' perfume in the silence of the orchard, we "see / in every fleeting human / shadow some disturbed Divinity" (Galassi). But this stab at transcendence is immediately cancelled when we are told in the opening lines of the last stanza that "the illusion fails" as we return to the quotidian reality of "noisy cities," "winter's tedium," and "miserly" light (Galassi). Finally, there is yet another turn in the dialectic of the poem, for (in Galassi's translation),

> one day through a half-shut gate
> in a courtyard, there among the trees,
> we can see the yellow of the lemons;
> and the chill in the heart
> melts, and deep in us
> the golden horns of sunlight
> pelt their songs.

Now, it is the color of the lemons rather than their odor that—recalling a phrase of the second stanza—"by some miracle" (*per miracolo*) warms the heart; the nature of this warmth demands explication and yet the lines resist close reading.

Compared with "The Lemon Trees," Montale's later lemon poem, "In the Greenhouse," is shorter, more compressed, and equally cryptic. Lemon trees (lemons) occur in the second line (*limonaia*) and the last line (*limoni*). Here are three English versions of the first stanza (in chronological order of publication):

Merrill:

> A pattering of moles
> filled up the lemon trees,
> in a rosary of cautious drops
> the scythe was glittering.

Arrowsmith:

> Filling the lemon tree,
> a skittering of mole paws.

> The sickle glistened, a rosary
> of cautious waterbeads.

Galassi:

> The lemon-house was being over-
> ridden by the moles' stampedes.
> The scythe shone in a rosary
> of wary waterbeads.

Notice that the three translators do not even agree on the number of lemon trees: for Merrill, there are many; for Arrowsmith, one; and for Galassi, presumably many—at least if a lemon-house is, like an orangery, devoted to cultivating citrus trees. A related question is how moles—famous for their earth-burrowing proclivities—can be pattering or skittering in trees at all; stampeding in the lemon-house makes more zoological sense. And this is confirmed in a prose translation of the first stanza (1986) by F. J. Jones, where *limonaia* becomes a "lemon grove": "The lemon grove was filled with a pattering of moles' feet."

Arrowsmith's and Galassi's versions include (like Montale's Italian) a pair of rhyming lines, but Merrill's version, without any rhymes, comes off better as a piece of poetry in its own right. It is likely that moles, lemon trees, and scythe, as well as the greenhouse setting, are among the concrete elements with which, in Galassi's words, "Montale returns to familial and childhood scenes, possibly with the aim of reinforcing values he sees as threatened in the postwar world." Montale seems to want to have it both ways: the drops of water on a scythe are, after all, only a quasi-rosary and yet, as Galassi suggests, "the image here immediately opens the scene to transcendent experience."

Looking now at the last major image of the poem—godhead descending (*Dio discendeva*)—we note first of all how this is expressed in the very enjambment of Montale's verse, as the words fall down the page, starting with the last two words of the third stanza, right on through to the isolated single line ("su me, su te, sui limoni . . .") fading out in an ellipsis, which ends the poem. All this is clear enough in all three translations:

Merrill:

> and the obscure
>
> idea of God descended
> upon the few living, among
> celestial soundings and infant drummings
> and hanging spheres of lightnings,
>
> upon me, and you, and the lemon trees . . .

Arrowsmith:

>   and the dark
>
>   idea of God descended
>   on the living few, sounds of heaven
>   all around, cherubic drummings,
>   globes of lightning hovering
>
>   over me, over you, over the lemons . . .

Galassi:

>   and the dark idea of God
>
>   descended on the living few
>   to celestial tones
>   and children's drums
>   and globes of lightning strung above
>
>   the lemons, and me, and you . . .

Among these versions, Galassi's perhaps stands out, though there may be some question about one of his trade-offs, which rhymes "few" with "you" at the expense of not ending the poem (as Montale does) with lemons. Again, though Montale reaches for the transcendent, it is at one crucial remove—not God but only the idea (*pensiero*) of God descends, and descends into a setting which is only quasi-religious, with its toy drums and lighted globes. That this divine descent touches the lemons equally with the merged lovers is certainly being affirmed, and yet Montale seems to leave unresolved his delicate balancing of the secular and the sacred. Thus, while it seems clear that there is, in Arrowsmith's words, "divine irradiation of the everyday object" and that, in Galassi's words, "the full experience of existence . . . is touched with divinity," it is not at all clear that anything like the reverse is also true; specifically, we need not credit Arrowsmith's "heavenly yearning of the earth-born lemons." Finally, one must wonder about the relationship between "the living few" of "In the Greenhouse" and "we the poor" of "The Lemon Trees." Or, to put it another way, is there any politics of lemons in Montale?

"Lemon" (1979), by Mario Satz (b. 1944)—born in Buenos Aires and now living in Israel—is a Spanish poem (translated by Willis Barnstone) that makes use of what may superficially appear to be some of the same images as Montale's two lemon poems but with entirely different effects. As for the images, there is the association of lemons with the sun (the last word of Montale's "I limoni" is *solarità*) and the quasi-religious exaltation of the lemon (though in "I limoni" the lemons' color melts the "chill in the heart," while, for Satz, the lemon's odor is "icy"):

> A lemon is a proof of faith, of faith in the sun;
>> and that aroma shot out with a burst of wind,
> a burst of seabreeze, a burst of muttering between hills,
>> is the lemon's voice talking to us.
> We ought to dance under the lemon tree's icy perfume

Like Montale, Satz ignores the taste of lemons but, unlike Montale, he alludes to their shape and texture:

> We ought to dance with our heart turned outward like the
>> lemon's navel, with its pores open during the day,
> closed at night; and we ought to see ourselves dancing!

Montale's lemon poems—and, of course, virtually all of his poetry—are evocative rather than assertive; Satz's "Lemon" is the reverse.

Another attempt to invest lemons with cosmic significance is by the American writer, editor, and translator of poetry, Clayton Eshleman (b. 1935), in his "Lemons" (1983). Before discussing the poem, we might look briefly at a kind of manifesto for Eshleman's approach to poetry formulated by Eliot Weinberger—himself a distinguished translator of poetry—in the introduction to a volume of Eshleman's poems selected from his many dozens of books, *The Name Encanyoned River* (1986). According to Weinberger, four things must—or should —characterize poetry today: first, "The poem is a becoming, not a being; and the poem, breaking out of its isolation, can no longer be contained by the traditional forms"; second, "the poem must be open to everything, and moreover . . . everything must come into the poem"; third, "A macrocosm without microcosm: in the poem all ages are contemporaneous, all events synchronous, each thing is itself and the metaphor of something else"; and last, "the poem has lost the language that speaks it" and "the poet must either wrestle the language back to (a temporary) meaning or surrender to meaninglessness, perhaps even revel in meaninglessness."

All four characteristics are clearly present in Eshleman's "Lemons." The poem begins with local and idiosyncratic detail: "These lovely freaks, skins / pulled tight about inner disturbance"—the opening lines of the first stanza. (Stanzaic form is one aspect of traditional poetry never eschewed by Eshleman.) In the third stanza, the local suddenly becomes "cosmic":

> Some are peaked like elves' shoes,
> Aladdin slippers, as the arabesque
> of cosmic charge tips
>> instead of curling on
>> into a seamless sphere

Continuing to quote the lines I like best, I conclude with the last two stanzas:

> It is good to be on earth.

Two fresh slit lemon halves
draw my heart out of its hiding heart space

Enter the mind of a lemon
the sweetness of rock
the soul of things that speak
only in the interface of us and them

The politically fraught lemons, apparently absent in Montale—and also in Satz and Eshleman—may be found in "Medicine," by Piotr Sommer (b. 1948), written in 1981–82, just after the imposition of martial law in Poland (and here translated by Stanislaw Baranczak and Clare Cavanagh):

I saw a real lemon again.
Ania brought it back from France.
She'd been wondering: come home or stay abroad?
And come to think of it, what keeps her here—
a few faces, a few words, this anxiety?
The lemon was yellow, it looked like the real thing.
You didn't have to put it in the window
to ripen alongside our pale tomatoes.
Or as we ourselves ripen
growing up and growing yellow over years.
No, it was already entirely itself
when she brought it, not even yellow, but gold,
and a little rough,
so I took it gratefully.
I want to wrap myself in the thick skin of the world,
I want to be tart, but good-tasting—
some child swallows me reluctantly
and I help to cure his cold.

What was it that Ania really brought back from France? Presumably, a taste of something long missing in Poland (freedom of expression?); and the poet wonders whether he can "grow up" not in the sense of growing yellow—which in human terms is associated with illness and death—but in the sense of becoming tough enough (thick-skinned), critical enough (tart), and persuasive enough (tasty) to serve as a worthy model for the younger generation.

In another poem by Sommer featuring a lemon, "Potatoes," the supreme power of imagination is again being celebrated, but not to the exclusion of recalcitrant reality (here translated by the poet himself and Charles Mignon):

My son won't write a poem about a coconut.
I'm running out of words myself.

> Still, if he wanted to paint a picture
> with the texture of a ripe orange,
> then by all means: let him get hold of a golden lemon,
> and in a wink a warm wind
> the colour of the setting sun will clothe it in a dress.
> Imagination, mother of our life,
> waft us more and more improbable landscapes!

To depict an orange, Sommer is saying, one can't start with potatoes or coconuts—not just any random metamorphosis will work—but a lemon might do for a starting point, provided one adds the proper transforming conditions ("a warm wind" and "the setting sun"). And the poet invokes the imagination with its promise of more and more "improbable" metamorphoses.

Unlike his odes to the apple and to the orange (which have been discussed earlier), Neruda's "Oda al limón" (Ode to the lemon, 1957) is resolutely apolitical and purely aesthetic in its appreciation of the lemon. The emphasis is on the shape of the fruit (compared successively to a house, a cathedral, a goblet, and a nipple), on its color (yellow, topaz, gold) and on its savor (in Margaret Peden's translation, "the most intense liqueur / of nature"). All these sensuous elements are present together in the final stanza, which begins not with a metaphor but with the everyday experience of squeezing some lemon juice onto something one is about to eat:

> So, when you hold
> the hemisphere
> of a cut lemon
> above your plate,
> you spill
> a universe of gold,
> a
> yellow goblet
> of miracles,
> a fragrant nipple
> of the earth's breast,
> a ray of light that was made fruit,
> the minute fire of a planet.

In his "Lemon Ode" (1980), "for Neruda," the American poet James Galvin ignores the physical qualities of lemons (until his penultimate line) and attends instead to their toughness and assertiveness, as in the first and last of six stanzas:

> Charmless and strange
> At the same time,
> The lemon can be opened
> To interpretations,

> Can encourage dispute,
> Ignore abuse, absolve itself
> From doubt.
> (Never doubt the lemon!)
>   [. . . . .]
> The lemon, as it burns, overflows.
> The lemon, which is sour,
> Makes demands.

Neruda's slice of lemon, which can have a transforming effect on food, is used with similarly piquant results in an untitled love poem (1930), by Fernando Pessoa (translated by James Greene and Clara de Azevedo Mafra):

> She brings the surprise of being.
> She is tall, of a dark blond.
> It does good only to think of seeing
> Her almost ripe body.
>
> If she lay down,
> Her high breasts would seem
> Two little hills which dawn
> Without need for twilight.
>
> And the hand is spread—
> Her white arm's fief—
> On the salience of a flank
> Of her clothed relief.
>
> Enticing as a boat;
> Like a piece of lemon [*gomo*, segment of orange or lemon].
> When, God, shall I embark?
> When, hunger, eat?

Keith Bosley's translation of the poem, incidentally, ignoring the citrus connotations of *gomo*, includes this version of the final stanza:

> As inviting as a boat,
> Like a fruit she glistens sweet.
> God, when shall I be afloat?
> Hunger, when am I to eat?

Until the twentieth century, children in more northern climes might have first encountered lemons and oranges in nursery rhymes (especially if fresh fruit was considered unhealthy for the young); in England, for instance, there was "The Bells of

London" with its opening lines: "Oranges and lemons, / Say the bells of St Clement's." And in the mid–twentieth century, for those fortunate enough to be acquainted with the children's verse of Eleanor Farjeon, there was "Oranges and Lemons":

> Oranges bright as the sun!
> Lemons as pale as the moon!
> Here they come, one after one,
> All to be harvested soon.
> Under the arch they go flinging,
> Bursting with laughter and singing
> With all the town bell-ringers ringing and swinging their tune.
>
> Candles and bed-time are near—
> Look! we have caught you, my dear,
> Now whisper low in my ear
> Which one will *you* be, which one?
> A lemon as pale as the moon and as clear,
> Or an orange as bright as the sun?
> *Don't let the other ones hear!*
>
> Now once again they go swinging,
> Swinging and springing along,
> And all the town steeples are ringing and flinging and
>   singing their song!

Lemons occupy an important place in the tradition of seventeenth-century Dutch *pronk* (sumptuous) still life painting, specifically in those concerned with food (see Sam Segal's *A Prosperous Past: The Sumptuous Still Life in the Netherlands, 1600–1700* [1988]). Svetlana Alpers, in her book *The Art of Describing* (1983), explains:

> Consider the lemon, one of the favored objects of Dutch vision. Its representation characteristically maximizes surface: the peel is sliced and unwound to reveal a glistening interior from which a seed or two is frequently discarded to one side. In the hands of Willem Kalf, particularly, the lemon offers a splendid instance of what I have termed division. The representation of the wrinkled gold of its mottled surface, with the peel here pitted, there swelling, loosened from the flesh and sinuously extended, totally transforms the fruit. We have never seen a lemon in this way before.

Alpers is alluding to Kalf's *Still Life with a Nautilus Goblet* (1660); for a black and white reproduction of the painting, see Alpers's book; for a color reproduction, see Schneider, *Still Life,* or Segal, *A Prosperous Past.*)

432   In 1864, Edouard Manet painted his *Still Life with Fish,* now in the Art Institute of Chicago, including oysters on the left and a lemon next to a knife on the right (oil on canvas, 28⅞ x 36¼ in.). The composition of the work derives from that of a still life by Chardin (see Charles S. Moffett, *Manet: 1832–1883* [1983]), and the presence of the lemon clearly reflects the practice of eating oysters with lemon juice. Later still life episodes by Manet include lemons with unwound peelings, such as *Still Life with Salmon* (1866) and *The Luncheon in the Studio* (1968), reminding one of Dutch still lifes of the seventeenth century. (For a reproduction of the first of these paintings, see Georges Bataille, *Manet* [1955]; for a reproduction of the second, see Bataille's *Manet* or *Manet: 1832–1883.*) The fascinating thing is that Manet had also begun to introduce lemons into portraits, such as that of Zacharie Astruc (1866; oil on canvas, 35½ x 45¾ in., Kunsthalle, Bremen), where in the still life cluster of books at the lower left there is a lemon with unwound peeling and a water goblet. The two latter items represent, according to Françoise Cachin, "an early instance of a Manet leitmotiv and a direct reference to Dutch still life, seemingly without special reference to Astruc" (who, incidentally, was primarily a writer at the time of the portrait, though he later became a well-known sculptor). Another portrait, *Woman with a Parrot* (1866), now in the Metropolitan Museum of Art in New York, repeats the lemon peel motif, which appears at the bottom of the parrot's perch near the woman's feet (oil on canvas, 72⅞ x 50⅝ in.). Finally, at the end of his life, Manet painted a single lemon now in the Musée D'Orsay, Paris (1880, oil on canvas, 5½ x 8¼ in.). (For reproductions of the last three paintings see *Manet: 1832–1883.*) All of Manet's lemons, according to Cachin, should be be understood "both as a signature—introducing an accent of color that progressively becomes an element in the oeuvre—and as a celebration of two guiding traditions, Flemish [Dutch?] painting and Spanish painting."

It is almost as if in response to the sumptuousness of those Dutch and French painted lemons that the American artist Donald Sultan (b. 1951) created his famous black lemons, where the volume, texture, and color of the fruit are all eliminated, leaving only the two-dimensional contour. (See, for example, *Black Lemon* [1984], pastel on paper, 50 x 48 in., in the Dunkin Donuts collection, Randolph, Mass., reproduced in *Art What Thou Eat,* ed. Linda Weintraub [1991].)

GRAPEFRUITS AND LIMES

The United States is now, perhaps uniquely in the world (certainly in the northern hemisphere), a land of citrus fruit, with many species and many varieties easily available throughout the country and throughout the year. The United States produces 15 percent of the world's oranges, 3 percent of its tangerines, 9 percent of its lemons and limes, and 50 percent of its grapefruit and pomelos. (The last figure is particularly surprising.) This abundance of citrus fruit seems to be what the American poet Kenward Elmslie (b. 1929) is both celebrating and somehow vaguely deploring in his "Fruit" (1971): five separate one-word lines of this twenty-five line poem are devoted to the

names of the five most common citrus fruits consumed by Americans. (Allusions to
"American youth" and to "the alleys of Kansas" make clear the American setting.)
Here are the opening and closing lines of the first stanza, the opening lines of the sec-
ond stanza, and the last lines of the last stanza:

> Oranges,
> someday the Negress who smears you with certified color
> will hear tap-taps and whines (the Giant Fruitbeast) in the swamplands
> arising like natural music, and she will shriek in her swoon
> [. . . . .]
> "City children, accept the perfume of your melons in the sun—
> Lemons."
>
> Limes,
> in spring you remind some men of little people's breasts.
>
> [. . . . .]
>
> Farm women in bed a-mornings,
> think of them in your bureau, then get up. A nation of you and you,
> Grapefruit,
> Tangerines,
> could only prove the all-nite cities have won. O lovely spring,
> the carnage! Oldsters with blinky chicken eyes resent your seeds,
> your sections, your juice and meats. Secretly in markets,
> they pinch you, hurry on and sniff their fingertips, estranged.

A similar uneasiness or ambivalence about the large-scale consumption of citrus
fruit by Americans—in this case by a single household—occurs at the beginning of
chapter 3 in *The Great Gatsby* (1925), by F. Scott Fitzgerald (1896–1940). Fitzgerald has
his narrator Nick Carraway, before he has ever met Gatsby, monitoring the things that
go in and out of his fabulous neighbor's house:

> Every Friday five crates of oranges and lemons arrived from a fruiterer in
> New York—every Monday these same oranges and lemons left his back
> door in a pyramid of pulpless halves. There was a machine in the kitchen
> which could extract the juice of two hundred oranges in half an hour if a
> little button was pressed two hundred times by a butler's thumb.

(In chapter 3 of a slightly earlier version of the novel—titled "Trimalchio"—there
are only three crates of oranges and lemons; the hitherto unpublished text is now
available in an edition by James L. W. West III and in annotated galley facsimile edited
by Matthew J. Bruccoli.) This traffic in citrus fruits and their reduction to juice by a special machine can easily stand for that thrilling mixture of pleasure and technology that

434   eventually drives Nick back from corrupt New York to a duller but presumably more innocent Middle West. But why no grapefruits in Gatsby's citrus supply from New York? Well, for one thing, it is hard to imagine a significant role for grapefruits in Gatsby's weekend parties, since few alcoholic drinks incorporate that fruit.

The surprising scarcity of literary references to grapefruits may stem in part from their uncertain status as food; as Alan Davidson puts it in *The Oxford Companion to Food:* "The rather bitter flavour is an acquired taste and the fruit is difficult to peel in the way that one might peel an orange." There are, then, the questions of when and how grapefruits are to be eaten: as the first course for breakfast (unembellished or sweetened with a little sugar); as the first or last course in some other meal (sweetened with brown or caster sugar, broiled, moistened with wine, adorned with a maraschino cherry). Another bothersome question is how grapefruits are to be prepared for eating: a peeled whole grapefruit is too large to eat gracefully out of the hand, an unsectioned half is too difficult to eat gracefully except with a special spoon, while sectioning requires time and care. (On this last subject, the food writer Leyland Cox has written a mildly amusing piece for *Gourmet* magazine called "The Perfect Half Grapefruit" [1978].) As for degree of tartness, grapefruits occupy a middle ground: less sour than lemons, less sweet than oranges. Furthermore, grapefruits seem to possess comic possibilities lacking in other citrus fruits, as in a memorable scene of an influential early sound film, *The Public Enemy* (1931), directed by William Wellman (1896–1975), where James Cagney smashes a grapefruit into the face of gang moll Mae Clarke. Grapefruits, then, are at once the most versatile and the most problematic of citrus fruits.

Paintings of grapefruits are also scarce; of the few I know, two by American artists stand out: *Grapefruit Picking Time* (1940s), by Ellis Ruley (1882–1959), and *Tables for Ladies* (1930), by Edward Hopper (1882–1967). (See plates 27 and 28.) Ruley was a self-taught painter who spent his entire life in Norwich, Connecticut, and was the first African American in the region to marry a white woman (his second wife). His picture (oil-based house paint on posterboard, 31½ x 25¼ in.), now in the Wadsworth Atheneum, Hartford, Connecticut, was almost certainly influenced in its composition by posed photographs of shapely young women picking fruit in such popular magazines as *Life;* for a reproduction of one such photograph, see Glenn Robert Smith's *Discovering Ellis Ruley* (1993). Hopper's painting of a typical middle-American restaurant (oil on canvas, 48¼ x 60¼ in.), now in the Metropolitan Museum of Art, New York, may be less bleak than many of his works, but the long line of grapefruits— nine and a half are visible—do suggest the endless repetitiveness of life for all the (four) people in the picture.

But let us turn to a few literary episodes. In her first novel, *Chilly Scenes of Winter* (1976), Ann Beattie (b. 1947) presents in the feckless Charles a protagonist—the very term is perhaps too strong for such a passive character—with little sense of the past and absolutely no sense of futurity. Thus, Charles "is amazed by people who can shop for a whole week's groceries on one day—that they know what to get, and how much of it, and that they will want to eat those things for sure during the next week." Not only Charles but also all the other characters have extreme difficulty in connecting the successive actions of their lives; they have little sense of causal efficacy, so that almost anything can accompany or be followed by anything else. Thus, in an early chapter, Charles wonders how he can talk to his girl friend Laura:

> Laura should be here. What is he going to say to her? He wants, somehow, to convey to her that her husband is a dull man. Since he is also dull, he wants to point out that she wouldn't be getting into anything unexpected; she would just be swapping a dull person who doesn't care much about her for one who does. That sounds awful. He will have to think harder.

Charles may be dull, but he appreciates little signs of the absence of dullness in Laura: "Another time in New York he bought two grapefruits at a fruit stand, and the next time he looked at her the grapefruit were under her sweater. It looked very nice. She was very nice." Still another time (in chapter 12), Charles buys a single grapefruit, along with apples, oranges, bananas, and a single pear, and leaves the bag of fruit at Laura's friend Betty's door to thank her for divulging Laura's new telephone number and to exonerate himself for exploiting Betty's friendship with Laura. Only one grapefruit so that Betty cannot repeat Laura's little caper? But is Charles even capable of making such a connection? Finally, in the last scene of the book, as Charles watches Laura preparing his favorite dessert—orange soufflé—she suddenly stops, "puts the whisk aside and walks over to his chair, sits in his lap. She smells like oranges." But this seemingly upbeat ending is partly negated, if not totally undercut, by Laura's last words, as she tells of a visit to her husband's institutionalized ex-wife, who sits staring at snowflakes: "It would be a waste of time just to stare at snowflakes, but she was counting, and even that might be a waste of time, but she was only counting the ones that were just alike."

In "Grapefruit" (1987), by Gerald Stern (b. 1925), a grapefruit is being eaten, but in a rather unconventional way, in the opening lines of the poem:

> I'm eating breakfast even if it means standing
> in front of the sink and tearing at the grapefruit,
> even if I'm leaning over to keep the juices
> away from my chest and stomach and even if a spider
> is hanging from my ear and a wild flea
> is crawling down my leg.

Gazing out at his garden through the window over the sink, at first all he can see are failures—lettuce, spinach, rhubarb, tomatoes—reminding him of some of the repellent tastes of his childhood, when even oranges could be unpleasant: "I hated / oranges when they were quartered, that was the signal / for castor oil—aside from the peeled

436   navel / I love the Florida cut in two." Note that the oranges are cut or peeled, while
the grapefruit has been torn. Later, lying on the ground in his garden among his corn-
flowers, his perspective changes, and the poem ends with a comic benediction:

> Blessed art Thou oh grapefruit King of the universe,
> Blessed art Thou my sink, oh Blessed art Thou
> Thou milkweed Queen of the sky, burster of seeds,
> Who bringeth forth juice from the earth.

A passing reference to grapefruit in "Incident on a Holiday" (1999), by Alan Brownjohn (b. 1931) is as perfunctory as everything else in the poem, whose setting is a holiday resort on some body of water. The "incident" in question is the torching of a
disco, which leaves the barber, the licensee, and the local cat unmoved; unlike these
others—dismissed in a line or two—the check-out girl, equally unmoved, gets an
entire stanza to herself:

> Not even the check-out girl taking one by one
> The grapefruit rolled down in a ritual
> To prick the boredom of her dreadful day
> And start her chatting—she doesn't as much as smile
> When I say, "Who would trash a lovely disco?"

However futile the attempt at humor, the intent has been to raise a smile with the aid
of grapefruits.

It is even harder to explain the scarcity of literary references to limes, which, in
contrast to oranges, flourish in tropical regions such as Sicily, the site of one of my two
examples. *Sicilian Limes* (Lumie di Sicilia) is the title of one of the earliest plays (one
act, first produced in Rome, 1910) of Luigi Pirandello (1867–1936), based on his own
short story. (I follow the translation by William Murray). The plot is simple. Two musically talented peasants have grown up together in a small town in Sicily: Micuccio
Bonavino, a piccolo player in the town band, and Teresina Marnis, a singer. Though
poor himself, Micuccio manages to pay for Teresina's music lessons and her eventual
enrollment in a conservatory. As the play opens in a city in northern Italy where
Teresina has made a notable reputation, Micuccio has come to visit her in hopes of
reviving an old love between them and also to return the thousand lire she sent him
when he was sick. The trip has taken two days on the train and during that time
Micuccio has had nothing to eat. The set consists of a waiting room sparsely furnished
with a table and chairs; through an exit in the rear one can see a splendidly furnished
salon with a sumptuously set dining table. Micuccio tells his story to two servants and
even starts to play a tune on his piccolo, at which the servants can hardly contain their
amusement. At this point, Sina—she has shortened her name—and her noisy party
arrive home, entering the salon from the rear. Sina's mother, Marta, joins Micuccio and
the servants and explains the occasion as a celebratory dinner for Sina and all her

admirers. As the guests eat in the salon, the food from each successive course is brought out for Micuccio and Marta. Finally, Sina herself appears, clad in an extremely low-cut gown and covered with jewels. She greets Micuccio perfunctorily and returns to her friends. Micuccio is stunned, as much by Sina's seminudity as by her cold welcome. After a series of disjointed and heartbroken speeches, Micuccio is about to leave when Sina returns. He picks up the filthy sack he has brought with him and empties its contents—limes—on the table. The limes remind Sina of home and she attempts to pick one up. Micuccio forcibly prevents her, then picks up a lime himself and, holding it under Marta's nose, says: "Smell it, smell the air of our town. . . . And now, what if I threw them, one by one, at the heads of all those fine gentlemen in there?" Marta pleads with him, and Micuccio leaves but not before stuffing his thousand lire down the front of Sina's dress, as she bursts into tears. Pirandello was evidently already a master of dramatic technique in this play. The simultaneous upstage and downstage dinners are a theatrical masterstroke, and the spilled limes suggest all sorts of dualities: southern and northern Italy, peasants and urban sophisticates, nature and culture.

In chapter 7, we discussed a series of literary mango episodes: one in French (by a Haitian), the others in English by writers most of whom grew up in Caribbean culture areas (Guyana, Miami, Puerto Rico, Cuba) during the second half of the twentieth century. This suggests that today's Hispano-American and Latino/a writers may soon be presenting us with a profusion of lime episodes. In any case, here is one such episode, in the form of a poem, "Lime Cure" (1992), by a writer born in Cuba and now living and teaching in the United States. Gustavo Pérez-Firmat (b. 1950) has the speaker in his poem attribute magical powers to limes: "I'm filling my house with limes / to keep away the evil spirits. / I'm filling my house with limes / to help me cope." But the speaker is clearly at home in the modern world (he owns a computer); we cannot take his lime cure entirely seriously, especially when he says things like: "I don't bathe, I marinade." But then the speaker adds:

> I taste the tart juice dripping on my tongue.
> I shudder.
> Then I sleep peacefully inside green dreams of lime
> and when I wake, I bask in the morning's lime light.

Could it be—for reasons that might be either profoundly cultural or idiosyncratically personal (or both)—that, for the speaker, the tartness of limes is upsetting but their green color is soothing? In any case, Pérez-Firmat's devotion to limes reminds one of the devotion to apples of the long list of American writers in chapter 1.

MELONS AND PAPAYAS

Fashions in food are constantly changing: a good illustration of this is the evolution of French attitudes towards eating melons. For consider what two quintessentially French writers, around a century apart, say about this fruit: in one of the two entries on fresh fruit in Flaubert's *Dictionary of Accepted Ideas* (the other, on apricots, has already been quoted) we read: "MELON. Nice topic for dinner-table conversation: is it a vegetable or a fruit? The English eat it for dessert, which is astounding." By contrast, here is one of Colette's memories from the summers of her childhood (first published in 1943 "in a deluxe edition in the darkest days of Nazi-occupied Paris," according to the editor's note by Robert Phelps): "Between the leaden galette and the pound cake there sits enthroned a cantaloupe, mysterious as a well, which has drunk a whole glass of port and two teaspoons of sugar" (translated by Matthew Ward). The exact identification of the galette (a sort of pancake) and pound cake need not detain us; the centerpiece of the desserts is clearly the melon. But let us turn to the poets.

Though the traditional ancient terms for melons sometimes confuse them with cucumbers and gourds, melons (in our sense) seem to have been known to the Romans. Thus, the third book of the fourth- or fifth-century C.E. compilation of recipes ascribed to Apicius—the only surviving cookbook from Classical times, preserved in two ninth-century manuscripts—gives a recipe for *pepones et melones* (long and round melons). But I doubt if anything written about melons in ancient times can prepare us for the astonishing passage of Latin hexameters in *De Cultura Hortorum* (Of gardening), by a writer straddling Roman and medieval literature, Walafrid Strabo (808/9–849). He was abbot of Reichenau, located on an island in Lake Constance (Bodensee) in Germany, just above the border with Switzerland. (In chapter 20, "Orchards, Groves, Gardens," we will encounter the apples and peaches of the dedicatory poem that Walafrid composed to accompany the gift of his little book to Grimold, abbot of St. Gall, south of Lake Constance in Switzerland.) Walafrid wrote the poem after he had retired from an exciting life caught up in imperial politics to become for the second time abbot of Reichenau (the first time he was expelled by a rival). From 842 until his sad death from drowning in the Loire, he seems to have quite literally cultivated his garden.

In the the 444 hexameter lines of *Hortulus* (The little garden)—as it is often called—Walafrid describes twenty-nine different plants, mostly medicinal herbs, but only one or two fruits: *cucurbita* (gourd) and *pepones* (melon-gourd). The former we shall return to in chapter 19, on wine; the latter is clearly identifiable, from its description, as what we call a melon. Walafrid explains how the melon grows (ll. 152–162) and how it tastes (ll. 173–180); in between, he invents a virtuosic comparison of the melon with—surprisingly—a soap bubble! Here are the lines, in a translation by Raef Payne (1966):

> In the same patch at the bottom of the garden where this fine crop
> My humble lines have just described is planted,
> You will see something else which looks like an eager vine creeping
> Over the dusty ground and nursing a rounded fruit.
> This one commonly lies on the dry ridges of earth
> And the growth it makes is beautiful—until the time when,
> Yellow and ripe with summer sun, it fills the gardener's basket.
> Some you will see are completely round and even;
> Others you'll find with a drooping oblong belly, the shape
> Of a nut or an egg—
>   Or like a soap bubble. You know how it is
> When you hold up a cake of soap: it gleams in your upraised hands
> As the slippery wetness runs over its surface, until by pouring
> More water on it you wash the fresh froth off.
> But when the fingers work on it, kneading and rubbing purposefully
> This way and that, it softens; and then, with your hands together
> And only a crack between, if you blow through narrowed lips
> Gently, gently, your breath will make the hollow suds
> Swell like blown glass, and the curve of the vaulted skin
> Meets to form a slippery center at the bubble's base.
> When a knife-blade finds the guts of a melon [*viscera pomi*] a gush
> Of juice comes out, and many seeds with it. Then
> Your lucky guest can divide by hand the hollow body
> Into several pieces and thus enjoy the luscious delicacy.
> Its freshness and savour [*candorque saporque*] delight the palate; nor can this food

In his unique and valuable anthology, *Poetry of the Carolingian Renaissance* (1985), Peter Godman includes six selections by Walafrid (for a total of sixteen pages, half Latin texts and half English translations). About the passage from *Hortulus* on gourds (ll. 99–151), Godman comments: "In this miniature *tour de force* the full range of Walahfrid's irony is given free play"; and, he adds, "the wit of this passage . . . has not stirred the interest of its critics, the majority of whom have been horticulturists." More generally:

De Cultura Hortorum is much more than "pure gardening literature" or a "cultural monument to the study of nature" in ninth-century Reichenau. It is an imaginative work of a high order, in which plants and vegetables, care and cultivation of the garden are presented in graphically human terms. The dense and intricate imagery of the passage [on gourds] is illustrative of Walahfrid's baroque fantasy, which can unite a profusion of similes and metaphors into a single coherent picture.

I presume Godman would agree that exactly the same thing is true of the passage on melons.

After Walafrid, the most extended poetic appreciation of melons I know is by Antoine-Girard de Saint-Amant (1594–1661) in the form of a long poem (332 lines), "Le Melon" (1631). (Saint-Amant's fellow countryman, Montaigne [1533–1592]—who died a couple of years before the poet was born—did remark laconically, in his very last essay (translated by Donald Frame), "Of Experience" (1587–88), "I am not excessively fond of either salads or fruits, except melons.") In a study of French baroque literature, Imbrie Buffum has singled out Saint-Amant's poem to illustrate the "familiar baroque effects of exaggeration and concrete sensual imagery . . . all the more striking when interspersed with humor." The first third of the poem—116 octosyllabics—describes the ecstasies of the author in the presence of a luscious, ripe melon, culminating in a catalogue of all of life's pleasures that are inferior to the taste of the melon (English prose translation by Geoffrey Brereton):

> Well, that's it. Now it is cut, and my hopes are not disappointed. O gods, the radiance that it casts leaves no doubt of its excellence! Who ever saw such a lovely hue! It is tinted a reddish yellow; it is firm right to the centre, it has few pips in its belly, and those few, I really believe, are so many grains of gold. It is not watery, its rind is thin: in short, a feast for a king. But, although I am not one, yet will I make a meal of it.
>
> Ha! Hold me up, I swoon! This delicious morsel tickles my very soul. It oozes a sweet juice which will steep my heart in ecstasy. My appetite is sated with a new and pure ambrosia, and all my senses, captivated by taste, are concentrated into one.
>
> No, neither the coconut, that delectable fruit which by itself provides the table with all the dishes which desire can imagine and choose, nor the kisses of a mistress when she herself caresses us, nor what is drawn from the [sugar] canes which Crete grows in its waters, nor the dear apricot which I love, nor the strawberry with cream, nor the manna which falls from heaven, nor the sacred pear of Tours, nor the green and sugared fig, nor the plum with delicate juice, nor even the muscat grape (strange indeed that *I* should say so), are more than gall and mud compared to this divine MELON, the glory of the Angevin clime.

The remaining two-thirds of the poem, in alexandrines (twelve-syllable lines), constitutes an ode dedicated to Apollo and features a burlesque banquet on Mount Olympus. As Buffum explains, "Each god has brought an especially delicious dish to the banquet, and each god is ironically described with a picturesque and grotesque epithet." The climax occurs when Thalia, the muse of comedy, presents a melon in honor of her master Apollo, who proceeds to carve a musical instrument out of a melon slice, thereby inventing the lute! More praise of the sensuous qualities of the melon ensues, including the lines:

> O beaucoup mieux que l'or, chef-d'oeuvre d'Apollon!
> O fleur de tous les fruits! O ravissant MELON!

> ~

O better far than gold, O Sun God's masterpiece! O flower of all fruits! O ravishing MELON!

And the ultimate sacrifice, in the last lines of the poem:

> Bref, O MELON sucrin, pour t'accabler de gloire,
> Des faveurs de Margot je perdrai la mémoire
> Avant que je t'oublie et que ton goût charmant
> Soit biffé des cahiers du bon gros SAINT-AMANT.

> ~

In short, O sugary MELON, to heap you with glory, I will lose the memory of Margot's favours before I forget you and your delightful taste is crossed off the books of good fat SAINT-AMANT.

Buffum remarks that there is mock-heroic irony in the telling of the story of the melon; at the same time, however, the melon seems to have been genuinely intended as an icon of pleasure—there is no ambivalence about that. Saint-Amant does not bother to say whether melons are consumed during meals, and if so, during which course.

Though Molly Bloom may be no Margot, Leopold's kissing of his sleeping wife's rump elicits from Joyce in *Ulysses* a literary performance rivalling Saint-Amant's in linguistic inventiveness if not in length:

> He kissed the plump mellow yellow smellow melons of her rump, on each
> plump melonous hemisphere, in their mellow yellow furrow, with obscure
> prolonged provocative melon-smellonous osculation.

A modern poet who had a special fondness for melons was Sylvia Plath. In general, she is ambivalent about food in her poetry; it was not that she didn't like food, for Anne Stevenson, in her biography of Plath, cites Olwyn Hughes's remembrance of Plath's "sheer delight in both cooking and eating." By the last months of her life in the

442   fall of 1962, however, cooking must have become as oppressive as anything else, for we find her writing, in "Lesbos" (1962), of "Viciousness in the kitchen! / The potatoes hiss," and, in "Mary's Song" (1962), that "The Sunday lamb cracks in its fat." Earlier, melons seem to have caught her attention, perhaps simply as ready-made icons of her own transitory states of intense excitement. Thus, among the five titles in Plath's juvenilia—that is, poems written prior to 1956—that seem to be about fruit (one about strawberries, one about apple blossoms, two about plums) there is one (which I have not read) titled "Green As a Melon My Sweet World Was." (Of the five poems, only "Bitter Strawberries" has been published, in Ted Hughes's edition of her collected poems). Again, in the spring of 1952, when Plath was about to finish her sophomore year at Smith, she wrote enthusiastically to her mother: "The world is splitting open at my feet like a ripe, juicy watermelon. If only I can work, work, work to justify all my opportunities." (Stevenson comments that the split watermelon was a favorite source of similes for Plath.) Later, in the summer of 1956 while honeymooning with Ted Hughes in Benidorm, a fishing village on the Mediterranean coast of Spain, Plath wrote "Southern Sunrise" (1956), the last lines of which are "And out of the blue drench / Of Angel's Bay / Rises the round red watermelon sun." At this same time, Plath wrote "Fiesta Melons," which Hughes has included as the title poem in a limited posthumous volume (1971) containing ten poems and fourteen pen drawings by Plath. It is a pleasant little poem, though not wholly convincing in the speaker's determination to roll melons "homeward to taste" or to strew melon seeds "like confetti" under the feet of fiesta-goers. But the melons are coolly and objectively observed: "with stripes / Of turtle-dark-green," "cream-smooth," "pink-pulped," and "bump-rinded." (This detached stance is maintained in her other Spanish poems, even when Plath is much more deeply engaged with her subject matter, which includes beggars, a bullfight, net-menders, and an old ladies' home.)

There is a certain poignancy in the fact that Hughes included in his volume *Crow*—published in the same year as Plath's *Fiesta Melons*—a poem called "Lovesong," containing these lines: "Their heads fell apart into sleep like the two halves / Of a lopped melon, but love is hard to stop."

By the time Plath came to write her next (and apparently last) fruit poem, "Blackberrying," in 1960, the subjectivity of her approach had deepened though she was still capable of acute and careful observation of her surroundings (see chapter 23, "Berries"). The underlying suicidal impulses of Plath's life and much of her writing are, of course, at the opposite extreme from the life-embracing and life-enhancing impulses that almost define Pablo Neruda. Neruda wrote many poems about food, and, like so many of his other poems, they seem to reflect the tastes of an omnivore—an omnivore not only with respect to food but with respect to experience as such. This omnivorousness appears at its purest and most lyrical in the *Odas Elementales* (Elementary odes), four volumes of which were published in 1954–59; already discussed are the odes to an apple, a lemon, and an orange, while other subjects include salt, tomatoes, onion, a fallen chestnut, plums, and a beautiful nude, as well as laziness, sadness, happiness, and autumn. Like most of the odes, the "Ode to the Watermelon" (Oda a la Sandía) is built up of many short lines—ninety-three lines, to be exact, some as short as one word, none more than eight words. Neruda begins by describing an intensely hot and dry summer, so that (in Robert Bly's translation) "we want to drink / waterfalls"; and then "the coolest of all / the planets crosses / the sky / the round, magnificent, / star-filled watermelon." The shape, color, and wateriness of the fruit are now deliriously characterized:

It's a fruit from the thirst-tree.
It's the green whale of the summer.
    [. . . . .]
its hemispheres open
showing a flag
green, white, red,
that dissolves into
wild rivers, sugar,
delight!
    [. . . . .]
When we're thirsty
we glimpse you
like
a mine or a mountain
of fantastic food,
but
among our longings and our teeth
you change
simply
into cool light
that slips in turn into
spring water
that touched us once
singing.

The sheer size of watermelons is the only thing that counts in a popular fable which the Algerian Arab writer Kaddour-Mermet probably composed in the late nineteenth century for recitation on the street. Couched in a North African patois, "La Zitoun y la Bastique" (The olive and the watermelon), like all but one of the twenty-eight fables in Kaddour's book *Fables et Contes en Sabir* (1916), is an adaptation from La Fontaine (1621–1695), in this case from "Le Gland et la Citrouille" (The acorn and the pumpkin). The speaker in the poem belongs to the Kabyle, one of the Berber peoples of northeastern Algeria; after some words of praise for the wisdom of Allah, an incident is recounted (translated by Norman R. Shapiro, 1992):

One fine day,
Certain Kabyle he look around
And see on ground
Big watermelon. Really big!
Kabyle he think: "How come such melon grow
On tiny twig?
Maybe this time, Allah he go
Be stupid dunce
For once!

In the remainder of the poem, Kabyle, lying under an olive tree and hit on the nose by a falling olive, is moved to exclaim:

"Instead of olive, what if melon fall?
It break my neck!!
Salamaleck!!!
Me only one who make mistake!" he bawl.
"Allah he never go screw up at all!"

A somewhat less assured celebration of the shape, color, and taste of watermelon is in "Watermelon," by the African American writer Ted Joans (b. 1928), who often recites his poems to jazz accompaniment:

Its got   a good shape/the outside color is green/its one of them
    foods from Africa
its got stripes sometimes like a zebra   or Florida prison pants
Its bright red inside/the black eyes are flat and shiney/it wont make you fat
Its got heavy liquid weight/the sweet taste is unique/some
    people are shamed of it/
I aint afraid to eat it/indoors or out/its soul food thing/Watermelon
    is what I'm
talking about   Yeah watermelon is what I'm talking about
    Watermelon

The speaker's defensiveness about his pleasure in eating watermelons stems, of course, from the maliciously humorous associations of watermelons and blacks in mainstream white American society. This malice was shockingly demonstrated in 1988 when a Texaco executive in Louisiana mocked one of his African American employees, who had just announced her pregnancy, by presenting her with a cake containing the iced inscription, "Happy Birthday, Sheryl. It must have been those watermelon seeds." The *New York Times* published a big picture of the cake on the front page of its Sunday business section for 10 November 1996 (as recounted in a book [1998] by Bari-Ellen Roberts).

Consider now an epigrammatic poem, "Watermelons" (1959), by Ron Loewinsohn (b. 1937):

> The pieces of watermelon
> lying shattered
> on the black pavement
> resemble strange jewels,
> jade & ruby clumped together,
> but they're pieces of watermelon.

And another, "Watermelons" (1974), by Charles Simic:

> Green Buddhas
> On the fruit stand.
> We eat the smile
> And spit out the teeth.

Loewinsohn first wants us to see the pieces of a shattered watermelon as jewels lying—as jewels are often exhibited—against a black background, but then resists this vision with the deflating "they're [only] pieces of watermelon"; Simic first has us attend to the tranquil expanse of green that is the watermelon's skin and that suggests the imperturbability of a Buddha, and then, rather brutally, has us eating a slice of the melon envisaged as a smile full of teeth. For Neruda, on the other hand, as we have seen, the watermelon is a whale: the largest fruit we eat reminds him of the largest living animal, while thickly clustered pits suggest the thickly clustered stars in the sky. Furthermore, Neruda uses the green of the watermelon rind as one stripe in his watermelon flag. But couldn't a poem be made about the rind itself? Precisely this is accomplished (for a cantaloupe rind) in the title poem of her first book *Ants on the Melon* (1996), by the American poet Virginia Hamilton Adair (b. 1913):

> Once when our blacktop city
> was still a topsoil town
> we carred to Formicopolis
> a cantaloupe rind to share
> and stooped to plop it down
> in their populous Times Square
> at the subway of the ants
>
> and saw that hemisphere
> blacken and rise and dance
> with antmen out of hand
> wild for their melon toddies

> just like our world next year
> no place to step or stand
> except on bodies.

"Formicopolis" is, of course, Adair's humorous coinage from *formica,* Latin for ant.

Another prominent trait of watermelons not alluded to in any of the poems cited so far is the sound they make—the thump—when struck. (There is, in fact, a summer festival called a "watermelon thump" in the small town of Luling, Texas, in the heart of watermelon country; among the featured events are an auction of the largest watermelon of the season and a watermelon-pit-spitting contest.) In "Watermelon," by the Russian poet Eduard Bagritsky (1895–1934), translated by Vera Dunham, occur these two lines: "On a melon, sonorous as a tambourine, / I'll cut the shape of a heart." The poem is ostensibly about the transportation of watermelons by ship from a port in the vicinity of the the Sea of Azov, which is mentioned in the first line. (The warm climate of the region surrounding the sea lends itself to the cultivation of watermelons.) Most of the poem is about the tumultuous sea voyage ending in shipwreck: "In the black hold watermelons collide"; then, "The waves / Rock a watermelon, marked by a heart"; and finally,

> The surf pounds the weed-covered reefs.
> A school of mackerel gambols.
> A low breeze rocks that watermelon
> And brings it to shore . . .
> Tossed no more by swell and storm,
> This will be the end of its journey.
> My sweetheart gathers it up.
>
> There is no one to suggest to her
> That she holds my heart in her hands.

In a recent poem by a Libyan living in the United States, "Watermelon Tales" (1993), by Khaled Mattawa (b. 1964), the *sound* of a struck watermelon is crucial. As the poem opens, the narrator is in exile in a cold climate, obsessed with thoughts of watermelons (I reproduce Mattawa's lineation scheme; its point escapes me):

> January. Snow. For days I have craved
> watermelons, wanted
> to freckle the ground with seeds, wanted
> to perform an ancient ritual:
> Noontime, an early
> summer Sunday, the village
> chief faces north, spits seven mouthfuls, then

> fingers a cycle
> around the galaxy of seeds.

In the third stanza Mattawa writes:

> His right ear pricked up
> close, my father taps on a
> watermelon, strokes as though it were
> a thigh. Then he slaps.
> "If it doesn't sound like your hands
> clapping at a wedding, it's not yours."

In the sixth stanza the sounding theme recurs:

> My father
> strokes, slaps, and when I lift the melon
> to my shoulder, says
> "Eleven years in America
> and you carry a watermelon
> like a damn peasant."

The eighth stanza repeats the magic pit theme:

> Her shadow twice her
> height, the village sorceress
> walks to where the chief has spit. She reveals
> size of the harvest,
> chance of drought, whose sons will wed
> whose daughters, and names of the ill whose
> ailments will not cease.

And, finally, in the eleventh stanza, the poem ends on a bitter note—with the loss of patriarchal authority and perhaps also of watermelon magic—when the sounding procedure of the narrator's father turns out to be all too fallible:

> I cut the watermelon we bought
> into cubes, strawberry red. But they were
> dry, almost bitter.
> After the third taste, my father
> dropped his fork. He gazed at the window
> for a while, then spent
> the rest of the day in bed.

That watermelons occupy a special place in the American diet was noted as long ago as the late 1820s by the Englishwoman Frances Trollope (1780–1863), who made

448   her observations during the course of a two-year stay in Cincinnati (1828–1830). Here is the relevant passage from her book *Domestic Manners of the Americans* (1832):

> Many waggon-loads of enormous water-melons were brought to market every day, and I was sure to see groups of men, women, and children seated on the pavement round the spot where they were sold, sucking in prodigious quantities of this watery fruit. Their manner of devouring them is extremely unpleasant; the huge fruit is cut into half a dozen sections, of about a foot long, and then, dripping as it is with water, applied to the mouth, from either side of which pour copious streams of the fluid, while, ever and anon, a mouthful of the hard black seeds are shot out in all directions, to the great annoyance of all within reach. When I first tasted this fruit I thought it very vile stuff indeed, but before the end of the season we all learned to like it. When taken with claret and sugar it makes delicious wine and water.

One wonders if Trollope ever encountered "spiked" (or "tipsy") watermelon, which one prepares by cutting a deep hole through the rind, pouring in some alcoholic beverage, resealing the opening, and then chilling the watermelon (as described by Ellen Ficklen in her account of watermelon folklore, *Watermelon* [1984]). Another trick was to open a watermelon by simply dropping it on the ground, the advantage of this procedure being that it released the "heart meat," which contains few seeds and is also supposedly the juiciest and tastiest part of the melon.

The heart meat of the watermelon was also preferred by those American painters who liked to depict the fruit. Thus, Sarah Miriam Peale (1800–1885), youngest daughter of one of the two founding fathers of America's greatest family of painters, the Peales of Philadelphia, in a work of 1822 (oil on panel, 13 ¼ x 19 ½ in.), represented a thin slice of watermelon sitting on a dish at the center of her painting, with a piece of the heart meat leaning on the right-hand edge of the dish (see plate 29). The painting, now in a private collection, is discussed in the catalogue *One Hundred and Fifty Years of Philadelphia Still-Life Painting* (1997), edited by Robert Devlin Schwarz. Sarah and her sister Anna Claypoole (1791–1878) were, by the way, the first women elected (in 1824) to the prestigious Pennsylvania Academy of the Fine Arts. Also, they collaborated on a series of portraits of public figures (including members of Congress), whom they painted in their respective Baltimore studios. Eventually, "fatigued by overwork and enervated by the stratified, conventional society of the East, Sarah decided to leave Baltimore," as Anne Sue Hirshorn explains in her contribution to the catalogue of a great Peale exhibition, *The Peale Family: Creation of a Legacy, 1770–1870* (1996) edited by Lillian B. Miller. Sarah moved in 1847 to the then frontier town of Saint Louis, where she had a successful career as a portrait painter, also returning to the still life subjects of her youth. Two of Sarah's paintings should not be missed: the utterly radiant early self-portrait of 1818 (oil on canvas, 24 ¹⁄₁₆ x 19 in.), now in the National Portrait Gallery, Washington, D.C.; and the superb late (ca. 1860) oval-shaped picture of raspberries, *Basket of Berries* (oil on canvas, 12 x 10 in.), now in a private collection (both of these paintings are reproduced in the catalogue).

Other American watermelon motifs—for example, on jewelry—may be found in Ellen Ficklen's *Watermelon* (1984). Also, since the early 1980s, the American stand-up comedian (Leo) Gallagher has used watermelons as a central prop in his performances. Gallagher ends each of his shows—such as his early "Melon Madness" (1985; available on video)—by wielding a large mallet to smash a variety of foods, including always a whole watermelon; he also maintains a website, "gallaghersmash.com," offering a range of products from watermelon bandanas to watermelon soap. A *New Yorker* cartoon by Donald Reilly (29 May 2000) may be alluding to what Gallagher calls his "sledge-o-matic" treatment of watermelons when it depicts a seated judge with a large mallet and a melon in front of him on his bench; one of the two men standing before the judge is saying to the other: "This judge is known as tough but fair, with a great sense of humor."

A watermelon is the subject of a wonderful painting, *Still Life: Watermelon* (1912), by the Italian Futurist Umberto Boccioni (1882–1916), now in the Sprengel Museum in Hannover (oil on canvas, 31¾ x 31¾ in.). Fruit still life may at first seem a surprising subject for a painter whose tastes (like those of his Futurist colleagues) ran rather to machines and other objects in rapid movement. But a remark by Ebert-Schifferer explains the attraction of the subject and also how it relates to an earlier tradition of Italian painting (she reproduces the painting in her book *Still Life*):

> The Italian Futurists were fascinated by the dynamism of modern technology and tried to capture the impression of movement in space by breaking up their subjects into partial planes. Boccioni here takes up the motif of the violently exploded watermelon, which he presumably knew from late Baroque Roman and Neapolitan still lifes. A centrifugal movement from an ideal center responds to the influence of the surrounding space, which causes the fruit to burst.

Two of America's greatest nineteenth-century writers, Henry Thoreau and Mark Twain, were enthusiastic admirers of native watermelons. In 1839, the twenty-two-year-old Thoreau and his older brother, John, planned a boat trip along the Concord and Merrimack Rivers. To celebrate their imminent departure on 29 August they gave a melon party, the first staging of what was to become a celebrated annual social occasion in Concord (for details, see Walter Harding, *The Days of Henry Thoreau* [1965]). Also, Thoreau often took watermelons along when he went on a trip, as he explains in the manuscript of his "Wild Fruits": "When I am going a-berrying in my boat or other carriage, I frequently carry watermelons for drink. It is the most agreeable and refreshing wine in a convenient cask, and most easily kept cool. Carry these green bottles of wine. When you get to the field you put them in the shade or in water till you want them."

Mark Twain wrote a tribute to the watermelon in the epigraph to chapter 14 of his novel *The Tragedy of Pudd'nhead Wilson* (1894), whose ostensible subjects are racial identity, slavery, and the influence of heredity and environment on the human individual:

> The true Southern watermelon is a boon apart, and not to be mentioned with commoner things. It is chief of this world's luxuries, king by the grace of God over all the fruits of the earth. When one has tasted it, he knows what the angels eat. It was not a Southern watermelon that Eve took: we know it because she repented.—*Pudd'nhead Wilson's Calendar.*

It may be that Twain is here deliberately undercutting the stereotypical association of the southern Negro with watermelons—a stereotype Twain must have been acquainted with, for by the end of the nineteenth century it had become widespread in blackface minstrel performances. One of the most celebrated of the minstrel performers, J. W. McAndrews, was actually called "The Watermelon Man" after his most famous act, which, according to M. B. Leavitt in his *Fifty Years in Theatrical Management* (1912), he "played with unvarying success" from 1856 until his death in 1899.

Watermelons continued to play an important role in the domestic economy of the American South in the twentieth century. In the magnificent comic novel by Eudora Welty (1909–2001), *Losing Battles* (1970), set in rural Mississippi in the 1930s, watermelons are not only straightforwardly present as food in the great feast celebrating Granny's ninetieth birthday, which constitutes the main action of the story, but they also appear repeatedly in similes:

> Little pink and yellow gravelstones, set like the seeds in long cuts of watermelon, banded all the banks alike, running above the road—more gravel than the road had ever received in its life.

> [Banner Road] ran deep between its banks that were bright as a melon at that instant split open.

> The two halves of a watermelon, eaten out, had been left beside the syrup stand like a pair of shoes beside a bed.

> Kneeling on the ground, Mr. Renfro had split open the first watermelon. He rose with the long halves facing outward from his arms, like the tablets of the Ten Commandments.

> He'd risen up still holding his watermelon to his cheek, harmonicalike.

> He ducked around Curly, hopped puddles to the truck. He started thumping its sides as if it were a watermelon and he were a judge of ripeness.

Finally, there is the powerful episode where Gloria is set upon by five aunts and numerous girl cousins (in a scene reminiscent of the goblins assaulting Lizzie in Rossetti's "Goblin Market"), who try to force watermelon down her throat:

> *"London Bridge is falling down,"* some voice sang, and a trap of arms came down over Gloria's head and brought her to the ground. Behind her came a crack like a firecracker—they had split open a melon.
>
> She struggled wildly at first as she tried to push away the red hulk shoved down into her face, as big as a man's clayed shoe, swarming with seeds, warm with rain-thin juice.
>
> They were all laughing. "Say Beecham!" they ordered her, close to her ear. They rolled her by the shoulders, pinned her flat, then buried her face under the flesh of the melon with its blood heat, its smell of evening flowers. Ribbons of juice crawled on her neck and circled it, as hands robbed of sex spread her jaws open.

Gloria is a young, red-haired, freckle-faced orphan who is determined to set herself apart from the Beechams—her mother-in-law's family and, possibly, her unknown father's (so she may be married to her first cousin). The scene permits us to observe in the horrifying torture of Gloria that streak of deep cruelty—especially in the female characters—which is otherwise expressed mostly verbally in the novel.

Two American visitors to Italy—one apparently just a tourist, one making a new home there—find Italian watermelon as luscious as any they have ever tasted. In "Ode to Italian Fruit," Barbara Hamby (b. 1952), in a loose, free-associative style—with, however, the regularity induced by eight ten-line stanzas—begins by emptying, more or less randomly, some of the contents of her mind into her first forty-odd lines, the only allusion to fruit coming in her description of her method of contraception: "using birth control, a type invented by the Egyptians, / a scooped out orange half, / the hemisphere of rind / a barrier against the sperm." Eventually (in line 47), we get to watermelon:

> All summer
> I have ended meals with a wedge of watermelon
> and in a not-so-slightly neurotic fashion have come
> to depend on the cool slivers of crimson,
> which you'd expect to be called *melone d'acqua* in Italian,
>
> but it's *cocomero,* a silly word but fun to say: *cocomero,*
> *cocomero.* The waiter says he has *lampone, frutti di bosco,*
> and *anguria.* My disappointment is ridiculous. I beat
> down the stiff-armed Mussolini rising inside of me,
> order *anguria* because I don't know what it is,
> and I can't have what I want, but the waiter brings

a plate of gorgeous red *cocomero,* so I say, "*Cocomero.*"
"*No, anguria,*" and suddenly, like Alice, I've fallen into
the Land of Anguria, as in Brueghel's painting
of the Land of Cockaigne, a world in which all things

are given like Moses' manna but infinitely more delicious:
rushing streams of wine, orchards of bread, topiaries
    of *gâteau,* and, in my case, a paradise
    of fruit: white peaches like globes
of perfume, *pesche gialle,* juicy and orange, grapes,
figs, green and purple, cherries, melons, then plates
    of *anguria:* crisp and succulent
    at the same time, like love, sex,
food and all things Egyptian and mysterious, which inhabit
their own worlds.

Frances Mayes we have already encountered in chapter 2, in her thoughts on figs. Here I want to quote her meditation on Italian watermelons (unlike Hamby, Mayes doesn't bother about the Italian names for the fruit):

> The watermelon hour—a favorite pause in the afternoon. Watermelon is arguably the best taste in the world, and I must admit that the Tuscan melons rival in flavor those Sugar Babies we picked hot out of the fields in South Georgia when I was a child. I never mastered the art of the thump. Whether the melon is ripe or not, the thump sounds the same to me. Each one I cut, however, seems to be at its pinnacle—toothy crispness, audacious sweetness. When we're sharing melon with the workers, I notice that they eat the white of the melon. When they finish, their rind is a limp green strip. Sitting on the stone wall, sun on my face, big slice of watermelon—I'm seven again, totally engrossed in shooting seeds between my fingers and spooning out circles from the dripping quarter moon of fruit.

For alimentary—if not botanical—reasons, papayas may be considered here with the melons (though green papayas resemble squash in needing to be cooked before eating them). Flowerdew's *Complete Book of Fruit* (1995) provides a compact characterization of the plant and its fruit:

> Papayas (also known as pawpaws) are small herbaceous "trees" which resemble palms as they are unbranched with ornate, acanthus-like foliage clustered on top and up to fifty green "melons" underneath. There are male, female, and hermaphrodite plants. The fruits uncannily resemble melons, turning yellow-orange as they ripen. The flesh is usually pink with a central hole full of small round seeds and can weigh up to 2 kg/5 lb.

It should be added that the "trees" bear fruit all year round. Among major producers
of papayas today are Hawaii, Brazil, Mexico, Indonesia, and Zaire. Brazilian papayas
(along with Brazilian pineapples) were represented in a painting by Albert Eckhout
already referred to in chapter 14.

The diversity of names for the papaya is a potential source of confusion, even
embarrassment, particularly in Spanish-speaking countries. Thus, "papaya" itself is a
Spanish version of the Carib word "ababaya" but in Mexico the name is *melon zapote,*
in Puerto Rico *lechosa,* in Cuba *fruta bomba.* It must be remembered, though, that
"papaya" in Cuba may be used as slang for the female genitalia, and in Brazil, on the
other hand, *mamão* (papaya) is closely related to *mama* (breast). In his poem "Mulata"
(1993), Ricardo Pau-Llosa (b. 1954)—who was born in Cuba and came to the United
States when he was six—relates the sad tale of a mixed-race Cuban prostitute whose
white client visits her every Wednesday afternoon, until, leaving her pregnant, he
departs for Miami with his wife and daughter. Pau-Llosa describes the lovemaking:

> His chest hairs swirled on her syrupy mameyes,
> her lips became slices of guayaba,
> and only American tourists order papaya
> instead of "bomb fruit" before blushing waitresses.
> Hunger and the corner cafe would make him come fast.

There are two different species of tropical fruit called "mameyes" in Cuba; it suffices
to know that they are both ovoid or subglobose in shape, three to eight inches in
diameter, and that one of them possesses (in the words of a publication by Harold
Lowry et al. on "miscellaneous" tropical fruits of Florida) "a slight nipple at the apex."
A "guayaba" is a guava.

Perhaps surprisingly, none of my next three literary episodes involving papayas
seems to have any obvious sexual overtones. In his mock-heroic epic, "The Battle of
the Summer Islands," Edmund Waller narrates a battle between the island of the
Bermudas and two whales. The first canto bears the epigraph, "What fruits they have,
and how Heaven smiles / Upon those late-discovered isles." Most of the canto of some
seventy-three lines is devoted to praise of the flora of the island. We have already
encountered, in chapter 15, the lemons and oranges; also mentioned are palm trees,
figs, tobacco, plaintains, melons, pineapple ("pine"), grapes, and potatoes. Especially
singled out for its rapid growth (in lines 52–55) is

> the fair papà,
> Now but a seed, (preventing nature's law)
> In half the circle of the hasty year
> Project a shade, and lovely fruit do wear.

Our second work containing papaya episodes is a bestselling French novel published in the year just prior to the beginning of the French Revolution, *Paul et Virginie*

454   (1788), by Bernardin de Saint-Pierre (1737–1814). It is difficult to exaggerate the quick success of the novel and its remarkable influence in Europe and America. John Donovan provides this summary:

> *Paul and Virginia* inspired songs and poems, plays, ballets, operas and musical entertainments. One of the most richly and variously illustrated of novels, it also provided the material for numerous sets of engravings and lithographs produced independently of the text, as well as paintings, theatrical posters and two silent films. Favourite scenes from the life of its hero and heroine regularly appeared on china, articles of clothing and miscellaneous decorative objects throughout the nineteenth century.

The setting of the novel is the Ile de France (Mauritius), a small island off the eastern coast of Madagascar. Bernardin had lived there while it was still a French colony in the years 1768–70, and he spends a good deal of time in his novel describing the topography and, especially, the flora and fauna of the island.

In Bernardin's preface to the first edition of his novel he states his goals very clearly (I cite Donovan's translation):

> I wrote this little book with great aims in view. In it I have tried to paint a soil and a vegetation different from those of Europe. Our poets have for long enough made their lovers rest on the banks of streams, in meadows and beneath the leaves of beeches. Mine were to sit on the seashore, at the foot of high rocks, in the shade of coconut-palms, banana-trees and lemon-trees in flower. . . . I wished to join to the beauty of nature between the tropics the moral beauty of a little society. It was also my purpose to exhibit a number of great truths, among them this one: that our happiness consists in living according to Nature and virtue.

He also tells us that he has read his novel in advance to selected individuals and that they have all concurred in their favorable responses, always manifested by the shedding of tears. And these real tears, be it noted, can have been as nothing compared to the torrents of tears—sometimes of joy, sometimes of sadness—shed by all the principal characters in the novel. Our concern is with the food grown and eaten by these characters. This food is largely fruitarian; as the old French settler, who tells the tragic tale of Paul and Virginia, recalls:

> How many times, in the shadow of these rocks, did I share your country fare, for which no animal had paid with its life? Gourds brimming with milk, fresh eggs, rice-cakes served on banana-leaves, baskets of sweet-potatoes, custard-apples, mangoes, oranges, pomegranates, bananas and pine-apples provided at once the most nourishing dishes, the gayest colours and the sweetest juices.

(When Paul and Virginia and their respective mothers come to visit the old settler, he entertains them with wine and seafood.) We first encounter pawpaws (*papayer*) when the twelve-year-old Paul and his mother's Negro slave, Domingue, are transplanting trees from the neighboring woods to the clearing where they live; among these trees is "the pawpaw whose trunk bristles with green melons instead of branches and rises to a capital of broad leaves like those of the fig-tree." Some years later, after Virginia has left for France to stay with a wealthy aunt, Paul notices the height of a pawpaw tree that Virginia planted from seed:

> At Virginia's departure this tree hardly came up to her knee, but it grows rapidly and two years later had reached a height of twenty feet with several rings of ripe fruit round the upper part of its trunk. Having gone to this place by chance, Paul was filled with joy when he beheld the tall tree which had grown from the small seed he had seen planted by his friend; at the same time a profound sadness came over him at this evidence of her long absence.

Finally, conversing with the old settler under that same tree, Paul becomes the mouthpiece for the ambivalent ideological sentiments of the author: "Oh, she who planted this pawpaw-tree gave to those who dwell in these forests a gift that is sweeter and more useful than a whole library of books." Books, of course, are still necessary in imperfect human society.

The Australian poet A. D. Hope (b. 1907), on the other hand, associates the pawpaw with the seductress Eve in his retelling of the Genesis story, "Imperial Adam." The fourth and fifth (of eleven) quatrains represent the moment after Adam first sees the newly created Eve:

> The pawpaw drooped its golden breasts above
> Less generous than the honey of her flesh;
> The innocent sunlight showed the place of love;
> The dew on its dark hairs winked crisp and fresh.

> This plump gourd severed from his virile root,
> She promised on the turf of Paradise
> Delicious pulp of the forbidden fruit;
> Sly as the snake she loosed her sinuous thighs.

A similar association of papayas with sex occurs in a full-page advertisement for Starwood Hotels in the *New Yorker* in 1999. Against a blazingly red background, a nude woman lies, with her eyes closed, in a split papaya that serves as her bed; she is partly covered with the tiny black pits of the fruit, which serve as her coverlet.

Jane Grigson, in her *Fruit Book,* notes that the papaya was introduced into Britain about ten years earlier (around 1972), though she "would not say it has caught

456   on as well as the mango—it is not such a stunning fruit." Certainly, today papayas are readily available in American supermarkets, so that it is possible for Tony Harrison, living in Manhattan, to celebrate papayas as his favorite breakfast fruit, in a long poem, "Fruitility" (1999). The poem, consisting of close to three hundred lines of iambic tetrameter rhymed couplets, begins with some twenty lines of praise for papayas and returns to papayas near the end for another ten lines; the long middle sections of the poem ramble on about life on Broadway at 73rd street, with particular attention to street people and to men with AIDS. (A reader not familiar with New York City may be confused by two references to "the Met": first it means the art museum and then the opera house.) But it is time to look at the papayas in some of the opening lines:

> What a glorious gift from Gaia,
> raspberries piled on papaya,
> which as a ruse to lift my soul
> I serve up in my breakfast bowl,
>   [. . . . .]
>   . . . in Nigeria, I'd grown
> what we called pawpaws of my own;
> picked, deseeded, served fridge-fresh
> I fed my kids their orange flesh.

The thought of feeding his children papayas leads the speaker to recall the fruits of his own childhood (apples and plums), which his mother "scrounged us in the war." And then, reflecting on the human condition, the speaker is led to coin a new word:

> I need to neologise to find
> the fruit in futile humankind,
> and *fruitility* is what I call
> the fate which falls upon us all.
> Meaningless our lives may be
> but blessed with deep fruitility.

    It is this idea—fruitility—that enables the speaker to survive the chaos and death around him, even though "day ends in a dying fire / hued like my rasps piled on papaya." The next morning, as garbage trucks haul away yesterday's "limp papaya skin," the speaker is:

> ready for the life-denier,
> tomorrow when my heart says *Yea*
> to darkness ripening into day,
> remembering my mother whose
> gifts of fruit taught me this ruse.

I know of no more heartfelt tribute to the life-enhancingness of fruit.

Are there any philosophical melons, as there are philosophical apples and philosophical pomegranates? Well, there is the mysterious melon that occurs in the first of
the three extraordinary dreams of René Descartes (1596–1650) on the night of 10–11
November 1619. Descartes thought the dreams were prophetic about his future philosophical career. In the earliest biography of Descartes, by Adrien Baillet, Descartes's
interpretation of the melon episode is reported as follows (translated by Alice
Browne): "The melon, which someone had wished to give him in the first dream, signified, he said, the charms of solitude, but presented by purely human solicitations"
(Le melon, dont on vouloit luy faire présent dans le prémier songe, signifoit, distoit il,
le charmes de la solitude, mais présentez par des sollicitations purement humaines).

If no one has yet provided convincing interpretations of Descartes's dreams, it
has not been for want of trying. Perhaps the lengthiest and most detailed set of interpretations to date are in a book by John R. Cole, *The Olympian Dreams and Youthful
Rebellion of René Descartes* (1992). Specifically in connection with Descartes's melon—
which has been interpreted as anything from the apple of Paradise to the forbidden
fruit of Genesis—Cole cites French and Dutch texts that might have been known to
Descartes and that assert a parallel between the difficulty of selecting a good melon
and the difficulty of selecting good friends. (Descartes had met his most important
intellectual mentor, the Dutchman Isaac Beeckman, exactly one year prior to the
dream day.) Thus, the entry for *melon* in Randle Cotgrave's French-English dictionary
(1st ed., 1611) cites as a proverb the saying, "A peine connoist on la femme, & le melon,"
or—a line cited by Cole—"a good woman is as hard to pick as a good melon." And,
Cole continues, a book of verse by the sixteenth-century author, Claude Mermet (ca.
1550–ca. 1601), *Le temps passé* (Paris, 1585), contains the following quatrain:

> Friends in the present day
> Have this in common with the melon,
> You've got to try fifty
> Before you get a good one.

> ~

> Les amis de l'heure *présente*
> Ont le naturel du *melon;*
> Il en faut essayer cinquante,
> Avant qu'en rencountrer un bon.

Finally, Cole cites a collection of versified Dutch proverbs, *Spiegel van den Ouden ende
Nieuwen Tijdt* (1632), by Jacob Cats (1577–1660), containing "a handsome plate of a
buxom melon vendor and her perplexed customer, who is trying to select a good
piece of fruit by its aroma," as well as a Dutch poem and two French poems on the
same theme (for a nineteenth-century version of Cats's melon vendor in a volume
edited by Richard Pigot, see fig. 12). Here are translations (by Cole) of the Dutch
and French poems from Cats's book, together with the original French texts:

Fig. 12: John Leighton (after Jacob Cats), "Like melons, friends . . . ," 1860

In choosing Friends, it's requisite to use
The self-same care as when we Melons choose:
No one in haste a Melon ever buys,
Nor makes his choice till three or four he tries;
And oft indeed when purchasing this fruit,
Before the buyer can find one to suit,
He's e'en obliged t'examine half a score,
And p'rhaps not find one when his search is o'er.
Be cautious how you choose a friend;
For Friendships that are lightly made,
Have seldom any other end
Than grief to see one's trust betray'd!

~

Friends are like melons.
In ten, you might not find a good one.

~

Amys sont comme le melon;
De dix souvent pas un est bon.

> ~
>
> Friends are like melons;
> You've got to try many to get a good one.
>
> ~
>
> Les amys sont comme le melon;
> Il faut essayer plusieurs pour rancontrer un bon.

The relevance of all this to Descartes's dream-life, according to Cole, is "a line of associations extending back from the *présent melon* in the dream through Descartes's memory of this proverbial maxim in poetic form to the painful infidelity of Isaac Beeckman, who had written so as to hurt, when his friend had needed help." (Descartes was to break with Beeckman some ten years later, but at the time of the dreams they were still friends.) What Cole is suggesting is Descartes's ambivalent feelings toward the older Dutch thinker, exacerbated perhaps by a letter from Beeckman of 6 May 1619 (some six months before the dreams) that might have offended Descartes—if he ever received it, which is not certain (and if he did not, that too would have been an affront, since Descartes had written asking Beeckman for assistance).

The most recent discussion of Descartes's dreams I have come across, by Alan Gabbey and Robert E. Hall, proposes an interpretation of the melon as "representing a complete world of knowledge, an integrated science of the whole, an entire science of the cosmos, a *sphérique encyclopédie,*" citing in support the following passage from the Italian philosopher Franceso Patrizi (1529–1597), whose work "Descartes surely read or knew about":

> But if from the beginning and end of each sign lines are prolonged through the surface of heaven all the way to each pole, they will divide it into twelve equal parts, like a melon. These parts must each have just as many parts of that empty space contiguous to them. And so the whole heaven and the whole world must be surrounded by an outermost space.

A kind of philosophical use of melons occurs in "In Defense of Adjectives" (1991), by Adam Zagajewski (b. 1945), one of a group of short essays—or prose poems—called "The New Little Larousse" (included in the volume *Two Cities* [1991], translated from Polish by Lillian Vallee [1995]). The essay begins with a common stylistic precept—"We are often told to scratch out adjectives"—that Zagajewski finds dubious; rather, he insists, more than the noun or the verb, "the adjective is the indispensable guarantor of the individuality of people and things." To illustrate what he has in mind, Zagajewski introduces an image of melons:

> I see a pile of melons at a fruit stand. For an opponent of adjectives, this matter presents no difficulty. "Melons are piled on the fruit stand." Meanwhile, one melon is as sallow as Talleyrand's complexion when he addressed

the Congress of Vienna; another is green, unripe, full of youthful arrogance; yet another has sunken cheeks, and is lost in a deep, mournful silence, as if it could not bear to part with the fields of Provence. There are no two melons alike. Some are oval, others are squat. Hard or soft. Smelling of the countryside, the sunset, or dry, resigned, exhausted by the trip, rain, strange hands, the gray skies of a Parisian suburb.

Subsequent illustrations are positive (any adequate characterization of a person requires "an entire list of adjectives") and negative ("The army limits the amount of adjectives"). Then, after another tribute to the adjective—"Long live the adjective! Small or big, forgotten or current. We need you, malleable, slim adjective that lies on objects and people so lightly and always sees to it that the vivifying taste of individuality not be lost"—Zagajewski concludes with the large claim that both ethics and memory are impossible without adjectives. Individuality, ethics, and memory are, of course, precisely what totalitarianism is determined to wipe out. It helps to understand Zagajewski to know that he writes as a politically committed opponent of totalitarianism but at the same time as a lone individual whose profound sense of privacy requires him to oppose the dogmas of anti-totalitarianism; he also writes, equally paradoxically, as a deeply skeptical mystic. (On both of these themes, see the brilliant review of Zagajewski's writing by Adam Kirsch in the *New Republic*.) But why the melons, and, indeed, why any fruit at all? It is the very arbitrariness of the choice of fruit and then, among possible fruits, of melons which is the point, I think. The pile of melons is simply a witty conceit and, in Kirsch's words, "with its rapid and unlikely juxtapositions, wit tends to undermine certainty."

19. Raphaelle Peale, *Still Life with Peach,* ca. 1816 [p. 234]

20. Georg Flegel, *Apricot Branch,* ca. 1630 [p. 281]

21. Joris Hoefnagel, medlar, *Mira Calligraphiae Monumenta,* late 1590s [p. 292]

P. BON CHRETIEN.

22. "P. Bon-Chretien," Joseph Decaisne, *Le Jardin fruitier du Museum,* vol. 3 (1860) [p. 333]

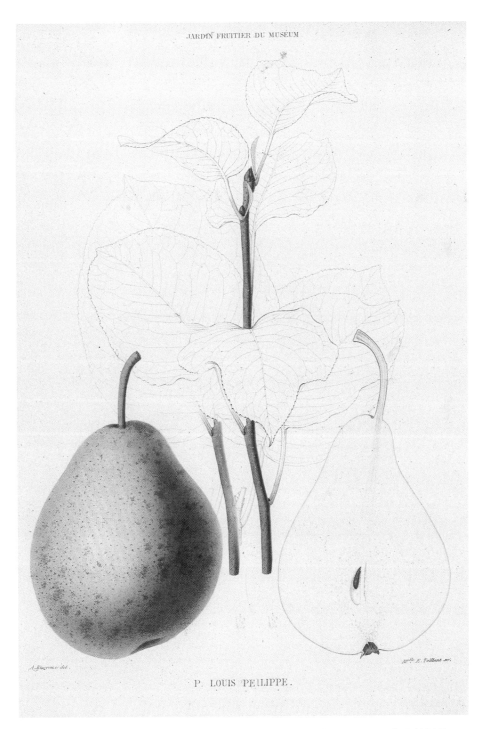

P. LOUIS PHILIPPE.

23. "P. Louis-Philippe," Joseph Decaisne, *Le Jardin fruitier du Museum,* vol. 4 (1861) [p. 333]

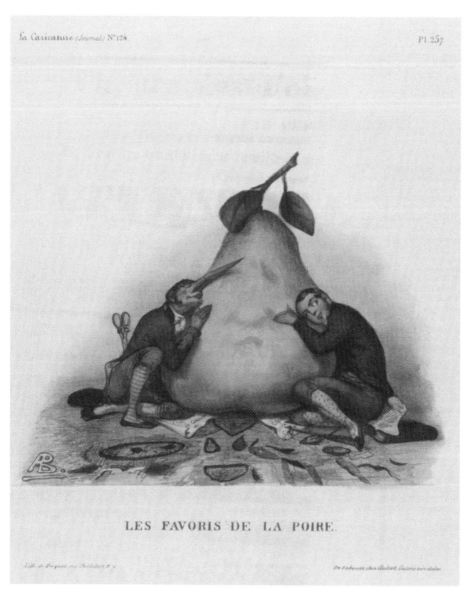

LES FAVORIS DE LA POIRE.

24. Auguste Bouquet, "Les Favoris de la Poire," 1833 [p. 359]

25. George Cruikshank, "Ah! sure such a pair . . . ," 1820 [p. 360]

26. Pineapple pavilion, Dunmore Park, Stirlingshire, Scotland, 1761 [p. 365]

27. Ellis Ruley, *Grapefruit Picking Time*, 1940s [p. 434]

28. Edward Hopper, *Tables for Ladies,* 1930 [p. 434]

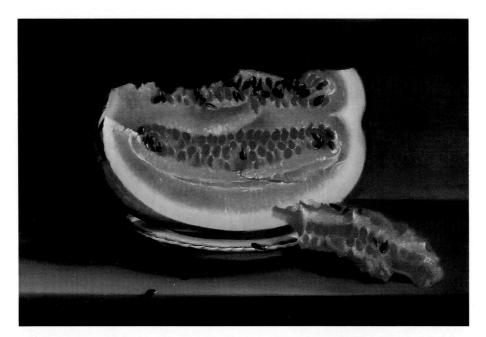

29. Sarah Miriam Peale, *Still Life with Watermelon,* 1822 [p. 448]

30. Philip Guston, *Cherries II,* 1976 [p. 491]

31. Pierre Labadie, "La Barrique d'Amontillado," mid–20th century [p. 591]

32. Gustave Caillebotte, *Nature Morte,* 1880–82 [p. 657]

33. "St Claus Brand,"
1920s–30s [p. 690]

HONEYSWEET

34. "Honeysweet," U. P. Hedrick, *Small Fruits of New York,* 1925 [p. 708]

35. Cadurcis Plantagenet Ream, *Blackberries Spilling from a Tin Cup,*
late 19th–early 20th century [p. 708]

CHAUTAUQUA

36. "Chautauqua," U. P. Hedrick, *Small Fruits of New York,* 1925 [p. 714]

Eve, and the Serpent, in the Garden, of Eden.

37. John H. Coates, "Eve, and the Serpent, in the Garden of Eden," 1916 [p. 735]

17

CHERRIES

Pliny the Elder, writing in the first century C.E., makes what seems to be a perfectly definite statement about the origin of cherry trees in Italy (*Natural History,* 15.102): "Prior to Lucius Lucullus' victory against Mithridates, that is, until [74 B.C.E.], there were no cherry-trees in Italy. Lucullus was the first to bring them back from Pontus [northwestern Turkey], and in the span of 120 years they have crossed the ocean and have spread as far as Britain." Pliny's term for cherry is *cerasus,* and, as Andrew Dalby explains, Pliny must be referring here to our *Prunus cerasus* rather than to our *Prunus avium,* the wild sweet-cherry, which is native to much of Europe; the latter was called *cornus,* and later, *cerasus silvatica,* by the Romans.

Lucullus (d. 57/6 B.C.E.) was a very successful general, but his career suffered from political intrigue, and when he returned to Rome, though he eventually received a triumphal procession, it was against the opposition of political enemies. Thereafter, Lucullus retired into private life, where he was known as something of a gourmet and bon vivant; he also collected manuscripts and was a patron of the arts. Summed up by his biographer, Plutarch, "It is true that in the life of Lucullus, as in an ancient comedy, one reads in the first part of political measures and military commands, and in the latter part of drinking bouts, and banquets, and what might pass for revel-routs, and torch-races and all manner of frivolity." Plutarch concludes that "one might deem Lucullus especially happy in his end, from the fact that he died before that constitutional change had come.... His country was in a distempered state when he lay down his life, but still she was free." (Plutarch, by the way, does not mention the cherry tree incident—nor, for that matter, does the *Oxford Classical Dictionary.*)

Bertolt Brecht, on the other hand, detected quite a different moral in Lucullus's life, in his radio play *Das Verhoer des Lukullus* (The trial of Lucullus; 1939; first performance, 1940). In the play, a jury of five dead souls in the underworld—including a farmer, a teacher, a fishwife, a baker, and a courtesan—are assembled to judge whether Lucullus's life was meritorious enough to qualify him to enter the Elysian Fields. But Lucullus needs a sponsor and, when it turns out that his first choice, Alexander the Great, is not available, a stone frieze depicting Lucullus's triumphal procession is enlisted. The jury then hears (in scene 8) from the following witnesses (in Frank Jones's translation):

A captured king with mournful gaze
A sloe-eyed queen with seductive thighs
A man with a little cherry tree, eating a cherry
A golden god, carried by two slaves, very fat
Two virgins with a tablet bearing the names of 53 cities
Two legionaries
One standing, one dying and saluting his general
A cook with a fish.

None of the testimony is favorable to Lucullus until the farmer's (in scene 13):

My friends, of all that has been conquered
In bloody war of hated memory
I call this the best. This little tree lives on.
A friendly newcomer, it takes its place
Beside the vine and the hard-working berry bush
And, growing with the growing generations
Bears fruit for them. And therefore I commend you
For bringing it to us. When all the plunder
Of both Asias has long turned to rot
This, the smallest of your trophies
Will stand upon the windy hills and wave
Each spring its bloom-white branches to the living.

Brecht's original text ends here, with the jury withdrawing to consider its verdict. Subsequently, in the form of a libretto for an opera by Paul Dessau (first performed in East Berlin, 1951), a new final scene was added in which the jury condemns Lucullus to "nothingness." (An earlier operatic version, with English libretto by H. R. Hays and music by Roger Sessions, had been performed in Los Angeles, in 1947.) The East German Communists were unhappy with the Brecht-Dessau opera and it was closed down after a single performance. Brecht made revisions—which again proved unsatisfactory to the authorities—softening the condemnation of war and altering the title to *The Condemnation of Lucullus*. (Details of the entire affair can be pursued in Martin Esslin's biography of Brecht [1971] and in Manheim and Willett's editorial notes to their edition of the collected plays [1972].)

Brecht uses the importation of the cherry tree to Italy as a mere peg on which to hang his ideological/aesthetic concerns (which are generally, at least in their pristine form, rather more complex—"dialectical"?—than some members of his first audiences would have preferred). I hasten now to consider literary episodes in which the actual attributes of cherries play a significant role. Cherries possess one outstanding attribute when it comes to eating them: their convenient size, which makes each cherry a comfortable mouthful, so that one may eat them rather carelessly while engaged in some other activity (though there is the problem of pit disposal). This relatively diminutive size is reflected in the proverb "It is no use making two bites of a cherry" (see the *Oxford English Dictionary* entry on "cherry"). A slight variation of this proverbial saying can be found in an episode in the fifth book of *Gargantua and Pantagruel* (which, though composed in the sixteenth century, is almost certainly not by—or, at least, not entirely by—Rabelais). Pantagruel and Panurge visit an island on which there is a monastery occupied by the order of the amusingly named "Semiquaver friars." (The semiquaver is the sixteenth note.) When Panurge catechizes one of the friars about the girls in the monastery, the answers to all the questions—there are well over a hundred—are extremely brief, and Panurge finally remarks (in Donald Frame's translation): "So this is the world's poor Semiquaver? Did you see how firm, summary, and succinct he is in his answers? He replies only in monosyllables. I think he'd take three bites for one cherry."

The relative tininess of cherries is also reflected in many of the literary uses of the fruit. Thus, in "These Words," by Jorge Teillier (translated by Mary Crow), the few brief words of the diminutive poetic form (with three of the lines in the first stanza simply repeated in the second) are singularly appropriate for the cherries (enclosed between two darknesses):

> These words want to be
> a handful of cherries,
> a whisper—for whom?—
> between one darkness and another.
>
> Yes, a handful of cherries,
> a whisper—for whom?—
> between one darkness and another.
>
> ~
>
> Estas palabros quieren ser
> un puñado de cerezas,
> un susurro—¿para quién?—
> entre una y otra oscuridad.
>
> Si, un puñado de cerezas,
> un susurro—¿para quién?—
> entre una y otra oscuridad.

Cherry stems, too, have their uses, as in this recipe for constructing a decorative cherry pyramid, from François Massialot's late-seventeenth-century cookbook, *Nouvelle instruction pour les confitures, les liqueurs, et les fruits* (1692; 1717):

One must have pyramidal tin funnels, of various sizes, to fit the porcelain dishes on which you will place them. You put a cherry at the bottom for the point.... On the second layer you put three, on the third, four or five, and thus to the end, according to the capacity of the mold, criss-crossing the stems toward the middle, which you fill up with some chopped worthless leaves, because your fruit will only be around the edges.... The whole being thus well arranged and solid, you put your dish at the opening of the mold, and having turned it over, you gently remove your mold, leaving the pyramid very well arranged and very tidy.

The translation is by Barbara Wheaton from her fine book on the history of French cuisine. One of Massialot's contemporaries, Madame de Sévigné (1626–1696), makes some amusing comments on such fruit pyramids in her description of a dinner party she had attended (translated by Leonard Tancock):

For the pyramids of fruit the doorways had to be raised. Our forefathers never foresaw mechanics like these, since they didn't imagine a door had to be higher than themselves. A pyramid wants to come in (one of those pyramids that mean you are obliged to write notes from one side of the table to the other, not that there is anything upsetting about that, on the contrary it is very pleasant not to see what they conceal). This pyramid, with twenty dishes, was so satisfactorily knocked down at the door that the din drowned the violins, oboes and trumpets.

One can also play games with cherries. Herrick uses a children's game involving cherries to write a poem, "Chop-Cherry" (H-364; 1648) about the game of love:

> Thou gav'st me leave to kisse;
> Thou gav'st me leave to wooe;
> Thou mad'st me thinke by this,
> And that, thou lov'dst me too.
>
> But I shall ne'r forget,
> How for to make thee merry;
> Thou mad'st me chop, but yet,
> Another snapt the Cherry.

Herrick's editor J. Max Patrick explains that "Chop-Cherry" is a "game of snatching with the mouth at cherries in water or hanging on strings." This looks like an easier version (perhaps for younger children?) of bobbing for apples.

As children grow up, a less literal association between lips and cherries may become appropriate, as in this anonymous Elizabethan lyric of 1595:

> Lady, those cherries plenty,
> Which grow on your lips dainty,
>   Ere long will fade and languish.

> Then now, while yet they last them,
>
> O let me pull and taste them.

The song was first published in *The First Booke of Balletts to Five Voyces* (1595) by the leading Elizabethan composer Thomas Morley (1557–1603?). Morley borrowed deeply from Italian sources for both his words and music; strictly speaking, "Lady, those cherries plenty" is not a "ballett" but a "canzonet," as indicated by the rhyme scheme (*aabcc*) of the text and the polyphonic musical style. There is a modern edition of the music by Edmund Fellowes (1965); the only recording I know of (long unavailable) is by Noah Greenberg's New York Pro Musica (first issued, 1955; reissued, 1966), whose brilliant performance is only a minute-and-a-quarter in duration—perfectly adapted to the fading and languishing referred to in the song.

Herrick's well-known version of the same theme is titled "Cherrie-Ripe" (H-53; 1648):

> CHerrie-Ripe, Ripe, Ripe, I cry,
>
> Full and faire ones; come and buy:
>
> If so be, you ask me where
>
> They doe grow? I answer, There,
>
> Where my *Julia's* lips doe smile;
>
> There's the Land, or Cherry-Ile:
>
> Whose Plantations fully show
>
> All the yeere, where Cherries grow.

Thomas Campion (1567–1620) had used the cherry/lips metaphor some three decades before Herrick in an untitled song (Fourth Book of Ayres, 7) for which he also composed the music, "There is a Garden in her face" (ca. 1617). (Campion was unusual among his contemporaries in composing the music for his own poems.) For Campion, there is no question of eating the cherries; the continual stream of images hardly leaves space for the literal meaning of the fruit. Each individual image is a commonplace, which has led John Hollander to characterize the poem as "a wonderful transformation of a whole series of commonplaces":

> There is a Garden in her face,
>
> Where Roses and white Lillies grow;
>
> A heav'nly paradice is that place,
>
> Wherein all pleasant fruits do flow.
>
> There Cherries grow, which none may buy
>
> Till Cherry ripe themselves doe cry.
>
> Those Cherries fayrely doe enclose
>
> Of Orient Pearle a double row;
>
> Which when her lovely laughter showes,

> They look like Rose-buds fill'd with snow.
> Yet them nor Peere nor Prince can buy,
> Till Cherry ripe themselves doe cry.
>
> Her Eyes like Angels watch them still;
> Her Browes like bended bowes doe stand,
> Threatning with piercing frownes to kill
> All that attempt with eye or hand
> Those sacred Cherries to come nigh,
> Till Cherry ripe themselves doe cry.

Hollander is particularly taken with the way "Campion's stanzaic development has served the imaginative purpose of taking seriously what might be, in a weaker song by a less serious and joyful singer, a bit of lyrical rhetoric." I must confess that I find the second stanza teetering on the edge of absurdity, especially when the beloved's teeth are compared to rows of pearls. But then Hollander asks us to see those pearls as rows in a garden, disregarding the fact that the only flowers in the stanza—the rose-buds—are identified with the beloved's lips (and her teeth with the snow). At this point, I believe all that can save the stanza, and perhaps the poem, is the view of C. S. Lewis (another great admirer of Campion) that Campion's poems are occasions "not for moral or intellectual activity but for the creation of a new experience which could occur only in poetry." With this understanding, Hollander's interpretation of the third stanza may stand: the "sacred" cherries are not forbidden apples but are rather to be associated with the golden apples of the Hesperides, and Campion's "heav'nly para-dice" (in the first stanza) is transformed into an "Earthly Paradise" of "beautiful"— if difficult—"sexual attainment."

Hollander says little about the music Campion composed to accompany his song, only that the repeated phrase, "Cherry ripe," is set to the notes of a London street vendor's cry, "through an ascending third." Walter R. Davis, on the other hand, thinks this bit of music "undercuts, with its earthy commercialism, the high Petrarchan style of the rest of the song." For the text and musical score of the song, see Davis's edition of Campion's *Works;* and for a performance of the song with lute accompaniment, one may listen to Steven Rickards (countertenor) and Dorothy Linell (lute) on a Naxos compact disc (1999).

An example of a "weaker" (Hollander's term) song than Campion's on the cherry/lips theme is this one by Francis Davison (1575?–1619), published some ten years earlier (1607):

> Since your sweet cherry lips I kissed,
> No want of food I once have missed;
> My stomach now no meat requires,
> My throat no drink at all desires;
> For by your breath, which then I gained,
> Chameleon-like my life's maintained.

Then grant me, dear, those cherries still,
O let me feed on them my fill;
If by a surfeit death I get,
Upon my tomb let this be set:
Here lieth he whom cherries two
Made both to live and life forgo.

Herrick's "Cherrie-ripe" may have been inspired by Campion's poem, which, according to Walter Davis, may itself have been inspired by the anonymous song (of 1595) cited earlier.

Cherry/lips *was* truly a commonplace; even Shakespeare used it but, significantly, for comic effect. In act 3, scene 2, of *A Midsummer Night's Dream* (1594)—"Another part of the wood" is the stage direction—Oberon's mischievous intervention in the loves of the four young Athenians causes Demetrius to shift his love from Hermia to Helena; his first words on awakening are those of a silly, besotted lover: "O Helen, goddess, nymph, perfect, divine! / To what, my love, shall I compare thine eyne? / Crystal is muddy! O, how ripe in show / Thy lips, those kissing cherries, tempting grow!" (137–40). Helena is highly offended by what she takes to be Demetrius's mockery, and when Hermia seems to be joining the cruel game, Helena responds with bitter allusions to their long and close friendship in a lengthy speech, during the course of which Shakespeare shows us what he can do in the way of producing an original cherry conceit (208–12):

So we grew together
Like to a double cherry, seeming parted,
But yet an union in partition,
Two lovely berries moulded on one stem;
So with two seeming bodies but one heart,

Rather more serious than any of the cherry poems we have just encountered are a set of prose episodes—by Jean-Jacques Rousseau (1712–1778), Tolstoy, and D. H. Lawrence—in which a lover picks cherries in an orchard. Toward the beginning of book 4 of part 1 of his *Confessions* (1782; 1789; 1798), Rousseau finds himself wandering on foot in the countryside south of Geneva; it is a summer morning, probably the first of July, 1730 (which would make Rousseau eighteen years old). He runs into two acquaintances on horseback, Mlle. Graffenried and Mlle. Galley, and helps them cross a stream. The girls are, respectively, twenty-one and twenty, and Mlle. Galley's mother owns a chateau in the vicinity, where the three young people end up spending the rest of the day together. After dinner, they decide to take their coffee, cake, and cream outside (as translated by Christopher Kelly):

and to keep our appetite at its peak we went into the orchard to finish our
dessert with cherries. I climbed up the tree and I threw them bunches
whose stones they returned to me through the branches. One time Mlle
Galley, putting forward her pinafore and pushing back her head, presented

herself so well, and I aimed so accurately, that I made a bunch fall in her bosom; and what laughter. I said to myself, "Why are my lips not cherries! How wholeheartedly would I throw them there?"

The two-way trafffic in cherries and pits I find puzzling: was it some sort of game? In any case, Rousseau is extravagantly enthusiastic about the innocent sexuality of the episode:

> I know that the remembrance of such a beautiful day touches me more, charms me more, returns more to my heart than that of any pleasures I have tasted in my life. I did not know very well what I wanted from these two charming persons, but both appealed to me very much. . . . However it might be, upon leaving them it seemed to me that I would not be able to live any longer without either of them. Who would have told me that I would never see them again in my life, and that our ephemeral love would end there?

Ian Hamilton Finlay has memorialized this famous episode from Rousseau's early life in a small monument erected in Finlay's famous garden in Lanarkshire, Scotland; the work is described as follows by Finlay: "On a small fluted column among the trees is a bronze or stone basket of cherries with the words *l'idylle des cerises*" (quoted in Susan Stewart's essay, "Garden Agon" [1998]).

A discreet but impassioned courting between lovers is the theme of our next two cherry-picking episodes, the first from Tolstoy's early short novel, *Family Happiness* (1859), and the second from D. H. Lawrence's early novel, *Sons and Lovers* (1913). If Rousseau never so much as sees his cherry-picking companions again, Tolstoy's cherry-tree lovers decide to marry soon after their cherry-picking episode, while Lawrence's cherry-tree lovers lose their virginity immediately after theirs.

The very title, *Family Happiness,* must remind us—as it could not, of course, have reminded Tolstoy's original readers—of the opening lines of the later novel *Anna Karenina* about happy and unhappy families. The two novels have this much in common: certain key elements in their respective plots turn on an adulterous relation—in the earlier case merely contemplated, in the later only too fulsomely realized—between a married woman and her lover. The story in *Family Happiness*—I follow the translation by Kyrila and April FitzLyon—is a reminiscence told by Maria Alexandrovna (Masha)—of how she was courted (part 1) and of her subsequent marriage, motherhood, and successfully resisted sexual temptation (part 2). (It should be noted that this instance of a female narrator is unique in Tolstoy's fiction.) She begins by mentioning the death of her own mother, which left her orphaned at seventeen. A neighbor and old friend of her father's, the thirty-six-year-old Sergey Mikhailovich, comes to visit the household, consisting now of Masha, her younger sister, Sonia, and Katia, the governess. Masha has, of course, known Sergey since her childhood; what she mostly associates him with is a remark of her mother's to the effect that such a man would make Masha a good husband. Not in Masha's eyes: "Then this idea had seemed extraordinary to me and even unpleasant; my ideal was quite different. I imagined my hero as thin and spare, pale and sad; whereas Sergey Mikhailovich was no longer in his first youth, was tall and thickset and, it seemed, to me, always cheerful." And now, six years since she has last seen him, "he had changed a great deal: he had become older and swarthier, and had grown side-whiskers which did not suit him at all." Masha does, however, very much respect his honesty and intelligence, even though this leads to him criticizing her for appearing bored and depressed: "'You must study more—and don't mope,' he said in a way which seemed to me too cold and forthright. 'And in spring I will set you an examination,' he added, letting go my hand and not looking at me."

Sergey duly returns in the spring and then proceeds to visit Masha's household several times a week throughout the summer. Finally, one afternoon at the beginning of autumn, Sergey arrives on horseback. In preparation for his arrival his favorite fruits—peaches and cherries—have been brought out into the garden. When he arrives, he is in a lively mood—one of "wild delight," as he calls it—and soon, "Catching sight of the plate of cherries, he seized it stealthily, and going up to Sonia under the lime tree, he sat down on her dolls. Sonia was annoyed at first, but he quickly made it up with her by racing her at eating cherries." Masha and Sergey then decide to pick some more cherries, but the cherry trees are growing inside a locked cage topped by a net (presumably to keep the birds out). One side of the cage is a wall, over which Sergey climbs to enter the cage. Unobserved herself, Masha then watches him as she stands on an empty tub looking over a lower wall that forms another side of the cage: "Hatless, and with his eyes closed, he was sitting in the fork of an old cherry tree and was carefully rolling a lump of resin into a little pellet." Masha hears him whisper her name feelingly several times. Then he notices her, first blushing and smiling but unable to speak, and finally admonishing Masha:

> "Climb down now—you'll hurt yourself," he said. "And tidy your hair—just look what a sight you are!"
>
> "Why does he pretend? Why does he want to hurt me?" I thought, vexed. And at the same instant I had an irresistible urge to disconcert him again and to test my power over him.
>
> "No, I want to pick the cherries myself," I said, and catching on to the nearest branch, I swung my legs over the wall. He had no time to catch me before I jumped on the ground inside the cage.
>
> "What stupid things you do do!" he said, blushing again and trying to cover his confusion with an air of annoyance. "You might have hurt yourself. And how are you going to get out of here?" . . .
>
> I, too, became confused, and blushing and trying to avoid him, not knowing what to say, I started to pick cherries, although I had nowhere to put them.

Sonia mercifully brings the key and releases the two lovers from their misery. The irritability of each of the lovers—arising, no doubt, from repressed sexual desire—has led to a tension between them that is only partially resolved later that evening when Sergey is able to convey his love for Masha by "every movement and look of his," though never in words.

The brief cherry-picking episode has taken over a full page to describe, with the action slowed down almost to a standstill: the effect on the reader is nevertheless electrifying, as the aches and ardors of first love are being so brilliantly depicted. Finally, though we never hear Sergey propose to Masha in so many words, they do decide a week later to get married, but during that week of intense anticipation Masha continues to agonize over her behavior during the cherry-picking: "the fact that I had jumped into the cherry-cage to him worried me." The hesitations and failed communications of the cherry-tree incident prefigure, I believe, the entire course of the future relationship between the lovers.

In the second half of the novel, Masha recalls the next three years of her—now married—life: trips to Moscow and Petersburg, the birth of a child, misunderstandings with her husband, always boredom and a vague sense of failed opportunities in her marriage. Once, while Masha is visiting a spa at Baden-Baden without her husband, an Italian marquis attempts to seduce her, kissing her (on the cheek): "'Je vous aimé, he whispered, in a voice that was so like my husband's. I remembered my husband and child as if they were dear things that had existed long ago, and as if all was over between them and me." But then Masha suddenly finds herself revolted by the marquis and decides to return immediately to her husband in Heidelberg. Sergey suspects something has happened, but when Masha tries to explain her feelings, he is utterly incapable of understanding. In the final section of the novel Masha recalls a day several years later, after the couple have had a second child, when she is home alone on an early spring evening and is reminded of the day that Sergey made his proposal of marriage. But now in the present: "The scent of lilac and cherry-blossom filled the garden and the terrace, as if all the air was in bloom; it came in waves, now stronger, now weaker, so that one wanted to close one's eyes and see nothing, hear nothing apart from that sweet scent." The activity of picking cherries has been replaced by a passive retreat into the near oblivion of a suffocatingly sweet atmosphere. When her husband arrives home, Masha finally confronts him with her unfulfilled hopes and the (for her) bewildering withdrawal of his love. For once, he seems to understand. Masha concludes with these reflections:

> From that day my romance with my husband was over, the old feeling became a dear, irretrievable memory, and a new feeling of love for my children and for the father of my children laid the foundation for another, this time completely different, happy life, which I am still living at the present moment.

Happy families may, indeed, be all alike, but is Masha's really a happy family? It is worth looking at two contrasting—if not diametrically opposed—interpretations of Tolstoy's novel, each of which confidently provides an answer to this question. (I am, of course, particularly interested in how each interpretation deals with the cherry tree episode.) Renato Poggioli devotes the entire penultimate chapter of his book, *The Oaken Flute* (1975), to the novel (chapter 13, "Tolstoy's *Domestic Happiness:* Beyond Pastoral Love"). In Poggioli's view, the first half of what he terms the "diptych" that constitutes the novel "is written in the key of a pastoral romance; the second, of realistic fiction." Poggioli's almost exclusive focus on the pastoral ideal certainly produces some important insights into aspects of Tolstoy's novel (such as the use of the four seasons as a structural framework in the first part), but, I'm afraid, it also obscures the continuity of the two parts of the novel—which, after all, share the same narrator—and, even more important, prevents him from noticing crucial situations and attitudes in the first part that are inconsistent with the pastoral ideal. Thus, Poggioli characterizes the cherry picking as "the charming episode in the orchard, when the girl climbs on the cherry tree to pick its fruits, while the man watches from below." Now, to begin with, this is a grossly inaccurate summary of the episode in question: it is Masha who watches Sergey in the cherry tree but he never seems to pick any cherries, while Masha does pick cherries but never climbs a tree. (Incidentally, Poggioli's summary of the Rousseau cherry-picking episode—which he adduces by way of contrast to Tolstoy's episode—is also grossly inaccurate: "Jean-Jacques simply shares a basket of cherries not with a single nymph of his choice but with two maidens met by chance in the woods.") Furthermore, as I have emphasized above, the dominant note of the entire episode is not adequately characterized as simply "charming." The pastoral ideal, of course, does not preclude tension between the lovers; indeed, without *some* tension pastoral becomes rather boring. For Masha and Sergey, however, the reality of their widely differing expectations and hopes for their marriage blights the joy of their love right from the beginning.

As to the question of what "happiness" means at the end of the novel, Poggioli concludes with the conventional, not to say trite, formula: "As soon as two lovers go beyond the boundaries of pastoral fantasy and romantic fancies they discover that love can last, and grow stronger and truer, only if and when it is circumscribed." This makes it sound as if Tolstoy were writing a marriage manual.

The second interpretation of Tolstoy's novel I want to discusss is in a book by Richard F. Gustafson on Tolstoy's fiction. Gustafson's fundamental assumption is that "Tolstoy's literary works cannot be separated from his religious world view; they are the verbal icons of it. . . . His narratives tell of the divine call to love and man's response to that call." Gustafson's critical method—"The primary rule in reading Tolstoy . . . is that the later clarifies the earlier"—is, I submit, only viable when balanced by an equal concern for the integrity of "the earlier," both in itself and as a guide to "the later."

More dubious I find Gustafson's idea that "the poetics of Tolstoy's fiction . . . are shown
to flow from the theological content." After reading this last claim I began wondering
about the possible theological basis of the cherry-picking episode in *Family Happiness.*
But in fact Gustafson simply ignores that episode, while for him Masha's "greatest
moment is in church"—actually, many moments, as she goes to the early morning
church service each day of the week after the cherry-picking episode and takes communion on one of the days (her birthday). I must confess I may undervalue the significance of Masha's sudden religious fervor, which I tend to see as all of a piece with
the rest of her surging emotions during the week in question.

Gustafson also ignores another aspect of the "poetics" of *Family Happiness,*
namely, the division of Masha's reminiscenses into two parts, before and after her marriage. For Gustafson, this division can have no great significance, since from the beginning to the end of her story Masha never escapes from "the abyss of self-love": her
"'understanding of life' is limited, and, although she changes, she does not grow toward
the discovery and seizure of the Divine." Happiness is hardly an issue; rather, Tolstoy's
concern is to refute "the modern assumption that romantic passion is the first step to
marital love and family life" and to explore "the age-old confusion between romantic
love and the Christian idea of love." Instead of a marriage manual, Tolstoy seems to
have been composing a theological treatise on the various meanings of love.

I prefer to interpret *Family Happiness* as the carefully modulated account by a
highly sensitive young woman of her stormy emotional life. At the very least, such an
interpretation forces one to examine carefully exactly what she says and does at each
critical point in her narrative. As for the cherry-picking episode, I make no claim that
it is the key to understanding Tolstoy's novel but only that it ought to be appreciated
for its superb literary quality (though I might also suggest that careful attention to the
details of the episode helps to rule out excessively narrow and tendentious interpretations of the work as a whole). And here I would appeal to Tolstoy's own view of his
literary method; the following quotation is from a letter of 23/26 April 1876 to N. N.
Strakhov (in R. F. Christian's translation), written in response to some comments on
Anna Karenina, which Strakhov was proofreading at the time:

> In everything, or nearly everything I have written, I have been guided by
> the need to gather together ideas which for the purpose of self-expression
> were interconnected; but every idea expressed separately in words loses its
> meaning and is terribly impoverished when taken by itself out of the con-
> nection in which it occurs. The connection itself is made up, I think, not
> by the idea, but by something else, and it is impossible to express the basis
> of this connection directly in words. It can only be expressed indirectly—
> by words describing characters, actions and situations.

Tolstoy's elusive "something else" may be identifiable with what the American critic
Philip Rahv calls "a glutinous substance" in his discussion (1946) of the novel:

The binding dogma in *Family Happiness* is the instability and deceptiveness of love as compared with a sound family life and the rearing of children in insuring the happiness of a married couple. Yet the didacticism of such ideas seldom interferes with our enjoyment of the Tolstoyan fiction. For the wonderful thing about it is its tissue of detail, the tenacious way in which it holds together, as if it were a glutinous substance, and its incomparable rightness and truthfulness.

Rahv goes on to explain how "*Family Happiness,* with its denigration of love and of equal rights for women, was conceived, quite apart from its personal genesis in Tolstoy's affair with Valerya Arsenev, as a polemical rejoinder to George Sand, then adored by virtually all the Petersburg writers, including Dostoevsky." The important point, though, is that Tolstoy's "early *nouvelles* can certainly be read and appreciated without reference to their historical context, to the ideological differences between him and his contemporaries."

I turn to D. H. Lawrence. Two-thirds of the way through *Sons and Lovers,* near the opening of chapter 11, "The Test on Miriam," the eight-year relationship between Paul and Miriam has reached the breaking point. He is twenty-four, she a few years younger; both are virgins. One evening when Paul is visiting Miriam at her home on Willey Farm, he and Edgar (one of Miriam's brothers) go out to pick cherries:

> There was a great crop of cherries at the farm. The trees at the back of the house, very large and tall, hung thick with scarlet and crimson drops, under the dark leaves. . . . Paul climbed high in the tree, above the scarlet roofs of the buildings. . . . The young man, perched insecurely in the slender branches, rocked till he felt slightly drunk, reached down the boughs where the scarlet beady cherries hung thick underneath, and tore off handful after handful of the sleek, cool-fleshed fruit. Cherries touched his ears and his neck as he stretched forward, their chill finger-tips sending a flash down his blood. All shades of red, from a golden vermilion to a rich crimson, glowed and met his eyes under a darkness of leaves.

But Lawrence is not content to delineate this episode in terms of cherries alone. There is a colorful sunset timed to coincide with the arrival of Miriam, who immediately discovers at her feet "four dead birds, thieves that had been shot. Paul saw some cherry-stones hanging quite bleached, like skeletons, picked clear of flesh": the air, we might say, is fraught with a sense of loss. And Lawrence goes on to describe Paul's view from high up in the cherry tree:

> She seemed so small, so soft, so tender, down there. He threw a handful of cherries at her. She was startled and frightened. He laughed with a low, chuckling sound, and pelted her. She ran for shelter, picking up some cherries. Two fine pairs she hung over her ears.

When the sun has finally set, Paul descends from the cherry tree (we never hear of Edgar again), and he and Miriam go for a walk in a dense grove of fir trees and pines. After some desultory conversation about the impending rain shower the two make love. Afterwards, neither is satisfied, though Lawrence takes us inside only Paul's mind: "He realized that she had not been with him all the time, that her soul had stood apart, in a sort of horror. He was physically at rest, but no more. Very dreary at heart, very sad."

During the years Lawrence was working on *Sons and Lovers,* he wrote two of his early, self-styled "rhyming poems" about the cherry-picking episode; one of these, "Cherry Robbers," was included in *Love Poems and Others* (1913), while the other, titled simply "Song," remained unpublished during Lawrence's lifetime. According to Lawrence, in his preface to *Collected Poems* (1928), the two are among his "Miriam poems," and between them they cover the same events as the cherry-picking episode in *Sons and Lovers.* In the childish "Song," the Paul-figure is up in a cherry tree raining cherries down on the Miriam-figure, who runs away. The published poem is more complex:

> Under the long dark boughs, like jewels red
> > In the hair of an Eastern girl
> Hang strings of crimson cherries, as if had bled
> > Blood-drops beneath each curl.

> Under the glistening cherries, with folded wings
> > Three dead birds lie:
> Pale-breasted throstles and a blackbird, robberlings
> > Stained with red dye.

> Against the haystack a girl stands laughing at me,
> > Cherries hung round her ears.
> Offers me her scarlet fruit: I will see
> > If she has any tears.

Many details differ from the version of the episode in *Sons and Lovers:* the number of dead birds—their species now named—is reduced from four to three; the cause of the birds' death is no longer specified; and, most important, in the poem the girl offers cherries to the speaker, whereas in the novel the young man throws cherries at the girl. The two versions need not, of course, have the same significance and, indeed, in her book on Lawrence's poetry, *Acts of Attention* (1972), Sandra Gilbert argues that "we might expect the novelist . . . to have been from the beginning a force at odds with the writer's poetic demon." This presumably explains why Gilbert ignores the *Sons and Lovers* version of the cherry-picking episode when interpreting "Cherry Robbers." According to Gilbert, "the chord coupling pain and beauty (or love) . . . is . . . the theme of the poem." As for the fruit, it is "more than the innocent cherries she hangs round her ears; and the young man who plucks the fruit of her sexuality—her virginity—will draw blood in more ways than one." On the other hand, the double loss of virginity—by both Paul and Miriam—emphasized in the novel implies a less one-sided view of the lovemaking than the bloody male aggressiveness which Gilbert takes to be the essence of the poem. Also, in the novel Miriam's anguished insight after the lovemaking is treated with considerable delicacy by Lawrence, as when he writes: "She had been afraid before of the brute in him: now of the mystic."

Another critic of the poem, Carol Dietrich, also ignores Lawrence's novel, as she offers a rather far-fetched interpretation of the cherries as "the fatal fruit in the Garden of Eden." I might add that the statement "I will see / If she has any tears" may not deserve Dietrich's charge of "cruelty": the girl's laughter in the presence of the dead birds might very well provoke curiosity in the speaker's mind as to whether she is also capable of (compassionate) tears.

I would assume that Lawrence was unaware of the vulgar equation of cherries with virginity, since the usage is missing from the leading compilation of British slang, Eric Partridge's *Dictionary of Slang and Unconventional English,* and enters the *OED* only in one of its recent supplements, where it is declared an Americanism, the earliest citation being a novel of 1926 by William Faulkner. For the American usage, we may consult the entry "cherry" in *The Random House Historical Dictionary of American Slang,* where the earliest citation is from 1918. In this latter entry, a couplet is quoted from a source specifically designated (by an asterisk) as non-American, namely, *The Fruit of That Forbidden Tree* (1975), an anthology of Restoration literature on love, edited by John Adlard (b. 1929): "Then be not affrighted, for thus we will do: / Thou shalt have my cherry, and cherry-stones, too." Turning to Adlard's book, we find an anonymous poem of eleven quatrains originally published in a collection called *Wit's Cabinet* (ca. 1700); the first five stanzas read:

> 'Now the weather is warm, let us laugh and be merry.
> My Betty, let us walk and taste of a cherry.
> Then be not affrighted, for thus we will do:
> Thou shalt have my cherry, and cherry-stones too.'
>
> 'Then use me not roughly, but prithee be kind;
> I thought to such tricks you had not been inclined;
> But since thou to me thy mind dost declare,
> We'll walk to the place where the cherry-trees are.'
>
> No sooner they came to sit under the boughs
> But Betty she taxed him with breaking of vows.
> Quoth Johnny, 'Don't say so, my love it is true:
> Thou shalt have my cherry, and cherry-stones too.

And this is a vow I am resolved to keep,
For a maidenhead I will have ere I do sleep.'
As soon as she heard him she quickly was won,
And under the cherry-tree there it was done.

Says Betty, 'Oh, will not these cherries prove ill
And be the cause for my belly to swell?
As many young maidens has [sic] cause for to rue,
For eating of cherries, and cherry-stones too.'

Clearly, the poem reveals a folk belief in cherries and cherry stones as causes of pregnancy (and not any identification of cherries with virginity, even though maidenhead is mentioned in the poem). Now, this folk belief Lawrence might very well have encountered. But is it plausible that he was thinking of the association of cherries and pregnancy when he wrote the two cherry-picking episodes?

Lawrence might also have known a very different set of verses associating cherries with pregnancy: a Christmas carol from the west of England, recorded in numerous versions by Francis James Child in his great compilation of English and Scottish popular ballads (1904). According to Child, the story on which the ballad is based stems from the pseudo-Matthew's Gospel (chapter 20), and there are Catalan and Provençal versions of the carol in which an apple replaces the cherry. Of the several English versions and variants, I quote the first nine of a dozen stanzas from Child's version A:

Joseph was an old man,
    and an old man was he,
When he wedded Mary,
    in the land of Galilee.

Joseph and Mary walked
    through an orchard good,
Where was berries and cherries,
    so red as any blood.

Joseph and Mary walked
    through an orchard green,
Where was berries and cherries,
    as thick as might be seen.

O then bespoke Mary,
    so meek and so mild:

"Pluck me me one cherry, Joseph,
    for I am with child."

O then bespoke Joseph,
    with words most unkind:
"Let him pluck thee a cherry
    that brought thee with child."

O then bespoke the babe,
    within his mother's womb:
"Bow down then the tallest tree,
    for my mother to have some."

Then bowed down the highest tree
    unto his mother's hand;
Then she cried, See, Joseph,
    I have cherries at command.

O then bespoke Joseph:
    "I have done Mary wrong;
But cheer up, my dearest,
    and be not cast down."

Then Mary plucked a cherry,
    as red as the blood,
Then Mary went home
    with her heavy load.

A versified version of the lovers picking cherries motif, also incorporating the pregnancy-cherries link, occurs in a balladlike poem by the Hungarian József Erdélyi (1896–1978); the first, fifth, ninth, and tenth of thirteen stanzas (in a version by Watson Kirkconnell) include the cherry-picking theme:

The cherry-blossoms may be white,
a pure and snowy flood:
but cherry-fruit will ripen red,
the hue of human blood.
    [. . . . .]
The cherries with pure drops of blood
shine bright upon the tree,
but where (they cry) are lad and lass

to pick the fruit for me?! . . .
[. . . . .]
The young lad shakes the tree above;
the lass picks up below;
her apron and her basket both
are full, and overflow.

She heaps the basket to the brim;
the heart is likewise filled;
and blessing on her womb's fair fruit
from gods of love instilled.

A particularly poignant reference to cherries occurs in the second poem of *A Shropshire Lad* (1896), by A. E. Housman (1859–1936), but there the concern is with cherry trees in bloom, a much more impressive phenomenon than the image of a single cherry:

Loveliest of trees, the cherry now
Is hung with bloom along the bough,
And stands about the woodland ride
Wearing white for Eastertide.

Now, of my threescore years and ten,
Twenty will not come again,
And take from seventy springs a score,
It only leaves me fifty more.

And since to look at things in bloom
Fifty springs are little room,
About the woodlands I will go
To see the cherry hung with snow.

Even though, however, Housman's tribute is to cherry trees in bloom and not to the fruit, the experience of the cherry blossoms must surely be affected by an anticipation of the fruit that will soon make its appearance. Beyond noting the appropriateness of the whiteness of the blossoms for the Easter season, all details of the experience of the cherry blossoms are suppressed by Housman; presumably, the emotions arising in the experience are either too overwhelming to be expressed at all or else so well known as to make any description redundant (or both). What the poem is about is the realization that no finite number of future repetitions of the experience will ever be enough; in other words, the poem is about the second-order experience constituted by this realization of human limitation. And this realization is hardly one that could come easily to a twenty-year-old, which implies that there is some dissonance between the youthfulness of the speaker and the sentiments expressed. So much for the charge that Housman succumbs to mere unreflective adolescent responses to nature.

(Dick Davis has pointed out, in the *TLS* [1998], another interesting and overlooked element in Housman's cherry blossom poem: an instance of arithmetical reckoning—seventy minus twenty equals fifty; such mathematical procedures, rare in English poetry, do occur in the work of the early-first-century B.C.E. Latin poet Manilius, the editing of whose versified astronomical treatise was Housman's greatest contribution to Classical scholarship.)

The cherry blossom poem is not much discussed and apparently not valued very highly by many of Housman's critics, though it has been set to music and is included among the eight Housman poems in Philip Larkin's *Oxford Book of Twentieth-Century English Verse* (1973). It is indeed a modest poem but the subtleties of the last stanza in particular should not be ignored: first, there is the generalization from cherry blossoms to anything in bloom; and, second, there is the characterization of the blossoms as snow, which suggests both an affinity between the seasons and the inevitability of their succession—a further dissonance in the feelings aroused in, and by, the poem.

Once again, we can ask our old question: Why cherry trees? If the two occurrences of "cherry" in the poem were to be replaced by "apple," the sounds and rhythms of the poem would be pretty much preserved; how about the "sense"? Apple trees in blossom are impressive (the apple blossom is the state flower of Arkansas and Michigan). Indeed, we have it on no less an authority than Colette that *any* fruit tree's blossoms are its glory, tending to overwhelm even its fruit (translated by Matthew Ward):

> A fruit tree's glory, the most lasting image it leaves us, the one we look back on most passionately, is the memory of its ephemeral flowering. The white sleeves slipped over the arms of the cherry trees, the early green-white stars of the plum trees, the pear trees' creamy white bristling with brown stamens, and finally, the apple trees white as roses, rosy as snow at dawn—that froth, those swans, those phantoms, those angels are born, billow, disappear, and die scattered. But those seven days blot out the more solid splendor, the durable and joyous season of fruit. Hand filled and hefting a big, long pear, we say, "Do you remember the day the pear trees on this hill all blossomed at once?"
>
> Because, though modest and small, and without much color, a blossom has all the qualities of an explosion, whereas, once put forth, the leaf has no choice but to grow. . . . The flower alone has its sex, its secret, its climax.

Not that Colette is insensitive to the particular beauties of the individual fruits; thus, she refers to "the Montmorency cherry with skin so fine that the pit shows through it against the light." In any case, perhaps Housman's point is that cherry trees are the earliest—or among the earliest—trees to blossom in the spring, something we know from another of his poems, where on the first of May the plum and the pear trees are

480   flowering but not the (earlier) cherry or the (later) apple ("The First of May," discussed below in chapter 20, "Orchards, Groves, Gardens").

Linda Pastan has commented on Housman's "Loveliest of trees, the cherry now" in her poem "Misreading Housman" (1991), whose thesis—not formulated until the second half of the work—is the confusion of today's weather (and, by implication, all of nature) and the futility of trying to do anything about it. I much prefer the first half of the poem:

> On this first day of spring, snow
> covers the fruit trees, mingling improbably
> with the new blossoms like identical twins
> brought up in different hemispheres.
> It is not what Housman meant
> when he wrote of the cherry
> hung with snow, though he also knew
> how death can mistake the seasons,
> and if he made it all sound pretty,
> that was our misreading
> in those high school classrooms
> where, drunk on boredom, we had to recite
> his poems.

One way of appreciating the special literary qualities of Housman's cherry blossom poem is by comparing it with similar poems on the same theme. There is, for example, the quatrain "The Cherry Trees," by Walter De la Mare (1873–1956), included in his little volume, *Memory* (1938):

> Under pure skies of April blue I stood,
> Where in wild beauty cherries were in blow;
> And, as sweet fancy willed, see there I could
> Boughs thick with blossom, or inch-deep in snow.

Here, the emphasis is not so much on the round of seasons as on the power of the poet's fancy, and the extra foot in the verse—five iambs instead of Housman's four—introduces a note of gravity that might otherwise be missing from such a brief poem. Moving, metrically, in the other direction, a German poem (in dimeters) about cherry blossoms suggests popular verse:

> Im morgen-taun
> Trittst du hervor
> Den kirschenflor
> Mit mir zu schaun,
> Duft einzuziehn
> Des rasenbeetes.

Fern fliegt der Staub . . .

Durch die natur
Noch nichts gediehn
Von frucht und laub—
Rings blüte nur . . .
Von süden weht es.

This untitled poem from the sixth section of a volume titled *The Seventh Ring* (1907), by Stefan George (1868–1933), is, in fact, one of the poet's deliberate "experiments in the folksong" (Ernst Morwitz). In their translation, Morwitz and Carol Valhope preserve the rhyme scheme (the final "s" of lines six and twelve is the equivalent of the feminine endings in George's German):

You came to view
The cherry tree
in bud, with me
In morning dew.
We drink the scent
Of grassy rows,
Dust far is swirled . . .
No leaves are sprung,
No fruit is spent
In Nature's world—
Just blooms are flung . . .
And southwind blows.

Once again, the earliness of the cherry tree's blossoming—before fruit and leaves [*frucht und laub*]—is prominent.

 D. J. Enright, relatively early in his long writing career, saw a single cherry tree growing in inhospitable soil and, noting its week-long blossoming, found a possible antidote to the despair of humans faced with their own mortality, in "Busybody under a Cherry Tree" (1960):

This tree reminds the busybody
That falling hopes are not so absolute as falling hairs,
That beauty needs and often gets no civic welcome,
That the half-educated still can love, and theirs
May be the whole which we shall never dare,

And that the cherry's body all year round is busy
Against one week of showered gifts without advice,
For it is silent, for its deeds suffice.
(ll. 8–15)

482 Any suspicions of the banality of the rhetoric are dissipated by an awareness of the poetic technique, with the obtrusive rhyme set off against an equally obtrusive metrical irregularity.

Gabriel Preil also associates a particular cherry tree with human mortality, but where Enright is quiet and resigned, Preil is passionate and willful in these lines from "Concerning the Cherry Tree" (1985; in a translation from the Hebrew by Robert Friend):

1

The cherry tree is red again
and the old man
who let me taste of it last year
is gone.
His fruit are darker now.
My fruit grow darker, too.

2

Whether the tree has felt
the old man's absence
I do not know,
but this is clear: this year its fruit ascend
in a rebellious roaring conflagration
proclaiming against death's night
life's repeating colors.

We turn next to a much larger-scale use of cherry blossoms, now in a novel. In *The Egoist* (1879; 1897), George Meredith (1828–1909) uses cherry blossoms to develop an important early episode of his novel. The episode clearly foreshadows the initially highly improbable union in marriage of two of the more attractive characters: Clara, who is engaged throughout most of the novel to "the egoist" (Sir Willoughby Patterne), to whom she finds herself emotionally riveted by means of her very revulsion against him; and Vernon, who, after a disastrous first marriage, seems temperamentally and in every other way unprepared for any further liaisons. The scene in question (in chapter 11, titled "The Double-Blossom Wild Cherry-tree") takes place in the vicinity of a double-blossom wild cherry tree located on the grounds of Willoughby's family estate, Patterne Hall. Our first acquaintance with the tree actually occurs earlier (in chapter 9) when Meredith describes an incident in which almost all the main characters of the novel are involved. To begin with, the young boy, Crossjay—who is innocently in love with Clara—has brought her a bouquet of wildflowers containing a sprig of blossoms from the cherry tree, an artfully arranged bouquet easily identified by Clara as Vernon's handiwork. Clara's father, the Classical scholar and parson Dr. Middleton, and Willoughby each make a significant comment about the tree, which is known to be Vernon's favorite. "'It is a gardener's improvement on the Vestal of the forest, the wild cherry,' said Dr. Middleton, 'and in this case we may admit the gardener's claim to be valid, though I believe that, with his gift of double-blossom, he has improved away the fruit. Call this the Vestal of civilization, then.'" ("Vestal," of course, refers to the white costumes of the vestal virgins of ancient Rome, and Dr. Middleton is alluding in his customary oblique way to the loss of the fruit entailed by the gardeners' success in breeding a tree with double-blossoms.) A moment later Sir Willoughby remarks to Clara that she "'can bear the trial'" of appearing near the tree. "'Few complexions can,'" he continues; "'it is to most ladies a crueller test than snow. Miss Dale, for example, becomes old lace within a dozen yards of it. I should like to place her under the tree beside you.'" Two of Meredith's themes are broached here, one universal (or philosophical), and the other specific to the plot of this novel: first, the way in which civilized human beings tend to lose touch with nature, and second, the contrast between the two potential brides for Willoughby. There is irony, also, in that Willoughby's slightly cruel remark about Laetitia Dale foreshadows a time when he will be forced to choose the lady with the less white complexion. The later episode, to which I now turn, also embodies a universal and a specific theme.

Crossjay, missing from the scene in chapter 9, is very much present in the episode, occupying one long paragraph, at the end of chapter 11. It must be explained that the freshness, sincerity, and honesty of Crossjay especially endear him to Clara precisely because she is not herself overly endowed with those virtues. Clara is out walking with the boy, who indicates where his tutor Vernon is asleep under the cherry tree; he is holding a book, and Clara attempts to see its title but then

> immediately, and still with a bent head, she turned her face to where the load of virginal blossom, whiter than summer cloud on the sky, showered and drooped and clustered so thick as to claim color and seem, like higher Alpine snows in noon sunlight, a flush of white. From deep to deeper heavens of white, her eyes perched and soared. Wonder lived in her. Happiness in the beauty of the tree pressed to supplant it, and was more mortal and narrower. Reflection came, contracting her vision and weighing her to earth. Her reflection was: "He must be good who loves to lie and sleep beneath the branches of this tree!"

Meredith's universal theme here is the sterility of a life without emotional outlets: like the beautiful but fruit-less tree, Vernon, for all his virtues, is nevertheless sterile, both as a scholar and as a man. The particular theme is, of course, Clara's privileging of Vernon above the other suitors for her hand (Willoughby, and the Irishman Horace De Craye), neither of whom appreciates the tree as Vernon does. Near the end of the novel Clara says explicitly she can love only Vernon.

A couple of later references reinforce the significance of the double-blossom wild cherry tree imagery. First, after she has decided to run away from Patterne Hall and all it represents, Clara muses (in chapter 19):

Happy the lady of the place, if happy she can be in her choice! Clara Middleton envied her the double-blossom wild cherry-tree, nothing else. One sprig of it, if it had not faded and gone to dust-colour like crusty Alpine snow in the lower hollows, and then she could depart, bearing away a memory of the best here!

But, of course, the blossoms will always fade eventually and, more important, Clara is at this point unable even to contemplate Vernon, the man with whom she has earlier associated the blossoms. Finally (in chapter 25), Clara and Crossjay, while on another stroll, again encounter the special tree:

> They were in time for a circuit in the park to the wild double cherry-blossom, no longer all white. Clara gazed up from under it, where she had imagined a fairer visible heavenliness than any other sight of earth had ever given her. That was when Vernon lay beneath. But she had certainly looked above, not at him. The tree seemed sorrowful in its withering flowers of the colour of trodden snow.

Clara is still unable to imagine a relationship with Vernon, though she eagerly welcomes Crossjay's fond praise of his tutor and friend. Meredith is preparing us for Clara's slow discovery of her real feelings for Vernon.

The blossoming cherry tree motif seems to have been suggested to Meredith by an old Chinese legend, as Margaret Harris explains:

> The designation of Sir Willoughby Patterne himself gives a clue to the dependence of the plot on the Chinese legend depicted on the blue-and-white Willow Pattern china which became popular in England in the eighteenth century. The story goes that the rich widowed mandarin who lives in the mansion on the right of the image intended to marry his daughter to a wealthy suitor of high degree. But the maiden loved a poor man, her father's secretary, whom she met in secret under the blossoming tree.

Double wild cherry trees (*Prunus avium plena*), by the way, are still recommended as ornamental garden trees by experts, such as Alan Mitchell and Allen Coombes in their book *The Garden Tree* (1998): "Globular flowers hang in dense lines beneath bright green new leaves and last well." On the other hand, while the ordinary wild cherry tree (or Gean) produces fruit of interest to birds, the double variant is, consistent with Dr. Middleton's opinion, "less likely to produce valuable fruit for native and migrating birds."

One of the more arresting pictures of cherry blossoms I know represents an incident that took place in Hamburg during the French military occupation of 1813. The French commander gave orders to cut down all trees in a wide swath around the fortified city, and some residents discovered that the branches of a felled cherry tree continued to blossom. A watercolor depicting the incident, *The Miracle of Blossoms* (ink and watercolor on paper, 8.6 x 13.6(8) in., private collection, Oldenburg), dating to 1814, was painted by Johann Heinrich Wilhelm Tischbein (1751–1829). On the back of the sheet of paper the artist has written an account of the incident in German; here is a translation (by Hinrich Sieveking) of the beginning and end of the passage:

> When the French destroyed the gardens surrounding Hamburg, cutting down their beautiful fruit trees in the winter and leaving them where they fell, some of them still sprouted leaves and fruit in the spring. It is even said that one owner of a cherry tree, which was still barely attached to the stump with a little bark, ate some cherries. . . . With such energy does nature strive to bring forth beauty once again. Could it be that the German greenhouses of the spirit and the beautiful spirits that are being trampled underfoot should also bloom again in time? They are like the plants, the inner power frequently brings forth blossoms, and now and then no doubt also a fruit.

Interestingly, a legend from Franconia, in Germany, ignores both the blossoms and the fruit of the cherry tree and features instead the wood of the tree and the cherry stone; the brief text of "The Treasure of Raueneck," in a translation by Norbert Krapf, reads:

> Under the ruins of the Raueneck mountain castle in the Hassgau lies a buried treasure guarded over by a restless ghost. A cherry sapling sprouts on the wall. After it has grown into a tree, it is cut down and a cradle is built from its wood. Whoever sleeps in the cradle as a Sunday's child will, if he remains pure in heart, during the noon hour free the ghost and release the treasure. He will then be so rich that he can once again rebuild Raueneck and all the castles around. But if the sapling withers or is broken by a storm, the ghost must wait again until a cherrystone, carried by the birds upon the wall, germinates and sprouts.

Cherry wood is, of course, highly valued in cabinetmaking, while a cherry stone is small enough to be carried in a bird's beak.

Jon Stallworthy uses this same sequence (including the bird)—from cherry to stone to cherry tree to wood to furniture—in his "Making a Table" (1986); the organizing motif is the circularity, literal and figurative, of natural and manmade objects: a cherry stone, successive spring seasons, a tree trunk, a round table, a round cork in a wine bottle, and, finally, "the coming together of wood and word, / the coming together of you and me, / the eternal convergence of things."

Donald Davie (1922–1995) has appropriated both the title and the initial line of Herrick's "Cherrie-ripe" for his own "Cherry Ripe" (1957), while turning Herrick's light and extraverted poem into something dark and inward-looking. Said to be "On a Painting by Juan Gris," the poem is, indeed, about art—more specifically, about "the ripening that is art's alone"—and the theme is developed in terms of a contrast between cherries and grapes. Davie must have noticed that, unlike grapes, cherries are rare in Gris's still life paintings—I know of only one which features cherries: *The Cherries* of 1915, now in the Richard S. Zeisler Collection in New York; for a reproduction, see Mark Rosenthal, *Juan Gris* (1983) —and Davie seems to be saying that it is cherries rather than grapes which satisfactorily figure the poetic process. The trouble with grapes (and many other fruits) is that they "have too much bloom of import," which I gloss as too heavy a freight of associations. The feelings engendered in the poet by grapes are too difficult to be "mastered by / Maturing rhythms, to compose a whole." But that such poetic mastering when it does occur may involve loss—terrible loss—is the burden of the last stanza (whose last line echoes the first line of the previous stanza, "And Cherry ripe, indeed ripe, ripe, I cry"):

> But how the shameful grapes and olives swell,
> Excrescent from no cornucopia, tart,
> Too near to oozing to be handled well:
> Ripe, ripe, they cry, and perish in my heart.

Sour cherries are not as deeply embedded in our literary tradition as sour grapes (see chapter 18) but there is an arresting instance by Heinrich Heine (1797–1856) in the form of a short untitled poem, which he wrote probably in 1844 but never published (here translated by Hal Draper):

> At home in dear Germany
> The trees of life grow free;
> Though cherries tempt us with their store,
> The scarecrows frighten us still more.
>
> Like sparrows we are then
> Bluffed off by bogeymen;
> However sweet the cherries spring,
> This song of abstinence we sing.
>
> Outside it's red, the cherry's skin,
> But death hides in its stone within;
> On high with the stars alone
> Are cherries without a stone.
>
> O Father, Son and Holy Ghost,
> Whose praise and glory is our boast:

Our poor German souls yearn sore
For that fruit evermore.

Only where angels wend
Springs joy without an end;
Down here all's sin and sore distress
And cherries soured with bitterness.

Heine is writing of the temptation to assume that human choices—imagined as cherries on the tree of life—are easily classifiable as morally good or bad. In fact, every human act is, from the moral standpoint, radically heterogeneous, like the cherry with its skin, flesh, and stone: though the first may be attractively red, the second is often sour, and the last is inedible if not poisonous.

Heine's metaphorical use of the distinct physical parts of a cherry is present also in "Wild Cherries" (1985), by Adam Zagajewski. After writing many openly political poems directed against the abuses of a repressive Communist regime in Poland, Zagajewski turned, with the imposition of martial law in 1981, to the cultivation of a more individual poetic voice in a series of what his translators Baranczak and Cavanagh call "rich, overflowing, almost baroque odes," which allude to moral and political issues only in a muted and indirect way. "Wild Cherries" has three sections; I quote the first and last about cherries, omitting the middle section about roses:

Wild cherries sprout on slim
stems, pits wrapped
in pink flesh. Here, sparrows can spend hours
confessing to a stern vicar's ear,
loudly betraying non-venial sins
perpetrated at dawn.
      [. . . . .]
The State is perfect, the weather fine.
When you leave, the door immediately
weighs heavier than denunciation.
Thirst can't be quenched.
Behind the soccer field, wild cherries
sprout on slim stems, tart
by day, sweet when asleep.

The Hungarian poet Gyula Illyés, in "Sour-Cherry Trees," personifies the trees, imagining them turned red by strangulation (translated by Emery George):

As is a face, the throat crushed,
so is a cherry tree deeply flushed.

That is the shade of red it turns;
the entire tree now chokes.

I can picture just the throat
which would tolerate such a threat,
and the strangler with the gall
to stalk these vineyards in the fall.

I come from below, stop here, on further,
look upon the scene of murder,
walk right on into the hill,
like one free to flee the kill.

Near, far, on these slopes, there are more
crimson trees than ever before.
Nightmare—I find strange consolation,
beauty in the very notion.

There is a puzzle in the translation of the second stanza: Why "vineyards," which can only refer to grapes? In my interpretation of the (translated) poem I prefer to read "orchards" for "vineyards," thereby preserving, I think, both the meter and the meaning. (But I am informed by the translator, in a personal communication, that "vineyards" accurately renders the Hungarian word.)

An even more extreme association of cherry trees with violence occurs in an early poem (1952) by Paul Celan (1920–1970). Living in Paris and writing, agonizingly, in the language of the people responsible for destroying Jewish communities throughout Europe (including his own parents), Celan was influenced by the imagery of Rilke and the French surrealists in these lines—the first and last stanzas of a brief poem (translated from the German by Michael Hamburger):

In the cherry-tree's branches a crunching of iron shoes.
Summer foams up for you out of helmets. The blacking cuckoo
with diamond spurs draws his image on to the gates of the sky.
[. . . . .]
But unshod through the air comes he who resembles you most;
iron shoes buckled on to his delicate hands
he sleeps through the battle and summer. It's for him that the cherry bleeds.

I want now to discuss a poem about the ripening of cherries that displays a fascination with the powerful forces inherent in plant growth (though the poem does not allude to it, these forces must, for example, overcome the downward pull of gravity). "The Cherry Tree" (1975) by Thom Gunn (b. 1929), uses the extended image of a cherry tree as a female being who produces hundreds of fat, pink babies. (There is also at the very beginning a suggestion of androgyny in the description of the tree trunk, "unmoving as the statue / of a running man," but this is never followed up.) First, the arboreal force and its physical manifestations:

> a need
>   to push
>   push outward
>   from the centre, to
>   bring what is not
>   from what is, pushing
>   till at the tips of the push
>   something comes about
>   and then
>   pulling it from outside
>   until yes she has them started
>   tiny bumps
>   appear at the ends of twigs.

Next come the cherry blossoms:

> Then at once they're all here,
> she wears them like a coat
> a coat of babies

And finally, the cherries themselves "shine among her leaves." The rest of nature responds:

> birds get them, men
> pick them, human children wear them
> in pairs over their ears
> she loses them all.

And the moral is that the cherry tree is importantly *not* like a human mother; the arboreal forces work inexorably and impersonally:

> That's why she made them,
> to lose them into the world, she
> returns to herself,
> she rests, she doesn't care.

Cherries occur prominently—but only as one among a host of disparate images—in a sequence of twenty-four prose poems by the Greek writer—both poet and novelist—Rhea Galanaki (b. 1947); titled *The Cake* (1980), its design, according to Galanaki's translator, Karen Van Dyck, is to track "a pregnant woman through her day as she weighs the ingredients for a cake." Galanaki's range of reference is wide: from

490   Euripides's *Bacchae,* early Christian bas-reliefs, and Galileo's definition of motion to the folklore of cocks in contemporary Greece; from the Chicago Haymarket riots of 1886 to Trotsky's murder in Mexico in 1940 and the least known of Luis Buñuel's trio of great films of the 1970s, *The Phantom of Freedom* (1974). The allusion to Buñel's film inevitably suggests surrealistic subversion, which turns out to be accurate enough as a characterization of Galanaki's work. But the subversion has a marked feminist inflection. Van Dyck puts it this way:

> Drawing on the formative experience of writing under an authoritarian regime, these women [Galanaki, Jenny Mastoraki, and Maria Laina] forged a poetics that established a gendered relation to censorship. The tactics for stabilizing signification upon which censorship relied were redeployed in their collections to unsettle and disrupt fixed meanings and sex roles.

Galanaki's very title is subversive; instead of either of the normal Greek terms for "cake," she simply transcribes the English word into Greek: *keik. The Cake* begins:

> 1. You hold the scales of pleasure with all the trays. The scale tips each time the slaughtered cock weighs it down.
>
>   [. . . . .]
>
> You push down with your slaughtered finger and it splatters blood on the kitchen table, where you weigh the right amount of flour, sugar, and butter for an anniversary; your body in its best dress is weighing, in its best dress gigantic, immobile, it is holding, it is as if you were already holding the cake in your hands.

By the twenty-first section, the cake has been adorned with cherries:

> 21. Their procession is arranged a man, then a woman, they are all friends and they hold a branch of cherry blossoms.
>
>   [. . . . .]
>
>   They wait and see. The pollen builds a martyr's tomb over the mortal remains. The pistils open their lips and receive the pollen's love. The flower center swells, the petals dry up and fall off. The new cherries are its hard, shiny fruit.
>
>   They eat the cake which is now decorated with lots of cherries in syrup. No one gets up to kiss. It has been awhile since the dead woman went to the neighboring lot to hang herself in the cherry tree. After she tested the syrup to see if it had set and found it adequate.

The last section—which "with its imagery (Phrygian drum, thyrsus, lion, and maenads) reworks Euripides's *Bacchae*" (Van Dyck)—ends with a birth:

> 24. My body is all the cardboard bodies of women and I arrive at the edge of an empty parking lot; and I arrive at the edge of myths. I wear my

cherry-colored veil and on top a deer hide. . . . In one of my palms the sugar, in the other the flour. My body in its best dress weighs, in its cherry-colored veil and the deer hide gigantic, immobile it weighs with the sensitive palm the right amount of flour, of sugar, and of butter. Then I toss the dough into the buttered pan in order to make a Phrygian cake with tiny cherries. . . . And I will drop twelve cherry questions in a circle around the top. To look like a speedometer. . . . And I will plant the maenad's clothes near a spring and the spring drawn on paper and the paper a page of language that wells up. And next to this I will lie down, calm and naked, and give birth.

Let us consider now some surprisingly dramatic roles for the seemingly modest cherry in a series of episodes in which grandiloquence occasionally spills over into absurdity. The first episode consists of the words which Herman Melville puts in the mouth of the second mate Stubb as his ship, the *Pequod,* is rapidly faltering under the onslaughts of the white whale, at the very end of *Moby-Dick* (1851): "Cherries! cherries! cherries! oh, Flask, for one red cherry ere we die!"; to which the third mate Flask replies: "Cherries? I only wish that we were where they grow."

Our second example is an installation in the sculpture garden outside the Walker Art Center in Minneapolis, Minnesota. *Spoonbridge and Cherry* (1988), by Claes Oldenburg (b. 1929) and Coosje van Bruggen (b. 1942), consists of an enormous spoon with a red cherry some nine feet in diameter fastened to its bowl. Constructed of stainless steel and painted aluminum ($29\frac{1}{2}$ x $51\frac{1}{2}$ x $13\frac{1}{2}$ ft.), the curved handle of the spoon spans a pool of water, while water rises through the cherry's stem and flows back over the cherry down into the bowl of the spoon. (For a photograph of the work, see the catalogue of the Walker Art Center [1990].)

Next, there are two large pictures of cherries, each now in a private collection, by Philip Guston (1913–1980). Painted (oil on canvas) in the same year (1976), in Guston's later—figurative—style, the cherries are lined up on a flat surface in *Cherries* ($68\frac{1}{2}$ x $116\frac{1}{2}$ in.) and piled up in a bowl in *Cherries II* (78 x 115 in.). (See plate 30.) Each cherry is around a foot in diameter and they are painted in that red hue so favored by Guston throughout his career. I also know of two later works by Guston depicting monstrous cherries (with their characteristic long, thick stems): *Curtain* (1977), a still life consisting of two cherries together with an open book and a giant mug (oil on canvas, 68 x 104 in.), belonging to the Philip Guston Estate; and the lithograph *Summer* (20 x 30 in.), produced by Guston in 1980 in collaboration with Gemini G.E.L., Los Angeles. (For reproductions, see *Cherries* in Dore Ashton's *A Critical Study of Philip Guston* [1976], *Curtain* in the catalogue of a retrospective exhibition of Guston at Bonn [1999], and *Summer* in Robert Storr's *Philip Guston* [1986].)

Another eloquent painted episode, this time with some tiny cherries at its focal point, is *Conversation Piece* (ca. 1851–2), by Lilly Martin Spencer (1822–1902), an oil on canvas ($28\frac{1}{4}$ x $22\frac{5}{8}$ in.) now in the Metropolitan Museum of Art, New York. (For a reproduction, see the issue of the Museum's bulletin describing acquisitions for 1998–99.) Spencer has painted herself seated and holding a baby in her lap, with her husband standing and looking rather foolish as he dangles a pair of cherries over the baby's outstretched arms. Tiny as they are, the cherries nevertheless immediately catch our eye: not only are they precisely centered horizontally but their redness stands out against the background of the father's dark suit. Some apt comments on the painting by Carrie Rebora Barratt unfortunately include the assertion that Spencer was "the only woman painter of note to pursue a career in America's antebellum period"—which ignores the many women painters of the Peale family (see Schwarz's *One Hundred and Fifty Years of Philadelphia Still-Life Painting;* we have already encountered Sarah Miriam Peale in chapter 16, "Melons").

An extended and effective use of cherries in an episode of black humor occurs in the latter half of an otherwise mediocre film, *The Witches of Eastwick* (1987), directed by George Miller (b. 1945). Though the script, by Michael Cristofer, is said to be based on John Updike's novel of the same name (1984), there are actually few resemblances between film and novel, apart from the names of the main characters. The cherries serve as one of several faux-occult episodes in which the magical powers both of the devil-figure Darryl Van Horne (Jack Nicholson) and of the three witch-figures, Alex (Cher), Jane (Susan Sarandon), and Sukie (Michelle Pfeiffer) are actualized. First, at a dinner party, Darryl, floating in his pool, offers his three guests cherries from an enormous bowl in his lap; as the three witches eat, their enemy Felicia Gabriel (Veronica Cartwright) agonizingly regurgitates the pits. (For many viewers, Cartwright's performance is the best thing in the film.) Later, the witches feed themselves cherries, thereby causing Darryl to regurgitate pits.

I have saved for last the briefest, simplest, and most poignant of all my literary allusions to cherries. Here is the full text of a letter (in English translation and the original Latin)—the fortieth in a collection of well over a hundred—written by an anonymous man to an anonymous woman during the first half of the twelfth century, probably in Paris:

> To a noble and very lovable friend: I beg you, be steadfast with me, as I want to be with you.
>
> Be with me, be my spirit, be my joy. Farewell, sweeter and more beautiful than the cherry.

~

> Amice nobili ac multam amabili: precor mecum sis stabilis, ut ego tecum volo.
>
> Tu mecum esto, meus animus esto, meum gaudium esto. Vale ceraso pulcrior et dulcior.

The quotations are from a book (1999) by the Australian medievalist Constant J. Mews containing a complete transcription of the correspondence (with translations by Mews and Neville Chiavaroli). The controversial thesis of the book is that the correspondence in question (drawn from a single manuscript copied by a monk named Johannes de Vepria [ca. 1445–ca. 1518]) consists of the early love letters of Peter Abelard (1079–1142) and Heloise (1100/1–1164). If Mews is right—and he has succeeded in convincing some knowledgable scholars—then the letter quoted above would presumably have been written during Abelard and Heloise's intense erotic/intellectual liaison of 1117–1119 (when he was in his late thirties and she was perhaps seventeen). It may be recalled that the known letters between Abelard and Heloise (readily available, in Betty Radice's translation, in Penguin Classics [1974]) were written after they had been separated for over a dozen years.

GRAPES

We might as well right off face the fact that much writing about grapes is either directly or obliquely about wine; here is an example by the Italian Renaissance humanist Andrea Navagero (whose lines on pears we have already cited in chapter 13). His formulaic six-line Latin tribute to a grapevine, "Damis' Vow to Bacchus on Behalf of His Vine," written in a conventional pastoral vein, has been turned into English prose by Alice Wilson:

> This vine which, ever fruitful with many bunches of grapes, has a habit of never disappointing its owner's prayers, is now consecrated, even now in its abundant prime, by the wine-dresser Damis, to thee, Bacchus. May thou, O God, ensure that this vine of yours disappoints not our hope and that the whole vineyard will fructify after its example.

Here, though, is an example in which the thought of making wine from grapes is at most a remote possibility; rather, we have in "The Goophered Grapevine" (1887), by Charles Waddell Chesnutt (1858–1932), a skillfully constructed short story about the commercial growing of grapes. Chesnutt was born in Cleveland, where he eventually practiced law, while becoming the first best-selling African American fiction writer. His first book, *The Conjure Woman* (1899)—a set of seven loosely connected tales, of which "The Goophered Grapevine" is the first—was published by the prestigious firm of Houghton Mifflin; the African American identity of the author was not disclosed. There is a frame narrator named John, an Ohio businessman, who has moved to North Carolina to take up grape cultivation and hired an elderly local ex-slave named Uncle Julius McAdoo as his coachman. The teller of all the tales (in carefully transcribed dialect) is Uncle Julius. Thus, as John Sekora points out, in his entry on "slavery" in the *Oxford Companion to African American Literature* (1997), "readers were faced with a modernist choice of two implied authors."

At the outset of "The Goophered Grapevine," sometime not long after the Civil War, John and his wife are visiting North Carolina to consider buying an old vineyard to develop for commercial grape-culture. In the vineyard they encounter Uncle Julius sitting on a pine log: "He held on his knees a hat full of grapes, over which he was smacking his lips with great gusto, and a pile of grapeskins near him indicated that the performance was no new thing." Uncle Julius advises against buying the vineyard on the grounds that the previous owner has had the vines bewitched ("goophered") by a local conjure woman in order to prevent people from stealing the grapes, because, in Uncle Julius's words, "ef dey's an'thing a nigger lub, nex' ter 'possum, en chick'n, en watermillyums, it's scuppernon's." (Scuppernong is a grape variety native to that region of the United States; as horticultural historian U. P. Hedrick explains: "Probably the great abundance of the Muscadine or Scuppernong grapes, *Vitis rotundifolia,* which run riot in all the southeastern states, and make a fair wine, was one reason why the early settlers in the Carolinas did not experiment with the European grape quite so enthusiastically.") Of course, after Uncle Julius has told several anecdotes illustrating the malign effects of the goophered grapevines, the would-be purchaser of the vineyard asks him how *he* manages to avoid the spell, and his unanswerable reply is that he "knows de old vimes fum de noo ones; but wid strangers dey ain' no tellin' w'at mought happen." Needless to say, the vineyard is purchased and the enterprise is highly successful (as appears in the later tales).

According to William L. Andrews, in his entry on Chesnutt in *The Oxford Companion to African American Literature,* "The Goophered Grapevine" (and other stories in *The Conjure Woman*) "portray slavery as a crucible that placed black people under almost unbearable psychological pressures, eliciting from them tenacity of purpose, firmness of character, and imaginative ingenuity in order to preserve themselves, their families, and their community." Andrews is emphasizing the extraordinary coping strategies developed by African American culture to deal with the harsh conditions of slavery. Without in any way disagreeing, another contributor to *The Oxford Companion,* Paula Gallant Eckard, in her entry on *The Conjure Woman,* tells us that the book "reveals the destructive and dehumanizing force of slavery," and that "the stories Julius tells subtly undercut the wholesome picture of the New South that John describes in his frame narration." Uncle Julius's "performance" (Chesnutt's term) when John and his wife first encounter him—eating grapes from his hat while carefully piling up the grapeskins nearby—seems to me to encapsulate neatly all of these larger interpretations of Chesnutt's work.

Over a century after Chesnutt's story, his grape varieties come up again in an eponymous poem by the American Donald Platt (b. 1957). "Scuppernong and Muscadine" (2000) is a remarkable pattern of allusions, in ten short stanzas, to the physical structure of the grape (a small sphere with tight skin, pits inside the juicy flesh), to its sensual characteristics (taste, color, explosiveness), and to its chief literary associations (an autumn harvest standing in for middle age, a plant of good and evil, a wifely erotic charge); and, as an unexpected bonus, the pleasure of pronouncing the two dactylic names of the grapes. The first two and the last four stanzas are particularly evocative:

> I take each swollen globe
> and crush it with my tongue against my hard palate's ridges
> so that the pale inner flesh
>
> bursts from the leathery skin and releases its unbearably

sweet, dusky juice
to make sunset in my mouth's dark.
[. . . . .]
It's October, and I have
the muscadine's dark

purple fruit flecked with russet stars and its cousin the scuppernong's
golden amber. I spit
skins and pits. What remains are two mere words,

three syllables each, dactyls
that I say over under my breath to savor their ripeness.
Muscadine, and the two half-moons

of my wife's small breasts rise slowly over the hem of of her descending
black velvet dress. Scuppernong,
her quick tongue in my ear. What more is there to hear?

One might have predicted that many of the literary uses of grapes would run to the offhand and lighthearted, as in a little poem, "Grapes" (1820), by the youthful Alexander Pushkin (1799–1837): the closing simile compares clusters of ripening grapes to (in A. D. P. Briggs's translation) "fingers on a young girl's hand." Or, this anonymous and undatable epigram (just fourteen words in the original, here translated by Dudley Fitts) from the *Greek Anthology* (5.304):

Green grape, and you refused me.
Ripe grape, and you sent me packing.
Must you deny me a bite of your raisin?

A similar association of love with grapes may be found in one of Horace's odes (2.5), in which advice is seemingly being offered to a friend about an impending amour: be patient, says the poet, and wait until the girl gets a little older, when she will not only return your passion but even pursue you. But though what I have said may for some purposes be acceptable as a reasonably accurate summary of the literal sense of the poem, serious misrepresentation occurs when Horace's metaphors are ignored. These metaphors first characterize the girl as a heifer not yet ready for the bull (stanzas 1 and 2) and then as a bunch of unripe grapes (stanza 3). The remaining three stanzas compare the subject of address successively to three young men from the world of myth, each of whom is doted on by all the girls who see him (stanzas 4–6). Our concern is with stanza 3:

tolle cupidinem
immitis uvae: iam tibi lividos

distinguet Autumnus racemos
purpureo varius colore.

A literal, word-for-word rendering comes out something like this: "Get rid of your desire for an unripe grape: soon will variegated Autumn mark off for you the dull blue clusters with purple color." Here are three English versions of the lines, by, successively, Thomas Creech (1684), James Michie (1963), and David Mulroy (1994):

> Forbear, design no hasty Rape
> On such a green, untimely Grape:
> Soon ruddy Autumn will produce
> Plump Clusters, ripe, and fit to use;

> ~

> Those grapes are crude:
> Deny yourself. Soon dapple-hued
> Autumn will give you the ripe cluster
> Tinged with the true dark-purple lustre.

> ~

> Resist your desire for sour
> berries. Purple imprinted by versatile
> Autumn will lend distinction
> soon to the leaden clusters.

There seem to be no great divergences in syntax or meaning among the three translations, but the color-words do, of course, present a problem, which one recent commentator on Horace's *Odes,* Daniel Garrison, addresses as follows: "*Lividus* is the leaden blue of the half-ripe grape. The metaphor therefore denotes progressing adolescence rather than full maturity"; "*Purpureus* varies from violet to scarlet depending on the amount of dye used"; "*varius:* many-colored."

Rukhl Fishman uses ripening grapes as a metaphor for her own demanding body in "More Heat" (1966; translated by Seymour Levitan):

> One shoulder high
> full open lips
> red back
> and pale green belly,
> I'm really most of all like
> a bunch of red grapes
> a week before picking-time.

> One week before picking
> you can't quiet them.

They want more sun, more heat, more love!
    [. . . . .]
Sweet red grapes:
Threaten! Demand!
One week before picking-time
no one so cruel
to say you nay.

Knowing even the barest particulars of Fishman's life—working on a kibbutz in Israel (where she presumably picked grapes) and suffering nine miscarriages—one can scarcely avoid reading an allusion to one of her pregnancies in the first stanza and an allusion to the threat of miscarriage in the last stanza. Her earlier "Grapes" (1960) associates grape picking with writing poems—the pain and joy of it, and the severe demands it makes on an unidentified friend or mate:

1
In the heat of conversation
one hot day
the grapes
told me their dream—
they want to be picked.
    [. . . . .]
2
If
picking the silent sunny grapes
leaves us sundazed, silent,
don't raise your eyebrow
when you see me sunned
to silence.

If
picking clear sunny grapes
leaves us lusting for words clear as clear,
comfort me when I cry,
I'm dreaming a poem
but its shadow is humpbacked.

If
joy pours into my veins
when I pick sweet sunny grapes,
let me laugh
the way we let rain come down

> when it rains,
> snow
> when it snows.

Grapes that are too sour to eat seem to possess a high potential for metaphorical elaboration. Two early and influential literary occurrences of sour grapes—both composed in the sixth century B.C.E., one in Greek, the other in Hebrew—are in Aesop's fable of the fox and the grapes and in the proverb quoted in Ezekiel 18:2: "The fathers have eaten sour grapes, and the children's teeth are set on edge." But *real* sour grapes played an important role in medieval cuisine. Verjuice, according to *The Oxford Companion to Food*, "literally 'green juice,' is an acid liquid obtained from crabapples, sour grapes, and other unripe fruit. It was much used in medieval European cooking, and lingered on until the 19th century." For a long list of medieval recipes including verjuice, see, for example, an English translation by James Prescott of one of the most important cookbooks of medieval France, *Le Viandier* (Food provider; 1373–80), by the chief cook of Charles V, Taillevent (ca. 1310–1395).

Relying on the versified Latin version of Aesop's prose by Phaedrus (ca. 15 B.C.E.–ca. 50 C.E.), Jean de La Fontaine composed a poetic version in French of the fable of the fox and the grapes for his first collection of fables (3.11), published in 1688. La Fontaine's version has in turn been translated many times into English (here by James Michie):

> A starving fox—a Gascon, Normans claim,
> But Gascons say a Norman—saw a cluster
> Of luscious-looking grapes of purplish lustre
> Dangling above him on a trellis-frame.
> He would have dearly liked them for his lunch,
> But when he tried and failed to reach the bunch:
> 'Ah well, it's more than likely they're not sweet—
> Good only for green fools to eat!'
>
> Wasn't he wise to say they were unripe
> Rather than whine and gripe?

Stephen Bann explains, in *The True Vine* (1989), how Charles Perrault (1628–1703) proposed a subtle interpretation of the allusion to Gascons and Normans: "This was a witty way of using provincial stereotypes to imply an ambiguity in the fox's motivation. He could have decided to rationalize his lack of access to the grapes either because of his Gascon pride or because of his Norman prudence."

About a century after La Fontaine's "The Fox and the Grapes," the French sculptor Pierre Julien (1731–1804) carved a marble memorial statue of La Fontaine (designed in 1783, now in the Louvre in Paris; for a picture of it, see Bann's book, or Michael Levey's *Painting and Sculpture in France, 1700–1789* [1993]). La Fontaine is seated, looking

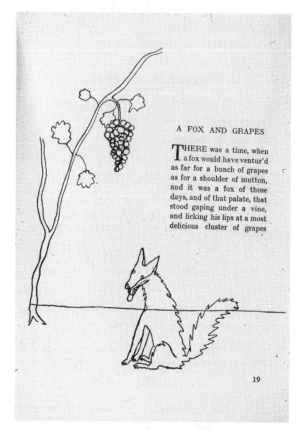

A FOX AND GRAPES

THERE was a time, when a fox would have ventur'd as far for a bunch of grapes as for a shoulder of mutton, and it was a fox of those days, and of that palate, that stood gaping under a vine, and licking his lips at a most delicious cluster of grapes

19

Fig. 13: Alexander Calder,
A Fox and Grapes, 1931

at a book on his lap: his own *Fables,* opened to "The Fox and the Grapes." Bann describes the statue in some detail, noting, in particular, how the location of fox and grapes—the former on the base near La Fontaine's right foot, the latter behind his left shoulder—would make it impossible for the fox to see the grapes and also impossible for the viewer to see fox and grapes in a single glance.

The fable of the fox and the grapes has been frequently illustrated—in the twentieth century, for example, by Marc Chagall (1887–1985) and Alexander Calder (1898–1976). Chagall painted his *Le renard et les raisins* in 1926–27 (now in a private collection in Paris) as one of a series of a hundred gouaches (ca. 20 x ca. 16 in.) of La Fontaine fables. (For a reproduction, see the beautifully designed volume, *Marc Chagall:The Fables of La Fontaine* [1997].) Calder made his *A Fox and Grapes* as one of fifty line drawings for a limited edition published in Paris in 1931 (see fig. 13).

In 1970, the American composer Ned Rorem (b. 1923) set five of La Fontaine's fables (in Marianne Moore's translation) to music—three singers with piano accompaniment—and called the work *Fables: Five Very Short Operas.* The first performance took place at the University of Tennessee at Martin in 1971. The fourth of the five pieces is "The Fox and the Grapes," and its vocal score (two minutes in duration) calls for two singers acting as chorus and a tenor as the Fox.

The great American satirical writer Ambrose Bierce (1842–1914?), in his "Fox and Grapes" (1890), composed a characteristically ironic variation on the traditional fable: "A Fox, seeing some sour grapes hanging within an inch of his nose, and being unwilling to admit that there was anything he would not eat, solemnly declared that they were out of his reach."

In chapter 6 of *The Way of All Flesh,* Samuel Butler literalizes the Ezekiel proverb to fit his theme, which is the overbearingness and cruelty of parents to their children. Overindulgence in food and drink, Butler suggests, can lead to dyspepsia and consequent mistreatment of one's children: "It is not as a general rule the eating of sour grapes that causes the children's teeth to be set on edge. Well-to-do parents seldom eat many sour grapes; the danger to the children lies in the parents eating too many sweet ones."

Wild grapes (along with most wild tree fruit) are mostly too tart to eat, and this is the main conceit in "Wild Grapes," by one of the outstanding Australian poets of the period between the world wars, Kenneth Slessor (1901–1971):

> The old orchard, full of smoking air,
> Full of sour marsh and broken boughs, is there,
> But kept no more by vanished Mulligans,
> Or Hartigans, long drowned in earth themselves,
> Who gave this bitter fruit their care.
>
> Here's where the cherries grew that birds forgot,
> And apples bright as dogstars; now there is not
> An apple or a cherry; only grapes,
> But wild ones, Isabella grapes they're called,
> Small, pointed, black, like boughs of musket-shot.
>
> Eating their flesh, half-savage with black fur,
> Acid and gypsy-sweet, I thought of her,
> Isabella, the dead girl, who has lingered on
> Defiantly when all have gone away,
> In an old orchard where swallows never stir.
>
> Isabella grapes, outlaws of a strange bough,
> That in their harsh sweetness remind me somehow
> Of dark hair swinging and silver pins,
> A girl half-fierce, half-melting, as these grapes,
> Kissed here—or killed here—but who remembers now?

This certainly fits Vincent Buckley's description of Slessor's writing as "neat, crisp, cadenced poems," but there is also a tension produced by the discrepancy between the balladlike subject matter and the irregular movement of the lines, some iambic (of four or five accents), some not.

A more subtle appreciation of the taste of grapes informs Jane Hirshfield's "Wine Grapes for Breakfast" (1997), in which the aftertaste suggests a "moral":

> Sweet
> at first
> on the tongue,
> hours later
> the red grapes
> still sting,
> as if trying
> to tell me something—
> what the hook
> tells the fish
> perhaps,
> or the wand
> or stick hears
> before conductor
> or mule driver
> brings it down.

Here now are some vineyard poems. Recalling Gunn's personification of the cherry tree and his close observation of the gradual development of the fruit, we may note that both are matched in Neruda's description of a vineyard in section 2 of his long poem, "The Fugitive," which is itself part 10 of his *Canto General* (1950), a book-length epic of America (which has been translated in its entirety by Jack Schmitt). The fugitive is Neruda himself, who had to go underground when the Chilean Communist Party was outlawed in 1946. The following translation is by James Wright and Robert Bly:

> It was the grape's autumn.
> The dense vinefield shivered.
> The white clusters, half-hidden,
> found their mild fingers cold,
> and the black grapes were filling
> their tiny stout udders
> from a round and secret river.

Like Gunn's cherry tree, Neruda's grapevines are feminized (grape/udders instead of cherry/babies), and the circular source of the grapes' nourishment corresponds to the cyclical force of the cherries' nourishment. One difference between the two poems is that Gunn's is a detached and autonomous lyric, while Neruda's is a lyrical interlude

in a disconcertingly verbose autobiographical narrative including numerous denunci-
ations of political enemies. There is just a hint of the wine that will be made from the
grapes in the allusion to the vine trunk's "simple goblet shape" (desnuda forma de
copa):

> The man of the house, an artisan
> with a hawk's face, read to me
> the pale earth book
> about the darkening days.
> His kindliness saw deep into the fruit,
> the trunk of the vine, and the work
> of the pruning knife, which returns to the tree
> its simple goblet shape.

In one of her loveliest short stories, "Grape Harvest" (1958), Colette surprises us
when she depicts a grape harvest in a French vineyard with not a drop of wine being
poured or drunk. Our surprise is, indeed, shared by Valentine, friend of the narrator,
who reveals herself as a city dweller precisely by her stereotypical conception of the
grape harvest as an excuse for heavy wine drinking. The entire story is about the experience of Valentine, during a few hours of grape harvesting, as filtered through the
refined sensibility of her unnamed friend from the country. Dressed in old clothes, the
two friends join the grape harvesters, who (it being wartime) are some ten very old
men. Eventually, everyone pauses for lunch "in the shelter of a tent made of reed thatch
draped with ecru sheets, pinned up by twigs with green acorns, blue convolvulus, and
pumpkin flowers" (Matthew Ward's translation). The food is substantial—chicken, beef,
bacon, and veal—and the beverage is cider; afterwards there is a maize *galette* (pancake)
and tepid coffee. Valentine then learns that there is no siesta during the grape harvest (as
there is during the wheat harvest). So, the men go back to work, while Valentine and her
companion rest in the shade of a hazelnut tree. But there is an interruption: the men are
enthusiastically greeting a pair of young women approaching across the fields.

> Unhurried, coquettish, one beneath a straw hat, the other beneath a white
> parasol, our two maids moved toward us. Mine was swinging above two
> little khaki-colored kid shoes a blue serge skirt which set off the saffron-
> colored lawn of her blouse. My friend's soubrette, all in mauve, was show-
> ing her bare arms through her openwork sleeves, and her belt, made of
> white suede like her shoes, gripped a waist which fashion might perhaps
> have preferred less frail.

The two ladies ruefully recognize the old dresses they have presented to their respective maids and, more significantly, they recognize some other things:

> The elegance, the Parisian touch, the chatelaine's dignity, of which we had
> deprived the grape harvest, were no longer missing, thanks to them, and

the rough workers once again became gallant, youthful, audacious, for them. . . .

A hand, that of a man kneeling, invisible, between the vine stocks, raised a branch laden with blue grapes up to our maids, and both of them, rather than fill any basket, plucked off what pleased them.

Then they sat down on their unfolded handkerchiefs on the edge of a slope, parasols open, to watch the harvesting of the grapes, and each harvester rivaled the other in ardor before their benevolent idleness.

The story ends with Valentine's words: "What I say is . . . bring back feudalism!"

A very different view of grape harvesting may be found in "The Vintage" (translated by Rae Dalven), by the short-lived Greek poet Kostas Krystallis (1868–1894). In the first place, the harvesters are now women:

> As a dense black swarm of bees pours out
> of rocks and lilies, deserts and gardens,
> to feed on the flowers, inhale their perfume,
> buzzing and droning in delight,
> so the village girls pour out of their homes,
> disperse to fields and mountains, run where there are vines,
> with wicker baskets, sickles, singing,
> with gladness when the vintage starts.

Krystallis's description of the grapes reads:

> the green vines reach out with the heavy grapes,
> black, gold and yellow, here forming black bunches, here glistening,
> under the first rays of the sun-heat rising,
> like black eyes or like thick clusters of pearls.

And in Krystallis's description of the harvesters' meal, it occurs not in the middle of the day but after night has fallen:

> they weave a hut; they sit around their frugal meal
> and a dim oil-lamp sheds light on their simple supper.
> Then in each vineyard, each slope, each vine,
> bright fires are lit in the dark expanse.
> Round and round the fires, the girls start a dance.

A modest but beautifully crafted poem about grape harvesting is "Vendemmia," by Robert Wells (b. 1947):

> And your dialect blurred with locality, I think,
> As the grapes with mist. We work along the rows
> Stripping the bunches from the vines, while I puzzle
> For sense in this tender meaningless conceit.

Grapes

505

The first line and a half all by itself constitutes an effective epigram in the pastoral mode, but to it Wells adds, first, a description of the setting from which that epigram might have emerged and, then, a self-conscious comment on the possible point of such an epigram.

At the other extreme, a virtually cosmic role for grapes may be found in a dramatic monologue by Anthony Hecht (b. 1923): "The Grapes" (1979) consists of a hundred and ten lines of blank verse, and the speaker is a chambermaid in a hotel called "Hôtel de l'Univers et Déjeuner," located on the lower eastern slope of a mountain (probably in the Alps). There is another hotel across the valley called the "Beau Rivage"; the time is some years after 1954. Early one morning in the dining room, as she gazes at a bowl of grapes in ice water, the chambermaid has an epiphany: she is no more than an isolated accident in the universe, living out a brief and insignificant life. Whatever poignancy the poem possesses derives from the voicing of such a "deep" insight by someone whose reading matter is restricted to out-of-date news magazines. The chambermaid's language is at first clipped and plain, but suddenly rises to eloquent heights in her description of the grapes:

> They were green grapes, or, rather,
> They were a sort of pure, unblemished jade,
> Like turbulent ocean water, with misted skins,
> Their own pale, smoky sweat, or tiny frost.
> I leaned over the table, letting the sun
> Fall on my forearm, contemplating them.
> Reflections of the water dodged and swam
> In nervous incandescent filaments
> Over my blouse and up along the ceiling.
> And all those little bags of glassiness,
> Those clustered planets, leaned their eastern cheeks
> Into the sunlight, each one showing a soft
> Meridian swelling where the thinning light
> Mysteriously tapered into shadow,
> To cool recesses, to the tranquil blues
> That then were pillowing the *Beau Rivage*.

Here, next, is another poem about love and grapes, but now dried grapes, or raisins, and the theme—by now we should no longer be surprised—is far from light-hearted. I quote the first twenty-five and the last nine lines (out of a total of forty-nine) of "Raisins" (1991), by the American Lorna Dee Cervantes (b. 1954):

> Raisins are my currency
> to date—slightly seedy,
> prickled as my nipples,
> black as pubis, colored
> as my opened eyelids.

I tongue you
frictives into vowels.
I suck you
to the scabs
you were, forbidden
fruit. Reminders.
Never mind
the way I found you
deserted in the depot
stall. No matter
how this small red box
was once a child's.
Lost wonder, you're
the gift of grace
swept up off
the bathroom floor.
You're my only food
today, the day I left
you, paper husband,
widowed name.
                [. . . . .]
Twenty-eight tips
of fate. Three good sweats
they soaked in sun
as you now soak
my spit, sweet
as acid, damp as rot.
This hunger, as your
memory, feeds
by chance.

It is obvious that the scenario of this poem could not have worked with any other fruit.

Drying grapes, by the way, must be as old as the cultivation of the grapes themselves, and the method is just to leave them in the sun. As David Masumoto explains,

> The industrial revolution and the miracles of technology have bypassed raisin vineyards. Green grapes are still picked in early September and spread out on trays that lie directly on the earth, exposed to the elements. A waiting game commences, and, as they have for generations, farmers pray for pale blue skies and hot days. . . . Within twenty days the sun dries the grapes into dark, sweet raisins, a simple and natural process done

entirely without equipment, machinery, or technology. I still make raisins in essentially the same way that my dad and his dad did.

There is one trick to the process of drying, however, and that is turning the raisins over:

> Two workers, one at each end of a tray, bend over, place an empty tray on top of the partially dried grapes, and, with good timing and a quick flip, turn the entire tray. Good turning teams work quickly and smoothly, their teamwork marked by a steady, unbroken rhythm. Bad teams are sloppy: the raisins fly and trays are crumpled and twisted, with grapes resting in piles instead of making even layers. Some people can work alone, using fast hands, good timing, and a steady cadence.
>
> Finally, the grapes become raisins, dark and meaty, the sun a wonderfully inexpensive dehydrator. Trays are then rolled like a cigarette, or with a few folds, a biscuit roll is created, the raisins wrapped safely inside. Teams then begin boxing by dumping the raisins out of the rolls into boxes or bins.

It may be mentioned that William Bartram, on his travels, observed some Indians drying grapes: "The Indians gather great quantities of them, which they prepare for keeping, by first sweating them on hurdles over a gentle fire, and afterwards drying them on their bunches in the sun and air, and store them up for provision."

An episode that would work with no fruit except a grape occurs in "Joy's Grape" (1998), by Michael Burns. (The title is a phrase from Keats's "Ode to Melancholy.") The speaker imagines himself with a toothache, and, seeking distraction "until my next Darvon," he first tries to write a pornographic poem. When that doesn't work, he says,

> I go
> get the grapes out of the refrigerator
> and wash them, carry them in to the TV
> in a dark green bowl. I place the roundness
> of one ripe grape right on top of the pain
> and then, as if testing the tightness of
> its skin and how much pressure it can stand
> upon my throbbing tooth before it splits,
> I bite. It bursts.

Only a grape possesses the right size and the requisite bursting power to perform this maneuver (though a small cherry tomato would, it seems, also do).

The image of a bursting grape may remind some readers of the powerful grape-bursting metaphor in the ninth poem of George Meredith's fifty-poem sequence, *Modern Love* (1862). The poems are often described as sonnets—this is Meredith's own term—but I find that misleading, since the four-quatrain, strictly rhymed stanzas *(abba cddc effe ghhg)* possess neither the bipartite structure of the Italian (or Petrarchan) sonnet nor the epigrammatic concluding couplet of the Elizabethan sonnet. (I find myself in agreement here with Lawrence Zillman, in his entry, "Sonnet," in the *Princeton Encyclopedia of Poetry and Poetics,* that "whether these 16–line poems should be admitted to the canon is questionable.") The subject of *Modern Love* is a married couple each of whom has taken a lover. (It is known that the situations described by Meredith are partly autobiographical and partly fictional.) By the opening of the ninth poem we have learned that the wife has been unfaithful and that the husband's hostility is rising. In a review of Daniel Karlin's Penguin anthology of Victorian poetry (1999)—which includes *Modern Love* in its entirety—Adam Hirsch singles out the fifth line of the ninth poem ("Had he not teeth to rend, and hunger too") for the manner in which it expresses "the wavering between the desire to do violence and the desire for sex—captured in the shift in meaning through the line." But in the penultimate line of the poem both the violence and the sex are combined in a concrete image—one of the very few in the entire sequence:

> Here thy shape
> To squeeze like an intoxicating grape—
> I might, and yet thou goest safe, supreme.

Another memorable image of violence, by the way, occurs when the wife recognizes a particular rose as having been associated with her husband's lover (in the forty-fifth poem of the sequence):

> Her whims
> Bid her demand the flower, which I let drop.
> As I proceed, I feel her sharply stop,
> And crush it under heel with trembling limbs.

A powerful nonphysical impact effected by a grape occurs when two disparate images are yoked together in the four lines of a fragment (1800–1805) by Friedrich Hölderlin (1770–1843); the translation is by Michael Hamburger:

> On fallow foliage rests
> The grape, the hope of wine, and so on the cheek rests
> The shadow of the gold ornament that hangs
> On the young woman's ear.

> ~

> Auf falben Laube ruhet
> Die Traube, des Weines Hoffnung, also ruhet auf der Wange
> Der Schatten von dem goldenen Schmuk, der hängt
> Am Ohre der Jungfrau.

In an equally brief Rumanian poem, "The Enveloping Echo," Ion Caraion (1923–1986) sharply separates the image of a bunch of grapes from the more banal

images of a day in the park; the translation is by Marguerite Dorian and Elliott
Urdang:

> A woman crossed the park and laughed.
> With hoop, with kite, with sling,
> the children ran about the sky.
> A woman crossed the park and sang.

> That fall was like a bunch of grapes.

We may turn next to Herrick, who wrote many "anacreontics" about the twin
pleasures of love and of imbibing wine, but once, more originally and surprisingly, represented his mistress as Bacchus in a poem in which wine is not even mentioned. In
"The Vine" (H-41; 1648), Herrick dreams of himself as a grape vine encircling his
Lucia. (Herrick, by the way, wrote more dream poems than any other seventeenth-
century English poet.) The poem possesses a highly erotic charge:

> Me thought, her long small legs and thighs
> I with my *Tendrils* did surprize;
> Her Belly, Buttocks, and her Waste
> By my soft *Nerv'lits* were embrac'd:
> About her head I writhing hung,
> And with rich clusters (hid among
> The leaves) her temples I behung:
> So that my *Lucia* seem'd to me
> Young *Bacchus* ravisht by his tree.
> 　　[. . . . .]
> But when I crept with leaves to hide
> Those parts, which maids keep unespy'd,
> Such fleeting pleasures there I took,
> That with the fancie I awook;
> And found (Ah me!) this flesh of mine
> More like a *Stock,* then like a *Vine.*

It is worth noting that some of the above images were considered too indecent to
print in the early twentieth century; the Everyman's Library volume of Herrick's
poems (first published in 1908 and reprinted in 1923), edited by Ernest Rhys (the
founder of Everyman's), excluded the first four and the last six of those lines.

A bunch of grapes makes a dramatic appearance in an utterly different poetic
inflection of the Classical tradition by Stéphane Mallarmé (1842–1898), in his most
famous poem, "L'Après-midi d'un faune" (The afternoon of a faun; 1876). Subtitled
"Églogue," the poem takes the form of a dramatic monologue in rhymed couplets,
recognizably belonging to the ancient pastoral tradition but now (in Keith Bosley's
words) "processed for city consumption" and attempting to "reconcile city and country

under a new simplicity, displacing its idealism on to the exotic." The encounter between the faun and two nymphs is, of course, long on gorgeously evocative rhetoric and short on definite action, but near the middle of the poem the faun does engage in a clear-cut act: he sucks dry a bunch of grapes, then lifts the residual hollow skins to the sky (as translated by Bosley):

> So, having sucked the brightness from the grapes,
> To banish a regret my laughter keeps
> At bay, I lift the cluster to the sky
> Empty, and puffing up its clear skins, dry
> For drunkenness, look through it till day dies.

> ~

> Ainsi, quand des raisins j'ai sucé la clarté,
> Pour bannir un regret par ma feinte écarté,
> Rieur, j'élève au ciel d'été la grappe vide
> Et, soufflant dans ses peaux lumineuses, avide
> D'ivresse, jusqu'au soir je regarde au travers.

I should add that the grapes have been transformed into wine in the penultimate line of the poem:

> Sans plus il faut dormir en l'oubli du blasphème,
> Sur le sable altéré gisant et comme j'aime
> Ouvrir ma bouche à l'astre efficace des vins!

> Couple, adieu; je vais voir l'ombre que tu devins.

> ~

> No more to do but sleep oblivious
> Of blasphemy, on the parched sand—what bliss
> To lap the effective star of wine!

> You two,
> Farewell; I'll see the shade that now is you.

Finally, it is perhaps worth citing Bosley's summary of the portion of the poem following the grapes episode: "Reality is now seen under its two Mallarméan aspects—first as absence, in the striking image of empty grape-skins, then as a threat, in the memory of an attempted abduction and its consequences; the faun cuts his losses and turns to wine, whose 'effective star' anticipates later symbols of the poetic process."

An early poem by Robert Frost has as its setting a birch tree with an entwined vine on which bunches of wild grapes are growing. Frost says he wrote "Wild Grapes" (1923) at the request of an old woman (his first editor, Susan Hayes Ward): "The birch of 'Wild Grapes' was one a girl swung in when she didn't weigh enough to bring it to earth. She told me about it eighty years later and asked me to write a poem about it for girls to match the other birch poem that she claimed was written for boys." Whatever Ward told Frost, she probably did not cast the episode, as Frost does, in terms of the Bible and ancient Greek myth. More specifically, the long, beautifully rendered central portion of the poem (seventy-three lines out of one hundred and three) takes the form of a woman's memory of a childhood episode in which a five-year-old girl, intent on gathering grapes growing on a birch tree, is helped by her older brother, who has "bent the tree to earth / And put it in my hands to pick my own grapes." When the boy leaves the tree, it snaps back and his sister is flung into the air; she refuses to let go, until finally her brother rescues her. The poem begins, however, with a passage of eighteen lines, also spoken by the woman, and containing an oblique allusion to the lines from Matthew 7:16 (already cited in the section "Biblical Figs" in chapter 2): "Are grapes gathered from thorns, or figs from thistles?" Frost's first two lines are: "What tree may not the fig be gathered from? / The grape may not be gathered from the birch?" The narrator then speaks of her rebirth:

> The day I swung suspended with the grapes,
> And was come after like Eurydice
> And brought down safely from the upper regions.

Of course, Orpheus was attempting to rescue Eurydice from the *lower* regions but one suspects this reversal of direction must have pleased Frost. Finally, the last section of the poem is the "moral"—reflections on her past and future life by the narrator (whose age is not revealed in the poem but who is old enough to be wise in self-knowledge):

> I had not learned to let go with the hands,
> As still I have not learned to with the heart,
> And have no wish to with the heart—nor need,
> That I can see. The mind—is not the heart.
> I may yet live, as I know others live,
> To wish in vain to let go with the mind—
> Of cares, at night, to sleep; but nothing tells me
> That I need learn to let go with the heart.

As a transition to the next chapter on wine, I refer now to the anonymous so-called Homeric *Hymn to Dionysus* (6th cent. B.C.E.), which includes a rather charming tale about the god of grapes and wine. (I cite the translation by Apostolos Athanassakis.) It seems that Dionysus (in disguise) is kidnapped by pirates, who intend to hold him for ransom. But as they set sail on "the wine-dark sea,"

> soon wondrous deeds unfolded before their eyes:
> first throughout the swift black ship sweet and fragrant wine

formed a gurgling stream and a divine smell
arose as all the crew watched in mute wonder.
And next on the topmost sail a vine spread about
all over, and many grapes were hanging down
in clusters. Then round the mast dark ivy twined,
luxuriant with flowers and lovely growing berries;

A "fearsome, loud-roaring lion" and a "shaggy bear" appear, terrifying the crew, who
leap overboard and are turned into dolphins. Milton, by the way, made use of this myth
when he invented a story for the birth of Comus [revelry], the central character of his
masque of the same name:

> Bacchus that first from out the purple grape,
> Crushed the sweet poison of misusèd wine
> After the Tuscan mariners transformed
> Coasting the Tyrrhene shore, as the winds listed,
> On Circe's island fell . . .
> [. . . . .]
> This nymph that gazed upon his clustering locks,
> With ivy berries wreathed, and his blithe youth,
> Had by him, ere he parted thence, a son
> Much like his father, but his mother more,
> Whom therefore she brought up and Comus named.

The metamorphosis of seamen into dolphins (omitting the lion and bear) is
depicted on an extraordinary black figure cup signed by the great vase painter Exekias
(mid-6th cent. B.C.E.). The only figure depicted in the painting is the god himself,
reclining on the deck of the ship as if it were a couch at a traditional drinking party,
or symposium; and, indeed, as Mark Davies tells us, "we know that Greek symposiasts
sometimes likened themselves to sailors, and their drinking-party to a ship on the high
seas." The painting is innovative in several ways, including the use of a special coral-
red glaze for the background, which "emphasizes the visual effect of the color of the
wine"—as explained by François Lissarrague, in his brilliant essay, *The Aesthetics of the
Greek Banquet: Images of Wine and Ritual* (1990). (For a colored reproduction of the
painting, see P. E. Arias, M. Hirmer, and B. Shefton, *A History of One Thousand Years of
Greek Vase Painting* [1961].)

19

WINE

PREHISTORY

Though the Greeks did not invent wine making and wine drinking, "it was in Greece that the wine-grape really came into its own, and it is significant that in classical texts one rarely hears of the grape being grown solely for eating. Greek legends claim that Dionysus fled thither from Mesopotamia, disgusted by its beer-drinking," say the Brothwells in their book on *Food in Antiquity*. In fact, the latest findings (reported by Patrick McGovern) concerning the prehistory of wine suggest that viticulture was already under way in northwestern Iran by 5400–5000 B.C.E. and in Mesopotamia by the late fourth millennium B.C.E. Recent evidence from Egypt enables us to date and locate quite precisely some of the earliest wine making in historical times. The evidence consists of some seven hundred wine jars from the burial chamber of an Egyptian king who lived around 3150 B.C.E. Advanced techniques of chemical analysis of residues in the jars prove they contained wine, and of the clay from the jars themselves prove they (and their contents) came from the area of present-day Israel and Jordan. A century later wine was being produced in Egypt itself. And some two millennia later, "Rameses III (1184–1153 B.C.) boasts of presenting 59, 588 jars of wine to the chief Egyptian deity, Amun, at his temple in Thebes, a favor that was expected to be returned in the hereafter." We now know, therefore, that the characteristic megalomania of Egyptian rulers extended to their offerings of wine to the gods. Similar analysis of Minoan and Mycenaean drinking vessels has demonstrated that wine mixed with pine resin was being drunk as early as around 1250 B.C.E. on Crete and mainland Greece (see Holley Martlew, "Minoans and Mycenaeans: Flavours of Their Time," in *Minerva* [1999]).

GREECE

A concern with the art of wine making goes back in ancient Greek literature at least to Homer, as evidenced by a famous episode from the *Odyssey* (9.353–59). A prisoner (along with some of his men) in the Cyclops's cave, Odysseus devises an ingenious means of escape, making use of the high-quality "honey-sweet red wine" he has been carrying around in a goatskin. (The wine was a gift from a man whose family Odysseus had saved.) After drinking some of the wine, here is the Cyclops's reaction, quoted in both Alexander Pope's (1725–26) and Richmond Lattimore's (1967) translations:

> He heard, he took, and pouring down his throat,
> Delighted, swill'd the large, luxurious draught.
> More! give me more, he cry'd: the boon be thine,
> Whoe'er thou art that bear'st celestial wine!
> Declare thy name; not mortal is this juice,
> Such as th' unblesst *Cyclopean* climes produce,
> (Tho' sure our vine the largest cluster yields,
> And Jove's scorn'd thunder serves to drench our fields)
> But this descended from the b<l>est abodes,
> A rill of Nectar, streaming from the Gods.

> "So I spoke, and he took it and drank it off, and was terribly
> pleased with the wine he drank and questioned me again, saying:
> 'Give me still more, freely, and tell me your name straightway
> now, so I can give you a guest present to make you happy.
> For the grain-giving land of the Cyclopes also yields them
> wine of strength, and it is Zeus' rain that waters it for them;
> but this comes from where ambrosia and nectar flow in abundance.'"

(A word about the Pope translation: half of the twenty-four books of the *Odyssey* were translated by his two collaborators, Elijah Fenton and William Broome, but—according to George Sherburn, who has made the fullest study of the subject—Pope himself actually translated book 9.) About the passage, Jean-Pierre Vernant makes this apt comment: "The Cyclops has barely drained the first cup of wine offered him by the Greek when immediately his tone changes. Having only tasted poor wine from wild grapes, the Cyclops is delighted and amazed by this divine nectar, the product of a refined culture, whose delights—and whose dangers—are completely new to him."

The importance of wine—its glories and its hazards—in ancient Greece is reflected in the fact that all city-states passed laws regulating its use. Sparta actually arranged, for the edification of its citizens, to periodically intoxicate its helots (or serfs) with quantities of wine as a cautionary example (reported by Plutarch in his life of Lycurgus). But the Spartans were perhaps exceptional in their attitude toward wine; for the Athenians, explains Lissarrague, "wine allows experience at another level: not only of another person, a neighbor, a drinking companion, but also of an otherness that each person feels in his own liberation and self-emancipation." Plato went so far in *The Laws* (his last and longest dialogue) as to formulate rules for the consumption of wine as a function of age (translated by Thomas Pangle):

> Won't we legislate as follows? First, children until the age of eighteen are
> not to taste wine at all. We will teach that one shouldn't pour fire into the
> fire that is already in the body and the soul until they've taken up their

tasks, and that they must be on their guard against the madness that is habitual in youth. After this, up until the age of thirty it will be permitted to taste wine with due measure; but drunkenness and copious wine drinking will be totally forbidden to the young man. As a man approaches forty he is to share in the enjoyment of the common meals, invoking the presence of the other gods, and especially Dionysus, at this mystery-rite and play of older men, which he has bestowed on human beings as a drug that heals the austerity of old age. Its effect is that we are rejuvenated, and the soul, by forgetting its despondency of spirit, has its disposition turned from harder to softer, so that it becomes more malleable, like iron when it is plunged into fire.

Should we be surprised at Plato's failure to mention women in this context? It is certainly true that women in ancient Greece did not participate in drinking parties (except as professional entertainers for the men) but in *The Laws* women citizens are expected to participate fully in communal feasts and as soldiers. As for political activities, again Plato assigns the same status to women and men (though women may hold office only after forty years of age, as compared with thirty for men).

Aristophanes (who was, of course, an older contemporary of Plato) often used the absence of socially sanctioned female drinking for comic effect. A single example—drawn from one of the less familiar Aristophanic comedies—may serve as illustration. A modern translator of Aristophanes, Kenneth McLeish, writes about *Women at the Thesmophoria* (411 B.C.E.) that "the plot is simple and of infinite potential, a farcical donnée of purest gold. Aristophanes' invention continues unflagging: in later times, only Feydeau ever created such an unstoppable escalation of logical, absurd disaster. . . . Aristophanes-lovers consider it one of the funniest of all his plays, its dazzle undimmed by age." It should be added, though, that difficulties of casting and staging the play (stemming at least in part from its extreme obscenity) have made it rarely performed in the modern theater.

The Thesmophoria was an annual festival, celebrated throughout Greece and honoring Demeter and Persephone; in Athens the festival lasted three days and came at the end of autumn. The two main characters in Aristophanes's comedy are the tragic playwright Euripides and his father-in-law (or kinsman) Mnesilochus. Euripides persuades Mnesilochus to dress up as a woman and to infiltrate the festival—which was strictly limited to married women—in order to discover a rumored plot to punish Euripides for the alleged misogyny of his plays. The gender of Mnesilochus is eventually revealed (by the uncovering of his male anatomy in the form of a comic phallus) and his rescue is effected by means of an enactment of the rescue scene from Euripides's tragedy *Andromeda* (with Mnesilochus playing the role of Andromeda and Euripides the role of Perseus—he comes flying in on his horse, Pegasus!).

At one point, in an effort to defend himself against the angry women, Mnesilochus seizes an infant from a nursing mother, Mikka, and takes refuge high up on an altar, where he threatens to kill his hostage if the women do not relent. Two different English versions of one of Mnesilochus's speeches (692–95) as he attempts to hold off the women surrounding the altar will give some idea of the varied linguistic resources called upon by translators; the first (by McLeish) is tough-guy colloquial, the second (by Jeffrey Henderson) is empurpled Elizabethan:

> Shout all you like. Take one more step,
> You won't see Diddums' fat little face again.
> With a single slice of this nice sharp knife
> I'll butcher the brat and that'll be that.
> We're talking blood, big blood.

> ~

> Scream away! You'll never feed it again if you don't let me go! Nay, right
> here and now, smitten to his crimson veins by this bodkin midst the thigh-
> bones, shall he begore the altar!

When the women gather firewood and threaten to set him ablaze, Mnesilochus unswaddles the baby, only to find—a wineskin (733–8; again, translations from McLeish and Henderson):

> A skin of wine. That explains the wrapping.
> Not to mention the tootsies. Ladies and gentlemen,
> Just look at this. Ah, women, god bless 'em,
> They're all the same. "Drink to me only,"
> "I don't mind if I do," "There's a tavern in the town"—
> And they do such a *profitable* Ladies' Night.

> ~

> The baby girl's turned into a skin full of wine, and wearing Persian booties
> to boot! Women, ye overheated dipsomaniacs, never passing up a chance
> to wangle a drink, a great boon to bartenders but a bane to us—not to
> mention our dishes and our woolens!

There follow some hilarious exchanges between Mnesilochus and the baby's (wine-skin's) mother (imbiber), with clever wordplay on the age of the child and the vintage of the wine. Finally, as Mnesilochus punctures the wineskin, Mikka begs to be allowed to save her baby's blood. What happens next depends on the imagination of the translator (and eventually, the director): Mnesilochus drains the wineskin either into his throat (McLeish) or into Mikka's bowl (Henderson). McLeish's alternative enables him to add some additional witty exchanges between Mnesilochus and Mikka:

> MIKKA.
> You bastard! There's nothing left.

How can you bear to see me so deprived!
MNESILOCHUS.
> Depraved, you mean. Here. Have this.
> *He throws the skin at her.*
MIKKA.
> What's that for?
MNESILOCHUS.
> I got the skinful, and you get the skin.
> Now go away.

The above scene has been recognized in a vase painting on an Apulian bell-krater (ca. 380 B.C.E.) in the Martin von Wagner Museum at the University of Würzburg (for a reproduction, see the frontispiece in Alan Sommerstein's translation of the play, or a plate in Oliver Taplin's *Comic Angels* [1993]). The identification is based on such features as the absence of a phallus: "Given its ubiquity on the comic vases, the best answer must be that the actor is wearing a woman's dress over it; and his rumpled hose indicates that he has a male costume beneath the female." There seems to be some stubble around the mouth on the actor's beardless mask, which would refer back to the earlier scene where Mnesilochus was shaved and dressed in a woman's costume (and presumably exchanged one mask for another); and there are even two little booties on the wineskin. The vase suggests that the *Thesmophoriazusai* was being performed in southern Italy in the early fourth century.

There were other significant groups of Greeks who, like upper-class women, did not participate in drinking parties: the plebeians (male and female) and slaves, all of whom, in James Davidson's words, "had to get their liquid refreshment elsewhere, in the tavern or *kapēleion,* a far more demotic and promiscuous space than the private and selective *andron* [men's room]"; and there must have been

> ranks among the taverns, running from high-quality *kapēleia* like the one dug up in the Agora [early 4th cent. B.C.E.], whose patrons could get hold of the best wines from the best producers, served in good ceramic ware by highly regarded barmen like Plato's Sarambus [in the *Gorgias*] through to the small stalls owned by the characters we encounter on the curse-tablets, some of which perhaps consisted of nothing more than a slave-girl and a cart by a spring.

The existence of such taverns in ancient Greece is well documented, though mostly ignored by Classical scholars.

The drinking party was important enough to have a name of its own: *symposion* (our "symposium")—literally, "a drinking together." A passage describing an idealized picture of the symposium's setting is quoted by Athenaeus (11.462c–f) from the philosopher Xenophanes (ca. 570–ca. 470 B.C.E.); the translation is Gulick's:

Now, at last, the floor is swept, and clean are the hands of all the guests, and their cups as well; one slave puts plaited wreaths on their heads, another offers sweet-smelling perfume in a saucer; the mixing-bowl stands full of good cheer; and other wine is ready, which promises never to give out—mellow wine in jars, redolent of its bouquet; and in the midst the frankincense sends forth its sacred fragrance; and there is water, cool and fresh and pure. The yellow loaves lie ready at hand, and a lordly table groans with the weight of cheese and luscious honey; an altar in the middle is banked all round with flowers, and singing and dancing and bounty pervade the house. But men of good cheer should first of all praise the god with pious stories and pure words; they should pour libations and pray for power to do the right (for that is the duty closer to hand); 'tis no sin to drink as much as you can hold and still get home without an attendant, unless you be very old.

Here are further details concerning the symposium as presented in an entry in the *Oxford Classical Dictionary* (much of the evidence is derived from vase paintings and archeological excavation):

The Greeks adopted the practice of reclining on the left elbow (one or two to a couch); from this evolved a characteristic shape of room, and a standard size for the drinking group of between fourteen and thirty: the *andron* or men's room was square, arranged with a door off centre to fit usually seven or fifteen couches. . . . Many such rooms have been recognized archaeologically. . . . They were supplied with low tables, cushions, decorated couches, and wall-hangings. . . . By the late 6th cent. a repertoire of vessels had been elaborated, including different cup shapes, jugs, wine coolers, and mixing-vessels: the decoration of these vases offers a set of self-conscious images related to the activities of the drinking group. . . . Water was mixed with the wine in a central crater to a strength determined by the president (usually three or four to one, or about the strength of modern beer); it was served by slave boys. . . . At the end of the session a procession (*komos*) in the streets would demonstrate the cohesion and power of the group.

The servers of the wine were not mere faceless servants, as is evident from this anecdote which Athenaeus (13.603e-604d) relates about Sophocles (496/5–406 B.C.E.):

Sophocles was fond of young lads, as Euripides was fond of women. . . . A Chian friend of his, Hermesilaus . . . entertained him, when there appeared, standing beside the fire, the wine-pourer, a handsome, blushing boy; Sophocles was plainly stirred and said: "Do you want me to drink with pleasure?" And when the boy said "Yes" he said, "Then don't be too rapid in handing me the cup and taking it away." . . . He asked him, as he was trying to pick off a straw from the cup with his little finger, whether he could see the straw clearly. When the boy declared he could see it Sophocles said, "Then blow it away, for I shouldn't want you to get your finger wet." As the boy brought his face up to the cup, Sophocles drew the cup nearer to his own lips, that the two heads might come closer together. When he was very near the lad, he drew him close with his arm and kissed him. They all applauded, amid laughter and shouting, because he had put it over the boy so neatly; and Sophocles said, "I am practising strategy, gentlemen, since Pericles told me that whereas I could write poetry, I didn't know how to be a general. Don't you think my stratagem turned out happily for me?"

Of central importance in the symposium was the practice of always drinking wine diluted with water. Decisive nonliterary evidence of this practice is the high incidence among surviving Greek vases of the type of mixing vessel called a *krater;* the term already occurs on a Linear B tablet from Mycenae dating from around 1400 B.C.E. A standard phrase, "the three kraters," refered to an ordered sequence of toasts to the Olympian gods, to the Heroes, and to Zeus Savior. Early literary evidence for water-wine mixing is to be found in a superstitious belief endorsed by Hesiod (in his *Works and Days,* lines 744–45): "Never put the wine-ladle on top / of the mixing bowl / when people are drinking. This brings / accursed bad luck with it" (translated by Lattimore). Further, literary, evidence is provided by Athenaeus (10.427a) when he quotes a poem by Anacreon (ca. 570–ca. 485 B.C.E.), here translated by David Mulroy:

> Come and bring a bowl,
> my boy, for me to drain
> in a single breath, but add
> ten ladles of water
> to five of wine. I want
> a nonviolent Bacchanal.

Athenaeus (15.693d) also quotes Theophrastus (4th cent. B.C.E.) from a work on drunkenness (translated by Gulick):

> "The unmixed wine [*akratistos,* unkratered] which is given upon ending the dinner and which they call a 'toast in honour of the Good Daemon' is taken only in small quantity, just as a reminder, through a mere taste, of the strength in the god's generous gift; and they offer it after they have been satisfied with food, so that the amount drunk may be very small."

So acute was Greek sensitivity to the niceties of wine mixing that it was seriously debated whether the wine should be poured onto the water or the water onto the wine; thus, Athenaeus quotes both Xenophanes and Theophrastus to the effect that in "antiquity" the wine was always poured onto the water in order to obtain a more watery mixture (see Dalby's *Siren Feasts*). Another serious question concerned the type of drinking vessel to use at different stages of the symposium; it seems to have been customary to begin with small cups and progress to larger ones.

Three types of wine were distinguished by Athenaeus (1.32c): white, amber (or yellow), and dark (presumably what we would call red). As for the significance of the time and place of a wine's origin, those too became matters of concern early on in the history of ancient Greek viticulture. First, on the superiority of aged wine: "If long storage of great quantities of wine was a sign of wealth and influence [as in certain passages of the *Odyssey*], then the appreciation of old wine might develop rather naturally, as had already happened in Egypt, where newly-sealed jars of wine were stamped with the regnal year, and where a jar of thirty-three-year-old wine was entombed (among more recent vintages) with King Tutankhamun about 1325 BC" (Dalby). By the early fifth century B.C.E., Pindar (518–438 B.C.E.) could write: "Wake for them the high strain of song, / and praise old wine, but the blossoms of poetry / that is young" (translated by Lattimore). On the presumed influence of locale on the quality of wine, there are many opinions expressed, especially in Athenian fifth- and fourth-century comedy; one of the more circumstantial passages is in a fragment from a lost play by Hermippus, an older contemporary of Aristophanes (translated by Dalby):

> Mendaen wine is what the gods piss in their soft beds. Sweet generous Magnesian, and Thasian over which the scent of apples plays, this I judge much the best of all the other wines after fine and unhurtful Chian. There is a certain wine that they call *Saprías,* from the mouths of whose jars when they are opened there is a smell of violets, a smell of roses, a smell of larkspur, a sacred smell through all the high-roofed hall, at once ambrosia and nectar. This is the nectar; of this I shall give to my friends to drink at the happy feast: to my enemies, Peparethan.

It is hard enough to identify the exact regions and varieties of grapes being graded in such passages, and the comic contexts do not make things any easier. What does seem clear is that the Greeks had some more or less exact conception of differences in the quality of different wines.

Another essential ritual of the symposium (as Lissarrague explains) was the choral performance, combining poetry, song, and dance, "similar to the mixing that takes place in the krater." Wine, indeed, became a familiar metaphor for poetry itself: "The poetic text circulates from the poet to the guests for whom it is intended; a poem can be offered like a drink, and verses are passed around like goblets," as in the lines "You are a true messenger . . . / sweet mixing bowl of vociferous song," by Pindar, or "Pour out the praise-songs like wine, for yourself and for us, / passing them from left to right," by Dionysos Chalchos (5th cent. B.C.E.).

Actual, nonidealized symposia—the kind often depicted on Greek vases—included some pretty wild behavior, but even this was generally of a traditional and ritualized order. Thus, there was a game called *kottabos,* in which a drinker would twirl on a finger the standard flat, two-handled wine cup (called a *kylix*), when it was almost empty, in order to fling some drops of wine across the room and hit a designated target (which might be a tiny saucer floating in a basin of water or a disk balanced on top of a tall pole). This was, however, not merely a game of skill, for, citing Lissarrague once more:

> When the balance is upset, something capsizes or falls with a crash, and this symbolizes that love has been assured. . . . The game requires an amatory partner, and before the throw one calls out to all the other guests the name of the person being targeted. The gesture always has an intended receiver, and the vases that carry such a person's name are not uncommon.

Before we leave the period of classical Greece, I want to quote from Davidson's summary of his brilliant chapter on drinking at Athens:

> One kind of consumption emphasizes the horizontal plane: the wine is blended expansively with water; it is sipped slowly from smaller shallower cups; there are as a result more rounds, more of those processes of circulation and distribution which make the symposium such a bonding experience; words join water in diluting the wine whose proper role is to facilitate conversation. . . . This is the wine of commensality, of Brillat-Savarin and the anthropologists. Opposed to this is the degenerate consumption of the vertical axis, the wine of Baudelaire and the alcoholists: the wine is *akratos,* thick, three-dimensional and strong; the cups are large and deep; drinking is long and breathless.

THE ANACREONTEA

Only a handful of Anacreon's poems have survived, but for well over two millennia he was much admired and imitated, and the generic term "anacreontic" came to be used for lighthearted poetry about drinking and love. In the first few centuries after he wrote—specifically, in the Hellenistic period—a genre of sympotic epigrams emerged, many of which, of course, involved wine. I will quote a selection of such epigrams by three Hellenistic poets who wrote in Ptolemaic Alexandria, in translations (with comments) drawn from Kathryn Gutzwiller's book on Hellenistic epigrams. First, here is an epigram by Asclepiades (b. 340/30 B.C.E.), "the undisputed founder of the erotic-sympotic epigram":

> Wine tests for love. As Nicagoras was denying his love
> to us, a series of many toasts betrayed him.
> He wept and hung his head and looked downcast,
> and his garland did not stay bound.

522   Asclepiades has substituted for the *in vino veritas* commonplace a small but concrete incident in which "wine tests for love."

Next, an epigram by Posidippus (ca. 300–ca. 250/40 B.C.E.), which probably introduced his collection of sympotic poems:

> Sprinkle, Cecropian jug, the dewy moisture of Bacchus,
>   sprinkle it. Let the toast that I contribute bedew us.
> Let Zeno, the wise swan, be silent, and Cleanthes' Muse,
>   and let bittersweet Eros be my topic.

Cecrops was a mythical king of Athens, Zeno and Cleanthes were leading Stoic philosophers; and, again quoting Gutzwiller, "by playfully substituting the Cecropian jug for Bacchus himself, Posidippus may here invent the practice of composing a hymnlike poem addressed to a wine jar." Another epigram by Posidippus (*Greek Anthology* 5.183) seems to reflect the altered nature of the symposium in Hellenistic times (translated by W. R. Paton):

> We are four at the party, and each brings his mistress; since that makes
> eight, one jar of Chian is not enough. Go, my lad, to Aristius and tell him
> the first he sent was only half full; it is two gallons short certainly; I think
> more. But look sharp, for we all meet at five.

Our third poet is Hedylus (3rd cent. B.C.E.), known for satirical poems about excessive eating and drinking such as this one:

> Let us drink, and so over wine I hope to invent
>   something new, some sweet and refined song.
> Drench me with amphoras of Chian wine and say, "Play,
>   Hedylus." I hate to live pointlessly, unintoxicated.

This—Hedylus's "signature piece"—is clearly self-satirical, as the poet (in Gutzwiller's formulation) "attributes the novelty of his own 'refined and sweet' verse to the inspiration gained from huge quantities of wine."

An undatable two-line epigram from the *Greek Anthology* (9.748), erroneously ascribed to Plato, is—and is about—a gem: "A Dionysus engraved in amethyst / either let it teach me to be sober or learn to get drunk." The translator, Alan Cameron, explains that the amethyst was supposed to protect against drunkenness and that therefore it was a paradox for the god of wine to be depicted on an amethyst. (This association of amethysts with disapproval of wine was based on a false etymology of "amethyst," as explained in chapter 12 in connection with Jacopo Sannazaro's Latin elegy on pomegranates.)

Finally, we may leave the Greek poets with a cautionary epigram (9) by Theocritus (translated by Hine):

Orthon the Syracusan enjoins you, stranger, not
To go out on a winter night when you have drunk a lot.
Such was my mistake, and instead of my
Native country, wrapped in foreign earth I lie.

ROME

If we turn now to the Latin poets, we may note first of all that, compared with most of the poets we have just been considering, the attitude of Virgil toward wine is generally far more serious, even didactic (like Hesiod), though he does let himself go a bit in the opening lines of his *Georgics* 2.1–8 (translated by C. Day Lewis):

> So far I have sung the tillage of earth, the lore of heaven:
> Now it's the turn of wine, and with it the trees that crowd
> In a woody copse, and the produce of the gradual-growing olive.
> Come, Lord of the wine-press—everything here is lavish
> By your largesse, for you the field's aflower and laden
> With bines of autumn, the vintage foams in vats overflowing—
> Come then, Lord of the wine-press, pull off your boots and paddle
> Bare-legged with me and dye your shins purple in the grape juice!

Later, in a strictly didactic vein, Virgil produces what is little more than a list of some thirteen wines (or grape varietals), and then concludes with a couple of meteorological metaphors:

> But to catalogue all the wines and their names would be quite beyond me
> And serve no useful purpose:
> If you wish to know their number, go and tot up the grains
> Of sand that are whirled around by a sand-storm in the Sahara,
> Or count the waves that break along Adriatic coasts
> When an easterly gale comes down in gusts upon the shipping.

Pliny, incidentally, a century after Virgil, lists some 185 wines (or grape varietals), in his *Natural History* (14.150). (Today there are more than eight hundred grape names in use for classifying wines; see *Jancis Robinson's Guide to Wine Grapes* [1996].) Pliny also warns us of the negative effects of overindulgence in wine:

> Even in the most favourable circumstances, the intoxicated never see the sunrise and so shorten their lives. This is a reason for pale faces, hanging jowls, sore eyes and trembling hands that spill the contents of full vessels; this the reason for swift retributions consisting of horrendous nightmares and for restless lust and pleasure in excess. The morning after, the breath reeks of the wine-jar and everything is forgotten—the memory is dead.

This is what people call "enjoying life"; but while other men daily lose their yesterdays, these people also lose their tomorrows.

With Virgil's contemporary, Horace, a rather different kind of poetry about wine emerged, as in a couple of his odes, in each of which the poet expresses anxiety about his social status vis-à-vis wealthy patrons. In *Odes* 1.20, the poet is inviting his patron, Maecenas, to share the mediocre wine which is all he can afford, with the implicit suggestion that, in return, Maecenas will receive the gift of a poetic tribute (here translated by David Mulroy):

> Your drink will be economical Sabine
> from little pots. I sealed it myself
> in a Grecian jar the day you received
> applause at the theater,
>
> cherished knight Maecenas, so loud
> that father Tiber's banks and Vatican
> Hill's delusive echo joined
> in the acclamation.
>
> A man like you is worthy of Caécuban
> or wine from the press at Cales, but neither
> Falernian vines nor the Formian hills
> are blent in my cups.

In *Odes* 3.21, Horace addresses Corvinus, another wealthy Roman literary patron, but now in the guise of addressing one of the poet's own wine jars (here translated by James Michie):

> Wine-jar whose birth-year, Manlius' consulship,
> Was mine as well, unstopper of elegies,
>   Jokes, quarrels, love's crazed fits and blessed
>   Effortless slumber (your kindest office),
>
> You've kept the choice old Massic in store for a
> Great moment: now, whatever occasion you
>   Foresaw, descend like Jove—my guest has
>   Called for a mellower wine from upstairs.
>
> *His* drink is Plato's wisdom of Socrates—
> Deep tipple; yet he'll never uncivilly
>   Snub *you:* they say old Cato often
>   Warmed his morale with an undiluted

Cup. Jar, you put brains stolid by nature to
Torment on your sweet rack; the philosopher's
   Dark thoughts are bared, his secret counsels
      Spilled at the prompting of jolly Bacchus.

You rally lost hopes back to the worry-worn,
You bring the poor man courage and confidence:
   Crowned kings can rage, call out their soldiers—
      After a taste of you, he'll defy them.

Friends keep you up late: Liber with Venus, when
She's gay, the three linked Graces who hate to let
   Go hands, and bright lamps burning on till
      Phoebus, returning, defeats the starlight.

Corvinus—his name is omitted in the translation—is properly flattered by being associated with the great Greeks, Socrates and Plato, and the great Roman, Cato, while the wonderful powers of wine are duly celebrated. Of particular interest is the phrase "undiluted cup," which corresponds to *mero* ("unmixed") in the Latin. It seems that the Romans, like the Greeks, only drank their wine neat on special occasions. In the context of Horace's ode we note that Corvinus is being granted license to drink his wine undiluted and even get drunk if he so desires.

Women as well as men, of course, drank wine in ancient Rome, but some strict moralists opposed the practice. Thus, Valerius Maximus (1st cent. C.E.), in his volume containing exemplary episodes drawn from Roman and Greek history, *Memorable Deeds and Sayings* (translated by Maureen Fant), related the following incident:

> Egnatius Metellus . . . took a cudgel and beat his wife to death because she had drunk some wine. Not only did no one charge him with a crime, but no one even blamed him. Everyone considered this an excellent example of one who had justly paid the penalty for violating the laws of sobriety. Indeed, any woman who immoderately seeks the use of wine closes the door on all virtues and opens it to vices.

Again, Aulus Gellius (b.125/8 C.E.) in his entertaining literary miscellany in twenty books, *Attic Nights* (ca. 180 C.E.), reports (in Fant's translation):

> Those who have written about the life and culture of the Roman people say that women in Rome and Latium "lived an abstemious life," which is to say that they abstained altogether from wine . . . and that it was the custom for them to kiss their relatives so they could tell by the smell whether they had been drinking. Women, however, are said to have drunk the wine of the second press, raisin wine, myrrh-flavoured wine and that sort of sweet drink.

As for plebeian drinking places, Davidson tells us that "in Pompeii [taverns] reached a density that compares with the frequency of bars and pubs in modern cities."

JEWS AND CHRISTIANS

The extremely high status of wine in Jewish life is reflected in the fact that wine is almost the only item not covered by the grace before meals and is rather assigned a special blessing ("Blessed are you . . . who created the fruit of the vine"). Furthermore, in rabbinic commentary the written law is often compared to water and the more exalted oral law to wine (although, of course, the oral law was itself eventually committed to writing). In the Hebrew Bible, words are sometimes compared to wine, as in this speech by Elihu from Job 32:17–19 (supposedly interpolated by a poet later than the sixth-century B.C.E. author of the main text):

> Now I also would have my say;
> I too would like to hold forth,
>   For I am full of words;
> The wind in my belly presses me.
>   My belly is like wine not yet opened,
> Like jugs of new wine ready to burst.

I should point out that the above translation differs from earlier English translations, which have "spirit" or "heart" instead of "belly" (see, for example, The New Oxford Annotated Bible).

The ancient Greek and Roman practice of mixing wine with water is used as the basis for a simile about literary style in the apocryphal book of Maccabees (in Greek, 2d cent. B.C.E.). Verses 2:15.38–9 close the book:

> At this point I shall bring my work to an end. If it is found to be well written and aptly composed, that is what I myself aimed at; if superficial and mediocre, it was the best I could do. For, just as it is disagreeable to drink wine by itself or water by itself, whereas the mixing of the two produces a pleasant and delightful taste, so too variety of style in a literary work charms the ear of the reader. Let this, then, be my final word.

With respect to the mixing of wine, it is of considerable interest that the earliest complete account of the *seder* (passover meal)—a tractate in the Mishnah written around 175–200 C.E.—specifies that each of the prescribed four cups be "mixed" (Hebrew: *mzg*), presumably with water (Mishnah Pesahim 10:2–7); as Baruch Bokser remarks, in his study of the early *seder:* "Otherwise it would be too strong and might make one drunk too quickly or even induce a Bacchic frenzy."

Positive connotations of wine are reflected in the conclusion of Amos (9:13–14) in the course of a prophecy of the restoration of the Davidic dynasty (a passage generally considered a later addition to the text):

          A time is coming
                         —declares the LORD—
When the plowman shall meet the reaper,
And the treader of grapes
Him who holds the [bag] of seed;
When the mountains shall drip wine
And all the hills shall wave [with grain].

     I will restore My people Israel.
They shall rebuild ruined cities and inhabit them;
They shall plant vineyards and drink their wine;
They shall till gardens and eat their fruits.

But the connotations of wine may also be deeply negative, as in the drunkenness of Noah (Gen. 9:20), who is said to have been the first to plant a vineyard. The danger of wine was subsequently fully recognized when (in Lev. 10:8) priests were forbidden to drink wine: "The LORD spoke to Aaron saying: Drink no wine or other intoxicant, you or your sons, when you enter the Tent of Meeting, that you may not die. This is a law for all time throughout the ages, for you must distinguish between the sacred and the profane, and between the unclean and the clean." Furthermore, as Gillian Feely-Harnik points out, "The Mishnah reflects this ambivalence toward wine by requiring at least four cups in the passover, but prohibiting extra cups between the third and fourth so as not to ruin the completion of the Hallel [the hymn of praise sung at the end of the passover]."

As for the intoxicating powers of wine, there is an incomparable depiction of the inebriated state at the end of Proverbs 23:

          Who cries, "Woe!" who, "Alas!";
     Who has quarrels, who complains;
     Who has wounds without cause;
     Who has bleary eyes?
          Those whom wine keeps till the small hours,
     Those who gather to drain the cups.
          Do not ogle that red wine
     As it lends its color to the cup,
     As it flows on smoothly;
          In the end, it bites like a snake;
     It spits like a basilisk.
          Your eyes will see strange sights;
     Your heart will speak distorted things.
          You will be like one lying in bed on high seas,
     Like one lying on top of the rigging.

> "They struck me, but I felt no hurt;
> They beat me, but I was unaware;
> As often as I wake,
> I go after it again."

The New Testament takes over from the Jews a deep preoccupation with wine and wine rituals. To begin with, Jesus' very first miracle involves the transformation of water into wine. The setting is a Jewish wedding in the town of Cana, near Nazareth, attended by Jesus, his mother, and his disciples. When the wine runs out, Jesus asks that six stone jars be filled with water, after which some liquid is withdrawn from one of the jars and taken to the steward of the feast. Tasting the liquid, the steward "called the bridegroom and said to him, 'Every man serves the good wine first; and when men have drunk freely, then the poor wine; but you have kept the good wine until now'" (John 2:10). The sheer supererogatory character of the miracle—not only turning water into wine but into *superior* wine—led later Christian commentators to associate the steward's comment with Jesus' revolutionary dictum (in Matthew, Mark, and Luke) that the first shall be last and the last first.

The most important occurrence of wine in the New Testament is, of course, during the Last Supper, where the synoptic Gospels have Jesus declaring, after a cup of wine has been shared by all his disciples, "This cup which is poured out for you is the new covenant in my blood" (Luke 22:20). The Gospel according to John, on the other hand, uniquely of the four gospels, has Jesus single out his betrayer, Judas Iscariot, by presenting him with a morsel of bread dipped in wine (John 13:26). Since John (13:1) sets the Last Supper *prior* to Passover, the morsel would seem to have been of ordinary, leavened bread. (The New Oxford Annotated Bible cites in this connection Ruth 2:14, in which Boaz reassures Ruth, the Moabite foreigner, by asking her to dip a morsel of bread in some wine.)

During the early centuries of Christianity other religions were also featuring wine rituals, sometimes in very tempting ways; so we find, for example, the Latin bishop of Lyon, Irenaeus (2d cent. C.E.), denouncing one Gnostic sect (in Fant's translation):

> [Marcus] pretends to say grace over a cup with wine in it; while he strings out his prayer at great length, he makes the wine turn red and purple, so that they will believe that the true Grace of the Company of the Most High is letting her blood drop into his cup during his prayer, and that those present should strongly desire to taste of that cup so that into them too Grace would drop, because she is summoned by that magician. Again, he gives women cups full of wine and orders them to say grace in his presence. When this is done he offers another cup much larger than the one over which the deceived woman has said grace; he then pours from the smaller cup (over which the woman said grace) into the much larger one

which he has brought forward; at the same time he says as follows: "May grace who is before all things, who cannot be known or imagined, fill your inner person and multiply in you her understanding, sowing her mustard seed in good soil." By saying this sort of thing he makes the poor woman insane, while he appears to be working wonders, since the bigger cup is filled up by the smaller cup, so that it spills over.

Presumably, Marcus was starting out with white wine. Turning red wine to white was easier: one had merely to follow the recipe in Apicius's *The Art of Cooking,* 1.5 (in the English version by Barbara Flower and Elisabeth Rosenbaum): "To Make White Wine Out of Red Wine. Put bean-meal or three egg-whites into the flask and stir for a very long time. The next day the wine will be white. The white ashes of vine have the same effect."

More difficult for Christians was the question of whether the wine in the Eucharist should be diluted with water. Greek practice, as we have seen, dictated diluting the wine, while some Gnostics rejected all wine drinking. Cyprian (d. 258), bishop of Carthage (248–258), defended the practice of diluting the wine with water on theological grounds, emphasizing the symbolism of the mixture: "When someone offers only wine, then the blood of Christ begins to exist without us; but when it is only water, then the people begin to exist without Christ" (translated by Francis Brunner).

Christian church fathers, like their pagan predecessors, worried about women drinking wine; Clement of Alexandria (late 2d–early 3d cent. C.E.) was an Athenian who converted to Christianity; his *Paedagogus* (Tutor) expounded the moral teachings of Christ but was also concerned with how a Christian should eat, drink, and dress. Clement formulated, in a particularly hilarious way, his worries about women drinking (Mary R. Lefkowitz's translation):

> (1) As far as women are concerned, it is undoubtedly because they wish to be attractive that they do not drink from wide-mouthed drinking-cups because they might cut their lips when opening their mouths wide, and so they drink out of narrow perfume-bottles that fit precisely in their mouths. When they drink they tilt back their heads in an unseemly fashion, and reveal their bare necks indecorously, as it seems to me, and they stretch out their throats to gulp down the drinks, as if to show everything they can to the other guests, and bring up belches like men. . . .
>
> (3) I do not forbid women to drink from perfume-bottles, but I condemn the desire to drink from these vessels exclusively. I advise the use of whatever vessels one has to hand, in order to put a stop to these desires before they can develop.
>
> (4) The passage of the air that gives rise to belching should be managed in silence. In no way should women be permitted to show any part of their bodies naked, lest both parties fall into sin.

Classical culture and institutions did not simply fade away as Christianity commenced its increasingly rapid expansion in late antiquity: we have been hearing this from many of the period's best scholars for quite some time now. We have already looked (in chap. 1) at some aspects of one of the outstanding texts (probably 3d century C.E.) belonging to a new genre of prose fiction in Greek, Longus's *Daphnis and Chloe,* which I want to return to now for its account of wine making. This occurs at the beginning of book 2; here are some of the carefully observed details (translated by Christopher Gill):

> Now the fruit season was at its height, and the grapes were ripe for harvesting. Everyone was working in the fields: some were getting wine-presses ready for use; some were cleaning out wine jars; some were plaiting wicker baskets. One man was attending to a small reaphook for cutting the bunches of grapes; another to a stone for squeezing the juice out of the grapes; another to a dry willow twig that had been battered into shreds to make a torch so that the sweet new wine [the partly fermented must] could be drawn off at night. Daphnis and Chloe too stopped looking after their goats and sheep and gave the others a helping hand. He carried bunches of grapes in baskets, put them in the winepresses and trod them, and drew off the wine into the jars. She prepared food for the grape pickers, poured out drinks of mature wine for them, and picked the grapes off the vines that were nearer the ground. In Lesbos all the vines are low; they do not grow up high and are not trained on trees, but they let their shoots hang down and are spread out like ivy. In fact, a baby who'd only just got his hands out of his shawl could reach a bunch.

The anacreontic tradition continued, as we have noted, for many centuries after the Hellenistic period. Here, for example, are two versions—the first by Fitts, the second by Skelton—of an epigram (*Greek Anthology* 7.32) by the Byzantine official Julian the Egyptian (5th cent. C.E.), taking the form of an imagined epitaph for Anacreon:

> I have sung this often,
> > even in the grave will I shout it:
> *Drink: for you must put on this mantle of dust.*

> I often said, and still I say
> "Drink up!" Like me, you'll soon be clay.

There is even a separate group of some sixty poems ascribed to Anacreon (but almost certainly not by him) preserved in the same tenth-century manuscript that contains the *Greek Anthology.* It is difficult to date these "Anacreontea"; as already noted, they range, like the poems of the *Greek Anthology* itself, from the first century B.C.E. to the fifth or sixth century C.E. Consider, for example, the lines: "Fine craftsman, make a springtime cup at once: the Seasons are bringing us the first delightful roses; beat the silver thin and make my drink delightful" (Anacr. 5; translated by Campbell). This is another example of what had already become a familiar genre: the wine poem featuring a drinking vessel. The poet in this case goes on to request the silversmith to engrave appropriate figures on the cup ("Loves unarmed and laughing Graces"). This poem, by the way, is considered late by the experts because of its crude prosody.

Let us look at one more of the Anacreontea (6) which has been ascribed to Julian the Egyptian; it is one of nine poems from the collection translated by Robert Herrick. Both Greek original (in the close prose translation by Campbell [1988]) and the rather free translation by Herrick, "Upon Cupid" (H-229; 1648), are playful; Herrick is somewhat less silly than the original:

> Once when I was weaving a garland I found Love among the roses. I held
> him by his wings and plunged him in my wine, then I took it and drank
> him down; and now inside my body he tickles me with his wings.

> AS lately I a Garland bound,
> 'Mongst Roses, I there *Cupid* found:
> I took him, put him in my cup,
> And drunk with Wine, I drank him up.
> Hence then it is, that my poore brest
> Co'd never since find any rest.

One particular literary product of late antiquity has seemed ripe for revaluation, and since it is an epic poem in Greek concerned with Dionysus, it deserves some extended consideration here. The *Dionysiaca* of Nonnos (mid-5th cent. C.E.) is, incidentally, the longest poetic text to survive from antiquity. Since 1940 there has been an English prose translation by W. H. D. Rouse of all forty-eight books of the *Dionysiaca*, published in three volumes of the Loeb Classical Library. The translation is preceded by H. J. Rose's "Mythological Introduction," which begins with the unpromising assertion that "The mythology of the *Dionysiaca* is interesting as being the longest and most elaborate example we have of Greek myths in their final stage of degeneracy." I suppose we are no longer so sure we can identify degeneracy when we see it, or, indeed, whether such a biological metaphor of downward development is in any case very useful.

First a few words—and a few words just about exhausts our knowledge—about Nonnos. He was born in Panopolis in Upper Egypt and probably lived in Alexandria. In Nonnos's time there was, in Neil Hopkinson's words, "a flourishing group of pagans" in Upper Egypt, and "it is this small number of intellectuals in Panopolis, Alexandria, and elsewhere, who must have been the intended audience for the *Dionysiaca*." Just about the only other thing we know about Nonnos is that he wrote a hexameter paraphrase of the Gospel according to John, "written in a style very similar to that of the longer poem, but without its expansiveness and abundant verbal facility." Was he converted *after* writing his polytheistic epic? Is the attribution of the Christian work to Nonnos a mistake? The consensus today seems to be that in fifth-century Egypt there was nothing very unusual about a practicing Christian having a deep interest in Classical polytheistic mythology.

In his epic with Dionysus as hero, Nonnos deliberately challenges Homer: twenty-four books on war (like the *Iliad*) and twenty-four on travel (like the *Odyssey*); Nonnos even gently reproves Homer for ignoring Dionysus! One thing which must be clearly understood is that there was nothing idiosyncratic or eccentric in Nonnos's choice of subject. By the fifth century C.E., Dionysus had long been celebrated in both literature and art, not, however, as the elderly and rather staid god of classical Greece but rather, in Glen Bowersock's language, as a "vigorous, flamboyant, drunken, surging, leaping, sexual divinity"; furthermore, since "Alexander had been a notorious devotee of the grape . . . Dionysos emerged as the most appropriate godly embodiment of his sensational career." Thus, in the *Dionysiaca*, the hero, like Alexander, makes a triumphal military campaign to India.

Stylistically, Nonnos is far from Homer—Hopkinson again: "Armed with such distinctively Alexandrian weapons as literary allusion, digression, eroticism, grotesquerie, and scientific and mythological learning." In his metrical techniques—a notoriously difficult subject, which it is impossible to discuss here—Nonnos is said to be profoundly innovative, effecting a transition from the purely quantitative meter of classical Greek to our familiar accentual meter.

After all these preliminaries, I can only hope that the passages to be quoted in Rouse's translation will not turn out to be too anticlimactic. I choose from two sections of the poem, the first dealing with the supernatural origin of the grapevine and of wine. The story revolves about Dionysus's favorite playmate, the beautiful youth Ampelos. Toward the end of book 11 (167–223), Ampelos has boldly mounted a wild bull, is thrown, and dies. Dionysus mourns his friend and is comforted by Eros—"in the horned shape of a shaggy Seilenos" (351–2)—who tells him a long story. At the beginning of book 12 (lines 23–28), the personified season of Autumn complains to Helios (the sun) that she alone makes no special contribution to the fruitfulness of the soil. Some hundred and fifty lines later, Autumn's wish is granted (lines 173–87):

> Then a great miracle was shown to sorrowful Bacchos witnessing. For Ampelos the lovely dead rose of himself and took the form of a creeping snake, and became the healtrouble flower. As the body changed, his belly was a long stalk, his fingers grew into toptendrils, his feet took root, his curlclusters were grapeclusters, his very fawnskin changed into the many-coloured bloom of the growing fruit, his long neck became a bunch of grapes, his elbow gave place to a bending twig swollen with berries, his head changed until the horns took the shape of twisted clumps of drupes. There grew rows of plants without end; there selfmade was an orchard of

vines, twining green twigs round the neighbouring trees with garlands of the unknown wineblushing fruit. . . .

Then Dionysos triumphant covered his temples with the friendly shady foliage, and made his tresses drunken with the toper's leaves. Now the boy grown plant was quickly ripening, and he plucked a fruit of the vintage. The god untaught, without winepress and without treading, squeezed the grapes firmly with hand against wrist, interlacing his fingers until he pressed out the inebriating issue, and disclosed the newflowing load of the purple fruitage, and discovered the sweet potation: Dionysos Tapster found his white fingers drenched in red! For goblet he held a curved oxhorn. Then Bacchos tasted the sweet sap with sipping lips, tasted also the fruit; and both so delighted his heart, that he broke out into speech with proud throat:

"O Ampelos! this is the nectar and ambrosia of my Zeus which you have made!"

But Nonnos is just beginning and he continues for some 210 more lines, which include the recital of "another and older legend"(12.293) about the origin of grapes and wine. And book 12 ends with sixty lines of revelry by a band of drunken Satyrs; here is a sample:

And one went bubbling the mindcharming drops of Bacchos as he turned his wobbling feet in zigzag jerks, crossing right over left in confusion as he wetted his hairy cheeks with Bacchos's drops. Another skipt up struck with a tippler's madness when he heard the horrid boom of the beaten drumskin. One again who had drunk too deeply of caredispelling wine purpled his dark beard with the rosy liquor. Another, turning his unsteady look towards a tree espied a Nymph half-hidden, unveiled, close at hand; and he would have crawled up the highest tree in the forest, feet slipping, hanging on by his toenails, had not Dionysos held him back.

Later, at the end of book 14 and the beginning of book 15, after a bloody victory near the shores of an Indian river, Dionysus "pitied his foes in his heart of merry cheer, and he poured the treasure of wine into the waters. So he changed the snowywhite waters to yellow, and the river swept along bubbling streams of honey intoxicating the waters. When this change came upon the waters, the breezes blew perfumed by the newly-poured wine, the banks were empurpled" (14.411–417). The predictable results follow (15.15–25):

And a great swarm drank at the ruddy stream, ladling out with ivy-wood cups a mass of the river-dew, as they held the rustic pot of the shepherds. And as the enemies belched vinously from wide-yawning throat, as their eyes gazed, the cliffs were doubled, and they thought to see through their eyelids a pair of waters in one yoke. And the bubbling outflow of the wineloving river gushed up a brown stream of carousal; and the fragrant banks poured up streams of the sweet drink of wine.

Thus the enemy were made drunken by the untempered stream.

All of these passages surely exemplify what Hopkinson calls "that curiously disconcerting mixture of serious and comic so characteristic of Dionysus and of the poem as a whole."

As a transition to medieval conceptions of wine, it is worth taking a brief look at an extraordinary and rather enigmatic Latin poem, some thirty-eight lines in length and probably from late antiquity, the *Copa Surisca,* so called from its first two words, translated by Helen Waddell as "Dancing Girl of Syria." The work is first mentioned in the fourth century and attributed to Virgil, but, as Waddell says, "its closeness to the Virgilian letter and extreme remoteness from the Virgilian spirit have left it one of the riddles of authorship." It is the note of ennui, even acedia (sloth, in the Christian reckoning of the deadly sins), that is so unusual, and this note is several times expressed in terms of wine. Early in the poem, the speaker asks: "And what's the use, if you're tired, of being out in the dust and the heat, / When you might as well lie still and get drunk on your settle?"; a few lines later: "And here's a thin little wine, just poured from a cask that is pitchy"; then: "If you have sense you'll lie still and drench yourself from your wine cup, / Or maybe you prefer the look of your wine in crystal?"; and finally the concluding couplet:

> Set down the wine and the dice, and perish who thinks of to-morrow!
> —Here's Death twitching my ear, "Live," says he, "for I'm coming."

> ~

> pone merum et talos. pereat qui crastina curat.
> Mors aurem vellens, "vivite," ait, "venio."

The last line, personifying, in Waddell's phrase, "this grim humorous Death who tweaks one's ear," is astonishing; the penultimate line was quoted in the Latin Middle Ages.

Some other transitional Latin poems on wine of a very different kind were composed in North Africa during the period of Vandal control (between 439 and 534 C.E.). Perhaps the best of these poems were by Luxorius (b. 488/90 C.E.), of whom next to nothing is known beyond his ninety or so surviving poems. In particular, the evidence as to his religious affiliation is uncertain, but his composition of obscene Latin epigrams by no means precludes his having been a Christian. (For a scholarly discussion of Luxorius's life and poetry, see Morris Rosenblum, *Luxorius: A Latin Poet among the Vandals* [1961].) Luxorius's poems form the largest surviving group by a single author among a coterie of fifteen poets from North Africa; their poems are included, along with many others, in the so-called Latin Anthology, which was known to eleventh- and twelfth-century Latin poets. Prose translations of two epigrams, "To a Drunkard

Who Eats Nothing but Is Forever Drinking," followed by "To a Drunken Woman Who
Passes Water Copiously" exemplify Luxorius's theme of excessive wine drinking:

> Since you alone often drink as many bowls of wine as all other men put
> together, and you never have enough at any hour, and scorn bread and care
> to take nothing but wine, Nerfa, I am no longer going to call you a man,
> but a wide-mouthed flagon filled to the brim.
>
> Because you drink wine and discharge all of it from your loins, your
> upper region should have been your thigh.
>
> You will drink holding your wine in (you will be able to do this, Fol-
> lonia), if you should grossly imbibe with your lower part.

THE WINE SONG IN ARABIC AND HEBREW

In discussing the flowering plum motif in Chinese culture we made the tacit assumption that one could safely ignore any connections with other, non-Chinese cultural
traditions. With respect to the Arabic and Hebrew literary traditions, they certainly
influenced each other (as we shall see) and we also know they interacted with the
Latin and Romance traditions, exhibiting a remarkable cross-fertilization of cultures—
what one school of Spanish historians has termed *convivencia* (loosely, "coexistence").
In its more positive aspects, there thus flourished, for example, in eleventh-century
Spain, what Alistair Forbes has memorably characterized as "the high and tolerant civilization of Córdoba and old Andalucia, in which the three related religions with their
successive Friday, Saturday, and Sunday sabbaths lived together as good neighbors."
Since we will be attending exclusively to some of the more positive aspects of this cultural cross-fertilization, we might do well to note at the outset that there were certainly negative aspects as well. As Thomas Glick explains, in his introductory note to
the catalogue of a museum exhibition titled "*Convivencia:* Jews, Muslims, and Christians in Medieval Spain" (1992), "The word, as we use it here, is loosely defined as
'coexistence,' but carries connotations of mutual interpenetration and creative influence, even as it also embraces the phenomena of mutual friction, rivalry, and suspicion." The title page illustration for the *Convivencia* catalogue, interestingly enough, is
an illustration from a manuscript of the *Book of Chess, Backgammon, and Dice* (1283), by
Alfonso X, the Wise (1221–1284), showing Jews and Muslims playing a game together
in a garden setting, which includes an orange tree and what looks like a pineapple
growing on a palm tree. (Pineapples were first encountered by Europeans in 1493
when Columbus landed on the island of Guadeloupe.)

Jane McAuliffe begins her careful study of attitudes toward wine in Islam with
the following summary statement:

> There are few things more widely known about Islam than its prohibition
> of intoxicants. Wine is the devil's work, proclaims the Qur'ān, so have
> nothing to do with it. . . . The penalties mandated by classical jurisprudence

for either drinking or trading in wine are severe. Its complete and life-long renunciation is demanded of every Muslim. Yet that renunciation need be no longer than life, for Muslims are promised a paradise whose rivers flow with wine. That which is forbidden on earth will be abundantly available in the Hereafter.

As for wine poetry in Arabic literature, it has a long history, predating Islam, but in the interest of brevity we shall look at just a few poets, the earliest of whom is Abu Nuwas (d. 813/15), who spent his youth in Basra and then moved to Baghdad. Abu Nuwas is generally regarded as having composed the finest of all poems in a genre of wine poetry that came to be called the *khamriyya*. Writing some two centuries after the founding of Islam, Abu Nuwas reflects both older celebratory attitudes toward wine as well as a certain obligatory ambivalence designed to deflect Koranic prohibitions against alcoholic beverages. Consider, for example, this eight-line poem (translated by Philip Kennedy; the bracketed additions are his):

> A censurer censured me, trying to produce a *bid'a* [heresy], and that, by
>   my life!, is a plan I cannot abide.
> He censured me that I might cease to drink wine, for it bequeaths—
>   [so he claimed]—a burden of sin upon all who taste it.
> My detractors have only made me more stubborn, for so long as I live
>   I shall be [wine's] companion.
> Should I reject [wine] when God has not eschewed its name, and
>   whilst our Caliph is its friend?
> It is the sun, though the sun burns, and our wine exceeds it in every
>   beauty.
> And even though for a brief moment we cannot live in Paradise, our
>   Paradise [in this world] is wine.
> So, my censurer, give me wine to drink and sing—for I am its sibling
>   until the time of my death:
> "When I die bury me by a vine whose roots can slake the thirst of my
>   bones."

In his book *The Wine Song in Classical Arabic Poetry* (1997), Philip Kennedy gives a detailed analysis of the poem but, as he admits, some problems of interpretation remain. The first and last lines are related in that the poet *does* finally produce a heresy, namely, the quotation in his last line of a "famous and consummately hedonistic verse" by one of his predecessors; but for this heresy, the poet implicitly blames the censurer! The argument of the fourth line turns, first, on the sophistical claim that the mere mention of wine in the Koran (mid-7th cent. C.E.) proves the acceptability of drinking it; as for the appeal to the Caliph—who had actually forbidden the drinking of wine—one can only assume that the association of the Caliph with God (and thereby with the Koran) makes the Caliph himself a friend of wine.

A much longer and even more complex wine poem by Abu Nuwas begins with a series of rhetorical flourishes:

> Splendid young blades, like lamps in the darkness, proud-nosed,
>   stiff-necked, keen—
> Who assaulted Fate with dalliance to which they clung assiduously, so
>   that their attachment to it could not be severed,
> For whom Time brought round its felicitous spheres and halted, bending
>   its tender neck over them—
> I drank with them sharp *Isfant* wine, imported from Takrit, clear and chilled;
> One of those whose hands we asked for in haste, when we roused the
>   owners of the wine-shops
> In a night-cohort, turbulent and swollen, like the sea which dazes the
>   sailor with fear.

After rousing the owner of a wine shop, who tries to put them off until morning, the carousers demand immediate satisfaction: "No, bring it now! / It is itself the morning; its clear radiance dispels the night when it shoots out sparks like rubies / As the patrolling angels do, when at night, they stone with the stars the rebellious Afrits [demons]." The brilliant description of the wine continues—how it pours, how it smells, how it mixes:

> It advanced in the cup as bright as the sun at day-break, poured from an
>   amphora upturned, bleeding at the waist.
>   [. . . . .]
> The odour that wafts from it to the drinkers was like the scent of crushed
>   musk from a newly slit vesicle;
> When mixed with clear rain-water it was like a network of pearls on a
>   ruby brocade.

A handsome youth distributes the wine; a lutenist performs:

> So he begins with accurate diction [to sing] polished and well-articulated
>   songs, keeping the time,
> Until when the sphere of the strings, together with the drums, spins us
>   round, we are left as if in a trance.
> We glorify in it in gardens thick with myrtle, acacia, pomegranate and
>   mulberry,
> Where the birds distract you from every other pleasure when they warble
>   in antiphonal strains.

There follows an ambiguous line that appears to refer to sexual dalliance, and then the shock of recognition—the poet is really old, after all:

> Until, lo! grey hair surprised me by its appearance—How hateful is the
>   appearance of cursed grey hair

In the eyes of beautiful women; when they see its appearance, they
    announce severance and separation from love.
Now I regret the mistakes I have made and the misuse of the times
    prescribed for prayer.
I pray to you, God, praised be Your name!, to forgive me just as You,
    Almighty One, forgave Him of the Fish (Jonah)!

The declaration of repentance (in the last two lines) is an instance of a conventional
element in one type of wine poem; often the declaration is understood to be insincere. The invocation of Jonah—the reluctant prophet—is peculiarly apt and, in addition, refers back to the young blades of the sixth line. Also, there is something
intriguing about finding a "minor" Hebrew prophet—who nevertheless has been so
elevated as to become the subject of the prophetic reading on the afternoon of Yom
Kippur—in an Arabic wine poem. It should be mentioned finally that the gender of
the love object in a *khamriyya* is more often than not a young boy. (For a fuller discussion of this poem, see Kennedy's book.)

I want to consider next some later Hispano-Arabic wine poems and some still
later Hebrew wine poems. A good deal is known about the arrangements of Andalusian Muslim wine parties, so we might begin with a summary account by Raymond
Scheindlin (his book is about medieval Hebrew poetry but he assures us that there is
every reason for believing that Jews modeled their wine parties on those of their Muslim neighbors):

> The Andalusian practice was to introduce the wine after dinner. As they
> did in antiquity, the drinkers sat on cushions placed around the room, with
> little tables by their side. The wine was ordinarily mixed with water.
> Sometimes each reveler had a crystal cup for his own use; other times, each
> drank from a common cup passed from drinker to drinker by a wine
> pourer known as the *sáki*. This servant, who played an important role in
> creating the desired atmosphere, was usually a young boy specially trained
> to perform his office with flirtatious charm and in accordance with pre-
> scribed rules of etiquette.

As at ancient Greek symposia, all the drinkers at a wine party were male, while musicians, singers, dancers (and even occasionally the *sáki*) were women. One important
contrast with the symposium was the setting: generally indoors for the Greeks, generally outdoors in a garden for the Andalusians. And since a favorite subject of the
Andalusian poets was the drinking of wine in these very gardens and since they often
recited their poems at the wine parties in the gardens, the reflexive possibilities in what
might be called *wine party performance* were potentially very rich. As Scheindlin puts it:

> When a wine party was held in a garden and a poet recited verse describ-
> ing a wine party in a garden, the poem functioned both as an instrument

of the evening's entertainment and as an idealized concretization of it, just as the garden is a concretization of nature. Such poems form a magic circle with their own social setting.

Let us look first at a poem by Ibn Hisn, composed in eleventh-century Seville. I quote a closely literal translation of "Reflection of Wine," from García Gómez's Spanish ("El Reflejo del Vino"), by Cola Franzen, resulting in what strikes me as a brilliant and limpid epigram:

> Light passing through wine
> reflects on the fingers
> of the cupbearer
> dyeing them red
> as juniper stains
> the muzzle of the antelope.

Another eleventh-century, epigramlike wine poem, "Los Vasos" (The goblets), by Ibn Al-Yamani, of Ibiza, has also been translated from García Gómez's Spanish by Cola Franzen:

> The goblets were heavy
> when they were brought to us
>
> but filled with fine wine
> they became so light
>
> they were on the point of flying away
> with all their contents
>
> just as our bodies are lightened
> by the spirits.

Here once more—and not for the last time—we have a wine vessel standing in for the wine itself.

Our last example of a Hispano-Arabic wine poem is by Ibn Quzman (ca. 1078–1160), who is, according to an eminent student of the subject, James Monroe, "one of the very greatest poets, not only of medieval Islam, but of all medieval literature." Ibn Quzman lived in Cordoba, and Monroe characterizes him as "a city poet of some sophistication, not a popular minstrel, [who] has suddenly become aware of the literary possibilities implicit in the teeming urban life that had hardly ever been reflected in poetry before." One of Ibn Quzman's most famous poems—a ninety-line *zajal* identified by its particular strophic form and its colloquial language—begins with a thirty-line bacchic passage, which smacks more of the tavern than of the traditional wine party. It is here translated by Monroe:

540 My life is spent in dissipation and wantonness!
O joy, I have begun to be a real profligate!
Indeed, it is absurd for me to repent
When my survival without a wee drink would be certain death.
Vino, vino! And spare me what is said;
Verily, I go mad when I lose my restraint!
My slave will be freed, my money irretrievably lost
On the day I am deprived of the cup.
Should I be poured a double measure or a fivefold one,
I would most certainly empty it; if not, fill then the *jarrón* [jar]!
Ho! Clink the glasses with us!
Drunkenness, drunkenness! What care we for proper conduct?
And when you wish to quaff a morning drink,
Awaken me before the *volcón* [the emptying of cups]!
Take my money and squander it on drink;
My clothes, too, and divide them up among the whores,
And assure me that my reasoning is correct.
I am never deceived in this occupation!
And when I die, let me be buried thus:
Let me sleep in a vineyard, among the vinestocks;
Spread [its] leaves over me in lieu of a shroud,
And let there be a turban of vine tendrils on my head!
Let my companion persevere in immorality, to be followed by every beloved one.
And remember me continuously as you go about it.
As for the grapes, let whomsoever eats a bunch,
Plant the [leftover] stalk on my grave!
I will offer a toast to your health with the large cup;
Take your bottle, lift it high and empty it!
What a wonderful toast you have been honored by.
Let whatever you decree against me come to pass!

The poem continues with the traditional erotic section (forty lines) and panegyric (twenty lines). Notable are the use of Spanish words like *vino, jarrón,* and *volcón,* whose effect Monroe explains: "Since the Romance words in this poem furthermore appear in the rhyme, their comic effect and foulmouthed realism, or better, negative idealism, receives even stronger emphasis."

The first Hebrew wine song was written by the Jewish poet Dunash ben Labrat (d. ca. 990), a native of Fez, who studied in Baghdad and settled in Cordoba. According to Carmi, Dunash "changed the course of Hebrew poetry by introducing quantitative metres and secular genres, verse-forms and images borrowed from the Arabic." The wine song in question has two parts, the first celebrating wine, the second seemingly taking it all back. The first half of the fruit part begins, in Carmi's prose translation:

He said: "Do not sleep! Drink old wine, amidst myrrh and lilies, henna and aloes, in an orchard of pomegranates, palms, and vines, full of pleasant plants and tamarisks, to the hum of fountains and the throb of lutes, to the sound of singers, flutes and lyres. There every tree is tall, branches are fair with fruit, and winged birds of every kind sing among the leaves.

In the second part, the "I" admonishes the previous speaker:

But I reproached him thus: "Silence! How dare you—when the Holy House, the footstool of God, is in the hands of the gentiles. . . . You have forsaken the study of the Supreme God's law. Even as you rejoice, jackals run wild in Zion. Then how could we drink wine, how even raise our eyes—when we are loathed and abhorred, and less than nothing?"

The old wine, the pomegranates, the lutes, the singers, the sounds of the birds, and, finally, the reproaches are all found in the wine song by Abu Nuwas cited above.

Scheindlin has translated Dunash's poem into verse, explaining in his commentary that the Hebrew text is in "Dunash's meter," with each verse divided into four lines, rhyming *aaax, bbbx,* etc., with the x-rhyme constant throughout. This particular prosodic scheme never caught on among later Jewish poets, but "it represents an experimental stage in the adaptation of Arabic prosody to Hebrew, and doubtless sounded like doggerel to ears accustomed to the long, grave, lines of Arabic verse." Scheindlin also explains that his translation does not succeed in maintaining the same x-rhyme throughout. I quote the passages already quoted above in prose translation:

> There came a voice: "Awake!
> Drink wine at morning's break.
> 'Mid rose and camphor make
> A feast of all your hours.
>
> 'Mid pomegranate trees
> And low anemones,
> Where vines extend their leaves
> And the palm tree skyward towers,
>
> Where lilting singers hum
> To the throbbing of the drum,
> Where gentle viols thrum
> To the plash of fountains' showers.
>
> On every lofty tree
> The fruit hangs gracefully.

And all the birds in glee
Sing among the bowers.
      [. . . . .]
I chided him: "Be still!
How can you drink your fill
When lost is Zion hill
To the uncircumcised.
      [. . . . .]
The Torah, God's delight
Is little in your sight,
While wrecked is Zion's height,
By foxes vandalized.

How can we be carefree
Or raise our cups in glee,
When by all men are we
Rejected and despised?"

As for the interpretation of the poem, several alternatives have been proposed by previous commentators: (1) the first part is seriously intended, the second part a mere perfunctory retraction; (2) only the second part is seriously intended; and—Scheindlin's view—(3) both parts are seriously intended and the dilemma is left unresolved.

Our next wine poem, by Samuel Hanagid—who wrote perhaps more wine poems than any other Jewish author of the Golden Age—is much more complex in tone than Dunash's poem, though the rhetorical structures of the two are superficially similar. Here is Scheindlin's version (one of seven wine poems by Hanagid he has translated and commented on):

My friend, we pass our lives as if in sleep;
      Our pleasures and our pains are merely dreams.
But stop your ears to all such things, and shut
      Your eyes—may Heaven grant you strength!—
Don't speculate on hidden things; leave that
      To God, the Hidden One, whose eye sees all.

But send the lass who plays the lute
      To fill the cup with coral drink,
Put up in kegs in Adam's time,
      Or else just after Noah's flood,
A pungent wine, like frankincense,
      A glittering wine, like gold and gems,

Such wine as concubines and queens
    Would bring King David long ago.

The day they poured that wine into the drum,
    King David's singer Jerimoth would strum
And sing: "May such a wine as this be kept
    Preserved and stored in sealed-up kegs and saved
For all who crave the water of the grape,
    For every man who holds the cup with skill,
Who keeps the rule Ecclesiastes gave,
    Revels, and fears the tortures of the grave."

This fascinating piece of writing is discussed in detail by Scheindlin, but I will restrict myself to just a few points. Scheindlin sees a turning point in verse 4 (lines 7 and 8, since a verse consists of two lines), when the organized alliterations in the Hebrew announce or coincide with the shift from an ascetic to a hedonistic ethos. In the translation, alliteration is replaced by a shift from pentameter to tetrameter. This shift is maintained throughout the next three verses, while the last four verses return to pentameter. The parodic nature of the poem is confirmed by the reference to absurdly ancient wine and by the characterization of King David as a paradigmatic drinker. (In his poetry, Hanagid often compares himself to King David.) Then, as Scheindlin explains, there is the obscure allusion to Jerimoth:

> Jerimoth was the fifth of the fourteen sons of Heman, one who was one of three Levites whom David appointed with their sons to serve as Temple singers. Mentioned only once in the Bible, in the midst of the stupefying list of names comprising Chapters 23 through 27 of I Chronicles, Jerimoth (as well as his thirteen brothers and numerous cousins) went unmentioned in the Jewish literature of the next 1300 years until revived by Samuel the Nagid, still as a musician, but with a distinctly secular function.

Finally, the poem ends puzzlingly with "the tortures of the grave"; Scheindlin comments: "I rather think that the ideal drinker is a man as complex as himself, who lives in both the profane and sacred worlds, and who drinks as if there were to be no final judgment—though he knows there is."

Let us close with Carmi's prose translation of an anonymous Hebrew song in praise of wine, using classical Hispano-Arabic meters and dating from some time between the thirteenth and sixteeenth centuries:

> Give me the cup that puts sorrow to flight, and let me have my share in the river of delights. Take a thousand in payment, and I shall add another hundred and twenty, and eighty more. And when I die before your very

eyes, my friend, dig my grave among the roots of vines. Do not scatter dust upon my grave; cover it with jugs instead of stones. And do not cry and mourn when I die; but make music with harp, lute and pipe. Fill my wash basin with grape-water, and embalm me in old grape husks. For Avshay is the father of all merriment. Remember his name through all generations.

There is a disguised allusion to the Hebrew Bible in the total payment of twelve hundred, which corresponds to separate payments of one thousand and two hundred in the Song of Songs (8:12). The plea to be buried among the roots of vines recalls the last line of Abu Nuwas's "A censurer censured me." Finally, Av(i)shay must be the author's name.

MEDIEVAL LATIN AND VERNACULAR

Earlier, in chapter 16, "Melons and Papayas," we had occasion to refer to Walafrid Strabo's extraordinary passage in his *Hortulus* on gourds (which were probably similar to our pumpkins). That passage begins with an extended simile comparing what, at first glance, must seem radically dissimilar plants—grapes and gourds. But Walafrid dwells on the fact that both plants require support (grapevines from tree trunks, gourds from a gardener's props). There follows a straightforward and detailed description of how a gourd may be dried out and used as a wine vessel (translated by Peter Godman):

> But if the gourd is allowed to stay on its parent tree
> to enjoy the breezes of the summer season and be cut down late
> in the year with a sickle, the same fruit can often be put to use
> as a vessel, when we scoop out the contents of its vast belly,
> easily shaving its sides with a lathe.
> Frequently a king-sized pint will go into this paunch,
> sometimes it holds the better part of a full measure,
> and, as a wine jar sealed with gummy pitch, it keeps
> the product of the noble vine in good condition for many a day.

Also in the ninth century, Christian monastic culture was generating poems about wine that were very different from the Classical hexameters of Walafrid. An example is the lively and jolly poem, "The Abbot of Angers," found in an anthology from Verona whose other poems are mostly religious in nature. Something of the eleven-syllable trochaic Latin verse (the first two lines: "Andecavis abas esse dicitur / ille nomen primi tenet hominum") is captured in the following English version of the first and last of five stanzas, by Howard Mumford Jones (1928):

> Angers,   one hears,   has a monk of mighty thirst,
> His name   the same   as Adam's was, of men the first;

Men think	his drink	runs to such vast quantities
No man	else can	run a score as large as his.

Praise him, praise him, praise him, praisc him!
Sing we Bacchus' praises now!
[. . . . .]

Shed tears,	Angers,	if death should get him in his grip;
No other	such brother	in all your city's fellowship!
Who'll quaff and laugh		and soak in wine as he has done?
Make eternal his diurnal		deeds in stone or paint, my son!

Praise him, praise him, praise him, praise him!
Sing we Bacchus' praises now!

In the ninth century, even philosophers and emperors were able to joke with one another about wine and drunkenness, if the following anecdote can be credited. The greatest philosopher of the time, John Scotus Eriugena (800/815–877?), was sitting across the table from his patron, Emperor Charles the Bald (823–877), when the following exchange occurred (as related by Helen Waddell in her book *The Wandering Scholars* [1932]):

> "What is there between *sottum et Scottum* [a drunkard and an Irishman]?" said Charles one night when the wine was in them both. "The breadth of the table, Sire," said John.

That John was Irish is pretty certain, since both of his surnames refer to Ireland.

By the twelfth century, Europe saw a proliferation of so-called goliardic poems in Latin; lighthearted and irreverent, these mostly anonymous writings were often about drinking wine. But the ancient Greek admonition never to drink wine neat was now precisely reversed, as in "Potatores exquisiti" (Topers all; found in the thirteenth-century manuscript called *Carmina Burana*); the first, fourth, fifth, and last of six stanzas are quoted both in Latin and in George F. Whicher's English in hopes of illustrating, even for the illatinate, the highly flexible syntax, the tremendous compression, and the resounding vowels of the original:

> Drinkers who revere your mission,
> Conoisseurs of wine's condition,
> Quenchless thirst be your ambition;
> Cups in ceaseless repetition
> May you quaff, with no contrition
> The morning after;

May your quips not breed suspicion,
    But endless laughter.
    [. . . . .]
When you drink for emulation,
Water not your pure potation;
Drink to shake the earth's foundation,
Drink to slur pronunciation,
Drink as if your soul's salvation
    On this depended:
To cause the swift evacuation
    Of jars up-ended.

God and goddess always bicker;
Wine scorns Water's flaccid ichor.
Liber (that's his name) is quicker,
Give him liberty, he'll trick her.
Joined with her, the god grows sicker
    In loathed communion.
Water shall not wed our liquor,
    We ban their union.

Let her pose as queen of ocean—
Goddess, if she likes the notion:
She'll not rouse our hearts' devotion
Mismatched with the stronger potion.
Ne'er by her, of his own motion,
    Was Bacchus lessened,
Nor with such presumptuous lotion
    Can he be christened.

    ~

Potatores exquisiti,
licet sitis sine siti,
et bibatis expediti
et scyphorum inobliti,
scyphi crebro repetiti
non dormiant,
et sermones inauditi
prosiliant.
    [. . . . .]
Cum contingat te prestare,
ita bibas absque pare,

ut non possis pede stare,
neque recta verba dare,
sed sit tibi salutare
potissimum
semper vas evacuare
quam maximum.

Dea deo ne iungatur,
deam deus aspernatur,
nam qui Liber appellatur,
libertate gloriatur,
virtus eius adnullatur
in poculis,
et vinum debilitatur
in copulis.

Cum regina sit in mari,
dea potest appelari,
sed indigna tanto pari,
quem presumat osculari.
Nunquam Bachus adaquari
se voluit,
nec se Liber baptizari
sustinuit.

A much longer poem, on the same theme and also from the *Carmina Burana,*
has been translated into English by David Parlett. The Latin begins: "Denudata veri-
tate / succinctaque brevitate / ratione varia"; the first and last of twenty-nine stanzas
vigorously denounce the mixing of water and wine:

Hear the truth! It's plain, unvarnished,
by long-windedness untarnished,
    and improved by various quotes:
Never mix in the same pitcher
substances together which are
    always at each other's throats.
        [. . . . .]
I (your poet, Peter) now declare a finish to this rowdy
    dispute. Here's the final score:
Whoso join these two together

may Christ from salvation sever
always and for evermore.
AMEN

Another thirteenth-century manuscript, now in Durham Cathedral, and written sometime before 1232 by Robert Grosseteste (ca. 1170–1253), contains a fascinating detail pertaining to the great Oxford scholastic philosopher's opinions on wine. Grosseteste is commenting on one of the psalms that mentions wine: "Good wine gives nourishment and health to the body; it clarifies the blood and opens the veins and purifies them; it expels the dark melancholy generated from the heart; it makes the soul forget its gloom and gives it joy and comfort; it gives the soul a happy boldness in undertaking subtle and difficult enquiries." Richard Southern, in his book on Grosseteste [1986], cites this as a comment on Psalm 59:5 (in Grosseteste's Latin Bible; 60:5 in the Hebrew Bible). To this, Southern adds: "By a happy coincidence the practical application of this doctrine can be found exemplified in a penance of a daily glass of good wine which Grosseteste imposed on a sullen friar"!

Turning to the vernacular, we may note that one unusual genre in Anglo-Saxon literature is the versified riddle. Like all Anglo-Saxon poetry, the riddles are written in a four-stress line with two of the stresses emphasized by alliteration. Here is the text of one such riddle, dating probably from the early eighth century (no. 11 in the Exeter Book; for the original, see Krapp and van Kirk Dobbie's edition [1936]) rendered into modern English by Kevin Crossley-Holland:

> My garb is ashen and in my garments
> bright jewels, garnet-coloured, gleam.
> I mislead muddlers, despatch the thoughtless
> on fool's errands, and thwart cautious men
> on their useful journeys. I can't think
> why, addled and led astray, robbed
> of their senses, men praise my ways
> to everyone. Woe betide addicts
> when they bring the dearest of hoards on high
> unless they've foregone their foolish habits.

The phrase "dearest of hoards" may refer to the soul. Crossley-Holland accepts *wine* as the most plausible solution to the riddle (other proposed solutions are *beaker of wine, night,* and *gold*) and explains the place of wine in eighth-century England as follows:

> Wine was a rarer commodity [than mead or ale], and a pupil in Ælfric's *Colloquy,* a dialogue used in monastery schools to teach Latin, comments, "I'm not rich enough to buy myself wine; and wine isn't a drink for children or the foolish, but for the old and wise." There were some vineyards in the South of England and much wine was imported from France and

Germany in large *amphorae* and in wooden barrels like those depicted in
the Bayeux Tapestry.

Drinking songs in the vernacular were also, of course, common in the Middle
Ages. Here is a Dutch example from around 1400, which Peter Potter, "a clerk in the
count's service [who] also dealt in wines and managed a tavern," jotted down together
with the tune in an archival document he happened to be writing: "Let us sing merrily
ho! and rejoice in the tears of the vine that gladden so many hearts. Let us not tarry,
therefore; pour and let go of your sorrow!" An (anonymous) English instance of the
genre—probably a fragment of a dance song—occurs in a manuscript dating from the
second quarter of the fourteenth century; this somewhat reconstructed version is due
to Thomas Duncan:

> Tabart is y-dronken,
>> Dronken, dronken,
> Y-dronken is Tabart,
> Y-dronken is Tabart
> Y-dronken attë [with] winë.

> Hay Robin, Malkin suster [sister],
>> Walter, Peter!
> Ye dronken allë depë [deeply],
> Ye dronken allë depë,
> And Ichullë ekë [and I shall too].

> Stondeth allë stillë
>> Stillë, stillë,
> Stillë stondeth allë,
> Stillë stondeth allë,
> Stille as any ston.

> Trippe a littel with thy fot [foot]
> And let thy body gon [go].

Next, here is an excerpt from an anonymous German popular song dating back
at least to the fifteenth century. As will be seen, all the lines have the same end-rhyme
(the prose translation is by Leonard Forster):

> Wein, Wein von dem Rhein,
> Lauter, klar und fein,
> Dein Farb gibt gar lichten Schein,
> Als Kristall und Rubein.
> Du gibst Medizein

Für Trauren. Schenk du ein!

Trink, gut Kätterlein,

Mach rote Wängelein!

Du söhnst die allzeit pflegen Feind zu sein,

Den Augustein

Und die Begein;

Ihnen beiden.scheiden.kannst du Sorg und Pein,

Dass sie vergessen Deutsch und auch Latein!

~

Wine, wine from the Rhine, pure, clear, and delicate, your colour shines brilliantly like crystal and ruby. You are a medicine against depression. Pour it out and drink, good Kate, and make your cheeks red! Wine, you make peace between those who are always at odds with one another, the Augustinians and the Beguines, and you can drive away all sorrow from both of them so that they forget both German and Latin!

Finally, to France. In the popular play *Le Jeu de Saint-Nicholas* (ca. 1200), by Jean Bodel, a clerk to the city governors of Arras, there occurs the following speech (lines 645–53), as translated by Richard Axton and John Stevens:

New wine, just freshly broached,

Wine in gallons, wine in barrels,

Smooth and tasty, pure full-bodied

Leaps to the head like a squirrel up a tree

No tang of must in it, or mold—

Fresh and strong, full, rich-flavored

As limpid as a sinner's tears

It lingers on a gourmet's tongue—

Other folks ought not to touch it.

This is the call of a "wine crier," according to Jane Williams in her book on the windows of the trades at Chartres cathedral. After quoting the above speech from Bodel's play, Williams explains that the crier's job was to "advertise the wine of each new barrel tapped in a tavern by calling out its price and quality at the crossroads, and by offering a sip of it to passersby from covered goblets called *hanaps*." Williams believes that from the twelfth century wine criers worked the nave in Chartres cathedral in an effort to divert buyers away from the competing taverns in the town. The cathedral's taverns were located in the cloister—an extensive region surrounding the cathedral, containing vineyards as well as the wheat fields which furnished the major source of income for the seventy-two canons, who "formed the largest and wealthiest cathedral chapter in France." Williams's evidence includes contemporary documents, as well as some of the stained glass windows of today's Gothic cathedral, which were

installed (after the Romanesque cathedral had been destroyed by fire in 1194) in the
years between 1205 and 1226. Of particular importance for the study of the wine
trade and wine rituals are the windows of the north aisle and north transept, about
which Williams remarks that she has "found no images like these of wine offering in
other thirteenth-century French cathedrals." One of these windows is devoted to the
legendary sixth-century bishop of Chartres, St. Lubinus—credited with founding both
the chapter and the school at Chartres—whose cult, by the thirteenth century, was second only to that of the cathedral's patron saint, the Virgin Mary. The cult of Lubinus—
best known in the thirteenth century for his healing powers—extended well beyond
Chartres; no fewer than sixteen regional churches were dedicated to him.

Williams's summary account of the Lubinus window reads:

> The Lubinus window has five interrelated themes about wine set out in
> geometrical order. At the base of the window, wine is advertised. In
> sequence up the center of the window, wine is transported, stored, and car-
> ried to the altar for mass. In the vertical borders, fourteen men offer gob-
> lets of wine to St. Lubinus, whose life is illustrated in the middle panels.

(By the advertising of wine Williams means the image of a wine crier; for a reproduction, see the second colored plate in her book.) But why this association of wine
with St. Lubinus, and who made the selection of images for the window dedicated to
the saint? The answer to the latter question—at least, prior to Williams's research—
has always been more or less that of Henry Adams (1838–1918), in his *Mont-Saint-
Michel and Chartres* (1904): "Saint Lubin . . . was, for some reason, selected by the wine-
merchants to represent them, as their interesting medallions show." Williams believes
otherwise. To begin with, she argues that the town wine merchants (or, better, tavern
keepers), having not yet formed their own confraternity, were licensed by the count
of Chartres. Furthermore, by the early thirteenth century there was a history of violent conflict between the count—more often, the countess, her husband being away
on crusade—and the cathedral chapter, even leading occasionally to homicide (as in
the bloody riot of 1210). As for the tavern keepers in the cloister, they were strictly
under the control of the cathedral chapter, which would, of course, have been ultimately responsible for selecting the themes of the windows. Other significant evidence
supporting Williams's claims are the probable location of the cloister tavern and the
chapter's wine cellar, both just north of the Lubinus window.

As for the question of why St. Lubinus should have been associated with wine,
Williams has two answers, one having to do with certain important liturgical practices
that took place on the north side of the cathedral (such as the presentation of wine at
the harvest feast of St. Lubinus), and the other with an attempt by the canons "to justify the chapter's large wine store by connecting it to the sacramental purpose of the
wine." In the Lubinus window, "sacred imagery of wine is combined with representation of wine-drinking for pleasure. This seems to be an attempt to amend contemporary

moral condemnation of such drinking" (such as, for example, the efforts of the Fourth Lateran Council of 1215 to control priests' excessive wine drinking). Along the same lines, the depictions of Noah and of the prodigal son in two other Chartres windows both omit any allusion to drunkenness, which leads Williams to conclude that "it seems that in these windows as well as the Lubinus windows, economic concerns motivated the alteration of religious imagery."

An anonymous dramatization of the prodigal son story, *Courtois d'Arras* (ca. 1200), by a contemporary of Jean Bodel, is of some interest, belonging, as it does, "to an Arras tradition of tavern realism," as Axton and Stevens explain. Much shorter than *Le Jeu de Saint Nicolas* (some 660 lines compared with over 1, 500), *Courtois d'Arras* is written, like Bodel's play, mostly but not entirely in octosyllabic couplets. There are nine speaking roles: Courtois, his father, and his brother; three tavern attendants; two "women of the town" (that is, whores); and a burgher. Exactly half of the lines are uttered in the tavern, where Courtois is plied with wine by the two whores and then fleeced, not only of his father's gift of money, but of the very clothes he is wearing. Here, in Axton and Stevens's translation, is the pot-boy crying his wine, at the beginning of the tavern scene (lines 103–9):

> This way, inside for Soissons wine!
> Sit on the grass or on rush mats—
> Wonderful drinking from silver tankards!
> Credit extends to everyone,
> Fools and wise men drinking inside—
> And no one has to leave a pledge!
> There's nothing to do but chalk it up.

A late-medieval English play of some 2, 143 lines, *Mary Magdalen* (Bodleian MS Digby 133), is considered an example of the decline of the genre of mystery plays by some scholars (such as Rosemary Woolf) whose criteria are primarily literary: "a hybrid curiosity, part mystery play, part saint's life, part morality play with realistic low-life elements." Other scholars, such as Baker, Murphy, and Hall (the most recent editors of the text of *Mary Magdalen*), being specially concerned with performance or theatrical values, take a more positive view of the play, calling it "physically the most elaborate single play in the English religious drama" and noting how "the sheer mechanical daring of the play matches its rhetoric." Dating from around 1500 and drawing on both New Testament and legendary sources, the play's plot is summarized by Darryll Grantley:

> It depicts Mary's fall into sin, her repentance and approach to Christ at the house of Simon the Leper, the resurrection of her brother Lazarus, Mary's sorrow after the crucifixion and her meeting with the risen Christ in the garden, her legendary disciplehood during which she converts the kingdom

of Marcyll [Marseilles], her last years spent in hermitage in the desert being fed by angels and her final assumption into heaven.

In an early scene in a tavern in Jerusalem Mary is first tempted to sin by the allegorical figure of Lechery; in the scene, the taverner speaks first (here in modernized spelling by the editors Baker, Murphy, and Hall):

> I am a taverner, witty and wise,
> That wines have to sell great plenty!
> Of all the taverners, I bear the prize,
> That be dwelling within the city!
> Of wines I have great plenty,
> Both white wine and red that [is] so clear.

> Here is wine of Mawt and malmeseyn,
> Clary wine, and claret, and other moo [more];
> Wine of Gylder, and of Gallys, that made at the Groine,
> Wine of Wyan and Vernage I say also—
> There be no better as far as ye can goo!

Ann Rycraft, in her essay "Food in Medieval Drama" (1999), identifies the wine place-names in a note: "'Mawt,' Malta; 'malmeseyn,' a sweet Greek wine, copied elsewhere; 'clary,' sweet wine, possibly with extra sweetening and spice; 'claret,' a light red wine from Bordeaux; 'Gylder,' perhaps Germany; 'Gallys,' Gascony; 'Groine,' La Coruña, Spain; 'Wyan,' probably Viana, Portugal; 'Vernage,' strong sweet Italian wine."

RENAISSANCE

The cynosure of Italian Renaissance neo-Latin poetry during his long life was Giovanni Pontano. (We have already encountered him as the author of a versified treatise on lemon growing.) Typical of the neo-Latin poets' deliberate emulation of ancient models is an early (mid-fifteenth century) poem by Pontano; as the translator Fred Nichols puts it, "*Ludit poetice* [He amuses himself, poetically] both imitates and carries on the movement of Propertius III, iii." In this Propertian elegy, the poet is admonished by Apollo not to attempt martial subject matter but to stick to love. As Nichols explains, Pontano not only echoes this theme in his opening lines but later actually mentions Propertius—who lived, like Pontano, in Umbria—and even repeats a couple of the older poet's phrases. Pontano's rhetorical strategy, however, is to begin with a tongue-in-cheek resolution to get down to serious writing, about war: "Enough now of idly amusing ourselves in the mild shade and offering what we've written to bands of nymphs. Now I'm pleased to lead the stout brothers into battle at Troy, and the Dardanian leaders back to arms." Suddenly, the poet is out in an Umbrian meadow and, far from getting away from nymphs, one appears abruptly with an offer of Apollo's lyre.

554   But then Bacchus puts in an appearance, and after frightening the nymph back into her spring, he goes on to dominate the latter half of the poem. Bacchus is surrounded by satyrs, nymphs, Silenus, and Priapus, as well as "red-faced Drunkenness and unwholesome Love" (Aebrietasque rubens: & malesanus Amor). Then, Arcadian Pan recites:

> Bacchus coming back from conquered India was the first to place new garlands on his own head. He was the first to teach how to press juice from the tendrilled grapevine and sweet honey from pure combs; and he first began to celebrate banquets with tables loaded with food, and unusual feasts with wine.

And the poet reverts to his old ways:

> Do war's encampments seem too hard for you, you who always cultivate leisure and delight? Clearly in us habit is the mistress: she in her genius generates this diligence, this skill. But if you'll get used to sweating a little under arms, soon you'll confidently feel a martial glow.

While in Mantua at the court of Francesco Gonzaga, another great Italian humanist and poet, Angelo Poliziano (1454–1494), composed a short pastoral drama (the first in Italian) called "The Fable of Orfeo"; it was successfully performed and eventually published in 1494. Some 340 lines in length, the work concludes with "A Chorus of Bacchantes," consisting of four six-line stanzas, each preceded and followed by the couplet: "Ognun segua, Bacco, te! / Bacco, Bacco, *euoè!*" Here is an English version by Joseph Tusiani in which I have slightly rearranged the two last stanzas:

> I am dying for some sleep.
> Am I drunk, say yes or no?
> Straight my legs no more can keep.
> It is you are drunk, I know.
> Everyone do as I do:
> everyone do as I do.
>
> Bacchus, let all follow you!
> Bacchus, Bacchus, *live anew!*
>
> Everyone shout Bacchus Bacchus,
> and still swallow more wine down,
> till our noise be weak and raucous.
> Drink! You too, you too, drink down!
> I can't dance another bout.
> *Live anew* let all men shout.
>
> Bacchus, let all follow you!
> Bacchus, Bacchus, *live anew!*

Leonardo da Vinci (1452–1519) might not have been amused by Poliziano's celebration of Bacchus; at least, one of his own humorous tales has a very different tone. In one of Leonardo's notebooks, the so-called Codex Atlanticus (ca. 1493), there is a tale about how Mahomet came to ban wine (translated by Jean Paul Richter):

> Wine, the divine juice of the grape, finding itself in a golden and richly wrought cup, on the table of Mahomet, was puffed up with pride at so much honour; when suddenly it was struck by a contrary reflection, saying to itself: "What am I about, that I should rejoice, and not perceive that I am now near to my death and shall leave my golden abode in this cup to enter into the foul and fetid caverns of the human body, and to be transmuted from a fragrant and delicious liquor into a foul and base one. . . . And it cried to Heaven, imploring vengeance for so much insult, and that an end might henceforth be put to such contempt; and that, since that country produced the finest and best grapes in the whole world, at least they should not be turned into wine. Then Jove made that wine drunk by Mahomet to rise in spirit to his brain; and that in so deleterious a manner that it made him mad, and gave birth to so many follies that when he had recovered himself, he made a law that no Asiatic should drink wine, and henceforth the vine and its fruit were left free.
>
> As soon as wine has entered the stomach it begins to ferment and swell; then the spirit of that man begins to abandon his body, rising as it were skywards, and the brain finds itself parting from the body. Then it begins to degrade him, and makes him rave like a madman, and then he does irreparable evil, killing his friends.

In a less serious vein than Leonardo's, Erasmus (d. 1536) composed a Latin satire on a friend who drank too much wine and had just died: "An Epitaph for a drunken jokester, in scazons" (1509–1511). "Scazons"—sometimes termed the "limping" meter—refers to a pattern of basically iambic lines in which the last foot of each line is a trochee (a reversed iamb) or a spondee (two accented syllables). Such metrical playfulness accorded with the subject matter, and, more generally, it must be understood that, by this time in his career, Erasmus had ceased writing serious poetry except, as his modern editor Harry Vredeveld explains, as "a pastime for himself, a service to his friends, a handmaiden to his prose." In the first eight of the fourteen Latin lines, the buried individual asks the passerby to read silently so as not to awaken him (1993, translated by Clarence Miller):

> and make my throat thirsty
> once again the minute I wake up. For I, the
> snoring jokester buried under this stone, was
> once a famous devotee of the mighty Bacchus,
> seeing that I drank my way through eight
> whole decades.

Line 11 exhibits some humorous wordplay: "Idem bibendi finis atque vivendi / Fuit" (I came to the end of drinking and / living at the same moment). The dead man was from Lisbon, and Vredeveld explains how "Erasmus mentions that some speakers, particularly those from Spain, say *b* for *v* and vice versa, pronouncing *'vivit* for *bibit* and *bibit* for *vivit.'*" The poem ends with another admonition to the passerby to depart silently.

The greatest poet of sixteenth-century France, Pierre de Ronsard (1524–1585), created some new poetic forms and wrote in virtually all the old ones, including odes inspired by Pindar, Horace, and the Anacreontic poets. Here is a literal translation (by Stanley Appelbaum, 1991) of some excerpts from Ronsard's *Odes* 2.10 (1550), together with the original French:

> Have my wine chilled so that
> It surpasses an icicle in coldness;
> [. . . . .]
> Page, replenish the wine in my cup,
> Let this tall glass be full to the brim.
> Curse the man who languishes in vain;
> I don't agree with these old Physicians:
> My brain is never fully sound
> Unless it is flooded with much wine.
>
> ～
>
> Fay refraischir mon vin de sorte
> Qu'il passe en froideur un glaçon;
> [. . . . .]
> Page, reverse dans ma tasse,
> Que ce grand verre soit tout plain.
> Maudit soit qui languit en vain,
> Ces vieux Medecins je n'appreuve:
> Mon cerveau n'est jamais bien sain,
> Si beaucoup de vin ne l'abreuve.

The two greatest prose writers of sixteenth-century France, François Rabelais and Michel de Montaigne, wrote about wine drinking in highly stimulating, though very different, ways. Toward the beginning of *The Most Horrific Life of the Great Gargantua* (1534), just before Gargantua is born, Rabelais composed, entirely in dialogue, a chapter entitled variously, in different English translations, "The Remarks of the Drunkards," "The Drunkards' Conversation," or "Palaver of the Potted." The text of the chapter (book 1, chapter 5) consists of more than a hundred remarks, mostly very brief, by a group of unnamed speakers. The dialogue begins as follows (translated by Donald Frame):

> "Draw!"
> "Pass it here!"

"Turn it on!"

"Mix it!"

"Let me have it without water. . . . That's it, my friend."

"Toss me off this glass gallantly."

"Come up with some claret for me, a weeping glass."

"A truce on thirst!"

Certain voices recur in the dialogue, as identified by their repeated use of theologico-religious, legal, or scientific jargon; here are some examples from each of the three categories: "Which came first, thirst or drinking?" "Thirst, for who could have drunk without thirst during our time of innocence?"; "You wine stewards, creators of new forms, from not drinking make me drinking!"; "I appear as appelant against thirst, even as against abuses. Page, draw up my appeal in due form"; "This stuff is going into my veins; the pissery won't get anything out of it." Some of the biblical allusions are at best irreverent and at worst blasphemous—for example, "I have the Word of God in my mouth: *Sitio* [I thirst]," where the Latin word translates Christ's penultimate word in John 19:28. It is only appropriate, then, that when Gargantua is finally born, in the next chapter, his first words are "'A drink, a drink, a drink!' as if inviting everybody to drink . . . he was heard in all the regions of Beusse and Bibarois."

The influential interpretation of Rabelais as a reflection of folk-carnival humor, in *Rabelais and His World* (Russian ed., 1965), by Mikhail Bakhtin (1895–1975), includes these comments on book 1, chapter 5 (translated by Hélène Iswolsky):

> This is a carnivalesque symposium. It has no external logical continuity, no unifying abstract idea or problem (as in a classic symposium). But the "Palaver of the Potulent" has a deep internal unity. It is one grotesque play of debasement carefully organized up to the minutest detail. Nearly every replica [*sic*] contains a formula from the higher level—ecclesiastical, liturgical, philosophical, or juridical—or some words of the scriptures applied to eating and drinking. The conversation is actually concerned with two topics: the ox tripes that are being consumed and the wine that washes down the food. But this material bodily lower stratum is travestied as images and formulas of the holy spiritual upper level.

Book 5 of *Gargantua and Pantagruel*—not, it will be recalled, authentic Rabelais—concludes with fifteen chapters (33–47) relating the quest for the oracle of the Bottle. The narrative drags and is not very funny, but chapter 44 offers something of interest—a shaped poem in the form of a wine flask. (Shaped poems go back to the Hellenistic period and are thought to have Persian or Turkish origins: see the entry "Pattern Poetry" by John L. Lievsay in the *Princeton Encyclopedia of Poetry and Poetics* [1974].) The travelers have reached an alabaster fountain of heptagonal form containing the sacred Bottle, and Bacbuc, the pontiff of wine, has ordered Panurge to "bow down and kiss the lip of the fountain, then get back up and dance around it three *ithymboi* [Bacchic dances]. That done, she ordered him to sit down between two stools prepared there, ass to the ground. Then she opened up her book of ritual, and, blowing into his left ear, had him sing a Bacchic ode."

One of Montaigne's early essays (1573–74, with later additions) is "Of Drunkenness" (2.2). Right in its middle the essay contains a long digression on Montaigne's father—which is naturally of exceptional biographical interest—but it is not so easy to make out exactly what Montaigne thinks about drunkenness. He begins by arguing that vices differ in degree and then asserts that drunkenness is "a gross and brutish vice. . . . The other vices affect the understanding; this one overturns it, and stuns the body" (translated by Donald Frame). Anyone who has studied the history of the cardinal sins may at this point recall that one traditional Christian view, of some influence in the Latin Middle Ages, deemed gluttony—which usually included drunkenness—the worst of sins, whereas other views placed gluttony among the lesser sins.

For Montaigne—in accord with his special version of Christian humanism—these medieval ideas seem to be elided without a trace, as he proceeds directly back to the ancients, informing us, "It is certain that antiquity did not strongly decry this vice." The great authority of antiquity in Montaigne's eyes then forces him to think again about drunkenness, and he discovers in himself a certain divided consciousness in the form of an opposition between his "taste and constitution" (which condemn drunkenness as "a loose and stupid vice") and his "reason" (which finds it "less malicious and harmful than the others"). Indeed, since reason seems to require of us that we seek pleasure, and since drinking is one generally acknowledged source of pleasure, we should drink in such a way as to maximize our pleasure. It follows, first, that we should learn to enjoy even inferior wines (because they are more readily available) and, second, that we should drink as frequently as possible (in order to increase the number of occasions on which we experience pleasure).

Surely Montaigne is being ironic, perhaps by letting us see the difficulties one gets into by following reason alone? It is not easy to say, for he goes on to argue that the diminished wine drinking by his contemporaries has necessarily been accompanied by an increase in lechery, and that this is on the whole a bad thing. In his father's generation, by contrast, sobriety was less valued and chastity more. (This, of course, is the rationale for introducing a portrait of Montaigne's father, ending with his marriage, "well along in age," at thirty-three. Montaigne himself was a year younger when he married; his wife was twenty.)

Montaigne was about forty when he started "Of Drunkenness" and perhaps it was then he first began to realize that becoming "a better drinker" might be a desirable hedge against the discomforts of old age, when wine is one of the few pleasures left to us. Nevertheless, Montaigne tells us, he can hardly understand "how people come to prolong the pleasure of drinking beyond their thirst, and forge themselves in their imagination an artificial and unnatural appetite." His own preference is to drink after eating (like the Greeks), so that his "last drink is almost always the biggest." Unless restrained by the idea of a "natural" limit, however, even Montaigne's disciplined drinking habits could turn out to serve merely as prelude to the kind of uncontrolled drinking bouts which he associates with the Germans. Montaigne, moreover, seems to recognize the origin of his own moderation more in his "stomach" (what he earlier termed his "taste and constitution") than in his reason.

This talk of the relative strength and value of the human faculties suggests something like the view—which Montaigne finds in Plato's *Laws*—that drunkenness is not virtuous or vicious in itself but only relative to the individual and to the situation. Montaigne does not engage directly with Plato's point, but he does assert unequivocally the highly un-Platonic doctrine that "wisdom does not overcome our natural limitations." Another Platonic doctrine that sees drunkenness as akin to "poetic frenzy and madness" is then cited, again without explicit approval or disapproval; and the essay ends abruptly on an uncertain note. Two comments should be added concerning these discussions of Plato: first, Plato was far from being one of Montaigne's favorite authors (except, of course, for the character of Socrates); and second, these discussions were late additions to the text of "Of Drunkenness," written at a time (after 1588) when we know Montaigne was reading Plato.

It is, of course, tempting to extract from Montaigne's essays definite doctrines on all major topics, and at least one leading Montaigne scholar has done just that with the drunkenness essay. Thus, M. A. Screech writes—what I see no reason to doubt—that "Montaigne detested drink taken to excess" but then adds that "it may have been this antipathy that led him to question the desirability of even those ecstasies of genius which were akin to drunkenness." But Montaigne does not simply repudiate those ecstasies: they fascinate him and they worry him, as he turns them about and about, examining them from different angles. Thus, in the very passage—a description of Torquato Tasso's madness in the essay "Apology for Raymond Sebond"—that Screech cites to illustrate Montaigne's impatience with abnormal mental states, Montaigne asks plaintively (in a sentence not quoted by Screech): "Of what is the subtlest madness made, but the subtlest wisdom?" In short, it seems to me that, in ignoring the twists and divagations, the ironies and modulations, of the essay on drunkenness, Screech has flattened out Montaigne's discussion, and all in support of Screech's own thesis that "in the end most ecstasies are firmly excluded from the wisdom the *Essays* gradually uncover."

At a far humbler literary level, another sixteenth-century Frenchman, Jean Le Houx—whom we have already met as a composer of songs about cider—composed many songs about wine. Here are two very different examples, the first crudely anatomical but not obscene, the second deploying a nice alchemical conceit (the translations are by James Patrick Muirhead):

> Fair nose! whose rubies many pipes have cost
> Of white and rosy wine,

Whose colours are so gorgeously embossed
    In red and purple fine;

Great nose! who views thee, gazing through great glass,
    Thee still more lovely thinks.
Thou dost the nose of creature far surpass
    Who only water drinks.

No Turkey-cock's proud throat thy tints outvies.
    How many wealthy folk
Have not so rich a nose! To paint such dyes,
    Much time must be bespoke.

~

The wine-glass is the brush, thy form to show;
    The colour is the wine,
Which paints thee with a more than cherry glow,
    Drinking from choicest wine.

They say it hurts the eyes.—Are they to choose?
    But wine doth always cure
My woes. I'd rather both the windows lose,
    Than the whole house, I'm sure.

'Tis here that I the quest desire
    Of philosophic stone;
My throat shall be my furnace-fire;
    Here be my bellows blown.

My sun shall be unwatered wine;
[Mon soleil, c'est le vin sans eau]
    Good cider, mercury;
        [Le bon sidre, c'est mon mercure.]
I'll put them in this fire of mine
    In native purity.

Should I on them expend my wealth,
    No alchemy but this
Would I desire for gold or health;
    For drinking is my bliss.

Quintessence of the apple-tree!
[O quintesse de pommier!]

Were I to drink thee dry,   *561*
Would that sufficient reason be
To doubt my sanity?

Sounding almost like a deliberate rejoinder to the uninhibited celebrations of wine and intoxication of Poliziano, Rabelais and Le Houx, the manual of manners by the papal diplomat and poet Giovanni della Casa (1503–1556) warns its readers against excessive drinking of wine. Della Casa's little book in Italian, *Galateo, or the Book of Manners,* posthumously published in 1558, is addressed less to the gentility—like the better-known *Courtier* (1528), by Castiglione—than to what we would call the middle classes. The penultimate twenty-ninth chapter, titled "Some particular instances of bad table-manners, and in this connexion, some remarks about excessive drinking," embroiders an incident from Plato's *Symposium* to help make its case (translated by R. S. Pine-Coffin, 1958):

> The practice of challenging others to drink, which is not an Italian cus-
> tom and is known by the foreign name of "brindisi," is in itself reprehen-
> sible and has not yet been adopted in our country, which is the reason why
> you should not do it. If anyone else challenges you, you can easily decline
> to accept by saying that you admit defeat, and you may thank him and
> even taste a little of the wine for the sake of politeness without drinking
> any more.
>
> These drinking bouts were an ancient custom of the Greeks, or so I
> have heard from several learned men, who are full of praise for a good man
> named Socrates, who lived in those days. He spent the whole length of a
> night in a drinking contest with another good man called Aristophanes,
> and at dawn the next day he worked out a difficult problem in geometry
> without a single mistake. In this way he proved that the wine had done
> him no harm. The learned also say that by frequently risking his life a man
> becomes fearless and sure of himself, and in the same way he learns sober
> and polite habits by growing used to the dangers of intemperance. They
> claim that drinking wine in this way, in excessive quantities, by way of a
> contest, is a great trial of the drinker's strength, and that it is done to test
> his powers so that he may learn to resist and overcome great temptations.
> Nevertheless, my own opinion is against this and I find these arguments
> extremely frivolous.

SEVENTEENTH CENTURY

We may confidently suppose that the popularity of *Galateo*—it was translated into French, Latin, Spanish, German, and English within twenty years of its first publica-tion—did not eradicate excessive drinking of wine among all its readers. We may also know for a certainty that poetic tributes to Bacchus continued to be written in Italy, since one of the most famous of these appeared in 1685. The author was the distinguished physician, scientist, poet, and bibliophile Francesco Redi (1626–1698), and his poem of some thousand lines was called *Bacco in Toscana*. The poem is subtitled a "dithyramb," which in ancient Greece at first meant a cult song with Dionysiac content but later came to refer to a poem whose form was highly irregular and whose content was highly passionate. Joseph Tusiani, who has translated a portion of Redi's poem into English, characterizes the original as "agile and carefree, light in meter and unassuming in tone, unusual for choice of rhymes and memorable for variety of accents" (1971). Tusiani puts into English something like the last 120 lines of Redi's poem. Here is a sample:

> Oh, what sudden dizziness
> wages war on me at once?
> Look, the earth begins to dance
> while my feet move less and less.
> But if the earth begins to quake and flee
> and, staggering about, spells threats to me,
> I'll leave the earth and jump into the sea.
> [. . . . .]
> He who drinks from a small flasket
> carries wealth in broken basket.
> You will never, never see
> in my dauntless, ever-free
> Dionysian bottlery
> little glasses of one shape.
> Glasses down with bottom up,
> glasses up with narrow top
> are utensils for sick men;
> and those flat and spread-out cups
> are for convalescent lips.

The poet, critic, and liberal political journalist Leigh Hunt (1784–1859) published an English version of the whole of Redi's poem in 1825. In his autobiography Hunt recounts the circumstances in which he made the translation. He was living just outside Florence, in 1823, and, too ill to write anything very demanding, he "had recourse to the lightest and easiest translation I could think of, which was that of Redi's *Bacco in Toscana*"; Hunt was also attracted by the challenge of translating a work that had always been considered untranslatable. Hunt summarizes the work as follows:

> A mock-heroical account of the Tuscan wines, put into the mouth of that god, and delivered in dithyrambics. It is ranked among the Italian classics, and deserves to be so for its style and originality. Bacchus is represented sitting on a hill outside the walls of Florence, in company with Ariadne and his usual attendants, and jovially giving his opinion of the wines, as he

drinks them in succession. He gets drunk after a very mortal fashion; but recovers, and is borne away into ecstasy by a draught of Montepulciano, which he pronounces to be the King of Wines.

At the opening of Hunt's translation, Bacchus is addressing Ariadne:

> Dearest, if one's vital tide
> Ran not with the grape's beside,
> What would life be, (short of Cupid?)
> Much too short, and far too stupid.
> You see the beam here from the sky
> That tips the goblet in mine eye;
> Vines are nets that catch such food,
> And turn them into sparkling blood.
> Come then—in the beverage bold
> Let's renew us and grow muscular;
> And for those who're getting old,
> Glasses get of size majuscular.

Next, about halfway through the poem:

> Pour then, pour, companions mine,
> And in the deluge of mighty wine
> Plunge with me, with cup and with can.
> Ye merry shapes of Pan,
> Ye furnishers of philosophic simile,
> The goatibeardihornyfooted family.
> Pour away, pour away,
> Fill your gasping clay
> With a pelting shower of wine.

And, finally, the last lines of the poem:

> Hearken, all earth!
> We, Bacchus, in the might of our great mirth,
> To all who reverence us, and are right thinkers;—
> Hear, all ye drinkers!
> Give ear, and give faith, to our edict divine—
> MONTEPULCIANO'S THE KING OF ALL WINE.
>   At these glad sounds,
> The Nymphs, in giddy rounds,
> Shaking their ivy diadems and grapes,
> Echoed the triumph in a thousand shapes.
> The Satyrs would have joined them; but alas!

> They couldn't; for they lay about the grass,
> As drunk as apes.

In a more sober vein, Johan van Beverwyck, a leading seventeenth-century Dutch physician and author, praised wine as the most healthful of beverages in his numerous immensely popular books of medical advice. One such passage (from *Schat der Gesontheyt* [Treasury of good health; first ed. 1636]) is here translated by art historian Julie Berger Hochstrasser; the Dutch original is in one of her notes.

> Wine is given as a medicine for the weak; and because there are few who have no weaknesses, so it has become a drink for all people. It strengthens the powers, moistens the body, maintains the spirits, helps the digestion and distribution of the foods, causes elimination of water, warms the nature of our body, induces sleep, is a remedy against the cold and dryness of age, quickens the courage, and makes one happy.

Hochstrasser quotes this passage to help make her point that the presence of wine in a Netherlandish still life painting may be read as medical advice rather than as a cautionary moral message. And when the wine is accompanied by fruit, it is often the latter that must be understood as risky to consume, with the wine serving as antidote; hence van Beverwyck's advice that "wine is the right remedy to help against the harm that can come from melons. But it must be strong wine: like Seck or other Spanish wine, and drunk a lot, to minimize the harmfulness of the melon and improve its digestion." Many other medical doubts about the advisability of eating raw fruit will be cited in chapter 22, "Enemies and Friends of Fruit."

Hunt had prefaced his translation of *Bacchus in Tuscany* with a song from Shakespeare's *Antony and Cleopatra* (1606?), and, indeed, this song comes as the climax of one of the great inebriation scenes in the history of theater. Recall the situation (beginning of act 2, scene 7): the three Roman triumvirs (Caesar, Lepidus, and Antony) at Pompey's invitation have boarded his galley near Mt. Misena, off the coast of Naples, for a "banquet" (which for the Elizabethans meant dessert with wine). One recent interpretation of the play (by John Wilders, 1995) opposes the "feeling and sensuality" of the Egyptian world to the "military and political action" of the Roman world. I would add that the ocean lying between Egypt and Rome both separates and connects the two worlds, so it is only appropriate that we find several powerful Romans behaving like Egyptians when they find themselves in this, so to speak, intermediate or neutral region. Leaving aside Lepidus—forever trying to reconcile his colleagues, who never take him seriously—no one of the remaining three has the slightest trust in the other two. After all, Caesar has already criticized Antony for desertion to the fleshpots of Egypt, and Antony is well aware of Caesar's hostility, while Pompey can never forget that Antony is occupying his family home. But after Lepidus is disposed of—he is carried ashore dead drunk—it is these three men who drink together, link hands under the direction of Antony and his chief follower, Enobarbus, and finally join in singing the chorus of a Bacchanalian song:

ANTONY   Come, let's all take hands
    Till that the conquering wine hath steeped our sense
    In soft and delicate Lethe.
ENOBARBUS   All take hands.
        Make battery to our ears with the loud music,
        The while I'll place you; then the boy shall sing.
        The holding every man shall beat as loud
        As his strong sides can volley.
                Music plays. Enobarbus places them hand in hand.

                            The Song
BOY   Come thou monarch of the vine,
                    Plumpy Bacchus with pink eyne!
                    In thy vats our cares be drowned;
                    With thy grapes our hairs be crowned.

ALL   Cup us till the world go round!
                    Cup us till the world go round!

The ironic tensions of the scene are capped by the refrain's allusion to "the world"—the world being precisely the prize for which all three are contending. Finally, it must be emphasized that the drunken revel portion of the scene on Pompey's galley seems to be Shakespeare's invention, since it does not occur in his principal source—North's Plutarch—nor in any of Shakespeare's other likely sources (see the material assembled in Bullough's *Narrative and Dramatic Sources of Shakespeare* [1964]); the scene may have been suggested by royal festivities in 1606 in which James I and Christian of Denmark feasted onboard ship. It must be said, though, that many directors of *Antony and Cleopatra* find the scene dispensable. (For a production history of the scene, from 1813 to 1995, see Richard Madelaine's edition of *Antony and Cleopatra* [1998].)

Samuel Palmer made an etching, *The Vine or Plumpy Bacchus* (1852), to illustrate *Anthony and Cleopatra* 2.7; the image is that of a bacchanal in a woodland setting and includes the printed text of "*The Song.*"

In another Shakespearean play, *The Tempest* (1611), the second scene of the second act contains a wonderfully comic inebriation scene (2.2.111–20). The "savage and deformed" Caliban encounters Trinculo and Stephano from the wrecked ship of the King of Naples. Stephano is already drunk on sack from the ship and has shared his bottle with Caliban:

CALIBAN (*aside*)   That's a brave god, and bears celestial liquor. I will kneel to him.

STEPHANO   How didst thou scape? How cam'st thou hither? Swear by this bottle how thou cam'st hither—I escaped upon a butt [barrel] of sack which the sailors heaved o'erboard—by this bottle, which I made of the bark of a tree with mine own hands since I was cast ashore.

CALIBAN   I'll swear upon that bottle to be thy true subject, for the liquor is not earthly.

The transformative powers of wine are seen operating on Stephano and Caliban—powers analogous to, but far less potent than—Prospero's magic. And some of the interrelated issues of the play—mastery, freedom, the status of monsters—are announced in a comic mode in the last lines of the scene (2.2.175–183):

STEPHANO   (*To Caliban*) Here, bear my bottle. Fellow Trinculo, we'll fill him by and by again.

CALIBAN   (*sings drunkenly*) Farewell, master, farewell, farewell!

TRINCULO   A howling monster; a drunken monster!

CALIBAN   No more dams I'll make for fish,
    Nor fetch in firing
    At requiring,
Nor scrape trenchering, nor wash dish:
    'Ban, 'Ban, Ca-Caliban
Has a new master—get a new man!
Freedom, high-day! High-day, freedom! Freedom, high-day, freedom!

STEPHANO   O brave monster! Lead the way!

A few years after the first production of *The Tempest,* Ben Jonson (1572–1637) published his tribute to Canary wine (obtained from the Mermaid tavern) in the course of "Inviting a Friend to Supper" (1616):

But that, which most doth take my Muse, and mee,
Is a pure cup of rich Canary-wine,
Which is the Mermaids, now, but shall be mine:
Of which had Horace, or Anacreon tasted,
Their lives, as doe their lines, till now had lasted.
Tabacco, Nectar, or the Thespian spring,
Are all but Luthers beere, to this I sing.

Now we know that Jonson frequented the Mermaid tavern during the years from about 1605 to about 1616—the period during which he was most active as a playwright—

along with a coterie of friends (including lawyers, scholars, a few courtiers, but probably not Jonson's writer friends, such as Beaumont, Fletcher, and Donne). Jonson's
biographer, David Riggs, suggests that "if the invitation refers to a specific supper
party, Jonson probably issued it between 1605 and 1612 while living at his house in
St. Anne's, Blackfriars." It is not certain when Jonson actually composed the poem, but
its publication (in his *Works* of 1613) followed by only three years an embarrassing
public episode of drunkenness in Paris where Jonson was accompanying Walter
Raleigh's young son, Wat, as his tutor. This may account for the line (35) immediately
following the tribute to Canary wine, which is otherwise something of a surprise in
that it promises no overindulgence in the beverage which has just been so extravagantly praised: "Of this we will sup free, but moderately" (where "sup" means sip).
Extravagantly, yes, but to call the lines, as the Jonson scholar Joseph Loewenstein does,
"egregious hyperbole" seems itself something of an egregious hyperbole. In any case,
by 1616, Jonson had good reasons for wishing to sound respectable, since he had
decided to stop writing plays and to seek financial support from the king, which
entailed, in Loewenstein's words, "for Jonson—ex-resident of debtors' prison, Catholic,
convicted felon—an ethics of moderation"; and, indeed, Jonson received a royal pen-
sion in 1616 and wrote his first masque for the court in 1617.

The unique character of particular wine vintages lies behind a little story told
by Sancho Panza to another squire, in chapter 13, part 2, of *Don Quixote de la Mancha*
(1605, 1615), by Cervantes (1547–1616). The two squires have been exchanging stories about their masters and their future prospects, and all the talk makes them thirsty.
The Knight of the Wood's squire supplies the wine and Sancho correctly identifies its
place of origin. Following up on this little triumph, Sancho boasts about his own and
his ancestors' wine tasting talents (translated by Samuel Putnam):

> On my father's side were two of the best winetasters La Mancha has known
> in many a year, in proof of which, listen to the story of what happened to
> them.
>
> The two were given a sample of wine from a certain vat and asked to
> state its condition and quality and determine whether it was good or bad.
> One of them tasted it with the tip of his tongue while the other merely
> brought it up to his nose. The first man said that it tasted of iron, the sec-
> ond that it smelled of Cordovan leather. The owner insisted that the vat
> was clean and that there could be nothing in the wine to give it a flavor
> of leather or of iron, but, nevertheless, the two famous winetasters stood
> their ground. Time went by, and when they came to clean out the vat they
> found in it a small key attached to a leather strap.

The anecdote, by the way, probably did not originate with Cervantes. In any
case, David Hume liked it well enough to borrow it from *Don Quixote* at a critical
point in his analysis of "delicacy of taste," in his only extended discussion of aesthetics,
"Of the Standard of Taste" (1757). After paraphrasing Cervantes, Hume asserts that

"the great resemblance between mental and bodily taste will easily teach us to apply this story," and goes on to explain delicacy of taste as "where the organs are so fine, as to allow nothing to escape them; and at the same time so exact as to perceive every ingredient in the composition." (Students of seventeenth-century European philosophy may recognize the two criteria characterizing delicacy—fineness and exactness—as corresponding to the Cartesian classification of ideas as clear/obscure and distinct/confused.)

One of the "sons of Ben," or poetic followers of Jonson, Robert Herrick, composed numerous poems about wine and love. There is the perfectly straightforward "Anacreontick Verse" (H-996; 1648):

> BRisk methinks I am, and fine,
> When I drinke my capring wine:
> Then to love I do encline;
> When I drinke my wanton wine:
> And I wish all maidens mine,
> When I drinke my sprightly wine:
> Well I sup, and well I dine,
> When I drinke my frolick wine:
> But I languish, lowre, and Pine,
> When I want my fragrant wine.

In commenting on Herrick's attitudes toward wine, Ann Baynes Coiro remarks that his "epigrams . . . are generally sarcastic about those who drink too much," whereas his "lyric poems use drunkenness as the primary metaphor for both poetic inspiration and the good life" (1988). Coiro believes that "perhaps Herrick's most successful lyric, certainly his most successful on the power of wine," is "His age, dedicated to his peculiar friend, Master John Wickes, under the name of Posthumus" (H-336; 1648). The "age" of the title means Herrick's old age; Wickes and Herrick were ordained together and remained close friends. "Posthumus" is the name of the addressee of one of Horace's most famous odes (2.14), which concerns the brevity of life and the inevitability of death. Herrick's poem consists of nineteen stanzas, the first ten of which elaborate the theme of Horace's ode and propose friendship (with Wickes) as the saving grace of Herrick's life. The remaining nine stanzas, however, go off in another direction, with Herrick describing in moving terms the descent into a decrepit old age of himself and his (imaginary) wife—fondly referred to as "Baucis . . . , / My old leane wife" (lines 83–4). For comfort, the poet calls on his (imaginary) son—fondly referred to as "my young / Iülus [Aeneas's son]" (lines 93–4)—to read aloud some of Herrick's favorite poems, including "The Lilly in a Christal," discussed above in chapter 4, "Strawberries (and Cream)." The last three stanzas are about wine—its capacity to cheer up the elderly, failing couple, and, finally, its soporific capacity to ease them into death:

> 17. Then the next health to friends of mine
>   (Loving the brave *Burgundian wine*)
>   High sons of Pith [mettle],

Whose fortunes I have frolickt with:
      Such as co'd well
Bear up the Magick bough, and spel:
And dancing 'bout the Mystick *Thyrse*,
Give up the just applause to verse:

18.   To those, and then agen to thee
     We'l drink, my *Wickes,* untill we be
          Plump as the cherry,
     Though not so fresh, yet full as merry
          As the crickit;
     The untam'd Heifer, or the Pricket [second year buck],
     Untill our tongues shall tell our ears,
     W'are younger by a score of years.

19.   Thus, till we see the fire lesse shine
     From th'embers, then the kitlings eyne,
          We'l still sit up,
     Sphering [circling] about the wassail cup,
          To all those times,
     Which gave me honour for my Rhimes,
     The cole once spent, we'l then to bed,
     Farre more then night bewearied.

The familiar association of wine with love also appears in this anonymous poem written around 1681:

Would you be a man of fashion?
     Would you lead a life divine?
Take a little dram of passion
     In a lusty dose of wine.
If the nymph has no compassion,
     Vain it is to sigh and groan.
Love was but put in for fashion,
     Wine will do the work alone.

The ancient metonymic association of wine with the vessel from which it is drunk is the motif of a poem by Rochester (1647–1680), "Upon his Drinking a Bowl" (after 1673), which appears to be a translation of an ode by Ronsard (see Frank Ellis's edition of Rochester [1994]). I quote just the quatrains that describe the bowl (the first, second, and fifth), omitting the last with its obscene language:

Vulcan, contrive me such a cup
     As Nestor used of old;

> Show all thy skill to trim it up,
>> Damask it round with gold.
>
> Make it so large that, filled with sack
>> Up to the swelling brim,
> Vast toasts on the delicious lake
>> Like ships at sea may swim.
>> [. . . . .]
> But carve thereon a spreading vine,
>> Then add two lovely boys;
> Their limbs in amorous folds intwine
>> The type of future joys.

This trifle by Henry Aldrich (1647–1710) comes from a few years later (1689):

> If all be true that I do think,
> There are five reasons we should drink:
> Good wine; a friend; or being dry;
> Or lest we should be by and by;
> Or any other reason why.

The subject of wine and love was presumably not fitting for a priest, but the German Jesuit, Jacob Balde (1604–1668), "the Horace of Germany" as he was called, seems to have had no difficulty in writing a Latin ode in the Horatian style in praise of wine. (It may be noted that there were hundreds of such neo-Latin poets among the Jesuits during the sixteenth, seventeenth, and eighteenth centuries.) Modeling his poetic compositions in every way on Horace, Balde wrote four books of odes and one book of epodes. Father James J. Mertz (1882–1979) of Loyola University in Chicago made a special study of neo-Latin Jesuit poetry and in his anthology may be found the Latin text and a rhymed English version of Balde's ode 1.2. Here is Jeffrey Kaimowitz's unpublished translation of the first and last of five stanzas of the ode, whose epigraph reads, "He Recommends the Wine of Flavius Leo":

> Wine sweeter than nectar Falernian,
> Wine such as Rhodos never has produced,
>> Often may you fill my glass, smooth
>>> Flowing, and pour forth an offering.
>>> [. . . . .]
> Perhaps in secret Juno sips you, and,
> With Juno unaware, glad Jupiter,
>> While Bacchus, leaving his own vintage,
>>> May prefer you and be reborn.

At a higher poetic level, John Dryden introduced wine and the god of wine in his "Alexander's Feast, or the Power of Music: An Ode in Honour of St. Cecilia's Day" (1697). Dryden thought this his best poem, and James Winn remarks that it "remains the standard by which English poems about music are judged." Written as a celebration of music for the annual dinner in commemoration of St. Cecilia, patroness of music, the initial performance of the work, scored for voices and orchestra, was on 22 November 1697; later, in 1736, the poem was set to music by Handel. It may be noted that in an earlier ode for St. Cecilia's Day (1687) Dryden made no mention of wine, whereas in "Alexander's Feast" wine is integral to Dryden's theme: the hollow character of Alexander the Great's military victories. The theme is embodied in a narrative about the royal musician, Timotheus, who has the power to control Alexander's passions by the music he performs. Wine is introduced in the third of the seven stanzas:

> The praise of Bacchus, then, the sweet musician sung;
> Of Bacchus ever fair, and ever young.
> The jolly god in triumph comes;
> Sound the trumpets, beat the drums;
> Flushed with purple grace
> He shows his honest face:
> Now give the hautboys breath; he comes, he comes.
> Bacchus, ever fair and young,
> Drinking joys did first ordain;
> Bacchus' blessings are a treasure,
> Drinking is the soldier's pleasure;
> Rich the treasure,
> Sweet the pleasure,
> Sweet is pleasure after pain.

Still under the influence of the wine, Alexander's depressed feelings reach a low point in the last lines of stanza 5: "At length, with love and wine at once oppressed, / The vanquished victor sunk upon her [Thais's] breast." Stanza 6 ends the narrative with martial music to the strains of which Alexander and his mistress Thais wantonly set fire to the homes of the conquered Persians. The last stanza recounts the invention of the organ by St. Cecilia, which widened the scope of music: "Enlarged the former narrow bounds, / And added length to solemn sounds."

Alexander's setting fire to the Persian capital is followed in Raymond Carver's poem "Wine" (1989) by the wanton slaying of one of Alexander's best friends:

> during a disagreement that turned ugly
> and, on Alexander's part, overbearing, his face flushed
> from too many bowls of uncut wine, Alexander rose drunkenly to his feet,

> grabbed a spear and drove it through the breast
> of his friend, Cletus, who'd saved his life at Granicus.

But Carver wishes us to see Alexander even further brutalized in his drunkenness:

> Finally he gave orders that the funeral
> rites described for Patroklos be followed to the letter:
> he wanted Cletus to have the biggest possible send-off.
> And when the pyre was burning and the bowls of wine were
> passed his way during the ceremony? Of course, what do you
> think? Alexander drank his fill and passed
> out. He had to be carried to his tent. He had to be lifted, to be put
> into his bed.

Exhortations to temperance in the consumption of wine continued to be heard (if not always heeded) throughout the century; perhaps the greatest of such exhortations in visual form is a stunning trompe l'oeil painting by the Netherlandish Johannes Torrentius (1589–1644). Torrentius was an unusual—and perhaps unusually intemperate—personality. First of all, he Latinized his name from "Beeck" (brook). Then, he was imprisoned for failure to pay alimony and for heresy and blasphemy, serving only five years of a twenty-year sentence when King Charles I requested his release so he could travel to England and work at the English court. Constantijn Huygens (in 1630) singled out Torrentius and his chief rival, Jacques de Gheyn (1565–1629), as the outstanding painters of "inanimate objects," employing the Latin term *inanimatus* for the first time in such a context. Torrentius's sole surviving painting seems to be a tondo (oil on wood, 20 ½ x 20 in.), *Allegory of Temperance* (1614), now in the Rijksmuseum in Amsterdam. The composition of the painting suggests the dilution of wine with water: from left to right, there are three vessels, a pewter pitcher presumably of wine, a glass only one-third full of liquid, and a stoneware jug presumably of water. Above the glass, a bridle (symbol of temperance) is suspended, while below the glass are a pair of downturned clay pipes and a sheet of music with Dutch words that say: "That which is without measure meets immeasurable evil." Here is how Chong, Kloek, and Wieseman conclude their extensive catalogue entry about the painting (which includes an excellent reproduction):

> The translucent shadows of the rim of the wineglass are particularly complex and subtle. Torrentius juxtaposes three rounded vessels, each of which catches the light in very different ways, as befits their materials. These soft reflections are rendered with remarkable verisimilitude. Moreover, there is a strong sense of symmetry in the composition. The bridle is positioned in the very center, exaggeratedly foreshortened; it is precisely echoed by the two clay pipes on either side of the central wineglass. Even the handle of the stoneware jug and the spout of the pitcher appear to radiate from the

center. The circular format underscores these symmetries as well as the
convex forms of the vessels.

It would be a really culpable omission to leave the seventeenth century without
even a mention of its greatest theological controversy (at least, among Christians): the
battle over what happens to the wine and the bread during the ritual of the mass (or
Eucharist). To simplify somewhat—and eschewing use of the technical terms "tran-
substantiation" and "consubstantiation"—the wine and bread could be (a) transformed
into the blood and body of Christ, or (b) coexist with the blood and body of Christ,
or (c) symbolically unite the believer with the blood and body of Christ. These three
positions were adopted, respectively, by Roman Catholics, Lutherans, and Calvinists.
Many Christians were repelled by the bitterness and (as they saw it) the scholastic hair-
splitting of the debate; among them was Constantijn Huygens (himself a Calvinist, of
course), whose Dutch sonnet "Prayer for the Holy Communion" (1642) expresses a
preference for a simple faith in "the universal, true, plain, old / And unsoiled usage of
your sacred words" (lines 9–10). Continuing to cite the translation of Davidson and
van der Weel, I quote the first eight lines of the sonnet:

> You made the water wine: a miracle
> Transparent as the water. You called bread
> Your flesh, and wine your blood. This was alone
> Commemoration. Thus I read. It stands.
> My soul's untroubled that far later times
> Make this the ground for an unending strife;
> Your miracle to celebrate or spurn,
> Are equal evils in intent or speech.

THE PARODIC AND THE TYPOLOGICAL

There are two other unusual genres of poems about wine that we have so far ignored:
one is parodic, the other typological, and each depends directly for its effectiveness on
the reader's familiarity with a specific earlier text or genre of texts. Among the most
popular kinds of parodies in the Latin Middle Ages were the liturgical ones, such as
the so-called drinkers' mass. Four complete drinkers' masses, in eight manuscripts, have
survived from the fifteenth and sixteenth centuries, as well as many fragments of such
masses from the thirteenth and fourteenth centuries; as Bayless explains, "the repeated
recombination of the phrases, puns, and images in disparate versions implies a huge
circulation of the form." Only those portions of the standard Catholic mass that could
be easily parodied were selected for inclusion in a drinkers' mass; to illustrate, we may
consider a few excerpts from a fifteenth century *Missa potatorum* (translated by Bayless):

> *Verse.*

> Blessed are they who live in your tavernacle [*tabernacula*], Bacchus,

They shall praise thee, cups without end.
No glory is mine
When I have nothing in my purse.

Deceit be with you. And with thy groaning.
Let us drink the full cup.
     [. . . . .]
     Hallelujah.. Drop down dew, ye goblets, from above, and let
the earth rain must, and produce drink. Hallelujah.
     [. . . . .]
     Sequence.

Good wine with savor
The abbot drinks with the prior,
And the monastery from the worse wine
     Drinks with sadness.

Hail, happy creature
Which the pure vine produced.
Every mind rests secure for thee
     In the cup of wine.

O how happy in color!
O how pleasing thou art in the mouth!
And sweet in savor,
     Sweet chain of the tongue.
     [. . . . .]
Fraud be with you. As above.
     [. . . . .]
Preface.

Cups without end. Straw.
Fraud be with you. And with thy groaning.
Contrary hearts we have toward Bacchus.
We give thanks to the lord Bacchus. Neat and must is it.

To appreciate the humor one must know exactly how the Latin of the drinkers' mass parodies the Latin of the traditional mass (a simple example: the recurring word "Straw" is a translation of the Latin *Stramen,* corresponding to *Amen*). The significance of such liturgical parodies is controversial. Mikhail Bakhtin's hypothesis—which finds the origins of such parodic humor in popular, specifically carnival, culture—seems unlikely here, given that only members of that small group of medievals who understood

Latin (basically, a churchly elite) could have produced and appreciated these parodies. For the most part Bakhtin avoids discussion of medieval Latin parodies; when he does mention them he either—implausibly—traces their origin to his beloved all-purpose explainer, the carnival, or relegates them to "the superficial forms of modern parodies and travesties." (For a more careful and nuanced discussion of the genre in question, see Bayless's book.)

The second genre of wine poems is illustrated by "The Bunch of Grapes" (1633), by George Herbert, which is a typological poem, defined by C. A. Patrides as "concerned with those events and persons in the Old Testament which are said to have foreshadowed the entry of Christ into history." Each of the four short stanzas has the same rhyme scheme *(ababbcc)* and the same metrically varied pattern (a sequence of four pentameter lines, one trimeter line, and two tetrameter lines); the first stanza may be quoted to exhibit the broad range of typological reference, the last to exhibit the role of the grapes, grape juice, and wine.

> Joy, I did lock thee up: but some bad man
> Hath let thee out again:
> And now, me thinks, I am where I began
> Sev'n yeares ago: one vogue and vein,
> One aire of thoughts usurps my brain.
> I did toward Canaan draw; but now I am
> Brought back to the Red sea, the sea of shame.
> [. . . . .]
> But can he want the grape, who hath the wine?
> I have their fruit and more.
> Blessed be God, who prosper'd *Noahs* vine,
> And made it bring forth grapes good store.
> But much more him I must adore,
> Who of the laws sowre juice sweet wine did make,
> Ev'n God himself, being pressed for my sake.

Canaan and the Red Sea allude to the journey of the Israelites from Egypt to the Promised Land, prefiguring Christ's and the poet's own life course, while the cluster of grapes (Num. 13:23) and Noah's vineyard (Gen. 9:20) prefigure Christ, the true vine (John 15:1). The last couplet, of course, alludes to the conversion of the Old Testament (the law) to the New Testament (salvation) by means of the crucifixion. What Herbert adds to the hermeneutics of typology is a personal, even autobiographical, dimension.

EIGHTEENTH CENTURY

"Wine" (1708) is the first poem published by John Gay (1685–1732); his theme is announced in the epigraph, a couple of lines from Horace (*Epistles* 1.19.2–3): "nulla placere diu nec vivere carmina possunt, / quae scribuntur aquae potoribus [no poems can please long, nor live / which are written by water-drinkers]." Gay's opening passage of eleven lines is an effective takeoff of the abstemious Milton's *Paradise Lost:*

> Of Happiness Terrestrial, and the Source
> Whence human pleasures flow, sing *Heavenly* Muse,
> Of sparkling juices, of th' enliv'ning Grape,
> Whose *quickning* tast adds *vigour* to the Soul,
> Whose sov'raign pow'r revives decaying nature,
> And thaws the frozen Blood of hoary Age
> A kindly warmth diffusing, Youthful fires
> Gild his dim Eyes, and paint with ruddy hue
> His wrizzled [wrinkled] Visage, ghastly wan before:
> Cordial restorative, to mortal Man
> With *copious* Hand by *bounteous* Gods bestow'd.

The tone and quality of the verse are not, however, maintained for the succeeding 267 lines, probably because, as Gay's editor Vinton Dearing sees it, Gay "attempted too much: he tried to burlesque John Philips as well as Milton, the bathetic as well as the sublime at the same time." Gay's parody of John Philips was, directed, of course, not at *Cyder* (see chapter 1) but at two earlier works by Philips. And, indeed, Gay himself went on to write a balladlike poem about cider.

A wonderful poem by Edward Taylor was inspired by the line from the Song of Songs 1:2, "Thy love is better than wine." I quote the first and last of eight stanzas from Meditation 98, Second Series, written in 1710 (but, of course, not published):

> A Vine, my Lord, a noble Vine indeed
>   Whose juyce makes brisk my heart to sing thy Wine.
> I have read of the Vine of Sibmahs breed,
>   And wine of Hesbon, yea and Sodoms Vine,
>   All which raise Clouds up when their Liquour's High
>   In any one: but thine doth Clarify.
>   [. . . . .]
> Lord make mee Cask, and thy rich Love its Wine.
>   Impregnate with its Spirits, Lord, my heart.
> And make its heat my heart and blood refine,
>   And Sweetness sweeten me in ery part.
>   Give me to drinke the juyce of this true Vine
>   Then I will sing thy Love better than Wine.

In his *Life of Johnson,* Boswell reports several lengthy conversations about drinking wine. It seems that after being a heavy drinker for much of his life, Dr. Johnson gave up drinking wine after an illness, as he explained to Boswell in March 1776 (when Johnson was sixty-seven years old): "I found myself apt to go to excess in it, and therefore, after having been for some time without it, on account of illness, I thought it better not to return to it." A month later, Johnson, Boswell, Sir Joshua Reynolds, and a few other friends were supping one evening at a tavern when the subject of drinking came up again. This was the occasion on which Johnson made his remark (already noted in chapter 11, "Medlars, Ripe and Rotten") comparing drunken men and rotten medlars. A couple of years later, dining with General Pasquale Paoli, the exiled Corsican patriot (in whose home Johnson and Boswell were frequent guests), there was, once more, talk of drinking wine. Boswell artfully arranges his account of the conversation in the form of a dialogue in which Johnson has by far the longest and most substantial speeches. Johnson begins—like Montaigne in his discussion of drunkenness, and just as surprisingly—by sounding like an Epicurean: "Wine gives great pleasure; and every pleasure is of itself a good." But, Johnson continues, pleasing oneself is not the same as pleasing others:

> The danger is, that while a man grows better pleased with himself, he may be growing less pleasing to others. Wine gives a man nothing. It neither gives him knowledge nor wit; it only animates a man, and enables him to bring out what a dread of the company has repressed. It only puts in motion what has been locked up in frost. But this may be good, or it may be bad.

Boswell then, characteristically, raises the issue of sociability: suppose your host—"a good worthy man"— wishes to show off his wine cellar by offering you a twenty-year-old vintage. Johnson will have none of this and his eloquence rises with his temper:

> As for the good worthy man; how do you know he is good and worthy? No good and worthy man will insist upon another man's drinking wine. As to the wine twenty years in the cellar,—of ten men, three say this, merely because they must say something;—three are telling a lie, when they say they have had the wine twenty years;—three would rather save the wine;—one, perhaps, cares. I allow it is something to please one's company: and people are always pleased with those who partake pleasure with them. But after a man has brought himself to relinquish the great personal pleasure which arises from drinking wine, any other consideration is a trifle.

Three years later, Johnson and Boswell were dining at Sir Joshua Reynolds's, where

> Johnson harangued upon the qualities of different liquors; and spoke with great contempt of claret, as so weak, that "a man would be drowned by it before it made him drunk. . . . No, Sir, claret is the liquor for boys; port for men; but he who aspires to be a hero (smiling,) must drink brandy. In the first place, the flavour of brandy is most grateful to the palate; and then brandy will do soonest for a man what drinking *can* do for him. . . . Florence wine I think the worst; it is wine only to the eye; it is wine neither while

you are drinking it, nor after you have drunk it; it neither pleases the taste, nor exhilarates the spirits." I reminded him how heartily he and I used to drink wine together, when we we were first acquainted; and how I used to have a head-ache after sitting up with him. He did not like to have this recalled, or, perhaps, thinking that I boasted improperly, resolved to have a witty stroke at me: "Nay, Sir, it was not the *wine* that made your head ache, but the *sense* that I put into it."

On a larger scale than any work about wine we have considered since Nonnos is a mock-epic (the first in Russian literature) by Vasilii Maikov (1728–1778), *Elisei, or Bacchus Enraged: A Poem* (1769–1770). The point of departure of the five-canto work is a quarrel, not the traditional one between wine and water, but between Bacchus and Ceres, the former wishing to promote drinking among the peasants and the latter to discourage it (in order to increase agricultural output). The "Elisei" of the title is a mock-heroic coachman; he is, as Evelyn Bristol puts it, "a drunkard, a lecher, and a brawler," who "is dressed by Bacchus as a woman and locked in a correctional home for prostitutes, where he has an affair with its directress."

The poem opens (in a prose translation by Harold Segel, 1967):

> I sing of the sound of glasses, I sing of that hero who, drunk, caused dreadful woes in many taverns for the pleasure of Bacchus; he beat up and got drunk wastrels and ox-cart drivers, broke cauldrons, buckets, goblets, bottles, and saucers. . . . O Muse! Keep not silent about this. Speak, or even mutter from inebriation if it is impossible for you to talk plainly.

One of Maikov's big set pieces occurs in the third canto, where Ceres and Bacchus present their respective positions before an assembly of the gods. Ceres argues that because of Bacchus's invention of wine "All mortals have now become addicted to drunkenness, and only brawling has resulted from it. . . . The peasants run away from their trade into the cities and find themselves in such great confusion that almost all of them peddle strawberries like old hags while each of them could have been plowing the earth." Bacchus counters by summarizing the beneficent effects of wine: "For mortals the best gift on earth is wine. Wine invigorates the heart, strengthens the stomach and, in a word, brings cheer to all people. All feasts would not be gay to them, all celebrations would be deprived of their amusement, if mortals did not know this gift."

In the last canto, Elisei breaks into a wine cellar; here are some excerpts from the description of the ensuing orgiastic scene:

> [He] saw there casks lined up everywhere against the walls. He also saw glasses and bottles, and big barrels of spirits by the dozens. He delighted himself with the sight of such things and flew at them like a falcon above a flock of timid birds. He beheld swans and jackdaws and tomtits. He then raced to the first bottle nearest him and grasped it to his embrace. Within

the wink of an eye, he popped out the plug and downed this little birdie in three swallows. Then he approached the biggest barrel there, uncorked it, and put his mouth to the middle slot, from which the liquid flowed into his throat. . . . Later on he used to say, if he was not fibbing, that it was just as though Bacchus himself were helping him along with his whole retinue, and were laboring together with him in this work. It was, he said further, just as though Silenus himself were uncorking the bottles and were himself swallowing the wine from them. It was just as though the Bacchi were dead drunk, as though the wet nurses and governesses were drawing the wine. Then suddenly such a roar tore through the entire cellar that all the glasses and bottles were upended. All the hoops quivered; the wine began pouring out of the casks, and not a single drop remained in any of them after a while. Soon this magnificent labor was at an end and they all left the cellar, leaving behind them a pond of wine.

The surreal character of the above scene contrasts with the ordinariness of the finale in which the authorities catch up with Elisei, shave his head "to his ears," and—worst of fates in eighteenth-century Russia—send him into military service. The "pond of wine" in the cellar, by the way, may recall a phrase from one of the most famous of Horace's odes (2.14), addressed to Postumus: "Et mero / tinget pavimentum superbo [and wine wets the splendid pavement]" (ll. 26–7). Evelyn Bristol's summary judgment of Maikov's work (1991) is worth quoting: "The poem's overall tone is deliberately crass, although its verse form is the elevated Alexandrine, or iambic hexameter."

Turning to Germany, we may note that just a few decades after the founding of Göttingen University (in 1737), it became for a brief period (1770–75) an important literary center. One of the talented student poets at Göttingen was Ludwig Heinrich Christoph Hölty (1748–1776), whose traditional carpe diem poem, ironically titled "Lebenspflichten" (Duties of life), ends with the two following stanzas (in a highly literal English version by Gustave Mathieu and Guy Stern, followed by the German):

> Our slumbering bones,
> sown into the tomb,
> do not feel the grove of roses
> which flutters round our grave;
>
> Do not feel the sound of joy
> of cups clinking together,
> nor the happy roundelay
> of carousers, made wise by wine.

~

> Unser schlummerndes Gebein,
> in die Gruft gesäet,

> fühlet nicht den Rosenhain,
> der das Grab umwehet;
>
> Fühlet nicht den Wonnenklang
> angestossner Becher,
> nicht den frohen Rundgesang
> weingelehrter Zecher.

The German inclination to construct compound words is well illustrated by *angestoss-ner* (together-clinking) and *weingelehrter* (wine-learned).

    Goethe's earliest poems are contemporary with Hölty's; the two authors were born just a year apart. Let us look first at a famous early poem by Goethe, "The King in Thule" (1774), about a golden wine goblet given to a king by his lover just before she dies. He continues to use the goblet until, at the point of death himself, he throws the goblet into the sea. This balladlike subject is given a balladlike form by Goethe, beautifully captured in the translation by John Frederick Nims (1983), of which I quote the first, fifth, and last of six stanzas, together with the German of the last stanza:

> There lived a king in Thule,
> Right faithful, to the grave.
> He loved a golden goblet
> His dying sweetheart gave.
>   [. . . . .]
> Then rose the snowy toper;
> A toast! to life's last glow!
> His sainted cup he catches,
> Flings to the foam below.
>
> He watched it falling, filling;
> He saw it settle, sink.
> His eyelids ebb; then never
> Another drop to drink.

The falling/filling, settle/sink, and sink/drink of Nims's translation may be compared with the trinken/sinken, Meer/mehr, trank/Tropfen pairings of Goethe's last stanza:

> Er sah ihn stürzen, trinken
> Und sinken tief ins Meer.
> Die Augen täten ihm sinken;
> Trank nie einen Tropfen mehr.

    A second, equally famous, poem by Goethe includes a striking wine episode (which, as we shall see, has Classical precursors). In the fifteenth of his *Roman Elegies,*

Goethe tells a little story about meeting his sweetheart ("die Liebste") one afternoon
in a Roman tavern; her mother and uncle are also present, lending a certain piquancy
to the situation. By carelessly spilling some wine on the table, the girl manages to communicate clandestinely the time of a rendezvous later that day (translated by David
Lukc):

> Raising her voice rather high for a Roman girl, she did the honours,
>> Gave me a sidelong look, poured the wine, missing her glass.
> Over the table it spilled, and with dainty finger she doodled—
>> There, on the wet wooden page, circles of moisture she traced.
> My name she mingled with hers; I eagerly followed her finger,
>> Watching its every stroke, and she well knew that I did.
> Quickly at last she inscribed a Roman "five," with an upright
>> "One" in front of it—then, when I had seen this, at once
> With arabesque-like lines she effaced the letters and numbers,
>> But left stamped on my mind's eye the delectable "IV."

(The hour of "four" refers to four hours after nightfall in an old system of time-
keeping.) Goethe was a year or two over forty (1788–90) when he wrote this, and
it undoubtedly reflects, at least in a general way, his two recent lengthy sojourns in
Italy. But the passage—and, indeed, the *Roman Elegies* in their entirety—also reflect
Goethe's turn to the Latin erotic poetry of Catullus, Propertius, and Tibullus (mentioned as the "triumvirate of Cupid" in the fifth elegy), "a quite un-Germanic stylistic
tradition," as David Luke puts it. The wine-writing device, in particular, can be found
in Propertius, Tibullus, and Ovid, though never spelled out in as much detail as in
Goethe; here, for example, is Ovid, in his *Amores,* 2.5.16–18, which I quote in Peter
Green's translation especially for his use of a delightful French word: "Those eyebrow-
signals, those eloquent nods, / *Œillades* and smiles, little messages traced on the table /
By your finger, in wine." Stylistically, Goethe adapts to German the Latin elegiac meter,
which consists, very roughly, of unrhymed distichs with a hexameter followed by a
pentameter, and Luke attempts to carry this over into English. (Incidentally, the elegy
we have been discussing, usually numbered "15," is numbered "18" in the book cited,
which includes four poems omitted by Goethe on first publication of the *Elegies* in
1795, because of concerns over excessive sexual frankness.)

NINETEENTH CENTURY

As we approach modern times, the accelerating growth of the pertinent literary corpus and the concomitant enlargement of my own areas of ignorance will necessarily
confine us to a few more or less randomly selected episodes. But it must be emphasized that in this period there are objective changes in the production and supply of
alcoholic beverages, which may be presumed to have affected the subjective aspects of
alcohol consumption and thereby imaginative writing about it (recall Samuel Johnson

on brandy); as Fernand Braudel, one of the few historians to take drink (and food) seriously, puts it: "The great innovation, the revolution in Europe was the appearance of brandy and spirits made from grain—in a word: alcohol. The sixteenth century created it; the seventeenth consolidated it; the eighteenth popularized it." Key inventions were some late-eighteenth-century improvements in the industrial still. In addition to brandy, the beverages in question included gin, rum, scotch, rye, and (especially in the United States) corn liquor. One uncannily astute recognition of what might be called the new regime of alcoholism occurs in a letter of 24 March 1814, from Byron to the Scots writer James Hogg, dismissing "the two tea-drinking Lake poets," Wordsworth and Southey:

> I doubt if either of them ever got drunk, and I am of the old creed of Homer the wine-bibber. Indeed I think you and Burns have derived a great advantage from this, that being poets, and drinkers of wine, you have had a new potation to rely upon. Your whiskey has made you original. I have always thought it a fine liquor. I back you against beer at all events, gill to gallon.

(One thing I will do by way of reducing the scope of this chapter's subject matter, is to discuss only literary episodes in which wine and wine drinking function more or less independently of other alcoholic beverages.)

Byron was not, of course, proposing that anyone give up wine in favor of whiskey, and, indeed, only four years after the letter to Hogg, Byron was composing a rousing poetical tribute to wine. This was in the the second canto of *Don Juan* (written in 1818), stanzas 178–80, taking the form of a digression from the subject at hand—which was Don Juan's first walk with his rescuer, the youthful and lovely Haidée, along the seashore of the Cycladic island where he had been shipwrecked. Byron reaches wine by the airiest of free associations—from ocean foam to the froth of a glass of champagne:

178

And the small ripple spilt upon the beach
   Scarcely o'erpassed the cream of your champagne,
When o'er the brim the sparkling bumpers reach,
   That spring-dew of the spirit! the heart's rain!
Few things surpass old wine; and they may preach
   Who please, —the more because they preach in vain, —
Let us have wine and woman, mirth and laughter,
Sermons and soda water the day after.
[. . . . .]
180

Ring for your valet—bid him quickly bring
   Some hock and soda-water, then you'll know

A pleasure worthy Xerxes the great king;
    For not the blest sherbet, sublimed with snow,
Nor the first sparkle of the desert-spring,
    Nor Burgundy in all its sunset glow,
After long travel, ennui, love, or slaughter,
    Vie with that draught of hock and soda-water.

Byron also alludes to champagne froth later on in *Don Juan* (15.65.7–8): "And then there was Champagne with foaming whirls, / As white as Cleopatra's melted pearls."

According to Vladimir Nabokov, in the commentary accompanying his English translation of *Eugene Onegin,* Alexander Pushkin read the first two cantos of *Don Juan* within a few years of its publication in 1819, in the mediocre French prose version of Amédée Pichot (Pushkin had no English to speak of). Pushkin then wrote his own work, *Eugene Onegin* —in eight "chapters" composed of fourteen-line stanzas—during the years 1823–31, originally referring to it as "a novel in verse in the style of Byron's *Don Juan.*" Leaving aside the question of just how Byron might have influenced *Eugene Onegin,* we may simply note that in chapter 4, Onegin's friend, the poet Lensky, comes to visit him, and immediately after his arrival in lines 4.44.13–14, Onegin delivers himself of a tribute to champagne (4.45) and then of what may be called an antitribute (4.46), explaining how the beverage no longer agrees with him:

> Of Veuve Clicquot or of Moët
> the blessèd wine
> in a befrosted bottle for the poet
> is brought at once upon the table.
> It sparkles Hippocrenelike;
> with its briskness and froth
> (a simile of this and that)
> it used to captivate me: for its sake
> my last poor lepton I was wont
> to give away—remember, friends?
> Its magic stream
> no dearth of foolishness engendered,
> but also what a lot of jokes, and verse,
> and arguments, and merry dreams!
>
> But it betrays with noisy froth
> my stomach,
> and I sedate Bordeaux
> have actually now preferred to it.
> For Ay I'm no longer fit,
> Ay is like a mistress

glittering, volatile, vivacious,
and wayward, and shallow.
But you, Bordeaux, are like a friend
who is, in grief and in calamity,
at all times, everywhere, a comrade,
ready to render us a service
or share our quiet leisure.
Long live Bordeaux, our friend!

The translation is by Nabokov and I have chosen it over the half dozen "poetic" versions I know for the simple reason that none of the latter gives the slightest evidence of the greatness every Russian reader ascribes to *Eugene Onegin*. Nabokov has carefully thought through the problems of translation and explains his own procedures in a foreword: "rendering, as closely as the associative and syntactical capacities of another language allow, the exact contextual meaning of the original." To acomplish his goal, rhyme and meter must be ignored, and also, of course, "the *EO* stanza" (Pushkin's invention), which Nabokov defines, in the course of his brilliant note on the subject, as follows: "It contains 118 syllables and consists of fourteen lines, in iambic tetrameter, with a regular scheme of feminine and masculine rhymes: ababeecciddiff." Nabokov's method of translation also requires the provision of an extensive commentary, so, for example, we are informed about "Ay" champagne: "The name of this glorious champagne comes from Aï or Ay, a town in the Marne Department, northern France, where the original vineyard was situated in the Marne watershed, near Epernay." "Hippocrene," he further explains, was "a fountain on Mount Helicon, in Bœotia, sacred to the Muses." Unfortunately, Nabokov does not gloss "lepton," a word more familiar today as the name for a group of elementary particles than as the name of a tiny unit of Greek currency.

Though in his commentary on 4.45 Nabokov cites the champagne foam of *Don Juan* 15.65.7–8 (quoted above), he reserves his most extended discussion for the possible influence of some lines by Pushkin's friend, the Russian poet Eugene Baratinski (1800–1844), whose elegy *The Feasts* was published in 1821 (later editions, 1826 and 1835). Nabokov translates a passage from the first edition:

Into plain cups the god of tippling
luxuriously to sons of glee
pours out his fondest drink, Ay:
courage within it is concealed;
its liquid, twinkling starrily,
is full of a celestial soul.
It sparkles free.
Like a proud mind, it cannot bear captivity;
it bursts its cork with sportive surf

and merrily its foam doth spurt

—a simile of youthful life

Now, when the 1826 edition was about to be published, the Russian censor objected to the inclusion of the seventh and eighth lines because of their allusion to freedom and pride: the explosiveness of champagne could, after all, be understood as a metaphor for political revolt (the Decembrist uprising against the regime had occurred the year before). The lines were then changed to: "It bubbles joyously. / Like a proud steed, it cannot bear captivity"! Furthermore, Nabokov suggests the possibility that Pushkin's lines 4.45.6–7—"with its briskness and froth / (a simile of this and that)"— constitute a veiled allusion to the censorship of his friend Baratinski's lines.

Returning to Britain, we might try balancing our account of the sobriety of Keats's ode "To Autumn" (in chapter 1) by attending to his exuberant approval of wine in some other poems and in some letters. We may note first of all that Keats, along with several other writers in his circle, were enthusiastic admirers of Robert Herrick, whose poetry—including the anacreontea—experienced something of a revival around 1800, and we can see the results in many of Keats's poems. (For a discusssion of the Herrick revival, see Anya Taylor, "Coleridge, Keats, Lamb, and Seventeenth-Century Drinking Songs" [1994].) In a slight poem, "Lines on the Mermaid Tavern," written probably during the last week of January, 1818, Keats celebrates the historic tavern (which we have encountered earlier, in a poem by Ben Jonson):

> Souls of poets dead and gone,
> What elysium have ye known,
> Happy field or mossy cavern,
> Choicer than the Mermaid Tavern?
> Have ye tippled drink more fine
> Than mine host's Canary wine?

On the other hand, just a few days later, Keats wrote a letter to his friend, J. H. Reynolds, including the following verses:

> Hence Burgundy, Claret & port
> Away with old Hock and Madeira
> Too couthly [earthly] ye are for my sport
> There's a Beverage brighter and clearer
> Instead of a pitiful rummer
> My Wine overbrims a whole Summer
> My bowl is the sky
> And I drink at my eye
> Till I feel in the brain
> A delphian pain—
> The[n] follow my Caius [Reynolds] then follow

> On the Green of the Hill
> We will drink our fill
> Of golden sunshine
> Till our brains intertwine
> With the glory and grace of Apollo!

Keats's ambivalence about wine is expressed here: while always affirming the joys of wine, he always at the same time knows they cannot match those of immersion in sun-saturated nature.

It must be emphasized that Keats was quite unequivocal regarding the joys of wine. This is clear from the wonderful lists he sometimes composes of his favorite experiences, as in this passage from a letter to his sister Fanny, 1 May (?) 1819:

> O there is nothing like fine weather, and health, and Books, and a fine country, and a contented Mind, and Diligent-habit of reading and think-ing, and an amulet against the ennui—and, please heaven, a little claret-wine cool out of a cellar a mile deep—with a few or a good many ratafia cakes—a rocky basin to bathe in, a strawberry bed to say your prayers to Flora in, a pad nag to go you ten miles or so; two or three sensible people to chat with; two or th[r]ee spiteful folkes to spar with; two or three odd fishes to laugh at and two or three numskuls to argue with.

Notice, though, that Keats asks for only a "little" wine. The entire context, critics have noted, recurs in Keats's "Ode to a Nightingale" (1819): "O, for a draught of vintage! that hath been / Cool'd a long age in the deep-delved earth, / Tasting of Flora and the country green." Furthermore, Keats has no puritanical ideas of limiting the wine consumption of his friends, since he elsewhere expresses a wish that "my friends should drink a dozen of Claret on my Tomb" (letter to Benjamin Bailey, 14 August 1819).

A somewhat different list of Keats's favorite experiences—once again, including the drinking of claret—occurs a couple of years later in a letter to Fanny Brawne of 24 (?) February 1820, in which Keats reports on the seriousness of his ill-health: "Like all Sinners now I am ill I philosophise aye out of my attachment to every thing, Trees, flowers, Thrushes, Sp[r]ing, Summer, Claret &c &c aye [e]verything but you—."

Keats's most extended tribute to claret occurs in a 19 February 1819 letter to his brother and sister-in-law:

> Now I like Claret whenever I can have Claret I must drink it.—'t is the only palate affair that I am at all sensual in—Would it not be a good Speck to send you some vine roots—could I [it] be done? I'll enquire—If you could make some wine like Claret to d[r]ink on summer evenings in an arbour! For really 't is so fine—it fills the mouth one's mouth with a gush-ing freshness—then goes down cool and feverless—then you do not feel it quarreling with your liver—no it is rather a Peace maker and lies as quiet as it did in the grape. . . . Other wines of a heavy and spirituous nature transform

a Man to a Silenus; this makes him a Hermes—and gives a Woman the soul and imortality of Ariadne for whom Bacchus always kept a good cellar of claret—and even of that he could never persuade her to take above two cups—I said this same Claret is the only palate-passion I have I forgot game.

Finally, there is the well-known anecdote by Keats's friend, the painter Benjamin Robert Haydon (1786–1846), recorded in his diary on 29 March 1821, a month after Keats's death. (It must be noted that Keats's biographers have expressed doubts about the significance, if not the authenticity, of the anecdote.)

> For six weeks he was scarcely sober, & and once to shew what a Man of
> Genius does, to gratify his appetites, when once they get the better of him,
> he covered his tongue & throat as far as he could reach with Cayenne pepper,
> in order as he said to have the "delicious coolness of claret in all its glory!"
> This was his own expression, as he told me the fact.

Anya Taylor, in her study of the influence of seventeenth-century drinking songs on Coleridge, Keats, and Lamb, has argued for important connections between Keats's lighthearted drinking songs and the profundities of his greatest poetry: "Clearly in the *carpe diem* mode popularized in the seventeenth century, Keats's warm-up exercises help to generate his later tragic hedonism, but also cast a new light on Bacchus's appearance in his major poems." It is worth quoting at some length a Bacchic passage from Keats's "Lamia" (1819), a deliberate experiment written just before the last of Keats's great odes. "Lamia" is in heroic couplets—modeled after, but also significantly departing from, Dryden and Pope—and at one point, as Anya Taylor puts it in her book *Bacchus in Romantic England* (1999), "Keats describes precisely how wine works to energize a party":

> Soft went the music the soft air along,
> While fluent Greek a vowel'd undersong
> Kept up among the guests, discoursing low
> At first, for scarcely was the wine at flow;
> But when the happy vintage touch'd their brains,
> Louder they talk, and louder come the strains
> Of powerful instruments . . .
>   [. . . . .]
> Now, when the wine has done its rosy deed,
> And every soul from human trammels freed,
> No more so strange; for merry wine, sweet wine,
> Will make Elysian shades not too fair, too divine.

> Soon was God Bacchus at meridian height

Unlike some of the writers among his contemporaries (such as Burns, Coleridge, and Charles Lamb), Keats himself was not addicted to alcohol. (In *Bacchus in Romantic England,* Anya Taylor shows how, until recently, the obvious alcoholism of many the leading British Romantics has tended to be downplayed, when not totally ignored, by their biographers.) Among Keats's most eminent literary acquaintances, as we have already noted, was Wordsworth, who seems to have been turned off wine by his very first experience of inebriation. The incident is recounted in *The Prelude,* book 3, "Residence at Cambridge," lines 296–305 (1850):

> Among the band of my compeers was one
> Whom chance had stationed in the very room
> Honoured by Milton's name. O temperate Bard!
> Be it confessed that, for the first time, seated
> Within thy innocent lodge and oratory,
> One of a festive circle, I poured out
> Libations, to thy memory drank, till pride
> And gratitude grew dizzy in a brain
> Never excited by the fumes of wine
> Before that hour, or since.

Charles Baudelaire (1821–1867) or Arthur Rimbaud (1854–1891) might have appreciated Keats's little experiment with pepper and claret—indeed, conceivably any one of these three poets might have written a poem about it. Baudelaire did write about wine, publishing no fewer than five poems on the subject in both the first and second editions of *Les Fleurs du mal* (1857, 1861): "The Soul of the Wine," "Ragpickers' Wine," "The Murderer's Wine," "The Solitary's Wine," and "Lovers' Wine." None of these is generally considered among Baudelaire's better poems. I quote from "The Soul of the Wine" the first and last stanzas (out of six) in both the French and Richard Howard's English version. (Howard makes the title part of the poem):

> Un soir, l'âme du vin chantait dans les bouteilles:
> "Homme, vers toi je pousse, ô cher déshérité,
> Sous ma prison de verre et mes cires vermeilles,
> Un chant plein de lumière et de fraternité!"
>   [. . . . .]
> En toi je tomberai, végétale ambroisie,
> Grain précieux jeté par l'éternel Semeur,
> Pour que de notre amour naisse la poésie
> Qui jaillira vers Dieu comme une rare fleur!"

> ~

> THE SOUL OF THE WINE
> sang by night in its bottles: "Dear mankind—
> dear and disinherited! Break the seal
> of scarlet wax that darkens my glass jail,

and I shall bring you light and brotherhood!
[. . . . .]
Into you I shall flow, ambrosia brewed
from precious seed the eternal Sower cast,
so that the poetry born of our love will grow
and blossom like a flower in God's sight!"

Neither in these two stanzas nor in the rest of the poem does Baudelaire express any really fresh sentiments about wine—simply the traditional and fairly conventional tribute to its joys and magical rejuvenative powers—but some of the images, and the sound throughout, are impressive.

Alban Berg (1885–1935) interrupted the composition of his opera *Lulu* to compose a musical setting of three of Baudelaire's wine poems on commission from the Czech soprano Ruzena Herlinger. Instead of Baudelaire's French, Berg used a translation into German by Stefan George. The resulting concert aria *Der Wein* (1929)—for soprano (or tenor) and orchestra—consists of three parts, "The Soul of the Wine," "Lovers' Wine," and "The Solitary's Wine," and takes about thirteen minutes to perform. Andrew Clements explains, in his notes for Anne Sofie von Otter's Deutsche Grammophon recording of *Der Wein,* directed by Claudio Abbado with the Vienna Philharmonic (1995), how the work

> became not only a study for the vocal lines in the opera but also for its sound world, in which saxophone and piano have prominent parts. . . . The verses are shaped into a ternary form—again prefiguring Lulu, in which classical forms would provide the framework for the drama—with the central "Der Wein der Liebenden" turned into a lopsided scherzo and the final "Der Wein des Einsamen" recapitulates the material of the opening "Die Seele des Weines."

Berg was thinking of his secret affair with Hanna Fuchs when he composed *Der Wein,* "referring obliquely through its title to Hanna's husband who was a great wine connoisseur and the owner of a famous cellar," as Douglas Jarman explains, in *The Cambridge Companion to Berg* (1997).

In the same year that *Les Fleurs du Mal* was first published, there appeared Flaubert's *Madame Bovary,* in which there is a small incident involving wine drinking that reflects a subtle but important social distinction (the time is 1837, the first year of the nine-year Bovary marriage). Shortly after their marriage, Charles and Emma are invited to a dinner party at the chateau of the local marquis, where Emma "was surprised to notice that several of the ladies had failed to put their gloves in their wine glasses" (part 1, sect. 8; Steegmuller's translation). Emma's reaction has baffled some readers (and some translators) but Steegmuller explains: "Provincial *bourgeoises* of that time, brought up in a spirit of genteel puritanism, considered it ladylike to eschew

wine at dinner parties; they proclaimed their intention by filling their wineglasses with
their flimsy evening gloves or with a lace handkerchief. Ladies of the old aristocracy
were freer in their behavior." Emma, of course, emulates the aristocrats: "Iced champagne was served, and the feel of the cold wine in her mouth gave Emma a shiver that
ran over her from head to toe."

We have already encountered a very different sort of dinner party in Zola's *L'Assommoir*, where Gervaise chooses to pawn some of her most prized possessions in order
to pay for the wine. Coupeau, her unemployed husband—injured in a fall, he can no
longer follow his roofing trade—pours the wine enthusiastically and with a certain
flair. The lengthy passage (exceeding an entire page) in which this is described illustrates to perfection what the French call *style indirect libre*, a kind of indirect discourse;
as Tancock explains in relation to this novel, "in a sense effacing the author with his
literary flights and expressing the whole through . . . the collective voice of the inhabitants of the rue de la Goutte d'Or":

> And the wine too, my boys—it flowed round the table like the waters of
> the Seine, or a stream when it's rained and the earth is parched. Coupeau
> poured from a great height so as to see the red stream foam, and when a
> bottle was empty he performed the trick of turning it upside down and
> pulling at the neck with the movements of a woman milking a cow. . . .
> Glasses were now being emptied at one go—you could hear the liquid
> poured in a stream down their throats making a noise like rainwater going
> down a drainpipe in a storm. It was raining wine, a wine that tasted at first
> of the cask, but that you soon got used to, until it finished by tasting nutty.
> Oh, Lord bless you, the Jesuits could say what they liked, but the juice of
> the vine was a damn good invention! . . . Wine cleaned you up and
> refreshed you after work, put some fire into your guts when you were feel-
> ing lazy, and then if the tricky stuff started playing you up, well, who the
> hell cared, you were on top of the world. . . . Then Gervaise suddenly
> remembered the half-dozen bottles of vintage wine she had forgotten to
> serve with the goose; she produced them and glasses were refilled.

It should be added, though, that Gervaise did *not* approve of Coupeau drinking spirits,
which, she had discovered, he was doing on the sly: "Wine, well, she didn't mind that
because wine builds a workman up, but spirits were an abomination, poison which
robbed a man of his taste for food itself. Oh, the government ought to prevent people
from making these beastly things!" Eventually, of course, Gervaise herself follows Coupeau in succumbing to spirits.

An American writer whose drinking episodes were most unfortunate—eventually
leading to his death—was Edgar Allan Poe (1809–1849), in one of whose Gothic horror tales wine is enlisted as a ruse in a ghastly murder. This is "The Cask of Amontillado," first published in November 1846 in the popular American magazine *Godey's
Magazine and Lady's Book*. The story has been much discussed by Poe scholars and is

widely considered one of his best. Thus, Thomas Ollive Mabbott writes in his collected Poe edition (1978): "This is one of the undeniably great stories, by some critics regarded as the finest of all Poe's tales of horror." The plot is simple: one aristocrat, Montresor, avenges himself (for undisclosed wrongs) on another, Fortunato—a great wine connoisseur—by luring him into Montresor's wine cellar with the prospect of tasting some precious amontillado wine. Having arrived at a niche deep inside the vaults, Montresor uses a conveniently located chain and padlock to fetter Fortunato to the rocky wall, and then immures him alive. Of course, the effectiveness of such a story depends on the details, and these Poe deploys brilliantly. Thus, at the very beginning we learn it is the carnival season, so that Fortunato is dressed in motley with cap and bells, while Montresor wears a cloak and a black mask. (For further discussion with many references, see the essay by David S. Reynolds, "Poe's Art of Transformation: 'The Cask of Amontillado' in Its Cultural Context" [1993].) Amontillado, by the way, is a special kind of sherry, to which aging has imparted a nutty taste and a golden color.

During the years 1848–65, Baudelaire wrote numerous enthusiastic appreciations of Poe's works, many of which he translated into French, including "The Cask of Amontillado" in 1857. (For an English translation of these critical writings by Baudelaire, see the volume *Baudelaire on Poe* [1952], by Lois Hyslop and Francis E. Hyslop Jr.) As a result, Poe's literary reputation has always been high in France. It is scarcely surprising, then, that an obscure twentieth-century French artist named Pierre Labadie (1896–1972) took "The Cask of Amontillado" as a subject for his *La Barrique D'Amontillado* (see plate 31). I have been unable to date the picture, which is now in my personal collection; it is executed in watercolor and pen and ink on paper (12 x 16⅞ in.), and the border consists of a separate paper frame glued to the main picture. Perhaps intended as an illustration for a printed version of Poe's story, the picture certainly conveys an atmosphere of horror and suspense.

With George Meredith's novel *The Egoist* we return to nineteenth-century England. In chapter 17, we have already encountered all the main characters of the novel in connection with the symbolism of the double-blossom wild cherry tree. One important twist in the plot requires that Dr. Middleton brush off all attempts by his daughter, Clara, to withdraw from her engagement to Sir Willoughby and to leave his house, Patterne Hall. Sir Willoughby conceals his difficulties with Clara from Dr. Middleton and at the same time seduces him into prolonging his stay at Patterne Hall by means of his wine cellar and, in particular, his old port. The better part of an entire chapter (20), titled "An Aged and a Great Wine," is devoted to Willoughby's maneuver. He has previously learned of Dr. Middleton's interest in wines, and "they kindled one another by naming great years of the grape" (chap. 15). But even wine did not disengage Dr. Middleton totally from his favorite subject; rather he found a profound isomorphism between the subject matters of wine and the Classics:

> Port is deep-sea deep. It is in its flavour deep; mark the difference. It is like
> a classic tragedy, organic in conception. An ancient Hermitage has the light
> of the antique; the merit that it can grow to an extreme old age; a merit.

Neither of Hermitage nor of Hock can you say that it is the blood of those long years, retaining the strength of youth with the wisdom of age. To Port for that! Port is our noblest legacy! Observe, I do not compare the wines; I distinguish the qualities. Let them live together for our enrichment; they are not rivals like the Idaean Three [Hera, Athena, and Aphrodite]. Were they rivals, a fourth would challenge them. Burgundy has great genius. It does wonders within its period; it does all except to keep up in the race; it is short-lived. An aged Burgundy runs with a beardless Port. I cherish the fancy that Port speaks the sentences of wisdom, Burgundy sings the inspired Ode. Or put it, that Port is the Homeric hexameter, Burgundy the Pindaric dithyramb.

Dr. Middleton accompanies Willoughby to the cellar, which, Willoughby explains, contains fifty-dozen bottles of a ninety-year-old port. Two bottles are removed for the evening—the rest of the company happily drink claret—and after five minutes of decanting Dr. Middleton has his first sip. Asked his opinion of the wine, Dr. Middleton handsomely replies: "I will say this—shallow souls run to rhapsody— I will say that I am consoled for not having lived ninety years back, or at any period but the present, by this one glass of your ancestral wine" (chap. 20). The question of quality is followed by one of quantity, as Dr. Middleton remarks that "old wine, my friend, denies us the full bottle!" (because some wine is lost to the decanting process). But Willoughby has anticipated this contingency, and another bottle of the port has been prepared. Dr. Middleton is not only impressed by Willoughby's generosity; he is also so affected by the wine that he woozily breaks his promise to accompany Clara to London in the morning. This is only the first of several crucial occasions on which Clara finds her father's mental and physical capacites disabled by Willoughby's port; as Clara later muses: "The strangeness of men, young and old, the little things (she regarded a grand wine as a little thing) twisting and changeing them, amazed her. And these are they by whom women are abused for variability! Only the most imperious reasons, never mean trifles, move women, thought she. Would women do an injury to one they loved for oceans of that—ah! pah!" (chapter 24).

Wine occupies an important place in many nineteenth-century novels. Thus, for example, according to Robert James Merrett in his survey of the uses of wine by some leading Victorian novelists, there is "a counterpoint between Port and Claret" in the Barsetshire novels of Anthony Trollope (1815–1882), though champagne, madeira, hock, and similar lesser wines also sometimes make their appearance.

Champagne is alluded to metonymically (*cette écume,* "this spume") in the very first line of what must be the greatest poetic toast of the nineteenth century—the sonnet called "Salut" (Toast; 1893), composed by Stéphane Mallarmé to be read at a banquet where a group of younger French poets were fêting him. (Later, Mallarmé placed this sonnet at the head of his collected poetry.) The second line alludes to the vessel (*la coupe,* the cup) that contains the champagne. The third and fourth lines refer to *sirènes* (sirens) carved into the glass of the vessel or imagined as emerging from the spume of the champagne (or both). The combination of a compressed and ambiguous syntax with an airy and almost offhand style makes the poem a difficult challenge to translators (English version by Frederick Morgan):

> Zero, this spume—a virgin verse
> that traces but the cup
> just as, far off, a copious troop
> of sirens drowns now wrong side up.

> ~

> Rien, cette écume, vierge vers
> À ne désigner que la coupe;
> Telle loin se noie une troupe
> De sirènes mainte à l'envers.

A clear and persuasive interpretation of the sonnet is provided by Roger Shattuck (along with his own translation) in a review in the *New Republic* (1994): "Every line refers directly or metaphorically to the literal scene of an older poet standing, champagne glass in hand, at the head of a tumultuous banquet table like a captain standing on the prow of his ship in stormy seas. The analogy of the dangerous sea voyage is both an elaborate joke and a serious literary device for making a toast to great poems still to be written."

Morgan's translation of seven of Mallarmé's poems, including "Salut," may be read in an elegant illustrated edition, *Breath* (1982), with four reproductions (of an etching, a charcoal drawing, a pastel, and a photograph of a glass sculpture)—all by Christopher Wilmarth (1943–1987)—accompanying each poem. In a preface, "Mallarmé, Friend of Artists," Dore Ashton discusses each of the seven sets of words and images; about "Salut" she says, "The champagne goblet and the prow of the ship with its ornate figurehead are the basic motifs Wilmarth chose for his sculpture. . . . In the etching, Wilmarth's image . . . ingeniously combines the shape of the champagne cup, the rocking movement of the sailing ship and the hint of the sea's horizon."

It would be difficult to find a more contrasting champagne episode—written just a few years after Mallarmé's sonnet—than the one we are about to examine. First of all, the author: she is Emilia Pardo Bazán (1851–1921), "one of the most important literary figures of nineteenth-century Spain [and] without doubt the most influential Spanish woman writer of that century, instrumental in promoting an awareness of French naturalism and Russian spiritual realism in the Spanish reading public" (in the words of Joyce Tolliver, 1996). Pardo Bazán wrote twenty novels, twenty-one novellas, two cookbooks, seven plays, almost six hundred short stories, and hundreds of essays. Her reputation was so high in her own day that a special chair was created for her at

594   the University of Madrid, and she became the first woman professor at any Spanish university. A brief story called "Champagne" was first published in 1898 in one of the volumes of Pardo Bazán's collected works (vol. 16, *Cuentos de amor* [Tales of love]). Unlike most of her stories, this one did not first appear in a popular journal, probably because the occurrence of a prostitute narrator with no moralizing commentary by another voice was deemed scandalous. The story is told in the colloquial speech of the lower classes by an anonymous prostitute to her client, Raimundo Valdés. (I follow the translation of Christina Urruela.) After he has seen "his evening companion's eyes darken as the cork was popped off the gold-sealed bottle," he is curious and asks her secret. She is in a mood to oblige. In brief, her stepmother had married her off to a man who was fortyish, wealthy, and proper. But she was already in love with an impoverished lieutenant, and unfortunately, under the influence of the wedding champagne, she revealed this to her husband on the way to their honeymoon. He immediately returned her to her parents, and to escape her oppressive stepmother, she took to the streets (the lieutenant having rejected her as well when he learned of her wedding). Her conclusion? "I think that if all women spoke their minds—as I did because of the champagne—a lot of them would be worse off than me." And the conclusion of the story? "Come on, give me more champagne. Now I can drink whatever I want. My lips have no more secrets to let out."

In about 1896 the young Hugo von Hofmannsthal (1874–1929) wrote an octosyllabic sonnet in German, "Die Beide" (The two), about a wine goblet, breaking all the traditional rhyming conventions for this verse form. Not only is the rhyme scheme unusual—*aabb acca ade ead*—but one of the rhyming words (*Hand*) is repeated no less than three times (in the first, fifth, and ninth lines). In his English version, Walter Kaufmann has succeeded in retaining von Hofmannsthal's rhyme scheme (except for interchanging the last two rhymes), even including three repetitions of the English word "hand":

> She bore the goblet in her hand—
> her chin and mouth firm as its band—
> her stride so weightless and so still
> that not a drop would ever spill.
>
> So weightless and so firm his hand:
> he rode a young horse for his pleasure
> and, looking like incarnate leisure,
> compelled it; trembling it must stand.
>
> But when he should take from her hand
> the goblet that she lifted up,
> the two were quivering so much

> that each hand missed the other's touch,
> and heavy grew the weightless cup
> till dark wine rolled upon the sand.

Kaufmann characterizes von Hofmannsthal's early writings as "distinguished by their languid beauty," but one may wonder if the poet's wilful violation of a traditional verse form does not also (like his later poetry) exhibit, in Kaufmann's words, a mark of "the weariness of the *fin de siècle* . . . given an existentialist twist."

Before leaving the nineteenth century, I want to look at a few memorable operatic toasts (or *brindisi*), the earliest from *Lucrezia Borgia* (1833), by Gaetano Donizetti (1797–1848). The libretto is by Felice Romani (1788–1865), based closely on a play by Victor Hugo that had opened in Paris in 1833. For me, one of the most interesting things about this opera is the way in which toasts dominate the action; in particular, after the prologue (often designated act 1), each of the two following acts culminates, musically and dramatically, with a toast in its second scene. In act 1, scene 2, Duke Alfonso (bass) is about to drink a toast fatal to Gennaro (tenor) while Lucrezia (soprano) is being forced to pour the so-called Borgia—that is, poisoned—wine. Lucrezia has, however, just realized that it is her son she is poisoning, and she tries to hold back. The Duke then sings in an aside to his wife (translated by Avril Bardoni):

> Woe if a gesture escape you
> or a word betray you!
> This man shall not leave
> my sight while still alive!

Lucrezia responds:

> Oh, if you knew how atrocious
> is the crime you force upon me,
> for all your brutal nature,
> you would be as appalled as I.

The innocent Gennaro joins them (as they repeat their lines) in a trio, whose music is hardly matched by any other number in the opera:

> Such benignness from them
> towards me I never expected;
> to meet with their forgiveness
> seems a dream to me.

William Ashbrook's discussion of *Lucrezia Borgia* in his book on Donizetti (1982) singles out for special praise "the superbly contrasted emotions of the trio 'Guai se ti sfugge un moto' [Woe if a gesture escape you]." I would just add that by having the Duke and Lucrezia first sing their lines from the trio as solos, Donizetti relieves the audience of having to hear the lines during the trio (which is often difficult to do). But the trio continues with fresh lines and these are not first introduced as solos. Now, however, it matters little whether we hear all the words of each singer, and, in any case, the critical words of each of them are repeated again and again: "Versa il liquor [Pour the wine]" (Duke Alfonso); "per pietà [have pity]" (Lucrezia); "Madre [Mother]" (Gennaro).

Act 2, scene 2, of *Lucrezia Borgia* is a supper party at the Princess Negroni's; it opens with five of Gennaro's friends singing tributes to wine—Madeira, Rhenish, and Cyprus wine are all praised. They then drink a toast to their hostess. When Gennaro's best friend, Orsini (contralto), proposes to sing a new drinking song he has composed, he is insulted by Gubetta, a secret agent of Lucrezia. Gennaro calms everyone down, and Orsini begins to sing what Ashbrook calls a "bumptious brindisi." Suddenly, we hear offstage tolling of bells and funereal chanting; Lucrezia enters dressed in black and announces that all the drinkers have been poisoned. Recognizing Gennaro, she utters what must be one of the (unintentionally) funniest lines in the history of opera: "Sei di nuovo avvelenato [You are poisoned again]!" As Ashbrook sees it, "The situation could easily be rendered ludicrous since it parallels that at the end of Act 1: again Gennaro has drunk poison unwittingly, and again Lucrezia offers him an antidote." Any impulse to laugh should be squelched, though, by the exchanges that follow between Lucrezia and Gennaro, reaching a climax in her coloratura aria "M'odi, ah m'odi [Listen, ah, listen to me]," and continuing on until the end of the opera. Ashbrook points out that "Verdi was in Milan as a student during the first run of *Lucrezia* and not the least of the lessons he absorbed was contained in this finale."

We turn next to the drinking song "Libiamo" from act 1 of *La Traviata,* by Giuseppe Verdi (1813–1901). Francesco Maria Piave (1810–1876) wrote the libretto and the opera was first performed in 1853, in Venice. The setting is a supper party at the home of the courtesan Violetta; among the guests are the Baron, whose mistress she is, and Alfredo, who is in love with her (up to this point, only from a distance). Tension arises almost immediately, as the Baron, sensing a rival, refuses to make a toast. After some persuasion—Violetta says it would please her—Alfredo rises, lifts his glass, and sings:

> Libiamo ne' lieti calici che la bellezza infiora;
> e la fuggevol ora s'innebri a voluttà.
> Libiam ne' dolci fremiti che suscita l'amore,
> poiché quell'occhio al core onnipotente va.
> Libiamo, amore, amor fra i calici più caldi baci avrà.

And here is a literal translation from an edition by Nico Castel of the complete libretti of Verdi's operas (1996, in both Italian and English):

> Let us drink from the happy goblets that beauty embellishes;
> and the fleeting hour let it intoxicate itself with pleasure.

Let us drink to the sweet trembling that arouses love,
(*Indicating Violetta*)
since that eye to the heart all-powerful goes.
Let's drink, love, love among the goblets warmer kisses shall have.

English translations of the libretto sometimes refer to wine, which is, however, not mentioned explicitly in the passage; also, later the chorus sings of "la tazza e il cantico," which is literally "the cup and the song."

Now, since Alfredo's "Libiamo" is one of the best-known arias in all of opera, it may be difficult to really *listen* to it or to say anything fresh about it. In this regard, some remarks by Joseph Kerman help. In the course of an essay, "Opera, Novel, Drama: The Case of *La Traviata*" (1978), Kerman finds the number lacking both in the way it is introduced—by a shout from the chorus and a tattoo from the orchestra— and in "the excess formality and grandiosity of the song itself, or the false quality of the chorus's participation in it." On the other hand, Kerman admires some of the original aspects of Verdi's treatment:

> For the soprano to take over the second stanza from the tenor was unusual,
> and for the tenor and soprano to share the third stanza, in such a way as to
> adumbrate their coming relationship, was both unusual and ingenious—
> and doubly ingenious in that the tune's original turn to the minor mode
> is now made to reflect Alfredo's subdued hint of his hopeless love.

Our third example is the operetta *Die Fledermaus* (The bat), by Johann Strauss Jr. (1825–1899), libretto by Carl Haffner (1804–1874/6) and Richard Genée (1823–1895), which had its premiere on 5 April 1874 in Vienna: here everyone seems to drink a lot of wine, but only a couple of men (the jailer and the prison governor) actually get drunk. Though not initially a success in Vienna, after a triumphant run of one hundred performances in Berlin, the opera has ever since attracted leading singers and conductors, as well as devoted audiences. And, of course, once one has listened to *Die Fledermaus,* one will find it difficult thereafter not to associate sociable drinking (especially of toasts) with some of its memorable arias: Alfred's "Trinke, Liebchen, trinke schnell, / Trinken macht die Augen hell" (Drink, my darling, drink up fast / Drinking makes your eyes so bright), in act 1; Prince Orlofsky's tribute to champagne, in act 2; Rosalinde's "Klänge der Heimat, / Ihr weckt mir das Sehnen" (Airs of my homeland / You waken my longing), in act 2; the concluding aria addressed to "King Champagne" by the entire company, in act 3. In addition, there is Frosch the jailer's great drunken scene—often simply mimed—at the beginning of act 3. This last, like the galley scene in *Antony and Cleopatra,* has been cut in some recent productions (such as one at the Royal Opera House, London, in January 1989, and another at the Metropolitan Opera, New York, in January 1999). In the former production, Frosch is given new lines to speak, addressed to the audience. Obviously, the taste for stage drunkenness changes; the translator of the Royal Opera production, John Mortimer, explains, "I don't find drunk scenes particularly funny." The general flavor of the long speech Mortimer composes for Frosch at the opening of act 3 should be conveyed by the following excerpt:

> Those of you who have been following the plot will have noticed that there has been an outbreak of drunken behaviour all over the shop! (*with excitement and relish*) A crime wave of mammoth proportions! . . . And what's this crime wave due to? I put it down to one thing. Champagne! Now, we're all grown up people here, on the whole. I shouldn't have to tell you that champagne is a very dangerous substance. It should not be abused! But would you believe it? There are champagne pushers at large in this very theatre!

This could be very funny, especially, of course, for an audience just returning, after intermission, from the opera bar.

TWENTIETH CENTURY

An early poem by Rilke, "The Song of the Drunkard," is the third in a sequence of ten about the *Dürftigen* (wretched/miserable/destitute). The sequence, called *The Voices: Nine Leaves with a Title Page,* was included in the second edition of *The Book of Pictures* (1906); besides the drunkard, there are the beggar, the blind man, the suicide, the widow, the idiot, the orphan girl, the dwarf, and the leper. In the first lines of the initial poem of the sequence, Rilke proclaims: "The rich and fortunate can well keep quiet, / nobody wants to know what they are. / But the destitute have to show themselves" (Edward Snow's translation). Here is Snow's English version of "Das Lied des Trinkers":

> It was not in me. It went out and in.
> Then I tried to hold it. Then the wine held it.
> (I don't know any more what it was.)
> Then the wine held me this and held me that,
> till I totally relied on it.
> I, fool.
>
> Now I am its game and it strews
> me scornfully about and loses me this day
> to that loutish swine, to Death.
> When he wins me, filthy card,
> he will scratch his gray scabs with me
> and toss me away in the dung.

With its abrupt and jagged style, the first stanza captures the progressive loss of control experienced by the drinker, while the second stanza expresses his fatalistic sense of death. Rilke's attitude is in no way reformist or even sympathetic to the plight of the drunkard, indeed, quite the contrary, as clearly appears from a letter of 1924, to Hermann Pongs, commenting on *The Voices:* "there is nothing that [the poet] would have to fear and refuse so much as a corrected world in which the dwarfs are stretched out and the beggars enriched. The God of completeness sees to it that these varieties do not cease, and it would be a most superficial attitude to consider the poet's joy in this suffering multiplicity as an esthetic pretense" (quoted in Stephen Mitchell's note on *The Voices*). What some will find unacceptable about Rilke's apparent complacency here, others may find admirable; most disturbing to me is Rilke's apparent belief that unfortunate human beings exist primarily as subject matter for his poetry.

Guillaume Apollinaire's *Alcools: Poems, 1898–1913* (1913), contains a group of poems written when he was twenty-two, during the year (1902) he spent in the Rhineland as tutor to a German girl. One of these poems, "Nuit rhénane" (Rhenish night), might be characterized as a Symbolist variation on a traditional bacchic theme, the thirteen lines beginning and ending with a wine glass (here translated by William Meredith, who adds punctuation where Apollinaire has none):

> My glass is filled with a wine that trembles like flame.
>
> ~
>
> Mon verre est plein d'un vin trembleur comme une flamme
> [. . . . .]
> My glass has shattered like a peal of laughter.
>
> ~
>
> Mon verre s'est brisé comme un éclat de rire

In the intervening lines, we are regaled with seven women sporting long green hair as they emerge from the river and cavort on its bank, while "the Rhine flows drunk with vine leaves trailing after."

A second poem about wine in *Alcools,* "Vendémiaire" (1909), is both longer and more ambitious, and, as the last poem in the book, serves as a pendant to the long opening poem, "Zone" (1912). Both opening and closing poems have been described (by Francis Steegmuller) as "highly colored urban poems [that] resemble the highly colored urban pictures that Delaunay and the futurists were painting at the time." Also, in each of the two poems we are to imagine a narrator walking through the city of Paris, but the narrator's mood is quite different in the two poems; quoting Steegmuller again: "*Alcools* . . . ends in a burst of grape-harvest gaiety and optimism, having opened with gravity and worries." Much of "Vendémiaire" takes the form of a conversation between the narrator and the cities and rivers of Europe (the actual place-names are all French or German). About the title: "Vendémiaire" is the French Revolutionary name for October, though Apollinaire refers only to September in the poem; Roger Shattuck, in the English version about to be quoted (1971), translates the title as "Vintage

600 Month," and, indeed, the poem's unifying conceit features grapes and wine. Near the end of the poem, there is a kind of summary passage, which, characteristically, combines fresh and unexpected imagery ("Des kilos de papier tordus comme des flammes") with intricate combinations of simple words ("Et tout ce que je ne sais pas dire / Tout ce que je ne connaîtrai jamais / Tout cela tout cela changé en ce vin pur"):

> The entire universe concentrated in this wine
> Which contained oceans animals plants
> Cities destinies and stars which sing
> Men on their knees on the bank of heaven
> And docile iron our good companion
> Fire which one must love as one loves oneself
> All the proud dead who are one under my brow
> The flash which lights up like a sudden thought
> All names by sixes and numbers one at a time
> Pounds of paper twisted like flames
> And those which will know how to whiten our bones
> The good immortal lines of verse which patiently bore themselves
> Armies drawn up in battle
> Forests of crucifixes and my lacustral dwellings
> Beside her eyes whom I love so
> Flowers which cry out from mouths
> And all I do not know how to say
> All that I shall never know
> All that all that changed into this pure wine
>
> What Paris was thirsty for
> Was presented to me then

And then, a few lines later, just before the poem's close, this Whitmanesque passage:

> I am drunk from having swallowed all the universe
> On the quay where I saw the darkness flowing and the barges sleeping
>
> Listen to me I am the gullet of all Paris
> And I shall drink the universe again if I want
>
> Listen to my songs of universal drunkenness

S. I. Lockerbie (1980) succinctly characterizes the style of these early poems: "Apollinaire's conception of poetry in [*Alcools*] is one that essentially derives from Symbolism. It is an introspective poetry in which the poet is concerned with the troubled depths of the psyche, the transitoriness of experience, and the quest for identity and permanence. The shadowy and obsessive nature of the poet's states of mind is reflected in elliptical, elusive, and sometimes hermetic expression."

In the period just before the First World War Apollinaire sought a poetic style adequate to what he perceived as the rapidly changing technology (radio, cinema) and revolutionary art (futurism, cubism, orphism) surrounding him. Abandoning the Symbolist aesthetic—or, better, inflecting it in new ways—he began (again quoting Lockerbie) "to abandon linear and discursive structures, in which events are arranged successively, in favor of what Apollinaire called *simultaneity:* a type of structure that would give the impression of a full and instant awareness within one moment of space-time." But the language of these new poetic structures—or perhaps we should call them antistructures—was now to consist of "the direct and forceful speech of contemporary life." An early example of a poem written in accord with these precepts was "Les Fenêtres" (Windows), which remained one of Apollinaire's favorites. The poem was first printed, in 1913, in the catalogue of a one-man show by the poet's friend, the painter and founder of orphism, Robert Delaunay (1885–1941). I quote, in Anne Hyde Greet's translation, the first two and the last two lines of thirty-seven, followed by some of Greet and Lockerbie's comments:

> From red to green all the yellow dies
> When the parakeets sing in their native forests
>   [. . . . .]
> The window opens like an orange
> The lovely fruit of light.

Delaunay's own observation that color is the fruit of light . . . transmuted in the poem or perhaps originating in it (that is, Delaunay may have picked up the metaphor from Apollinaire), becomes a comment on both painting and poetry and a final focusing on the present moment. Apollinaire seemingly resolves conflicting color theories by offering Delaunay and us an orange: it harmonizes with both red and yellow and it embodies light, an element essential to painters and poets. On a deeper level the whole poem, with its colors, its noises and voices, its far-flung lands, leads, in the last lines, to an intensely lyrical invocation of the poem—perhaps also of a painting—as a window opening onto life.

Apollinaire's stylistic experiments were accelerated by the advent of the war and his enlistment in the French artillery. On 7 February 1916, Apollinaire sent Madeleine Pagès (a woman he had offered to marry) "Le Vigneron Champenois" (The Vinegrower of champagne). First published in November 1917, the poem was eventually included in *Calligrammes* (1918). It is here translated by Greet:

> The soldiers are coming
> The village is almost asleep in the perfumed light

602

A priest wears a helmet
A bottle of champagne is artillery yes or no
Vine stocks like ermine on a coat of arms
Hello soldiers
I saw them running to and fro
Hello soldiers you bottles of champagne in which the blood ferments
You'll linger a few days and then return to your lines
Arranged in echelon like the vine plants
I hurl my bottles everywhere like charming artillery shells

The night is a blonde oh blonde wine
A vine grower sang bowed over his vineyard
A mouthless vinegrower in the depths of the horizon
A vinegrower who was himself the living bottle
A vinegrower who knows what war is
A vinegrower of Champagne who is also an artilleryman
Now it's evening they're playing blackjack
Then the soldiers will depart for the front
Where the Artillery uncorks its frothy bottles
Let's be off Goodbye friends try to come back
But no one can tell the outcome

About the central images of the vinegrower and the explosive champagne, Greet and Lockerbie have this to say:

> This figure is a larger-than-life deity who presides over the war from a standpoint beyond the notions of death and destruction. In the bountiful vision of such a deity the artillery can appropriately be likened to a sparkling, explosive wine, for it represents a manifestation of vitality and exuberance, transcending its death-dealing function to become an expression of the life spirit.

The poet Constantine Cavafy (1863–1933) was an older contemporary of Apollinaire's, but though both took the turn toward modernism, the resulting poetry of the one (in Greek) was necessarily importantly different from that of the other (in French). In Peter Bien's words, Cavafy rejected "the grand rhetorical style then in vogue in Greece" in favor of "flatness and anticlimax," and "found models for what he needed in the ancient Alexandrian epigrammists and writers of mime." Furthermore, Cavafy cultivated "frugality, terseness, realism, dramatic objectivity, scholarly exactitude in the realm of technique" and "disillusion, weary paganism, obsession with thwarted hopes and with wilting of the senses in the realm of theme." Though Cavafy was saturated in ancient history—in particular, the history of his native Alexandria from its founding in the fourth century B.C.E. to the late nineteenth century—his poems are by no means devoid of contemporary reference. Thus, for example, Cavafy himself commented about his great early poem "Waiting for the Barbarians" (written 1898; published 1904) that "the barbarians are a symbol" and consequently the setting is "not necessarily Roman" (cited by George Savidis in a note on the poem).

A somewhat later poem, in twenty-two rhymed couplets, "The Retinue [crew, procession] of Dionysos" (written 1903; published 1907), is about wine; more precisely, about an imaginary ancient Greek—probably Hellenistic—sculptor named Damon who is carving a marble relief of Dionysus accompanied by seven other figures, each of them intimately related to the ritual of wine drinking: Acratus (pure wine), Methe (intoxication), Hydrooenus (sweet wine), Molpus (melody), Hydemeles (sweet singer), Comus (festive hymn), and Telete (sacred rite). One question faced by any translator of this poem is whether to transliterate or to translate the Greek names. Of the three English translations I know, two (by Rae Dalven and by Memas Kolaitis) simply transliterate and then explain the meaning of each name in a note, while one (by Edmund Keeley and Philip Sherrard) translates with no indication of the Greek proper names. The three translations also differ in the English term they use for the Greek word *synodeia,* which occurs in the title but also in the third line of the poem. There are certainly subtle semantic differences between "retinue" (which suggests a leader and his subordinates), "crew" (which suggests a group of rowdy drinking companions), and "procession" (which suggests a religious ritual), but all three meanings seem to fit comfortably within the semantic network of the the poem as a whole.

After the poem shifts dramatically in tone in the middle of the fifteenth line, the three translations no longer differ significantly: the "flatness and anticlimax" referred to above take over as the master sculptor is no longer exercising his skill but rather thinking of his large fee and how it will enhance his social status and political power (translated by Keeley-Sherrard):

> And as he works
> his thoughts turn now and then
> to the fee he's going to receive
> from the king of Syracuse:
> three talents, a large sum.
> Adding this to what he has already,
> he'll live grandly from now on, like a rich man,
> and—think of it—he'll be able to go into politics:
> he too in the Senate, he too in the Agora.

The farthest thing from Damon's mind would seem to be celebrating his achievement in a symposium—presumably an accurate measure, in Cavafy's view, of the changes that have occurred in ancient Greek culture by the Hellenistic period.

With a precisely datable setting of 175 B.C.E., another of Cavafy's poems about wine is "Craftsman of Wine Bowls" (1921), consisting of twelve lines (each really a double line). Here the craftsman works in silver, and he is making a wine bowl (*krater*) to commemorate a beloved young man who died in battle fifteen years earlier. Once again, the poem shifts in the middle of the seventh line from a lovingly detailed description of the bowl's decoration to the flat report of a casualty in a military defeat in the last nine lines (translated by Keeley-Sherrard):

> notice these graceful flowers, the streams, the thyme.
> In the center I put this beautiful young man,
> naked, erotic, one leg still dangling
> in the water. O memory, I begged
> for you to help me most in making
> the young face I loved appear the way it was.
> This proved very difficult because
> some fifteen years have gone by since the day
> he died as a soldier in the defeat at Magnesia.

Jaroslav Seifert—the modern Czech poet we have already encountered in chapter 1—wrote a couple of poems about wine and war. The first, "A Ballad from the Champagne" (1926), is about the First World War. The poem's translator, Dana Loewy, thinks it likely that Seifert's poem deliberately echoes Apollinaire's "Vigneron Champenois." Seifert's poem, however, bears an epigraph that points to the "moral" of the poem, a quotation from the French newspaper *Le Temps:* "4,000 French poets fell in the world war." The poet addresses "Josephine," whose "father was a vintner":

> On the palate you taste wine
> and in wine I delight,
> tell me Josephine,
> how do you like the Champagne?

The war is over now and Josephine's brother is the vintner:

> Softly singing, he studies the grapevine,
> fragile stalks he ties up with bast.
> How heavy full bunches of grapes are,
> when they ripen.

Josephine is then addressed again:

> He is eating supper silently drinking wine,
> in the paper he is looking quietly reading.
> Have you seen yet, dear Josephine,
> how many poets fell in France?
>
> Four thousand!
> The things that war will perpetrate!

Josephine is silent. In the silence,
now and then between teeth a glass of wine will resound.

She reminisces. Half smiles, half tears
make her lips tremble lightly.
—How many others there must have been
who did not know how to write poetry!

Ten years later, during the Spanish Civil War, Seifert wrote a not very subtle antiwar poem, "Spanish Vineyards" (1936); I quote the last seven (out of twelve lines) in Ewald Osers's translation:

Oh charming villages which give renown
and name to those sweet juices swelling out
the grapes that bow the slender branches down.

It's April now and drops of crimson blood
are spattered over simple smock and hand.
Ah, Spanish grapes, who will be here to pick you
the day there is no fighting in this land?

Not all French poets have been fixated on champagne. Thus, the octosyllabic sonnet, "Le Vin perdu" (The lost wine; 1922), by Paul Valéry, is based on the highly original image of someone throwing drops of (red) wine into the sea in a ritual gesture described, literally, as an "offering to nothingness." The French phrase, *offrande au néant*, is translated "oblation to vacancy" in the following English version of the poem by David Paul:

Once on a day, in the open Sea
(Under what skies I cannot recall),
I threw, as oblation to vacancy,
More than a drop of precious wine. . . .

Who decreed your waste, oh potion?
Did I perhaps obey some divine?
Or else the heart's anxiety,
Dreaming blood, spilling the wine?

Its habitual clarity
After a mist of rosiness
Returned as pure again to the sea. . . .

The wine lost, drunken the waves! . . .

> I saw leaping in the salt air
> Shapes of the utmost profundity.

In brilliantly compressed fashion, Valéry has alluded to familiar rituals involving wine (such as the Eucharist), to the intoxicating power of wine, and to the physical process by which one liquid diffuses into another.

As for Valéry's rhyme-scheme—*abab cdcd eef gfg*—it is, as in von Hofmannsthal's sonnet just above, highly irregular: though the first eight lines set up expectations of a Shakespearean sonnet, the last six lines defeat such expectations. Paul's translation, in its quest for almost word-for-word equivalences to the French text, ends up with several nonrhyming lines. I believe it is worth looking at an older translation, "Wasted Wine," (1947), by Olga Marx, that rhymes throughout and yet manages to avoid fatal infidelities of meaning:

> One day I poured into the sea
> —But where it was, I do not know—
> A jet of noble wine, as though
> To placate blank immensity.
>
> Who willed this waste? Did I obey
> An augur, or perhaps a sign
> Of my tormented heart, at play
> With dream of blood, with gush of wine?
>
> The crystal of the ocean, stained
> With smoky rose, regained
> Its clear accustomed hue.
>
> Spent wine and drunken waters! Through
> The bitter wind I saw the bound
> Of symbols featured and profound.

Paul's "salt air" and Marx's "bitter wind," by the way, correspond to the French phrase *l'air amer,* which is literally "bitter air": opposite choices have been made by Paul and Marx as to which word to translate literally and which not so literally.

In an age when diluted wine smacks of adulteration or catering to children, the notion of watering wine can easily have comic connotations, as in the much-anthologized "Wine and Water" (1914), by G. K. Chesterton (1874–1936). Noah is the ostensible subject of a poem that consists of three six-line stanzas; it will suffice to quote the refrain: "But I don't care where the water goes if it doesn't get into the wine." This absolute bar against diluting wine is recent even in France, as explained by Theodore Zeldin in his excellent discussion (1980) of eating and drinking in France during the period 1848–1945: "Adding water was harmless—indeed it was very common

for people to dilute even good wines in the nineteenth century, the prohibition on
this by the connoisseurs being quite recent."

A much funnier poem involving wine is James Joyce's parody of T. S. Eliot's *The Waste Land* (1922), which he enclosed in a letter of 15 August 1925 to his great patron and benefactor, Harriet Weaver. The Joyces had gone on holiday to Normandy after his vision had not improved much from the recent (seventh) operation on his eyes. He and Nora had encountered bad weather in Rouen, pushing them further south to Arcachon. The parodied passages are drawn from several sections of Eliot's poem:

> Rouen is the rainiest place getting
> Inside all impermeables, wetting
> Damp marrow in drenched bones.
>   [. . . . .]
> But the winepress of the Lord thundered over that grape of Burgundy
> And we left in a hurgundy.
>   (Hurry up, Joyce, it's time!)
>   [. . . . .]
> Mr Anthologos, the local gardener,
> Greycapped, with politeness full of cunning
> Has made wine these fifty years
> And told me in his southern French
> *Le petit vin* is the surest drink to buy
> For if 'tis bad
> *Vous ne l'avez pas payé*
>   (Hurry up, hurry up, now, now, now!)
>
> But we shall have great times,
> When we return to Clinic, that waste land
> O Esculapios!
>   (Shan't we? Shan't we? Shan't we?)

Joyce's favorite wine, by the way, was a Swiss white called Fendant de Sion, which he first discovered in 1919. Ellmann relates the circumstances: "After drinking it with satisfaction, he lifted the half-emptied glass, held it against the window like a test tube, and asked [Ottocaro] Weiss, 'What does this remind you of?' Weiss looked at Joyce and at the pale golden liquid and replied, '*Orina.*' '*Si,*' said Joyce laughing, '*ma di un'arciduchessa*' ('Yes, but an archduchess's'). From now on the wine was known as the Archduchess, and is so celebrated in *Finnegans Wake* [1939]." Here is the whole of the passage, which is about Shem, one of the chief characters of *Finnegans Wake,* notable for his low tastes in food and drink:

> No likedbylike firewater or firstserved firstshot or gulletburn gin or honest
> brewbarrett beer either. O dear no! Instead the tragic jester sobbed himself

wheywhingingly sick of life on some sort of a rhubarbarous maundarin yellagreen funkleblue windigut diodying applejack squeezed from sour grapefruice and, to hear him twixt his sedimental cupslips when he had gulfed down mmmmuch too mmmmany gourds of it retching off to almost as low withswillera, who always knew notwithstanding when they had had enough and were rightly indignant at the wretch's hospitality when they found to their horror they could not carry another drop, it came straight from the noble white fat, jo, openwide sat, jo, jo, her why hide that, jo jo jo, the winevat, of the most serene magyansty az arch-diochesse, if she is a duck, she's a douches, and when she has a feherbour snot her fault, now is it? artstouchups, funny you're grinning at, fancy you're in her yet, Fanny Urinia.

According to Ellmann, Joyce was not really the wine connoisseur he fancied himself, though he once said (referring to wine), "I'd like to have seven tongues and put them all in my cheek at once."

The French poet Robert Desnos (1900–1945) went through several changes in style during his relatively brief writing career. At first, beginning in 1922, he was at the center of Paris surrealism, with its "automatic" writing during trancelike "sleeps." Then, in 1926 he turned to journalism, writing by preference about the popular arts of film and recorded music; he was eventually read out of the Surrealist movement by André Breton for refusing to join the Communist Party. Desnos's poetic style became more straightforward and lyrical, as in these opening stanzas of "Coming Harvests" (1937–8), here translated by Carolyn Forché and William Kulik:

> Hail, coming harvests, scented, bloody,
>   intoxicating harvests of the coming autumn
> Hail, groaning winepresses, echoing barrels,
>   bung holes, cellars, hail
>
> Hail bottles, corks, and glasses
> Hail drinkers of future years
> Drinkers who'll drink greedily
> Drinkers who'll drink learnedly

Much more interesting, I believe, is a later poem about wine, "Verse on the Glass of Wine" (1942), in which Desnos's old Surrealism is once more evident (Forché-Kulik translation):

> When the train leaves don't wave
> Your hand, your handkerchief, or your parasol
> But rather fill a glass of wine
> And toss the long flame of wine

toward the train whose slatted sides are singing
The bloody flame of wine like your tongue
And share with it
The palace and the bed
Of your lips and your mouth.

This was written in German-occupied France, where Desnos was a member of the Resistance. In 1944, he was arrested and died in Terezin, Czechoslovakia, just after Russian troops liberated the concentration camp.

In the long tradition of wine poems that dwell on the vessel containing the precious fluid—Cavafy's "Craftsman of Wine Bowls," von Hoffmannsthal's "The Two," Mallarmé's "Toast," Baudelaire's "The Soul of the Wine," Goethe's "The King in Thule," Rochester's "Upon his Drinking a Bowl," Rabelais's bottle poem, Al-Yamani's "The Goblets," Walafrid Strabo's *Hortulus,* Horace's *Ode* 3.21, and Posidippus's "Sprinkle, Cecropian jug, the dewy moisture of Bacchus," are eleven we have already encountered—H. D. (1886–1961) chooses to imagine the process of constructing a "crater" in the ancient Greek style, in "Wine Bowl" (1931). Written in her characteristic literary mode—over ninety short, clipped lines, with a choppy rhythm interrupted by occasional longer lines that slow the pace—the poem describes a chiseled wine bowl. The first nine lines are repeated as the conclusion:

> I will rise
> from my troth
> with the dead,
> I will sweeten my cup
> and my bread
> with a gift;
> I will chisel a bowl for the wine,
> for the white wine
> and red.

Perhaps the most effective sequence is lines 19–44, combining precise visual detail with emotional intensity:

> I will cut round the rim of the crater,
> some simple
> familiar thing,
> vine leaves
> or the sea-swallow's wing;
> I will work at each separate part
> till my mind is worn out
> and my heart:
> in my skull,

where the vision had birth,

will come wine,

would pour song

of the hot earth,

of the flower and the sweet

of the hill,

thyme,

meadow-plant,

grass-blade and sorrel;

in my skull,

from which vision took flight,

will come wine

will pour song

of the cool night,

of the silver and blade of the moon,

of the star,

of the sun's kiss at mid-noon.

Next, I quote from a collection of love poems (in Arabic and English), by Nizar Kabbani (1923–1998), edited by Frangieh and Brown. In this case, the mere presence of a goblet, regardless of its physical character, is decisive:

I am afraid

To express my love to you

Wine loses its fragrance

When poured into a goblet.

Kabbani, it must be noted, was an extraordinarily popular, even populist, poet in the Arabic-speaking world. Nevertheless, the idea of wine—or love—losing its savor just as it is about to be consumed could hardly have appealed to readers devoted to the classical Arabic wine poem tradition. But this was only the beginning of Kabbani's anti-traditionalism, since he went so far as "express[ing] himself in the first-person feminine." Along with his feminism (or perhaps part of it) was an apparent obsession with women's breasts, the subject of two of his most famous—and notorious—poems. Furthermore, though he served as a Syrian diplomat for over twenty years, eventually Kabbani moved abroad, spending the last years of his life in London; and yet, when he died, he was given a state funeral in Damascus.

Now, for a poem that mentions the containing vessel (the "flute") only glancingly but dwells on the vinous contents: Diane Wakoski's "Champagne Light" (1995). The opening sentence—"Morning sunshine is like champagne / that you inhale"—immediately gives us pause because literally, champagne can, and cannot, be inhaled (one can inhale the bubbles of carbonation, not the liquid itself) but it is not clear how sunshine can be inhaled either literally or figuratively. So, in what sense *is* sunshine like champagne?

> The flute holding this light
> gives you energy, you sip it,
> no task seems impossible.

In other words, both morning sunshine and champagne are sources of *energy* (an abstract term that applies equally to both of them). The remainder of the poem traces the gradual degradation of this energy in the feelings of "heaviness" one experiences as the day wears on. And then the cycle repeats:

> You know
> the pleasure of giving up, of falling asleep early under the blanket,
> and then, throwing it off in the night, waking up to champagne
> light, strawberries for breakfast; it's not just that the light
> is beautiful, it's that you are light, unweighted, not even thinking
> about the champagne hangover, the heaviness of limb.

The literal meaning of champagne, in danger of being lost as the poem develops, is revived with the mention of strawberries and hangover. And the poem concludes with a thud: "And you might be made of moon rocks / instead of moonlight."

A serious drinker of champagne will supplement an awareness of the bubbles with an appreciation of the color and savor of the liquid, as in a passage from "A Good Appetite" (1959), by A. J. Liebling (1904–1963), the first chapter of *Between Meals* (1962). Originally published (like the rest of the book) in the *New Yorker*, the piece deals with Liebling's year (1926–27) studying at the Sorbonne. He is attending a dinner party in the home of a French acquaintance, where the food is mediocre and the wine worse than mediocre, but finally one of the guests, a certain M. Clicquot (so called because he was "the grand manitou of Veuve Clicquot champagne") "retrieved the evening, oenologically, by producing two bottles of a wine 'impossible to find in the cellars of any restaurant in France'":

> The Veuve Clicquot '19 was tart without brashness—a refined but effective understatement of younger champagnes, which run too much to rhetoric, at best. Even so, the force was all there, to judge from the two glasses that were a shade more than my share. The wine still had a discreet *cordon*—the ring of bubbles that forms inside the glass—and it had developed the color known as "partridge eye." I have never seen a partridge's eye, because the bird, unlike woodcock, is served without the head, but the color the term indicates is that of serous blood or a maple leaf on the turn.

The short stories "Taste" (1951), by Roald Dahl, and "The Last Bottle in the World" (1968), by Stanley Ellin (1916–1986), both feature an exceedingly rare vintage French wine. (The stories may be conveniently read in one of the best of the many anthologies of writings about wine: Alexis Bespaloff's *Fireside Book of Wine* [1977].) Set, respectively, in London and Paris, each story is concerned with a marriage: in

612   Dahl's, a possible marriage is the stake in a wager involving the attempt to identify a 1934 vintage Bordeaux; in Ellin's, a marriage is saved (and a man killed) by a 1929 vintage Burgundy. There is no point in rehearsing here either of the rather contrived plots, except to say that the uncorking of the bottle plays a crucial part in each case. Dahl's description of the event is worth quoting:

> It takes enormous strength to draw a cork which has not been pierced through from a bottle of wine which it has sealed for decades. The bottle must be kept upright and immobile, the pull must be straight up and steady without any of the twisting and turning that will tear a cork apart. The old-fashioned corkscrew which exerts no artificial leverage is the instrument for this, because it allows one to feel the exact working of the cork in the bottleneck.
>
> The hand Kassoulas had round the bottle clamped it so hard that his knuckles gleamed white. His shoulders hunched, the muscles of his neck grew taut. Strong as he appeared to be, it seemed impossible for him to start the cork. But he would not give way, and in the end it was the cork that gave way. Slowly and smoothly it was pulled clear of the bottle-mouth, and for the first time since the wine had been drawn from its barrel long years before, it was now free to breathe the open air.

According to Hugh Johnson—described by his publishers as "the world's leading authority on wine"—a traditional corkscrew "demands unnecessary exertion." (For pictures and explanations of seven mechanically more efficient corkscrews, see Johnson's *How to Enjoy Wine* [1985].)

Also set in Paris is "Wine," by Doris Lessing (b. 1919). Nothing could be more trite than the setting: two jaded lovers sitting in a Paris cafe at midday and watching the passing crowd. But Lessing makes something vivid and convincing out of her slight sketch. The two order coffee and ignore it when it arrives. They look at each other: "Desire asleep, they looked. This remained: that while everything which drove them slept, they accepted from each other a sad irony; they could look at each other without illusion, steady-eyed. He orders wine, and she responds, 'What, already?' When he lifts his glass, she responds 'Not yet.'" The ritual they must go through before they can drink the wine is his declaration that he has never loved anyone but her, backed up by the story of an encounter with a young girl many years before (really, a non-encounter, since though he kisses the girl, he rebuffs her sexual advances). His present listener is indignant:

> "It's terrible," she said. "Terrible. Nothing could ever make up to her for that. Nothing, as long as she lived. Just when everything was most perfect, all her life, she'd suddenly remember that night, standing alone, not a soul anywhere, miles of damned empty moonlight."

The exchange over, they can drink; he bends over and kisses her, puts the wine glass into her hands, "and she lifted it, looked at the small crimson globule of warming liquid, and drank with him."

One genre of fiction where a contrived plot is a virtual necessity is that of the mystery or suspense story. In his brief "In Vino Veritas" (1949), A. A. Milne (1882–1956) manages to compress into just a few pages as many twists and surprises as the average full-length mystery novel. To give away the plot would be a minor crime; suffice it to say that a gift of a magnum of poisoned Tokay wine plays a central role. (Tokay is the town in Hungary where this aromatic wine originated.)

John Hollander has written several poems about gifts of wine. His "Thanks for the Bottle" (1984) takes the form of a graceful and grateful note to the giver, "Dear Angus." The poem, consisting of thirty-five lines of rhymed couplet tetrameters (with a final tercet), has an appealing emotional trajectory: first the "lovely bottle of Beychevelle," vintage 1967, is opened; the wine is tasted and its various subtastes distinguished (grapes, wood, glass); then the writer recalls his own history during the seven-year interval since the wine was bottled—a history of "ravages and tears" and the arrival of middle age; the atmosphere gets even gloomier as the bottle is finally drained, but the thought of his friend brings some welcome light in the last six lines:

> It is dark. Emptiness is all
> Toward which we stare with eyes yet bright
> That make a little, glooming light,
> Recalling, just before the end
> (As the last breaths of flame descend)
> The gift, the giver and the friend.

For those who are not wine connoisseurs, the following entry on "Chateau Beychevelle" from *The New Sotheby's Wine Encyclopedia* (1997), by Tom Stevenson, may be helpful: "RED Medium- to full-bodied wines of good colour, ripe fruit, and an elegant oak and tannin structure. They can be quite fat in big years."

An earlier poem of Hollander's, in his volume *Movie-Going and Other Poems* (1962), "For a Thirtieth Birthday with a Bottle of Burgundy," was written to accompany the gift of a bottle of wine to a friend; the printed text has the shape of a burgundy bottle and is one of Hollander's first shaped poems (see fig. 14). Notable in the poem is the pun on "tears," which has a special technical meaning for wine connoisseurs. As Emile Peynaud explains:

> When a glass of wine has just been swirled, one's attention is caught by the streams running down the sides of the glass. A liquid film creeps up the sides, several centimetres above the wine's surface, and then starts to form droplets which fall back in uneven runs. The wine is said to be weeping and the drops are its tears; alternatively, they are called legs, arches or

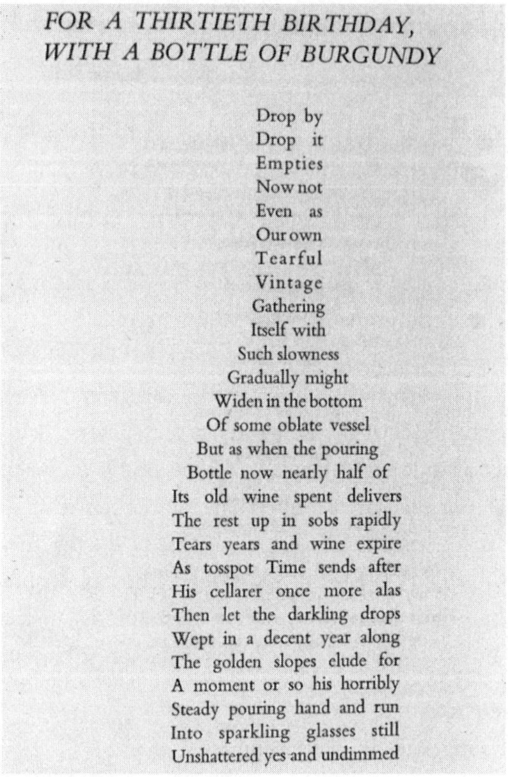

614

FOR A THIRTIETH BIRTHDAY, WITH A BOTTLE OF BURGUNDY

Drop by
Drop it
Empties
Now not
Even as
Our own
Tearful
Vintage
Gathering
Itself with
Such slowness
Gradually might
Widen in the bottom
Of some oblate vessel
But as when the pouring
Bottle now nearly half of
Its old wine spent delivers
The rest up in sobs rapidly
Tears years and wine expire
As tosspot Time sends after
His cellarer once more alas
Then let the darkling drops
Wept in a decent year along
The golden slopes elude for
A moment or so his horribly
Steady pouring hand and run
Into sparkling glasses still
Unshattered yes and undimmed

Fig. 14: John Hollander, "For a Thirtieth Birthday," 1962

arcs.... This phenomenon ... was first correctly explained by James Thomson in 1855. Briefly, because alcohol is more volatile than water, a thin layer of more aqueous liquid forms on the surface of the wine and on the sides of the glass moistened by the wine; this fine film has a higher surface tension. Capillary action causes the liquid to rise up the sides of the glass, and the increase in surface tension tends to form tears which eventually flow back down into the wine. The higher the alcoholic content of the wine, the more tears there are, and they are generally colourless.

Peynaud complains that many wine connoisseurs quite mistakenly take the presence of tears as a criterion of high quality in a wine. In his volume *Types of Shape* (1991)—a collection of shaped poems—Hollander reprints his poem with the following comments: "The bottle shape (like that of the flask-shaped poem in Book 5 of Rabelais's *Pantagruel*) is trivial, but the connections discovered that link aging past thirty (when years pour by more quickly), rates of pouring from actual filled and half-filled bottles, and ultimately the pace at which the poem's syntax extends along printed lines of verse anticipate the emblematic levels of my later figured poems."

Another poem about wine by Hollander is even more adventurous. Wine talk can embrace a wide range of historical and cultural topics, and "Blue Wine" (1979)

manages to canvass many of the possibilities, in spite of—or, perhaps, because of—the
fact that the wine in question is imaginary. Hollander tells us he wrote the poem, dedicated to the artist Saul Steinberg, after he had "visited Saul Steinberg one afternoon and
found that he had pasted some mock (or rather, visionary) wine labels on bottles, which
were then filled with a substance I could not identify. This poem is an attempt to make
sense out of what was apparently in them." With its long lines stretching right across the
page, the poem is divided into eleven (numbered) sections, each largely devoted to one
of the principal discursive categories often exemplified in talk about wine:

(1) the fermenting process
(2) color ("it is a profound red in the cask, but reads as blue / In the
    only kind of light that we have to see it by")
(3) water ("the organized / Reflective blue of its body remembered
    once the sky / Was gone")
(4) ancient literature ("Plutarch's lost essay 'On Blue Wine'")
(5) games ("Is blue / Wine derived from red or white?")
(6) personal memories ("the famous blue / Color of the stuff could come
    to mean so little, could change / The contingent hue of its
    significance")
(7) sociability
(8) epic poetry ("In huge casks half-buried there lay aging the wine of
    the / Island and, weary half to madness, they paused there to drink"
(9) hospitality ("the youngest / Child came forth holding with both hands
    a jug of the local wine")
(10) rituals ("Under the Old Law it was seldom permitted to drink / Blue
    wine, and then only on the Eight Firmamental / Days")
(11) names ("*Das Rheinblau, Chateau / La Tour d'Eau, Romanée Cerulée,*
    even the funny old / Half-forgotten *Vin Albastru*")

All in all, a delightful poem, and—the highest possible praise—fully worthy of Saul
Steinberg.

Blue wine occurs, it may be recalled, in Arthur Rimbaud's most famous poem, "Le
Bateau ivre" (The drunken boat; 1871), that great virtuoso performance by a youth not
yet seventeen years old. The *vin bleu* is in the fifth stanza (translated by Oliver Bernard):

> Plus douce qu'aux enfants la chair des pommes sures,
> L'eau verte pénétra ma coque de sapin
> Et des taches de vins bleus et des vomissures
> Me lava, dispersant gouvernail et grappin.

Sweeter than the flesh of sour apples to children, the green water penetrated my pinewood hull and washed me clean of the splashes of blue
wine and vomit, carrying away both rudder and anchor.

I can see no significant connection in either content, style, or mood between Hollander's "Blue Wine" and Rimbaud's "The Drunken Boat": Rimbaud's speaker writes like someone drunk on blue wine, while Hollander's writes like an excited but sober chronicler of the beverage.

From imaginary wine to an imaginary poetic persona: on 13 June 1926—exactly thirty-eight years after the birth of Fernando Pessoa—one of his three main poetic personae (or "heteronyms"), Ricardo Reis, wrote an ode about wine, in Portuguese but in the style of Horace:

> Not only wine but its oblivion I pour
> In my cup, and I will be happy, because happiness
>   Is ignorant. Who, remembering
>   Or foreseeing, ever smiled?
>
> Let us, with our thinking, obtain not the life
> But the soul of animals, taking refuge
>   In the impalpable destiny
>   Which neither hopes nor remembers.
>
> With mortal hand I raise the fragile cup
> Of fleeting wine to my mortal mouth,
>   Eyes clouded,
>   Ready to stop seeing.

This amounts to a not very original disquisition on the theme of "ignorance is bliss," an example, in the translator Richard Zenith's words, of one of those "terse Horatian odes on themes reminiscent especially of the Augustan poet's second book of odes," in which, however, "Reis was less concrete than Horace, never referring to the events of his time and the more prosaic details of daily life."

In a much more deeply despairing poem on the same theme (written under his own name and dated 1935, the year of his death), Pessoa delays introducing wine until the very last line (as translated by Edwin Honig and Susan Brown): "Let me have more wine, life is nothing." The poem begins with "sicknesses worse than sicknesses" and "pains that do not ache, not even in the soul, / Yet are more painful than all the others," and continues in this vein for a dozen more lines, until the bleak conclusion.

More lighthearted is a Serbian poem addressed to wine, by Aleksandar Ristovic (b. 1933). Alluded to in the title, "Old Motif," is the poem's theme, the energizing—and largely beneficent—effects on behavior of drinking wine, a message evident in these four of six stanzas, translated by Charles Simic:

> For whom are you intended, wine in the corked bottle
> on a white tablecloth,

next to some swaying flowers,
while a young girl sweeps the still-empty room?

You'll untie the tongue of the silent one,
make the fool into a wise man,
and to the weakling you'll give courage
to act on his secret desire.

Out of the wise man you'll make a foolish one
who squanders his wealth among the much-pampered servants and flunkies
and who promises the big-breasted cashier
a house with pine needles on the floor.
    [. . . . .]
For whom are you intended, wine in the corked bottle?
Through whose veins will you send your merry little flame,
making him see the most ordinary things
in many strange and unaccustomed ways?

Louise Bogan's "To Wine" (1937) actually mentions wine only in its title:

> Cup, ignorant and cruel,
> Take from the mandate, love,
> Its urgency to prove
> Unfaith, renewal.
>
> Take from the mind its loss:
> The lipless dead that lie
> Face upward in the earth,
> Strong hand and slender thigh;
> Return to the vein
> All that is worth
> Grief. Give that beat again.

Jacqueline Ridgeway objects to "the neurotic concern with infidelity and reassurance [that] mars the first stanza, as the sense of cynicism—that wine can provide 'all that is worth grief'—mars the entire poem." But Bogan did choose to include it in the selected poems of her final book, *The Blue Estuaries*.

Dispirited in a different way is "Over Wine" (1962), by the Polish poet Wislawa Szymborska (b. 1923). The speaker is sitting opposite someone out to flatter her for reasons undisclosed (love or politics? both?): "He glanced, gave me extra charm / and I took it as my own. / Happily I gulped a star." Here are the third, fourth, and last (of seven) stanzas in an English version by Stanislaw Baranczak and Clare Cavanagh:

The chair's a chair, the wine is wine,
in a wineglass that's the wineglass
standing there by standing there.
Only I'm imaginary,
make-believe beyond belief,
so fictitious that it hurts.

And I tell him tales about
ants that die of love beneath
a dandelion's constellation.
I swear a white rose will sing
if you sprinkle it with wine.
      [. . . . .]
When he isn't looking at me,
I try to catch my reflection
on the wall. And see the nail
where a picture used to be.

Eating and drinking have always been (and, of course, continue to be) highly gendered activities; we have already encountered numerous literary episodes in which the drinking of wine exemplifies the truth of this generalization (for example, wine drinking in ancient Greece). Here is a Yiddish poem about women and wine, "Havdolah Wine," by Miriam Ulinover (1890–1944), who was born in Lodz and died in Auschwitz. ("Havdolah" is part of the Sabbath ceremony; the translation is by Seth L. Wolitz.)

Everyone drinks Havdolah wine
So I drink a few drops too.
Says Grandma sweetly earnest:
"My dear child: I must warn you

A girl who drinks Havdolah wine
Will grow a beard in no time,
So is it written in books
Over there in the bookcase."

I break into a cold sweat
And tap the edge of my chin:
Oh Thank God, still smooth and soft . . .
Only fright can make it bristle.

But let us conclude our short succession of twentieth-century wine poems on a quieter, even playful, note with a pair of triplets from Eugenio Montale's fourth book of poetry, *Satura* (Miscellany; 1971), which the poet himself characterized as "diaristic" and "spontaneous." The Italian is included along with Arrowsmith's translation so as to exhibit the sound effects that are so essential to Montale's humor:

> The wine peddler poured you a thimble
> of Inferno. And you, shrinking back: "Must I drink it?
> Isn't it enough to simmer in the stuff?"
>
> "And Paradise? Is there a paradise too?"
> "I think so, Signora, but nobody likes
> those sweet dessert wines anymore."
>
> ~
>
> Il vinattiere ti versava un poco
> d'Inferno. E tu, atterrita: "Devo berlo? Non basta
> esserci stati dentro a lento fuoco?"
>
> "E il Paradiso? Esiste un paradiso?."
> "Credo di sì, signora, ma i vini dolci
> non li vuol più nessuno."

The translator provides a note for each poem about the wine in question:

> *Inferno:* red Lombard wine from Valtellina made from the Nebbiolo grape.
> In Milan local wines were commonly peddled door to door by tradesmen
> or peasants.
>
> *Paradiso:* sweet or semisweet dessert wine also from Valtellina, produced by
> the Fattoria Paradiso.

We must, finally, acknowledge the existence of a large-scale and thriving branch of writing devoted to the perpetuation and enhancement of what can only be called "the mystique of wine." With genres ranging from histories to guides to companions to travel books to encyclopedias, the writing is too often pretentious and jargon-ridden, sometimes wilfully obscurantist, and usually tedious to read except for committed oenophiles. Colette is one great exception: on wine, as on most subjects, she is direct and down-to-earth. It is, therefore, tempting to quote at length from her discussion of wine in *Prisons et paradis* (1932), but I will offer just a sample from her recollections of how she was introduced to wine by her parents (translated by Derek Coltman):

> I was very well brought up. As a first proof of so categorical a statement, I
> shall simply say that I was no more than three years old when my father
> poured out my first full liqueur glass of an amber-colored wine which was
> sent up to him from the Midi, where he was born: the muscat of Frontignan.
>
> The sun breaking from behind clouds, a shock of sensuous pleasure, an
> illumination of my newborn tastebuds! This initiation ceremony rendered

Wine Descriptors Encountered in the Literature—Preliminary List

acetic	clean	ethereal	full-bodied	humble	nutty	redolent	smooth	tannic
acidic	cloying	empty	full-flavored	immature	oaky	refreshing	soft	tart
acrid	coarse	evolved	gassy	insipid	oily	respectable	solid	taut
aged	common	exhilerating	gay	has legs	odd	rich	sophisticated	tender
alcoholic	has come on	faded	gentle	light	off	ripe	sound	thick
aloof	complex	fat	generous	lingering (finish)	old	robust	sour	thin
aromatic	cooked	feminine	grapy	little	ordinary	roguish	spicy	tough
astringent	corked	fermenting	graceful	lively	original	round	has stamina	transcendental
attenuated	corky	fierce	grandiose	luscious	ostentatious	rounded	stalky	twiggy
austere	creamy	fiery	great	maderized	overripe	rough	steely	unbalanced
baked	crisp	fine	has grip	has majesty	oxidized	rugged	stemmy	unharmonious
balanced	dead	finesse	green	manly	pebbly	salty	stiff	unripe
beery	decrepit	finish	gun flint	mature	penetrating	sappy	stony	vegy (vegetable)
big	delicate	firm	hale	meager	peppery	savory	sturdy	velvety
has bite	developed	flabby	hard	mealy	perfumed	scented	strong	vigorous
bitter	deep	flamboyant	harmonious	meaty	piquant	semisweet	stylish	vinous
bouquet	disciplined	flat	harsh	medium	plump	senile	suave	vulgar
bland	discreet	flattering	heady	mellow	has poise	sensuous	succulent	warm
blurred	distinctive	fleshy	hearty	mettlesome	positive	serious	subtle	watery
has body	distinguished	flinty	heavy	mineral	powerful	sharp	sugary	weak
breed	dry	flowery	herby	moldy	pretentious	short (finish)	superficial	wild
brisk	dull	foxy	herbaceous	mossy	pricked	silky	supple	withered
buttery	dumb	fragile	hollow	musky	prickly	silly	sweet	woody
caramel	durable	fragrant	honest	musty	puckery	simple	swallowable	yeasty
chalky	dusty	fresh	hot	neutral	pungent	skunky	syrupy	young
has character	eartly	frolicsome	huge	noble	racy	small	tangy	zestful
charming	elegant	fruity		nose	rare	smoky		

Fig. 15: "Wine Descriptors," Adrienne Lehrer, *Wine and Conversation,* 1983

me worthy of wine for all time. A little later I learned to empty my goblet of mulled wine, scented with cinnamon and lemon, as I ate a dinner of boiled chestnuts. At an age when I could still scarcely read, I was spelling out, drop by drop, old light clarets, and dazzling Yquems. Champagne appeared in its turn, a murmur of foam, leaping pearls of air providing an accompaniment to birthday and First Communion banquets, complementing the gray truffles from La Puisaye. . . . Good lessons, from which I graduated to a familiar and discreet use of wine, not gulped down greedily but measured out into narrow glasses, assimilated mouthful by spaced-out, meditative mouthful.

There are three books on wine I can unreservedly recommend. One is *The Grapes of Ralph* (1992), by Ralph Steadman (b. 1936)—though admittedly more for the pictures than the text—a brilliantly satirical performance by an outstanding illustrator. The second book is by a linguist interested in the nature of the language used to describe wines. In her *Wine and Conversation* (1983), Adrienne Lehrer (b. 1937) begins by collecting in a table all the terms for taste (some 241 of them) that she can find in a sampling of the literature (in English) on wine (see fig. 15). She stresses the fact that her list is open-ended and easily extended in obvious ways, such as by adding one of the following suffixes to an appropriate noun: -*y, -like , -ish, -ic, -ful, -ous.* Some possible examples (my own) would be: *citrusy, berrylike, candyish, metallic, forceful, malicious.* Applications of this vocabulary are usually a matter of degree: too much or too little (with negative connotations) and just right (with positive connotations). For example, along the dimension of acidity, one can say *sour* (too much), *bland* (too little), or *crisp* (just right). But the dimension of sweetness is somewhat different: though one can say *cloying* (too much) or *dry* (just right), there appear to be no terms for too little sweetness.

The most common way of extending the vocabulary of terms for describing the taste of wine is by a process linguists call "semantic extension," that is, the extension of meaning from one semantic field to another (where a semantic field is, roughly speaking, a particular subject matter or conceptual sphere). Some of the main semantic fields that have been extended to wine tasting include touch and feel (*sharp, flat, hard, flabby*), spatial dimension (*big, deep, huge*), shape (*angular*), age (*decrepit, senile*), and flexibility (*stiff, supple, taut*). The semantic field in which perhaps the greatest lexical innovation among wine tasters occurs is that of personality, behavior, and character (*respectable, serious, silly, naive, suave, sincere*). I might just add that even my casual perusal of some recent books on wine conoisseurship has turned up many terms not mentioned by Lehrer, such as *weedy, disjointed, diffuse, shallow, four-square, chunky, loosely-knit, tarry, corpulent,* and *plausible.*

A good part of Lehrer's book is taken up with reporting her attempts to determine whether there is any consensus among three different groups of experimental subjects on the application of wine-tasting terms, and whether such consensus can be improved with practice. Her answers are negative for both questions, at least for the two groups of ordinary, nonexpert subjects. But even a group of wine scientists had problems with arriving at unanimous judgments. Lehrer concludes:

> The task of encoding into language the perceptual properties of complex and varied stimuli, such as wines, and subsequently decoding such messages, is an extremely difficult one, even for people with great knowledge and experience. Contrary to popular opinion, the language provides rich resources for talking about taste and smell. . . . But each speaker has a different set of educational and personal experiences and all this contributes to the variability found in speakers' linguistic behavior.

The third book I would recommend is Peynaud's *Taste of Wine,* from which I have already quoted. Though rigorous—even "scientific"—whenever possible, Peynaud is no skeptic when it comes to accepting the reality of the trained oenologists's skills. His taxonomy of taste-words for characterizing wines is expressed in a diagram containing over seventy-five terms, well over half of which are in Lehrer's list (Peynaud is working, of course, with a French vocabulary). But Peynaud is also capable of writing skeptically about detecting the odor (or "nose") of wine: "The evocative search for smells is akin to the sensual delights of the imagination; but here, as in poetry, where are the limits of sincerity? And beyond these limits how big a part is played by autosuggestion and bluff? Irrelevance and exaggeration are the beginner's standard mistakes."

I have recently come across gratifying evidence that contemporary writing about wine can be exact, elegant, and imaginative. One of my three examples is by a scholar of Renaissance art who is also an amateur oenologist. I have already cited Leonard Barkan in his first role, in connection with a passage by Vasari describing the painting of a Priapean scene by Giovanni da Udine. Now, I want to quote from a long, brilliant paragraph by Barkan explaining with no mystification at all a view of the general significance of wine in civilization:

> Grapes grow and then ferment more or less automatically; where and how they do it will affect the result even with no intervention. European civilization has fussed more about grapes than most other crops not only because they produce alcohol pretty reliably but also because grapes have an extraordinary responsiveness to every aspect of both nature and nurture that goes into their production. Consequently, for at least three or four millennia, individuals have chosen to intervene, both by closely watching nature and by inventing technologies to improve nurture, which in this instance includes everything from soil management to bottling. The grape, in other words, is remarkable for its ability to *express* all the nature and culture that went into it, that is, to contain and reflect everything that earth and sun, winemaker and technologist have implanted. In a grand symmetry, individuals who taste the wine, as they convert their experience into language are, once again, *expressing* all that interlocking heritage of origins; and they are building metaphors and metonymys of association in response. Wine is art because it is heightened reality in need of expression.

My second example is a long poem about grape growing and wine making by the American poet George Bradley (b. 1953). "A Georgic for Doug Crase" consists of some 540 lines addressed to a close friend of the poet's, describing in meticulous detail some of the main procedures used in growing grapes and making wine in Bradley's vineyard on Long Island. Following his most famous predecessor in georgic poetry, Bradley writes, like Virgil, in hexameters. (The meter is very different in the two languages, Latin prosody being based on long and short syllables, English prosody usually on stressed and unstressed syllables. It is impossible to discuss the subject here, but a brief and enjoyable introduction may be recommended: John Hollander's *Rhyme's Reason* [1989].) Bradley's line has six stresses, five dactyls followed by a trochee: ‑˘˘/‑˘˘/‑˘˘/‑˘˘/‑˘˘/‑˘ . Here are two characteristic passages, one about growing grapes and one about the different procedures for making white and red wine:

> So much requires your attention that resting is out of the question:
> Have you uncovered the base of each vine to increase its aeration?
> Have you supported the grapes, so the branches don't break with their burden?
> Have you been keeping the weeds down? And what about fences for wildlife?
> Rabbits and deer make a banquet of bark that they strip from your seedlings.
> Then there's the spray—with the poison you use, you'll outlive Mithridates!—

Byleton, Captan, cuprated lime, Malathion and Sevin and Ferbam . . .
All of it's probably carcinogenic, and none of it's lovely
For the environment. Isn't that typical nurturing for you?
Trying to make something grow wants suppressing whatever's around it.

White grapes are pressed in advance of fermenting, the way that I've outlined;
Red ones, however, are crushed and fermented along with the grapeskins,
Taking on color, and only at this point are pressed for their tannin.
Reds that are left on their lees for too long will refuse to develop,
Harsh from the start and unpleasant well after their fruit is exhausted.
(Frankly, a white wine's for neophytes, easy to make and too easy,
Not to say boring, to drink.
      [. . . . .]
Here on Long Island, the chardonnay thrives and the diet is seafood:
White wines don't count, I agree, but a white wine is what I'm producing.)

My third example is a novel by the New Zealand writer Elizabeth Knox (b. 1959), *The Vintner's Luck* (1998). The vintner of the title is a French peasant, Sobran Jodeau, whose life is narrated in fifty-six episodes—ranging in length from three words to thirty-seven pages—one per year, from 1808 (when he is eighteen years old) until his death in 1863. Sobran is a shrewd, literate, but fairly ordinary man, whose inner life is transformed when he encounters an angel on the moonlit night of 27 June 1808, after drinking two bottles of wine from his own vineyard:

> Someone had set a statue down on the ridge. Sobran blinked and swayed. For a second he saw what he *knew*—gilt, paint and varnish, the sculpted labial eye of a church statue. Then he swooned while still walking forward, and the angel stood quickly to catch him.
>
> Sobran fell against a warm, firm pillow of muscle. He lay braced by a wing, pure sinew and bone under a cushion of feathers, complicated and accommodating against his side, hip, leg, the pinions split around his ankle. The angel was breathing steadily, and smelled of snow.

Sobran marries, has children, becomes a successful vintner, has a love affair with an atheist baroness (whose disbelief is challenged when she too encounters angels); but the most important thing in his life is the friendship—which becomes a love affair—with the angel. Sobran learns that the angel is named Xas (pronounced "sass"). The angel visits Sobran regularly once a year, usually on the anniversary of their initial encounter, and they always drink together—wine from Cru Jodeau. On their twentieth anniversary, Xas reveals that he is a fallen angel, and a distraught Sobran now believes he himself is damned. But he continues to love Xas. In 1835, Sobran finds Xas unconscious, with a gaping, bleeding wound in his chest: he has been punished for "trespassing." The archangel Lucifer arrives and surgically removes Xas's wings, and the angel recovers.

One way in which wine enters the novel is in the titles of the sections, each one taking the form of a French phrase relating to viniculture. Some of the more arresting phrases are these: 1809 Vin de Coucher (nuptial wine); 1811 Vin Tourné (turned wine); 1814 Vin Capiteux (a spirited, heady wine); 1817 Vin de Cru (wine from the grapes of a single vineyard); 1818 Vin du Clerc (wine offered by a plaintiff to the court clerk if the tribunal finds in the plaintiff's favor); 1823 Vin de Goutte (poor-quality wine from the last pressing of the grapes); 1831 Cru (the soil in which vines are grown); 1842 Epluchage (the picking out of rotten and black grapes from the picked bunch); 1843 Epondage (pruning dead twigs and suckers off the vine). The last section of the novel jumps to 1997 at the Chateau Vully l'Ange du Cru Jodeau, where Xas is mingling with a group of tourists from New Zealand and Britain who are being shown around by a guide on "a lovely day, at the height of the tourist season" (we can guess that it is 27 June). The guide explains "about *Phylloxera vastatrix,* the vine louse that devastated the vineyards of Europe between 1863 and 1890. The vines here were grafted onto American vinestock in the 1870s. Only the rootstock of its Grand Cru was spared—just one walled vineyard between Mâcon and Chagny, Clos Jodeau, which lies three miles south of Vully." Quite abruptly, then, the identity of the narrator appears to change as we hear Xas speaking to Sobran, telling him of his own recent life, of certain things Xas concealed from Sobran, and of Xas's acquaintance with God and Lucifer. In the last lines of the book, Xas recalls his first encounter with Sobran:

> You fainted and I caught you. It was the first time I'd supported a human.
> You had such heavy bones. I put myself between you and gravity.
> Impossible.

ORCHARDS, GROVES, GARDENS

SOME EARLY FRUIT ORCHARDS AND GARDENS

Some of the earliest descriptions of fruit orchards occur in Egyptian literature of the New Kingdom (1550–1080 B.C.E.), in particular, in three love songs from the Turin Papyrus. The texts are fragmentary but it is clear that the voice in each song is a tree in an orchard. I quote a few lines from the first and the third songs:

> [The pomegranate] says:
> Like her teeth my seeds,
> Like her breasts my fruit,
> [foremost am I] of the orchard
> since in every season I'm around.
> 　　[. . . . .]
> All, all pass away,
> except for me, from the fields.
> Twelve months I spend
> [within the park] waiting.
>
> 　　　　～
>
> The little sycamore,
> which she planted with her hand,
> sends forth its words to speak.
>
> The flowers [of its stalks]
> [are like] an inundation of honey;
> beautiful it is, and its branches shine
> more verdant [than the grass].
>
> It is laden with the ripeness of notched figs,
> redder than carnelian,
> like turquoise its leaves,
> like glass its bark.

626   There are two descriptions of orchards in the *Odyssey* and each occurs at a decisive juncture in the story, the first in book 7, when the shipwrecked Odysseus sees the fruit orchards near the palace of King Alkínoös in Phaiákia. (I use the Fitzgerald translation.) Concealed by Athena in "a sea fog around him," Odysseus, "who had borne the barren sea, / stood in the gateway and surveyed this bounty. / He gazed his fill, then swiftly he went in." Odysseus has good reason to gaze his fill: he has not eaten or even seen fruit during his long sea voyage. As for the food provided Odysseus just a little earlier, in book 6, by Alkínoös's daughter Nausikaa and her maids, it is difficult to decide whether or not it included fruit—Fitzgerald specifies "bread and wine," and other translators mention merely "food and drink"; we do know that Odysseus is still ravenously hungry when he arrives at the palace. But Odysseus has another reason for gazing at the orchard: it reminds him of home (and in a particularly wrenching way, as readers familiar with the *Odyssey* will understand if they remember the recollected orchard scene in book 24). In any case, this is what Odysseus sees near Alkínoös's palace:

> To left and right, outside, he saw an orchard
> closed by a pale—four spacious acres planted
> with trees in bloom or weighted down for picking:
> pear trees, pomegranates, brilliant apples,
> luscious figs, and olives ripe and dark.

And Homer continues with what Odysseus could not have known:

> Fruit never failed upon these trees: winter
> and summer time they bore, for through the year
> the breathing Westwind ripened all in turn—
> so one pear came to prime, and then another,
> and so with apples, figs, and the vine's fruit
> empurpled in the royal vineyard there.

It seems that the royal gardeners have learned how to ensure that *all* the fruits of the orchard grow *all* year round (an arrangement, as we shall see, that is repeated again and again in later representations of the Golden Age or the Earthly Paradise). When Odysseus arrives back home in Ithaca there is a long suspenseful episode before he reveals himself to his aged father, Laërtes. Odysseus first sees his father working in his orchard: "On a well-banked plot / Odysseus found his father in solitude / spading the earth around a young fruit tree," and at the sight of the old man, "the son paused by a tall pear tree and wept." When Odysseus finally reveals himself, his father doubts his identity. To convince his father, Odysseus gives two proofs: first, a scar inflicted by a wild boar, and, second, his faithful recollection of a childhood gift of fruit trees and grape vines from Laërtes:

I was a small boy at your heels, wheedling
amid the young trees, while you named each one.
You gave me thirteen pear, ten apple trees,
and forty fig trees. Fifty rows of vines
were promised too, each one to bear in turn.
Bunches of every hue would hang there ripening,
weighed down by the god of summer days.

627

Only the pomegranates of Alkínoös's orchard are missing; were these considered somehow inappropriate for a young boy?

The young Alexander Pope singled out Homer's description of Alkínoös's garden for translation into heroic couplets. The thirty-four lines, titled "The Gardens of Alcinous" (1713), were first published independently and later took their place in Pope's translation of the *Odyssey*. Here are the lines corresponding to the passage quoted above:

Close to the gates a spacious garden lies,
From storms defended, and inclement skies:
Four acres was th' allotted space of ground,
Fenc'd with a green enclosure all around.
Tall thriving trees confess'd the fruitful mold;
The red'ning apple ripens here to gold,
Here the blue fig with luscious juice o'erflows,
With deeper red the full pomegranate glows,
The branch here bends beneath the weighty pear,
And verdant olives flourish round the year.
The balmy spirit of the western gale
Eternal breathes on fruits untaught to fail:
Each dropping pear a following pear supplies,
On apples apples, figs on figs arise:
The same mild season gives the blooms to blow,
The buds to harden, and the fruits to grow.
  Here order'd vines in equal ranks appear
With all th' united labours of the year,
Some to unload the fertile branches run,
Some dry the black'ning clusters in the sun,
Others to tread the liquid harvest join,
The groaning presses foam with floods of wine.
Here are the vines in early flow'r descry'd,
Here grapes discolour'd on the sunny side,
And there in autumn's richest purple dy'd.

628   Homer's eleven lines have been expanded to twenty-five, as Pope copes with his relatively wordy linguistic medium and the demands of his heroic couplets.

There is an interesting allusion to Alkínoös's orchard in a poem by Martial (8.68)
already mentioned in connection with the discussion, in chapter 4, "Strawberries (and
Cream)," of Herrick's "The Lilly in a Chrystal." Martial first describes how Entellus
has outwitted nature by getting grapes to ripen in winter inside a greenhouse; the
appearance of the grapes under glass then reminds the poet of the look of a woman's
body sheathed in silk and also of stones seen under water. Three rather different modern translations are worth quoting, the first, by Peter Whigham, close but artful (and
hence, like the Latin, not so easy to make out); the second, by Shackleton Bailey, very
literal; and the third, by Rolfe Humphries, who needs double the number of lines to
achieve its rhymes:

> Your country-house—its garden—far outstrips
> 　　the orchards of *Alcinous.*
> Vexed winter cannot nip your purpling grape,
> 　　nor frost tipple *Bacchus'* gifts.
> Treasured 'neath transparent glass the vine-crop
> 　　protects, while it displays, itself.
> A woman's body dawns through silken clothes.
> 　　Smallest stones are clear in clearest streams.
> At mankind's skill Nature yields, conjuring
> 　　sterile winter issue autumn's fruits.

~

He who has seen the orchards of Corcyra's king will prefer the country
inside your city mansion, Entellus. Lest envious winter bite the purple
clusters, and chill frost devour the gifts of Bacchus, the vintage lives
enclosed in transparent glass and the blooming grape is covered, yet not
hidden. So a woman's body shines through silk, so pebbles are counted in
clear water. What license has nature not willed for ingenuity? Barren winter is bidden to bear an autumn.

~

> The orchards of Corcyra's king
> Are less spectacular than those,
> Entellus, which your walls enclose.
> Here, lest the hateful northers bring
> Cold winter-burning to the vine,
> Or lest the chilly frost consume
> The gift of Bacchus, future wine,

Your vineyards, with protected bloom,

Behind transparent window walls,
Flourish protected, fair to see,
And fortunate, whate'er befalls.
So, through her silken drapery,
One sees the radiance and gleam
Of a girl's limbs; so one may look
Below the slowly moving brook
And count the pebbles in the stream.
Nature from one ingenious wit
Withholds invention; here we find
The barren winter benefit
Autumn, obedient to man's mind.

The connection between Corcyra and Alkínoös (Alcinous) is that the latter's island kingdom was presumed by Homer's readers in antiquity to be Corcyra (Corfu) off the northwestern coast of Greece.

By the second century C.E. even Homer was ripe for parody, practiced very effectively by Lucian (c. 120–c. 180 C.E.) in *A True Story*, written in a close imitation of classical Greek prose, and described by Lionel Casson as a "tall-tale travelogue to end all tall-tale travelogues." In the second (and last) part of the work the narrator and his companions find themselves in the Elysian Fields. The description of the fruit orchards is an obvious—perhaps rather too obvious—satire on what Odysseus sees in book 7 of the *Odyssey:* "The vines bear twelve times a year and are harvested monthly. The pomegranate, apple, and other fruit trees bear, we were told, thirteen times a year since they bear twice during Minosmonth, as it's called in the local calendar" (2.13). A good deal funnier is an episode in part 1, where the travellers encounter "vines of a fabulous type":

> The part growing out of the ground, the stalk proper, was well set up and thick. But the part above that was a perfect replica of a female body from hips to head, looking somewhat like Daphne in those paintings where she's shown turning into a tree as Apollo lays his hands on her. The women had branches bearing clusters of grapes growing out of the tips of their fingers and, instead of hair, actual shoots with leaves and grapes. They called out to welcome us as we came up, some in Lydian, some in Indian, but most in Greek. They also started kissing us on the lips, and everyone they did this to immediately became drunk and began to reel. We weren't able to pick the grapes because, as we pulled them off, the women would cry out in pain. They were burning with desire to have intercourse with us. Two of my men tried it—and couldn't be pried loose: they were held fast by the penis; it had grown into, become grafted onto, the vines.

630   One of the most notable postclassical gardens in European literature is that described by Walafrid Strabo in *De cultura hortorum* (which we have already cited for its melon and gourd episodes). Helen Waddell gives the following appreciation of the poem as a whole:

> [Walafrid's] Gloss on Holy Writ, a kind of biblical encyclopedia, was one of the first mediaeval books which the Renaissance thought it worth while to print; it went into fresh editions, even in the seventeenth century. But the work that keeps his memory green is not the *Glossa Ordinaria,* but the garden that he made in the wilderness of academic verse, his plot of ground at Reichenau, of sage and rue and southern-wood, poppy and penny-royal, mint and parsley and radishes, and, for love's sake only, gladioli and lilies and roses, even though only plain German roses, no Tyrian purple nor the scarlet splendour of France.

There is a sixteen-line verse dedication at the end of Walafrid's poem (lines 429–44) addressed to Grimold, head of Walafrid's old school at the abbot of St. Gall; it is, in Helen Waddell's words, in her *Mediaeval Latin Lyrics* (1968), "perhaps the most famous dedication in medieval Latin." Walafrid envisages Grimold sitting in his own garden (Waddell's translation):

> So might you sit in the small garden close
> In the green darkness of the apple trees,
> Just where the peach tree casts its broken shade,
> And they would gather you the shining fruit
> With the soft down upon it; all your boys,
> Your little laughing boys, your happy school,
> And bring huge apples clasped in their two hands.

And Walafrid exhorts "my father" to read his book and "prune it of its faults," while wishing him "the green / Unwithering palm of everlasting life."

Another connection between Reichenau and St. Gall during this same period is of surpassing interest. A manuscript known as the Plan of St. Gall was copied between 820 and 830 C.E. in the scriptorium at Reichenau by tracing it on parchment from a lost original. The plan was designed as a guide to the architecture of an ideal Benedictine monastery; its recommendations were never realized in actual buildings, and this particular copy of the plan—the only one that seems to have survived—was for centuries hidden away in the library of St. Gall. Rediscovered by scholars in 1604, it only began to be seriously studied in 1844. In 1978, a great edition of the manuscript, in three quarto volumes, was published by the University of California Press. Among the elements of the plan—and explaining our interest in it here—is a monks' cemetery and garden, containing designated spaces for fourteen burials and thirteen trees (or groups of trees) in a careful alternating geometrical arrangement. (Both the

numbers thirteen and fourteen, by the way, have sacred associations.) The trees specified in the plan are flowering species—suggestive of resurrection—and include apple,
pear, plum, service tree, medlar, bay laurel, chestnut, fig, quince, peach, hazel, almond,
mulberry, and walnut. Fig and laurel, while not suited to northern climates, have Classical literary associations, which may account for their presence.

A fruit orchard can, of course, have quite different metaphorical connotations
than resurrection. Thus, harvesting a ripe fruit orchard has been used as a metaphor
for sex with a young woman, in "Seeing Herself Beautiful and Nubile," by Qasmuna,
who lived in twelfth-century Granada and is one of over thirty known Hispano-
Arabic women poets.

> I see an orchard
> Where the time has come
> For harvesting,
> But I do not see
> A gardener reaching out a hand
> Toward its fruits.
> Youth goes, vanishing; I wait alone
> For somebody I do not wish to name.

The translation—from the Spanish of García Gómez—is by Middleton and Garza-
Falcón.

THE GARDEN AS EARTHLY PARADISE

In the Jewish tradition of biblical commentary, much attention was bestowed on the
Garden of Eden (Gan Eden), usually interpreted as the Paradise or heavenly abode of
the righteous, with the happiness of the residents often envisaged in terms of wonderful banquets. The food was occasionally identified as the flesh of Leviathan, rather
than as fruit in the Garden of Eden. On the other hand, the garden itself was described
in extravagant terms, as in a thirteenth-century compilation commenting on Genesis
20 and ascribed to the third-century scholar R. Joshua b. Levi (translated by A.
Cohen):

> In every corner of Gan Eden there are eighty myriad species of trees, the
> most inferior of them being finer than all the aromatic plants (of this
> world); and in each corner are sixty myriads of ministering angels singing
> in pleasant tones. In the centre is the Tree of Life, its branches covering the
> whole of Gan Eden, containing five hundred thousand varieties of fruit all
> differing in appearance and taste.

In the Koran, "Good food," as van Gelder explains, "is one of the essential pleasures of Paradise." Fruit is especially singled out: "In the Hereafter the believers may
expect 'of every fruit two kinds.'" And the emphasis on fruit is extended even to Hell,

632   "where the food is the fruit of the zaqqum tree that boils in the bowels"! (For the Arabic original and a modern translation, see Ahmed Ali's *Al-Qur'an*. [1988].)

Let us look now at a few paradisal gardens in medieval and Renaissance epics. The great popularity of *The Romance of the Rose*—the initial (shorter) part by Guillaume de Lorris, the final part by Jean de Meun (d. 1305)—in the late Latin Middle Ages is amply evidenced by the survival of over two hundred manuscripts, many richly illustrated. Though written in a style that is straightforward compared to, say, the six cantos on the earthly paradise of Dante's *Purgatorio,* the interpretation of the *Romance* is by no means simple or obvious. Modern commentators on the *Romance* tend to agree that sorting out the rhetorical strategies (such as irony) in the work is crucial for adequate understanding. I want to deal only with the garden setting of the *Romance,* as described by the twenty-year-old narrator (who is soon identified as "the Lover"). Early in the first book, he tells us he is recounting a dream, in which he entered a garden and thought he was in "the earthly paradise [paradis terrestre]" (634). After describing the men and women in the garden—with names like Idleness, Diversion, Joy, and Courtesy—he says he "will tell in a full and orderly way about the appearance of the garden" (694–97). The description of the garden occupies some eighty-eight lines (1321–1408), of which the first fifty-two (1321–72) are almost entirely about trees. Here, in Dahlberg's prose translation, are some of the passages concerning fruit trees:

> The garden was a completely straight, regular square, as long as it was wide. Except for some trees which would have been too ugly, there was no tree which might bear fruit of which there were not one or two, or perhaps more, in the garden. There were apple trees, I well remember, that bore pomegranates, an excellent food for the sick. There was a great abundance of nut trees that in their season bore such fruit as nutmegs, which are neither bitter nor insipid. There were almond trees, and many fig and date trees were planted in the garden. . . .
>
> There were the domestic garden fruit trees, bearing quinces, peaches, nuts, chestnuts, apples and pears, medlars, white and black plums, fresh red cherries, sorb-apples, service-berries, and hazelnuts. . . . There were so many different trees that one would be heavily burdened before he had numbered them.

There is no suggestion that any of these trees is anything but luxuriantly covered with foliage and fruit—in other words, no suggestion of a denuded tree like Dante's tree of the knowledge of good and evil (see chapter 3, "Missing Fruit"). What the Lover discovers instead as he explores the garden is, first, "the true fountain of the fair Narcissus" (1511) and then, climactically, a rose garden surrounded by a hedge. All that keeps him from picking one of the most beautiful of the rosebuds is fear of "the sharp and piercing thorns" (1673). We have been introduced to the theme, in Dahlberg's words, of "the Lover's headstrong folly in his pursuit of the rose-sanctuary-*con*." As for rhetorical

strategies, de Lorris has his Lover deduce a moral from the story of Narcissus, which   633
by deftly reversing the sexes is converted into an appeal to the "ladies" (*dames*) to save
the lives of their "sweethearts" (*amis*) by not withholding their love (1505–08).

Almost exactly three centuries after the completion of *The Romance of the Rose*, a
quite different version of the earthly paradise appeared in Portuguese, *The Lusiads* (1570),
by Luís de Camões (1524/5–1580). Designed to glorify the author's native Portugal by
an account of Vasco da Gama's voyage to India in 1497–98, the poem's epic qualities
are—depending on one's critical standpoint—either enhanced or drastically weakened
by its apparatus of Classical gods and goddesses. In any case, the two last cantos of the
work (9, 10) are given over to a visit by da Gama's fleet to an island of love—a kind of
glorified brothel—conjured up by the Portuguese navigator's divine patroness, Venus, as
a reward to the intrepid sailors. As the ships approach the island, in stanza 9.56,

> Trees beyond number climbed to the sky
> With luscious, sweet-smelling fruits;
> The orange with its bright lanterns,
> The colour of Daphne's hair;
> Citron-trees, brushing the ground
> With the weight of their yellow burden;
> And fragrant, moulded lemons which, when pressed,
> Are curved and nippled like a maiden's breast.

The translation—a modern one by Landeg White—retains rhyme only for the concluding couplet of de Camões's *ottawa rima* (Italian: *ottava rima; abababcc*). The next
stanza is devoted to other trees (poplar, laurel, myrtle, pine, cypress) and then we return
to fruit in stanzas 9.58–59:

> Cherries, as purple as *amoras,*
> (Or mulberries, with their name of love);
> The peach, that apple found in Persian fields,
> But grown in exile gives much better yields.
>
> Pomegranates gaped, exposing jewels
> Richer, redder than any rubies;
> Vines threaded the boughs of the elm
> With hanging clusters, purple and green;
> And pear trees were so heavily laden
> They took the shape of pyramids,
> Yielding to a myriad of birds, deft
> With their ravenous beaks, intent on theft.

I might just add that, as a transition to his description of the flowers on the island,
Camões refers (like de Lorris) to the story of Narcissus.

The pyramidal pear trees, by the way, correspond to the Portuguese phrase *peras piramidais,* which might better be translated "pyramidal pears" (since *pera* means pear, while pear tree is *pereira*). Furthermore, I do not see why heavily laden pear trees would necessarily take on a pyramidal shape, while it does make sense to describe individual pears as pyramidal (as in an earlier English translation by Leonard Bacon). Another easily available translation of *The Lusiads* —William C. Atkinson's prose version—seems to refer to the *boughs* of the pear tree as pyramidal: "and so mightily did the pear-tree flourish that its laden boughs, like pyramids, constrained it to welcome the depredations of the birds." On the other hand, the American horticulturist Patrick Barry (whom we have already cited several times) remarks in "The Pear, as a Pyramid": "The pear is eminently *the* tree for the pyramidal form, either on the free stock, or on the quince"; and he illustrates with a picture of a pyramidal pear tree.

Not quite a dozen years after *The Lusiads,* Torquato Tasso (1544–1595) published a historical epic in Italian, *Jerusalem Delivered* (1581), about the Christian capture of Jerusalem from the Muslims in 1099 during the First Crusade. The twenty cantos of Tasso's poem (like *The Lusiads,* in *ottava rima*) culminate with the rescue of the hero, Rinaldo, from the enchantress Armida's clutches by two Christian knights. In the sixteenth canto, the knights enter the garden of Armida's palace, where, such are her magical powers, nature imitates art. One sign of the reigning enchantment is that time is suspended; the resulting confusion is the theme of stanzas 16.10–11 (the Italian is so convoluted that it is helpful, I believe, to quote two translations, Tusiani's in verse and Ralph Nash's in prose, along with the concluding couplets in Italian):

> Artlessness and great art so finely blend
> that ornament and site seem nature's way.
> Nature, it seems, in jest is vying with
> the very art that vies with all her deeds.
> The very air is but her stratagem—
> the air that livens every tree: eternal
> among eternal blooms the sweet fruit lasts,
> for when one is full ripe, another blasts.

~

> co' fiori eterni eterno il frutto dura,
> e mentre spunta l'un, l'altro matura.

> From the same trunk and on the selfsame leaf
> over the new-born fig the fig grows old.
> Both fruits hang from one bough, the new with green,
> the old one with a lucent, aureate rind.
> The twisted vine crawls high in lusciousness,
> and, where the garden is most sunlit, blooms:

among its buds some grape is not yet sweet,
and some, red nectar for the gods to eat.

~

qui l'uva ha in fiori acerba, e qui d'òr l'have
e di piropo, e già di nèttar grave.

~

You would judge (so mingled is negligence with care) both the grounds
and their improvements only natural. It seems an art of nature, that for her
own pleasure playfully imitates her imitator. The very breeze (not to speak
of the rest) is the work of the sorceress, the breeze that causes the trees to
be in flower: with blossoms eternal eternal lasts the fruit, and while the
one buds forth, the other ripens.

On the same tree and among the selfsame foliage, above the nascent fig
the fig grows old: from a single bough hangs down new apple and
matured, the one with golden skin, the other green; luxuriant twines aloft
and fruits the twisted vine where the garden plot is sunniest: here it has
green grapes among its flowers, and here of gold and pyrope, and already
heavy with nectar.

The temporal confusion signified by the impossible botany is a small but telling
instance of Tasso's wild, overheated, and rich imagination.

In his "To Penshurst" (1612), Ben Jonson attempts (as his biographer David
Riggs explains) to replace the actual country house estate of Robert Sidney, Lord
Lisle, with the idealized image of "a self-sufficient agrarian paradise." The poem of 102
heroic couplets "transforms the architectural signifier into a verbal one," and for two
reasons: first, of course, to flatter a potential patron, but also because Jonson genuinely
believed that the traditional aristocratic way of life "represented an alternative to the
fluid, anxiety-ridden world of court politics." An irony of Jonson's literary enterprise
consisted in the deep discontinuity between the medieval founders of Penshurst and
the Sidney family, who had owned the estate for only sixty years—"Lisle's father had
bribed the heralds to fake a genealogy for them in 1568"! But if the architecture Jonson praises in the opening lines ("an ancient pile") was fake Gothic, perhaps at least
the orchards were authentic:

> Then hath thy orchard fruit, thy garden flowers,
> Fresh as the ayre, and new as are the houres.
> The earely cherry, with the later plum,
> Fig, grape, and quince, each in his time doth come:
> The blushing apricot, and wooly peach
> Hang on thy walls, that every child may reach.

A vision of fruit as an element of tranquil, stable country life in early-seventeenth-century England occurs in the ode (published in 1648) by Sir Richard Fanshawe (1608–1666), which is similar ideologically to Jonson's "To Penshurst." Fanshawe's ode was occasioned by the dismissal of Parliament by King Charles I in 1630. (No session of Parliament was called for the next eleven years, but then the so-called Long Parliament remained in session from 1640 until 1660.) In a lengthy series of occasionally enjambed quatrains—thirty-four of them—Fanshawe rather complacently contrasts English peace with Continental strife. Along the way, the "ladies" are assured how much better their lot is in the country than in town. (Elaine Hobby notices, in the essay "The Politics of Gender" [1993], how Fanshawe's allusion to the myth of Philomela—raped by her brother-in-law and then metamorphosed into a nightingale—serves to put women in their place.) The poem concludes, appropriately enough, with the comforting and restorative value of flowers and, in the last two stanzas, of fruit—fruit, indeed, in three different states (fresh, preserved, and converted into emollient):

> Plant Trees you may, and see them shoote
> Up with your Children, to be serv'd
> To your cleane boards, and the fair'st Fruite
>   To be preserv'd:
>
> And learne to use their severall gummes,
> "'Tis innocence in the sweet blood
> Of Cherryes, Apricocks and Plummes
>   To be imbru'd."

The fruit is not climactic but neither is it anticlimactic: it simply completes Fanshawe's encompassing image of the patriarchal state, estate, and family.

Later country-house poems were written by the English poets Thomas Carew (1594?–1640) and Robert Herrick (two each), and Andrew Marvell ("Upon Appleton House"). Marvell's poem of 776 lines is much longer than any of the others, each of which is under 200 lines. More important, "Upon Appleton House" resembles in its structure Netherlandic country-house poems, such as Constantijn Huygens's 2,824–line *Hofwijk* (the name of Huygens's country estate near the Hague); as Peter Davidson explains (in his *TLS* article, "Green Thoughts" [1999]), both poems take the form of "a discursive and conversational walk around an estate." And while there is no definite evidence that Marvell and Huygens ever met, Huygens knew English, and Marvell knew Dutch and visited the Netherlands in the 1640s. Davidson has even found some lines in another poem by Huygens—"Do I sit in a green shade / or in a cool greenness?" ("Batava Tempe," lines 447–48)—that recall Marvell's most famous lines: "Annihilating all that's made / To a green thought in a green shade" ("The Garden," lines 47–48).

As for Marvell's and Huygens's country-house poems—both of which were probably started in 1651—we can pause to consider only one of the significant details they share. First, though, the overall structure of Huygens's actual country estate must be outlined (in Davidson and van der Weel's words; they also provide a reproduction of the plan of Hofwijk included in the first publication of Huygens's poem, in 1653):

> The garden was laid out as an elongated rectangle (125 x 410 m) which was intended to represent the symmetry and proportion of the Vitruvian human figure (most famously represented by Leonardo Da Vinci's well-known drawing of a man simultaneously occupying a square and a circle). . . . The villa, surrounded by a moat, represented the head. An orchard, flanked by avenues of trees, represented the chest and arms; a wooded area represented the legs.

The account of the orchard is amplified by Davidson in the comparison he draws in his *TLS* article between Marvell's and Huygens's poems:

> Marvell's celebrated lines which imagine the garden in military terms, with flowers as artillery, the bee as sentinel, and the garden walls as ramparts find an echo in Huygens's poem where the shelter-belt of poplars are the guard which protects the citizenry of herbs, flowers and fruit trees.

For the orchard flanked by avenues of trees, we now turn to Huygens himself (*Hofwijk,* lines 907–14, translated by Davidson and van der Weel):

> Look up at my white poplars, gaze up to their crests,
> You'll see no split or fissure, not the slightest trace
> Of bending at the onslaught of the fierce south-western wind,
> Or to the spoiling northerly which threatens orchard trees.
> White poplars, old grey folk, old warriors, I said true;
> Well you have guarded us through all the battle's heat,
> Which is the ice-borne wind; you have protected well
> Apples and pears with pikes of timber, shields of leaves:

The seventeenth-century poems we have been considering have begun to depart from the idea of the garden as an earthly paradise, which, as Giamatti sees it, ends with the Renaissance; in the modern period, "real gardens embody man's ideals; actual landscapes animate song, and figure forth the rational principles by which the sane man lives. When the living landscape can reflect what you believe, why invoke the earthly paradise?"

Real gardens can also be—if not full-blown commercial enterprises—a welcome source of income to their owners. Here is an instance of a quite ordinary seventeenth-century fruit garden, which we know about from the letters of a daughter to her father; he is away from home and she writes him (on 24 July and 13 August 1633) just before and just after a devastating summer storm (translated by Dava Sobel):

The lemons that hung in the garden all dropped, the last few remaining ones were sold, and from the 2 *lire* they brought I had three masses said for you, Sire, on my own initiative.

~

The grapes in the vineyard already looked frightfully scarce before two violent hailstorms struck and completed their ruination. A few grapes were gathered in the heat of July before the arrival here of the highway-men, who, not finding anything else to steal, helped themselves to some apples. On the feast day of San Lorenzo there came a terribly destructive storm that raged all around these parts with winds so fierce that they wreaked great havoc . . . knocking over one of those terra-cotta flower pots that held an orange tree. The tree is transplanted in the ground for the time being, until we have word from you as to whether you want another pot purchased to hold it. . . .

The other fruit trees have borne practically nothing; particularly the plums, of which we have not a single specimen; and as for those few pears that were there, they have been harvested by the wind.

The writer is Sister Maria Celeste (1600–1634) of the convent of San Matteo, at Arcetri, just outside Florence, and her father is Galileo Galilei (1564–1642), recuperating at the residence of the archbishop of Siena from the ordeal of his trial and condemnation by the Roman Inquisition. (Galileo's daughter certainly preserved his letters to her, but they were probably destroyed after her death by her mother abbess.)

ORCHARDS IN THE THEATER

Obviously, an orchard or garden cannot be easily presented on stage, but it can be glimpsed through an open window or door, and this may be more effective dramatically than a close-up inspection. The most famous example must be that of *The Cherry Orchard* (1904) by Anton Chekhov (1860–1904). It seems, as Donald Rayfield explains in his biography of Chekhov, that "the image of cherry blossom had recurred in Chekhov's prose for fifteen years. In autumn 1901 he first mentioned it to Stanislavsky as a setting for a future play." Then, in a letter of 5 February 1903 to Stanislavsky, Chekhov writes: "It's already completed in my head. It's called *The Cherry Orchard,* it has four acts and in Act One cherry trees can be seen in bloom through the windows, the whole orchard a mass of white. And ladies in white dresses." In the play, the orchard not only forms the imaginative setting of the entire action, but also serves as a symbol of the old order that is being destroyed by the forces of modernization—though I do *not* mean to suggest that the play is intended as anything like an elegy for that order. And it is totally contrary to Chekhov's intentions to make the merchant Lopakhin into a symbol of the vulgarity and inhumanity of the new order, for in a letter to Stanislavsky of 30 October 1903 Chekhov wrote: "True, Lopakhin is a merchant, but he's a decent person in the full sense of the words and his bearing must be that of a completely dignified and intelligent man."

Here I wish only to gather together the various descriptions of the orchard by different characters in the play. To begin with, in his stage directions for the first act, Chekhov specifies the time as a frosty morning in May with the cherry trees in bloom, and this is confirmed by the clerk, Yepihodov, when he enters, at the very beginning of the act. A little later, Lopakhin remarks that the only thing really remarkable about the cherry orchard is its size (which is confirmed by Gayev's response that the orchard is mentioned in "the encyclopedia," presumably some standard reference work of the time). Lopakhin also notes that there is no one to buy the biannual cherry crop. This leads Firs to reminisce about the wonderful cherry jam and dried cherries that used to be products of the orchard, and, in response to a query from Ranyevskaya, he says that the recipe for the dried cherries is now lost. Later, Gayev opens a window and remarks on the whiteness of the orchard; his sister happily looks out and professes to see her dead mother walking through the orchard in a white dress. Immediately, however, she explains the apparition as simply the appearance of one particular cherry tree bent down under the weight of its blossoms. Each of these allusions to the cherry orchard contributes something vital to the delineation of the characters in the play and of the socio-cultural milieu in which the characters are placed. Thus, Richard Gilman, in his book on Chekhov's plays, notes that the exchange between Ranyevskaya and Firs about the recipe for dried cherries implies "that nobody seems to have maintained the orchard in one of its chief material functions and that consequently it has taken on a purely decorative existence."

After act 1, there are just a few more—but critically important—allusions to the cherry orchard. In act 2, in the second of his lengthy speeches, directed to the seventeen-year-old Anya, Trofimov (a student and one-time tutor of Ranyevskaya's dead little boy) tries to blot out Anya's image of the cherry orchard in favor of a vague conception of all of Russia as an orchard. But, after a pause, Trofimov returns to the image of the cherry orchard, which he uses to condemn Russian serfdom by suggesting that each cherry tree somehow embodies or reminds us of the soul of a suffering serf. Trofimov's image of the cherry trees is fantastic, but it is explained at least in part by Chekhov's dilemma: political censorship prevented him from depicting Trofimov openly as a budding revolutionary. Presumably, that is what lies behind Chekhov's reservations about "a certain sketchy quality in the role of Trofimov, the student . . . [who] is constantly being expelled from the university" (letter of 19 October 1903 to his wife, Olga Knipper). In any case, just after Trofimov's outburst, Varya is heard calling for Anya, and, to escape her, Trofimov and Anya decide to go down to the river. They do not mention the cherry orchard, but if my understanding of the topography is correct, they would have to traverse the orchard—to walk among the cherry trees—to get to the river. We have here, then, a necessary and important extension of the audience's spatial imagination beyond the actual stage set.

The final—only indirect—allusions to the cherry orchard occur in act 4. It is a warm October day, as announced by Lopakhin, who adds that it is good weather for building (thereby reminding everyone within earshot of the imminent fate of the cherry orchard). There is also meteorological irony in the contrast between the unseasonable cold of May in act 1 and the unseasonable warmth of October in act 4. This emphasis on the season of the year may have thematic significance: according to Laurence Senelick, "Chekhov was interested in examining how human beings behave when caught up in an historic process. For him, the passage of time was a natural occurrence, an unalterable law to be accepted, no crueller than the change of seasons." In any case, after the stage has cleared, with only the old servant Firs remaining, the sound of an axe striking a tree is heard in the distance.

The place of the cherry orchard—both physically (on the stage) and conceptually (in the mind of the director)—will go far in determining the character of the production of Chekhov's play. This is well worth thinking about, and much fascinating material on the topic has been assembled by Senelick in his book *The Chekhov Theatre* (1997). Two examples from the history of recent Russian productions of *The Cherry Orchard* will have to suffice by way of illustration. In 1965, Mariya Knebel staged the play at the Soviet Army Theater in Moscow and three years later at the Abbey Theater in Dublin; here is her interpretation of the symbolism of the cherry orchard:

> It seems to me that in this last of his plays Chekhov understood very well what it means to *lose* something infinitely beloved. . . . Each of us has lost and will lose our own "cherry orchard." Each of us is trying to hold on to it. The moment when you lose "the cherry orchard" you think you lose everything. But ahead lies life, a thousand times richer than any loss.

Then, in 1982, Igor Ilinsky staged the play at the Maly Theater in Moscow "in a gaudy, noisy *mise-en-scène*, with enormous flowering trees that grew shorter in each act." Chekhov, of course, specifies in his stage directions for act 1 only that "the cherry trees are in bloom" and "the windows of the room are shut" (in Ronald Hingley's translation), while a photograph of the set for act 1 in the original production of 1904 by the Moscow Art Theater shows some cherry blossoms between the window drapes (see Senelick's book for a reproduction of the photograph).

Just three years after the opening of *The Cherry Orchard*, August Strindberg (1849–1912) wrote a series of four so-called chamber plays designed for production in a tiny performance space in Stockholm seating just 161 people and named the "Intimate Theater." The second of these plays was *The Burned House* (1907), whose opening scene includes the specification: "Back left, the walls of a one-story house gutted by fire; the wallpaper and porcelain stoves still visible. In the distance a fruit orchard in flower." (I cite the Seabury Quinn Jr. translation.) As a dramatic expository device Strindberg uses a police inspector questioning a local resident (a bricklayer). We quickly learn that the fire has occurred the night before. But why were the apple trees not destroyed, asks the inspector. The bricklayer responds: "They're just in bud, and it had rained yesterday. The heat forced the buds into bloom in the middle of the night. Little early, I guess. If we have a frost now, the gardener's in for it." About a third of the way into the first scene the Stranger enters, who turns out to be Arvid Valstrom, the brother of Rudolf Valstrom, the dyer who owns the burned house. Most of the last half of the scene is given over to a conversation between the two brothers, who have not seen each other in thirty years. They reminisce, and, in the longest speech of the scene, Arvid recalls how he was once forced to take the blame for some apples Rudolf had stolen:

> I can see that very apple tree from where I'm sitting. That's what brought
> it back to me. It's still standing over there. The apples were pale gold. If you
> want to look, you'll see the scar of a sawed-off branch. . . . I didn't get
> angry with you, you see, for my unjust punishment, but it happened that
> I did get angry with the tree, and I cursed it. Two years later that huge
> branch died and was sawed off. The story of the fig tree Our Saviour
> cursed came to my mind but I didn't draw any presumptuous conclusions.
> Even today I know all the trees in our orchard by heart. Once when I was
> lying in bed with yellow fever, in Jamaica, I rehearsed the names of every
> one of them. Most of them are still there. I can still see the red-streaked
> apple where the mockingbird nested, and the melon apples outside the
> attic window where I used to study engineering. There's the red fall
> astrakhan, the poplar tree that's like a pyramid, and the preserving pears
> that never got ripe. Mother loved them but they disgusted us. There was
> a wry-necked cuckoo in that old tree . . . she twisted her head around and
> screeched in a horrid voice. . . . That's fifty years ago!

(The "Astrachan Large Fruited," according to Morgan and Richards, was "found 1850s nr Stockholm by E. Lindgren; introduced by him early 1860s"; it is "Large, creamy yellow. Sharp. Cooks to quite sweet purée.") Arvid then recalls something else about the orchard: "I remember once we rented out that garden, but we still had the right to stroll in it. It seemed to me we'd been driven out of paradise and there was the Tempter behind every tree. In the fall, when the apples lay ripe on the ground, I gave in to temptation . . . it was irresistible." So, Arvid was stealing apples in his own garden! Strindberg shows masterful control here in his use of biblical allusions.

In the second (and last) scene, the walls of the burned building have been removed and consequently the orchard is observed in full bloom. This could conceivably be breathtaking for the audience as they see the entire orchard in full bloom for the first time at the opening of the scene. Just how this vision of the orchard was managed in the Intimate Theater is not, however, easy to imagine; as Margery Morgan puts it, in her book on Strindberg (1985): "[the chamber plays'] settings offer problems for a small stage which demand imaginative solutions."

SPATIAL AND TEMPORAL ORDER
IN FRUIT ORCHARDS AND GARDENS

In ordinary English today "orchard" and "grove" generally refer interchangeably to extensive plantings of fruit trees, but there are local variations; thus, John McPhee tells us that "in . . . Florida, citrus plantations are called groves; in California, they are generally called orchards." Gardens, on the other hand, while they may contain trees, and especially fruit trees, usually also contain smaller plants, such as vegetables or flowers. In any case, an orchard, grove, or garden always possesses an artificially imposed order (if only a contrived disorder). In the seventeenth century, one preferred type of order in gardens was geometrical, as illustrated by the nineteen diagrams which make up the anonymous compilation *Certain Excellent and New Invented Knots and Mazes, for Plots for Gardens* (1623).

In his essay "Of Gardens" (1625), Francis Bacon is concerned not so much with the spatial as with the temporal ordering of gardens—what he calls the "royal ordering of gardens" in which "there ought to be gardens for all the months in the year; in which severally [separately] things of beauty may be then in season." To obtain, "for the climate of London," the desired "*ver perpetuum*" (perpetual spring), Bacon lists scores of flower species and their flowering times but also numerous fruit trees, with their flowering and fruiting times. Bacon's monarch could not enjoy an orchard like that of King Alkínoös, with ripe fruit of all kinds available all the time—but, then, London is not Phaiákia!

We have already noted the importance of knowing the flowering time of cherry trees for the interpretation of one of Housman's poems; in another, later, Housman poem flowering time is again important. In "The First of May" (first published in *Last Poems* of 1922) we are asked to imagine an aging narrator on the last day of April, presumably far from Ludlow, site of the next day's county fair; the narrator's theme is "The sumless tale of sorrow"—a line in the last stanza—symbolized by, but also enacted by, this annual civic event. The narrator himself imagines fresh groups of young people each year walking the same roads to the fair, while they think the same thoughts and say the same words as the narrator and his friends, most of them now buried under Ludlow tower. The cycle of futility is underscored by the regular movement of the iambic trimeter verse; there are occasional lines with a missing or an extra syllable, but the prominent terminal lines of each of the four stanzas are all regular.

Just halfway from home to Ludlow are the orchards, always in blossom on the first of May: "The plum broke forth in green / The pear stood high and snowed," while "Between the trees in flower / New friends at fairtime tread." The "trees in flower" are clearly intended to serve as a rebuke to the heedless youth:

> Dressed to the nines and drinking
> And light in heart and limb,
> And each chap thinking
> The fair was held for him.

But why do not those same trees serve as an implicit rebuke to Housman's narrator and his easy moralizing? After all, the orchards do continue to bloom every year. And, indeed, this very fact is appealed to by Jorge Teillier in the poem addressed to his father, "Portrait of My Father, Militant Communist" (1961); the translation is by Carolyne Wright:

> Because his hope has been beautiful
> as cherry trees blooming forever
> at the side of the road,
> I ask that he may live to see the time
> he's always hoped for.

More truly bleak than the cherry blossoms of Housman's "First of May" are those of Edward Thomas's "The Cherry Trees" (written May 1916; first published 1920):

> The cherry trees bend over and are shedding
> On the old road where all that passed are dead,
> Their petals, strewing the grass as for a wedding
> This early May morn when there is none to wed.

Thomas would certainly have known Housman's "Loveliest of trees, the cherry now" though not, of course, "First of May." For Thomas, war and the possibility of becoming a war casualty were real enough in May 1916, almost a year after he had enlisted in the British army; future generations of young men were hardly the point when members of the present generation were being wantonly slaughtered. And Thomas's somber sentiments are echoed in the somber movement of his verse, where the first two lines of fairly regular iambic pentameter (one with a feminine ending) are followed by two less easily scanned lines (one with a feminine ending).

GRAFTING FRUIT TREES

A memorable line (50) in the ninth of Virgil's eclogues (39–38 B.C.E.) is part of a song whose words the youthful Lycidas recalls: "Graft trees, Daphnis. Grandchildren will pick your fruit [insere, Daphni, piros: carpent tua poma nepotes]" (translated by Guy Lee). By Virgil's time, fruit trees had long been grafted to improve the quality and yield of the crop, and so successfully that by the first century C.E. we find Pliny the Elder writing, "Grafting has long since been perfected, since people have tried every possibility— Virgil mentions the grafting of nuts on to an arbutus, apples on to a plane-tree, and cherries on to an elm. Nothing more can be devised—at any rate, it is now a long time since any new variety of fruit has been discovered." Pliny, of course, was simply being complacent in assuming that grafting could no longer yield further improvements in the quality and variety of fruit.

There is another, longer, passage about grafting trees in Virgil's *Georgics* 2.73–82 (29 B.C.E.), but to appreciate its subtleties, it helps to know something about the work as a whole. To begin with, any modern student of the *Georgics* will be reading it with at least an echo of Dryden's striking judgment in mind—"the best work of the best poet"; in other words, no critic today is likely to underestimate the sheer literary skill evident in every aspect of the *Georgics,* from its diction to its overall composition and structure. Then, there is the question of genre. We know the subject matter is farming from the very title—"georgics" is derived from a Greek term meaning "the facts of farming"—and this is confirmed by the opening passage (1.1–5) addressed to Virgil's patron Maecenas (in Smith Palmer Bovie's translation):

> What makes the crops rejoice, beneath what star
> To plough, and when to wed the vines to elms,
> The care of cattle, how to rear a flock,
> How much experience thrifty bees require:
> Of these, Maecenas, I begin to sing.

But as L. P. Wilkinson explains in his "critical survey" of the *Georgics,* "The chief obstacle to appreciation of the *Georgics* has been its ostensible *genre*: it was deceptive and has abundantly deceived. This is no more a didactic poem than Ovid's *Ars Amatoria*: it simply masquerades as such. . . . If the *Georgics* has to be assigned to a *genre,* it is Descriptive Poetry." It would seem to follow that among the criteria for evaluating the poem should *not* be its utility as a manual of agricultural information or advice. On the other hand, Virgil himself "has insisted," as Richard Jenkyns points out in his *Virgil's Experience* (1998), "that he is not writing fiction [non . . . carmine ficto]."

Let us examine what Virgil says about tree grafting, in Jenkyns's straightforward prose translation:

> Nor are the methods of grafting and budding the same. For where the buds push out from the bark and break their fine sheaths, a narrow slit is made right on the knot; here they insert a shoot from an alien tree and teach it to grow into the moist sapwood. Alternatively, knotless trunks are cut back, a path is cleft deep into the core with wedges, and then the fruitful slips are put in. It is not long before a mighty tree has shot up heavenwards with prosperous branches, wondering at its unfamilar leaves and fruits [*poma*] not its own.

To understand this passage properly one should know some elementary facts about grafting procedures, and here the detailed commentary of R. A. B. Mynors (1990) is most helpful. First of all, Mynors explains how Virgil must have been aware of other procedures than the two he describes—budding and what is today called crown-grafting—and, in any case, Virgil "reduces [grafting] to a symmetrical pair of alternatives, of which he represents one (most unfairly) as coarse and clumsy and the other as elegance itself." Following Mynors, Jenkyns spells this out by showing how Virgil's choice of words gives "the impression of careful exactitude" for the budding procedure ("the pathetic fallacy of 'docent' [teach]," for example) and the opposite impression for the crown-grafting procedure (the "rude, rugged business" of the *cuneus* [wedge], for example). Furthermore, Virgil says nothing at all "of the subsequent tying and plastering of the wound," a vital part of both procedures.

How are we to respond to the inaccuracies in Virgil's account of horticultural grafting? Jenkyns apparently wishes us to embrace them as part of Virgil's style: "The contrast between the subtle and the rude kinds of grafting has its own charm." And, Jenkyns adds, "No one will understand or appreciate the *Georgics* who cannot allow the poet this much freedom." I am not sure this settles the question, since everyone who admires the *Georgics*—including, of course, Jenkyns—wishes to ascribe a high degree of accuracy or truth to at least certain portions of the work. In the absence of a satisfactory answer, I am content to note, as a curious feature of the passage, how Virgil concludes his description of horticultural grafting with a bit of literary grafting—specifically, the insertion of a rhetorical flourish that anthropomorphizes the new growth and that, for me, easily justifies all that has gone before. Here are two very different translations of the lines (2.80–82), each impressive in its own way, by John Dryden (1697–98) and C. Day Lewis (1940):

> The battening bastard shoots again and grows;
> And in short space the laden boughs arise,
> With happy fruit advancing to the skies.
> The mother plant admires the leaves unknown
> Of alien trees, and apples not her own.

~

> before long
> That tree ascends to heaven in a wealth of happy branches,
> Surprised at its changeling leaves and the fruits that are not its own.

The exhilarating sense of power that may be associated with the horticultural procedure of grafting is celebrated by Abraham Cowley in the penultimate stanza (10) of "The Garden" (1667):

> We no where Art do so triumphant see
> As when it Grafts or Buds the Tree:
> [. . . . .]
> Who would not joy to see his conqu'ring Hand
> O'er all the Vegetable World command?

> And the wild Giants of the Wood receive
>   What Law he's please'd to give?
> He bids th' ill-natur'd Crab produce
>   The gentler Apple's Winy Juice;
>   The Golden Fruit, that worthy is
>   Of *Galatea's* purple Kiss;
> He does the savage Hawthorn teach
>   To bear the Medlar and the Pear;
>   He bids the rustick Plum to rear
>   A noble Trunk, and be a Peach.
>   Ev'n *Daphne's* Coyness he does mock,
>   And weds the Cherry to her Stock,
>   Tho' she refus'd *Apollo's* suit;
>   Ev'n she, that chaste and Virgin Tree,
>   Now wonders at her self, to see
> That she's a Mother made, and blushes in her Fruit.

Very different are the feelings animating Colette's account of grafting (translated by Matthew Ward):

> The scion, spliced and left to rest and soften in a damp, dark place, then inserted into the slit in the wild or worn-out subject, then dressed with grafting wax, its stump bandaged with cloth and raffia, then adopted by the tree it revives—I can assure the uninformed that a proud pounding of the heart greets the moment when the dormant bud of the scion, which had been sleeping on the foreign stem, wakes, turns green, asserts its paradoxical nature, and enjoins [*sic:* conjoins?] the eglantine with its rose, the plum tree with its peach, its nectarine.

Not joy but a sense of awe, not power but a sense of nurturing, are what Colette seems to be feeling.

Different again is the attitude toward the grafting of fruit trees expressed by Marvell in one of his poems. In "The Mower Against Gardens" (1650–52) Marvell writes a brilliant variation on the traditional topic of art versus nature. Marvell opts for nature and uses horticulture as his source of examples, mentioning, with mild though evident disapproval, pinks "double" bloomed, roses with "strange perfumes," and tulips "taught to paint." Marvell then turns to a more objectionable artifice, the grafting of fruit trees:

> And yet these rarities might be allowed
>   To man, that sovereign thing and proud,
> Had he not dealt between the bark and tree,
>   Forbidden mixtures there to see.

No plant now knew the stock from which it came;
    He grafts upon the wild the tame:
That th' uncertain and adulterate fruit
    Might put the palate in dispute.
His green seraglio has its eunuchs too,
    Lest any tyrant him outdo.
And in the cherry he does nature vex,
    To procreate without a sex.

This poem's forty-line alternation of decasyllable and octasyllable couplets—Marvell's only use of this metrical pattern—was probably stimulated by a poem about seduction with the same pattern and the same art versus nature theme, "Upon Love Fondly Refus'd for Conscience Sake" (first published posthumously), by Thomas Randolph (1605–1635). Unlike Marvell, Randolph defends art against nature and, more specifically, he derives an (ironic?) argument for the legitimacy of adultery from the grafting techniques of gardeners:

If the fresh Trunke have sap enough to give
    That each insertive branch may live;
The Gardner grafts not only Apples there,
    But addes the Warden and the Peare,
The Peach, and Apricock together grow,
    The Cherry, and the Damson too.
Till he hath made by skilfull husbandry
    An intire Orchard of one Tree.
So least our Paradise perfection want,
    We may as well inoculate as plant.

At virtually the same time that Thomas Randolph was writing about a Paradise resulting from the grafting of fruit trees, George Herbert, in "Paradise" (1633), was wittily describing a very different sort of Paradise, a spiritual one, in which pruning rather than grafting is the figured horticultural procedure, and whose results are reflected in the spacing of the words of the poem:

I blesse thee, Lord, because I GROW
Among thy trees, which in a   ROW
To thee both fruit and order   OW.

What open force, or hidden CHARM
Can blast my fruit, or bring me HARM,
While the enclosure is thine   ARM?

Inclose me still for fear I START.
Be to me rather sharp and TART,
Then let me want thy hand & ART.

When thou dost greater judgements SPARE,
And with thy knife but prune and PARE,
Ev'n fruitfull trees more fruitfull ARE.

Such sharpnes shows the sweetest FREND:
Such cuttings rather heal than REND:
And such beginnings touch their END.

Something must be said about the fruit in Andrew Marvell's most famous poem, "The Garden," if only because of the violent differences in interpretation among recent critics. One thing is clear: nothing could be further from the poet's mind than any such practical questions as how to order the plants in a garden or how to graft or prune fruit trees. Marvell's is a garden of the mind—the mind turned in on itself, "annihilating all that's made / To a green thought in a green shade." Some of the components of Marvell's ideal garden are trees (oak, laurel, apple, peach, nectarine), grape vines, melons, a fountain, and a sundial. The fruits are all mentioned in stanza 5:

What wondrous life is this I lead!
Ripe apples drop about my head;
The luscious clusters of the vine
Upon my mouth do crush their wine;
The nectarene, and curious peach,
Into my hands themselves do reach;
Stumbling on melons, as I pass,
Ensnared with flowers, I fall on grass.

(The "melons" in line 7 can hardly be apples—from Greek *melon* [apple]—as Empson suggests, first, because apples have already been mentioned in line 2, and, second, because "stumbling" on apples, rather than the larger melons, is implausible; also, in Marvell's "Bermudas"—already discussed in chapter 15, "Citrus Fruits"—there is a similar reference to "the melons at our feet.") About Marvell's fruit, it seems right to say, with Frank Kermode and Keith Walker, that "the catalogue of readily available fruit is a commonplace with a long history."

The Marvell stanza is quoted in a lecture by Helen Reed, the female protagonist of David Lodge's *Thinks* . . . (2001), in one of the climactic episodes near the end of the novel. Reed, a novelist teaching creative writing for a term at (fictional) Gloucester University, presents the quotation to her audience in the form of an overhead projection (her first use of the technique) during her closing remarks at a three-day academic conference on consciousness (jocularly known as "Con-Con"), in which she is the lone representative of the humanities. Helen has been invited to speak by Lodge's male protagonist, Ralph Messenger, the director of the conference and an internationally known cognitive scientist, who also happens to be Helen's crass but exciting lover. Lodge actually presents the entire text of Reed's fifteen-minute talk, the gist of which is how literature treats the sensuous "qualia" that cognitive science can only understand as, alternatively, "mind events or brain events." Pointing to "a paradox about Marvell's verse," Helen explains:

> Although he speaks in the first person, Marvell does not speak for himself alone. In reading this stanza we enhance our own experience of the qualia of fruit and fruitfulness. We see the fruit, we taste it and smell it and savour it with what has been called "the thrill of recognition" and yet it is not there, it is the virtual reality of fruit, conjured up by the qualia of the poem itself, its subtle and unique combination of sounds and rhythms and mean-ings which I could try to analyse if there were world enough and time, to quote another poem of Marvell's—but there is not.

Helen goes on to quote and explicate the next two stanzas of "The Garden," con-cluding that Marvell's poem suggests an important—even essential—role for literature in a world that Messenger and most of his colleages can see only as an agglomeration of real and virtual machines.

ORCHARDS AND DISCOURSE

It takes a particularly curmudgeonly personality to disapprove of orchards. But in Basil Bunting (1900–1985) we have such a man, who was also a powerful poet. In his *First Book of Odes* (1965), we find successive excoriations of "a Poet who advised me to pre-serve my fragments and false starts" (poem 11), a Lady who questioned Bunting's draw-ing-room attire (poem 12), artists and writers who exploit a new tiger in the zoo (poem 13), and those responsible for a Scottish farmer's displacement from his land (poem 18). We are not entirely unprepared, then, when we read, in the untitled poem 19:

> Fruits breaking the branches,
> sunlight stagnates in the rift;
> here the curl of a comma,
> parenthesis,
>
> (Put the verb out of mind, lurking
> to jar all to a period!)
> discourse interminably
> uncontradicted
>
> level under the orchards'
> livid-drowsy green:

> this that Elysium
> they speak of.

> Where shall I hide?

So, Bunting has added yet another cautionary example to the collection of people and situations he deplores and abhors. But he must be understood, I believe, as wishing to hide, not from orchards, but from those who find in orchards a pretext for endless and uncritical discourse about nature-induced states of bliss. (That Bunting himself finds no reason to refrain from celebratory discourse about nature—he even seems to embrace the so-called pathetic fallacy—is clear from the initial poem, of 1924, in the *First Book of Odes;* this could almost be a rejoinder to some of Housman's poems, such as "The First of May," for we read of weeping oaks, mournful chestnuts, and "sad . . . spring" equated with "everlasting resurrection.") How the subtle play of sounds (rift/ parenthesis, curl/comma, lurking/interminably, period/uncontradicted, level/livid, Elysium/of) interacts with the "meaning" of the orchards is, of course, the right question to ask, no matter the difficulty of answering it. One part of the answer may be that Elysium resides more in such verbal sound patterns than in fancy writing about orchards. The only discussion of Bunting's poem I have found, by the way, addresses itself to the significance of the parenthesis—both the sign and its name, or, rather, the conjunction of the two; this is in John Lennard's remarkable book, *But I Digress: The Exploitation of Parentheses in English Printed Verse* (1991). Lennard suggests that the sentence parenthesized is itself a "measure of stagnation" but at the same time "refutes [its] own imperative" by "including a verb and concluding with an exclamation mark"; the net result is that "Bunting ironizes and deepens the question to which the poem leads."

Bunting's confrontation between discourse and orchard appears also in a poem by Wallace Stevens, "The Reader" (1935), except that the orchard is now a garden and the discourse now takes the material form of a book:

> All night I sat reading a book,
> Sat reading as if in a book
> Of sombre pages.

> It was autumn and falling stars
> Covered the shrivelled forms
> Crouched in the moonlight.

> No lamp was burning as I read,
> A voice was mumbling, "Everything
> Falls back into coldness,

> Even the the musky muscadines,

The melons, the vermilion pears
Of the leafless garden."

The sombre pages bore no print
Except the trace of burning stars
In the frosty heaven.

The time is a moonlit night in autumn—season of falling stars, falling fruit, and falling leaves—and the place is a fruit garden; the "shrivelled forms / Crouched in the moonlight" may be the fallen grapes, melons, and pears. In the middle of all this is the reader, who is not really reading at all—indeed, there is nothing to read because his book contains only "the trace of burning stars / In the frosty heaven." Instead, the reader is contemplating the passage of time in nature as signaled by the changes in the garden and even in the stars. But without "print" things are "sombre" and "frosty": nature requires poetic invocation, if not celebration, for the redemption of autumn. And the apparent redundancy of "musky" as a modifier of "muscadines" (which already connotes musky) may be one way of valorizing sound over meaning (exactly as in Bunting's poem).

Another poet who takes orchards, so to speak, personally is William Carlos Williams, comparing himself, in "Drink" (1916), to a wild tree defending itself against the onslaught of orchards:

My whiskey is
a tough way of life:
The wild cherry
continually pressing back
peach orchards.

ORCHARDS AND THE SEASONS

The seasonal cycle of fruit trees is the leading motif of "End of a Summer" (1955), by the German poet Günter Eich (1907–1972). The poem begins (in Patrick Bridgwater's version) with two stark exclamations: "Who would live without the consolation of the trees! / How good it is that they partake of death!" The poet then turns to those experiences of nature that have provoked his exclamations: the growth of fruit trees ("The peaches have been gathered, the plums are taking on colour") and flights of migrating birds ("Their distances grow visible in the foliage in the form of a dark compulsion, the movement of their wings colours the fruits"). But though the birds "calmly measure off their share of eternity," our human status is less clear: we are offered only an admonition to "have patience" and a hollow-sounding promise that "soon the birds' writing will be deciphered." Perhaps the experience of an endless round of seasons constitutes our own share of eternity—but who is to say the round is truly endless? The ripening fruit may make the waiting easier, and the desired consummation perhaps even unnecessary.

We have now encountered poems about fruit orchards in spring (the blossoms), summer (the ripe fruit), and autumn (the falling fruit). What could a poem about a fruit orchard in winter have as its subject matter? One answer is provided by Richard Wilbur (b. 1921) in "Orchard Trees, January" (1987):

> It's not the case, though some might wish it so
> Who from a window watch the blizzard blow
>
> White riot through their branches vague and stark,
> That they keep snug beneath their pelted bark.
>
> They take affliction in until it jells
> To crystal ice between their frozen cells,
>
> And each of them is inwardly a vault
> Of jewels rigorous and free of fault,
>
> Unglimpsed by us until in May it bears
> A sudden crop of green-pronged solitaires.

The poem depends upon the biological necessity for a certain amount of cold weather to enable certain varieties of fruit trees to blossom (in May), the blossoms being identified with jewels ("solitaires," often diamonds) in metal settings.

ORCHARDS IN ART

In the 1890s, numerous painters in France (including Puvis de Chavannes, Berthe Morisot, Maurice Denis, and the American Theodore Robinson) were working with the theme of women harvesting fruit; an unusually large-scale treatment of this subject was created by Mary Cassatt (1844–1926) for the main exposition hall of the Woman's Building at the World's Columbia Exposition of 1893 in Chicago. The building itself was designed by Sophia Hayden (1868–1953), one of the first professionally trained woman architects in the United States, while two American painters living in France, Mary Cassatt and Mary MacMonnies (1858–1946), were commissioned to paint murals for the two end walls of the main exhibition hall. Despite the vehement opposition of Degas—a close friend and an admirer, who objected to Cassatt's wasting her "infinite talent" on a mere decorative project—Cassatt agreed to paint a triptych called *Modern Woman* (oil on canvas, 14 x 58 ft.) to fit in the south tympanum of the hall. The central part of this triptych, titled *Young Women Plucking the Fruits of Knowledge,* showed ten women of various ages picking apples, pears, and cherries. (MacMonnies did a corresponding triptych called *Primitive Woman* for the north tympanum.) Cassatt spend about half a year on the painting and received a fee of $3,000. In May of 1893 the exposition opened, and when it closed six months later the murals were removed, subsequently disappeared, and have never been recovered. (We know what the painting looked like from contemporary photographs and from some of Cassatt's preparatory studies.) Leading Cassatt specialist Nancy Mowll Mathews provides, in the introduction to her volume *Cassatt: A Retrospective* (1996), the following summary account of the painting and its reception:

> "Modern Woman" [was] painted in brilliant colors in a light-filled outdoor setting. She dressed her models in the latest fashions, but portrayed them plucking fruit as if in a solemn ceremony. The mural was declared a success by Cassatt's associates in Paris and by the more sophisticated critics in Chicago, but to many others it was considered incomprehensible, even "cynical." The negative reactions so far outweighed the positive that a reproduction of the mural in the guide to the fair was eliminated in the second edition. Cassatt seems to have been insulated from the negative reactions; she declined an invitation to Chicago and spent the summer of the fair painting peacefully in the French countryside.

Cassatt, in fact, spent the summer preparing for her first major retrospective exhibition (in Paris, in the fall of 1893), which turned out to be both a critical and commercial success. Two other Cassatt critics, Carolyn Carr and Sally Webster, in their article on the sad fate of the Cassatt and MacMonnies murals, comment on the "radical" significance of Modern Woman: "Cassatt's depiction of women passing the fruits of knowledge from one generation to the next can be seen as a direct assault on traditional religious interpretations of the story of Adam and Eve in the Book of Genesis." (For reproductions of the pertinent visual material, see Mathews's *Cassatt: A Retrospective*, or the catalogue of a major Cassatt exhibition at the Art Institute of Chicago, *Mary Cassatt: Modern Woman*, ed. Judith A. Barter [1998].)

FRUIT,
CONJOINED AND DISJOINED

SPATIALLY CONJOINED FRUITS (CORNUCOPIAS)

Up to this point we have been mostly concerned with literary episodes in which a specific kind of fruit occurs; the fruit may be many or few but they have generally been
all of the same kind. Now, the grammar of nouns or, more deeply, the logical algebra of
classes suggests that different kinds of fruit may be indefinitely *conjoined* or *disjoined*, either
in space or in time (apples and pears and oranges and . . . ; apples or pears or oranges
or . . .). One type of conjunction of different kinds of fruit in space is the cornucopia.
The idea of the "horn of plenty" goes back to Classical mythology. In one version,
Hercules must battle the river god, Achelous, for the hand in marriage of Deianira.
As Ovid tells it (*Metamorphoses* 9.85–92), Achelous changes himself successively into a
snake and a bull; and then (Achelous is speaking; the translation is A. D. Melville's):

> He grasped my strong stiff horn in his fierce hand,
> Broke it, and wrenched it off—my brow was maimed!
> My Naiads filled it full of fragrant flowers
> And fruits, and hallowed it. From my horn now
> Good Plenty finds her wealth and riches flow.

One splendid use of the myth is in depicting the winning of the American West in
Achelous and Hercules (1947), a painting in tempera and oil on canvas (62 ⅞ x 264 ⅛ in.),
by Thomas Hart Benton (1889–1960), in the National Museum of American Art,
Washington, D.C. (For a reproduction, see the museum catalogue edited by Elizabeth
Broun [1995].)

A piling up of fruit of many different kinds occurs in a key scene in chapter 45
of Jane Austen's *Pride and Prejudice* (1813), when Elizabeth Bennet and her aunt, Mrs.
Gardiner, are making their first social visit to Mr. Darcy's great estate at Pemberley. At
the opening of the scene there are no less than six ladies awkwardly trying to make
conversation. The situation is not helped by the fact that the lady serving as hostess is
the shy and slightly inept Georgiana, sister and ward of Mr. Darcy, or that one of the
women, Miss Bingley, is openly hostile to Elizabeth. (The other ladies present are Miss

Bingley's married sister, Mrs. Hurst, and Mrs. Annesley, Georgiana's companion.)
Before any of the gentlemen arrive, there are some embarrassing pauses in conversation among the six far from congenial ladies, until finally food arrives in the form of
"cold meat, cake, and a variety of all the finest fruits in season. . . . There was now
employment for the whole party; for though they could not all talk, they could all eat;
and the beautiful pyramids of grapes, nectarines, and peaches, soon collected them
round the table." Maggie Lane describes the fruit as "hot-house," which seems wrong
if we adopt the usual meaning of "in season." The time of the scene, we know, is summer, and nectarines and peaches do ripen by late July or August. Seasonal grapes are
more problematic, since they tend not to ripen until autumn; so perhaps Austen had
hothouse fruit in mind after all.

Lane draws attention to the probable importance of the above scene in that it
represents "the only mealtime set-piece in any of Jane Austen's novels which is
described straightforwardly by the narrator as impinging on the heroine's consciousness." Lane's explanation of how the scene functions in the novel is complex and
overdetermined. First of all, "the pyramids of fruit are symbolic of the rigid social
pyramid which the love between Elizabeth and Darcy must find the will to topple."
This argument would be more persuasive if the pyramids of fruit had been described
as possessing a hierarchical arrangement of some sort. Second, she says, "In the pyramid of fruits at Pemberley nature and artifice are held in perfect balance: the produce
of nature shaped by man. The shape itself is suggestive of the shape of the novel,
placed as the scene is exactly at the point where Elizabeth's antagonism tips over into
self-acknowledged love. The apex of the pyramid is the fulcrum of the plot." Finally,
Elizabeth "has tasted the fruit of Pemberley . . . fruit is a potent symbol of sexual attraction and love."

In one of the great set pieces in Flaubert's *L'Education sentimentale* (1869) we
again encounter those pyramids of fruit, this time definitely of the hothouse variety.
The occasion is a celebration, at the home of the banker M. Dambreuse, of the defeat
of the June 1848 insurrection in Paris (which makes the early summer day of the banquet too early for most ordinary seasonal fruit). The butler announces dinner, and the
guests are treated to an impressive spread (translated by Robert Baldick):

> Under the green leaves of a pineapple, in the middle of the tablecloth, a
> dolphin lay with its head pointing to a haunch of venison and its tail touch-
> ing a mound of crayfish. Figs, huge cherries, pears, and grapes, all grown in
> Parisian hothouses, were piled in pyramids in baskets of old Dresden china;
> here and there bunches of flowers were interspersed with the gleaming
> silver; the white silk blinds, lowered over the windows, filled the room with
> a soft light; the air was cooled by two fountains containing pieces of ice;
> and tall servants in knee-breeches waited on the guests. All this was the
> more refreshing for the excitement of the past few days. The guests were
> enjoying once more the things which they had been afraid of losing.

656   The congruity between the expensive hothouse fruit and the rest of the luxurious trappings with the victory of the wealthy and privileged classes is almost too obvious to mention, but perhaps one should also consider here Maggie Lane's suggestion that a fruit pyramid may stand for the social pyramid.

The image of the fruit pyramid is invested with quite a different significance in "In the Street of the Fruit Stalls" (1963), by Jon Stallworthy: "Melon, guava, mandarin, / pyramid-piled like cannon-balls, / Glow red-hot, gold-hot, from within" and, again: "melon, guava, mandarin— / the moon compacted to a rind, / the sun in a pitted skin." Instead of the destructive explosiveness of cannon balls, the fruit brings light to the "dark children" who eat it: "They take it, break it open, let / a gold or silver fountain wet / mouth, fingers, cheek, nose, chin."

In Zola's *Le Ventre de Paris* (The belly of Paris; 1874), chapter 5 contains mounds of fruit—some pyramidal—far surpassing anything we have encountered so far. But Zola's fruit is for "the people"—at least, if they can afford to buy it in the then newly built food market of Paris, Les Halles, the site of the action of the novel. In fact, Zola's novel—I follow Vizetelly's translation—is composed of numerous great set pieces on food ("symphonies" is the term some critics have used), one per chapter, in roughly the order of the courses in a French dinner: *charcuterie,* or delicatessen (chap. 1), meat and poultry (chap. 2), fish (chap. 3), vegetables (chap. 4), fruit and cheese (chap. 5), liqueurs and tobacco (chap. 6). The plot of the novel, briefly, revolves about a wild insurrectionary plan of a pork butcher's older brother, Florent, for taking over the city of Paris. For allegedly participating in the resistance to Louis Napoleon's coup d'etat in 1851 (he is actually entirely innocent), Florent had been transported to French Guiana; after seven years of imprisonment, he escapes and returns to Paris, just as the novel begins. He is so hungry he cannot even eat when his sister-in-law offers him food and he never regains his appetite. Working as an assistant to the municipal inspector of fish, Florent begins to see Les Halles as a symbol of what is wrong with society: "Those colossal markets and their teeming odoriferous masses of food had hastened the crisis. To Florent they appeared symbolical of some glutted, digesting beast, of Paris, wallowing in its fat and silently upholding the Empire." Florent's scrawniness and lack of interest in eating fuel his revolutionary ideology:

> Believing in a call to avenge his leanness upon the city which wallowed in food while the upholders of right and equity were racked by hunger in exile, he took upon himself the duties of a justiciary, and dreamt of rising up, even in the midst of those markets, to sweep away the reign of gluttony and drunkenness.

In the end, Florent is informed on by his stout, prosperous sister-in-law; he is re-arrested and once more sentenced to transportation.

In terms of sheer diversity the most extensive aggregations of food Zola shows us in *The Belly of Paris* are the twenty kinds of cheese and the thirty kinds of fruit (three

varieties of melons, two of peaches and apricots, three of cherries, seven of apples, five   657
of pears, three of plums and currants, wild and garden strawberries, and raspberries).
There is a partial visual equivalent of Zola's conjunction of fruits in the oil painting
(30⅛ x 39⅜ in.) by Gustave Caillebote (1848–1894) in the Boston Museum of Fine
Arts, *Nature morte* (1880–82), which depicts some eleven varieties of fruit. As Kirk
Varnedoe explains, "the image is at once a random slice of commercial presentation,
seen every day in Parisian fruit-stands, and a highly ordered structure" (see plate 32).

Zola's description of the fruit constitutes much more than a mere list. To begin
with, the fruit seller, La Sarriette ("the tasty one"), is herself characterized in terms of
a series of fruit-derived metaphors: vine branches (the disarray of her hair), peaches
and cherries (the color of her arms and neck), plums (the perfume of her gown), and
strawberries (the odor of her kerchief). Furthermore, she has hung some black cherries on her ears and she is eating red currants. There follows a page and a half of passages "humanizing" the appearance of the fruit. Here is a sample:

> Piles of apples and pears, built up with architectural symmetry, often in
> pyramids, displayed the ruddy glow of budding breasts and the gleaming
> sheen of shoulders, quite a show of nudity, lurking modestly behind a
> screen of fern leaves.

After the color and shape of the fruit comes the odor:

> La Sarriette lived in an orchard, as it were, in an atmosphere of sweet, intox-
> icating scents. The cheaper fruits—the cherries, plums, and strawberries—
> were piled up in front of her in paper-lined baskets, and the juice oozing
> from their bruised ripeness stained the stall front and steamed, with a
> strong perfume, in the heat. She would feel quite giddy on those blazing
> July afternoons when the melons enveloped her with a powerful, vaporous
> odor of musk.

But if La Sarriette and her fruit are one, the same is true of her neighbor, another fruit
seller—"an old woman, a hideous old drunkard, [who] displayed nothing but wrinkled apples, pears as flabby as herself, and cadaverous apricots of a witch-like sallow-
ness." Not everyone is as enchanted as La Sarriette is with her fruit; the character
Monsieur Jules, for example, tells her that the intense scent of her new shipment of
mirabelle plums gives him a headache.

Among the most curious of sixteenth-century paintings are those by the
Milanese painter, Giuseppe Arcimboldo (1527–1593), consisting of human heads composed of various botanical elements. Thus, two of his four personified seasons—
Summer and *Autumn*—are largely composed of fruit: the cheek of *Summer,* for example, is a rosy apple, and the nose of *Autumn* is a ripe pear. (There are four versions of
Summer and two of *Autumn,* the originals dating to 1563 and copies to 1572–73; the
paintings are oil on canvas or wood, approximately 2½ x 2 ft. For reproductions, see

658   Werner Kriegeskorte, *Giuseppe Arcimboldo* [1988], or Diana Craig, *The Life and Works of Arcimboldo* [1996].) Arcimboldo's masterpiece in this genre, though, is his *Vertumnus* (1590–91), the Roman god of vegetation. (The painting, oil on wood, 3 x 2 ft., is presently in a Swedish gallery; for a reproduction, see Kriegeskorte or Craig.) Like many of Arcimboldo's paintings, this one was made for Rudolph II and it is, in fact, a likeness of the emperor, whom the artist served in other capacities as well (engineer, costume designer). Arcimboldo's good friend, Gregorio Comanini, wrote a long poem (over two hundred lines) about the *Vertumnus,* translated in the English edition of Kriegeskorte's book, from which some of the lines about fruit may be quoted:

> Grapes are hanging from my temples,
> Softly contoured, warmly painted,
> Gently stroked by rays of sunshine,
> By the sun's great brush conceived,
> Painted red and painted yellow,
>   [. . . . .]
> By the river, at the spring,
> Then the melon will refresh us,
>   [. . . . .]
> With its tough and wrinkled skin,
> It produces wrinkles on my
> Forehead . . .
>   [. . . . .]
> Behold the apple and the peach:
> See how my two cheeks are formed,
> Round and full of life.
> Also have a good look at my eyes,
> Cherry-coloured one and mulberry the other
>   [. . . . .]
> Also, friend, I beg you, take
> Notice of this fig which ripened,
> Then burst open and now dangles
> From my ear

For some reason, the enormous pear nose and the cherry lips are omitted.

These paintings by Arcimboldo may remind one of some dialogue from an early scene (1.2.12ff.) in Ben Jonson's *Bartholomew Fair* (first performed in 1614). At Littlewit's urging, Winwife has just kissed Littlewit's wife, Win; boasting about his wife, Littlewit comments, "I envy no man my delicates, sir," to which Winwife replies, "Alas, you ha' the garden where they grow still! A wife here with a strawberry-breath, cherry-lips, apricot-cheeks, and a soft velvet head, like a melicotton." (A "melicotton" is a cross between a peach and a quince, and Winwife is here referring to the hat Win is wearing.)

Winwife is courting Win's widowed mother, which leads him to comment: "But my taste, Master Littlewit, tends to fruit of a later kind: the sober matron, your wife's mother." These are the earliest references to food in a play loaded with—even built up out of—alimentary episodes; one strand of the plot, for instance, hinges on the pregnant Win's feigned desire for some of the roast pig sold by a central character, Ursula the pig-woman. It is worth mentioning also that one of the (extremely minor) characters in the play is a costermonger whose main stock in trade seems to be pears; in one episode (4.2.28), he is tripped up by the ballad singer Nightingale and the pears spill out of his basket, which distracts the foolish Bartholomew Cokes (previously characterized as "a ravener after fruit," at 1.5.109) long enough for Nightingale and his confederate the cutpurse Edgworth to make off with Cokes's hat and cloak. (A "costard," incidentally, is a variety of apple, but by Jonson's time costermongers peddled an assortment of fruits and vegetables.)

Sidewalk fruit sellers in Padua (*Padova*) are the subject of James Wright's prose poem, "The Fruits of the Season" (1977), which begins: "It is a fresh morning of late August in Padova. After the night's rain, the sun is emerging just enough so far to begin warming the grapes, melons, peaches, nectarines, and the other fruits that will soon fill this vast square." The transience of the fruit is contrasted with the staying power of another kind of fruit in "a huge exhibit of paintings, the enduring fruits of five hundred years." But the poet defiantly proclaims in conclusion that the real fruit "will last long enough. I would rather live my life than not live it. The grapes in a smallish stall are as huge and purple as smoke. I have just eaten one. I have eaten the first fruit of the season, and I am in love." Perhaps such a slight poem should be as transient as the momentary pleasure of eating a grape.

A fashionable Dublin fruiterer, Thornton's, is the setting for an episode in the ninth section of the tenth chapter ("Wandering Rocks") of Joyce's *Ulysses,* where we find Blazes Boylan, Molly Bloom's theatrical manager, sending her a basket of assorted fruit as a first step in his planned seduction. But the artfully arranged fruits in the shop have a powerful aphrodisiacal effect on Boylan himself, as the blond girl clerk "bestowed fat pears neatly, head by tail, and among them ripe shamefaced peaches," while Boylan "walked here and there in new tan shoes about the fruitsmelling shop, lifting fruits, young juicy crinkled and plump red tomatoes, sniffing smells." Boylan also notices someone outside the shop examining books for sale from a hawker; this turns out to be Bloom, also looking for a gift for Molly in the form of a pornographic novel. Boylan continues to flirt with the clerk as she "reckoned again fat pears and blushing peaches." The brief episode makes its own contribution to what Clive Hart refers to, in his analysis of this chapter of *Ulysses,* as "Joyce's most direct, most complete celebration of Dublin, demonstrating succinctly his conception of the importance of physical reality, meticulously documented, as the soil from which fictions may best grow."

A more overt sexual encounter, late at night in the produce department of a nearly empty American supermarket, opens a novel of the soft-porn genre, *Eat Me*

(1997), by Linda Jaivin (b. 1955). Here the heroine is an excitable young women, who masturbates with a selection of the fruits on display (including figs, strawberries, grapes, kiwifruit, and bananas) and eats the resulting pulp; she then forces a leering security guard to "eat" her, while she penetrates him from behind with a handy cucumber. We learn in the second chapter that this entire episode is the first chapter of a novel being written by Phillipa, one of four women friends who are the protagonists of Jaivin's novel. On the other hand, Molly Bloom's erotic fantasies, in her soliloquy that concludes *Ulysses,* extend only to a banana, and at that she is "afraid it might break and get lost up in me somewhere."

A so to speak *miniaturized* cornucopian vision of fruit is depicted in the youthful poem "Satirical Opus" (1901), by Paul Klee (1879–1940), translated by Harriett Watts and followed by the German text:

> The happy man, a half idiot,
> for whom everything flourishes
> and bears fruit.
> Standing on his little acre,
> one hand clasps the watering can,
> the other points at himself,
> the navel of the world.
>
> Everything blossoms and thrives,
> fruit-laden branches bend down upon him.

~

> Der Glückliche, das ist ein halber Idiot,
> dem alles gedeiht und Früchte trägt.
> Steht auf seinem kleinem Besitz,
> die eine Hand hält die Giesskanne,
> die andere zeigt auf sich selber,
> als den Nabel der Welt.
>
> Es grünt und blüht.
> Von Früchten schwere Zweige neigen sich auf ihn.

This could almost be a description of one of Klee's paintings, or a recipe for such a painting.

An exuberant cornucopian vision of fruit shadowed by the realities of inevitable decay in all living things may be found in "This Compost" (1856; 1881), by Walt Whitman (1819–1892). In the first section of the poem, Whitman worries about the way the earth is being polluted by the continual burial of human carcasses, "those drunkards and gluttons of so many generations." The second, and longer, section celebrates triumphantly and yet reverently the transformation of foul and decayed matter into compost and thence into the fresh life of plants and animals:

What chemistry!   *661*

    [. . . . .]

That blackberries are so flavorous and juicy,

That the fruits of the apple-orchard and the orange-orchard, that

    melons, grapes, peaches, plums, will none of them poison me,

That when I recline on the grass I do not catch any disease,

Though probably every spear of grass rises out of what was once

    a catching disease.

An even more passionate, indeed ecstatic, invocation of fruit is central to the theme of a religious sonnet, "Concerning the Fruit-bringing Autumn Season" (1662), by the Austrian poet Catharina Regina von Greiffenberg (1633–1694). Greiffenberg believed, Gerald Gillespie tells us, in "Austria's manifest destiny to reunite Christendom," by means of her poetry as well as by direct intervention of the Hapsburg emperor. She had trouble with the authorities of her own Reformed faith when she decided to marry her father's half brother and was accused of incest. It is amusing to note that one of the leading German literary associations of Greiffenberg's time— which, like all such associations, barred female members—was called the *Fruchtbringende Gesellschaft* (Fruitbearing Society). The baroque hypertrophy of vocabulary, with its fertile invention of composite words, is illustrated in the very first line of Greiffenberg's sonnet (translated by George Schoolfield):

Freud'-erfüller/Früchte-bringer/vielbeglückter Jahres-Koch/

        ~

Glee-fulfiller, fruit-producer, cook who glad the year can feed

A fruit cornucopia makes its appearance—"Shake from out your copious horn [*reichen Horn*] highly hoped rejoicing's fruit"—at the beginning of the sestet, which concludes with the couplet:

Lass die Anlas-Kerne schwarz Schickungs-Aepffel safftig werden:

    dass man Gottes Gnaden-Frücht froh geniest und isst auf Erden.

I take *Anlas-Kerne* (literally, "causal-kernels") to be apple pips, and translate the lines as follows: "May the black causal-kernels become juicy fate-apples: / That God's gracious fruit be happily savored and eaten on Earth."

A spilled cornucopia with fruit rolling in all directions is the central image of Gabriela Mistral's "Fruit," from her collection of children's poems, *Tenderness*. The poem is addressed to an infant (by a poet who adopted her nephew but otherwise never had any children of her own). In Giachetti's translation, here are the third and fifth of the five brief stanzas:

Crawling, you pursue the fruits

as though they were little girls,

scattering in all directions:

> melting loquats
> and hard, tattooed pineapples . . .
> [. . . . .]
> Touch them, kiss them, whirl them,
> and learn their faces.
> Dream, child, that your mother
> has ripened features;
> the night is a black basket
> and that the Milky Way is an orchard.

Finally, one of Philip Roth's earliest publications, the long story *Goodbye, Columbus* (1957) contains a memorable variant of the cornucopia motif. The story has to do with the tensions arising in the brief summer romance between Neil Klugman and Brenda Patimkin, each born in Newark, New Jersey, to middle-class Jewish parents. Neil, a twenty-three-year-old graduate of the Newark branch of Rutgers University and a philosophy major, still lives with his family and is currently employed in the Newark Public Library. Brenda lives with her family in Short Hills, a suburb of Newark some distance up, both topographically and socially, from Newark, and is currently a student at Radcliffe. Fruit occurs prominently in the first seven of the eight sections of the story: (1) Neil's favorite dessert is fruit; (2) under the twin oak trees outside the Patimkin home the family's assorted athletic equipment looks like fruit that has dropped from the branches; (3) Neil surreptitiously discovers in the basement of the Patimkin home an old refrigerator full of fruit; (4) Neil and Brenda gorge themselves on the fruit from that refrigerator, Neil eventually suffering an upset stomach; (5) after each consuming a grapefruit, Neil and Brenda run timed laps before breakfast; (6) while eating a handful of grapes alone one afternoon, Neil has a premonition of the imminent breakup of the affair when Brenda returns to college; (7) while waiting on Fifth Avenue in Manhattan for Brenda to be fitted with a diaphragm, Neil muses (in St. Patrick's Cathedral) as to which features of his new "wedded" life might meet with divine approval (he concludes that God must approve of everything "gold dinnerware, sporting-goods trees, nectarines, garbage disposals, bumpless noses, Patimkin Sink, Bonwit Teller"). Soon thereafter, a real wedding (of Brenda's brother) ends, depressingly for Neil, with the spectacle of drunken guests and congealed left-over cherry jubilee (the only particularized food mentioned in Roth's account of the wedding, and prepared, of course, from dried—juiceless—cherries). The eighth section of the story, which is free of fruit imagery, is dominated by Brenda's mother's discovery of the diaphragm, and the inevitable end of the love affair. The (almost) carefree idyll of shared juicy fruits drawn from the cornucopic refrigerator of the upwardly mobile Patimkin family has been overwhelmed by the demanding and threatening Patimkin ethos—encapsulated in their demonizing of the diaphragm—which has no place for someone like Neil. The diaphragm, incidentally, which has been exalted by Neil as a symbolic wedding ring, may also be seen as just another piece of "sporting-goods,"

as in the characterization of the couple's awkward initial post-diaphragm sex as resembling a "lousy double-play combination."

Roth's description of the fruit refrigerator is worth quoting in full:

> I opened the door of the old refrigerator; it was not empty. No longer did
> it hold butter, eggs, herring in cream sauce, ginger ale, tuna fish salad,
> an occasional corsage—rather it was heaped with fruit, shelves swelled
> with it, every color, every texture, and hidden within, every kind of pit.
> There were greengage plums, black plums, red plums, apricots, nectarines,
> peaches, long horns of grapes, black, yellow, red, and cherries, cherries
> flowing out of boxes and staining everything scarlet. And there were
> melons—cantaloupes and honeydews—and on the top shelf, half a huge
> watermelon, a thin sheet of wax paper clinging to its bare red face like a
> wet lip. Oh Patimkin! Fruit grew in their refrigerator and sporting goods
> dropped from their trees!

Citrus fruit—consumed primarily at breakfast—is presumably stored in the kitchen
refrigerator. Another common fruit missing from the contents of the cornucopia is
bananas, which are usually not refrigerated but which are also a non-juicy fruit.

FRUIT STILL LIFES—PAINTED, SCULPTED, PHOTOGRAPHED

Visual arrangements of fruit in the form of pure still life paintings are often thought
of as beginning, in post-Renaissance Europe, with Caravaggio's somewhat mysterious
Basket of Fruit, probably commissioned by Archbishop Federico Borromeo in Rome
shortly after 1597. (Slightly earlier and considerably more conventional paintings of
fruit—in Hartford and Rome—have also been ascribed, though controversially, to
Caravaggio; for reproductions of all these paintings, see *The Age of Caravaggio* [1985]
or Giorgio Bonsanti's *Caravaggio* [1991].) We know that Borromeo was enthralled
with the richness and infinite variety of the divine creation evoked in some slightly
later still life paintings of flowers by Jan Brueghel the Elder, but Caravaggio's picture
(oil on canvas, 12 ³⁄₁₆ x 18 ½ in., Pinacoteca Ambrosiana, Milan) is rather different. For
one thing, it contains only a few pieces of quite ordinary-looking fruit, and none of
that "disguised symbolism" (in Erwin Panofsky's phrase) such that "every ordinary
plant, architectural detail, implement, or piece of furniture could be conceived as a
metaphor." (Insects and other small animals should certainly be added to Panofsky's list.)
It is true that some of Caravaggio's fruits—there are grapes, apples, figs, a pear, and a
quince—contain blemishes and worm holes, but somehow even these are not evocative
of the transitoriness and vanity of human life—that favorite theme of seventeenth-
century Dutch still life painting. I should report, though, that a biographer of Federico
Borromeo thinks otherwise; Pamela Jones writes that "Caravaggio's vigorous still life,
cut off from any context and lit independently from its pale, flat background, must have
appealed to Borromeo as a discrete vision of meditational prayer. Moreover, Archbishop

664   Federico presumably interpreted the worm-eaten fruit and desiccated leaves in the basket as allusions to the transitory character of God's earthly gifts."

Nor does Caravaggio's picture seem to be simply an exercise in the realistic representation of material objects; rather, as Helen Langdon puts it, "the immediate appearance of realism is comprehensively interpenetrated by ambiguities, which have the effect of checking and blocking many ways of responding to the painting before, as it were, they have had time to gather momentum. Nothing is quite what it seems." Some of the peculiarities of the picture are its uniform gold background, the fact that most objects cast no shadows, and, in Langdon's words, "the astonishing virtuoso rendition of water drops that rest on the fruit and leaves and yet simultaneously appear to have been scattered on the surface of the painting." An analogous virtuosity was exhibited in other media, such as the luxurious inlaid semiprecious stones, that were a specialty of the Medici workshop in Florence. A rare example of this technique, taking the form of a tabletop and dating from the first quarter of the seventeenth century, is located in the Castle of Rosenborg, Denmark. In the colored reproduction found in a catalogue of the Medici collection one can easily make out, besides the flowers and birds, apples, pears, grapes, cherries, plums, and peaches (see *The Treasures of Florence* [1997], edited by Cristina Acidini Luchinat).

To sum up, since Caravaggio's time—and especially in the nineteenth and twentieth centuries—there may not have been any more popular subject for painters than the pure still life of—or prominently featuring—fruit. (And, as we have just seen, not only painted canvas was being employed to depict fruit but other media as well, eventually including ceramics, fabrics, wallpaper, and photographs.) Fruit still life paintings, of course, continue to be produced today in depressingly large numbers and at every conceivable level of skill—by professionals, Sunday painters, folk artists, outsiders. All this has moved one contemporary art critic, Martin Gayford, to deplore "the reputation still life has had, early and late, as something essentially frivolous. Even these days, many artists and dealers talk of pictures of fruit as suspiciously saleable. . . . Ergo, these images of eatables on tables must represent rather an undemanding source of visual gratification." (Literary still lifes of fruit, on the other hand, seem to be quite rare; a few will be discussed in the next section.)

One way of countering the low reputation of the fruit still life is to satirize the very motif itself. An effective satire of this kind comes from a most unlikely source, a self-taught American folk artist named Henry Church (1836–1908), from Chagrin Falls in northern Ohio. Church learned blacksmithing from his father, but he was self-taught in sculpture and painting; he was also a musician, constructing his own harp and bass fiddle. Probably Church's most impressive piece of art is the ensemble of high-relief sculptures carved into a massive fallen cliff called Squaw Rock, some twelve miles outside Cleveland. Church chiselled his name and the date 1885 into the rock, which was intended to be part of a sanctuary on the theme "The Rape of the Indian Tribes by the White Man." When the partially completed project was discovered, Church ceased working on it, but Squaw Rock is now a popular tourist attraction in the Cleveland area.

Church built a small museum, in 1888, to exhibit his paintings; he charged admission but never succeeded in selling any. Most of his paintings were burned by his daughter when she moved to a smaller house; fortunately, a few of the best survived, including *Still Life* and *The Monkey Picture* (both ca. 1895–1900). The former painting (oil on canvas, 26 x 38 in.) belongs to Church's granddaughter; the latter (oil on canvas, 28 x 44 in.) is in the Abby Aldrich Rockefeller Folk Art Center, Williamsburg, Virginia. (For reproductions, see Sam Rosenberg's essay on Church in *American Folk Painters of Three Centuries* [1980], or *Self-Taught Artists of the Twentieth Century* [1998].) *Still Life* shows a pretty traditional spread of fruit across a tabletop: at the center a large segment of watermelon, two glass compotes (peaches, cherries, and purple plums in one, raspberies in another), lemons, strawberries, green plums, purple and yellow grapes, a pineapple, a pear, an apple, four bananas, and—the only nonfruits—a glass compote of cookies, a pitcher and glass of lemonade. (With the exception of the bananas and pineapple, all of these fruits were presumably readily available in Ohio in the late nineteenth century.) *The Monkey Picture* is closely similar to *Still Life,* with, however, the bananas replaced by an opened canteloupe on which is inscribed "II. Church, Pixt.—Painter" (and the painting is also signed at the bottom: "H. Church—Painter—Blacksmith"). The fruit, however, is now scattered and fallen to the floor, the compotes and pitcher are overturned, and a gesticulating policeman may be seen in the backgound. The agents responsible for the havoc are two monkeys, evidently escaped from a cage just visible near the policeman, and now cavorting wildly on the table (the monkey on the left is pulling the tail of its companion, which is eating a banana). Sidney Janis interprets the painting as an example of Church's subversiveness:

> It does not require great imagination to believe that one of the reasons Church painted *The Monkey Picture* was to ridicule the abundance of staid Victorian fruit still lifes that found their way even to remote sections of the country at the time colored lithography was first in flower.
>
> With great disrespect and no little glee, he has literally turned the tables. The prize fruits assembled here in all their glorious colors, their bloom and lusciousness, are deliberately scattered, trampled upon and tumbled in all directions. Withal, thay are tenderly treated as they remain uncrushed in the melee.

One other painting by Church should not be missed: a superb oval-shaped allegorical self-portrait, ca. 1880 (oil on composition board, 29¾ x 23½ in.), now owned by the Joan T. Washburn Gallery, New York. The half-length figure of Church is backed by angels (the muses of painting, music, sculpture, and blacksmithing) and lying before him are three large peaches and a pear, as well as a fruit knife and some roses. (For a reproduction, see *American Folk Painters of Three Centuries* or *Self-Taught Artists of the Twentieth Century.*)

666   Possible directions for revitalizing fruit still life painting may be found in works by two relatively neglected modern masters and, improbably, in works of the 1980s by an acclaimed figurative sculptor: a stylistically late work by André Derain (1880–1954), a stylistically transitional work by Hans Hofmann (1880–1966), and five low reliefs by George Segal (1924–2000). Derain's still life of 1939, now in the Santa Barbara Museum of Art, *Nature morte au potiron* (Still life with pumpkin; oil on canvas, 40¾ x 52¾ in.), features especially pears in addition to the title fruit. The artist uses his post-Fauvist palette of browns, grays, ochers, and greens, plus what John Ashbery calls "a rich, limpid lampblack [which] became his signature." The color scheme, Ashbery finds, in a review originally titled "France's Forgotten Man" (1980), "for all its reserve . . . is endlessly evocative: of distances, volumes, atmosphere and above all of some secret relation among the intrinsic natures of things." (For a reproduction of the painting, see Gaston Diehl, *Derain* [1977] or the catalogue of a major Derain retrospective in Paris in 1994, *André Derain: Le peintre du "trouble moderne."*)

As for Hofmann, his *Fruit Bowl* (1950) represents a transition from cubism to his final wholly abstract style, for, as William Seitz reminds us, "the formative period of Hofmann's development . . . was in the milieu of early cubism." In the painting (oil on canvas, 29⅞ x 38 in.), now in the Sheldon Memorial Art Gallery, Lincoln, Nebraska, the bowl and its fruit—set against a black rectangle in the upper-left corner—are delineated by means of thin black lines tracing geometric shapes. The remainder of the painting consists mostly of large overlapping polygonal shapes of uniform color (yellow, red, green). What John Russell remarks of a stylistically similar painting—an interior with still life—of the same period, *Magenta and Blue* (1950), applies equally to *Fruit Bowl,* namely, that it "looks back to the classic French interiors which Matisse for one had brought to perfection; but it also looks forward to the day when Hofmann would be able to structure his paintings in terms of large flat rectangles of pure color." (For a reproduction of *Fruit Bowl,* see *Art What Thou Eat* [1991].)

Finally, there is George Segal's Cézanne-apples series, each of which is a low-relief painted plaster rendition of a Cézanne painting—the first entirely nonfigural sculptures in Segal's mature oeuvre. Segal explained to the interviewer Marla Price (in 1988) how the idea of transforming Cézanne's paintings of apple still lifes into three dimensional sculptures

> goes back to Meyer Schapiro's lectures, where Cézanne was advertised to be this inventor of planes and the father of Cubism. And the wall on which the painting hung was the back wall of the painting and all the planes advanced forward, so that any analysis of a Cézanne painting involved a succession of planes that marched forward from that wall. So that almost demanded, logically, working in a relief style. . . . And I was literally constructing plywood planes. They looked quite abstract before I painted them and put a cloth on them and plaster casts of fruit.

About the fruit itself Segal adds, "I constructed a sloping plane. Then I had to cast fruit
and go to the supermarket and buy perfect fruit. Each fruit had to have a different
shape and then I had to make a cast of it." Pictures of the first four sculptures, along
with Marla Price's interview, may be found in her *George Segal: Still Lifes and Related
Works* (1990), and pictures of all five sculptures in Sam Hunter and Don Hawthorne's
George Segal (1984).

A few unusual comic visual cornucopias are worth mentioning. First, there is
"The Lady in the Tutti-Frutti Hat" scene in the technicolor film by Busby Berkeley
(1895–1976), *The Gang's All Here* (1943), featuring Carmen Miranda with her cornucopian headdress (for a black and white still, see Tony Thomas and Jim Terry with
Busby Berkeley, *The Busby Berkeley Book* [1973], or Martin Rubin, *Showstoppers: Busby
Berkeley and the Tradition of Spectacle* [1993]). Then, there is Alexis Smith's vision of a
cornucopian hat in a mixed-media collage (21¼ x 16 in.) called *Tokyo Rose* (1982); the
torso and head of the cartoonlike figure consist of a peeled banana, with the words
"Sometimes men went crazy from the heat" printed over her skirt. Finally, there is the
marvelous drawing of a snail shell as the horn of a cornucopia (1968), one of some
thirty variations by Ronald Searle on the snail theme (see Searle, *The Square Egg*
[1968]).

FRUIT STILL LIFES IN LITERATURE

Of particular interest are two poems specifically about fruit arrangements of the type
usually found in still life paintings. "Still Lifes—I" was written by the Yiddish poet
Reuben Iceland (1884–1955); the translation is by Etta Blum:

> Like cool ample breasts
> hiding a secret ardor,
> the heavy grapes lie near
> the brown virile pears.
> Consumed by redness,
> two apples with brazen femininity
> nestle close to a glistening,
> ripe-with-wisdom orange.
> A pair of bananas gape like clumsy yokels.
> Eagerly,
> like a girl after her first kiss,
> a cherry breaks away from its red stem.

The humorous twist here, of course, is that tenor and vehicle are being reversed from
the usual direction of fruit/human metaphors—breasts, for example, are not like grapes
but grapes are like breasts—thereby serving to endow the different pieces of fruit with
human traits.

668   Our second poetic still life of fruit, by Eavan Boland, constitutes the penultimate
poem in an eleven-poem sequence called *Domestic Interior* (1982). Unlike "Fruit on a
Straight-Sided Tray," the other ten poems are intimately concerned with infancy—
teddy bears, nappies, and maternal milk being prominently featured; also, in the fruit
still life poem the short, one- to five-word lines of the other ten poems are replaced
with mostly eight- to nine-word lines, while retaining the occasional rhymes of the
other poems. The "true subject" of the fruit still life poem is "the geometry of the visible," though at the very end, almost as an afterthought, an analogy with the mother-
child relationship appears:

> When the painter takes the straight-sided tray
> and arranges late melons with grapes and lemons,
> the true subject is the space between them,
>
> in which repose the pleasure of these ovals
> is seen to be an assembly of possibilities;
> a deliberate collection of cross purposes.
>
> Gross blues and purples. Yellow and the shadow of bloom.
> The room smells of metal polish. The afternoon sun
> brings light but not heat and no distraction from
>
> the study of absences, the science of relationships
> on which the abstraction is made actual: such as
> fruit on a straight-sided tray; a homely arrangement.
>
> This is the geometry of the visible, physical tryst
> between substances, disguising for a while the equation
> that kills: you are my child and between us are
>
> spaces. Distances. Growing to infinities.

A more extended appearance of literary fruit still life occurs in A. S. Byatt's *Still
Life* (1985). To begin to understand the role of still life in this novel—which was followed by the third in a tetralogy, *Babel Tower,* discussed in chapter 12, "Pomegranates"
—one must note Byatt's reflections in the novel itself on her own literary intentions.
Thus, the author tells us at one point that she would have liked to have "written . . .
without, as far as possible, recourse to simile or metaphor." And repeatedly throughout the novel, Byatt draws explicit analogies of literature with painting (often quoting at length from Vincent van Gogh's letters). On the other hand, Byatt recognizes
that a literal, purely descriptive style is impossible even in painting: "As Vincent Van
Gogh said, in our world, olive trees may stand for themselves, maybe must stand for

themselves, and so with cypresses, sunflowers, corn, human flesh. (Though he could not divest any of these of the cultural metaphors that come close and intrinsic as their shadows, replacing, as he almost said, the old halo)." Instead, Byatt has recourse to two different literary strategies in her approach to still life: she has her characters discuss particular still life paintings, and she constructs fictional episodes in which "communication . . . [is] centered in, conducted through, things." I cite an episode of each type in which fruit figures prominently.

Still Life is set in the England of the 1950s (just as *Babel Tower* is set in the England of the 1960s), but there is a prologue called "Post-Impressionism: Royal Academy of Arts, London, 1980." This section refers to an actual exhibition, which opened in the fall of 1979. Present in the prologue are three of the main characters of the novel: Frederica, her widowed brother-in-law Daniel, and her old friend Alexander Wedderburn, who has written *The Yellow Chair,* a play about van Gogh. (John House, the real-life organizer of the exhibition, also makes a cameo appearance.) One of the paintings in the exhibition which Frederica and Alexander discuss is Gauguin's "*Still-Life, Fête Gloanec 1888* in which various inanimate objects, two ripe pears, a dense bunch of flowers, swam across a bright red tabletop rimmed with a black ellipse. The painting was signed 'Madeleine Bernard.'" Frederica informs Alexander "from the catalog that the vegetation was supposed to be a jocular portrait by Gauguin of Madeleine, the pears her breasts, the dense flowers her hair." Frederica has been citing the entry by John House in the catalogue of the exhibition, *Post-Impressionism, Cross-Currents in European Painting* (1979); the one variant from the source is that the signature is "Madeleine B," referring indeed to the seventeen-year-old daughter of Gauguin's friend, the painter Emile Bernard. (For a reproduction of the painting—an oil on canvas mounted on panel, 15 x 21 in., Musée des Beaux-Arts, Orléans—see *Paul Gauguin* [1993], by Michael Gibson, or *Gauguin: His Life and Works* [1998], by Anna Maria Damigella.)

Midway through *Still Life,* we find Alexander Wedderburn renting a room in the flat of his good friend Thomas Poole, who has a wife, Elinor, and three young children. One morning, breakfasting with the family, Alexander realizes that "he had no real idea what Elinor thought about Thomas, or Anthea [Thomas's one-time lover], or indeed himself, but he knew exactly what she thought about potatoes, coffee, wine." The breakfast fruit particularly is associated with Elinor: "The fruit changed with the seasons: dark burgundy cherries, gold-green greengages, wax-gold spotted pears, plums misted on purple-black. He watched Elinor arrange the fruits and then watched the fruits." While Elinor arranges and rearranges the breakfast objects, Alexander simply observes, at one point concentrating on "the not-yet-dead plums, with their breathing skins . . . the germ waiting inside the stone." And, being a writer, he speculates about words:

> How would one find the exact word for the color of the plum-skins?
> (There was a further question of *why* one might want to do so, why it was
> not enough to look at, or to eat and savor the plum, but Alexander did not

wish to address himself to that, not just now. It was a fact that the lemons and the plums, together, made a pattern that he recognized with pleasure, and the pleasure was so fundamentally human it asked to be noted and understood.)

Alexander is finishing his play, *The Yellow Chair,* and he is "obsessed" with a still life of van Gogh's that depicts a breakfast table, a painting van Gogh describes in a letter to his brother Theo as a study in blues, yellows, and oranges. Not long afterward, Alexander—who is not very interested in sex—is seduced by Elinor. Their lovemaking is gentle, silent, and fulfilling for both of them. The affair continues, and Alexander becomes more and more integrated into the family, even while his "life became both more intensely pleasurable and more unreal." The punning implications of Byatt's title are more evident than ever.

The most recent literary treatment I know of a fruit still life occurs in "Death by Fruit" (2000), by the American poet Kay Ryan (b. 1945). The point of the poem is that the subtler painters of *vanitas* still lifes—which are intended to express the vanity of human life—will ignore too obvious items like skulls in favor of fruit; the last ten (of twenty-nine) lines succinctly state this argument:

> The greatest masters
> preferred the subtlest *vanitas*
> modestly trusting to fruit baskets
> to whisper *ashes to ashes,*
> relying on the poignant exactness
> of oranges to release
> like a citrus mist
> the always fresh fact
> of how hard we resist
> how briefly we're pleased.

I wonder if anyone has written a poem—someone should—about the still lifes of the north Italian painter Evaristo Baschenis (1617–1677), eighteen of whose paintings were displayed, in one of the most stunning recent shows of a "rediscovered" old master, at the Metropolitan Museum of Art in New York (2000–01); the excellent catalogue of the show, *The Still Lifes of Evaristo Baschenis: The Music of Silence* (2000), was edited by Andrea Bayer and contains reproductions of all the paintings. The priest-musician Baschenis had two subjects when he painted: kitchen scenes, generally restricted to dead fowl, bread, pots, and jugs; and arrangements of musical instruments, generally not being played (hence the subtitle of the catalogue). Several of Baschenis's most outstanding paintings, however, escape these two categories: the early *Still Life with a Basket of Apples, Melons, Pears, and a Plate of Plums* (ca. 1640) and his masterpiece, the so-called Agliardi Triptych (ca. 1665), of which two of the paintings depict performing musicians. Baschenis seems to have invented the musical instrument motif, which

was widely imitated by later painters. One curious feature of Baschenis's versions of
this motif is the frequent presence of one or two pieces of decaying fruit (peaches,
pears, or apples). What is more extraordinary is the frequent representation on the surface of a musical instrument of a trompe l'oeil layer of dust marked by the swipe of a
wandering hand—an unmistakable allusion to the *vanitas* theme, which is occasionally
alluded to yet again by the broken strings of a musical instrument.

EXOTIC FRUIT LISTS

A lighthearted celebration of fruit (and other foods) is the title poem, "Food and
Drink" (1932), of one of the collections of the American poet and critic Louis Untermeyer (1885–1977). Untermeyer begins by deploring the comparative rarity of such
poetic celebration: "Why has our poetry eschewed / The rapture and response of
food?" He includes several lines on fruit:

> The sapid catalogue of fruits;
> Plebeian apple, caustic grape,
> Quinces that have no gift for shape,
> Dull plums that mind their own affairs,
> Incurably bland and blunted pears,
> Fantastic passion-fruit, frank lemons
> With acid tongues as sharp as women's,
> Exotic loquats, sly persimmons,
> White currants, amber-fleshed sultanas
> (Miniature and sweetened mannas)
> Expansive peaches, suave bananas,
> Oranges ripening in crates,
> Tight-bodied figs, sun-wrinkled dates,
> Melons that have their own vagaries;
> The bright astringency of berries

Some of Untermeyer's fruits are slightly exotic (the passion fruit, the loquats, the
persimmons), but the names are not unfamiliar and the fruits themselves were probably available in Untermeyer's time—as they certainly are today—in fancy food stores.
What are we to make, though, of a poem alluding exclusively to exotic fruits, which
many likely readers will never have tasted, seen, or even heard of? Such a poem is
"Songs of the Fruits and Sweets of Childhood," by Lorna Goodison. Her poem is, in
fact, about both fruits and "sweets" (such as guava cheese and various candies); the
fruits include mackafat, roseapple, jimbelin, stinking toe, coolie plums, naseberry, and
starapple. The very names themselves tantalize us with the promise of novel olfactory,
gustatory, and visual experiences:

> Cream pink pomander
> like a lady's sachet

is the the genteel roseapple
scenting the breath.

Jade green lantern
light astringent
is the tart taste
of the jimbelin.
[. . . . .]
The starapple
wears a thick coat
of royal purple
and at its center
sports a star
of many points.

Like lists of exotic place-names—which have been put to good use by poets as far back as Homer and the Hebrew Bible—lists of the names of exotic fruits possess a strong semantic charge. Exotic fruits reduced to such a list occur in a poem by Blaise Cendrars (1887–1961), the sixth of eight exotic "Menus," in his volume *Kodak* (1924); Ron Padgett's English version is followed by the original French:

Canned beef from Chicago and German delicatessen
Crayfish
Pineapples guavas loquats coconuts mangoes custard apple
Baked breadfruit

~

Conserves de bœuf de Chicago et salaisons allemandes
Langouste
Ananas goyaves nèfles du Japon noix de coco mangues pomme-crème
Fruits de l'arbre à pain cuits au four

The eight menu poems have been characterized by Jay Bochner as "an unexpectedly sublime ending to the album, a magical decantation of all the disparate localities that have supplied the travelogue's poems." It comes, then, as something of a surprise when we learn that "the only trip Cendrars took for these snapshots is through a book by someone else, a writer of popular novels he knew named Gustave Le Rouge"; the menu poems are composed of words found in one of Le Rouge's novels.

Exoticism is, of course, a relative matter, so that to Soviet Russians, for example, bananas and pineapples might very well have appeared to be exotic fruits. I want to consider in this light a poem by Boris Slutsky (1919–1986), "The State of Serfdom," first published in 1990 but written many years earlier. It is worth pointing out, to begin with, that Slutsky published his first poem in 1941 and not another for fifteen years—1956 being the year in which a Communist Party congress declared Stalinism an aberration. Slutsky, however, remained a Leninist and a party member throughout his life, though, unlike most of his contemporaries in the arts, he refused any committment to the dogmas of socialist realism. Furthermore, Slutsky dealt critically in some of his poems with the issue of anti-Semitism. For all these reasons, it was not until 1990 that Yurii Boldyrev published in Moscow "the first substantial collection to bring together the unpublished and published work, surely one of the dozen best books of Russian poetry this century" (the words of Gerald Smith, who published the first volume of English translations of Slutsky's poetry in 1999).

"The State of Serfdom" begins by emphasizing how profound and tenacious is the presence of servitude in Russian history:

> The state of serfdom, tougher and more true
> than any of its abolitions, that old scab
> of villeinage, —not easy to pick off

Anyone familiar with the history of Russian libertarianism would recognize the "abolitions" as referring to the many attempts (beginning in the eighteenth century) at providing limitations on legal coercion by the Russian state, including the three Soviet constitutions of 1924, 1936, and 1977. The latter half of the poem (lines 10–17 in the English translation) is given over to two extended metaphors—a rarity in Slutsky's work—relating, respectively, to the senses of hearing and taste:

> From time to time the sleeper is awakened
> by caterwauling from a drunken tocsin,
> or proclamation of a constitution.
> From time to time, as if having a fit,
> in plot common-or-garden, history
> grows some bananas, even pineapples.
> She brings them forth; but then, late or soon,
> she says indifferently: "Bad move!"

An exotic fruit list may even reduce to a single item, as in the brilliant essay in natural history by Amy Clampitt, "Cloudberry Summer" (1985), which is about an exotic variety of the ordinary raspberry. (In chapter 23, "Berries," we will look at two other berry poems by Clampitt, one about gooseberries and one about blueberries.) The poem is about a berry commonly called, as Clampitt explains in the poem, either "heathberry" ("Down East") or "cloudberry" ("farther north"). (*The New Oxford Book of Food Plants* reveals that the berry is *Rubus chamaemorus,* "a small, low, perennial herb with golden or orange fruit. It is rarely cultivated but grows wild in Scandinavia, Arctic Russia, Siberia, northern Britain, and Canada, and the fruit can be stewed or used in jam.") With a great sense of discovery, the poet finds the berries in mid-July growing in a bog:

> these strangely sallow-
> tinged, blandly-baked-apple-
> flavored thimble nubbins, singly borne, no
> more than inches from the bog's sour surface

Constructing her eleven seven-line stanzas out of a mixture of close moral observations and ideas drawn from "the dank / sector of organic / chemistry," Clampitt surprises us some two-thirds of the way though her poem by announcing an even more astonishing discovery—that same bog, in June, almost a year later, with the cloudberry plants in bloom:

> a thriving
> cloudberry spring: revisited, the
> bog's sunken floor a dapple of such countless,
> singly borne, close-to-the-
> ground corollas, each of a whiteness
> so without flaw
>
> I thought, for
> half a second, *Snow.* But no. Some new
> species, then?

And the finale: "Days later . . . / the whole unstable, illusory van of pleasure / had moved on."

TEMPORALLY CONJOINED FRUITS

We have been considering arrangements (sometimes mere lists) of different kinds of fruit juxtaposed in space, whether real, physical space or some sort of abstract space. But fruits may also be conjoined in time. In its simplest form, such a temporal arrangement might occur as one walks through an orchard of varied fruit trees, as in James Thomson's stroll through the Dorset seat of his patron, George Bubb Dodington:

> And, as I steal along the sunny Wall,
> Where Autumn basks, with Fruit empurpled deep,
> My pleasing Theme continual prompts my Thought:
> Presents the downy Peach; the shining Plumb,
> With a fine blueish Mist of Animals
> Clouded; the ruddy Nectarine; and dark,
> Beneath his ample Leaf, the luscious Fig.
> The Vine here too her curling Tendrils shoots;
> Hangs out her Clusters, glowing to the South;
> And scarcely wishes for a warmer Sky.

An imaginary survey of his estate was composed by one of the so-called libertine poets, Théophile de Viau (1590–1626), while in prison; written in 1624 and addressed to his brother, the poem consists of thirty-three ten-line stanzas with a strictly observed rhyme scheme *(abab cc dede)*. The two stanzas about fruit—the twenty-second and twenty-third—are particularly appealing (the English prose translation is Geoffrey Brereton's):

> Je cueillerai ces abricots,
> Ces fraises à couleur de flammes
> Dont nos bergers font des écots
> Qui seraient ici bons aux dames,
> Et ces figues et ces melons
> Dont la bouche des aquilons
> N'a jamais su baiser l'écorce,
> Et ces jaunes muscats si chers
> Qui jamais la grêle ne force
> Dans l'asile de nos rochers.
>
> Je verrai sur nos grenadiers
> Leurs rouges pommes entr'ouvertes,
> Où le ciel, comme à ses lauriers,
> Garde toujours des feuilles vertes
> Je verrai ce touffu jasmin
> Qui fait ombre à tout le chemin
> D'une assez spacieuse allée,
> Et la parfume d'une fleur
> Qui conserve dans la gelée
> Son odorat et sa couleur.

~

I shall pick those apricots, those flame-coloured strawberries from which our shepherds make snack meals which here would be good enough for the ladies, and those figs and melons whose skin the mouth of the cold winds has never been able to kiss, and those precious yellow muscat grapes which the hail never violates in the shelter of our rocks.

I shall see the red, half-opened fruit on our pomegranate-trees, on which heaven, as with its own laurels, always keeps green leaves. I shall see that leafy jasmine which shades the whole length of quite a broad garden-walk and scents it with a flower which keeps its fragrance and its colour through the frosts.

De Viau includes in his survey fruits that in all likelihood would never be ripe at the same time, but one could, of course, imagine a succession of seasonal fruits—which is precisely what Elinor Wylie does in the first three sonnets of her frequently anthologized sonnet sequence "Wild Peaches" (1921). The first sonnet begins:

> When the world turns completely upside down
> You say we'll emigrate to the Eastern Shore
> Aboard a river-boat from Baltimore;
> We'll live among wild peach trees, miles from town.

Most of the clothing (homespun), food (salted herrings), flora (wild peaches), and fauna (pigs, garter snakes) on offer to the speaker as part of a proposed new lifestyle would seem close to the hearts of native New Englanders and yet are vehemently rejected (in the fourth sonnet) as incompatible with the speaker's "Puritan marrow of my bones"; instead, the sterile stasis of winter seems to be embraced ("And sleepy winter, like the sleep of death"). Only the lovingly enumerated seasonal fruits may be seen as reflecting "this richness that I hate": the spring strawberries and plums, the summer cherries and peaches, the autumn grapes and persimmons. It is difficult to resist interpreting the incoherence of the poem's expressed tastes as a reflection of the incoherence of Wylie's actual feelings and attitudes, in particular, the tension between the sensuous and ascetic strains in her personality, which is well documented by her biographers.

One of Wylie's biographers, Judith Farr, cites two lines from Wylie's second novel, *The Venetian Glass Nephew* (1925), as evidence of the author's "taste," so "charming" and "mannered." (It happens that both lines involve fruit: "His suave voice delicately divided silence, as one cuts a precious fruit"; "Upon the day of her birth a golden peach knocked at the door and a white rose flew into the window.") Another Wylie biographer, Stanley Olson, explains that her "favorite foods were the simplest and the most delicious: spring lamb, asparagus, artichokes, new potatoes, and scones" (fruit being significantly absent from the list). Both biographers tell us of Wylie's taste for the high-fashion gowns of a leading Paris designer, Paul Poiret. So, was she in any sense a Puritan? Not by descent (both her father's and mother's families came from Pennsylvania) and not by environment (she was born in New Jersey, grew up in Pennsylvania and Washington, D.C., and never spent much time in New England). Her professed Puritanism was a pose, and an inconsistent one at that.

FRUITARIAN MEALS

Another way in which fruits may be conjoined in time is in the form of a meal consisting entirely of fruit courses. But who ever ate, or eats, such a meal? Are there such people as fruitarians (or frugivores), that is, individuals who eat nothing but fruit? From the fact that Epicurus taught his disciples in a garden, Abraham Cowley infers that no foods can be eaten with more pleasure than those grown in a garden:

The wanton Taste no Fish, or Fowl can chuse,
For which the Grape or Melon he would lose,
Tho' all th'Inhabitants of Sea and Air
Be listed in the Glutton's Bill of Fare;
       Yet still the Fruits of Earth we see,
Plac'd the third Story high in all her Luxury.

Another answer as to the identity of the fruitarians is that suggested by Prest in *The Garden of Eden:* for "many seventeenth century writers . . . fruit [is] the original food of mankind." Milton, for example, is quite explicit about this in *Paradise Lost* (5.482–83): "flowers and their fruit / Man's nourishment." Though Milton was following tradition in having Adam and Eve subsist entirely on fruit, he was quite heterodox in having his angels also eat fruit (since for Christian orthodoxy angels are entirely spiritual and do not eat at all). A famous example of the corporeal appetite of Milton's angels occurs when Adam and Eve have the archangel Raphael over for lunch (at least, the meal begins at noontime). God has sent Raphael to warn Adam and Eve of Satan's wiles (and thereby to guarantee that their eventual fall will be enacted strictly of their own free will). With this VIA about to arrive bearing an important message from God on high, Adam is understandably agitated and, in accordance with the gendered division of labor already in place in Eden, he asks Eve to "go with speed, / And what thy stores contain, bring forth and pour / Abundance, fit to honour and receive / Our heavenly stranger" (5.313–16). Eve's prudent and housewifely answer is that freshly picked food is far better (except, she meticulously—and, in the context, hilariously—notes, "what by frugal storing firmness gains / To nourish, and superfluous moist consumes" [5.324–25]). She then proceeds to gather fresh fruit of all kinds. And here Milton refuses the obvious literary gambits, neither constructing a list of many of the delicious fruits already known to his readers nor regaling them with fruity odors, tastes, and textures; instead, he limits his description to the outer appearance of what we must take to be some uniquely Edenic fruit: "In coat, / Rough, or smooth rind, or bearded husk, or shell / She gathers" (5.341–43). On the other hand, Milton is more inventive about the drinks: "For drink the grape / She crushes, inoffensive must, and meads / From many a berry, and from sweet kernels pressed / She tempers dulcet creams" (5.344–47). And Raphael enjoys his meal; at least in this Adam and Eve are successful.

The fruitarian meal Eve prepares for Raphael is not often depicted by illustrators of Milton's *Paradise Lost,* but William Blake's watercolor design for book 5 (see plate 6) does show a bowl of fruit sitting on a table between Adam and Eve on the left and the angel on the right, while directly above the bowl stands a serpent-encircled tree bearing flat, pink ovals (as already noted in chapter 1, "Apples").

It is worth emphasizing that mounds of fruit possess a wide range of significations in Euro-American painting, sometimes serving to call attention to a culture of conspicuous consumption, as in innumerable seventeenth-century Dutch still lifes, and

678   sometimes to the painters' virtuosic representational skills, as in the work of such artists
as the Dutch Willem Kalf (1619–1693), the Spanish Luis Meléndez (1716–1780), and
the American Levi Wells Prentice (1851–1935). A rather unexpected signification of a
painted bowl of fruit occurs in *Philemon and Baucis, Entertaining Jupiter and Mercury* (ca.
1615–25), by the Dutch painter Abraham Janssens Van Nuyssen (ca. 1575–1632), in
the Davis Museum of Wellesley College. (For a reproduction, see Lucy Flint Gohlke,
Davis Museum and Cultural Center, History and Holdings [1993].) The subject, from
Ovid's *Metamorphoses,* concerns a visit by Jupiter and Mercury, in disguise, to the humble home of the elderly peasants Philemon and Baucis. The couple is supposed to provide the visitors with what meager fare they have available, and in Van Nuyssen's
painting there is a small bowl of fruit placed at the very center of the table (also the
very center of the picture), which we are presumably to interpret as in keeping with
the poverty of the host and hostess. In a somewhat later painting (1658) of the same
subject by Rembrandt (1606–1669), in the National Gallery (Washington, D.C.), the
bowl of fruit is even more meager. (For a reproduction, see A. Bredius and H. Gerson,
Rembrandt: The Complete Edition of the Paintings [1971].)

If we turn to Ovid's gently humorous account of the myth (*Metamorphoses*
8.618–724), we find that the food provided by Baucis turns out to include all three
courses of a conventional full-scale Roman meal: first, olives, pickled cornel-cherries,
endives, radishes, cream cheese, and roasted eggs; second, cabbage and bacon; and, for
dessert (in Frank Justus Miller's translation), "nuts and figs, with dried dates, plums
and fragrant apples in broad baskets, and purple grapes just picked from the vines;
in the centre of the table was a comb of clear white honey" (674–77). We can see
that fresh fruit, even in older painting or poetry, is not always a sign of luxury. And
this conclusion is confirmed by an account of the cuisine of Baucis and Philemon
provided by Johannes de Hauvilla in his *Arch-weeper*—an account that adds many
details not in Ovid in about twice as many Latin hexameter lines. The voice is
the Arch-weeper's, and this is part of his denunciation of gluttony (translated by
Wetherbee):

> She brings fruits whose taste is close to both honey and vinegar, fruits
> whose cheeks are covered with the fresh down of youth, and fruits fur-
> rowed with wrinkles, daughters of time, the twisting scars of gnarled old
> age. Each fruit is still clad in its rind, and neither he nor she plucks away
> this garment by the artful use of a sharp knife. To divest a fruit of its outer
> covering in a single twisting spiral is not a cottager's lot; the rural courtier
> has no such arts.
>
> She offers pears, cornel-cherries flushed with a delicate red, and figs.
> She brings plums, some clad in rosy purple; some imbued with a yellow
> more delicate than white gold; some over whose surface float shadows of
> rusty red; and some which Nature in her zeal has painted with a variety
> of colors, a charming discord pleasing to the eye.

Another fruitarian meal occurs in a futuristic fantasy called "The New Adam and Eve" (1843), by Nathaniel Hawthorne (1804–1864). Having asked us to imagine our present world stripped of all living creatures but otherwise intact, Hawthorne then contrives to introduce into this imagined world—and specifically, into the city of Boston—a pair of freshly minted and innocent human beings, a "new" Adam and Eve, whose cognitive and affective faculties are exactly like our own but whose ignorance of the human past is total. This donnée is, unfortunately, fatally undercut by the difficulties inherent in all counterfactual historical assumptions, and in particular by the difficulty of eliminating any single factor of the real historical world without at the same time eliminating the presuppositions and consequences of that factor. (In Hawthorne's story, the factor in question is, of course, the actual human race.) It makes little sense to imagine a world without human beings—not even dead human beings—but with two new inhabitants whose instincts just happen to coincide with the more or less parochial prejudices of a mid-nineteenth-century Boston elite, so that, for example, Adam and Eve unhesitatingly decide that "sculpture, in its highest excellence, is more genuine than painting" and Eve "instinctively thrusts the rosy tip of her finger into a thimble." In fact, what the story amounts to is simply a lightly disguised attack on all those aspects of his age that Hawthorne abhors and a rather jejune plea for love as the cure for sin and as the defining purpose of human existence. In any case, one of the high points of Adam and Eve's exploration of the churches, law courts, prisons, banks, and shops of the city comes when they enter a grand mansion in which the dining room is all set for a banquet. Adam and Eve do not recognize as food the turtle soup, the haunch of venison, the Parisian pasty; indeed, "fish, fowl, and flesh, . . . to their pure nostrils, steam with a loathsome odor of death and corruption." Fortunately, they discover the dessert table, where Eve

> receives a red-cheeked apple from her husband's hand, in requital of her predecessor's fatal gift to our common grandfather. She eats it without sin, and, let us hope, with no disastrous consequences to her future progeny. They make a plentiful, yet temperate meal of fruit, which, though not gathered in Paradise, is legitimately derived from the seeds that were planted there. Their primal appetite is satisfied.

Hawthorne's delight in fruit is clearly exhibited by his affection for the orchard at the "Old Manse" in Concord (the ancestral property of the Emerson family that Hawthorne rented for three and a half years after his marriage in 1842). In his preface to the collection of stories called *Mosses from an Old Manse* (1846)—which contains "The New Adam and Eve"—Hawthorne discourses eloquently for over a page and a half on the delights of the orchard. He begins by recalling the man who planted the trees—"the old minister, [who] before reaching his patriarchal age of ninety, ate the apples from this orchard during many years." The minister "loved each tree, doubtless, as if it had been his own child"; and, Hawthorne continues:

680   There is so much individuality of character, too, among apple-trees, that it
gives them an additional claim to be the objects of human interest. One
is harsh and crabbed in its manifestations; another gives us fruit as mild as
charity. One is churlish and illiberal, evidently grudging the few apples that
it bears; another exhausts itself in free-hearted benevolence. The variety of
grotesque shapes, into which apple-trees contort themselves, has its effect
on those who get acquainted with them; they stretch out their crooked
branches, and take such hold of the imagination that we remember them
as humorists and odd fellows.

This, of course, must remind us of Thoreau's paean to apples (discussed above, in
chapter 1), written just a decade and a half later. But Hawthorne goes on to mention other fruits:

Throughout the summer, there were cherries and currants. . . . And,
besides, there were pear-trees, that flung down bushels upon bushels of
heavy pears, and peach-trees, which, in a good year, tormented me with
peaches, neither to be eaten nor kept, nor, without labor and perplexity,
to be given away. The idea of an infinite generosity and exhaustless
bounty, on the part of our Mother Nature, was well worth obtaining
through such cares as these. That feeling can be enjoyed . . . by a man
long habituated to city-life, who plunges into such a solitude as that of
the Old Manse, where he plucks the fruit of trees that he did not plant,
and which therefore, to my heterodox taste, bear the closest resemblance
to those that grew in Eden.

Hawthorne's psychological explanation of his pleasure in freely gathering fruit planted
by other hands is based on keen introspection, and provides a good measure of the
secularizing currents in the intellectual life of the nineteenth century.

Far from Paradise or the rural haunts of the Old Manse, in Paris just prior to
World War II, Colette develops a pivotal scene in her novella, *Julie De Carneilhan*
(already referred to above in chapter 1), with the help of a lunch consisting entirely of
fruit (well, almost entirely: some ham is inadvertently included, as we shall see). Julie
has been summoned by her ex-husband, Herbert, Comte d'Espivant, to visit him after
his heart attack. She is excited to return to the very house where she used to live but
baffled as to Herbert's motive in inviting her. After she arrives, in his chauffeured automobile, she responds to his proposal of lunch with the apparently casual remark (translated by Fermor): "Just anything, then. Some fruit. . . . It's my day for fruit." Julie's
choice of fruit for lunch is anything but casual: sensual and expensive, it also turns out
to stimulate what Colette calls a "spiteful complicity" between the two ex-spouses, at
the expense of his present wife and provoked by the latter's poor taste in interior decoration. The lunch begins

when two tables laden with fruit were wheeled in. Julie found it all fault-less: late cherries, rose-coloured peaches, thin-skinned Marseilles figs, cloudy hot-house grapes that had been carefully protected from the wasps. . . .

"Who asked for this ham, Herbert? Nobody wants it."

Herbert answers that it must have been his wife, Marianne. A moment later, he

chose the best of the peaches, still adorned with its living green leaf, and let it rest in the palm of his hand.

"How lovely it is . . ." he sighed. "Take this one. Do you still drink your coffee while you're eating fruit?"

This reminder of their old life together caught Julie unawares. She flushed, and steadied herself by drinking a glass of champagne.

Herbert cuts a peach, puts it down, and picks up a handful of cherries; holding them to the light, he remarks:

"Look, they're so clear you can almost see the stones inside! What have I ever had of my own after all? All I'll have to say goodbye to amounts to just about this."

He dropped the cherries and waved towards the little sunlit table. His gesture did not exclude the tall fair-haired woman sitting slant-wise in her chair, facing the light, and feeling as happy as a wasp in the sun.

Now, the plot has begun to emerge: Herbert, with little money of his own, has married a widow possessed of great wealth, but has no real control over his wife's fortune. But what has Julie to do with this unhappy situation? When Julie leaves, "the yellow rose-bud pinned to her lapel was beginning to droop. 'One of Marianne's roses.'" That rose is a sign that Julie has succumbed to Herbert's—as yet unclear—designs on Marianne's money. A second visit by Julie reveals his utterly unscrupulous scheme for obtaining a million francs from his wife at the expense of Julie's reputation. Julie, not quite believing Herbert capable of such a nasty trick, goes along and eventually receives one hundred thousand francs—"'It's ten percent; what a middle-man or a house agent would get,' she said out loud, on what she hoped was a cynical and bantering note. But the sound jarred on her." Much food is consumed in *Julie de Carneilhan,* but the lunch between Julie and Herbert is special in that it not only provides a clue as to what will happen next but is instrumental in making it happen.

INTERCHANGEABLE FRUITS

The second fundamental logical operation that may be performed on classes (or kinds) is *disjunction,* the *or*-operation, as we have already noted at the outset of this chapter. Is there then a literary form or genre in which different kinds of fruit are semiotically interchangeable? Certain folktales seem to fit the criterion. Consider, as an illustration, the folktale called "The Three Oranges." The story—termed "essentially South European, sporadically worldwide" by the folklorist Stith Thompson—occurs in dozens of versions, with lemons, citrons, or pomegranates substituted for the oranges. The story involves numerous metamorphoses—orange to woman, woman to dove, dove to orange tree, and orange once more to woman. It seems that virtually any tree fruit would work in the story, and this may account for the proliferation of the different versions.

A case of the interchangeability of fruit trees occurs in a remarkably subtle and graceful *cossante* (stanza) by the late-medieval Spanish poet Diego Hurtado de Mendoza (1364–1404). Though fruit (*las frutas*) is only explicitly mentioned in its penultimate line, it has been foreshadowed from the beginning by repeated references to a flowering tree (the translation is by Eugenio Florit):

> That tree whose leaves are trembling
> is yearning for something [*algo se le antoja*].
>
> That tree so lovely to look at
> acts as if it wants to give flowers [*flores*]:
> it is yearning for something.
>
> That tree so lovely to see
> acts as if it wants to flower [*florecer*]:
> it is yearning for something.
>
> It acts as if it wants to give flowers:
> they are already showing; come out and look:
> it is yearning for something.
>
> It acts as if it wants to flower:
> they are already showing; come out and see:
> it is yearning for something.
>
> They are already showing: come out and look.
> Let the ladies come and pick the fruits:
> it is yearning for something.

Clearly, it is important that the tree be a fruit tree; and just as clearly, it is not important which kind of fruit tree.

Another poem in which fruit trees are interchangeable is "Never May the Fruit Be Plucked" (1924), by Millay:

> Never, never may the fruit be plucked from the bough
> And gathered into barrels.

He that would eat of love must eat it where it hangs.
Though the branches bend like reeds,
Though the ripe fruit splash in the grass or wrinkle on the tree,
He that would eat of love may bear away with him
Only what his belly can hold,
Nothing in the apron,
Nothing in the pockets.
Never, never may the fruit be gathered from the bough
And harvested in barrels.
The winter of love is a cellar of empty bins,
In an orchard soft with rot.

Here, eating fruit stands in for loving, the point of the poem being that love exists only in the act of loving and—unlike fruit, which can be "gathered" or "harvested" for the winter—cannot be retained beyond the act. Obviously, the exact nature of the fruit is irrelevant to Millay's rather straightforward—indeed, banal—thesis.

A closely related but much more striking fruit-tree metaphor may be found in the fourth poem of the nineteen *Laments* (1580), which the Polish poet Jan Kochanowski (1530–1584) wrote on the death of his two-and-a-half-year-old daughter, Ursula:

> Ungodly Death, my eyes have been defiled
> By having had to watch my best loved child
> Die! watch you like a robber stalk the house
> And shake the green fruit from her parents' boughs.

The beautiful translation is by Stanislaw Baranczak and Seamus Heaney. Often considered the "inventor" of modern Polish poetry, Kochanowski was defying the classical conventions of the elegy in writing about the death of a small child. Lament 4 has eighteen lines; the others possess a variety of lengths and forms. Lament 5 compares Ursula to a young olive tree grown from a seed. For a classically inclined writer like Kochanowski, an olive tree is especially apposite to his theme, but in terms of the conceit developed in the poem any other fruit tree that grows from seed would do.

In a poem published in 1658—"On the Death of Mr Persall's Little Daughter in the Beginning of the Spring, at Amsterdam"—an anonymous seventeenth-century English author rejects the comparison of the death of the infant to the blighting of the blossoms of a fruit tree:

> Say not, because no more you see
> In the fair arms of her mother tree
> > This infant bloom, the wind of time
> > Has nipped the flower before the prime;
> Or whate'er autumn promised to make good
> In early fruit is withered in the bud.

684 The second stanza's explanation of what one *should* think (or "say") about this only apparently premature death takes the form of a metaphysical conceit drawn from alchemy but remaining within the botanical realm, and the poem ends with a third stanza directly addressing the parents' grief:

> But, as when roses breathe away
> Their sweet consenting souls, none say
>   The still deflowers those virgin leaves,
>   But them extracts, exalts, receives,
> Even so has heaven's almighty chemic here
> Drawn this pure spirit to its proper sphere.

> Sad parents, then, recall your griefs:
> Your little one now truly lives,
>   Your pretty messenger of love,
>   Your new intelligence above;
> Since God created such immortal flowers
> To grow in his own paradise, not ours.

Adam Zagajewski uses fruit, paradoxically, as a symbol of unattainability in his "Fruit" (1985). Here are the first nine lines of fifteen (the last six are weakened, I believe, by excessive abstractness):

> How unattainable life is, it only reveals
> its features in memory,
> in nonexistence. How unattainable
> afternoons, ripe, tumultuous, leaves
> bursting with sap; swollen fruit, the rustling
> silks of women who pass on the other
> side of the street, and the shouts of boys
> leaving school. Unattainable. The simplest
> apple inscrutable, round.

In one sense, fruit is, of course, easily attainable, and it is only after Zagajewski has explained that afternoons and rustling silks and the shouts of boys are also unattainable that we begin to grasp what he is driving at. What we cannot achieve is to arrest a valued experience so as to savor its special qualities; an exact delineation of the features of any such experience can only take place in memory, which implies that the experience is no more. This is not a very original thought and, furthermore, we are given no particular reason for singling out fruit as the paradigm for this recognition of the transience of things with the consequent epistemological dilemmas.

More obscure is the meaning of the fruit in some sonnets by Rainer Maria Rilke. In his *Sonnets to Orpheus* (1922), three in the first series (13–15) are all about fruit. To isolate these sonnets from the others in the sequence—there are twenty-six sonnets in the first series and twenty-nine in the second—must be in some respects to distort their meaning; this is a risk we shall have to take. (It is not, after all, as if the questions of whether and how the sonnets relate to each other had clear-cut answers.) Two facts about the sonnet sequence as a whole are, however, worth recalling. First, the sequence is dedicated to the memory of a woman, Vera Ouckama Knoop, who was a dancer and died young; second, in the *Sonnets*—written during February 1922 while Rilke was finishing his *Duino Elegies*—the purely transcendent angels of the Elegies are replaced by the figure of Orpheus, representing some sort of intermediary between the human and the transcendent. One other preliminary point: I know at least seven English versions of the *Sonnets to Orpheus;* the two I choose to quote from stay close to the German, employ rhymes and near rhymes, and read fairly fluently. Here, then, is Sonnet 13 in David Young's translation together with the German text:

> Ripe apple, pear and banana,
> gooseberry . . . They speak of life and death
> as soon as they get in our mouths . . .
> Try watching a child's face: you can
>
> see the far-off knowledge as he tastes it.
> What's going on in your mouth? Something nameless,
> slow. Instead of words, a flood of discoveries,
> startled loose from the flesh of the fruit.
>
> Do you dare tell what we mean by "apple"?
> This sweetness that first condenses itself
> so that when you lift it to take a bite
>
> it will be pure, wide-awake, transparent,
> two-meaninged, sunlike, earthlike, all presence—:
> Oh experience, sensation, happiness—, *immense!*

> ~

> Voller Apfel, Birne und Banane,
> Stachelbeere . . . Alles dieses spricht
> Tod und Leben in den Mund . . . Ich ahne . . .
> Lest es einem Kind vom Angesicht,
>
> wenn es sie erschmeckt. Dies kommt von weit.
> Wird euch langsam namenlos im Munde?
> Wo sonst Worte waren, fliessen Funde,
> aus dem Fruchtfleisch übberrascht befreit.

686

Wagt zu sagen, was ihr Apfel nennt.
Diese Süsse, sie sich erst verdichtet,
um, im Schmecken leise aufgerichtet,

klar zu werden, wach und transparent,
doppeldeutig, sonnig, erdig, hiesig—:
O Erfahrung, Fühlung, Freude—, riesig!

A few comments about the diction of the translation. The German word *ahne* ("suspect" or "guess") has been omitted and with it the double ellipsis indicating suspension or hesitation. The German word *hiesig* (Young's "all presence") is difficult to translate; it means, literally, "local" or "here and now"; other translators of Sonnet 1.13, use "real" or "ours." The fruits mentioned in the first two lines seem to have been chosen simply for variety (which perhaps explains why one translator felt free to substitute "melon" and "peach" for "pear" [*Birne*]). There is, however, clearly something special about the apple (recall the "apple-pose" in Rilke's much earlier sonnet on Eve, quoted in chapter 1), for it becomes the subject of the entire sestet; and, indeed, Rilke seems to have had some near-mystical experiences while munching apples, as he reports in a letter of 16 January 1912 to Princess Marie von Thurn und Taxis-Hohenlohe (translated by Stephen Mitchell): "At various times I have had the experience of feeling apples, more than anything else—barely consumed, and often while I was still eating them—being transposed into spirit. Thus perhaps the Fall. (If there *was* one.)"

Mitchell also mentions as a source for the first three lines of Rilke's sonnet "Le Cimetière Marin" (The graveyard by the sea; 1920), lines 25–27, by Paul Valéry; Rilke actually translated these lines into German. Valéry's lines deserve quotation in their own right, along with the second half of his stanza to complete the simile (here cited both in C. Day Lewis's English translation and the original French):

Even as a fruit's absorbed in the enjoying,
Even as within the mouth its body dying
Changes into delight through dissolution,
So to my melted soul the heavens declare
All bounds transfigured into a boundless air,
And I breathe now my future's emanation.

~

Comme le fruit se fond en jouissance,
Comme en délice il change son absence
Dans une bouche où sa forme se meurt,
Je hume ici ma future fumée,
Et le ciel chante à l'âme consumée
Le changement des rives en rumeur.

Rilke returns to the taste of fruit in the fifteenth sonnet, but first in the fourteenth he questions the earth which is the source of fruit (and flowers and vine leaves): is fruit the product of "the earth-nourishing dead"? And the larger question: are we "masters" of this fruit or its "slaves"? (The myth of Orpheus is, of course, relevant here insofar as it deals with his tragically limited control over the powers of the earth.) It would seem that here fruit stands for the whole life of nature, and we humans must ask where we fit into that life—though an answer may never be forthcoming, and the sonnet ends on an interrogative note (translated by David Young):

> Are *they* the masters, asleep among roots,
> and grudging us from their surpluses
> this crossbred thing of speechless strength and kisses?

Sonnet 15 finally is about young women dancing and about the taste of fruit, with the startling admonition in the fourth line to "dance the taste of the fruit you have known" (tanzt den Geschmack der erfahrenen Frucht!). What follows is a passage of ten lines passionately celebrating oranges—their juice and their rind, their taste and scent and succulence (translated by Stephen Mitchell):

> Dance the orange. Who can forget it,
> drowning in itself, how it struggles through
> against its own sweetness. You have possessed it.
> Deliciously it has converted to you.
>
> Dance the orange. The sunnier landscape—
> fling it *from* you, allow it to shine
> in the breeze of its homeland! Aglow, peel away
>
> scent after scent. Create your own kinship
> with the supple, gently reluctant rind
> and the juice that fills it with succulent joy.

We may recall that a disjunctive use of fruit sometimes occurs in Renaissance paintings of the Madonna. In such paintings, apples, oranges, grapes, cherries, and pomegranates often occur, some perhaps with specific religious connotations, but in addition almost any other fresh fruit may be present, because, as Panofsky explains: "The fruit, beautifully fresh and intact, suggests by this very intactness the *gaudia Paradisi* lost through the Fall of Man but regained, as it were, through Mary, the 'new Eve.'" Christian commentators on Genesis also associated Eve and Mary through the idea of wilderness (representing sin)—the region to which Eve was banished from Eden and from which the Virgin ascended to Heaven. And the wilderness itself is (perhaps) sometimes symbolized by a bear reaching for fruit from a tree, as in two outstanding Italian marble relief sculptures: the late-Gothic *Adam and Eve in the Wilderness* (1334–37), by Andrea Pisano (d. 1348), in the Museo dell'Opera del Duomo, Florence; and the early-Renaissance *Assumption of the Virgin* (1414–22), by Nanni di Banco (ca. 1374–1421), in Santa Maria del Fiore, Florence. The bear-fruit motif is, however, rare and obscure; in

Mary Bergstein's cautionary words, in her book on Nanni's sculpture, "the meaning of this bear has eluded all known commentators from Renaissance times to the present, representing one of the most intriguing iconographic puzzles in Italian art." (For a discussion, with illustrations, see Bergstein's *The Sculpture of Nanni di Banco* [2000].)

Dealing with the iconography of fruit in her massive volume *The Garden of the Renaissance: Botanical Symbolism in Italian Painting* (1977)—dedicated, by the way, to the memory of Erwin Panofsky—Mirella Levi D'Ancona shows that, in general, fruit may refer to Christ, to various saints, or to the Old and New Testaments (baskets of fruit to the left and right of the Virgin Mary). It seems clear that specific fruits (such as peaches and pears) almost never have unique significations in Renaissance art; like dream symbolism, fruit symbolism is inherently equivocal.

One use of the word "fruit" (in American slang) is to refer to male homosexuals. In her novel *The Last Resort* (1998), Alison Lurie (b. 1926) has her heroine, Jenny Walker, cleverly deflate the contemptuous connotations of the term by constructing a disjunction of desirable fruits and at the same time extending the denotation to women (Jenny herself and her new friend, Lee):

> Though if Jacko were a fruit, she thought sleepily, it would probably be a peach, because of the warm tanned bloom of his skin, and the slight down on his arms and legs. Whereas if she, Jenny, were a fruit she'd be an apple: a McIntosh, or one of those white-fleshed Cortlands that were so good in salad. And Lee would be something more exotic: maybe a papaya, or a South American melon like the ones they sometimes had at the Waterfront Market. They smelled heavenly, and weighed heavy and warm in the hand; and when opened they showed firm, brilliant rose-orange flesh and exuded a rich sweetness. As Lee might if—

It is particularly appropriate for Jenny to have these thoughts, since she has been married to an overbearing man for twenty-five years and it is his use of the insulting epithet "fruit" that has set off her meditation on its meaning. She has also just found herself in love with Lee (though Jenny's choice of fruit to associate with Lee seems to be innocent of the erotic meaning of "papaya" referred to in chapter 16, "Melons and Papayas").

ENEMIES AND FRIENDS OF FRUIT

One might wonder if the dangerous fruit of "Goblin Market" in any way reflects the idea that fresh fruit is unhealthy for children—a belief underlying the experiences of two Englishmen whose respective childhoods chronologically bracket the composition and publication (1859–61) of Rossetti's poem. In *Præterita* (1885–89), John Ruskin (b. 1819) undertakes in his second chapter "to mark what advantage and mischief, by the chances of life up to seven years old, had been irrevocably determined for me." The advantages—which, in Ruskin's account, derive almost entirely from the careful nurturing by his parents—turn out to include "peace, obedience, faith; these three for chief good; next to these, the habit of fixed attention with both eyes and mind" and "lastly, an extreme perfection in palate and all other bodily senses, given by the utter prohibition of cake, wine, comfits, or, except in carefullest restriction, fruit; and by fine preparation of what food was given me." There was certainly no shortage of fresh fruit from his mother's orchard in the household of Ruskin's childhood; as Ruskin's biographer, Tim Hilton, explains, "At the back of the house she had the best pear and apple trees in the neighbourhood. The orchard was seventy yards long, a whole world to the small child who followed his mother while she planted and pruned, plucked the peaches and nectarines."

I might just add that, though there is no occasion to go into it here, I cannot help recalling the sense of shock when I read for the first time the next two sentences from Ruskin's *Præterita* :

> Such I esteem the main blessings of my childhood;—next, let me count the equally dominant calamities.
>
> First, that I had nothing to love.

Our other Englishman is Bertrand Russell (1872–1970), in the first chapter of whose *Autobiography* (1967–69) we read that "in the matter of food, all through my youth I was treated in a very Spartan manner, much more so, in fact, than is now considered compatible with good health." Since the two families—Ruskin's and Russell's —were socially worlds apart (Ruskin's father was a wine merchant, Russell's a titled aristocrat), their similar attitudes towards food for children may have been peculiarly British and Victorian. In any case, Russell goes on to explain that in his family "there was an unalterable conviction that fruit is bad for children." He illustrates with a couple of incidents, one involving oranges and another blackberries. He remembers once at dinner when only the adults were served oranges for dessert. Another time, he was accused of eating blackberries while his governess briefly left him alone near some blackberry bushes, and he was caught out (in what he recalls as his first lie!) when forced to show his tongue.

Russell's orange incident, by the way, is in sharp contrast to what Gillian Saunders describes in the Victoria and Albert Museum catalogue *Oranges and Lemons* (1985) as "the Victorian custom of putting oranges in children's Christmas stockings." Saunders's illustration of the custom—an orange wrapper depicting Santa Claus with a sack of oranges and lemons—dates, in fact, from the early 1920s or 30s. The wrapper, labeled "St Claus Brand," was used by a Sicilian exporter, and since it is only five inches square in size (information provided by the Victoria and Albert Museum), it seems it could only wrap a rather small orange. (For a reproduction of the wrapper, see plate 33.) Such wrappers were introduced in the nineteenth century to protect the oranges from destructive molds. Saunders quotes Thackeray, in an essay of 1860, in praise of their artistic quality. By the mid-twentieth century, the use of protective wax on the rind of oranges and "new fungicides in the orchard, rinses at the factory, and better control of temperature and humidity in storage further diminished the need for paper protection" (as David Karp explains in the essay "Orange Wrappers" [1999]).

A couple of Victorian paintings support the idea that fresh fruit was not only eagerly sought but even medicinally recommended for children. One of the paintings, *The Boy with Many Friends* (oil on canvas, Bury Art Gallery and Museum, Lancaster), by Thomas Webster (1800–1886), depicts a new boy at school surrounded by other boys eager to share his mound of fruit and other goodies; the second painting, *Feeling Much Better* (1901; oil on canvas, Ackermann & Johnson Ltd., London), by George Bernard O'Neill (1828–1917), depicts a boy reclining on a chaise longue, the table next to him furnished with a glass of water and a dish of fresh fruit. (Both paintings are reproduced in Richard O'Neill's *The Art of Victorian Childhood* [1996].)

Literary evidence indicates that by the mid-nineteenth century in England fruit was a part of normal dining, at least for adults, as in the dinner which Jaggers gives for Pip and his three friends in Charles Dickens's *Great Expectations* (published in 1860–61 but set some decades earlier): "The table was comfortably laid . . . and at the side of his chair was a capacious dumb-waiter, with a variety of bottles and decanters on it, and four dishes of fruit for dessert" (chapter 26). Later in the novel, the refreshments provided for the mourners at Pip's sister's funeral include "cut-up oranges" (chapter 35).

One wonders if either Ruskin's or Russell's family was familiar with Dr. Johnson's remark, in his life of Jonathan Swift (1779), about the alleged risks of eating fruit: "Before [Swift] left Ireland he contracted a disorder, as he thought, by eating too much fruit. The original of diseases is commonly obscure. Almost every boy eats as much fruit as he can get, without any great inconvenience." Johnson is sensible as always (and we should recall his own extreme fondness for peaches and oranges, as described in chapters 7 and 15); nevertheless, when Johnson generalizes about boys, he should not be taken as formulating a universal truth about human appetites, since the enthusiasm for eating fruit in England seems to have begun only in the seventeenth century. Thus, Prest cites as something novel the remark of Sir William Temple that "all men eat fruit that can get it," while at the same time emphasizing that "the gardening literature of the period is filled with fruit."

Also in the seventeenth century but on the Continent, we know from the first biographer of Giovan Lorenzo Bernini (1598–1680) that the great Italian baroque artist was a devotee of fruit: "His moderate eating habits helped maintain his good health. Ordinarily he allowed nothing to be prepared for him except a small dish of meat and a great quantity of fruit. He used to say in jest that this craving for fruit was the original sin of those born in Naples."

Perhaps the earliest recorded instance of fear of fruit goes back to the second century C.E., when the great physician Galen (129–199/216 C.E.), in his *Hygiene* (ca. 180 C.E.) cautioned against the consumption of fresh fruit (including apples, pears, apricots, peaches, and nectarines) as tending to produce a bad balance among the four fundamental qualities of the body (warmth, coolness, dryness, and moisture). Galen— whose influence pervaded European and Arabic medicine for a millenium and a half—had inherited from the Hippocratic medical tradition, dating from as early as 400 B.C.E., the theory that foods dominated by coolness and dryness (such as barley) were most digestible and most nutritious, whereas among fruits, pears and apples were too cool, while green figs and grapes were recommended. Galen's negative opinion of most fruits was, however, further supported by his own experience of acute digestive pain after eating fresh fruit. Vivian Nutton, in some comments on Galen's dietary principles (1995), argues that "whatever the cause [of Galen's discomfort]—and one might also adduce other examples of various types of ailments brought on by ingesting unripe or over-ripe fruits—this is a good example of the way in which Galen jumps to conclusions." On the other hand, Galen recommends apples, pears, and also pomegranates for treating patients whose humors (combinations of the four qualities) are out of balance. Properly administered, such fruit remedies can cure, for example, either costiveness or diarrhea; this possibility Galen explains by the convenient assumption that "quite a few things are composed of opposite qualities." The quotation is from Galen's *On the Powers of Food,* a work somewhat later than the *Hygiene,* of which the second part is devoted to fruits and vegetables (the translation is by Mark Grant in his book *Galen on Food and Diet* [2000]).

Some of Galen's successors claimed that apples and pears possessed distinct dietary properties, as in Athenaeus's conclusion (3.81b): "And in general apples are less digestible than pears, as is shown by the fact that though we may eat fewer apples, we digest them less easily, whereas we may take a larger quantity of pears and digest them better" (translated by Gulick). According to the historian of medicine Erwin

692   Ackerknecht, this medical prohibition against many or most fruits lasted until the eighteenth century, at which time alternative (and equally dubious) nutritional theories, some favoring fruits, began to replace the humoral theory.

The encyclopedic-minded Robert Burton (1577–1640) cites, in addition to Galen, some seven, mostly sixteenth-century, medical authorities, who attribute melancholy to (among many other things) the eating of fruit; some authorities forbid all fruit, others only certain fruits, still others only raw fruit (*The Anatomy of Melancholy* [1628], partition 1, section 2, member 2, subsection 1: "Bad Diets a Cause. Substance"). When Burton comes to consider cures for melancholy, his dietary recommendations with respect to fruit are generally rather moderate (partition 1, section 2, member 1, subsection 1: "Diet Rectified in Substance"):

> *Crato* . . . censures all manner of fruits, as subject to putrefaction, yet tolerable at some times, after meales, at second course, they keepe downe vapors, and have their use. Sweet fruits are best, as sweet cherries, plummes, sweet apples; peare-maines, and pippins, which *Laurentius* extols, as having a peculiar property against this disease, and *Plater* magnifies, *omnibus modis appropriata conveniunt* [they are agreeable to all], but they must bee corrected for their windinesse; ripe grapes are good, & raysins of the Sun, muske-millions well corrected, and sparingly used. Figges are allowed, and almonds blanched. . . . Pomegranates, Lemons, Oranges are tolerated if they be not too sharpe.

Two best-selling sixteenth-century medical writers not cited by Burton in his discussion of fruit and melancholy are his own countrymen, Sir Thomas Elyot (ca. 1490–1546), and Bartolomeo Sacchi (Platina), whom we have already encountered in chapter 1. Elyot's *Castel of Helthe* (1539), according to Samuel Tannenbaum, "a medical book for laymen, achieved the phenomenal success of going through not less than fifteen editions between the years 1539 and 1610." Chapter 14 of the second book of Elyot's work is devoted to fruit (melons, cucumbers, dates, figs, grapes and raisins, cherries, peaches, apples, quinces, pomegranates, pears, medlars, prunes, olives, oranges, and various nuts), preceded by the following interesting evolutionary speculation concerning human eating habits:

> For as moche as before that tyllage of corne was inuented, and that deuouringe [devouring] of fleshe and fyshe was of mankynde used, men undoubtedlye lyued by fruites, and Nature was therewith contented and satisfied: but by chaunge of the diete of our progenytours, there is caused to be in our bodyes, such alteration frome the nature, whiche was in men at the begynnynge, that nowe all fruites generally are noyfull [noxious] to manne, and do ingender yll humours, and be ofte tymes the cause of putrified feuers, if they be moche and continually eaten. Not withstanding unto

them, which haue abundaunce of coler, they be somtime conuenient, to
represse the flame, which procedeth of coler. And some fruites which be
styptike [acidic], or bynding in tast, eaten before meales, do bynd the bely,
but eten after meales, they be rather laxative.

About cherries, Elyot has this to say: "Cheries, if they be swete, they do soone slyp
downe into the stomake, but if they be soure or sharpe, they be more holsome, and
do louse, if they be eaten freshe, and newly gathered. they be cold and moist in the
first degree." As for oranges:

> The ryndes taken in a lyttell quantitie, do comfort the stomake, where it
> digesteth, specially condite [preserved] with sugar, and taken fastynge in a
> smalle quantitie. The iuyce of orenges hauinge a toste of breadde put unto
> it, with a lyttell powder of myntes, sugar, and a lyttell cynamom, maketh a
> very good sauce to prouoke appetite. The iuyce eaten with sugar in a hotte
> feuer, is nat to be discommended, The rynde is hotte in the firste degree,
> and drye in the seconde. The iuyce of theym is colde in the seconde degre,
> and dry in the fyrst.

During the very period when Elyot's book was presumably being widely read
in Britain, a portrait of the family of Henry Brooke, Lord Cobham (oil on panel, 36⅛
x 47¼ in.), was painted (by an unknown artist); dating from 1567, the picture shows
six children (their ages specified above their heads: two, one, six, five, five, and four)
seated around a dinner table with their parents and Lady Cobham's sister in the background. Two pet birds and a little dog are present and on the table is a plate for each
child and a platter of fruit—the only food on view. The recognizable fruits include
grapes, apples, pears, and quinces, and the children have clearly been eating the fruit:
several have grapes on their plates; one has half an apple. There is certainly no fear of
fruit expressed in the painting. (For a colored reproduction of the painting, now in
a private collection, see *Dynasties: Painting in Tudor and Jacobean England, 1530–1630*
[1995], ed. Karen Hearn; a second version of the painting with an additional son is also
in a private collection.)

More evidence from art about attitudes toward eating fruit comes from seventeenth-century Dutch still life painting. Citing still lifes by Clara Peeters (1583–1657)
and Osias Beert (ca, 1580–1623), Norbert Schneider generalizes: "Fruit was always one
of the last courses in a banquet. In the cuisine of the landed gentry and the merchant
classes, great emphasis was therefore placed on the more refined fruits: wild fruit from
the woods, fields and meadows were considered inferior, as they were smaller and had
less taste."

Platina was the important Italian humanist Bartolomeo Sacchi, whose sobriquet
derives from the Latin name of his birthplace (Piadena, near Cremona). We have
already encountered, in chapter 1, Platina's most popular work, *De honesta voluptate et*

694   *valetudine* (*On Right Pleasure and Good Health*), of which "about forty percent" is borrowed from an Italian cookbook by Martino de Rossi, first employed by the dukes of
Milan and subsequently the celebrated chef of Cardinal Ludovico Trevisan. For the
medical portions of his book, Platina drew heavily on the Arabic medical tradition,
while "the source of most of Platina's information on plants and animals is Pliny's *Natural
History,* which is unmentioned in the preface and only sporadically credited in the
individual chapters." In spite of all his borrowings, the leading expert on Platina, Mary
Ella Milham, finds originality in his concern for "the esthetic and psychological
dimensions of pleasurable dining."

Fresh fruit occupies a prominent place in Platina's first two books. In book 1, he
tells us that eating should begin with "whatever is of light and slight nourishment, like
apples and pears"; book 1, in fact, begins with the following passage on cherries (and
continues with plums, mulberries, melons, cucumbers, quinces, and figs):

> Of all the fruit-bearing trees in our region, the cherry [*cerasa*] . . . ripens
> first and is first served for eating. L. Lucullus brought this tree to Italy after
> his Mithridatic victory in the year of the city 680. Its productiveness has
> been so great that it has been carried as far as the Ocean and into Britain.
> Some cherries are tart, some sour, some sweet. The sour ones constrict
> the bowels and upset the stomach; tart ones cut phlegm, repress yellow
> bile, quench thirst, and stimulate the appetite. Sweet ones are bad for the
> stomach, for they generate intestinal worms and foul humors in the bow-
> els. If they are eaten in the morning, fresh and with their pits, they move
> the urine and the bowels.

In book 2, Platina discusses the beneficial and ill effects of eating apples, pears, grapes,
pomegranates, quinces, citrons, dates, medlars, service berries, cornel cherries, and
peaches. The citron passage also contains a discussion of oranges (*narantia*):

> Almost the same things can be said about those citron or medicinal apples
> which are commonly called oranges; really because some are sweet, some
> tart, the reason for eating is repeated from the earlier recipes. The sweet
> ones are good for the stomach if eaten at any time before a meal. They are
> not tart if they have been dipped in sugar, which is done when the peel is
> removed and the membranes taken out.

One of the principal Arabic writers on the medical aspects of food was Ibn Butlan
(born in Baghdad, died after 1068), though it is not clear how his writings (in Latin
versions dating to the eleventh or twelfth century) were transmitted to Platina. A direct
influence of the Arab physician can be traced, however, on the textual annotations in
a remarkable group of five illustrated late-medieval Latin health handbooks. (These are
discussed, with reproductions, in Luisa Cogliati Arano's *The Medieval Health Handbook:
Tacuinum Sanitatis* [1976].) Each of the handbooks takes the form of an illuminated

text either of the late fourteenth century (four manuscripts from Lombardy) or early fifteenth century (one manuscript from Tuscany). The manuscripts are examples of a genre called *tacuinum sanitatis,* or "health table," and the illustrations depict things that influence health: foods, emotional states (anger, for example), physical influences (such as seasons of the year, bathing, wind directions, clothing). Among the foods, fruit is very prominent: sweet and sour apples; sweet and sour cherries; pears; oranges; sweet and sour pomegranates; grapes; figs; peaches; plums; quinces; apricots; medlars; dates; watermelons and cucumbers; sweet and tasteless melons. The Latin annotations written beneath each picture follow a formula that includes "usefulness" and "dangers"—each fruit possesses some of both; for example (in translations by Oscar Ratti):

> Sour Cherries (*Ceresa Acetosa*)
> *Nature:* Cold at the end of the first degree, humid in the first. *Optimum:* The pulpy ones with a thin skin. *Usefulness:* Good for phlegmatic stomachs burdened with superfluities. *Dangers:* They are digested slowly. *Neutralization of the dangers:* By eating them on an empty stomach.

> Oranges (*Cetrona id est Narancia*)
> *Nature:* The pulp is cold and humid in the third degree, the skin is dry and warm in the second. *Optimum:* Those that are perfectly ripe. *Usefulness:* Their candied skin is good for the stomach. *Dangers:* They are difficult to digest. *Neutralization of the dangers:* Accompanied by the best wine.

It will be noted that all three of the last three medical texts mentioned—Elyot's, Platina's, and the *Tacuinum Sanitatis*—agree that sweet cherries are unwholesome and that sweet oranges are wholesome.

Like Burton, Ackerknecht cites only medical theorists as sources of evidence, and yet, as we have already seen, in one example after another, writings of all kinds in the literary traditions we have been considering are full of favorable references to fruit. Let me cite just one more piece of literary evidence from thirteenth-century France. In his book *Aristocratic Life in Medieval France* (2000), John Baldwin refers to the shadowy late-twelfth-century French composer of romances, Jean Renart (probably a pseudonym), for episodes in which aristocratic hosts provide fruit and wine to their guests before they retire. In two other of Renart's episodes, "when the empress wishes to ingratiate herself with her husband, she has chamberlains serve them in bed with wine and fruit, both raw and cooked," and "the count of Saint-Gilles customarily joins the ladies in the *chambre aux dames* to relax by the fire, while his pears and apples are stewing." We have, of course, ample independent evidence of large-scale fruit growing in orchards and gardens: someone must have been eating all that fruit! It is possible, though, that in Victorian England some surviving remnant of an older medical tradition might have contributed to a superstitious fear of raw fruit, especially for children.

696   What were American attitudes toward eating raw fruit in the middle of the nineteenth century? I will cite a piece of advice—which I can only assume is not atypical—quoted from *Hall's Journal of Health,* in a farm periodical published in Boston in 1859:

> EATING FRUIT.—No liquid of any description should be drank within an hour after eating fruits, nor any thing else be eaten within two or three hours afterwards—thus time being allowed for them to pass out of the stomach, the system derives from them all their enlivening, cooling and opening influences. The great rule is, eat fruits in their natural state, without eating or drinking any thing for at least two hours afterwards. With these restrictions, fruit and berries may be eaten with moderation during any hour of the day, and without getting tired of them, or ceasing to be benefited by them during the whole season. It is a great waste of lusciousness that fruits and berries, in their natural state, are not made the sole dessert of our meals, for three-fourths of the year; human enjoyment, and health, and even life, would be promoted by it.

Like most generalizations about nutrition, each opinion about the effects of eating fruit has its supporters and its opponents. In a funny poem, "Eat Fruit," Marge Piercy recounts her mother's admonition to "eat fruit" and her own faithful adherence to the precept. The seventh and last stanza wittily explains her reward:

> However, I tell you smugly, I am regular in Nome,
> in Paducah, in both Portlands and all Springfields.
> While you are eating McMuffins I am savoring a bruised
> but extremely sophisticated pear that has seen five
> airports and four cities and grown old in wisdom.

Diane Wakoski, on the other hand, is not interested in anything so mundane as the effects of eating fruit on nutrition or digestion. Is there anything intelligent or subtle about fruit?, she has been asking, and finally, somewhat surprisingly, finds an affirmative answer in framboise (the liqueur derived from raspberries):

> It was at your house
> that I first drank
> that clear heady liquor,
> framboise,
> an eau de vie, promising
> that fruit did not have to be
> fresh-cheeked, fat or stupid,
> that it could read Proust,
> or learn differential
> equations.

> The Saturnian taste
> of old raspberries
> [. . . . .]
> The pebbled surface
> of a raspberry

There are, of course, nonhuman friends and enemies of fruit. One of the earliest extant descriptions of a devastating insect invasion of fruit orchards is by the Jewish prophet Joel (ca. 400–350 B.C.E.), who interprets what must have been a plague of locusts as a manifestation of God's judgment on a sinful Israel (1:4–12). Although the meaning of some of the Hebrew terms is uncertain, it seems that Joel begins with a designation of the different developmental stages of the insect:

> What the cutter has left, the locust has devoured;
> What the locust has left, the grub has devoured;
> And what the grub has left, the hopper has devoured.

The incursion of the locusts is compared to an invading army and the individual insects to lions:

> Vast beyond counting,
> With teeth like the teeth of a lion,
> With the fangs of a lion's breed.

Wheat and barley crops have been destroyed, as well as cattle and sheep pastures; as for the fruit:

> The vine has dried up,
> The fig tree withers,
> Pomegranate, palm, and apple—
> All the trees of the field are sear.
> And joy has dried up
> Among men.

Earlier, in chapter 2, we encountered the fig wasp, responsible for pollinating fig trees. But there are other wasps that feed on pears; the process is described by Colette in "Flora and Pomona" (translated by Matthew Ward):

> Below the the sparsely leaved, scaly Messire Jean trees exposed to the wind, other early pears would begin to ripen in July, quickly turning mealy if not picked on time, and craftily emptied out by the wasps. They would bore a single hole in the pears, then busy themselves inside while the fruit retained its shape. How many times have I crushed a yellow, wasp-filled Montgolfier in my hand?

698   One of the most interesting representations of a pear I know of in modern painting is the superb oil on canvas (36¾ x 38⅝ inches) *Wasp and Pear* (1927), by the American Gerald Murphy (1888–1964), in the Museum of Modern Art. The painting was done while Murphy was living in France and, no doubt, he saw, or knew of, the pear-wasp relationship described by Colette. (For a reproduction, see Elizabeth Hutton Turner et al., *Americans in Paris (1921–1931): Man Ray, Gerald Murphy, Stuart Davis, Alexander Calder* [1996].)

As noted earlier, both Stevens and Preil were attentive to the riot of colors in certain varieties of pears. These colors are beautifully captured in Joseph Decker's painting *Pears,* a small (9½ x 10⅝ in.) close-up study of some seventeen pears artfully disposed among branches and leaves; the pears are full of spots and imperfections and one of them has a large, brown, scooped-out region produced by two enterprising wasps. (For a reproduction of the painting, now in a private collection, see William H. Gerdts, *Joseph Decker: Still Lifes, Landscapes, and Images of Youth* [1988].)

Not a wasp but "a huge golden bee" is discovered, in James Wright's "The First Days" (1977),

> ploughing
> His burly right shoulder into the belly
> Of a sleek yellow pear
> Low on a bough.

The pear falls to the ground and the bee is immobilized in the flesh of the pear. The poet releases him by slicing open the fruit, and then wonders whether perhaps he should have left the bee to die happy, "drowning in his own delight." The final six lines include an English version of the Latin tag from Virgil that serves as epigraph—"The best days are the first / To flee"—and, finally, the disclosure that the city where this little drama is being enacted is Mantua (Virgil's birthplace).

We have already noted the problems of early American fruit growers with plant pests. Jefferson learned of the fruit curculio from the writings of William Bartram, who had described the life cycle of the insect as early as 1789 in a lecture to the Philadelphia Society for Promoting Agriculture:

> This is the mischievous insect which destroys all our stone fruit, plumbs, pears, nectarins, cherries &c. and I believe apples, the European walnut, and other fruits. But it is not in the fly or beetle state that they do this mischief, but in that of the caterpillar or worm. In the spring when the young fruit is about half grown or younger, the female is furnished with a sharp spatula or gauge at the extremity of her abdomen, somewhat like the point of a lancet, with which she pierces the rind of the tender green fruit, at the same instant depositing an egg or knit just under the raised cuticle of the wound, which is like to that made by the nib of a pen. This egg soon hatches, and the little larva immediately eats inward, descending to the

stone or kernel of the fruit, round about which it feeds, between it and
the pulpy rind, or enters the kernel, which is yet very tender and delicate;
but in this last circumstance, the destroyer generally falls a victim to his
own intemperance and gluttony, for such fruit generally drop before they
are half ripe, and consequently before the metamorphosis of the grub, but
such as feed only on the interior pulp round about the stone, continue on
the tree until the ripening of the fruit , and thus live out their time. . . .
Such is the prolific nature of this insect, that each female lays many hundred eggs, and a few flies are abundantly sufficient to destroy the fruit of a
large tree.

Listen to this prolonged cry of horticultural despair from a prominent Pennsylvania fruit grower named Richard Peters (1744–1828)—who also happened to be a
frequent correspondent of Thomas Jefferson's—as he eloquently agonizes over his failures at peach culture, in an essay published in 1808:

I have failed in many things, in which others are said to have succeeded.
Straw . . . surrounding the trees, from the root, at all distances, from 5
inches, to 3 or 4 feet—white washing, painting, urinous applications,
brine, soot, lime, frames filled with sand, oil, tar, turpentine, sulphuric acid
or oil of vitriol, nitrous mixtures, and almost every kind of coating. I
ruined several trees, by cutting them down, and permitting the stump to
throw up new shoots, and branch at pleasure. All teguments kept the exsu-
dation [exudation] from evaporating with freedom. The pores being
closed, or too open, were alike injurious. Teguments of straw or bass made
the bark tender; and threw out under the covering, sickly shoots. The
more dense coating stopped the perspiration. The oil invited mice and
other vermin, who ate the bark thus prepared for their repast and killed
the tree. I planted in hedge rows and near woods, I paved, raised hillocks
of stone—I have suffered them to grow from the stone only, grafted on
various stocks and budded, hilled up the earth in the spring and exposed
the butt in the fall, sometimes I have used the knife freely—frequently
have left the tree to shoot in every direction—I have scrubbed the stocks
or trunks. . . . I had temporary success, but final disappointment.

Paul Muldoon (b. 1951) is much more succinct in his haiku on the ills of peaches:

That peach bears the brunt
of the attacks by mildew,
black rot, smuts, and bunts.

"Smut" and "bunt," by the way, both refer to parasitic fungoids that convert parts of an
infected plant into a mass of black powdery spores. Such threats to peach growers are
hardly a thing of the past; in October of 1999, for example (according to an Associated

Press dispatch in the *New York Times*), the so-called plum pox virus was identified for the first time in North America, in some peach orchards in central Pennsylvania: the virus "affects stone fruit trees, including peach, plum, nectarine, apricot and almond. The affected fruit is not harmful, but it becomes ugly, mottled with rings and unmarketable. The infected trees eventually stop producing fruit." The only solution is to destroy and burn the infected trees.

A consideration of the general problems of protecting fruit crops from their chief enemies (at least, from the human point of view)—the insects—has been turned, against all probability, into an effective poem, by James Fenton (b. 1949). Many of the statements and phrases in Fenton's "The Fruit-Grower in War-time (and some of his enemies)" (1968–70) are taken, as he explains in a note, from a Penguin book by Raymond Bush, *The Fruit-Grower;* the quoted passages are italicized by Fenton. The poem consists of eight stanzas, each of a dozen lines, and the stress pattern is identical throughout: a four-stress line, four five-stress lines, two two-stress lines, four five-stress lines, and a four-stress line. There is enjambment between many of the stanzas and occasional rhymes. The only fruit mentioned in the poem is the apple, but there is a long list of "enemy" insects: weevil, sawfly, codling moth, Capsid bug, Wooly Aphis ("called American Blight"), and winter moth. The third and fourth stanzas detail the constant attack of the pests:

> He knows that what few apples survive attack
> From weevils and mature have only to face
> Further depredations from the sawfly and
> Codling moth. Often, walking down orchard rows
> > In summer where such pests
> > Are prevalent, he has
> Heard the sharp clicks as the innumerable
> Apple-suckers jump from the apple leaves at
> His approach, a pest whose winged generation
> Can cloud the windscreens of bus-drivers in Kent.
> > No wonder then that he cultivates

> > Such minute accuracy. *Settling*
> *Herself at the edge of the calyx cup, where*
> *Two sepals join, the sawfly faces into*
> *The centre of the flower, bends her body down*
> *And inserts her ovipositor into*
> > *The side of the fruitlet.*
> > The eggs of the Codling
> Moth are *noticeable only when the sun*
> *Glints on them.* To control the grubs he will need
> Not a single spray at petal fall (which is

Useless over a length of time) but a wash   701
    Between the 1st and 10th of July.

By the time Fenton gets to his penultimate stanza he has begun to worry about
the long-term effects of insecticides:

             We find it hard,
Knowing that a bad harvest or a poor crop
    Can overthrow a state,
    To overestimate
The value of his work. But something remains
Which gives us pause. We think of all those gallons
Of arsenate of lead being pumped over
Our native soil. How can we help comparing
    Ourselves to the last idiot heirs
    Of some Roman province, still for the
Sake of form eating off lead platters? With each
Bug destroyed and apple saved we are nearer
Discovering what we are about. Meanwhile
We must observe the fruit-grower with caution
    But remember his friend's
    Stern charge that *it is you*
Who when you eat into an apple do not like to
Bite into a bug, that have led him into
His bloodthirsty way of life. One cannot doubt
That this is so and that in similar or
    Related cases the paradigm holds true.

A closer look at the effects of apple blight is provided in a poem (1996) by Paul
Zimmer that takes its title from the disease:

    Blighted apples will not shine.
    Though they are buffed by winds
    As diligent as Caesar's valets,
    The fog has settled in their skins.

    Branches bow down low to death,
    Dragged by blighted apples.
    Cold leaves curl about the wind,
    Strangled by dull apples.

    Though apples host the cruelest worms,
    The hardest beetles, still they shine,

But when the sickness sweeps the tree
They will not shine, they will not shine.

Human beings cultivate fruit and consume it—indeed, they mostly cultivate fruit in order to consume it—but in adverse circumstances these same human beings are only too prone to destroy wantonly any fruit they perceive as belonging to their enemies; and this too has been written about by poets. Thus, the anonymous twelfth-century author of an English poem about the war waged by Henry II against Scotland writes (in modernized English):

They did not lose within, I assure you I do not lie,
As much as amounted to a silver denier.
But they lost their fields, with all their corn,
Their gardens ravaged by those bad people.
And he who could not do any more injury took it in his head
To bark apple trees—it was bad vengeance.

As for praise of fruit, I know of few writers more eloquent and none more systematic than Ralph Austen. In his treatise on fruit trees, Austen distinguishes the profits and pleasures of planting such trees. The profits are five in number (with subdivisions): to a man's estate, to his body, to his mind, to his name, and to others. The pleasures also number five:

First to the Eare, and that in two respects, first, by sweete tunes of singing birds: secondly, by gentle motion of Boughes, and leaves.

Secondly, Here's Pleasure to the Touch, and that in two respects, first, by coole fruits, Boughes, and Leaves: secondly, by coole fresh Aires.

Thirdly, Here's Pleasure to the Eye, and that in two respects, first, by exact, and decent formes of Trees, Alleyes, Walkes, Seates, and Arbours: secondly, by curious colours of the blossomes, Leaves, and fruits.

Here's Pleasure to the smell, and that in two respects: first, from fresh Earth digged up: secondly, from the Leaves, and Blossomes.

Fift[h]ly, Here's Pleasure to the Tast, and that in two respects: first from ripe, and raw fruits. Secondly, from dishes and drinkes made of them.

And Austen concludes: "And as there is a mutuall consent and concurrence of all the *Profits* among themselves, and of all the *Pleasures* among themselves, soe likewise there is a mutuall consent and concatenation of the *Profits* with the *Pleasures* one imbracing another, one supporting, and upholding each other."

That enthusiastic and knowledgable home gardener Eleanor Perényi might agree with Ralph Austen in principle, but in practice she knows better. Her little essay on fruit, in *Green Thoughts,* confesses wistfully: "The truth is that I am no hand at raising fruit and seriously doubt that many home gardeners are." There are just too many

variables one must control, as well as those out of one's control (such as the weather):
a dwarf nectarine tree planted too deeply, which returned to a standard; a nonbearing
pear tree; an apricot tree destroyed by borers; birds eating the cherries, squirrels the
peaches; picked pears which rot before they ripen; apricots killed by a late frost or a
dry summer. Her conclusion:

> That I go on ordering fruit trees represents, as was said of second mar-
> riages, the triumph of optimism over experience, and I persist in believ-
> ing that somehow, someday, a bowl of ripe, home-grown fruit will come
> to rest on the kitchen table. I know in my heart that it won't, but mean-
> while I go on watering and mulching and pruning the little trees, and they
> do look pretty when they bloom in spring. Next year, I may get a with-
> ered plum or two and that would be a novelty. But it's too early to tell.

BERRIES

"the berries: that which is attractive or pleasing; the height of excellence"

Historical Dictionary of American Slang

Why are berries singled out in American slang as a synonym for superlative quality? Well, to begin with, berries possess perhaps the most varied and intense tastes of all fruits. Furthermore, berrying is for many Americans one of the great pleasures of childhood, with the added delight that wild berries are usually quite the equal of, and frequently superior to, the cultivated varieties (by contrast, wild tree fruits, such as apples or plums, are often inedible). The sometimes almost willed pleasure of berrying in childhood is precisely the point of Virginia Hamilton Adair's poem "Blueberry City" (1996), where the mother reduces her daughter to tears after a bout of strenuous berry picking on a cold, snowy day, with her remark: "I said to my little girl, Remember / this: maybe the happiest hour of our life."

For another American poet, Maxine Kumin (b. 1925), wild berries—picking them, eating them, cooking them up into jam—are evidently ingredients in many of the peak experiences of her life. All of these experiences involve intimate relations with members of her family (father, mother, husband, daughter). We may begin with her father in "Appetite" (1985):

> I eat these
> wild red raspberries
> still warm from the sun
> and smelling faintly of jewelweed
> in memory of my father
>
> tucking the napkin
> under his chin and bending
> over an ironstone bowl
> of the bright drupelets
> awash in cream
>
> my father

with the sigh of a man
who has seen all and been redeemed
said time after time
as he lifted his spoon

men kill for this

Jewelweed, by the way, is a wildflower also known as touch-me-not, while drupelets are the individual seed-containing sacs of the raspberry. In another poem, "Making the Jam Without You" (1970), Kumin thinks of her absent daughter (the dedicatee of the poem) while "crushing blackberries / to make the annual jam / in a white cocoon of steam." Kumin wishes for her daughter to find a man to help with the picking of "plum size" berries, "the buckets / crooked on his angel arms," and for their "two heads" to

touch over the kettle,
over the blood of the berries
that drink up sugar and sun,
over that tar-thick boil
love cannot stir down.

Finally, the poet withdraws from the scene she has conjured up, leaving further intimacies to the imagined couple themselves:

At this time
I lift the flap of your dream
and slip out thinner than a sliver
as your two mouths open
for the sweet stain of purple.

The clear lines of continuity from one generation to the next are vividly identified for Kumin with her family tradition of gathering wild berries and then almost ritualistically making jam of them.

As for her husband and mother, they have leading roles in Kumin's brief essay "Enough Jam for a Lifetime" (1994). Her husband is "an addicted picker . . . whose enthusiasm became my labor," while reminiscences of her mother stimulate a long account of the jam-making techniques she has inherited from her mother, ending with the remark:

There is no quality control in my method. Every batch is a kind of revisionism. It makes its own laws. But the result is pure, deeply colored, uncomplicated, and unadulterated blackberry jam, veritably seedless, suitable for every occasion.

Yet another American poet, Cary Waterman, also writes about making jam from wild berries: she has not picked them herself but the picker must be someone she is

706   intimately acquainted with—a family member or a friend. Here are the three central
       stanzas from her "Elderberry Jam" (1982):

Now you come back,
stand in the doorway,
your hair wet with dew.
And in your hand
a brown bag in which
the elderberries are captive,
still rigid,
still resisting on
their hooks of stem.

After we clean them
I start the jam.
In an old pot
the berries burst into purple.
They are like little skulls of stain.
I add sugar,
that white iceberg,
and a scant touch of water
to start the boil.
Now the fruit is becoming tender,
the juice begins to flow.

At the moment of mashing
they rise up
vengefully,
shaking fists,
boiling and turning
like hot rock
and pushing to the center,
to smother,
to go down
in the purple face of the pot.

It seems there is something violent about picking the wild berries and perhaps doubly
violent about boiling them up into jam. It should be added that the first and last framing stanzas emphasize the darkness encompassing the house, which heightens the
transgressive atmosphere still further. This troubling mixture of pleasure and disqui-
etude will recur in most of our remaining berry episodes.

Before we go on to consider further berry-picking episodes, however, it is important to remind ourselves that not all children have the privilege of going berrying during their childhood. Gwendolyn Brooks (1917–2000) is presumably writing, in the epigram "Old Mary" (1960) of someone who spent her childhood in the inner city:

> My last defense
> Is the present tense.
>
> It little hurts me now to know
> I shall not go
>
> Cathedral-hunting in Spain
> Nor cherrying in Michigan or Maine.

In the last line, "berrying" could be substituted for "cherrying" without any loss, as far as I can see. Unlike the former term, however, which according to the *OED* goes back at least to 1871, Brooks's term seems to be unknown to the editors of modern dictionaries of English (including the revised *OED* of 1989 and its two supplements of 1993). Michigan, by the way, produces almost three-quarters of the world's supply of cherries, while Maine is more famous for blueberries.

If there is any question about the high quality of America's wild berries, we may call as historical witness the redoubtable Frances Trollope, certainly no uncritical eulogist of things American. Here is a passage on blackberries, which she chose not to publish, from one of her notebooks (1830):

> I am almost sure I shall be laughed at if I say that the blackberries of North America are almost the finest fruit I ever tasted of the berry kind, but so it is. They are as large as moderate-sized mulberries, and as juicy. They are less acid and the flavour is incomparably richer. As a sweetmeat they are much finer than either raspberries or strawberries.

Did Trollope really omit this passage from her book to avoid being laughed at? In any case, about a century later, U. P. Hedrick, in his *Small Fruits of New York* (1925), finds European and American blackberries equally fine: "The blackberry is about the commonest wild fruit of Europe and the fruit of some species is quite as delectable as that of our American blackberries." Hedrick also observes that "the blackberry, in one or another of its many species, is indigenous in most temperate parts of the northern hemisphere, and in this great zone might almost be said to be at once the best and most abundant wild fruit. Their abundance is proverbial"—as in this line from a speech of Falstaff's in Shakespeare's *Henry IV,* Part 1 (2.4.248–50): "If reasons were as plentiful as blackberries, I would give no man a reason upon compulsion, I." One may add another Shakespearean line to the same effect from *Troilus and Cressida* (1602), in a speech by Thersites (5.4.11): "Ulysses, is proved not worth a blackberry."

Something more should be said about Hedrick's volume on "small fruits," which deals only with berries: bramble fruits (raspberries, dewberries, and blackberries), bush fruits (currants and gooseberries), and strawberries. Hedrick expresses his regret that he cannot include cranberries or blueberries, even though both of them were beginning to be commercially cultivated; neither would grow successfully on the grounds of the New York State Agricultural Experimental Station. In this, the last of the New York State fruit volumes, the illustrative plates are especially fine; my favorite plate shows life-sized Honeysweet black raspberries at various stages of ripeness (see plate 34). Black raspberries, as Hedrick explains, are also called "blackcaps" or "thimbleberries." Honeysweets possess "a rich, honey-like, distinct flavor, made more delectable by an enticing aroma. The berries are of large size, glossy black, very handsome, so that, with the high quality they are nearly perfect in fruit character."

American painters did not ignore the native blackberries; indeed, rarely has anyone painted blackberries more beautifully than the Chicago artist Cadurcis Plantagenet Ream (1837–1917), who specialized in fruit subjects. Ream's *Blackberries Spilling From a Tin Cup* (oil on board, 9½ x 11⅜ in.) is in a private American collection (see plate 35; on Ream, see the account by Susan Danly and Bruce Weber in the catalogue of the Gerdts collection, *For Beauty and For Truth* [1998]). Ream's painting is notable for the beautifully rendered metallic sheen on the tin cup and for the circular arrangement of highlights on the drupes of each berry.

Also worth mentioning is a remarkable but considerably earlier (ca. 1813) American painting of blackberries by Raphaelle Peale, now in the Fine Arts Museum of San Francisco (oil on panel, 7¼ x 10¼ in.). In his book on Raphaelle Peale's still lifes, *The Body of Raphaelle Peale: Still Life and Selfhood, 1812–1824* (2001), Alexander Nemerov has devoted his first three chapters to an extended analysis of the "strangeness" or "uncanniness" of this painting. Nemerov's analysis consists partly of a fascinatingly detailed look at the painting's compositional and optical properties. The main thrust of Nemerov's treatment (and of his entire book) is, however, to relate these aesthetic (or formal) elements to the culture of early nineteenth-century Philadelphia and, more especially, to the phenomenology peculiar to Peale's painterly practices. As Nemerov puts it,

> What interests me most is the phenomenological sense of embodiedness these object project. . . . The body in question, in turn, is that of the artist himself. Raphaelle's paintings simulate the artist's own physical existence projected into the objects of perception. They do so as a way of uncannily breaking down the position of a secure subject standing apart from the things he beholds.

More briefly: "What Raphaelle imagines is this: a primordial embodied space, set off hermetically from the surrounding world, in which a 'self' does not exist." (These few words convey, of course, only the conclusion of Nemerov's study; a sense of the intricate and sometimes convoluted argumentation is missing.)

Writing in his own notebook some decade and a half after Trollope, Thoreau would have thoroughly agreed with her observations on American berries: in "Wild Fruits," Thoreau is breathless, almost incoherent, in his praise of wild black huckleberries. Before proceeding with Thoreau, a few words should be said about huckleberries. The name seems to be an American dialect variant (from as early as 1670) of the Middle English hertleberry or whortleberry. All these names refer to berries belonging to either one of two different genera: *Vaccinium* (the blueberry genus) and *Gaylussacia* (the huckleberry genus). Blueberries and huckleberries look pretty much alike but can be distinguished by the texture of their flesh: "If it looks like a blueberry and tastes like a blueberry, but it's small and dark and grainy with seeds, it's a huckleberry," says *Taylor's Guide to Fruits and Berries*. Thoreau is at his best in his alert scrutiny of the qualities of huckleberries, which, he tells us, "are of various forms, colors, and flavors: some round, some pear-shaped, some glossy black, some dull black, some blue with a tough and thick skin (though they are never of the peculiar light blue of blueberries with a bloom), some sweeter, some more insipid, and so on—more varieties than botanists take notice of."

Thoreau is, of course, interested in black huckleberries as food: "This crop grows wild all over the country—wholesome, bountiful, and free, a real ambrosia." But he is equally interested in the fact of their wildness and the resultant "pleasure of gathering" them. Thus, Thoreau relates how sometimes in his boyhood he was sent out on a summer morning to pick enough black huckleberries for a pudding. Even more memorable was another occasion when what I am going to call the family romance of picking wild berries took one of its more grotesque forms:

> I once met with a whole family—father, mother, and children—ravaging a huckleberry field in this wise. They cut up the bushes as they went and beat them over the edge of a bushel basket till they had it full of berries, ripe and green, leaves, sticks, and so forth; and so they passed along out of my sight like wild men.

Thoreau also, rather implausibly, attributes a potent moral and educational function to picking wild berries: "Liberation and enlargement—such is the fruit which all culture aims to secure." And he goes on to deplore the loss of wildness: "What sort of a country is that where the huckleberry fields are private property?"

A decade or so after Thoreau was writing about huckleberries, his compatriot Mark Twain wrote one of his early journalistic pieces, "Morality and Huckleberries," for the San Francisco newspaper *Alta California* (September 1868). Twain reports his first sight of the berries on a visit to Hartford, while delivering to his publisher the manuscript of what was to be his first successful book, *The Innocents Abroad* (1869). Justin Kaplan, in his biography of Twain, explains the significance of the huckleberry incident:

Now he saw children gathering buckets of them on the hillsides, and by the slow process of unconscious creation the huckleberry, a Hartford fact, was to become a talisman for recapturing the Hannibal past. What had happened was that, in Hartford, the sight of a promised land, and, in New York, his first meetings with Olivia Langdon [Twain's future wife] caressed and quickened memory and aspiration.

In his Mark Twain dictionary (1995), R. Kent Rasmussen explains in the entry "huckleberry" that the term is "nineteenth-century slang for an inconsequential person" but that the huckleberry "is not native to the Missouri region, where Huckleberry Finn got his name." After relating the Hartford huckleberry incident, Rasmussen goes on to point out that in Twain's novel *Huckleberry Finn* (1884) only two characters call Huck by his full name, Miss Watson four times and the King once.

Here now are some twentieth-century North American poets going berrying or observing others berrying: Robert Frost ("Blueberries," 1914), Irving Layton ("Berry Picking," 1958), Robert Haas, ("Picking Blackberries with a Friend Who Has Been Reading Jacques Lacan," 1979), Amy Clampitt ("Gooseberry Fool," 1985; "Blueberrying in August," 1990), Yusef Komunyakaa ("Blackberries," 1989), Susan Ludvigson ("Blackberries," 1993), Claudia Rankine ("The Man. His Bowl. His Raspberries," 1994), and Wally Swist ("Aftermath," 1999). The poems form a set of variations on the family romance of picking wild berries (the idealized version of the romance consists of one or more children plus one or more adults): some poems discover tensions in the romance, while others reduce the romance to just two individuals, or even focus on the lone berry picker.

Frost characterized his "Blueberries" as an eclogue (as reported in Jeffrey Cramer's *Robert Frost Among His Poems* [1996]) and the poem does indeed take the form of a conversation, in a pastoral setting, between two unidentified people (call them the first and second interlocutor—they may plausibly be understood as husband and wife); the poem is 105 lines in length, in rhymed couplets with an occasional triplet. The two interlocutors talk about blueberries and, especially, about the Loren family (husband, wife, and numerous young children), who know where all the best wild berries grow and who are very jealous about revealing their secrets to others. The interlocutors resent the Lorens' secrecy, while reluctantly conceding it may be necessary for their way of life, which apparently consists mostly of eating and selling berries. (For the Lorens, the family romance of picking wild berries has become a way of life.) The poem opens and closes with the first interlocutor's enthusiastic but careful observations of wild blueberries (lines 3–7, 103–5):

> "Blueberries as big as the end of your thumb,
> Real sky-blue, and heavy, and ready to drum
> In the cavernous pail of the first one to come!
> And all ripe together, not some of them green

And some of them ripe! You ought to have seen!"
[. . . . .]
"You ought to have seen how it looked in the rain,
The fruit mixed with water in layers of leaves,
Like two kinds of jewels, a vision for thieves."

Of the two speakers, the first is clearly the more knowledgable about blueberrying in their present neighborhood—but not nearly as knowledgable as the Loren family. On the other hand, the second understands something rather special about so-called low-bush blueberries: they are very tolerant of fire, so that if one clears an area containing such bushes by burning all the vegetation, the blueberry bushes will reappear almost immediately (lines 13–21). This burning trick, by the way, was already used by native Americans to cultivate lowbush blueberries; it depends on the fact that the plants spread by means of underground stems called rhizomes, which are impervious to the fire above. (Lee Reich, in a chapter called "Lowbush Blueberry: More American Than Apple Pie," in his *Uncommon Fruits Worthy of Attention,* explains how lowbush blueberries may be cultivated in a home garden.)

"Blueberries," written in 1912, was probably inspired by Frost's recollection of the summer of 1895 (he was thirteen) when, after the recent death of his father, the family had moved back to New England and was spending the summer on a New Hampshire farm belonging to his great-uncle and great-aunt. The latter—like the Lorens in "Blackberries"—picked berries to supplement their income from the farm. Frost and his sister themselves hunted for both high- and low-bush blueberries. (See the account in Cramer's book.)

Like Frost, Irving Layton in "Berry Picking" devises a scenario involving a married couple, but now the wife is engaged in picking blueberries, while her husband (the poet) seems only to be watching. In the very first stanza, the husband is, in fact, enacting his literary role, seeing the "darkgreen . . . leaves" as "full of metaphors" and seeing one particular metaphor in the berries: "Now lit up is each tiny lamp of blueberry." Turning from the berries to the picker, the husband explains, in the second stanza, how much he admires his wife: "Berries or children, patient she is with these." The next two stanzas contrast, respectively, the distancing and uncertain rewards of poetry with the immediate and unalloyed sensual pleasure of eating berries:

> I only vex and perplex her; madness, rage
> Are endearing perhaps put down upon the page;
> Even silence daylong and sullen can then
> Enamour as restraint or classic discipline.
>
> So I envy the berries she puts in her mouth.
> The red and succulent juice that stains her lips;

> I shall never taste that good to her, nor will they
> Displease her with a thousand barbarous jests.

There is a puzzle here, for blueberry juice is not red; however, the last line of the poem refers to the wife's lips as "redder than the raspberries." Are we perhaps meant to assume that she is picking one kind of berry and eating another (perhaps because there are simply too few raspberries to be worth collecting)? In any case, the growing complexity of feeling in the poem is accompanied by—perhaps reflected in—the growing remoteness of the end-rhymes and the failure of the last two quatrains to repeat the pattern established in the first four: furze/metaphors/blueberry/free; bush/leaves/hush/these; rage/page/then/discipline; mouth/lips/they/jests. In the last two stanzas, two new rhyme schemes are introduced: *abbb* (take/hers/stares/answers) and *aaba* (deceives/yes/off/raspberries).

The act of berry picking in Layton's poem represents, and exacerbates, the emotional gulf between husband and wife, but, of course, the same act can serve to bring two people together, as in the unpublished "Aftermath" (1999), by the American poet Wally Swist (b. 1953):

> We talk cautiously of differences:
> how the fragrance of roses
> opens in the heat of the afternoon,
> how honey locust blossoms
> are most fragrant in evening coolness,
> how the shape of the beech leaf
> opposes the chestnut, the first
> saw-toothed, the latter elliptical,
> notched, the tips tapered.
> We remark how ferns uncurl
> their green fists into fronds.
> We walk back through the meadow,
> find patches of strawberries
> growing in the sand that we pluck
> by the handful. You dispose
> one after another in my mouth.
> The tart sweetness sears my tongue.
> Beneath the bluest possible sky,
> the whole field burns with blossoms.

The poem by Robert Haas (b. 1941) about picking berries is notably light-hearted, not least in its slightly mocking title. Haas describes picking blackberries with his friend Charlie; they have been discussing "subject and object / and the mediation of desire" in a book by Lacan, when suddenly Charlie recalls a time "twenty years ago / and raspberries and Vermont." The two cease their conversation, "And Charlie, /

laughing wonderfully, / beard stained purple / by the word *juice,* / goes to get a bigger pot." Picking and eating and thinking about wild berries overwhelm philosophical speculation.

Perhaps the first thing to note about "Gooseberry Fool" (1985) by Amy Clampitt is the punning title, which can mean either someone excessively devoted to gooseberries or—in British English—the dessert prepared from stewed gooseberries and heavy cream; both meanings, as we discover, are intended. There are three stanzas to the poem, totaling fifty lines, with an irregular pattern of end-rhymes. Clampitt's lines are short and frequently feature enjambment, even, à la Marianne Moore, the splitting of words at the ends of lines (it happens four times). The first two stanzas—over three-quarters of the poem—expatiate upon the negative features of wild goose-berries (such as the fact that their leaves harbor a "blister rust" fatal to pine tress) and how even "gooseberry virtues / take some getting / used to, much as does trepang, / tripe à la mode de Caen, / or having turned thirteen" (lines 16–20). (Trepang may be more familiar as sea cucumber and the tripe dish mentioned features cider and apple liqueur.) It is only in the last stanza that we hear how the speaker has just ". . . stumbled into / this trove" of wild gooseberries (lines 39–40), and wishes to make a gift of them to her (thirteen-year-old?) friend, "a gleeful Ariel" (line 44). But the speaker faces a dilemma: the gathered gooseberries are ". . . tart as any / kindergarten martinet" (lines 3–4) or, alternatively, they possess "The acerbity of all things green / and adolescent" (lines 21–22). (So, both are sour: the teacher of young children—unless "kindergarten martinet" refers to a child—and the children themselves when they grow older.) The speaker's solution (lines 35–38) is a promise to prepare tomorrow for Ariel a demonstration of

> the mingling into one experience
> of suave and sharp, whose supremely im-
> probable and far-fetched culinary
> embodiment is a gooseberry fool.

But the preparation of the dessert seems also to be both an exorcism for the speaker of "the disarray of an / uncultivated childhood" (lines 30–1) and an occasion for recognizing the limits of her powers: "the great globe itself's too much to carry" (line 50), adapting Shakespeare's phrase from *The Tempest* (4.1.148).

Highly prized in Great Britain and northern Europe, gooseberries and the closely related currants—both belonging to the genus *Ribes*—have had an abortive commercial career in North America owing to the fungus fatal to white pine trees and hosted by many *Ribes* plants. To help protect the American timber industry, planting of gooseberries and currants became subject to strict legislative controls in the early 1900s. Amateur American gardeners continue, of course, to cultivate gooseberries, which are easy to grow even in small gardens, attractive to look at (the fruit can be green, white, yellow, and all shades of red from pink to purple), and, most important,

714   productive of delicious crops. All of the American horticultural writers we have
encountered so far describe and illustrate numerous recommended gooseberry cultivars: Ebenezer Emmons (1851), ten; U. P. Hedrick (1925), 244; Lee Reich (1991), fifty-
two; and Roger Holmes (1996), twenty-five. (See plate 36 for a life-sized picture of
Chautauqua gooseberries from Hedrick's *Small Fruits of New York*.)

To encourage Americans to cultivate gooseberries, Lee Reich quotes the opinion of the English food writer Edward Bunyard, from his *Anatomy of Dessert:* "the
Gooseberry is of course the fruit *par excellence* for ambulant consumption." And the
cultivation of gooseberries does seem to have reached some sort of horticultural summit in Great Britain. There is, of course, gooseberry fool, which the English food
writer Elizabeth David recommends in her booklet *Syllabubs and Fruit Fools* (1969):

> Soft, pale, creamy, untroubled, the English fruit fool is the most frail and
> insubstantial of English summer dishes. . . . In this selection of old and
> modern recipes I give precedence to those dishes made from the goose-
> berry, because green gooseberry fool is—to me at any rate—the most deli-
> cious as well as the most characteristic of all these simple, almost childlike,
> English dishes.

But one main direction that gooseberry cultivation took in England was the quest for
larger and larger fruit, as explained by Charles Darwin, who himself cultivated no
fewer than fifty-four varieties:

> The most interesting point in the history of the gooseberry is the steady
> increase in the size of the fruit. . . . This gradual and on the whole steady
> increase of weight from the latter part of the last century to the year 1852,
> is probably in large part due to improved methods of cultivation, for
> extreme care is now taken; the branches and roots are trained, composts
> are made, the soil is mulched, and only a few berries are left on each bush;
> but the increase no doubt is in main part due to the continued selection
> of seedlings which have been found to be more and more capable of yield-
> ing such extraordinary fruit. Assuredly the "Highwayman" in 1817 could
> not have produced fruit like that of the "Roaring Lion" in 1825; nor could
> the "Roaring Lion," though it was grown by many persons in many places,
> gain the supreme triumph achieved in 1852 by the "London" Gooseberry.

Alan Davidson has written about what he terms "the craze which began in the
eighteenth century for growing giant gooseberries," in his essay "On the Trail of Giant
Gooseberries" (1986). Davidson is describing the annual Egton Bridge Old Gooseberry Competition, in Yorkshire, for 1985:

> This is no simple competition for the one heaviest gooseberry. There are
> separate classes for red, green, white (very pale green) and yellow berries.
> Since all the berries are green until ripe, and it is hard to ensure that

berries attain full ripeness on the exact day of the competition, most of
the berries look green; but many of them are really reds, yellows or whites,
and part of the judges' skill consists in correctly classifying them. "Maidens," as new members are known, have their own prizes, and there are also
prizes for the heaviest twelve and the heaviest six. A complex rule-book
ensures that no one wins too many prizes, and that a high proportion of
the contestants win something.

Davidson reports that the single heaviest gooseberry in the competition he witnessed
was of the yellow variety Woodpecker, which "at 30 drams 22 grains, was breath-
takingly close to two ounces (a figure as talismanic to gooseberry growers as the
four-minute mile once was for athletes)." We will return to gooseberries—Russian
ones—later on in this chapter.

Compared with "Gooseberry Fool," a later poem by Clampitt, "Blueberrying in
August," is shorter, tighter, and in a way less ambitious, occupied really with just the
single transcendent experience of picking blueberries on an island in August:

> Sprung from the hummocks
> of this island, stemmed,
> sea-spray-fed chromosomes
> trait-coded, say, for eyes
> of that surprising blue
> some have, that you have:
> they're everywhere, these
> mimic apertures the color
> of distances, of drowning—
>
> of creekside bluebells
> islanded in the lost world
> of childhood; of the
> illusory indigo that moats
> these hillocks when
> the air is windless.
>
> Today, though, there is
> wind: a slate sag occludes
> the afternoon with old,
> hound-throated mutterings.
> Offshore, the lighthouse
> fades to a sheeted
> sightless ghost. August
> grows somber. Though the blue-

eyed chromosome gives way,
living even so, minute to
minute, was never better.

Somewhat arbitrarily, I choose as a starting point for the explication of this poem the two words "hummocks" and "hillocks," which, if not strictly synonyms, seem to refer to the same topographical features in the landscape of the poem. Why, then, two different words? The easy answer is that Clampitt does not want to repeat herself, but why then repeat the notion of "small hills" at all? I believe we are supposed to take special note of the synonymy of meaning of the two words and at the same time their differences in *sound* and *spelling*. For consider the respective phonological and orthographical environments of the two words: "hummocks" sounds like "sprung" and looks like "stemmed"; "hillock" sounds and looks like "illusory" and sounds like "windless." May not the echoing of certain sounds and the repetition of certain orthographical features help define the subject matter of the poem—blueberrying, all right, but exactly what about it?

To begin with, there is, as in so many berrying episodes, the almost obligatory—in this case, merely glancing—reference to childhood, but there are no literary or mythological or culinary references, and indeed the mood is objective, almost "scientific," what with the chromosomes and the exacting attention to color hues ("blue," "indigo," "slate"). There is, to be sure, the single personal reference to "you" with "eyes / of that surprising blue," but these eyes simply take their place in a sequence of blue objects: berries, eyes, bluebells, atmosphere ("distances"), water ("sea," "drowning," "moats"). As for sound, the blowing of the wind is characterized as "old, / hound-throated mutterings," with "old" echoing "occludes" and "throated." The poem is, in fact, about subtle and not-so-subtle resemblances of color and of sound in an August afternoon of island blueberrying.

"Blackberries," by Yusef Komunyakaa (b. 1947), begins as if it were going to be just another exercise in nostalgia for a past episode of berrying, though with a certain puzzling tinge of guilt tarnishing the childhood innocence:

> They left my hands like a printer's
> Or thief's before a police blotter
> & pulled me into early morning's
> Terrestrial sweetness, so thick
> The damp ground was consecrated
> Where they fell among a garland of thorns.

Immediately, however, in the next two lines, we note how the nostalgia is going to be mixed with longer historical memories of a very different sort:

> Although I could smell old lime-covered
> History, at ten I'd still hold out my hands

> & berries fell into them. Eating from one
> & filling a half gallon with the other,
> I ate the mythology.

The ten-year-old boy is envisaged in retrospect as "limboed between worlds": on the one hand (in the first two-and-a-half stanzas), the "consecrated" natural world of a "terrestrial sweetness" where even the thorns of the blackberry bushes may be seen as a "garland," and on the other hand (in the concluding stanza and a half), the world bordered by "City Limits Road" where the picked berries are to be exchanged for money, but at the expense of fever ("sweat") and chills ("wintertime") provoked by the sight of a "big blue car" whose occupants include a "boy / & girl my age, in the big backseat / Smirking." We realize now that this latter moment of crisis has been prefigured in the first two lines of the poem, when the poet wonders if the blackberry picker is worthy—even admirable—like a printer, or whether he is simply a thief. (This reference of Komunyakaa to a thief may remind us of the last line of Frost's "Blueberries" with its description of wet blueberry bushes as "a vision for thieves.") We return to the boy's stained fingers in the final two lines of the poem, seemingly stretched out for emphasis: "Smirking, & it was then I remembered my fingers / Burning with thorns among berries too ripe to touch." The narrator has remembered the anguish of his childhood self, when the smirking children forced him to recall the earlier pain in his fingers from the thorns and the present stain on his fingers from the berries. The pain and the stain inevitably suggest the boy's nascent racial consciousness.

The speaker in the poem by Susan Ludvigson (b. 1942) has evidently been picking wild blackberries for several days running and suffering scratches and falls in the process. But the pain only makes her think of "sudden love." Then, in the second stanza, we get a closer look at the berries themselves:

> The ripest ones
> will drop into your hand
> at a brush of the branch.
> I can spot them now, the ones
> so black they're almost blue,
> crow colored. That ready,
> they don't cling to their pods,
> but wish themselves into the air,
> onto the tongue.

Finally, in the last four lines of the third stanza, she notices her burning right hand:

> It makes me dream of blackberries.
> I tell you, they ache for pastry
> to hold them, for the mouth
> I put now to my humming hand.

The voice in "The Man. His Bowl. His Raspberries," by Claudia Rankine (b. 1963), is that of an omniscient narrator, who is privy to the minutest detail of the man's behavior as he picks raspberries and also to the future pleasure of the woman when she eats them:

> The bowl he starts with
> is too large. It will never be filled.
>
> Nonetheless, in the cool dawn,
> reaching underneath the leaf, he frees
> each raspberry from its stem
> and white nipples remain suspended.
>
> He is being gentle, so does not think
> *I must be gentle* as he doubles back
> through the plants
> seeking what he might have missed.
> At breakfast she will be pleased
> to eat the raspberries and put her pleasure
> to his lips.
>
> Placing his fingers beneath a leaf
> for one he had not seen, he does not idle.
> He feels for the raspberry. Securing, pulling
> gently, taking, he gets what he needs.

Now, whatever else berries may be, or may stand for, their primary use is as *food*, but food that plays radically different roles in the poems we have been considering: for Frost, blueberries serve as nutrition essential to the very subsistence of an eccentric and irritating, but in certain respects admirable, family; for Layton, berries are gathered and consumed only by the wife, whose husband seems barred from these activities by his very role as poet; for Swist, the shared actions of picking and eating strawberries serve to resolve "differences"; for Haas, picking and eating blackberries serve to turn the poet and his friend away from philosophical speculation and back to the sensuous present and to memories of a sensuous past; for Clampitt, gooseberries serve as food for delectation but also for personal moral growth, while the mere experience of picking blueberries on one particular occasion is so overwhelming that the question of eating them does not even arise; for Komunyakaa, blackberries are gathered with one hand and eaten with the other, generating the tension between the two worlds of the poem; for Ludvigson, the supreme destiny of her blackberries is in pastry; for Rankine, raspberries as a gift of food from the man to the woman serve to reveal the gentle but intimate character of their relationship.

I would not want to sound unduly chauvinistic about the superior quality of American berries or the sensitive temper of American berry pickers, so here are two further blackberrying poems, one set in England, one in Ireland: "Blackberrying" (1961), by Sylvia Plath, and "Blackberry-Picking" (1966), by Seamus Heaney (b. 1939). The berries in each poem are lushly plump and juicy, but only traces of the family romance associated with picking wild berries in North America remain, and each poem culminates in bleak disappointment.

Sylvia Plath wrote "Blackberrying" on 23 September 1961 in Devon, England, where she and her husband, Ted Hughes, and their baby daughter had settled in their newly purchased house on the last day of August 1961. The poem was first published in the *New Yorker* in 1962 and then in Plath's posthumous volume, *Crossing the Water*, in 1971. In his edition of Plath's *Collected Poems* (1981) Hughes has a note specifying more exactly where the poem was written: "in a cliff cove looking out on to the Atlantic." The berrier is alone, as she twice states, except for some choughs and their "voice, protesting, protesting." (Is it because the birds are being deprived of their food?) The only real description of the blackberries is in the last five lines of the first stanza:

> Blackberries
> Big as the ball of my thumb, and dumb as eyes
> Ebon in the hedges, fat
> With blue-red juices. These they squander on my fingers.
> I had not asked for such a blood sisterhood; they must love me.
> They accomodate themselves to my milkbottle, flattening their sides.

"Big as the ball of my thumb" recalls Frost's "big as the end of your thumb" in the third line of his "Blueberries." One wonders if Plath was unconsciously echoing Frost's poem. We learn in Stevenson's biography of Plath that she heard him read his poems at Smith College in 1952 and spent an evening with him at Peter Davison's apartment in 1958. On the other hand, Frost's exact phrase occurs in Thoreau's "Wild Fruits"—which, of course, Frost could not have known—as a characterization of wild blackberries: "the finest of the high blackberries, as big as the end of your thumb, however big that may be."

More important than this minor matter of a possible borrowing is the harmonious sound of Plath's verse, in such sharp contrast to the increasingly harsh nature of the thought, reaching finally "nothing but a great space" and an incessant metallic "beating." The poem consists of three stanzas, each of nine lines, and the aural harmony is nowhere more evident than in the lines quoted above: "big/ball," "thumb/dumb," "Ebon/hedges," "blue-red/juices," "These/they," "squander/on/fingers," "blood/sisterhood," "accomo-date themselves," "my/milkbottle/flattening." There are also many line-ending harmonies; in the first stanza alone we find "blackberries/Blackberries/eyes/sides," "mainly/sea/me," "fat/fingering." Plath was very aware of her ear for the music of verse (for actual music her ear was not so good); as she was reported saying, "the music behind verse was always with her." As for the "meaning" of "Blackberrying," we may cite Plath's sister-in-law, Olwyn Hughes (quoted by Anne Stevenson):

> "Blackberrying," at first reading a superb evocation of a windy, clifftop cove, on closer inspection invokes the poet's reluctant hold on life, and how a horror of meaninglessness waits for her around the corner.... Huge blackberries ... squander menstrual juices as they're picked.... The berries present an exquisite vision of corruption.

Heaney's "Blackberry-Picking"—an early poem, from his first book, *Death of a Naturalist* (1966)—is, like Plath's "Blackberrying," full of harmonious sounds but otherwise far from her free verse, with his twelve rhymed couplets in iambic pentameter. Like Plath's blackberries, Heaney's are satisfyingly fat and juicy, and also delicious: "You ate that first one and its flesh was sweet / Like thickened wine." But that sweetness of the first berry picked is swiftly overtaken by an obsessive and frantic attempt to pick every berry in sight, until "our hands were peppered / With thorn pricks, our palms sticky as Bluebeard's"—words that illustrate the harsh metrical roughnesses and strained slant rhymes, as also the associations of violence and death, characterizing many of the lines. Once the berries are picked, they must be stored, and then disaster overtakes the pickers:

> We hoarded the fresh berries in the byre.
> But when the bath was filled we found a fur,
> A rat-grey fungus, glutting on our cache.
> The juice was stinking too. Once off the bush
> The fruit fermented, the sweet flesh would turn sour.
> I always felt like crying. It wasn't fair
> That all the lovely canfuls smelt of rot.
> Each year I hoped they'd keep, knew they would not.

As Helen Vendler remarks, "The youthful Heaney was beset, always, by moral riddles that suggested symbols in everything, even ... the ooze of frog spawn"—or, as in this case, even blackberry fungus. It is worth noting how Plath and Heaney move in opposite directions in their identification of berry juice with blood: for Plath, that blood is experienced inwardly as a sign of her own corruption, while for Heaney the blood is "summer's," staining the tongue and hands but subject to its own peculiar and inexorable natural laws. Finally, Heaney, like Plath, is not really interested in eating the picked berries, in sharp contrast to most of our previous poets.

Another wonderful blackberrry-picking poem about childhood, with a European ambiance, is "Brambleberries, Blackberries," by Ruth Pitter; published posthumously in 1996, it is described by the poet as "from the Provençal":

> Brambleberries, blackberries—
> Grown without our pain or powers;

> Brambleberries, beggars's gain,
> Oh how strongly bring again
> Hedgerow searchings, eager hours.
>
> When brown Pomona after heat
> Brings lovely and elusive days,
> The poor fruit from the past can raise
> The taste of childhood, bittersweet.

Another North American poem about picking blackberries takes as its point of departure other previously published poems about picking blackberries. Here are some of the more striking lines in "Many Have Written Poems about Blackberries" (1995), by the Canadian poet Stephanie Bolster (b. 1969):

> but few have gotten at the multiplicity of them, how each berry
> composes itself of many dark notes, spherical,
> swollen, fragile as a world. A blackberry is the colour of a painful
> bruise on the upper arm, some internal organ
> as yet unnamed.
> > [. . . . .]
> The bushes themselves ramble like a grandmother's sentences,
> giving birth to their own sharpness.
>
> Picking blackberries must be a tactful conversation
> of gloved hands. Otherwise your fingers will bleed
> the berries' purple tongue; otherwise the thorns
> will pierce your own blank skin.
> > [. . . . .]
> The flavour is its own reward, like kissing the whole world
> at once, rivers, willows, bugs and all, until your swollen
> lips tingle. It's like waking up
> to discover the language you used to speak
> is gibberish, and you have never really
> loved.

Bolster thinks the taste of freshly picked blackberries startles and confuses conventional language; another poem, published a few years earlier by the American poet Jack Myers (b. 1941), relates the beginnings of such language in a young child to the sight of blackberries. Here are the first eight lines from "Jake Addresses the World from the Garden" (1991):

> It's spring and Jake toddles to the garden
> as the sun wobbles up clean and iridescent.

He points to the stones asleep and says, "M'mba,"
I guess for the sound they make, takes another step

and says, "M'mba," for the small red berries crying
in the holly. "M'mba" for the first sweet sadness

of the purplish-black berries in the drooping monkey grass,
and "M'mba," for the little witches' faces bursting into blossom.

Quite different from the moral growth associated with Clampitt's gooseberries, moral stasis is associated with these berries in a story by Chekhov. "Gooseberries" (1898) is one of a triad of stories, among the last, and best, Chekhov wrote. The stories are told by a group of three old friends to one another; for our purposes, the first and third story and the framing narrative for all three stories can be ignored. I cannot, however, resist saying a few words about the complex narratological structure of "Gooseberries," much of which is devoted to an embedded story in which money plays a big part; at one point in the embedded story there is a further embedding of two striking but digressive anecdotes about money. The main embedded story in "Gooseberries" is told by a veterinarian named Ivan Ivanych to his good friend, a high school teacher named Burkin, and to their host, a gentleman farmer named Alyohin; during the narration, the men partake of the tea and jam brought in by a beautiful servant, Pelageya. Alyohin is tall and fat, innocently happy like a child, and rather eccentric; his friends' visit is occasioned by their need to find shelter from a heavy rainstorm, which has interrupted their hunting expedition. Alyohin urges his friends to bathe in his bathhouse on the river before they change into dry clothes; he himself takes the opportunity to have his first bath in months—as he repeatedly announces to his guests—and then swims out into the river in the rain.

The story in question is about Ivan Ivanych's only brother, Nicolay Ivanych, by occupation a petty bureaucrat, of whom Ivan is very fond. The brothers grew up in the country and, though never stated explicitly, it is this fact that makes Nicolay, the enforced city dweller, perpetually dream of retiring to a country estate with a gooseberry patch. Eventually, Nicolay contracts a loveless marriage with an elderly, homely widow, and when his miserliness causes her literally to die of starvation, he inherits her money. He buys a miserable estate with no gooseberry bushes, so he plants some. Ivan then tells about his recent visit to his brother's estate and how physically repulsive and morally vacuous he found his brother's present way of life. (His brother's dog, his brother's cook, and his brother himself all remind Ivan Ivanych of pigs.) In the evening, the brothers are served tea together with gooseberries from the first crop of Nicolay very own bushes. Here is how Nicolay reacts (translated by Avrahm Yarmolinsky):

> My brother gave a laugh and for a minute looked at the gooseberries in
> silence, with tears in his eyes—he could not speak for excitement. Then

he put one berry in his mouth, glanced at me with the triumph of a child
who has at last been given a toy he was longing for and said: "How tasty!"
And he ate the gooseberries greedily, and kept repeating: "Ah, how delicious! Do taste them!"

In fact, the berries are "hard and sour," but for Nicolay it does not matter: he has achieved
his goal and is happy. Ivan underscores the irony here by a quotation from Pushkin:

> The falsehood that exalts we cherish more
> Than meaner truths that are a thousand strong.

And Nicolay's behavior at tea is repeated at intervals during a night that is wakeful for
both brothers: "He would get up again and again, go to the plate of gooseberries and
eat one after another." That Nicolay is a despicable character is beyond question, but
that can hardly be the point of the story; Donald Rayfield's comment, in his biography of Chekhov, that "'Goosberries' is against avarice" also seems off the mark.

The real point of the gooseberry incident, it seems to me, is how it affects Ivan
Ivanych, and the remainder of his story consists of a long meditation on the nature of
happiness. Ivan realizes that in his own way he too has been unthinkingly happy. Now,
however, he says, "I am afraid to look at the windows, for there is nothing that pains
me more than the spectacle of a happy family sitting at table having tea," and in a final
outburst he admonishes his sleepy host that "there is no happiness and there should be
none, and if life has a meaning and a purpose, that meaning and purpose is not our
happiness but something greater and more rational. Do good!" Here we recognize
the doctrine, or better, the sentiments, of *Uncle Vanya* (1897) and *The Three Sisters*
(1900–01), which bracket the date of composition of "Gooseberries." And if we have
learned to appreciate Chekhov's characterization of *The Seagull* and *The Cherry
Orchard* as comedies, we should equally be able to recognize the comic in such a character as Ivan Ivanych, who, after all, has made himself ridiculous and unhappy to no
purpose. A fondness for sour gooseberries may indeed signify a debased taste, but it is
much healthier and, indeed, more satisfying just to acknowledge this and move on.
One way of putting this is suggested by the ending of Clampitt's "Gooseberry Fool,"
where "the green globe of an unripe berry" evokes another globe—"the great world
itself"—whose claims are dismissed as "too much to carry." Now, it happens that right
near the beginning of Ivan Ivanych's story he too had foolishly imagined an extension
of the human reach to impossibly global dimensions: "Man needs not six feet of earth,
not a farm, but the whole globe, all of Nature, where unhindered he can display all
the capacities and peculiarities of his free spirit." This absurd spiritual overreaching
should not be mistaken for boldness of imagination.

But, of course, that Chekhov wishes us to judge Ivan Ivanych himself evenhandedly
and not too harshly is suggested by the remarkably apt and satisfying conclusion to the
framing story, as the two friends try to fall asleep in "two old wooden beds decorated
with carvings," in a room where "in the corner [was] an ivory crucifix":

"Lord forgive us sinners!" [Ivan Ivanych] murmured, and drew the bed-clothes over his head.

His pipe, which lay on the table, smelled strongly of burnt tobacco, and Burkin, who could not sleep for a long time, kept wondering where the unpleasant odor came from.

The rain beat against the window panes all night.

Ivan appropriately asks for forgiveness. Burkin, like the two brothers in Ivan's story, is now an insomniac, aware that something is disturbing him but unable to locate its source (is it perhaps the story he has just heard?); and the impersonal natural forces of wind and rain, beating relentlessly on, recall the cleansing effects of the water on Alyohin earlier in the day.

The American poet Stephen Berg (b. 1934) has responded to his reading of Chekhov's story with a dreamlike poem, "Gooseberries" (1975), in which the speaker and his friend in turn merge with one another and with the characters in the Chekhov story:

After reading the Chekhov Story

I can't sleep tonight, can you?
It is the voice of Gooseberries whispering
we are not good enough to be happy.
Near sleep, when your face gazes at itself
through a window or against a pale floor,
I hear you scratching on the wall of my room.
Forget about happiness. Tomorrow, when we
meet outside on the steps of our houses,
show me how to kiss your sad lips, tell me
what I can give you.
The fat owner who is happy is not you,
eating jam near the glue factory, drinking
tea, bathing in the river,
his wet hands lifted to the dying sun.
In a dish the gooseberries do not wait
and the doctor who did not believe in God
still asks forgiveness, and he is you.
I can smell the clean sheets where Burkin lay down,
suspicious of burnt tobacco.
He thought the stink came from something else.
It was hours before he could sleep and touch you.
Rain beat against the windowpanes all night.

The fat Alyohin has been conflated with the fat Nicolay Ivanych (who does indeed live near a stream on one of whose banks there is a glue factory); Ivan Ivanych, whose dis-belief in God is never mentioned by Chekhov, has been elevated to a doctor; and, of course, the "I" and the "you" are personae invented by the poet. It is not at all clear to me that Berg's "we are not good enough to be happy" is a sentiment Chekhov would endorse, but what we most miss is the subtle role of the gooseberries in Chekhov's extraordinarily subtle story.

For reasons already noted, berries are especially suited to recapture childhood memories; the psychological process is depicted with great clarity and immediacy in a poem of Brecht's about elderberries, "Difficult Times" (1955), here translated by Michael Hamburger:

> Standing at my desk
> Through the window I see the elder tree in the garden
> And recognize something red in it, something black
> And all at once recall the elder
> Of my childhood in Augsburg.
> For several minutes I debate
> Quite seriously whether to go to the table
> And pick up my spectacles, in order to see
> Those black berries again on their tiny red stalks.

> ~

> Stehend an meinem Schreibpult
> Sehe ich durchs Fenster im Garten den Holderstrauch
> Und erkenne darin etwas Rotes und etwas Schwarzes
> Und erinnere mich plötzlich des Holders
> Meiner Kindheit in Augsburg.
> Mehrere Minuten erwäge ich
> Ganz ernsthaft, ob ich zum Tisch gehn soll
> Meine Brille holen, um wieder
> Die schwarze Beeren an den roten Zweiglein zu sehen.

This is one of Brecht's last poems, written in a style he called "rhymeless verse with irregular rhythms." The hesitation is left unresolved about whether he should get his spectacles in order to see the elderberries better. But also left unresolved is why he hesitates: is it because he thinks it is not worth the effort, or is it because the past of his childhood may be too disquieting to contemplate in the difficult present?

Alexander Pushkin apparently called for some berries on his deathbed in St. Petersburg, according to Serena Vitale's biography:

> He really seemed to be sleeping when all at once he opened his eyes and asked for cloudberries. There were none in the house; someone hurried out to buy some. Pushkin, impatient, almost irate, kept saying, "*Moroshki, moroshki!*" He wanted his wife to feed them to him. Kneeling beside the sofa, Natalya Nikolaevna brought the small spoon to his lips, helped him to eat two or three berries and drink a bit of juice.

Cloudberries, belonging to the same genus, *Rubus,* as blackberries, are golden or orange in color and grow wild only in far northerly climates, such as Scandinavia and (presumably) St. Petersburg. (On cloudberries, see the entry, including an illustration, in *The New Oxford Book of Food Plants.*) In another biography of Pushkin, by Henri Troyat, the acount of the deathbed incident mentions blackberries and associates them with the country estate (outside Moscow) where Pushkin spent the summers of his childhood.

Consider now two British poems about raspberries. In the 4 July 1975 issue of the *New Statesman,* Peter Porter announced the joint winners of the paper's recent poetry competition: John Fuller (b. 1937) and Laurence Lerner (b. 1925), each for a poem about raspberries. Porter was fully aware of the broad scope for sarcastic response to his announcement but bravely explained that "the great difference between the ways Messrs Fuller and Lerner treat raspberries in their poems will offset the faintly ludicrous coincidence of their titles." In fact, Fuller's title was "Wild Raspberries," while Lerner's was "Raspberries," a crucial difference, since Fuller's poem is about collecting, and Lerner's about eating, the berries. Both poems are about love, more specifically, about the loss of love. Fuller describes in hectic neo-Gothic language the look of the berries and the activity of gathering them ("faery casques," "the dulled red of lanterns," "Little lanterns," "waiting chaises," "Plump facets paddled like dusty cushions," "the coach swaying"), and concludes that what is left of his love is "nothing at all but raspberries." Lerner is haunted by the taste of the berries ("On the always edge of decay, on the edge of bitter," "Tasting of earth and of crushed leaves," "Tasting of earth and the thought of you as earth") and with a love "unfolded" in that taste, a love now threatened by the illness of the beloved, as the lover eats raspberries and awaits the "impending news."

Raspberries also figure in a wonderful scene near the beginning of part 6 of *Anna Karenina.* (I cite Joel Carmichael's translation.) The setting is a balcony on the Levin estate and the characters are all women: the pregnant Kitty, Levin's wife; her sister, Dolly; their mother, the Princess Shcherbatsky; and Miss Agatha, an old servant of Levin's. Urged on by Kitty, Agatha is preparing raspberry jam by the most up-to-date technique: heating the fruit without water in "a preserving pan over the brazier with a rotating movement." (Agatha has, disobediently, already prepared the strawberry jam in the traditional way; she distrusts the novel recipe and hopes it will fail.) When a scum begins to appear on the surface of the sugar and berry concoction, Kitty wants to remove it herself but because of Kitty's condition her mother objects, and finally Dolly does the job:

> She began carefully moving the spoon over the bubbling sugar; now and then, to remove what stuck to it she would tap it against a plate that was already covered by the varicolored, yellowish-pink scum, with its blood-red streaks of syrup. How they'll lick it up with their tea! she said to herself, thinking of her children and recalling how when she was a child

herself she used to be astonished at grown-ups' not eating the best part—
the scum.

The women have been arguing about whether it is better to give money or
presents to servants, and many contemporary readers may be offended by this apparent insensitivity to the presence of the servant, Agatha; in fact, however, we learn a little
later that the women have all along been conversing in French (which will be con-
strued as another form of the same insensitivity by those same readers). The scene continues for several more pages, with a new topic of conversation: the possibility of a
match between Kitty's friend, Varenka, and Levin's half-brother, Koznyshov, which
leads to a discussion of the courtship of the sisters' parents, Vronsky's abortive courting of Kitty, and his subsequent affair with Anna. Levin then returns and inquires
whether the new method for making jam is any good. Agatha grudgingly replies: "I
suppose so. . . . We would think it overcooked"; to which Kitty responds that this way,
even without refrigeration—and their ice is now all melted—the jam won't ferment.
To cheer Agatha up, Kitty praises her pickling and at the same time adjusts the old
woman's kerchief. Agatha's response is surprisingly forthright:

> Miss Agatha gave Kitty an angry look.
> "There's no need to comfort me, ma'am. The moment I look at you
> and him together I feel cheerful," she said; the coarse way she had of say-
> ing *him* touched Kitty.

With its skillful interweaving of the details of culinary progress with poignant childhood reminiscences, subtle peasant-aristocrat relationships, and feminine views of male
sexual jealousy, the scene recapitulates many of the central themes of the novel. It must
be reported, however, that this scene is omitted both from the rather pedestrian plot
summary in a book by Gary Adelman (*Anna Karenina: The Bitterness of Ecstasy* [1990])
and from the brilliant and detailed commentary on the novel by Vladimir Nabokov.
The reason perhaps is that, until Levin's arrival at the end of the scene, the characters
are all women and none is central to the plot of the novel.

Finally, here are three poems about raspberries that span the distance between
macrocosm and microcosm, between deity and human: from God the companion to
the wonder of five billion years of terrestrial evolution to that slightest and lightest
form of human communication, the love letter.

In "The Berries" (1983), the American poet William Heyen (b. 1940) meditates
on the death of a neighbor's elderly father as he approaches the bereaved home with
a gift of raspberry jam. Here are the second and last of the four stanzas:

> In my left coat pocket, a jar
> of raspberry jam. . . . I remembered
> stepping into the drooping canes, the ripe

raspberry odor. I remembered bending over,
or kneeling, to get down under the leaves
to hidden clusters.

    [. . . . .]

When I was a boy, the Lord I talked to
knew me. Where is He now? I seem to have
lost Him, except for something
in that winter air, something insisting on being
there, and here—that summer's berries, that mind's
light against my hip, myself kneeling again
under the raspberry canes.

The religious imagery—the kneeling, the hiddenness, the light—is perhaps not fresh
enough to achieve the poet's professed goal in his comments on the poem: "Its images
of ice- and berry-light, its three tenses (present, past, and a further past remembered
during present and past), move toward a single word, 'except,' and a faith true to the
poem's own thoughtfulness."

"Ripeness" (1999), by another American poet, Robert Pack (b. 1929), is the
twelfth of forty-eight so-called sonnetelles, constituting the book *Rounding It Out*
(1999); the four sections of the book are "Morning," "Mid-Day," "Evening," and
"Night," and "Ripeness" is the last poem of "Morning." A sonnetelle is a hybrid poetic
form of sixteen lines, part sonnet, part villanelle, basically iambic pentameter but with
occasional groups of lines containing either a missing or an extra foot. The rhyme
schemes vary somewhat; that of "Ripeness" is *abab cbcb dbdb ebee.* Also, the first line of
each sonnetelle returns as the last line (sometimes slightly altered), and the second line
recurs (sometimes slightly altered), usually as the eighth or ninth line.

Pack's poetic sequence begins with the sun—its present age of some five billion
years and its life expectancy of another five billion. The imagery is both cosmic (the
evolutionary process) and down to earth (flowers, trees, birds). "Ripeness" is one of the
more successful poems, with its controlling image of ripening raspberries observed in
an August dawn:

> Familiar summer now seems strangely new
> As this faint chill of languid August dawn
> Shivers the clustered berries in the dew
> As if completed ripeness has been born
> From ripeness recollected ripening,
> Ripeness again repeated, here and gone,
> Presence and loss together as both bring
> A scented chill to languid August dawn.
> Five billion years of evolution on our earth

Produced this momentary ripeness in the sun,
This rounded revelation at the birth
Of sweet acceptance in the fruitful one
Prolific meaning earth can offer you,
Ripeness to smell, to taste, to meditate upon,
Red raspberries becoming redder in your view
Which makes familiar summer strangely new.

Like Heyen, Pack has commented on his objectives: "The poems faithfully (as in a vow) employ meter and rhyme, assonance and alliteration, taking delight and finding consolation in the sensuousness of our native tongue even in the face of inevitable and ongoing loss in a universe of ceaseless flux, changing, as I see it, without sponsored purpose or destination, indifferent to human longing and aspiration."

As for the love letter, Paul Muldoon connects one with raspberries in this haiku:

Raspberries. Red-blue.
A paper cut on the tongue
from a billet-doux.

We have seen how the planting of an apple tree can serve as a kind of living memorial for someone who has died. Would other types of trees serve as well? It would seem the only really essential quality is longevity. The youthful Tennyson, sometime while he was a student at Cambridge (1827–1831), wrote a poem about such a tree—except that in his case the tree was supposed to have been planted by the memorialized figure himself. In the poem (which Tennyson never published) the tree itself is imagined to be speaking:

Look what love the puddle-pated squarecaps have for me!
I am Milton's mulberry, Milton's Milton's mulberry—
But they whipt and rusticated him that planted me,
Old and hollow, somewhat crookèd in the shoulders as you see,
Full of summer foliage yet but propt and padded curiously,
I would sooner have been planted by the hand that planted me,
Than have grown in Paradise and dropped my fruit on Adam's knee—
Look what love the tiny-witted trenchers have for me.

There was a tradition at Cambridge in Tennyson's time about the suspension of Milton from the university ("rustication"); "squarecaps" and "trenchers" refer to academic caps. As for mulberry trees, they are long-lived and "can become big, gnarled and picturesque in advanced old age," according to Bob Flowerdew in his *Complete Book of Fruit*. The common black mulberry resembles a raspberry but is darker in color. In this one instance, I will offer a recipe, quoting Flowerdew's for "Mulberry No Fool" (really, after all, a null recipe!):

730

Crème fraiche or heavy cream
some honey
a pot of tea
biscuits
a mulberry tree in fruit and a sunny day off

Take a cereal bowl with a large portion of cream, and the tea and biscuits. Sit peacefully under the mulberry tree, savoring the tea and biscuits while waiting for enough fruits to fall to fill your bowl. Then eat them with the cream and honey.

CONCLUSION
Words and Fruit

As good a way as any, I suppose, to end what might be regarded as an orgy of words about fruit is with some claims about the affinity between words and fruit. I might first recall the epigrammatic opening lines from "Ars Poetica" (1926), by Archibald MacLeish (1892–1982): "A poem should be palpable and mute / As a globed fruit." It is interesting that a couple of decades later Angela Figuera (Aymerich) used the Spanish equivalent of "globed fruit" (*fruto redondo*) as the title of one of her earliest published poems, translated as "The Round Fruit" (1948):

> Yes, I'd also like to be a naked word.
> A featherless wing in an airless sky.
> A weightless streak of gold, a rootless dream,
> an incorporeal sound . . .
> But my verses are born round like fruit [*redondo comos frutos*]
> wrapped in the hot pulp of my flesh.

Figuera's translator, John Wilcox, explains how her poem is an echo and an implicit critique of certain ideas and phrases of her great contemporary Juan Ramón Jiménez (1883–1958), who went into exile after Franco's victory in the Spanish Civil War and died in Puerto Rico after receiving the Nobel Prize for literature. To begin with, the title of Figuera's poem alludes to a poem by Jiménez published in 1936 and called "El otoñado" (Replete with autumn fullness; translated by Eloïse Roach):

> I am fulfilled with nature,
> in full dusk of gold maturity,
> high wind transfixed upon the green.
> Rich hidden fruit, I hold
> in me the elemental great (earth,
> water, fire, and air) the infinite.
>
> Light streams from me: I gild the darkened place;
> I seep fragrance: the shadow smells of god;
> I distill sound: space is profound music;

I filter savor: the mass drinks up my soul;
I delight the touch of solitude.

I am treasure supreme, unfettered,
with the dense roundness of a limpid opal,
from the bosom of action. And I am all:
The all that is the peak of nothingness,
the all that is enough and that is served
with what is still but ambition.

The gold, the incorporeal sound, the roundness of Figuera's poem all refer back to phrases in Jiménez. What is more, Jiménez evokes the emptiness and impersonality of infinite space, whereas Figuera evokes "the hot pulp of my flesh." In short, "Jiménez likens his poetic maturity to a ripe fruit or sphere gracefully circling through infinite space" while Figuera "gives birth to poems the way women give birth to children."

For the American poet George Oppen (1907–1984), a poem is not mutely and passively complacent like MacLeish's piece of fruit; rather, according to "The Gesture" (1965), a poem resembles a gesture—but what kind of gesture?

The question is: how does one hold an apple
Who likes apples

And how does one handle
Filth? The question is

How does one hold something
In the mind which he intends

To grasp and how does the salesman
Hold a bauble he intends

To sell? The question is
When will there not be a hundred

Poets who mistake that gesture
For a style.

The salesman's intended selling of a bauble is identified with the handling of filth; the intended grasp of something by the mind is identified with how an apple is grasped by the hand of someone fond of apples. We are not provided with a means for positively identifying "poetic" gestures, and this is surely because any such criterion would be self-defeating—after all, even people fond of apples do not all grasp them in the same way. We are provided only with an important negative criterion: poems are not baubles being offered for sale.

In his fourteen-line, one-sentence poem "Blackberry Eating" (1980), Galway Kinnell (b. 1927), out picking blackberries early one September morning, notices how

> lifting the stalks to my mouth, the ripest berries
> fall almost unbidden to my tongue,
> as words sometimes do, certain peculiar words
> like *strengths* or *squinched,*
> many-lettered, one-syllabled lumps,
> which I squeeze, squinch open, and splurge well
> in the silent, startled, icy, black language
> of blackberry-eating in late September.

"Squinched" is a peculiar word, all right—not only phonetically by also semantically: originating in the early nineteenth century, as a hybrid of "squeeze" (or "squint") and "pinch"(?), it means to squeeze together or contract. Kinnell's "squinch open" seems oxymoronic. What I find even more perplexing is the notion that for Kinnell eating blackberries is apparently a "language," albeit a "silent" one.

A detailed correspondence between berries and words occurs in one of the prose poems of Francis Ponge, "Ripe Blackberries" (first published in 1936, here translated by C. K. Williams).

> In the typographical thickets that go into the making of a poem, along a road that leads neither beyond things nor to the mind, certain fruits are formed by an agglomeration of spheres, each filled with a drop of ink.
>
> * * *
>
> Black, pink, and khaki clustered together, they offer the spectacle of a haughty family at various times of life more than a very strong temptation to pick them.
>
> > Given the disproportion of pips to pulp, birds don't much care for them; so little remains after the voyage from beak to anus.
>
> * * *
>
> But the poet on his professional outing finds food in them for thought. "Thus," he reflects, "the patient efforts of a flower, very fragile, albeit defended by a forbidding tangle of brambles, are in large measure fulfilled. With few other qualities, the blackberries (*mûres*) become perfectly ripe (*mûres*), just as this poem has ripened."

What one might notice first about Williams's translation is how, in the last paragraph, he is forced to convey the pun implicit in the French title by adding (in parentheses) the word *mûres* after each of the two English words "blackberries" and "ripe." Perhaps by way of compensation, Williams introduces a pun in his English version that is not present in the original when he translates the assertion *ce poème est fait* as "this poem has ripened." As for the second paragraph, what is perhaps most striking is the image of a "haughty family" (*une famille rouge*) constituted by a multicolored aggregation of

734   blackberries at different stages of ripeness—Ponge's color terms are *noir, rose,* and
kaki—beautifully captured in the cluster of Honeysweet blackberries in plate 34.
About the first paragraph, Ian Higgins comments, in his edition (1979) of Ponge's *Le
Parti pris des choses,* that it "seems to go round in a circle, like each blackberry and each
globule of each blackberry. The blackberries are words, their black juice is ink."

"Ripe Blackberries" is about, and at the same time exemplifies, Ponge's ideas
on the relation between words and things. As Ponge himself defines his goal, one
should "by a manipulation, a fundamental disrespect for words etc. give the impression of a new idiom that will produce the same effect of surprise and novelty as the
object we are looking at" (quoted from another of Ponge's translators, Margaret Guiton).
But, of course, any such procedure is circular and hence, strictly speaking, impossible,
because the "surprise and novelty" in a perceived object is itself a function of its
poetic re-creation in language. This is why Ponge can write that *his* (poetic) blackberries have ripened along with the completion (or ripening) of *his* poem. And this
is also perhaps why Ponge's blackberries have but a single fundamental quality—their
color or degree of ripeness (the "pips" and "pulp" are dross matter, not even of interest
to birds).

Ponge's emphasis on the freedom inherent in the poet's use of language seems
in line with the thesis of Irving Layton's evocatively titled "The Fertile Muck" (1956),
the first of whose stanzas makes great claims for the poet vis-à-vis apples:

> There are brightest apples on those trees
> but until I, fabulist, have spoken
> they do not know their significance
> or what other legends are hung like garlands
> on their black boughs twisting
> like a rumour. The wind's noise is empty.

With respect to apples, we are told, only the poet—this particular poet—can provide
significance, dispel rumors, impart meaning to mere noise. And this aggressive proclamation of the high claims of the poet as fabulist is extended in the second, third, and
fourth stanzas to insects (and therefore presumably to the animal realm generally) and
to human habitations (and therefore presumably to the realm of human constructions
generally). The last stanza, however, in a gentler mood, reminds us that not just the
poetic imagination but also love can "dominate reality," and there may even be some
chance for the coexistence of love and imagination:

> How to dominate reality? Love is one way;
> imagination another. Sit here
> beside me, sweet; take my hard hand in yours.
> We'll mark the butterflies disappearing over the hedge
> with tiny wristwatches on their wings:
> our fingers touching the earth, like two Buddhas.

A poem that has begun with apples—or, rather, with "the fertile muck" in which all fruits have their origin—has ended with love. At this point we have also, incidentally, returned to our own starting point—the topic of apples in literature. But in Layton's poem, apples and love, separated by the space of three stanzas, seem very different from the pristine apples and innocent love of, say, the Song of Songs or *Daphnis and Chloe*. Despite the "hard hand" of the poet, though, there is some hope in the image of the (momentarily?) tranquil Buddha-like lovers, their fingers, like Antaeus, drawing strength from contact with the "earth" (which in one of its guises is none other than "the fertile muck").

The most recent work I know by the American poet Michael McClure (b. 1932)—who, like Layton, throughout a long career has always attempted to flout polite conventionalities—is a long poem, "Haiku Edge" (1999), composed as a sequence of fifty-eight haiku. (But, McClure explains, he has "abandoned seventeen syllables, which is over-ample in English." Also, it may be noted that McClure reads his haiku in public performances accompanied by piano.) Things mentioned in the fifty-eight haiku range from a snail, a cat, a deer, and a spider web to assault rifles, pine boards, a garbage can, and a train whistle. And just three fruits: blackberry (twice), strawberry, and apple.

Here may be the right place to introduce my final illustration, returning to the images of our first chapter with an American version of Edenic apples in the form of a delightful drawing, *Eve, and the Serpent, in the Garden, of Eden* (pen and ink on paper-board, 28 x 21⅞ in.), now in the Smithsonian American Art Museum, Washington, D.C. (see plate 37). Neither life dates nor place of activity are known for the artist; at lower right is an inscription "by Prof John H Coates; 1916." The words "REAL PEN WORK" suggest the picture may have been designed for a penmanship manual. (See the catalogue of an exhibition of folk art at the Smithsonian: Lynda Roscoe Hartigan, *Made with Passion: The Hemphill Folk Art Collection in the National Museum of American Art* [1990].)

I want next to refer to an eloquent passage about fruit (and vegetables) from Joyce's *Ulysses*, in which apples and berries are yet again conjoined. The twelfth chapter ("Cyclops") of Joyce's novel consists of two radically different kinds of literary material: on the one hand, dialogue among some thirteen men (including Bloom) in two low Dublin pubs, and, on the other hand, interrupting the dialogue, a series of some thirty-three extended authorial asides, most of them parodies of various nineteenth-century adaptations of earlier literary styles. What the dialogue and the asides share stylistically is *excess*—what Joyce himself, according to Stuart Gilbert, called "gigantism" (appropriate enough, since the Cyclops were, of course, giants). The second of these asides interrupts the narrative just as a pair of characters leave one (unnamed) pub for another (Barny Kiernan's), and it parodies James Clarence Mangan's "Irish revival" translation of a seventh-century Irish poem called "Aldfrid's Itinerary." The passage begins with the words, "In Inisfail the fair there lies a land, the land of holy Michan."

736   Now, St. Michan's in *Ulysses* is the name of the parish in which both of the afore-mentioned pubs are located, so here we see how the two disparate types of literary material are sometimes related thematically. After a longish mock-heroic paragraph about a sea voyage—corresponding to Odysseus's journey to the island of the Cyclops—the second (and concluding) paragraph of the aside is devoted largely to a list of the vegetables and fruit being transported across the sea. The only individual mentioned in this passage is "O'Connor Fitzsimon," "a chieftain of chieftains"—and this is the name of the man who was the superintendent of the Dublin food market in 1904 (the year in which the action of the novel takes place). Two unusual adjectives near the end of the passage—"pomellated" (dappled) and "pelurious" (furred or hairy)—seem to be characteristic Joycean coinages (and are cited as such in the second edition of the *Oxford English Dictionary*), which signifies, I believe, that the style has been modulating away from mere parody. After what David Hayman, in his interpretation of the Cyclops chapter, calls a catalogue of improbable "flora and fauna" (the fish and trees of St. Michan's "nonexistent streams" and "missing forests"), comes a list of what must have been to Dubliners at the time perfectly familiar vegetables and fruits. But the "pomellated" apples and the "pelurious" berries are described with an exuberance that transcends parody and celebrates not only fruit but the very prose style itself. As another interpreter of the Cyclops chapter, Marilyn Reizbaum, puts it, "The ambiguity and excess of Joyce's text, threatening, dangerous as it may seem, like Bloom, is finally redeeming, if not redeemed."

> Thither the extremely large wains bring foison of the fields, flaskets of cauliflowers, floats of spinach, pineapple chunks, Rangoon beans, strikes of tomatoes, drums of figs, drills of Swedes, spherical potatoes and tallies of iridescent kale, York and Savoy, and trays of onions, pearls of the earth, and punnets of mushrooms and custard marrows and fat vetches and bere and rape and red green yellow brown russet sweet big bitter ripe pomellated apples and chips of strawberries and sieves of gooseberries, pulpy and pelurious, and strawberries fit for princes and raspberries from their canes.

And how better to conclude than with a fruit-oriented prayer for help? Many perceptive readers of modern poetry see Zbigniew Herbert (1924–1998) as one of the greatest poets of the second half of the twentieth century. His verse possesses the lucidity and precision of first-rate expository prose but also a vein of vivid and inventive fantasy. In our concluding fruit episode, "Prayer" (here translated from the Polish by John and Bogdana Carpenter, in *The Paris Review* [2000]), we are challenged to imagine a fruit constituted by the fundamental dualities of sweet and salt, dark and light, height and depth, high notes and low notes, free invention and blind destiny:

> Lord,
> > help us to invent a fruit
> > a pure image of sweetness

as well as the meeting of two surfaces
dusk and dawn
to extract from the folds of the sea
the bass of pure depth
and also a girl
blind as destiny
a girl who sings—*belcanto*

REFERENCES

INTRODUCTION

Paul Schmidt, "'As If a Cookbook Had Anything to Do with Writing.'—Alice B. Toklas," *Prose* 8 (spring 1974): 179–203.

Robert Palter, "Reflections on Food in Literature," *Texas Quarterly* (autumn 1978): 6–32.

Geert Jan van Gelder, *God's Banquet: Food in Classical Arabic Literature* (New York: Columbia University Press, 2000), 5.

Random House Dictionary of the English Language, s.v. "fruit."

Harold McGee, *On Food and Cooking: The Science and Lore of the Kitchen* (New York: Charles Scribner's Sons, 1984), 124–25.

Salve Millard, "Filipino Food," chap. 18 in *The Asian Pacific American Heritage: A Companion to Literature and the Arts,* ed. George J. Leonard (New York: Garland, 1999), 198.

Oxford Companion to Food, s.v. "pomology."

Jeffrey Steingarten, "Ripeness Is All," in *The Man Who Ate Everything* (New York: Knopf, 1998), 74–88.

Margaret Visser, *The Rituals of Dinner: The Origins, Evolution, Eccentricities, and Meaning of Table Manners* (New York: Penguin, 1991).

Sybille Ebert-Schifferer, *Still Life: A History,* trans. Russell Stockman (New York: Harry N. Abrams, 1999).

Alan Chong and Wouter Kloek, ed. *Still-Life Paintings from the Netherlands, 1550–1720* (Zwolle, Netherlands: Waanders, 1999).

Arie Wallert, ed., *Still Lifes: Techniques and Style, An Examination of Paintings from the Rijksmuseum* (Zwolle, Netherlands: Waanders, 1999).

CHAPTER 1: APPLES

Some Apple Facts

Plutarch, *Table-Talk* 5.8.683D; *Plutarch's Moralia,* vol. 8, trans. Herbert B. Hoffleit (London: William Heinemann, 1969), 435.

Greek Anthology 5.80; in *Poems from the Greek Anthology,* trans. Dudley Fitts (New York: New Directions, 1956), 33; in *The Greek Anthology and Other Ancient Greek Epigrams,* ed. Peter Jay (New York: Oxford University Press, 1973), 46.

740   *Oxford Classical Dictionary,* 3d ed., s.v. "anthology."

Harold McGee, *The Curious Cook* (San Francisco: North Point Press, 1990), 61.

S. A. Beach, *The Apples of New York,* 2 vols. (Albany, N.Y.: J. B. Lyon, 1905).

Creighton Lee Calhoun, Jr., *Old Southern Apples* (Blacksburg, Va.: McDonald and Woodward, 1995), 5.

H. A. Baker, "Growing Apples," in *The Apple Book* by Rosanne Sanders (New York: Philosophical Library, 1988), 134.

Edward A. Bunyard, *The Anatomy of Dessert* (New York: E. P. Dutton, 1934), 3–34.

Joan Morgan and Alison Richards, with paintings by Elisabeth Dowle, *The Book of Apples* (London: Ebury Press, 1993).

Roger Yepsen, *Apples* (New York: W. W. Norton, 1994).

Mark Rosenstein, *In Praise of Apples: A Harvest of History, Horticulture, and Recipes* (Asheville, N.C.: Lark Books, 1996), 9–13.

Edward Behr, "14. A Multiplicity of Apples," in *The Artful Eater* (New York: Atlantic Monthly Press, 1992), 169.

Praxilla frag. 747, "Hymn to Adonis"; in *Greek Lyric,* vol. 4, trans. David A. Campbell (Cambridge: Harvard University Press, 1992), 375.

Nazim Hikmet, "The Cucumber," in *Selected Poetry,* trans. Randy Blasing and Mutlu Konuk (New York: Persea Books, 1986), 149.

Homer, *Odyssey* 11.588–90; in *Odyssey,* trans. Robert Fitzgerald (New York: Anchor, 1963), 204.

Andrew Dalby, *Siren Feasts: A History of Food and Gastronomy in Greece* (London: Routledge, 1996), 79.

Theocritus, *Idylls* 7.115–19; in *Theocritus: Idylls and Epigrams,* trans. Daryl Hine (New York: Atheneum, 1982), 31.

Lucy Baldwyn, "Blending In: The Immaterial Art of Bobby Baker's Culinary Events," *Drama Review* (winter 1996): 47, with illustration.

The Classical Tradition

Apples as Love Tokens

Sextus Propertius, *Elegies* 1.3, in *The Poems of Propertius,* trans. Ronald Musker (London: J. M. Dent and Sons, 1972), 48; in *Elegies,* trans. G. P. Goold (Cambridge: Harvard University Press, 1990), 51–53; in *The Poems of Sextus Propertius,* trans. J. P. McCulloch (Berkeley and Los Angeles: University of California Press, 1972), 15; in *Propertius: The Poems,* trans. Guy Lee (Oxford: Clarendon Press, 1994), 6.

Charles Spaak and Jean Renoir, *La Grande Illusion,* trans. Marianne Alexandre and Andrew Sinclair (London: Villiers, 1968), 99.

Maurice Scève, "While we were chatting one evening, my lady said to me," in *Delia, object of highest virtue,* trans. Geoffrey Brereton, in *Sixteenth to Eighteenth Centuries,* vol. 2 of *The Penguin Book of French Verse,* ed. Brereton (Harmondsworth, England: Penguin, 1958), 14.

Mary Ella Milham, ed. and trans., *Platina: On Right Pleasure and Good Health* (Tempe: Arizona State University, 1998), 135.

Mythological Apples

Sappho frag. 2; in *Archaic Greek Poetry,* ed. and trans. Barbara Hughes Fowler (Madison: University of Wisconsin Press, 1992), 130.

Catullus 2; in *Catullus,* 2d ed., trans. G. P. Goold (London: Duckworth, 1989), 32–33; in *Latin Lyric and Elegiac Poetry: An Anthology of New Translations,* ed. Diane J. Rayor and William W. Batstone, trans. Jane Wilson Joyce (New York: Garland, 1995), 4.

Ovid, *Metamorphoses* 10.636–651, 665–680; in *Ovid's Metamorphoses,* trans. Charles Boer (Dallas: spring, 1989), xiii, 224–25.

John Frederick Nims, introduction to *Ovids's Metamorphoses,* trans. Arthur Golding (New York: Macmillan, 1965), xiv.

Ovid, *Metamorphoses* 10.778–797; trans. Arthur Golding, in *Shakespeare's Ovid: Being Arthur Golding's Translation of the Metamorphoses,* ed. W. H. D. Rouse (Carbondale: Southern Illinois University Press, 1961), 216.

Ted Hughes, *Tales from Ovid* (New York: Farrar Straus Giroux, 1997), 128–29.

Oxford Classical Dictionary, 3d ed., s.v. "Atalanta."

Lexicon Iconographicum Mythologiae Classicae (LIMC), s.v. "Atalanta," vol. 2, pts. 1 and 2 (Zurich and Munich: Artemis Verlag, 1984).

Jane Davidson Reid and Chris Rohmann, eds., *The Oxford Guide to Classical Mythology in the Arts, 1300–1990s* (New York and Oxford: Oxford University Press, 1993), vol. 1, 237–40.

Guido Reni, *Atalanta and Hippomenes,* in *Guido Reni: A Complete Catalogue of His Works with an Introductory Text* by D. Stephen Pepper (New York: New York University Press, 1984), col. pl. 5; in *Guido Reni, 1575–1642* (Bologna: Pinacoteca Nazionale di Bologna, 1988), 75, 77.

Natale Conti, "Atalanta," bk. 10 of *Natale Conti's Mythologies: A Select Translation,* trans. Anthony DiMatteo (New York: Garland, 1994), 374.

Henri de Linthaut, *Commentaire de H. de Linthaut de Mont-Lion sur le Trésor des trésors* (Lyon, 1610), quoted by François Secret in *Roman and European Mythologies,* ed. Yves Bonnefoy and Wendy Doniger, trans. John Leavitt (Chicago: University of Chicago Press, 1992), 216.

Francis Bacon, *On the Wisdom of the Ancients,* "Author's Preface," in *The Philosophical Works of Francis Bacon,* ed. Robert Leslie Ellis, James Spedding, and John M. Robertson (London: George Routledge, 1905), 822, 848.

James Spedding, preface to "Of the Wisdom of the Ancients," in *The Philosophical Works of Francis Bacon,* ed. Robert Leslie Ellis, James Spedding, and John M. Robertson (London: George Routledge, 1905), 816.

Ron Nyren, "Ordinary Apples," *Missouri Review* 21, no. 2 (1998): 161, 150, 155.

Beach, *Apples of New York,* vol. 1, 56–60.

Pietro Andrea di Bassi, *The Labors of Hercules,* trans. W. Kenneth Thompson (Barre, Mass.: Imprint Society, 1971), 61, 63.

Anon., Farnese Hercules, in *Taste and the Antique: The Lure of Classical Scholarship* by Francis Haskell and Nicholas Penny (New Haven: Yale University Press, 1982), fig. 118.

Hendrik Goltzius, *Farnese Hercules,* in Haskell and Penny, *Taste and the Antique,* fig. 5.

Willem Danielsz van Tetrode, *Hercules Pomarius,* in *Vermeer and the Delft School* by Walter Liedtke (New York: The Metropolitan Museum of Art, 2001), 523.

James David Draper, "Willem Danielsz van Tetrode, *Hercules Pomarius,*" in Liedtke, *Vermeer and the Delft School,* 522.

Alfred, Lord Tennyson, "The Hesperides," in *The Poems of Tennyson,* 2d ed., vol. 1, ed. Christopher Ricks (Berkeley and Los Angeles: University of California Press, 1987), 463, 467.

Emily Dickinson, "Except the smaller size," in *The Complete Poems of Emily Dickinson,* ed. Thomas H. Johnson (Boston: Little, Brown and Co., 1960), 485.

742   Malcolm Davies, *The Epic Cycle* (Bristol, England: Bristol Classical Press, 1989).

Conti, *Mythologies,* bk. 6, chap. 23, "Paris," in *Natale Conti's Mythologies: A Select Translation,* trans. Anthony DiMatteo (New York: Garland, 1994), 339–40, 342.

Julius S. Held, *The Marriage of Peleus and Thetis,* in *The Oil Sketches of Peter Paul Rubens: A Critical Catalogue,* vol. 2 (Princeton: Princeton University Press, 1980), plate 217.

Paul Henry Láng, *Music in Western Civilization* (New York: W. W. Norton, 1941), 352, 405.

András Batta, *Opera: Composers, Works, Performers,* trans. Paul Aston et al. (Cologne: Könemann, 2000), 338–39).

Raphael, *The Three Graces,* in *Raphael* by Roger Jones and Nicholas Penny (New Haven: Yale University Press, 1983), fig. 10.

Eduard Mörike, "Offering," in *Friedrich Hölderlin, Eduard Mörike: Selected Poems,* trans. Christopher Middleton (Chicago: University of Chicago Press, 1972), 206–7.

Women and Apples

Sappho frag. 105a; in *Archaic Greek Poetry,* ed. and trans. Barbara Hughes Fowler (Madison: University of Wisconsin Press, 1992), 141.

Catullus 65; in *Catullus,* 2d ed., trans. G. P. Goold (London: Duckworth, 1989), 165.

Theocritus, *Idyll* 7.114; in *Theocritus: Idylls and Epigrams,* trans. Daryl Hine (New York: Atheneum, 1982), 31.

Martial 3.65; in *Epigrams of Martial,* trans. Palmer Bovie (New York: New American Library, 1970), 145.

Longus, *Daphnis and Chloe* 1.23–4, 3.33; in *Collected Ancient Greek Novels,* ed. B. P. Reardon, trans. Christopher Gill (Berkeley and Los Angeles: University of California Press, 1989), 298n. 16, 299, 332.

J. R. Morgan, "The Greek Novel: Towards a Sociology of Production and Reception," in *The Greek World,* ed. Anton Powell (London: Routledge, 1995), 143.

Dickinson, "'Heaven'—is what I cannot reach!" in *The Complete Poems of Emily Dickinson,* ed. Thomas H. Johnson (Boston: Little, Brown and Co., 1960), 109.

Lorenz Hart, "On Your Toes," in *The Complete Lyrics of Lorenz Hart,* ed. Dorothy Hart and Robert Kimball (New York: Knopf, 1986), 224.

J. R. Morgan, "Greek Novel," 145.

Gavin Ewart, "Eve and the Apple," in *Selected Poems, 1933–1988* (New York: New Directions, 1988), 67.

Women's Breasts as Apples

Jeffrey Henderson, *The Maculate Muse: Obscene Language in Attic Comedy,* 2d ed. (New York: Oxford University Press, 1991), 149.

Theocritus, *Idyll* 27.49–50; in *The Greek Bucolic Poets,* ed. J. M. Edmonds (Cambridge: Harvard University Press, 1950), 340; in *The Idylls of Theocritus,* trans. Thelma Sargent (New York: W. W. Norton, 1982), 114.

Rufinus 5.60; in *The Greek Anthology and Other Ancient Greek Epigrams,* ed. Peter Jay, trans. Alan Marshfield (New York: Oxford University Press, 1973), 299; in *The Greek Anthology,* vol. 1, trans. W. R. Paton (London: William Heinemann, 1916), 159; in *Hellenistic Poetry: An Anthology,* ed. and trans. Barbara Hughes Fowler (Madison: University of Wisconsin Press, 1990), 310.

Peter Jay, ed., *The Greek Anthology* (New York: Oxford University Press, 1973), 24–25, n.

Rufinus 5.62; in *Hellenistic Poetry: An Anthology,* ed. and trans. Barbara Hughes Fowler (Madison: University of Wisconsin Press, 1990), 309.

Robin Skelton, ed. and trans., *Two Hundred Poems from the Greek Anthology* (Seattle: University of Washington Press, 1971), 62.

John Updike, *Bech at Bay: A Quasi-Novel* (New York: Knopf, 1998), 151.

Susan Hauptman, *Self-Portrait,* in *Narcissism: Artists Reflect Themselves* (Escondido, Calif.: Center for the Arts, 1996), 49.

Johannes de Hauvilla, *Architrenius,* trans. Winthrop Wetherbee (Cambridge: Cambridge University Press, 1994), xvi, 144–45, 32–33.

Ludovico Ariosto, *Orlando Furioso* 7.14; in *Orlando Furioso,* ed. Lanfranco Caretti (Torino, Italy: Giulio Einaudi, 1966), 150; in *Orlando Furioso,* vol. 1, trans. Barbara Reynolds (Harmondsworth, England: Penguin, 1975), 245.

Ariosto, *Orlando Furioso* 7.14; in *Orlando Furioso,* vol. 2, trans. William Stewart Rose (London: John Murray, 1824), 7.

Ariosto, *Orlando Furioso* 10.96; in *Orlando Furioso,* vol. 1, trans. Reynolds, 340.

Ariosto, *Orlando Furioso* 10.96; in *Orlando Furioso,* ed. Caretti, 253.

Pierre Ronsard, *Sonnets* 1.55; in *Œuvres Complètes de Ronsard,* vol. 2 (Paris: Librairie Garnier Frères, 1923), 248; quoted in Humbert Wolfe's translation, in *Ronsard* by D. B. Wyndham Lewis (New York: Coward-McCann, 1944), 251–52.

Stuart Peachey, *Fruit Variety Register, 1580–1660,* vol. 1 (Bristol: Stuart Press, 1995), 18.

Johann Wolfgang von Goethe, *Faust* pt. 1, 4128–4135; in *Faust I and II,* trans. Stuart Atkins (Princeton: Princeton University Press, 1994), 106.

Sigmund Freud, *Die Traumdeutung,* 8th ed. (1930); Freud, *The Interpretation of Dreams,* trans. James Strachey (London: George Allen and Unwin, 1954), 287.

James H. Marrow and Alan Shestack, *Hans Baldung Grien: Prints and Drawings* (New Haven: Yale University Art Gallery, 1981), 120–21.

H. Diane Russell and Bernardine Barnes, *Eva/Ave: Women in Renaissance and Baroque Prints* (Washington, D.C.: National Gallery of Art, 1990), 123–25.

Random House Historical Dictionary of American Slang, s.v. "apple."

Colette, *Julie de Carneilhan* and *Chance Acquaintances,* trans. Patrick Leigh Fermor (London: Secker and Warburg, 1952), 56.

Anne Sexton, "Jesus Suckles," in *The Complete Poems* (Boston: Houghton Mifflin, 1981), 337.

Marjorie Barnard, *The Persimmon Tree* (London: Penguin Books-Virago Press, 1985), 22, 23, 25.

Oxford Dictionary of Modern Slang, s.v. "melon."

Sarah Lucas, *Au Naturel,* in *Sensation,* ed. Brooks Adams et al. (London: Thames and Hudson, 1997), 115.

Jaroslav Seifert, "Abacus," in *The Early Poetry of Jarolav Seifert,* trans. Dana Loewy (Evanston, Ill.: Hydra Books, Northwestern University Press, 1997), 135.

Seifert, *Reminiscences,* in *The Poetry of Jaroslav Seifert,* trans. George Gibian (North Haven, Conn.: Catbird Press, 1998), 220.

Joan Lebold Cohen, *The New Chinese Painting, 1949–1986* (New York: Harry N. Abrams, 1987), fig. 172.

Man Ray, *Ciné-sketch: Adam et Eve,* in *Man Ray, 1890–1976,* ed. Manfred Heiting (Cologne: Taschen, 2000), 69.

744 Frédéric Brenner, *Survivors, Los Angeles, California, 1994,* in *Jews/America/A Representation* (New York: Harry N. Abrams, 1996), 28.

The Biblical Tradition

Apples in the Song of Songs

Harold N. Moldenke and Alma L. Moldenke, *Plants of the Bible* (New York: Ronald Press, 1952), 185.

Ariel Bloch and Chana Bloch, trans., *The Song of Songs* (New York: Random House, 1995), 149n.

Bloch and Bloch, trans., *Song of Songs,* 55–57, 103, 111.

J. N. Postgate, "Notes on Fruit in the Cuneiform Sources," *Bulletin on Sumerian Agriculture* 3 (1987): 115–44.

Andrew Dalby, *Siren Feasts* (London: Routledge, 1996), 77–78.

M. A. Powell, "Classical Sources and the Problem of the Apricot," *Bulletin on Sumerian Agriculture* 3 (1987): 153–56.

Song of Songs 7:9; in *Song of Songs,* trans. Marvin H. Pope (New York: Doubleday, 1977), 593, 636, 20.

Cantica Canticorum, in *The Voice of My Beloved: The Song of Songs in Western Medieval Christianity* by E. Ann Matter (Philadelphia: University of Pennsylvania Press, 1990), xvi–xxxiii.

Stanley Stewart, *The Enclosed Garden: The Tradition and the Image in Seventeenth-Century Poetry* (Madison: University of Wisconsin Press, 1966), 10.

Francis Quarles, *Emblemes: Divine and Moral,* 5.2 (London: Thomas Tegg, 1845), 253–54.

Peachey, *Fruit Variety Register,* vol. 1, 9, 16.

Mathias Casimire Sarbiewski *Odes* 4.21; in *The Odes of Casimire,* trans. G. Hils (London: Humphrey Moseley, 1646; reprint, Los Angeles: Augustan Reprint Society, 1953), 86–87.

John Mason, "My Jesus is an Apple-Tree" and "What are the common Trees o'th'Wood," quoted in *The Enclosed Garden: The Tradition and the Image in Seventeenth-Century Poetry* by Stewart, 202n. 30.

Louis L. Martz, foreword to *The Poems of Edward Taylor,* ed. Donald E. Stanford (New Haven: Yale University Press, 1960), xxxvi, xxix, xxiii.

Edward Taylor, Meditation 161A, B, in *The Poems of Edward Taylor,* ed. Stanford, 375, 377.

Edenic Apples in Biblical Contexts

Monika Brazda, *Zur Bedeutung des Apfels in der Antiken Kultur* (Bonn: Rheinische Friedrich-Wilhelms-Universität, 1977), 121–29.

A. N. Doane, *The Saxon Genesis: An Edition of the West Saxon* Genesis B *and the Old Saxon* Vatican Genesis (Madison: University of Wisconsin Press, 1991), x, 143n. 6, 223, 361.

Anon., *Le Mystère d'Adam,* translated as "Adam and Eve," in *Medieval French Plays,* trans. Richard Axton and John Stevens (Oxford: Basil Blackwell, 1971), 3–36.

Martha Bayless, *Parody in the Middle Ages: The Latin Tradition* (Ann Arbor: University of Michigan Press, 1996), 47, 48, 209, 241, 255.

Markham Harris, trans., *The Cornish Ordinalia: A Medieval Dramatic Trilogy* (Washington, D.C.: Catholic University of America Press, 1969), xxviii, 7, 12–13.

Quarles, *Emblemes,* 1.1 (1845), 5, 7.

John Milton, *Paradise Lost,* in *John Milton,* ed. Stephen Orgel and Jonathan Goldberg (Oxford: Oxford University Press, 1991), 537–38.

Edenic Apples in Nonbiblical Contexts

Bartholomaeus Anglicus, *On the Properties of Things,* vol. 1, ed. M. C. Seymour, trans. John Trevisa (Oxford: Clarendon Press, 1975), 300–301.

Bridget Ann Henisch, *The Medieval Calendar Year* (University Park: Pennsylvania State University Press, 1999), 147, 202.

Edmund Spenser, *The Faerie Queene,* "Letter," bk. 1, 1.2.1, 11.48.2, 11.47.6–9; in *The Poetical Works of Edmund Spenser,* ed. J. C. Smith and E. De Selincourt (London: Oxford University Press, 1926), 407, 4, 62.

John Donne, "The Progress of the Soule," in *The Complete English Poems,* A. J. Smith, ed. (Harmondsworth, England: Penguin, 1981), 177.

John Carey, *John Donne: Life, Mind, and Art,* new ed. (London: Faber and Faber, 1990), 134–44.

Donne, canto 9 of "Progress of the Soule," 180.

Timothy Oelman, ed., *Marrano Poets of the Seventeenth Century* (London and Toronto: Associated University Presses, 1982), 206.

Antonio Enríquez Gómez, "The Sin of the First Pilgrim," in *Marrano Poets of the Seventeenth Century,* ed. Oelman, 152–53, 206n. 50, 207n. 54.

Robert Graves, *The Greek Myths,* vol. 1 (Baltimore: Penguin, 1955), 21–22.

Graves, *The White Goddess: A Historical Grammar of Poetic Myth,* amended and enlarged ed. (New York: Farrar, Straus and Giroux, 1966), 316.

Graves, "Apple Island," in *Collected Poems, 1975* (New York: Oxford University Press, 1988), 205.

Edenic Apples in Art

Anon., Fall of Adam and Eve, Escorial Beatus, fol. 18, in *Early Spanish Manuscript Illumination* by John Williams (New York: George Braziller, 1977), plate 25; in John P. O'Neill, ed., *The Art of Medieval Spain,* A.D. 500–1200 (New York: Metropolitan Museum of Art, 1993), 157.

Anon., Adam and Eve, Bible, Provincial Library of Burgos, MS 846, fol. 12v, in *Art of Medieval Spain,* ed. O'Neill, 299.

Anon., Adam and Eve, Paris Psalter, Bibliothèque Nationale, MS. lat. 10434, fol. 10, in *French Miniatures from Illuminated Manuscripts* by Jean Porcher (London: Collins, 1960), color plate 44.

Anon., The Fall, Morgan Old Testament, MS M.638, fol. 1v, in *Old Testament Miniatures: A Medieval Picture Book with 283 Paintings from the Creation to the Story of David* by Sydney C. Cockerell (New York: George Braziller, 1975), 29.

Anon., Tree of Vices, De Lisle Psalter, fol. 128v, in *The Psalter of Robert de Lisle in the British Library* by Lucy Freeman Sandler (London: Harvey Miller, 1983), 48, plate 8.

Paul, Herman, and Jean Limbourg, The Garden of Eden, Très Riches Heures of Jean, Duke of Berry, fol. 25v, in *The Très Riches Heures of Jean, Duke of Berry* by Jean Longon and Raymond Cazelles (Secaucus, N.J.: Wellfleet Press, 1969), plate 20.

Boucicaut Master, Adam and Eve, in *De cas de nobles hommes et femmes,* by Boccaccio, Getty Museum, MS 63, in "Boccaccio's *Des cas des nobles hommes et femmes* at the Getty Museum" by Thomas Kren, *Apollo* (Sept. 1996): 77.

746   Ingo F. Wather, ed., *Painting in the Gothic Era* (Cologne: Taschen, 1999), 40, 38.

Masolino, *The Temptation of Adam and Eve,* in *The Brancacci Chapel, Florence* by Andrew Ladis (New York: George Braziller, 1993), 38.

Masolino, *The Temptation of Adam and Eve,* in *Masolino da Panicale* by Perri Lee Roberts (Oxford: Clarendon Press, 1993), 75, color plate 3.

Raphael, *The Temptation and Fall of Adam and Eve,* in *Raphael: The Stanza della Segnatura* by James Beck (New York: George Braziller, 1993), 32–33, plate. 3.

Nicolas Bocquet, *Adam and Eve on the Brink of Disobedience,* in *Adam et Eve de Dürer à Chagall: Gravures de la Bibliothèque Nationale* (Paris: Réunion des Musées Nationaux, 1992), plate 66.

Joseph-Théodore Richomme, *Adam and Eve on the Brink of Disobedience,* in *Adam et Eve de Dürer à Chagall,* plate 77.

Max J. Friedländer and Jakob Rosenberg, *The Paintings of Lucas Cranach* (Ithaca, N.Y.: Cornell University Press, 1978), monochrome plates 191–99, color plate 194.

Robert A. Koch, *Hans Baldung Grien: Eve, the Serpent, and Death* (Ottawa: National Gallery of Canada, 1974), 28–29.

Lucas Cranach the Elder, *Cupid Complaining to Venus,* in *Early Netherlandish and German Paintings* by Alistair Smith (London: National Gallery, 1985), plate 38.

Lucas Cranach the Elder, *Adam and Eve,* in *The Courtauld Institute Galleries, University of London* by Dennis Farr et al. (London: Scala Publications, 1990) 45.

Anon., Adam and Eve, in *Italian Majolica, 15–18 Centuries* by A. N. Kube, O. E. Mikhailova, and E. A. Lapkovskaya (Moscow: Iskusstvo Art Publishers, 1976), plate 32.

Anon., Fall of Man, in *Five Centuries of Italian Majolica* by Giuseppe Liverani (New York: McGraw-Hill, 1960), plate 73.

Anon., Virgin and Child, in *Romanesque Art Guide* (Barcelona: Museo Nacional d'Art de Catalunya, 1998), 110–11, cat. nos. 105, 108, 109.

Anon., Virgin and Child, in "Recent Acquisitions: A Selection, 1998–1999," *Metropolitan Museum or Art Bulletin* 57 no. 1 (fall 1999), 17.

Tilman Riemenschneider, *Adam,* in *Tilman Riemenschneider: Master Sculptor of the Late Middle Ages,* ed. Julian Chapuis (New Haven: Yale University Press, 1999), 243, cat. 20.

Tullio Lombardo, *Adam,* in *Italian Renaissance Sculpture* by John Pope-Hennessy (New York: Random House, 1985), plate 141.

Nicolò Roccatagliata, *Adam and Eve,* in *Renaissance Master Bronzes from the Collection of the Kunsthistorisches Museum, Vienna* by Manfred Leithe-Jasper (Washington, D.C.: Scala Books, 1986), 183.

Anon., The Fall of Man, in *J. Pierpont Morgan, Collector* by Linda Horvitz Roth (Hartford, Conn.: Wadsworth Atheneum, 1987), 106–8.

Rainer Maria Rilke, "Eva," in *Translations from the Poetry of Rainer Maria Rilke,* trans. M. D. Herter Norton (New York: W. W. Norton, 1938), 184–85.

William Blake, *The Temptation and Fall of Eve,* in *William Blake at the Huntington* by Robert N. Essick (New York: Harry N. Abrams, 1994), 116, plates 47, 50.

Revelation 12:1, New Oxford Annotated Bible.

Giambattista Tiepolo, *The Immaculate Conception,* in *The Glory of Venice: Art in the Eighteenth Century,* ed. Jane Martineau and Andrew Robison (New Haven: Yale University Press, 1994), 184.

Francisco de Zurbarán, *The Immaculate Conception,* in *Zurbarán,* ed. Jeannine Baticle (New York: 747
  Harry N. Abrams, 1987), 33, 55, 59, 70.
Johannes Vermeer, *Allegory of the Faith,* in *Vermeer and the Delft School,* ed. Liedtke, 401.

Edenic Apples Allegorized

Abraham Cowley, "The Tree of Knowledge," in *Poems,* ed. A. R. Waller (Cambridge: Cam-
  bridge University Press, 1905), 45.
Philip Booth, "Original Sequence," in *Chapters into Verse,* vol. 1, ed. Robert Atwan and Laurance
  Wieder (New York: Oxford University Press, 1993), 39.
Linda Pastan, "A Symposium: Apples," in *Carnival Evening: New and Selected Poems, 1968–1998*
  (New York: W. W. Norton, 1998), 84–85.
Pastan, "On the Question of Free Will," in *The Imperfect Paradise* (New York: W. W. Norton,
  1988), 75.
D. J. Enright, "Paradise Illustrated: A Sequence, 11" and "In a Corner," in *Collected Poems,*
  1948–1998 (Oxford: Oxford University Press, 1998), 243–44, 449.
Robert Friend, "In the Orchard," in *A Geography of Poets: An Anthology of the New Poetry,* ed.
  Edward Field (New York: Bantam, 1979), 506.
Jorie Graham, "Self-Portrait as the Gesture between Them," in *The Dream of the Unified Field:*
  Selected Poems, 1974–1994 (Hopewell, N.J.: Ecco Press, 1995), 52–54.
Angela Figuera, "Impertinent Exhortation to My Sister Poetesses," in *Women Poets of Spain,*
  1860–1990: Toward a Gynocentric Vision, trans. John C. Wilcox (Urbana: University of Illi-
  nois Press, 1997), 192–93.
Angela Figuera Aymerich, "Exhortación impertinente a mis hermanas poetisas," in *Obras Com-*
  pletas (Madrid: Hiperión, 1986), 302–3.
Gloria Fuertes, "Otra versión," in *Historia de Gloria (Amor, humor y desamor),* 3d ed. (Madrid:
  Cátedra, 1981), 370.
Fuertes, "Another Version," in *Women Poets of Spain, 1860–1990: Toward a Gynocentric Vision,*
  trans. John C. Wilcox (Urbana: University of Illinois Press, 1997), 217.
Christopher Maurer, ed., *Federico García Lorca: Selected Verse* (New York: Farrar Straus Giroux,
  1995), xi.
Federico García Lorca, "Initium," in *Federico García Lorca: Selected Verse,* ed. Christopher Maurer,
  trans. Jerome Rothenberg (New York: Farrar Straus Giroux, 1995), 58–61.
Rhina P. Espaillat, "If You Ask Me," in *Where Horizons Go* (Kirksville, Mo.: New Odyssey Press,
  1998), 1.
Maurya Simon, "Claiming the Apostrophe," *Georgia Review* 53, no. 3 (fall 1999), 527.
Ted Hughes, "Apple Tragedy," in *Crow* (New York: Harper and Row, 1971), 66.
Helen Vendler, *The Odes of John Keats* (Cambridge: Harvard University Press, 1983), 250.
John Ehle, chaps. 11–12 in *The Cheeses and Wines of England and France* (New York: Harper and
  Row, 1972).
Anya Taylor, "Coleridge, Keats, Lamb, and Seventeenth-Century Drinking Songs," in *Milton, the*
  Metaphysicals, and Romanticism, ed. Lisa Low and Anthony John Harding (Cambridge:
  Cambridge University Press, 1994), 223.
John Keats, "O blush not so! O blush not so," in *John Keats: Complete Poems,* ed. Jack Stillinger
  (Cambridge: Harvard University Press, 1982), 167–68.

748   Emily Schlesinger, "An Allegory," in *Making the Alphabet Dance: Recreational Wordplay,* ed. Ross Eckler (New York: St. Martin's Press, 1996), 14–15.

Anne Sexton, "Rats Live on No Evil Star," in *The Complete Poems* (Boston: Houghton Mifflin, 1981), 359–60.

Demystified Edenic Apples

Tadeusz Rózewicz, "The Apple," in *Post-War Polish Poetry,* trans. Czeslaw Milosz (Harmondsworth, England: Penguin, 1970), 72–73, 69.

Mark Twain, *The Diaries of Adam and Eve* (New York: Oxford University Press, 1996), 13–14, 17, 41, 89, 107, 109.

Ursula K. Le Guin, introduction to *The Diaries of Adam and Eve* by Mark Twain, xl–xli.

The Secularization of Biblical Apples

Dan Pagis, *Hebrew Poetry of the Middle Ages and the Renaissance* (Berkeley and Los Angeles: University of California Press, 1991), 69.

Moses Ibn Ezra, "The Apple," in *The Penguin Book of Hebrew Verse,* ed. and trans. T. Carmi (New York: Penguin, 1981), 326.

Ibn Ezra, "Beautiful as the pomegranate is the white face," in *Selected Poems of Moses Ibn Ezra,* 2d ed., trans. Solomon Solis-Cohen (Philadelphia: Jewish Publication Society of America, 1945), 71.

Solomon Ibn Gabirol, "An Apple for Isaac," in *The Jewish Poets of Spain, 900–1250,* ed. and trans. David Goldstein (Harmondsworth, England: Penguin, 1965), 77.

Solomon Ibn Gabirol, *Selected Poems,* trans. Peter Cole (Princeton: Princeton University Press, 2000), 53, 73, 81, 207.

Guillaume de Lorris and Jean de Meun, *The Romance of the Rose,* 3d ed., trans. Charles Dahlberg (Princeton: Princeton University Press, 1995), 41; Félix Lecoy, ed., *Le Roman de la Rose,* vol. 1 (Paris: Librairie Honoré Champion, 1965), ll. 802–3.

Rafael Alberti, "Red," in *Selected Poems,* trans. Ben Belitt (Berkeley and Los Angeles: University of California Press, 1966), 172–73.

Jehudah Halevi, "By an Apple Tree," in *Selected Poems of Jehudah Halevi,* ed. Heinrich Brody, trans. Nina Salaman (Philadelphia: Jewish Publication Society of America, 1952), 56.

Pagis, *Hebrew Poetry,* 64–68.

Halevi, "The Apple," in *The Jewish Poets of Spain, 900–1250,* ed. and trans. David Goldstein (Harmondsworth, England: Penguin, 1965), 150; Pagis, trans., *Hebrew Poetry,* 38.

Raymond Scheindlin, "Hebrew Poetry in Medieval Iberia," in *Convivencia: Jews, Muslims, and Christians in Medieval Spain,* ed. Vivian B. Mann, Thomas F. Glick, and Jerrilynn D. Dodds (New York: George Braziller/The Jewish Museum, 1992), 47.

Paul the Silentiary, 5.290, in *The Greek Anthology,* vol. 1, trans. W. R. Paton (London: William Heinemann, 1916), 280–81; in *Two Hundred Poems from the Greek Antology,* ed. and trans. Skelton, 47.

George Martin, trans., "Apple Girl," in *Italian Folktales,* ed. Italo Calvino (New York: Pantheon, 1980), 308–9.

Secularized Apples

Samuel Hanagid, "The Apple," nos. 1–3, in *Selected Poems of Shmuel HaNagid,* trans. Peter Cole (Princeton: Princeton University Press, 1996), 167, 12.

Secularized Apples in Art 749

Thomas Kren, preface to *Mira Calligraphiae Monumenta,* ed. Lee Hendrix and Thea Vignau-Wilberg (Malibu: J. Paul Getty Museum, 1992), viii–ix.

Lee Hendrix, "The Writing Model Book," in *Mira Calligraphiae Monumenta,* ed. Hendrix and Vignau-Wilberg, 41.

Claudia Swan, *The Clutius Botanical Watercolors: Plants and Flowers of the Renaissance* (New York: Harry N. Abrams, 1998), 11.

Norbert Schneider, *Still Life: Still Life Painting in the Early Modern Period* (Cologne: Benedikt Taschen, 1994).

Thomas Da Costa Kaufmann, *The Mastery of Nature: Aspects of Art, Science, and Humanism in the Renaissance* (Princeton: Princeton University Press, 1993), 17.

Zurbarán al Museo Nacional d'Art de Catalunya (Barcelona: Museo Nacional D'Art de Catalunya, 1998), 245–47, cat. no. 21–22, 23–26.

Ann Sutherland Harris, "Garzoni, Giovanna," in *The Dictionary of Art,* ed. Jane Turner (New York: Grove, 1996), 169–70.

Gerardo Casale, *Giovanna Garzoni: "Insigne miniatrice," 1600–1670* (Milan: Jandi Sapi, 1991).

Silvia Trkulja and Elena Fumagalli, *Giovanna Garzoni: Nature Morte* (Paris: Bibliothèque de l'Image, 2000).

Gillian Riley, *Renaissance Recipes* (San Francisco: Pomegranate Artbooks, 1993), 78.

Pierre Rosenberg, *Chardin, 1699–1779* (Cleveland: Cleveland Museum of Art, 1979).

William B. Jordan and Peter Cherry, *Spanish Still Life from Velázquez to Goya* (London: National Gallery, 1995).

Frédéric Desbuissons et al., *Courbet et la commune* (Paris: Réunion des Musées Nationaux, 2000), plates 1–7.

Sarah Faunce and Linda Nochlin, *Courbet Reconsidered* (Brooklyn: Brooklyn Museum, 1988), 195–99.

Pastan, "Courbet's 'Still Life with Apples and Pomegranate,'" in *An Early Afterlife* (New York: W. W. Norton, 1995), 40.

Virginia Woolf to Nicholas Bagenal, 15 April 1918, in *The Letters of Virginia Woolf,* ed. Nigel Nicolson and Joanne Trautmann, vol. 2 (New York: Harcourt Brace Jovanovich, 1976), 230.

John Rewald, ed. *The Paintings of Paul Cézanne: A Catalogue Raisonné,* vol. 1 (New York: Harry N. Abrams, 1996), 232.

Paul Cézanne, *Still Life with Apples,* in *Cézanne* by Françoise Cachin et al., trans. John Goodman (New York: Harry N. Abrams, 1996), fig. 49.

W. H. Auden, "Letter to Lord Byron," in *Collected Longer Poems* (New York: Random House, 1975), 61.

Christopher Middleton, "A Cart with Apples," in *111 Poems* (Manchester: Carcanet New Press, 1983), 72.

Les Murray, "Five Postcards," *Times Literary Supplement,* 26 June 1998, 34.

Meyer Schapiro, "The Apples of Cézanne: An Essay on the Meaning of Still-Life," *Art News Annual* 34 (1968): 34–53; reprinted in *Modern Art, Nineteenth and Twentieth Centuries: Selected Papers* by Meyer Schapiro (New York: George Braziller, 1978).

Schapiro, "Apples of Cézanne," in *Modern Art,* 15, 26, 30.

750   Schapiro, *Paul Cézanne* (New York: Harry N. Abrams, 1952), 98–99.

Schapiro, "Apples of Cézanne," 11, 6, 30–2.

Philostratus the Elder, *Imagines* 1.6, "Cupids"; in *Philostratus: "Imagines" and "Callistratus": Descriptions,* trans. Arthur Fairbanks (London: William Heinemann, 1931), 21–29.

Schapiro, "Apples of Cézanne," 6.

Titian, *The Worship of Venus,* in *Titian* by David Rosand (New York: Harry N. Abrams, 1978), plate 17.

Julius S. Held, "Rubens and Titian," in *Titian: His World and His Legacy,* ed. David Rosand (New York: Columbia University Press, 1982), 312, figs. 7.23, 7.24.

Peter Paul Rubens, *The Worship of Venus,* in *Peter Paul Rubens: Man and Artist* by Christopher White (New Haven: Yale University Press, 1987), 273, plate 244.

George Mauner, *Cuno Amiet, Giovanni Giacometti, Augusto Giacometti: Three Swiss Painters* (Lausanne: Presses Centrales, [1973]), 15, 16.

Peter Selz, *German Expressionist Painting* (Berkeley and Los Angeles: University of California Press, 1974), 97.

Cuno Amiet, *The Apple Harvest,* in *Die Künstlergemeinschaft Brücke* by Lothar-Günther Buchheim (Tübingen: Buchheim Verlag, 1956), fig. 403.

Gustav Klimt, *Apple Tree I* and *Apple Tree II,* in *Klimt* by Catherine Dean (Ann Arbor: Borders Press, 1996), 42–43.

Bonnie Yochelson, "Clarence H. White, Peaceful Warrior," in *Pictorialism into Modernism: The Clarence H. White School of Photography,* ed. Marianne Fulton (New York: Rizzoli, 1996), 16.

Clarence H. White, *The Orchard,* in *Pictorialism into Modernism: The Clarence H. White School of Photography,* ed. Fulton, 13.

Man Ray, untitled, in *The Machine As Seen at the End of the Mechanical Age* by K. G. Pontus Hultén (New York: Museum of Modern Art, 1968), 158.

Heiting, ed., *Man Ray, 1890–1976,* 150.

History and Apples

Adriaen Van der Donck, *A Description of the New Netherlands,* 2d ed., trans. Jeremiah Johnson (n.p.: 1656; reprint, Syracuse: Syracuse University Press, 1968), 24.

Ann Leighton, *American Gardens in the Eighteenth Century: "For Use or Delight"* (Boston: Houghton Mifflin, 1976), 225.

Rosella Rice, "Johnny Appleseed," in *A Treasury of North American Folk Tales,* ed. Catherine Peck (New York: Book-of-the Month-Club, 1998), 103–5, 376.

Amelia Simmons, *American Cookery* (Hartford, Conn.: Hudson and Goodwin, 1796); reprint, ed. Iris Ihde Fry (Greens Farms, Conn.: Silverleaf Press, 1984), 26–27.

Henry David Thoreau, *Wild Apples* (Bedford, Mass.: Applewood Books, n.d.); Bradley P. Dean, ed., *Wild Fruits* (New York: W. W. Norton, 1999), 74–92, 244–48.

Henry James, chap. 1, "New England: An Autumn Impression," in *The American Scene* (New York: Harper and Brothers, 1907); *Henry James, Collected Travel Writings: Great Britain and America* (New York: Library of America, 1993), 370.

James, chap. 5 in *William Wetmore Story and His Friends, from Letters, Diaries, and Recollections,* vol. 1 (New York: Grove Press, 1957), 295–96.

Leon Edel, *Henry James: A Life* (New York: Harper and Row, 1985), 566.

Bruce Weber, *The Apple of America: The Apple in Nineteenth Century American Art* (New York: Berry-Hill Galleries, 1993).

Thomas Philipott, *Poems* (London: John Wilcox, 1646), ed. L. C. Martin (Liverpool: University Press of Liverpool, 1950), 9.

Iona Opie and Peter Opie, *The Oxford Nursery Rhyme Book* (New York: Oxford University Press, 1955); Opie and Opie, *A Family Book of Nursery Rhymes* (New York: Oxford University Press, 1964).

"Here's to thee, good apple tree" and "Up in the green orchard there is a green tree," in Opie and Opie, *A Family Book of Nursery Rhymes,* 29.

Iona Opie, "Apple, apple," in *The People in the Playground* (Oxford: Oxford University Press, 1993), 233.

Robert Francis, "Remind Me of Apples," in *The Orb Weaver* (Middletown, Conn.: Wesleyan University Press, 1960), 26; Francis, *Collected Poems, 1936–1976* (Amherst: University of Massachusetts Press, 1976), 178.

Susan Stewart, "Apple," in *The New Bread Loaf Anthology of Contemporary American Poetry* (Hanover and London: University Press of New England, 1999), 301.

Beach, *The Apples of New York,* vol. 1, *Index to Varieties.*

David Guterson, "The Kingdom of Apples," *Harper's,* Oct. 1999, 54–55, 56.

Dave Smith, "Winesaps," in *The Roundhouse Voices* (New York: Harper and Row, 1985), 139.

Michael S. Harper, "History as Apple Tree," in *Images of Kin* (Urbana: University of Illinois Press, 1977), 143.

Brendan Galvin, "Brother Francisco Anthony Eats an Apple," in *The Strength of a Named Thing* (Baton Rouge: Lousiana State University Press, 1999), 4–5.

Ivan Bunin, "Apple Fragrance," in *Shadowed Paths,* trans. Olga Shartse (Moscow: Foreign Languages Publishing House, n.d.), 7–8.

Morgan and Richards, *Book of Apples,* 182.

Hans J. Rindisbacher, *The Smell of Books: A Cultural-Historical Study of Olfactory Perception in Literature* (Ann Arbor: University of Michigan Press, 1992), 140.

Seifert, "Moscow," in *The Poetry of Jaroslav Seifert,* trans. Ewald Osers (North Haven, Conn.: Catbird Press, 1998), 34; Seifert, *The Early Poetry of Jarolav Seifert,* trans. Dana Loewy (Evanston, Ill.: Hydra Books, Northwestern University Press, 1997), 195, 220.

George Gibian, introduction to *The Poetry of Jaroslav Seifert,* trans. Osers, 3.

Seifert, "An Apple Tree with Cobweb Strings," in *The Early Poetry of Jarolav Seifert,* trans. Loewy, 188–89.

Apples: Shape and Weight

Jonathan Swift, "On the Words 'Brother Protestants and Fellow Christians,'" in *Jonathan Swift, The Complete Poems,* ed. Pat Rogers (New Haven: Yale University Press, 1983), 537–38, 879–80.

Random House Historical Dictionary of American Slang, s.v. "apple."

Paul Zimmer, "In Apple Country," in *Introspections: American Poets on One of Their Own Poems,* ed. Robert Pack and Jay Parini (Hanover and London: University Press of New England, 1997), 319–23.

Jorge Teillier, "Gift," in *From the Country of Nevermore,* trans. Mary Crow (Hanover and London: University Press of New England, 1990), 60–61.

752   William Stukeley, *Memoirs of Sir Isaac Newton's Life,* ed. A. Hastings White (London: Taylor and Francis, 1936), 19–20.

Voltaire, "Letter Fifteen: On the System of Attraction," in *Philosophical Letters,* trans. Ernest Dilworth (Indianapolis: Bobbs-Merrill, 1961), 68.

Voltaire, *Lettres philosophiques,* ed. Frédéric Deloffre (Paris: Gallimard, 1986), 104.

George Gordon, Lord Byron, *Don Juan* 10.1–2; in *Lord Byron: The Complete Poetical Works,* vol. 5, ed. Jerome J. McGann (Oxford: Clarendon Press, 1986), 37.

Vladimir Soloukhin, "The Apple," in *Twentieth-Century Russian Poetry,* ed. John Glad and Daniel Weissbort, trans. Daniel Weissbort (Iowa City: University of Iowa Press, 1992), 204–5.

Lev Mak, "Eden," in *Voices within the Ark: The Modern Jewish Poets,* ed. Howard Schwartz and Anthony Rudolf, trans. Daniel Weissbort (New York: Avon, 1980), 1105–6.

Imants Ziedonis, "I Love an Apple," in *Shifting Borders: East European Poetries of the Eighties,* ed. Walter Cummins, trans. Inara Cedrins (London and Toronto: Associated University Presses, 1993), 104.

Ziedonis, "Try to Find," in *Shifting Borders: East European Poetries of the Eighties,* ed. Cummins, trans. Cedrins, 105.

John Hollander, "Granny Smith," in *The Night Mirror* (New York: Atheneum, 1971), 72.

Charles Simic, "Dear Isaac Newton," in *Austerities* (New York: George Braziller, 1982); reprinted in *Verse and Universe,* ed. Kurt Brown (Minneapolis: Milkweed Editions, 1998), 297–98.

David Young, "Four about Apples, 3," in *Models of the Universe: An Anthology of the Prose Poem,* ed. Stuart Friebert and David Young (Oberlin, Ohio: Oberlin College Press, 1995), 232.

René Magritte, *The Post Card* and *The Listening Room,* in *Magritte,* ed. David Larkin (New York: Ballantine Books, 1972), plates 6, 26.

Magritte, *The Post Card* and *The Idea,* in *Magritte* by Suzi Gablik (Boston: New York Graphic Society, 1976), figs. 143, 145.

Magritte, *The Listening Room,* in *Magritte* by Jacques Meuris, trans. J. A. Underwood (London: Greenwich Editions, 1994), fig. 237.

Hollis Frampton and Marion Faller, *Apple Advancing (var. "Northern Spy"),* in *Hollis Frampton, Recollections, Recreations* by Bruce Jenkins and Susan Krane (Cambridge: Massachusetts Institute of Technology Press, 1984), 77–85.

Sheer Number of Apples

Metrodorus, 14.118, in *The Greek Anthology,* vol. 5, trans. W. R. Paton (London: William Heinemann, 1916–1918), 87; in *Briefly Singing,* trans. Skelton (Victoria, B.C.: Sono Nios Press, 1994), 172.

Jean Follain, "Vie," trans. Keith Waldrop, in *The Random House Book of Twentieth-Century French Poetry,* ed. Paul Auster (New York: Random House, 1982), 386–87.

Follain, "La Pomme rouge," in *Poems and Texts,* trans. Serge Gavronsky (New York: October House, 1969), 72–73.

Follain, "Ces Trois pommes dernières," in *D'Après Tout: Poems by Jean Follain,* trans. Heather McHugh (Princeton: Princeton University Press, 1981), 174–75.

Follain, "Ève," trans. W. S. Merwin, in *The Random House Book of Twentieth-Century French Poetry,* ed. Paul Auster (New York: Random House, 1982), 388–89.

Robert Frost, "After Apple-picking," in *Robert Frost: Collected Poems, Prose, and Plays* (New York: 753
    Library of America, 1995), 70–71.

Richard Poirier, *Robert Frost: The Work of Knowing* (New York: Oxford University Press, 1977),
    299.

Pablo Neruda, "Ode to the Apple," in *Neruda's Garden: An Anthology of Odes,* trans. Maria Jacketti
    (Pittsburgh: Latin American Literary Review Press, 1995), 191–93.

Bernd Heinrich, *The Trees in My Forest* (New York: HarperCollins, 1997), 133, 135.

Apples, Peeled and Sliced

Yehuda Amichai, "With Her in an Apple," in *Yehuda Amichai: A Life of Poetry, 1948–1994,* trans.
    Benjamin Harshav and Barbara Harshav (New York: HarperCollins, 1994), 378.

Charles Tomlinson, "Paring the Apple," in *Selected Poems, 1955–1997* (New York: New Direc-
    tions, 1997), 16, xiv.

Frank McCourt, *Angela's Ashes: A Memoir* (New York: Scribner, 1996), 154–55, 161.

Robert Francis, "Apple Peeler," in *The Orb Weaver* (Middletown, Conn.: Wesleyan University
    Press, 1960), 11.

Lawrance Thompson and R. H. Winnick, *Robert Frost: The Later Years, 1938–1963* (New York:
    Holt, Rinehart and Winston, 1976), 205–6.

Biancamaria Frabotta, "The apple you teach me is to double the half of self," in *Italian Woman
    Poets of the Twentieth Century,* trans. Catherine O'Brien (Dublin: Irish Academic Press,
    1996), 242–43, 232.

Hikmet, "We are one half of an apple," in *Poems of Nazim Hikmet,* trans. Randy Blasing and
    Mutlu Konuk (New York: Persea Books, 1994), 102.

Eaten Apples

Elinor Wylie, "Green Apple," in *Last Poems,* ed. Jane D. Wise (New York: Alfred A. Knopf, 1943),
    6–7.

Shirley Kaufman, "Apples," in *Gold Country* (Pittsburgh: University of Pittsburgh Press, 1973),
    40.

Roger Weingarten, "Apples," in *Shadow Shadow* (Boston: David R. Godine, 1986), 3–4.

Ralph Gustafson, "My Love Eats an Apple," in *Selected Poems* (Toronto: McClelland and Stewart,
    1972), 67.

Robert Isaacson, "The Evolution of Bouguereau's Grand Manner," *Minneapolis Institute of the
    Arts Bulletin* 62 (1975): 77.

William Bouguereau, *Temptation,* in *William Bouguereau, 1825–1905* (Montreal: Montreal Museum
    of Fine Arts, 1984), 217–18, cat. no. 91.

Cary Waterman, "Temptation," in *The Salamander Migration* (Pittsburgh: University of Pitts-
    burgh Press, 1980), 37–38.

William Bouguereau, *Temptation,* in *Bouguereau* by Fronia E. Wissman (San Francisco: Pome-
    granate Artbooks, 1996), plate 25.

Mark Steven Walker, "Bouguereau at Work," in *William Bouguereau, 1825–1905* (Montreal:
    Montreal Museum of Fine Arts, 1984), 73.

Michael Palma, preface to *The Man I Pretend to Be: The Colloquies and Selected Poems of Guido
    Gozzano,* trans. Palma (Princeton: Princeton University Press, 1981), xii.

754   Guido Gozzano, "The Colloquies, 1" and "Parable," in *The Man I Pretend to Be: The Colloquies and Selected Poems of Guido Gozzano*, trans. Palma, 5, 187.

Cooked Apples

Maggie Lane, *Jane Austen and Food* (London: Hambledon Press, 1995), 153.

Jane Austen, *Emma*, chaps. 3 and 27; ed. Fiona Stafford (London: Penguin, 1996), 19–20, 195–97.

Lane, *Jane Austen and Food*, 165.

Margaret Gibson, "Apples," in *Signs* (Baton Rouge and London: Louisiana State University Press, 1979), 43.

Anon., *The Adventures of A, Apple Pie, Who Was Cut to Pieces and Eaten by Twenty Six Young Ladies and Gentlemen* (New York: George Burgess, ca. 1835; reprint, New York: Dover, 1973).

Gloria T. Delamar, *Mother Goose: From Nursery to Literature* (Jefferson, N.C.: McFarland, 1987), 76–80.

Oxford Dictionary of Nursery Rhymes, 2d ed., s.v. "A."

Leonard Welsted, "Of Apple-Pyes," *Petits Propos Culinaires* 64 (Apr. 2000): 49–51.

Jane Hirshfield, "Mele in Gabbia," in *The Lives of the Heart* (New York: HarperCollins, 1997), 65.

Raymond Carver, "Bright Red Apples," in *No Heroics, Please*, ed. Tess Gallagher (New York: Vintage, 1992), 60–61.

Gallagher, ed., *No Heroics, Please*, 15.

Carver, "My Daughter and Apple Pie" and "To My Daughter," in *All of Us: The Collected Poems* (New York: Alfred A. Knopf, 1998), 86–87, 70.

Sara Maitland, "Gluttony," in *The Seven Deadly Sins*, ed. Alison Fell (London: Serpent's Tail, 1988), 160–61.

Fermented Apples: Cider

James Patrick Muirhead, ed. and trans., *The Vaux-de-Vire of Maistre Jean Le Houx, Advocate, of Vire* (London: John Murray, 1875), lvi, 174–75, 201.

Gustave Flaubert, *Madame Bovary*, pt. 2, sect. 8; trans. Francis Steegmuller (New York: Random House, 1957), 151–52.

James A. Galloway, "Driven by Drink? Ale Consumption and the Agrarian Economy of the London Region, c. 1300–1400," in *Food and Eating in Medieval Europe*, ed. Martha Carlin and Joel T. Rosenthal (London and Rio Grande, Ohio: Hambledon Press, 1998), 88.

Isaac Newton to Oldenburg, 2 September 1676, *The Correspondence of Isaac Newton*, vol. 2, ed. H. W. Turnbull et al. (Cambridge: Cambridge University Press, 1960), 93–94.

Stuart Peachey, "Red Strakes," in *Fruit Variety Register*, vol. 1 (Bristol: Stuart Press, 1995), 16.

Newton to Oldenburg, 14 November 1676, *The Correspondence of Isaac Newton*, vol. 2, 181.

Mavis Batey, *Oxford Gardens: The University's Influence on Garden History* (Amersham: Avebury, 1982), 37.

John Philips, *Cyder*, 2.665–69, in *The Poems of John Philips*, ed. M. G. Lloyd Thomas (Oxford: Basil Blackwell, 1927), 87.

Samuel Johnson, "John Philips," in *Lives of the English Poets*, vol. 1 (London: Everyman, J. M. Dent, 1946), 274, 276–77.

Philips, *Cyder* 1.486–90, 1.512–23, 1.530–36, in *Poems of John Philips*, ed. Thomas, 58–60.

Thomas Hardy, "Great Things," in *The Complete Poems of Thomas Hardy*, ed. James Gibson (New York: Macmillan, 1976), 474–75.

Peter Redgrove, "Eve's Apple," *Paris Review* 122 (spring 1992): 91–92.

Imperfect Apples: Cores and Rot

Émile Zola, *L'Assommoir*, trans. Leonard Tancock (Harmondsworth, England: Penguin, 1970), 348.

William Shakespeare, *The Merchant of Venice* 1.393–97; ed. John Russell Brown (London: Methuen, 1977), 26–27.

Clarence Major, "Apple Core," in *The Garden Thrives: Twentieth-century African-American Poetry*, ed. Clarence Major (New York: HarperCollins, 1996), 168–69.

Young, "Four about Apples, 4," in *Models of the Universe*, 233.

Philip Larkin, "As Bad as a Mile," in *The Whitsun Weddings* (New York: Random House, 1964), 32; in *Collected Poems*, ed. Anthony Thwaite (New York: Farrar, Straus and Giroux, 1989), 125.

David Ignatow, "To an Apple," in *Poems, 1934–1969* (Middletown, Conn.: Wesleyan University Press, 1970), 193.

Ludvík Vaculík, "Cidering," trans. Slavic 116, University of California–Berkeley, Oct. 1981, in *Formations* 1, no. 1 (spring 1984), 130–31.

William Empson, "Value Is in Activity," in *Collected Poems* (New York: Harcourt Brace, 1949), 4, 93.

Franz Kafka, *The Metamorphosis*, trans. Stanley Corngold, in *The Metamorphosis by Franz Kafka*, trans. and ed. Corngold (New York: Bantam Books, 1972; reprinted 1986), 3, 39.

Hellmuth Kaiser, "Kafka's Fantasy of Punishment," in *The Metamorphosis by Franz Kafka*, ed. Corngold, 155–56.

William Empson, "A Family Monster," in *Argufying: Essays on Literature and Culture*, by Empson, ed. John Haffenden (Iowa City: University of Iowa Press, 1987), 470–71.

David Eggenschwiler, "*Die Verwendung*, Freud, and the Chains of Odysseus," in *Franz Kafka's "The Metamorphosis,"* ed. Harold Bloom (New York: Chelsea House, 1988), 71, 79–80.

Worms in Apples

Gonzalo Millan, "Clinical Bulletin," trans. John Upton, *Triquarterly* 13–14 (fall–winter 1968–1969): 383.

Reinhard Döhl, "Wurm in Apfel," in *An Anthology of Concrete Poetry*, ed. Emmett Williams (New York: Something Else Press, 1967).

Eugène Guillevic, "The Worm," in *The Fabulists French: Verse Fables of Nine Centuries*, trans. Norman R. Shapiro (Urbana: University of Illinois Press, 1992), 217–18.

Linda Pastan, "Routine Mammogram," in *Carnival Evening: New and Selected Poems, 1968–1998* (New York: W. W. Norton, 1998), 183–84.

Sue Owen, "The Worm in the Apple," in *My Doomsday Sampler* (Baton Rouge: Lousiana State University Press, 1999), 14.

Poisoned Apples

Dante Gabriel Rossetti, "The Orchard-Pit," in *The Collected Works of Dante Gabriel Rossetti*, vol. 1, ed. William M. Rossetti (London: Ellis and Elvey, 1890), 427, 377.

Oswald Doughty, ed., *Dante Gabriel Rossetti: Poems* (London: J. M. Dent, 1957), 307n. 1.

756   Jack Zipes, trans., "Snow White," in *The Complete Fairy Tales of the Brothers Grimm* (New York: Bantam Books, 1987), 202.

Olga Broumas, "Snow White," in *Beginning with O* (New Haven: Yale University Press, 1977), 71, 70.

Alojz Ihan, "Apple," trans. Tom Lozar, in *Verse* 13, 2/3: *Younger Slovene Poets* (1996), 178.

Apples, Blossoming and Falling

John Clare, "The Crab Tree," in *John Clare: Poems of the Middle Period, 1822–1837,* ed. Eric Robinson et al., vol. 4 (Oxford: Clarendon Press, 1998), 189.

Eric Robinson and Geoffrey Summerfield, ed., *Selected Poems and Prose of John Clare* (Oxford: Oxford University Press, 1967), 163–64, xxviii–xxix.

Christina Rossetti, "An Apple-Gathering," in *Christina Rossetti: Poems and Prose,* ed. Jan Marsh (London: Everyman, J. M. Dent, 1994), 61.

William Morris, *Pomona,* in *Textiles by William Morris and Morris and Co., 1861–1940* by Oliver Fairclough and Emmeline Leary (London: Thames and Hudson, 1981), 56.

William Morris, "Pomona," in *The Everyman Book of Victorian Verse: The Pre-Raphaelites to the Nineties,* ed. Donald Thomas (London: Everyman, J. M. Dent, 1993), 33.

Christina Rossetti, "A Birthday," in *Christina Rossetti: Poems and Prose,* 60–61.

Dante Gabriel Rosetti, *A Vision of Fiametta,* in *Dante Gabriel Rossetti* by Alicia Craig Faxon (New York: Abbeville Press, 1989), figs. 236, 235.

Dante Gabriel Rossetti to Frederic Shields, April 1878, quoted in *The Paintings and Drawings of Dante Gabriel Rossetti (1828–1882): A Catalogue Raisonné* by Virginia Surtees, vol. 1 (Oxford: Clarendon Press, 1971), 149.

Dante Gabriel Rossetti, "A Vision of Fiammetta," quoted in Surtees, *The Paintings and Drawings of Dante Gabriel Rossetti, 1828–1882: A Catalogue Raisonné,* vol. 1, 148.

William Carlos Williams, "Portrait of a Lady," in *The Collected Poems of William Carlos Williams,* vol. 1, ed. A. Walton Litz and Christopher MacGowan (New York: New Directions, 1986), 129, 492.

Linda Welsheimer Wagner, *The Poems of William Carlos Williams: A Critical Study* (Middletown, Conn.: Wesleyan University Press, 1964), 77–78.

Fragonard, *The Happy Hazards of the Swing* and *The Swing,* in *Jean-Honoré Fragonard: Life and Work* by Jean-Pierre Cuzin (New York: Harry N. Abrams, 1998), figs. 125, 251.

James Wright, "The Revelation," in *Above the River: The Complete Poems* (Middletown, Conn.: Wesleyan University Press, 1990), 66–67.

Robert Frost, "The Cow in Apple Time," in *Robert Frost: Collected Poems, Prose, and Plays* (New York: Library of America, 1995), 121.

Pastan, "The Apple Shrine," in *An Early Afterlife* (New York: W. W. Norton, 1995), 66.

Janet Holmes, "Seven Lyrics of Autumn," in *The Physicist at the Mall* (Tallahassee: Anhinga Press, 1994), 45.

John Hollander, "Something for the Fall Wind" and "Long after the End of Fall," in *Harp Lake* (New York: Alfred A. Knopf,1988), 65, 67.

Apple Orchards

Vita Sackville-West, *The Land and the Garden* (London: Michael Joseph, 1989), 38, 101.

Robert Frost, "A Prayer in Spring," in *Robert Frost: Collected Poems, Prose, and Plays* (New York: Library of America, 1995), 21.

Eleanor Farjeon, *Edward Thomas: The Last Four Years* (Oxford: Oxford University Press, 1979),
254.

Farjeon, *Martin Pippin in the Apple Orchard* (New York: Frederick A. Stokes, 1922), 2, 236, 252.

Naomi Lewis, *A Book for Eleanor Farjeon: A Tribute to Her Life and Work, 1881–1965* (New York: Henry Z. Walck, 1966), 2.

Samuel Palmer, *The Magic Apple Tree*, in *Apples: A Social History* by Sally Twiss (London: The National Trust, 1999), 3.

John Irving, *The Cider House Rules* (New York: Ballantine, 1993), 441, 506.

Jaqueline Ridgeway, *Louise Bogan* (Boston: Twayne, 1984), 58.

Louise Bogan, "The Crossed Apple," in *The Blue Estuaries: Poems, 1923–1968* (New York: Farrar, Straus and Giroux, 1975), 45–46.

Elizabeth Frank, *Louise Bogan: A Portrait* (New York: Alfred A. Knopf, 1985), 123.

Rachel Hadas, "Pomology," in *Halfway down the Hall: New and Selected Poems* (Hanover and London: Wesleyan University Press, 1998), 10.

Angie Estes, "Apples in August," in *The Uses of Passion* (Salt Lake City: Gibbs Smith, 1995), 36.

James Merrill, "For a Second Marriage," in *New Poets of England and America,* ed. Donald Hall, Robert Pack, and Louis Simpson (New York: Meridian, 1957), 213–14; "Upon a Second Marriage," in *Collected Poems, James Merrill,* ed. J. D. McClatchy and Stephen Yenser (New York: Alfred A. Knopf, 2001), 72.

Samuel Johnson, "Abraham Cowley," in *Lives of the Poets,* vol. 1 (London: Everyman, 1946), 29–31.

The Resanctification of Apples

Vernon Watkins, "Music of Colours—White Blossoms . . . ," in *Selected Poems* (New York: New Directions, 1967), 43–44.

Jim Harrison, "Suite to Appleness," in *Selected and New Poems, 1961–1981* (New York: Dell, 1982), 37–40.

Banal, or Philosophical, Apples

Edna St. Vincent Millay, "Recuerdo," in *Collected Poems* (New York: Harper, 1956), 128.

Millay, "Now, I could very easily tell," quoted by Amy Clampitt in "Two Cheers for Prettiness," *New Republic,* 6/13 Jan. 1992, 45.

Macrobius, *The Saturnalia,* trans. Percival Vaughan Davies (New York: Columbia University Press, 1969), 505–6.

Arild Nyquist, "Apple Stealing," in *Modern Scandinavian Poetry: The Panorama of Poetry, 1900–1975,* trans. Martin Allwood (Oslo: Dreyers Forlag, 1982), 224.

Jacques Prévert, "Picasso's Promenade," in *Selections from "Paroles,"* trans. Lawrence Ferlinghetti (Harmondsworth, England: Penguin, 1965), 124–27.

Charles Brackett, Billy Wilder, and D. M. Marshman Jr., *Sunset Boulevard* (Berkeley and Los Angeles: University of California Press, 1999), 104–6.

Magritte, *The Treachery of Images* and *This is not an Apple,* in *Magritte* by Meuris, figs. 92–94, 50.

CHAPTER 2: FIGS

Some Fig Facts

Don Brothwell and Patricia Brothwell, *Food in Antiquity: A Survey of the Diet of Early Peoples,* expanded ed. (Baltimore: Johns Hopkins University Press, 1998), 145.

Oxford Classical Dictionary, 3d ed., s.v. "fig."

758   Jared Diamond, *Guns, Germs, and Steel: The Fates of Human Societies* (New York: W. W. Norton, 1997), 124–25.

Ananios, quoted in "The Sources and Sauces of Athenaeus " by John Wilkins and Shaun Hill in *Food in Antiquity,* ed. John Wilkins, David Harvey, and Mike Dobson (Exeter: University of Exeter Press, 1995), 430.

Mishnah, *Ketubot,* 5.8, cited in "Food and Archaeology in Romano-Byzantine Palestine" by Shimon Dar, in *Food in Antiquity,* 327–28.

Philostratus the Elder, *Imagines* 1.31, "Xenia"; in *Philostratus: "Imagines" and "Callistratus": Descriptions,* trans. Arthur Fairbanks (London: William Heinemann, 1931), 123.

Barbara Ferguson, ed., *All about Growing Fruits, Berries, and Nuts* (San Ramon, Calif.: Ortho Books, 1987), 70.

Daniel H. Janzen, "How to Be a Fig," *Annual Review of Ecology and Systematics* 10 (1979): 14–15, 47.

Frances Mayes, *Under the Tuscan Sun: At Home in Italy* (San Francisco: Chronicle Books, 1996), 71–72.

Richard Dawkins, *Climbing Mount Improbable* (New York: W. W. Norton, 1996), 4, 300, 320–21.

Song of Songs 4:12, New Oxford Annotated Bible.

Hilary Wilson, *Egyptian Food and Drink* (Haverfordwest, Wales: C. I. Thomas and Sons, 1988), 27.

Karen Polinger Foster, "The Earliest Zoos and Gardens," *Scientific American* (July 1999): 67.

Wayne H. Davis, "A Fig Tree in Kentucky," *Pomona* 29, no. 4 (fall 1996): 55.

Aristophanes, *The Birds* 588–91; in *Three Comedies by Aristophanes: The Birds, The Clouds, The Wasps,* trans. William Arrowsmith (Ann Arbor: University of Michigan Press, 1987), 44.

Pliny the Elder, *Natural History* 15.21.79–81; in *Natural History,* vol. 4, trans. H. Rackham (London: William Heinemann, 1945), 343–45.

Samuel Butler, *The Way of All Flesh,* chap. 61; ed. James Cochrane (Harmondsworth, England: Penguin, 1966), 291.

Marilyn Hacker, "Late August," in *Selected Poems, 1965–1990* (New York: W. W. Norton, 1994), 217.

Biblical Figs

Penny Howell Jolly, *Made in God's Image? Eve and Adam in the Genesis Mosaics at San Marco, Venice* (Berkeley and Los Angeles: University of California Press, 1997), plate 1, fig. 20.

Victor Perera, *The Cross and the Pear Tree: A Sephardic Journey* (New York: Alfred A. Knopf, 1995), 9.

The Anchor Bible: Jeremiah, 24:1–10, trans. John Bright (New York: Doubleday, 1965), 192.

The Works and Days of Hesiod, 679–82, in *Hesiod,* trans. Richmond Lattimore (Ann Arbor: University of Michigan Press, 1973), 99.

Song of Songs 2:11–13, in *The Song of Songs,* trans. Ariel Bloch and Chana Bloch (New York: Random House, 1995), 59.

Mark 13:28, New Oxford Annotated Bible.

Matthew 7:16, 21:18–19, 22, New Oxford Annotated Bible.

Luke 13:8–9, New Oxford Annotated Bible.

Leviticus 19:23–25, New Oxford Annotated Bible.

Alastair Fowler, ed. *The New Oxford Book of Seventeenth Century Verse* (Oxford: Oxford University Press, 1991), xl.

Mildmay Fane, "Shamed by the Creature," in *New Oxford Book of Seventeenth Century Verse,* 362–63.

W. F. R. Browning, "fig," in *A Dictionary of the Bible* (Oxford: Oxford University Press, 1996), 136.   *759*

Donald Hall, "A Small Fig Tree," in *Old and New Poems* (New York: Ticknor and Fields, 1990), 31.

John Ruskin, 3 July 1872, letter 20 in *Fors Clavigera* (Orpington, Kent: G. Allen, 1871–1884); E. T. Cook and Alexander Wedderburn, ed., *The Works of John Ruskin,* vol. 27 (London: George Allen, 1907), 335–36.

Wolfgang Kemp, *The Desire of My Eyes: The Life and Work of John Ruskin,* trans. Jan van Heurck (New York: Noonday Press, 1990), 378.

Classical Figs

Jeffrey Henderson, *The Maculate Muse: Obscene Language in Attic Comedy,* 2d ed. (New York: Oxford University Press, 1991), 134–35.

Archilochus, "On a Willing Woman," in *Greek Lyrics,* 2d ed., trans. Richmond Lattimore (Chicago: University of Chicago Press, 1960), 2.

Aristophanes, *Peace* 1214–23, 1346–48, 1351–52, in *Aristophanes: Clouds, Wasps, Peace,* trans. Jeffrey Henderson (Cambridge: Harvard University Press, 1998), 582–83, 600–601.

Henderson, *Maculate Muse,* 118.

Propertius, elegy 4.5.75–78; in *Elegies,* trans. G. P. Goold (Cambridge: Harvard University Press, 1990), 400–401.

Propertius, elegy 4.5.75–78; in *The Poems of Propertius,* trans. John Warden (Indianapolis: Bobbs-Merrill, 1972), 207.

Maurice Olender, "Priapus: The Last of the Gods," in *Roman and European Mythologies,* ed. Yves Bonnefoy and Wendy Doniger, trans. Gerald Honigsblum (Chicago: University of Chicago Press, 1992), 139–40.

Horace, *Satires* 1.8.1–7; in *Priapea: Poems for a Phallic God,* trans. W. H. Parker (London: Croom Helm, 1988), 15.

Peter Stewart, "Fine Art and Coarse Art: The Image of Roman Priapus," *Art History* 20, no. 4 (Dec. 1997): 575–88.

Charles Avery, *Bernini: Genius of the Baroque* (Boston: Little, Brown, 1997), fig. 24.

Leonard Barkan, "Feasts for the Eyes, Foods for Thought," *Social Research* 66, no. 1: "Food: Nature and Culture" (winter 1998): 233–34.

Givanni da Udine, *Loggia of Psyche* (detail), in *Raphael* by Roger Jones and Nicholas Penny (New Haven: Yale University Press, 1983), plate 196.

Martial, *Satires,* 7.25; in *Epigrams of Martial Englished by Divers Hands,* ed. J. P. Sullivan and Peter Whigham, trans. Olive Pitt-Kethley (Berkeley and Los Angeles: University of California Press, 1987), 269.

Pliny the Elder, *Natural History* 14.74–75; in *Natural History: A Selection,* trans. John F. Healy (London: Penguin, 1991), 200–201.

F. J. Meijer, "Cato's African Figs," *Mnemosyne* 37, no. 1–2 (1984): 123–24.

The Fig Gesture

Dante Alighieri, *The Divine Comedy, Inferno* 24.4–5, 82–84 and 25.1–3; in *The Divine Comedy, Inferno 1: Italian Text and Translation,* trans. Charles S. Singleton (Princeton: Princeton University Press, 1970), 246–47, 252–53, 258–59.

Joan M. Ferrante, "Canto XXIV, Thieves and Metamorphoses," in *Lectura Dantis, Inferno,* ed. Allen Mandelbaum, Anthony Oldcorn, and Charles Ross (Berkeley and Los Angeles: University of California Press, 1998), 316–27.

760   Anthony Oldcorn, "Canto XXV, The Perverse Image," in *Lectura Dantis, Inferno,* 331.

Charles S. Singleton, *Divine Comedy, Inferno 2: Commentary* (Princeton: Princeton University Press, 1970), 428.

Eugene Paul Nassar, *Illustrations to Dante's* Inferno (London and Toronto: Associated University Presses, 1994), 285–86, 282–83, 288.

William Blake, *Inferno,* Canto 25, in *Blake's Dante: The Complete Illustrations to the* Divine Comedy by Milton Klonsky (New York: Harmony Books, 1980), plate 52; in David Bindman, *William Blake, The Divine Comedy* (Paris: Bibliothèque de l'Image, 2000), 123.

Dante, *Dante's Inferno,* trans. and illustrator Tom Phillips (London: Thames and Hudson, 1985), 203.

Tom Phillips, *A Humament: A Treated Victorian Novel,* 1st rev. ed. (London: Thames and Hudson, 1987).

Johanna Drucker, *The Century of Artists' Books* (New York: Granary Books, 1995), 111.

François Rabelais, *Gargantua and Pantagruel,* bk. 4, chap. 45; in *The Complete Works of François Rabelais,* trans. Donald M. Frame (Berkeley and Los Angeles: University of California Press, 1991), 534.

Geoffrey Barraclough, *The Origins of Modern Germany,* 2d ed. (New York: W. W. Norton, 1984), 230.

Shakespeare, *Henry V,* 3.6.56–58; ed. T. W. Craik (Watton-on-Thames Surrey: Thomas Nelson, 1997), 236.

Ovid, *Fasti* 5.433–34; in *Fasti,* vol. 5, trans. James George Frazer (Cambridge: Harvard University Press, 1926), 292–93.

Eric Partridge, "fig," in *Dictionary of Slang and Unconventional English,* 5th ed. (New York: Macmillan, 1961), 274.

Edward Taylor, "A Fig for Thee Oh! Death," in *The Poems of Edward Taylor,* ed. Donald E. Stanford (New Haven: Yale University Press, 1960), 488.

Andrea Vincenzo de Jorio, *Gesture in Naples and Gesture in Classical Antiquity,* trans. Adam Kendon (Bloomington: Indiana University Press, 2000), 215.

Modern Poetic Figs

D. H. Lawrence, "Figs," in *The Complete Poems of D. H. Lawrence,* ed. Vivian de Sola Pinto and Warren Roberts (Harmondsworth, England: Penguin, 1977), 282–84.

Lawrence, "Breadalby," chap. 8 in *Women in Love,* ed. Charles L. Ross (Harmondsworth, England: Penguin, 1982), 139.

Michael Burns, "To D. H. Lawrence," *Paris Review* (summer 1998): 183–84.

Lawrence, "Bare Fig-Trees," in *The Complete Poems of D. H. Lawrence,* 299–300.

André Gide, *Fruits of the Earth,* trans. Dorothy Bussy (London: Secker and Warburg, 1949), 80.

Rainer Maria Rilke, *Duino Elegies,* elegy 6; in *The Penguin Book of German Verse,* trans. Leonard Forster (Harmondsworth, England: Penguin, 1959), 400–401.

Rilke, *Duino Elegies,* elegy 6; in *Duino Elegies and the Sonnets to Orpheus,* trans. A. Poulin, Jr. (Boston: Houghton Mifflin, 1977), 42–43.

Federico García Lorca, "Bacchus," in *Federico García Lorca: Selected Verse,* ed. Christopher Maurer, trans. Alan S. Trueblood (New York: Farrar Straus Giroux, 1995), 144–47.

Maurer, "Notes to the Poems," in *Federico García Lorca: Selected Verse,* 312.

Geraldine Cleary Nichols, *Miguel Hernández* (Boston: Twayne, 1978), 131, 39, 99.

Miguel Hernández, "You were like a young fig tree," trans. Timothy Baland, in *Miguel Hernán-*   *761*
dez *and Blas de Otero, Selected Poems,* ed. Timothy Baland and Hardie St. Martin (Boston:
Beacon, 1972), 86–87.

Ágnes Nemes Nagy, "Figtrees," trans. Bruce Berlind, in *Contemporary East European Poetry,* ed.
Emery George (New York: Oxford University Press, 1993), 259–60.

Naomi Shihab Nye, "My Father and the Fig Tree," in *Anthology of Modern Palestinian Literature,*
ed. Salma Khadra Jayyusi (New York: Columbia University Press, 1992), 356–57.

Felix Stefanile, "A Fig-Tree in America," *Poetry 99,* no. 4 (Jan. 1962): 220.

Francis Ponge, *Comment une figue de paroles et pourquoi* (Paris: Flammarion, 1977), 14, 87.

Gabriela Mistral, "The Fig," trans. Maria Giachetti, in *A Gabriela Mistral Reader,* ed. Marjorie
Agosin, (Fredonia, N.Y.: White Pine Press, 1993), 169.

Modern Fictional Figs

James Joyce, *A Portrait of the Artist as a Young Man,* chap. 5; ed. Hans Walter Gabler with Walter
Hettche (New York: Garland, 1993), 204, 268, 277.

James Joyce, *Stephen Hero,* ed. Theodore Spencer (New York: New Directions, 1944), 118.

Sylvia Plath, *The Bell Jar* (New York: Harper and Row, 1971), 65, 91.

Linda Wagner-Martin, *The Bell Jar* (New York: Twayne, 1992), 38.

Katherine Anne Porter, "The Fig Tree," in *The Collected Stories of Katherine Anne Porter* (New
York: Harcourt Brace Jovanovich, 1965), 354–58, 361–62.

V. S. Pritchett, "The Fig Tree," in *Collected Stories* (Harmondsworth, England: Penguin, 1984),
435, 438, 441–42, 457.

Roger Angell, "Marching Life," *New Yorker,* 22–29 Dec. 1997, 132.

CHAPTER 3: MISSING FRUIT

Yehuda Amichai, "The Singer of the Song of Songs," trans. Chana Bloch and Chana Kronfeld,
New Republic, 26 Apr. and 3 May 1999, 98.

Charles Tomlinson, "A Thousand Waterdrops," *Times Literary Supplement,* 15 Oct. 1999, 13.

Classical Greek Literature

Athenaeus, *The Deipnosophists or Banquet of the Learned,* vol. 3, trans. C. D. Yonge (London: Henry
G. Bohn, 1854), 1227–52.

Athenaeus, *The Deipnosophists* 14.653f; in *The Deipnosophists,* vol. 7, trans. Charles Burton Gulick
(Cambridge: Harvard University Press, 1937), 7.

Andrew Dalby, *Siren Feasts* (London: Routledge, 1996), 76, 22–23.

James Davidson, *Courtesans and Fishcakes: The Consuming Passions of Classical Athens* (New York:
HarperCollins, 1998), 12–20.

Classical Roman Literature

Emily Gowers, *The Loaded Table: Representations of Food in Roman Literature* (Oxford: Clarendon
Press, 1993), 17, 109, 43, 145.

Horace, *Satires* 2.8.31–32, 2.4.22–23; in *Horace: Satires and Epistles; Persius: Satires,* trans. Niall
Rudd (Harmondsworth, England: Penguin, 1979), 123, 107.

Smith Palmer Bovie, trans., *Satires and Epistles of Horace* (Chicago: University of Chicago Press,
1959), 88.

762   Niall Rudd, *The Satires of Horace* (Berkeley and Los Angeles: University of California Press, 1982), 212.

Horace, *Satires* 2.4.22–23, 70–71; in *Horace: Satires and Epistles; Perseus: Satires,* trans. Rudd, 107–8.

Martial, *Epigrams* 5.78; in *Martial: Epigrams,* vol. 1, trans. D. R. Shackleton Bailey (Cambridge: Harvard University Press, 1993), 418–21; in *Epigrams of Martial Englished by Divers Hands,* ed. J. P. Sullivan and Peter Whigham, trans. Peter Whigham (Berkeley and Los Angeles: University of California Press, 1987), 216–19.

Gowers, *Loaded Table,* 250–53, 263.

Martial, *Epigrams* 1.43; in *Epigrams of Martial,* trans. Palmer Bovie (New York: New American Library, 1970), 54, 53.

Peter Howell, *A Commentary on Book One of the Epigrams of Martial* (London: Athlone Press, 1980), 203–5.

Gowers, *Loaded Table,* 265.

Juvenal, *Satires* 11.99, 72–76 and 5.149–55; in *The Satires of Juvenal,* trans. Rolfe Humphries (Bloomington: Indiana University Press, 1958), 139, 138, 61.

Juvenal, *Satires* 5.149–55; in *Juvenal: The Sixteen Satires,* trans. Peter Green (Harmondsworth, England: Penguin, 1967), 122.

Petronius, *The Satyricon* 31.11, 60.4, 66.4; in *Petronius the Satyricon and Seneca the Apocolocyntosis,* rev. ed., trans. J. P. Sullivan (London: Penguin, 1986), 54, 75, 80.

Dante

Dante, *Inferno* 13.4–6; in *The Divine Comedy, Inferno 1: Italian Text and Translation,* trans. Charles S. Singleton (Princeton: Princeton University Press, 1970), 128–29.

Dante, *The Divine Comedy,* in *Divine Comedy, Inferno 2: Commentary,* trans. Charles S. Singleton (Princeton: Princeton University Press, 1970), 205n. 6.

Dante, *Purgatorio* 28.2, 28.78, 28, 130; in *The Divine Comedy, Purgatorio 1: Italian Text and Translation,* trans. Charles S. Singleton (Princeton: Princeton University Press, 1970), 302–3.

Dante *Purgatorio* 27.115–17; in *The Divine Comedy, Purgatorio 1: Italian Text and Translation,* trans. Singleton, 298–99.

Dante, *The Divine Comedy,* in *Purgatorio 2: Commentary,* trans. Singleton, 685n. 120.

Dante, *Purgatorio* 32.38–39; in *The Divine Comedy, Purgatorio 1: Italian Text and Translation,* trans. Singleton, 352–53.

Dante, *The Divine Comedy, Purgatorio 2: Commentary,* trans. Singleton, 786n. 39.

Dante, *Purgatorio* 32.73–84; in *The Divine Comedy of Dante Alighieri, Purgatorio,* trans. Allen Mandelbaum (New York: Bantam, 1984), 301.

Matthew 17:1–8, quoted in *The Divine Comedy, Purgatorio 2: Commentary,* trans. Singleton, 792.

CHAPTER 4: STRAWBERRIES (AND CREAM)

Robert Herrick, "Upon the Nipples of *Julia's* Breast," in *The Complete Poetry of Robert Herrick,* ed. J. Max Patrick (New York: Anchor, 1963), 221.

Herrick, "Fresh Cheese and Cream," in *The Complete Poetry of Robert Herrick,* ed. Patrick, 244.

Christopher Ricks, *Keats and Embarrassment* (Oxford: Oxford University Press, 1974), 103, 105–8.   *763*

Herrick, "The Lilly in a Christal," in *The Complete Poetry of Robert Herrick,* ed. Patrick, 107–9.

J. B. Broadbent, "The Imperious Empiricist," *Times Literary Supplement,* 25 July 1975, 836.

Denis Diderot and Jean D'Alembert, eds., "Fraisier," in *Encyclopédie,* vol. 7 (Paris: 1757), 277; reprint, vol. 2 (Elmsford, N.Y.: Pergamon, n.d.), 90.

Thomas Tusser, *Five Hundred Pointes of Good Husbandrie, 1580,* ed. W. Payne and Sidney J. Herrtage (London: Trubner, 1876), 41, 64.

Jane Austen, *Emma,* chap. 42; ed. Fiona Stafford (London: Penguin, 1996), 296.

Peter J. Hatch, *The Fruits and Fruit Trees of Monticello* (Charlottesville: University Press of Virginia, 1998), 170.

William Bartram, pt. 3, chap. 3 in *Travels through North and South Carolina, Georgia, East and West Florida* (Philadelphia: James and Johnson, 1791); Bartram, *William Bartram: Travels and Other Writings* (New York: Library of America, 1996), 291–92.

Bartram, "Observations on the Creek and Cherokee Indians," chap. 5 in *William Bartram: Travels and Other Writings* (New York: Library of America, 1996), 536.

P[atrick] Barry, *The Fruit Garden: A Treatise* (Auburn and Rochester: Alden and Beardsley, 1855), 344–46.

Barbara Ferguson, ed., *All about Growing Fruits, Berries, and Nuts* (San Ramon, Calif.: Ortho Books, 1887), 98–101.

John Ruskin, "Fontainebleu," chap. 4 in *Præterita: Outlines of Scenes and Thoughts Perhaps Worthy of Memory in My Past Life* (London: Rupert Hart-Davis, 1949), 285.

Margot Arce de Vazquez, *Gabriela Mistral: The Poet and Her Work* (New York: New York University Press, 1964), 43–45.

Mistral, "The Wild Strawberry," trans. Maria Giachetti, in *A Gabriela Mistral Reader,* ed. Marjorie Agosin (Fredonia, N.Y.: White Pine Press, 1993), 74.

Langston Hughes, "Dinner Guest: Me," in *The Collected Poems of Langston Hughes,* ed. Arnold Rampersad (New York: Vintage, 1995), 548, 19.

Eleanor Perényi, *Green Thoughts: A Writer in the Garden* (New York: Vintage, 1983), 213–14.

Jane Grigson, "Strawberry," in *Jane Grigson's Fruit Book* (London: Penguin, 1982), 416.

Émile Zola, *L'Assommoir,* chap. 7; trans. Leonard Tancock (Harmondsworth, England: Penguin, 1970), 197, 221.

David Baguley, *Emile Zola: L'Assommoir* (Cambridge: Cambridge University Press, 1992), 65.

Zola, *Nana,* chap. 6; trans. Douglas Parmée (Oxford: Oxford University Press, 1998), 152–53.

Marcel Proust, "Combray," *Swann's Way,* in vol. 1, *In Search of Lost Time,* trans. C. K. Scott-Moncrieff and Terence Kilmartin (New York: Vintage, 1981), 152.

Alistair Elliot, "Erdbeeren, Fragole, Fraises," *Times Literary Supplement,* 19 Jan. 1996, 29.

Jon Silkin, "The Strawberry Plant," in *Poems New and Selected* (Middletown, Conn.: Wesleyan University Press, 1966), 66.

John Kinsella, "In the Best Interest of Strawberries," *Poems, 1980–1994* (Newcastle upon Tyne: Bloodaxe Books, 1998), 116.

Walter W. Skeat, "strawberry," in *A Concise Etymological Dictionary of the English Language,* new ed. (Oxford: Clarendon Press, 1901), 523.

Gayle Ross, "Strawberries," in *Treasury of North American Folk Tales,* ed. Catherine Peck (New York: Book-of-the Month-Club, 1998), 322, 380.

764   Thoreau, *Wild Fruits,* ed. Bradley P. Dean (New York: W. W. Norton, 1999), 10–12.

Laurence Stapleton, *Marianne Moore: The Poet's Advance* (Princeton: Princeton University Press, 1978), 142.

Marguerite Young, "An Afternoon with Marianne Moore," in *Festschrift for Marianne Moore's Seventieth Birthday,* ed. Tambimuttu (New York: Tambimuttu and Mass, 1964), 63–64.

Marianne Moore, "Nevertheless," in *The Complete Poems of Marianne Moore* (New York: Macmillan/Viking, 1981), 125–56.

Ruth Pitter, "The Strawberry Plant," in *Collected Poems* (London: Enitharmon Press, 1996), 83.

Grace Paley, "When the wild strawberry leaves turn," in *Begin Again: Collected Poems* (New York: Farrar, Straus, and Giroux, 1999), 63.

Marina Tsvetaeva, "The Kirillovnas," trans. Collyer Bowen, in *Pages from Tarusa: New Voices in Russian Writing,* ed. Andrew Field (Boston: Little, Brown, 1964), 294, 297, 300.

Pamela Chester, "Strawberries and Chocolate: Tsvetaeva, Mandelstam, and the Plight of the Hungry Poet," in *Food in Russian History and Culture,* ed. Musya Glants and Joyce Toomre (Bloomington: Indiana University Press, 1997), 148–49, 159nn. 3–4, 153.

Henry Ward Beecher, "Strawberries and Cream," in *Eyes and Ears* (Boston: Ticknor and Fields, 1863), 376–77.

J. B. S. Chardin, *Basket of Wild Strawberries,* in *Chardin, 1699–1779* by Pierre Rosenberg (Cleveland: Cleveland Museum of Art, 1979), 325, color plate 18; *A Basket of Wild Strawberries,* in *Chardin* by Philip Conisbee (Lewisburg, Pa.: Bucknell University Press, 1985), fig. 193.

J. Carter Brown, foreword to Nicolai Cikovsky, Jr., *Raphaelle Peale Still Lifes* (New York: Harry N. Abrams, 1988), 7; *Strawberries and Cream,* fig. 45.

Pierre Bonnard, *Strawberries,* in *Pierre Bonnard,* ed. Willem de Looper and Kevin Grogan (Washington, D.C.: Phillips Collection, 1979), plate 19.

Walter S. Gibson, *Hieronymus Bosch* (London: Thames and Hudson, 1973), 80.

John Rowlands, *The Garden of Earthly Delights, Hieronymous Bosch* (New York: E. P. Dutton, 1979), n.p.

Wilhelm Fränger, *The Millennium of Hieronymus Bosch: Outlines of a New Interpretation,* trans. Eithne Wilkins and Ernst Kaiser (Chicago: University of Chicago Press, 1951), 116.

CHAPTER 5: PLUMS

Keats, "On Fame," in *John Keats, Complete Poems,* ed. Jack Stillinger (Cambridge: Harvard University Press, 1982), 278.

Grace Stone Coates, "Wild Plums," in *The Best American Short Stories of the Century,* ed. John Updike and Katrina Kenison (Boston: Houghton Mifflin, 1999), 102, 104.

Bartram, pt. 3, chap. 7 in *Travels through North and South Carolina; William Bartram: Travels and Other Writings,* 342–43.

Joseph Restele, *Wild Plum,* in *Drawn from Nature: The Botanical Art of Joseph Prestele and His Sons* by Charles Van Ravenswaay (Washington, D.C.: Smithsonian Institution Press, 1984), plate 26.

Mani Leyb, "A Plum," trans. John Hollander, in *The Penguin Book of Modern Yiddish Verse,* ed. Irving Howe, Ruth R. Wisse, and Khone Schmeruk (New York: Penguin, 1987), 134–35.

William Carlos Williams, "This Is Just to Say," in *Collected Poems of William Carlos Williams,* vol. 1, ed. A. Walton Litz and Christopher MacGowan (Middletown, Conn.: Wesleyan University Press, 1964), 372, 536.

Charles Altieri, "Presence and Reference in a Literary Text: The Example of Williams' 'This is   *765*
Just to Say,'" *Critical Inquiry* 5, no. 3 (spring 1979): 499–501.

Paul Mariani, *William Carlos Williams: A New World Naked* (New York: McGraw-Hill, 1981).

William Carlos Williams, "To a Poor Old Woman," "Spring," and "The Widow's Lament in
Springtime," in *Collected Poems of William Carlos Williams,* vol. 1, ed. A. Walton Litz and
Christopher MacGowan (Middletown, Conn.: Wesleyan University Press, 1964), 383, 158,
171.

Moyshe-Leyb Halpern, "Never Again Will I Say," in *Onions and Cucumbers and Plums,* trans.
Sarah Zweig Betsky (Detroit: Wayne State University Press, 1958), 50–53.

Ruth R. Wisse, *A Little Love in Big Manhattan* (Cambridge: Harvard University Press, 1988), 117.

Bertolt Brecht, "The Plum-Tree," trans. Edwin Morgan, in *Modern European Poetry,* ed. Willis
Barnstone et al. (New York: Bantam, 1966), 154.

Brecht, "Erinnerung an die Marie A." and "Der Orangenkauf," in *Die Gedichte von Bertolt Brecht
in einem Band* (Frankfurt am Main: Suhrkamp, 1981), 232, 540–41.

Brecht, "Remembering Marie A.," trans. John Willett, in *Bertolt Brecht: Poems, 1913–1956,* ed.
John Willett, Ralph Manheim, and Eric Fried (New York: Methuen, 1976), 35–36, 527.

Brecht, "Buying Oranges," trans. Naomi Replansky, in *Bertolt Brecht: Poems, 1913–1956,* ed.
John Willett, Ralph Manheim, and Eric Fried (New York: Methuen, 1976), 231, 557.

William Dickey, "Plum," in *The Education of Desire* (Hanover, N.H.: Wesleyan University Press,
1996), 28.

Random House Historical Dictionary of American Slang, vol. 1, s.v. "fisting."

Jon Silkin, "The Plum-tree," in *The Little Time-keeper* (New York: W. W. Norton, 1976), 38.

Helen Thomas, "Poets' Holiday in the Shadow of War," *(London) Times,* 3 August 1963, 8.

Edward Thomas, "Two Houses," in *The Collected Poems of Edward Thomas,* ed. R. George
Thomas (Oxford: Clarendon Press, 1978), 243.

Jay Meek, "Plums," in *Windows* (Pittsburgh: Carnegie Mellon University Press, 1994), 29–30.

Edward Thomas, "There's nothing like the sun," in *The Collected Poems of Edward Thomas,* ed.
R. George Thomas (Oxford: Clarendon Press, 1978), 249.

Josephine Miles, "Conservancies," in *A Geography of Poets: An Anthology of the New Poetry,* ed.
Edward Field (New York: Bantam Books, 1979), 89–90.

Marge Piercy, "The Pernickety Plum Tree," in *The Twelve-Spoked Wheel Flashing* (New York:
Alfred A. Knopf, 1978), 63.

Robin Skelton, "Plums," in *The Collected Shorter Poems, 1947–1977* (Victoria, B.C.: Sono Nis
Press, 1981), 23.

Gary Soto, "The Plum's Heart," in *Black Hair* (Pittsburgh: University of Pittsburgh Press, 1985), 5–6.

Faye George, "Plum," *Poetry* 170, no. 1 (Apr. 1997): 35.

Alan Shefsky, "It Is the Ripe Red," *TriQuarterly* 103 (fall 1998): 140–41.

Robert Winner, "Plums," in *The Sanity of Earth and Grass: Complete Poems* (Gardiner, Maine:
Tilbury House, 1994), 63.

CHAPTER 6: THE FLOWERING PLUM

Hui-Lin Li, "Mei Hua: a Botanical Note," in *Bones of Jade, Soul of Ice: The Flowering Plum in Chinese Art,* ed. Maggie Bickford et al. (New Haven: Yale University Press, 1985), 246, fig. 138.

Craig Clunas, *Fruitful Sites: Garden Culture in Ming Dynasty China* (Durham, N.C.: Duke University Press, 1996), 44.

766   Maggie Bickford, *Ink Plum: The Making of a Chinese Scholar-Painting Genre* (Cambridge: Cambridge University Press, 1996), 31.

Bickford, *Bones of Jade, Soul of Ice,* figs. 18, 27.

Bickford, *Ink Plum,* 63.

Anon., "Falling are the plums," trans. Hans H. Frankel, in *Bones of Jade, Soul of Ice,* 153.

Wang Anshi, "The flowering plums on Lone Hill," trans. Frankel, in *Bones of Jade, Soul of Ice,* 167.

Li Qingzhao, "Last night I was very drunk and careless in undressing" and "Year after year when it snowed," trans. Frankel, in *Bones of Jade, Soul of Ice,* 175.

Bickford, *Ink Plum,* 45.

Bickford, *Bones of Jade, Soul of Ice,* 43, 106, 134–35.

James Cahill, *The Painter's Practice: How Artists Lived and Worked in Traditional China* (New York: Columbia University Press, 1994), 23–24.

CHAPTER 7: PEACHES, MANGOES, AND OTHER JUICY FRUITS

Roberto Roversi, "Afternoon," trans. William Fense Weaver, in *An Anthology of New Italian Writers,* ed. Marguerite Caetan (New York: New Directions, 1950), 353–54.

T. S. Eliot, "The Love Song of J. Alfred Prufrock" and "The Hippopotamus," in *The Complete Poems and Plays, 1909–1950* (New York: Harcourt, Brace and World, 1952), 7, 30.

Saul Bellow and Isaac Rosenfeld, "Nu-zhe, kum-zhe, ikh un du," in Mark Shechner, "Dear Mr. Einstein: Jewish Comedy and the Contradictions of Culture," in *Jewish Wry, Essays on Jewish Humor,* ed. Sarah Blacher Cohen (Detroit: Wayne State University Press, 1987), 149–50.

Christopher Driver, "J. Alfred's Appetite," quoted in *On Fasting and Feasting* by Alan Davidson (London: Macdonald, 1988), 64.

Elizabeth Gaskell, *Cranford* with *Mr Harrison's Confessions* and *The Cage at Cranford,* ed. Graham Handley (London: Everyman, J. M. Dent, 1995), 29, xix.

Iris Murdoch, *The Sea, the Sea* (New York: Viking, 1978), 87.

John Keats to C. W. Dilke, 22 Sept. 1819, *The Letters of John Keats,* vol. 2, ed. Hyder Edward Rollins (Cambridge: Harvard University Press, 1958), 179.

John Keats to Fanny Keats, 28 Aug. 1819, Rollins, ed., *Letters of Keats,* vol. 2, ed. Rollins, 149.

Stuart Peachey, *Fruit Variety Register,* vol. 2 (Bristol: Stuart Press, 1995), 54–55, 57–64.

Charles Darwin, chap. 10 in *Variation of Animals and Plants under Domestication,* 2d ed. (London: John Murray, 1875), vol. 1, 362; Darwin, *The Works of Charles Darwin,* vol. 19, ed. Paul H. Barrett et al. (New York: New York University Press, 1988), 317.

Wallace Stevens, "A Dish of Peaches in Russia," in *Parts of a World* (New York: Alfred A. Knopf, 1942), 78–79; in *Wallace Stevens, Collected Poetry and Prose* (New York: Library of America, 1997), 206.

Massimo Montanari, *The Culture of Food,* trans. Carl Ipsen (Oxford: Blackwell, 1994), 86.

P. W. Hammond, *Food and Feast in Medieval England,* corr. ed. (Stroud, Gloucestershire: Alan Sutton, 1995), 26, 28–29, 36.

Gregorio Comanini, "On the Painting of Certain Very Naturalistic Peaches," in *Caravaggio: A Life* by Helen Langdon (New York: Farrar, Straus and Giroux, 1998), 32.

Ambrogio Figino, *Still Life with Peaches,* in *Spanish Still Life from Velázquez to Goya* by William B. Jordan and Peter Cherry (London: National Gallery, 1995), fig. 2.

Ambrogio Figino, *Still Life with Peaches,* in *Still Life* by Sybille Ebert-Schifferer (New York: Harry N. Abrams, 1999), fig. 53.

Ambrogio Figino, *Still Life with Peaches,* in *Giovan Ambrogio Figino* by Roberto Paolo Ciardi (Florence: Marchi and Bertolli, 1968), color plate 2.

Fede Galizia, *Peaches in a White Ceramic Basket,* in Ebert-Schifferer, *Still Life,* fig. 54.

H. Frederic Janson, *Pomona's Harvest: An Illustrated Chronicle of Antiquarian Fruit Literature* (Portland, Oreg.: Timber Press, 1996), 221–22, 224.

René Rapin, *The Orchard,* bk. 4 of *Of Gardens,* 3d ed., trans. James Gardiner (London: Bernard Lintot, 1728), 158–59.

Peachey, *Fruit Variety Register,* vol. 2, 57.

Samuel Johnson, quoted in "Manners, Meals, and Domestic Pastimes" by Dorothy Marshall, in *Johnson's England,* vol. 1, ed. A. S. Turberville (Oxford: Clarendon Press, 1933), 348.

Waverly Root and Richard de Rochemont, *Eating in America: A History* (New York: William Morrow, 1976), 237.

Naomi Shihab Nye, "Going for Peaches, Fredericksburg, Texas," in *Grape Leaves: A Century of Arab American Poetry,* ed. Gregory Orfalea and Sharif Elmusa (Salt Lake City: University of Utah Press, 1988), 270–71.

Philip Roth, *American Pastoral* (Boston: Houghton Mifflin, 1997), 304–5.

Peter J. Hatch, *The Fruits and Fruit Trees of Monticello* (Charlottesville, Va.: University Press of Virginia, 1998), 79, 83.

Gordon Dunthorne, *Flower and Fruit Prints of the Eighteenth and Early Nineteenth Centuries* (Washington, D.C.: Gordon Dunthorne, 1938; reprint, Staten Island: Maurizio Martino, n.d.).

U. P. Hedrick, *A History of Horticulture in America to 1860* (New York: Oxford University Press, 1950; reprint, Portland, Oreg.: Timber Press, 1988), 487.

Ebenezer Emmons, "Early Crawford," in *Agriculture of New-York,* vol. 3 (Albany: C. Van Benthusen, 1851), 158.

Emmons, *Agriculture of New-York,* vol. 3 (illustrations), iv.

U. P. Hedrick, *The Peaches of New York* (Albany: J. B. Lyon Co., 1917), v.

Hedrick, "Early Crawford" and "Elberta," in *The Peaches of New York,* 205, 209.

Bob Flowerdew, *The Complete Book of Fruit* (New York: Penguin, 1996), 43.

Hedrick, *The Peaches of New York,* vi.

Nicolai Cikovsky, Jr., *Raphaelle Peale Still Lifes* (New York: Harry N. Abrams, 1988), 103, 122, 50, 34, 56, 47.

Matthew Arnold, "Civilisation in the United States," in *The Last Word,* vol. 11 of *The Complete Prose Works of Matthew Arnold,* ed. R. H. Super (Ann Arbor: University of Michigan Press, 1977), 354, 488–89.

David Mas Masumoto, *Epitaph for a Peach: Four Seasons on My Family Farm* (San Francisco: HarperCollins, 1995), x, 45, 117–18, 215–16.

James Bethuel Smiley, *Modern Manners and Social Forms,* quoted by John F. Kasson, in "Rituals of Dining: Table Manners in Victorian America," in *Dining in America, 1850–1900,* ed. Kathryn Grover (Amherst: University of Massachusetts Press, 1987), 135–36.

768   Anon., *Civilité française* (Liège: n.p., 1714?), 48; quoted in *The Civilizing Process: The History of Manners* by Norbert Elias, trans. Edmund Jephcott (New York: Urizen Books, 1978), 95.

Ted Hughes, "Fulbright Scholars," in *Birthday Letters* (New York: Farrar Straus Giroux, 1998), 3.

Roald Dahl, *James and the Giant Peach* (New York: Penguin, 1996), 24–25, 55–56.

Christina Rossetti, "Goblin Market," in *Christina Rossetti: Poems and Prose,* ed. Jan Marsh (London: Everyman, J. M. Dent, 1994), 162–63, 165–66, 172–74, 176.

W. J. Rorabaugh, "Beer, Lemonade, and Propriety in the Gilded Age," in *Dining in America, 1850–1900,* 35.

Ellen Moers, *Literary Women* (New York: Doubleday, 1976), 102.

D. M. R. Bentley, "The Meretricious and the Meritorious in *Goblin Market:* A Conjecture and an Analysis," in *The Achievement of Christina Rossetti,* ed. David A. Kent (Ithaca: Cornell University Press, 1987), 57–81.

Paula Marantz Cohen, "Christina Rossetti's 'Goblin Market': A Paradigm for Nineteenth-Century Anorexia Nervosa," *University of Hartford Studies in Literature,* 17, no. 1 (1985): 1–18.

Richard Menke, "The Political Economy of Fruit *Goblin Market,*" in *The Culture of Christina Rossetti: Female Poetics and Victorian Contexts,* ed. Mary Arseneau et al. (Athens: Ohio University Press, 1999), 109, 126.

William Taylor, diary for January 1875, quoted by Joan Morgan and Alison Richards, in *A Paradise out of a Common Field: The Pleasures and Plenty of the Victorian Garden* (New York: Harper and Row, 1990), 136–37.

Erica Jong, "Adam naming the fruit," in *Fruits and Vegetables* (New York: Holt, Rinehart and Winston, 1974), 10.

Aretino's Dialogues, part 2, Day 3, trans. Raymond Rosenthal (New York: Stein and Day, 1976), 309; reprint, New York: Marsilio, 1994.

Raymond Rosenthal, preface, *Aretino's Dialogues,* 10.

Pietro Aretino, *Sei Giornate,* ed. Giovanni Aquilecchia (Bari: Gius. Laterza, 1969), 283; *Scritti Scelti,* ed. Giuseppe Guido Ferrero, 2d ed. (Turin: UTET, 1970), 444.

Lawrence, "Peach," in *The Complete Poems of D. H. Lawrence,* ed. Vivian de Sola Pinto and Warren Roberts (Harmondsworth, England: Penguin, 1977), 279, 12.

Philip Roth, *Portnoy's Complaint* (New York: Bantam, 1970), 177.

Sandra Cisneros, "Ass," *My Wicked Wicked Ways* (New York: Random House, 1987), 53.

Francis Ponge, "The Apricot," in *Selected Poems,* trans. John Montague (Winston-Salem, N.C.: Wake Forest University Press, 1994), 196–97.

Roger Holmes, ed., *Taylor's Guide to Fruits and Berries* (Boston: Houghton Mifflin, 1996), 364.

J. J. Ochse, foreword to Mortimer J. Soule, Jr., *A Bibliography of the Mango* (Coral Gables: Florida Mango Forum and University of Miami, 1950), iii.

John Agard, "English Girl Eats Her First Mango (a kind of love poem)," in *Mangoes and Bullets* (London: Pluto Press, 1985), 39–40; reprinted in *The Heinemann Book of Caribbean Poetry,* ed. Stewart Brown and Ian McDonald (Oxford: Heinemann, 1992), 1, 4.

Richard Blanco, "Mango, Number 61," in *City of a Hundred Fires* (Pittsburgh: University of Pittsburgh Press, 1998), 10.

Duracine Vaval, "The Mangoes," trans. Donald Devenish Walsh, in *Anthology of Contemporary Latin-American Poetry,* ed. Dudley Fitts (Norfolk, Conn.: New Directions, 1942), 446–47.

Pat Mora, "Mangos y limones," in *The Best American Poetry, 1996,* ed. Adrienne Rich (New York: Scribner, 1996), 142–43, 270.

Judith Ortiz Cofer, "Tales Told under the Mango Tree," in *Hispanic American Literature,* ed. Nicolás Kanellos (New York: HarperCollins, 1995), 34, 38–39, 41, 44.

Vivian Leal, "Mangoes," in *New World: Young Latino Writers,* ed. Ilan Stavans (New York: Delta, 1997), 9, 17, 12, 34.

Shirley Geok-lin Lim, "Mango," in *What the Fortune Teller Didn't Say* (Albuquerque, N.Mex.: West End Press, 1998), 26.

Lorna Goodison, "The Mango of Poetry," in *Turn Thanks* (Urbana and Chicago: University of Illinois Press, 1999), 43–44.

Neal Bowers, foreword to Laurie Kutchins, *Between Towns* (Lubbock: Texas Tech University Press, 1992), xii.

Laurie Kutchins, "Mangoes," in *Between Towns,* 73.

Margaret Gibson, "Mango," *Georgia Review* 53, no. 2 (summer 1999): 246–47.

Charles Lamb, "The Last Peach," in *The Complete Works and Letters of Charles Lamb* (New York: Modern Library, 1935), 366–67.

Jack Gilbert, "Peaches," in *The Great Fires: Poems, 1982–1992* (New York: Alfred A. Knopf, 1997), 57.

Rita Dove, "The Peach Orchard," in *On the Bus with Rosa Parks* (New York: W.W. Norton, 1999), 60–61.

Dave Morice, "Peaches," in *None of the Above: New Poets of the USA,* ed. Michael Lally (Trumansburg, N.Y.: The Crossing Press, 1976), 84–85.

Siv Cedering, "Peaches" and "Mother Is," in *Letters from the Floating World: Selected and New Poems* (Pittsburgh: University of Pittsburgh Press, 1984), 71, 52.

CHAPTER 8: BANANAS

Prudence Leith-Ross, *The John Tradescants: Gardeners to the Rose and Lily Queen* (London: Peter Owen, 1984), 97.

Jeanette Winterson, *Sexing the Cherry* (New York: Vintage Books, 1989), 5–6.

Edmond De Langhe and Pierre de Maret, "Tracking the Banana: Its Significance in Early Agriculture," in *The Prehistory of Food: Appetites for Change,* ed. Chris Gosden and Jon Hather (London: Routledge, 1999), 378–80, 392, 388.

Wilfrid Blunt, *The Compleat Naturalist: A Life of Linnaeus* (New York: Viking, 1971), 107–8.

John Singleton, *A General Description of the West-Indian Islands,* in *Caribbeana: An Anthology of English Literature of the West Indies, 1657–1777,* ed. Thomas W. Krise (Chicago: University of Chicago Press, 1999), 266.

Andrés Bello, "Ode to Tropical Agriculture," in *Selected Writings of Andrés Bello,* trans. Frances M. López-Morillas (New York: Oxford University Press, 1997), 29–37.

Thomas Pynchon, *Gravity's Rainbow* (New York: Viking, 1973), 8–10.

Steven Weisenburger, *A* Gravity's Rainbow *Companion: Sources and Contexts for Pynchon's Novel* (Athens: University of Georgia Press, 1988).

Anthony Powell, chap. 1 of *A Buyer's Market,* in *A Dance to the Music of Time,* vol. 1, *Spring* (New York: Popular Library, 1976), 29.

Powell, chap. 1 of *A Question of Upbringing,* in *A Dance to the Music of Time,* vol. 1, *Spring* (New York: Popular Library, 1976), 10–11.

Powell, chap. 1 of *A Buyer's Market,* 34, 72.

770   William Faulkner, *As I Lay Dying,* in *The Sound and the Fury* and *As I Lay Dying* (New York: Modern Library, 1946), 531–32.

Olga W. Vickery, *The Novels of William Faulkner: A Critical Interpretation* (Baton Rouge: Lousiana State University Press, 1959), 63.

Erica Jong, "But the poem about bananas has not yet been written," in *Fruits and Vegetables* (New York: Holt, Rinehart and Winston, 1974), 8.

Ferreira Gullar, "Rotten Bananas," in *Brazilian Poetry 1950–1980,* ed. and trans. Emanuel Brasil and William Jay Smith (Middletown, Conn.: Wesleyan University Press, 1983), 6, 25.

Cyn. Zarco, "Flipochinos," in *American Poetry since 1970: Up Late,* 2d ed., ed. Andrei Codrescu (New York: Four Walls Eight Windows, 1989), 273.

Michael Benedikt, "The Moralist of Bananas," in *The Prose Poem: An International Anthology,* ed. Michael Benedikt (New York: Dell, 1976), 544.

Wallace Stevens, "Floral decorations for Bananas," in *Harmonium,* enlarged ed. (New York: Alfred A. Knopf, 1931), 71–72; in *Wallace Stevens: Collected Poetry and Prose* (New York: Library of America, 1997), 43–44.

Laurence Lieberman, "The Banana Dwarf" and "The Banana Madonna," in *New and Selected Poems, 1962–92* (Urbana and Chicago: University of Illinois Press, 1993), 165–67, 193–95.

Evan Jones, "The Song of the Banana Man," in *Breaklight: The Poetry of the Caribbean,* ed. Andrew Salkey (New York: Anchor, 1973), 102.

Virginia Scott Jenkins, *Bananas: An American History* (Washington, D.C.: Smithsonian Institution Press, 2000), 173–76.

Linda Nochlin, "Eroticism and Female Imagery in Nineteenth-Century Art," in *Woman as Sex Object,* ed. Thomas B. Hess and Linda Nochlin (New York: Art News Annual 38, 1972), 12–13; Nochlin, *Women, Art, and Power and Other Essays* (New York: Harper and Row, 1988), 138, 142.

Alexis Smith, "Me Tarzan, You Jane," in Richard Armstrong, *Alexis Smith* (New York: Whitney Museum of American Art, 1991), 159.

Aharon Shabtai, "Finding It Hard to Fall Asleep," in *Love and Selected Poems,* trans. Peter Cole (Riverdale-on-Hudson, N.Y.: Sheep Meadow Press, 1997), 214.

Phyllis Rose, *Jazz Cleopatra: Josephine Baker in Her Time* (New York: Doubleday, 1989), 97, 114.

Anon., picture postcard, in *1000 Nudes: Uwe Scheid Collection* by Michael Koetzle (Cologne: Benedikt Taschen, 1994), 358.

Marina Warner, "Going Bananas," chap. 16 in *No Go the Bogeyman: Scaring, Lulling, and Making Mock* (New York: Farrar, Straus and Giroux, 1999), 356, 351.

Philip Levine, "The Mercy," in *The Mercy* (New York: Alfred A. Knopf, 1999), 73.

Clive Hart, "Wandering Rocks," in *James Joyce's Ulysses: Critical Essays,* ed. Clive Hart and David Hayman (Berkeley and Los Angeles: University of California Press, 1974), 191.

James Joyce, "Wandering Rocks," chap. 10 in *Ulysses;* new ed. (New York: Random House, 1961), 233.

Samuel Beckett, *Krapp's Last Tape,* in *Collected Shorter Plays* (New York: Grove Weidenfeld, 1984), 54–63.

Hugh Kenner, *A Reader's Guide to Samuel Beckett* (New York: Farrar, Straus and Giroux, 1973), 169.

Michael Feingold, "At the Minimum," *Village Voice,* April 1993, 89.

Gabriel Egan, *Times Literary Supplement,* 4 July 1997, 20.

Beckett, *Krapp's Last Tape,* in *Collected Shorter Plays,* 57–58, 62.

Jim McCue, "Deadpan Bed Pan Man," *Times Literary Supplement,* 29 Jan. 1993, 18.

James Knowlson, ed., *Krapp's Last Tape,* vol. 3 of *The Theatrical Notebooks of Samuel Beckett* (New York: Grove Press, 1992), 16.

Miguel Angel Asturias, *Strong Wind,* trans. Gregory Rabassa (New York: Delacorte Press, 1968), 20–21, 69–70.

Asturias, *The Green Pope,* trans. Gregory Rabassa (New York: Delacorte Press, 1971), 107, 139, 153.

Richard J. Callan, *Miguel Angel Asturias* (New York: Twayne, 1970), 107.

Alain Robbe-Grillet, *Jealousy,* trans. Richard Howard (New York: Grove Press, 1965), 39–41, 50–53.

CHAPTER 9: APRICOTS, RIPE AND UNRIPE

Shakespeare, *Hamlet,* 3.2.174–203; ed. G. R. Hibbard (Oxford: Oxford University Press, 1987), 259–60.

C. J. Driver, "A Psalm," *Times Literary Supplement,* 12 Jan. 1996, 4.

Peter Davidson and Adriaan van der Weel, eds., preface to *A Selection of the Poems of Sir Constantijn Huygens, 1596–1687* (Amsterdam: Amsterdam University Press, 1996), ix.

Constantijn Huygens, "On the Death of Tesselschade's Eldest Daughter, and on Her Husband Thereafter Bleeding to Death," in *A Selection of the Poems of Sir Constantijn Huygens, 1596–1687,* ed. Davidson and van der Weel, 86–87.

John Parkinson, *Theatrum Botanicum: The Theater of Plants; or, An Herball of a Large Extent* (London: Tho. Cates, 1640), 1, 511.

Stuart Peachey, *Fruit Variety Register,* vol. 1 (Bristol: Stuart Press, 1995), 27.

Richard Crashaw, "Upon two greene Apricockes sent to *Cowley* by Sir *Crashaw,*" in *The Complete Poetry of Richard Crashaw,* ed. George Walton Williams (New York: W. W. Norton, 1974), 494–95.

Jan Breugel the Elder, *Garden of Eden,* in *The Garden of Eden* by John Prest (New Haven: Yale University Press, 1981), 4–5.

Barbara Pym, *A Few Green Leaves* (New York: Harper and Row, 1981), 126, 131, 250.

John Webster, *The Duchess of Malfi* 2.1.70–71; 1.1.286–87; 2.1.143–44, 146–47, 154; 2.2.1–3; in *The Duchess of Malfi,* ed. John Russell Brown (Manchester: Manchester University Press, 1976), 43, 25, 47–49, 6.

Ian Sansom, "Grubs in the Night," *Times Literary Supplement,* 19 Jan. 1996, 23.

John Russell Brown, "Techniques of Restoration: The Case of *The Duchess of Malfi,*" in *Shakespearean Illuminations,* ed. Jay L. Halio and Hugh Richmond (Newark, Del.: Associated University Presses, 1998), 330.

Thomas Middleton and William Rowley, *The Changeling* 4.1–2; in *The Changeling,* ed. N. W. Bawcutt (Cambridge: Harvard University Press, 1958), 68–74, 80–81.

Shakespeare, *Measure for Measure* 2.1.86–87, ed. N. W. Bawcutt (Oxford: Oxford University Press, 1991), 114.

Shakespeare, *Richard II* 3.4.29–66, ed. Peter Ure (London: Arden Shakespeare, 2000), 118–121.

Jane Austen, *Mansfield Park,* chap. 6; ed. Kathryn Sutherland (London: Penguin, 1996), 47ff.

Maggie Lane, *Jane Austen and Food* (London: Hambledon Press, 1995), 147.

Lionel Trilling, "Jane Austen and Mansfield Park," in *From Blake to Byron: The Pelican Guide to English Literature,* vol. 5, ed. Boris Ford (Baltimore: Penguin, 1969), 117.

Claudia L. Johnson, *Jane Austen, Women, Politics, and the Novel* (Chicago: University of Chicago Press, 1988), 96.

Tony Tanner, "The Quiet Thing: *Mansfield Park,*" chap. 5 in *Jane Austen* (Cambridge:Harvard University Press, 1986), 150.

772   P. Barry, *The Fruit Garden* (Auburn and Rochester: Alden and Beardsley, 1855), 320.

J. G. Vaughan and C. Geissler, *The New Oxford Book of Food Plants* (Oxford: Oxford University Press, 1997), 79.

Gustave Flaubert, "Apricots," in *Dictionary of Accepted Ideas,* trans. Jacques Barzun (New York: New Directions, 1968), 15.

Alan Davidson and Jane Davidson, eds. and trans., *Dumas on Food: Selections from* Le Grand Dictionnaire de Cuisine *by Alexandre Dumas* (London: Folio Society, 1978), 47.

Diane Ackerman, "The Consolations of Apricots," in *I Praise My Destroyer* (New York: Random House, 1998), 60.

Gyula Illyés, "The Apricot Tree," trans. Christine Brooke-Rose, in *In Quest of the "Miracle Stag": The Poetry of Hungary,* ed. Adam Makkai (Chicago: Atlantis-Centaur,1996), 628–29.

Norman Manea, "Portrait of the Yellow Apricot Tree," trans. Cornelia Golna, *Paris Review* 122 (spring 1992): 185–88.

Jacques Linard, *Apricots and Moths,* in *French Painting from Le Nain to Fragonard* by Jacques Thuillier and Albert Châtelet, trans. James Emmons (Geneva: Skira, 1964), 41.

Christopher Wright, *The French Painters of the Seventeenth Century* (Boston: Little, Brown, 1985), 232–33.

Louise Moillon, *Bowl of Apricots, Apricots on a Blue Porcelain Plate,* and *Basket of Apricots,* in *Le Grand Siècle de la Nature Morte en France* by Michel Faré (Fribourg, Switzerland: Office du Livre, 1974), 58, 62, 64.

Christopher Middleton, "Louise Moillon's Apricots (1635)," in *The Pursuit of the Kingfisher* (Manchester: Carcarnet Press, 1983), 179.

Kurt Wettengl, *Georg Flegel, 1566–1638, Stilleben* (Stuttgart: Verlag Gerd Hatje, 1999), 128.

Ebert-Schifferer, *Still Life,* 99.

CHAPTER 10: PITS AND SEEDS

The Perils of Pits

Sholom Aleichem, "The Search," trans. Norbert Guterman, in *A Treasury of Yiddish Stories,* ed. Irving Howe and Eliezer Greenberg (New York: Schocken, 1973), 75, 182–87.

Irving Layton, "Family Portrait," in *The Darkening Fire: Selected Poems, 1945–1968* (Toronto: McClelland and Stewart, 1975), 88; Layton, *The Selected Poems of Irving Layton* (New York: New Directions, 1977), 20.

Flaubert, pt. 2, sect. 13 and pt. 1, sect. 5, 7 in *Madame Bovary,* trans. Francis Steegmuller (New York: Random House, 1957), 232–33, 36, 51.

Francis Ponge, "The Apricot," in *Selected Poems,* trans. John Montague (Winston-Salem, N.C.: Wake Forest University Press, 1994), 198–99.

A Digression on Nature from Within

Les Murray, "Stone Fruit," in *Translations from the Natural World* (New York: Farrar, Straus and Giroux, 1992), 48.

Alberto Caeiro, *The Keeper of Flocks,* poem 28, trans. Keith Bosley, in *A Centenary Pessoa,* 2d ed., rev., ed. Eugénio Lisboa with L. C. Taylor (Manchester: Carcanet Press,1995), 58.

Richard Ellmann, introduction to *Selected Writings, Henri Michaux: The Space Within* (New York: New Directions, 1968), xvi.

Henri Michaux, "Magic," in *Selected Writings, Henri Michaux: The Space Within,* trans. Richard   773
    Ellmann, 186–89, 192–93.

Pits and Games

Jacques Stella, "16, Cherry Pit," in *Games and Pleasures of Childhood,* trans. Stanley Appelbaum
    (New York: Dover, 1969), n.p.

Randle Cotgrave, *A Dictionarie of the French and English Tongues* (London: Adam Islip, 1611;
    reprinted, Columbia: University of South Carolina Press, 1950), s.v. "noyau."

Sandra M. Gilbert, "Eating Your Words," *Poetry* (March 1982): 338.

CHAPTER 11: MEDLARS, THE RIPE AND THE ROTTEN

Matthew 7:18–20, New Oxford Annotated Bible.

J. Newton Davies, "Matthew," in *The Abingdon Bible Commentary,* ed. Frederick Carl Eiselen et
    al. (New York: Abingdon Press, 1929), 968.

Amos 8:1–2n. 8:1–3 New Oxford Annotated Bible.

Ludovico Ariosto, *Orlando Furioso* 7.71–72; in *Orlando Furioso (The Frenzy of Orlando),* vol. 1,
    trans. Barbara Reynolds (Harmondsworth, England: Penguin, 1975), 259–60.

A. Bartlett Giamatti, *The Earthly Paradise and the Renaissance Epic* (Princeton: Princeton Uni-
    versity Press, 1966), 160.

Schneider, *Still Life,* 121.

Wallace Stevens, "Sunday Morning," in *Harmonium,* 92; *Wallace Stevens: Collected Poetry and Prose*
    (Library of America), 55.

Shorter Oxford English Dictionary, 3d ed., s.v. "medlar."

Random House Dictionary of the English Language, s.v. "medlar."

Anon., *A Book of Fruits and Flowers* (London: Tho. Jenner, 1653), 45; C. Anne Wilson, introduction
    to facsimile edition of Anon., *A Book of Fruits and Flowers* (London: Prospect Books, 1984), v.

Lee Reich, *Uncommon Fruits Worthy of Attention: A Gardener's Guide* (Reading, Mass.: Addison-
    Wesley, 1991), 45.

J. G. Vaughan and C. Geissler, *The New Oxford Book of Food Plants* (Oxford: Oxford University
    Press, 1997), 68.

George Birkbeck Hill and L. F. Powell, eds., *Boswell's Life of Johnson* (Oxford: Clarendon Press,
    1934), 12 Apr. 1776; *Boswell's Life of Johnson,* ed. R. W. Chapman (London: Oxford Uni-
    versity Press, 1953), 746.

Sackville-West, "The Garden: Autumn," in *The Land and the Garden* (London: Michael Joseph,
    1989), 175–76.

Lawrence, "Medlars and Sorb-apples," in *The Complete Poems of D. H. Lawrence,* ed. Vivian de
    Sola Pinto and Warren Roberts (Harmondsworth, England: Penguin, 1977), 280–81.

Mary Taylor Simeti, *On Persephone's Island: A Sicilian Journal* (New York: Alfred A. Knopf, 1986), 216.

Giacomo Castelvetro, *The Fruit, Herbs, and Vegetables of Italy: An Offering to Lucy, Countess of Bed-
    ford,* trans. Gillian Riley (London: Viking, 1989), 120–21.

Geoffrey Chaucer, "The Reeve's Prologue," ll. 3869–875, in *Canterbury Tales,* ed. A. C. Craw-
    ley (New York: Everyman's Library, 1992).

Anon., "The Flower and the Leaf," in *Chaucerian and Other Pieces,* ed. Walter W. Skeat (Oxford:
    Oxford University Press, 1897), 364.

774   John Dryden, "The Flower and the Leaf; or, the Lady in the Arbour: A Vision," in *John Dryden,* ed. Keith Walker (Oxford: Oxford University Press, 1987), 753.

Anon., The Unicorn Tapestries, panel 2, in *The Unicorn Tapestries* by Margaret B. Freeman (New York: E. P. Dutton, 1976), 18, 125; in *The Unicorn Tapestries at the Metropolitan Museum of Art* by Adolfo Salvatore Cavallo (New York: Harry N. Abrams, 1998), 52.

Anon., *The Englishman's Doctor; or, The Schoole of Salerne; or, Physicall Observations for the Perfect Preserving of the Body of Man in Continuall Health* (London: John Helme and John Busby, 1607; reprinted as *Regimen Sanitatis Salernitanum: A Poem on the Preservation of Health in Rhyming Latin Verse,* Oxford: D. A. Talboys, 1830), 133.

Shakespeare, *Romeo and Juliet,* 2.1.33–38; ed. Brian Gibbons (London: Routledge, 1980), 126n. 38.

Shakespeare, *As You Like It,* 3.2.123–128; 2.7.26–7, 97–99; ed. John F. Andrews (London: Everyman, J. M. Dent, 1991)., 111–13, 83, 89.

Caroline F. E. Spurgeon, *Shakespeare's Imagery and What It Tells Us* (Boston: Beacon Press, 1958), 119.

George Chapman, *Bussy D'Ambois,* 3.2.237–41, 267–69; ed. Nicholas Brooke (London: Methuen, 1964), 73–76, 76n. 20.

Henry Howard, Earl of Surrey, "The Frailty and Hurtfulness of Beauty," in *Poetry of the English Renaissance, 1509–1660,* ed. J. William Hebel and Hoyt H. Hudson (New York: F. S. Crofts, 1932), 28.

Shakespeare, *King Lear,* 5.2.8–11; ed. Jay L. Halio (Cambridge: Cambridge University Press, 1992), 243–44.

CHAPTER 12: POMEGRANATES

Vassos Karogeorghis, ed., *Ancient Art from Cyprus: The Cesnola Collection* (New York: Metropolitan Museum of Art, 1999), 69 cat. 110.

Martin Henig, ed., *A Handbook of Roman Art* (Oxford: Phaidon, 1983), plate 5; *Pompeii, A.D. 79,* vol. 1 (Boston: Museum of Fine Arts, 1978), 74.

James Hall, *Dictionary of Subjects and Symbols in Art,* rev. ed. (New York: Harper and Row, 1979), s.v. "pomegranate," 249.

Botticelli, *Madonna of the Pomegranate,* in *Alessandro Botticelli, 1444/45–1510* by Alexandra Grömling and Tilman Lingesleben (Cologne: Könemann, 1998), fig. 85.

David Shterenberg, *Still Life with Pomegranates,* in *100 Years of Russian Art,* ed. David Elliott and Valery Dudakov (London: Lund Humphries, 1989), 120.

Random House Dictionary of the English Language, s.v. "pomegranate."

Anon., "To Demeter," in *The Homeric Hymns,* trans. Apostolos N. Athanassakis (Baltimore: Johns Hopkins University Press, 1976), 12.

Helene P. Foley, ed., *The Homeric* Hymn to Demeter: *Translation, Commentary, and Interpretive Essays* (Princeton: Princeton University Press, 1994), 30–31, 151–69.

Ovid, *Metamorphoses* 5.543–4; trans. A. D. Melville (Oxford: Oxford University Press, 1987), 115.

Ovid, *Fasti* 4.607; in vol. 5, trans. James George Frazer (Cambridge: Harvard University Press, 1926), 233.

A. S. Byatt, *Babel Tower* (New York: Random House, 1996), 4, 78–79, 81–82.

Song of Songs 4:3, 6:7; in *Song of Songs,* trans. Ariel Bloch and Chana Bloch (New York: Random House, 1995), 73, 93, 170n.

James Elkins, *The Object Stares Back* (New York: Simon and Schuster, 1996), 163–64.

Song of Songs 4:3, 6:7; in *The Voice of My Beloved: The Song of Songs in Western Medieval Chris-tianity* by E. Ann Matter (Philadelphia: University of Pennsylvania Press, 1990), xxii–xxiii, xxx–xxxi.

Menachem Kellner, *Commentary on Song of Songs: Levi ben Gershom (Gersonides)* (New Haven: Yale University Press, 1998), vii, xxi, 73.

Marvin H. Pope, *Song of Songs: A New Translation with Introduction and Commentary* (New York: Doubleday, 1977), 567, 192–205.

Rabbi Nosson Scherman, ed., *Tanach, The Torah, Prophets, Writings: The Twenty-four Books of the Bible Newly Translated and Edited* (Brooklyn: Mesorah Publications, 1996), 1681, 1691, 1690n.

Marvin H. Pope, *Song of Songs,* 17.

Jacopo Sannazaro, "Pomegranates," *Elegy* 2.10, in *The Major Latin Poems of Jacopo Sannazaro,* trans. Ralph Nash (Detroit: Wayne State University Press, 1996), 145–46, 175–76.

Richard Jenkyns, *Virgil's Experience, Nature and History: Times, Names, and Places* (Oxford: Claren-don Press, 1998), 157–58, 167–68.

Andrew Marvell, "Bermudas," in *Andrew Marvell: The Complete Poems,* ed. Elizabeth Story Donno (Harmondsworth, England: Penguin, 1972), 116.

Alan Davidson and Jane Davidson, ed. and trans., *Dumas on Food* (London: Folio Society, 1978), 226.

André Gide, *Fruits of the Earth,* trans. Dorothy Bussy (London: Secker and Warburg, 1949), 79–80.

Gide, *Les Nourritures terrestres et Les Nouvelles Nourritures* (Paris: Gallimard, 1947), 89.

Paul Valéry, "Pomegranates," trans. David Paul, in *Poems: On Poets and Poetry,* vol. 1 of *The Col-lected Works of Paul Valéry,* ed. Jackson Mathews (Princeton: Princeton University Press, 1971), 206–7.

Rachel Hadas, "Pomegranates," in *Other Worlds Than This* (New Brunswick, N.J.: Rutgers Uni-versity Press, 1994), 131.

Louis Dudek, "The Pomegranate," in *The Oxford Book of Canadian Verse,* ed. A. J. M. Smith (Toronto: Oxford University Press, 1960), 362–63; Dudek, "The Pomegranate," in *The Penguin Book of Canadian Verse,* ed. Ralph Gustafson (Harmondsworth, England: Penguin, 1958), 216–17.

Kellyn Bardeen, "Pomegranate," in *Movin': Teen Poets Take Voice,* ed. Dave Johnson (New York: Orchard Books, 2000), 47.

T. Carmi, "To the Pomegranate Tree," in *T. Carmi and Dan Pagis; Selected Poems,* trans. Stephen Mitchell (Harmondsworth, England: Penguin, 1976), 56.

Carmi, "To the Pomegranate," in *The Modern Hebrew Poem Itself,* ed. Stanley Burnshaw, T. Carmi, and Ezra Spicehandler, trans. Harold Schimmel (New York: Schocken,1966), 168–70.

M. L. Rosenthal, introduction to *T. Carmi and Dan Pagis: Selected Poems,* trans. Mitchell, 11.

Octavio Paz, "A Tree Within," trans. Eliot Weinberger, in *Twentieth-Century Latin American Poetry,* ed. Stephen Tapscott (Austin: University of Texas Press, 1996), 264.

Rukhl Fishman, "Full as a Pomegranate," in *I Want to Fall Like This,* trans. Levitan, 34–37.

David G. Roskies, introduction to *I Want to Fall Like This,* trans. Levitan, 12–13.

Yehuda Amichai, "Jerusalem," trans. Chana Bloch and Chana Kronfeld, *Tikkun* 14, no. 5 (Sept.–Oct. 1999): 52.

776   Patricia Storace, *Dinner with Persephone* (New York: Pantheon, 1996), 217–19.

Yannos Ritsos, "Persephone," in *The Fourth Dimension,* trans. Peter Green and Beverly Bardsley (Princeton: Princeton University Press, 1993), xvi, 177, 182, 184, 189.

Bruce Bond, "Pomegranate," *Paris Review* 138 (spring 1996): 111.

George Seferis, "Young Fate," in *Collected Poems, 1924–1955,* trans. Edmund Keeley and Philip Sherrard (Princeton: Princeton University Press, 1967), 93.

Odysseus Elytis, "The Mad Pomegranate Tree," in *Voices of Modern Greece,* trans. Edmund Keeley and Philip Sherrard (Princeton: Princeton University Press, 1981), 146–47.

Jeffrey Carson, introduction to *The Collected Poems of Odysseus Elytis* (Baltimore: Johns Hopkins Press, 1997), xviii.

Aharon Shabtai, "Love," in *Love and Selected Poems,* trans. Peter Cole (Riverdale-on-Hudson, N.Y.: Sheep Meadow Press, 1997), 3, 7, 40–41.

Shabtai, "The Domestic Poem," in *Love and Selected Poems,* trans. Cole, 128, 130–31, 133, 137.

Eavan Boland, "The Pomegranate," in *In a Time of Violence* (New York: W. W. Norton, 1994), 26–27.

Concha Méndez Cuesta, "Lo mismo que una granada," in *Surtidor: Poesias* (Madrid: Argis, 1928), 25; John C. Wilcox, trans., *Women Poets of Spain, 1860–1990: Toward a Gynocentric Vision* (Urbana and Chicago: Illinois University Press, 1997), 99, 87–88.

Mistral, "Mother Pomegranate," trans. Maria Giachetti, in *A Gabriela Mistral Reader,* ed. Marjorie Agosin (Fredonia, N.Y.: White Pine Press, 1993), 84, 85.

Siv Cedering, "Pomegranates," in *Letters from the Floating World: Selected and New Poems* (Pittsburgh: University of Pittsburgh Press, 1984), 37.

Dante Gabriel Rossetti, *Proserpine,* in *Essential Pre-Raphaelites* by Lucinda Hawksley and Juliet Hacking (Bath: Parragon, 1999), 123.

Virginia Surtees, *The Paintings and Drawings of Dante Gabriel Rossetti (1828–1882): A Catalogue Raisonné,* vol. 1 (Oxford: Clarendon Press, 1971), 131.

Dante Gabriel Rossetti, *Proserpine,* in Alicia Craig Faxon, *Dante Gabriel Rossetti,* fig. 212.

Husain Haddawy, trans., "The Story of the Three Apples" and "The Story of the Two Viziers," in *The Arabian Nights* (New York: W. W. Norton, 1990), 176, 190, 195, 197–99, 206.

Robert Irwin, *The Arabian Nights: A Companion* (London: Penguin, 1994).

Diogenes Laertius, *Lives of Eminent Philosophers,* vol. 2, trans. R. D. Hicks (New York: G. P. Putnam, 1925), 285.

CHAPTER 13: QUINCES AND PEARS

Pyrus Fruits

Frost, "The Rose Family," in *Robert Frost: Collected Poems, Prose, and Plays* (New York: Library of America, 1995), 225.

Lawrence, "Grapes," in *The Complete Poems of D. H. Lawrence,* ed. Vivian de Sola Pinto and Warren Roberts (Harmondsworth, England: Penguin, 1977), 285.

Roger Holmes, ed., "Quinces," in *Taylor's Guide to Fruits and Berries* (Boston: Houghton Mifflin, 1996), 314.

Propertius, Elegy 3.13.27; in *Elegies,* trans. G. P. Goold (Cambridge: Harvard University Press, 1990), 306–7.

Johannes de Hauvilla, *Architrenius* 4.3.44; in trans. Winthrop Wetherbee (Cambridge: Cambridge University Press, 1994), 90–91.

Thoreau, *Wild Fruits,* ed. Bradley P. Dean (New York: W. W. Norton, 1999), 208.

Edward Lear, "The Owl and the Pussy Cat," in *Nonsense Songs, Stories, Botany, and Alphabets* (London: Robert Bush, 1871); Lear, "The Owl and the Pussy Cat," in *The Complete Nonsense of Edward Lear,* ed. Holbrook Jackson (New York: Dover, 1951), 62.

Ibycus, "In the spring flourish Cydonian quince-trees," in *Greek Lyric,* vol. 3, trans. David A. Campbell (Cambridge: Harvard University Press, 1992), 255.

Al-Mushafi, "The Quince," in *Andalusian Poems,* trans. Christopher Middleton and Leticia Garza-Falcón (Boston: David Godine, 1993), 4–5.

Chafar ben Utman al-Mushafi, "El Membrillo," in *Poemas Arabigoandaluces,* 7th ed., ed. Emilio García Gómez (Madrid: Espasa-Calpe, 1982), 96.

Middleton and Garza-Falcón, introduction to *Andalusian Poems,* ix–x, xiii.

Jeremy Warren, "Fortnum and the Della Robbia," *Apollo* (May 1997): 57.

Federico García Lorca, *Two Quinces,* in *Line of Light and Shadow: The Drawings of Federico García Lorca* by Mario Hernández, trans. Christopher Maurer (Durham, N.C.: Duke University Press, 1991), 262, cat. 240.1.

Martin S. Soria, "Sánchez Cotán's 'Quince, Cabbage, Melon, and Cucumber,'" *Art Quarterly* 8, no. 3 (summer 1945): 227.

Gillian Riley, "Gastronomy in the Still-Life Paintings of Luis Meléndez," in *Food in the Arts,* ed. Harlan Walker (Devon, England: Prospect Books, 1999), 154.

Juan Sánchez Cotán, *Still Life with Quince, Cabbage, Melon and Cucumber,* in *Spanish Still Life from Velázquez to Goya* by William B. Jordan and Peter Cherry (London: National Gallery, 1995), 26; Ebert Schifferer, *Still Life,* 78 fig. 55.

The Taste of, and for, Pears

Edward A. Bunyard, *Anatomy of Dessert* (New York: E. P. Dutton, 1934), 110–11.

Virgil, *Georgics* 2.88; in *The Eclogues, The Georgics,* trans. C. Day Lewis (Oxford: Oxford University Press, 1983), 72.

de Hauvilla, *Architrenius,* trans. Wetherbee, 90–91, 259–60 n. 8.

Andrea Navagero, "Iolas," in *An Anthology of Neo-Latin Poetry,* trans. Fred J. Nichols (New Haven: Yale University Press, 1979), 56, 386–87, 57.

Anon., "On the Nativity of the Lord," in *Analecta Hymnica Medii Aevi,* vol. 45B (Leipzig, 1886–1922), 131.

John Suckling, "A Ballad upon a Wedding," in *The Works of Sir John Suckling,* ed. A. Hamilton Thompson (New York: Russell and Russell, 1964), 30.

Stuart Peachey, *Fruit Variety Register,* vol. 2. (Bristol: Stuart Press, 1995), 72.

H. Frederic Janson, *Pomona's Harvest* (Portland, Ore.: Timber Press, 1996), 117.

Jean de La Quintinie, *The Complete Gard'ner . . . in Six Books,* trans. John Evelyn (London: Matthew Gillyflower and James Partridge, 1693; facsimile reprint, New York: Garland, 1982), 70, 79–80, 126.

Terence M. Russell and Ann-Marie Thornton, *Gardens and Landscapes in the Encyclopédie of Diderot and D'Alembert,* vol. 1 (Aldershot, England: Ashgate, 1999), 183.

778   Pierre Daubenton, "Poirier" in *Encyclopédie,* vol. 12 (1757), and "Pommier," vol. 13 (1765); Russell and Thornton, trans., *Gardens and Landscapes in the Encyclopédie of Diderot and D'Alembert,* vol. 2, 481, 490.

William H. Gerdts, *Painters of the Humble Truth: Masterpieces of American Still Life, 1801–1939* (Columbia and London: Philbrook Art Center and University of Missouri Press, 1981), 20.

Wesley Vernier, *The Great California Pear,* in Gerdts, *Painters of the Humble Truth,* 26.

U. P. Hedrick, *History of Horticulture in America to 1860* (Oxford: Oxford University Press, 1950); reprint Portland, Ore: Timber Press, 1988), 235.

Sandra Raphael, *An Oak Spring Pomona* (Upperville, Va.: Oak Spring Garden Library, 1990), xxxi.

P. Barry, *The Fruit Garden* (Auburn and Rochester: Alden and Beardsley, 1855), 297, 319.

Joseph Decaisne, *Le Jardin fruitier du Muséum,* 9 vols. (Paris: F. Didot, 1862–75).

Jane Hirshfield, "Heart Grown Stubborn on Nectar," in *The Lives of the Heart* (New York: HarperCollins, 1997), 21.

Pears and Apples

John Clare, "The Flitting," in *John Clare: Poems of the Middle Period, 1822–1837,* vol. 3, ed. Eric Robinson et al. (Oxford: Clarendon Press, 1998), 480.

Margaret Grainger, ed., *The Natural History Prose Writings of John Clare* (Oxford: Clarendon Press, 1983), 109–10n. 4.

Henry David Thoreau, *Journal,* 11 October 1860, in *The Writings of Henry David Thoreau,* ed. Bradford Torrey (Boston: Houghton Mifflin, 1906), vol. 20, 113–14; Thoreau, *Wild Fruits,* ed. Dean, 127.

François Pierre de la Varenne, quoted in *The Cross and the Pear Tree: A Sephardic Journey* by Victor Perera (New York: Alfred A. Knopf, 1995), 140.

Pieter Bruegel the Elder, *The Harvesters,* in *From Van Eyck to Bruegel: Early Netherlandish Painting in the Metropolitan Museum of Art,* ed. Maryan W. Ainsworth and Keith Christiansen (New York: Harry N. Abrams, 1998), 388–89.

Mary Sprinson de Jesus, "The Harvesters," in *From Van Eyck to Bruegel: Early Netherlandish Painting in the Metropolitan Museum of Art,* ed. Ainsworth and Christiansen, 390.

Nadine M. Orenstein, "Bruegel, the Land, and the Peasants," in *From Van Eyck to Bruegel,* ed. Ainsworth and Christiansen, 385.

Ethan Matt Kavaler, *Pieter Bruegel: Parables of Order and Enterprise* (Cambridge: Cambridge University Press, 1999), 178, 1.

Jules Renard, "In the Garden," in *Natural Histories,* trans. Richard Howard (New York: Horizon Press, 1966), 201.

Bruce Bawer, review of Guy Davenport, *Apples and Pears and Other Stories,* in *New Criterion 3,* no. 4 (Dec. 1984): 11–14.

Guy Davenport, "Quagga," in *Apples and Pears and Other Stories* (San Francisco: North Point Press, 1984), 179.

Pablo Picasso, *Apple and Pear,* in *Objects on a Table: Harmonious Disarray in Art and Literature* by Guy Davenport (Washington, D.C.: Counterpoint, 1998), 71.

Patricia Goedicke, "Montana Pears," in *As Earth Begins to End: New Poems* (Port Townsend, Wash.: Copper Canyon Press, 2000), 109–11.

David Levine, *Julia Child* (December), in *David Levine: 1999 Calendar* (New York: *New York Review of Books,* 1998).

René Magritte, *Memory of a Journey,* in *Painters of the Mind's Eye: Belgian Symbolists and Surrealists* (New York: The New York Cultural Center, 1974), fig. 110.

Magritte, *Common Sense,* in *Magritte* by Suzi Gabelik (Boston: New York Graphic Society, 1976), fig. 75.

Luc de Heusch, *Magritte or the Object Lesson,* in Gabelik, *Magritte,* fig. 73; Jacques Meuris, *Magritte,* trans. J. A. Underwood (London: Greenwich Editions, 1994), 210, fig. 339.

Jean Dypréau, *Magritte,* in Meuris, *Magritte,* 211, fig. 341.

E. H. Gombrich, "Tradition and Expression in Western Still Life," in *Meditations on a Hobby Horse and Other Esaays on the Theory of Art* (London: Phaidon, 1963), fig. 38.

Eric Partridge, *Dictionary of Slang and Unconventional English,* 5th ed. (New York: Macmillan, 1961), s.v. "apples and pears."

The Shapes of Pears

Stephen Jay Gould, "When Fossils Were Young," *Natural History* (Oct. 1999): 72.

Jean Bauhin and Jean Henri Charler, *Historia plantarum universalis, nova, et absolutissima cum consensu et dissensu,* vol. 1 (Yverdon, Switzerland: n.p., 1650–1651), 27–59.

Linda Pastan, "Pears," in *Setting the Table* (Washington, D.C. and San Francisco: Dryad Press, 1980), n.p.

Pastan, "Espaliered Pear Trees," in *An Early Afterlife* (New York: W. W. Norton, 1995), 5.

Wallace Stevens, "A Study of Two Pears," in *Parts of a World* (New York: Knopf, 1942), 12–13; *Wallace Stevens: Collected Poetry and Prose* (Library of America), 180–81.

Wallace Stevens, "Three Academic Pieces, 1," in *Wallace Stevens: Collected Poetry and Prose* (Library of America), 690.

Wallace Stevens, "In the Clear Season of Grapes," *Wallace Stevens: Collected Poetry and Prose* (Library of America), 92.

Gabriel Preil, "A Pear, For Instance," in *Sunset Possibilities and Other Poems,* trans. Robert Friend (Philadelphia: Jewish Publication Society, 1985), 23.

Andrei Voznesensky, "The Triangular Pear, Prelude I," in *Antiworlds and the Fifth Ace: Poetry by Andrei Voznesensky,* ed. Patricia Blake and Max Hayward, trans. William Jay Smith (New York: Anchor, 1967), xxii, 151.

John Updike, "A Pear Like a Potato," in *Collected Poems, 1953–1993* (London: Penguin,1995), 205–6.

Pears As Sexual Objects

Anon., "I have a newe garden," MS Sloane 2593, British Library, London; in *Medieval English Lyrics, 1200–1400,* ed. Thomas G. Duncan (Harmondsworth, England: Penguin, 1995), 171, xxxvii.

Peachy, *Fruit Variety Register,* vol. 2, 81–84.

Giovanni Boccaccio, "Day 7," story 9, in *Decameron,* trans. G. H. McWilliam (London: Penguin, 1972), 577–79.

Edmond Pognon, *Boccaccio's Decameron Fifteenth Century Manuscript* (Cordoba: Graficromo, S.A., 1978), 88.

780   Eric Jager, *The Tempter's Voice: Language and the Fall in Medieval Literature* (Ithaca, N.Y.: Cornell University Press, 1993), 251, 270–71, 277, 279–81.

Geoffrey Chaucer, "The Merchant's Tale," 2138–49, 2352–53, 2374, 2421, in *Geoffrey Chaucer: Canterbury Tales,* ed. A. C. Cawley (New York: Everyman's Library, Alfred A. Knopf, 1992), 281, 287, 289.

Lee Patterson, *Chaucer and the Subject of History* (Madison: University of Wisconsin Press, 1991), 341.

Larry D. Benson, ed. *The Riverside Chaucer,* 3d ed. (Boston: Houghton Mifflin,1987), 885.

Leo Tolstoy, pt. 1, sect.1, in *Anna Karenina,* trans. Joel Carmichael (New York: Bantam Books, 1960), 2.

Anon., "In the green garden a pear tree," in *Russian Folk Lyrics,* trans. Roberta Reeder (Bloomington: Indiana University Press, 1993), 131.

Peter Brown, *Augustine of Hippo* (Berkeley and Los Angeles: University of California Press, 1967), 172.

James J. O'Donnell, *Augustine Confessions,* vol. 2 (Oxford: Clarendon Press, 1992), 1–7, 126.

Augustine, *Confessions,* trans. Henry Chadwick (Oxford: Oxford University Press), 29.

Max J. Friedländer and Jakob Rosenberg, *The Paintings of Lucas Cranach* (Ithaca, N.Y.: Cornell University Press, 1978), plates 201–2, 212–13, 261–62.

Sigmund Freud, *Interpretation of Dreams,* trans. James Strachey (London: George Allen and Unwin, 1954), 372–73.

Pears As Literary Devices

Charles Dickens, *David Copperfield,* chap. 39; ed. Nina Burgis (Oxford: Oxford University Press, 1997), 563–64.

Vinícius de Moraes, "The Pear," trans. Ashley Brown, in *An Anthology of Twentieth-Century Brazilian Poetry,* ed. Elizabeth Bishop and Emanuel Brasil (Middletown, Conn.: Wesleyan University Press, 1972), 98–99

Ferreira Gullar, "The Pears," in *Brazilian Poetry, 1950–1980,* ed. and trans. Emanuel Brasil and William Jay Smith (Middletown, Conn.: Wesleyan University Press, 1983), 15.

Pamela Stewart, "The Pears," in *The Pushcart Prize: 5,* ed. Bill Henderson (New York: Pushcart Press, 1980), 435–36.

Konrad Bayer, "the pear," in *German Writing Today,* ed. and trans. Christopher Middleton (Harmondsworth, England: Penguin, 1967), 103–5.

Niccolò Tucci, *The Sun and the Moon* (New York: Alfred A. Knopf, 1977), 346–48.

Roy Kiyooka, "The Pear Tree Pomes," in *Pacific Windows: Collected Poems of Roy K. Kiyooka,* ed. Roy Miki (Burnaby, B.C.: Talonbooks, 1997), 197, 201, 204, 210, 217, 222.

Stanley Kunitz, "My Mother's Pears," in *Passing Through: The Later Poems, New and Selected* (New York: W. W. Norton, 1995), 141–42.

Colette to Léon Hamel, Sept. 1912, quoted in *Colette: A Taste for Life* by Yvonne Mitchell (New York: Harcourt Brace Jovanovich, 1975), 121.

Pears As Visual Metaphors

John M. Merriman, "Philipon versus Philippe: The July Monarchy and Its Enemies," in *The Pear: French Graphic Arts in the Golden Age of Caricature* by Elise K. Kenney and John M. Merriman (South Hadley, Mass.: Mount Holyoke College Art Museum,1991), 22.

Robert Justin Goldstein, *Censorship of Political Caricature in Nineteenth-Century France* (Kent,   *781*
Ohio: Kent State University Press, 1989), 132, 129–31.

Kenney and Merriman, *The Pear: French Graphic Arts in the Golden Age of Caricature,* 63, cat. 26.

Ian Hamilton Finlay, "Au Pair Girl," in *Speaking Pictures,* ed. Milton Klonsky (New York: Crown, 1975), 247.

Erik Satie, "Trois Morceaux en forme de poire," in *Erik Satie* by Alan M. Gillmor (New York: W. W. Norton, 1988), 126–27.

CHAPTER 14: PINEAPPLES

Joseph de Acosta, *The Natural and Moral History of the Indies,* bk. 4, chap. 19; trans. Edward Grimston (n.p., 1604; reprinted London: Hakluyt Society, 1880), vol. 1, 236.

Vaughan and Geissler, *New Oxford Book of Food Plants,* 102–3.

Albert Eckhout, *Pineapples and Papayas,* in *Still-Life Paintings from the Netherlands, 1550–1720,* ed. Alan Chong and Wouter Kloek (Zwolle, Netherlands: Waanders, 1999), 193.

Johan Maurits to Louis XIV, 1679, quoted in *Still-Life Paintings from the Netherlands, 1550–1720,* ed. Chong and Kloek, 193.

John Evelyn, *The Diary of John Evelyn,* vol. 3, ed. E. S. de Beer (Oxford: Clarendon Press, 1955), 293, 513–14.

Sandra Raphael, *An Oak Spring Pomona* (Upperville, Va.: Oak Spring Garden Library, 1990), xxxiii.

Jeanette Winterson, *Sexing the Cherry* (New York: Vintage Books, 1989), 117–18.

Lady Mary Wortley Montagu to her sister Frances, 17 December 1716, in *The Complete Letters of Lady Mary Wortley Montagu,* ed. Robert Halsband, vol. 1 (Oxford: Oxford University Press, 1965), 290.

Theodore Netscher, *Pineapple,* in *Gardening in Britain* by Miles Hadfield (London: Hutchinson, 1960), 167.

Bernard Mandeville, *The Fable of the Bees; or, Private Vices, Publick Benefits,* vol. 1 (Oxford: Clarendon Press, 1924), 194.

G. S. Rousseau, "Pineapples, Pregnancy, Pica, and *Peregrine Pickle,*" in *Tobias Smollett: Bicentennial Essays Presented to Lewis M. Knapp,* ed. G. S. Rousseau and P.-G. Boucé (New York: Oxford University Press, 1971), 101.

Alexander Pope to William Fortescue, 22 March 1734/5, in *The Correspondence of Alexander Pope,* ed. George Sherburn, vol. 3 (Oxford: Oxford University Press, 1956), 453.

James Thomson, *Summer,* ll. 685–89, in *James Thomson: The Seasons,* ed. James Sambrook (Oxford: Clarendon Press, 1981), 94.

Sylvia Saudan-Skira and Michael Saudan, *Orangeries: Palaces of Glass—Their History and Development* (Cologne: Benedikt Taschen Verlag, 1998), 121, 122–23.

John Singleton, *A General Description of the West-Indian Islands,* ll. 163–65, 175–79, 184–95, in *Caribbeana: An Anthology of English Literature of the West Indies, 1657–1777,* ed. Thomas W. Krise (Chicago: University of Chicago Press, 1999), 266–69.

Tobias Smollett, in *The Adventures of Peregrine Pickle,* chap. 5; rev. ed., ed. James L. Clifford and Paul-Gabriel Boucé (Oxford: Oxford University Press, 1983), 21–23.

Richard Sheridan, *The Rivals,* 3.3.16–20, in *Sheridan's Plays,* ed. Cecil Price (Oxford: Oxford University Press, 1975), 43.

782   William Cowper, "The Bee and the Pine Apple," in *The Poems of William Cowper,* vol. 1, ed. John D. Baird and Charles Ryscamp (Oxford: Clarendon Press, 1980), 216–17, 418–19, 494, 551.

Jane Austen, *Northanger Abbey,* chap. 22; ed. Marilyn Butler (London: Penguin, 1995), 155.

Maggie Lane, *Jane Austen and Food* (London: Hambledon Press, 1995), 95.

Flaubert, *Madame Bovary,* pt. 1, sect. 8, trans. Steegmuller, 55.

Manuel de Zequeiray y Arango, "A la piña," in *Literatura Hispanoamericana* by Enrique Anderson Imbert and Eugenio Florit (New York: Holt, Rinehart and Winston, 1960), 183–84.

John Locke, *An Essay Concerning Human Understanding,* bk. 3, chap. 4, sect. 11; ed. Peter H. Nidditch (Oxford: Clarendon Press, 1975), 424.

David Hume, *A Treatise of Human Nature,* bk. 1, pt. 1, sect. 1; ed. Ernest C. Mossner (London: Penguin, 1984), 53.

Wallace Stevens, "Someone Puts a Pineapple Together," in *Wallace Stevens: Collected Poetry and Prose* (New York: Library of America, 1997), 693–97.

Beverly Maeder, *Wallace Stevens' Experimental Language: The Lion in the Lute* (New York: St. Martin's Press, 1999), 65, 67.

Stevens, "Poem Written at Morning," in *Wallace Stevens* (Library of America), 198.

CHAPTER 15: CITRUS FRUITS

Citron or Etrog

Roger Holmes, ed., *Taylor's Guide to Fruits and Berries* (Boston: Houghton Mifflin, 1996), 158.

Harold Schwartz, ed. and trans., "The Tale of the Etrog," in *Gabriel's Palace: Jewish Mystical Tales* (New York: Oxford University Press, 1993), 265, 354.

Fillipo Napoletano, *Two Citrons, Shown Life-size,* in Ebert-Schifferer, *Still Life,* 64, fig. 44.

Citrus Trees: Blossoms and Fruit

John Prest, *The Garden of Eden* (New Haven and London: Yale University Press, 1981), plate 49.

John Webster, *The Duchess of Malfi* 2.2.14–17; ed. John Russell Brown (Manchester: Manchester University Press, 1976), 49–50.

Edmund Waller, "The Battle of the Summer Islands," canto 1, ll. 40–43, in *Poems,* ed. G. Thorn Drury (London: George Routledge, n.d.), vol. 1, 67.

Alexander Pope, "Cowley: The Garden," in *The Poems of Alexander Pope,* ed. John Butt (New Haven: Yale University Press, 1963), 13.

Ruth Pitter, "Other People's Glasshouses," in *Collected Poems* (London: Enitharmon Press, 1996), 143.

Yehuda Amichai, "Poem in an Orange Grove," in *Poems,* trans. Assia Gutmann (New York: Harper and Row, 1969), 20.

James Merrill, "The Will," in *From the First Nine: Poems, 1946–1976* (New York: Atheneum, 1982), 345.

The Genus *Citrus*

Pinhas Spiegel-Roy and Eliezer E. Goldschmidt, *Biology of Citrus* (Cambridge: Cambridge University Press, 1996), 42–43.

Waverly Root, *The Food of Italy* (New York: Atheneum, 1971), 577.

Kenneth Carpenter, *The History of Scurvy and Vitamin C* (Cambridge: Cambridge University Press,1988), 92.

Patrick O'Brian, *Desolation Island* (New York: W. W. Norton, 1978), 271–72.

H. Frederic Janson, *Pomona's Harvest* (Portland, Ore.: Timber Press, 1996), 113.

Lance Walheim, *Citrus* (Tuscon: Ironwood Press, 1996), 31.

Oxford Companion to Food, s.v "kumquat."

Tony Harrison, *A Kumquat for John Keats* (Newcastle upon Tyne: Bloodaxe Books, 1981).

Goethe, letter of 13 December 1786, retrospect of April 1788; Goethe, *J. W. Goethe: Italian Journey, 1786–1788,* trans. W. H. Auden and Elizabeth Mayer (New York: Schocken, 1968), 138, 487–88.

Spiegel-Roy and Goldschmidt, *Biology of Citrus,* chaps. 5–6.

Francis Haskell and Henrietta McBurney, "General Introduction to Catalogue Raisonné," in *Citrus Fruit,* pt. 1 of David Freedberg and Enrico Baldini, *The Paper Museum of Cassiano dal Pozzo: Series B, Natural History* (London: Harvey Miller, 1997), 8.

David Freedberg, "Cassiano, Ferrari and Their Drawings of Citrus Fruit," in *Citrus Fruit,* pt. 1 of Freedberg and Baldini, *Paper Museum of Cassiano dal Pazzo,* 66, 78, 74–76; figs. 75, 215, 233, 299–300.

Thomson, *Summer,* ll. 657–66, in *James Thomson: The Seasons,* ed. James Sambrook (Oxford: Clarendon Press, 1981), 92

John Singleton, *A General Description of the West-Indian Islands,* ll. 119–28, 163–65, in *Caribbeana: An Anthology of English Literature of the West Indies, 1657–1777,* ed. Thomas W. Krise (Chicago: University of Chicago Press, 1999), 266–67.

Oxford English Dictionary, 2d ed., vol. 6, s.v. "forbidden."

Oranges

S. Tolkowsky, *Hesperides: A History of the Culture and Use of Citrus Fruits* (London: John Bale, 1938).

Ben Sara, "El Naranjo," in *Poemas Arabigoandaluces,* 7th ed., ed. Emilio García Gómez (Madrid: Espasa-Calpe, 1982), 78, 35.

Boccaccio, introduction to "Day 3," in *Decameron,* trans. G. H. McWilliam (London: Penguin, 1972), 232.

Harold N. Moldenke and Alma L. Moldenke, *Plants of the Bible* (New York: Ronald Press, 1952), 286.

Francisco de Zubarán, *Still Life with Basket of Oranges,* in Jordan and Cherry, *Spanish Still Life from Velázquez to Goya,* fig. 74.

Christopher Wright, *The French Painters of the Seventeenth Century* (Boston: Little, Brown, 1985), 99.

Edouard Manet, *A Bar at the Folies-Bergère,* in *Manet, 1832–1883,* ed. Françoise Cachin et al. (New York: Metropolitan Museum of Art and Harry N. Abrams, 1983), 479–80.

William McEvoy, "Honourably Discharged," review of *Blue/Orange* by Joe Penhall, *Times Literary Supplement,* 28 Apr. 2000, 20.

André Barret, *Tintin and the Blue Oranges,* trans. Leslie-Lonsdale-Cooper and Michael Turner (London: Methuen, 1967).

784   John Baldessari, *Millennium Piece (With Blue Apple), 1999,* in *Blind Spot* 14 (1999), n.p.

Jack Bankowsky, "Editor's Note," *Art Forum* (Dec. 1999): 29.

Tolkowsky, *Hesperides,* plate 82.

Dorothy Osborne, letters 13, 18, 22 in *Dorothy Osborne: Letters to Sir William Temple,* ed. Kenneth Parker (London: Penguin, 1987), 67, 76, 84.

Jonathan Swift, "Verses Made for the Women Who Cry Apples, etc.: Oranges," in *Jonathan Swift: The Complete Poems,* ed. Pat Rogers (New Haven: Yale University Press, 1983), 563.

George Birkbeck Hill and L. F. Powell, ed., *Boswell's Life of Johnson,* 1 April 1775, vol. 2 (Oxford: Clarendon Press, 1934), 330–31, 331n. 1.

Bruce Redford, ed., *The Letters of Samuel Johnson,* vol. 1 (Princeton: Princeton University Press, 1992), 76n. 1.

Samuel Johnson to Hill Boothby, 31 Dec. 1755; Redford, ed., *Letters of Samuel Johnson,* vol. 1, 120–21.

J. M. Thompson, *Robespierre,* vol. 1 (New York: D Appleton-Century, 1936), 186n. 4.

Norman Hampson, *The Life and Opinions of Maximilien Robespierre* (London: Duckworth, 1974), 88.

Marie-Catherine d'Aulnoy, "The Bee and the Orange Tree," in *Beauties, Beasts, and Enchantment: Classic French Fairy Tales,* trans. Jack Zipes (New York: Meridian,1991), 296, 434–35, 297.

John Harold Wilson, *Nell Gwyn, Royal Mistress* (New York: Pellegrini and Cudahy, 1951), 26–27.

Arthur Bryant, *The England of Charles II* (London: Longmans, Green, 1934), 36.

Samuel Pepys, *Diary,* 2 Nov. 1667; Robert Latham, ed., *The Shorter Pepys* (Berkeley and Los Angeles: University of California Press, 1985), 846.

John McPhee, *Oranges* (Toronto: Macfarlane Walter and Ross, 1991), 67.

Tolkowsky, *Hesperides,* 109.

Edward Gibbon, *The History of the Decline and Fall of the Roman Empire,* chap. 45; ed. David Womersley (London: Allen Lane, The Penguin Press, 1994), vol. 2, 851, 853.

Gibbon, *The History of the Decline and Fall of the Roman Empire,* ed. J. B. Bury (London: Methuen, 1911), vol. 5, 10n. 20.

Waverly Root, *The Food of Italy* (New York: Atheneum, 1971), 604.

Princeton Encyclopedia of Poetry and Poetics, enlarged ed., s.v. "Spanish poetry."

Lope de Vega Carpio, "The girl throws me little oranges," in *The Penguin Book of Spanish Verse,* trans. J. M. Cohen (Harmondsworth, England: Penguin, 1960), 238–39.

Salvador Jacinto Polo de Medina, "The Orange-trees," in *The Penguin Book of Spanish Verse,* trans. Cohen, 306–7.

Anon., "A branch of orange blossom," in *The Wind Cried,* trans. Paul Hecht (New York: Dial, 1968), 172.

A. R. Ammons, "Communication," in *The Really Short Poems of A. R. Ammons* (N.Y.: W. W. Norton, 1990), 157.

Federico García Lorca, "Adelina out Walking," "The Moon Appears," "Two Evening Moons, 2," and "Song of the Dead Orange Tree," trans. Alan S. Trueblood, in *Federico García Lorca: Selected Verse,* ed. Christopher Maurer (New York: Farrar Straus Giroux, 1995), 141, 153, 155, 167.

Hasan al-Buhairi, "Orange Blossoms," in *Anthology of Modern Palestinian Literature,* ed. Salma Khadra Jayyusi, trans. Salwa Jabsheh and John Heath-Stubbs (New York: Columbia University Press, 1992), 137.

Neruda, "Ode to the Orange," in *Neruda's Garden: An Anthology of Odes,* trans. Maria Jacketti (Pittsburgh: Latin American Literary Review Press, 1995), 201–3.

Jacques Prévert, "Alicante," in *Selections from "Paroles,"* trans. Lawrence Ferlinghetti (Harmondsworth, England: Penguin, 1965), 14–15.

Prévert, "Tangerine," in *Words for All Seasons,* trans. Teo Savory (Greensboro, N.C.: Unicorn Press, 1980), 35.

Jack Gilbert, "The Four Perfectly Tangerines," in *Views of Jeopardy* (New Haven: Yale University Press, 1962), 28–29.

Francis Ponge, "The Orange," trans. Lane Dunlop, in *The Prose Poem: An International Anthology,* ed. Michael Benedikt (New York: Dell, 1976), 174–75.

Ian Higgins, ed., *Francis Ponge: Le Partis Pris des choses* (London: The Athlone Press, 1979), 113n. 6, 114n. 6.

Gilbert Sorrentino, "Across this water sits a shore," "That the mouth speak not daggers," and "Remember the story of Columbus and the orange?" in *The Orangery* (Austin and London: University of Texas Press, 1978), 24, 38, 22.

McPhee, *Oranges,* 10.

Spiegel-Roy and Goldschmidt, *Biology of Citrus,* 101.

Andrew Marvell, "Bermudas," in *Complete Poems,* ed. Elizabeth Story Donno (Harmondsworth: Penguin, 1976), 116, 266n.

Edmund Waller, "The Battle of the Summer Islands," in *The Poems of Edmund Waller,* ed. G. Thorn Drury (London: George Routledge, 1904), vol. 1, 66.

Christopher Ricks, "Literature and the Matter of Fact," in *Essays in Appreciation* (Oxford: Clarendon Press, 1996), 298–99.

George MacBeth, "The Orange Poem," in *The Oxford Book of Comic Verse,* ed. John Gross (Oxford: Oxford University Press, 1994), 433.

Carlos Fuentes, *The Orange Tree,* trans. Alfred MacAdam (New York: Farrar, Straus and Giroux, 1994), 37, 207, 215–16.

David Park, "Oranges from Spain," in *The Vintage Book of Contemporary Irish Fiction,* ed. Dermot Bolger (New York: Vintage, 1995), 317–18.

Karen Tei Yamashita, *Tropic of Orange* (Minneapolis, Minn.: Coffee House Press, 1997),182.

David Ignatow, "The Orange Picker," in *Poems, 1934–1969* (Middletown, Conn.: Wesleyan University Press, 1970), 132.

Diane Wakoski, "Image Is Narrative," in *The Rings of Saturn* (Santa Rosa: Black Sparrow Press, 1986), 81–82.

Ron Silliman, ed., *In the American Tree* (Orono, Maine: National Poetry Foundation,1986), xvi.

John Mason, "Red Fred exhumed the orangepeels," in *In the American Tree,* ed. Silliman, 405.

Lisa Ruddick, *Reading Gertrude Stein: Body, Text, Gnosis* (Ithaca: Cornell University Press, 1990), 192–93, 241–42, 231–32.

Gertude Stein, *Tender Buttons; Gertrude Stein Writings, 1903–1932* (New York: Library of America, 1998), 343.

Denise Riley, "Lure, 1963," in *Out of Everywhere: Linguistically Innovative Poetry by Women in North America and the UK,* ed. Maggie O'Sullivan (London: Reality Street Editions, 1996), 86.

Derek Walcott, "In a Green Night," in *Collected Poems, 1948–1984* (New York: Farrar, Straus and Giroux, 1986), 50–51.

786 Rei Terada, *Derek Walcott's Poetry: American Mimicry* (Boston: Northeastern University Press, 1992), 49–50.

Asher Barash, foreword to *A Selection of the New Hebrew Poetry,* (Tel Aviv, 1938), quoted in "'Our Poetry Is Like an Orange Grove': Anthologies of Hebrew Poetry in Erets Israel" by Hannan Hever, *Prooftexts* 17, no. 2: *The Jewish Anthological Imagination,* pt. 2 (May 1997): 199.

Arthur Miller, act 2 of *Death of a Salesman,* ed. Gerald Weales (New York: Viking, 1967), 82.

Eleanor Clark, "Old Glamour, New Gloom," in *Death of a Salesman,* ed. Weales, 222.

Alistair Elliot, "Reasons for Happiness in San Francisco," in *My Country: Collected Poems* (Manchester: Carcanet, 1989), 34.

James Merrill, "Oranges," *New York Review of Books* 45, no. 20 (17 Dec. 1998): 23; *Collected Poems, James Merrill,* ed. J. D. McClatchy and Stephen Yenser (New York: Knopf, 2001), 856.

Margot Arce de Vazquez, *Gabriela Mistral* (New York: New York University Press, 1964), 20.

Gary Soto, "Oranges," in *Black Hair* (Pittsburgh: University of Pittsburgh Press, 1985), 8.

Alexis Smith, "Same Old Eden," in *Alexis Smith* by Richard Armstrong (New York: Whitney Museum of American Art, 1991), 194–95.

Barbara Barrick McKie, *Fanfare for an Orange,* in "Quilted Constructions: The Spirit of Design," by Suzannah Schatt, *Folk Art* 26, no. 3 (fall 2001): 28.

Karl Krolow, "Three oranges, two lemons," in *Twentieth-Century German Verse,* trans. Patrick Bridgwater (Harmondsworth, England: Penguin, 1963), 261–62.

Lemons

Gil Vicente, "In the garden is born the rose," in *The Penguin Book of Spanish Verse,* trans. Cohen, 102–3.

Philip Levine, "The Trade," in *The Simple Truth* (New York: Alfred A. Knopf, 1994), 16–17.

Jack Spicer, "The rind (also called the skin)," in *The Collected Books of Jack Spicer,* ed. Robin Blaser (Santa Rosa: Black Sparrow Press, 1996), 249.

Gérard de Nerval, "Delphica," in Peter Jay, trans., *Nerval: The Chimeras* (Redding Ridge, Conn.: Black Swan Books, 1984), 22–23.

Norma Rinsler, ed., *Gérard de Nerval: Les Chimères* (London: Athlone Press, 1973), 58, 18–25, 10, 31.

J. W. Kneller, "Delfica," in *The Poem Itself,* ed. Stanley Burnshaw (New York: Schocken, 1960), 4.

Richard Holmes, "A Letter on a Line by Nerval," in *Nerval: The Chimeras,* trans. Peter Jay, 45–46, 48, 53.

Rinsler, ed., *Gerard de Nerval: Les Chimères,* 80.

Walcott, "Sunday Lemons," in *Collected Poems, 1948–1984,* 298–99.

Cowley, "Written in Juice of Lemmon," in *Poems,* ed. A. R. Waller (Cambridge: Cambridge University Press, 1905), 72.

Ian Higgins, ed., *Francis Ponge: Les Partis Pres des choses,* 14.

Alain Bosquet, "The Lemons," trans. Susan Alliston, *Modern Poetry in Translation* 2 (summer 1966), 17.

Bosquet, "The Lemons," trans. Edward Lucie-Smith, *Modern Poetry in Translation* 2 (summer 1966), 18.

William Frawley, "Translator's Introduction," in *Instead of Music: Poems by Alain Bosquet* (Baton Rouge and London: Louisiana State University Press, 1980), xi, 2–3.

Miguel Hernández, "Me tiraste un limón," in *Poemas* (Barcelona: Plaza and Janes, 1967), 28.

Hernández, "You threw me a lemon" and "Your heart?—it is a frozen orange," trans. Robert Bly, in *Miguel Hernández and Blas de Otero: Selected Poems,* ed. Timothy Baland and Hardie St. Martin (Boston: Beacon Press, 1972), 10–11, 16–17.

Hernández, "Your hand that tossed me such a bitter lemon," in *The Unending Lightning: Selected Poems of Miguel Hernández,* trans. Edwin Honig (Riverdale-on-Hudson, N.Y.: Sheep Meadow Press, 1990), 5.

Hernández, "You threw a bitter lemon at me so austere," in *Six Masters of the Spanish Sonnet,* trans. Willis Barnstone (Carbondale and Edwardsville: Southern Illinois University Press, 1993), 285, 262.

Jonathan Galassi, trans., *Eugenio Montale: Collected Poems, 1920–1954* (New York: Farrar, Straus and Giroux, 1998), 444.

Eugenio Montale, "The Lemon Trees," trans. Irma Brandeis, in *Eugenio Montale: Selected Poems* (New York: New Directions, 1965), 2–5.

Montale, "The Lemon Trees," in *Eugenio Montale: Cuttlefish Bones, 1920–1927,* trans. William Arrowsmith (New York: W. W. Norton, 1993), 6–9.

Montale, "The Lemon Trees," in *Eugenio Montale: Collected Poems, 1920–1954,* trans. Galassi, 8–11, 447.

Glauco Cambon, *Eugenio Montale's Poetry: A Dream in Reason's Presence* (Princeton: Princeton University Press, 1982),11, 9.

Joseph Cary, *Three Modern Italian Poets: Saba, Ungaretti, Montale,* 2d ed. (Chicago: University of Chicago Press, 1993), 252–54.

Claire de C.L. Huffman, *Montale and the Occasions of Poetry* (Princeton: Princeton University Press, 1983), 82, 86.

Montale, "In the Greenhouse," trans. James Merrill, in *Eugenio Montale: Selected Poems,* 131.

Montale, "In the Greenhouse," in *Eugenio Montale: The Storm and Other Things,* trans. William Arrowsmith (New York: W. W. Norton, 1985), 110–11.

Montale, "In the Greenhouse," in *Eugenio Montale: Collected Poems, 1920–1954,* trans. Galassi, 358–59.

F. J. Jones, *The Modern Italian Lyric* (Cardiff: University of Wales Press, 1986), 483.

Galassi, trans., *Eugenio Montale: Collected Poems, 1920–1954,* 576–77.

Arrowsmith, *Eugenio Montale: The Storm,* 192.

Mario Satz, "Lemon," in *Voices within the Ark: The Modern Jewish Poets,* ed. Howard Schwartz and Anthony Rudolf, trans. Willis Barnstone (New York: Avon, 1980), 1164.

Eliot Weinberger, introduction to Clayton Eshleman, *The Name Encanyoned River: Selected Poems, 1960–1985* (Santa Barbara: Black Sparrow Press, 1986), 9–10.

Eshleman, "Lemons," in *The Name Encanyoned River: Selected Poems, 1960–1985,* 205–6.

Piotr Sommer, "Medicine," in *Polish Poetry of the Last Two Decades of Communist Rule: Spoiling Cannibals' Fun,* trans. Stanislaw Baranczak and Clare Cavanagh (Evanston: Northwestern University Press, 1991), 171–72.

Sommer, "Potatoes," in *Things to Translate and Other Poems,* trans. Piotr Sommer and Charles Mignon (Newcastle upon Tyne: Bloodaxe Books, 1991), 39.

Neruda, "Ode to the Lemon," in *Selected Odes of Pablo Neruda,* trans. Margaret Sayers Peden (Berkeley and Los Angeles: University of California Press, 1990), 327.

James Galvin, "Lemon Ode," in *Resurrection Update: Collected Poems, 1975–1997* (Port Townsend, Wash.: Copper Canyon Press, 1997), 47–48.

Fernando Pessoa, "She brings the surprise of being," in *The Surprise of Being,* trans. James Greene and Clara de Azevedo Mafra (London: Angel Books, 1986), 34–35.

788   Pessoa, "She surprises just by being," in *A Centenary Pessoa,* ed. Eugénio Lisboa and L. C. Taylor, trans. Keith Bosley (Manchester: Carcanet, 1997), 39.

Iona Opie and Peter Opie, "The Bells of London," in *A Family Book of Nursery Rhymes* (New York: Oxford University Press, 1964), 46.

Eleanor Farjeon, "Oranges and Lemons," in *Something I Remember: Selected Poems for Children by Eleanor Farjeon,* ed. Anne Harvey (London: Penguin, 1989), 64.

Sam Segal, *A Prosperous Past: The Sumptuous Still Life in the Netherlands, 1600–1700* (The Hague: SDU Publishers, 1988).

Svetlana Alpers, *The Art of Describing* (Chicago: University of Chicago Press, 1983), 91, fig. 59.

Willem Kalf, *Still Life with Nautilus Goblet,* in *Still Life: Still Life Painting in the Early Modern Period* by Norbert Schneider (Cologne: Benedikt Taschen, 1994), 109; Segal, *A Prosperous Past,* 182.

Charles S. Moffett, "Still Life with Fish," in *Manet, 1832–1883,* ed. Françoise Cachin et al. (New York: Metropolitan Museum of Art and Harry N. Abrams, 1983), 216, fig. 81.

Manet, *The Luncheon in the Studio* and *Still Life with Salmon,* in *Manet* by Georges Bataille, trans. Austryn Wainhouse and James Emmons (New York: Skira, 1955), 79–81.

Manet, *Portrait of Zacharie Astruc, The Luncheon in the Studio,* and *Lemon,* in *Manet, 1832–1883,* ed. Françoise Cachin et al. (New York: Metropolitan Museum of Art and Harry N. Abrams, 1983), 248, 250, 255, 291, 452.

Donald Sultan, *Black Lemon August 24, 1984,* in *Art What Thou Eat: Images of Food in American Art,* ed. Linda Weintraub (Mount Kisco, N.Y.: Moyer Bell, 1991), 52.

Grapefruits and Limes

Kenward Elmslie, "Fruit," in *From the Other Side of the Century: A New American Poetry, 1960–1990,* ed. Douglas Messerli (Los Angeles: Sun and Moon Press, 1994), 862–63.

F. Scott Fitzgerald, *The Great Gatsby,* chap. 3; ed. Matthew J. Bruccoli (New York: Scribner, 1995), 43–44.

James L. W. West III, chap. 3 in *Trimalchio: An Early Version of "The Great Gatsby,"* F. Scott Fitzgerald (Cambridge: Cambridge University Press, 2000), 33; see also *Trimalchio* by F. Scott Fitzgerald, ed. Matthew J. Bruccoli (Columbia: University of South Carolina Press, 2000).

Oxford Companion to Food, s.v. "grapefruit."

Leyland Cox, "The Perfect Half Grapefruit," *Gourmet,* October 1978, 48–51.

Glenn Robert Smith, *Discovering Ellis Ruley* (New York: Crown, 1993), 43, fig. 7.

Ann Beattie, *Chilly Scenes of Winter* (New York: Vintage, 1991), 35, 34, 279–80.

Gerald Stern, "Grapefruit," in *This Time: New and Selected Poems* (New York: W. W. Norton, 1998), 203–4.

Alan Brownjohn, "Incident on a Holiday," *Times Literary Supplement,* 26 Nov. 1999, 6.

Luigi Pirandello, *Sicilian Limes,* in *Pirandello's One-Act Plays,* trans. William Murray (New York: Doubleday, 1964), 59.

Gustavo Pérez-Firmat, "Lime Cure," in *Hispanic American Literature,* ed. Nicolás Kanellos (New York: HarperCollins, 1995), 256–57.

CHAPTER 16: MELONS AND PAPAYAS

Gustave Flaubert, "Melon," in *Dictionary of Accepted Ideas,* trans. Jacques Barzun (New York: New Directions, 1968), 63.

Colette, "Flora and Pomona," in *Flowers and Fruit,* trans. Matthew Ward (New York: Farrar Straus Giroux, 1986), viii, 127.

Apicius, *The Art of Cooking* 3.7; in *The Roman Cookery Book,* trans. Barbara Flower and Elisabeth Rosenbaum (London: George G. Harrap, 1958), 79.

Walafrid Strabo, *Hortulus;* trans. Raef Payne (Pittsburgh: Hunt Botanical Library, 1966), 38–41.

Peter Godman, ed. and trans., *Poetry of the Carolingian Renaissance* (London: Duckworth, 1985), 38–39.

Michel de Montaigne, "Of Experience," in *The Complete Essays of Montaigne,* trans. Donald M. Frame (Stanford, Calif.: Stanford University Press, 1958), 846.

Antoine-Girard de Saint-Amant, "Le Melon," in *Oeuvres,* vol. 2, ed. Jean Lagny (Paris: Librairie Marcel Didier, 1967–1979), 14–31.

Imbrie Buffum, *Studies in the Baroque from Montaigne to Rotrou* (New Haven: Yale University Press, 1957), 136–37.

Antoine-Girard de Saint Amant, "The Melon," in *Sixteenth to Eighteenth Centuries,* vol. 2 of *The Penguin Book of French Verse,* ed. and trans. Geoffrey Brereton (Harmondsworth, England: Penguin, 1958), 189–92.

James Joyce, "Ithaca," chap. 17 in *Ulysses,* new ed. (New York: Modern Library, 1961), 734–35.

Anne Stevenson, *Bitter Fame: A Life of Sylvia Plath* (Boston: Houghton Mifflin, 1989), 110, 30, 41.

Plath, "Lesbos," "Mary's Song," "Bitter Strawberries," "Southern Sunrise," and "Fiesta Melons," in *The Collected Poems of Sylvia Plath,* ed. Ted Hughes (New York: Harper and Row, 1981), 227, 257, 299–300, 26, 46–7.

Plath, "Fiesta Melons," in *Fiesta Melons* (Exeter: The Rougemont Press, 1971), 15.

Ted Hughes, "Lovesong," in *Crow* (New York: Harper and Row, 1971), 77.

Neruda, "Ode to the Watermelon," in *Neruda and Vallejo: Selected Poems,* ed. Robert Bly (Boston: Beacon Press, 1976), 146–51.

Kaddour-Mermet, "The Olive and the Watermelon," in *The Fabulists French: Verse Fables of Nine Centuries,* trans. Norman R. Shapiro (Urbana and Chicago: University of Illinois Press, 1992), 186–87.

Ted Joans, "Watermelon," in *Black Pow-Wow* (New York: Hill and Wang, 1969), 40.

Bari-Ellen Roberts, *Roberts vs. Texaco: A True Story of Race and Corporate America* (New York: Avon, 1998), 273.

Ron Loewinsohn, "Watermelons," in *Meat Air: Poems, 1957–1969* (New York: Harcourt, Brace, and World, 1977), 6.

Charles Simic, "Watermelons," in *Selected Poems, 1963–1983* (New York: George Braziller, 1985), 53.

Virginia Hamilton Adair, "Ants on the Melon," in *Ants on the Melon* (New York: Random House, 1996), 25.

Eduard Bagritsky, "Watermelon," trans. Vera Dunham, in *Twentieth Century Russian Poetry: Silver and Steel,* ed. Albert C. Todd and Max Hayward (New York: Doubleday, 1993), 309–10.

Khaled Mattawa, "Watermelon Tales," in *The 1994/1995 Pushcart Prize, 19,* ed. Bill Henderson (Wainscott, N.Y.: Pushcart Press, 1995), 252, 254.

Frances Trollope, *Domestic Manners of the Americans,* ed. Donald Smalley (New York: Alfred A. Knopf, 1949), 85.

Robert Devlin Schwarz, *One Hundred and Fifty Years of Philadelphia Still-Life Painting* (Philadelphia: The Schwarz Gallery, 1997), 33.

Anne Sue Hirshorn, "Anna Claypoole, Margaretta, and Sarah Miriam Peale: Modes of Accomplishment and Fortune," in *The Peale Family: Creation of a Legacy, 1770–1870,* ed. Lillian B. Miller (New York: Abbeville Press, 1996), 240.

790   Ellen Ficklen, *Watermelon* (Washington, D.C.: American Folklife Center, Library of Congress, 1984), 36.

Donald Reilly, "This judge is known as tough but fair . . ." (cartoon caption), *New Yorker,* 29 May, 2000, 116.

Umberto Boccioni, *Still Life: Watermelon,* in Ebert-Schifferer, *Still Life,* fig. 243.

Walter Harding, *The Days of Henry Thoreau* (New York: Knopf, 1965), 89–90.

Thoreau, *Wild Fruits,* ed. Dean, 107.

Mark Twain, *The Tragedy of Pudd'nhead Wilson and the Comedy Those Extraordinary Twins* (New York: Oxford University Press, 1996), 179.

M. B. Leavitt, *Fifty Years in Theatrical Management* (New York: Broadway Publishing Co., 1912), 31.

Eudora Welty, *Losing Battles* (New York: Random House, 1970), 100, 102, 154, 195, 198, 415–16, 269.

Barbara Hamby, "Ode to Italian Fruit," in *The Alphabet of Desire* (New York: New York University Press, 1999), 76–77.

Frances Mayes, *Under the Tuscan Sun* (San Francisco: Chronicle Books, 1996), 63.

Bob Flowerdew, *The Complete Book of Fruit* (New York: Penguin Press, 1995), 153.

Richard Pau-Llosa, "Mulata," in *Paper Dance: 55 Latino Poets,* ed. Victor Hernández Cruz et al. (New York: Persea Books, 1995), 136–38.

Harold Lowry et al., bulletin 156A, Agricultural Extension Service, *Miscellaneous Tropical and Subtropical Florida Fruits* (June 1958), 36, 79.

Edmund Waller, "The Battle of the Summer Islands," canto 1, ll. 52–55, in *The Poems of Edmund Waller,* ed. Drury, vol. 1, 68.

Jacques-Henri Bernardin de Saint-Pierre, *Paul and Virginia,* trans. John Donovan (London: Peter Owen, 1982), 9, 37, 59, 64, 100, 105.

A. D. Hope, "Imperial Adam," in *King Solomon's Garden: Poems and Art Inspired by the Old Testament,* ed. Laurance Wieder (New York: Harry N. Abrams, 1994), 32.

Jane Grigson, *Jane Grigson's Fruit Book* (London: Penguin, 1982), 284–85.

Tony Harrison, "Fruitility," *London Review of Books* 21, no. 21 (28 Oct. 1999): 12–13.

Alice Browne, "Descartes's Dreams," *Journal of the Warburg and Courtauld Institutes,* 40 (1977): 266.

John R. Cole: *The Olympian Dreams and Youthful Rebellion of René Descartes* (Urbana and Chicago: University of Illinois Press, 1992), 143, 264n. 16.

Randle Cotgrave, *A Dictionarie of the French and English Tongues* (London: Adam Islip, 1611; reprinted, Columbia: University of South Carolina Press, 1950), s.v. "melon."

Richard Pigot, trans. and ed., *Moral Emblems with Aphorisms, Adages, and Proverbs, of All Ages and Nations, from Jacob Cats and Robert Farlie* (New York: D. Appleton, 1860), 225–26.

Alan Gabbey and Robert E. Hall, "The Melon and the Dictionary: Reflections on Descartes's Dreams," *Journal of the History of Ideas* 59, no. 4 (Oct. 1998): 662, 661.

Adam Zagajewski, "In Defense of Adjectives," in *Two Cities: On Exile, History, and the Imagination,* trans. Lillian Vallee (New York: Farrar, Straus, Giroux, 1995), 263.

Adam Kirsch, "The Lucid Moment," *New Republic,* 23 Mar. 1998, 40.

CHAPTER 17: CHERRIES

Pliny the Elder, *Natural History* 15.102; in *Natural History: A Selection,* trans. John F. Healy (London: Penguin, 1991), 202.

Andrew Dalby, *Siren Feasts,* 230–31n. 111.

Plutarch, "Lucullus" 39.1–2; in *Plutarch's Lives,* vol. 2, trans. Bernadotte Perrin (London: William Heinemann, 1924), 597.

Plutarch, "Comparison of Lucullus and Cimon" 1.1; in *Plutarch's Lives,* vol. 2, trans. Perrin , 611.

Bertolt Brecht, *The Trial of Lucullus,* in *Collected Plays,* vol. 5, ed. Ralph Manheim and John Willett, trans. Frank Jones (New York: Vintage Books, 1972), 115, 128, 306–30.

Martin Esslin, *Brecht: The Man and His Work,* new rev. ed. (New York: Anchor Books, 1971), 182–86.

Oxford English Dictionary, 2d ed., vol. 3, s.v. "cherry."

Rabelais, *Pantagruel* 5. 27; in *The Complete Works of François Rabelais,* trans. Donald M. Frame (Berkeley and Los Angeles: University of California Press, 1991), 675.

Jorge Teillier, "These Words," in *From the Land of Nevermore: Selected Poems of Jorge Teillier,* trans. Mary Crow (Hanover, N.H., and London: University Press of New England, 1990), 12–13.

François Massialot, *Nouvelle instruction pour les confitures; les liqueurs, et les fruits,* quoted trans. in *Savoring the Past: The French Kitchen and Table from 1300 to 1789* by Barbara Ketcham Wheaton (Philadelphia: University of Pennsylvania Press, 1983), 188.

Mme. de Sévigné to Mme de Grignan, 5 Aug. 1671, in *Madame de Sévigné: Selected Letters,* trans. Leonard Tancock (Harmondsworth, England: Penguin, 1982), 108.

Herrick, "Chop-Cherry," in *The Complete Poetry of Robert Herrick,* ed. J. Max Patrick (New York: Anchor, 1963), 193.

Anon., "Lady, those cherries plenty," in *The New Oxford Book of Sixteenth Century Verse,* ed. Emrys Jones (Oxford: Oxford University Press, 1991), 619.

Herrick, "Cherrie-ripe," in *The Complete Poetry of Robert Herrick,* ed. Patrick, 30.

Thomas Campion, "There is a Garden in her face," *Fourth Booke of Ayres,* 7 [ca. 1617], in *The Works of Thomas Campion,* ed. Walter R. Davis (New York: W. W. Norton, 1970), 174–76.

John Hollander, introduction to *Selected Songs of Thomas Campion,* ed. W. H. Auden (Boston: David Godine, 1973), 20, 22.

C. S. Lewis, *English Literature in the Sixteenth Century, Excluding Drama* (Oxford: Oxford University Press, 1954), 556.

Walter R. Davis, ed., *The Works of Thomas Campion* (New York: W. W. Norton, 1970), 174n. 28.

Thomas Campion, "There is a Garden in her face," in *Thomas Campion, Lute Songs* (Naxos compact disc 8.553380, 1999).

Francis Davison, "Since your sweet cherry lips I kissed," in *English Madrigal Verse, 1588–1632,* ed. E. H. Fellowes, 2d ed. (Oxford: Clarendon Press, 1929), 109.

Davis, *Works of Thomas Campion,* 174n. 28.

Thomas Morley, "Lady, those cherries plenty," in *First Booke of Balletts to Five Voyces* by Thomas Morley (1595; 2d ed., 1600), in *The English Madrigalists,* vol. 4, no. 16, ed. Edmund H. Fellowes, rev. Thurston Dart (London: Stainer and Bell, 1965), 63–67.

William Shakespeare, *A Midsummer Night's Dream,* 3.2.137–40, 208–12; Trevor R. Griffiths, ed. (Cambridge: Cambridge University Press, 1996), 159, 162.

Jean-Jacques Rousseau, *Confessions,* pt. 1, bk. 4, trans. Christopher Kelly, in *The Collected Writings of Rousseau,* vol. 5, ed. Christopher Kelly et al. (Hanover and London: University Press of New England, 1995), 115–16.

Rousseau, *Les Confessions,* pt. 1, bk. 4, in *Oeuvres Complètes* by Jean-Jacques Rousseau, ed. Bernard Gagnebin and Marcel Raymond (Paris: Gallimard, 1959), vol. 1, 137.

Susan Stewart, "Garden Agon," *Representations* 62 (spring 1998): 138n.14, fig. 4.

792   Leo Tolstoy, *A Landowner's Morning, Family Happiness, and The Devil: Three Novellas by Leo Tolstoy,* trans. Kyrila FitzLyon and April FitzLyon (London: Quartet Books, 1984), 70–1, 75, 87–8–9, 90, 140–1, 146, 153.

Renato Poggioli, *The Oaken Flute: Essays on Pastoral Poetry and the Pastoral Ideal* (Cambridge: Harvard University Press, 1975), 266, 273, 282.

Richard F. Gustafson, *Leo Tolstoy, Resident and Stranger: A Study in Fiction and Theology* (Princeton: Princeton University Press, 1986), xii, 7, xiv, 117, 115, 110.

Leo Tolstoy to N. N. Strakhov, 23/26 April 1876; in *Tolstoy's Letters,* trans. R. F. Christian (New York: Charles Scribner's Sons, 1978), vol. 1, 296.

Philip Rahv, preface to *The Short Novels of Tolstoy,* trans. Aylmer Maude (New York: Dial Press, 1946), xvi–xvii; in *Essays on Literature and Politics 1932–1972,* ed. Arabel J. Porter and Andrew J. Dvosin (Boston: Houghton Mifflin, 1978), 217–18.

D. H. Lawrence, *Sons and Lovers* (Harmondsworth, England: Penguin, 1948), 347–49, 350.

Lawrence, "Song" and "Cherry Robbers," in *Complete Poems,* ed. De Sola Pinto and Roberts, 859–60, 36–37.

Lawrence, foreword to *Collected Poems* (1928); in *Complete Poems,* ed. De Sola Pinto and Roberts, appendix 1, 850.

Sandra M. Gilbert, *Acts of Attention: The Poems of D. H. Lawrence* (Ithaca, N.Y., and London: Cornell University Press, 1972), 23, 50–51.

Carol E. Dietrich, "The Raw and the Cooked: The Role of Fruit in Modern Poetry," *Mosaic* 24, no. 3/4 (summer/fall 1991), 133–34.

Oxford English Dictionary Additions Series, vol. 1, ed. John Simpson and Edmund Weiner (Oxford: Oxford University Press, 1993), s.v. "cherry," 48.

Anon., "Now the weather is warm," in *The Fruit of That Forbidden Tree: Restoration Poems, Songs, and Jests on the Subject of Sensual Love* by John Adlard (Cheadle, England: Carcanet, 1975), 62–63.

Francis James Child, *The English and Scottish Popular Ballads,* vol. 2 (Boston and New York: Houghton Mifflin and Co., 1904), 2.

József Erdélyi, "Cherry-Tree," trans. Watson Kirkconnell, in *In Quest of the "Miracle Stag": The Poetry of Hungary,* ed. Adam Makkai (Chicago: Atlantis-Centaur, 1996), 559–60.

A. E. Housman, "Loveliest of trees, the cherry now," in *A Shropshire Lad* (1896); in *The Collected Poems of A. E. Housman* (New York: Holt, Rinehart and Winston, 1965), 11.

Dick Davis, "Blue Remembered Hills," *Times Literary Supplement* (5 June 1998), 3–4.

Colette, "Flora and Pomona," in *Flowers and Fruit,* trans. Matthew Ward (New York: Farrar, Straus and Giroux, 1986), 119.

Linda Pastan, "Misreading Housman," in *Heroes in Disguise* (New York: W. W. Norton, 1991), 72; Pastan, *Carnival Evening,* 254.

Walter De la Mare, "The Cherry Trees," in *Memory and Other Poems* (New York: Henry Holt, 1938), 66.

Stefan George, "Im morgen-taun," in *Poems,* trans. Carol North Valhope and Ernst Morwitz (New York: Pantheon, 1943), 174–75, 30.

D. J. Enright, "Busybody under a Cherry Tree," in *Collected Poems, 1948–1998* (Oxford: Oxford University Press, 1998), 52.

Gabriel Preil, "Concerning the Cherry Tree," in *Sunset Possibilities and Other Poems,* trans. Robert Friend (Philadelphia: Jewish Publication Society, 1985), 135.

George Meredith, chaps. 9, 11, 19, 25 of *The Egoist: A Comedy in Narrative,* rev. ed., ed. Margaret Harris (Oxford: Oxford University Press, 1992), 78–79, 117–18, 189, 262–63.

Harris, introduction to *The Egoist: A Comedy in Narrative,* xi–xii.

Alan Mitchell and Allen Coombes, *The Garden Tree* (London: Weidenfeld and Nicolson, 1998), 215.

Johann Heinrich Wilhelm Tischbein, *The Miracle of Blossoms,* in *Fuseli to Menzel: Drawings and Watercolors in the Age of Goethe from a German Private Collection* by Hinrich Sieveking (Munich: Prestel, 1998), cat. no. 16, 68, 69.

Anon., "The Treasure of Raueneck," in *Beneath the Cherry Sapling: Legends from Franconia,* ed. and trans. Norbert Krapf (New York: Fordham University Press, 1988), 132–33.

Jon Stallworthy, "Making a Table," in *The Anzac Sonata: New and Selected Poems* (New York: W. W. Norton, 1987), 131–32.

Donald Davie, "Cherry Ripe," in *Collected Poems* (Chicago: University of Chicago Press, 1991), 69.

Juan Gris, *The Cherries,* in *Juan Gris* by Mark Rosenthal (New York: Abbeville, 1983), 68.

Heinrich Heine, "At home in dear Germany," in *The Complete Poems of Heinrich Heine: A Modern English Version,* trans. Hal Draper (Boston: Suhrkamp/Insel, 1982), 766.

Heine, "Im lieben Deutschland daheime," in *Neue Gedichte,* ed. Elisabeth Genton, vol. 2 of *Heinrich Heine: Historisch-kritische Gesamtausgabe der Werke,* vol. 2 (Würzburg: Hoffmann und Campe, 1973), 186–87.

Stanislaw Baranczak and Clare Cavanagh, trans., *Polish Poetry of the Last Two Decades of Communist Rule: Spoiling Cannibals' Fun* (Evanston: Northwestern University Press, 1991), 12.

Adam Zagajewski, "Wild Cherries," in *Canvas,* trans. Renata Gorczynski, Benjamin Ivry, and C. K. Williams (New York: Farrar Straus Giroux, 1991), 68.

Gyula Illyés, "Sour-Cherry Trees," trans. Emery George, in *Contemporary East European Poetry,* ed. Emery George (New York: Oxford University Press, 1993), 240.

Paul Celan, "In the Cherry-Tree Branches . . . ," trans. Michael Hamburger, in *Paul Celan: Selected Poems* (Harmondsworth: Penguin, 1972), 26.

Thom Gunn, "The Cherry Tree," in *Jack Straw's Castle* (New York: Farrar, Straus and Giroux, 1976), 69–70; Gunn, *Collected Poems* (New York: Noonday Press, 1994), 294–96.

Karen Van Dyck, ed. and trans., *The Rehearsal of Misunderstanding: Three Collections by Contemporary Greek Women Poets* (Hanover and London: University Press of New England, 1998), xviii–xix.

Rhea Galanaki, *The Cake,* in *The Rehearsal of Misunderstanding: Three Collections by Contemporary Greek Women Poets,* ed. and trans. Van Dyck, 7, 59–61, 75–77.

Herman Melville, *Moby-Dick,* chap. 135; in *Redburn, White Jacket, Moby-Dick* (New York: Library of America, 1983), 1405.

Claes Oldenburg and Coosje van Bruggen, *Spoonbridge and Cherry,* in *Walker Art Center: Painting and Sculpture from the Collection* (Minneapolis: Walker Art Center, 1990), 412–13.

Philip Guston, *Cherries,* in *A Critical Study of Philip Guston* by Dore Ashton (Berkeley and Los Angeles: University of California Press, 1976), color plate 11.

Guston, *Curtain,* in *Gemälde 1947–1979,* ed. Christoph Schreier (Bonn: Hatze Cantz, 1999), 111.

Guston, *Summer,* in *Philip Guston* by Robert Storr (New York: Abbeville Press, 1986), fig. 109.

Lilly Martin Spencer, *Conversation Piece,* in Carrie Rebora Barratt, "Lily Martin Spencer, Conversation Piece," *Metropolitan Museum of Art Bulletin* 57, no. 2 (fall 1999): 52.

Robert Devlin Schwarz, *One Hundred and Fifty Years of Philadelphia Still-Life Painting* (Philadelphia: The Schwarz Gallery, 1997), 47.

794   Constant J. Mews, *The Lost Love Letters of Heloise and Abelard: Perceptions of Dialogue in Twelfth-Century France* (New York: St. Martin's Press, 1999), 220–21.

Betty Radice, trans., *The Letters of Abelard and Heloise* (Harmondsworth, England: Penguin, 1974).

CHAPTER 18: GRAPES

Andrea Navagero, "Damis' Vow to Bacchus on Behalf of his Vine," trans. Alice E. Wilson, in *Renaissance Latin Poetry,* ed. I. D. McFarlane (Manchester: Manchester University Press, 1980), 29, 223.

The Oxford Companion to African American Literature, s.v. "slavery," "Chesnutt, Charles Waddell," and "The Conjure Woman."

Charles W. Chesnutt, *The Conjure Woman* (Ridgewood, N.J.: Gregg Press, 1968), 8–9, 13, 34.

U. P. Hedrick, *History of Horticulture in America* (Oxford: Oxford University Press, 1950); reprint, Portland, Ore: Timber Press, 1988), 124.

Donald Platt, "Scuppernong and Muscadine," *New Republic,* 7 August 2000, 46.

Alexander Pushkin, "Grapes," in *Alexander Pushkin,* trans. A. D. P. Briggs (London: Everyman Dent, 1997), 38.

Anon., *Greek Anthology,* 5.304; in *Poems from the Greek Anthology,* trans. Dudley Fitts (New York: New Directions, 1956), 49.

Horace, *Odes* 2.5; trans. Thomas Creech, in *The Oxford Book of Classical Verse in Translation,* ed. Adrian Poole and Jeremy Maule (Oxford: Oxford University Press, 1995), 339.

Horace, *Odes* 2.5; in *The Odes of Horace,* trans. James Michie (New York: Orion, 1963), 113.

Horace, *Odes* 2.5; in *Horace's* Odes *and* Epodes, trans. David Mulroy (Ann Arbor: University of Michigan Press, 1994), 105.

Daniel H. Garrison, *Horace, Epodes and Odes: A New Annotated Latin Edition* (Norman and London: University of Oklahoma Press, 1991), 266.

Rukhl Fishman, "More Heat" and "Grapes," in *I Want to Fall Like This,* trans. Seymour Levitan (Detroit: Wayne State University Press, 1994), 113, 25–27.

Ezekiel 18:2, New Oxford Annotated Bible.

Oxford Companion to Food, s.v. "verjuice."

James Prescott, trans., *Le Viandier de Taillevent,* 2d ed. (Eugene, Oregon: Alfarhaugr Publishing Society, 1989).

Jean de La Fontaine, "The Fox and the Grapes," in *La Fontaine: Selected Fables,* trans. James Michie (New York: Viking, 1979), 85.

Stephen Bann, *The True Vine: On Visual Representation and the Western Tradition* (Cambridge: Cambridge University Press, 1989), 60, 62–63.

Pierre Julien, *La Fontaine,* in *Painting and Sculpture in France, 1700–1789* by Michael Levey (New Haven: Yale University Press,1993), fig. 247.

Marc Chagall, *The Fox and the Grapes,* in *The Fables of La Fontaine* (New York: The New Press, 1997), 65.

Ned Rorem, *4. The Fox and the Grapes,* in *Fables, Five Very Short Operas* (New York: Boosey and Hawkes, 1974), 20–22.

Ambrose Bierce, "Fox and Grapes," in *The Collected Fables of Ambrose Bierce,* ed. S. T. Joshi (Columbus: Ohio State University Press, 2000), 150.

Samuel Butler, *The Way of All Flesh,* chap. 6; ed. James Cochrane (Harmondsworth: Penguin, 1971), 54.

Kenneth Slessor, "Wild Grapes," in *The Faber Book of Modern Australian Verse,* ed. Vincent Buck-   795
ley (London: Faber and Faber, 1991), 7–8.

Buckley, ed., *The Faber Book of Modern Australian Verse,* xxi.

Jane Hirshfield, "Wine Grapes for Breakfast," in *The Lives of the Heart* (New York: Harper-
Collins, 1997), 66.

Pablo Neruda, *Canto General,* trans. Jack Schmitt (Berkeley and Los Angeles: University of California Press, 1991).

Neruda, "It was the grape's autumn," in *Neruda and Vallejo: Selected Poems,* ed. Robert Bly, trans.
James Wright and Robert Bly (Boston: Beacon, 1976), 113.

Colette, "Grape Harvest," trans. Matthew Ward, in *The Collected Stories of Colette,* ed. Robert
Phelps (New York: Farrar, Straus and Giroux, 1983), 66, 68.

Kostas Krystallis, "The Vintage," in *Modern Greek Poetry,* trans. Rae Dalven (New York: Gaer
Associates, 1949), 162–63.

Robert Wells, "Vendemmia," in *Selected Poems* (Manchester: Carcanet, 1986), 49.

Anthony Hecht, "The Grapes," in *The Venetian Vespers* (New York: Atheneum, 1979), 5.

Lorna Dee Cervantes, "Raisins," in *New American Poets of the '90s,* ed. Jack Myers and Roger
Weingarten (Boston: David R. Godine, 1991), 23–24.

David Mas Masumoto, *Epitaph for a Peach* (San Francisco: HarperCollins, 1995), 132, 134.

William Bartram, *Travels and Other Writings* (New York: Library of America, 1996), 326.

Michael Burns, "Joy's Grape," *Paris Review* 147 (summer 1998), 182.

Princeton Encyclopedia of Poetry and Poetics, enlarged ed., s.v. "Sonnet."

George Meredith, *Modern Love,* IX: "He felt the wild beast in him betweenwhiles," and XLV:
"It is the season of the sweet wild rose," in *The Poems of George Meredith,* vol. 1, ed. Phyllis B. Bartlett (New Haven: Yale University Press, 1978), 121, 142.

Adam Hirsch, "Modern Love," *New Republic,* 1 November 1999, 45.

Friedrich Hölderlin, "Auf falben Laube ruhet," in *Poems and Fragments,* trans. Michael Hamburger (Cambridge: Cambridge University Press, 1980), 514–15.

Ion Caraion, "The Enveloping Echo," trans. Marguerite Dorian and Elliott Urdang, in *Contemporary East European Poetry,* ed. Emery George (New York: Oxford University Press,
1993), 322.

Herrick, "The Vine," in *The Complete Poetry of Robert Herrick,* ed. J. Max Patrick (New York:
Anchor, 1963), 26.

Stéphane Mallarmé, "A Faun's Afternoon, An Eclogue," in *Mallarmé: The Poems, A Bilingual Edition,* trans. Keith Bosley (Harmondsworth, England: Penguin, 1977), 27, 121–23, 124–25.

Robert Frost, "Wild Grapes," in *Robert Frost: Collected Poems, Prose, and Plays* (New York: Library
of America, 1995), 847–48, 182–83, 185.

Anon., *Hymn to Dionysus,* in *The Homeric Hymns,* trans. Apostolos N. Athanassakis (Baltimore:
Johns Hopkins University Press, 1976), 56–57.

Milton, "A Masque of the Same Author Presented at Ludlow Castle, 1634, before the Earl of
Bridgewater Then President of Wales," ll. 46–49, 54–58, in *John Milton,* ed. Stephen Orgel
and Jonathan Goldberg (Oxford: Oxford University Press, 1991), 46.

Mark I. Davies, "Sailing, Rowing, and Sporting in One's Cups on the Wine-Dark Sea," in
Athens Comes of Age, From Solon to Salamis (Princeton: Archaeological Institute of America, 1978), 76.

796   François Lissarrague, *The Aesthetics of the Greek Banquet, Images of Wine and Ritual,* trans. Andrew Szegedy-Maszak (Princeton: Princeton University Press, 1990), 122.

Exekias, Dionysus Crossing the Sea, in *A History of 1000 Years of Greek Vase Painting* (New York: Harry N. Abrams, 1961) by P. E. Arias, Max Hirmer, and Brian Shefton, col. pl. 16.

CHAPTER 19: WINE

Prehistory

Don Brothwell and Patricia Brothwell, *Food in Antiquity,* expanded ed. (Baltimore: Johns Hopkins University Press, 1998), 168–69.

Patrick E. McGovern, "Wine For Eternity" and "Wine's Prehistory," *Archaeology* (July–Aug. 1998): 32.

Holley Martlew, "Minoans and Mycenaeans: Flavours of Their Time," *Minerva,* 10, no. 5 (Sept.–Oct. 1999): 33–36.

Greece

Homer, *Odyssey* 9.353–59; trans. Alexander Pope, in *The Odyssey of Homer,* books I–XII, ed. Maynard Mack (London: Methuen & Co., 1967), 323; trans. Richmond Lattimore, in *The Odyssey of Homer* (New York: Harper Perennial, 1991), 146.

George Sherburn, "The Ethics of Collaboration," chap. 9 in *The Early Career of Alexander Pope* (Oxford: Clarendon Press, 1934), 260.

Jean-Pierre-Vernant, "Odysseus in Person," *Representations* 67 (summer 1999): 9.

Lissarrague, *Aesthetics of the Greek Banquet,* 10.

Plato, *The Laws* 2.666a–c; in *The Laws of Plato,* trans. Thomas L. Pangle (New York: Basic Books, 1980), 47.

Kenneth McLeish, "Translator's Introduction," in *Aristophanes, Plays: Two* (London: Methuen, 1993), xxviii.

Aristophanes, *Thesmophoriazousai* 692–95, 733–38; Aristophanes, *Festival Time,* in *Aristophanes, Plays: Two,* trans. Kenneth McLeish, 269, 271, 273; Aristophanes, *Women at the Thesmophoria,* trans. Jeffrey Henderson (New York: Routledge, 1996), 120, 121–22.

Alan H. Sommerstein, trans., *Thesmophoriazusae,* vol. 8. of *The Comedies of Aristophanes* (Warminster, U.K.: Aris and Phillips, 1994), frontispiece.

Oliver Taplin, *Comic Angels and Other Approaches to Greek Drama through Vase-Paintings* (Oxford: Clarendon Press, 1993), plate 11.4.

James N. Davidson, *Courtesans and Fishcakes: The Consuming Passions of Classical Athens* (New York: HarperCollins, 1997), 53, 58–59.

Athenaeus, 11.462c–f; in *The Deipnosophists,* vol. 5, trans. Charles Burton Gulick (Cambridge: Harvard University Press, 1937), 15–17.

Oxford Classical Dictionary, 3d ed., s.v. "symposium."

Athenaeus 13.603e–604d; in *The Deipnosophists,* vol. 6, trans. Gulick, 253–57.

Hesiod, *The Works and Days,* ll. 744–45; in *Hesiod, The Works and Days,* trans. Richmond Lattimore (Ann Arbor: University of Michigan Press, 1959), 107.

Athenaeus 10.427a, quoting Anacreon, "Come and bring a bowl," in *Early Greek Lyric Poetry,* trans. David Mulroy (Ann Arbor: University of Michigan Press, 1992), 130.

Athenaeus 15.693d, quoting Theophrastus, in *The Deipnosophists,* vol. 7, trans. Gulick, 213.

Andrew Dalby, *Siren Feasts* (London: Routledge, 1996), 103, 93–4, 99–100.

Pindar, *Olympian* 9.48; in *The Odes of Pindar,* trans. Richmond Lattimore (Chicago: University of Chicago Press, 1947), 28.

Lissarrague, *Aesthetics of the Greek Banquet,* 123–24.

Davidson, *Courtesans and Fishcakes,* 68.

The Anacreontea

Kathryn J. Gutzwiller, *Poetic Garlands: Hellenistic Epigrams in Context* (Berkeley and Los Angeles: University of California Press, 1998), 120.

Asclepiades, "Wine tests for love," in Gutzwiller, *Poetic Garlands,* 125.

Posidippus, "Sprinkle, Cecropian jug," in Gutzwiller, *Poetic Garlands,* 157.

Gutzwiller, *Poetic Garlands,* 157–58.

Posidippus, *Greek Anthology* 5.183; "We are four at the party," in *The Greek Anthology,* vol. 1, trans. W. R. Paton (London: William Heinemann, 1916), 219.

Hedylus, "Let us drink," in Gutzwiller, *Poetic Garlands,* 179.

Gutzwiller, *Poetic Garlands,* 181–82.

Plato the Younger, *Greek Anthology* 9.748; trans. Alan Cameron, in Cameron, *The Greek Anthology from Meleager to Planudes* (Oxford: Clarendon Press, 1993), 269.

Theocritus, *Epigrams* 9; in *Theocritus: Idylls and Epigrams,* trans. Daryl Hine (New York: Atheneum, 1982), 114.

Rome

Virgil, *Georgics* 2.1–8, 103–8; in *The Eclogues, The Georgics,* trans. C. Day Lewis (Oxford: Oxford University Press, 1983), 69, 72.

Jancis Robinson, *Jancis Robinson's Guide to Wine Grapes* (Oxford: Oxford University Press, 1996), 4.

Pliny the Elder, *Natural History* 14.142; in *Natural History: A Selection,* trans. John F. Healy (London: Penguin, 1991), 192–93.

Horace, *Odes* 1.20; in *Horace's Odes and Epodes,* trans. David Mulroy (Ann Arbor: University of Michigan Press, 1994), 79–80.

Horace, *Odes* 3.21; in *The Odes of Horace,* trans. James Michie (New York: Orion, 1963), 230–33.

Valerius Maximus, *Memorable Deeds and Sayings* 6.3.9, trans. Fant, in *Women's Life in Greece and Rome: A Source Book in Translation,* 2d ed., ed. Mary R. Lefkowitz and Maureen B. Fant (Baltimore: Johns Hopkins University Press, 1992), 96.

Aulus Gellius, *Attic Nights* 10.23, trans. Fant, in *Women's Life in Greece and Rome: A Source Book in Translation,* ed. Lefkowitz and Fant, 97.

Davidson, *Courtesans and Fishcakes,* 54.

Jews and Christians

Job 32:17–19; in *Sacred Writings, Judaism: The Tanakh,* new JPS trans. (New York: Book-of-the-Month Club, 1992), 1385.

Maccabees 2:15.38–39; in *The Apocrypha and the New Testament: The Revised English Bible* (New York: Quality Paperback Book Club, 1992), 205.

798   Baruch M. Bokser, *The Origins of the Seder: The Passover Rite and Early Rabbinic Judaism* (Berkeley and Los Angeles: University of California Press, 1984), 63.

Amos 9:13–14; in *Sacred Writings, Judaism: The Tanakh,* new JPS trans., 1031.

Leviticus 10:8; in *Sacred Writings, Judaism: The Tanakh,* new JPS trans., 167.

Gillian Feely-Harnik, *The Lord's Table: The Meaning of Food in Early Judaism and Christianity* (Washington. D.C.: Smithsonian Institution Press, 1994), 156.

Proverbs 23:29–35; in *Sacred Writings, Judaism: The Tanakh,* new JPS trans., 1323–24.

John 2:10, 13:1, 13:26, New Oxford Annotated Bible.

Luke 22:20, New Oxford Annotated Bible.

Irenaeus, *Against Heresies* 1.13.1–4, trans. Fant, in *Women's Life in Greece and Rome: A Source Book in Translation,* ed. Lefkowitz and Fant, 323.

Apicius, *The Art of Cooking* 1.5; in *The Roman Cookery Book,* trans. Barbara Flower and Elisabeth Rosenbaum (London: George G. Harrap, 1958), 47.

Cyprian, Epistle 63, to Caecilius, quoted in Joseph A. Jungmann, *The Mass of the Roman Rite: Its Origin and Development,* trans. Francis A. Brunner and Charles K. Riepe (Westminster, Md.: Christian Classics, 1959), 333.

Clement of Alexandria, *Christ the Educator* 2.33.1–4, trans. Lefkowitz, in *Women's Life in Greece and Rome: A Source Book in Translation,* ed. Lefkowitz and Fant, 324–25.

Late Antiquity

Longus, *Daphnis and Chloe* 2.1; in *Collected Ancient Greek Novels,* ed. B. P. Reardon, trans. Christopher Gill (Berkeley and Los Angeles: University of California Press, 1989), 303.

Julian the Egyptian, *Greek Anthology* 7.32; in *Poems from the Greek Anthology,* trans. Dudley Fitts (New York: New Directions, 1956), 141; in *Two Hundred Poems from the Greek Anthology,* trans. Robin Skelton (Seattle: University of Washington Press, 1971), 25.

Anacreontea 5; in *Greek Lyric,* vol. 2, trans. David A. Campbell (Cambridge: Harvard University Press, 1988), 167–69.

Anacreontea 6; in *Greek Lyric,* vol. 2, trans. Campbell, 169.

Herrick, "Upon Cupid," in *The Complete Poetry of Robert Herrick,* ed. J. Max Patrick (New York: Anchor, 1963), 134.

H. J. Rose, "Mythological Introduction," in *Dionysiaca,* by Nonnos, vol. 1, trans. W. H. D. Rouse (Cambridge: Harvard University Press, 1995), x.

Neil Hopkinson, introduction to *Studies in the* Dionysiaca *of Nonnus,* ed. Neil Hopkinson, supp. vol. 17 (Cambridge: Cambridge Philological Society, 1994), 5.

Glen Bowersock, "Dionysos as an Epic Hero," in *Studies in the* Dionysiaca *of Nonnus,* ed. Hopkinson, supp. vol. 17, 156.

Hopkinson, "Nonnus and Homer," in *Studies in the* Dionysiaca *of Nonnus,* ed. Hopkinson, supp. vol. 17, 9.

Nonnos, *Dionysiaca* 11.351–52; in *Dionysiaca,* vol. 1, trans. W. H. D. Rouse (Cambridge: Harvard University Press, 1995), 383.

Nonnos, *Dionysiaca* 12.23–28, 12.173–87, 193–208, 293, 363–75; in *Dionysiaca,* vol. 1, trans. Rouse, 399, 411, 413, 419, 423–25.

Nonnos, *Dionysiaca* 14.11–17; in *Dionysiaca,* vol. 1, trans. Rouse, 501.

Nonnos, *Dionysiaca* 15.15–25; in *Dionysiaca,* vol. 1, trans. Rouse, 503–5.

Hopkinson, "Nonnus and Homer," 9.

Anon., "Dancing Girl of Syria," trans. Helen Waddell, in *Mediaeval Latin Lyrics*, 4th ed. (Harmondsworth, England: Penguin, 1968), 13–15, 294.

Luxorius, "To a Drunkard Who Eats Nothing But Is Forever Drinking" and "To a Drunken Woman Who Passes Water Copiously," in *Luxorius: A Latin Poet among the Vandals* by Morris Rosenblum (New York: Columbia University Press, 1961), 127, 157.

The Wine Song in Arabic and Hebrew

Alistair Forbes, "Tales from Old Tangier," *Times Literary Supplement,* 30 Nov. 1979, 56.

Thomas F. Glick, "Convivencia: An Introductory Note," in *Convivencia: Jews, Muslims, and Christians in Medieval Spain,* ed. Vivian B. Mann, Thomas F. Glick, and Jerrilynn D. Dodds (New York: George Braziller/The Jewish Museum, 1992), 1.

Jane D. McAuliffe, "The Wines of Earth and Paradise: Qur'anic Proscriptions and Promises," in *Logos Islamikos,* ed. Roger M. Savory and Dionisius A. Agius (Toronto: Pontifical Institute of Mediaeval Studies, 1984), 159.

Abu Nuwas, "A censurer censured me . . . ," in *The Wine Song in Classical Arabic Poetry: Abu Nuwas and the Literary Tradition* by Philip F. Kennedy (Oxford: Clarendon Press, 1997), 266, 175.

Nuwas, "Splendid young blades . . . ," in Kennedy, *The Wine Song in Classical Arabic Poetry: Abu Nuwas and the Literary Tradition,* 268–70, 232–36.

Raymond P. Scheindlin, "Wine," chap. 1 in *Wine, Women, and Death: Medieval Hebrew Poems on the Good Life* (Philadelphia: Jewish Publication Society, 1986), 19–20, 11.

Ibn Hisn, "El Reflejo del Vino" and "Los Vasos," in *Poemas Arabigoandaluces,* 7th ed., ed. Emilio García Gómez (Madrid: Espasa-Calpe, 1982), 66, 125.

Ibn Hisn, "Reflection of Wine," in *Poems of Arab Andalusia,* trans. Cola Franzen (San Francisco: City Lights Books, 1989), 6.

Ibn al-Yamani, "The Goblets," in *Poems of Arab Andalusia,* trans. Cola Franzen (San Francisco: City Lights Books, 1989), 13.

James T. Monroe, *Hispano-Arabic Poetry: A Student Anthology* (Berkeley and Los Angeles: University of California Press, 1974), 41–42.

Ibn Quzman, "My life is spent in dissipation and wantonness," trans. James T. Monroe, in *Hispano-Arabic Poetry: A Student Anthology,* ed. Monroe, 260–64.

Dunash ben Labrat, "The Poet Refuses an Invitation to Drink," in *The Penguin Book of Hebrew Verse,* trans. T. Carmi (New York: Penguin, 1981), 97, 280.

Dunash ben Labrat, "There came a voice: 'Awake!,'" in Scheindlin, *Wine, Women, and Death: Medieval Hebrew Poems on the Good Life,* 41–42.

Samuel Hanagid, "My friend, we pass our lives as if in sleep," in Scheindlin, *Wine, Women, and Death: Medieval Hebrew Poems on the Good Life,* 55, 58–59.

Anon., "The Drunkard's Testament," in *The Penguin Book of Hebrew Verse,* trans. Carmi, 448–49.

Medieval Latin and Vernacular

Walafrid Strabo, *De Cultura Hortorum,* in *Poetry of the Carolingian Renaissance,* trans. Peter Godman (London: Duckworth, 1985), 225.

Howard Mumford Jones, trans., "The Abbot of Angers," in *The Romanesque Lyric: Studies in Its Background and Development from Petronius to the Cambridge Songs 50–1050* by Philip Schuyler Allen (Chapel Hill: University of North Carolina Press, 1928), 239, 352.

Helen Waddell, *The Wandering Scholars,* 6th ed. (Garden City, N.Y.: Doubleday Anchor, 1955), 56.

800   Anon., "Potatores Exquisiti," trans. George F. Whicher, in *The Goliard Poets: Medieval Latin Songs and Satires,* ed. Whicher (New York: New Directions, 1949), 234–37.

Anon., "Hear the truth! It's plain, unvarnished," trans. David Parlett, in *Selections from the Carmina Burana: A Verse Translation,* ed. Parlett (Harmondsworth, England: Penguin, 1986), 158–64.

R. W. Southern, *Robert Grosseteste: The Growth of an English Mind in Medieval Europe* (Oxford: Clarendon Press, 1986), 178–79.

George Philip Krapp and Elliott van Kirk Dobbie, ed., riddle 11 in *The Exeter Book* (New York: Columbia University Press, 1936), 186, 327.

Kevin Crossley-Holland, trans., riddle 11 in *The Exeter Book of Riddles,* rev. ed. (London: Penguin, 1993), 15, 89.

Peter Potter, "Let us sing merrily ho!," trans. Frits Pieter van Oostrom, in *Court and Culture: Dutch Literature, 1350–1450,* trans. Arnold J. Pomerans (Berkeley and Los Angeles: University of California Press, 1992), 267.

Anon., "Tabart is y-dronken," in *Medieval English Lyrics, 1200–1400,* ed. Thomas G. Duncan (Harmondsworth, England: Penguin, 1995), 244.

Anon., "Wine, wine from the Rhine," in *The Penguin Book of German Verse,* ed. and trans. Leonard Forster (Harmondsworth, England: Penguin, 1972), 79.

Jean Bodel, *Le Jeu de Sainte-Nicholas,* ll. 645–53, in *Medieval French Plays,* trans. Richard Axton and John Stevens (Oxford: Basil Blackwell, 1971), 99.

Jane Welch Williams, *Bread, Wine, and Money: The Windows of the Trades at Chartres Cathedral* (Chicago: University of Chicago Press, 1993), 80, 77, 34, 82, col. pl. 2.

Henry Adams, *Mont Saint Michel and Chartres,* chap. 10; in *Henry Adams: Novels, Mont San Michel, The Education* (New York: Library of America, 1983), 507.

Williams, *Bread, Wine, and Money,* 101, 100.

Anon., *Courtois d'Arras,* ll. 103–9, in *Medieval French Plays,* trans. Axton and Stevens, 144.

Rosemary Woolf, "The Decline of the Plays," chap. 14 in *The English Mystery Plays* (Berkeley and Los Angeles: University of California Press, 1972), 312.

Donald C. Baker, John L. Murphy, and Louis B. Hall, *The Late Medieval Religious Plays of Bodleian MSS Digby 133 and E Museo 160* (Oxford: Oxford University Press, 1982), xlvi–xlvii.

Darryll Grantley, "Saints' Plays," in *The Cambridge Companion to Medieval English Theatre,* ed. Richard Beadle (Cambridge: Cambridge University Press, 1994), 278–79.

Anon., *Mary Magdalen,* ll. 470–80, in Baker, Murphy, and Hall, *The Late Medieval Religious Plays of Bodleian MSS Digby 133 and E Museo 160,* 39.

Ann Rycraft, "Food in Medieval Drama," in *Food in the Arts,* ed. Harlan Walker (Devon, U.K.: Prospect Books, 1999), 171n. 27.

Renaissance

Giovanni Pontano, "He Amuses Himself, Poetically," in *An Anthology of Neo-Latin Poetry,* trans. Fred J. Nichols (New Haven: Yale University Press, 1979), 19, 143, 145, 147.

Angelo Poliziano, *Testi,* vol. 1 of *Angelo Poliziano, Poesie Volgari,* ed. Francesco Bausi (Rome: Vecchiarelli, 1997), 55–56.

Poliziano, "Bacchanal," in *Italian Poets of the Renaissance,* trans. Joseph Tusiani (Long Island: Baroque Press, 1971), 99.

Leonardo Da Vinci, *The Notebooks of Leonardo Da Vinci,* vol. 2, ed. and trans. Jean Paul Richter (New York: Dover, 1970), 348.

Harry Vredeveld, introduction to *Poems,* vol. 85 of *Collected Works of Erasmus* (Toronto: University of Toronto Press, 1993), xxiv.

Desiderius Erasmus, "An epitaph for a drunken jokester, in scazons," in *Poems,* vol. 85 of *Collected Works of Erasmus,* trans. Clarence Miller, 122–23.

Vredeveld, *Notes to Poems,* line 11, in *Collected Works of Erasmus,* vol. 86 (Toronto: University of Toronto Press, 1993), 522.

Pierre de Ronsard, *Odes* 2.10; in *Introduction to French Poetry,* trans. Stanley Appelbaum (New York: Dover, 1991), 46–47.

Rabelais, *Gargantua and Pantagruel* 1.5; in *The Complete Works of François Rabelais,* trans. Donald M. Frame (Berkeley and Los Angeles: University of California Press, 1991), 15–17, 20.

Mikhail Bakhtin, *Rabelais and His World,* trans,. Hélène Iswolsky (Bloomington: Indiana University Press, 1984), 224.

Princeton Encyclopedia of Poetry and Poetics, enlarged ed., s.v. "pattern poetry."

Rabelais, *Gargantua and Pantagruel* 5.44; in *The Complete Works of François Rabelais,* trans. Frame, 706–8.

Montaigne, "Of Drunkenness," in *The Complete Essays of Montaigne,* trans. Donald M. Frame (Stanford, Calif.: Stanford University Press, 1958), 245–51.

M. A. Screech, *Montaigne and Melancholy:The Wisdom of the Essays* (London: Penguin, 1991), 40–41.

Montaigne,"Apology for Raymond Sebond," in *The Complete Essays of Montaigne,* trans. Frame, 363.

Jean Le Houx, "Fair nose: whose rubies many pipes have cost" and "The wine-glass is the brush thy form to show," in *Vaux-de-Vire of Maistre Jean Le Houx,* ed. and trans. James Patrick Muirhead (London: John Murray, 1875), 10–11, 13, 123.

Giovanni della Casa, *Galateo, or the Book of Manners,* trans. R. S. Pine-Coffin (Harmondsworth, England: Penguin, 1958), 99–100.

Seventeenth Century

Francesco Redi, "Bacchus in Toscany," in *From Marino to Marinetti: An Anthology of Forty Italian Poets Translated into English Verse,* trans. Joseph Tusiani (New York: Baroque Press, 1974), 30–31, 34.

J. E. Morpurgo, ed., *The Autobiography of Leigh Hunt* (London: Cresset Press, 1949), 374–75.

Redi,"Bacchus in Toscany," trans. Leigh Hunt, in *The Poetical Works of Leigh Hunt,* ed. H. S. Milford (London: Oxford University Press, 1923), 468, 475, 481.

Johan van Beverwyck, *Schat der gesontheyt, Schat der ongesontheyt,* quoted by Julie Berger Hochstrasser in "Feasting the Eye: Painting and Reality in the Seventeenth-century 'Bancketje,'" in *Still-Life Paintings from the Netherlands, 1550–1720,* ed. Alan Chong and Wouter Kloek (Zwolle, Netherlands: Waanders, 1999), 75, 83n. 20.

William Shakespeare, *Antony and Cleopatra,* ed. John Wilders (London: Routledge, 1995), 55.

Shakespeare, *Antony and Cleopatra* 2.7.106–18; in *Antony and Cleopatra,* ed. Wilders, 169–70.

Geoffrey Bullough, ed., *Narrative and Dramatic Sources of Shakespeare,* vol. 5 (London: Routledge and Kegan Paul, 1964), 278–79.

Richard Madelaine, ed., *Antony and Cleopatra* (Cambridge: Cambridge University Press, 1998), 203.

Shakespeare, *The Tempest* 2.2.111–20, 169–83; in *The Tempest,* ed. Stephen Orgel (Oxford: Oxford University Press, 1987), 148–49, 151.

Ben Jonson, "Inviting a Friend to Supper," in *Poems of Ben Jonson,* ed. George Burke Johnston (Cambridge: Harvard University Press, 1962), ll. 28–34.

802 David Riggs, *Ben Jonson: A Life* (Cambridge: Harvard University Press, 1989), 230.

Joseph Loewenstein, "Jonsonian Corpulence; or, The Poet as Mouthpiece," *English Literary History* 53, no. 3 (fall 1986): 504, 501.

Miguel de Cervantes, *Don Quixote de la Mancha*, pt. 2, chap. 13; trans. Samuel Putnam (New York: Viking, 1949), 589–90.

Hume, "Of the Standard of Taste," in *David Hume, Essays, Moral, Political, and Literary*, rev. ed., ed. Eugene F. Miller (Indianapolis: Liberty Classics, 1987), 235.

Herrick "Anacreontick Verse," in *The Complete Poetry of Robert Herrick*, ed. J. Max Patrick (New York: Anchor, 1963), 407–8.

Ann Baynes Coiro, *Robert Herrick's* Hesperides *and the Epigram Book Tradition* (Baltimore: Johns Hopkins University Press, 1988), 125–27.

Herrick "His age, dedicated to his peculiar friend, Master John Wickes, under the name of *Posthumus*," ll. 83–4, 93–4; in *The Complete Poetry of Robert Herrick*, ed. Patrick, 181–83.

Anon., "Would you be a man of fashion?," in *Seventeenth Century Lyrics*, 2d ed., ed. Norman Ault (New York: William Sloane, 1950), 422.

Rochester, "Upon His Drinking a Bowl," in *John Wilmot, Earl of Rochester: The Complete Works*, ed. Frank H. Ellis (London: Penguin, 1994), 335, 38.

Henry Aldrich, "If all be true that I do think," Ault, ed. *Seventeenth Century Lyrics*, 443.

Jacob Balde, "In Praise of Wine to Flavius Leo," in *Jesuit Latin Poets of the 17th and 18th Centuries: An Anthology of Neo-Latin Poetry*, trans. James J. Mertz (Wauconda, Ill.: Bolchazy-Carducci, 1989), 105.

James Anderson Winn, *John Dryden and His World* (New Haven: Yale University Press, 1987), 493.

John Dryden, "Alexander's Feast or the Power of Music," in *John Dryden*, ed. Keith Walker (Oxford: Oxford University Press, 1987), 546, 548, 550.

Raymond Carver, "Wine," in *All of Us: The Collected Poems* (New York: Alfred A. Knopf, 1998), 246–47.

Johannes Torrentius, *Allegory of Temperance*, in *Still-Life Paintings from the Netherlands, 1550–1720*, ed. Alan Chong, Wouter Kloek, and Betsy Wieseman (Zwolle, Netherlands: Waanders, 1999), 132–34.

Constantijn Huygens, "Prayer for the Holy Communion," in *A Selection of the Poems of Sir Constantijn Huygens, 1596–1687*, ed. Peter Davidson and Adriaan van der Weel (Amsterdam: Amsterdam University Press, 1996), 113.

The Parodic and the Typological

Anon., "Blessed Art They Who Live in Your Tabernacle," in *Parody in the Middle Ages: The Latin Tradition* by Martha Bayless (Ann Arbor: University of Michigan Press, 1996), 99, 342–43.

Mikhail Bakhtin, *Rabelais and His World*, trans. Iswolsky, 14, 295.

C. A. Patrides, ed., *The English Poems of George Herbert* (London: Dent, 1974), 26.

George Herbert, "The Bunch of Grapes," in *The English Poems of George Herbert*, ed. Patrides, 139–40.

Eighteenth Century

Horace, *Epistles* 1.19.2–3; in *Horace Satires, Epistles and Ars Poetica*, trans. H. Rushton Fairclough (London: William Heinemann, 1929), 380–81.

John Gay, "Wine," in *John Gay Poetry and Prose* , vol. 1, ed. Vinton Dearing and Charles E. Beck-   803
with (Oxford: Clarendon Press, 1974), 21, 5–6.

Edward Taylor, Meditation 98, 2d series; in *The Poems of Edward Taylor,* ed. Donald E. Stanford
(New Haven: Yale University Press, 1960) 258–59.

Boswell's Life of Johnson, 16 Mar. 1776, 28 Apr. 1778, 7 Apr. 1779; ed. R. W. Chapman (London:
Oxford University Press, 1965), 687, 974–75, 1016.

Vasilii N. Maikov, *Elisei, or Bacchus Enraged: A Poem,* in vol. 2 of *The Literature of Eighteenth-Century
Russia,* ed. and trans. Harold B. Segel (New York: Dutton, 1967), 130–31, 154–55, 171–72.

Evelyn Bristol, *A History of Russian Poetry* (New York: Oxford University Press, 1991), 64–65.

Ludwig Hölty, "Duties of Life," in *Introduction to German Poetry,* trans. Gustave Mathieu and Guy
Stern (New York: Dover, 1991), 36–37.

Johann Wolfgang von Goethe, "The King in Thule," in *Selected Poems,* ed. Christopher Middleton, trans. John Frederick Nims (London: John Calder, 1983), 34–35.

Goethe, "Roman Elegy XV (XVIII)," trans. David Luke, in *Johann Wolfgang von Goethe, Roman
Elegies and The Diary* (London: Libris, 1988), 79.

David Luke, ed. and trans., *Goethe* (Harmondsworth, England: Penguin, 1985), xxvii.

Ovid, *Amores* 2.5.16–18; in *Ovid: The Erotic Poems,* trans. Peter Green (Harmondsworth, England: Penguin, 1982), 117.

Nineteenth Century

Fernand Braudel, *The Structures of Everyday Life: The Limits of the Possible,* vol. 1 of *Civilization
and Capitalism 15th–18th Century,* trans. Miriam Kochan and Siân Reynolds (New York:
Harper and Row, 1981), 241.

Lord Byron to James Hogg, 24 Mar. 1814, *Byron's Letters and Journals,* vol. 4, ed. Leslie A. Marc-
hand (Cambridge: Harvard University Press, 1975), 85.

Lord Byron, *Don Juan* 2.178–80, 15.65.7–8; in *Lord Byron: The Complete Poetical Works,* vol. 5,
ed. Jerome J. McGann (Oxford: Clarendon Press, 1986), 144–45, 608.

Vladimir Nabokov, trans., commentary, pt. 1 in *Eugene Onegin: A Novel in Verse by Aleksandr
Pushkin,* rev. ed., vol. 2 (Princeton: Princeton University Press, 1975), 161, viii, 10.

Pushkin, *Eugene Onegin* 4.45–6; in *Eugene Onegin: A Novel in Verse by Aleksandr Pushkin,* rev. ed.,
vol. 1, 196.

Eugene Baratinski, *The Feasts,* ll. 129–39; in *Eugene Onegin,* vol. 2., trans. Vladimir Nabokov,
481–82.

Anya Taylor, "Coleridge, Keats, Lamb, and Seventeenth-Century Drinking Songs," in *Milton, the
Metaphysicals, and Romanticism,* ed. Lisa Low and Anthony John Harding (Cambridge:
Cambridge University Press, 1994).

Keats, "Lines on the Mermaid Tavern," in *John Keats, Complete Poems,* ed. Jack Stillinger (Cambridge: Harvard University Press, 1982), 166.

Keats, "Hence Burgundy, Claret & port," in *The Letters of John Keats,* vol. 1, ed. Hyder Edward
Rollins (Cambridge: Harvard University Press, 1958), 220–21; Keats, "Hence burgundy,
claret, and port," in *John Keats, Complete Poems,* ed. Jack Stillinger (Cambridge: Harvard
University Press, 1982), 168.

Keats to Fanny Keats, 1 May (?) 1819; Rollins, ed., *Letters of Keats,* vol. 2, 56.

Keats, "Ode to a Nightingale," in *John Keats, Complete Poems,* ed. Stillinger, 280.

Keats to Benjamin Bailey, 14 Aug. 1819; Rollins, ed., *Letters of Keats,* vol. 2, 139.

804   Keats to Fanny Brawne, 24 (?) Feb. 1820; Rollins, ed., *Letters of Keats,* vol. 2, 265.

Keats to George and Georgiana Keats, 19 Feb. 1819; Rollins, ed., *Letters of Keats,* vol. 2, 64.

Willard Bissell Pope, ed., *The Diary of Benjamin Robert Haydon,* vol. 2 (Cambridge: Harvard University Press, 1960), 317.

Anya Taylor, "Coleridge, Keats, Lamb, and Seventeenth-century Drinking Songs," in *Milton, the Metaphysicals, and Romanticism,* 232.

Anya Taylor, *Bacchus in Romantic England: Writers and Drink, 1780–1830* (London: Macmillan, 1999), 187.

Keats, "Lamia," pt., 2, ll. 199–205, 209–213; in *John Keats, Complete Poems,* ed. Stillinger, 356.

William Wordsworth, *The Prelude* [1850], bk. 3, ll. 296–305; in *William Wordsworth: The Prelude, A Parallel Text,* ed. J. C. Maxwell (Harmondsworth, England: Penguin, 1971), 117, 119.

Charles Baudelaire, "The Soul of the Wine," in *Les Fleurs du Mal,* trans. Richard Howard (Boston: David R. Godine, 1982), 113, 291.

Andrew Clements, record notes to *Alban Berg, 3 Orchesterstücke op. 6, 7 frühe Lieder, Der Wein,* Deutsche Grammophon 445 846-2, 1995.

Douglas Jarman, "Secret Programmes," in *The Cambridge Companion to Berg,* ed. Anthony Pople (Cambridge: Cambridge University Press, 1997), 170.

Flaubert, pt. 1, sect. 8 of *Madame Bovary,* trans. Francis Steegmuller (New York: Random House, 1957), 54, vi, 55.

Émile Zola, *L'Assommoir,* trans. Leonard Tancock (Harmondsworth, England: Penguin, 1970), 17, 217–18, 194.

Edgar Allan Poe, "The Cask of Amontillado," in *Tales and Sketches, 1843–1849,* ed. Thomas Ollive Mabbott, vol. 3 of *Collected Works of Edgar Allan Poe* (Cambridge, Mass.: Harvard University Press, 1978), 1252.

David S. Reynolds, "Poe's Art of Transformation: 'The Cask of Amontillado' in Its Cultural Context," in *New Essays on Poe's Major Tales,* ed. Kenneth Silverman (Cambridge: Cambridge University Press, 1993), 93–112.

Lois Hyslop and Francis E. Hyslop, Jr., *Baudelaire on Poe* (State College, Pa.: Bald Eagle Press, 1952).

George Meredith, *The Egoist,* rev. ed., ed. Margaret Harris (Oxford: Oxford University Press, 1992), 148, 198, 202, 249.

Robert James Merrett, "Port and Claret: The Politics of Wine in Trollope's Barsetshire Novels," *Mosaic* 24, no. 3/4 (summer/fall 1991): 122.

Stéphane Mallarmé, "Salut," in *Mallarmé: The Poems, A Bilingual Edition,* trans. Keith Bosley (Harmondsworth, England: Penguin, 1977), 54.

Mallarmé, "Toast," in *Breath,* ed. Christopher Wilmarth, trans. Frederick Morgan (New York: Christopher Wilmarth, 1982), 36.

Roger Shattuck, "Worlds within Words," *New Republic,* 14 Nov. 1994, 40.

Dore Ashton, "Mallarmé, Friend of Artists," in Wilmarth, *Breath,* 22.

Joyce Tolliver, introduction to Emilia Pardo Bazán, *Torn Lace and Other Stories,* trans. María Christina Urruela (New York: Modern Language Association of America, 1996), ix.

Emilia Pardo Bazán, "Champagne," in *Torn Lace and Other Stories,* trans. Urruela, 69, 74.

Hugo von Hofmannsthal, "The Two," in *Twenty-five German Poets,* trans. Walter Kaufmann (New York: W. W. Norton, 1975), 189, 186.

Gaetano Donizetti, *Lucrezia Borgia,* libretto by Felice Romani, trans. Avril Bardoni, dir. Richard Bonynge (New York: Decca, 1979), 21, 27.

William Ashbrook, *Donizetti and His Operas* (Cambridge: Cambridge University Press, 1982),   *805*
82, 348, 351.

Giuseppe Verdi, "Libiamo," act 1 of *La Traviata,* vol. 4 of Nico Castel, trans., *The Complete Verdi Libretti* (Geneseo, N.Y.: Leyerle Publications, 1996), 256–58.

Joseph Kerman, "Opera, Novel, Drama: The Case of *La Traviata,*" *Yearbook of Comparative and General Literature* 27 (1978): 49.

Johann Strauss, Jr., Carl Haffner, and Richard Genée, *Die Fledermaus, or The Bat's Revenge,* trans. John Mortimer (New York: Viking, 1989), 12, 118–19.

Twentieth Century

Rainer Maria Rilke, "The Drunkard," in *The Voices, The Book of Images,* rev. ed., trans. Edward Snow (New York: Farrar, Straus and Giroux, 1994), 185, 190–91.

Rilke to Hermann Pongs, 21 Oct. 1924, in *Ahead of All Parting: The Selected Poetry and Prose of Rainer Maria Rilke,* trans. Stephen Mitchell (New York: Modern Library, 1995), 217.

Guillaume Apollinaire, "Rhenish Night," in *Alcools: Poems, 1898–1913,* trans. William Meredith (New York: Anchor, 1965), 156–57.

Francis Steegmuller, "Notes," in *Alcools: Poems, 1898–1913,* trans. Meredith, 231, 253.

Apollinaire, "Vendemiaire" (Vintage Month), in *Selected Writings of Guillaume Apollinaire,* trans. Roger Shattuck (New York: New Directions, 1971), 136–39.

S. I. Lockerbie, introduction to *Guillaume Apollinaire: Calligrammes, Poems of Peace and War, 1913–1916,* trans. Anne Hyde Greet (Berkeley and Los Angeles: University of California Press, 1980), 1–2, 3, 5.

Apollinaire, "Windows," in *Guillaume Apollinaire,* trans. Greet, 26–29, 354–55.

Apollinaire, "The Vine Grower of Champagne," in *Guillaume Apollinaire,* trans. Greet, 302–5, 483.

Peter Bien, *Constantine Cavafy* (New York: Columbia University Press, 1964), 42, 44.

George Savidis, note on "Waiting for the Barbarians," in *C. P. Cavafy: Collected Poems,* rev. ed., trans. Edmund Keeley and Philip Sherrard (Princeton: Princeton University Press, 1992), 221.

Constantine Cavafy, "The Retinue of Dionysos," in *C. P. Cavafy: Collected Poems,* trans. Keeley and Sherrard, 24.

Cavafy, "Dionysos and His Crew," in *The Complete Poems of Cavafy,* trans. Rae Dalven (New York: Harcourt, Brace and World, 1961), 23.

Cavafy, "The Procession of Dionysos," in *The Canon,* vol. 1 of *The Greek Poems of C. P. Cavafy,* trans. Memas Kolaitis (New Rochelle, N.Y.: Aristide D. Caratzas, 1989), 24.

Cavafy, "Craftsman of Wine Bowls," in *C. P. Cavafy: Collected Poems,* trans. Keeley and Sherrard, 119.

Jaroslav Seifert, "A Ballad from the Champagne," in *The Early Poetry of Jarolav Seifert,* trans. Dana Loewy (Evanston, Ill.: Hydra Books, Northwestern University Press, 1997), 184–85.

Seifert, "Spanish Vineyards," in *The Poetry of Jaroslav Seifert,* trans. Ewald Osers (North Haven, Conn.: Catbird Press, 1998), 50.

Paul Valéry, "The Lost Wine," in *Poems, On Poets and Poetry,* vol. 1 of *The Collected Works of Paul Valéry,* ed. Jackson Mathews, trans. David Paul (Princeton: Princeton University Press, 1971), 208–9, 462.

Valéry, "Wasted Wine," trans. Olga Marx, *Quarterly Review of Literature* 3, no. 3 (1947): 265.

G. K. Chesterton, "Wine and Water," in *A G. K. Chesterton Anthology,* ed. P. J. Kavanagh (San Francisco: Ignatius Press, 1985), 353–54.

806   Theodore Zeldin, *France, 1848–1945: Taste and Corruption* (Oxford: Oxford University Press 1980), 412.

James Joyce, "Rouen is the rainiest place getting," in Joyce to Harriet Shaw Weaver, 15 Aug. 1925; Richard Ellmann, ed., *Selected Letters of James Joyce* (New York: Viking, 1976), 309.

Richard Ellmann, *James Joyce,* rev. ed. (Oxford: Oxford University Press, 1983), 572, 455.

Joyce, *Finnegans Wake* (New York: Viking, 1939), 171.

Robert Desnos, "Coming Harvests" and "Verse on the Glass of Wine," in *The Selected Poems of Robert Desnos,* trans. Carolyn Forché and William Kulik (New York: Ecco Press, 1991), 131, 142.

H. D., "Wine Bowl," in *Collected Poems, 1912–1944,* ed. Louis L. Martz (New York: New Directions, 1983), 241–42.

Nizar Kabbani, "I am afraid," in *Arabian Love Poems,* trans. Bassam K. Frangieh and Clementina R. Brown (Boulder: Lynne Rienner, 1999), 219, 5.

Diane Wakoski, "Champagne Light," in *The Emerald City of Las Vegas* (Santa Rosa, Calif.: Black Sparrow Press, 1995), 167–69.

A. J. Liebling, "A Good Appetite," in *Between Meals: An Appetite for Paris* (San Francisco: North Point Press, 1986), 21, 24, 26.

Roald Dahl, "Taste," in *Someone Like You* (New York: Alfred A. Knopf, 1953); Alexis Bespaloff, ed., *The Fireside Book of Wine: An Anthology for Wine Drinkers* (New York: Simon and Schuster, 1977).

Stanley Ellin, "The Last Bottle in the World," in Bespaloff, ed., *The Fireside Book of Wine,* 399.

Hugh Johnson, *How to Enjoy Wine* (New York: Simon and Schuster, 1985), 14–15.

Doris Lessing, "Wine," in *Stories* (New York: Alfred A. Knopf, 1978), 87, 91–92.

A. A. Milne, "In Vino Veritas," in *Murder and Other Acts of Literature,* ed. Michele Slung (New York: Barnes and Noble, 1997), 297–313.

John Hollander, "Thanks for a Bottle," in *Harp Lake* (New York: Alfred Knopf, 1988), 47.

Tom Stevenson, "Chateau Beychevelle," in *The New Sotheby's Wine Encyclopedia* (New York: DK Publishing, 1997), 83.

Hollander, "For a Thirtieth Birthday with a Bottle of Burgundy," in *Movie-Going and Other Poems* (New York: Atheneum, 1962), 37.

Emile Peynaud, *The Taste of Wine: The Art and Science of Wine Appreciation,* trans. Michael Schuster (San Francisco: Wine Appreciation Guild, 1987), 35.

Hollander, *Types of Shape,* new and expanded ed. (New Haven: Yale University Press, 1991), xiv.

Hollander, "Blue Wine," in *Blue Wine and Other Poems* (Baltimore: Johns Hopkins University Press, 1979), back cover, 3–6; Hollander, *Selected Poetry* (New York: Alfred A. Knopf, 1995), 109–12, 334.

Arthur Rimbaud, "The Drunken Boat," in *Rimbaud,* trans. Oliver Bernard (Harmondsworth, England: Penguin, 1962), 166.

Ricardo Reis, "Not only wine but its oblivion I pour," in *Fernando Pessoa and Co.: Selected Poems,* ed. and trans. Richard Zenith (New York: Grove Press, 1998), 126, 97.

Pessoa, "There are sicknesses worse than sicknesses," in *Poems of Fernando Pessoa,* trans. Edwin Honig and Susan M. Brown (New York: The Ecco Press, 1986), 157.

Aleksandar Ristovic, "Old Motif," in *The Horse Has Six Legs: An Anthology of Serbian Poetry,* trans. Charles Simic (Saint Paul, Minn.: Graywolf Press, 1992), 158.

Louise Bogan, "To Wine," in *The Blue Estuaries: Poems, 1923–1968* (New York: Farrar, Straus and Giroux, 1975), 71.

Jaqueline Ridgeway, *Louise Bogan* (Boston: Twayne, 1984), 85.

Wislawa Szymborska, "Over Wine," in *Poems New and Collected, 1957–1997*, trans. Stanislaw Baranczak and Clare Cavanagh (New York: Harcourt Brace, 1998), 46.

Miriam Ulinover, "Havdolah Wine," trans. Seth L. Wolitz, in *Voices within the Ark: The Modern Jewish Poets*, ed. Howard Schwartz and Anthony Rudolf (New York: Avon, 1980), 366.

Eugenio Montale, "The wine peddler poured" and "And Paradise?" in *Satura, 1962–1970*, trans. William Arrowsmith (New York: W. W. Norton and Co., 1998), 26–27, 216.

Colette, "Wines," in *Earthly Paradise*, ed. Robert Phelps, trans. Derek Coltman (New York: Farrar, Straus and Giroux, 1966), 274.

Ralph Steadman, *The Grapes of Ralph: Wine According to Ralph Steadman* (New York: Harcourt Brace, 1992).

Adrienne Lehrer, *Wine and Conversation* (Bloomington: Indiana University Press, 1983), 5–7, 129–35.

Peynaud, *Taste of Wine*, 170.

Leonard Barkan, "Feasts for the Eyes, Foods for Thought," *Social Research* 66, no. 1, *Food: Nature and Culture* (winter 1998), 238.

George Bradley, "A Georgic for Doug Crase," in *The Fire Fetched Down* (New York: Alfred A. Knopf, 1996), 57, 66.

Hollander, *Rhyme's Reason: A Guide to English Verse*, new and enlarged ed. (New Haven: Yale University Press, 1989).

Elizabeth Knox, *The Vintner's Luck* (New York: Farrar, Straus and Giroux, 1998), 6, 280–81, 284.

CHAPTER 20: ORCHARDS, GROVES, GARDENS

Some Early Fruit Orchards and Gardens

Anon., "Turin Love Songs," trans. William Kelly Simpson, in *The Literature of Ancient Egypt: An Anthology of Stories, Instructions, and Poetry* (New Haven: Yale University Press, 1972), 312, 314.

Homer, *Odyssey* 7.15, 133–35, 112–22; 24.226–27, 234, 337–44; in trans. Robert Fitzgerald (New York: Anchor, 1963), 111, 115, 114, 452, 455.

Alexander Pope, "The Gardens of Alcinous," in *The Poems of Alexander Pope*, ed. John Butt (New Haven: Yale University Press, 1963), 59–60.

Martial, *Epigrams* 8.68; in *Epigrams of Martial Englished by Divers Hands*, ed. J. P. Sullivan and Peter Whigham, trans. Peter Whigham (Berkeley and Los Angeles: University of California Press, 1987), 300–301.

Martial, *Epigrams* 8.68; in *Martial: Epigrams*, vol. 2, trans. D. R. Shackleton Bailey (Cambridge: Harvard University Press, 1993), 216–19.

Martial, *Epigrams* 8.68; in *Martial: Selected Epigrams*, trans. Rolfe Humphries (Bloomington: Indiana University Press, 1963), 82–83.

Lucian, *A True Story*, in *Selected Satires of Lucian*, trans. Lionel Casson (New York: Norton, 1962), 13, 38, 16–17.

Helen Waddell, *The Wandering Scholars* (New York: Doubleday Anchor, 1955), 58.

Walafrid Strabo, "Of Gardening," in *Mediaeval Latin Lyrics* by Helen Waddell, 4th ed. (Harmondsworth, England: Penguin, 1968), 323, 127.

808   Walter Horn and Ernest Born, *The Plan of St. Gall: A Study of the Architecture and Economy of, and Life, in a Paradigmatic Carolingian Monastery,* vol. 2 (Berkeley and Los Angeles: University of California Press, 1979), 211–12.

Qasmuna, "Seeing Herself Beautiful and Nubile," in *Andalusian Poetry,* trans. Christopher Middleton and Leticia Garza-Falcón (Boston: David Godine, 1993), 48.

The Garden as Earthly Paradise

R. Joshua B. Levi, "Commentary on Genesis," in *Everyman's Talmud,* trans. A. Cohen (London: J. M. Dent, 1949), 388.

Geert Jan van Gelder, *God's Banquet* (New York: Columbia University Press, 2000), 22–23.

Koran 44:43–46; trans. Ali Ahmed, in *Al-Qur'an: A Contemporary Translation* (Princeton: Princeton University Press, 1988), 425.

de Lorris and de Meun, *The Romance of the Rose* 1.634, 694–97, 1321–38, 1345–50, 1360–62, 1511, 1673; in *The Romance of the Rose,* 3d ed., trans. Charles Dahlberg (Princeton: Princeton University Press, 1995), 39–40, 48–49, 51, 53.

Dahlberg, introduction to *The Romance of the Rose,* trans. Dahlberg, 10.

Luís Vaz de Camões, *Os Lusíadas* 9.56, 58–59; in *The Lusíads,* trans. Landeg White (Oxford: Oxford University Press, 1997), 188.

de Camões, *Os Lusiadas* 9.59.6; in *Os Lusiadas,* Frank Pierce, ed. (Oxford: Oxford University Press, 1973), 213.

de Camões, *The Lusiads of Luiz de Camões* 9.59.5; in trans. Leonard Bacon (New York: Hispanic Society of America, 1950), 329.

de Camões, *The Lusiads,* 9.59.5; in trans. William C. Atkinson (London: Penguin, 1952), 210.

P[atrick] Barry, *The Fruit Garden* (Auburn and Rochester: Alden and Beardsley, 1855), 329. fig. 101.

Torquato Tasso, 16.10–11; in *Torquato Tasso's Jerusalem Delivered,* trans. Joseph Tusiani (Cranbury, N.J.: Fairleigh Dickinson University Press, 1970), 340.

Tasso, 16.10–11; in *Jerusalem Delivered,* trans. Ralph Nash (Detroit: Wayne State University Press, 1987), 341.

Tasso, *Gerusalemme Liberata* 16.10–11; in *Opere di Torquato Tasso,* 3d ed., vol. 1, ed. Bortolo Tommaso Sozzi (Torino: Tipografia Capretto and Macco, 1974), 487.

David Riggs, *Ben Jonson: A Life* (Cambridge, Mass.: Harvard University Press, 1989), 180, 185.

Jonson, "To Penshurst," in *Poems of Ben Jonson,* ed. George Burke Johnston (Cambridge: Harvard University Press, 1962), 77.

Richard Fanshawe, "An Ode Upon occasion of His Majesties Proclamation in the yeare 1630. Commanding the Gentry to reside upon their Estates in the Country," in *The Poems and Translations of Sir Richard Fanshawe,* vol. 1 (Oxford: Clarendon Press, 1997), 59.

Elaine Hobby, "The Politics of Gender," in *The Cambridge Companion to English Poetry: Donne to Marvell,* ed. Thomas N. Corns (Cambridge: Cambridge University Press, 1993), 46–47.

Peter Davidson, "Green Thoughts, Marvell's Gardens: Clues to Two Curious Puzzles," *Times Literary Supplement,* 3 Dec. 1999, 14–15.

Huygens, "Hofwijk," ll. 907–14, in *A Selection of the Poems of Sir Constantijn Huygens, 1596–1687* by Peter Davidson and Adriaan van der Weel (Amsterdam: Amsterdam University Press, 1996) 142–45.

A. Bartlett Giamatti, *The Earthly Paradise and the Renaissance Epic* (Princeton: Princeton University Press, 1966), 356.

Sister Maria Celeste (Virginia Galilei) to Galileo, 24 July and 13 Aug. 1633, in *Galileo's Daughter: A Historical Memoir of Science, Faith, and Love* by Dava Sobel (New York: Walker, 1999), 293, 298.

Orchards in the Theater
Donald Rayfield, *Anton Chekhov, A Life* (New York: Henry Holt, 1997), 572.

Anton Chekhov to K. S. Stanislavsky, 5 Feb. 1903, in *The Oxford Chekhov,* vol. 3, trans. Ronald Hingley (London: Oxford University Press, 1964), 318.

Chekhov to K. S. Stanislavsky, 30 Oct. 1903, in *The Oxford Chekhov,* vol 3, trans. Hingley, 327.

Richard Gilman, *Chekhov's Plays: An Opening into Eternity* (New Haven: Yale University Press, 1995), 220.

Chekhov to Olga Knipper, 19 Oct. 1903, in *Anton Chekhov's Life and Thought: Selected Letters and Commentary,* trans. Michael Henry Heim and Simon Karlinsky (Berkeley and Los Angeles: University of California Press, 1973), 456.

Laurence Senelick, *The Chekhov Theatre: A Century of the Plays in Performance* (Cambridge: Cambridge University Press, 1997), 71–72, 219, 225.

Chekhov, act 1 of *The Cherry Orchard,* in *The Oxford Chekhov,* vol.3, trans. Hingley, 145.

August Strindberg, *The Burned House,* trans. Seabury Quinn, Jr., in *The Chamber Plays,* 2d ed., trans. Evert Sprinchorn, Seabury Quinn, Jr., and Kenneth Petersen (Minneapolis: University of Minnesota Press, 1981), 53, 55, 69–70.

Joan Morgan and Alison Richards, "Astrachan Large Fruited," in *The Book of Apples* (London: Ebury Press, 1993), 183.

Margery Morgan, *August Strindberg* (New York: Grove Press, 1985), 132–33.

Spatial and Temporal Order in Fruit Orchards and Gardens
John McPhee, *Oranges* (Toronto: Macfarlane and Ross, 1991), 19.

Anon., *Certain Excellent and New Invented Knots and Mazes, for Plots for Gardens* (London: John Marriott, 1623; reprinted as *The English Landscape Garden,* ed. John Dixon Hunt (New York: Garland, 1982).

Francis Bacon, "Of Gardens," in *Francis Bacon,* ed. Brian Vickers (Oxford: Oxford University Press, 1996), 430–31.

Housman, "The First of May," in *Last Poems,* xxxiv; Housman, *Collected Poems of A. E. Housman,* 140–41.

Jorge Teillier, "Portrait of My Father, Militant Communist," in *In Order to Talk with the Dead: Selected Poems of Jorge Teillier,* trans. Carolyne Wright (Austin: University of Texas Press, 1993), 109.

Edward Thomas, "The Cherry Trees," in *The Collected Poems of Edward Thomas,* ed. R. George Thomas (Oxford: Clarendon Press, 1978), 313.

Grafting Fruit Trees
Virgil, *Eclogues* 9.50; in *Virgil: The Eclogues,* trans. Guy Lee (London: Penguin, 1984), 98–9.

Pliny the Elder, *Natural History* 15.57; in *Natural History: A Selection,* trans. John F. Healy (London: Penguin, 1991), 199.

Virgil, *Georgics* 1.1–5; in *Virgil's Georgics: A Modern English Verse Translation,* trans. Smith Palmer Bovie (Chicago: University of Chigago Press, 1956), 3.

810   L. P. Wilkinson, *The Georgics of Virgil: A Critical Survey* (Cambridge: Cambridge University Press, 1969), 3–4.

Richard Jenkyns, *Virgil's Experience, Nature, and History: Times, Names, and Places* (Oxford: Clarendon Press, 1998), 308.

Virgil, *Georgics* 2.73–82; trans. Richard Jenkyns, in *Virgil's Experience, Nature and History: Times, Names, and Places,* 308.

R. A. B. Mynors, ed., *Virgil Georgics* (Oxford: Clarendon Press, 1990), 110.

Jenkyns, *Virgil's Experience,* 309.

Virgil, *Georgics* 2.80–82; in *John Dryden,* ed. Keith Walker (Oxford: Oxford University Press, 1987), 483; in *Virgil: The Eclogues, The Georgics,* trans. C. Day Lewis (Oxford: Oxford University Press, 1983), 71.

Abraham Cowley, "The Garden," stanza 10, in *The Complete Works in Verse and Prose of Abraham Cowley,* ed. Alexander B. Grosart, vol. 2 (Edinburgh: 1881; reprint, New York: AMS Press, 1967), 329.

Colette, "Flora and Pomona," in *Flowers and Fruit,* trans. Matthew Ward (New York: Farrar Straus Giroux, 1986), 154.

Marvell, "The Mower against Gardens," ll. 19–30, in *Andrew Marvell: The Complete Poems,* ed. Elizabeth Story Donno (Harmondsworth, England: Penguin, 1972), 105.

Thomas Randolph, "Upon Love Fondly Refus'd for Conscience Sake," quoted in *The Art of Marvell's Poetry* by J. B. Leishman, 2d ed. (New York: Minerva Press, 1968), 133.

George Herbert, "Paradise," in *The English Poems of George Herbert,* ed. C. A. Patrides (London: Dent, 1974), 143–44.

Marvell, "The Garden," in *Andrew Marvell: The Complete Poems,* ed. Donno, 101.

Frank Kermode and Keith Walker, eds., *Andrew Marvell* (Oxford: Oxford University Press, 1990), 299n.

David Lodge, *Thinks . . .* (New York: Viking, 2001), 317.

Orchards and Discourse

Basil Bunting, "Fruits breaking the branches," in *The Complete Poems,* ed. Richard Caddel (Oxford: Oxford University Press, 1994), 89, 90, 91, 96–97, 79.

John Lennard, *But I Digress: The Exploitation of Parentheses in English Printed Verse* (Oxford: Clarendon Press, 1991), 232.

Wallace Stevens, "The Reader," in *Wallace Stevens, Collected Poetry and Prose* (New York: Library of America, 1997), 118.

William Carlos Williams, "Drink," in *The Collected Poems of William Carlos Williams,* vol. 1, ed. A. Walton Litz and Christopher MacGowan (New York: New Directions, 1986), 53.

Orchards and the Seasons

Günter Eich, "End of a Summer," in *Twentieth-Century German Verse,* trans. Patrick Bridgwater (Harmondsworth, England: Penguin, 1963), 229.

Richard Wilbur, "Orchard Trees, January," in *New and Collected Poems* (New York: Harcourt Brace Jovanovich, 1988), 27.

Orchards in Art

Nancy Mowll Mathews, ed., introduction to *Cassatt: A Retrospective* (n.p.: Hugh Lauter Levin Associates, 1996), 24.

Carolyn Kinder Carr and Sally Webster, "Mary Cassatt and Mary Fairchild MacMonnies: The   *811*
Search for Their 1893 Murals," *American Art* 8, no. 1 (winter 1994), 60.

Judith A. Barter, ed., *Mary Cassatt: Modern Woman* (Chicago and New York: The Art Institute of
Chicago and Harry N. Abrams, 1998).

CHAPTER 21: FRUIT, CONJOINED AND DISJOINED

Spatially Conjoined Fruits (Cornucopias)

Ovid, *Metamorphoses* 9.85–92; in trans. A. D. Melville (Oxford: Oxford University Press, 1987), 201.

Thomas Hart Benton, *Achelous and Hercules,* in *National Museum of American Art* by Elizabeth
Broun (Washington, D.C.: Smithsonian Institution, 1995), 98–99.

Jane Austen, *Pride and Prejudice,* chap. 45; ed. Vivien Jones (London: Penguin, 1996), 219.

Maggie Lane, *Jane Austen and Food* (London: Hambledon Press, 1995), 146–47.

Gustave Flaubert, *Sentimental Education,* trans. Robert Baldick (Harmondsworth, England: Penguin, 1964), 338.

Jon Stallworthy, "In the Street of the Fruit Stalls," in *The Anzac Sonata: New and Selected Poems*
(New York: W. W. Norton, 1987), 27.

Émile Zola, *The Belly of Paris,* trans. Ernest Alfred Vizetelly (Los Angeles: Sun and Moon Press,
1996), 182, 286, 300–301.

Kirk Varnedoe, *Gustave Caillebotte* (New Haven: Yale University Press, 1987), 158–59.

Werner Kriegeskorte, *Giuseppe Arcimboldo* (Cologne: Benedikt Taschen Verlag, 1988), 15, 46–47.

Diana Craig, *The Life and Works of Arcimboldo* (New York: Smithmark,1996), 38, 41.

Jonson, *Bartholomew Fair,* 1.2.12–20; 4.2.28, 43–44, 56–59, 66–68; 1.5.109–12, ed. Eugene M.
Waith (New Haven: Yale University Press, 1963), 38, 127–29, 54–55.

James Wright, "The Fruits of the Season," in *Above the River: The Complete Poems* (Middletown,
Conn: Wesleyan University Press, 1990), 313–14.

James Joyce, "Wandering Rocks," chap. 10 in *Ulysses* (New York: Modern Library, 1961), 227–28.

Clive Hart, "Wandering Rocks," in *James Joyce's "Ulysses": Critical Essays,* ed. Clive Hart and
David Hayman (Berkeley and Los Angeles: University of California Press, 1974), 181.

Linda Jaivin, *Eat Me* (New York: Broadway Books, 1997), 1–8.

Joyce, "Penelope," chap. 18 in *Ulysses,* 760.

Paul Klee, "Satirical Opus," in *Three Painter-Poets: Arp, Schwitters, Klee,* trans. Harriett Watts (Harmondsworth, England: Penguin, 1974), 128.

Klee, *Gedichte,* ed. Felix Klee (Zürich: Verlag Die Arche, 1960), 47.

Walt Whitman, "This Compost," in *Leaves of Grass by Walt Whitman: The 1892 Edition* (New
York: Bantam Books, 1983), 296–97.

Gerald Gillespie, *German Baroque Poetry* (New York: Twayne, 1971), 146.

Catharina Regina von Greiffenberg, "Concerning the Fruit-bringing Autumn Season," trans.
George C. Schoolfield, in *German Poetry from the Beginnings to 1750,* ed. Ingrid Walsøe-
Engel (New York: Continuum, 1992), 262–65.

Gabriela Mistral, "Fruit," trans. Maria Giachetti, in *A Gabriela Mistral Reader,* ed. Marjorie
Agosin (Fredonia, N.Y.: White Pine Press, 1993), 73.

Philip Roth, *"Goodbye, Columbus" and Five Short Stories* (Boston: Houghton Mifflin, 1959), 43.

Fruit Still Lifes—Painted, Sculpted, Photographed

Metropolitan Museum of Art, *The Age of Caravaggio* (New York: Metropolitan Museum of Art,
1985), 207, 210, 263.

812   Giorgio Bonsanti, *Caravaggio* (New York: Riverside Book Co., 1991), 4, 8.

Erwin Panofsky, *Early Netherlandish Painting: Its Origins and Character,* vol. 1 (New York: Harper and Row, 1971), 142.

Pamela M. Jones, *Federico Borromeo and the Ambrosiana: Art Patronage and Reform in Seventeenth-Century Milan* (Cambridge: Cambridge University Press, 1993), 81–82.

Helen Langdon, *Caravaggio: A Life* (Boulder, Colo.: Westview Press, 1998), 118–19.

Cristina Acidini Luchinat, ed., *The Treasures of Florence: The Medici Collection, 1400–1700,* trans. Eve Leckey (Munich: Prestel, 1997), 134–35.

Martin Gayford, "A Magical Realism," *Modern Painters* 8, no. 1 (spring 1995): 30.

Henry Church, *Still Life, The Monkey Picture,* and *Self-Portrait,* in "Henry Church 1836–1908" by Sam Rosenberg, in *American Folk Painters of Three Centuries,* ed. Jean Lipman and Tom Armstrong (New York: Hudson Hills Press, 1980), 178–79, 181; in *Self-Taught Artists of the 20th Century: An American Anthology* by Gerald C. Wertkin et al. (San Francisco: Chronicle Books, 1998), 45–47.

Sidney Janis, *They Taught Themselves,* quoted in *American Folk Painters of Three Centuries,* ed. Lipman and Armstrong, 179.

John Ashbery, "France's Forgotten Man," *Newsweek,* 21 Feb. 1983, 71; reprinted in *Reported Sightings: Art Chronicles, 1957–1987,* ed. David Bergman (New York: Alfred A. Knopf, 1989), 153.

André Derain, *Still Life with Pumpkin,* in Gaston Diehl, *Derain,* trans. A. P. H. Hamilton (New York: Crown, 1977), 83.

André Derain, *Nature morte au potiron* (Still life with pumpkin), in *André Derain: Le peintre du "trouble moderne"* (Paris: Musée d'Art Moderne de la Ville de Paris, 1994), 261, 484.

William C. Seitz, *Hans Hofmann* (New York: Museum of Modern Art, 1963), 24.

John Russell, *The Meanings of Modern Art* (New York: Museum of Modern Art and Harper and Row, 1981), 302.

Hans Hofmann, *Fruit Bowl,* in *Art What Thou Eat,* ed. Linda Weintraub (Mount Kisko, N.Y.: Moyer Bell, 1991), 50.

Marla Price, *George Segal: Still Lifes and Related Works* (Fort Worth: Modern Art Museum of Fort Worth, 1990), 4, 6, 14–17.

Sam Hunter and Don Hawthorne, *George Segal* (New York: Rizzoli, 1984), 70–71, 259.

Tony Thomas and Jim Terry with Busby Berkeley, *The Busby Berkeley Book* (New York: New York Graphic Society, 1973), 153.

Martin Rubin, *Showstoppers: Busby Berkeley and the Tradition of Spectacle* (New York: Columbia University Press, 1993), plate 71.

Alexis Smith, *Tokyo Rose,* in *Alexis Smith* by Richard Armstrong (New York: Whitney Museum of American Art, 1991), 109.

Ronald Searle, *The Square Egg* (Brattleboro, Vt.: Stephen Greene Press, 1968), 89.

Fruit Still Lifes in Literature

Reuben Iceland, "Still Lifes—I," trans. Etta Blum, in *A Treasury of Yiddish Poetry,* ed. Irving Howe and Eliezer Greenberg (New York: Schocken, 1976), 115.

Eavan Boland, "Fruit on a Straight-Sided Tray," in *An Origin Like Water: Collected Poems, 1967–1987* (New York: W. W. Norton, 1996), 149.

A. S. Byatt, *Still Life* (New York: Simon and Schuster, 1985), 116, 324, 175, 6–7.

Paul Gauguin, *Still-Life, Fête Gloanec 1888,* in *Post-Impressionism, Cross-Currents in European Painting* by John House (London: Weidenfeld and Nicolson, 1979), 75.

Gauguin, *Still Life, Fête Gloanec 1888,* in *Paul Gauguin* by Michael Gibson (New York: Rizzoli, 1993), fig. 18; in *Gauguin: His Life and Works* by Anna Maria Damigella (Philadelphia: Running Press, 1998), 94.

Byatt, *Still Life,* 175–76, 184.

Kay Ryan, "Death by Fruit," *Partisan Review* 67, no. 3 (summer 2000), 488–89.

Andrea Bayer, *The Still Lifes of Evaristo Baschenis: The Music of Silence* (Milan: Olivares, 2000).

Exotic Fruit Lists

Louis Untermeyer, "Food and Drink," in *Food and Drink* (New York: Harcourt, Brace, and Co., 1932), 4.

Lorna Goodison, "Song of the Fruits and Sweets of Childhood," in *To Us, All Flowers Are Roses* (Urbana and Chicago: University of Illinois Press, 1995), 18–19.

Blaise Cendrars, "Menus," in *Complete Poems,* trans. Ron Padgett (Berkeley and Los Angeles: University of California Press, 1992), 135, 303.

Jay Bochner, introduction to Cendrars, *Complete Poems,* trans. Padgett, xxviii–xxix.

Boris Slutsky, "The State of Serfdom," in *Things That Happened,* trans. G. S. Smith (Moscow and Birmingham: GLAS, 1999), 271.

G. S. Smith, "The Texts," in *Things That Happened,* trans. Smith, 24.

Amy Clampitt, "Cloudberry Summer," in *The Collected Poems of Amy Clampitt* (New York: Alfred A. Knopf, 1997), 112–14.

J. G. Vaughan and C. Geissler, *New Oxford Book of Food Plants* (Oxford: Oxford University Press, 1997), 84.

Temporally Conjoined Fruits

James Thomson, "Autumn," ll. 673–82, in *James Thomson: The Seasons,* ed. James Sambrook (Oxford: Clarendon Press, 1981), 170.

Théophile de Viau, "Lettre de Théophile, à son frère," in *Œuvres Poétiques,* vol. 3, ed. Jeanne Streicher (Geneva: Librairie Droz, 1958), 185–97.

Théophile de Viau, "Letter to His Brother," in *The Penguin Book of French Verse,* vol. 2, *Sixteenth to Eighteenth Centuries,* ed. and trans. Geoffrey Brereton (Harmondsworth, England: Penguin, 1958), 173.

Elinor Wylie, "Wild Peaches," in *Collected Poems* (New York: Alfred A. Knopf, 1932), 11–13.

Judith Farr, *The Life and Art of Elinor Wylie* (Baton Rouge: Louisiana State University Press, 1983), 2–3, 13.

Stanley Olson, *Elinor Wylie: A Life Apart* (New York: Dial Press, 1979), 189, 268.

Fruitarian Meals

Abraham Cowley, "The Garden," in *Poems,* ed. A. R. Waller (Cambridge: Cambridge University Press, 1905), 328.

John Prest, *The Garden of Eden* (New Haven and London: Yale University Press, 1981), 70.

Milton, *Paradise Lost* 5.482–83, 313–16, 324–25, 341–43, 344–47; in *John Milton,* ed. Stephen Orgel and Jonathan Goldberg (Oxford: Oxford University Press, 1991), 458, 454.

Abraham Janssens Van Nuyssen, *Philemon and Baucis, Entertaining Jupiter and Mercury,* in *Davis Museum and Cultural Center: History and Holdings* by Lucy Flint Gohlke (Wellesley, Mass.: Wellesley College, 1993), fig. 64.

Rembrandt, *Jupiter and Mercury Visiting Philemon and Baucis,* in *Rembrandt: The Complete Edition of the Paintings* by A. Bredius and H. Gerson, 4th ed. (London: Phaidon, 1971), 390.

814   Ovid, *Metamorphoses* 8.674–77; in vol. 1, trans. Frank Justus Miller (London: William Heinemann, 1946), 453.

Johannes de Hauvilla, *Arch-Weeper* 2.448–60; in trans. Winthrop Wetherbee (Cambridge: Cambridge University Press, 1994), 57.

Nathaniel Hawthorne, "The New Adam and Eve," in *Nathaniel Hawthorne: Tales and Sketches* (New York: Library of America, 1982), 754–56.

Hawthorne, "The Old Manse," in *Nathaniel Hawthorne: Tales and Sketches,* 1130–31.

Colette, chaps. 2, 7 in *Julie de Carneilhan,* trans. Patrick Leigh Fermor (London: Secker and Warburg, 1952), 27–29, 42, 126.

Interchangeable Fruits

Stith Thompson, "The Three Oranges," in *One Hundred Favorite Folktales* (Bloomington: Indiana University Press, 1974), 436.

Diego Hurtado de Mendoza, "Stanza," in *Introduction to Spanish Poetry,* trans. Eugenio Florit (New York: Dover, 1991), 12–13.

Edna St. Vincent Millay, "Never May the Fruit Be Plucked," in *Collected Poems,* ed. Norma Millay (New York: Harper, 1956), 185.

Jan Kochanowski, "Lament 4" and "Lament 5," in *Laments,* trans. Stanislaw Baranczak and Seamus Heaney (New York: Farrar, Straus and Giroux, 1995), 8–9, 10–11.

Anon., "On the Death of Mr. Persall's Little Daughter in the Beginning of the Spring, at Amsterdam," in *New Oxford Book of Seventeenth Century Verse,* ed. Alastair Fowler (Oxford: Oxford University Press, 1991), 660.

Adam Zagajewski, "Fruit," in *Canvas,* trans. Renata Gorczynski, Benjamin Ivry, and C. K. Williams (New York: Farrar Straus Giroux, 1991), 80.

Rainer Maria Rilke, "Sonnets to Orpheus, 1.13," in *Sonnets to Orpheus,* trans. David Young (Middletown, Conn.: Wesleyan University Press, 1987), 26–27.

Rilke to Princess Marie von Thurn und Taxis-Hohenlohe, 16 Jan. 1912, quoted and translated in *The Sonnets to Orpheus: Rainer Maria Rilke* by Stephen Mitchell (New York: Simon and Schuster, 1985), 168.

Paul Valéry, "The Graveyard by the Sea," in *Selected Writings of Paul Valéry,* trans. C. Day Lewis (New York: New Directions, 1950), 42–43.

Rilke, "Sonnets to Orpheus, 1.14," in *Sonnets to Orpheus,* trans. Young, 29.

Rilke, "Sonnets to Orpheus, 1.15," in *Ahead of All Parting: The Selected Poetry and Prose of Rainer Maria Rilke,* ed. and trans. Stephen Mitchell (New York: Modern Library, 1995), 439.

Erwin Panofsky, *Early Netherlandish Painting* (New York: Harper and Row, 1971), vol. 1, 144.

Mary Bergstein, *The Sculpture of Nanni di Banco* (Princeton: Princeton University Press, 2000), 156.

Mirella Levi D'Ancona, *The Garden of the Renaissance: Botanical Symbolism in Italian Painting* (Florence: Leo S. Olschki, 1977), 152–53, 294–99.

Alison Lurie, *The Last Resort* (New York: Henry Holt, 1998), 196.

CHAPTER 22: ENEMIES AND FRIENDS OF FRUIT

Ruskin, *Præterita: Outlines of Scenes and Thoughts Perhaps Worthy of Memory in My Past Life* (London: Rupert Hart-Davis, 1949), 33, 35.

Tim Hilton, *John Ruskin: The Early Years 1819–1859* (New Haven and London: Yale University Press, 1985), 10.

Bertrand Russell, "Childhood," chap. 1 in *The Autobiography of Bertrand Russell* (London: Unwin, 1975), 22–23.

Anon., "St. Claus Brand," in *Oranges and Lemons* by Gillian Saunders (London: Victoria and Albert Museum, 1985), plate 13.

David Karp, "Orange Wrappers," in *Food in the Arts*, ed. Harlan Walker (Devon, U.K.: Prospect Books, 1999), 122.

Thomas Webster, *The Boy with Many Friends*, in *The Art of Victorian Childhood* by Richard O'Neill (London: Smithmark, 1996), 14–15.

George Bernard O'Neill, *Feeling Much Better*, in O'Neill, *The Art of Victorian Childhood*, 48–49.

Charles Dickens, chaps. 26, 35 in *Great Expectations*, ed. Angus Calder (Harmondsworth, England: Penguin, 1965), 234, 299.

Samuel Johnson, "Jonathan Swift," in *Lives of the English Poets*, vol. 2 (London: Dent, 1946), 247.

John Prest, *The Garden of Eden* (New Haven and London: Yale University Press, 1981), 75.

Filippo Baldinucci, *The Life of Bernini by Filippo Baldinucci*, trans. Catherine Enggass (University Park and London: Pennsylvania State University Press, 1966), 72.

Vivian Nutton, "Galen and the Traveller's Fare," in *Food in Antiquity*, ed. John Wilkins et al. (Exeter: University of Exeter Press, 1995), 367.

Mark Grant, *Galen on Food and Diet* (London: Routledge, 2000), 122.

Athenaeus, *The Deipnosophists* 3.81b; in vol. 1, trans. Charles Burton Gulick (Cambridge: Harvard University Press, 1937), 349.

Erwin H. Ackerknecht, *Therapie von den Primitiven bis zum 20. Jahrhundert* (Stuttgart: Ferdinand Enke, 1970), 174–75.

Robert Burton, "Diet Rectified in Substance," partition 1, sect. 2, member 1, subsect. 1, in *The Anatomy of Melancholy*, vol. 2, ed. Nicolas K. Kiessling et al. (Oxford: Clarendon Press, 1990), 23.

Samuel A. Tannenbaum, introduction to Thomas Elyot, *The Castel of Helthe* (London, 1541; New York: Scholars' Facsimiles and Reprints, 1937), iii, 23v–24r, 25v, 27v.

Anon., *William Brooke, 10th Lord Cobham and His Family*, in *Dynasties: Painting in Tudor and Jacobean England, 1530–1630*, ed. Karen Hearn (New York: Rizzoli, 1995), 100.

Norbert Schneider, *Still Life* (Cologne: Benedikt Taschen, 1994), 121.

Platina, *On Right Pleasure and Good Health*, ed. and trans. Mary Ella Milham (Tempe: Arizona State University, 1998), 12, 50–51, 56, 123, 145–47.

Anon., *Sour Cherries* and *Oranges*, in Luisa Cogliati Arano, *The Medieval Health Handbook: Tacuinum Sanitatis*, trans. Oscar Ratti and Adele Westbrook (New York: George Braziller, 1976), plates 7–8.

John W. Baldwin, *Aristocratic Life in Medieval France: The Romances of Jean Renart and Gerbert de Montreuil, 1190–1230* (Baltimore: Johns Hopkins University Press, 2000), 178.

Anon., "Eating Fruit," *New England Farmer* 11, no. 1 (Jan. 1859): 37–38.

Marge Piercy, "Eat Fruit," in *Available Light* (New York: Knopf, 1988), 15.

Diane Wakoski, "Braised Leeks and Framboise," in *The Rings of Saturn* (Santa Rosa: Black Sparrow Press, 1986), 34–35.

Joel 1:4, 6, 12; in *Sacred Writings, Judaism: The Tanakh*, new JPS trans. (New York: Book-of-the-Month Club, 1992), 1005–6.

Colette, "Flora and Pomona," in *Flowers and Fruit*, trans. Matthew Ward (New York: Farrar Straus Giroux, 1986), 152.

816   Gerald Murphy, *Wasp and Pear*, in *Americans in Paris, 1921–1931: Man Ray, Gerald Murphy, Stuart Davis, Alexander Calder* by Elizabeth Hutton Turner et al. (Washington, D.C.: Counterpoint, 1996), 91.

Joseph Decker, *Pears*, in *Joseph Decker: Still Lifes, Landscapes, and Images of Youth* by William H. Gerdts (New York: Coe Kerr Gallery, 1988), plate 2.

James Wright, "The First Days," in *Above the River: The Complete Poems* (Middletown, Conn: Wesleyan University Press, 1990), 312.

Bartram, "Observations on the Pea Fly or Beetle, and Fruit Curculio," in *William Bartram: Travels and Other Writings* (New York: Library of America, 1996), 590–91.

Richard Peters, quoted in *The Fruits and Fruit Trees of Monticello* by Peter J. Hatch (Charlottesville, Va.: University Press of Virginia, 1998), 84–85.

Paul Muldoon, "xxx," in *Hay* (New York: Farrar Straus Giroux, 1998), 61.

"Incursion by Plum Pox Alarms U. S. Growers," *New York Times,* 23 Nov. 1999, F12.

James Fenton, "The Fruit-Grower in War-time (and Some of His Enemies)," in *Children in Exile: Poems, 1968–1984* (New York: Random House, 1984), 86, 88.

Paul Zimmer, "Apple Blight," in *Crossing to Sunlight: Selected Poems* (Athens, Ga.: University of Georgia Press, 1996), 5.

Anon., "They did not lose within," in *The Medieval Garden* by Silvia Landsberg (London: Thames and Hudson, 1996), 17.

Ralph Austen, *A Treatise of Fruit-Trees* (Oxford: Tho. Robinson, 1653; facsimile, New York: Garland, 1982), 40–41.

Eleanor Perényi, "Fruit," in *Green Thoughts: A Writer in the Garden* (New York: Vintage, 1983), 69–70.

CHAPTER 23: BERRIES

Random House Historical Dictionary of American Slang, s.v. "the berries."

Virginia Hamilton Adair, "Blueberry City," in *Ants on the Melon* (New York: Random House, 1996), 109.

Maxine Kumin, "Appetite," in *The Long Approach* (New York: Viking, 1985), 9.

Maxine Kumin, "Making the Jam Without You," in *The Nightmare Factory* (New York: Harper and Row, 1970), 39–41.

Kumin, "Enough Jam for a Lifetime," in *Women, Animals, and Vegetables: Essays and Stories* (New York: W. W. Norton, 1994), 63, 66.

Cary Waterman, "Elderberry Jam," in *The Salamander Migration* (Pittsburgh: University of Pittsburgh Press, 1980), 21.

Gwendolyn Brooks, "Old Mary," in *Blacks* (Chicago: Third World Press, 1992), 332.

Frances Trollope, *Domestic Manners of the Americans,* ed. Donald Smalley (New York: Alfred A. Knopf, 1949), 426.

U. P. Hedrick, *The Small Fruits of New York* (Albany: J. B. Lyon, 1925), 181, 180, 164.

Shakespeare, *Henry IV,* Part 1, 2.4.248–50, ed. Barbara A. Mowat and Paul Werstine (New York: Washington Square Press, 1994), 87.

Shakespeare, *Troilus and Cressida,* 5.4.11, ed. Kenneth Muir (Oxford: Oxford University Press, 1984), 182.

Alexander Nemerov, *The Body of Raphaelle Peale: Still Life and Selfhood, 1812–1824* (Berkeley and Los Angeles: University of California Press, 2001), 2, 27.

Roger Holmes, ed., *Taylor's Guide to Fruits and Berries* (Boston: Houghton Mifflin, 1996), 336. *817*

Henry David Thoreau, "Wild Fruits," *Harper's,* Oct. 1999, 36, 38; Thoreau, *Wild Fruits,* ed. Bradley P. Dean (New York: W. W. Norton, 1999), 38, 56–57.

Justin Kaplan, *Mr. Clemens and Mark Twain* (New York: Simon and Schuster, 1966), 64–65.

R. Kent Rasmussen, "Huckleberry," in *Mark Twain: A to Z* (New York: Oxford University Press, 1995), 216.

Jeffrey S. Cramer, *Robert Frost among His Poems* (Jefferson, N.C.: McFarland and Co., 1996), 29, 37–38.

Frost, "Blueberries," in *Robert Frost: Collected Poems, Prose, and Plays* (New York: Library of America, 1995), 62–65.

Lee Reich, "Lowbush Blueberry: More American Than Apple Pie," in *Uncommon Fruits Worthy of Attention: A Gardener's Guide* (Reading, Mass.: Addison-Wesley, 1991), 185–96.

Irving Layton, "Berry Picking," in *The Selected Poems of Irving Layton* (New York: New Directions, 1977), 24–25; Layton, *Selected Poems,* ed. Wynne Francis (Toronto and Montreal: McClelland and Stewart, 1974), 59–60.

Robert Haas, "Picking Blackberries with a Friend Who Has Been Reading Jacques Lacan," in *Praise* (New York: Ecco Press, 1979), 36.

Clampitt, "Gooseberry Fool," in *The Collected Poems of Amy Clampitt* (New York: Alfred A. Knopf, 1997), 115–16.

Ebenezer Emmons, chap. 9, "Gooseberries," in *Agriculture of New-York* (Albany, N.Y.: C. Van Benthuysen, 1851), vol. 3, 184–85; vol. 3 (illustrations), plates 59–60.

Hedrick, *The Small Fruits of New York,* 323–54.

Reich, "Gooseberry Cultivars," in *Uncommon Fruits Worthy of Attention,* 29–33.

Holmes, "Recommended Varieties of Gooseberries," in *Taylor's Guide to Fruits and Berries,* 253–57.

Elizabeth David, "Syllabubs and Fruit Fools," in *An Omelette and a Glass of Wine* (New York: Viking, 1985), 237–38.

Darwin, chap. 10 in *Variation of Animals and Plants under Domestication,* 2d ed. (London: John Murray, 1875), vol. 1, 378; Darwin, *Works of Charles Darwin,* vol. 19, ed. Paul H. Barrett et al. (New York: New York University Press, 1988), 331.

Alan Davidson, "On the Trail of Giant Gooseberries," in *A Kipper with My Tea: Selected Food Essays* (San Francicso: North Point Press, 1990), 14, 16.

Clampitt, "Blueberrying in August," in *The Collected Poems of Amy Clampitt* (New York: Alfred A. Knopf, 1997), 307.

Yusef Komunyakaa, "Blackberries," in *New American Poets of the '90s,* ed. Jack Myers and Roger Weingarten (Boston: David R. Godine, 1991), 206.

Susan Ludvigson, "Blackberries," in *Everything Winged Must Be Dreaming* (Baton Rouge: Lousiana State University Press, 1993), 25.

Claudia Rankine, "The Man. His Bowl. His Raspberries," in *The Garden Thrives: Twentieth-century African-American Poetry* (New York: HarperCollins, 1996), 428–29.

Sylvia Plath, "Blackberrying," in *Collected Poems,* ed. Ted Hughes (New York: Harper and Row, 1981), 291, 168–69.

Anne Stevenson, *Bitter Fame* (Boston: Houghton Mifflin, 1989), 30, 154, 228.

Thoreau, *Wild Fruits,* ed. Dean, 53.

818   Seamus Heaney, "Blackberry-Picking," in *Selected Poems, 1966–1987* (New York: Farrar, Straus and Giroux, 1990), 7.

Helen Vendler, "Choices," *New Yorker,* 15 Apr. 1991, 99.

Ruth Pitter, "Brambleberries, Blackberries," in *Collected Poems* (London: Enitharmon Press, 1996), 292.

Stephanie Bolster, "Many Have Written Poems about Blackberries," in *Breathing Fire: Canada's New Poets,* ed. Lorna Crozier and Patrick Lane (Madeira Park, B.C.: Harbour, 1995), 8–9.

Jack Myers, "Jake Addresses the World from the Garden," in *New American Poets of the '90s,* ed. Jack Myers and Roger Weingarten (Boston: David R. Godine, 1991), 267.

Chekhov, "Gooseberries," in *The Portable Chekhov,* trans. Avrahm Yarmolinsky (New York: Viking, 1947), 380, 382, 375, 383.

Donald Rayfield, *Anton Chekhov: A Life* (New York: Henry Holt, 1997), 460.

Stephen Berg, "Gooseberries," in *New and Selected Poems* (Port Townsend, Wash.: Copper Canyon Press, 1992), 45.

Bertolt Brecht, "Schwierige Zeiten," in *Gedichte,* vol. 7 (Berlin: Suhrkamp, 1955), 119; Brecht, "Difficult Times," trans. Michael Hamburger, in *Bertolt Brecht: Poems, 1913–1956,* ed. John Willett, Ralph Manheim, and Eric Fried (New York: Methuen, 1976), 449.

Serena Vitale, *Pushkin's Button,* trans. Ann Goldstein and Jon Rothschild (New York: Farrar, Straus and Giroux, 1999), 253.

J. G. Vaughan and C. Geissler, "Cloudberry," in *New Oxford Book of Food Plants* (Oxford: Oxford University Press, 1997), 84–85.

Henri Troyat, *Pushkin,* trans. Nancy Amphoux (London: George Allen and Unwin, 1974), 585.

John Fuller, "Wild Raspberries," *New Statesman,* 4 July 1975, 31.

Laurence Lerner, "Raspberries," *New Statesman,* 4 July 1975, 31.

Leo Tolstoy, pt. 6, sect. 2 in *Anna Karenina,* trans, Joel Carmichael (New york: Bantam, 1960), 592, 596.

Gary Adelman, *Anna Karenina: The Bitterness of Ecstasy* (Boston: Twayne, 1990), 91–98.

Vladimir Nabokov, *Lectures on Russian Literature,* ed. Fredson Bowers (New York: Harcourt Brace Jovanovich, 1981), 137–236.

William Heyen, "The Berries," in *The Generation of 2000: Contemporary American Poets,* ed. William Heyen (Princeton: Ontario Review Press, 1984), 128, 119.

Robert Pack, "Ripeness," in *Rounding It Out: A Cycle of Sonnetelles* (Chicago: University of Chicago Press, 1999), 14.

Bob Pack, "Rounding It Out," *Middlebury Magazine* 73, no. 4 (fall 1999): 33.

Paul Muldoon, "xxxv," in *Hay* (New York: Farrar Straus Giroux, 1998), 62.

Tennyson, "Look what love the puddle-pated squarecaps have for me!," in *The Poems of Tennyson,* 2d ed., vol. 1, ed. Christopher Ricks (Berkeley and Los Angeles: University of California Press, 1987), 305.

Bob Flowerdew, "Mulberries," in *The Complete Book of Fruit* (New York: Penguin, 1996), 52–53.

CONCLUSION

Archibald MacLeish, "Ars Poetica," in *Collected Poems, 1917–1982* (Boston: Houghton Mifflin, 1985), 106.

Angela Figuera Aymerich, "El Fruto Redondo," in *Obras Completas* (Madrid: Hiperión, 1986), 54; Aymerich, "The Round Fruit," in *Women Poets of Spain, 1860–1990: Toward a Gynocentric*

Vision, trans. John C. Wilcox (Urbana and Chicago: Illinois University Press, 1997),   *819* 187–88.

Juan Ramón Jiménez, "Replete with Autumn Fullness," *Three Hundred Poems, 1903–953,* trans. Eloïse Roach (Austin: University of Texas Press, 1962), 168.

George Oppen, "The Gesture," in *Collected Poems* (New York: New Directions, 1975), 80.

Galway Kinnell, "Blackberry Eating," in *Mortal Acts, Mortal Words* (Boston: Houghton Mifflin, 1980), 24.

Francis Ponge, "Ripe Blackberries," trans. C. K. Williams, in *Francis Ponge, Selected Poems,* ed. Margaret Guiton (Winston-Salem, N.C.: Wake Forest University Press, 1994), 15, xii.

Ian Higgins, ed., *Francis Ponge, Le Parti pris des choses* (London: Athlone Press, 1979), 85.

Irving Layton, "The Fertile Muck," in *Selected Poems,* ed. Wynne Francis (Toronto and Montreal: McClelland and Stewart, 1974), 47.

Michael McClure, "Haiku Edge," in *Rain Mirror* (New York: New Directions, 1999), viii, 3–31.

Lynda Roscoe Hartigan, ed., *Made with Passion* (Washington, D.C.: Smithsonian Institution Press, 1990), 174.

Stuart Gilbert, *James Joyce's "Ulysses"* (New York: Vintage, 1930), 30.

Joyce, "Cyclops," chap. 12 in *Ulysses,* new ed. (New York: Random House, 1961), 293–94.

Oxford English Dictionary, 2d ed., vols. 11, 12, s.v. "pomellated" and "pelurious."

David Hayman, "Cyclops," in *James Joyce's* Ulysses: *Critical Essays,* ed. Clive Hart and David Hayman (Berkeley and Los Angeles: University of California Press, 1974), 269.

Marilyn Reizbaum, "When the Saints Come Marching In: Re-Deeming 'Cyclops,'" in *Ulysses—En-Gendered Perspectives: Eighteen New Essays on the Episodes,* ed. Kimberly J. Devlin and Marilyn Reizbaum (Columbia: University of South Carolina Press, 1999), 184.

Zbigniew Herbert, "Prayer," trans. John and Bogdana Carpenter, *Paris Review* 154 (spring 2000): 31.

INDEX OF WORKS CITED

INDEX OF ARTISTS, AUTHORS, AND TRANSLATORS

PERMISSIONS

ILLUSTRATION ACKNOWLEDGMENTS

Grateful acknowledgment is made to the following institutions and collectors for permission to reproduce images in this volume.

Figures 1, 8, 9, 10, and plates 7, 12, 13, 15, 16, 17, 18, 24, 31, collection of Robert Palter.

Figure 2, Hans Baldung Grien, *Adam and Eve,* Rosenwald Collection, photograph copyright 2000 Board of Trustees, National Gallery of Art, Washington, D.C.

Figure 3, Northwestern University Press, Evanston, Ill.

Figure 5 and plate 14, Collection of Rachel Lambert Mellon, Oak Spring Garden Library, Upperville, Virginia.

Figures 6, 7, 12, and plates 22, 23, 34, 36, Trinity College Library, Hartford, Connecticut.

Figure 13, *Fables of Aesop According to Roger L'Estrange, with Fifty Drawings by Alexander Calder, 1967* (Mineola, New York: Dover Publications).

Figure 14, Yale University Press, New Haven, Conn.

Figure 15, Indiana University Press, Bloomington, Ind.

Plate 1, Pierpont Morgan Library, New York, N.Y.

Plate 2, British Library, London

Plates 3, 8, 9, 21, J. Paul Getty Museum, Los Angeles, Calif.

Plate 4, National Gallery of Canada, Ottawa

Plate 5, National Gallery, London

Plate 6, Huntington Library, Art Collections, and Botanical Gardens, San Marino. Calif.

Plate 10, Giovanna Garzoni, Italian, 1600–1670, *Still Life with Birds and Fruit,* watercolor with graphite on vellum, 25.8 x 41.7 cm.. Copyright The Cleveland Museum of Art, 2000, bequest of Mrs. Elma M. Schniewind in memory of her parents, Mr. and Mrs. Frank Geib, 1955. 140.

Plate 11, private collection, Berry-Hill Galleries, New York, N.Y.

Plate 19, San Diego Museum of Art, San Diego, Calif. (Museum purchase through Earle W. Grant Acquisition Fund).

Plate 20, Hessisches Landesmuseum, Darmstadt, Germany

Plate 25, Richard A. Vogler, ed., *Graphic Works of George Cruikshank* (Mineola, N.Y.: Dover Publications, 1979).

Plate 26, Michael Saudan.

Plate 27, Wadsworth Atheneum, collection of the Amistad Foundation, Hartford, Conn.

872   Plate 28, Photograph copyright 1983 The Metropolitan Museum of Art, New York, N.Y.,
          George A. Hearn Fund, 1931 (31.62).

Plate 29, private collection, courtesy Schwarz Gallery, Philadelphia, Pa.

Plate 30, estate of Philip Guston, courtesy McKee Gallery, New York, N.Y.

Plate 32, Museum of Fine Arts, Boston, Mass.

Plate 33, Victoria and Albert Museum, London.

Plate 35, private collection, New York, N.Y.

Plate 37, Smithsonian Museum of American Art, Washington, D.C.